Web Sites

- How-to videos help students understand and solve homework problems
- Hundreds of character-building and parenting articles and videos
- Sites for everyone from preschool through parenthood

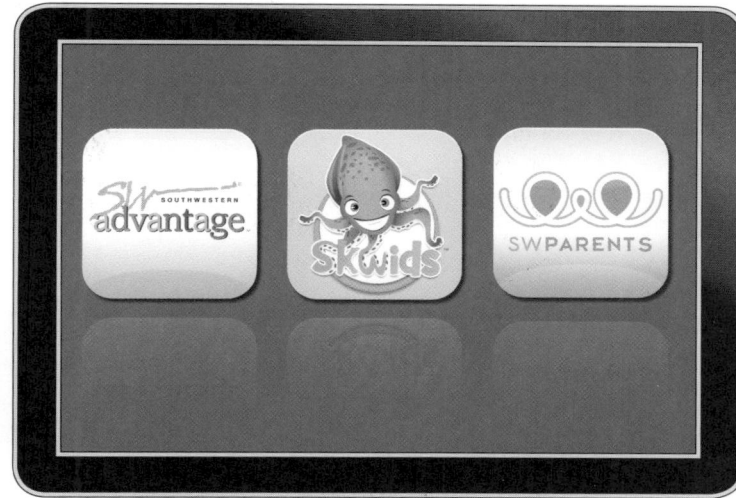

SOUTHWESTERN
advantage
Learning System

Software

- Younger education packages introduce children to computers and give them games to encourage learning
- Older students can use the software to edit and research reports, practice revision techniques, and write practice papers
- The College Prep Pack is specially designed to help college-bound students

www.SWadvantage.com

Books

- Essential tools to help students excel in school as well as prepare for life
- Easily accessible, yet authoritative for the most important academic subjects
- Designed to teach children through exciting activity-based learning

Sharing the Advantage

Southwestern Advantage is an effective learning system and an important key to a better education and achieving success in life. Our mission is to share education and learning skills with every child and every family, regardless of their circumstances, through qualified nonprofit partnerships and local community involvement with organizations focused on helping young people. Southwestern Advantage will also donate one SWadvantage.com membership for each one purchased.

Thank you for helping us Share the Advantage!

SCIENCE

SOUTHWESTERN
advantage.

www.SWadvantage.com

Printed on Recycled Paper

SCIENCE

SOUTHWESTERN
advantage

Southwestern Advantage

Henry Bedford
Chief Executive Officer, Southwestern/Great American, Inc.

Dan Moore
President, Southwestern

Dave Kempf
President, Southwestern Publishing Group, Inc.

Sales Directors

Chris Adams	Robin Mukherjee
Dave Causer	Mark Rau
Lester Crafton	Tim Ritzer
Grant Greder	Chris Samuels
Kevin Johnson	Nate Vogel

Printed in the United States of America by
R. R. Donnelley

*Front cover "monogram" art and back cover "Southwestern Advantage
logo" are both proprietary trademarks of Southwestern/Great
American, Inc., dba The Southwestern Company*
Front cover art created by Travis Rader

Editorial

Executive Editor and President
Dan Moore

Editorial Director
Mary Cummings

Managing Editor
Judy Jackson

Senior Editor
Barbara J. Reed

Editor
Alison Nash

Section Editors
Julee Hicks
Cathy Ropp
Tanis Westbrook

Design

Senior Art Directors
Steve Newman
Starletta Polster

Senior Designer
Travis Rader

*Composition and
Production Design*
Jessie Anglin
Sara Anglin

Production

Production Manager
Powell Ropp

Production Coordinator
Wanda Sawyer

Preface

Welcome to *Southwestern Advantage Science*. We are pleased to bring you this unique, user-friendly reference book. It has been designed in such a way that students can spend "more time learning, less time looking." The pages are open and inviting and organized into information boxes, bulleted lists, and other easily usable and understandable pieces.

How Does That Work boxes contain capsule summaries of particular processes or other information. **The Basics** boxes outline information essential to the topic at hand. **How Do We Know That** boxes give brief recaps of how scientists discovered certain things or formulated or proved various theories. **FYI** boxes give additional small nuggets or bits of information.

Students (or their parents) can also go to **SWadvantage.com**, where they will find additional, more in-depth information on a wide range of subject matter.

We hope you will find this book both useful and enjoyable. Every effort has been made to ensure that the information in this book is as accurate as possible. If errors should be found, however, we would appreciate hearing from you. Please send your comments or suggestions to editor@southwestern.com or to Editor, The Southwestern Company, P.O. Box 305142, Nashville, TN 37230.

How to Use Southwestern Advantage

SOUTHWESTERN

How to Use This Book

This book has been designed so that information can be accessed easily. Science has been divided into six "strands": Biology; Chemistry; Earth Science; Ecology; Physics; and Space Science. Each strand is then divided into smaller units.

The first navigational tool is the detailed, color-coded Table of Contents. The contents pages also indicate separately where the special features of the book can be found, such as the Table of Physics Formulas and Constants and the Space Science time line.

BIOLOGY

CHEMISTRY

EARTH SCIENCE

Next, above the heading on the right-hand text pages, you will see color bars that tell you exactly where you are in the book. The bar that extends all the way to the edge of the page is the color of the unit you are in; the other bar denotes the strand you are in. The strand color is repeated in a tab at the bottom of the page. When the book is closed, you can tell at a glance where each strand and unit begins and ends.

When the book is open, headings on the pages also help to tell you exactly where you are in the book, for example, the Life section of Biology.

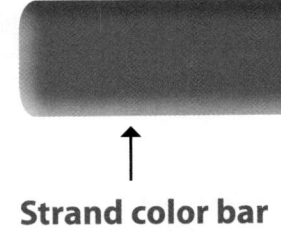

Strand color bar

The human body has more than 10 trillion cells!

How to Use Southwestern Advantage Online (www.SWadvantage.com)

An integral part of Southwestern Advantage is the accompanying Web site. Organized by subject areas, it is a comprehensive suite of online study helps, additional in-depth subject matter, tips for parents, and coaching for students on how to get better at life.

ECOLOGY

PHYSICS

SPACE SCIENCE

SPECIAL ADVANTAGES

Periodic Table of Elements 320

Alphabetical Table of Elements 326

Laws of Motion 762

Physics Practice Problems 868

Time Line of Space Exploration 976

Cells LIFE **BIOLOGY**

↑ **Unit within Biology**

↑ **Name of strand Biology strand**

↑ **Unit color bar**

Spotlight on...

GREGOR JOHANN MENDEL

1822–1884

Gregor Johann Mendel was an Austrian botanist and monk who formulated the basic laws of heredity; he

- used the gardens of the abbey to pursue his passion for studying nature

THE basics

CELLS

All cells have certain characteristics in common.

✔ cells are alive—as alive as you are

HOW DOES THAT WORK

RNA IS FORMED

Messenger RNA is a copy of the DNA blueprint for the polypeptide chain of the protein to be produced. mRNA forms in three steps:

1. First, the DNA splits lengthwise between its bases. Half the ladder serves as a mold to form mRNA.

FRANKENFOODS

Today, scientists genetically modify a variety of crops and animals, called *GMOs* (genetically modified organisms).

↑ **Features**

Strand color tab →

Contributors and Advisors

We gratefully acknowledge the invaluable contributions of these educators and writers to the development and production of this book. Their academic awards are testament to their breadth of knowledge and excellence in the classroom, and the accomplishments listed here are merely highlights from their careers.

Joan Brummond
M.A., Lesley College
B.A., University of Wyoming
26 years as a classroom teacher, K–Grade 3; Wyoming Teacher of the Year; developed new programs in guided reading; coached and consulted for a migrant workers education program; developed a before-school early-bird library program; tutors middle school students; coaches early literacy teachers

Kent Crippen
Ph.D., M.Ed., and B.S., University of Nebraska
Associate professor, Curriculum and Instruction, UNLV; coauthor of "Computer Uses in Chemical Education" in *The New ChemSource*; associate editor of the *Journal of Science Education and Technology*; associate director, Center for Mathematics and Science Education, University of Nevada, Las Vegas; his research involves the design and implementation of Web-based learning systems to support self-regulated learning

Denise Croker
M.Ed., Peabody College of Vanderbilt University
B.A., University of Kansas
more than 20 years as a classroom teacher, in English and Journalism; advisor to award-winning student newspaper and news site; frequent contributor to such scholarly publications as the *English Journal*, which gave her their Paul and Kate Farmer writing award; State Media Adviser of the Year; named a Dow Jones Newspaper Fund Special Recognition Adviser; frequent speaker at regional and national conferences

Arthur R. Echerd, Jr.
Ph.D., M.A., and B.A., University of North Carolina
25 years as a classroom teacher, in European History, AP Comparative Government, AP U.S. Government, World Religions; Tennessee Humanities Council Outstanding Teacher Award; Presidential Scholar's Inspirational Teacher Award; past holder of the Ellen Bowers Hofstead Chair in the Humanities

Jesus Garcia
Ed.D. and M.A., University of California, Berkeley
B.A., San Francisco State University
Professor, Curriculum and Instruction, UNLV; coauthor of *Field Experience: Strategies for Exploring Diversity in School, Social Studies for Children: A Guide to Basic Instruction,* and *Contexts of Teaching: Methods for Middle and High School Instruction*; past president, National Council for the Social Studies

Sherri Gould
M.Ed. and B.S., University of Maine
28 years as a classroom teacher, in English and Literacy; department chair; Maine Teacher of the Year; UMPI Alumni Educator of the Year; frequent speaker at conferences and workshops; former secretary and former vice president of National State Teachers of the Year Association; supervisor and trainer of preservice teachers

Pat Graff
B.S., Oklahoma State University
29 years as a classroom teacher, in Journalism, Humanities, and Social Studies; New Mexico Teacher of the Year; Governor's Award for Outstanding New Mexico Woman; Distinguished Service Award, National Council of Teachers of English; Medal of Merit, Journalism Education Association

Dale A. Grote
Ph.D., University of Wisconsin
M.A., University of Iowa
B.S., Cornell University
Associate professor, Classics, University of North Carolina; author of *A Comprehensive Guide to Wheelock's Latin*; president of the North Carolina Classical

Association; frequent speaker at education conferences; conducts study tours to Greece and Rome

Barry Hertz
M. Ed, University of Alberta
M.S. and B.S., South Dakota State University
21 years as a classroom teacher, in Biology, Chemistry, Physics, and IB (International Baccalaureate) Biology; Prime Minister's Award for Teaching Excellence

Keil Hileman
M.S. and B.S., University of Kansas
more than 20 years as a classroom teacher, Social Studies/Museum Studies; Kansas Teacher of the Year; 2004 National Teacher of the Year finalist; creator of the Museum Connections class, which has amassed more than 20,000 teaching artifacts; teaches museum courses for other social studies teachers

Rollie J. Myers
Ph.D., University of California
M.S. and B.S., California Institute of Technology
Emeritus professor, Chemistry, University of California, Berkeley; Guggenheim Fellow; ACS International Award Fellow; former visiting professor, Harvard University; former faculty senior scientist, Lawrence Berkeley National Laboratory; author of, among other books, *University Chemistry* and *Molecular Magnetism and Magnetic Resonance Spectroscopy*

James A. Roe
Ph.D., University of California, Berkeley
B.S., Williams College
Associate professor, Chemistry and Biochemistry, Loyola Marymount University; contributor to such scholarly publications as *Journal of Biological Chemistry* and *Free Radical Biology and Medicine*

Edna Rogers
M.S. and B.S., University of Tennessee
33 years as a classroom teacher, in Pre-K, Grade 2, and Grade 5; Tennessee Teacher of the Year; National Teachers Hall of Fame; Tennessee Educators Association Friend of Education Award; Presidential

Award for Excellence in Science and Mathematics; Governor's Outstanding Tennessean Award; on the boards of, among others, the Dollywood Foundation and Berkshire Education Scholarship Foundation; director of Dolly Parton's Chasing Rainbows Award

Ernest Schiller
Ph.D. and M.S., University of Iowa
B.S., Iowa State University
33 years as a classroom teacher, in Biology and Advanced Biology; Iowa Teacher of the Year; Outstanding Young Iowan Educator Award; Excellence in Teaching Science Award; Presidential Award in Secondary Science; Christa McAuliffe Award

Michael Seidel
Ph.D., M.A., and B.A., University of California, Los Angeles
Emeritus Jesse and George Siegel Professor in the Humanities, Columbia University; Department Chair; associate editor of *Columbia History of British Fiction, Columbia World of Quotations*, and *The Works of Daniel Defoe*; author of, among other books, *Epic Geography: James Joyce's Ulysses* and *Streak: Joe DiMaggio and the Summer of '41*; frequent contributor to such scholarly publications as *Eighteenth-Century Fiction* and *James Joyce Quarterly*

Mary Elizabeth Spalding
Ph.D., Indiana University
M.A. and B.A., West Virginia University
Editor, *Journal of Teacher Education*; frequent contributor to such scholarly publications as *Educational Forum, English Education, English Journal*, and *Teaching and Teacher Education;* member, executive committee, Conference on English Education of the National Council of Teachers of English; her research interests include performance and portfolio assessment, learning communities in teacher education, and secondary English teaching and teachers

Contents

INTRODUCTION

The Nature of Science **18**
What Is Science?, History of Science,
Scientific Methods

BIOLOGY

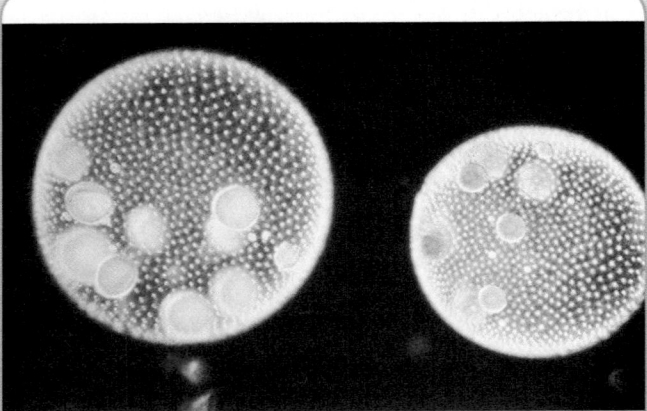

Life on Earth 30
Origins and Development, The Origin of Life,
Great Diversity

Evolution 36
Theory of Evolution, Causes of Change

Explaining Existence 40
Theory of Creationism

Intelligent Design 42
Theory of Intelligent Design

Cells 44
Cell Theory, Types of Cells, Inside Cells,
In the Cytoplasm, Cell Functions, Cell Division,
Mitosis vs. Meiosis, Multicellular Organisms

Genetics 62
Heredity, Chromosomes and DNA, Producing Protein,
Genetic Variation, Classical Genetics, Mendel's Laws,
Mendelian Crosses, Genetics and Technology, Mapping
Genes, **Genetics Practice Problems and Answers**

BIOLOGY (CONT.)

Scientific Classification **90**
Sorting Life, Archaea and Bacteria, Protists and Fungi,
Plants and Animals

Plants **98**
Ancient Plants, Early Land Plants

Plants and People **102**
Myth and Medicine, Botany's Rebirth

Plant Taxonomy **106**
Classification of Plants

Plant Divisions **108**
The Lower Plants, Bryophytes, Ferns and Fern Allies,
Naked Seed Plants, Flowering Plants

Plant Anatomy **118**
Plant Cells, Plant Tissues

Plant Organs **122**
Roots, Stems, Leaves, Flowers, Fruits

Plant Physiology **132**
Water Transport, Photosynthesis, Respiration and
Digestion, Stimulus and Response

Plant Growth **142**
Hereditary Factors, Hormones, Plant Life Cycles

Fungi **148**
Fungi Form and Function, Importance of Fungi

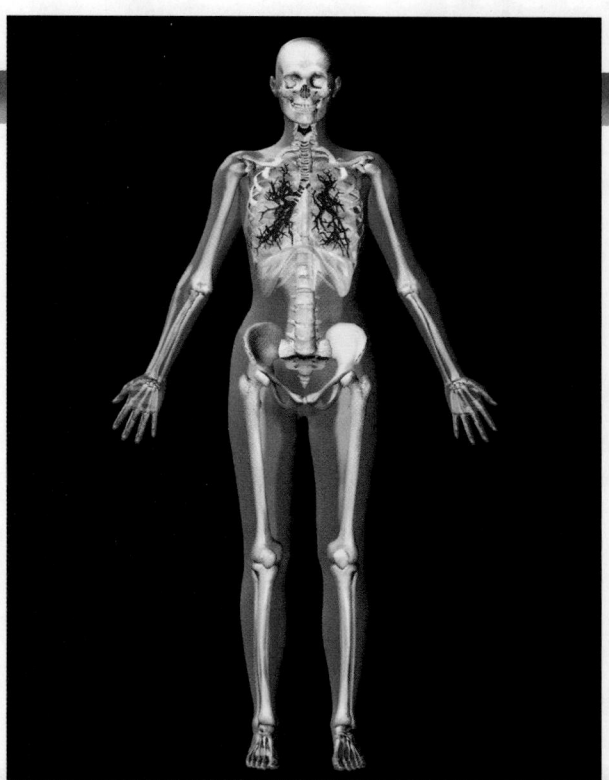

First Life 152
Signs of Life, Breaking the Water Barrier,
Vertebrates Reach Dry Land

The Mesozoic and Cenozoic Eras 158
Reign of the Dinosaurs, Varieties of Dinosaurs,
Rise of the Mammals

History of Zoology 164
Beginnings of Zoology, Insights into Animal Anatomy,
Deep Time and Changing Forms

Classification of Animals 170
Grouping Animals

Kingdom Animalia 172
Sponges to Jellyfish, Flatworms to Lampshells,
Cephalopods to Insects, Starfish to Vertebrates

Morphology of Animals 180
Animal Building Blocks, Cells to Tissues to Organs,
How Animals Move, Varieties of Animal Life Cycles

Physiology of Animals .188
Animal Building Blocks

Digestive Systems 190
How Animals Process Food

The Circulatory and Respiratory Systems . . .192
Transporting Blood, Processing Oxygen

The Reproductive System 196
New Generations, Reproduction

Homeostasis 200
Maintaining Balance, Regulating the Animal Body,
Perceiving the Outside World

Animal Life Spans 206
How Long Do They Live?

Animal Behavior 208
Varieties of Rhythms, Innate Behaviors,
How Animals Learn

Social Behavior 214
How Animals Interact, Conflict and Courtship,
Social Interactions

Animal Intelligence 220
From Ganglia to Brains, Intelligence in the Great Apes

Human Anatomy 224
The Human Body, Skeletal System, Muscular
System, Nervous System, Circulatory System,
Respiratory System, Digestive System,
Reproductive System, Endocrine and Urinary
Systems, Integumentary System

Sense Organs 244
Eye, Ear and Skin, Nose and Tongue

Human Anatomy Diagrams 250
Brain and Skeletal System, Nervous and
Circulatory Systems, Muscular System, Organs

Health and Nutrition 258
Physical Health, Nutrition, Fat, Cholesterol,
Diet and Health, Vitamins and Minerals, Vitamins,
Minerals, Nutrition Information, Calories and Fat

Fitness 280
Exercise, Weight Control, Eating Issues

Mental Health 286
Stress, Emotional Health

Health Issues 290
Healthy Decisions, Disease, Heart Disease,
Cancer and Diabetes, Alcoholism and Drug Abuse,
Sexually Transmitted Diseases, Immunity to Disease

Biology Glossary 304

Contents

SOUTHWESTERN

CHEMISTRY

Material of the Universe. 312
Matter and Energy, Atoms, Atomic Structure,
Electron Cloud Model

Elemental Organization. 320
Periodic Table, Chemical Elements, **Table of Elements**

Chemical Bonds 344
Attracted Atoms, Molecules, Molecules and Matter

States of Matter 350
Solids, Liquids, Gases, Gas Laws

Compounds. 358
Formulas and Reactions, Naming Compounds,
Equations and Energy, Balancing Equations

Reactions and Equilibrium 368
Reaction Rates, Equilibrium

Matters of Scale 372
Types of Measurements, Molar Mass and Volume,
Stoichiometry

Thermochemistry 378
Heat, Bond Energy and Thermodynamics

Solutions 382
Dissolving Substances, Solution Calculations

Acids and Bases 386
Properties of Acids and Bases, The pH Scale

Electrochemistry 390
Electrochemical Reactions, Galvanic Cells, Batteries

Inorganic Chemistry 396
Oxidation and Reduction, Inorganic Compounds,
Transition and Lanthanide Metals

Nuclear Chemistry. 402
Radioactivity, Nuclear Energy, Types of Nuclear Reactions

Organic Chemistry. 408
Hydrocarbons, Hydrocarbon Structure and Names,
Organic Reactions

Biological Polymers. 414
Nucleic Acid, Lipids and Fatty Acids, Amino Acids,
Enzymes

Chemistry Tools 422
Mass Spectrometry, Magnetic Resonance Imaging

Chemistry Practice 426
Problems, Solutions

Chemistry Glossary 436

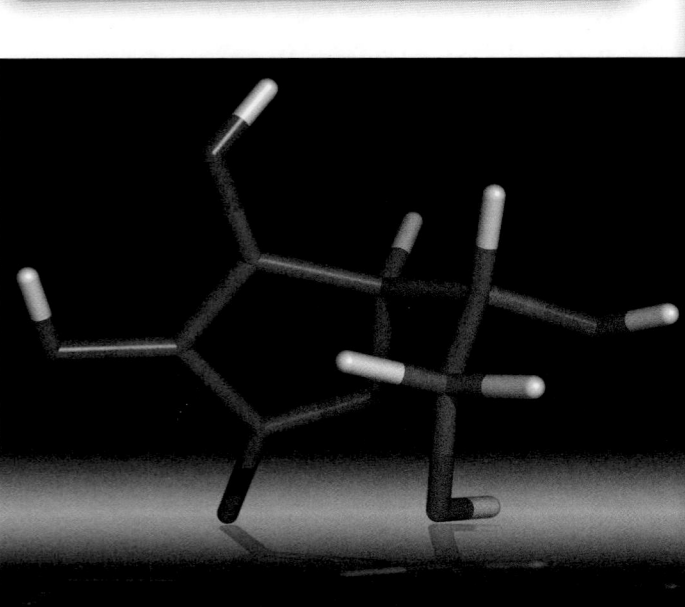

EARTH SCIENCE

Physical Geology 442
Earth's Interior, Earth's Layers, Earth's Density

Plate Tectonics 448
Continental Drift, Plate Movement, Volcanoes,
Hot Spots, Earthquakes

Minerals 460
Mineral Facets, More about Minerals

Rocks 466
Igneous Rocks, Sedimentary Rocks,
Metamorphic Rocks, The Rock Cycle

Historical Geology 474
Earth's Changing Surface

Geologic Time 476
Dating Rocks, Fossils, Geologic Time Scale,
Precambrian Time, Cambrian and Ordovician,
Silurian and Devonian, Carboniferous,
Permian and Triassic, Jurassic, Cretaceous,
Paleogene and Neogene, Quarternary

Earth in Space 502
Earth's Magnetic Field, Mapping Earth

Lithosphere 506
Weathering and Erosion, Running Water,
Glaciers, Wind, Mass Movement

Earth's Shifting Crust 522
The Broken Crust, Mountain Building

Natural Resources 528
Metal Ores, Rocks and Fuels, Soil

Atmosphere 534
Layers of Air

Weather 536
Wind Systems, Water Cycle, Air Masses,
Hurricanes, Thunderstorms and Twisters

Predicting Weather 550
Radar, Satellites and Computers

Climate 554
Factors Affecting Climate

Climate Zones 558
Tropical Climates, Middle Latitudes,
Polar Climates

Hydrosphere 564
Groundwater, Streams and Lakes

Oceans 568
Salty Seas; Physical Oceanography;
Water in Motion; Currents, Tides, and Waves;
Ocean Waves; The Seafloor; Ocean Life

Earth Science Glossary 582

Contents

ECOLOGY

Introduction to Ecology .590
An Intricate Structure, Populations, Population Controls

Communities. 596
Forms of Interaction, Invasions from Other Ecosystems

Ecosystems 600
The Biotic and Abiotic; Energy's One-Way Path;
Trophic Levels; Water, Carbon, and Nitrogen

Classification of Major Ecosystems 608
Types of Ecosystems, Savannas and Deserts, Grasslands
and Forests, Life on the Tundra and in the Water

Animals and Humans 616
Taming the Wild

Plants and the World. .618
Habitat and Niche, Geography and Succession,
Biomes of North America

Plants and Humans 624
Domesticating Plants, Controlling Plants,
Reshaping Plants

The Environment 630
The Biosphere, Changing the Environment

The Growing Population 634
Population Explosion; More People, Less Space

Conservation. 638
Plants and Animals, Species in Trouble,
Wildlife Conservation

Fossil Fuels 644
Conserving Fossil Fuels, Alternative Energy

Health and the Environment. 648
The Human Cost, Indoor Pollution,
Occupational Hazards

Protecting the Earth 654
History of Environmentalism, A Role for Everyone

Pollution 660
Air Pollution, Smog

Acid Rain 666
Causes of Acid Rain, Effects of Acid Rain

The Greenhouse Effect 670
Greenhouse Gases, Climate Change,
Slowing Climate Change

The Ozone Layer. 678
The Ozone Hole

Radiation 682
Harmful Radiation

Noise Pollution. 684
From Sound to Noise, Effects of Noise Pollution

Polluted Land 688
Waste: Where It Comes From, Taking Out the Trash,
Recycling, Hazardous Wastes, Radioactive Wastes,
Radioactive Cleanup

Habitats in Peril 700
Wetlands, Forests, Conserving Forests,
Protecting Habitats

Agriculture 708
Threatened Soils, Soil Conservation, Fertilizers and
Pesticides, Alternatives to Pesticides, Genetic Diversity

Water Pollution 718
The Water Supply, Water Pollution, Types of Water
Pollution, Oil Pollution, Costs of Water Pollution,
Protecting Water Supplies, Water Conservation

Energy 734
Fossil Fuels, Nuclear Energy, Water Power,
Hydrogen Power, Solar Energy, Other Energy Sources

Ecology Glossary 746

PHYSICS

Physics 752
What Is Physics?, Types of Physics

Energy 756
Forms of Energy, Mechanical Energy

Mechanics 760
Measurement, **Motion,** Force, Gravitation,
Torque, Work, Machines, Momentum,
Density

Matter 778
Properties, Solids, Liquids and Gases

Heat 784
Heat Energy, Heat Sources, Temperature,
Thermodynamics, Heat Transfer, Heat Transfer Methods,
Cryogenics

Waves 798
Waves and Vibrations, Wave Motion

Sound 802
Sound Waves, Sound Properties,
Acoustics, Acoustic Applications

Electricity and Magnetism 810
Electromagnetism, Static Electricity,
Flowing Current, AC/DC

Magnetism 818
Magnets: How They Work, Electromagnets,
Current in a Coil

Electronics 824
Electronic Development

Semi- and Superconductors 826
Semiconductors, Semiconductor Devices,
Transistors, Superconductors

Light 834
The Nature of Light, How Light Behaves,
Interference and Diffraction

Optics 840
Geometrical Optics, Lenses, Polarized Light,
Measuring Light, Spectra and Atomic Structure, Lasers

Theories of Relativity 852
Special and General Relativity

Nuclear Physics 854
Atomic Structure, Accelerators,
Fission and Fusion

Subatomic Particles 862
New Particles, Forces and Grand Theories,
Formulas and Constants

Physics Practice 868
Problems, Answers

Physics Glossary 892

Contents

SPACE SCIENCE

Astronomy...............................900
History of Astronomy, Early Concepts of the Universe,
Making Progress, Among the Stars

Astronomical Instruments.................908
Telescopes, Spectroscopy, Invisible Astronomy,
Beyond the Telescope

The Solar System 916
Theories of Origin, Around the Sun

Terrestrial Planets 920
Mercury and Venus, Earth's Satellite,
Eclipses, Mars

Gas Giants 928
Jupiter, Saturn and Uranus, Neptune and Dwarf Planets

Other Objects 934
Small Bodies

The Sun and Stars 936
The Sun: A Typical Star, Solar Activity

The Stars 940
Stellar Distance; Star Light, Star Bright;
Classifying the Stars; Life of a Star; Supernovas and
Neutron Stars; Black Holes and Binary Stars

The Milky Way............................952
A Spiral Galaxy, A Dusty Galaxy

The Universe.............................956
Galaxies, Vast Distances, Quasars

Cosmology...............................962
Origins and Age, Nature of the Universe,
The Search for Life

Space Exploration **968**
Rockets, Rocket Flight

Humans in Space **972**
The Space Race, The Final Frontier,
Time Line of Space Exploration

Space Science Glossary **988**

SPECIAL ADVANTAGES

What Is Science? 18

In the Cytoplasm 50

Mitosis vs. Meiosis 58

Genetics Practice Problems 82

Human Anatomy Charts 224

Human Anatomy Diagrams 250

Periodic Table of Elements 322

Alphabetical Table of Elements 326

Chemistry Practice Problems 426

Biomes of North America 622

Laws of Motion 762

Physics Formulas and Constants 866

Physics Practice Problems 868

Time Line of Space Exploration 976

Index 1000

THE NATURE OF SCIENCE

Science has taught us much of what we know about the world. Through science, we've learned that tiny living things cause diseases, that Earth's continents move, and that gravity can bend light.

But science has its limits. For instance, science can only explain the workings of the natural world. Also, science is not definitive. Any scientific knowledge can be challenged or changed when new information becomes available.

In fact, many scientists feel that this is when science gets truly exciting—when new information comes along that changes what we thought we knew about the world!

What Is Science?

Science covers the broad field of knowledge that deals with observed facts and the relationships among those facts. The word *science* comes from the Latin word *scientia,* which means knowledge.

Scientists study a wide variety of subjects. For example, some scientists search for clues to the origin of the universe. Other researchers examine the structure of molecules in the cells of living plants and animals. Still others investigate why we act the way we do, or try to solve complicated mathematical problems. But in whatever field they work, all scientists explore the workings of the world.

Systematic Study

Scientists use systematic methods of study to make observations and collect facts. They then develop theories that help them order or unify related facts.

Scientific theories consist of general principles or laws that attempt to explain how and why something happens or happened. Science advances as scientists accumulate more detailed facts and gain a better understanding of these fundamental principles and laws.

The Large Hadron Collider (LHC) is the largest machine ever built. It is a 27-kilometer (17-mile) tube that smashes together two circulating beams of high-energy particles. Scientists hope the experiments at the LHC will help them improve their understanding of the behavior of subatomic particles.

Knowledge Through Consensus

A theory developed by a scientist cannot be accepted as part of scientific knowledge until it has been verified by the studies of other researchers. In fact, for any knowledge to be truly scientific, it must be repeatedly tested with experiments and found to be true. This characteristic of science sets it apart from other branches of knowledge.

Constant Change

Science also differs from other types of knowledge in that scientific progress depends on new ideas expanding or replacing old ones. Great works of art produced today do not take the place of masterpieces of the past. But the theories of modern scientists have revised many ideas held by earlier scientists. Repeated observations and experiments lead scientists to update existing theories and to propose new ones.

As new discoveries continue to be made, even many recent scientific theories will become outdated and will have to be replaced by better theories that can explain more facts. In this way, scientific knowledge is always growing and improving.

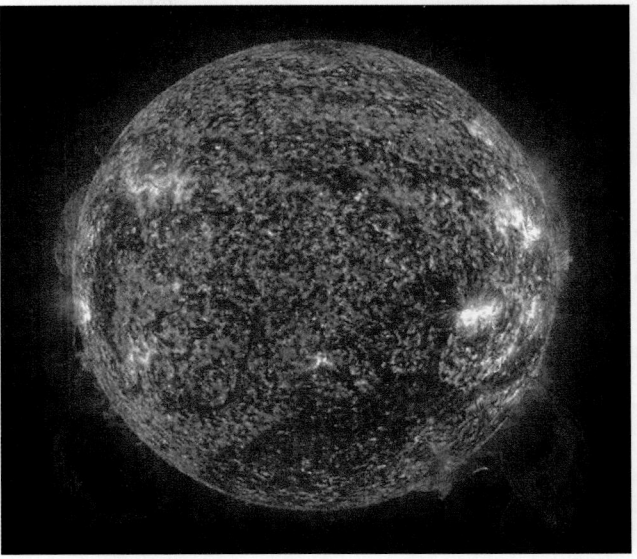

The Sun. The methods used by scientists have revealed many secrets of the universe, including the fact that light travels at 299,792 kilometers (186,282 miles) per second. It takes about 8 minutes for light from the sun to reach Earth.

HOW SCIENTISTS COMMUNICATE

Scientific knowledge spreads quickly when people exchange new ideas. Scientists exchange knowledge in several ways.

- **Science Networks.** Scientists depend on informal and formal networks to communicate their ideas. Through these networks, they are able to discuss their experiments with other scientists, who in turn pass on the information.

- **Science Publications.** Special magazines known as *scientific journals* enable scientists to formally announce the results of their work. Journal editors may send articles to a *peer review board* of experts in the field who help decide if they should be published.

- **Scientific gatherings** provide scientists with a formal place to discuss the latest discoveries and to meet other experts in their field. Some countries jointly sponsor research institutes as a way of sharing the cost of expensive laboratory equipment.

The Limits of Science

Science is concerned with understanding the natural world. It is important to understand that science cannot provide an answer or explanation for every question. Supernatural phenomena, for example, cannot be explained by science.

The World and How It Works. Science seeks to understand how the natural world works and how it came to be the way it is. In order for an explanation to be considered scientific, it must be testable. This means that experiments can be done that will prove that the explanation is—or is not—consistent with the laws of nature.

For example, the *humanities,* which include religion, philosophy, and the arts, deal with ideas about human nature and the meaning of life. Such ideas cannot be scientifically proven. There is no test that tells whether a philosophical system is "right." No one can determine scientifically what feeling an artist tried to express in a painting. Nor can anyone perform an experiment to check for an error in a poem.

History of Science

Highlights in the History of Science	
c. 400 BC	Hippocrates taught that diseases have natural causes.
c. 300 BC	Euclid organized geometry as a single system of mathematics.
200s BC	Archimedes proved the law of the lever and invented the compound pulley.
AD 100s	Ptolemy proposed that Earth is the center of the universe.
AD 100s	Galen developed the first medical theories based on experiments.
800s and 900s	Arab scientists mapped the heavenly bodies and made major advances in mathematics, medicine, and optics.
c. 1500	Leonardo da Vinci studied anatomy, astronomy, botany, and geology.
1543	Nicolaus Copernicus of Poland published *On the Revolutions of the Heavenly Spheres*. The book, which proposed a sun-centered theory of the universe, revolutionized astronomy.
1543	The first scientific text on human anatomy, *On the Structure of the Human Body* by Andreas Vesalius, appeared.
1609	Johannes Kepler established astronomy as an exact science.
1628	William Harvey published his theory of how the blood circulates.
Early 1600s	Human vision was explained in geometric terms by René Descartes. He held that mathematics was a model for all sciences.
Mid-1600s	Robert Hooke used the microscope to uncover the world of cells.
Mid-1600s	Robert Boyle helped establish the experimental method in chemistry.
Late 1600s	Experiments with prisms conducted by Sir Isaac Newton of England began the modern study of optics. Newton demonstrated that sunlight is a mixture of light of all colors.
Mid-1700s	Carolus Linnaeus of Sweden began scientific classification of plants and animals.
1752	Benjamin Franklin proved that lightning is electricity.
1770s	Carl Scheele and Joseph Priestley independently discovered oxygen.
1777	Antoine Lavoisier discovered the nature of combustion.
1830s	Drawings of cells by Theodor Schwann of Germany helped prove cells make up all organisms.
1830	Charles Lyell showed that Earth has changed slowly through the ages.

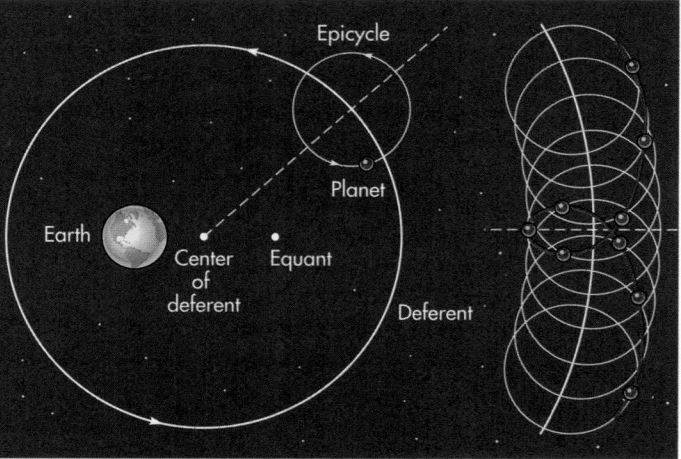

Ptolemy's Universe. Ptolemy's hypothesis that Earth was the center of the universe changed when Copernicus observed that the planets revolve around the sun.

Isaac Newton used a prism to demonstrate that sunlight is a mixture of all colors.

Genetics Is Born. In the mid-1800s Gregor Mendel used observation, logic, and experiments to discover the basic laws of heredity.

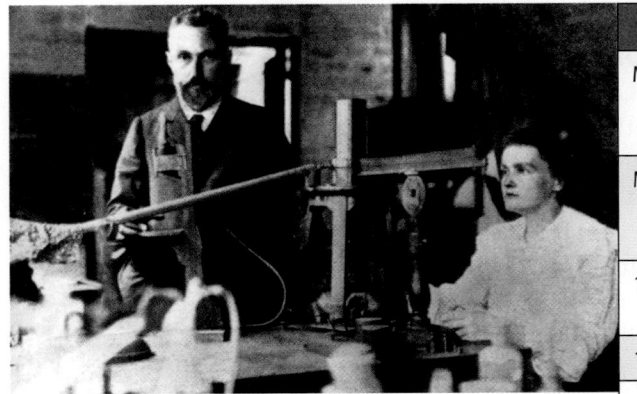

Radioactivity. In 1898, Marie and Pierre Curie discovered the radioactive element *radium,* as well as *transmutation,* a process through which atoms of one element can transform into atoms of another element.

Nuclear Energy. Scientists, including Enrico Fermi, first released nuclear energy on a large scale in 1942. This work led to the development of both the atomic bomb and nuclear power plants.

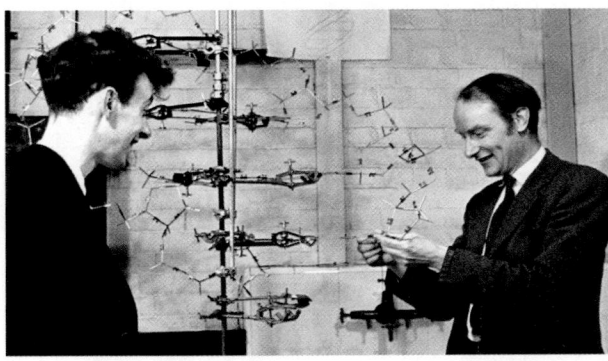

Twisted Ladder. In 1953, James Watson and Francis Crick discovered the twisted ladder—or *double helix*—structure of DNA, the substance that makes up genes.

Highlights in the History of Science	
Mid-1800s	Gregor Mendel, an Austrian monk, discovered the basic laws of heredity. He studied the inheritance of various traits in garden pea plants.
Mid-1800s	Louis Pasteur of France started modern microbiology with his discovery that certain kinds of microscopic organisms cause disease.
1859	Charles Darwin set forth his theory of evolution in *The Origin of Species*.
1860s	James Clerk Maxwell developed his electromagnetic theory.
1869	Dmitri Mendeleev published his periodic table of the elements.
1879	Wilhelm Wundt founded one of the first psychological laboratories.
1898	Marie and Pierre Curie and Gustave Bémont discovered the element radium.
c. 1900	Sigmund Freud established the field of psychoanalysis.
c. 1900	Paul Ehrlich originated the treatment of diseases with chemicals.
1900	Max Planck, a Germany physicist, advanced his quantum theory, which states that energy is given off in a stream of separate units called quanta.
1905	Albert Einstein, a German-born physicist, published his special theory of relativity, which revolutionized scientific thinking about space and time.
1911	Ernest Rutherford put forth his theory of atomic structure.
1928	Alexander Fleming discovered penicillin, the first antibiotic.
1942	Enrico Fermi and others at the University of Chicago achieved the first controlled nuclear chain reaction, starting the atomic age.
1953	Jonas Salk produced the first effective polio vaccine.
1953	A ladderlike model of DNA, the substance that controls heredity, was built by James Watson of the United States and Francis Crick of England.
1957	The Soviet Union launched the first artificial satellite.
1969	Astronauts of the U.S. Apollo 11 mission became the first human beings to walk on the moon.
1974	Researchers developed the first successful recombinant DNA procedure.
1981	The United States launched *Columbia*, the first reusable spacecraft carrying a crew.
1983	Researchers in France isolated the virus that causes AIDS.
1991	The first Web browser allowed public access to the Internet.
2003	The Human Genome Project was completed.

Scientific Methods

Scientists use a number of methods in making discoveries and in developing theories. Most scientific research involves some or all of these methods. They include the following:

1. **observing nature**
2. **classifying data**
3. **using logic**
4. **conducting experiments**
5. **forming a hypothesis (proposed explanation)**
6. **expressing findings mathematically**
7. **modeling with computers**

HAPPY ACCIDENT

It's not an official method, but even chance can play a role in the scientific process. Sir Alexander Fleming, a British bacteriologist, discovered penicillin accidentally in 1928, when he noticed that a bit of mold of the genus *Penicillium* had contaminated a laboratory dish containing bacteria. Examining the dish, Fleming saw that the bacteria around the mold had been killed.

Observing Nature

Observing nature is one of the oldest scientific methods. For example, the ancient Egyptians and Babylonians studied the motions of heavenly bodies and so learned to predict the changes of seasons and the best times to plant and harvest crops.

In the 1830s, Charles Darwin carefully observed plants and animals in many parts of the world while serving as a naturalist with a British scientific expedition aboard the H.M.S. *Beagle*. Study of the specimens collected on the voyage helped Darwin develop his theory that modern species had evolved from a few earlier ones. (See pages 36–39.)

Classifying Data

The relationships among observed facts can be revealed through the classification of data. In the mid-1800s, Dmitri Mendeleev, a Russian chemist, classified the elements into families or groups in a chart called the *periodic table*. On the table, elements with similar properties appeared at regular intervals. Gaps in the table indicated elements that were not yet known. Scientists later proved the importance of Mendeleev's systematic classification when they discovered the existence and chemical properties of new elements that filled the gaps. (See pages 320–323.)

The ancient Egyptians carefully observed the motions of the objects in the sky.

The Periodic Table

Using Logic

Scientists use logic to draw conclusions from existing information. In the late 1800s, a German physicist named Wilhelm Wien studied the relationship between temperature and the energy radiated by heated solids and liquids. After studying many specific examples, he noted that multiplying the temperature of a heated solid or liquid by the wavelength of greatest intensity radiated at that temperature always produced the same number. Although Wien could not test all solids and liquids, he used inductive reasoning (reasoning from specific cases to a general rule) to conclude that this number was a universal constant which was the same for all heated solids and liquids, regardless of their physical or chemical makeup.

Conducting Experiments

Conducting experiments is one of the most important tools in developing and testing scientific theories. The Italian astronomer and physicist Galileo was one of the first scientists to recognize that systematic experimentation could help reveal the laws of nature. During the late 1500s, Galileo began performing carefully designed experiments to study the basic properties of matter in motion. By rolling balls of different weights down inclined planes, Galileo discovered that all objects fall to the ground with the same acceleration (rate of increase in speed), unless air resistance or some other force slows them down.

AN EXPERIMENT WITH HEART

In the early 1600s, William Harvey, an English physician, used the experimental method to learn how blood circulates through the body.

Harvey made careful studies of the human pulsebeat and heartbeat and dissected (cut up) human and animal corpses for examination. Harvey concluded that the heart pumps blood through the arteries to all parts of the body and that the blood returns to the heart through the veins.

The Circulatory System ▶

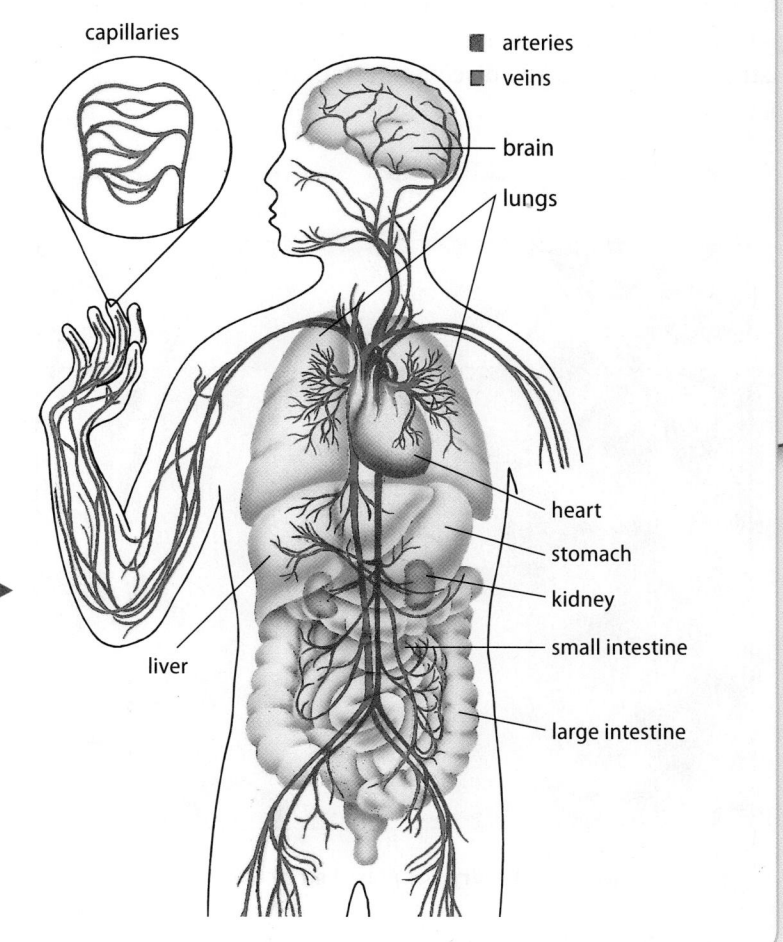

capillaries

■ arteries
■ veins

brain

lungs

heart

stomach

kidney

small intestine

large intestine

liver

Scientific Methods

Forming a Hypothesis

A *hypothesis* is a proposed explanation for a scientific question. Forming a hypothesis requires talent, skill, and creativity. Scientists base their proposed explanations on existing information. They strive to form hypotheses that help explain, order, or unify related facts. They then use experimentation and other means to test their hypotheses.

The discovery of the planet Neptune in the mid-1800s resulted from the formation of a hypothesis. Astronomers noticed that Uranus, which they thought was the most distant planet, was not always in the position predicted for it by the laws of gravitation and motion.

Some astronomers concluded that the laws did not hold at such great distances from the sun. But other astronomers hypothesized that the force of gravity from an unknown planet might cause the variations in the orbit of Uranus. By calculating where such a planet would have to be located to affect the orbit, astronomers eventually discovered Neptune. (See page 932.)

Expressing Findings Mathematically

Expressing findings mathematically can yield valuable insights about how the world works. Galileo used mathematics to express the results of his experiments with falling bodies and to enable him to determine the distance an object would fall in a certain amount of time.

The English scientist Sir Isaac Newton developed a mathematical theory of gravitation in the 1600s that explained many types of motion, both on Earth and throughout the universe. (See pages 762–763.)

In addition to the development of the law of universal gravitation, Isaac Newton also discovered that sunlight is a mixture of light of all colors and invented the branch of mathematics called the calculus.

▲ **The heliocentric theory** was published by Copernicus in 1543.

WHAT IS A THEORY?

In our everyday use of the term, *theory* means something unproven, perhaps an educated guess. When scientists use the term *theory,* they mean something quite different.

In science, a theory is a set of statements or concepts based on a vast number of observations about nature that explains many related facts. When a set of concepts has withstood many scientific challenges and has solid evidence supporting it, scientists begin to refer to those concepts as a theory.

Like all scientific knowledge, theories may be refined by future findings or discoveries. A scientific theory represents the most reasonable explanation science has to offer about how nature works.

One important criterion for a theory is that it must be testable—that is, we can specify what observations or experiments would show that the theory is false. Theories also help scientists find fruitful new questions to investigate.

Modeling with Computers

Modeling with computers helps scientists quickly analyze large amounts of data. A *model* is a set of mathematical equations that describes relationships between data. In the past, scientists computed these equations on paper or with a calculator. Many models were too difficult or time-consuming to attempt. But the development of highly powerful computers in the late 1970s enabled scientists to formulate complex models at great speeds.

Using computer models, scientists can easily vary data to test scientific hypotheses. This use of a model is known as *simulation*. Scientists commonly simulate experiments that would be impossible to carry out in a laboratory.

For example, meteorologists simulate the development of thunderstorms to test how changes in atmospheric pressure affect cloud movement. An engineer may simulate an airplane's flight to find ways of improving its design. Simulations are also used to predict voting results, population growth, and stock market prices.

EUREKA!

In the early 1900s, the German-born physicist Albert Einstein found that mass is related to energy by the mathematical equation $E=mc^2$. The equation states that energy (E) is equivalent to mass (m) multiplied by the speed of light squared (c^2). This equation later provided the basis for the development of nuclear energy. (See page 853.)

Examples of successful scientific theories include the *heliocentric theory* (the theory that the sun is the center of the solar system), the *germ theory of disease* (the theory that diseases can be caused by microorganisms), and *cell theory* (the theory that the cell is the basic structural and functional unit of all living things).

▲ **Cell theory** was developed in the 1830s.

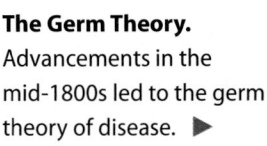

The Germ Theory. Advancements in the mid-1800s led to the germ theory of disease. ▶

Science
Advantage

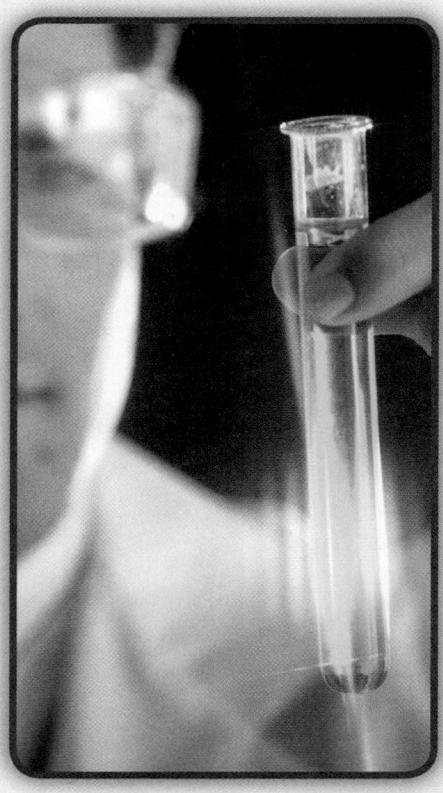

Biology

Chemistry

Earth Science

Ecology

Physics

Space Science

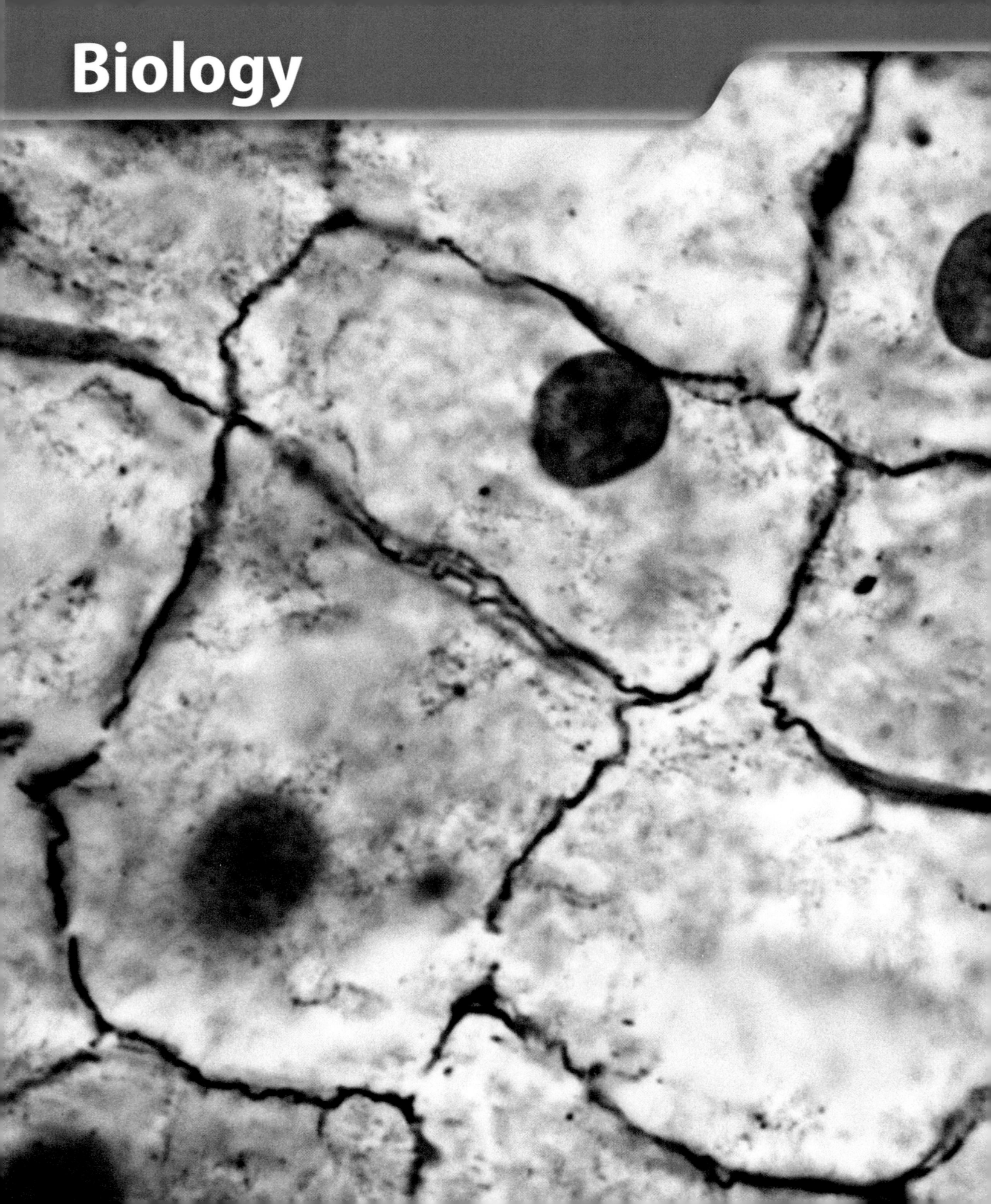

Life 30

Plants and Fungi 98

Animals 152

Humans 224

Glossary 304

LIFE ON EARTH

Throughout history people have attempted to explain how and why the universe, Earth, and life exist. Explanations include both natural and supernatural phenomena. Several of these explanations are explored in the following pages.

Below are summaries of these explanations: scientific theories on how life originated on Earth, the theory of evolution, creationism, and intelligent design.

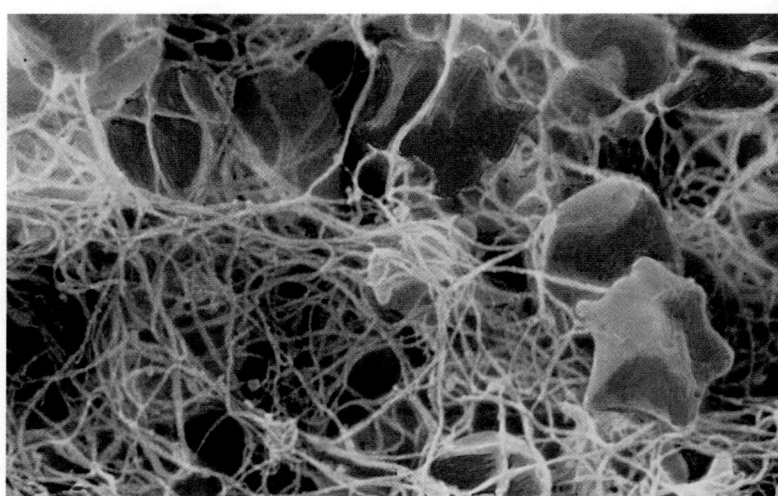

Theories on the Origin of Life

Most scientists favor the idea that life originated on Earth through a process of chemical evolution: simple organic compounds formed naturally early in Earth's history.

These simple compounds combined with one another to form the complex structures that make up living things. There are several theories for how chemical evolution may have taken place.

Oparin-Haldane Hypothesis. States that the first living organism arose out of large quantities of organic chemicals that were present in the oceans of the primitive Earth.

Miller-Urey Experiments. Re-created the Oparin-Haldane model of Earth's early atmosphere in a laboratory. The experiments resulted in the creation of amino acids that are necessary for life.

Panspermia. States that life began elsewhere in the solar system or universe and was carried to Earth from outer space, on a comet or meteorite.

Clay-Life Hypothesis. States that life developed in deposits of clay.

The Theory of Evolution

Evolution is a process of change over time. The basic idea behind the theory of evolution states that species undergo changes in their inherited characteristics over time.

Causes. Mutations produce random variation in species, causing permanent changes in the hereditary material of organisms. Through a process called natural selection, the organisms best suited to their environment are most likely to leave offspring.

New Species. New species evolve based on three factors.

1. Reproductive isolating factors, which are biological factors that prevent different species from mating.
2. Geographically isolated groups, which evolve differently because their environments differ and different mutations occur.
3. Rapid speciation, which often occurs when a population settles in a new habitat.

Evidence. Evidence that supports the theory of evolution is found in fossils, in the way species are distributed, in organisms' anatomical similarities and differences, and in direct observation of rapid evolutionary change.

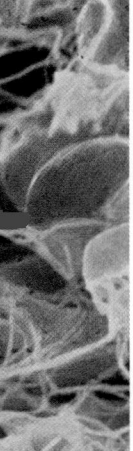

◄ **Irreducible Complexity.** According to intelligent design, the system by which blood clots is so complex that it could not have evolved without an intelligent designer.

Fossils. According to evolution, the fossil record shows a progression from one-celled life to multicelled organisms, and to the many simple and complex organisms living now. This is the fossilized arm of an extinct arthropod. Its spikes (the points on the arm's underside) made it a fearsome predator. ►

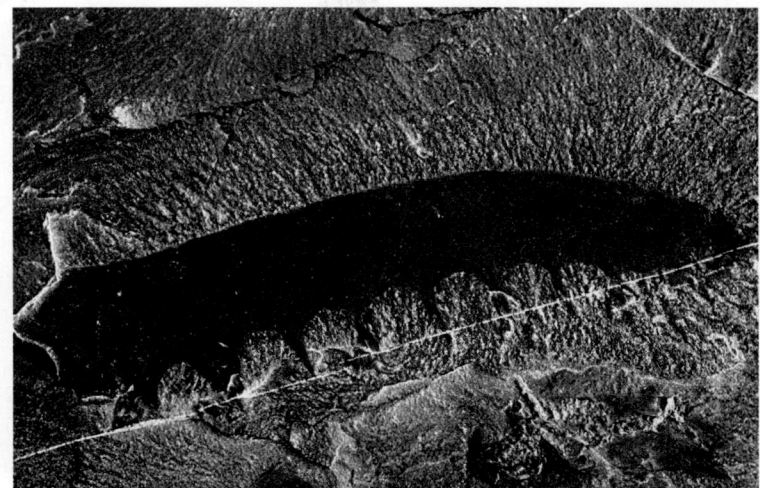

Creationism

Creationism is a set of beliefs based on the idea that a Supreme Being brought into existence Earth and all its life through a direct act of creation. Most proponents of creationism base their beliefs on the Bible's account of the Creation.

Creationism states that all life forms remain relatively unchanged over time. Each species remains essentially as it was created.

Strict Creationism. States that a Supreme Being created the universe as described in the Bible's book of Genesis. According to Genesis, God created the universe less than ten thousand years ago, and He created all life forms in a 6-day period.

Scientific Creationism. States that a Supreme Being has always existed, and that this being created the universe, Earth, and all life. States that:

1. The universe was created in a state of perfect organization and complexity. Changes can only maintain or decrease that degree of organization.
2. The universe operates within a set of fixed laws at a relatively uniform rate.
3. The perfect order of the universe was disrupted sometime after its creation, causing negative changes that lead to imperfections in the world.

Intelligent Design

Intelligent design is the idea that, because of the complexity of certain features of nature, an "intelligent designer" must have played a role in the development of life. Supporters of intelligent design argue that living beings are too complex to have developed through purely natural processes.

Irreducible Complexity. States that any organism that possesses irreducible complexity could not have evolved through natural selection. Irreducible complexity describes a system within a living thing that is made up of parts that work together and have no necessary function on their own.

Specified Complexity. States that if a natural occurrence is both complex and specified, it must have come from an intelligent designer. Defines *complex* as a pattern that is unlikely to occur by chance, and *specified* as something requiring a complex set of instructions that is not part of a pattern.

A Designed Universe. Intelligent design states that the laws the universe operates under— factors like electromagnetism, nuclear forces, and the gravity that holds fundamental particles together—are so complex that they cannot be explained by chance.

The Origin of Life

Scientists who study the fossil record believe that life first appeared on Earth a little over 3 billion years ago. They and other thinkers are still working to understand how that life began.

Nearly all religions have creation stories to explain the origin of life. Modern religious thinkers interpret these stories in various ways. Some people believe life was created exactly as the writings or traditions of their religion say. Other people interpret the texts symbolically.

The material presented here addresses several varying efforts to explain the origins of life on Earth.

Origin Theories

Most scientists favor the idea of *chemical evolution* as the best explanation for life's origin. According to this idea, simple organic compounds formed naturally, early in Earth's history. These simple compounds combined with one another to form the complex structures associated with living things.

Chemical evolution was first proposed by two scientists working separately in the 1920s.

Oparin-Haldane Hypothesis

In 1924, the Russian biochemist Alexander I. Oparin suggested that the first living organism arose out of large quantities of organic chemicals that he proposed were present in the oceans of the primitive Earth. British biologist J. B. S. Haldane independently came to the same conclusion in 1929. This is the theory.

1. The primitive atmosphere contained hydrogen (H_2), ammonia (NH_3), methane (CH_4), and water (H_2O).

2. These compounds collected in clouds and were carried down to the primordial ocean by precipitation.

3. A combination of lightning and ultraviolet light caused a reaction of the compounds that formed simple organic compounds.

4. The simple organic molecules in that mixture, or primordial soup, reacted with one another to form structures of greater complexity, until finally something was formed that could be characterized as having life.

Sparks of Life. According to the Oparin-Haldane hypothesis, life formed in primitive oceans when lightning and ultraviolet light from the sun caused atmospheric compounds to transform into organic material.

Panspermia

Panspermia is the idea that life began elsewhere in the solar system or the universe. According to this idea, hardy organisms could have been carried to Earth from outer space, perhaps by a comet or meteorite. But even if such a journey is possible, panspermia leads to the question of how life began elsewhere.

NEW FINDINGS ON THE OLD ATMOSPHERE

The Oparin-Haldane hypothesis and the Miller-Urey experiments assumed that the primitive atmosphere was rich in hydrogen.

Recent geological findings suggest that molecular hydrogen might actually have been quite scarce, and that carbon dioxide (CO_2) was in abundance instead.

Employing an atmosphere that took this new evidence into account, Cyril Ponnamperuma of the University of Maryland has achieved results similar to those of Miller and Urey.

Clay-Life Hypothesis

A 1960s theory posits that life developed in deposits of clay. Researchers studying common ceramic clay have discovered properties in the material suggesting that it would have acted as a chemical catalyst in, and might even have directed, the evolution of molecules from simple to complex.

Clays trap and store light energy in their internal crystalline structure. That energy can move to a site where it might alter trapped compounds. Defects commonly found within the crystals of a clay could have acted not unlike genes in living organisms that code for the synthesis of proteins.

PRIMORDIAL SOUP

In 1953, Stanley Miller and Harold Urey of the University of Chicago conducted a series of experiments to test the Oparin-Haldane model by re-creating Earth's early atmosphere in a laboratory.

- They circulated a mixture of hydrogen, ammonia, methane, and water vapor between two electrodes discharging 60,000 volts, simulating lightning. The process was repeated continuously for 1 week.

- Any of the mixture that condensed was collected and any organic material trapped.

- When the material that had collected in the trap was examined, it was found that the amino acids glycine, alanine, glutamic acid, and aspartic acid had been created. These amino acids are important in the synthesis of proteins.

- Other organic compounds, such as *purine* and *pyrimidine*—bases found in nucleic acids—were synthesized as well.

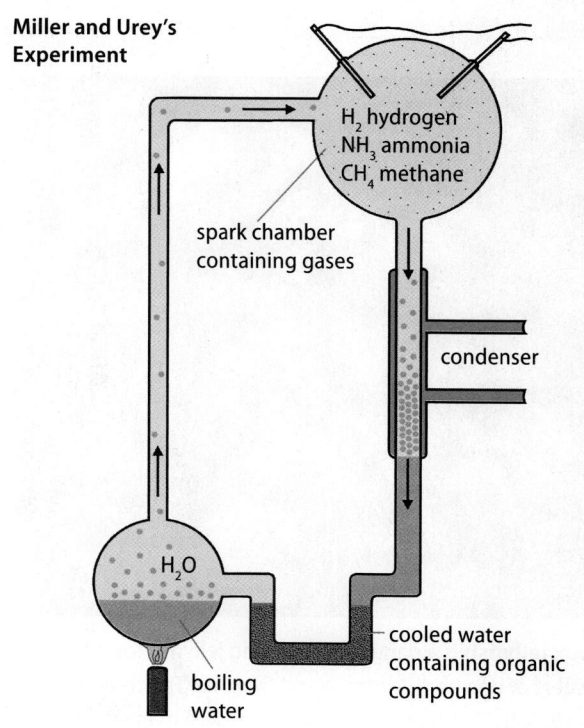

Miller and Urey's Experiment

H_2 hydrogen
NH_3 ammonia
CH_4 methane

spark chamber containing gases

condenser

H_2O

boiling water

cooled water containing organic compounds

Great Diversity

There are more than 10 million species of living things on Earth. They range in size from microscopic bacteria to huge blue whales and towering redwood trees.

Living things differ greatly in where and how they live. However, all forms of life share certain characteristics that set them apart from nonliving things.

- They take in and process materials from their surroundings.
- They grow and reproduce.
- They respond and adapt to their environment.

Biodiversity

The vast array of life—the great variety that exists among organisms and their environments—is called *biodiversity*.

From the primitive box jellyfish, a marine animal with stinging tentacles up to 3 meters (10 feet) long but no brain, to the chimpanzee, a primate noted for its intelligence and curiosity, Earth is home to creatures of all shapes and sizes.

Historical Diversity. Fossils found in Earth's surface reveal even greater diversity in the planet's history. Scientists studying the fossil record have learned that giant dinosaurs roamed Earth millions of years ago, and that tiny, single-celled organisms lived more than 3 billion years ago. (See pages 480–481.)

Importance of Diversity. Biodiversity is important to the overall health of any environment. With a range of species, and variety within those species, living things are more likely to survive changing environmental conditions.

Conserving species diversity is important to save potentially useful organisms. Otherwise, sources of new drugs or food crops might be wiped out before they are discovered.

Biodiversity also should be maintained for its beauty. Each kind of species and ecosystem differs from every other and adds to the loveliness of our world.

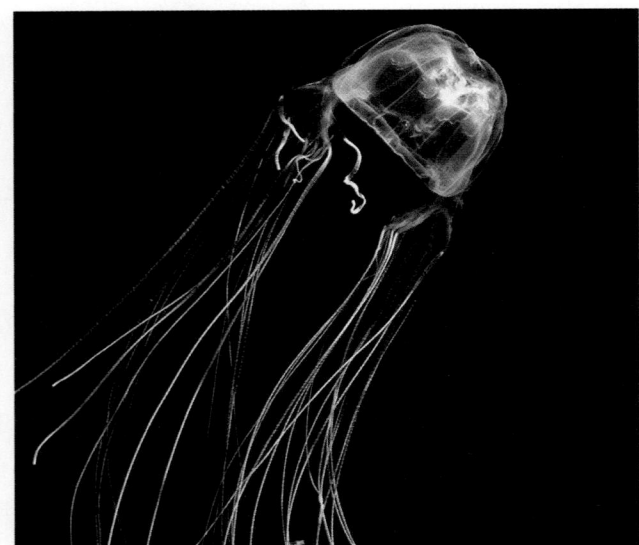

The box jellyfish is a dangerous stinging jellyfish found in the waters of northern Australia and Oceania. The tentacles of a box jellyfish contain billions of tiny capsules, many of which hold a poisoned barb.

The chimpanzee is one of the five major kinds of apes. Its scientific name is *Pan troglodytes*. The adult male weighs about 50 kilograms (110 pounds). Chimpanzees, bonobos, gorillas, and orangutans are known as *great apes*.

A coral reef is a complex, biologically rich *ecosystem*—that is, a community of living things and their environment. Many of the world's most colorful animals live in coral reefs.

WHAT IS LIFE?

It is usually easy to tell living things from nonliving things. A butterfly, a horse, and a tree are obviously alive. A bicycle, a house, and a stone are obviously not alive. But to define what life actually is can be more difficult.

Scientists have a difficult time establishing an exact dividing line between living and nonliving things, but they agree that all living organisms share certain basic characteristics:

1. They have a higher degree of internal structure and functional organization than are found in nonliving matter.

2. They use energy from the environment to maintain life through chemical processes called *metabolism*.

3. They respond to environmental stimuli.

4. They adapt to changes in the environment.

5. They can reproduce and pass on to the resulting new organisms all the information they possess for growth, development, maintenance of life, and reproduction.

Sally lightfoot crab

TEEMING WITH LIFE

The Galapagos Islands are an island chain located near the equator in the Pacific Ocean. The Galapagos are known for their wide variety of animal and plant life. Many of these animals and plants exist nowhere else.

The many rare creatures of the Galapagos Islands include marine iguanas—the only lizards that feed in the sea—and giant tortoises that weigh more than 230 kilograms (500 pounds). Other peculiar animals include cormorants that cannot fly and the Galapagos penguin, which lives farther north than any other penguin.

The large variety of species living on the Galapagos makes the islands an important location for biologists studying the diversity of life.

Blue-footed booby

Giant tortoise

Penguin

Marine iguana

EVOLUTION is a process of change over time. The word evolution may refer to various types of change. For example, many astronomers think that the stars and planets evolved from a huge cloud of hot gases. Anthropologists study the evolution of human culture from hunting and gathering societies to complex, industrialized societies.

Most commonly, however, evolution refers to the formation and development of life on Earth. The idea that all living things evolved from simple organisms and changed through the ages to produce millions of species is known as the *theory of evolution*.

Theory of Evolution

The basic idea behind evolutionary theory states that species undergo changes in their inherited characteristics over time.

Competition and Fitness

The most important mechanism of evolution is *natural selection,* a process by which the individuals better suited to their environment tend to leave more descendants. All living organisms must compete for a limited supply of food, water, space, mates, and other things they need to successfully reproduce. Scientists use the term *fitness* to refer to an individual's overall ability to reproduce.

Main Types of Change

There are two main types of change in organic evolution.

- *anagenesis:* change within species
- *cladogenesis:* the splitting of one species into two

Anagenesis refers to changes that occur within a single species over time. Because of anagenetic change, the forms and traits of many species today differ from the forms and traits of their ancestors.

Cladogenesis refers to the splitting of one species into two or more descendant species. This branching process, also called *speciation,* can be repeated to create many species.

Current evolutionary theory holds that all species evolved from a single form of life that lived more than 3.5 billion years ago. Over time, repeated speciation events and anagenetic changes have produced the more than 10 million species inhabiting Earth today.

◀ **Out of the Sea.** In 2006, scientists found 375-million-year-old fossils of a species they named *Tiktaalik.* Scientists believe that *Tiktaalik* spent most of its life in the water but used its leglike fins to crawl onto land to find food or escape predators.

Common Ancestors

Related to speciation is the idea of *common ancestry*. Because all organisms evolved from one basic life form, any two species once had a common ancestor. Closely related species share a more recent common ancestor, but distantly related species must trace their ancestry far into the past to find a common ancestor.

For example, mammals evolved from a common ancestor—a shrewlike animal—that lived about 150 million years ago, while the common ancestor of mammals and reptiles lived about 300 million years ago.

The Tempo of Change

The rate at which evolutionary changes occur depends on many factors. Scientists have identified two patterns related to the tempo of evolutionary change.

Gradualism is the idea that some evolutionary changes occur continuously over long stretches of time.

Punctuated equilibrium is the idea that some evolutionary changes take place in relatively short periods, from tens to hundreds of generations, followed by longer periods of little change called *stasis*.

Both gradual and punctuated patterns can occur for different traits. The theory of evolution holds that evolution continues today at rates comparable to those of the past.

◄ **Natural selection** favors hummingbirds with bills that are the correct size and shape for the flowers in its environment.

THE basics

THEORY OF EVOLUTION

Theory of Evolution: species undergo changes in their inherited characteristics over time. All species developed from a single form of life that lived more than 3.5 billion years ago.

Causes
- Mutations: permanent changes in hereditary material of organisms produce random variation in the biology of a species
- Natural Selection: organisms best suited to their environment are most likely to leave offspring

Evolution of New Species
- Reproductive Isolating Factors: species remain distinct within an area because of factors that prevent different species from mating

- Geographically Isolated Groups: populations isolated geographically evolve differently because their environments differ and different mutations occur
- Rapid Speciation: the relatively rapid development of a new species; often occurs when a population settles in a new habitat

Evidence
- Fossils: show progression from earliest types of one-celled life to first simple, multicelled organisms, and then to the many simple and complex organisms living today
- Distribution of Species: oceanic islands—never connected to continents—provide important evolutionary evidence
- Anatomy: structural similarities and differences in organisms help scientists determine evolutionary history
- Direct Observation: evolutionary change that occurs rapidly allows scientists to directly observe the process

Causes of Change

Much evolutionary change results from the interaction of two processes.

1. **Mutation** produces random variation in the biological makeup of a species or a population— that is, individuals of the same species living in the same area.

2. **Natural selection** sorts out these random changes according to their value in enhancing the individual's reproduction and survival.

Mutations

Mutation is a permanent change in the hereditary material of an organism. Mutations may produce changes in the inherited characteristics of an organism. To understand how mutations produce these changes, one must understand how characteristics are inherited. (See also pages 68–69.)

How Characteristics Are Inherited. Hereditary characteristics of organisms are carried by threadlike structures called *chromosomes* in cells. Chromosomes carry large numbers of *genes,* the basic units of heredity.

Among most animals and plants, each body cell has a full set of paired chromosomes. Human body cells, for example, have 46 chromosomes arranged in 23 pairs. Offspring inherit half a set of chromosomes from each parent.

Fertilization. Parents pass on their chromosomes to their offspring during sexual reproduction. Egg and sperm cells have half the number of chromosomes found in all other cells in the body. During reproduction, a sperm and an egg unite in the process called *fertilization,* and the fertilized egg then has the full number of chromosomes.

Recombination. Sometimes, the genes from one of a pair of chromosomes change places with genes on the other pair as a sperm or egg cell forms. This change in the arrangement of genes, called *recombination,* can result in new combinations of inherited traits.

GOOD MUTATIONS

Mutations that help an organism survive will be passed on. A plant in a dry area might have a mutant gene that causes it to grow longer roots. Since this plant's roots could reach deeper for water, it would have a better chance of survival than others of its species. And because it has a better chance of survival, it is more likely to reproduce and pass its genes on to the next generation.

How Mutations Change a Species. Mutations introduce new hereditary characteristics. For this reason, they are the building blocks of evolutionary change and of the development of new species.

Mutations may be caused by environmental factors, such as chemicals and radiation, which alter the DNA in genes, or by errors in the copying of DNA during cell division.

After a gene has changed, it duplicates itself in its changed form. If these mutant genes are present in the egg or sperm cells of an organism, they may alter some inherited characteristics.

Unfavorable Traits. Mutations occur regularly but are usually infrequent, and most of them produce unfavorable traits. In most cases, such mutant genes are eliminated by natural selection because most individuals that inherit them die before producing any offspring.

Favorable Traits. Some mutations, however, help organisms adapt better to their environment. These beneficial mutations provide the raw material for evolutionary change.

Natural Selection

The theory of *natural selection* was first explained in detail in the 1850s by the British naturalist Charles Darwin. Natural selection is a process in nature by which the organisms best suited to their environment are the ones most likely to leave offspring. This process has been called *survival of the fittest,* though a more accurate term would be *reproduction of the fittest.*

Plants and animals produce many offspring, but some of the young die before they can become parents. According to Darwin's theory, natural selection determines which members of a species die prematurely and which ones survive and reproduce.

Variation. The theory of natural selection is based on the great variation among even closely related individuals. In most cases, no two members of a species are exactly alike. Each has a unique combination of such traits as size, color, and ability to withstand cold or other harsh conditions.

Competition. In any environment, the members of a species with traits that allow them to catch food—or escape predators—will be more likely to survive and reproduce. ▼

Competition. Only a limited supply of food, water, and other necessities of life exists for all the organisms that are produced. Therefore, the organisms must constantly compete for these necessities. They also struggle against such dangers as being destroyed by animals that prey on them or by unfavorable weather.

In any environment, some members of a species have combinations of traits that help them. Other members have traits that are less suitable for that environment. The organisms with the favorable traits are most likely to survive, reproduce, and pass on those traits to their young. Organisms that are less able to compete are likely to die prematurely or to produce few or inferior offspring. As a result, the favorable traits replace the unfavorable ones in the species. (See pages 216–217.)

Different Environments. If the environment changes, different traits or combinations of traits may become favorable to survival, and the overall character of a species might change. In this way, a species adapts to its environment and avoids extinction. If two populations of a species live in different environments, they will probably develop differently. Eventually, they may differ so much that they become two separate species.

EXPLAINING EXISTENCE

Creationism and *intelligent design* are two related explanations for how the universe, Earth, and the life on it came to be. Both explanations state that a Supreme Being, or intelligent designer, created the universe.

Creationism states that the universe was created in a state of perfect organization and complexity. Since it began in a perfect state, this organization and complexity can only be maintained or decreased.

Intelligent design states that the universe, Earth, and life are too complex to have developed through natural processes. An intelligent being must have played a role.

Earth's Surface. According to creationism, the formations on Earth's surface were formed by a devastating worldwide flood that occurred thousands of years ago. ▼

Theory of Creationism

Creationism is a set of beliefs based on the idea that a Supreme Being brought into existence Earth and all its life through a direct act of creation. Most proponents of creationism base their beliefs on the Bible's account of the Creation.

There is considerable variation in creationist beliefs, but there are two main types of creationism.

- strict creationism
- scientific creationism

Strict Creationism

Strict creationism states that a Supreme Being created the universe as described in the Bible's Book of Genesis. According to Genesis, God created the universe less than 10 thousand years ago, and He created all life forms in a 6-day period.

Strict creationism—like all creationism—states that all life forms remain relatively unchanged over time. Each species remains essentially as it was created. Creationism does not agree that life evolved from simple beings into more complex beings.

Some proponents of creationism interpret the Bible more loosely. For example, some think the universe is millions or billions of years old, but that human beings were created thousands of years ago.

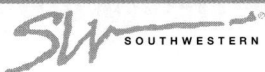
SOME TENETS OF SCIENTIFIC CREATIONISM

- The universe, including space, time, matter, and energy, has not always existed. A Supreme Being is the only thing that has existed for eternity. The Supreme Being created the universe supernaturally.

- Life did not arise by natural processes from nonliving matter. The Supreme Being created life supernaturally.

- Each species was created functionally complete. No species evolved from some other species. Changes that have occurred in certain species from the time of their creation have been either horizontal changes, which add variation within a species, or downward changes, such as harmful mutations or extinctions.

- Human beings were created fully formed. They did not evolve from an animal lineage. The spiritual side of humans—self-awareness, morality, abstract reasoning, language, will, and religious nature—is distinct from the biological side. The spiritual side of human beings was created supernaturally.

- Earth's surface has been mainly formed by short-term, intense catastrophes. Earth's history, as recorded in rock layers and fossils, cannot be explained as the result of gradual, uniform natural processes. There is scientific evidence that Earth and the universe were created relatively recently. There is scientific evidence that rock layers and the fossil record were formed and deposited by a worldwide flood.

Scientific Creationism

Scientific creationism attempts to use scientific evidence to explain the existence of Earth and all its life in a way that remains consistent with creationist beliefs. Scientific creationism states that a Supreme Being has always existed, and that this being created the universe, Earth, and all life.

Complexity. According to scientific creationism, the basic systems of nature were brought into existence fully formed in a state of organization and complexity. Since the universe was created by a Supreme Being, it began in a state of perfection. All changes that have occurred since that time have either maintained that degree of organization and complexity, or decreased it.

Fixed Laws. Today the natural world operates within a set of fixed natural laws at a relatively uniform rate, so the level of organization and complexity generally does not decrease at a dramatic rate.

Harmful genetic mutations can cause changes of decreased complexity within a species. Global catastrophes can cause larger changes, such as extinction.

Disrupted Order. According to creationism, the perfect order was disrupted sometime after the creation. Aging, disease, extinction, and other imperfections in the natural world are caused by the negative changes that occur as a result of this disruption.

▲ **Creationism** states that all life forms remain relatively unchanged over time, existing just as the Supreme Being created them.

COMPLEXITY, MORE OR LESS

The theory of evolution states that all living things developed from simple organisms. Natural processes such as mutations cause both increases and decreases in complexity.

According to creationism, the universe was created in perfection by a Supreme Being, so the level of complexity can only remain the same or decrease. The rate of decrease might be very small during peaceful times, and very high during catastrophes.

INTELLIGENT DESIGN is the idea that, because of the complexity of certain features of nature, an "intelligent designer" must have played a role in the development of life. Supporters of intelligent design argue that living beings are too complex to have developed through purely natural processes.

Intelligent design differs from creationism in that it does not base its tenets on the Biblical story of creation. It does not assert that Earth is less than 10 thousand years old and does not attempt to explain the nature of the intelligent designer.

Theory of Intelligent Design

Irreducible Complexity

Irreducible complexity describes a system within an organism that is made up of multiple parts that do not work if all parts are not present. According to intelligent design, any organism that possesses irreducible complexity could not have evolved through natural selection.

- An irreducibly complex system is made up of individual parts that work together and have no necessary function on their own.
- The individual parts would not have been useful to an organism that had not fully evolved the entire system.
- The useless parts would not have survived through the generations necessary to evolve the entire complex system.

Complex Examples. Supporters of intelligent design point to several examples in nature that they understand to be irreducibly complex (see table below).

System	Description	Irreducible Complexity Argument
Bacterial flagellum	*Flagella* are tail-like structures that project from the body of certain cells. Bacterial flagella are made up of 30 to 35 different proteins, organized into a rotor that spins like a propeller, rotating the bacteria's tail and allowing it to move.	According to intelligent design, there are many parts that work together intricately, and if any one of these parts is removed, the entire system becomes useless.
Blood clotting	*Blood clotting* is the coagulation of blood that causes a wound to stop bleeding. It is a complex process requiring several different proteins. When a blood vessel is damaged, each of the proteins responds, causing platelets to stick to the damaged surface and to one another, forming a plug.	Clotting is intricate and complex. If blood clots did not form, a tiny cut could cause a person to bleed to death. If clots formed at the wrong time, they would block circulation and cause heart attacks and strokes. According to intelligent design, the clotting system is so complex that it could not have evolved without an intelligent designer.
The immune system in mammals	The *immune system* is a collection of cells, molecules, and tissues that help defend the body against diseases and other harmful invaders, such as bacteria, fungi, parasites, and viruses. The immune system consists of a complex collection of interconnected parts that must work together for the system to function properly.	According to intelligent design, each of the individual parts of the immune system would not have been necessary to an organism except as part of the system. Therefore, the immune system is an example of irreducible complexity.

Specified Complexity

Specified complexity is the argument that if something that occurs in nature is both *complex* and *specified,* it must have originated from an intelligent designer. Intelligent design defines these terms as follows:

- complex: describes a pattern that is unlikely to occur by chance
- specified: something that requires a complicated set of instructions but is not part of a pattern

The example often used to illustrate specified complexity is the written word. An individual letter is specified but not complex. A long string of random letters is complex but not specified. A poem is both specified and complex.

According to intelligent design, details within living things, such as the sequence of genetic information contained within DNA, exhibit specified complexity. Therefore, living things—and DNA—must have been created by an intelligent designer.

A LONG HISTORY

The intelligent design argument in its current form gained popularity in the late 1980s and 1990s. But the central ideas of intelligent design date back thousands of years.

Ancient Greek philosophers Plato and Aristotle both argued that the first cause of the cosmos must be an intelligent creator. Marcus Tullius Cicero of ancient Rome wrote that evidence of a divine power could be seen throughout the natural world.

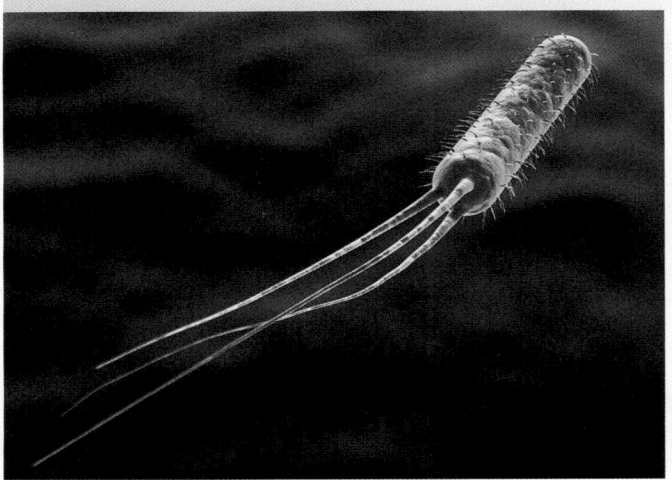

The Fine-Tuned Universe

Intelligent design goes beyond the origins of life to argue that the universe and the laws it operates under are so complex that they cannot be explained by chance.

This argument states that factors like electromagnetism, nuclear forces, and the gravity that holds fundamental particles together must have been set in motion by an intelligent designer.

If any of these features were slightly different, it would have been impossible for galaxies, solar systems, and planets to form in the first place.

COSMIC WATCHMAKER

In the 1800s, theologian William Paley stated that if a person who had never seen a watch found one on the ground, then based on the complicated inner workings of the watch, the person would conclude that it could not exist by accident—that an intelligent being must have designed it.

Paley used this example to argue that a similar conclusion can be drawn from looking at the complexity of the world.

◀ **The bacterial flagellum,** according to intelligent design, is an example of irreducible complexity. The tail-like structure acts as a rotary motor, allowing bacteria to move about.

CELLS are the basic units of all life. Every living organism consists of either a single cell or a collection of many interdependent cells. Bacteria are examples of single-celled, or *unicellular,* organisms. *Multicellular* organisms, composed of many cells, include most plants, fungi, and animals.

While some cells—frog eggs and certain nerve cells, for example—can be seen with the naked eye, most cells can only be seen using a microscope. It would take about 40,000 red blood cells to fill this letter *O.* It takes millions of cells to make up the skin on the palm of your hand.

Cell Theory

Human beings, and every multicellular organism, develop from a single cell. That cell grows to a certain size and then divides. Each new cell grows and divides, over and over again, until it forms a complete organism.

The theory that every form of life is made up of cells was developed in the 1800s. Cell theory consists of three basic principles:

1. The cell is the fundamental unit of all life.
2. All living organisms are made up of cells.
3. Every cell is the product of the division of a previously existing cell.

Today, many different scientific specialists study the cell. Cell biologists deal with cells on every level. Cytologists study cell structure. Biochemists and biophysicists investigate cell *physiology,* or function. Histologists study tissues, which are collections of similar cells, such as muscles and blood.

BLOOD CELLS
red blood cells

white blood cells

basophil

eosinophil

lymphocyte

monocyte

neutrophil

MUSCLE CELLS
striated (voluntary)

smooth (involuntary)

cardiac

NERVE CELL

BONE CELL

REPRODUCTIVE CELL

GLAND CELL

Cell Size	
human nerve cell	up to 2 m in length
chicken egg cell	approx. 30 mm in diameter
frog egg cell	approx. 1 mm in diameter
human egg cell	approx. 100 μm* in diameter
human red blood cell	approx. 8 μm in diameter
average eukaryotic cell	approx 10–100 μm in diameter
average plant body cell	approx. 30–50 μm in diameter
average animal body cell	approx 10–20 μm in diameter
average true bacteria	approx. 1 μm in diameter
average prokaryotic cell	approx. 1–10 μm in diameter
mycoplasma	approx. 0.16 μm in diameter
*μm = micron (one micron = 0.000001 meters)	

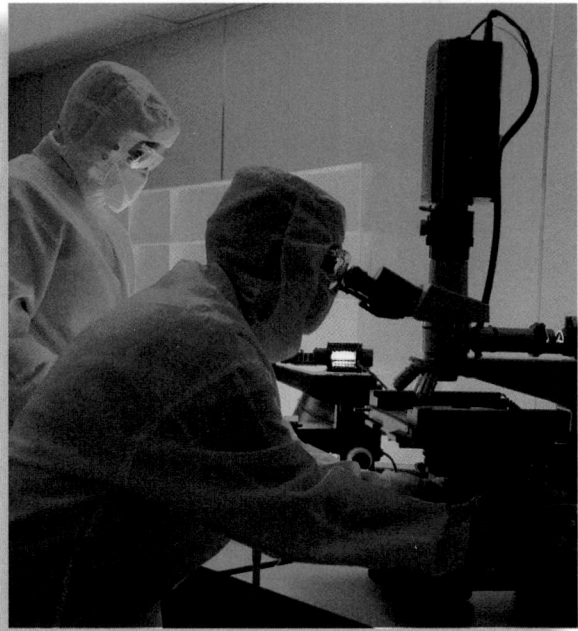

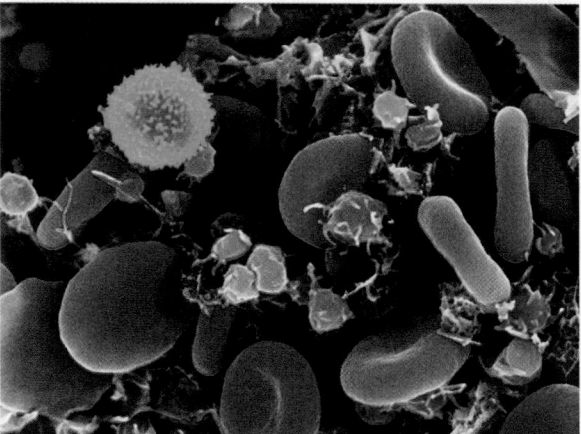

Microscopes allow scientists to study the details of a cell. The scanning electron microscope (*left*) can magnify an image up to 200,000 times. At this magnification, the minuscule features of human blood (*below*) are clear, bright, and vivid.

THE basics

CELLS

All cells have certain characteristics in common.

✔ cells are alive—as alive as you are

✔ cells "breathe," take in food, get rid of wastes, grow, reproduce, and, in time, die

✔ cells have a *membrane,* a thin covering that encloses every cell

✔ complete contents of a cell are called the *protoplasm*

✔ most cells have a structure called the *nucleus,* which contains the cell's genetic program, the master plan that controls almost everything the cell does

✔ the part of the protoplasm outside the nucleus is called the *cytoplasm*

The human body has more than 10 trillion cells!

HOW DO WE KNOW THAT ?

CELLS

● **1665** English physicist Robert Hooke coins the term "cell" after observing that a thin section of cork he was examining through a primitive microscope was made up of tiny chambers, like cells in a monastery.

● **1674** Dutch naturalist Anton van Leeuwenhoek observes unicellular organisms, recognizing that the miniscule cells were not plants but functioning animals. He calls the bacteria and protozoa "animalcules."

● **1805** German naturalist Lorenz Oken claims that every form of life is made up of cells.

● **1838** German botanist Matthias Jakob Schleiden studies plants under a microscope, shows that all plants are made up of cells.

● **1838** German zoologist Theodor Schwann confirms that animals are also made of cells and that living things grow when cells multiply.

Types of Cells

Cells can be one of two types.

- **prokaryotic,** meaning *before the nucleus.* Prokaryotic cells are unicellular organisms like bacteria. They do not have a nucleus.
- **eukaryotic,** meaning *having a true nucleus.* All multicellular animals and plants consist of eukaryotic cells, as do fungi and some unicellular organisms.

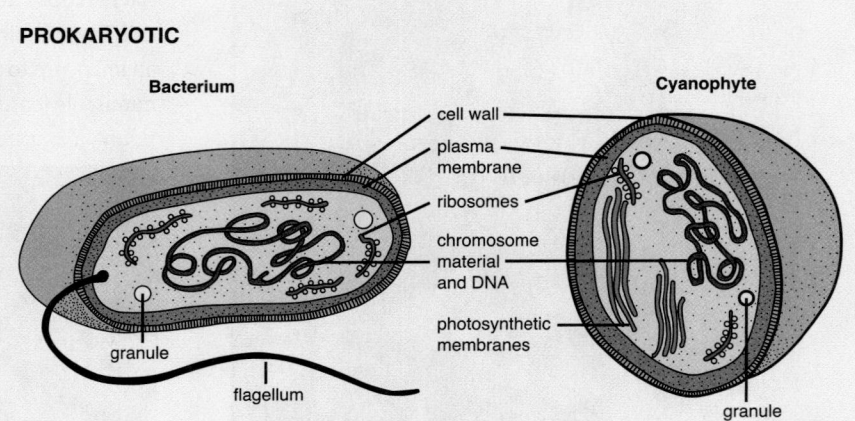

Prokaryotic Cells

All prokaryotic cells are unicellular organisms. They live alone or in clusters called *colonies.* Most scientists classify all living things in three large groups called *domains.* Prokaryotes make up two of these domains: *Bacteria* and *Archaea.*

Domain Bacteria includes true bacteria and the algaelike *cyanobacteria,* sometimes called blue-green algae. Domain Archaea consists of prokaryotes that resemble bacteria but differ from them genetically in important ways.

Prokaryotic cells lack a true membrane-enclosed nucleus. Instead, they have a *nucleoid,* or nuclear region, with a single large strand of *DNA (deoxyribonucleic acid),* the substance that controls heredity. Also lacking are many of the membrane-bound *organelles,* structures that perform specialized functions in eukaryotic cells.

Common to both cell types but considerably smaller in prokaryotes are *ribosomes,* structures within the cell that function as sites for protein synthesis.

Prokaryotic cells are surrounded by a protective double-layered cell wall that in composition and physical characteristics is completely different from the membrane that surrounds eukaryotic cells.

THE OLDEST LIFE FORM?

Archaea are a group of single-celled organisms that make up one of the three basic divisions of life. They rank among the oldest forms of life on Earth. Some scientists believe these organisms are similar to the original ancestors of all modern life.

Archaea live in such harsh conditions as oil wells, deep-sea hydrothermal vents (hot springs), and anaerobic (oxygen-free) environments. (See Seafloor Spreading, page 450.) Other archaea grow in soils and within various living organisms. People have archaea living harmlessly in their digestive systems.

Archaea have developed unusual properties. Some kinds can consume acetic acid, hydrogen, or sulfur. Some archaea can even produce the gas methane.

Pyrolobus fumarii, a member of Domain Archaea, has been found living in deep-sea underwater vents at temperatures of 113°C (235°F).

Eukaryotic Cells

Eukaryotic cells are much larger than prokaryotic cells and far more complex. Single-celled algae and fungi and all protozoa are eukaryotic unicellular organisms. All multicellular organisms, such as plants, animals, and all multicelled fungi and algae, are composed of eukaryotic cells.

Eukaryotic cells have a true membrane-bound nucleus containing the genetic information of the cell in structures called *chromosomes*. Surrounding the nucleus are numerous and varied organelles with a wide range of specialized functions.

EUKARYOTIC
Plant cell

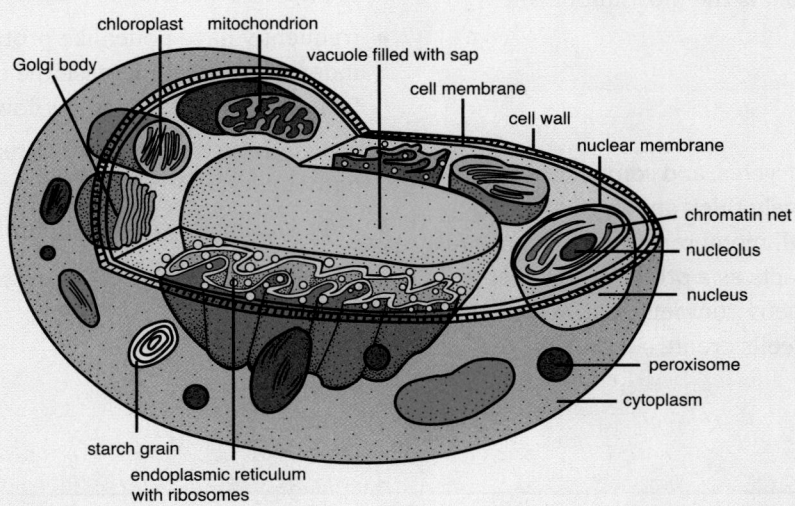

Animal cell

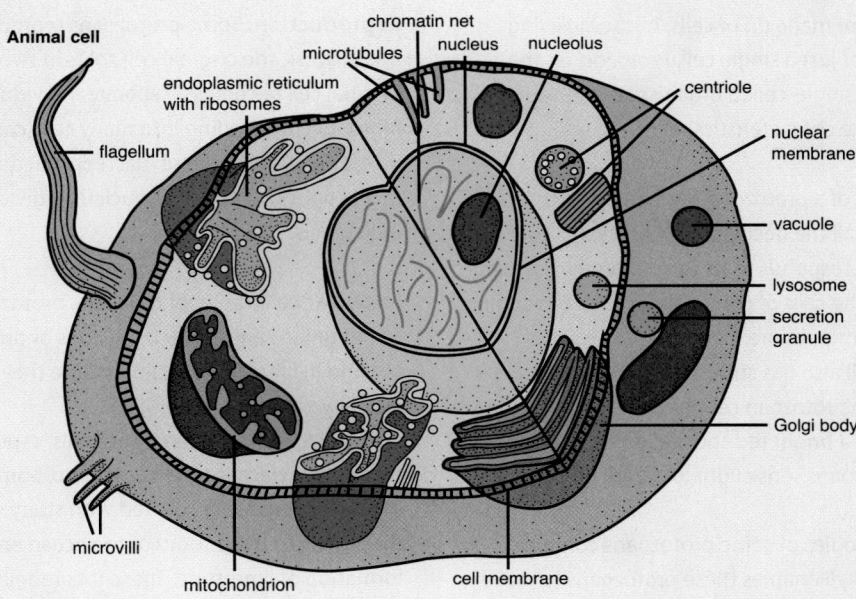

Inside Cells

Cells vary greatly, in size, shape, and in the special jobs they do. But all cells share certain features. All cells have *cytoplasm,* an outer *membrane,* and either a *nucleus* or a less distinct *nuclear region.* Plant cells, most prokaryotes, and some other unicellular organisms have external *cell walls.*

All cells have various kinds of *organelles,* or specialized internal structures, within the outer membrane. Prokaryotes have only a few. In eukaryotic cells, they can be quite numerous. The nucleus, or nuclear region, is the most important of a cell's organelles.

Cell Wall

Plant cells, most prokaryotes, and some unicellular eukaryotes have a relatively thick and rigid cell wall surrounding the outer cell membrane. In unicellular organisms, the cell wall acts as a protective barrier against the surrounding environment. Cell walls around individual plant cells create support for the entire organism.

Plant cell walls are composed mainly of carbohydrates in the form of cellulose. Prokaryotic cell walls are made up primarily of *murein,* an arrangement of sugars and amino acids.

Cell Membrane

Surrounding every cell is a thin, double-layered membrane that gives the cell its structure and determines the substances that can enter and exit. Cell membranes

- are flexible and elastic.
- frequently have pouchlike protrusions and indentations that increase the surface area to facilitate the inflow and outflow of materials.
- are made up mainly of proteins, lipids, and carbohydrates.
- are typically less than a millimicron (one 1,000th of a micron) in thickness.

PLANT OR ANIMAL?

All living things are made up of cells, but some living things are made up of just a single cell. *Protozoan* is the common name for a single-celled organism that may have plantlike or animallike characteristics.

Structure. The body of a protozoan is made up of just one cell, which performs all the necessary life processes by itself. It eats, breathes, and responds to its surroundings. It has the same basic parts as the cells of plants and animals, including the nucleus and cell membrane.

The protozoan cell also has structures not found in plant or animal cells. Some protozoan cells have cell mouths for feeding. Others have a bright red spot called an eyespot. The eyespot helps protozoans sense light and dark but cannot form images.

Like plants, the bodies of some protozoans contain chlorophyll. Chlorophyll enables these protozoans to make their own food through photosynthesis.

Reproduction. Some protozoans reproduce by mitosis. In this process, the original cell splits in two. Each half of the original cell becomes a separate individual. Certain protozoans reproduce by dividing into many cells called *spores.* Other protozoans engage in sexual reproduction. In all these forms of reproduction, the cell's nucleus is divided among the new individuals.

Importance. In spite of their size, protozoans are important to both humans and animals. Millions of protozoans swim in the sea and in lakes and streams, where they help keep the water clean by eating bacteria.

Protozoans are eaten by animals, especially by larval (young) fish and crustaceans such as shrimp. Some protozoans, such as the foraminifera, are covered with stony shells. When they die, they settle to the bottom of the ocean and contribute to the formation of limestone. These fossil shells are partly responsible for the chalk cliffs that are found in southern England.

Nucleus

The largest organelle in a cell is the nucleus. The nucleus controls the life processes of a cell. A cell's nucleus

- is bounded by a porous membrane that allows substances to move between it and the cytoplasm.
- contains the *nucleolus,* a discrete body composed of RNA and protein, which produces the ribosomes that direct protein synthesis in the cell.
- contains *chromosomes,* long, threadlike strands of a substance called *chromatin.*

Some cells have more than one nucleus, and some nuclei have more than one nucleolus.

Cytoplasm

Cytoplasm is all of the cell material between the outer membrane and the nucleus. Most of the cytoplasm consists of water with proteins, carbohydrates, lipids, smaller organic molecules, and inorganic salts and minerals. Contained within the cytoplasm, and considered part of it, are the many and varied discrete organelles that perform many of the vital functions of the cell.

Information about these organelles can be found on the following two pages.

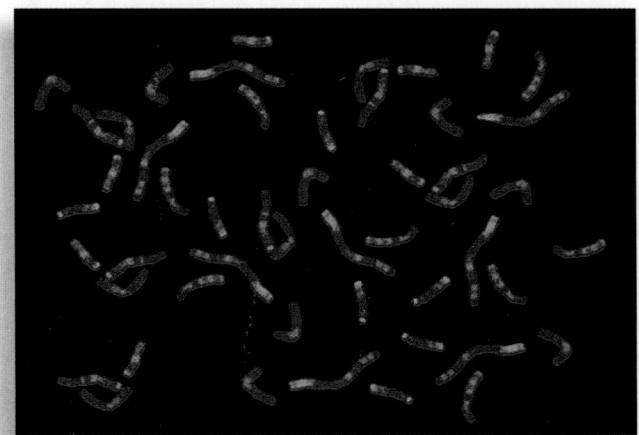

CHROMOSOMES

Chromosomes are long, threadlike strands of chromatin. Chromatin consists of DNA and proteins. DNA makes up the genes, which are the basic units of heredity. Chromosomes, therefore, are responsible for passing the hereditary information of the cell on to the next generation of cells. ▶

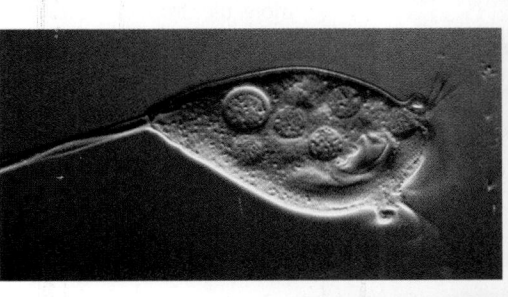

▲ **Ciliates:** Vorticella

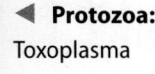

◀ **Protozoa:** Toxoplasma

Single-Celled Life. There are tens of thousands of species of protozoans, most of them so small that they can be seen only through a microscope.

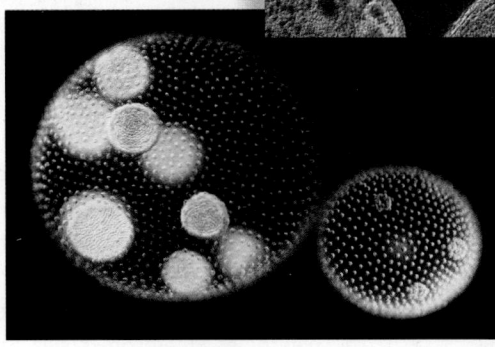

▲ **Green algae** colonies

Sarcodine: Radiolaria ▼

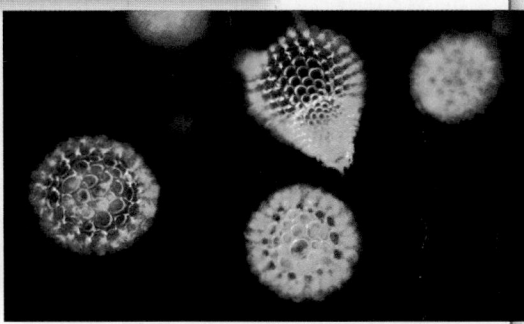

In the Cytoplasm

The organelles contained within the cytoplasm of a cell each have a certain function to perform.

Vacuoles are membrane-bound cavities in the cytoplasm that vary greatly in size. Many plant cells contain one or more large vacuoles; in some, a single large vacuole takes up almost the entire interior space. Plant vacuoles may contain water, stored food, pigments, salts, gases, sugars, and other materials. Substances toxic to the cell may also be safely stored there. Vacuoles in animal cells are generally much smaller than those found in plants. Materials may enter and leave the cell by way of vacuoles.

TYPICAL PLANT CELL

Plastids. Found in most plant cells and in photosynthetic unicellular organisms, plastids are intricate, self-replicating organelles containing their own DNA, RNA, and ribosomes. The most important plastids are *chloroplasts,* where photosynthesis occurs in plants. *Chromoplasts* manufacture and store the pigments that give fruits, vegetables, leaves, and flowers their color. *Leucoplasts* are the sites where fats and proteins are stored and glucose is converted to starch.

Endoplasmic reticulum is an intricate system of membranes that contains flattened tubules and interconnecting channels and winds its way through the cytoplasm. The endoplasmic reticulum acts as a transport system for the distribution of molecules from one part of a cell to another.

Microfilaments, *(not shown)* or *fibrils,* are much thinner than microtubules. They are thought to be composed of fibers of protein and seem to have the ability to contract like muscle. Microfilaments are found in some plant and animal cells and may account for the movement of the cytoplasm and the movement of the cell itself.

Microtubules *(not shown)* are a series of long, thin cylinders that support, stiffen, and give shape to cells. They consist primarily of the protein *tubulin* and are found throughout the cytoplasm. In addition to providing internal structural support for the cell, microtubules are thought to play a role in the sorting out of chromosomes during cell division. They are the basic components of centrioles, kinetosomes, cilia, and flagella.

Mitochondria are the power plants of the cell. They are relatively large, sausage-shaped, fluid-filled sacs scattered throughout the cytoplasm. They provide the cell with its supply of chemical energy in the form of adenosine triphosphate (ATP). A double-layered membrane separates each mitochondrion from the surrounding cytoplasm. Each membrane encapsulates an inner membrane that is highly convoluted to form partitions called *cristae*. The cristae provide a large surface area on which chemical reactions take place.

Lysosomes are small membranous sacs of varying size and shape containing powerful digestive enzymes. These enzymes break down carbohydrate, protein, and fat molecules into simpler substances. Lysosomes can fuse with and digest foreign particles or organisms that invade the cell. For example, it is the lysosomes in white blood cells that fight pathogenic bacteria by digesting it.

TYPICAL ANIMAL CELL

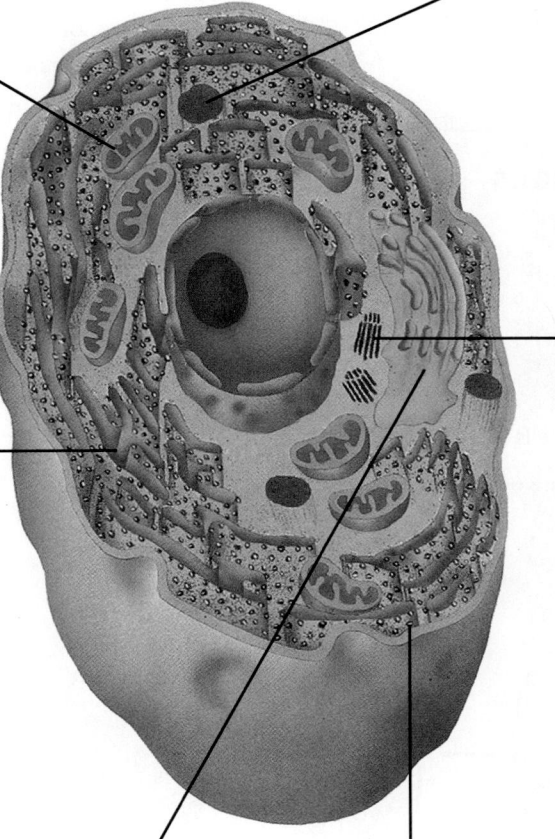

Centrioles are located near the nucleus and found in the cells of animals, most unicellular eukaryotes, fungi, and lower plants. They are a pair of small, rodlike bodies that lie at right angles to each other. The centrioles assist in the distribution of the chromosomes during the process of cell reproduction.

Golgi Apparatus. Located near the nucleus and continuous with the endoplasmic reticulum, the Golgi apparatus is a stacked arrangement of small, flattened membrane-bounded sacs. They synthesize carbohydrates and package proteins in *vesicles,* or membranous sacs, for transport to the surface of the cell, where they are secreted.

Ribosomes. Attached to membranes of the endoplasmic reticulum, ribosomes are the extremely small sites within the cytoplasm where proteins are synthesized. The number of ribosomes in a cell varies with the amount of protein the cell is required to produce. In some cells, there are millions of ribosomes. They attach themselves to messenger RNA from the nucleus and construct proteins from amino acids according to the coded instructions of the messenger RNA.

Cell Functions

Every cell takes the raw materials it needs for life from its outside environment, uses those materials to carry out chemical processes within its interior, and then returns waste products generated by those processes back into the environment.

The cell membrane, the boundary between the cell and its environment, plays a key role in maintaining the harmonious balance required for functioning. The movement of materials into and out of a cell through the cell membrane is accomplished by any of several processes that are either passive or active.

VARIOUS CELL FUNCTIONS

cell growth
reproduction
repair
maintenance
movement
muscle contraction
communication between nerve cells

Passive Processes

Passive processes are influenced by physical laws of nature and require no output of energy from the cell. They include *diffusion* and *osmosis*.

Permeability. Most cell membranes are selectively permeable, that is, they permit some materials to enter readily while denying entry to, or slowing down, others. Whether a molecule can pass through the membrane, or the degree of ease with which it can pass through, is determined by two factors:

- the size of the molecule
- its solubility in lipid, which is the major component of the membrane

Water, oxygen, carbon dioxide, and small ions (such as those of sodium, chlorine, and potassium) move through with relative ease. Small organic monomers (such as glucose and amino acids) pass through more slowly. Large organic polymers (such as fats and proteins) do not enter by means of diffusion.

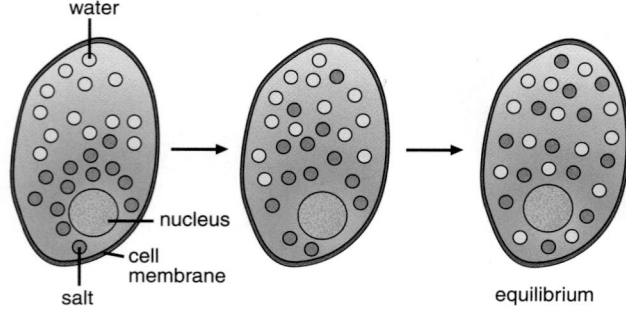

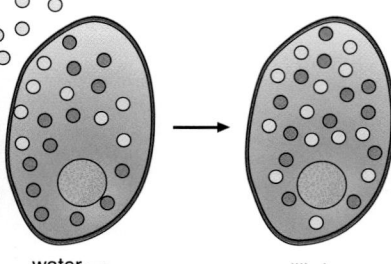

DIFFUSION

Diffusion is the movement of a substance from an area of high concentration to an area of low concentration. Diffusion is a physical process that allows movement within a cell as well as across the membrane of a cell.

As molecules move inside or outside of a cell, they will attempt to pass through the cell membrane if doing so will achieve uniformity of distribution.

OSMOSIS

Osmosis is a form of diffusion in which water or another solvent moves through a semipermeable membrane. The water moves through the membrane from a more dilute solution to a more concentrated solution. The *solutes* in a solution, dissolved or suspended solids, do not pass through the membrane.

Active Processes

Active processes, which do call for the expenditure of energy and the contribution of certain chemical substances by the cell, include *active transport* and two processes called *pinocytosis* and *phagocytosis.*

Active Transport.
Cells do not rely exclusively on the effects of physical laws to regulate the passage of substances into and out of the cytoplasm. Active transport mechanisms, either augmenting or working against the effects of those laws, are constantly occurring as well. This active transport process calls on the cell to supply

- energy
- enzymes
- a carrier molecule

The carrier molecule, using the energy supplied and assisted by the enzyme, binds with the molecule that needs to be transported through the membrane and then carries it in or out by chemically opening the membrane to effect passage.

Energetic Cells

Cells need energy to carry out their functions. They get this energy from a compound called *adenosine triphosphate* (ATP). All cells manufacture ATP.

Manufacturing ATP. Energy is made available to living organisms through the metabolism of carbohydrates, fats, and proteins. Living organisms process and utilize energy through photosynthesis and cellular respiration. (See pages 135–137.)

1. In the cell's cytoplasm, the simple sugars are broken down into pyruvic acid. A small amount of ATP is produced.

2. The amino, fatty, and pyruvic acids enter the mitochondria.

3. Enzymes break down these substances further in a series of chemical reactions that produce carbon dioxide, water, and many molecules of ATP.

4. The ATP molecules leave the mitochondria.

5. The ATP provides energy where it is needed in the cell. As the energy is needed, special enzymes break the ATP phosphate bonds and release the energy.

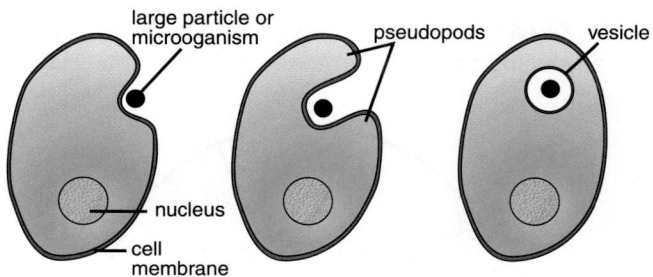

PHAGOCYTOSIS

Cells take in large particles of material using a process called phagocytosis. The cell produces extensions of the cytoplasm that literally reach out and surround the material to be taken in. The particle is engulfed by the cell and enclosed in a pocket, called a vesicle, to be digested. Large particles of material and even entire organisms, such as bacteria, are acquired by cells in this fashion.

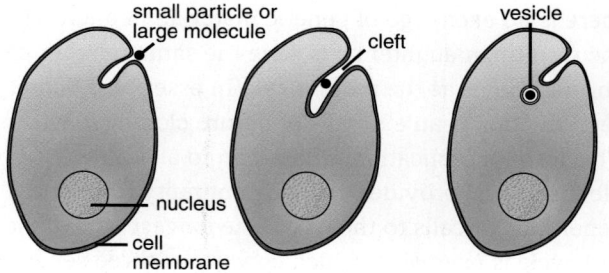

PINOCYTOSIS

Pinocytosis is similar to phagocytosis. In pinocytosis, the cell also engulfs the object to be ingested, but the material is usually a fluid or very small particle. The cell encloses the material in intracellular vesicles. A deep indentation forms in the membrane. When the substance to be taken in enters the indentation, the membrane pinches off to form a bubblelike vesicle with the ingested material inside.

Cell Division

Human beings and other multicellular organisms develop from a single cell. After the cell grows to a certain size, it divides and forms two cells. These two cells remain attached to each other. They grow and divide, forming four cells. The cells grow and divide over and over again, and during this process they begin to specialize. A dog, a fish, a human being, or some other multicellular organism finally develops from the single cell.

Cell division involves two processes. In the first process, called *nuclear division,* the nucleus divides. In the second process, called *cytokinesis,* the cytoplasm divides, and the cell splits in half. There are two types of nuclear division: *mitosis* and *meiosis.*

A CELL SPLITS

New cells are formed by cell division, in which one cell splits to become two cells. Cell division involves two processes. In the first, called nuclear division, the nucleus divides. In the second process, cytokinesis, the cytoplasm divides, producing two cells.

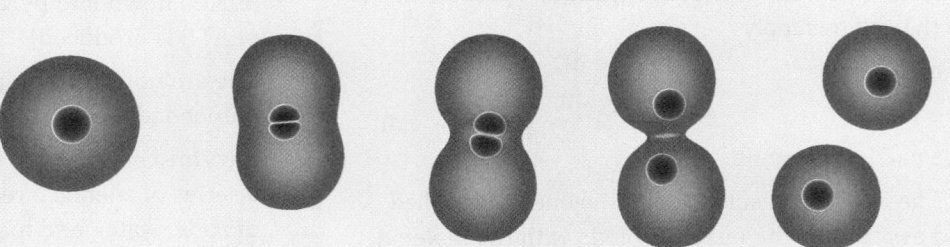

The Cell Cycle

All cells except those producing sex cells follow the cell cycle. It is a form of asexual reproduction, as there is no exchange of genetic material. In addition, the resulting daughter cells have the same number of chromosomes as the mother cell. In essence, asexual reproduction is an example of nature cloning itself. This form of replication is common to all known life forms and provides genetic continuity from one generation of cells to the next. The longest part of the cell cycle is *interphase,* which consists of three separate phases:

1. **G_1 phase:** Cells grow and carry out a various and a specific function; for example, a pancreatic cell produces the hormone insulin.

2. **S phase (synthesis):** Each chromosome or DNA molecule is doubled. The process of doubling cannot be viewed directly. This is because the genetic material is in a noncondensed, amorphous state known as chromatin. Also, the double-stranded chromosomes (two sister chromatids) formed during synthesis do not become visible until mitosis.

3. **G_2 phase:** The cell prepares for division by producing enzymes, proteins, and other materials.

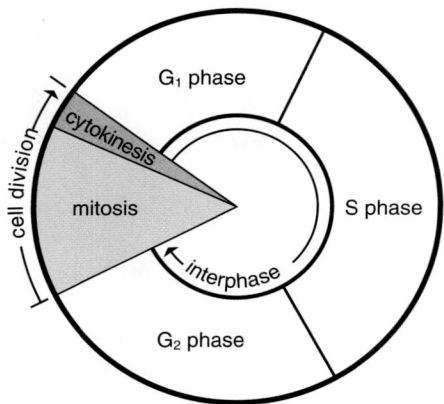

The Cell Cycle. Cells that follow the cell cycle make identical copies of themselves.

Reproduction

Organisms reproduce in one of two ways.

- asexual reproduction
- sexual reproduction

Asexual Reproduction. Organisms that form through asexual reproduction have the same exact DNA structure as their parent, and each daughter organism carries the exact hereditary information that is found in the parent.

Sexual Reproduction. Organisms that form through sexual reproduction receive DNA from two separate parents. These organisms produce specialized cells called *gametes,* or sex cells. A male gamete, called a *sperm,* unites with a female gamete, called an *egg,* to create a new individual. Gametes are produced through a special kind of cell division called *meiosis.*

Each gamete produced contains one-half the number of chromosomes of a normal body cell. This is essential for sexual reproduction, because if sperm cells and egg cells had the same number of chromosomes as normal cells, the chromosome number of a species would double with each generation.

Meiosis produces organisms that are genetically different. *Crossing over,* when chromosome pairs become entangled and exchange sections of DNA, and the random assortment of chromosomes ensure that each daughter cell will be different. Additional genetic mixing will occur at fertilization when the chromosome number is restored. (See pages 238–239.)

TYPES OF ASEXUAL REPRODUCTION

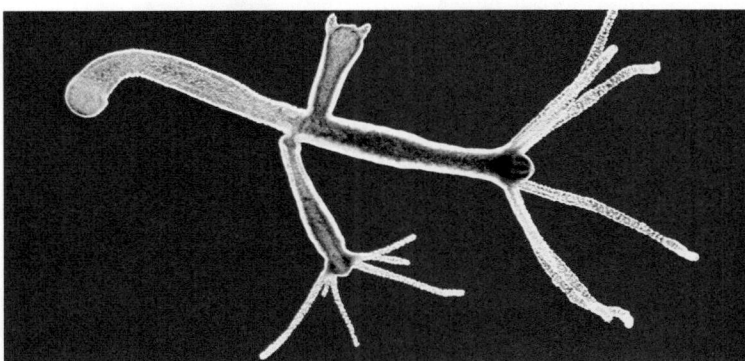

Spores. Many plants, such as this fern, reproduce by spores, which are special cells that grow into new plants when they reach a suitable environment.

Vegetative Reproduction. Both plants and some animals can reproduce "vegetatively." The hydra, a tiny water animal, grows buds that break off to form "daughter" hydras.

Regeneration. Many plants and a few animals, such as the sea star, can reproduce through regeneration. If a sea star is cut into several pieces, each piece may develop into a new sea star.

Mitosis vs. Meiosis

Mitosis

All eukaryotic cells except the sex cells divide through the duplication of the nucleus with its DNA and chromosomes. This process is called mitosis. The time between cell divisions is called *interphase.* Mitosis then takes place in four phases: *prophase, metaphase, anaphase,* and *telophase.*

Interphase. The cell grows and carries out its regular functions. Each cell begins to grow to mature size. Each chromosome duplicates itself to form identical sister chromatids. The DNA is duplicated and proteins are synthesized. The cell becomes ready to divide and interphase ends.

Prophase. The chromosomes condense or coil into short, thick structures. The nuclear membrane breaks down and disappears. The centrioles migrate to opposite regions of the cell, forming two poles. A football-shaped structure, the spindle, made of tubelike fibers, then forms between the poles.

Metaphase. The double-stranded chromosomes migrate to the center of the cell, apparently pushed or pulled along by the spindle fibers.

Anaphase. The sister chromatids separate from each other. Each daughter chromosome, as they are now called, migrates toward opposite poles.

Telophase. The daughter chromosomes are at opposite poles of the spindle, and the spindle starts to break down. The individual chromosomes become thinner and longer. The nuclear membrane re-forms around each set of chromosomes.

Cytokinesis, the division of the cytoplasm, usually begins during telophase. A furrow or groove appears in the membrane of animal cells and a cell plate forms in plant cells. In animal cells, the furrow curves inward until a complete membrane separates the two daughter cells. In plant cells, the plate expands until a wall is formed that separates the two cells. A new interphase then begins in each daughter cell.

Mitosis

Parent Cell

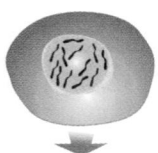

Prophase
Chromatin condenses into chromosomes. Nuclear envelope disappears.

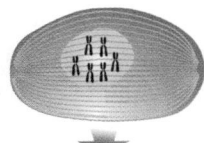

Metaphase
Chromosomes align at the equatorial plate.

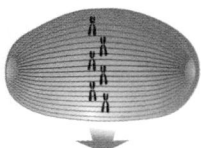

Anaphase
Sister chromatids separate. Centromeres divide.

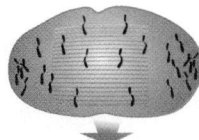

Telophase
Chromatin expands. Cytoplasm divides.

Two identical daughter cells

THE basics

MITOSIS
- All eukaryotic cells except sex cells divide through mitosis.
- The nucleus divides and forms two identical nuclei.
- The cytoplasm usually divides soon after mitosis.
- End result is two daughter cells with identical nuclei.
- Takes place in four stages:
  prophase
  metaphase
  anaphase
  telophase

Meiosis

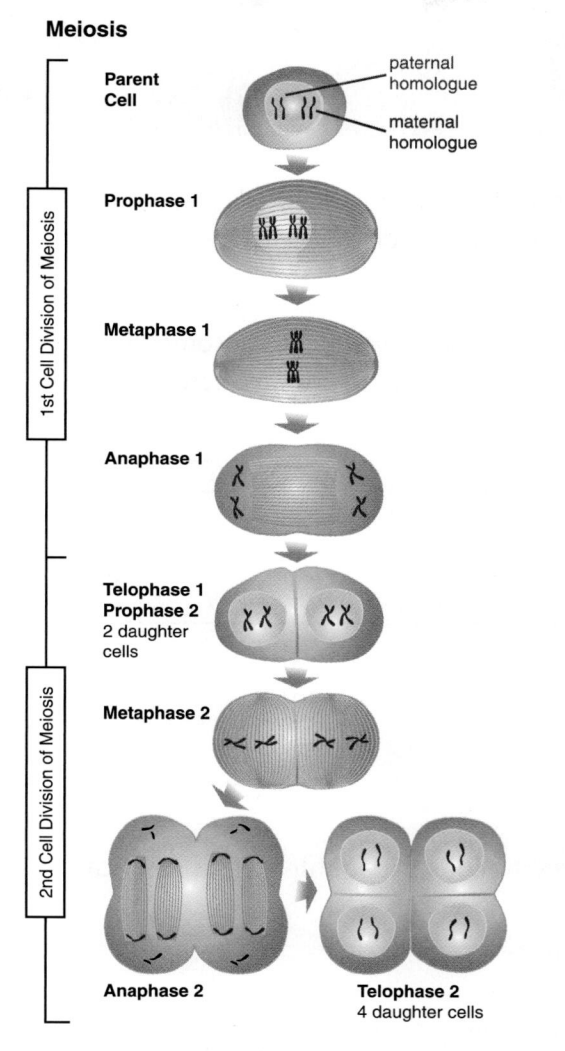

Meiosis

Parent Cell — paternal homologue — maternal homologue

1st Cell Division of Meiosis

Prophase 1

Metaphase 1

Anaphase 1

Telophase 1
Prophase 2
2 daughter cells

2nd Cell Division of Meiosis

Metaphase 2

Anaphase 2

Telophase 2
4 daughter cells

MEIOSIS

- Only sex cells divide through meiosis.
- Sex cells are called gametes.
- The female gamete is the egg and the male gamete is the sperm.
- Consists of two cell divisions that result in four daughter cells.
- Each daughter cell has half the chromosomes of the species.
- Those chromosomes will combine with the chromosomes of another gamete during reproduction.
- Meiosis produces organisms that are genetically different.

Meiosis

Organisms that form through sexual reproduction receive DNA from two separate parents. These organisms produce specialized cells called *gametes,* or sex cells. A male gamete, called a *sperm,* unites with a female gamete, called an *egg,* to create a new individual. Gametes are produced through a special kind of cell division called meiosis.

Meiosis differs from mitosis in a number of ways. In meiosis, there are two cell divisions resulting in four daughter cells. The chromosomes can exchange parts. The chromosomes duplicate only once, even though there are two cell divisions. The chromosomes line up and randomly move to either pole. In this way, each gamete is unique and has one-half the chromosome number of its species. Meiosis occurs in two stages.

First Meiotic Division. Each chromosome has duplicated itself. Each replicated chromosome seeks out its sister. The duplicated chromosomes pair up, forming a four-stranded group called a tetrad. Exchange of genetic material may happen at this time. As tetrads are forming, the nuclear membrane is breaking down and spindle fibers are forming. The tetrads migrate toward the center and line up randomly. Complete chromosomes gather at each pole and the cytoplasm divides either by furrowing or forming a cell plate. Each new cell now has half the chromosome number of its species. Humans, for example, have 46 chromosomes, so each gamete has 23 chromosomes after the first division.

Second Meiotic Division. This phase is very similar to mitosis. Spindle fibers form, the paired chromosomes line up at the center of the cell, and the spindle fiber begins to draw the chromosomes apart. The chromosomes group and migrate together at each pole. The cytoplasm again divides. Four daughter cells have formed, each with half the chromosome number. Usually in male organisms the cytoplasm divides evenly and all four cells function as sperm cells. In females, the cytoplasm divides unequally with one cell receiving the majority of the cytoplasm. This cell becomes the functioning gamete.

Mitosis vs. Meiosis

Mitosis

Parent Cell

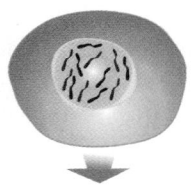

Prophase
Chromatin condenses into chromosomes. Nuclear envelope disappears.

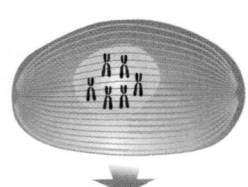

Metaphase
Chromosomes align at the equatorial plate.

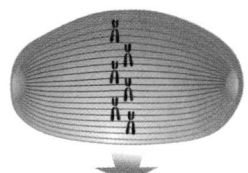

Anaphase
Sister chromatids separate. Centromeres divide.

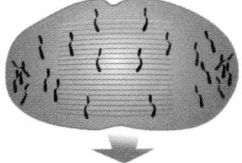

Telophase
Chromatin expands. Cytoplasm divides.

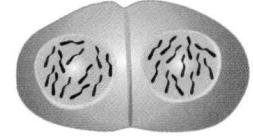

Two identical daughter cells

Mitosis
Produces body (somatic) cells with two sets of chromosomes (diploid cells)
Homologous (paired) chromosomes line up independently at the center (equatorial plate) of the cell.
Occurs in all cells
Uses spindle fibers
Genetic code of daughter cells is identical.
Two daughter cells produced
One nuclear division per cycle
Chromosome pairs are replicated before mitosis.
Products (daughter cells) of mitosis are capable of further division.

Meiosis

Produces sex (sperm and egg) cells with one set of chromosomes (haploid cells)

Homologous chromosomes or tetrads line up together at the equatorial plate.

Occurs only in sex organs or gonads

Uses spindle fibers

Genetic code varies due to crossing over and random assortment of chromosomes.

Four daughter cells produced in males; one daughter cell produced in females

Two nuclear divisions per cycle

Chromosome pairs are replicated before meiosis

Meiotic products are not capable of further meiotic division but may divide again through mitosis.

Meiosis

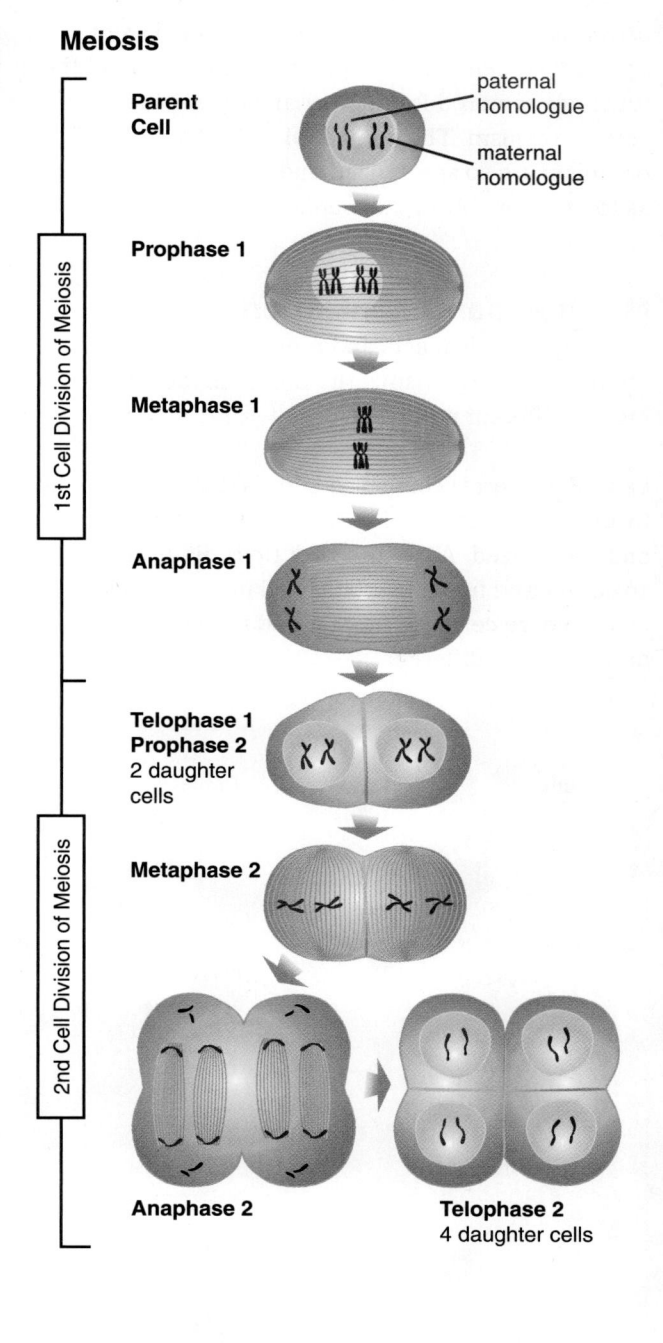

Parent Cell — paternal homologue, maternal homologue

1st Cell Division of Meiosis

Prophase 1

Metaphase 1

Anaphase 1

Telophase 1
Prophase 2
2 daughter cells

2nd Cell Division of Meiosis

Metaphase 2

Anaphase 2

Telophase 2
4 daughter cells

Multicellular Organisms

Most species of animals and plants are *multicellular organisms*. A multicellular organism consists of specialized cells that cooperate to carry out all the functions required for maintenance of the life of the entire organism. The individual cells of a multicellular organism are so specialized and mutually dependent as to be incapable of independent survival outside the organism.

Multicellular Organization

Every organism acts and functions as a unit. In multicellular organisms, the unit is made up of visibly different parts.

Cells. Each part is composed of cells that have different forms and functions. These cells are differentiated and specialized. A cell in a root tip is different in both structure and function from a cell in the surface of a leaf. A nerve cell, muscle cell, and red blood cell in a human are all different.

Tissues. Each cell type is grouped with many others of its type and shares the same life processes. A muscle is composed of thousands of cells, similar in shape and function. A group of cells and the material between the cells is called *tissue*. *Simple tissue* is made up of the same types of cells, while *composite tissue* is made up of two or more types of cells.

Organs. In complex organisms, groups of tissues are combined to form *organs*. An organ is a group of tissues that works together to perform a special function for the benefit of the organism.

Organ Systems. Organs can become interacting parts of an anatomical and physiological system. The human digestive system is a sequence of organs from the mouth through the esophagus, the stomach, and the small and large intestine to the anus. Each organ is different, but each interacts with the others to accomplish the process of digestion.

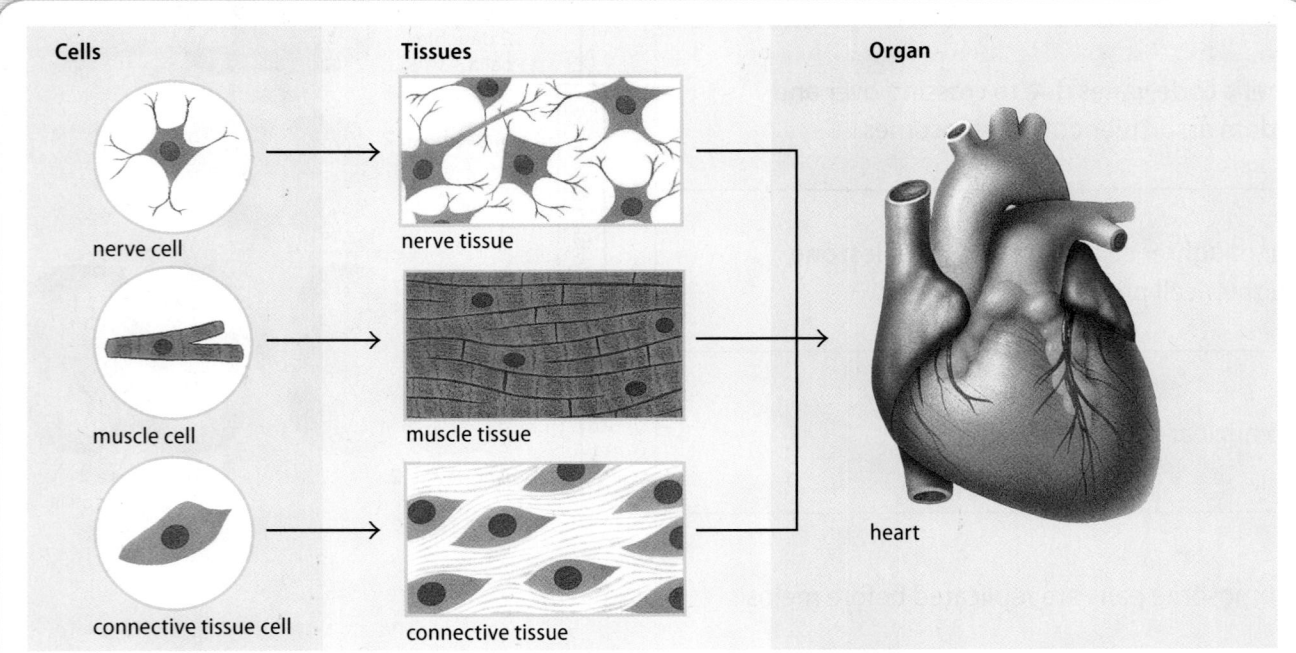

SPECIALIZED CELLS

Multicellular organisms have many specialized kinds of cells. Cells that are similar in structure and function make up a tissue. Tissues, in turn, are grouped together and form organs, which are the basic structural and functional units of higher plants and animals.

Organ Systems

Complex multicellular animals such as humans and other mammals have 10 organ systems. (See Human Anatomy, pages 224–257.)

1. Integumentary system encloses or covers the animal. Hair, skin, nails, scales, feathers, and hooves are parts of the integumentary system.

2. Skeletal system provides support, protection, and help in movement.

3. Muscular system provides for movement of the animal and its internal organs.

4. Respiratory system moves gases in and out of the organisms.

5. Excretory system eliminates the liquid wastes from the body. A kidney is a key organ in this system.

6. Nervous system receives stimuli from the environment and causes organs to respond.

7. Endocrine system through its hormones, regulates and controls the growth, development, and functions of the organism.

8. Digestive system changes food into a form that can be used by the individual cells.

9. Circulatory system moves food, hormones, and other materials throughout the body.

10. Reproductive system produces gametes to continue the species of organism.

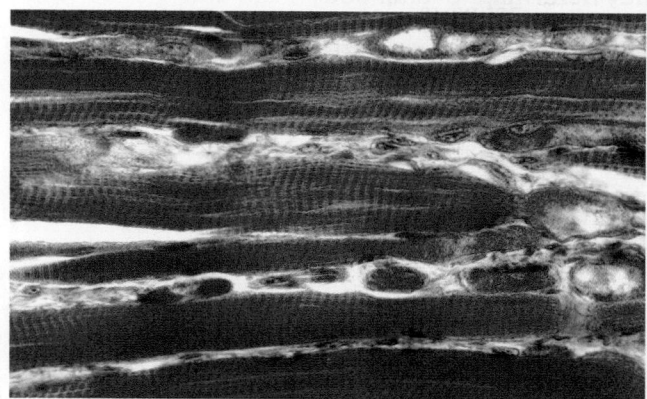

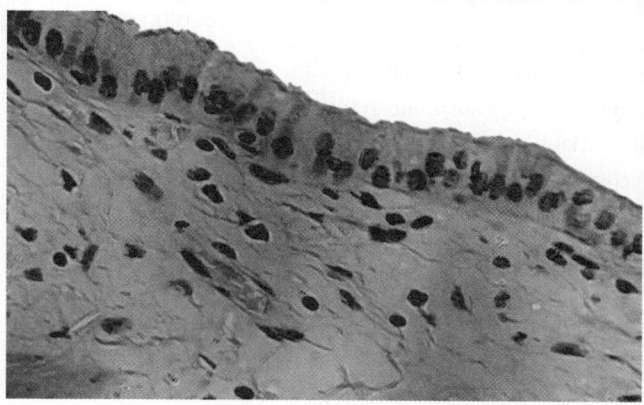

Specialized Tissue. Some examples of the range of cell diversity are shown in these microphotographs of animal tissue. *Top,* compact bone, spongy bone, and viable blood vessels. *Middle,* skeletal muscle. *Bottom,* simple columnar epithelium.

FROM ONE CELL TO MANY

Until about 600 million years ago, single-celled organisms were the only life forms on Earth. Some unicellular organisms began to live together in colonies. They became partially dependent on one another and eventually some cells acquired a special talent for performing certain specialized tasks, such as obtaining food, locomotion, and reproduction.

As more cells became more specialized, their dependence on other cells increased, as did the efficiency of the entire group in dealing with the environment. It is not hard to imagine how the success of such a colony might have led to the development of what we now define as a multicellular organism.

ORGANIZATION OF MULTICELLULAR ORGANISMS

cells ⟶ tissues ⟶ organs ⟶ organ systems

GENETICS is the scientific study of *heredity*, the passing on of characteristics of living organisms from one generation to the next. Geneticists investigate the structure, function, and transmission of *genes*. Genes are the basic units of heredity and are present in the cells of all organisms. For example, each of the cells in the human body has about 20,000 to 30,000 genes. They determine overall body build and such traits as eye, hair, and skin color.

Heredity

Heredity is the passing on of biological characteristics from one generation to the next. The process of heredity occurs among all living things—animals, plants, and even microscopic organisms. Heredity explains why a human mother always has a human baby and why a mother dog has puppies—not kittens. It is also the reason offspring look like their parents.

Through heredity, living things inherit *traits*, or characteristics, from their parents. You resemble your parents because you inherited your hair color, nose shape, and other traits from them.

Genes

Tiny biochemical units called *genes* inside each cell carry traits from one generation to the next. Genes are made of a chemical called *DNA (deoxyribonucleic acid)*. They are found in long chains of DNA in structures known as *chromosomes*. (See pages 48–49.)

Genes exist inside every cell of all living things. They are found in the cell's nucleus, on chromosomes, which are made up of long chains of DNA and certain proteins. Each cell contains tens of thousands of genes.

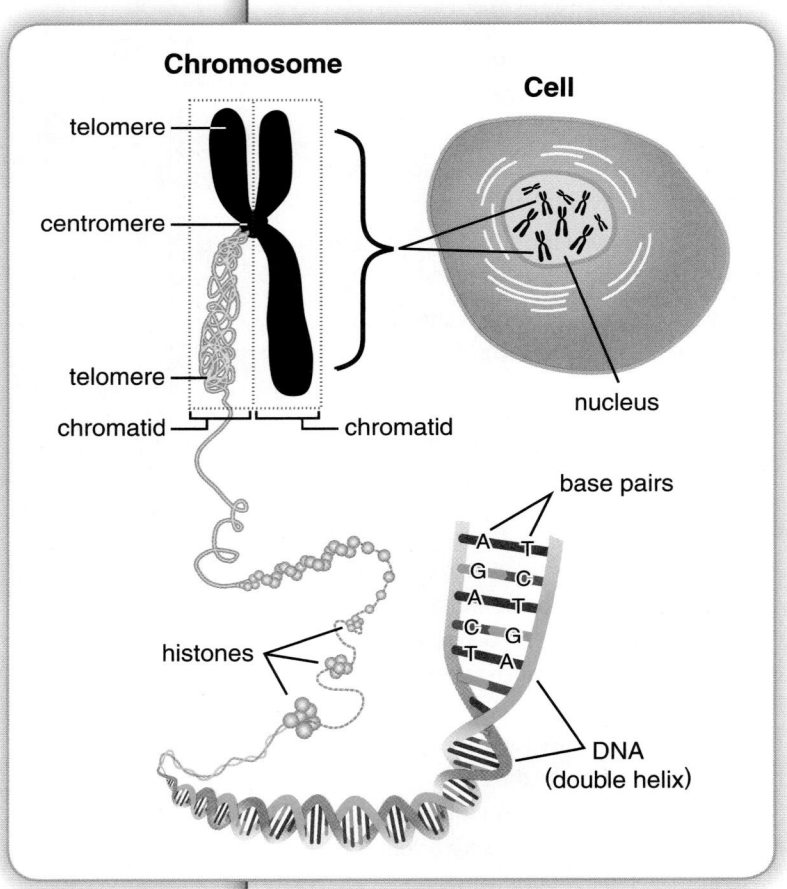

Chromosome

telomere

centromere

telomere

chromatid — chromatid

Cell

nucleus

base pairs

histones

DNA (double helix)

THE basics

THE BASICS: GENES

✔ Similar to blueprints for building a house, genes carry the plans for building cells, tissues, organs, and bodies.

✔ Genes have the instructions for making the thousands of chemical building blocks in the body. These building blocks are called *proteins*.

✔ Some proteins are responsible for the size, shape, and structure of the parts making up your body.

✔ Other proteins, known as *enzymes,* make possible the thousands of chemical reactions that occur constantly in all living things.

✔ *Gene expression* is the process by which the cell makes a protein according to the instructions carried by a gene.

Genes and the Environment

A gene gives the potential for the development of a trait. How this potential is achieved depends on the interaction of the gene with other genes. But it also depends partly on the environment. In fact, most characteristics result from a combination of heredity and environment.

For example, a person may have a genetic tendency toward being overweight. But the person's actual weight will depend on such environmental factors as how much and what kinds of food the person eats. Or, you may have inherited a talent for playing the piano. But you will not be able to play unless you take lessons and practice. The talent is hereditary. The lessons and practice are environmental.

GENETICS TIME LINE

1865–1869	1941–1948	1950–1953	1997–2003
1865 Gregor Mendel, **Discovery** Described and explained inheritance of dominant-recessive traits (factors) from parent to offspring in the common garden pea	**1941** Beadle and Tatum **Discovery** One gene–one polypeptide hypothesis	**1950** Erwin Chargaff **Discovery** Sequence of nitrogen bases varies widely, but certain bases are always in 1:1 ratio.	**1997** Ian Wilmut/Roslin Institute **Discovery** Reproductive cloning of an adult sheep
1869 Friedrich Miescher **Discovery** Nucleic acids are composed of a simple sugar, phosphate, and nitrogen-containing bases.	**1943** Oswald Avery **Discovery** DNA carries the genetic information. **1948** Linus Pauling **Discovery** Many proteins are helical in shape.	**1952** Rosalind Franklin and Maurice Wilkins **Discovery** Used X-ray crystallography to elucidate the helical structure of DNA **1953** James Watson and Francis Crick **Discovery** Described the double-stranded, helical nature of DNA, bonded together by complementary base pairs	**2003** International group of scientists **Discovery** Completion of Human Genome Project— described and located 20,000+ genes in human chromosomes

Chromosomes and DNA

In most organisms, chromosomes are found in a cell's nucleus. Chromosomes are tiny, threadlike structures made largely of DNA and proteins. Chromosomes generally occur in pairs. The two chromosomes in a pair resemble each other in size and shape. They also contain similar hereditary information.

Each species of animal and plant has a characteristic number of chromosomes in its body cells. Body cells, often called *somatic cells*, are the cells that make up such body parts as muscles and bones. Human beings typically have 46 chromosomes, arranged in 23 pairs, in their body cells. Dogs have 78 (39 pairs), and corn has 20 (10 pairs). The fruit fly *Drosophila melanogaster*, which is widely used in genetic research, has only 8 chromosomes (4 pairs).

Genes are the basic units of heredity. Each gene consists of a section of an extremely long DNA molecule found in a chromosome.

DNA

DNA, often referred to as the genetic code, contains most of the information needed to make new cells. For each chromosome pair, one chromosome originates from the maternal side of the family, the other from the paternal side. Each chromosome contains one DNA molecule wrapped around protein spheres called *histones*. Nucleotides within the DNA combine to make up the various genes that code for specific amino acids, the building blocks of protein. A gene provides the blueprint, or plan, for a specific job or function in the cell. Scientists estimate that human beings have 20,000 to 30,000 different genes. A set of all the genes a species has in its chromosomes is called its *genome*.

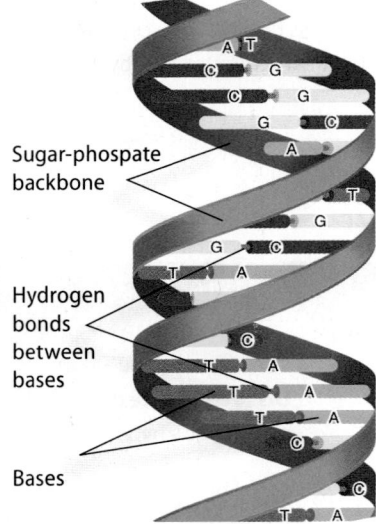

Sugar-phospate backbone

Hydrogen bonds between bases

Bases

DNA is a double-stranded macromolecule, located in the nucleus of eukaryotic (plant and animal) cells and in the organelles, mitochondria, and chloroplasts.

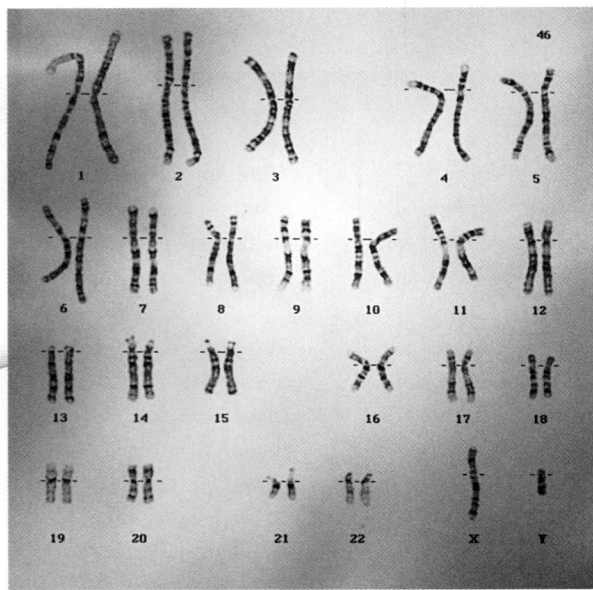

Karyotyping. A karyotype is a microphoto of chromosomes organized according to shape and size. A characteristic karyotype exists for every species. Normal human male (*above*) and female (*right*) karyotypes show 46 chromosomes, the diploid number for humans. There are 22 homologous pairs, called autosomes. The remaining pair are sex chromosomes.

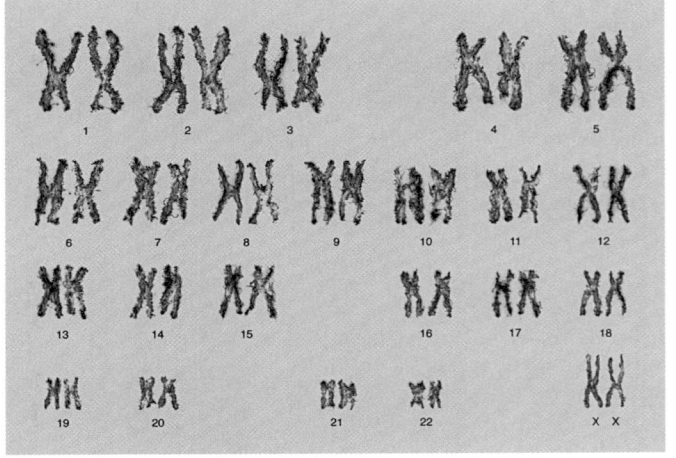

The Structure of DNA

DNA is a thin, chainlike molecule made up of smaller chemical units called *nucleotides*. Each nucleotide is composed of

- a pentose sugar called *deoxyribose*.
- an oxygen-phosphorus chemical group called a *phosphate*.
- one nitrogen-containing base.

The sugar and phosphate are the same in all DNA nucleotides, but the bases vary. There are four DNA bases.

- two purine bases: *adenine* and *guanine*
- two pyrimidine bases: *thymine* and *cytosine*

In DNA, adenine bonds to thymine and guanine to cytosine. The four bases are universal—they are present in the DNA of all living things, as well as in viruses.

The nitrogenous base pairs are the "rungs" of the twisted DNA ladder. A deoxyribose sugar is attached to each end of a base pair, along with a phosphate on either side of the sugar. These last two components contribute to the "uprights" of the ladder.

DNA replicates itself during the S phase of the cell cycle in what is described as semiconservative replication, which is to say that one-half of the original DNA molecule ends up in each resulting daughter cell.

MUTATIONS

Sometimes bases are mismatched during DNA replication. Repair mechanisms within the cell correct most of these errors. Mistakes that remain in the base sequence are known as *mutations*.

Not all mutations are harmful to the organism or species. Some changes in code may be beneficial because they provide for a new variation or adaptation. In times of environmental change, natural selection may favor this new trait because it helps the species survive and evolve. (See page 38.)

DNA REPLICATION

DNA replication requires the following basic components:

- the original DNA molecule
- free nucleotides of the four bases (adenine, thymine, guanine, and cytosine)
- DNA polymerases (enzymes that catalyze DNA synthesis) and other enzymes
- ATP (cellular energy necessary for forming chemical bonds)

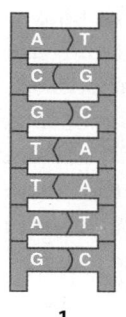

1

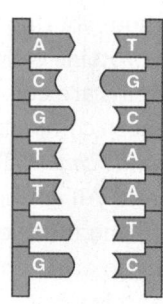

2

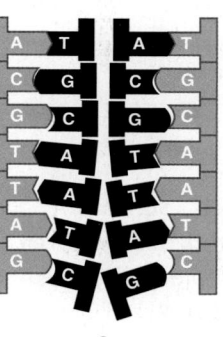

3

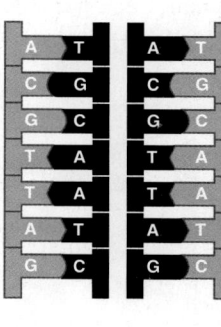

4

DNA replication occurs as follows:

1. DNA uncoils.

2. The DNA molecule chemically unzips (bonds between complementary base pairs are broken) using the enzyme helicase, resulting in two single strands. SSBs (single-stranded binding proteins) keep the separated strands from rebonding.

3. With the use of nucleoside triphosphates and DNA polymerases, free nucleotides are attached to complementary bases on each single strand.

4. Two identical DNA molecules result. The newly formed double-stranded chromosomes re-coil.

Producing Protein

A section of DNA that codes for a particular trait is known as a *gene.* Genes determine the traits of an organism by directing the production of proteins.

All living things contain proteins. The structures of a cell are built largely of proteins. The proteins called *enzymes* speed up the chemical reactions of life. They help digest your food, help produce energy, and assist in building other proteins. A single cell may contain hundreds of different kinds of enzymes. Many *hormones,* the substances that regulate chemical activities throughout your body, are proteins. The body also makes proteins called *antibodies* to fight disease germs.

Proteins are complex, three-dimensional substances composed of one or more long, folded *polypeptide chains.* These chains consist of amino acid units. All amino acids contain carbon, hydrogen, oxygen, and nitrogen, and some also contain sulfur. The amino acids link together in a line to form polypeptide chains. (See page 260.)

DNA contains blueprints for all the proteins made in a cell. Each gene contains a blueprint for a specific polypeptide.

TWO STEPS TO MAKE PROTEINS

Protein synthesis is divided into two processes.

Transcription (takes place within the nucleus)

- A gene uncoils and unzips.
- Free RNA nucleotides bond to complementary bases on the active DNA template.
- Single-stranded messenger RNA (mRNA) is produced.

Translation (takes place within the cytoplasm)

- mRNA moves through the nuclear pores to the cytoplasm.
- mRNA temporarily bonds to complementary transfer RNA (tRNA) at the ribosome.
- Individual amino acids are bonded together according to base sequence in gene.
- Specific polypeptide is produced for use by the organism.

Protein Synthesis

Most protein synthesis takes place during the G_1 phase of the cell cycle. Making protein requires additional substances, including two new nucleic acids, *mRNA* and *tRNA*. RNA is different from DNA—RNA does not contain thymine. Instead, adenine bonds to a base known as *uracil.*

mRNA

- messenger RNA
- a single-stranded nucleic acid transcribed from DNA
- consists of a coding segment of three nucleotides referred to as the *codon*
- since there are four bases in DNA, there are 64 possible combinations of bases for the codons
- different codons code for the same amino acid
- for each gene, there is an initiator codon and a stop codon

tRNA

- transfer RNA
- a cloverleaf shape, responsible for carrying specific amino acids to the ribosome, the site of protein synthesis
- referred to as the *anticodon*

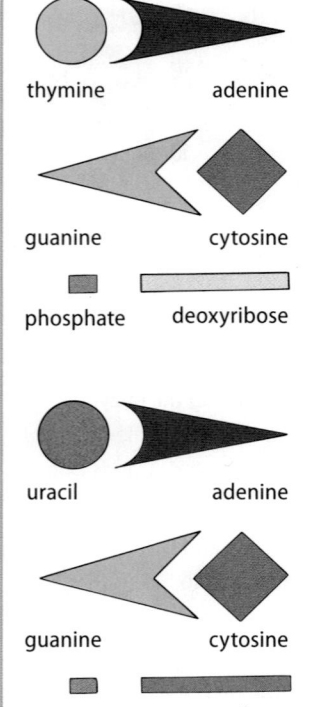

◀ **DNA's Six Parts.** A DNA molecule consists of *phosphate,* a sugar called *deoxyribose,* and four bases—*adenine, cytosine, guanine*, and *thymine.*

thymine | adenine
guanine | cytosine
phosphate | deoxyribose

◀ **RNA's Six Parts.** RNA differs from DNA in two chief ways. The sugar in RNA is *ribose,* and RNA contains *uracil* instead of thymine.

uracil | adenine
guanine | cytosine
phosphate | ribose

PRODUCING PROTEINS

The proteins a cell produces determine the cell's form and function. Proteins are made up of tiny units called amino acids. DNA contains the blueprints for all the proteins made in a cell. These blueprints direct the order in which the amino acids will be linked together to form particular proteins.

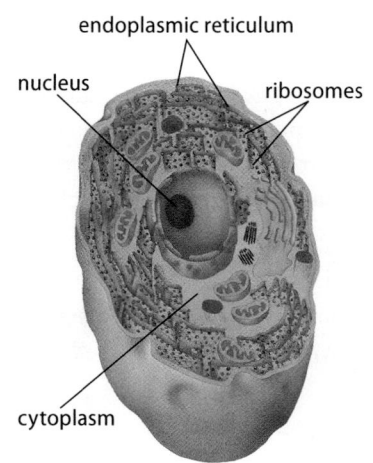

endoplasmic reticulum

nucleus

ribosomes

cytoplasm

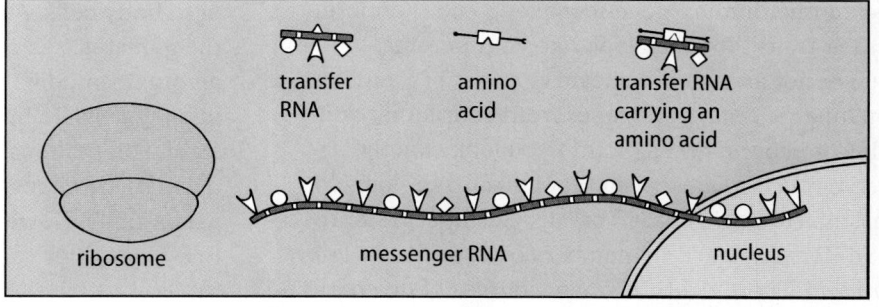

transfer RNA

amino acid

transfer RNA carrying an amino acid

ribosome

messenger RNA

nucleus

When a protein is to be made, an RNA copy of the DNA blueprint for that protein is made in the nucleus. This mRNA then goes to a ribosome, a tiny body on the surface of the endoplasmic reticulum in the cytoplasm. The mRNA lines up amino acids in the proper order. Another type of RNA—tRNA—collects amino acids in the cytoplasm.

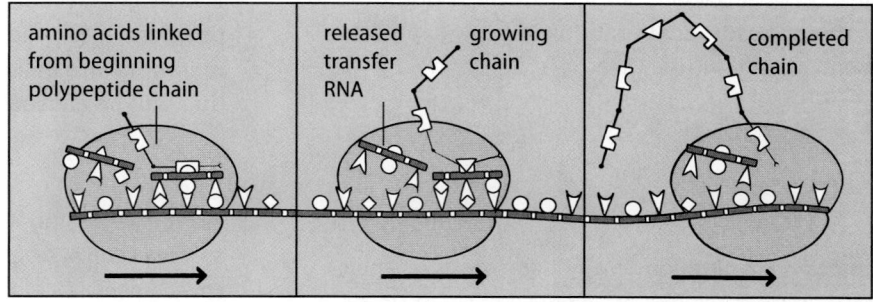

amino acids linked from beginning polypeptide chain

released transfer RNA

growing chain

completed chain

The ribosome moves along the mRNA. The tRNA, carrying amino acids, lines up with the mRNA in the ribosome. The amino acids link together, and the tRNA is released, *left*. As the ribosome moves down the mRNA, a polypeptide chain forms, *center*. The final segment of mRNA, *right,* signals that the chain is complete.

HOW DOES THAT WORK ?

RNA IS FORMED

Messenger RNA is a copy of the DNA blueprint for the polypeptide chain of the protein to be produced. mRNA forms in three steps:

1. First, the DNA splits lengthwise between its bases. Half the ladder serves as a mold to form mRNA. Free RNA bases, with their attached sugars and phosphates, match up with the exposed DNA bases. A strand of mRNA thus begins to form.

2. As mRNA forms, it becomes a reverse copy of the DNA blueprint and begins to peel off the DNA mold. As it breaks away, bases of the DNA ladder start to rejoin.

3. The completed mRNA leaves the nucleus and goes to the ribosomes. It will serve as a mold on which amino acids will be linked into a protein chain.

Genetic Variation

Individual members of a species differ widely from one another in their genetic makeup and therefore in their traits. You may look like your parents, but you are not an exact duplicate of either of them. You inherited half your genes from your father and half from your mother. Nor do you look exactly like your classmates, even though you and your classmates are all human beings. Scientists refer to the differences among members of a species as *genetic variation*. There are three main sources of diversity among individual members of a species—*mutation, independent assortment,* and *genetic recombination*.

Mutations

A mutation is a permanent change in the amount, structure, or sequence of the DNA in an organism's cells. It can result in alterations in gene expression that can change traits. (See page 38.)

Types of Mutations. Mutations can occur in sex cells or in body cells. A *germinal mutation* affects the DNA in the gametes (sex cells) and is therefore passed on from an organism to its offspring. A *somatic mutation* occurs in body cells. In human beings and other animals, somatic mutations do not affect the gametes. Consequently, the changes are not inherited by succeeding generations. However, the changes are passed along to the daughter cells of the original mutant cell.

Causes of Mutations. Scientists do not know what causes most mutations, even though these changes occur at known rates. Some mutations are caused by such agents as ultraviolet light, X-rays, and certain chemicals. Others are caused by transposable elements—certain segments of DNA that can change position within the chromosomes. Agents that cause mutations are called *mutagens*. The type of mutation that will be caused by a mutagen cannot be predicted.

MUTATIONS

Chromosomal mutations: Many mutations affect entire chromosomes. In some cases, an organism has too many or too few chromosomes. Down syndrome is a chromosomal disorder of autosomes in which the individual has an extra chromosome 21. In this case, meiosis has failed to take place properly, a phenomenon known as nondisjunction, or trisomy. The Down syndrome individual has three copies of chromosome 21, with a total of 47 chromosomes in each body cell. Sometimes the structure of a chromosome is abnormal. For example, a mutation called translocation occurs when part of one chromosome breaks off and attaches to another.

Gene mutations: Gene mutations, or point mutations as they are sometimes called, are caused by a change at the base level within the DNA. Often, there may be but one base difference between the normal form of a gene and the mutant gene. A base may be substituted, deleted, or added to the code of a particular gene. This single base difference may have a significant impact on the subsequent protein for which it codes, as a change in the base sequence can alter the triplet coding for the amino acid.

Multifactorial mutations: In multifactorial disorders, there is an interaction of several genes in addition to the added effect of environmental factors.

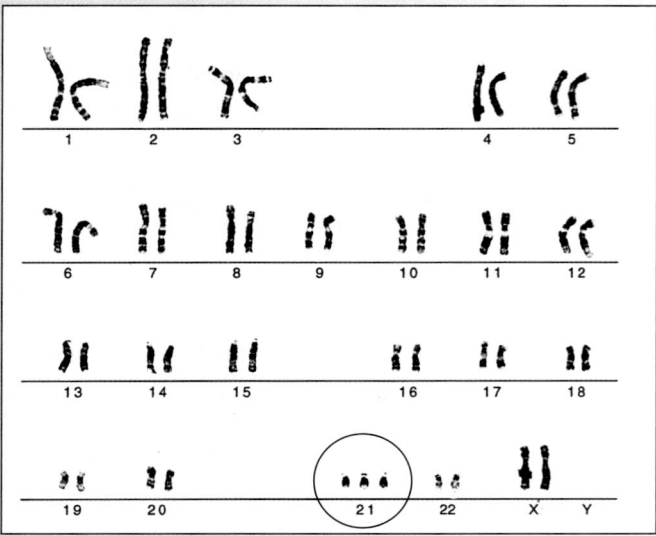

Chromosome 21 appears three times in a person with Down syndrome, resulting in 47 chromosomes in each body cell.

GENE MUTATION: SICKLE CELL ANEMIA

- an inherited blood disorder found on chromosome 11
- abnormal hemoglobin—the oxygen-carrying molecule found in red blood cells
- hemoglobin abnormality due to a substitution of one nucleotide—adenine to thymine
- results in a change of one amino acid out of 146, altering hemoglobin's structure
- red blood cells containing the mutant hemoglobin are sickle-shaped
- may block flow of blood through capillaries
- blockages cause recurrent episodes of pain
- red blood cells live only 10 to 20 days instead of the normal 120 days
- insufficient number of red blood cells; decreased oxygen-carrying capacity

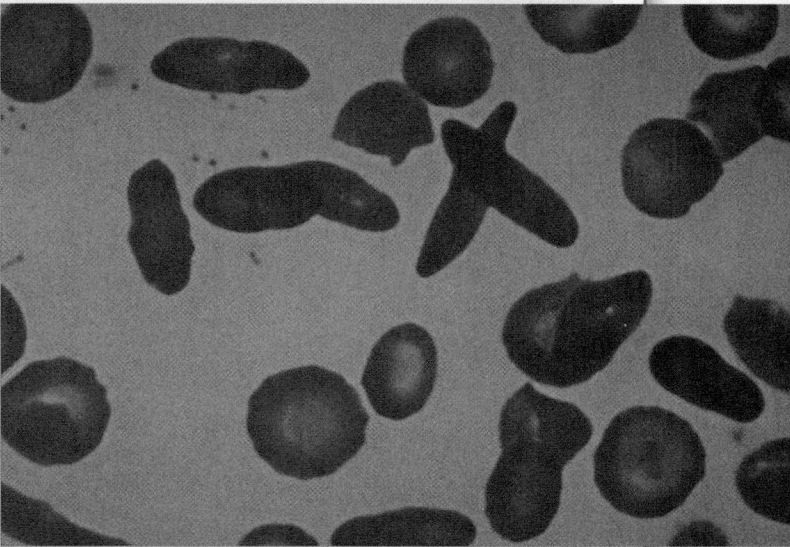

Red blood cells in an individual who has sickle cell anemia.

Independent Assortment

The Law of Independent Assortment states that chromosomes and their genes are distributed when a sex cell divides to form eggs or sperm.

- An immature sex cell contains two of each chromosome—one from the individual's father and one from the mother.
- During meiosis, each pair of chromosomes separates, and each egg or sperm receives one chromosome from each pair.
- The chromosomes separate in a random manner, so each egg or sperm receives some chromosomes from the individual's mother and some from the father.
- This reshuffling of chromosomes and genes can result in new combinations of traits in offspring.

Genetic Recombination

Genetic recombination is the exchange of genes between two partner chromosomes. Genes on separate chromosomes are inherited in a random and independent manner. But genes located close to each other on the same chromosome are generally inherited together. In other words, genes that are closely linked on a parent's chromosome largely remain linked in offspring.

Sometimes, however, linked genes are not inherited together. This situation arises because of *crossing over*. Just before immature sex cells divide to form sperm or eggs, each chromosome of a pair lines up side by side with its partner chromosome. During a crossing-over event, groups of genes from one chromosome change places with groups of genes from its partner chromosome. As a result, different sperm or eggs may carry different combinations of linked genes.

Classical Genetics

Today genetics research is usually done at the molecular level. But classical genetics, based on the work of Gregor Mendel, a 19th-century Austrian monk, remains the foundation for all areas of genetics study.

Classical genetics is concerned with the ways in which genetic traits are transmitted over generations in plants and animals. In the 1800s, Mendel proved that hereditary traits are transmitted by pairs of distinct units, later called *genes*, which reshuffle, segregate, and redistribute, rather than blend, in offspring.

Mendel's Experiments

Mendel used garden peas in his experiments because they hybridize easily. When a purebred tall plant was crossed with a purebred short plant, all hybrid offspring were tall, no matter which type was the mother and which the father.

The hybrids self-fertilized. Mendel counted the offspring and found 787 tall plants and 277 short plants, a ratio of about three to one. When the short plants self-fertilized, they produced only short offspring, but when the tall plants self-fertilized, there were two types of offspring: one-third had only tall offspring, and two-thirds produced both tall and short in a ratio of three to one.

Mendel found the results to be approximately the same when he crossed six other characteristics.

- round and wrinkled peas
- colored and uncolored flowers
- yellow and green peas

Spotlight on... GREGOR JOHANN MENDEL

1822–1884

Gregor Johann Mendel was an Austrian botanist and monk who formulated the basic laws of heredity; he

- used the gardens of the abbey to pursue his passion for studying nature
- performed his heredity experiments on the common garden pea
- controlled the fertilization of the pea plants by manipulating the reproductive structures of the plant's flower
- classified traits as dominant or recessive
- formulated the Law of Segregation and the Law of Independent Assortment
- discovered how organisms transfer traits from parent to offspring

Mendel's peas were self-pollinating—they had both male and female reproductive parts. Mendel removed the stamens from the flowers so that he could control the fertilization.

MENDEL'S EXPERIMENTS ON HEREDITY

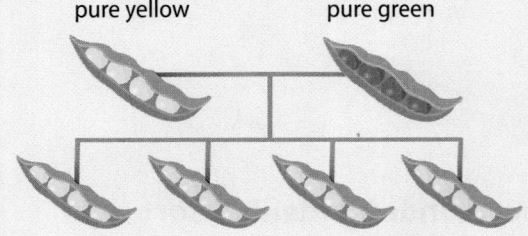

pure yellow   pure green

first generation (hybrid yellow)

Mendel first experimented with purebred strains of pea plants—one with yellow seeds and one with green. He crossed these strains, and all the resulting hybrid seeds were yellow. He concluded that yellow seed color was the dominant trait.

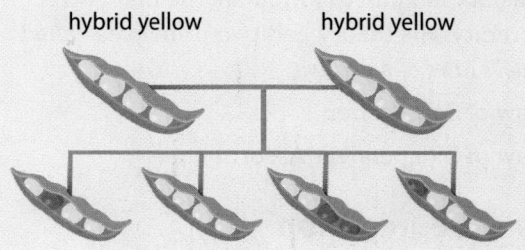

hybrid yellow   hybrid yellow

second generation

Plants grown from the hybrid yellow seeds produced yellow and green seeds in a ratio of about three to one. The inheritance patterns Mendel discovered in this experiment and similar ones led him to formulate the first correct theory of heredity.

Dominant and Recessive Genes

Most genes occur in pairs. Each pair of genes is contained in a pair of matching chromosomes, with one copy of a gene in each chromosome. Some hereditary traits are determined by a single pair of genes. But many other traits, called *polygenic traits*, are influenced by a number of pairs of genes. Tens or hundreds of pairs of genes are involved in the inheritance of such traits as height, weight, and intelligence.

The two genes in a pair may differ in the effects they produce. Different forms of the same gene are called *alleles*. Some alleles are *dominant*, and others are *recessive*. A dominant allele masks the effects of its recessive partner. In other words, the dominant allele is expressed, and the recessive allele is not.

How Traits Are Expressed. A trait that results from a recessive allele is evident only in an individual that has two recessive alleles for that trait. For example

- Mendel showed that in pea plants the allele that produces violet flowers (symbolized by V) is dominant over the one that causes white flowers (v).

- pea plants that have two dominant alleles for violet flowers (VV) or one allele for violet flowers and one for white flowers (Vv) will have violet flowers.

- only those with two recessive alleles (vv) will have white flowers.

THE basics

GENOTYPE VS. PHENOTYPE

- **Genotype:** the underlying genetic makeup of a trait.

- **Phenotype:** the way the trait is expressed—the actual appearance of the trait.

- For example, in the diagram on the following page, the phenotype of both the pure yellow and the hybrid yellow peas is the same—yellow. But the genotype is different—YY for the pure yellow peas, and Yy for the hybrid yellow peas.

Mendel's Laws

Mendel's studies of pea plants in the garden of his monastery led him to formulate the first correct theory of heredity. His theory had two principles called *Mendel's laws of heredity.*

- Law of Segregation
- Law of Independent Assortment

Law of Segregation

Mendel's first law, the *Law of Segregation,* has three parts:

1. Hereditary characteristics are determined by separate units (now called genes).

2. These units occur in pairs.

3. The genes in a pair *segregate,* or separate, during the division of *gametes,* or sex cells. Each sperm or egg is *haploid,* meaning it receives only one member of the pair. Once the gametes unite to form the *zygote,* or fertilized egg, the zygote is called *diploid,* or double.

Law of Independent Assortment

Mendel's second law is called the *Law of Independent Assortment.* It states that each pair of genes behaves independently of all other pairs in the production of sex cells. Therefore, each gene pair is inherited independently of all other genes.

Geneticists now know that independent assortment applies only to genes that are on different chromosomes or far apart on the same chromosome. Genes that are linked, or near each other on the same chromosome, tend to be inherited together.

LAW OF SEGREGATION

Parental Generation (P)

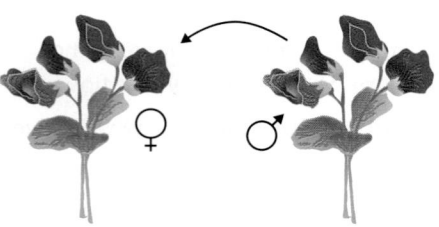

Phenotype: yellow seeds   green seeds
Genotype: YY   yy

First Filial Generation (F₁)

Phenotype: yellow seeds (for all seeds)
Genotype: Yy (for all seeds)

Second Filial Generation (F₂)

Phenotype: ¾ yellow seeds   ¼ green seeds
Genotype: ¾ Yy   ¼ yy

Each true-breeding parent plant carries a pair of identical alleles. The yellow seed allele is dominant (YY). The green seed allele is recessive (yy). The allele pairs separate when sex cells form. Each sex cell contains a single Y or a single y allele.

The offspring receive one allele from each parent. All seeds in this generation have a genotype of Yy. They are all yellow, since green is recessive.

Plants from F₁ are now crossed. The possible genotype combinations for the second filial generation are YY, Yy, yY, and yy. There is a one in four chance that two recessive y alleles will combine, so only one offspring out of four will have green seeds.

Fruit Flies. In 1908, geneticist Thomas Hunt Morgan and his team began breeding fruit flies. They studied the inheritance of eye color and wing shape, making important genetic discoveries, such as crossing over and sex-linked traits.

MENDEL LOST AND FOUND

Mendel published his work in 1866, but it went unnoticed for years. Then, in 1900, three European botanists each redis-covered Mendel's work. They conducted their own experiments that each supported Mendel's conclusions.

Many important genetic discoveries followed in the early 1900s. Scientists studying fruit flies showed that genes were located on chromosomes, made the first genetic map, and demonstrated the inheritance of genes on sex chromosomes.

LAW OF INDEPENDENT ASSORTMENT

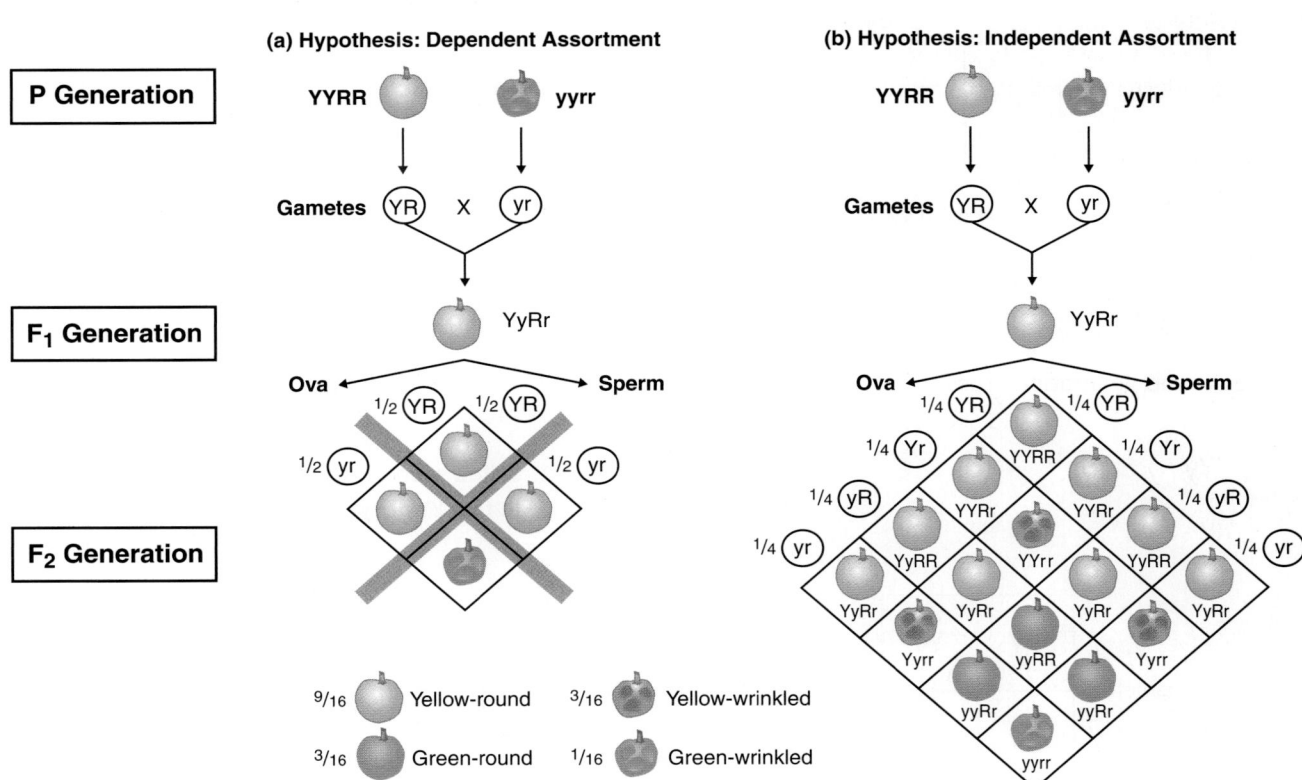

Two sets of true-breeding parents carry two pair of identical alleles. One is for color: YY (yellow) or yy (green). One is for shape: RR (round) or rr (wrinkled).

(a) If the two traits were inherited together, the F₁ hybrids can only produce two different sex cells. The phenotype ratio of the F₂ generation would be 3:1.

(b) If the two traits are inherited separately, the F₁ hybrids will produce four different gametes. The phenotype ratio of the F₂ generation will be 9:3:3:1.

Mendel's experiments supported the Independent Assortment hypothesis.

Mendelian Crosses

In the early 1900s, a mathematical tool known as the Punnett square was devised to demonstrate which gametes were present in a particular cross, as well as the expected or probable genotypes of the offspring. With Mendelian crosses, it is all a matter of probability as to which genetic outcomes are possible. For example, in the parental cross used previously with yellow and green

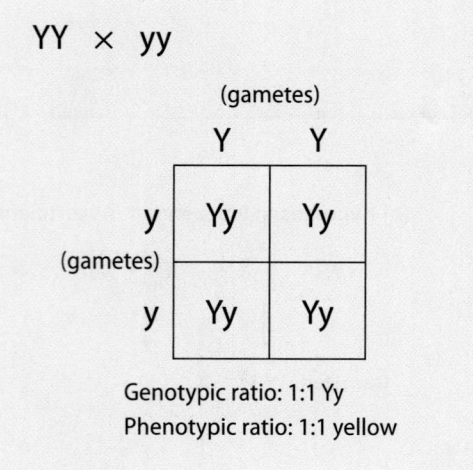

YY × yy

(gametes)

	Y	Y
y	Yy	Yy
y	Yy	Yy

(gametes)

Genotypic ratio: 1:1 Yy
Phenotypic ratio: 1:1 yellow

The second generation cross

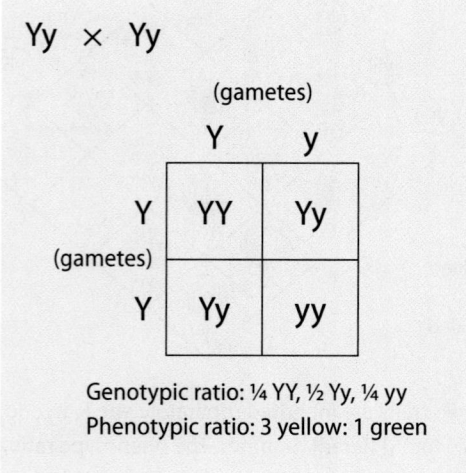

Yy × Yy

(gametes)

	Y	y
Y	YY	Yy
Y	Yy	yy

(gametes)

Genotypic ratio: ¼ YY, ½ Yy, ¼ yy
Phenotypic ratio: 3 yellow: 1 green

Test Crossing

Plant and animal breeders often need to determine the genotype of an organism that exhibits a dominant trait. This is especially true when they are attempting to develop a pure breeding line.

For instance, if a pea plant produces yellow seeds, a plant breeder will want to know if the plant is homozygous (YY) or heterozygous (Yy) for seed color. Carrying out a test cross will determine the actual genotype of the yellow-seeded plant.

In the test cross, the unknown genotype is crossed with a homozygous recessive (yy). If any offspring show the recessive trait, the yellow-seeded plant must have been heterozygous. If no recessive trait is expressed, the yellow-seeded parent must have been homozygous. For example

1. possible outcomes:

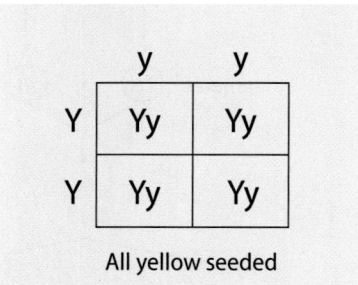

	y	y
Y	Yy	Yy
Y	Yy	Yy

All yellow seeded

2. Yellow seed × Green seed
(either YY or Yy)   (yy)

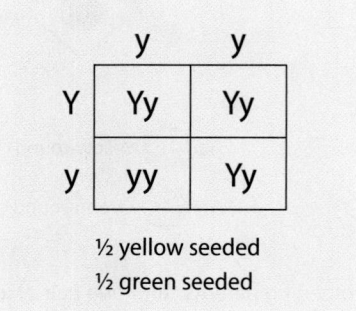

	y	y
Y	Yy	Yy
y	yy	Yy

½ yellow seeded
½ green seeded

By using the test cross, breeders are able to artificially select the traits they want, thereby ensuring that the offspring are homozygous for the trait. This approach is the basis of all purebred lines of plants and animals.

The Results of Mendel's F₁ Crosses for Seven Characteristics in Pea Plants

Character	Dominant Trait	X	Recessive Trait	F2 Generation Dominant:Recessive	Ratio
Flower color	Purple	X	White	705:224	3.15:1
Flower position	Axial	X	Terminal	651:207	3.14:1
Seed color	Yellow	X	Green	6022:2001	3.01:1
Seed shape	Round	X	Wrinkled	5474:1850	2.96:1
Pod shape	Inflated	X	Constricted	882:299	2.95:1
Pod color	Green	X	Yellow	428:152	2.82:1
Stem length	Tall	X	Dwarf	787:277	2.84:1

THE basics

GENETICS TERMS TO KNOW

- **chromosomes:** tiny, threadlike structures found in the cells of living things. Carriers of heredity-bearing genes.
- **homologous:** having the same genes arranged in the same order.
- **genes:** basic unit of inheritance, made up of long sequences of DNA molecules.
- **alleles:** a pair of genes at the same positions (loci) on paired chromosomes. Alleles can be dominant or recessive.

- **homozygous:** having two identical alleles on paired chromosomes. That is, they are both dominant or both recessive.
- **heterozygous:** having two different alleles on paired chromosomes. That is, one is dominant and the other recessive.
- **dominant:** a gene which masks the recessive allele on paired chromosomes.
- **recessive:** a gene which, in the presence of its dominant allele, does not express itself.
- **loci:** the positions of genes on the chromosome.

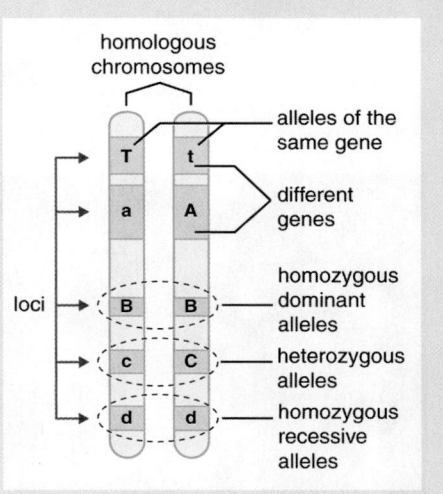

Mendelian Crosses

Incomplete Dominance

With many traits, there exists what is known as incomplete dominance. In such situations, the heterozygous form will express a "blended," or "in-between," phenotype, a combination of the effects of having both alleles present.

When incomplete dominance is the mode of inheritance, a letter symbol with superscript is used to identify the allele and trait.

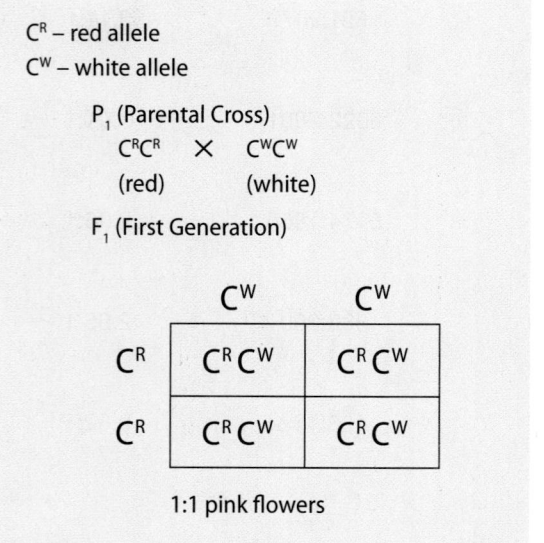

C^R – red allele
C^W – white allele

P_1 (Parental Cross)
$C^R C^R$ × $C^W C^W$
(red)   (white)

F_1 (First Generation)

	C^W	C^W
C^R	$C^R C^W$	$C^R C^W$
C^R	$C^R C^W$	$C^R C^W$

1:1 pink flowers

With incomplete dominance of this nature, there will be three phenotypes possible. In the F_2 cross, the following offspring would be possible:

$C^R C^W$ × $C^R C^W$
(pink)   (pink)

1 red: 2 pink: 1 white

Blood Typing

Incomplete dominance comes in many forms. Human blood typing involves multiple alleles of types A, B, and O, with A and B being codominant and O being recessive. Thus, there are six genotypes and four phenotypes possible.

Genotype	Phenotype
$I^A I^A$	A
$I^A i$	A
$I^B I^B$	B
$I^B i$	B
$I^A I^B$	AB
ii	ii

Crosses involving human blood types are similar to other monohybrid crosses. For instance, a cross of an individual with A (heterozygous) and another with B (heterozygous) would allow for the equal probability of any of the four phenotypes.

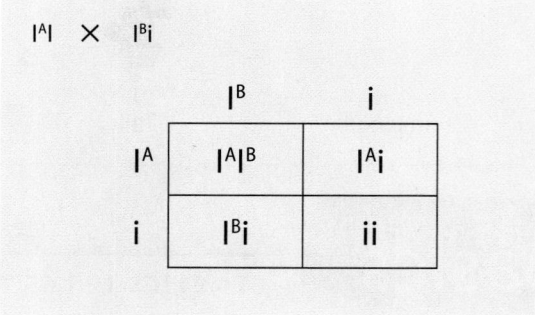

$I^A I$ × $I^B i$

	I^B	i
I^A	$I^A I^B$	$I^A i$
i	$I^B i$	ii

The four o'clock flower is a good example of incomplete dominance. ▼

Sex-Linked Traits

Genes on sex chromosomes are called *sex-linked genes*. Humans have over 250 genes on the X chromosome that can cause hereditary disorders such as hemophilia and muscular dystrophy. Most of these disorders are recessive.

Males have one X chromosome and one Y chromosome while females have two X chromosomes. Therefore, recessive sex-linked traits are much more common in males. This can be seen by showing the results of a cross between a female who is heterozygous for color blindness with a normal-vision male.

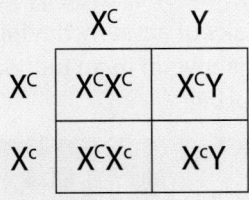

X^C – normal-vision allele
Y – no gene for vision present
X^c – colorblind allele

$$X^C X^c \quad \times \quad X^C Y$$

(carrier female)   (normal-vision male)

	X^C	Y
X^C	$X^C X^C$	$X^C Y$
X^c	$X^C X^c$	$X^c Y$

All female offspring in this case would have normal vision. There is a one in four chance that male offspring will be color-blind. For a female offspring to be color-blind, the mother would have to be heterozygous and the father would need to be color-blind. Thus, each parent could donate a recessive allele.

PEDIGREE CHARTS

It is possible to construct a *pedigree chart*, or a family tree, using Mendel's principles of inheritance.

Analyzing pedigree charts for the mode of inheritance involves looking for patterns as to who is affected. With sex-linked traits, females seldom show the recessive trait. They may be carriers, though, and pass the trait to their offspring.

Genetic counselors construct pedigree charts by gathering information about harmful genes in a family's history. In plant and animal breeding programs, pedigree charts are invaluable for tracking both desirable and undesirable traits.

Dihybrid Crosses

A *dihybrid cross*, a cross involving two traits, may be approached in the same manner as a monohybrid cross. What is most important here is to know whether or not two traits, such as seed color (yellow and green) and seed shape (round and wrinkled), are located on different pairs of chromosomes.

If the traits in question are located on different chromosomes, they are classified as unlinked genes. Although Mendel knew nothing about genes or chromosomes, he was able to infer their "independence" based on the results of his crosses. (See Law of Independent Assortment, page 69.)

In contrast, if the two above-mentioned traits were linked, the F_2 generation would carry the same gametes as the parental cross. With independently assorting genes, however, there are four types of gametes possible, resulting in four different phenotypes. With dihybrid crosses, the Punnett square may again be used to obtain the probable offspring.

YyRr × YyRr
(both yellow-seeded, round)

	YR	Yr	yR	yr
YR	YYRR	YYRr	YyRR	YyRr
Yr	YYRr	YYrr	YyRr	Yyrr
yR	YyRR	YyRr	yyRR	yyRr
yr	YyRr	Yyrr	yyRr	yyrr

9 Yellow-round: 3 Yellow-wrinkled:
3 Green-round: 1 Green-wrinkled

Though Mendel studied only traits with two contrasting forms, modern geneticists now know that few types of inheritance are this simple. Many traits are polygenic in nature, involving the interaction of a number of different genes located on different chromosomes.

Genetics and Technology

As our knowledge of chromosomes and DNA has increased, so have the advances in the application of this knowledge. *Biotechnology*, especially as it applies to genetics, is on the cutting edge of new discoveries regarding our understanding of inheritance at the cellular and molecular levels. Techniques in manipulating and working with DNA have been vitally important in probing the mechanism and secrets of the replication of life itself.

Extracting DNA

To work directly with DNA, scientists must first separate and isolate it from other cell materials. Biochemists, along with cell biologists, were instrumental in devising a simple technique to extract DNA.

STEPS TO EXTRACT DNA

1. To extract DNA, scientists first need to free the chromosomes from the confines of the cell. They do this by physically breaking the cell wall and/or membranes using lab equipment similar to a kitchen blender.

2. Scientists add chemicals to the chopped-up mixture, allowing the strands of DNA to separate and float to the top.

3. The DNA is removed and manipulated. Most often, scientists want large amounts of a small part of a chromosome. In this case, *endonucleases*, or restriction enzymes, are added to the isolated DNA. Endonucleases chemically cut out a particular section of the DNA, allowing for the isolation of a smaller part of the genetic code.

4. Scientists use *PCR (polymerase chain reaction)*, or DNA amplification, to make many copies of the small sample. Millions of identical copies can be made within the short space of an hour or two, giving scientists the large amount of DNA they need to perform their experiments.

5. *Gel electrophoresis*, or DNA fingerprinting, is used to compare the genes of two members of a species or that of two different species. The resulting DNA profile can determine the relationship between two organisms or the actual identity of an individual organism.

Uses of DNA Profiling

Once the techniques used to extract and profile DNA were developed, scientists and society quickly found uses for the technology.

Forensic Science. DNA profiling is used in forensic science to identify or eliminate possible suspects in criminal proceedings. Investigators may compare DNA found at the crime scene with DNA from a suspected criminal. On the basis of this comparison, the suspect can be included or excluded as a possible source of the DNA found at the scene of the crime.

Population Genetics. DNA profiling is also used in population genetics to delineate relationships between and within a species. In the latter case, pedigree charts (family trees) may be constructed and their evolutionary relationship determined. Single-gene disorders within an individual can also be identified. This type of information is used by genetic counselors to analyze the risks of actually having a particular genetic disorder show up in an individual or that individual's offspring.

Copycats. The first cloned cat was created in 2001 using genetic material from an adult donor. Although the cats share the same DNA, each cat uses it differently, resulting in differences in markings and personality.

Ethical Concerns

DNA Profiling. Critics of DNA profiling feel that the practice raises privacy issues. The genetic information gathered could potentially be used in a discriminatory manner. A health insurance company might charge an individual higher rates or refuse to sell him or her insurance because the person carries a specific gene.

Cloning can help scientists to develop treatments for a wide variety of diseases and conditions, including cancer and birth defects. However, many people worry that these procedures are not safe and may be used unethically.

Scientists soon may be able to use cloning techniques to reproduce human beings. However, cloned animals often suffer from developmental problems and do not survive long. Most scientists consider the cloning of humans to be unethical, and many countries have laws prohibiting it.

CLONING

Cloning is the production of an organism with genetic material identical to that of another organism. The first successful cloning of an animal was of a tadpole in 1952.

In recent years, scientists have used a technique known as *SCNT (somatic cell nuclear transfer)* to clone animals. In SCNT

- the nucleus is removed from the cell of one organism.

- the removed nucleus is placed inside the *enucleated* (DNA removed) cell of another organism.

Cloning technology may yield important benefits to people. The cloning of such animals as cattle or sheep could enable scientists to create livestock with desirable genetic traits. Such livestock might produce higher quality meat, milk, and wool.

There are numerous problems with cloning technology. It has a low success rate (one out of 276 tries for Dolly). Many cloned mice become extremely obese or develop other life-threatening disabilities. Also, cloning by SCNT does not produce exact genetic copies.

Even Dolly was not totally identical, since only DNA from the donor cell's nucleus had been transferred. DNA from the recipient cell's cytoplasm (mitochondrial DNA) also contributed traits to Dolly.

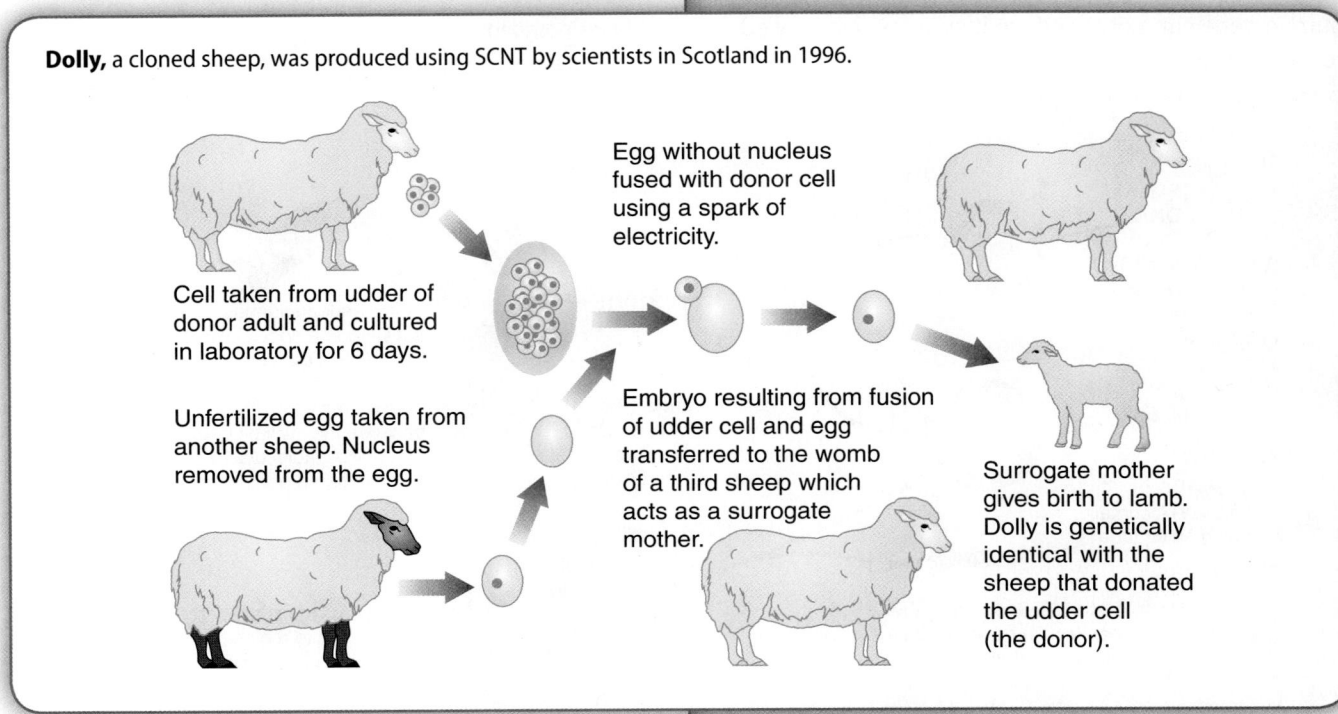

Dolly, a cloned sheep, was produced using SCNT by scientists in Scotland in 1996.

Cell taken from udder of donor adult and cultured in laboratory for 6 days.

Unfertilized egg taken from another sheep. Nucleus removed from the egg.

Egg without nucleus fused with donor cell using a spark of electricity.

Embryo resulting from fusion of udder cell and egg transferred to the womb of a third sheep which acts as a surrogate mother.

Surrogate mother gives birth to lamb. Dolly is genetically identical with the sheep that donated the udder cell (the donor).

Mapping Genes

A *genome* is the sum total of all the genes found within a species. *DNA profiling* has been used extensively for mapping the locations of nearly all of the genes present in the human genome, as well as in a number of other important species. Gene mapping has provided a relatively quick way for scientists to gather information on how certain types of diseases cause illness, providing a possible approach to successful treatment.

Genetic Engineering

Scientists use certain techniques to alter the genes or combination of genes in an organism. This is called *genetic engineering*. DNA profiling has been used in conjunction with other techniques such as gene splicing. In this case, scientists genetically engineer an organism that produces a desired substance or performs a specific job.

Designer Life Forms. In one example of engineering, a small portion of the *plasmid* (DNA) of a bacterial cell can be replaced with the human gene responsible for insulin production. The resulting plasmid contains what is known as *recombinant DNA*, since its DNA is from two different species. Bacteria that contain this human gene can now produce insulin, which is used to treat people afflicted with diabetes, and this insulin came from animals.

Organisms such as the bacteria described at left that have foreign genes spliced into their DNA are known as *transgenic organisms*. Another example of these designer species is a tomato that contains an Arctic cod gene. The fish gene codes for a particular protein that allows the plant to grow in cooler climates without succumbing to frost. Other examples are bacteria engineered to digest oil spills and plants with a built-in resistance to herbicides.

FRANKENFOODS

Today, scientists genetically modify a variety of crops and animals, called *GMOs* (genetically modified organisms).

Genetic engineering enables scientists to increase the quality and productivity of crops and livestock. In some cases, scientists can even design GMOs with genetic resistance to pests and diseases, reducing the amount of pesticides needed to grow them.

Critics of GMOs refer to them as "frankenfoods," implying that they are dangerous to the public health. For example, plants with herbicide resistance may pose a serious threat to the environment if they are able to establish themselves somewhere other than where they were intended.

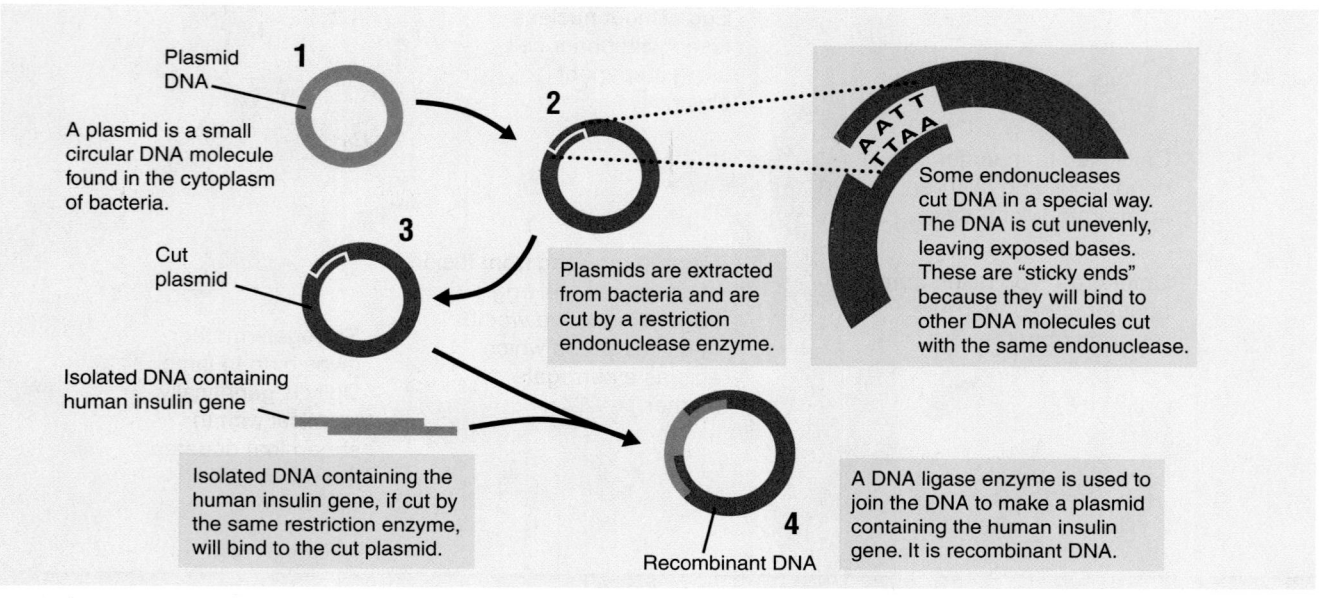

Plasmid DNA **1**

A plasmid is a small circular DNA molecule found in the cytoplasm of bacteria.

2 Some endonucleases cut DNA in a special way. The DNA is cut unevenly, leaving exposed bases. These are "sticky ends" because they will bind to other DNA molecules cut with the same endonuclease.

Cut plasmid **3**

Plasmids are extracted from bacteria and are cut by a restriction endonuclease enzyme.

Isolated DNA containing human insulin gene

Isolated DNA containing the human insulin gene, if cut by the same restriction enzyme, will bind to the cut plasmid.

4 Recombinant DNA

A DNA ligase enzyme is used to join the DNA to make a plasmid containing the human insulin gene. It is recombinant DNA.

HUMAN GENOME PROJECT

Begun in 1990 and completed in April 2003, the Human Genome Project was an international scientific program that helped analyze the human genome, the chemical instructions located on the 3 billion pairs of bases in human DNA.

Scientists located precisely where most human genes occur within the genome, providing a nearly complete human gene map. They used these findings to determine that a human genome has about 25,000 genes. Scientists also found that the sequences of many human genes closely resemble the sequences of corresponding genes in such simple organisms as worms, flies, and bacteria.

Human Genome Project data are helping experts determine various genes' roles in normal body processes and in disease. Such work involves analyzing individual differences among genomes, and it may lead to effective disease treatments.

▲ **The Human Genome Project** mapped the genomes of the fruit fly, house mouse, and a roundworm, in addition to human beings.

MAIN STAGES OF DNA PROFILING

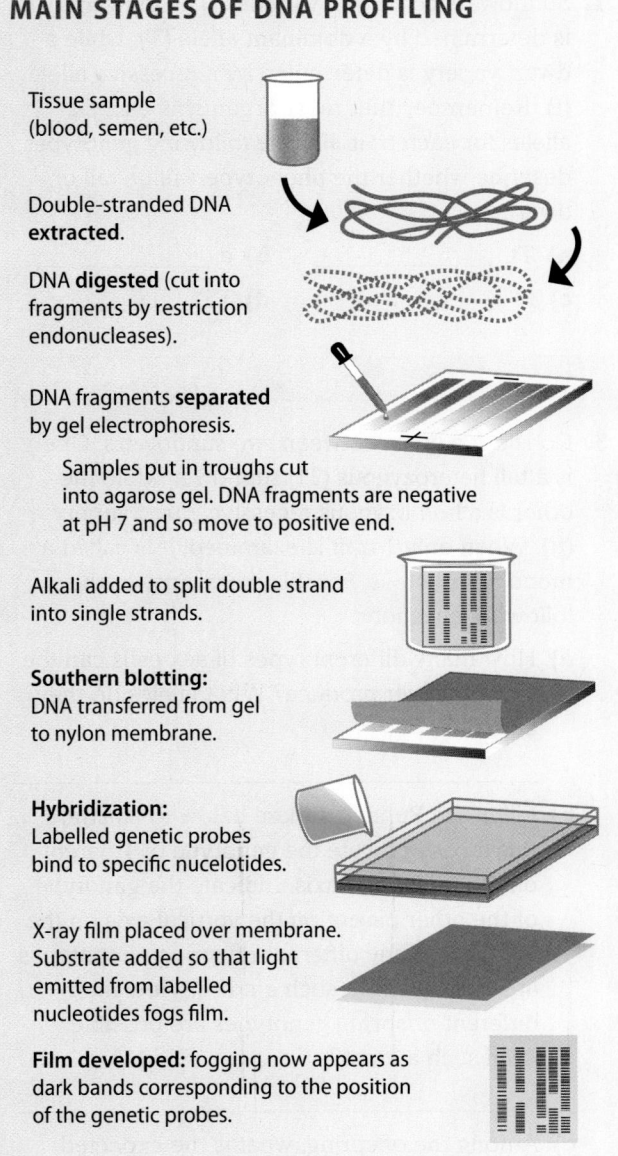

Tissue sample (blood, semen, etc.)

Double-stranded DNA **extracted**.

DNA **digested** (cut into fragments by restriction endonucleases).

DNA fragments **separated** by gel electrophoresis.

Samples put in troughs cut into agarose gel. DNA fragments are negative at pH 7 and so move to positive end.

Alkali added to split double strand into single strands.

Southern blotting: DNA transferred from gel to nylon membrane.

Hybridization: Labelled genetic probes bind to specific nucelotides.

X-ray film placed over membrane. Substrate added so that light emitted from labelled nucleotides fogs film.

Film developed: fogging now appears as dark bands corresponding to the position of the genetic probes.

Junk DNA. Recent findings suggest that more than 95 percent of the human genome consists of DNA that does not code for proteins, and in fact has no known function. This DNA is referred to as noncoding or junk DNA.

Some geneticists believe that junk DNA may prove vital for the survival of an organism, especially during early embryological development. Others believe that these sequences may be the DNA of failed viruses, which became part of our genome through a process called *reverse transcription*, or that they may even be remnants of failed genes.

Genetics Practice Problems

1. Sunflowers come in 2 varieties. The tall variety is determined by a dominant allele (T), while a dwarf variety is determined by a recessive allele (t). Remember that most organisms carry 2 alleles for each trait. For the following genotypes, describe whether the phenotype will be tall or dwarf.

   a) Tt _____   b) tt _____

   c) tT _____   d) TT _____

2. Is there any difference between the heterozygous genotypes Tt and tT?

   _____

3. Consider a cross between two sunflowers. One is a tall heterozygous (Tt) sunflower while the other is a homozygous recessive dwarf variety (tt). When only 1 trait is examined, it is called a monohybrid cross. For this cross, answer the following questions.

   a) How many different types of sex cells can the tall sunflower produce? What alleles do they contain?

   _____

   b) Fill in the Punnett square below to illustrate this cross. Indicate the genotype of 1 parent on the horizontal axis. Indicate the genotype of the other parent on the vertical axis on the left. How many different offspring phenotypes are possible from such a cross? How many different offspring genotypes are possible from such a cross?

   _____

   c) Among the offspring, what is the expected ratio of tall plants to dwarf plants?

   _____

   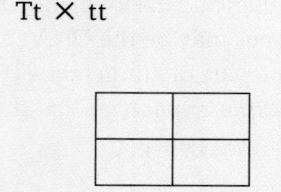

   Tt × tt

4. Howler monkeys come in 2 varieties. There is a long-tailed variety and a short-tailed variety. These characteristics are caused by the action of a single gene. The long-tailed variety is dominant (L), while the short-tailed variety is recessive (l).

   In the Punnett square below, illustrate a cross between a homozygous long-tailed monkey (LL) and a heterozygous long-tailed monkey (Ll). Then answer the following questions:

   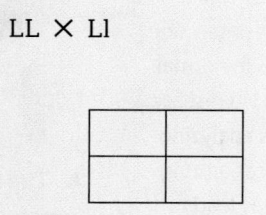

   LL × Ll

   a) Out of 16 offspring from this cross, how many would be expected to have long tails?

   _____

   b) Out of 16 offspring from this cross, how many would be expected to have short tails?

   _____

   c). Out of 16 offspring from this cross, how many would be expected to be heterozygous?

   _____

Howler monkeys use their long, powerful tails for balance and sometimes for swinging.

5. In howler monkeys, black fur is a dominant trait (B). Brown fur is a recessive trait (b). Consider a cross between two heterozygous (Bb) howler monkeys and answer the following questions.

a) What is the phenotype of each parent in terms of fur color?

_____

b) Each sex cell produced by each parent contains only 1 allele. How many different sex cell varieties can each parent produce? What are they?

_____

c) Illustrate this cross in the Punnett square below. Out of 16 offspring, how many can be expected to have black fur? Do you expect any of the offspring to have brown fur?

_____

d) Out of 16 offspring, how many can be expected to have a heterozygous genotype? How many offspring can be expected to have a homozygous genotype?

_____

Bb × Bb

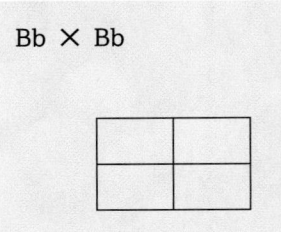

6. In a cross between two homozygous dominant howler monkeys (BB), what percentage of the offspring can be expected to have black fur?

_____

Illustrate your answer in the Punnett square below. Will any offspring have brown fur?

_____

BB × BB

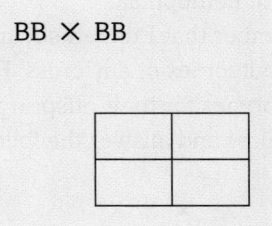

7. In a cross between two heterozygous howler monkeys (Bb × Bb), how many genotypes can result from this cross? Illustrate your answer in the Punnett square below.

_____

Bb × Bb

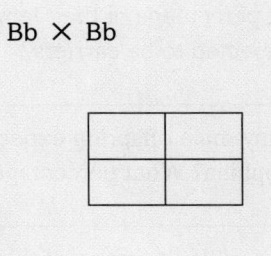

a) Express the number of genotypes as a ratio:

_____ BB _____ Bb _____ bb

b) Express the number of phenotypes as a ratio:

_____ Black _____ Brown

c) Remember, the Punnet square illustrates all possible outcomes of a cross. Is it possible that all of the offspring of this cross have brown fur?

_____

Genetics Practice Problems

8. Hemophilia is a genetic condition where an individual's blood lacks the ability to clot. In humans, the gene that causes hemophilia is an X-linked trait and is recessive. Use an X^H to indicate the normal condition and X^h to indicate the hemophilia trait. Consider a cross between a normal male (X^HY) and a female who is a carrier for hemophilia (X^hX^h). Keep in mind that the male sex chromosome Y carries information only for gender, not hemophilia.

Remember that Punnett squares illustrate the possible outcomes of any cross. Fill in the possible genotypes for their offspring in the Punnett square below and answer the following questions:

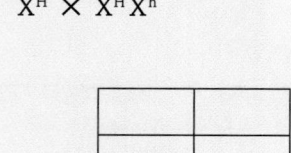

$$X^H \times X^HX^h$$

a) What percentage of their offspring can be expected to be female?

_____

b) What percentage of their female offspring can be expected to be carriers?

_____

c) Are any male offspring expected to have hemophilia? What percentage?

_____

d) Is it possible that none of their children will be carriers or have hemophilia?

_____

Blood does not clot normally in a person with hemophilia. ▶

9. In human beings, the MN blood group has 2 alleles that demonstrate incomplete dominance. A person with a homozygous genotype (MM or NN) will have that blood type as the phenotype. A heterozygous individual will have an MN blood type as the phenotype.

Consider a cross between 2 heterozygous (MN) individuals. Fill in the possible genotypes for their offspring in the Punnett square below and answer the following questions:

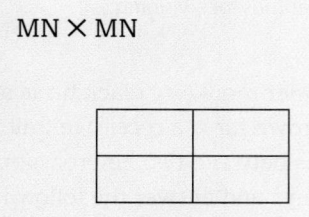

$$MN \times MN$$

a) What percentage of their offspring can be expected to be heterozygous (MN)?

_____

b) Can any of their offspring be homozygous MM?

_____

c) What is the ratio of homozygous individuals (MM or NN) to heterozygous individuals (MN) among expected offspring?

_____

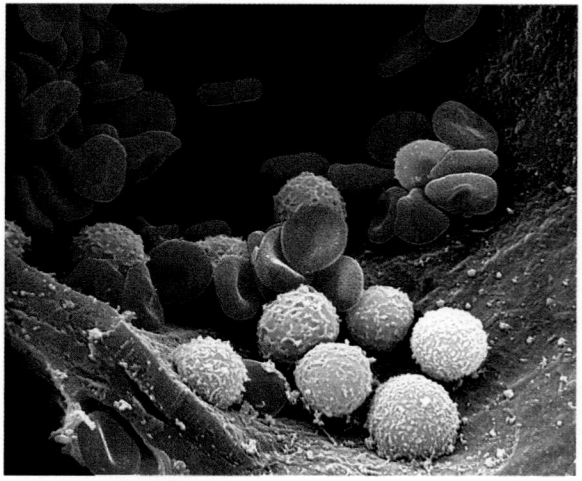

Hamsters inherit such traits as fur color and ear length from their parents.

10. In hamsters, brown fur is a dominant trait (B) while black fur is recessive (b). Also in hamsters, short ears (S) are dominant over longer ears (s). The gene for fur color is at a different *locus*, on a chromosome separate from the gene for ear length. Describe the phenotype in terms of fur color and ear length for the hamsters that have the following genotypes.

BBSs _____

Bbss _____

BBSS _____

bbss _____

bbSS _____

BbSs _____

    Remember that sex cells carry only one allele for each trait. For a hamster with the genotype BbSs, how many different sex cell can this hamster produce?

_____

11. A male hamster with the genotype bbSS is crossed with a female hamster with the genotype BbSs. Since 2 separate traits, each with 2 alleles, are being examined, this is called a dihybrid cross. Fill in the Punnett square below and answer the following questions.

	bS	bS	bS	bS
BS				
Bs				
bS				
bs				

a) Of the 16 possible genotype combinations for the offspring, how many have black fur and short ears? _____

b) Of the 16 possible genotype combinations for the offspring, how many have brown fur and long ears? _____

c) Of the 16 possible genotype combinations for the offspring, how many have black fur and long ears? _____

d) Of the 16 possible genotype combinations for the offspring, how many have brown fur and short ears? _____

e) Of the 16 possible genotype combinations for the offspring, what phenotype is most common?

_____

_____

_____

Genetics Problems — Answers

1. a) Tt ___tall___   **b)** tt ___dwarf___

  c) tT ___tall___   **d)** TT ___tall___

Explanation: A dominant allele will always mask the effects of a recessive allele. To determine the phenotype from the genotype, simply check to see if one of the two alleles is a dominant (T) allele. The presence of even a single dominant allele will result in a tall genotype. If no dominant allele is present, the sunflower will have 2 copies of the recessive dwarf allele. The phenotype for this plant will be dwarf, since no dominant allele is present.

2. ___No. They are identical.___

Explanation: The position of each allele in a pair has no effect. The only factor that will affect phenotype is the combination of dominant and recessive alleles. However, the uppercase (dominant allele) is always stated first, so Tt is expressed correctly, while tT is not.

3. a) ___2; T and t___

Explanation: The tall sunflower is heterozygous, so it has one of each of the two alleles (T and t). When producing sex cells for reproduction, each parent contributes only one allele to each sex cell. Thus, the heterozygous sunflower can contribute either a tall allele (T) or a dwarf allele (t).

  b) ___2; 2___

Explanation:

Tt × tt

	T	t
t	Tt	tt
t	Tt	tt

  c) ___1 : 1___

Explanation: As seen in the Punnett square, there are only 2 possible genotypes for the offspring in such a cross. One genotype is heterozygous (Tt) and will produce only tall flowers. This is due to the presence of the dominant tall allele (T). The other possible genotype is homozygous recessive (tt). Since the dominant tall allele is not present, this will produce only dwarf flowers.

4.

LL × Ll

	L	L
L	LL	LL
l	Ll	Ll

  a) ___16___

Explanation: The Punnett square illustrates all possible outcomes from the cross in each of the four boxes. Since individual outcomes occur randomly, each outcome has a 1 in 4 chance of occurring. For 16 offspring, you would expect 4 offspring to possess the genotype of each box within the Punnett square. However, in this particular cross, each box in the Punnett square contains at least one dominant allele (L). Thus, the phenotype for all four genotypes possible will be the same. The phenotype for all offspring will be the same—the dominant long tail.

  b) ___0___

Explanation: See above. Since a dominant allele (L) is present in all four possible outcomes of this cross, none of the offspring can show the recessive phenotype (ll) of a short tail. Only homozygous recessive individuals will have a short tail.

4. (cont'd.)

c). _____ 8 _____

Explanation: Here we must distinguish between the genotype and the phenotype among the outcomes in the Punnett square. While all of the offspring will have the same phenotype (long tails), they will not have the same genotype. As seen in the boxes, one half of the possible outcomes will have one of each allele (Ll). These are *heterozygous*. One half will have two identical alleles (LL) and are called *homozygous*. Since half of the expected outcomes are heterozygous, we should expect half of the actual outcomes to have a heterozygous genotype. The actual number of outcomes, however, may be different, since outcomes are random.

5.

Bb × Bb

	B	*b*
B	*BB*	*Bb*
b	*Bb*	*bb*

a) _____ *black* _____

Explanation: If each parent is heterozygous, they each possess one dominant allele (B). The dominant allele will mask the expression of any recessive allele present. So, both parents will have the black fur phenotype.

b) _____ *2; B, b* _____

Explanation: Each parent is heterozygous, meaning they possess one of each of the two alleles (Bb). Each parent contributes only one allele to each offspring, so each parent can contribute either the dominant (B) allele or the recessive (b) allele. The alleles are randomly selected from each parent.

5. (cont'd.)

c) _____ *12; yes, 4* _____

Explanation: The Punnett square shows all possible outcomes from such a cross. Remember, the outcomes of Punnett squares are probabilities. Each outcome is random and has a 1 in 4 chance of actually occurring. Thus, out of 16 offspring, we would expect ¾ of them to possess at least one dominant (B) allele. These outcomes will have black fur. Three-fourths of 16 is 12. Of the possible outcomes, ¼ are homozygous recessive. These individuals will have brown fur, as the recessive trait is not masked by a dominant allele. One-fourth of 16 is 4. So, out of 16 offspring, we would expect 4 to have brown fur.

d) _____ *8; 8* _____

Explanation: Each outcome is random and has a 1 in 4 chance of actually occurring. Of the four outcome boxes, two are homozygous (BB and bb) and two are heterozygous (Bb and bB). Thus, out of 16 offspring, we would expect half (8) to be homozygous for either allele and half (8) to be heterozygous, possessing one of both alleles.

6. _____ *100%; no* _____

BB × BB

	B	*B*
B	*BB*	*BB*
B	*BB*	*BB*

Explanation: There is only one possible outcome from such a cross. Each parent can only contribute one dominant allele (B) to the offspring. Thus, the offspring must be homozygous for the dominant allele. Since no parent can contribute a recessive (b) allele for brown fur, there is no possibility that any offspring will show this trait.

7. _____ *3* _____

Explanation: Each parent contributes 1 of 2 alleles to the offspring. Alleles are contributed randomly. Thus, each parent can contribute either a dominant (B) allele or a recessive (b) allele. All possible combinations of outcomes are shown in the Punnett square. Of those, 2 are homozygous (BB and bb). The other 2 are heterozygous (Bb). Thus, there are 3 possible genotype outcomes: BB, bb, and BbbB.

Bb × Bb

	B	**b**
B	**BB**	**Bb**
b	**Bb**	**bb**

a) __*1*__ BB __*2*__ Bb __*1*__ bb

Explanation: All possible genotype combinations are shown in the Punnett square. Of those, two are homozygous (BB and bb). Two are heterozygous Bb. So, the ratio of BB : Bb or bB : bb is 1 : 2: 1.

b) __*3*__ Black __*1*__ Brown

Explanation: Phenotype is determined by the presence or absence of the dominant allele (B) in any outcome. There are 4 possible combinations. Of those, 3 of 4 have at least one dominant allele (B). Thus, 3 of 4 will have black fur. Only one outcome is homozygous recessive (bb). Thus, 1 of 4 outcomes will have brown fur. Expressed as a ratio, the outcomes are 3:1 black fur to brown fur.

c) _____ *Yes.* _____

Explanation: Remember that the outcomes shown in the Punnett square are probable outcomes. Actual outcomes are random. For example, the probability of a flipped coin landing on heads or tails is equal (50 percent). But, it is possible to flip a coin 5 times and have it land on tails each time. It may not be likely, but it is possible. So, it is possible (but highly improbable) that all the offspring from such a cross can be homozygous recessive (bb) genotype and brown fur.

8.

$X^H Y \times X^H X^h$

	X^H	Y
X^H	$X^H X^H$	$X^H Y$
X^h	$X^H X^h$	$X^h Y$

a) What percentage of their offspring can be expected to be female?

_____ *50%* _____

Explanation: Remember that each parent contributes 1 allele to the offspring. Females can only contribute an X sex chromosome. Males produce sperm with an X chromosome in numbers equal to sperm with a Y chromosome. As a result, about half of all babies are boys, and half are girls.

b) What percentage of their female offspring can be expected to be carriers?

50% ($X^H X^h$)

Explanation: The female in this cross contributes one X sex chromosome to the offspring. Since the female possesses two X chromosomes, but only one has the hemophilia trait, the chance that a female offspring will inherit that chromosome is 1 out of 2, or 50 percent.

c) Are any male offspring expected to have hemophilia? What percentage?

Yes; 50% (25% of total offspring could be $X^h Y$)

Explanation: The female in this cross contributes 1 X sex chromosome to the offspring. For male offspring, the Y chromosome must come from the father. Since the female possesses 2 X chromosomes, but only 1 has the hemophilia trait, the chance that a male offspring will inherit that chromosome is 1 out of 2, or 50 percent of male offspring (25 percent of total offspring).

d) Is it possible that none of their children will be carriers or have hemophilia?

_____ *Yes.* _____

8. (cont'd.)

Explanation: Remember that the outcomes shown in the Punnett square are probable outcomes. Actual outcomes are random. For example, the probability of a flipped coin landing on heads or tails is equal (50 percent). But, it is possible to flip a coin 5 times and have it land on tails each time.

9.

MN × MN

	M	*N*
M	*MM*	*MN*
N	*MN*	*NN*

a) What percentage of their offspring can be expected to be heterozygous (MN)?

50%

Explanation: In the Punnett square, 2 outcome squares contain 1 of each allele (M and N). In a co-dominant trait, these individuals will have the phenotype MN. They represent 50 percent of possible outcomes.

b) Can any of their offspring be homozygous MM?

Yes.

Explanation: As seen in the Punnett square, 1 out of the 4 possible outcomes is the homozygous MM genotype.

c) What is the ratio of homozygous individuals (MM or NN) to heterozygous individuals (MN) among expected offspring?

1:1

Explanation: As seen in the Punnett square, there are 2 outcomes that are heterozygous and 2 outcomes that are homozygous. Expressed as a ratio, this is 1:1.

10. BBSs _____ *brown fur, short ears* _____

Bbss _____ *brown fur, long ears* _____

BBSS _____ *brown fur, short ears* _____

bbss _____ *black fur, long ears* _____

bbSS _____ *black fur, short ears* _____

BbSs _____ *brown fur, short ears* _____

Explanation: The presence of a dominant allele in any combination will show that phenotype. Recessive traits only show in homozygous combinations.

_____ *BS Bs bS bs* _____

Explanation: Each sex cell contains only 1 of 2 alleles for each trait.

11.

	bS	bS	bS	bS
BS	*BbSS*	*BbSS*	*BbSS*	*BbSS*
Bs	*BbSs*	*BbSs*	*BbSs*	*BbSs*
bS	*bbSS*	*bbSS*	*bbSS*	*bbSS*
bs	*bbSs*	*bbSs*	*bbSs*	*bbSs*

a) ___*8*___

b) ___*0*___

c) ___*0*___

d) ___*8*___

e) Of the 16 possible genotype combinations for the offspring, what phenotype is most common?

The Punnett square predicts an equal number of hamsters with brown fur and short ears, and black fur and short ears.

Explanation: Once the Punnett square is filled in, all possible outcomes are shown. Count which phenotypes are the most common possible outcomes.

SCIENTIFIC CLASSIFICATION is the

method scientists have developed to arrange all of the world's organisms into groups. Scientists base their classification system on the biological similarities that exist among *species* (kinds) of organisms. Classification creates a method for organizing facts about organisms and groups of organisms.

Some scientists estimate that about 10 million different species of living organisms exist. The number of extinct organisms is even greater. Some 1.5 million living organisms have been classified by taxonomists.

Sorting Life

Recorded attempts to classify living organisms go back as far as the ancient Greek philosophers Plato and Aristotle. Aristotle developed a rudimentary system of classification that some say provided the foundation for present-day schemes. Both established a concept of species—the basic unit of classification of living organisms.

Not until the advent of the microscope, and Anton van Leeuwenhoek's observations of microscopic forms in the mid-17th century, did scientists recognize that the living world is composed of more than what the naked eye can see, and that macroscopic nonmotile plant and motile animal life forms represent only a part of that world.

SCIENTIFIC CLASSIFICATION

Taxonomy: the scientific discipline that deals with the identification, naming, and classification of organisms.

Systematics: concentrates on *phylogeny*, or origin and development, of organisms as a major factor in their classification.

Linnaean Classification

In the Linnaean classification scheme, living organisms are grouped according to similar visible and anatomical structures. Linnaeus arranged these groups in a hierarchical order, beginning with the most inclusive and largest group, which was the *kingdom,* and ending with the smallest unit of classification, the *species*. Species are groups of organisms that share certain characteristics and are able to interbreed.

Linnaeus classified organisms into one of two kingdoms—one for plants and one for animals—and then further divided each kingdom into four subdivisions. (See Plant Taxonomy, pages 106–107; History of Zoology, pages 164–165.)

Spotlight on...

CAROLUS LINNAEUS

1707–1778

Perhaps the best-known taxonomist is the Swedish naturalist Carolus Linnaeus.

- wrote extensively on plant and animal classification
- wrote the classic works *Systema naturae* (1735) and *Genera plantarum* (1737)
- developed a practical system for naming and classifying all living organisms
- became known as the father of modern taxonomy

Classification Today

Linnaeus's two kingdoms have been added to as scientists learn more about living organisms. The highest group is now called the *domain*. Most taxonomists divide all living things into three domains: *Archaea*, *Bacteria*, and *Eukaryota*. Archaea and Bacteria have *prokaryotic cells*, which do not have a nucleus. All other living things have *eukaryotic cells*, which have a nucleus.

There are different classification systems in use today, but most taxonomists agree on the same basic framework. Living things are now subdivided into eight groups, with domain ranking as the highest level and largest group, and species ranking as the lowest and smallest. Taxonomists do research to determine the placement of each group within the overall classification framework.

1. Domain
2. Kingdom
3. Phylum
4. Class
5. Order
6. Family
7. Genus
8. Species

Kingdom Protista. This tiny, unicellular paramecium uses cilia to move through freshwater.

SIX KINGDOMS OF LIFE

Today many scientists classify living things into three domains and six kingdoms.

Domain	Kingdom
Archaea	Archaea
Bacteria	Bacteria
Eukaryota	Protista
	Fungi
	Plantae
	Animalia

NAMING ORGANISMS

Linnaeus developed a system for naming organisms that is still used today, called binomial nomenclature. Each species is given its own unique scientific name consisting of two Latin or Greek words. The first word identifies the *genus,* a group of closely related species to which the organism belongs. The second word identifies the particular species. When writing the binomial, the first letter of the genus is capitalized and both names are italicized.

The scientific name for humans is *Homo sapiens*. The genus name *Homo* means *man* in Latin. The species name *sapiens* means *wise*. The classification for humans is as follows.

Domain Eukaryota

Kingdom Animalia

Phylum Chordata

Class Mammalia

Order Primata

Family Hominidae

Genus Homo

Species sapiens

Classification of Living Things		
Domain	**Kingdom**	**Types of Organisms**
Archaea	Archaea	organisms that inhabit harsh environments like deep-sea hydrothermal vents
Bacteria	Bacteria	all bacteria and many other soil and water microbes
Eukaryota	Protista	simple, mostly unicellular animals
	Fungi	mushrooms, bread molds, mildews, yeasts, and lichens
	Plantae	mosses, ferns, conifers, and flowering plants
	Animalia	mammals, fish, insects, and worms

Archaea and Bacteria

SOUTHWESTERN

Kingdom Archaea

For this group of single-celled organisms, *Archaea* is the name of both the domain and the kingdom. Scientists had traditionally classified archaea with bacteria because of their similar cell structures. But beginning in the 1970s, close analyses of their genes revealed that archaea and bacteria are too different to be grouped together. In many respects, archaea more closely resemble eukaryotes than they do bacteria.

- *Archaea* comes from a Greek word meaning *ancient* or *primitive*.

- Archaea rank among the oldest forms of life on Earth.

- Some scientists believe these organisms are similar to the original ancestors of all modern life.

- Archaea have prokaryotic cells, meaning they do not have a nucleus.

- Various kinds of archaea can consume acetic acid, hydrogen, or sulfur.

- Some can produce the gas methane.

- Many are categorized as chemosynthetic autotrophs because they are capable of obtaining energy by breaking down inorganic molecules such as hydrogen sulfide. The energy is used to make carbon compounds similar to those produced by photosynthetic organisms.

- Many live in such harsh conditions as oil wells, deep-sea hydrothermal vents (hot springs), and anaerobic (oxygen-free) environments. (See Seafloor Spreading, page 450.)

- Other archaea grow in soils and within various living organisms.

- Archaea live harmlessly in human digestive systems.

Grand Prismatic Spring in Yellowstone National Park is marked by brilliant ribbons of color caused by *thermophiles,* which are archaea and bacteria.

E. coli

Streptococcus

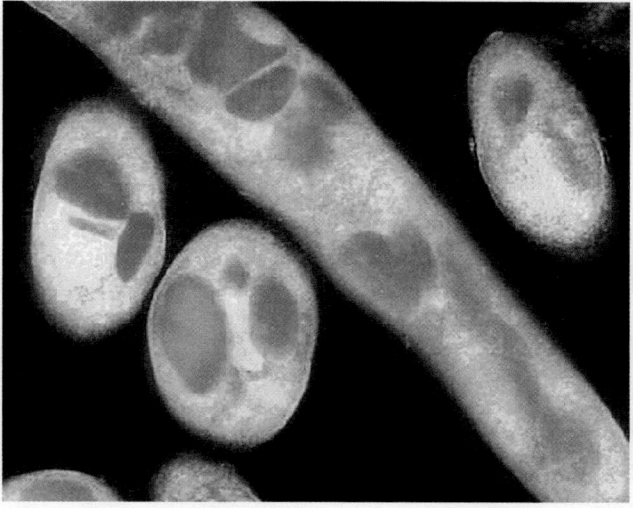
Anthrax

Kingdom Bacteria

There are more bacteria in the world than any other living thing. There are thousands of species of bacteria. Bacteria are grouped into two phyla: true bacteria and *cyanobacteria,* or blue-green bacteria.

- Bacteria are tiny organisms that generally consist of a single prokaryotic cell.
- Bacteria generally reproduce by a process called fission. In fission, one cell simply divides, producing an offspring.

Phylum Schizophyta: Bacteria

- Bacteria exist in three different shapes: spherical bacteria are called cocci; rod-shaped bacteria are called bacilli; spiral-shaped bacteria are called spirilla.
- Some bacteria possess a flagellum, a long hairlike structure that propels the bacterium.
- Some bacteria are decomposers, breaking down the remains of plants or animals and releasing vital substances such as oxygen, carbon, and sulfur into the atmosphere.
- Some bacteria cause serious illnesses, such as tuberculosis, cholera, typhoid fever, and tetanus. (See Disease, page 292.)

Phylum Cyanophyta: Cyanobacteria

- Cyanobacteria are sometimes called blue-green bacteria or blue-green algae.
- They carry on photosynthesis, but their chlorophyll is not contained in chloroplasts as it is in other photosynthetic organisms.
- Blue-green bacteria may be single-celled or multicellular.
- They grow mainly in a freshwater environment.

THE STUDY OF BACTERIA

Late 1800s

- Louis Pasteur shows that bacteria cause certain chemical changes such as the souring of milk.
- Robert Koch becomes the first bacteriologist to show that specific bacteria cause certain diseases. He finds that the bacterium *Bacillus anthracis* causes anthrax in cattle and people.

1930s

- The development of the electron microscope enables bacteriologists to study the interior of bacterial cells.

Today

- Bacteriologists work with bacterial genes to learn more about how bacteria cause disease.
- They also use bacteria to help control water pollution and treat sewage and industrial wastes.

Protists and Fungi

Kelp

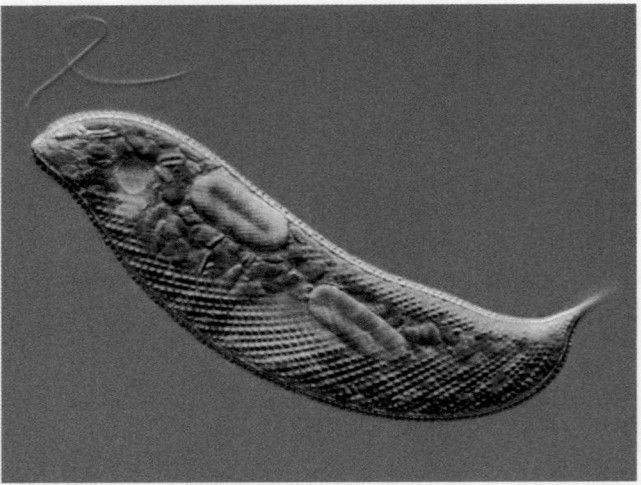

Euglena

Kingdom Protista

The members of this kingdom range from tiny single-celled organisms to giant seaweed. Protists are comprised of eukaryotic cells that contain a distinct nucleus as well as other cell bodies.

Phylum Protozoa. *Protozoa* are like animals because they move and obtain their food from outside sources. They reproduce sexually and asexually. There are perhaps 30,000 species of protozoa.

The remaining phyla consist of photosynthetic organisms. There are perhaps 25,000 species of such algae. Most are found in water environments.

Phylum Euglenophyta. The *euglena* have characteristics of plants and animals. They contain chlorophyll and can make their own food through photosynthesis. They can also capture their own food.

Phylum Chrysophyta. In golden algae, chlorophyll is masked by yellow to brown pigments, giving these organisms their characteristic color. *Diatoms* are single-celled algae. They are among the living things that comprise plankton—tiny organisms that float along the water's surface. Plankton serves as food for many marine animals.

Protistan Cell

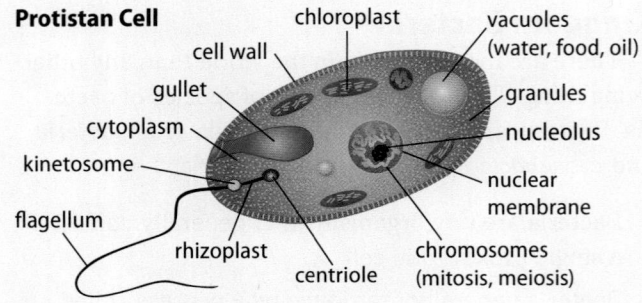

Phylum Pyrrophyta consists of organisms called *dinoflagellates*. One species creates the so-called "red tide" that occurs in the Gulf of Mexico, produced by a large number of dinoflagellates whose pigments create the red color. Red tides kill many types of marine life.

Phylum Chlorophyta. These are the green algae. Members of this phylum are various shapes and sizes. There are single-celled algae such as *chlamydomonas* and *desmids*. *Spirogyra* is a long filament that makes up the scum that covers ponds. The multicellular algae have specialized cells that perform various functions.

Phylum Phaeophyta and Phylum Rhodophyta. Phylum Phaeophyta consists of brown algae, and Phylum Rhodophyta consists of red algae. These are multicelled algae known as seaweeds. The brown algae are the largest and include the giant kelp. Some of the kelps are over 40 feet in length.

Kingdom Fungi

A fungus is an organism that produces spores and gets its food by absorbing it from dead or living organisms. (See pages 148–151.)

- Kingdom Fungi includes about 80,000 species of fungi.
- Along with bacteria and protozoa, fungi act as decomposers.
- Fungi reproduce by sexual and asexual means.
- Some species of fungi can cause diseases such as ringworm and athlete's foot.

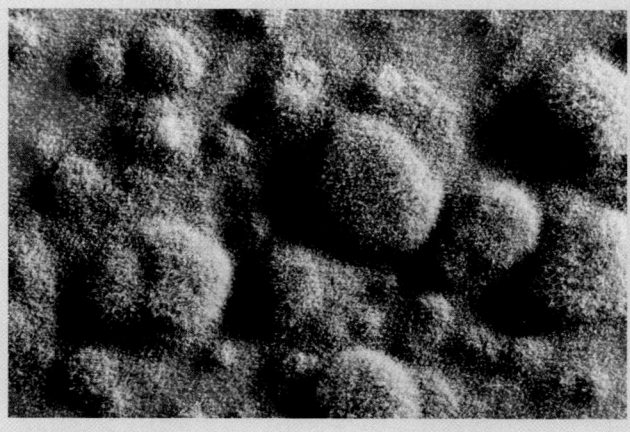

Penicillium mold

Amanita muscaria

Phylum Basidiomycota. This class includes mushrooms and toadstools as well as rusts and smuts. Some mushrooms are edible, but others are poisonous and should be avoided. Only that part of the mushroom involved in reproduction appears above the surface; the rest remains below ground. Rusts and smuts are parasites that attack wheat, trees, and other plants.

Phylum Deuteromycota. Among these fungi are the *Penicillium* molds. Species of this mold are the source of the drug penicillin. Some species are also used in the production of cheeses. Many types of molds spoil food; for example, the *Trichothecium* grows on apples and produces rot.

Phylum Mycomycota. A *lichen* is composed of a species of algae and a species of fungi living together. The algae manufacture food, while the fungi form a framework that protects the algae. Lichens are hearty organisms that can survive in inhospitable environments, such as the icy conditions of Antarctica, where lichens can be found living inside the outer layers of some rock formations.

GOURMET FUNGUS

A *truffle* is a type of fungus that is valued as a food delicacy. Truffles grow wild throughout the world. They grow underground near the roots of oak, hazel, and other trees. Because of the scent truffles produce, pigs and dogs are used to hunt for them.

Plants and Animals

Kingdom Plantae

This kingdom consists of multicellular, photosynthetic organisms that range in size from tiny mosses to giant sequoia trees. Reproduction among the plants is both sexual and asexual.

Phylum Bryophyta. The *bryophytes* are small, nonflowering plants.

- made up of Class Musci (mosses), Class Hepaticae (liverworts), and Class Antherocerotae (hornworts)
- bryophytes are *nonvascular*—do not possess a system of specialized cells for carrying water and food through the plants
- frequently found near water, and they remain small
- over 23,000 species of bryophytes

Class Musci

- consists of about 14,000 species of mosses
- tiny plants that grow in clumps
- leaflike parts above ground and rootlike structures, called rhizoids, that absorb water and nutrients
- among the first species to inhabit harsh environments
- on rocky surfaces, mosses break up the rocks and create fertile soil where other plants can survive

Pine trees are conifers.

Phylum Tracheophyta. *Tracheophytes* are any of about 260,000 species of *vascular* plants. Vascular systems allow plants to grow very tall.

- have a system of roots, stems, and leaves
- roots absorb water and minerals from the ground, transport them to the rest of the plant
- stems transport nutrients, provide sturdiness and support for the plant's leaves and branches
- leaves manufacture food through photosynthesis

Class Pteridopsida

- consists of about 11,000 species of seedless plants called *ferns*

Class Gymnospermopsida

- consists of the *gymnosperms,* one of two large groups of seed-bearing plants
- gymnosperm means "naked" or "exposed" seed—the seed is not enclosed by a fruit
- includes about 550 species of cycad trees, over 500 species of conifers, and one species of ginkgo

Division Anthophyta

- consists of the *angiosperms,* or flowering plants
- flowers contain plants' reproductive organs
- flowering plants are divided into two classes: the *monocots,* with one seed leaf; and the *dicots,* with two seed leaves
- monocots include grasses, lilies, orchids, and palms
- dicots include oaks, maples, beeches, willows, mustards, roses, poppies, and mints

Ginkgo. Only one species of ginkgo exists today.

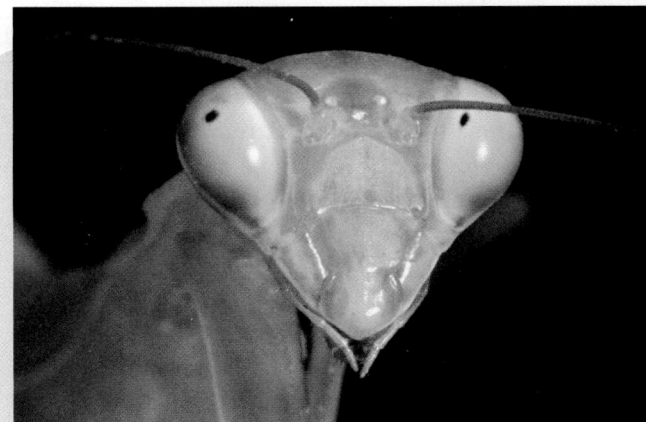

Praying Mantis. Scientists have classified about 1 million insects.

Kingdom Animalia

Animals are multicelled organisms that do not produce their own food and must obtain it by ingesting organic materials. Most animals move. Members of this kingdom fall into two large groups: invertebrates, animals without backbones; and vertebrates, animals with backbones.

Phylum Porifera (sponges)

- consists of over 4,000 species of sponges, which live on the floors of oceans and lakes

Phylum Cnidaria (cnidarians or coelenterates)

- includes hydras, jellyfish, corals, and sea anemones
- animals with definite tissues and a saclike digestive cavity surrounded by special organs such as tentacles

Phylum Platyhelminthes (flatworms)

- have three tissue layers and definite organs
- many flatworms are parasites that live in humans and animals

Phylum Nematoda (roundworms)

- consist of an outer tube enclosing a digestive system
- some are parasites

Phylum Annelida (segmented worms)

- majority of these worms live in marine habitats, but the best known is the earthworm

Phylum Molluska (mollusks)

- largest group of water animals—110,000 species
- soft body and a foot protruding from it; some mollusks also have a shell
- includes clams, mussels, oysters, snails, slugs, squids, and octopuses

Phylum Echinodermata (echinoderms)

- about 6,000 species of spiny-skinned animals found in marine environment
- includes starfish, sea urchins, sea cucumbers, and sand dollars

Phylum Arthropoda (arthropods)

- the largest phylum in the animal kingdom—around 1 million species
- have jointed legs, segmented bodies, and an exoskeleton—an outside shell
- includes insects, crustaceans, and arachnids

Phylum Chordata (chordates)

- phylum consists primarily of the vertebrates
- includes amphibians, birds, mammals, and reptiles, as well as hagfishes, lampreys, and bony fishes

Gorilla

PLANTS grow in almost every part of the world. We see such plants as flowers, grass, and trees nearly every day. Plants also grow on mountaintops, in the oceans, and in many desert and polar regions.

Without plants, people could not survive. Plants provide the oxygen we breathe. The food we eat comes from plants or the animals that eat plants. People rely on plants to clothe them, shelter them, and treat aches, pains, and diseases.

It is no wonder that humans began to observe and appreciate plants at a very early date. *Botany* is the study of plants, including their structure, life processes, historical origins, geographic distribution, and roles in the ecosystem.

Ancient Plants

The first life on Earth appeared about 3.5 billion years ago. It was simple in the extreme, consisting of single-celled *prokaryotic* (lacking a nucleus) marine bacteria. According to paleobotanists, these bacteria were the ancestors of all the complex plant life—and animals as well—that exists today.

Plants' Early Ancestors

Prokaryotes gave way about a billion years later to the first microscopic *eukaryotic* organisms, which were single-celled, like the bacteria, but the cells contained a nucleus. (See pages 46–47.)

These primal eukaryotes, or *protists,* as they are generally termed, are by nature extremely diverse, and include some organisms that are animal-like (amoebas), some that are plantlike (diatoms), and some that resemble nothing more than fungi (euglenas).

The appearance of the true fungi marked the next significant step in plant evolution. Fungi are more complex than their predecessors, but they share characteristics of both plants and animals. Once generally treated as primitive plants, fungi are now neatly segregated in their own group.

PALEOBOTANY

The study of ancient, fossilized plants is called *paleobotany.* Paleobotanists examine the fossil record to understand how and when the first generations of plants came into existence, and how they evolved over time. Paleobotanists study the remains of ancient plants found

- in sedimentary rock.
- in primeval tar pits.
- in bits of amber (the resin of ancient trees).
- in bogs or other places where materials remain in a state of preservation.
- in fossil fuels (coal, oil, or natural gas), which retain the chemical residues of decayed plant products.
- as petrifications, the mineralized and often perfectly preserved replacements of ancient plant parts found in some rocks.

◄ **Ancient plant remains** can be found fossilized in sedimentary rock.

Green algae, which usually grow in lakes, ponds, and along seashores, are believed to be the first plants to make the transition from water to land.

The First Plants

The first true plants appeared early in the Paleozoic era, the time in which the continents were formed. These were multicellular algae, which are further grouped according to color. Of these, the green algae are the most important historically and genetically.

The Move to Land. Based on the known fossil record, paleobotanists believe that some species of green algae made the revolutionary transition from water to land some 450 to 500 million years ago. They washed up on shore and gained a foothold on a rocky eminence that was all but soilless.

The transition from water to land required substantial changes in the way these organisms functioned. Earthbound plants had to develop new ways to gain access to needed resources, which were no longer so readily available. Special structures were needed now to transport the water and minerals below the surface of the soil and to collect light and air above the soil.

The air itself had also changed. Scientists believe that Earth's atmosphere had been accumulating oxygen and a protective envelope of ozone for 2.5 billion years, since the first blue-green algae had begun to respire oxygen. Only when that ozone layer had reached a sufficient concentration to absorb some of the harmful radiation of the sun could the organisms survive out of water and be directly exposed to the sun.

BRANCHES OF BOTANY

Botany has developed from a science concerned mainly with *taxonomy,* or the grouping and naming of organisms, into a vast field of interrelated specialties.

- **morphology:** the science of physical forms
- **anatomy:** that part of morphology that focuses on structure
- **histology:** the study of tissues
- **physiology:** which deals with life processes
- **cytology:** the study of the anatomy and physiology of the individual cell
- **genetics:** the study of inheritance and breeding
- **ecology:** the study of the relationship of living organisms to their various environments
- **phytogeography:** the study of the distribution of plants
- **phytopathology:** the science of plant diseases
- **phytosociology:** the study of the interrelationships of plants within a plant community
- **ethnobotany:** the study of folk uses of plants through history
- **paleobotany:** the study of fossilized plants and the development of plants from simpler to more complex forms

Early Land Plants

The challenges of growing on land spawned two sets of solutions and two main branches of the plant kingdom's ancestral tree.

- mosses and mosslike plants
- vascular plants

Mosses

The mosses and mosslike plants were rudimentary plants that lacked true leaves, stems, and roots. They also had no efficient means of moving nutrients and water very far internally, a factor that kept all their species short and close to the ground.

Though they appeared perhaps 300 million years ago, the limited evolutionary possibilities of mosses have kept them from changing much through the ages. They took hold chiefly in moist, shady places, not so different from those favored by their marine ancestors.

In terms of historical development, the mosses appeared more or less coincident with the evolutionary debut of some amphibians and bony fish.

SETTING THE STAGE FOR COMPLEX PLANTS

Mosses played an important role in the very slow process of soil-building. They contributed organic materials to Earth's surface through their capacity to hold large quantities of water and in the endless cycle of growth and decay. As mosses (or any organisms) die and decompose, they release minerals and other nutrients. In fact, mosses were essential to the creation of an environment in which the more advanced, rooted, vascular plants could flourish. (See Soil, pages 532–533.)

Vascular Plants

The second branch of early plants—the *vascular* plants—developed an efficient and specialized internal system for moving water and nutrients. This radical improvement put them at a distinct advantage over most other plants. They not only succeeded impressively, but diversified rapidly, taking over many kinds of habitats. Vascular plants appeared about 400 million years ago.

- three primitive vascular groups appear in succession: 1. *Rhyniophyta* 2. *Trimerophyta* 3. *Zosterophyllophyta*
- all three groups leafless and lacking conventional roots
- each represents a somewhat improved set of adaptations over its predecessors
- first three vascular plant divisions become extinct between 400 and 360 million years ago, according to fossil evidence
- probably driven out by more vigorous seedless vascular plants developing in the Carboniferous period, 360 to 280 million years ago
- four relatively new divisions of vascular plants appear about that time: 1. *Lycophyta* 2. *Sphenophyta* 3. *Psilophyta* 4. *Pterophyta*
- during the Carboniferous period, great forests of these complex plants, including lycophyte trees, ferns, and horsetails cover Earth
- their descendants remain viable to this day

◄ **Mosses** usually live on land, in moist, shady places. They often form soft, dense mats on rocks, trees, or soil.

Vascular plants appeared during the later stages of the Paleozoic era, when the global climate was stable and mild, much like that of the subtropics today.

Development of Seed-Bearing Plants		
Plant Type	**Time Period**	**Features**
Gymnosperms	Mesozoic era (about 240 million years ago)	• first plants to bear seeds • better adapted than spore-producing plants • could survive extreme climates • effective seed dispersal—seeds are winged and drift with the slightest breeze when released • dominated landscape soon after first appearance • present-day survivors include gingkos, cycads, and conifers • developed at same time as dinosaurs, small mammals, flying reptiles, and the first birds
Angiosperms	Cenozoic era (about 65 million years ago); become abundant at end of Cenozoic era (about 7 million years ago)	• flowering plants • seeds contained within flower or fruit • appeared at the time the dinosaurs became extinct and the continents split apart • present-day survivors of earliest angiosperms include the magnolia, willow, sycamore, and water lily • as the climate moderated, forests of gymnosperms and angiosperms gave way to vast grasslands (also angiosperms) • in the Pliocene epoch, angiosperms became abundant, adapted to diverse climates • wild grains evolved

PLANTS AND PEOPLE

People have always been interested in plants and have used them in many ways. Prehistoric people gathered wild plants for food and used plants to build shelters. By about 8000 BC, people in several locations around the world had begun to raise plants and animals for food.

Prehistoric people also raised plants for their beauty and used plants for medicine and in religious ceremonies. Sacred festivals and rites involving plants developed, sacred groves were set aside, and gods of fertility, flowers, the vine, and the fields were worshiped.

Myth and Medicine

The sciences of botany and pharmacology were linked early, as scholars from ancient civilizations in the Near East, Egypt, India, China, and elsewhere turned to studying plants for their medicinal virtues.

The Near East

In the Near East, the agricultural traditions of Egypt had permeated many cultures. As early as 700 BC, the Assyrians had compiled an *herbal,* or guidebook, to medicinal plants that contained the names and descriptions of over 900 plants.

In the fourth century BC, the princes of India and Persia maintained pleasure gardens in which plants were admired and studied.

The Far East

In the Far East, the Chinese had a remarkably diverse plant world available to them. With their early traditions of scholarship, they studied and wrote about plants extensively.

- As early as the fourth century AD, Chinese naturalists experimented with breeding improved strains of plants for particular climates.

- Chinese explorers also introduced many new plants to China as they discovered them in their travels.

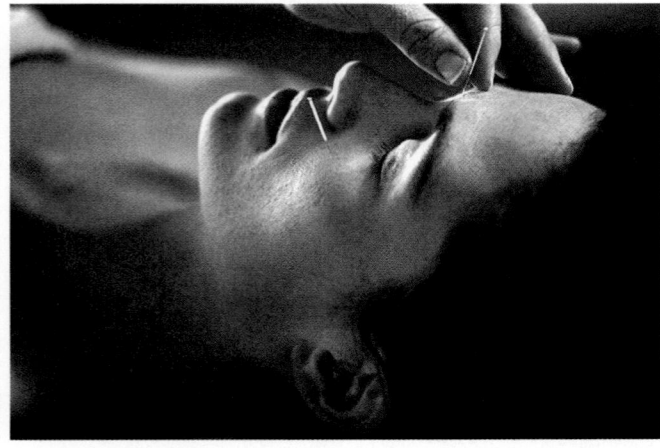

Acupuncture is an ancient Chinese medical procedure to relieve pain and treat a variety of diseases.

TRADITIONAL CHINESE MEDICINE

The medical system used in China is one of the oldest in the world. Going back at least 2,200 years, traditional Chinese medicine is centered on the idea that the human body has enormous powers to heal itself, as long as the forces within the body remain in balance.

Traditional Chinese medicine uses *herbs,* or plants whose leaves or stems are used for medicine, and *acupuncture,* a procedure in which needles are stuck into certain parts of the body in order to relieve pain and activate the body's healing potential.

Acupuncturists believe that disease and pain occur because of an imbalance of two forces of nature called *yin* and *yang.* Insertion of acupuncture needles is meant to restore the balance between these forces.

Pliny the Elder was a first century Roman who wrote many historical and technical works, but only his *Natural History* has survived. *Natural History* is a 37-volume compilation of ancient Greek and Roman wisdom on the subject of plants, animals, and other aspects of the natural world. Books 12 through 19 deal with botany, and books 20 through 27 deal with the subject of plant pharmacology. *Natural History* remained an authority on scientific matters from the time it was written in the first century AD up to the Middle Ages.

 *With the fall of Rome in the fifth century AD, very little progress was made in the field of botany until after the Middle Ages, which lasted through the 1400s. The few botanical works that were produced were mostly rewrites of Pliny and Dioscorides.*

The West

In the West, the first individual to study plants according to a quasi-scientific method was Theophrastus (c. 371–c. 287 BC), a Greek philosopher and disciple of Aristotle. Theophrastus, who kept a kind of botanical garden outside of Athens, distinguished himself in the natural sciences with such works as *Inquiry into Plants* and *Growth of Plants*.

Theophrastus classified some 550 plants known to the classical world on the basis of observed form and structure. He divided them into three categories: trees, bushes, and herbs.

De Materia Medica. Theophrastus's approach became a model of sorts for Dioscorides of Tarsus, a Greek army physician of the first century AD. Dioscorides, who traveled about the Mediterranean with the armies of the emperor Nero, surveyed each region's botanical treasures chiefly as a source of medicines.

Dioscorides collected his data in the five-part *De Materia Medica,* which remained for 1,500 years the principal authority on Western botany and medicinal plants. His writings featured descriptions of more than 600 plants.

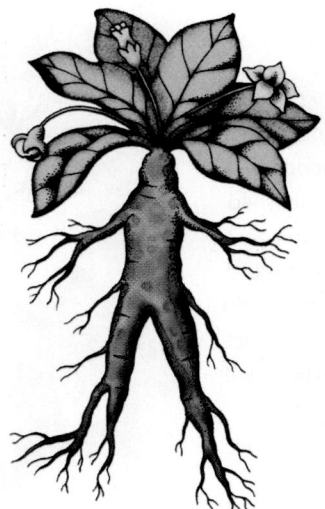

Mandrake, a plant that grows in southern Europe and Asia, has long been thought to have magical properties. Mandrake has two chemicals that can be used as medicine or poison, and ancient peoples used them to make "love potions."

Botany's Rebirth

After the Middle Ages, the development of modern botany began during the Renaissance, a 300-year period of European history that started in the AD 1300s. Interest in plants revived with the general rise in scientific curiosity.

THE AGE OF EXPLORATION

During the Renaissance, European exploration of the world greatly stimulated the study of botany and other sciences. Explorers discovered many new types of plants and brought them to scholars to examine and identify.

The Age of Exploration brought a new awareness that the world—including the world of plants—is far larger and more complex than had previously been imagined.

Form, Function, and Names

As part of the effort to organize the information that was being gathered on a scale previously unimagined, various means were sought to describe plants more accurately and to discover the bases of their interrelationships. In this way, modern botanical gardens and botanical studies were born.

Modern botany developed around such basic research areas as the classification of plants and the study of their form and function. The study of plant form made tremendous advances during the 1600s, after the development of the compound microscope.

During the mid-1700s, the Swedish naturalist Carolus Linnaeus developed a system of naming plants that eventually became accepted as a standard classification system. This system has been modified and expanded into the modern classification system used today.

Classification and the study of plants' form and function gradually expanded into many specialized fields as botanists focused on more specific aspects of plant life.

Herbals, large books with descriptions of plants and handsome woodcut illustrations, were published following the invention of the printing press in the 15th century. Though these works contributed little to botanical knowledge, several included illustrations drawn from nature rather than from the imagination.

Early Botanical Gardens		
Founded	**Garden**	**Founder**
1540s	Padua and Pisa, Italy	under the patronage of Cosimo de Medici
1635	*Jardin des Plantes Medicinales* in Paris, France	Guy de la Brosse, physician to Louis XIII
1673	Chelsea, England	Society of Apothecaries
before 1700	European cities of Zurich, Bologna, Leiden, Leipzig, Breslau, Basel, Heidelberg, and Berlin	Not known
c. 1700	Royal Botanic Gardens at Kew, England	British Royal Family (First manager: botanist William Aiton; initiated a farsighted plan of plant exploration, sending botanists to collect new specimens in distant parts of the world.)

Modern Scientific Approaches to the Study of Plants	
Scientist	**Work**
Marcello Malpighi (1628–1694), Italy	began fundamental studies in plant anatomy and morphology
Nehemiah Grew (1641–1712), England	also studied plant anatomy and morphology
Robert Hooke (1635–1703), English experimental philosopher	discovered cells in cork, and thereby initiated the study of plant cytology
Rudolph Jacob Camerarius (1665–1721), German physician and botanist	beginnings of plant genetics; first to demonstrate that plants have sexuality, and that pollen is necessary for fertilization and the formation of seeds
Joseph Gottlieb Koelreuter (1733–1806), German botanist	experiments in plant hybridization
Stephen Hales (1677–1761), British physiologist and inventor	built on the work of William Harvey's blood circulation studies; made important beginnings in plant physiology, particularly the movement of the sap
Joseph Priestley (1733–1804), British theologian and scientist	contributed the first scientific understanding of the role of plants in producing oxygen
Hugo von Mohl (1805–1872), German botanist	discovered the functional structure of vascular tissues in stems, roots, and leaves; differentiated the protoplasmic substance of a cell's body from its nucleus using a microscope
Karl Gustav Sanio (1832–1891), Polish botanist	discovered the origin of the vascular cambium; showed how it produces annual rings in the course of tree growth

PLANT TAXONOMY

is the science of naming and classifying plants. Botanists classify plants by grouping them according to their shared similarities. This provides a logical way to organize information about plants and to show how different plants are related to each other.

Most botanists group plants by their overall appearance, their internal structure, and the form of their reproductive organs. One frequently used classification system classifies plants into two large *groups* and several *divisions*.

Classification of Plants

Plant classification and form provides the framework for almost all fields of botany. In studying a plant, a botanist must first know what type of plant it is. Botanists who specialize in *systematics* identify and name plant species.

Given the complexity of their task, it is not surprising that continued revision of earlier taxonomic divisions goes on. Plants can now be examined for differences and similarities at their molecular level, rather than solely on the basis of external appearance, form, and structure. This new information is also altering some taxonomic presumptions about family lineage.

Fortunately, the system of plant classification that has evolved over the centuries is flexible, and its organizational framework is now capable of incorporating not only the 350,000 or so known plant species, but the estimated 100,000 plants that will be discovered in the future. (See pages 90–91.)

Two Main Groups

The plant kingdom is separated into two large groups: those that do not have *vascular tissue* and those that do. Vascular tissue is tissue that carries water and nutrients throughout the plant.

Nonvascular Plants. The nonvascular plants lack *xylem* and *phloem* tissues. These are the vascular tissues that carry water and food from one part of the plant body to another. Nonvascular plants do not have true roots, stems, or leaves. They are usually low to the ground and live in moist, shady places.

Vascular Plants. All other divisions of the plant kingdom are made up of vascular plants that contain xylem and phloem tissues.

- xylem: the tissue that carries water throughout a vascular plant
- phloem: the tissue that carries food throughout a vascular plant

◄ **Elm trees,** like all trees, are vascular plants. They have true roots, stems, and leaves. Their water and nutrients are transported by xylem and phloem tissues.

DIVISIONS OF THE PLANT KINGDOM

The divisions of Kingdom Plantae are mostly organized in ascending order of complexity.

Chlorophyta
Single celled or multicelled, chlorophyll present, mostly freshwater

Rhodophyta
Multicelled, red pigments cover green of chlorophyll, mostly marine

Phaeophyta
Multicelled, brown pigments cover green of chlorophyll, mostly marine

Bryophyta
Multicellular reproductive structures, no true phloem or xylem

Lycophyta
True leaves have a single vein and are photosynthetic, variously branched stems

Sphenophyta
Nonphotosynthetic, leaves are reduced to scales, jointed stems

Psilophyta
Vascular, without true leaves, stems branch by forking

Pterophyta
Leaves have more than one vein, spores are produced on leaves

Cycadophyta
Gymnosperms, leaves are pinnate and palmlike, sperm are motile

Ginkgophyta
Gymnosperms, strong cambial growth, small fan-shaped leaves, motile sperm

Gnetophyta
Gymnosperms, seeds are produced in cones, wood contains vessels, nonmotile sperm

Pinophyta
Gymnosperms, wood contains no vessels, strong cambial growth, nonmotile sperm

Anthophyta
Flowering, seeds borne within fruits

Modern Classification

Each plant is described in a series of rankings, going from the most general to the most specific, and reflecting the progressive diversification of life from certain common ancestors to ever-greater specialization.

The evolutionary pathways by which plants have progressed over millions of years becomes an integral part of the description.

- Starting at the largest and most inclusive category, every living organism is assigned membership in a *kingdom*.

- The plant kingdom is subdivided into *divisions* (called *phyla* in the animal kingdom) according to certain perceived similarities and differences among their populations.

- Divisions are further divided into distinct *classes*.

- Classes are divided into *orders*.

- Orders are divided into *families*.

- Families are divided into *genera* (singular *genus*).

- Genera are divided into *species*.

Naming Species

Each individual species is officially known by its two-part species name. The first name is the species' Latin or Greek generic, or genus, which is capitalized, and the second, its species epithet or descriptor, which is uncapitalized. The species name usually describes some unique characteristic such as color, form, habit of growth, native origin, or the individual who first introduced it to the Western world.

RULES OF BOTANICAL NOMENCLATURE

Consistency is important in science. It allows scientists around the world to share information. In 1930, the International Rules of Botanical Nomenclature were accepted by botanists of virtually all nations, making it possible for scientists to communicate accurately with each other as new species are added or known species are reevaluated and their taxonomic descriptions modified.

PLANT DIVISIONS

Botanists classify plants by grouping them according to their shared similarities. Most botanists group plants by their overall appearance, their internal structure, and the form of their reproductive organs.

The most widely accepted approach describes 13 divisions. The 13 divisions can be further divided into five subkingdoms.

FIVE SUBKINGDOMS OF KINGDOM PLANTAE

The five subkingdoms are, in order of complexity:

- the *thallophytes,* or lower plants, comprising three divisions
- the *bryophytes,* consisting of a single division
- the *ferns* and *fern allies,* consisting of four divisions
- the *gymnosperms,* or naked seed plants, consisting of four divisions
- the *angiosperms,* or flowering plants, consisting of a single division

The Lower Plants

The *thallophytes* are called the lower plants because all three divisions within the subkingdom are relatively primitive. They have little or no specialization of parts. They do not have stems, roots, or leaves. *Thallophyta* translates roughly as "sprout plant."

Thallophytes are divided into three divisions.

- Division **Chlorophyta**
- Division **Rhodophyta**
- Division **Phaeophyta**

Division Chlorophyta

Commonly known as green algae, this division includes a diverse 7,000 or so species of algae, most of which are freshwater plants found growing in and on ponds and lakes.

- Green pigment bodies called *chlorophyll* give green algae their distinctive color and the ability to manufacture their own food molecules using the sun's energy. (See pages 134–135.)
- Some chlorophytes are single-celled and *colonial*— they live together as a single unit but without any division of labor or specialization of parts.
- Many chlorophytes are multicellular, but simple in structure and function.
- A minority possess microscopic *cilia,* whiplike organs that give them some mobility.

◀ **The plant kingdom** is made up of primitive water plants, spore-bearing mosses and ferns, and seed-bearing gymnosperms and angiosperms.

- Green algae typically reproduce asexually in one of two ways:

    1. The mother cell divides into two daughter cells, each of which becomes an identical new plant.

    2. Some species reproduce through *fragmentation*, the mechanical breaking apart of a chlorophyte through some event such as wave action.

- Since death of the parent cell does not normally occur, these species of green algae are in a sense immortal.

- Still other species of chlorophytes reproduce through sexual reproduction, the fusing of two motile cells to form a new cell.

- Green algae is often found in association with a fungus, a combination that is known as a *lichen*.

- The most familiar genus is pond scum, *Spirogyra*, the bloom that turns many stagnant ponds bright green in warm weather.

Division Rhodophyta

Red algae, the common name of Rhodophyta, consists of some 4,000 species of simple multicellular plants.

- Rhodophytes are generally red or purple in color due to the red pigment *phycoerythrin* that masks the green chlorophyll that is also present.

- Red algae are typically found in marine habitats, favoring relatively warm waters such as those of the Mediterranean.

- Rhodophytes anchor themselves to rocks by means of a rootlike *holdfast*.

- They often display fine frondlike branches of a slick, leathery texture.

- Rhodophytes are found at the tide line and in some cases as much as 100 meters (330 feet) below the water's surface.

- Their red pigments give them the ability to capture the faint rays of orange to red sunlight that can penetrate to this depth, and they are able to carry out food production to sustain themselves.

Giant kelps grow off the Pacific coast of North America and reach lengths of 70 meters (230 feet) or more.

Division Phaeophyta

Phaeophyta, or brown algae, includes roughly 1,500 species of brown-colored algae.

- They range in size from tiny seaweeds and rockweeds to the giant kelps.

- Brown algae are the dominant marine plant life of many parts of the temperate world.

- The phaeophytes attach themselves firmly to the rocky coastline with holdfasts.

- Fan kelp, sea collander, and rockweed or bladderwrack are among the most familiar phaeophytes.

PRACTICAL ALGAE

Red algae—the rhodophytes—have many uses for humans. It constitutes a significant part of the diet of many coastal peoples. Irish moss, *Chondrus crispus,* has commercial value as the source of *carrageenan,* a gelatinous substance used in cosmetics, soaps, and puddings, and in general manufacturing. Tengusa, *Gelidium corneum,* is the principal source of *agar,* used in pharmaceuticals, and also is the most important edible seaweed in the Japanese diet.

Bryophytes

A single division, the bryophytes are ranked as developmentally higher in the kingdom's hierarchy because they are *terrestrial:* they grow on land.

Bryophytes are traditionally made up of **liverworts**, **mosses**, and **hornworts**. Many scientists consider mosses to be the only true bryophytes, but the term is still used to refer to hornworts, liverworts, and mosses, which share many characteristics.

Division Bryophyta

This division includes about 24,000 species of mosses, liverworts, and hornworts. Small, green, and flowerless, the bryophytes are multicellular plants with pigments and food manufacturing and storage capabilities similar to those of the green algae.

- Bryophytes are *nonvascular,* which means they have no specialized water transport systems such as roots or stems.

- They draw water and nutrients chiefly through rootlike structures known as *rhizoids.*

- Because bryophytes have given rise to no more advanced plant forms, they are often considered a terminal evolutionary group.

PEAT MOSS

Peat is partly decayed plant matter that has collected in swamps and marshes over long periods of time. It is generally the first stage in the formation of coal.

Peat moss is a kind of moss from which peat is formed. Peat mosses make up a genus called Sphagnum. They have a spongy texture and are absorbent. Many gardeners use them to keep young plants from drying out. In the past, some American Indians made diapers out of peat mosses. During World War I (1914–1918), peat mosses were used as dressings for wounds.

▲ **Peat moss**

Peat ▶

Mosses play an important part in the lives of many small animals. Certain mites and spiders live in mosses. Some birds use moss fibers to build or line their nests. Weevils have been found with mosses growing on their backs, serving as camouflage.

Liverwort is a type of small, nonflowering plant. There are thousands of species of liverworts, hundreds of which grow in the United States and Canada.

Mosses

- True mosses grow erect but are usually no more than 5 centimeters (2 inches) in height.
- Communities of moss can cover large areas—sometimes many acres—in carpets of green.
- Mosses grow and reproduce in two phases—as *sporophytes* and *gametophytes*. This kind of life cycle is called *alternation of generations*.
- The gametophyte is the plant familiarly recognized as moss.
- In the second phase of the moss life cycle, a zygote develops into a sporophyte that remains attached to the gametophyte. Microscopic structures called *spores* form in the sporophyte.
- A sporophyte may contain from four to more than a million spores, depending on the species.
- *Sphagnum* mosses, consisting of some 300 species, create vast peat bogs and grazing fields for moss-eating herds in colder, temperate regions.
- Peat grows at the rate of about 30 centimeters (12 inches) per hundred years, and is harvested as fuel in some parts of the world.

Liverworts and Hornworts

- Liverworts are small and resemble some seaweeds in appearance.
- Liverworts are found in polar, mild, and tropical regions.
- Liverworts have *thalli*—flat, dark green, veinless leaves that look something like a liver.
- They contain chemicals called terpenoids, which give some liverworts a spicy aroma.
- Liverworts generally are inedible to people and many animals.
- Hornworts constitute hundreds of species.
- They are found throughout the world but are especially common in tropical regions and in warm, moist climates.

Hornworts grow mainly on bare, damp, shaded soil. They are often found along roadsides or near edges of streams or lakes.

Ferns and Fern Allies

The four divisions of ferns and fern allies, and the remaining higher divisions, are all vascular plants, or *tracheophytes*. They have separate and specialized structures for transporting water and foods throughout the plant body. The seedless vascular divisions include the club mosses, horsetails, whisk ferns, and true ferns.

Division Lycophyta

Lycophyta, or club mosses, are flowerless, mostly evergreen land plants that resemble mosses but tend to be larger.

- Two hundred and fifty million years ago lycophytes included giant lycopod trees that grew in coal-forming swamps.

- Today only 400 species remain, including some tropical *epiphytes*, plants that rely on other plants for support but are not parasitic.

- Some species such as ground pine are native to the temperate forest floor. Others grow in the Arctic.

- Lycophytes include the quillwort, an aquatic plant with quill-shaped leaves.

Like mosses, ferns and fern allies reproduce via spores and a cyclical process known as *alternation of generations*.

ALTERNATION OF GENERATIONS

The life cycle of ferns and fern allies involves two distinct stages—asexual and sexual.

The asexual stage

1. This stage begins with the sporophyte, which is the familiar fern plant with its fronds, stems, and roots.

2. Spore-producing cases appear on the undersides of the fertile fronds, clustering in dots, rows, or masses. Each species has its own characteristic distribution pattern.

3. Large numbers of microscopic single-celled spores are produced within the cases.

4. When the spores mature, the protective membrane over the cases shrivels, the individual cases split open, and the spores, often by the millions, are catapulted through the air.

5. The spores fall to the moist ground, some of them germinating to form gametophytes.

The sexual stage

1. The gametophytes are thin, flat, heart-shaped plants of no more than 2 centimeters (0.5 inch).

2. They produce both male and female sex organs in which sperm and egg are developed.

3. The sperm of one gametophyte swims along the damp ground to fertilize an egg on another gametophyte while the stationary egg is similarly fertilized from elsewhere.

4. A new, young sporophyte springs up from each fertilized gametophyte.

5. Once the new generation is self-sufficient, the gametophyte decomposes and disappears.

◀ **The resurrection plant** is a lycophyte. This remarkable plant closes up and appears to die during periods of desert drought and then springs to life again when water is available.

Division Sphenophyta

Horsetails, or Sphenophyta, survive as a single genus, with perhaps 35 species.

- Sphenophytes grow in wet places all over the world, except for the countries of Australia and New Zealand.

- Their distinctive stems, jointed and unbranched, ringed with circles of small, black scalelike leaves and topped with a brushy spore-filled tip, give the horsetails their popular name.

- Fossil records indicate that extinct horsetails may have grown to over 27 meters (90 feet) in height, but modern species rarely exceed 1 meter (39 inches).

- The stems of horsetails, which are suffused with silica, are sometimes used in polishing metals.

Horsetails

Whisk ferns

Ferns

Division Psilophyta

Psilophyta, or whisk ferns, contains just two living genera with a total of perhaps nine species.

- They grow in humid, subtropic, and tropical conditions.

- Psilophytes reproduce by spores, and appear in clumps as rootless, leafless, branching plants of fernlike delicacy.

Division Pterophyta

Pterophyta, which is made up of the ferns, is the only division of the ancient vascular seedless plants to continue to flourish in modern times. There are some 12,000 living species of ferns.

- Ferns are worldwide in distribution, though most are adapted to grow in tropical regions.

- Fern *fronds,* or leaves, come in many shapes and sizes, often feathery in form.

- Fronds expand by unfurling from the base. At this immature stage, they are called *fiddleheads* because of their resemblance to the neck and scroll of a violin.

- Pterophytes are the first in evolutionary terms to have true roots.

- Ferns growing in tropical climates may attain heights similar to those of trees, but most temperate species are seldom more than 1 meter (39 inches) in stature.

Naked Seed Plants

Gymnosperms, or naked seed plants, are one of two large groups of seed-bearing plants. They are somewhat more primitive than the *angiosperms,* the second group of seed-bearers. Unlike angiosperms, gymnosperms do not produce flowers. Most gymnosperms bear their seeds in cones. Gymnosperms are divided into four divisions.

- **Division** Cycadophyta
- **Division** Ginkgophyta
- **Division** Gnetaphyta
- **Division** Pinophyta

Ephedra is a wiry gnetophyte shrub native to the deserts of the American Southwest.

Division Cycadophyta

The Cycadophyta, or *cycads,* are plants that resemble tree ferns, with fernlike leaves and large seed cones.

- Cycads were the dominant vegetation in the time of the dinosaurs.
- Today they number only 100 species.
- This group is generally confined to the tropics and subtropics.
- Pollen and seed cones are borne on separate male and female plants.

Division Ginkgophyta

Ginkgophyta—or gingkos—is represented in modern times by a single species, the maidenhair or ginkgo tree.

- The ginkgo tree exists only in domesticated varieties—none exist in the wild.
- Ginkgos are recognizable by their fan-shaped leaves and fleshy seeds borne at the ends of branches.

Division Gnetophyta

Gnetophyta is represented by about 70 seed-bearing species, most of them highly unusual in form and adaptation.

- The *Welwitschia,* which is native to the deserts of South Africa, does most of its growing underground.
- The two straplike leaves of the Welwitschia split lengthwise repeatedly to create a tangled pile of vegetative debris on the desert surface.

SACRED TREE

Gingkos thrived during the Mesozoic era but, according to botanists, would probably have naturally gone extinct thousands of years ago. They were saved, however, by ancient Chinese and Japanese Buddhist monks, who considered gingko trees sacred, and planted them around ancient temple grounds.

◀ **Gingko tree**

The giant redwood trees of the Pacific Coast Range, which are conifers, are the tallest plants on Earth. One tree in Redwood National Park, California, reaches over 115 meters (379 feet).

Division Pinophyta

The trees of Pinophyta, sometimes called Coniferophyta, are commonly called conifers. They comprise all the conifers, of which there are currently about 550 species.

- The conifers include pines, firs, cedars, yews, hemlocks, larches, spruces, redwoods, cypresses, and junipers.

- Most bear soft, berrylike cones.

- Conifers are primarily evergreen, although a few species are *deciduous*, meaning they shed their leaves each year.

- The leaves of conifers are distinctive in that they are generally needle-shaped, a specialized adaptation designed to resist extremes of dryness and cold.

- The needles are grouped in *fascicles,* or clusters, of two, three, or five, depending upon species.

- Individual fascicles remain alive and attached for two or more years before separating, giving rise to the common term *evergreen* for most conifers.

- The dominant land plants 200 million years ago, conifers are less extensive today, except in many northern regions and at high altitudes where their ability to prosper in poor or shallow soil and reduced moisture gives them an advantage.

CONIFER REPRODUCTION

Each conifer produces both smaller pollen (male) cones and larger seed (female) cones on the same plant. The male cones occur on the lower branches and the more conspicuous female cones occur on the higher branches. Each female cone is a concentration of scales.

1. Seeds develop at the base of the scales of the female cone.

2. When the seeds are ripe, the scales open, and wind-borne male pollen falls down among them.

3. The pollinated cone closes up again and fertilization occurs.

4. Countless embryos begin to develop.

5. As much as 2 years after the cycle begins, the scales spread apart for a second time, and paper-thin winged seeds are disseminated on the wind, ready to take root as new organisms if they find a congenial patch of soil.

Flowering Plants

The *angiosperms* are the flowering plants. They are the dominant and most varied division of plants on Earth today. There are more than 300,000 species of angiosperms, with more being constantly added. Among the most important angiosperms are broadleaf trees and crop plants.

Fruits and Enclosed Seeds

Angiosperms are distinctive from all other plant divisions because they have enclosed seeds. Their seeds develop within the sexual structures of the flower.

Angiosperm flowers contain both male reproductive organs called *stamens* and female reproductive organs called *carpels*. Stamens produce pollen grains that carry *sperm* (male sex cells) to the carpels. Carpels contain *ovules*, or eggs, that become seeds after fertilization by sperm.

The carpels develop into fruits. The fruits develop after fertilization as a means for covering, surrounding, and further protecting the seeds.

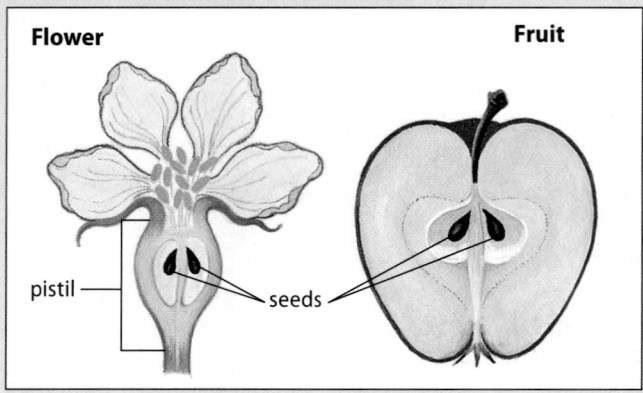

The flower and fruit of an angiosperm contain the plant's seeds.

Angiosperms include a huge variety of plants, from the oak tree to the orchid. They grow in most of the world's environments, including Arctic tundra, deserts, and rain forests.

Monocots and Eudicots

Angiosperms consist of a single division: division Anthophyta. Scientists divide the angiosperms into several classes. The two largest classes are:

1. the *monocotyledons*, or *monocots*

2. the *eudicotyledons*, or *eudicots*

Seed Leaves. Monocots grow from seeds that contain one seed leaf called a *cotyledon*. All other angiosperms, including the eudicots, have two cotyledons in their seeds. Flowers with two cotyledons are sometimes called *dicotyledons*, or *dicots*.

Scientists once treated all dicots as belonging to their own class. They now know that many dicots are only distantly related to others.

Dicots, like this snapdragon, have flower parts that appear in multiples of four or five.

Monocotyledon seeds, such as this corn seed, have one cotyledon.

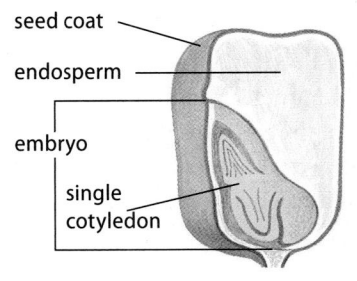

seed coat

endosperm

embryo

single cotyledon

Dicotyledon seeds, such as this bean seed, have two cotyledons.

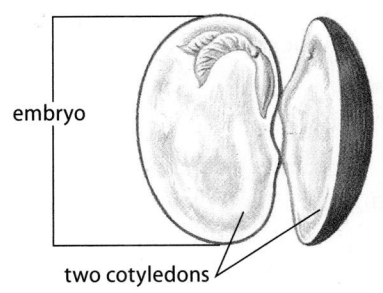

embryo

two cotyledons

	Monocots	Dicots
Flower parts	found in multiples of three	found in multiples of four or five
Stem structure	soft	often woody
Vascular system	consists of scattered channels	consists of an orderly circle of channels
Species	about 65,000	about 190,000
Families	about 60	about 250
Examples	Grasses, tropical palms, orchids, lilies, onions, and garlic	Broadleaf trees, sunflowers, legumes (including beans, alfalfa, soybeans, peanuts, and peas), broccoli, cabbage, mustard, turnips, brussels sprouts, and cottton

PLANT ANATOMY

There is an enormous amount of diversity in the plant world. A plant can be so tiny as to be almost invisible or as large as a giant redwood. It can go through its entire life cycle in a matter of days or live for centuries. There are plants that can live in seawater, in freshwater, in soil, or suspended in air in the forest canopy.

With all these differences, the *anatomy,* or physical structure, of each and every plant is dedicated to delivering and processing the materials that all plants need to survive: water, carbon dioxide, sunlight, and mineral nutrients.

Plant Cells

All plants—like all living things—are made up of cells. The most primitive plants are single-celled organisms, while the more complex plants are aggregates, often of many millions of living and nonliving cells organized into specialized tissues, each performing one or more activities that contribute to the life of the plant. (See pages 48–51.)

Size and Shape

The size and shape of an individual plant cell is determined by its function. Cells can range from spherical to angular or stringlike. Some are as wide as they are long, while others—certain fiber cells—reach lengths of as much as 60 centimeters (24 inches) but have virtually no crosswise dimension.

Whatever their function, plant cells are so small that they need to be studied with the aid of a microscope, and in some cases, with a high-magnification electron microscope.

Cell Wall

Plant cells and animal cells have much in common, but plant cells are unique in having an external wall that gives each cell—and the plant itself—a degree of rigidity and self-support. Cell walls

- consist chiefly of a substance called cellulose, but also of the substances lignin and pectin.
- secrete materials that bind one cell to the next to hold the plant together and form channels for the circulation of fluids within the plant and for communication between cells.
- vary greatly in thickness with the age and type of cell.

A primary cell wall is the cell wall of a young, growing cell. It is typically thin and only partially rigid to allow the cell to reach its full size. As the cell matures, it lays down a secondary wall whose composition and structure reflect a degree of specialization.

Typical Plant Cell

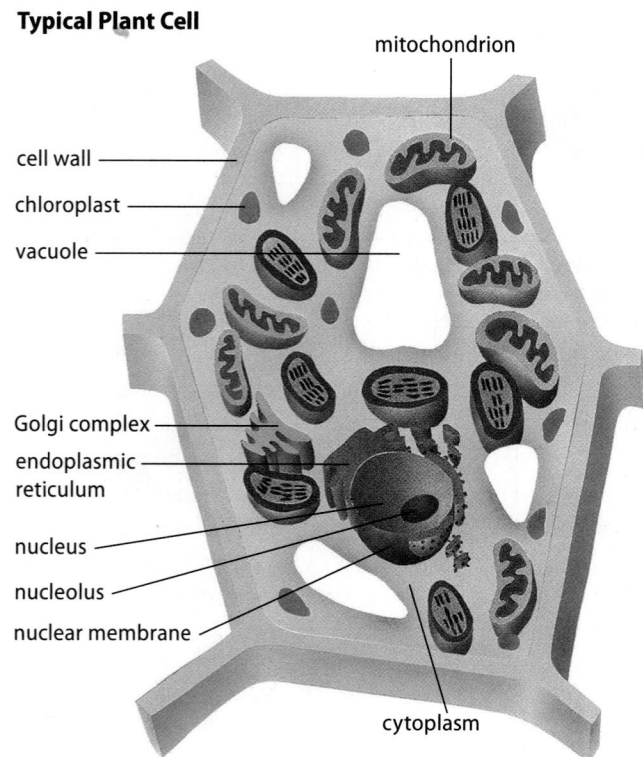

- mitochondrion
- cell wall
- chloroplast
- vacuole
- Golgi complex
- endoplasmic reticulum
- nucleus
- nucleolus
- nuclear membrane
- cytoplasm

Inside the Cell

Within the cell wall are the nucleus, cytoplasm, and organelles. The *nucleus* controls and directs cellular activity, taking its cues from the genes strung along its chromosomes. *Cytoplasm* is all the cell material—besides the nucleus—that is contained within the cell wall. It consists chiefly of a viscous, transparent substance composed of 85 to 90 percent water in which are suspended proteins, sugars, fats, acids, and salts.

Organelles. Also within the cytoplasm are the *organelles*, or specialized structures, that perform vital functions for the cell and ultimately the plant. The organelles include *plastids*, *vacuoles*, and *mitochondria*.

Plastids are specialized disc-shaped bodies.

- **chloroplasts:** Green-colored plastids that contain the pigment chlorophyll. Chloroplasts are the sites of photosynthesis, the process by which plants harness sunlight to synthesize food molecules.

- **chromoplasts:** Plastids that synthesize and store red, yellow, and orange pigments. They are responsible for the coloration of petals, leaves, and fruits in many species.

- **leucoplasts:** Colorless plastids that store glucose in the form of starch until needed by the plant.

Vacuoles are envelopes filled with a watery substance known as cell sap. In young cells, vacuoles are small and multiple. In mature cells, they are large and centralized in a single cavity. The vacuole acts as a catch basin for stored foods, water, salts, and materials that would be toxic to the cell if allowed to seep out. They also help maintain the cell's internal pressure, keeping the cell firm and rigid.

Mitochondria are the cell's power centers, using atmospheric oxygen to convert sugars into carbon dioxide and water and releasing adenosine triphosphate (ATP). ATP is the major source of chemical energy for biochemical reactions, from synthesis to growth. Mitochondria are often present in large numbers—up to a thousand per cell.

The organs of flowering plants include the roots, stem, leaves, flowers, seeds, and fruits.

THE basics

PLANT ANATOMY

Plants are made up of cells, tissues, and organs.

Cells

- different from animal cells—have a cell wall that gives the plant rigidity and self-support

- groups of specialized cells form tissue, work together to perform certain functions

Tissue

- plants consist of different types of simple and complex tissue

- all plants except bryophytes have vascular tissue, which carries water, minerals, and other nutrients throughout the plant

- xylem tissue consists of cells that carry water and minerals from the roots to the leaves

- phloem tissue consists of cells that carry food made by photosynthesis in the leaves to other parts of the plant

Organs

- vegetative organs involved with basic growth

- vegetative organs consist of the roots, stem, and leaves

- reproductive organs specialized for reproduction

- reproductive organs consist of the flowers, seeds, and fruits

Plant Tissues

In the simplest photosynthesizing organisms—the red algae living in water—there is no need for specialized tissues. Each cell is at the plant's surface and makes direct contact with its environment, where it absorbs essential water and nutrients and discharges wastes. But in higher, vascular plants, the individual cells cannot function autonomously. Many are deep within the massive, multicelled body, and they can survive only through cooperation and division of labor among many different sorts of cells in many different locations.

UNLIMITED GROWTH

The growing tips of a plant are called the *apical meristems*. The apical meristems contain the cells that divide and grow to form new leaves, flowers, and stems.

Apical meristems have a property that is unique to the plant kingdom: *open growth*. Unlike the cells of creatures in the animal kingdom, for whom vertical growth is finite, the meristematic tissues of plants continue to grow throughout the life of the plant.

As apical meristems elongate, they gradually alter their structure to become one of several different kinds of specialized tissue types, as the plant may require.

Simple Tissues

These tissues are composed of a single, uniform type of cell.

Epidermis is analogous to the skin of organisms in the animal kingdom.

- one layer of cells thick
- protects underlying tissues
- carries out exchanges of water, minerals, oxygen, and carbon dioxide, depending on the part of the plant where it is found
- forms the surface layers of roots, stems, leaves, and flowers
- epidermis cells are usually flattish, with large vacuoles, a relatively small amount of cytoplasm, and a cell wall covered with cutin, a waxy, waterproofing substance

Parenchyma is the tissue that acts as the site of chloroplasts (for photosynthesis) and of storage.

- parenchyma cells are more or less spherical in shape
- contain a thin primary wall and no secondary wall
- develop from the ground meristem
- found chiefly in the cortex, which forms the bulk of stems, roots, leaves, and fruits
- important in wound healing and the regeneration of plant parts after injury or pruning

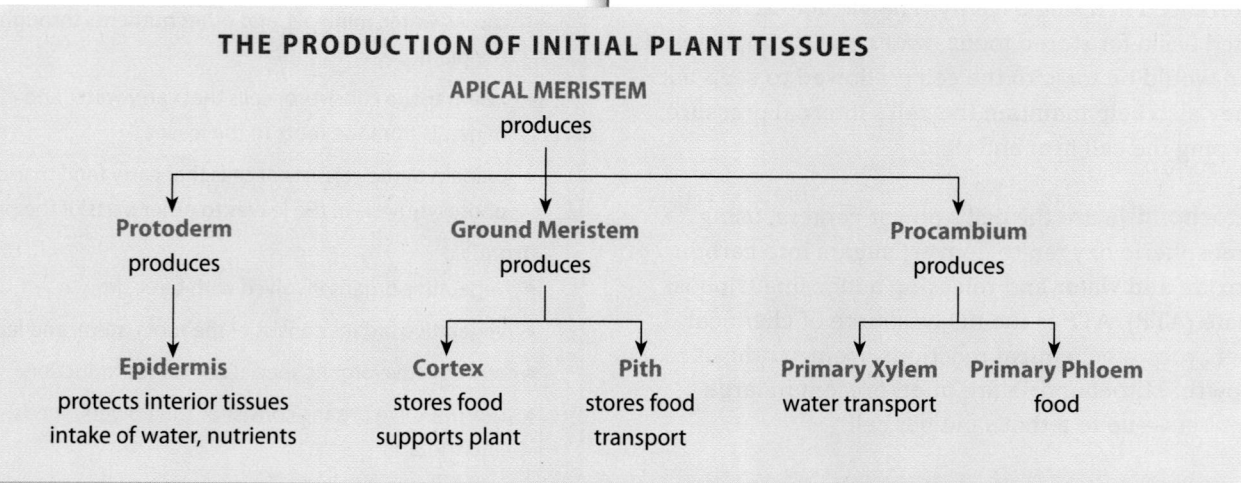

THE PRODUCTION OF INITIAL PLANT TISSUES

APICAL MERISTEM produces

Protoderm produces → Epidermis: protects interior tissues, intake of water, nutrients

Ground Meristem produces → Cortex: stores food, supports plant; Pith: stores food, transport

Procambium produces → Primary Xylem: water transport; Primary Phloem: food

The cork tree produces an uncommonly large amount of cork tissue that can be harvested as a renewable crop.

Cork cells serve chiefly as a waterproofing tissue.

- have thick walls impregnated with *suberin*, a waxy material
- found in many older woody plants
- produced by the stretching and tearing of the epidermis as the stem's girth increases year by year

Collenchyma tissue cells make up a young plant's primary supportive tissues.

- combine flexibility with tensile strength
- cells are elongated
- evolved from ground meristem cells
- usually concentrated directly beneath the epidermis in stems and bordering the veins of dicot leaves

Sclerenchyma cells strengthen mature plant parts.

- have thick primary walls
- secondary walls are often impregnated with lignin
- cells vary greatly in size and shape depending on whether they are further specialized into *fibers* or *sclerids*
- fiber sclerenchyma are elongated, tapered cells that aggregate into long, tough strands
- sclerids are more irregular in shape, resembling stars, stones, columns, hourglasses
- sclerids give strength to such things as nut shells, the hard parts of seeds, and the texture of certain fruits

Complex Tissues

The complex tissues are the vascular tissues. They are specialized for conducting water, minerals, and dissolved foods throughout the plant.

Xylem is the tissue that carries water and minerals from a plant's roots to its leaves.

- characterized by long tubular and nontubular cells that conduct water and nutrients and provide support
- forms countless pathways for water transport through the roots, stems, leaves, flowers, and fruits
- as the plant matures, more xylem tissue is found toward the inside of the plant, near the nonfunctioning center of a trunk or branch

Phloem is the tissue that carries food made by photosynthesis in the leaves to other parts of the plant.

- runs parallel with the elongated strands of xylem tissue
- designed to transport food, primarily sugars, generally downward from the site of photosynthesis in the leaves
- fundamental cells are sieve tubes, which form a transport network throughout the body of the plant
- movement in the xylem is generally upward and movement in the phloem is generally downward
- in actual practice either tissue may channel movement laterally, along branches, for example
- as the plant matures, more phloem is found toward the outer, dermal area, or in the case of trees, toward the bark side of the plant

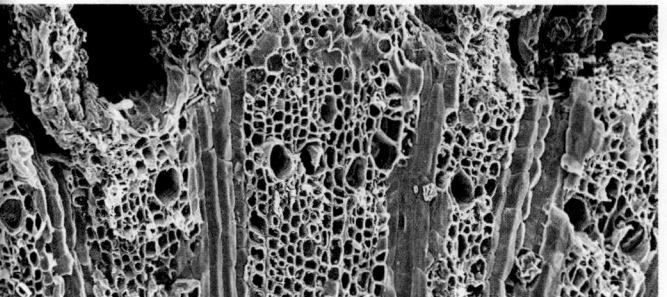

Xylem tissue carries water and minerals throughout the body of the plant. Sugar maple sap rises through xylem.

PLANT ORGANS

Plants are made up of several important parts called *organs*. Plant organs include *roots, stems, leaves, flowers,* and *fruits*. Each organ is a combination of two or more kinds of tissue, and each is more complex than their tissue parts. These interacting organs combine, in turn, into systems that carry out a major process, such as digestion, circulation, respiration, or reproduction.

The *vegetative organs*—the roots, stems, and leaves—are involved with the growth of the plant.

The *reproductive organs*—the flowers, seeds, and fruits—are specialized for reproduction.

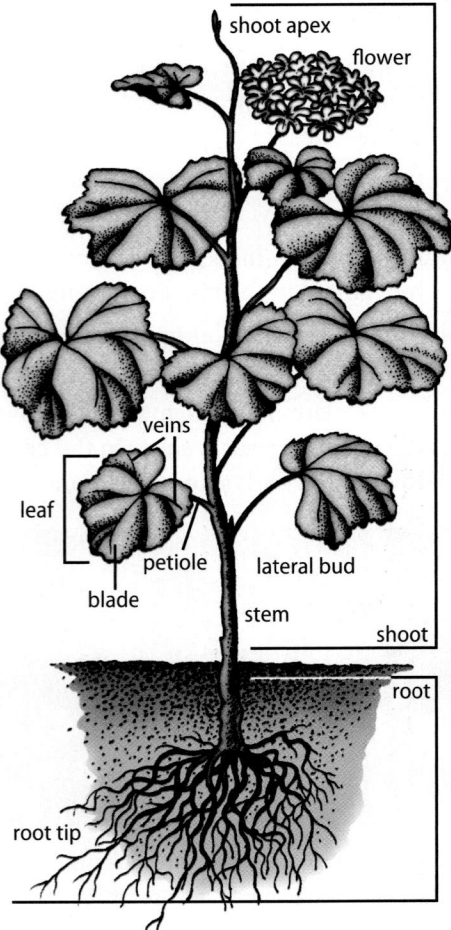

Roots

Plants absorb water and waterborne nutrients through their roots. Most roots are long and round and grow underground. The roots anchor the plant to its site by sending branching extensions deep and wide. Many roots also store food for later use by the plant.

Kinds of Roots

The first root to develop from a seed is the *primary root*. It produces many branches called *secondary roots*. The secondary roots produce branches of their own.

There are two main kinds of root systems:

- taproot
- fibrous

Factors such as depth and quality of soil, and the amount of rainfall, make one type of root system more advantageous than another.

Taproot System

- the primary root is the main, longest, and thickest root of the mature plant
- examples: dandelion, carrot, beet, and the vastly larger walnut tree
- taproot system of the grape vine may reach several meters into the soil

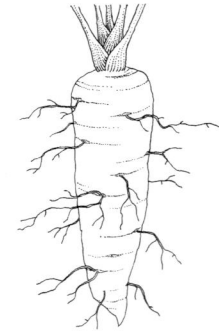

Taproot (Carrot)

Fibrous System

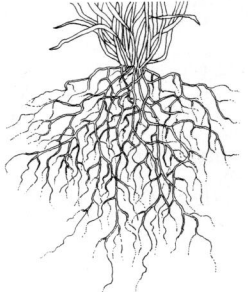

Fibrous (Grass)

- the primary root ceases to grow when the plant is young
- several new, secondary roots of roughly equal size grow in various directions
- secondary roots reach different soil depths and water sources to maximize uptake
- fibrous roots can make up more than half the plant body

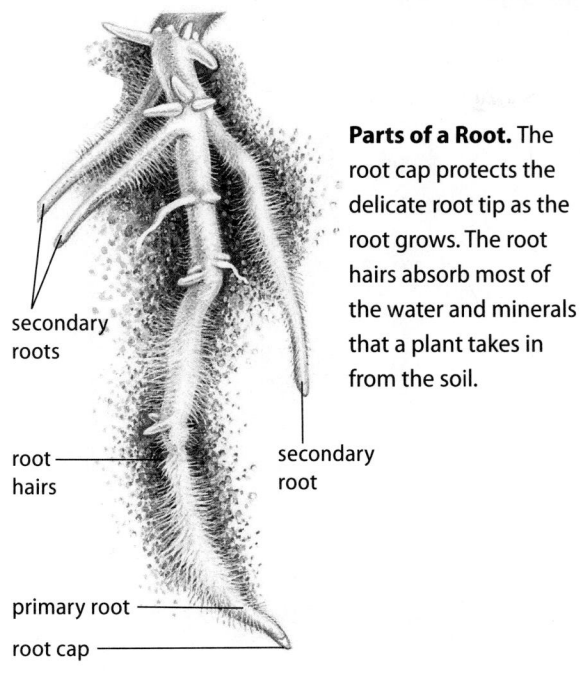

Parts of a Root. The root cap protects the delicate root tip as the root grows. The root hairs absorb most of the water and minerals that a plant takes in from the soil.

secondary roots

root hairs

secondary root

primary root

root cap

SOIL PROTECTOR

Roots take water and minerals from the soil, but they also give something back: protection. The dense network of roots of grasses, trees, and other plants hold soil in place, preventing erosion by wind and water.

Plants called legumes, which include clover, peas, and soybeans, help enrich the soil. Their roots contain bacteria that convert nitrogen from the air into compounds that are useful to the plant.

Root Structure

Root Tip. The apical meristem is covered by a dome-shaped cell mass called a *root cap*. The root cap is adapted to regenerate as fast as it is worn down by the rough and resistant soil through which it advances.

Outer Tissues. The roots' epidermis protects the tissues beneath. Tiny, hairlike extensions called *root hairs* grow from the epidermis. The root hairs absorb water and minerals from the soil. In most kinds of plants, the root hairs live only a few days.

The cortex lies just inside the epidermis. The cells of the cortex contain stored food and water. The inner layer of cells of the cortex makes up the *endodermis*.

The core, or *stele*, is the root's central portion. Its outer layer of cells is called the *pericycle*. Branch roots grow from the pericycle, which contains the vascular tissue.

Xylem includes rows of dead, tubular cells called *vessels*, which conduct water and minerals up to the stem and leaves.

Phloem consists largely of rows of long, living cells called *sieve tubes*. These cells transport food down from the leaves for use or storage by the root.

Secondary tissues add to the thickness of a root. Secondary-tissue growth produces the large, woody roots in trees and other plants that live for many years.

CROSS SECTION OF A ROOT

Seen in cross section, the internal structure of root tissues consists of three concentric layers.

1. **The epidermis** is very thin. Epidermal cells enclose the outer surface of the root and are specially adapted to absorb water and minerals from the soil, chiefly through their extremely fine hairlike projections known as root hairs.

2. **The cortex** is thicker. It is made up chiefly of parenchyma cells, but because the root is typically subterranean, it lacks the chloroplasts found in aboveground parenchyma tissue cells. Rather, it functions chiefly as a site of food storage. The cortex is also permeated with air spaces.

3. **The vascular cylinder** consists of xylem and phloem tissue and serves the stem's conduction needs.

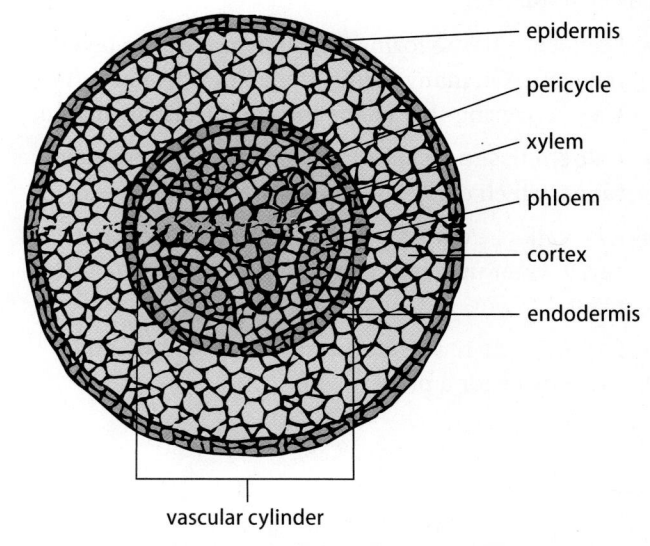

epidermis

pericycle

xylem

phloem

cortex

endodermis

vascular cylinder

Stems

The stem is the part of a plant that produces and supports the buds, leaves, flowers, and fruit. The stem holds leaves in a position to receive the sunlight needed for photosynthesis. It transports materials to and from the roots. Some plants store food or water in their stems, and others, like cacti, carry on photosynthesis in their stems.

All plants have stems except mosses, liverworts, and hornworts. Most stems grow erect above the ground, but some grow underground or horizontally along the ground.

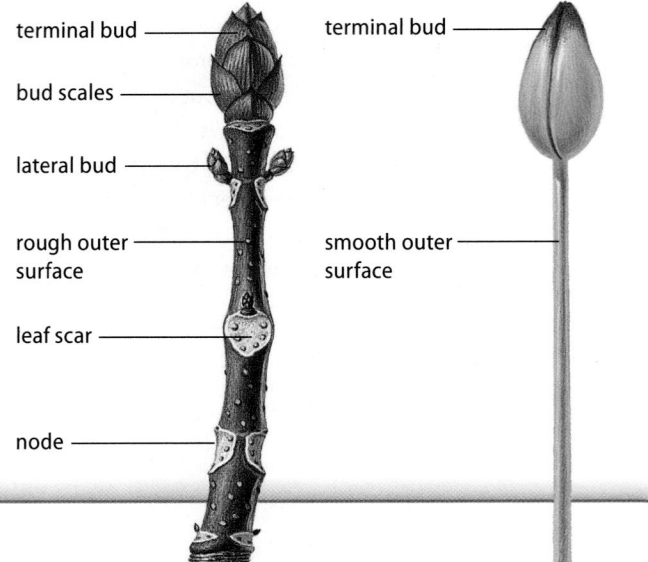

Woody Stem **Herbaceous Stem**

terminal bud —
bud scales —
lateral bud —
rough outer surface —
leaf scar —
node —

terminal bud —
smooth outer surface —

▲ **Stems.** A woody stem, *left,* has a rough, brown surface. A herbaceous stem, *right,* has a smooth, green surface.

Types of Stems

There are two main types of stems.

- herbaceous stems
- woody stems

Herbaceous stems are typically soft, flexible, and green. They do not grow substantially thicker from year to year. In most cases they die and decompose within a single season.

Most grasses are herbaceous. So are many horticultural flowering plants, their parts either dying altogether or dying back to the roots each autumn.

Herbaceous stems consist of *primary tissues,* which include the epidermis, the phloem, the xylem, and the parenchyma.

- Epidermis tissue forms the outer protective layer of the stem. On many stems, the epidermis has a thin waxy covering that keeps the stem from drying out.
- Phloem tissue includes living cells that form sieve tubes, which carry sugar down from the leaves.
- Xylem tissue consists mainly of dead tubes that carry water up from the roots to other parts of the plant.
- Parenchyma tissue stores food and various other substances for a plant.

Woody stems have rough surfaces that are brown or gray. They are rigid and durable. All gymnosperms have woody stems. The trees and shrubs of the angiosperm division have woody stems as well.

Woody stems grow thicker each growing season, followed by a period of dormancy. During their first year of growth, woody stems begin to develop *secondary tissues* that support or replace primary tissues by producing wood and bark.

Woody stems increase greatly in diameter over time because they develop new layers of secondary tissues each year. As the stem grows in width, the epidermis and cortex are pushed outward. These tissues break up and fall away.

A cross section of a mature woody stem shows circular layers of the primary and secondary tissues.

The *primary xylem* and *secondary xylem* form a core of wood, which makes up the greatest part of a woody stem. During each growing season, the *cambium* produces a *growth ring,* or new layer of secondary xylem that can be distinguished from previous layers.

Cell division in the cambium produces secondary xylem and *secondary phloem.*

Phelloderm and *cork* are produced by cell division in the *cork cambium.*

Stem Structure. Herbaceous stems have only primary tissues, which develop from cell division at the tip of the stem. Woody stems have both primary and secondary tissues. Secondary tissues cause woody stems to develop wood and bark and to grow thicker.

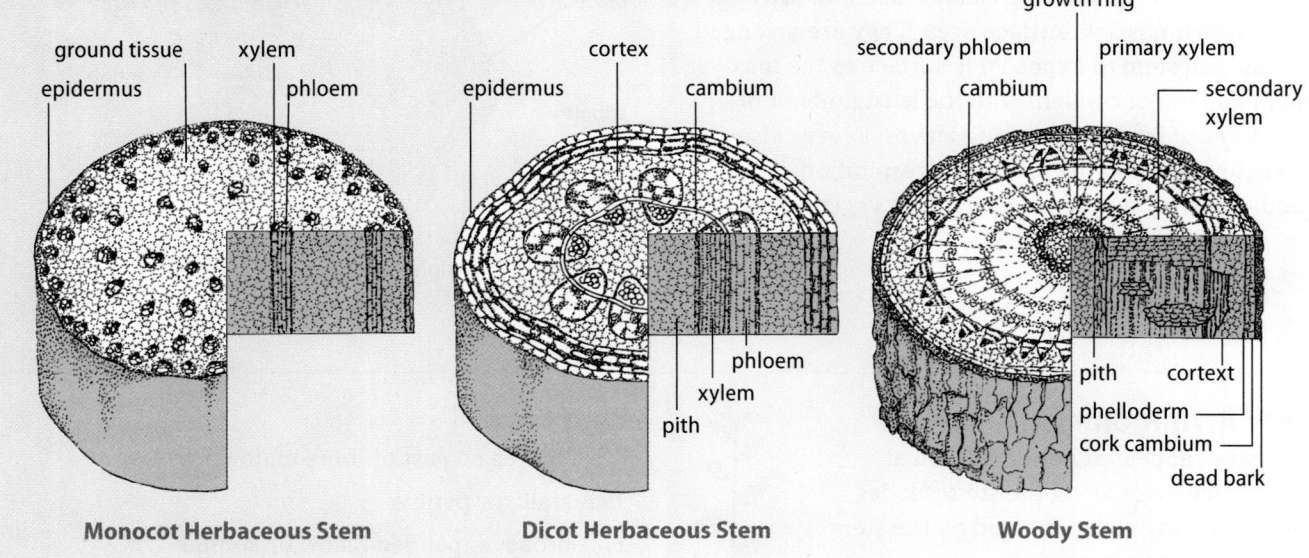

Monocot Herbaceous Stem   **Dicot Herbaceous Stem**   **Woody Stem**

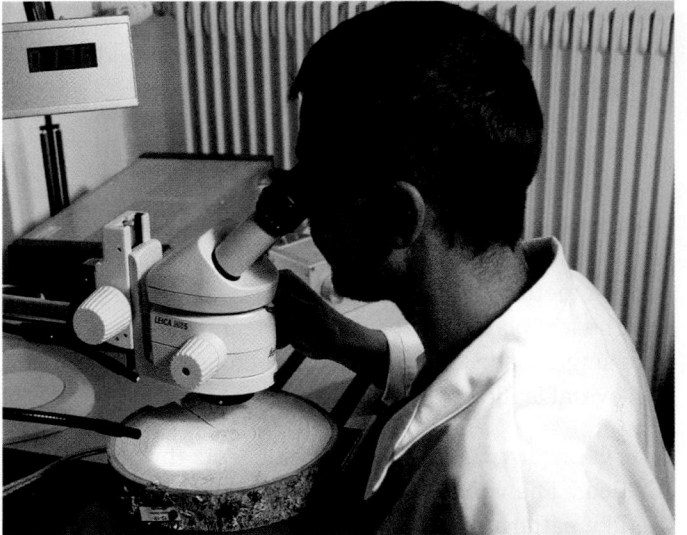

GROWTH RINGS

The approximate age of a woody stem can be determined by counting the growth rings. New cells produced in spring are softer and lighter in color than the new cells produced later in the season, which accounts for the distinct bicolor concentric rings visible when the trunk is cut crosswise.

The thickness of each double ring is also an index of growing conditions. A thick ring generally indicates a season with abundant rain and a thin ring offers a clue to a season of drought, with its necessarily slower growth rate. (See page 480.)

Specialized Stems		
Stem Type	**Features**	**Examples**
bulb	cone-shaped stems surrounded by scalelike leaves modified to store food	onions, tulips
corm	often confused with bulbs, underground modification of stem buds	gladiolas, crocuses
rhizome	fleshy, horizontal stems growing beneath the surface	irises, violets
tuber	enlarged tips of rhizomes, specialized for food storage	potatoes
runner	horizontal stem growing on the soil surface, produces roots and shoots at nodes	strawberries, Bermuda grass
tendril	modified stems of climbing plants, coil around or stick to objects	grape, Virginia creeper

Leaves

Leaves are the plant structures that are specialized primarily for the manufacture of food through photosynthesis. Most leaves are constructed to provide the greatest possible surface area. They are arranged around the stem to expose this surface to the maximum amount of sunlight with the least amount of interference from neighboring leaves. Leaves also exchange gases in the process of respiration, store food, and may reproduce new plants vegetatively.

The Parts of a Leaf

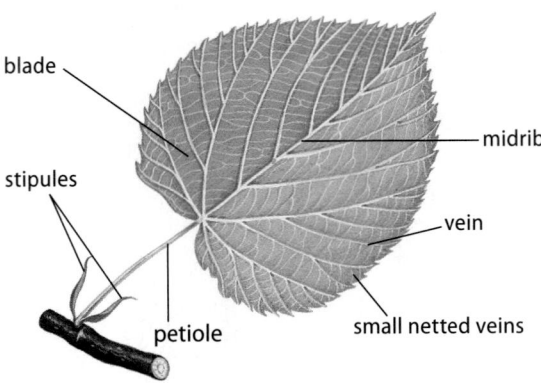

Leaf Arrangement

Leaves appear at nodes, spaced at regular intervals along the stem. Nodes and their leaves are arranged on the stem in one of three patterns.

1. Alternate arrangement. The most common pattern, a single leaf appears at each node and the leaves form a continuous ascending spiral on the stem.

2. Opposite arrangement. Two leaves are attached at the same node and directly across the stem from each other.

3. Whorled pattern. Three or more leaves develop at the same node, but at well-spaced positions around the stem.

Alternate

Opposite

Whorl

Vein Patterns

pinnately veined
(lower side of blue beech)

palmately veined
(lower side of sweet gum)

parallel veined
(upper and lower sides of rye)

center veined
(cross section of white pine)

Leaf Form

Most leaves consist of three main parts.

1. A stalk, or petiole
2. A broad, expanded blade, or lamina
3. An arrangement of veins

The petiole joins the leaf blade to the stem. It is usually, but not always, fairly slender, short, and inconspicuous.

The blade is the broad, flat part of the leaf. Photosynthesis occurs in the blade. Blades come in many shapes and sizes, from broad fronds to tiny scales and needles. They can have smooth edges or small, jagged teeth.

The leaf blade may be simple, meaning it consists of a single blade, or compound, meaning it consists of several leaflets.

The veins distribute water and nutrients throughout the leaf. The veins of most broad leaves form a netlike pattern. There are two main types of net-vein patterns: *pinnate* and *palmate*.

- Pinnately net-veined leaves have one large central vein, called the *midrib*, which extends from the base of the blade to its tip. Other large veins branch off on each side of the midrib.

- Palmately net-veined leaves have several main veins of about equal size, all of which extend from a common point at the base of the blade.

HOW DOES THAT WORK

FALLING LEAVES

The falling of deciduous leaves occurs as the result of chemical changes. In autumn, the level of the hormone *auxin* in the leaf naturally decreases. A special layer of cells, called the *abscission layer*, forms at the base of the petiole and blocks the continued flow of water and nutrients to the leaf. Chlorophyll ceases to be produced, and the green color of the leaf fades, replaced by the brilliant oranges, reds, and yellows of autumn. Meanwhile, the petiole becomes progressively weaker and eventually breaks off the stem, leaving only a leaf scar.

Fall colors ▶

Leaf Structure

Epidermal Layer
- covers top and bottom surface of leaf
- one cell thick
- epidermal cells secrete waterproof waxy cuticle to slow down water evaporation
- openings in cuticle called stomata allow CO_2 to enter the leaf and O_2 to exit the leaf

Mesophyll
- multilayered region between the upper and lower epidermis
- composed chiefly of parenchyma cells with numerous chloroplasts
- site of most, if not all, photosynthesis
- upper tier populated with cells arranged in tightly ranked palisades
- lower tier designated the spongy mesophyll because of irregularly fitting, loosely assembled parenchyma cells

Vascular Tissue
- vascular tissue, or veins, is interwoven through the mesophyllic cell and very conspicuous on the leaf's surface.

A Typical Leaf Blade. Palisade and spongy cells serve as food producers. In the veins, xylem tissue distributes water, and phloem tissue carries away food.

upper epidermis   palisade tissue   phloem tissue   chloroplasts

xylem tissue

section of the leaf enlarged at the left

pore closed   pore open

guard cells

Guard cells regulate the amount of carbon dioxide and water vapor that pass through a stoma. The stomata are usually open while the leaf is making food.

lower epidermis   stomata   supporting fibers   vein   spongy tissue

Flowers

Roots, stems, and leaves are all vegetative organs pertaining to asexual growth processes. By contrast, flowers are organs of sexual reproduction, producing the male and female gametes (pollen and eggs) that will unite to produce the next generation of plants.

Only angiosperms have flowers. The flower and its resulting fruit and seed are the structures that have made angiosperms—the youngest division of the plant kingdom—the most successful in evolutionary terms.

Flower Parts

All flowers are based on the same structural design. The flower stands atop a flower stalk, known as a *pedicel*, which terminates in an enlarged *receptacle*. Attached to the receptacle in orderly succession are four floral organs: the *calyx*, the *corolla*, the *stamens*, and the *carpels*.

PARTS OF A FLOWER

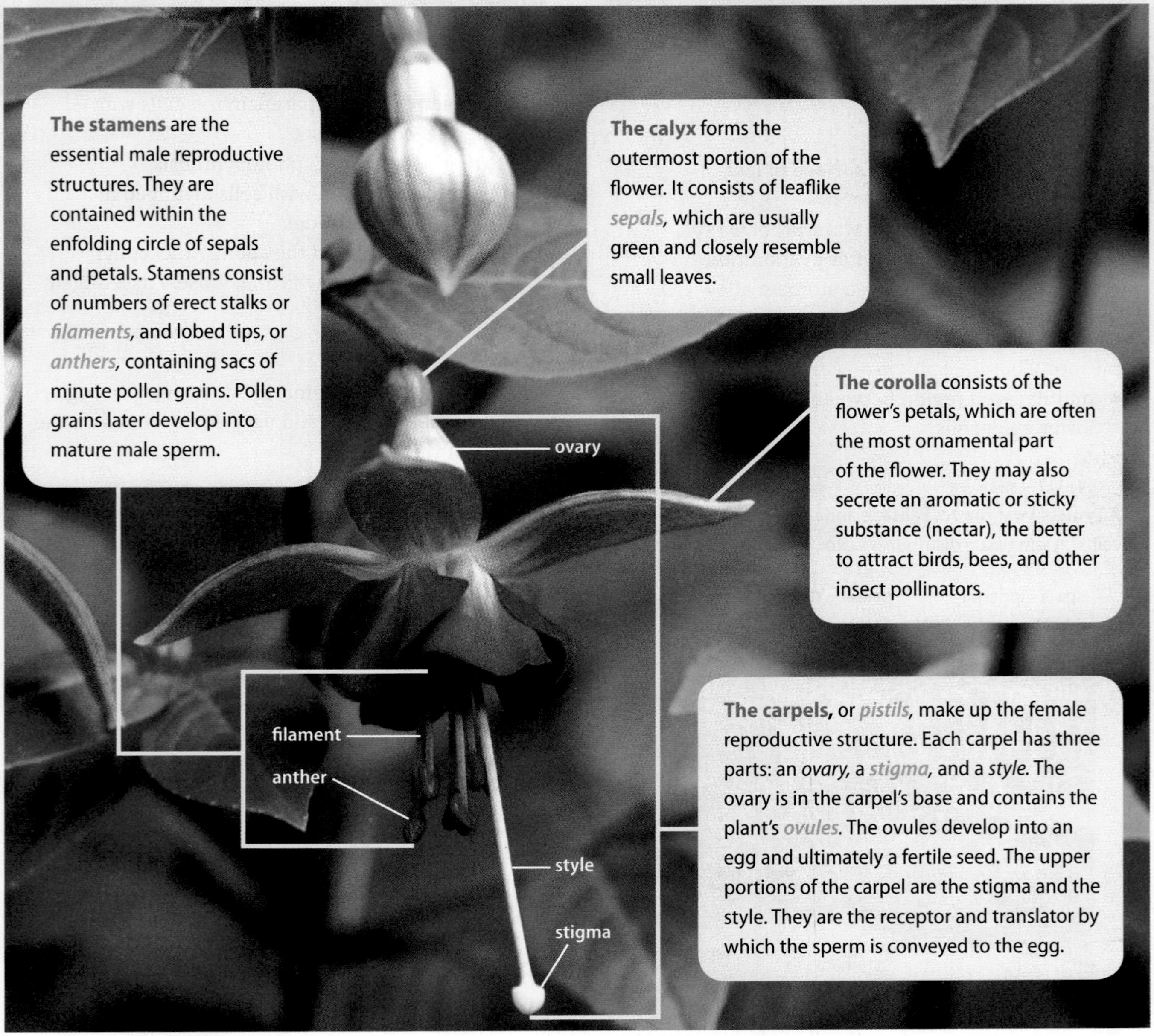

The stamens are the essential male reproductive structures. They are contained within the enfolding circle of sepals and petals. Stamens consist of numbers of erect stalks or *filaments*, and lobed tips, or *anthers*, containing sacs of minute pollen grains. Pollen grains later develop into mature male sperm.

The calyx forms the outermost portion of the flower. It consists of leaflike *sepals*, which are usually green and closely resemble small leaves.

The corolla consists of the flower's petals, which are often the most ornamental part of the flower. They may also secrete an aromatic or sticky substance (nectar), the better to attract birds, bees, and other insect pollinators.

The carpels, or *pistils*, make up the female reproductive structure. Each carpel has three parts: an *ovary*, a *stigma*, and a *style*. The ovary is in the carpel's base and contains the plant's *ovules*. The ovules develop into an egg and ultimately a fertile seed. The upper portions of the carpel are the stigma and the style. They are the receptor and translator by which the sperm is conveyed to the egg.

ovary

filament

anther

style

stigma

128

Reproduction

Flowering plants reproduce sexually in two main steps: *pollination* and *fertilization*. Pollination is the transfer of pollen from a stamen to a pistil. Fertilization is the union of a sperm with an egg cell.

Pollination

There are two methods of pollination: *self-pollination* and *cross-pollination*. In self-pollination, pollen is transferred from a stamen to a pistil of the same flower or to a pistil of another flower on the same plant. Cross-pollination involves the transfer of pollen from a stamen on one plant to a pistil on another plant.

Self-Pollination. A flower with both stamens and carpel is said to be perfect because it contains male and female parts. A perfect flower is capable of self-pollination. About half of all species of plants normally pollinate themselves.

Cross-Pollination. Most flowering plants are pollinated through cross-pollination. Pollen is transferred from one flower to another mainly by insects, but also by birds, bats, and the wind.

Many insects depend on flowers for food. Bees live on nectar and pollen. Butterflies and moths also live on nectar, and certain beetles and flies feed on both nectar and pollen. As an insect travels from flower to flower in search of food, pollen grains stick to its body. Some or all of these grains may brush off onto the stigmas of some flowers that the insect visits. One or more of these flowers may thus become cross-pollinated.

FLOWER POWER

When searching for food, an insect could easily fail to visit a particular kind of flower unless the insect was attracted to it. Most flowers that depend on insects for pollination are brightly colored or heavily scented. Each kind of pollinating insect is attracted by certain colors or odors and so visits certain flowers rather than others.

Fertilization

A pollen grain that lands on a stigma may grow a *pollen tube*. The tube pushes its way down the style to an ovule in the ovary. Sperm from the pollen grain travel down the tube to the ovule. Fertilization occurs when a sperm unites with an egg cell in the ovule. A seed then begins to develop. The ovary itself develops into a fruit that encloses the seed.

Busy Bees. More flowers are pollinated by bees than by any other insect. Bees become covered in pollen when they drink nectar from flowers. A bee will leave some of this pollen at other flowers it visits, pollinating them.

Fruits

Botanists define a *fruit* as the part of a flowering plant that contains the seeds. The role of fruits in the reproductive cycle is seed dispersal. Fruits come in two basic forms: *simple* and *compound*. The diversity represented within those two categories is substantial, reflecting modifications to suit many different natural environments and many different dispersal modes.

Dispersal

Dispersal mechanisms are diverse and selective. Small, lightweight fruits, such as the parachute-like tuft of the dandelion, are designed to travel on the slightest waft of air when released. The fruits of the maple tree are carried on the wind by their winged projections. Other fruits are buoyant and water-resistant and can float short or long distances before taking hold in soil and germinating. The saltwater-resistant coconut, for example, can take to the sea and colonize sandy shorelines all over the tropics, and the seed of grass plants constantly washes down slopes with the rain to seed raw banks of earth.

Animals play a key role in fruit dispersal. Aromatic, highly visible, fleshy fruits attract birds and animals that eat and distribute them in their droppings throughout their migratory range. In fact, the seeds of certain plants must pass through an animal's digestive tract to be prepared for germination. Gatherers like mice, squirrels, or pack rats collect and scatter seeds. Burrs and other adhering fruits stick to the fur, feathers, or feet of animals that later drop them far away.

SIMPLE FRUITS

Simple fruits typically form from a single carpel. They are classified as either *dry* or *fleshy*. Dry fruits include the fruits of the pea plant and the sunflower. Fleshy fruits include the *berries*, *drupes*, and *pomes*.

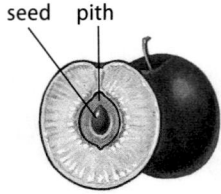

Plum

Orange

Berries consist entirely of fleshy tissue, and most species have many seeds. The seeds are embedded in the flesh. This group includes only a few of the fruits that are commonly known as berries.

Drupes are fleshy fruits that have a hard inner stone or pit and a single seed. The pit encloses the seed.

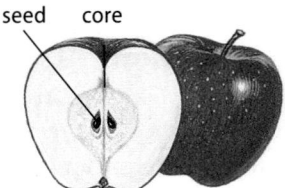

Apple

Pomes have a fleshy outer layer, a paperlike core, and usually 5 to 10 seeds. The seeds are enclosed in the core.

COMPOUND FRUITS

Compound fruits consist of a cluster of seed-bearing fruits. They are classified as *aggregate* or *multiple*.

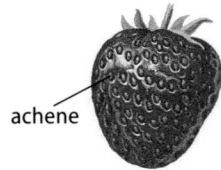

Strawberry

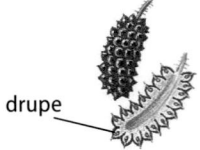

Mulberry

Aggregate fruits develop from the numerous but separate carpels of a single flower and form a clustered fruit such as a strawberry or raspberry.

Multiple fruits are formed from carpels of several associated fruits whose ovaries grow together into a mass during maturation. Examples include the fruits of the pineapple, mulberry, and fig.

Sleeping Seeds

Seeds exhibit *dormancy*, a control mechanism that keeps the seed in a state of suspended animation until the time of the year in which its chances for survival are best.

The trigger that causes the seed to sprout after dormancy depends on the species. Some end their dormant phase with the release of certain hormones. Others are triggered by the length of the day and amount of sunlight. A period of below-freezing weather followed by a period of warmth will cause some seeds to germinate.

When all the critical conditions for germination readiness are met, the seed coat ruptures. The seed inside becomes moist and soft and the embryo resumes growth.

Seeds typically remain dormant for several months before germinating, but under certain circumstances some can survive for hundreds, even thousands, of years. When scientists thawed lupine seeds that had been frozen in the Arctic tundra for 10,000 years, they were found to be capable of germinating within 48 hours of planting.

Ecballium elaterium

SPITTING SEEDS

Like fruits, seeds display a variety of adaptive features to assist in dispersal by wind, water, and animals. One spectacular adaptation is found in the squirting cucumber, *Ecballium elaterium*. The fruit of this plant explodes open at the moment of maturity, shooting its seeds as far as 3 to 6 meters (about 10 to 20 feet).

Seeds

Seeds consist of the *embryo*, *food storage tissue*, and the *seed coat*.

- **The embryo** develops from the fertilized egg. It contains the parts that form a new plant.
- **Food storage tissue:** The cotyledons absorb and digest food from the food storage tissue of the seed. In angiosperm seeds, this tissue is called the *endosperm*.
- **The seed coat** develops from the outermost layers of the ovule. It protects the seed from injury, insects, and loss of water.

Sprouting Conditions

Ripe seeds sprout through a process called *germination*. Conditions required for a seed to germinate include:

- abundant water
- an adequate supply of oxygen
- proper temperatures

Dicotyledon Seed (Bean)

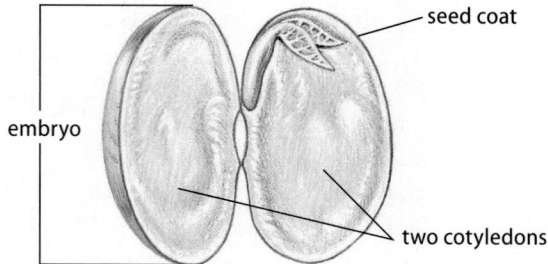

A seed consists of an embryo, food storage tissue, and a seed coat. The two cotyledons in this bean seed absorb and digest food from the food storage tissue.

PLANT PHYSIOLOGY is the study

of how plants function. Scientists examine how different parts of plants work together to achieve a particular function.

Plant physiology is closely tied to plant anatomy. Since each part of a plant has evolved to carry out a certain task or tasks, closely studying the structure of each plant part can reveal that part's function.

Plant physiology involves the study of the vital processes that occur within plants, including the transport of water and nutrients, photosynthesis, digestion, respiration, stimulus and response, and how plants grow.

Water Transport

Water helps plants stand up straight by supporting the cells, making each relatively firm. Water is essential in chemical reactions, from photosynthesis, to respiration, to the dissolution and diffusion of carbon dioxide through cell walls.

Water is the solvent whose fluctuating levels within each cell regulate the varying concentrations of minerals in the plant. Water also enables minerals to pass from the soil and enter the roots. Lastly, water is the internal transport system by means of which food and energy are enabled to circulate throughout the plant.

Absorption

Plants take in almost all the water they receive through their root systems. For absorption to occur, it is essential that a plant's root system reach soil that holds enough water. Available water enters the plant as water molecules. These molecules pass through individual cell walls along the roots' epidermal layer in a complex mechanism known as *osmosis*.

HOW DOES THAT WORK ?

OSMOSIS

Osmosis is the process by which a fluid of lower concentration passes through a membrane into a solution of higher concentration. The steps in plant osmosis are

1. water and certain minerals move from the soil through the cell wall of the epidermal cell into the cytoplasm inside the cell.

2. as each cell absorbs its limit of water, the cell interior swells, becoming firm, or turgid, in what is called *turgor pressure*.

3. surrounding cells, with lower concentrations of water and higher concentrations of solutes, become successive targets of osmosis.

4. eventually, some of the water reaches the primary transport system within the cambium and begins to move upward through the stem.

◄ **Plant osmosis** is the process by which a plant's roots take water in from the soil. The water is absorbed through the plant's tiny root hairs.

Essential Plant Nutrients Carried by Water		
Macronutrients	**Function**	**Symptoms of Deficiency**
Carbon, Oxygen, Hydrogen	Component of all organic compounds	
Nitrogen	Part of chlorophyll, amino acids, proteins	Loss of color in leaves, stunted growth
Potassium	Activates enzymes, used in formation of sugar and starch	Yellowing of leaves, particularly at edges
Calcium	Used in cell growth and division, part of cell wall	Dying roots, dead or dying terminal buds
Magnesium	Part of chlorophyll, activates enzymes	Leaves yellow between green veins
Phosphorus	Used in ATP and ADP	Purplish leaves, stunted growth
Sulfur	Part of amino acids and proteins	Yellow or light green leaves
Micronutrients	**Function**	**Symptoms of Deficiency**
Iron	Used in photosynthesis	Yellowing of leaves
Chlorine	Aids in root growth	Plants wilt
Boron	Affects reproduction	Leaves become brittle, terminal buds die
Copper	Used in chlorophyll, activates enzymes	Growth is stunted, terminal buds die
Manganese	Part of chlorophyll, activates enzymes	Dead spots on leaves, veins remain green
Zinc	Used in auxins, activates enzymes	Roots grow abnormally
Molybdenum	Used in nitrogen fixation	Leaves become rolled and pale green

Transpiration

Transpiration is the process by which plants continually lose water through their leaves. The process causes plants to suck the water absorbed through osmosis up through stems and trunks. Once the water reaches the leaves and has yielded up all the mineral nutrients required, the plant allows much of it to escape through the millions of small pores, or stomata, on its leaf surface.

The rate of transpiration is dependent upon the amount of moisture in the air (humidity), air temperature, and wind speed. Stomata open and close to maintain favorable water pressure within the leaf.

Through absorption and transpiration, many plants maintain enough water to make them 75 to 80 percent water by weight.

THE BASICS: PLANT PHYSIOLOGY

Water Transport. Plants need a continuous supply of water to perform necessary life processes. They absorb water and essential nutrients through their roots, via osmosis. They continually give off water through transpiration.

Photosynthesis is the process by which plants capture sunlight and use it to make food.

Digestion is the process by which a plant uses enzymes to break down stored food for use by the plant.

Respiration breaks down food made through photosynthesis and releases energy for the plant. The plant uses energy for growth, reproduction, and repair.

Stimulus and Response. Plants react to stimuli in their environment. They move toward or away from a stimulus through reactions called *tropisms. Nastic movements* are physiological responses to specific stimuli, such as the closing of a tulip or morning glory at night.

Growth. Like all living things, plants follow a life cycle. The life cycle of a plant includes germination and seedling development, maturation and flowering, and aging and death.

Photosynthesis

Photosynthesis is a food-making process that occurs in green plants, algae, and certain microscopic organisms. Photosynthesis is the chief function of leaves. The word *photosynthesis* means *putting together with light*.

Green plants use sunlight to combine carbon dioxide and water to make food. This process converts light energy into the chemical energy of food. Plants use the food to grow, or they store it for later consumption.

Photosynthesis has been called the single most important chemical process in the world. It provides food for plants, and plants in turn support all the animals in the food chain, including humans.

The Importance of Photosynthesis

Photosynthesis provides the critical link between inorganic chemicals and the living world. The food that photosynthesis produces nourishes the plants and the plants in turn support all other organisms higher on the food chain.

Food and Materials. Photosynthesis is extremely efficient. A plant needs no more than one-sixth of the energy it produces for its own maintenance, leaving as much as five-sixths available to make food, fuel, and the other materials useful to the rest of the natural world, including the human economy.

Oxygen. Equally important to life on Earth, photosynthesis enables the release of free oxygen molecules. Before there were photosynthesizing plants on Earth, the atmosphere consisted largely of ammonia (NH_3), water (H_2O), and methane (CH_4). The development of a vast biomass of green plants with its unique and powerful system of gas exchange has literally created the oxygenated air that supports the great number of other living organisms, including humans.

After Photosynthesis

Once photosynthesis has done its work, the simple sugars and the other organic compounds go to sites all over the plant. Some of the product is used to synthesize proteins within the cell. Some is stored locally in the form of starch.

Most of the sugars, however, are transported from the cell and the leaf to other parts of the plant by way of the vascular system. These sugars will be stored, used to produce new plant parts, or broken down to produce energy for the plant's immediate use.

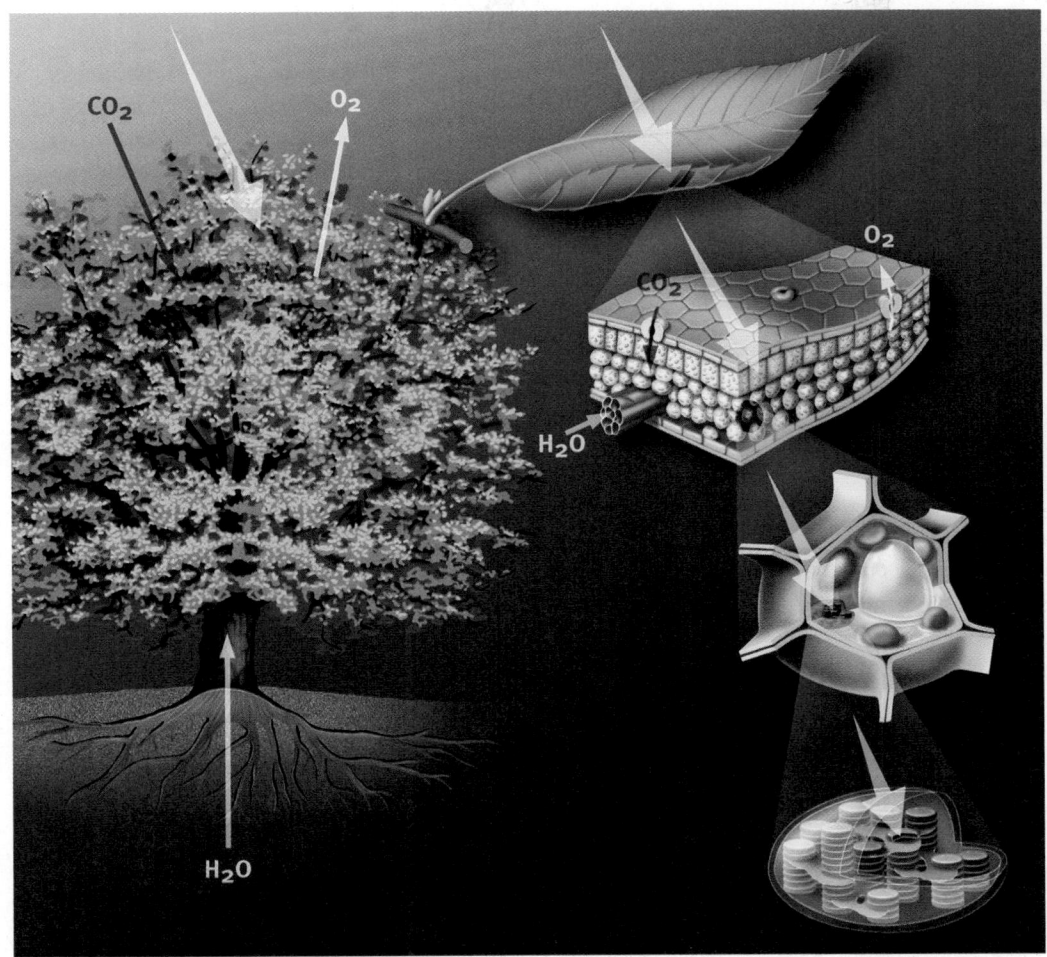

Green plants capture light energy to first break down water into oxygen molecules and hydrogen. The captured energy is then used to attach the hydrogen to carbon dioxide, thus producing chemical energy in the form of a simple sugar known as glucose.

PHOTOSYNTHESIS

The energy and nourishment created by photosynthesis provide all the food that people and other animals eat. Animals either eat plants directly, or eat animals that eat the plants.

1. The process begins when light strikes the leaf's *chloroplasts*. Chloroplasts are small green bodies found in the plant's cells. They can occur in the slender cells of the plant's palisade tissue, or in the broad, irregularly-shaped cells of the spongy tissue.

2. Energy from the light is absorbed by *chlorophyll*, which is the green *pigment,* or coloring matter, in the chloroplasts.

3. Partly surrounding each cell of the palisade and spongy tissues is an air space filled with carbon dioxide, water vapor, and other gases. The energy absorbed by the chlorophyll splits the water molecules in these spaces into molecules of hydrogen and oxygen.

4. The hydrogen then combines with carbon dioxide to produce a simple sugar.

5. The excess oxygen enters the air through the *stomata,* or pores, of the leaf. People, animals, and all other living organisms need oxygen in order to live.

6. The sugar produced by photosynthesis is carried throughout the plant in *phloem*. Phloem is tissue made up of special tubelike cells.

7. The sugar can be burned in order to release energy for the plant's growth, or it can be combined with various minerals. These minerals enter the plant through the roots.

8. The combination of sugar and minerals produces vital compounds, such as proteins and vitamins. These compounds provide nourishment for the plant.

Respiration and Digestion

The end result of photosynthesis is the simple sugar that plants use for food. After photosynthesis, plants convert that sugar into energy through two processes.

- respiration
- digestion

REVERSE RESPIRATION

Photosynthesis is sometimes thought of as "reverse respiration." This is because respiration involves chemical reactions that break down the simple sugar *glucose*. Photosynthesis, of course, results in the creation of glucose.

Respiration

Respiration, in its simplest description, is the reversal of the chemical reactions that take place in photosynthesis. (See pages 134–135.)

Respiration provides the means by which plant cells break down foods, chiefly carbohydrates, but also fats, proteins, and organic acids, through oxidation, and turn them back into plant-building energy with carbon dioxide and water as by-products. Another name given to respiration is *carbohydrate metabolism*.

ATP and Respiration. Like photosynthesis, respiration is carried out chiefly in the leaves. It is centered in the countless mitochondria within each cell. These tiny powerhouses are the sites of a series of reactions, mediated by still other specialized enzymes, which cause molecules to be broken down into smaller molecules of *adenosine triphosphate (ATP)*.

The ATP molecules then become convenient packages of energy, easily shunted about, and available to perform myriad activities of cell maintenance, repair, and construction.

PHOTOSYNTHESIS AND RESPIRATION

Mitochondria use energy released by the breakdown of carbohydrates and fats to make ATP. Cells use ATP to power movement, transport substances into or out of the cell, and create chemicals that cells need to grow and divide.

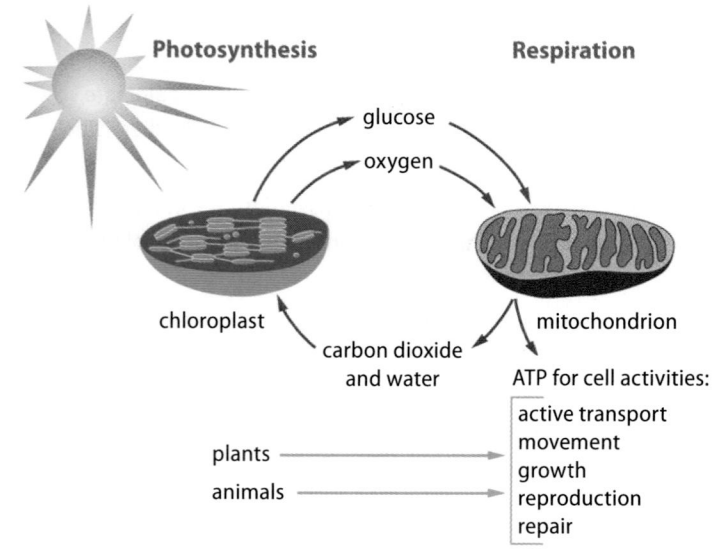

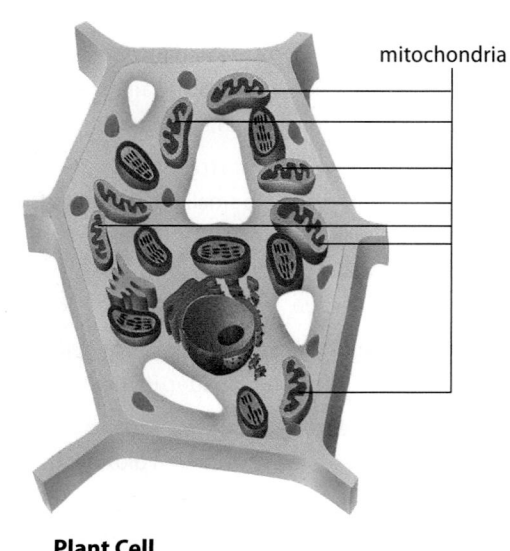

Plant Cell

ATP

ATP is the molecule from which all cells obtain their required energy. A molecule of ATP consists of an adenosine group with three phosphate groups bonded to it and forming a "tail."

The bond between the second and third phosphate groups is the high-energy bond. When this bond is broken, energy is released and the third phosphate group is freed. *ADP (adenosine diphosphate)* is formed. When energy is available, ADP will combine with a free phosphate, reforming ATP. Energy is thus stored for future use.

ATP

Digestion

In plants, *digestion* is the breaking down of large molecules of stored food into smaller molecules.

The sugar produced during photosynthesis becomes available to form new chemical compounds important to the cell and to the plant as a whole. Not all of these compounds are used right away. Many of them are stored for long periods of time as carbohydrates, fats, and proteins.

After a period of dormancy, it takes time for a plant to produce adequate supplies of new food. During this time, the plant uses the stored food to sustain growth. The stored food is made soluble and transportable through digestion.

Enzymes. The digestive process relies on *enzymes*, proteins that aid in biochemical breakdown. Each group of stored macromolecules has its own set of digestive enzymes.

- **Amylases** convert starch into soluble glucose.
- **Proteases** change proteins into amino acids.
- **Lipases** convert lipids into fatty acids.

Once available in solution, the foods can be oxidized and the energy released through respiration.

Important By-products

In addition to the production of the primary plant compounds—the carbohydrates, fats, proteins, and nucleotides—many plants also produce significant amounts of *secondary compounds*. While the latter are not important to a plant's metabolism, they sometimes have considerable importance to a plant in terms of its value in the environment.

Tannins are astringent, aromatic compounds found in the leaves, bark, wood, and fruit of many plants. Also deterrents to herbivores, they flavor tea, wine, and some fruits. Tannins are useful in curing leather.

Alkaloids are nitrogen-containing compounds. They include atropine, colchicine, morphine, nicotine, quinine, tubocurarine, opium, caffeine, and strychnine. Alkaloids serve plants as defenses against grazing animals. They are used by people as medicinal drugs, hallucinogens, poisons, and in the case of caffeine, found in the coffee bean, as stimulants.

Terpenes include volatile, or essential, oils, resins, and *polyterpenes*, the key ingredient of rubber.

Flavonoids are the basic building blocks of many pigments, and thus they play a role in coloring flowers and in attracting insects that carry out pollination.

Stimulus and Response

Living things sense and respond to changes in their surroundings. Changes that produce responses in organisms are called *stimuli*. Such factors as light and temperature can serve as stimuli.

In the animal kingdom, the capacity to respond to a stimulus is centered in the sensory neurons and nervous system. Plants, while less highly organized, are also very responsive, though the rate of movement involved is often very gradual. There are many stimulus-response patterns in the plant world. These include

- tropisms
- nastic movements
- responses to climate

Tropisms

A *tropism* is a movement toward or away from the direction of a stimulus. Most tropisms involve true plant growth and once expressed become a permanent part of the plant's physical size and shape.

Phototropism is a response by a plant to the stimulus of light. Plants bend toward a light source. ▼

Phototropism. The best-known, most widely observed tropism is *phototropism*, in which a plant grows toward light, the source of photosynthesis and the plant's self-generating food supply.

- Phototropism occurs when sunlight reaches one side of the *apical meristem*, or growing plant tip, in greater intensity and over longer periods than it reaches the other. (See Unlimited Growth, page 120.)
- Sunlight causes the hormone *auxin* to move from the illuminated side to the shaded side.
- Auxin then moves downward to the stem cells, and particularly the epidermal cells immediately below.
- The higher concentrations of auxin cause the shaded side to become progressively more elongated than the cells opposite.
- The plant stem as a whole curves toward the light, putting itself and its leafy extensions in greater exposure to the sun.
- Phototropism also causes the leaves to turn so as to place blades at an angle perpendicular to the sun, the angle of maximum exposure.

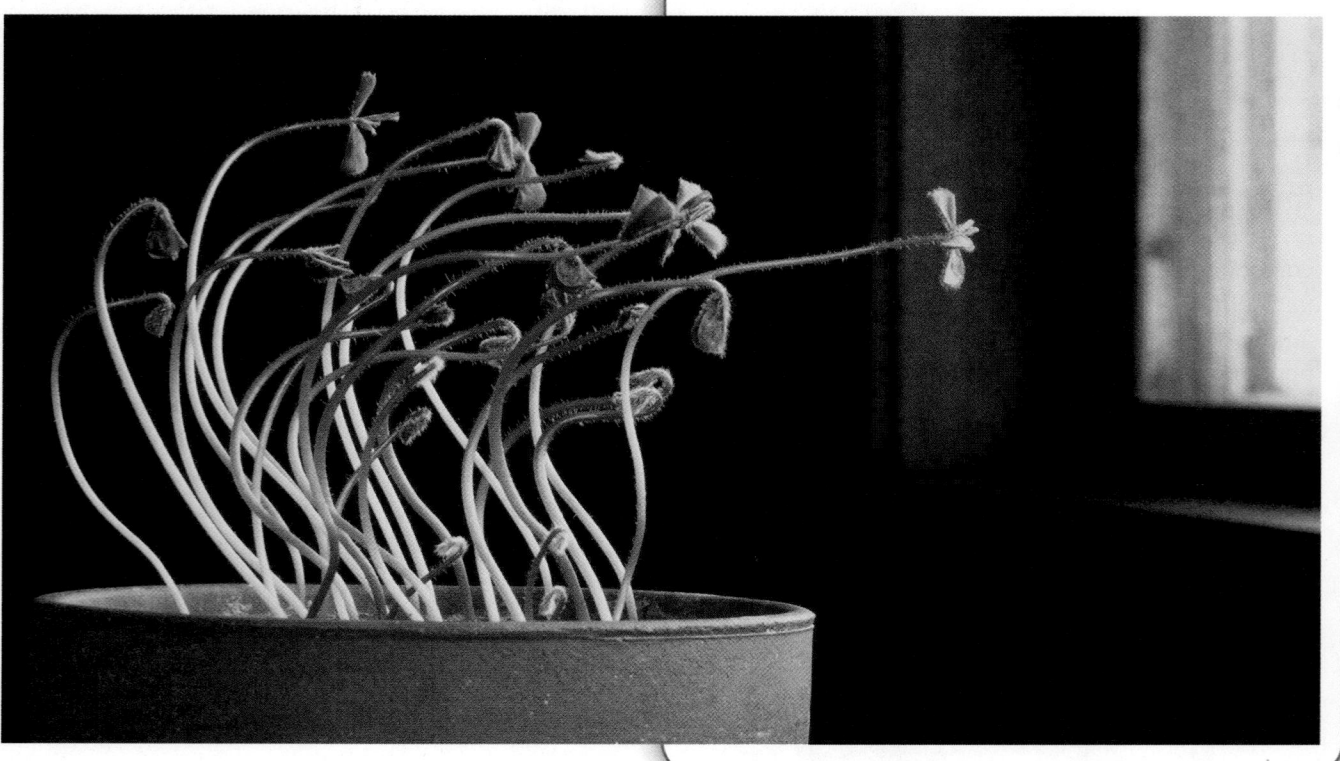

Geotropism. The pull of Earth's gravity is responsible for *geotropism*. When, for example, a seedling is laid horizontally in the dark, with no cues from sunlight to guide its direction, the stem will immediately begin to bend and grow upward and the root to bend and grow downward.

- Geotropism causes the roots of plants on the steep side of a mountain to grow straight down into the soil.

- Geotropism helps plants growing in locations where sunlight is hard to capture to strike a viable compromise between growing sideways and growing upright.

- Geotropism occurs because gravity causes the cell-elongating hormone auxin to concentrate on the lower side of the plant part.

- In roots, this causes the cells higher up to grow longer than the lower cells, so the roots grow downward.

- The same concentration of auxin causes the opposite reaction in the stem.

- In the stem region, the lower cells grow longer than higher cells.

- This prompts the stem to turn upward.

Geotropism. Gravity causes the roots of a plant to grow straight down into the ground, no matter how steep the slope. Geotropism causes the opposite reaction in the stem of a plant, causing it to grow straight up.

Thigmotropism (from the Greek word *thigma*, meaning "touch") is a tropism resulting from physical touch.

- Some plants, particularly those with twining vines and tendrils—such as peas and grapes—undergo selective cell elongation wherever the stem touches a supporting surface such as a stick or tree trunk or arbor.

- The one-sided elongation, which takes place on the side away from contact, causes the stem to curl as best it can around whatever it touches.

Thigmotropism causes the stem to grow around and along the stick, trunk, or trellis that supports it.

FALSE TROPISM

Hydrotropism, or the growing of plant roots toward a water source, was once listed among the tropisms but it is no longer so classified. Roots grow in regions of greater moisture because the environment is especially favorable to root growth and not as the result of a hormone-mediated tropic response.

Nastic Movements

In contrast to tropisms, *nastic movements* are nondirectional and involve no plant growth.

Nastic movements are physiological responses to specific stimuli. Some examples of nastic movement are

- the tulip, morning glory, and dandelion flowers, which close at night.
- the tobacco and four-o'clock flowers, which close in intense sunlight and only open again when light intensity lowers.
- plant leaves that fold at twilight and open again after dawn.

Biological Clock. The daily rhythm of these plants is so much a part of their nature that it persists independently of actual lighting conditions. Experiments have shown that when one of these light-conditioned plants is artificially subjected to continued darkness, the folding and unfolding continue for several days. The movements occur at precisely the same hours as they did when exposed to sunshine.

The function of these sleep positions in plants has not been determined, though one popular theory is that it slows heat loss from the leaves, the folded leaves helping to insulate against the colder external air of the night.

TOUCH-ME-NOT

When a leaflet of the tropical *Mimosa pudica* is touched, it folds up, and the long petiole drops down. If a very strong stimulus is applied to the shrub, even leaflets at some distance from the contact may fold and drop down. This kind of adaptation is believed to offer protection against excessive water loss.

Touchy Plants. Some plants react to touch. Nastic movements triggered by touch are known as *thigmonasty*. The *Mimosa pudica* folds up when touched, and the Venus's-flytrap snaps shut.

Both responses result from changes in *turgor pressure*. Oversized cells filled with water act as hinges. By a complicated sequence of events, the touch causes water pressure to drain away instantly and the cell to wilt or collapse, closing the hinge. The trigger cocks again only after the impulse has passed and the target cell refills with water at its normal turgid pressure.

PREDATOR PLANT

Venus's-flytrap also displays thigmonasty when it snaps shut, usually around an insect unfortunate enough to have lighted on its trigger mechanism. This touch response is the plant's means of providing itself with nutrients. Enzymes secreted by the plant digest the captured insect, thereby providing nitrogen and other nutrients lacking in the bogs and swamps that are the plant's native habitat.

Venus's-flytrap

Climate

Daily temperatures, transient water shortages, changes in humidity, and even wind play a small part in the individual metabolism of each plant. Every plant species has a genetically determined range of tolerances to weather. Within this range, a plant develops efficiently. Individual plants may grow somewhat beyond those tolerances, but it is usually at the price of lowered vitality.

Temperature. Extreme temperatures can greatly affect plant metabolism. Very high temperatures cause metabolic processes to occur at a very high rate. A heat wave can cause a developmental stage to be so rushed that it fails to complete itself.

Low temperatures slow biochemical reactions. If the temperature drops enough, some physiological functions—such as water transport or digestion—may become impossible.

Temperatures also influence the germination and flowering of certain plants. Some plants require low temperature stimulation, or *vernalization*, at a stage in their development. This need is demonstrated in the fact that plants such as rye and wheat require a period of cold in order to germinate naturally.

PHOTOPERIOD

The photoperiod is determined by Earth's seasonal tilt and by latitude. Near the equator, photoperiods vary little from one season to the next. Days and nights are roughly 12 hours each all year round. (See The Spinning Earth, page 502.)

But photoperiods in regions near the North and South poles change substantially with the seasons, approaching 24-hour-long spans of daylight or darkness around the time of the solstices.

Sunlight. The growth of plants is also affected by the length of the periods of light and dark they receive.

- *Long-day* plants, like lettuce and spinach, bloom only when the *photoperiod* (period of daylight) is long.

- These species flower in late spring and summer, and then only if the daylight is 14 to 18 hours long.

- *Short-day* plants, like asters, chrysanthemums, and poinsettias, flower in early spring or fall, when the daylight period is less than 10 or 11 hours daily.

- If their growth is delayed because of weather or other reasons, and they are in an immature state when day lengths exceed the photoperiodic limit, flowering cannot occur, no matter how perfect other conditions are.

- *Day-neutral* plants, like marigolds and tomatoes, are not affected by the length of the photoperiod.

Extreme Cold. The briefest encounter with below-freezing temperature can cause ice crystals to form in plant tissues, bursting fragile cell walls and tearing plant organs, sometimes even killing the plant.

REVIEW: Stimulus-Response Patterns	
Pattern	Description
Tropism	A movement toward or away from the direction of a stimulus; involves growth
Nastic movement	Physiological response to direct stimuli; does not involve growth
Climate response	Plant development affected by surrounding conditions; involves growth

PLANT GROWTH

A plant cannot continue to live without continuous growth. A plant's growth is shaped by hereditary and environmental interactions. Plants grow upward, downward, and sideways. They generate seeds that can travel on the wind, float on running water, or be carried in the digestive systems of animals. They produce flowers and fruits capable of attracting other organisms that do move. In these ways, plants extend their physical presence and thereby enable the survival of their species.

Hereditary Factors

One of the most striking facts about all life forms is that offspring resemble their parents. In lower plants, which reproduce asexually, there is almost perfect resemblance between generations. In the higher plants, offspring are the product of sexual reproduction.

Reproduction and Heredity

The daughter plants that result from sexual reproduction derive their heritable traits from two parents, combining features of each in predictable ways. (See pages 62–63.)

Variation. Sexual reproduction ensures that all individuals are different in detail from the previous generation and even slightly different from others of the same generation.

This variability results in the adaptability of a plant species. The offspring that are better suited to the environment are more likely to survive and reproduce than offspring with traits that are not suited to the environment. This adaptability is an enormous advance in terms of long-term survival.

Chromosomes. The source of a plant's traits and the predictable patterns of inheritance that occur can be traced to the moment of *fertilization*, or union between the parent plants' sperm and egg cells. Within the nucleus of each of these cells are tiny *chromosomes*, along which *genes*, the packages of hereditary blueprints, are aligned.

The chromosomes are present in matching pairs. The numbers of genes carried on these chromosomes vary, but they number in the thousands.

In sexual reproduction, the genetic blueprints of each parent are joined to produce new chromosome pairs and different offspring. *Mutations*, spontaneous errors in the transcription of genetic codes, may also occur, adding to genetic variability.

◀ **Adder's tongue fern,** *Ophioglossum reticulatum,* has more chromosomes than any other plant: 630 pairs for a total of 1,260.

Plants grow continuously. This little seedling is the first sprouting of growth that will continue throughout the life of the plant. ▶

Inheritance Patterns

Underlying each trait (stem length, pod color, seed coat texture, flower bicolor, etc.) in sexually reproducing organisms are two genes or, in some instances, groups of linked genes. Each gene has different forms, called *alleles*. For example, a gene for flower color can have an allele for purple flowers and an allele for blue flowers.

An allele can be *dominant* or *recessive*. If a plant receives two dominant alleles, or one dominant and one recessive allele, it will display the dominant trait. If it receives two recessive alleles, it will display the recessive trait.

If the plant receives one dominant and one recessive allele, the recessive allele has a chance of being expressed in the next generation if it is matched during sexual reproduction with an identical recessive gene from another plant.

With a few exceptions, each trait is transmitted to offspring independently of all other traits, so that in the new generation they can theoretically combine in many ways.

PLANT GROWTH

Hereditary Factors

- Lower plants favor asexual reproduction though some can also reproduce sexually.

- Higher plants reproduce both sexually and asexually.

- Sexual reproduction ensures genetic variation. Each offspring receives genes from two different parents.

- Genetic variation increases adaptability.

Plant Life Cycles

The life cycle of a plant occurs in four stages.

1. germination
2. seedling development
3. maturation and flowering
4. aging and death

Hormones

- Hormones are substances made within a plant that play a part in regulating plant growth.

- Hormones keep the plant's physiological processes in harmony as they stimulate activity in one area or inhibit it in another.

- Hormones control such activities as the growing of roots and the production of flowers and fruit.

There are five known classes of plant hormones.

Growth promoters:
1. auxins
2. gibberellins
3. cytokinins

Growth inhibitors:
4. abscisic acid
5. ethylene

Hormones

Hormones are substances made within a plant that play a part in regulating plant growth. They act as messengers, moving through the plant, keeping the plant's physiological processes in harmony as they stimulate activity in one area or inhibit it in another. Hormones control such activities as the growing of roots and the production of flowers and fruit.

There are five known classes of plant hormones, all of them small molecules that travel along the plant's transport system and penetrate cell walls to reach their target cells. The five classes of hormones are:

Growth Promoters
- auxins
- gibberellins
- cytokinins

Growth Inhibitors
- abscisic acid
- ethylene

▲ **Into the Light.** Auxin tends to be destroyed by exposure to light. The shoot's dark side therefore grows more rapidly than the light side. The shoot's tip bends toward the light source.

Growth Promoters

Auxins are the prime growth-promoting hormone.

- Auxins cause cell elongation.
- They are synthesized in the meristematic areas of the shoot and root, where they remain in high concentration.
- They promote continuous and rapid growth of the plant.
- Auxins promote the turning of plants toward the light.
- Auxins are concentrated in the cambium layer of stems and trunks to produce rapid cell division.
- They are concentrated in the base of stems to cause formation of adventitious and lateral roots.
- They are concentrated in the flower buds to develop female flower parts and fruits.
- Auxins produce the characteristic shapes of particular plants through *apical dominance*—the lateral growth of the plant is repressed in favor of vertical growth, resulting in a particular branching pattern.
- Apical dominance is strong in many conifers, as expressed in their tall, upright growth.

SYNTHETIC HORMONES

Scientists have been able to synthesize auxins in the laboratory for use in agricultural and horticultural applications. The auxins induce stronger rooting, override certain inhibitory hormones, and kill certain kinds of weeds selectively by upsetting their normal growth patterns.

THE FLOWERING HORMONE

There is another type of hormone that is believed to be responsible for inducing a plant to flower. Called *florigen*, this hormone has not yet been isolated chemically, though its existence has been postulated since 1937.

Recent experiments suggest that florigen may not, after all, be a separate hormone but a compound of gibberellins and some other hormone or hormones.

Gibberellins are a second group of growth-promoting hormones.

- Gibberellins induce cell elongation, particularly in stem cells.
- The absence or insufficiency of gibberellins results in dwarf or miniature varieties of some plants.
- Gibberellins help in leaf growth.
- They inhibit root formation.
- They stimulate the development of male flower parts.
- They play a role in developmental processes controlled by temperature and light, such as seed stalk formation and plant and seed dormancy.
- The gibberellin compounds are produced chiefly in the chloroplasts of young leaves, from which they are distributed throughout the plant.

Cytokinins are the hormones that promote cell division.

- Cytokinins are produced in the roots.
- They are distributed through the xylem tissue to actively dividing tissues such as those found in germinating seeds, fruits, and new root growth.
- In high concentrations, cytokinins slow the process of *senescence,* or aging, in leafy green vegetables and other plants.

Growth Inhibitors

Abscisic acid is a growth inhibitor produced in mature leaves. (See page 127.)

- Abscisic acid is concentrated in high levels in leaf petioles in autumn.
- It is responsible for seasonal *abscission*, or the detaching of leaf stems.
- It inhibits plant growth by promoting a state of dormancy over the winter.
- Its levels fall with the onset of spring, coincident with rising concentrations of growth promoter hormones.

Ethylene is the only gaseous growth-regulating hormone.

- Ethylene causes changes in color, texture, and chemical composition that relate to ripening.
- As a gaseous hormone, it travels through the plant and the air around the plant.
- Ethylene can affect the tissues of plants some distance away.
- The presence of ethylene accounts for the fact that one bad apple can spoil a whole barrel.

Abscisic acid causes leaves to fall in the autumn and ensures that a plant becomes dormant in winter.

Plant Life Cycles

The life cycle of a plant occurs in four stages.

1. Germination

Once a seed has matured, it goes into a state of *dormancy*, or inactivity. *Germination* marks the end of dormancy and the revitalization of the embryo.

The environmental requirements needed for a seed to sprout include oxygen, moisture, a proper temperature, and in some cases, light.

Germination begins when moisture enters the seed coat, commencing a physical process called *imbibition*. The dry seed soaks up the water, causing the tissues to swell dramatically and the seed coat to burst open. As seed tissues become hydrated, metabolism speeds up. The seed begins to break down stored food in the endosperm to fuel growth and respiration.

At this point, adequate levels of oxygen become critical. If the soil becomes flooded, or if it is compacted, the seed can suffocate and rot. If too little water is available, germination may take place very slowly or not at all.

Primary Root. If conditions are favorable, a *radicle*, a tiny but vigorous primary root, protrudes and begins developing downward into a root system. The radicle, like the secondary roots that will follow, has an apical meristem, where growth takes place, covered at the tip by a protective root cap. With the radicle's appearance, germination is complete.

2. Seedling Development

A plant is considered a *seedling* from the end of germination until it ceases to depend on its stored food reserves.

A hypocotyl, or lower part of the seedling, grows from the juncture of radicle and seed and makes a channel through the soil as it forces its way upward.

The cotyledons, the embryonic leaves, follow in the wake of the hypocotyl.

Breaking the Surface. When the cotyledons reach the soil surface, light causes them to unfold and the hypocotyl hook to straighten. The seedling now has an aboveground shoot, or *epicotyl*.

For several days, the cotyledons supply the seedling's growth needs through stored energy and photosynthetic energy. But when the shoot sets its first true leaves, the cotyledons wither and drop away.

germination

seedling development

3. Maturation and Flowering

Once a plant has left the seedling stage, it turns its dynamic energies toward the flowering process and the production of flowers, seeds, and fruits.

Annuals are plants that reach maturity within the same growing season. Annuals live only a year, having fulfilled their reproductive cycle.

Biennials take 2 years and two growth seasons to complete the reproductive cycle, developing vegetative growth in the first year and flowering, fruiting, and finally dying in the second.

Perennials are plants that grow and renew themselves over a period of 3 years or more.

4. Aging and Death

Preparations for the reproductive stage of growth—the formation of flowers, fruits, and seeds—place an especially heavy demand on the plant. This demand, chiefly in the form of a drain of nutrients, can sometimes be observed in the premature yellowing of vegetative parts of the plant that have performed their functions.

This process is termed *senescence*. It is a natural part of a plant's life history as moderated by hormonal changes. It is distinctly different from the premature death that plants may suffer from a traumatic environmental insult, such as starvation, unseasonal drought, or freezing.

maturation and flowering

aging and death

FUNGI are organisms that obtain food by absorbing it from other living organisms or from parts of formerly living things. According to *mycologists* (scientists who study fungi), thousands of fungus species exist. Some of the most common fungi include mildews, molds, mushrooms, rusts, and smuts.

A number of fungi are too small to be seen without a microscope. But many types can be seen with the unaided eye. In fact, the largest-known living organism in the world is a fungus that grows in a forest in Oregon.

Small golden mushrooms that emerge from the ground every autumn are the only surface signs of the giant fungus.

Fungi Form and Function

Many fungi are *decomposers*, meaning they feed on the dead remains of organisms and organic waste. They play an important role in the ecosystem because they cycle nutrients from the remains back into the environment and slow the accumulation of waste.

Scientists gain a better understanding of fungi by studying their *anatomy*, or physical form, and *physiology*, or how they function.

Parts of a Fungus

- The main part of a fungus consists of thousands of threadlike cells called *hyphae* (except for one-celled fungi such as yeasts and chytrids).
- These tiny, branching cells sometimes form a tangled mass called a *mycelium*.
- Mycelium often grows beneath the surface of the material on which the organism is feeding.
- The umbrella-shaped growth known as a *mushroom* is actually the fruiting body of the fungus.
- *Spores* are cells that develop into new hyphae, enabling the fungus to reproduce. Spores are smaller and simpler than the seeds of plants.
- Some types of molds bear spores in tiny structures called *sporangia*.
- Such fungi as the green mold *Penicillium notatum* produce chains of spores from branched hyphae called *conidiophores*.
- Other fungi, such as cup fungi, produce spores that they shoot into the air from individual saclike cells.

HUMONGOUS FUNGUS

The world's largest-known living organism is a fungus in the Malheur National Forest in eastern Oregon. The fungus, a tree-killing specimen called *Armillaria ostoyae*—popularly known as the honey mushroom—is approximately 5.6 kilometers (3.5 miles) across and extends into the ground about 1 meter (3 feet).

The fungus was not discovered until August 2000, because the only signs on the surface are clumps of mushrooms that grow each autumn. Beneath the surface, a web of threadlike filaments called a *mycelium* spreads from tree to tree, drawing water and nutrients. The fungus is at least 2,400 years old.

How a Fungus Lives

Since fungi cannot produce their own food, they take carbohydrates, proteins, and other nutrients from the living organisms or dead organic matter on which they live. Fungi discharge chemicals called *enzymes* into the material on which they feed. The enzymes break down complex carbohydrates and proteins into simple compounds that the hyphae can absorb.

Fungi live almost everywhere on land and in water.

- *Saprophytes*, a large group of fungi that includes mushrooms, live on dead or decaying matter.

- Parasitic fungi, such as mildews and smuts, feed on living organisms.

- Some fungi live together with other organisms in ways that are mutually beneficial.

The fruiting body of a mushroom produces spores, which develop into new hyphae.

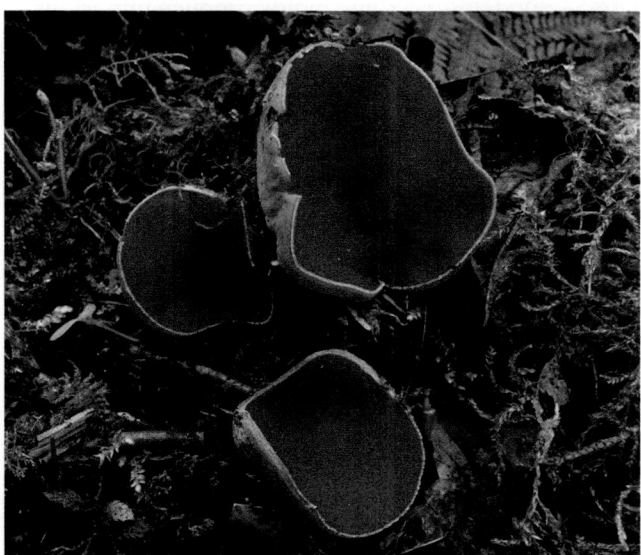

Cup fungi forcefully shoot their spores into the air from saclike cells. A spore that lands in a favorable location *germinates* (starts to grow) and eventually produces a new mycelium.

Reproduction. Fungi generally reproduce by forming spores.

- Some spores are produced by the union of *gametes* (sex cells).

- *Asexual*, or *imperfect*, spores develop without the union of gametes.

- Many fungi produce spores both sexually and asexually.

Spreading Spores. Numerous spores are scattered by the wind, and others are transported by water or by animals. Mushrooms, cup fungi, and some other fungi forcefully discharge their spores.

BUDDING

Yeasts can reproduce by forming sexual spores, but many kinds of yeasts reproduce by *budding*. When a yeast buds, a bulge forms on the cell. A cell wall grows and separates the bud from the original yeast cell. The bud then develops into a new cell. Budding produces a large number of yeast cells rapidly.

Importance of Fungi

Fungi are found in soil, in the air, in water, on plants and animals, and within plants and animals. Fungi break down dead organisms and waste matter. They are the ingredients that cause bread to rise and beer and wine to ferment. They are used for food and medicine, but they can also be poisonous and cause disease.

Useful Fungi

Many fungi break down complex animal and plant matter into simple compounds. This process of decomposition enriches the soil and makes essential substances available to plants and other organisms in a usable form. Through decomposition, fungi also return carbon dioxide to the atmosphere, where green plants can reuse it to make food.

Edible Fungus. Fungi play a major role in a number of foods. For example, many people consider mushrooms and truffles to be delicacies. (See page 95.)

Cheese manufacturers add molds to Camembert and Roquefort cheeses to ripen them and provide their distinctive flavors.

Yeasts cause the fermentation that produces alcoholic beverages. In the fermentation process, yeasts break down sugar into carbon dioxide and alcohol. Baker's yeast causes bread to rise by producing carbon dioxide from the carbohydrates in the dough. The carbon dioxide gas enlarges very small bubbles already present in the dough, causing the rise. Some people eat yeasts as a rich source of protein and B vitamins.

Penicillium notatum is one of several green molds that produce penicillin, which physicians use in treating many diseases caused by bacteria.

Life-Saving Fungus. Some molds produce important drugs called *antibiotics*. Antibiotics weaken or destroy bacteria and other organisms that cause disease. For example, *penicillin* is a powerful drug used to treat infections caused by bacteria. It was the first antibiotic used successfully to treat serious diseases in human beings.

Various forms of the drug, called penicillins, have become widely available for medical use since the mid-1940s. Penicillins have played a major role in treating pneumonia, rheumatic fever, scarlet fever, and other diseases.

The development of penicillins had a tremendous impact on medicine and encouraged research that led to the discovery of many other antibiotics.

Mold is purposefully added to certain cheeses to give them their flavor. Other molds, however, can spoil food or be poisonous to humans.

HOW DO WE KNOW THAT? ANTIBIOTICS

In 1928, a British bacteriologist named Alexander Fleming made one of the greatest discoveries in the history of medicine. And it happened by accident.

Fleming was studying bacteria, searching for a substance that could kill disease-causing bacteria without harming humans. His work required him to create various cultures in laboratory dishes. While a tidier researcher may have discarded these dishes, Fleming kept a large number of them in his work area for several weeks at a time.

Harmful Fungi

Some fungi may cause extensive damage.

- Parasitic fungi destroy many crops and other plants. Important parasitic fungi that attack plants include mildews, rusts, and smuts.

- Other fungi produce diseases in animals and people. Fungal diseases in humans are called mycoses. They can cause a mild respiratory infection or be severe, infecting the blood and every organ system.

- Some mushrooms are poisonous and can cause serious illness or death if eaten. There are 70 to 80 known mushroom species that are poisonous to humans.

- Molds spoil many kinds of food, and they may also prove poisonous.

- In damp climates, mildews and other fungi can ruin clothing, bookbindings, and other materials. Fungi may also cause wood to decay or rot.

Amanita phalloides is a mushroom also known as the "death cap." If eaten, toxins in the mushroom cause vomiting, abdominal pain, damage to the liver, kidneys, and central nervous system, and even death.

Looking at old cultures before throwing them away, Fleming noticed that an unexpected mold had grown in a dish containing staphylococcus bacteria. In the area around the mold, the colonies of bacteria had been dissolved.

The mold turned out to be a rare one: ***Penicillium notatum***. Fleming found that the mold effectively killed the bacteria that caused pneumonia, cerebral meningitis, diphtheria, anthrax, and gangrene.

In the late 1930s and early 1940s, two other scientists—Lord Florey and Ernst Boris Chain—used Fleming's research to create penicillin, the first antibiotic.

Fleming, Florey, and Chain shared the 1945 Nobel Prize in Medicine for their work.

Alexander Fleming

FIRST LIFE

The young Earth was rich in carbon and other minerals and had an abundance of water. The temperature on the surface of Earth was neither so hot that water evaporated away nor so cold that it froze solid permanently. This moderation was crucial for the origination of life.

Life began in the oceans, where it was shielded from the sun's radiation but still had access to the sun's radiant energy. The first fossils of a living organism date from 3.5 billion years ago. They were prokaryotic, photosynthetic cells similar to today's cyanobacteria. (Prokaryotes are the most primitive cells, lacking the specialized units called organelles found in later, more complex cells.)

Signs of Life

Age of Bacteria

Nothing dated earlier than 3.5 billion years ago has been found, but the fact that fossil cells were already well developed leads scientists to believe that the first living things began much earlier—possibly 3.8 billion years ago, soon after Earth's crust solidified. One hypothesis is that the first cells were *heterotrophs* (organisms that need to feed on organic matter), and the ability to photosynthesize came somewhat later.

- For 2.5 billion years, the cyanobacteria were the dominant form of life on Earth, giving off oxygen and causing a buildup of that gas in the atmosphere.

- Oxygen-using organisms developed by 1.5 billion years ago, when the first eukaryotic cells (cells with a nucleus and other organelles) appeared.

- By about 1.2 billion years ago, some eukaryotes are believed to have taken in smaller photosynthetic cells or cell units that went on existing inside their new hosts in a symbiotic union beneficial to both.

Thus began the strain that would become plants, also known as *autotrophs* (organisms that can make their own food). Some of the eukaryotic cells that remained heterotrophs became the ancestors of animals.

Some Major Differences Between Animals and Plants		
Activity	**Animals**	**Plants**
Nutrition	Heterotrophic	Autotrophic
Major mode of obtaining nourisment	Ingestion	Photosynthesis
Requirements	Oxygen, water, minerals	Carbon dioxide, water, minerals
Waste	Carbon dioxide	Oxygen (carbon dioxide from metabolism)
Extent of growth	Predetermined	Indeterminate
Movement	Mostly mobile	Mostly immobile
Nervous system	Present in most	Absent

▲ **Stromatolites** are reeflike mounds of rock created by a community of microbes. They rank among the oldest known fossils. This specimen, found in Namibia, is between 760 and 830 million years old. Some have been found that are 3 billion years old. "Live" stromatolites still exist today.

▲ **Cell Colony.** This azure vase sponge clings to a coral reef.

Multicellularity

The most likely way that multicellular animals arose is with the aggregation of formerly independent and free-living one-celled organisms in the form of a colony. As members of a colony, the cells began to specialize and ultimately lose the ability to live on their own. (See page 60.)

Size and Mobility. One advantage that multicellular organisms have over their one-celled counterparts is size. They are bigger; therefore, they are more likely to eat than be eaten. Multicellular organisms have greater control over their environment than do microorganisms. Their much greater mobility allows animals to get away from noxious environments, to escape from predators, or to defend against them.

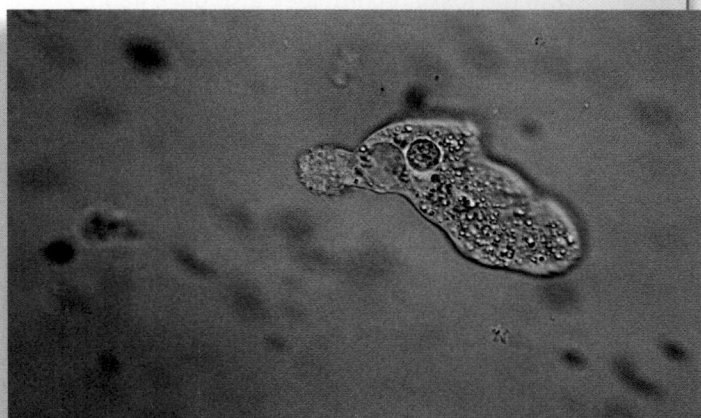

▲ **An example** of a present-day eukaryotic organism: an amoeba is a protozoan that moves by extending fingerlike pseudopods (false feet).

SPONGES

A sponge, the simplest of animals, can be used as a living example. If a piece of a sponge is cut off and strained through a cloth to separate all the cells, the cells will begin to move about randomly. Whenever they come into contact with one another, they will stop moving and form clusters. When enough cells have rejoined to form a sufficient mass, every cell seems to remember its original position and function. The cells jostle about until they are back to their proper places so that a tiny sponge is operating again.

Breaking the Water Barrier

Animals Emerge

The earliest traces of multicellular animals are worm burrows in rocks about a billion years old.

Starting about 670 million years ago, marine life began to proliferate. These creatures were complex invertebrates, inhabiting shallow waters near shore; some were free floating, while others were anchored to the ocean floor.

The Cambrian Explosion. The Cambrian period began about 570 million years ago with a striking diversification of invertebrates within a few million years—the blink of an eye in geological time. So conspicuous was this spread of forms and numbers that it has been called the Cambrian Explosion. Most major phyla, the largest subdivisions in the animal kingdom, first start to appear in the fossil record. (See also page 486.)

Trilobites. The most common fossils from this period are trilobites, ancient arthropods that ranged in size up to 45 centimeters (18 inches) long and in weight up to about 4.5 kilograms (10 pounds). Like all arthropods, the trilobite had a segmented body, in this case a head region, a thorax, and a tail section with a pair of appendages extending from each segment. Also like other arthropods, trilobites had an external skeleton. Some species of trilobites had the most complex eyes of any Cambrian organism.

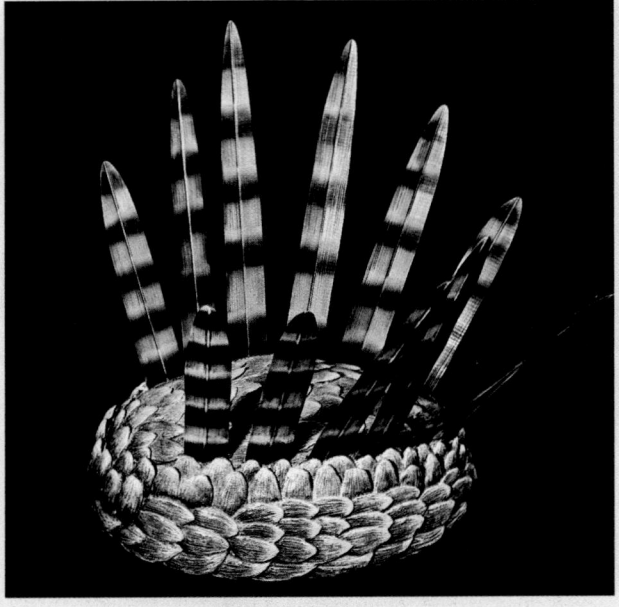

▲ **Wiwaxia.** This reconstruction shows a worm with spines.

WHY THIS SUDDEN OUTBURST OF LIFE?

There are several theories for the sudden appearance of a wide variety of complex life forms at the beginning of the Cambrian period.

- The level of atmospheric oxygen increased at the beginning of the Cambrian period.

- The climate improved at the beginning of the Cambrian period, which followed the end of a global ice age.

- The earliest complex animals arose before the pre-Cambrian period but were too tiny to have been detected easily in the fossil record.

- It was not so much the sudden appearance of complex multicellular life, but rather the sudden widespread appearance of external hard parts, which provided protection from predators, that made the body much more susceptible to fossilization.

- The melting glaciers at the tail end of an ice age transferred deposits of calcium and other minerals into the oceans, providing the raw materials necessary for animal life to evolve protective shells.

Paleontologists have found more than 10,000 species of trilobites in the fossil record. Some trilobites were predators, preying on other marine animals. Some were scavengers. Some lived off plankton.

The Paleozoic era saw the development of many kinds of animals and plants in the seas and on land. Fossil evidence of the earliest known land plants is about 470 million years old.

Plants Colonize Dry Land

The Cambrian period ended about 500 million years ago, at a point when Earth's land areas remained devoid of life. At about the middle of the Ordovician period—between 500 and 440 million years ago—plants began the invasion of land.

Living things required several adaptations in order to make the move from water to land.

- increased protection from the ultraviolet rays of the sun

- structural support to make up for the lack of buoyancy that water provides

- a change in the methods of respiration, since aquatic plants and animals derive these vital materials directly from the water in which they live

- a change in the way eggs are fertilized during sexual reproduction

Pterygotus, a giant arthropod commonly known as a sea scorpion, flourished in the Silurian period. Pterygotus could reach 2.3 meters (7 feet.). ▶

The Silurian Period. It was not until the Silurian period, from about 440 to 410 million years ago, that animals followed plants onto land. (See page 488.) The first invaders were arthropods—ancestral scorpions and wingless insects. Among the oldest terrestrial animal fossils found so far is a bristletail resembling today's silverfish.

Arthropods, with their exoskeletons, were able to adjust to the pull of gravity, and they were able to overcome the other great transitional difficulty, obtaining oxygen from the air.

- Insects developed tracheae, small tubes that branched into the body with adjustable openings in the exoskeleton.

- Land crabs and spiders developed something like an internal gill immersed in a protective sac.

LAND PLANTS

Land plants during the Silurian period included mosses and other similar plants. They were short, probably reaching no more than 1 foot (30 centimeters) in height. They also required the damp conditions found along riverbanks and in swamps. Away from such areas, the land remained barren.

Age of Fishes

While the long, slow conquest of land was taking place, certain life forms in the ocean were evolving a new kind of skeleton: an internal skeleton to help support and strengthen the creatures' gelatinous bodies. Vertebrates are so-named because the vertebral column is the beginning of, and central to, this skeleton, with a new kind of body organized around it.

The skeletons of some vertebrates—sharks, for example—were and are made of cartilage, a dense, tough connective tissue. The skeletons of most vertebrates, however, are made of bone, a combination of strong protein fibers and crystals made from calcium, phosphate, and carbonate minerals.

In studying the fossil record, paleontologists had long suspected that primitive ancestors of bony fish, known as lobe-fins, might have been the transitional forms between fish and amphibians. Lobe-fins developed a pouchlike primitive lung that in some species evolved into a swim bladder used to regulate buoyancy and that was passed on to later bony fish. But some lobe-fins that remained in shallow pools sometimes were stranded by receding waters, and the lung was put into use to breathe air.

The earliest known vertebrates are a class of fish called agnaths. They probably came into existence about the time the first plants were making their move onto land.

Another candidate for the vertebrate land pioneer is the lungfish. As its name implies, the lungfish has a dual breathing system. It can extract oxygen from water through gills or rise to the surface and breathe air through mouth or nasal passages.

A LIVING FOSSIL

Until 1938, it was believed that the only surviving examples of lobe-finned fish were several species of lungfish. Theories about the link between fish and amphibians centered on another group of lobe-finned fish: the coelacanths, which were believed to have become extinct 80 million years ago.

However, in 1938, a fisherman caught a coelacanth in the Indian Ocean off the coast of South Africa. The coelacanth has two pairs of lobe fins that project away from its body and which move as pairs, in a manner common to four-legged animals but not to fish.

The modern coelacanth is a large, ocean-going fish. However, the ancient coelacanths were smaller and lived in shallow waters, where these powerful lobe fins would have been useful for crawling along the bottom of shallow waters.

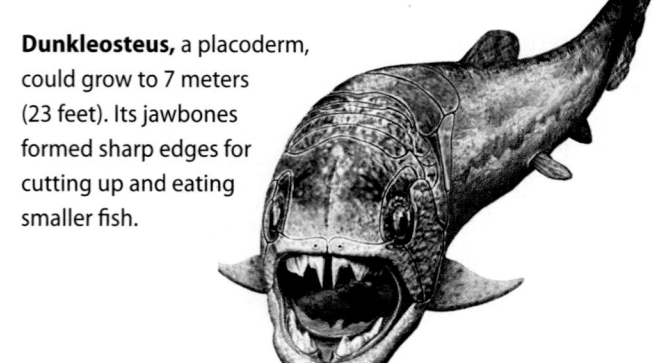

Dunkleosteus, a placoderm, could grow to 7 meters (23 feet). Its jawbones formed sharp edges for cutting up and eating smaller fish.

JAWS

Jaws were a pivotal mechanism in the history of vertebrates. Fish that developed jaws came to dominate the seas. One early group with primitive jaws, called placoderms, was heavily armored with bony plates. For a while, placoderms were the top predators, but their heavy armor eventually proved more of a liability than an advantage. Placoderms virtually disappeared by the close of the Devonian period and became extinct.

By the close of the Devonian period, the oceans were inhabited by the two types of fish we know today: the cartilaginous fish best known as sharks and rays, and the so-called real fish. They are designated bony fish.

Age of Amphibians

The invasion of land by vertebrates was in full swing in the Carboniferous period. Climates were moist and warm with heavy rains, favoring the growth of lush swamp forests of tree ferns and mosses.

An Incomplete Transition. Despite their success, the amphibians were still not fully adapted to life on land. Their simple lungs were insufficient to provide all the oxygen necessary for a land animal, and they had to get some of their oxygen through their skin. In order to function in this way, the skin must be kept moist. Furthermore, amphibians must deposit their sperm and eggs in water in order to reproduce. The fertilized egg then develops into an aquatic larva that, through the process known as metamorphosis, then matures into a terrestrial animal. It is by this transformation that amphibians get their name—in Greek, *amphi* means "both" and *bios* means "life."

The amphibians reigned on land for the better part of 100 million years. But the cooling and drying out of the environment in the subsequent Permian period restricted the range of amphibians and opened opportunities for their successors, the reptiles.

ICHTHYOSTEGA

Fossil skeletons of Ichthyostega, a creature that lived about 360 million years ago, provide evidence that tetrapods (four-legged animals) evolved from fish. Ichthyostega had legs, enabling it to live on land. Ichthyostega's leg bones, however, were similar to the fin bones of fish. It also had fishlike teeth and a broad, finned tail for swimming. Later tetrapods lost these fishlike traits.

End of an Era

By the end of the Permian period, gigantic upheavals were taking place. Over tens of millions of years, Earth's movable tectonic plates had been pushing the landmasses into one supercontinent, called *Pangaea*. Collisions of these blocks of land upthrust mountain chains, such as the Appalachians and Urals, rearranging habitats—sealing off some, opening up others, causing the spread of deserts, and reducing the environmental diversity conducive to the variety of species. The shifting plates induced earthquakes and powerful volcanic eruptions. The coming together of land bodies radically decreased coastlines, with their shallow waters so hospitable to marine animals.

There may have been other causes, such as meterorite impacts, but these known convulsions seem sufficient to explain the greatest devastation of life that has ever occurred at one time. More than half the families of animals disappeared. More than 90 percent of all species of marine animals living in shallow water, vertebrates and invertebrates alike, were extinguished. The trilobites, which had persevered from the beginning of the Cambrian period, were wiped out. Amphibians, already in decline, soon nearly disappeared.

Animal life of the Paleozoic era included an abundance of species. Animals from the Permian period at the end of that era, shown here, included the reptiles Dimetrodon and Edaphosaurus, which had large sail-like fins on their backs. Such amphibians as the large Eryops, triangular-headed Diplocaulus, and smaller Seymouria lived on land and sea.

THE MESOZOIC AND CENOZOIC ERAS

Discontinuities are not only endings but also beginnings. The reptiles, who had already outcompeted the amphibians as the dominant large land animals in the Permian period, were poised to evolve into a dizzying array of creatures as the Mesozoic era began some 250 million years ago. One group of dinosaurs, the sauropods, became the largest land vertebrates of all time. The Mesozoic era became the Age of Reptiles, especially dinosaurs.

Reign of the Dinosaurs

Age of Reptiles

Reptiles completed the transition to land begun by the amphibians. They reduced their dependence on water in four ways.

1. Reptiles developed copulation, in which the sex cells are fertilized in the moist—and safe—environment of the female's reproductive tract.

2. Reptiles produced an egg that could be laid on land, even in a dry place.

3. Horny scales developed, preventing water loss from the skin.

4. Reptiles had a better respiratory system, with ribs that performed like bellows.

Rulers of the Seas. Dinosaurs were not the only giant reptiles to dominate their habitats. Ichthyosaurs readapted to aquatic life, much as mammalian seals and dolphins have done. Their bodies were streamlined and had limbs resembling fins, a dorsal fin, and a fishlike tail. Giant mosasaurs and plesiosaurs also roamed the ocean during the Mesozoic era.

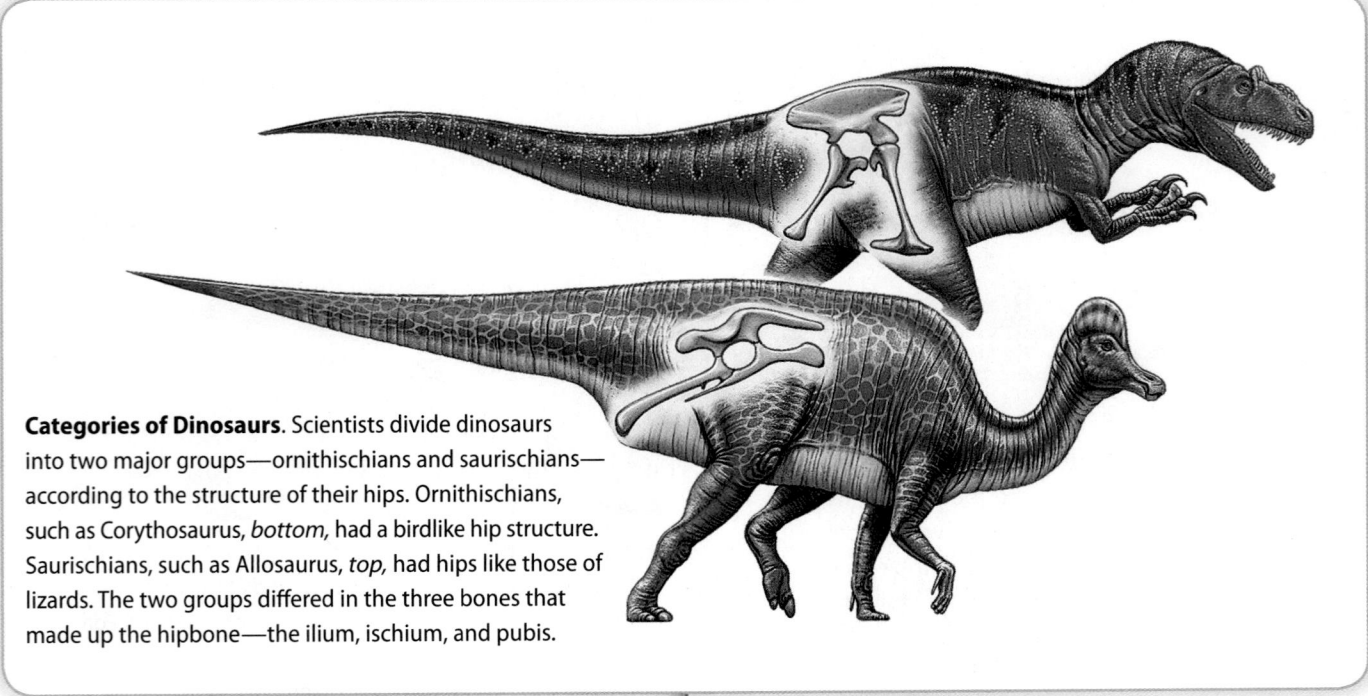

Categories of Dinosaurs. Scientists divide dinosaurs into two major groups—ornithischians and saurischians—according to the structure of their hips. Ornithischians, such as Corythosaurus, *bottom,* had a birdlike hip structure. Saurischians, such as Allosaurus, *top,* had hips like those of lizards. The two groups differed in the three bones that made up the hipbone—the ilium, ischium, and pubis.

SOUTHWESTERN

Rulers of the Sky. Reptiles took to the air in such forms as pterodactyls and pterodons of the order Pterosauria. The wings were made of skin that stretched from the forelimbs to the hind legs. None of these wings had feathers, but archaeopteryx, about the size of a crow, had a long feathered tail, a beak lined with teeth, big feathered forelimbs resembling wings, and a feathered body. The theory is that the feathers served as insulation to retain body heat and, therefore, that the animal was warm-blooded, or endothermic. It is such characteristics that have made archaeopteryx the favored progenitor of modern birds.

Dinosaurs were the most spectacular reptiles of the Jurassic and Cretaceous periods. Brachiosaurus was once believed to be the most massive of all, at a weight of up to 77 metric tons (85 tons). Smaller herbivores were the heavily armored stegosaurus and three-horned triceratops, weighing in at 10 metric tons (11 tons). Tyrannosaurus rex, the most fearsome of the meat-eating predators, was 12 meters (40 feet) long and weighed the staggering total of about 15 metric tons (17 tons). (See pages 494–497.)

Dinosaurs of the Jurassic period (200 million to 145 million years ago) included the huge Diplodocus and the meat-eating Allosaurus, *center.* Another Jurassic dinosaur, Stegosaurus, *background,* had stiff bony plates along its back. Camptosaurus, *far left,* could walk on its two hind legs.

Ammonites were a group of cephalopods that thrived in the oceans for more than 300 million years, only to be wiped out at the end of the Cretaceous period.

Cataclysm

The Cretaceous period concluded 65 million years ago with a calamity that brought an end to the dinosaurs and many other animals. In the seas, the victims ranged from large marine reptiles, to a group of large marine invertebrates known as ammonites, down to microscopic plankton. On land, no animal weighing more than about 27 kilograms (60 pounds) survived.

What Happened? The most compelling explanation has been the suggestion that a meteorite 9.5 kilometers (6 miles) in diameter struck Earth with a force sufficient to hurl trillions of tons of dust and steam into the upper atmosphere. Evidence for this impact can be found in a thin layer of iridium in clay deposits 65 million years old, which has been found at about 40 sites. Iridium is a rare element on Earth's surface, but it is more common in meteorites.

Dire Effects. According to the theory, the matter thrown up by the searing impact spread into an immense shroud that cast Earth's surface into darkness. Temperatures plummeted. Hardest hit by such an event would have been large animals adapted to a warm climate and requiring substantial amounts of food. Some small animals, such as mammals, were able to survive this long, cataclysmic winter.

Varieties of Dinosaurs

WHEN DINOSAURS LIVED

Dinosaurs lived during the Mesozoic era, which is divided into three periods—the Triassic (about 251 million to 200 million years ago), the Jurassic (200 million to 145 million years ago), and the Cretaceous (145 million to 65 million years ago). Pictured here are dinosaurs from each of these periods.

Procompsognathus
3 feet (0.9 meters) long
Late Triassic Period

Heterodontosaurus
3 to 4 feet (0.9 to 1.2 meters)
Early Jurassic Period

Plateosaurus
20 feet (6 meters) long
Late Triassic Period

Stegosaurus
25 feet (7.6 meters) long
Early Jurassic Period

Scelidosaurus
12 feet (3.7 meters) long
Late Jurassic Period

Brachiosaurus
70 feet (21 meters) long
Late Jurassic Period

Apatosaurus
70 feet (21 meters) long
Late Jurassic Period

Ornitholestes
6 feet (1.8 meters) long
Late Jurassic Period

Camptosaurus
15 feet (4.8 meters) long
Late Jurassic Period

Compsognathus
2.5 feet (0.8 meters) long
Late Jurassic Period

Allosaurus
30 feet (9 meters) long
Late Jurassic Period

Iguanodon
30 feet (9 meters) long
Early Cretaceous Period

Deinonychus
9 feet (2.7 meters) long
Early Cretaceous Period

Tyrannosaurus
40 feet (12 meters) long
Late Cretaceous Period

Ornithomimus
14 feet (4.3 meters) long
Cretaceous Period

Ankylosaurus
30 feet (9 meters) long
Cretaceous Period

Velociraptor
6 feet (1.8 meters) long
Late Cretaceous Period

6 feet
(1.8 meters)

Corythosaurus
30 feet (9 meters) long
Late Cretaceous Period

Pentaceratops
25 feet (7.6 meters) long
Late Cretaceous Period

Rise of the Mammals

Age of Mammals

Mammals are believed to have evolved from a group of reptiles known as therapsids (order Therapsida) that had mammal-like features. (They may have been endotherms and homeotherms, creating their own heat and maintaining an even temperature.) Therapsids were hard hit by the holocaust that ended the Paleozoic era. Of 50 genera of this order, only a few survived into the Mesozoic era. One of these groups gave rise to true mammals. The earliest mammals were small, probably living in trees and mostly nocturnal, and would not have competed directly with dinosaurs and other reptiles. So the mammals bided their time all through the Jurassic and Cretaceous periods, gradually evolving into a variety of forms.

In the early Cenozoic era, the placental mammals had one distinct advantage over their biggest competition, the birds: they gave birth to live young. The fetus develops inside the mother's womb, protected by an amniotic sac (which can also be found in reptile and bird eggs). After a live birth, the young get their nourishment by drinking milk from the mother's mammary glands, a distinguishing feature of the class and the origin of the word mammal. (See pages 498–499.)

REIGN OF THE MAMMALS

Mammals reached their greatest variety during the Miocene epoch (23 million to 5.3 million years ago). The number of mammalian species began to decline during the Pliocene epoch (5.3 million to 2.6 million years ago). The Pleistocene epoch, which began about 2.6 million years ago, brought enormous changes in climate. Several waves of glaciers advanced over much of the land. Many mammals—including ground sloths, mammoths, saber-toothed cats, and woolly rhinoceroses—died out.

Coryphodon, an early mammal

The Mammalian Edge. Mammals (as well as birds) are warm-blooded, meaning that they can maintain the same internal body temperature, regardless of the temperature of their surroundings. This enabled mammals to thrive in a wide variety of climates. Scientists refer to warm-blooded animals as endothermic or homeothermic.

Mammals' speed and agility resulted from a more advanced nervous system and a better design for locomotion. The two pairs of legs shifted from the sides, as in a crocodile, to underneath the body, as in a cheetah. Additional changes were an improved jaw with teeth shaped for specific tasks—sharp incisors in front for cutting, canines long and pointed for piercing and tearing, and flat molars for grinding. These improvements have made mammals some of the most successful of all animals, inhabiting every part of the planet.

Rise of the Hominids

One order of mammals, the primates, is of particular interest because it includes the human species. Primates consist of four groups: prosimians (the most primitive primates), monkeys, apes, and human beings. Fossils of tree shrews, the first prosimians, are about 80 million years old. Insect-eating tree shrews were small, four-legged animals, but their paws were veering toward hands for grasping branches. Over the next 50 million years, their descendants evolved into forms similar to modern lemurs, tarsiers, and monkeys.

About 30 million years ago, monkeys split off from the line ancestral to hominids. The last division, of chimpanzees and humans, took place anywhere from 5 to 8 million years ago.

The first hominids—bipedal, walking upright—appeared about 4 million years ago or perhaps somewhat earlier.

- The human genus *Homo* appeared about 2.5 million years ago.
- The earliest known member of this genus was *Homo habilis*, and it was distinguished by its use of tools.
- *Homo erectus* appeared about 1.6 million years ago, and that species existed until 250,000 years ago.

Cranium capacity

- *H. habilis* had a cranium capacity of from about 500 to 800 cubic centimeters (30 to 50 cubic inches).
- *H. erectus* had a cranial size of from 750 to 1,225 cubic centimeters (compared with 1,000 to 2,000 cubic centimeters in modern human beings).

While *H. habilis* fossils have been found only in Africa, *H. erectus* ranged far more widely. This species started using fire about 500,000 years ago or perhaps somewhat earlier, began living in caves, and about 400,000 years ago began to make artificial shelters from branches.

Homo sapiens. Our species, *Homo sapiens*, emerged 300,000 or more years ago. But modern human beings are a much more recent development, appearing in Africa perhaps 125,000 to 250,000 years ago and in Europe perhaps as recently as 40,000 years ago.

Homo sapiens possesses the most highly developed brain of any animal. The human brain gives people many special abilities, the most outstanding of which is the ability to speak. Language has enabled human beings to develop culture, which consists of ways of behaving and thinking.

The human brain helps make people the most adaptable of all creatures.

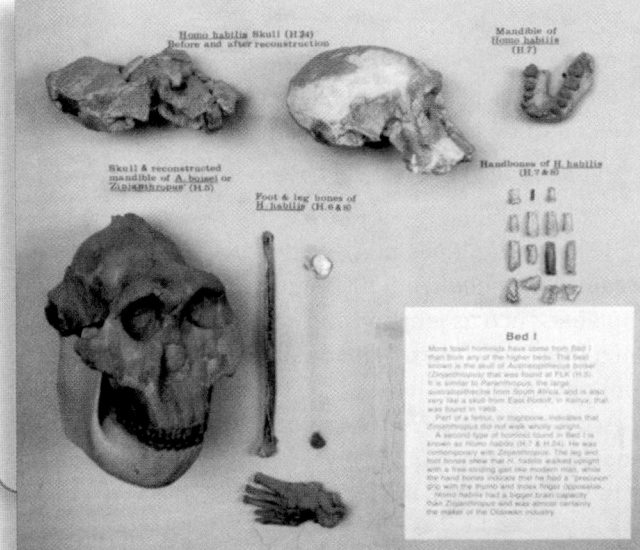

◄ **The first** *Homo habilis* fossils were found at Olduvai Gorge, Tanzania, in 1960, in an expedition led by the British anthropologist Louis Leakey. This collection of *Homo habilis* and *Homo erectus* fossils is displayed at the Leakey Museum in Tanzania.

HISTORY OF ZOOLOGY

While human beings share the planet with a great many kinds of living things, there is no complete inventory of life on Earth. Slightly more than 1 million species of animals have been catalogued.

Of these, 875,000 are arthropods, including 750,000 insects. In contrast, about 43,000 vertebrates have been described. If plants, algae, fungi, and microorganisms are added, the total number of known species is about 1.4 million. But so much remains to be investigated that scientists believe there could be from 5 to 30 million species, most of them animals.

Aristotle began the science of biological classification that we call taxonomy.

Aristotle (384–322 BC)

Aristotle believed it was feasible to work out a logical classification of animals. He originated the term *species,* meaning a group in which all members have common attributes.

According to Aristotle, living things possess a number of attributes.

Beginnings of Zoology

Classification

Human observers through the ages have been awed by the profusion of living things and have felt a need to name them and to arrange them in some kind of systematic way: to impose order on the diversity of life.

ARISTOTLE'S CLASSIFICATION OF ANIMALS

1. **Blooded animals**
   - A. Hairy, live-birth quadrupeds (mammals)
   - B. Birds
   - C. Cetacea (sea mammals)
   - D. Fish
   - E. Snakes
   - F. Egg-laying quadrupeds (most reptiles and amphibians)

2. **Bloodless animals**
   - A. Malakia (squid, octopus, soft-shelled crustaceans)
   - B. Crustacea
   - C. Testacea (mollusks and other hard-shelled marine animals)
   - D. Insects

- At the top level are human beings, who possess all the attributes of animals below them plus the power to think.
- At the next level, animals have the ability to feed themselves plus, in varying degrees, faculties for locomotion, sensing, and desire.
- Plants at the lowest level have only one attribute: self-nutrition.

Below the animals in Aristotle's classification were organisms he could not distinguish as wholly animals or plants, such as jellyfish and sponges. At the bottom of the scale were higher plants, lower plants, and nonliving matter.

Aristotle's system of classification remained the model for more than 2,000 years. It came to be known as the *scala naturae,* ladder of nature.

Conrad Gesner (1516–1565)

Swiss physician and naturalist Conrad Gesner (1516–1565) laid the foundations for scientific zoology. He set out to compile all recorded knowledge of animals and at the same time separate observed facts from myths and popular errors that had accumulated over the years. The end result was a huge volume, *Historiae animalium,* produced in 1551, on animals that bear live young, followed by books on egg-laying animals, birds, fish, and serpents. The accuracy of his facts was supported and advanced by numerous woodcut illustrations of the animals.

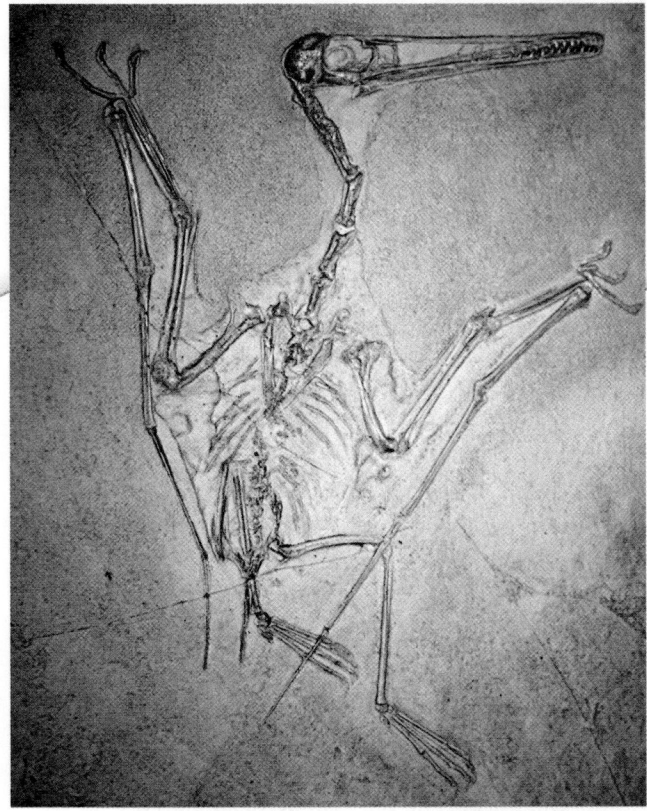

▲ **Fossils perlexed** naturalists in the 18th and early 19th centuries because they represented species that did not exist at that time, suggesting the possibility that different animals lived in the past and that these animals had since become extinct. Shown here is a fossil of a Pterodactylus, a type of pterosaur.

Carolus Linnaeus (1707–1778)

The discovery of the Americas was followed by the discovery of new kinds of animals and plants. These newly found species began to flow into Europe in bewildering varieties. They both overwhelmed and undermined Aristotle's system of classification.

As the situation approached chaos, Swedish botanist Carolus Linnaeus struck on the idea of labeling every kind and group of organism in Latin. The descending levels of hierarchy in the Linnaean kingdom were

- class
- order
- genus
- species

This immediately provided a clarity and consistency that were lacking in previous attempts to improve on Aristotle's system. (See page 90.) Linnaeus also developed the binomial system. Each organism is designated first by its genus, which is capitalized, and then by its species. It was Linnaeus who labeled the human species *Homo sapiens.*

Georges-Louis Leclerc de Buffon (1707–1788)

Georges-Louis Leclerc de Buffon gained fame among his fellows by publishing the 36-volume *Natural History*. Buffon distrusted Linneaus's emphasis on identification and nomenclature. His *Natural History* emphasized living animals and their life histories, habits, and habitats.

By this time, an increasing number of fossils were being uncovered. Some of these fossils were of animals that no longer existed. This raised questions. What had happened to the animals? Why did they not still exist? What about the idea that everything is immutable from the beginning? Buffon was a man of wide learning and he opened up discussion on the origin of Earth and the possibility that it might be much older than supposed, the problem of animal extinction, and the possibility that animals might evolve. However, he did not believe in evolution. If a species is a succession of similar individuals that breed together, according to Buffon, then one species cannot evolve into another.

Insights Into Animal Anatomy

Comparative Anatomy

Georges Cuvier made the next advance in classification by demonstrating the importance of comparative anatomy. In order to appreciate Cuvier's contribution, some background is needed.

Galen of Pergamum (129–c. 199 BC)

Galen of Pergamum, a Greek physician, recorded all the medical knowledge of the ancient world in an encyclopedic work. It contained numerous misconceptions and errors. For instance, Galen said that blood pulses back and forth in the body in a tidal action and that the heart is a suction device. For 13 centuries, physicians accepted the word of Galen even as it contradicted evidence from their own observations.

Andreas Vesalius (1514–1564)

The work of a Belgian, Andreas Vesalius, laid Galen's anatomy to rest forever. At Padua, site of the leading medical school in Europe, Vesalius had access to the cadavers of executed criminals for dissection. From these studies he published in 1543 *De fabrica humani corporus* (*On the Structure of the Human Body*), illustrated by artists from the school of Titian in Venice.

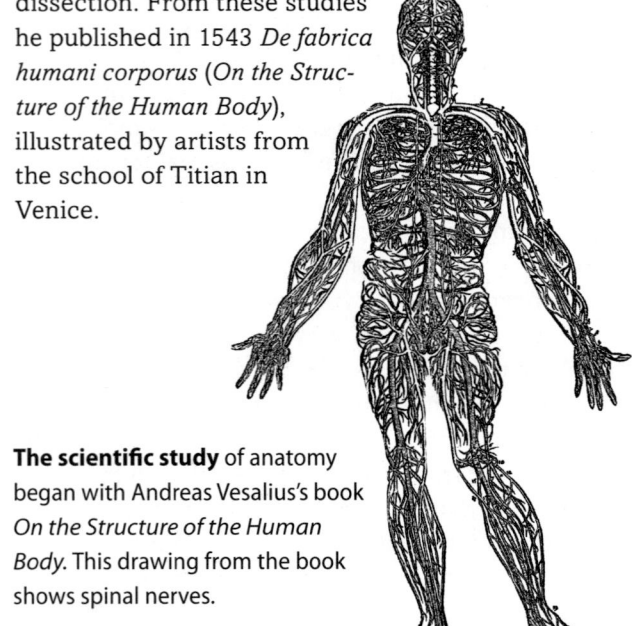

The scientific study of anatomy began with Andreas Vesalius's book *On the Structure of the Human Body*. This drawing from the book shows spinal nerves.

William Harvey of England (1578–1657)

William Harvey of England is credited with solving the mystery of the circulation of blood. Harvey concluded in 1628 that blood movement is circulatory. Blood is thrust from the heart through the arteries and returned through the veins. The pulse results from the propulsive action of the heart. The valves in the veins, as in the legs, are to prevent the blood from coursing backward. (See pages 232–233.)

William Harvey, an English physician, discovered how blood circulates in mammals, including human beings. In this engraving, Harvey demonstrates his ideas to King Charles I.

Georges Cuvier (1769–1832)

Frenchman Georges Cuvier demonstrated the importance of comparative anatomy. His field of interest and study was invertebrates. His aim was to discover general principles from the knowledge of comparative structures.

Before Cuvier, the parts and organs of animals were seen as a hodgepodge of independent bits and pieces. Cuvier showed that what is important is the correlation of the parts. The parts of an organism are so interdependent that a skilled anatomist can decide the nature of other features from a single section.

Cuvier dismissed Aristotle's categories of blooded and bloodless animals, renaming them vertebrates and invertebrates. He also created the category of phylum, making it the major subdivision under kingdom, and he gave invertebrates their own phyla.

Composition

The next great advance was made with the use of the microscope. The discovery of the principle of the compound telescope and microscope—viewing an object through two lenses—probably occurred in the Netherlands about 1600.

Anton van Leeuwenhoek (1632–1723)

Anton van Leeuwenhoek in 1674 opened the window on microorganisms. As a cloth merchant, Leeuwenhoek used a magnifying glass to inspect the quality of the cloth. He built a single magnifying lens of extraordinary power. With such an instrument, he was able to see, in a drop of water, thousands of "animacules," creatures far smaller than the tiniest organisms visible to the naked eye.

DISCOVERING THE CELL

One of the fundamental insights of modern biology is the discovery that all living things are made up of cells.

- In 1665, English scientist Robert Hooke examined cork, which is dead plant tissue, through a microscope. He saw that it was honeycombed with cavities. Hooke called these little units cells, in the first use of the word to denote components of living matter.

- When German botanist Matthias Schleiden (1804–1881) decided to use the microscope to understand what plants are made of, his discovery astounded the world. Plants, he announced in 1838, are made entirely of smaller living units, cells.

- Schleiden's findings were reinforced a year later when German physiologist Theodor Schwann (1810–1882) declared that animals also are composed of cells.

Gregor Mendel, an Austrian botanist and monk, formulated the basic laws of heredity. His experiments with the breeding of garden peas led to the development of the science of genetics.

Marcello Malpighi (1628–1694)

In Italy, Marcello Malpighi was developing microscopic anatomy. With his microscope, Malpighi discovered the minute capillaries connecting arteries to veins, thus completing the loop in Harvey's circulatory system. He described the optic nerve and minute structures of the brain. He was the first to see red blood cells and understand that they give blood its characteristic color. He studied the microscopic structure of the liver, kidneys, bones, and skin layers.

Gregor Mendel (1822–1884)

Gregor Mendel, an Augustinian monk at Altbrunn, Austria, set out to unravel the riddle of heredity, a problem that had stumped some of the most prominent scientists in Europe. Mendel chose to decipher the strange language of heredity in the garden pea. He spent 2 years collecting 34 varieties of peas and then in 1856 began to crossbreed contrasting varieties.

After a series of experiments in which the plants were mated in certain ways or allowed to self-fertilize, Mendel noted that characteristics appeared in ratios that reflected the expression of dominant over recessive traits. (See also pages 70–71.)

Before Mendel, heredity had been compared to a vat of paint with endless blending of colors and tints. Mendel showed that heredity is not a blend, but a mosaic of separate units. Those units are genes and eventually they would be found to exist in the DNA (deoxyribonucleic acid) inside the nucleus of each cell.

Deep Time and Changing Forms

Heritage

As new discoveries presented an ever more detailed view of the fossil record, it became clear that the diversity of animal life extended far back into time and that it included animals that no longer existed.

Cuvier pointed out that as one digs deeper into the earth, one comes upon different strata of rocks and that each tier has its particular set of species. The highest layers of strata contain fossils similar to living animals, but as one descends, the fossils become more and more dissimilar to modern forms.

Cuvier believed that there had been a succession of catastrophes, like the biblical flood, that caused each set of extinctions. But the question remained: where did the new species come from?

▲ **According to Lamarck's** theories on evolution, giraffes who need to stretch their necks to reach leaves in tall trees will give birth to offspring with longer necks.

GOT TO KNOW !

DARWIN'S THEORY OF NATURAL SELECTION

- Small, incremental changes in the environment cause small, incremental adaptations in organisms.

- The sum total of these adaptaions will transform one species into another.

James Hutton (1726–1797)
Charles Lyell (1797–1875)

Geologist James Hutton presented, and his successor, Charles Lyell, championed, two iconoclastic proposals.

1. Earth is extremely old. Hutton and Lyell argued that there is no trace of a beginning and no prospect of an end. Earth is eternal. This was a shocking departure from contemporary belief that Earth's history could be measured in thousands of years.

2. Geologic changes have been going on continually throughout the history of Earth. Weathering wears away mountains, floodwaters lay down sediments, and volcanoes throw up lava that cools into solid rock.

Hutton and Lyell offered *uniformitarianism*—a geological doctrine that Earth's surface changes gradually, in ways that are imperceptible over short periods of time (such as a human lifetime) but that result in environmental transformations over eons.

Jean-Baptiste Lamarck (1744–1829)

The problem of extinction also intrigued Jean-Baptiste Lamarck (1744–1829). In his studies of mollusks, Lamarck noticed anatomical relationships between fossils of extinct animals and living species. "May it not be possible," Lamarck wrote, "that the fossils in question belonged to species still existing, but which have been converted into the similar species we now actually find?"

Lamarck theorized that living things change their forms to adapt to their environment, and that these changes are then passed along to their offspring. However, discoveries in genetics have since shown that acquired characteristics of an organism cannot be genetically transmitted to its offspring.

Lamarck's seminal contribution was to break with the age-old belief that life is fixed and static. The living world is dynamic, changing to meet the requirements of a dynamic physical world.

Charles Darwin, a British naturalist, became famous for his theories on evolution. Darwin, shown in this photographic portrait, believed that all species of plants and animals had evolved over millions of years from a few common ancestors.

On the Galapagos Islands, Darwin observed these several finches (and many others) in 1835. His observations and subsequent analysis of the birds' beak shapes and diet helped him formulate his theory of natural selection.

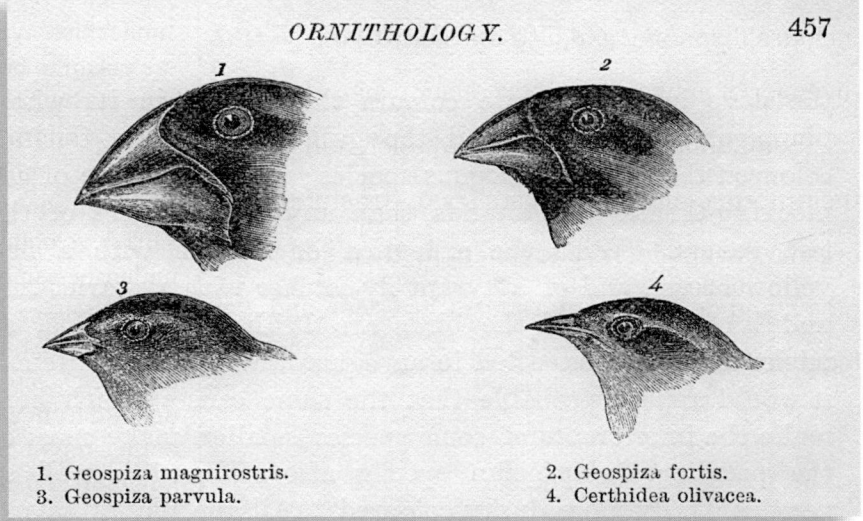

ORNITHOLOGY.   457

1. Geospiza magnirostris.   2. Geospiza fortis.
3. Geospiza parvula.   4. Certhidea olivacea.

Charles Darwin (1809–1882)

Charles Darwin provided the key insight as to how evolution could really work. Darwin spent years observing nature, collecting specimens, and formulating his ideas before presenting them publicly. Part of his hesitation was based on the controversy he knew his ideas would spark.

Darwin's theory of natural selection follows this logic. (See also pages 36–39.)

- Environmental conditions present challenges to species.

- Certain individuals will possess characteristics that make them more likely to survive in that environment than those individuals who lack those characteristics.

- They will survive long enough to reproduce and pass on those characteristics to their offspring.

- If those same environmental pressures continue over many generations, the selection for those characteristics will be reinforced generation after generation.

Synthesis. Of course, how the changes in an organism occur still was not known in 1859, when Darwin published *The Origin of Species by Means of Natural Selection or the Preservation of Favored Races in the Struggle for Life*. Mendel was learning the secret of heredity, but his discoveries would not become known until the 20th century. However, when that finally happened, the science of genetics was born. Among its early revelations was the phenomenon of genetic mutation, caused by radiation, some other environmental influence, or errors in reproduction. The remarkable thing about mutations is that they occur at random and they take place with a certain regularity. Most mutations are deleterious, in which case the individual's ability to survive is diminished and so is the likelihood of the genes being passed on. But when a mutation is beneficial, it enhances the individual's chances of survival and procreation. The change is preserved and spreads through offspring.

Scientists began to realize that findings in genetics meshed with what had been discovered in evolutionary biology, and in the 1930s and 1940s a synthesis of the two sciences took place.

CLASSIFICATION OF ANIMALS

The science of classifying is called taxonomy, from the Greek word *taxis,* meaning "arrangement." The term *systematics* often is used interchangeably with taxonomy, but systematics is broader; it includes taxonomy and also the study of the diversity of animals and their relationships.

Today, animals are classified by such traits as their morphology (an animal's form, structure, organic development, and function); their embryology; and developmental stages, behavior, and biochemical similarities.

Grouping Animals

Analogy and Homology

An excellent way to illustrate how ancestry shows closeness or distance in animal relationships is through the phenomena of analogy and homology.

When animals of different ancestries live in the same environment, they often develop anatomical similarities. When some land animals returned to the ocean to become whales and dolphins and seals, they evolved the same streamlined contours as fish. These kinds of similarities are *analogous* structures. They are not derived from the same ancestors, but are adaptations to meet environmental conditions. This developing of similarities by unrelated animals under the same environmental conditions is known as convergence.

In contrast, the wings of a pterodactyl, a bird, and a bat are *homologous*. These structures are variations derived from a common ancestor—just as the legs of the amphibians probably evolved from the fins of lobe-finned fish. The matter of common descent is a key element in the classification of animals.

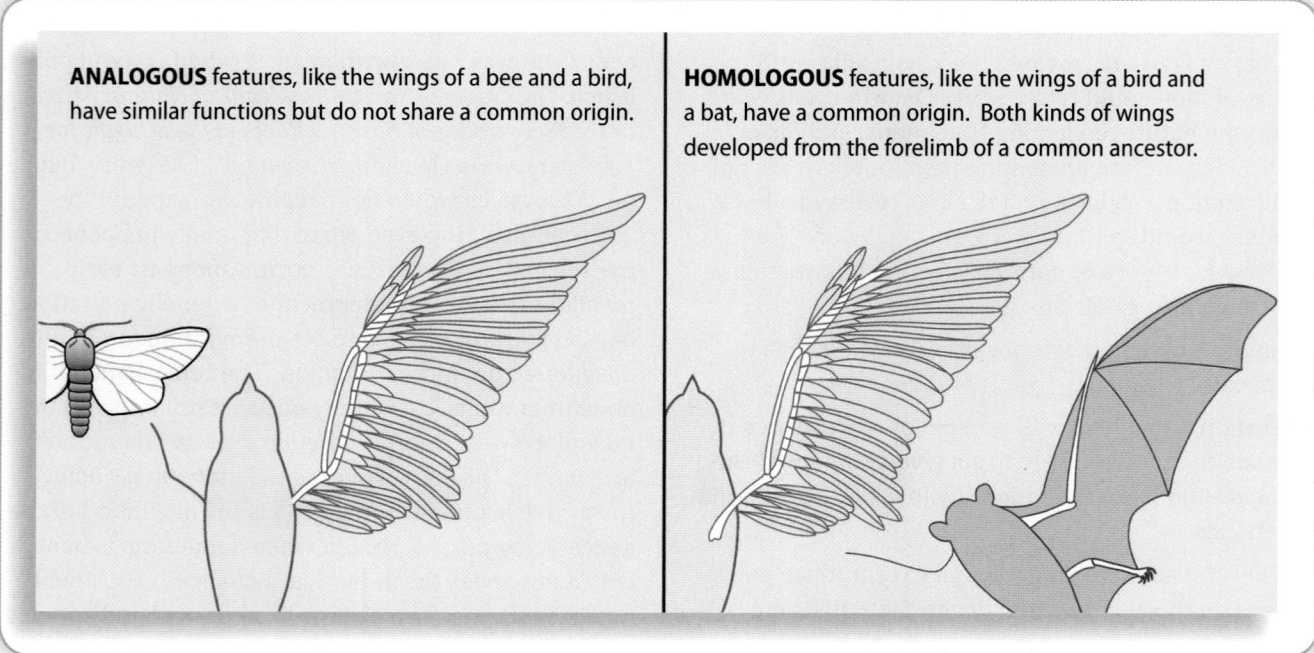

ANALOGOUS features, like the wings of a bee and a bird, have similar functions but do not share a common origin.

HOMOLOGOUS features, like the wings of a bird and a bat, have a common origin. Both kinds of wings developed from the forelimb of a common ancestor.

PHENETICS AND CLADISTICS

Phenetic systematics compares as many traits as possible among living organisms and groups them according to the number of similarities.

Cladistic systematics is based entirely on how long ago two species shared a common ancestor. A *clade* is a series of organisms descended from a common ancestor, a set of populations descending through time after having split off as a distinct species.

Modern Classification

Biological classification forms a hierarchy. Each *taxon*, the term for any classified group, includes all the groups under it. The standard taxonomic hierarchy follows. (See also pages 90–91.)

Kingdom—the highest and most inclusive taxon

Phylum—contains all organisms with a common ancestor and the same basic structural layout. It is like the trunk of a big tree.

Class—the bigger branches of the tree. Classes of vertebrates are fish, amphibians, reptiles, birds, and mammals.

Order—the next subdivision, still in large groups. For example, mammals are divided into the marsupials, carnivores, insectivores, rodents, and primates.

Family—a more restricted grouping, such as the cat family Felidae, including all the felines, or Canidae for dogs, wolves, foxes, and jackals

Genus—includes only closely related species (plural: genera)

Species—populations of male and female animals that can mate and reproduce fertile offspring

Biochemical Analysis

Taxonomists were better able to isolate genetic relationships with the development of biochemical analysis. One method examines the sequence of amino acids in proteins. Hemoglobin and other blood proteins are frequently used for this kind of analysis. Another, and probably better, method is to use short segments of DNA, the molecule of heredity in the cell nucleus.

 *Genus and species is the signature of a particular kind of animal. When a subspecies is added, such as* Canis lupus accidentalis, *the northern timber wolf seen now mainly in Canada and Alaska, the standard binomial designation becomes trinomial.*

CLASSIFICATION OF A HORSE

KINGDOM: Animalia
PHYLUM: Chordata
CLASS: Mammalia
ORDER: Perissodactyla
FAMILY: Equidae
GENUS: Equus
SPECIES: caballus

KINGDOM ANIMALIA

Animals range in size from smaller than unicelled microorganisms to the 150-ton blue whale. More than 95 percent of all animals are invertebrates. Vertebrates, animals with a backbone and spinal cord, are restricted to the phylum Chordata. Only members of two phyla, Chordata and Arthropoda (insects, spiders, and other arachnids), are fully adapted to living on land. Species of other phyla live on land, but like earthworms, they require constant moisture. Like amphibians, they have not gained full independence of the aqueous environment.

Sponges to Jellyfish

Gradations

The phyla that are described below are presented in order of increasing anatomical complexity. As one progresses among the phyla, there are certain fundamental differences that have been used by taxonomists to separate and distinguish them.

Sponges are so different from the other phyla that they have been placed into a different subkingdom. Sponges have no tissues and thus no organs, and they take various indeterminate shapes.

The next phyla—the coelenterates, such as jellyfish, corals, and sea anemones—are characterized by radial symmetry. They have a top and a bottom, but no front or back. The rest of the phyla show bilateral symmetry—they have a front and a back, a top and bottom, a left side and a right.

The bilaterals can be divided into three grades.
- those without a body cavity like the flatworms
- those with an unlined body cavity like rotifers
- nematodes, and those with a lined body cavity. In human beings, this lining is known as the peritoneum.

The embryos of all bilateral animals develop three tissue layers known as the endoderm, mesoderm, and ectoderm (inner, middle, and outer layers). The organ systems develop from these cells. In general, the intestine and other digestive organs come from the endoderm, muscles and skeleton from the mesoderm, and nerves and skin from the ectoderm. In animals with a true or lined body cavity, known as a coelom, the mesodermal lining encapsulates the digestive, reproductive, and other organs.

◀ **Kingdom Animalia** is wondrously diverse, both in the wide range of body types that animals possess, and in the adaptations animals have made to radically different environments. This water spider "breathes" by carrying air bubbles on its abdomen. The water spider also encloses its underwater web in air bubbles.

Porifera: sponge

Phylum Porifera

Porifera, meaning pore bearer, is the phylum comprising the sponges. Sponges date from early in the Cambrian period, 550 million or more years ago. They come in many shapes (tubes, fans, cups, crusts), sizes (from microscopic to more than 90 centimeters, or 3 feet), and colors (white, red, orange, yellow, green, blue, purple, brown). There are four classes and about 10,000 species. All but about a hundred freshwater species live in saltwater.

Most sponges are stationary, attached permanently to some object. Many coat rocks and logs and are not recognized as animals because of their formlessness. Nevertheless, they ingest their food, are heterotrophs, and so are classified as animals.

A sponge has thousands of pore holes, many opening into canals through which water flows, bringing food and oxygen. The oxygen diffuses through the body walls, while plankton and bits of organic matter are taken in by cells lining the canals. Wastes diffuse out through the body walls or through a single large opening. Sponges are noteworthy in their ability to regenerate. Commercial sponge collectors rebuild their supply by planting sponge fragments and allowing them to grow to harvest.

Cnidaria: coral

Phylum Cnidaria

Cnidaria are among the oldest animals, dating back nearly 700 million years. Members of the phylum exhibit radial symmetry and come in two basic kinds.

- jellyfish, free-floating animals shaped like a bell or umbrella with mouth and tentacles facing downward
- corals and sea anenomes, which have a cylindrical body around a hollow digestive sac open at one end, while the other end is attached to a surface, holding the creature in place

Cnidarians range in size from the microscopic to the Portuguese man-of-war, with a gas-filled body up to 30 centimeters (1 foot) long and with strands of polyps up to 50 meters (about 165 feet) in length. Cnidarian tentacles come with stinging structures designed to paralyze fish or other prey.

CORAL REEFS

Corals have had a profound effect on the oceans and marine life. Coral reefs are the underwater limestone ridges formed by secretions from corals and in which the soft-bodied animals live. When the animals die, the structures remain, and the new corals continue to build on top. The reefs provide sheltered habitats for so many species of fish, invertebrates, and protists that they have been called oases of the sea. When the reefs push through the surface, dry land accumulates.

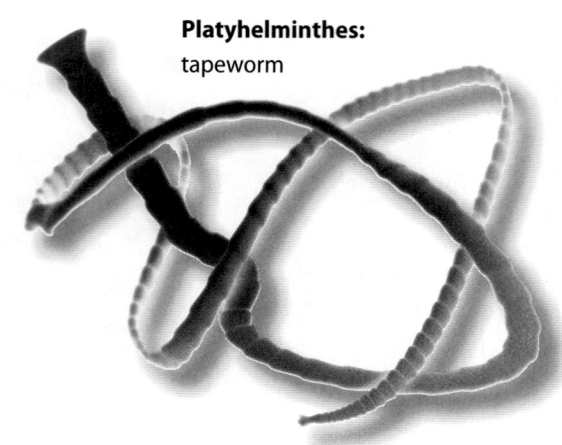

Platyhelminthes:
tapeworm

Phylum Platyhelminthes

These animals look like flattened worms. They are the least complex of all animals with heads, having a mouth that leads to a gut, but no rear exit, so wastes must be voided through the mouth. Members of the phylum range in size, with the smallest barely visible to tapeworms of more than 9 meters (30 feet).

There are about 15,000 species in three classes: flatworms, flukes, and tapeworms.

Flatworms are free-living; some are marine creatures while others live in moist soil or fresh water. These free-living forms have eyespots grouped in the head. Other nerve endings in the head can detect food, chemicals, objects, and water currents. Flatworms are carnivores and scavengers, eating insects, crustaceans, worms, and smaller organisms. With a tubular pharynx that may project through the mouth, they suck out the soft parts of their prey.

Flukes are internal or external parasites of animal hosts, attaching themselves by means of hooks and suckers.

Tapeworms are internal parasites of vertebrates and other animals, gaining entry as larvae secreted in animals on which the hosts feed.

Members of the phylum have two notable capabilities. One is a great power to regenerate. Slices of some species reform into entire worms. Platyhelminthes can tolerate a temperature range of from −50° to 47°C (−58° to about 117°F).

Phylum Rotifera

Rotifers are among the smallest animals, some being smaller than a single-celled amoeba and requiring a hundred-fold magnification to be seen. Nevertheless, each rotifer has between 500 and 1,000 cells. Despite the miniature dimensions, the rotifer has a more complete organ system than the flatworm: The mouth and gut rest in a body cavity and end with an anus, so waste can pass. Its eyespots are more advanced than those in flatworms.

The rotifer is recognized by a crown of hairs, called *cilia*, surrounding the mouth. When in motion, the cilia give the crown the appearance of a rapidly rotating wheel, hence the name rotifer, from a Latin word meaning "wheel-bearer." The cilia sweep particles of food into a set of jaws that grind the food. Most rotifers live in fresh water, but some are marine creatures and some live on land, but only in moist environments.

There are about 2,000 rotifer species, and most of them can be found all over the world. The major ecological contribution of rotifers is to serve as a major source of food for freshwater animals and to help in decomposing soil.

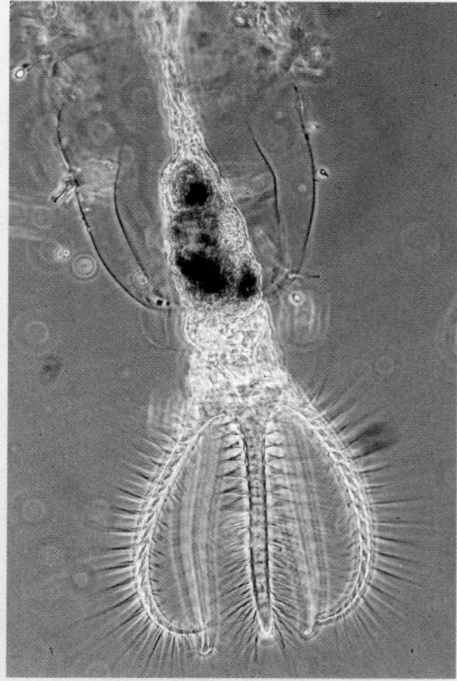

Rotifera:
rotifer

Nematoda:
roundworm

Phylum Nematoda

Nematodes, from the Greek for "thread," are known as roundworms because many of them have rounded ends. They range in length from a few millimeters to 1 meter (40 inches). They are not segmented like earthworms and have a tough smooth inelastic skin, known as a cuticle, that straitjackets the animal. The result is that roundworms cannot inch along by extending and contracting. They move by bending or flipping. They live as scavengers, plant feeders, and parasites.

This does not limit nematodes in numbers. There are some 80,000 known species. A single rotting apple can contain 90,000 roundworms. Rich farmland topsoil has about 3 billion nematodes in an acre.

Reproduction always is sexual and prodigious. Females have been found with 27 million eggs, depositing them at a rate of 200,000 a day.

Human beings eat and drink enormous numbers of nematodes, usually without ill effect. But one species, *Trichinella spiralis*, is responsible for the disease trichinosis. The larvae of the worms live in the muscles of pigs and other animals. If pork is not cooked thoroughly, the larvae can survive and enter the human body, develop, and encyst in muscles, causing great pain in joints. Many other nematodes can become parasites in humans, including the hookworm, which grips an intestinal wall with special mouth parts.

Phylum Brachiopoda

Anyone who has walked along a beach is familiar with the attractive symmetrical fan-shaped shell of these animals. Brachiopods, from the Latin for "arm-foot," with their strong calcium carbonate shells, look like clams, but the valves—halves of the complete shell—of a clam form the left and right sides, whereas the valves are the front and back of a brachiopod.

This animal, nicknamed lampshell, constitutes a big advance in complexity over the nematode. A brachiopod has a coelom, a fully lined body cavity. In it are a stomach as well as an intestine and a tiny heart. There are no blood vessels; the blood is pumped though the tissues. Lampshells also have three pairs of muscles. One pair opens and closes the valves. The other two pairs attach to a peduncle, an appendage used to anchor the animal to a rock. The muscles enable the brachiopod to turn about on the peduncle.

Brachiopoda:
lampshell

 *Lampshells got their name because, when found dead, their valves often are locked together, and to some people they resemble an antique oil lamp with a hole (where the peduncle comes out) for the wick.*

Mollusca:
snail

Phylum Mollusca

There are about 110,000 known species of mollusks, grouped into seven classes.

- bivalves (two-sided shells), including clams, oysters, mussels, and scallops

- gastropods, including snails and slugs

- cephalopods, including octopuses, squid, and nautiluses

- scaphopods, also called tooth shells

- Chitons or Polyplacophora

- Monoplacophora

- Aplacophora

All mollusks share some features. One is a muscular foot that is variously adapted for creeping or burrowing and that is part of the head-foot complex. A mantle, which is a sheet of tough specialized material, covers the internal organs like a body wall. The outer surface of the mantle secretes the shell familiar in snails, clams, oysters, and other mollusks.

Cephalopods are the most mobile of mollusks. They have eyes that, in octopuses, squid, and cuttlefish, come close to resembling vertebrate eyes. Cephalopods have the largest and most highly developed brains of any invertebrate. Octopuses in captivity have shown an impressive ability to learn.

Phylum Annelida

Annelids, from the Latin for "little ring," are segmented worms. Annelids come in three classes: marine worms, leeches, and earthworms.

The little rings of the name are visible externally as ringlike depressions. Internally, the segments are a series of identical doughnut-shaped rings separated by thin partitions. This allows annelids to increase body size with a minimum of new genetic information, since the layout for each segment is the same. There are some special segments, however, including a head with a well-developed brain and a mouth, and an anus at the other end of the alimentary canal.

The partitions divide the body cavity into a series of compartments filled with fluid. By contracting segment muscles, one or a series of segments can be made rigid. Burrowing is accomplished by waves of contractions that sweep along the body. Crawling is effected by lifting a section free of the surface and moving it forward, then lowering it and grasping the ground and pushing backward. Improved movement was one of the significant achievements of annelids.

Annelids are among the oldest animal forms, with fossil traces that may be 700 million years old. There are about 8,700 kinds of segmented worms, from microscopic size to a giant tropical earthworm 3.6 meters (12 feet) long.

Annelida:
earthworm

Arthropoda: scorpion

Arthropoda: blue butterfly

Phylum Arthropoda

Arthropods, from the Greek for "jointed foot," are horseshoe crabs, arachnids, crustaceans, and uniramians—insects, centipedes, and millipedes.

In both numbers of individuals and of species, arthropods—insects in particular—are the dominant animals on Earth. Upward of 900,000 species of arthropods are known, and the total number of species living today could be as high as 10 million.

Body. Arthropods are believed to have evolved from annelids because of their segmented bodies. But the segments in arthropods are quite individualized. In general, the arthropod body consists of a small head area plus a thorax and abdomen that make up 80 to 90 percent of the body. In insects, one pair of leg appendages extends from each segment. Arachnids have four pairs of legs, and crustaceans have five pairs, with the forward pair enlarged into usually uneven claws. In addition, there is a long pair of sensory antennae extending forward from the head. Uniramians have jawlike mandibles on either side of the mouth for biting and holding food. Arthropods' legs also are segmented and jointed for flexibility.

Exoskeleton. Arthropods improved on annelids by protecting their soft bodies with an exoskeleton made of a tough material called *chitin*. In terrestrial arthropods, the waxy covering guards against dehydration, while specialized respiratory and excretory systems enable sustained activity in arid conditions. An elaborate muscular system is attached to the exoskeleton and makes arthropods among the most agile of the land invertebrates.

Behavior. The instinctive behavior of arthropods is far more complex than that of annelids. Scorpions perform a courtship ritual before mating, and a number of species live in complex social systems.

Eyes. Many arthropods have image-resolving eyes; honeybees have color vision. Large compound eyes evolved in trilobites, crustaceans, and insects, but even the simpler eyes of spiders enable them to leap on prey with accuracy.

Range. These improvements, plus the possession of wings by insects, have enabled arthropods to spread over Earth more successfully than any other animal. There is a species of spider that is a permanent dweller on Mount Everest at an altitude of 6,000 meters (19,680 feet), and one crab species lives in the ocean at depths of 2,500 meters (8,200 feet).

Starfish to Vertebrates

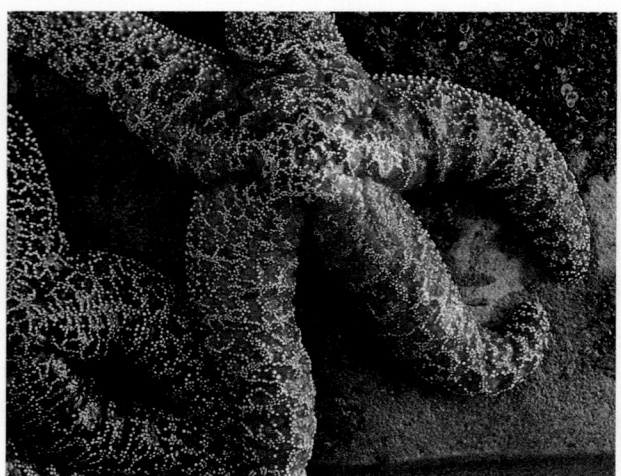

Echinodermata: starfish

Phylum Echinodermata

Echinoderms, from the Greek for "sea urchin skin," are the starfish, sea urchins, sand dollars, and sea cucumbers, among others. They have a bewildering diversity of forms, and all live on the ocean floor. There are five classes of echinoderms and a total of about 6,000 species.

Embryonic development indicates that this phylum and chordates originated from common ancestors that split off from other animals eons ago. Otherwise, echinoderms have little in common with vertebrates, although these marine animals do have an endoskeleton made of protective plates of calcium carbonate found under the outer skin.

- Most echinoderms can regenerate lost parts.
- Adults lack heads, brains, and segmentation.
- Most are radially symmetrical.
- The body usually has five arms.

STARFISH

On the five arms and body of a starfish, for example, are the most distinctive features of echinoderms, from which they get their name. These are little protuberances known as tube feet. There are hundreds of these tube feet along the surface. Through elongation and contact, the tube feet can be used for either locomotion or seizing prey. When hundreds of the tube feet act in concert, a starfish can grasp a clam in its arms and gradually pull the shell apart to expose the tender flesh inside.

Chordata: timber wolf

Phylum Chordata

Chordates, from the Greek for "string," are the phylum of animals that are best known to human beings, except for two marine invertebrate groups—tunicates and lancelets. They are grouped with the vertebrates as chordates because they share certain unique features with all the members of this great phylum.

Most of these characteristics have to do with what is commonly referred to as the backbone.

- a notochord, a stiff but flexible rod that extends the entire length of the body, providing an attachment site for muscles
- a dorsal nerve cord, which at the front end has developed into a brain for all vertebrates
- a tail (in human beings it is the vestigial coccyx)
- gill grooves, which are located in the pharynx. Even human beings have gill grooves during one brief stage of their embryonic development.

In vertebrates, the embryonic notochord is replaced during development by a vertebral column or backbone that is made of bone or cartilage. The backbone, in fact, is part of a living skeleton that is capable of growth and self-repair. Vertebrates include amphibians, birds, fish, mammals, and reptiles.

THE basics

Mammalia: zebra

SEVEN CLASSES OF VERTEBRATES
(SUBPHYLUM VERTEBRATA):

Agnatha (lampreys, hagfish) 63 species

Chonrichthyes (cartilaginous fish: sharks, rays, skates) 850 species

Osteichthyes (bony fish) about 18,000 species

Amphibia (frogs, toads, salamanders) 4,200 species

Reptilia (crocodiles, alligators, turtles, snakes, lizards) about 6,300 species

Aves (birds) about 9,000 species

Mammalia (mammals) about 4,300 species, including these orders:

  Monotremata (duck-billed platypus, echidnas [spiny anteaters]) 4 species

  Marsupialia (kangaroos, wallabies, opossums, koala) about 170 species in Australia and neighboring islands; 72 New World species, mostly in South America

  Insectivora (shrews, moles, hedgehogs) about 400 species, three-quarters of them shrews

  Chiroptera (bats) some 900 species

  Primata (prosimians, monkeys, apes, human beings) 180 species

Edentata (armadillos, sloths, anteaters) 31 species

Lagomorpha (rabbits, hares, pikas) about 50 species

Rodentia (mice, rats, squirrels, chipmunks, marmots, woodchucks, guinea pigs, beavers, muskrats, gophers) 2,400 species

Carnivora (dogs, cats, bears, raccoons, weasels, badgers, otters, skunks, hyenas, seals, walruses) 274 species

Cetacea (whales, dolphins, porpoises) 83 species, including 31 species of tooth whales, 13 species of baleen whales, 32 species of dolphins, 7 species of porpoises

Proboscidea (elephants) 2 species

Sirenia (manatees, dugong) 4 species

Perissodactyla (odd-toed ungulates: horses, zebras, asses, rhinoceroses, tapirs) 15 species

Artiodactyla (even-toed ungulates: cattle, sheep, deer, antelope, pigs, camels, bison, hippos, giraffes) about 150 species

Reptilia: lizard

Osteichthyes: goliath grouper

MORPHOLOGY OF ANIMALS

Historically, animals have been identified and grouped morphologically, by gross (large) anatomical features. Other criteria—such as cells and cellular components, relationships of body parts, comparisons among animals, and ancestral derivations—all helped to refine scientific evaluations. But structure remains the primary, and virtually only, way of classifying fossils.

Animal Building Blocks

Components of Organization

There are distinct levels of organization in the morphology of all animals, and they build one upon the other. While each level has its own characteristic nature, it incorporates the lower levels of organization, so that the levels in effect are gradations in increasing complexity, competence, and capacity to accomplish.

Molecules. The chemical joining of atoms to form molecules is the first level of organization. Animals are made up of the molecules of carbohydrates, fats, proteins, and nucleic acid—DNA (deoxyribonucleic acid) or RNA (ribonucleic acid). These molecules, particularly proteins and DNA, are relatively huge and complex.

There are many molecular or structural units in a cell, known as organelles, each designed to carry out specific biochemical activities. At one time, the fluid and jellylike substance that make up a cell's contents was called protoplasm and was regarded as the basic (or lowest-level) living material. Today, all of the cellular content exclusive of the nucleus is called cytoplasm and may only be considered alive as part of a functioning cell.

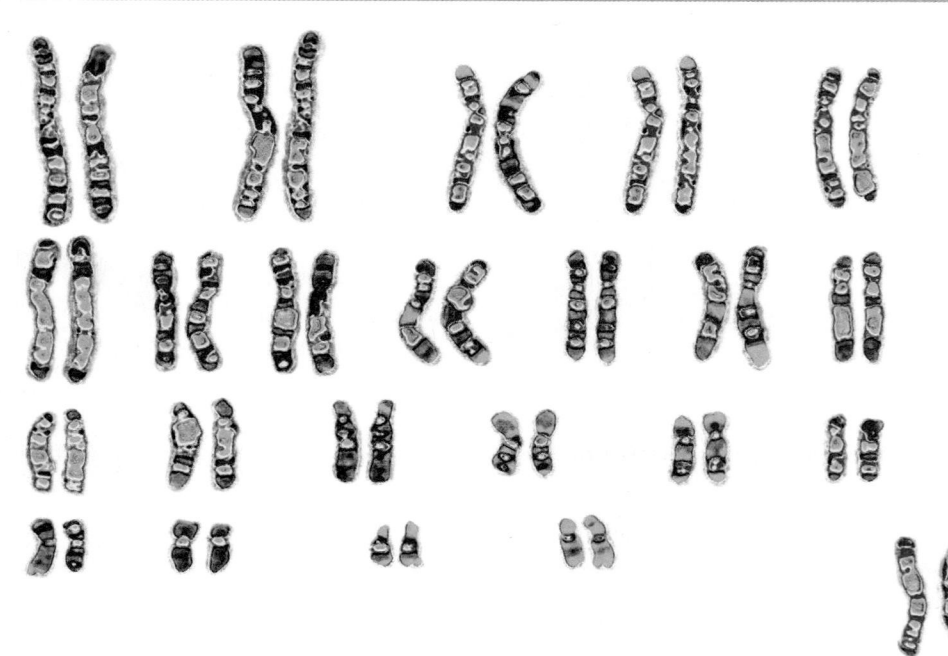

Chromosomes, made up of long strands of tightly coiled DNA, generally occur in pairs. This photograph shows the 23 pairs of chromosomes that occur in most human body cells.

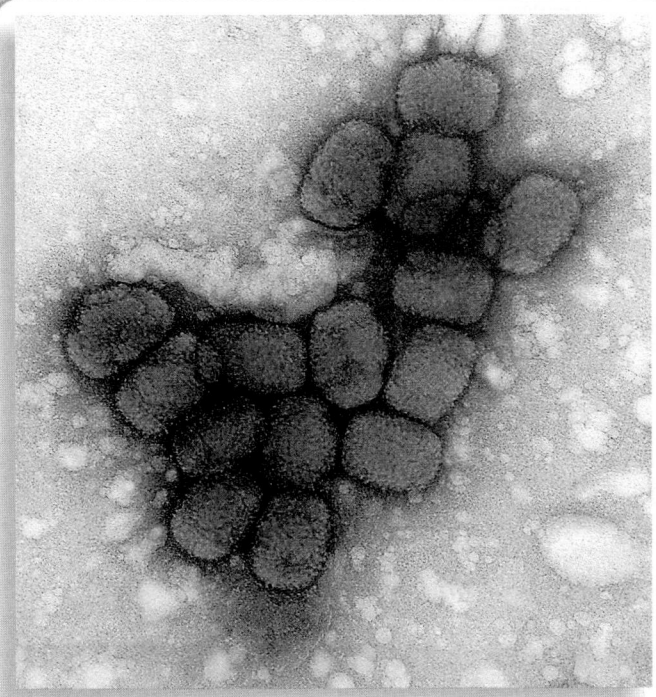

▲ **Smallpox viruses** appear flat in this enhanced-color transmission electron microscope image because the electrons pass right through them.

Viruses. Viruses represent an intermediate level of organization but are not in the main line in the organization of life. When viruses were first discovered, they were not regarded as living agents. At best, they were considered a bridge between living and inanimate things.

Viruses are stripped-down entities consisting of only a small amount of DNA or RNA wrapped in a covering of protein, called a *capsid*. When outside an animal cell, viruses are inert, usually assume a crystalline form, and are known as *virions*. But when they enter a cell, they are able to commandeer its machinery and compel the cell to make viral nucleic acid, which then accomplishes a crucial function of living beings—it reproduces new viruses. Because viruses cannot move, grow, reproduce, or metabolize on their own, they are considered degenerate or parasitic life forms. Nevertheless, they are accepted as alive, and at least 15 families with hundreds of kinds of viruses have been described.

Cells. Cells are the basic living units. They can utilize energy, grow, and reproduce—everything necessary to carry on life. A cell can compose a complete, free-living organism in itself or it can be part of a larger multicelled organism.

Cells in multicellular organisms differentiate into various kinds and, through markers or receptors on the cell surface or through other means, are able to recognize members of their own kind as well as aliens. This is the basis for embryogenesis, in which cells migrate and form aggregations at certain locations. These cells have the ability not only to seek out like cells but to adhere to certain different kinds of cells as well. For example, in a mixture of mouse liver, muscle, and skin cells, the liver cells are the most cohesive. They cluster together. The muscle cells are attracted to certain other cells. They form a layer around the core of liver cells. The epidermal cells are the least adhesive. They can barely tolerate touching one another and dislike contact with other cells even more. They end up as a layer just one cell thick on the outside. This remarkable activity and selectivity suggest the solution to a longtime mystery, the miracle of the way a body forms itself.

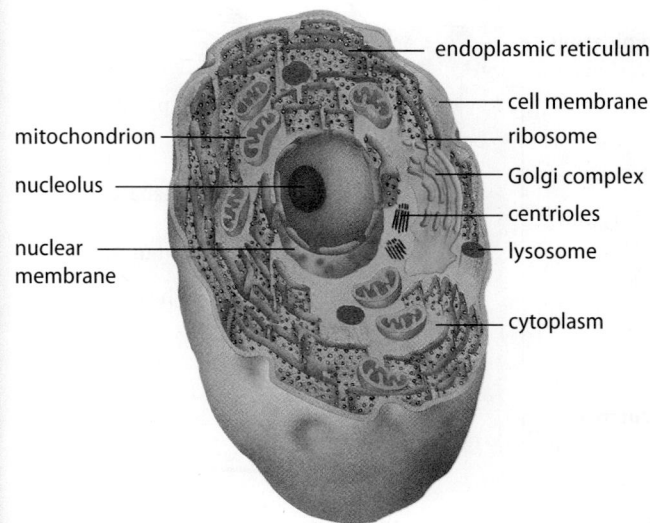

▲ **Typical Animal Cell.** These labeled components, described in detail on pages 50–51, are found in most animal cells. Plant cells possess other, specialized components.

Cells to Tissues to Organs

SOUTHWESTERN

Tissues. The aggregation of like cells leads to the formation of tissues, the next level of organization of living systems. Tissues are integrated masses of similar cells. Specialized tissues provide more efficient responses to an organism's needs.

There are four broad categories of tissues in vertebrates.

- Epithelial tissues are made up of cells that cover the body with skin and the internal organs with membranes.
- Endothelial tissues line the inside of organs.
- Stroma tissues serve as a matrix in which other cells are embedded.
- Connective tissues, composed of both cells and extracellular material, provide connecting matter between other tissues.

Tissues also can be grouped into the kinds of work they do. One kind involves the systems that bring nutrients and oxygen to cells and remove wastes from them. The digestive tract is made of muscle tissues lined by epithelial cells with nervous tissues and blood vessels in between.

A second group of tissues is employed in bodily coordination. These primarily are nervous and sensory tissues that operate the nervous system and endocrine tissues. Nervous activity regulates internal glands and skeletal muscles.

A third group of tissues contributes to the body's support and movement. These are connective tissues that surround and interpenetrate bones and muscles and help to hold them together. Examples of these tissues are tendons, which connect muscles to bones, and ligaments, which join bones together. Bone and cartilage are other major structural tissues.

A fourth tissue group consists of cells that are constituents of blood, such as hemoglobin, which form lymph and other bodily fluids and compose the reproductive tissues.

Organs. The various organs, composed of different specialized tissues to carry out specific vital functions, represent the next level of organization of living systems. The pharynx, esophagus, stomach, intestine, pancreas, and liver are all quite different organs performing distinctly different functions, but all operate in concert or cooperate as part of the digestive system.

Organs are coordinated into organ systems. The 10 organ systems of higher animals are noted below.

Finally, all these levels of organization merge in the plateau that is the animal organism, the unit of independent action.

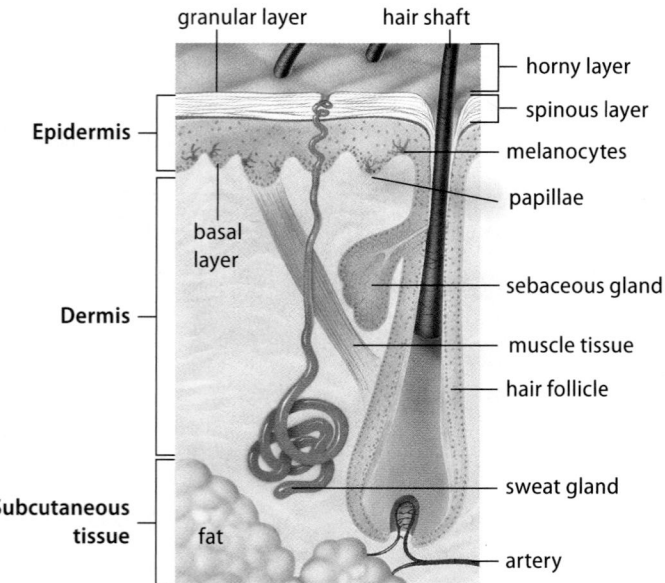

granular layer · hair shaft · horny layer · spinous layer · melanocytes · papillae · sebaceous gland · muscle tissue · hair follicle · sweat gland · artery · Epidermis · basal layer · Dermis · Subcutaneous tissue · fat

Skin is the organ that covers the bodies of human beings and many other animals. Human skin has three layers of tissue—the epidermis, the dermis, and subcutaneous tissue. The epidermis consists of four layers of cells—horny, granular, spinous, and basal. The skin also has hair and two kinds of glands, sebaceous and sweat.

THE basics

TEN ORGAN SYSTEMS

1. Integumentary system (skin, armor, horns, offering protection)
2. Skeletal system
3. Muscular system
4. Digestive system
5. Circulatory system
6. Respiratory system
7. Excretory system
8. Nervous system
9. Endocrine system (hormone-producing glands)
10. Reproductive system

Size and Shape

The single most important factor affecting animal size and form is surface-to-volume ratio. As the size of an animal increases, the surface area of its body shrinks dramatically in relation to the body volume or, conversely, the inner area expands more rapidly than the surface with growth in size.

This phenomenon has consequences for living organisms. A bacterium has ample surface through which to take in all the nutrients it needs and get rid of its wastes. A larger cell has much more internal substance to be maintained but relatively less access to resources to maintain it. This places a limit on size and explains why cells have remained small.

Small Animals. Proportionately, a small animal loses more heat through body surface than a larger animal. For endothermic (warm-blooded) birds and mammals, this means that the smaller the body, the higher the metabolic rate required to keep up the necessary body temperature to sustain life. This imposes a minimum limit to size. A shrew, the smallest mammal, weighing less than an ounce, must eat nearly its body weight in food every day.

SURFACE AREA LIMITATIONS

Animals have developed an effective solution to the limitations that surface area imposes on an animal's size— wrinkles. It is amazing how much a surface area can be stretched and expanded by folds, bumps, and indentations. Our lungs are only a few inches wide but their surface—the lining exposed to the vital air of the external environment—if laid out flat would cover the floor of a room 7.5 by 13.5 meters (25 by 45 feet). The surface of the digestive tract would cover half an acre.

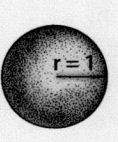 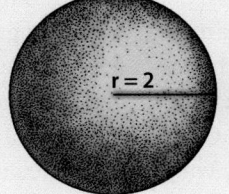 

The ratio of surface area to volume decreases as the size of a sphere increases. Wrinkles increase the surface area considerably.

▲ **A Bald Eagle.** Wingspreads of different species range from about 0.9 to 2.4 meters (3 to 8 feet), and yet most eagles weigh only about 3.2 to 5.4 kilograms (7 to 12 pounds).

The Inconvenience of Gravity. A major force affecting size in land animals is gravity, although it is not nearly as important for aquatic creatures. Gravity limits the size of an animal to the mass that can be supported. The support system is skeletal. Only about 4 percent of a shrew's mass is skeleton. In a cat, about 7 percent is skeleton. A human being is about 8.5 percent skeleton, a horse 10 percent, an elephant 13 percent.

Animals have dealt with gravity in various ways. Birds that fly need to be as light as possible. As a result, the bones of birds are hollow. The shafts that support the feathers are also hollow. The hollow-shaft principle is seen as well in the wing veins of insects and appendages of spiders.

How Animals Move

A fish moves with a lateral wave motion of its body. The amphibious salamander, although it has legs, retains the same kind of motion. ▶

One challenge to animal movement is friction. The amount of frictional drag depends on how smoothly water or air flows around a body in motion. As a result, the fastest moving animals are streamlined fish, slender-bodied birds, and sleek, narrow land animals. (See Friction, pages 763.)

Water

The length of a dolphin is five times its diameter, close to optimal proportions for streamlining, and the maximum diameter occurs slightly back of center, the optimal position for reducing turbulence. A dolphin can cut through water at a speed of 7.5 meters (25 feet) per second and, if it could maintain that pace, 27 kilometers (17 miles) in an hour.

Locomotion. The most primitive and the oldest method of locomotion in water probably is the lateral wriggle, a wave motion that increases in width as it moves from head to tail. Lampreys, eels, and some sharks use this lateral slithering motion. A modification of the full-body slither is a wavelike motion that is confined to the tail area. Half-body waving improves acceleration with less energy expenditure; this motion is used by trout, salmon, barracuda, bass, and perch, among others.

Constriction. A further improvement in fish design is a constriction between the main body of the fish and the tail fin to cut down on body recoil. Finally, a specially designed crescent-shaped tail fin marks the fastest swimmers in the ocean—tuna, striped marlin, sailfish, and swordfish.

Land

When animals departed from water onto land, they were confronted with new travel problems. The original wriggle, though, could be adapted to moving on land. When snakes cross loose pebbles or a waterway, they undulate just like an eel.

But land is not as homogeneous an environment as water. Meeting a furrow too narrow for horizontal wriggling, a snake undulates vertically. When it crawls through a hole, contraction waves run along the snake's body. A serpent also can crawl like a worm by alternate stretches and pushes.

Legs. The ultimate breakthrough in land travel came with the appearance of legs. These appendages took advantage of the laws of leverage—short muscle movements producing big movements of bodies. Lifting the body off the ground reduces friction drag, making a bumpy or rutted surface less of a problem to maneuver.

Primates. Primates were accustomed to living in trees, and some of them became very good at grasping branches. Gibbons and chimpanzees excel at swinging from branch to branch with arms overhead in what is known as brachiation. On the ground, chimpanzees as well as gorillas usually walk on the soles of their feet and knuckles of their hands, and sometimes bipedally, although their bodies are not structurally erect enough for them to be good at it. Full bipedalism became a distinguishing mark of human beings.

Air

The key to flight is the asymmetrical wing. A wing in motion forces onrushing air to flow past the upper edge faster than the air flowing past the underside. This creates lift. The air moving faster and farther on top acts as suction, while the slower-moving air on the bottom contributes by pushing upward.

Insects, the first ones into the air, get by on rapid wing strokes—200 per second for bees and houseflies, 400 per second for mosquitoes, up to 1,000 for a gnat—and their small size, which gives them relatively strong muscles in a light body.

Birds are the masters of the air, due primarily to the aerodynamic and physical properties of feathers. Feathers are the lightest construction in the vertebrate world, yet they are durable, elastic, and flexible. Birds need well-designed wings to maximize laminar flow, the smooth streamlined flow of air over the wing surface.

- Wings are designed for different speeds and purposes.
- Wings with a large surface generate lift but also cause drag, so birds like eagles and owls are slow fliers.
- Long wingspan provides lift and narrow wings reduce drag, so a bird like the albatross, with extremely long, narrow wings, is a fast and powerful flyer.

HOW WING SHAPE AFFECTS FLYING SKILLS

The shape of a bird's wings relates to the type of flying that the bird does best. Gulls, *left*, and other birds with long, pointed wings excel at soaring and gliding. Most fast fliers, such as swifts, *center*, have narrow, tapered wings. Pheasants, *right*, and most other fowllike birds have short, broad, rounded wings. These birds can take off quickly but can fly fast only for a short distance.

▲ **Flies** are among the fastest of all flying insects. The buzzing of a fly is the sound of its wings beating. A housefly's wings beat about 200 times a second, and some midges move their wings 1,000 times a second. Houseflies fly at an average speed of 7.2 kilometers (4.5 miles) per hour.

Varieties of Animal Life Cycles

Construction

Two of the hallmarks of all living things are growth and the replacement of individuals. The continual creation of new individuals is a necessity for life to go on, not only because of the attrition of existing creatures but because new types are required to keep up with an ever-changing environment.

Living things reproduce in many ways.

Reproduction. Asexual reproduction occurs in many animals, but sexual reproduction has the advantage of promoting diversity through genetic recombination. (See page 55.)

In one form of asexual reproduction, a coral can divide to form two smaller but complete individuals that take up independent lives. This is reproduction by fission. Some annelids and flatworms reproduce by regeneration. They divide and then regenerate the missing half; for the tail end, this means reconstituting the head and brain.

Many sponges and coelenterates reproduce by budding: A miniature version of the animal grows on the parent's body and, when large enough, breaks off.

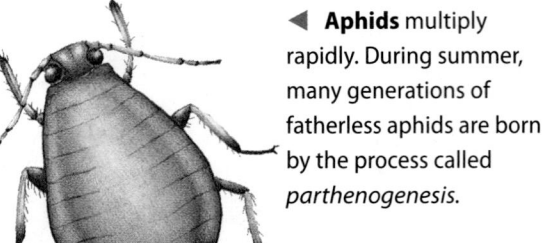

◄ **Aphids** multiply rapidly. During summer, many generations of fatherless aphids are born by the process called *parthenogenesis.*

Finally, there is parthenogenesis, in which unfertilized eggs develop into adults. This method of reproduction is common among invertebrates, but many of these species also are capable of sexual reproduction. Parthenogenetic animals usually are females, although male honeybees come from unfertilized eggs, while their sisters develop from fertilized eggs. Parthenogenesis takes place in rotifers, insects like ants, wasps, and bees, among others.

The bodies of tapeworms and many pond snails produce both sperm and eggs. They are known as hermaphrodites. Some, but not all, can fertilize themselves.

In most cases of sexual reproduction, sperm comes from the male and eggs from the female. External fertilization, or spawning, is the common method for reproduction among fish, many other marine animals, and amphibians. The sperm and eggs are released into the water and must find one another to unite. The job is made easier by the enormous numbers of these sexually receptive gametes at the spawning site and a seasonal timing for breeding. With frogs, sperm and eggs are deposited in water at the same time.

The reproductive method used by insects and the later forms of vertebrates—reptiles, birds, and mammals—is internal fertilization. Through copulation the male deposits sperm in the female's reproductive tract.

◄ **Portuguese Man-of-War.** Although it resembles a jellyfish, it actually consists of a colony of hundreds of members. The colony begins with just one larval member. As it grows, this original member produces new members of several different types, by a process called budding.

METAMORPHOSIS

Metamorphosis is a process in which an immature stage of the animal, the larva, emerges from the egg and then at some point undergoes a transformation in structure and behavior into a strikingly different adult. Metamorphosis is especially conspicuous in two kinds of animals that had to make tremendous transitions during the course of their evolution: amphibians changed from aquatic to terrestrial animals, and insects developed the ability to fly.

Development. Development of most animals begins, after the union of sperm and egg to form a zygote, with cell division, morphogenesis (shaping the body and its parts), cell differentiation, including the dermal layers, and formation of a body cavity.

Amphibians. Fertilized frogs' eggs usually are laid in water. The tadpole, the name given to this larva, is a completely aquatic animal with external gills. Soon, the gills are shielded by a covering. The tadpole lives like a kind of fish, propelling itself through the water with its tail. Then tiny hind limbs appear, followed by a pair of forelimbs. Ultimately, the tadpole metamorphoses into a land animal, losing its gills, tail, and aquatic mouth parts and assuming the familiar figure of a frog.

▲ **The development** of a frog from egg to adult is an example of metamorphosis.

Insects. Some form of metamorphosis takes place in all flying insects. In grasshoppers, the process is known as gradual metamorphosis. The grasshopper larva, known as a nymph, progresses through several molts from the wingless nymph to the adult with wings. Gradual metamorphosis occurs when the larval form is relatively similar to that of the adult.

A more decisive transformation is seen in dragonflies and damselflies. The larva, known as a naiad, while somewhat resembling the adult form, is aquatic, with gills and without wings. In one abrupt molt after the naiad has crawled out of the water, the aquatic larva changes into an air-breathing, winged adult.

Four-stage transformation is characteristic of insects like flies, beetles, and butterflies, in which the larva is totally different from the adult. The distance to be bridged by the transformation is so great that another, intermediate stage is required. The metamorphosis entails going from egg to larva to pupa before finally arriving at the adult form. The pupa stage is a cocoon or, in the case of a butterfly, a chrysalis—a protected state during which the larval organs are destroyed and replaced with the adult parts.

▲ **This dragonfly nymph** resembles the adult form—the body is long and the eyes are large—but wings have not yet formed.

PHYSIOLOGY OF ANIMALS

Physiology is concerned with how animal bodies work and the processes of living.

Operation processes come under the broad heading of metabolism: getting and using materials and energy in order for the body to grow and carry out its necessary activities. Maintaining the body in good working order is known as homeostasis. It incorporates self-regulating processes that enable the animal to remain in a relatively stable condition even as the animal continually adjusts to various environmental stresses.

Animal Building Blocks

Metabolism

Animals require food and the oxygen needed to metabolize the food into a usable form. The complex organic molecules of carbohydrates, fats, and proteins are broken down into simpler component molecules of sugars, fatty acids, and amino acids. Metabolism is the sum of the chemical processes by which cells produce the materials and energy necessary for life.

The materials that animal bodies make come in four broad categories: nucleic acids, carbohydrates, lipids, and proteins.

Carbohydrates are the water-soluble sugars. Glucose, the most common sugar in animal systems, is a small, single molecule known as a monosaccharide. It forms chains of sugars called polysaccharides. Polysaccharides often are used for structural materials such as chitin, which forms the exoskeletons of insects, spiders, and crabs.

Interesting Facts About Animals
Kinds of Animals. No one knows exactly how many kinds of animals there are. New kinds are found every year. So far, scientists have identified more than 1.5 million types of animals. About 1 million of these are insects, and there are thousands of kinds of fish, amphibians, reptiles, birds, and mammals.
Largest Ears and Eyes. The largest ears of all animals are those of the African elephant. Elephant ears grow as large as 1.2 meters (4 feet) across. The largest eyes of all animals are those of the giant squid. They measure about 25 centimeters (10 inches) wide.
The flying dragon is another name for the draco lizard. This lizard can spread out folds of skin to form "wings" that it uses to glide through the air from tree to tree. It lives in Asia and the East Indies.
Lives of animals range from several hours to many years. An adult mayfly survives only a few hours or days. Some giant tortoises have lived more than 100 years.
The world's only known poisonous bird is the hooded pitohui, which lives on the island of New Guinea. This brilliantly colored orange-and-black bird has poison on its feathers and skin. This poison serves as a defense against hawks, snakes, and other enemies. It is the same type of poison as that carried by the deadly poison-dart frog of South America.
The hummingbird can fly straight up like a helicopter. It can hover in front of a flower to suck the nectar. The bee hummingbird, which grows to only 5 centimeters (2 inches) long, is the smallest of all birds.
The chameleon's tongue is as long as its body. This lizard swiftly shoots out its tongue to capture insects for food. Certain chameleons can change color quickly and even develop spots and streaks that make them seem to be part of their background.
A tree-climbing crab lives on many tropical islands. It is called the coconut crab because it cracks coconuts with its powerful claws and eats the sweet meat.
The platypus, a mammal, has a bill like a duck and lays eggs as birds do. But it nurses its young with milk as do other mammals. It lives only on mainland Australia and the island of Tasmania.

Lipids are fats when they are solid at room temperature, oils when liquid at room temperature. They are composed of two types of building blocks: glycerol and fatty acids. Lipids are insoluble in water, which makes them good material for cell membranes because they help to keep cell contents inside and to bar external fluids from entering the cell.

Proteins are made up of smaller molecules called amino acids. About 20 different amino acids join in various ways to constitute all the proteins. Some proteins are enzymes that guide all the chemical reactions taking place in a cell. There is a separate enzyme tailored to each biochemical reaction. In addition, proteins are used to make structural materials, such as muscles or hair or horns or spider webs, for hormones and antibodies, and can store energy.

MAKING ATP

Glucose, a blood sugar, has a high content of chemical energy and is the cell's, and animal's, primary energy source. In order for animals to make use of the energy, however, it must be converted to the common carrier of accessible energy, ATP, the molecule adenosine triphosphate. (See Energetic Cells, page 53.) But energy production from fat is only about half that from glycogen, so if the switch occurs during sustained exertion, muscle performance falls off noticeably.

Glycolysis. ATP can be formed in two ways. One process of glucose metabolism is known as glycolysis; it takes place in the cytosol, the fluid part of the cell's cytoplasm in all cells, eukaryotic and prokaryotic. Glycolysis is a primitive and less efficient way of converting glucose into usable energy. Glycolysis can produce only two ATP molecules from one glucose molecule. While glycolysis can take place in the presence of oxygen, it does not require oxygen.

Cellular Respiration. In animal cells, the products of glycolysis go into an organelle known as a mitochondrion. There the breakdown process is completed through a much more efficient process of oxidation called cellular respiration. This produces 36 more ATP molecules, so cellular respiration is 18 times more efficient than glycolysis in producing energy molecules. Animals have become dependent on this huge bonus of energy to meet their needs from cellular respiration. They cannot live without it.

Body weight of animal

Puma
97 pounds
(44 kilograms)

Locust
0.035 ounce
(1 gram)

Penguin
88 pounds
(40 kilograms)

African elephant
5.9 tons
(5,400 kilograms)

Etruscan shrew
0.07 ounce
(2 grams)

Amount of food eaten by animal

**54 pounds
(24.5 kilograms)
in a week**

**14 ounces
(3.5 grams)
in a week**

**1.23 tons
(560 kilograms)
in a week**

**2.7 tons
(2,443 kilograms)
in a week**

1.5 ounces (42 grams) in a week

A living thing's metabolic rate is the speed with which it turns food into the energy and materials it needs to live and grow. The higher the metabolic rate, the more food a living thing must consume to maintain its metabolism. This chart compares the metabolic rates of several different animals. Smaller animals tend to have higher metabolic rates than larger animals.

DIGESTIVE SYSTEMS

Early cells that existed independently lived by diffusion. Food from the sea came in through the cell membranes, and wastes moved out in the same way. But as animal bodies became larger, most of the cells no longer had access to the outside world and its nutrients. Therefore, it became necessary for more complex animals to bring the external environment with its food resources to the cells.

How Animals Process Food

In sponges, the simplest of animals, there is no organized digestive system. Sponges rely on their individual cells to digest and convert food to forms that can be used by the cells. This decentralized system of ingesting food limits the size of nutrients to what can be managed by each cell. As large as a sponge may be, its menu is restricted to microscopic particles.

Cnidarians. Cnidarians, such as jellyfish, hydras, and sea anemones, have a mouth that opens into a gastrovascular cavity. This is a sac into which glandular cells secrete enzymes so that the food is broken down and partial digestion takes place. The reduced nutrients are engulfed by cells lining the gastrovascular cavity and canals leading from it, where the process of digestion is completed.

Parts of the Digestive System

Mouth — Salivary glands

Esophagus

Liver

Gallbladder

Stomach

Pancreas

Small intestine

Large intestine

Rectum

Stomach

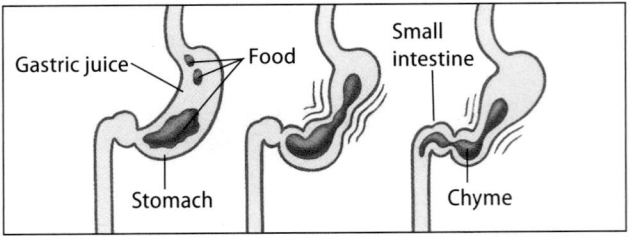

Gastric juice — Food — Small intestine

Stomach — Chyme

Bile and pancreatic juice

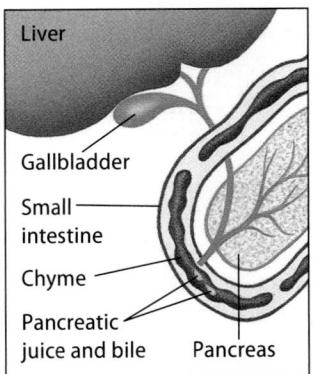

Liver

Gallbladder

Small intestine

Chyme

Pancreatic juice and bile — Pancreas

Digested food

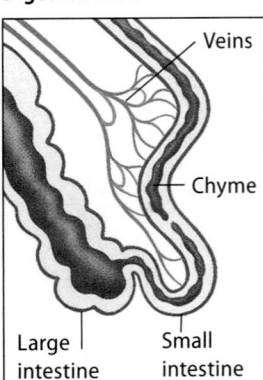

Veins

Chyme

Large intestine — Small intestine

Digestion is the process that breaks food down into simple substances the body can use. The digestive system includes all the organs and tissues involved in this process. (See pages 236–237.)

Beyond Cnidarians and Flatworms. Most animals have a digestive system that is basically a tube running through the body from mouth to anus, so that there is a process of progressive digestion as the food moves from its entry point to exit.

In the earthworm, a pharynx draws in soil and vegetation from the mouth and passes it to an esophagus. From there it goes to a crop, which collects food and gradually moves it to a gizzard. In the gizzard, muscles use bits of sand to grind the food into smaller particles. When these small pieces move into the intestine, enzymes reduce the food to simple molecules that can be absorbed by cells lining the intestine wall. Birds, especially grain-eating birds, also have gizzards that help them to break up and grind solid food.

This is essentially the same process at work in human beings and other vertebrates. The food is first broken down physically and then reduced chemically for cell absorption. In human beings and higher mammals, the digestive system consists of the mouth, teeth, tongue, throat or pharynx, esophagus or gullet, stomach, small intestine, large intestine (consisting of three colons), rectum, and anus. The saliva glands in the mouth, gastric glands in the stomach lining, and the pancreas, liver, and gallbladder all supply digestive juices.

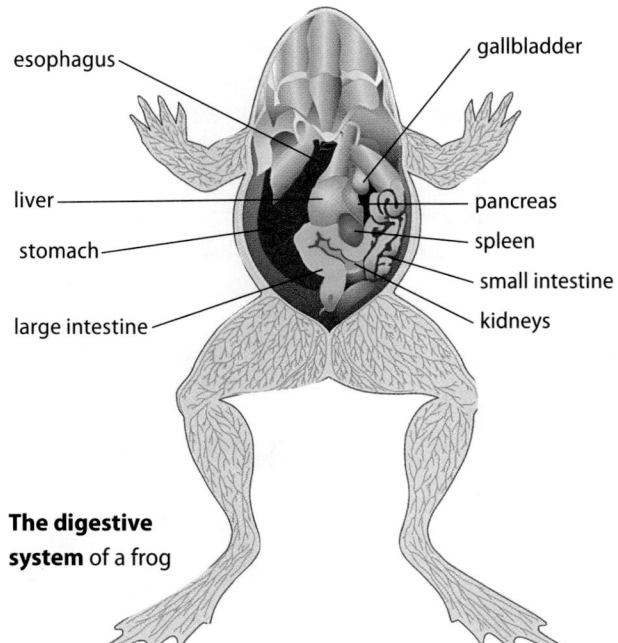

esophagus

gallbladder

liver

pancreas

stomach

spleen

small intestine

large intestine

kidneys

The digestive system of a frog

Ruminants. Most animals cannot digest cellulose, the tough polysaccharide that forms the cell walls of plants, because animals have no enzymes to deal with it. But animals such as cows, sheep, goats, and camels—ruminants—have a unique digestive system.

In ruminants, it is not the animal's enzymes but symbiotic microorganisms and their enzymes that convert cellulose into a digestible food. Ruminants have a digestive system with what amounts to a four-chambered stomach. The first of these compartments, larger than the other three combined, is the rumen, housing microorganisms that break down the cellulose. The animal packs masses of vegetation into the rumen, where it is reduced to cud. The cud is regurgitated, chewed, and then returned to the rumen for further treatment. Only then does the material begin to pass though the other three chambers, where still other microorganisms and their enzymes go to work to complete the digestion process.

HOW DOES THAT WORK ?

THE GIZZARD

The gizzard is a muscular organ of the digestive system of birds and a few other animals. It breaks up and grinds hard, solid foods. The gizzard in birds is associated with the stomach and is lined with thick, tough plates. The breakdown of food in the gizzard is aided by gravel that the bird has swallowed. Food enters a pouch of the gullet called the crop and is moistened there. It passes from the crop to the glandular part of the stomach, where it is mixed with gastric juices. The food then passes into the gizzard, where it is crushed by the movements of the muscular walls and the gravel. Gizzards of grain-eating birds are well developed, and those of fruit-eating birds are often poorly developed.

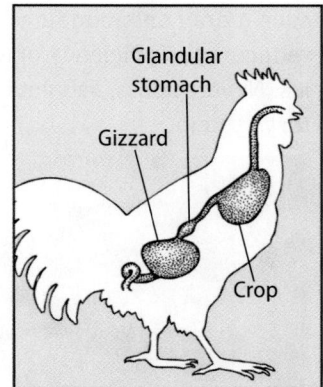

Glandular stomach

Gizzard

Crop

THE CIRCULATORY AND RESPIRATORY SYSTEMS

The circulatory system is a network that carries blood throughout the body. All animals except the simplest kinds have some type of circulatory system.

In some invertebrates (animals without a backbone), the circulatory system consists of a simple network of tubes and hollow spaces. Other invertebrates have pumplike structures that send blood through a system of blood vessels. In human beings and other vertebrates (animals with a backbone), the circulatory system consists primarily of a pumping organ—the heart—and a network of blood vessels.

Transporting Blood

Circulatory Systems

For the larger and more complex animals, circulatory systems are needed to complete the bringing of nutrients and oxygen to cells and the removal of wastes.

Open Systems. The simplest transport systems are known as open systems. In the nematode worm, blood fills the whole internal cavity, bathing the organs and sloshing around when the animal moves. Insects and other arthropods also have an open system, but it is more complex. A tubular kind of heart runs along the creature's back, pumping and emptying rhythmically. Blood vessels with valves to control the direction of flow may be attached to the long heart vessel.

Closed Systems. The closed circulatory system appears with earthworms. All closed vascular systems have hearts to drive the blood through the system. An earthworm can have multiple hearts to drive the blood through two longitudinal vessels that traverse the body along what we would call the back and belly of the animal. These major vessels connect to smaller ones, which in turn feed capillaries, where the exchange of gases, nutrients, and wastes occurs.

Fish have two-chambered hearts. An atrium takes in the returning blood and passes it to the ventricle, which pumps the blood out again. But the blood must pass through two sets of capillary beds—one at the gills to pick up oxygen and expel the animal's carbon dioxide, the other to exchange those gases along with nutrients and their waste products with the rest of the body's cells. The first capillary system at the gills puts such a drag on blood flow that pressure is lowered, reducing the efficiency of trades with system capillaries. Nevertheless, fish get by with this kind of circulatory system.

Shoal of crescent-tail bigeyes

Amphibians and reptiles have two circulatory pathways—one to the lungs to oxygenate the blood and one back to the heart to be pumped through the system. But the hearts in amphibians and most reptiles have only three chambers. Two atria take in blood. One receives oxygenated blood from the lungs, and the other receives deoxygenated blood and waste products from the rest of the system. Both chambers empty into one ventricle, so blood that is only half refreshed goes back to the body.

Paradise tree snake

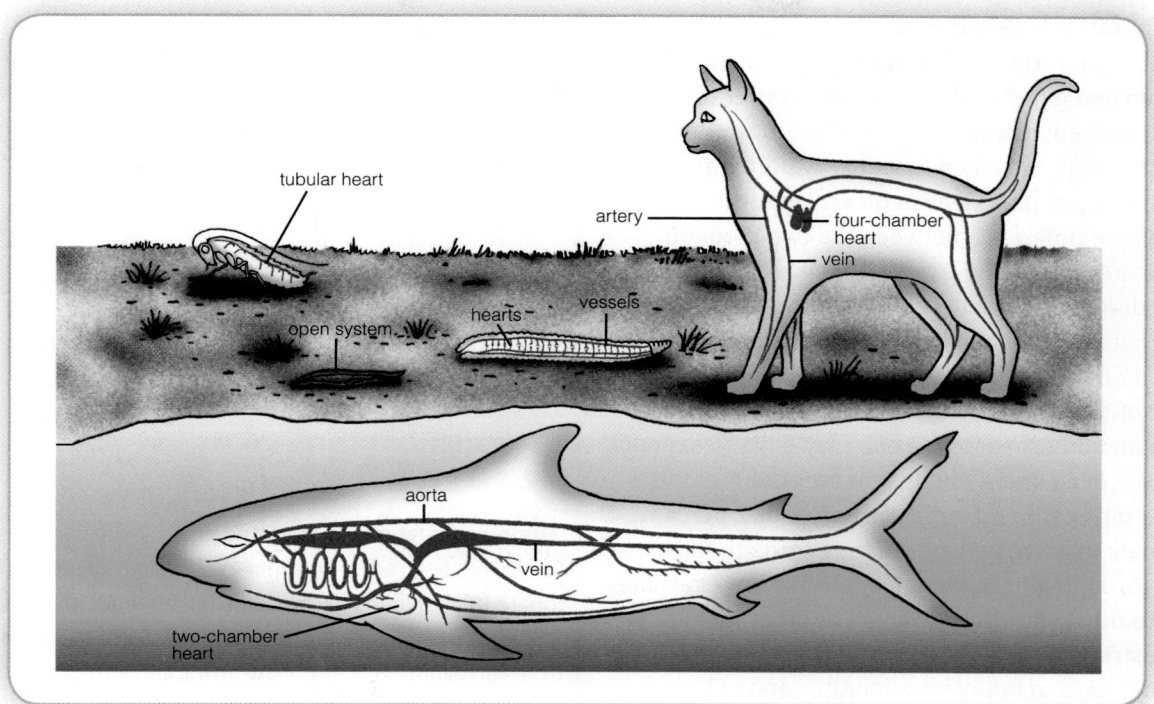

▲ **Circulatory systems** vary considerably in different kinds of animals.

Birds and mammals (and reptilian crocodiles and alligators) are the only animals that have four-chambered hearts. Blood returning from the system with wastes is received by the right atrium, moved to the right ventricle, where it is pumped to the lungs for carbon dioxide removal and a fresh cargo of oxygen, returned to the left atrium, and then into the left ventricle to be sent on its way to the system capillaries.

Cephalopods like the octopus and squid solved the pressure problem by developing two booster hearts to force the blood efficiently through each of the gills and then back to the main heart, where the blood is driven through the system capillaries.

California bigeye octopus

Grizzly bear

Processing Oxygen

Respiratory Systems

Respiration is the process by which animals take in oxygen and expel carbon dioxide in order to meet energy requirements. In the case of animals, the external environment can be either water or air. In terms of oxygen, as well as in other ways, there is considerable difference between the two mediums. There is only about one-twentieth the amount of free oxygen dissolved in well-oxygenated water as there is in air. That means that a fish must process a much greater amount of water in order to extract the same amount of oxygen that a mammal can take from air. For this and other reasons, a fish may have to expend 20 percent of its energy budget in order to breathe, whereas the cost to mammals is only 1 or 2 percent.

Animals that live in water respire through the skin and/or through gills, although a few fish are alternately able to inhale air through lungs or other means.

Terrestrial animals get their oxygen from air
- through skin in many invertebrates and amphibians.
- through book lungs in spiders.
- through tracheae in insects.
- through lungs in amphibians, reptiles, birds, and mammals.

Single-celled organisms such as these diatoms exchange oxygen and carbon dioxide directly with the environment through their cell membranes. In higher animals, however, each cell lacks direct contact with the environment. A system of specialized structures or organs is required to carry out respiration in these animals.

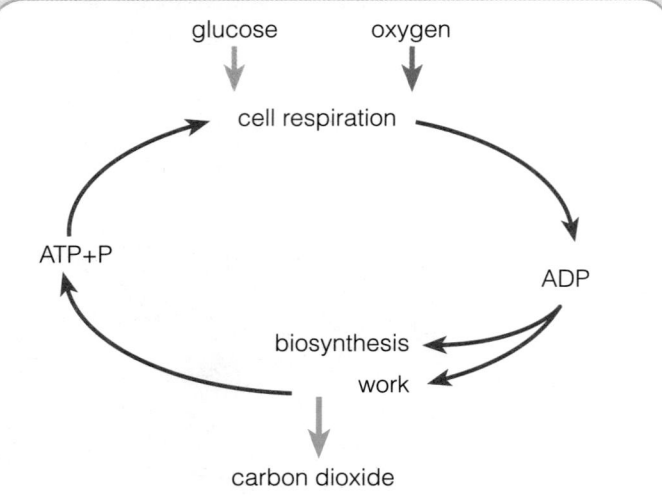

During cellular respiration, energy is used to join phosphate molecules to an adenosine molecule to form adenosine triphosphate (ATP). When energy is needed for work, the bonds between a phosphate molecule and the adenosine are broken, leaving adenosine diphosphate (ADP), and energy is released.

OPERATING PRINCIPLE

Despite the radical differences between water and air, the fundamental operating principle for these respiratory organs is exactly the same. The gas molecules cross through extremely thin membranes. The oxygen molecules diffuse directly into cells or the blood-stream (to be carried to cells) because there are more oxygen molecules outside than inside. And the carbon dioxide diffuses out because there is more of it inside than outside.

Skin. Respiration by diffusion through the skin can serve many animals if, as in nematode worms, the skin is kept moist and the animal is small enough so that the gases do not have far to go to accommodate all the cells. Diffusion through the skin also works if the body is flattened, as in flatworms, so that most cells are near the surface, or if the body has a low demand for energy, as in a jellyfish.

While breathing through the skin serves both aquatic and terrestrial animals, it is not efficient enough all by itself for large animals. These animals developed specialized respiratory organs that would speed up the process and enlarge their oxygen supply.

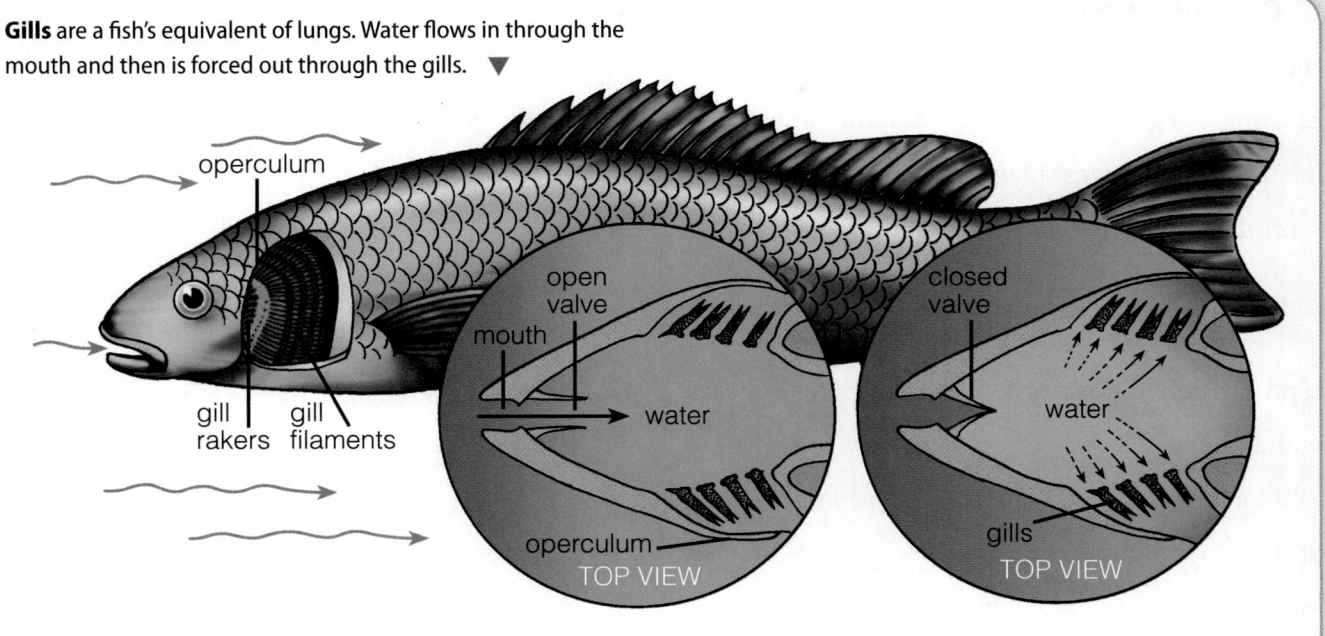

Gills are a fish's equivalent of lungs. Water flows in through the mouth and then is forced out through the gills. ▼

operculum

gill rakers

gill filaments

open valve

mouth

water

operculum

TOP VIEW

closed valve

water

gills

TOP VIEW

Gills. Fish and other aquatic animals use gills. A gill consists of branched or feathery tissues teeming with tiny blood vessels near the surface. In fish, gills are housed in cavities behind the head and safeguarded by a flesh-covered bony flap called an operculum. The fish gulps water through its mouth and ejects the water out through the opercular opening to maintain a steady flow of oxygenated water over the gills. The water flow is increased when a fish swims with its mouth open. Fast-swimming fish like tuna or mackerel, which need enormous amounts of oxygen, must swim constantly in order to remain alive.

Book Lungs. Spiders and some other arachnids, such as scorpions, developed book lungs, a series of moist membranes that lie side by side like pages in a book. The air is brought in through slits in the abdomen that are closed when not in use and, therefore, reduce dehydration.

Tracheae. Insects have tracheae, a system of branching tubes that bring oxygen to cells throughout the body. Because of this, insects do not have to use their blood circulation to transport oxygen and carbon dioxide.

Lungs. With lungs, the moist gas-exchange membranes are safeguarded deep within the body. Whereas gills are a modification of an animal's body surface, lungs are a modification of its gut.

Lungs essentially are elastic bags with extremely thin linings to facilitate gas exchange. Their great advantage is a relatively huge gas-exchange surface. The book lungs of arachnids and lungs of vertebrates are contained in an airtight compartment. By the muscular expansion of this compartment, the chest cavity in human beings, air is drawn into the lungs (inspiration); with relaxation of the muscles and collapse of the cavity, air is forced out (expiration).

Oxygen from inhalation (inspiration) diffuses into the oxygen-poor blood that has come from the body and is circulating through the lungs. At the same time, carbon dioxide, the waste product of respiration, diffuses into the lungs and is expelled during exhalation.

HOW ORGANISMS REPRODUCE

Cell reproduction is the process by which living things create more of their own kind. All types of living creatures reproduce, from the tiniest bacteria to the largest plants and animals. Without reproduction, all forms of life would die out.

Most organisms make new cells or replace old, worn-out cells through mitosis, a form of asexual reproduction. Mitosis produces two daughter cells with identical DNA.

Many organisms also use sexual reproduction at some point in their life cycle. The end products of meiosis are sex cells, which differ from the parent cell since they contain only half the original amount of DNA. Each sex cell is genetically different from all others. Human sex cells (sperm and egg) combine through fertilization to produce a new organism. The zygote grows, replicates DNA, and divides again and again by mitosis. At some point, meiosis and fertilization produce another generation. The new generation is similar but not identical to its parent.

New Generations

Asexual Reproduction

All cells are derived from other cells. In eukaryotic cells, which include all plants and animals, the major type of cell reproduction is mitosis. In this case, identical copies of each molecule of DNA are synthesized prior to mitotic division so that each resulting daughter cell has the same "blueprint," or genetic code. Because of mitosis, all body cells of an organism have identical molecules of DNA, and the number of chromosomes characteristic of each species remains constant.

Mitosis, a four-phase process, is repeated a finite number of times throughout the life of an organism.

Mitosis

Interphase. This is the time between mitotic cell divisions. The amount of time a cell spends in interphase varies with the species, its age, temperature, and other factors. Most cells divide on a regular basis in order to repair or replace other cells. During interphase, each cell begins to grow to mature size, and RNA and protein synthesis occurs. DNA replication begins when the cell reaches a particular size. Each chromosome duplicates itself to form identical sister chromosomes. The DNA is duplicated, more proteins are synthesized, and the cell continues to increase in size. The cell becomes ready to divide and interphase ends.

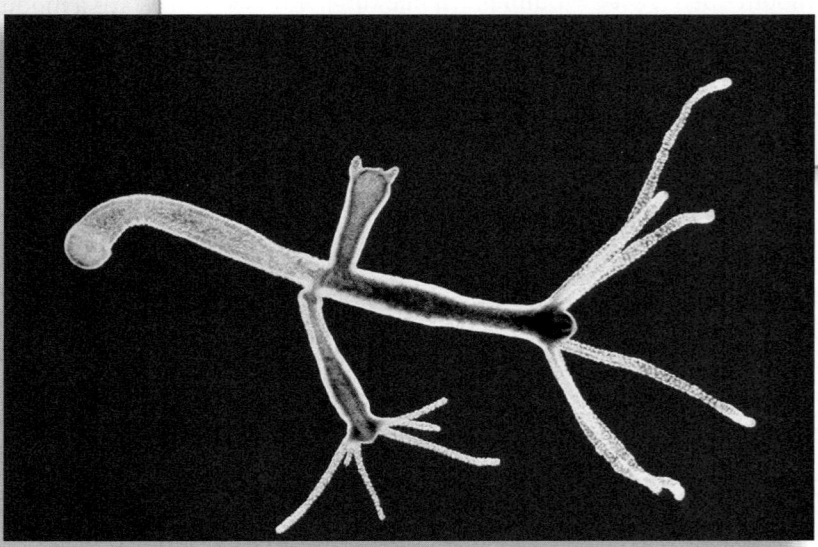

Vegetative reproduction. The hydra, a tiny water animal related to jellyfish and coral, grows buds that break off to form "daughter" hydras.

Mitosis

Parent Cell

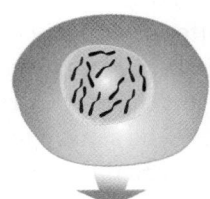

Prophase

Chromatin condenses into chromosomes. Nuclear envelope disappears.

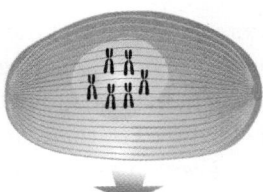

Metaphase

Chromosomes align at the equatorial plate.

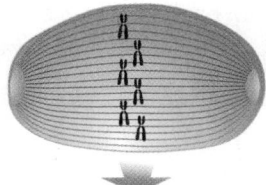

Anaphase

Sister chromatids separate. Centromeres divide.

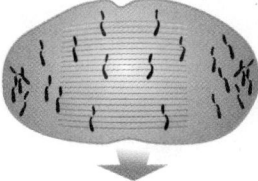

Telophase

Chromatin expands. Cytoplasm divides.

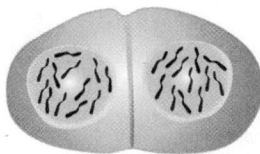

Two identical daughter cells

Prophase. The chromosomes condense or coil into short, thick structures that become visible under a light microscope. The membrane around the nucleus breaks down and disappears. If centrioles are present, they begin to migrate to opposite regions of the cell, forming two poles. A football-shaped structure, the spindle, made of tubelike structures, then forms. The spindle fibers form between the poles. The spindle forms in plant cells without centrioles. The chromosomes begin to move toward the middle of the spindle.

Metaphase. The chromosomes line up along the middle of the spindle, apparently pushed or pulled along by the spindle fibers.

Anaphase. The sister chromosomes separate from each other. Each daughter chromosome, as they are now called, migrates toward opposite poles. The chromosomes often have a V or J shape.

Telophase. The daughter chromosomes are at opposite poles of the spindle, and the spindle starts to break down. The individual chromosomes become thinner, longer, and less visible. The nuclear membrane re-forms around each set of chromosomes. The centrioles replicate. A furrow or groove appears in the membrane of animal cells and a cell plate forms in plant cells. The animal cell furrow curves inward until a complete membrane separates the two daughter cells. The plant cell plate expands until a wall is formed that separates the two cells. A new interphase then begins in each daughter cell.

New Generations

Types of Asexual Reproduction

Binary Fission. There are several types of asexual reproduction. Prokaryotic cells, such as bacteria, reproduce by *binary fission*. The parent cell pinches in half to form two new cells. The pinched off cells contain identical DNA but division by mitosis has not occurred.

Budding is common to some organisms, including the small aquatic animal hydra, as well as yeast cells, which are fungi. In each case, a small bud develops on the parent cell or organism. The bud contains a copy of the parent cell's DNA. Eventually the bud breaks off to become a new hydra or yeast cell. These new cells are essentially clones of the parent organism.

Vegetative reproduction is common to many plants and some animals. In vegetative reproduction, another organism will develop from a portion of an organism that separates or has been removed from it. For example, potato tubers can be cut up and planted to produce a number of new potatoes; a branch of a willow tree can grow a new root system and develop into a new tree; the animal hydra develops buds. The buds are special collections of cells that develop into new hydra and eventually separate and become independent organisms.

Regeneration means the regrowth of missing parts. If a starfish or a planarian is cut into several pieces,

each may develop into an independent organism. Some organisms can only regenerate missing parts, however.

Regeneration. Many plants can reproduce by regeneration. A few animals, such as the starfish, can also regenerate. Since starfish prey on oysters, oyster fishermen used to catch starfish and tear them to pieces. This practice was stopped when the fishermen realized that each piece regenerated into a new starfish.

Spores. Some organisms produce specialized cells that can grow into complete organisms. These cells are called *spores*. Bread mold and mushrooms reproduce thousands of organisms by this method. The smoky cloud emitted by fungi known as puffballs is actually a cloud of extremely tiny spores.

Organisms that have formed from asexual reproduction have the same exact DNA structure as their parent, and each daughter organism carries the exact hereditary information that is found in the parent.

Many organisms produce specialized cells that differ from spores in that they do not develop directly into a new organism. These cells, called *gametes*, will form a new individual only after they have fused or become fertilized by another gamete. Fertilization is the key event in sexual reproduction. Organisms formed by sexual reproduction are truly new and different from their parents, since the organism receives DNA from each parent. To accomplish this, another form of cell division, called *meiosis*, is required.

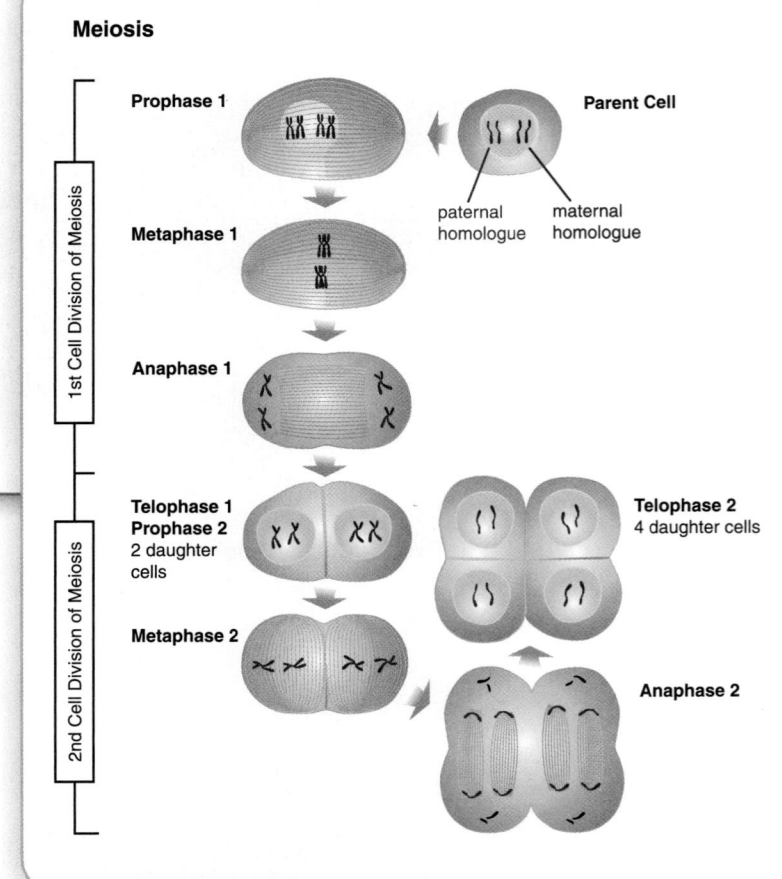

Meiosis

Prophase 1 — Parent Cell

paternal homologue — maternal homologue

1st Cell Division of Meiosis

Metaphase 1

Anaphase 1

2nd Cell Division of Meiosis

Telophase 1 Prophase 2 2 daughter cells

Metaphase 2

Telophase 2 4 daughter cells

Anaphase 2

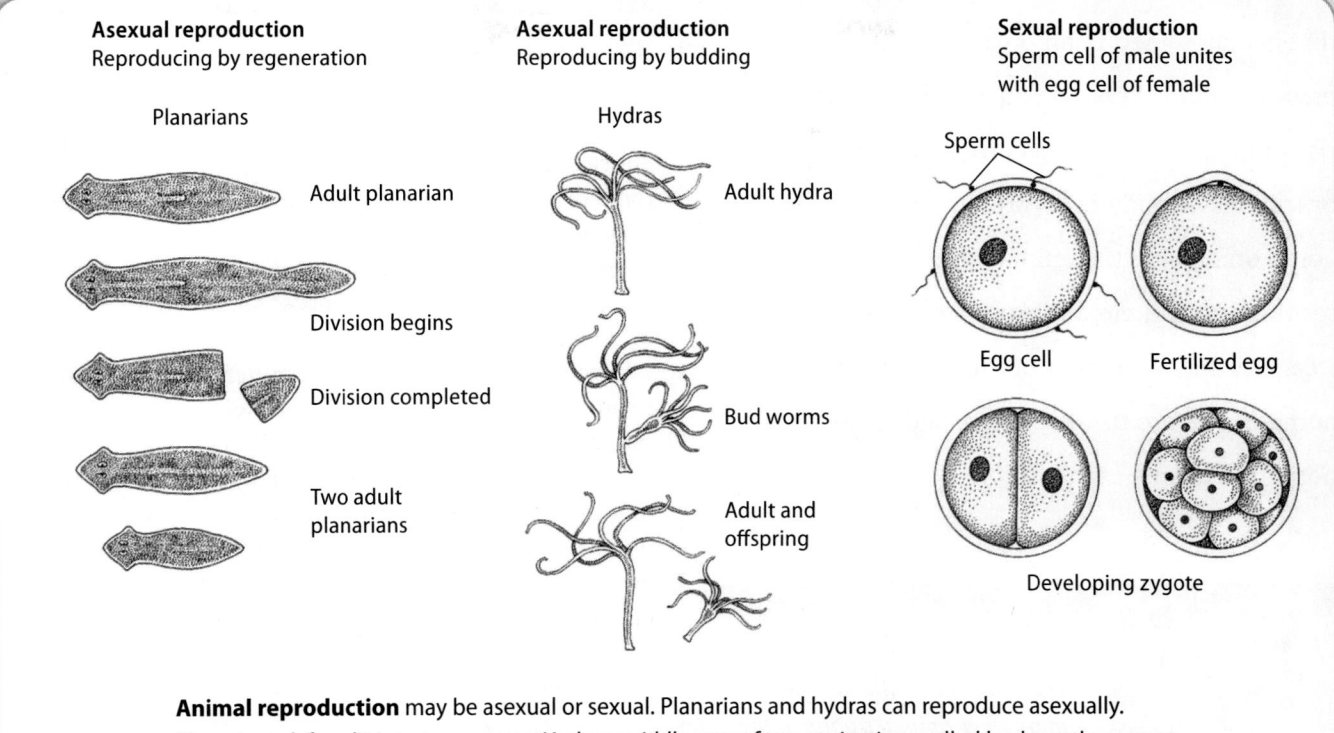

Asexual reproduction
Reproducing by regeneration

Planarians

Adult planarian

Division begins

Division completed

Two adult planarians

Asexual reproduction
Reproducing by budding

Hydras

Adult hydra

Bud worms

Adult and offspring

Sexual reproduction
Sperm cell of male unites with egg cell of female

Sperm cells

Egg cell

Fertilized egg

Developing zygote

Animal reproduction may be asexual or sexual. Planarians and hydras can reproduce asexually. Planarians, *left*, split into two worms. Hydras, *middle*, grow from projections called buds on the parent. In sexual reproduction, *right*, a sperm cell fertilizes an egg, which develops into a new animal.

Meiosis

The chromosomes in each cell occur in pairs. In humans there are 46 chromosomes, or 23 pairs. If the gametes (usually called egg and sperm) fuse, the chromosome number would double. Meiosis is a process of cell division unique to gametes where the chromosome number is halved. Meiosis occurs in two stages.

First Meiotic Division. Each chromosome has duplicated itself. Each replicated chromosome seeks out its sister. Frequently, chromosome pairs will become entangled and exchange sections of DNA. This process is called *crossing over*. The duplicated chromosomes pair up, forming a four-stranded group called a *tetrad*.

As tetrads are forming, the nuclear membrane is breaking down and spindle fibers are forming. The tetrads migrate toward the center and line up randomly. Complete chromosomes gather at each pole and the cytoplasm divides either by furrowing or forming a

cell plate. Each new cell now has half the chromosome number of its species (in humans, 23).

Second Meiotic Division. This phase is very similar to mitosis. Spindle fibers form, the paired chromosomes line up at the center of the cell, and the spindle fiber begins to draw the chromosomes apart. The chromosomes group and migrate together at each pole. The cytoplasm again divides. Four daughter cells, each with half the chromosome number, have formed. Usually in male organisms the cytoplasm divides evenly and all four cells function as sperm cells. In females, the cytoplasm divides unequally with one cell receiving the majority of the cytoplasm. This cell becomes the functioning gamete.

Meiosis produces organisms that are genetically different. Crossing over and the random assortment of chromosomes ensure that each daughter cell will be different. Additional genetic mixing will occur at fertilization when the chromosome number is restored.

HOMEOSTASIS

Homeostasis signifies the state of balance that is maintained in an organism. The internal environment is kept constant with just the right amount of materials provided to millions or trillions of body cells, no matter what is going on outside the animal. The digestive, respiratory, and circulatory systems all play a role. But the main parts of the body involved in homeostasis are the excretory, endocrine, and nervous systems.

Pheromones are chemical secretions that influence cells in another animal's body; if the chemical is directed to cells in the same body, it is a hormone.

Maintaining Balance

Excretory System

The excretory system does much more than simply remove metabolic wastes. The mammalian body's entire supply of blood is constantly going through the pair of kidneys to be monitored in a never-ending surveillance. The kidneys divert out waste materials, keep in important foodstuffs, regulate water balance, and maintain the proper levels of sodium and other inorganic ions that cells need to function.

The regulation of water and mineral salts is closely related. In the process of osmosis, water molecules diffuse through semipermeable cell membranes that block dissolved substances, but salt particles will tend to move through the membrane in the opposite direction. If an organism is unable to get rid of excess salts or toxic materials, it will die. At the same time, too little or too much water can be fatal. So the kidneys' ability to maintain the proper levels of water and salts in the blood is a matter of life and death.

Hormones. The prerequisite for bodily regulation is cellular communication. Cells must be able to communicate needs to one another. In multicellular animals, cells usually are unable to move around to communicate by physical contact, but they can send vital chemical messages.

Hormones make up a system for communication and for coordination of functions in animal bodies. Hormones are manufactured in a number of endocrine glands and enter the bloodstream to be taken to other parts of the body. In the circulatory system, the released hormones come into contact with virtually all cells. But only cells with the proper receptors receive and respond to the hormonal message. There are many different messengers. Mammals, for instance, have about 30 different kinds of hormones.

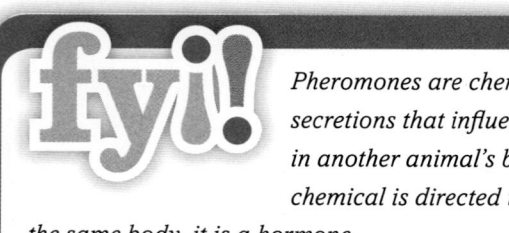

Hormone Producing Cells / target cell / capillary / hormone

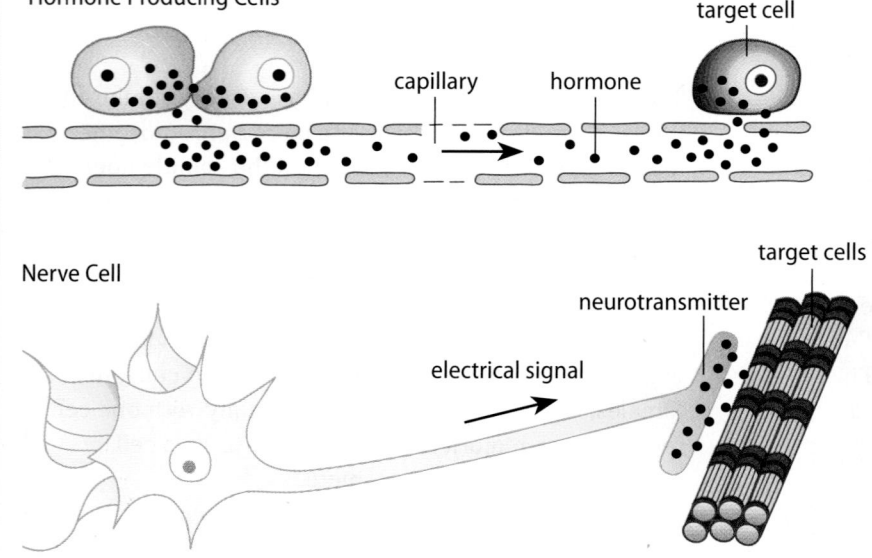

Nerve Cell / neurotransmitter / target cells / electrical signal

Control of the body is shared by the nervous and hormonal systems.

Salt. Freshwater fish gain water osmotically and lose salts by diffusion through their skin. In freshwater lakes and ponds, water is continually moving into fish while necessary salts tend to move out. Fish are able to overcome an always impending imbalance by drinking no water and releasing great amounts of dilute urine to conserve salt loss.

For marine fish, the situation is reversed, with water molecules flowing out and salts entering. Marine fish drink copiously to maintain water balance and urinate little, but the small amount of urine that is excreted has a high concentration of salts. In freshwater fish, the kidney reabsorbs the salts and returns them to the blood, while allowing water to pass through. The kidneys of marine fish reverse the process.

Saltwater fish drink copiously to maintain water balance. They urinate little, but the small amount of urine that is excreted has a high concentration of salts.

Blue trunkfish

Clown triggerfish

Blue tang surgeonfish

Moorish idol

In freshwater lakes and ponds, water is continually moving into fish while necessary salts tend to move out. Freshwater fish are able to overcome an always impending imbalance by drinking no water and releasing great amounts of dilute urine to conserve salt loss.

Rainbow darter

Common shiner

Southern redbelly dace

Creek chub

Nitrogen. The major metabolic waste produced by all animals is one that contains some kind of nitrogen. Freshwater fish and aquatic invertebrates such as sponges and jellyfish get rid of the nitrogen in the form of ammonia. Ammonia is highly toxic, but it also is highly soluble, and these creatures, bathed in water, release it easily. Animals without such access to water cannot let ammonia accumulate in their bodies, so they convert it to a less toxic form, urea.

Marine fish, amphibians, and mammals must carry the waste nitrogen in their bodies for longer periods of time, so it is excreted in the less toxic form of urea. For birds, reptiles, and insects, all of which have a great need to preserve water, the ammonia is converted to its least toxic form, uric acid. This is also the least soluble form and is typically excreted as a solid, as in the whitish material in bird droppings. (See page 607.)

Regulating the Animal Body

Negative feedback. Since hormones exert powerful effects, their duration must be regulated. On a hot day, an animal has lost water from its body through exertion. The pituitary gland releases the antidiuretic hormone (ADH), which causes the kidneys to conserve water and reabsorb it into the blood. Now the animal comes to a stream and begins to drink. When the body's water level returns to normal, the secretion of ADH stops and the kidneys switch from the conservation mode and return to normal function.

This is called negative feedback—the secretion of the hormone causes effects that will lead to cancellation of further hormone production. This kind of control is a prime mechanism of homeostasis.

Nerves. The hormonal system shares control of the body with the nervous system. Nerve cells, known as *neurons*, flash messages to various parts of the body via electrical signals traveling through chains of *neurons*. But the messages must be conveyed from neuron to neuron by chemical messengers, called *neurotransmitters*.

In vertebrates, the central nervous system consists of

- the brain, where conscious communications originate.
- the spinal cord, the main distribution trunk for conscious communications as well as the short-circuit dispatcher of reflex commands that must be sent especially quickly.

The autonomic nervous system, which is regulated by the hypothalamus in the brain, is charged with complete homeostatic control of the body. It regulates all the functions that keep the body performing well, such as

- proper heartbeat, blood pressure, and pulse for the appropriate physical situation.
- dilation of the pupil of the eye as light dims and contraction of the pupil as light brightens.
- sweating in humans or panting in dogs when the internal temperature rises too high.

The autonomic system also prepares an animal for emergencies, for situations requiring a great expenditure of energy, or for any kind of stressful event. Because of these two kinds of activities—normal maintenance and the meeting of challenges and

IMPORTANT MAMMALIAN HORMONES

Some other hormones important in metabolism and homeostasis in mammals include:

- cortisol, a long-term stress hormone that increases blood glucose levels by causing the breakdown of proteins and fats
- glucagon, which raises the level of blood glucose by causing the liver to break down glycogen stores
- insulin, which lowers blood glucose by increasing blood glucose intake into cells
- calcitonin, which decreases the calcium level in the blood by promoting storage in bone and excretion of urine
- parathormone, which increases the calcium level in the blood by causing its release from storage in the skeletal system
- thyroxine, which is responsible for increasing the body's metabolic rate

threats—the autonomic system is composed of two largely independent systems or nervous pathways.

1. The parasympathetic nervous system takes over and runs things when an animal is at rest.

- Breathing slows and heartbeat is less forceful and the rate slows.
- Blood pressure goes down.
- Blood flows to the body's surface and to the viscera, activating the digestive tract, and various digestive juices are stimulated.

2. The sympathetic nervous system takes control when an animal is confronted with any stressful or threatening situation.

- Heart rate and blood pressure are increased.
- Digestive activity stops.
- Blood is diverted from the viscera and skin to the skeletal muscles.
- The coagulative factor in blood increases and breathing is enhanced, providing more oxygen.
- The rate of metabolism increases and the animal becomes mentally alert.
- Pupils dilate to provide greater visual acuity.
- Hair becomes erect and affords mammals greater protection.

To stay alive, lizards and other reptiles must avoid extremely high or low temperatures. Most reptiles that are active during the day keep moving from sunny places to shady spots. Many species of reptiles that live in hot climates are active mainly at night.

Thermoregulation. Still another way that the autonomic nervous system keeps the bodies of birds and mammals in balance is by regulating the temperature of their bodies. Birds and mammals are homeothermic and are commonly called warm-blooded. Invertebrates, fish, amphibians, and reptiles are ectothermic and are referred to as cold-blooded. The body temperature of ectothermic animals varies with their environment, remaining just a few degrees above the temperature of their surroundings. These animals require outside heat for their metabolic functioning, which is why a frog or lizard must sit in the morning sun for a while before it goes about its day's business.

Warm-blooded birds and mammals are endothermic, in that they create their own inner heat through metabolism, as well as homeothermic, even-temperatured. Because birds need a higher metabolic rate in order to sustain flight, avian temperatures range between 40° and 42°C (104° to 108°F), while most mammals are between 37° and 39°C (98° and 101.5°F). Because of their inner-generated, stable body temperatures, birds and mammals are less dependent on environmental warmth and can be wider ranging.

Temperature. Heat is lost and temperature lowered chiefly through blood vessels near the surface of the body. If a warm-blooded animal is in a cold environment, the autonomic system largely shuts down surface blood flow. If the reduction in heat loss is insufficient to maintain core temperature from metabolic processes, additional heat is generated. The autonomic system causes the muscle activity recognized as shivering.

Muscle activity generates body heat, so if the body becomes overheated from exertion or because of a hot environment, the autonomic system opens surface blood vessels and enlarges the diameters of those vessels. If that is insufficient, the system initiates sweating in humans and panting in other mammals, both efficient ways to lose heat through evaporation.

HOW DOES THAT WORK ?

Temperature is the primary factor in mammalian hibernation. A creature such as the bear can eat enough during the summer months to build a reserve of nutrient-rich fat. As the days grow short, the animal settles into its burrow, sinks into a deep sleep with body temperature dropping as the outside temperature declines until it is within a few degrees of freezing. The brain temperature remains at a normal level and the temperature sensors work to maintain a level to prevent freezing but continue deep hibernation.

Woodchucks eat large amounts of food in the fall before hibernating. The extra food is changed to fat in their bodies, and the woodchucks live on this fat during their winter sleep. This additional fat may account for as much as 15 to 20 percent of its body weight.

Perceiving the Outside World

External Communications

Sensory systems enable an animal to monitor, and thus function in, the external environment through appropriate functions in its internal environment.

The development of bilateral symmetry in animals resulted in a front end of the body where sensory nerve cells congregated to allow an animal to know what kind of environment it was getting into. Nerves that centered in the head among the most primitive bilaterals began the centralization of the nervous system. These nerve cells included

- chemoreceptors used to detect various kinds of chemical substances dissolved in water.
- photoreceptors to detect light.
- rheoreceptors to detect water currents.
- various types of receptors for touch.

Certain snakes, such as rattlesnakes, can literally see heat. They have holes on either side of the head between the eyes and nostrils. At the back of each depression is a tiny opening like a pinhole camera—but one that registers infrared radiation, or heat, instead of light radiation. The system is sensitive enough to detect temperature changes as small as 0.003°. What emerges is a heat picture that is relayed to the area of the brain that deals with vision and is analyzed like signals from the eye. For this reason, the snake can see and strike its mammalian prey in pitch dark.

CHEMORECEPTORS

Chemoreceptors undoubtedly were the earliest sensors, enabling unicellular organisms to move toward food and a potential mate, and away from noxious materials or a dangerous enemy or competitor. Terrestrial vertebrates have two chemical senses, the sense of smell for airborne molecules, and the sense of taste for chemicals dissolved in water or saliva. Smell, or chemical detection, is the main way of knowing the world for many kinds of animals. Insects locate mates this way. The female emits a pheromone, and the male at a distance detects the chemical.

COMPLEX EYE

The most advanced eye, the complex eye, evolved independently in vertebrates and organisms such as the octopus and squid. In mammals such as chimpanzees and humans, the lens changes shape as the viewed object comes closer or moves farther away. In the cephalopods, as well as in fish, amphibians, and snakes, the lens has a fixed shape but is telescoped in similar fashion to the telephoto lens of a camera. The complex eye has three distinguishable tissue layers—an outer layer, the sclera, which protects the eye and differentiates into the cornea at the front of the eye; a middle layer known as the choroid coat which provides nutrients and oxygen via blood vessels; and the inner layer, or retina, which contains the photoreceptors, cones, and rods.

◀ **The rattlesnake's** infrared detection pits are responsible for its designation as a pit viper. Pit vipers include about 30 species of rattlesnakes, water moccasins, copperheads, and the fer-de-lance.

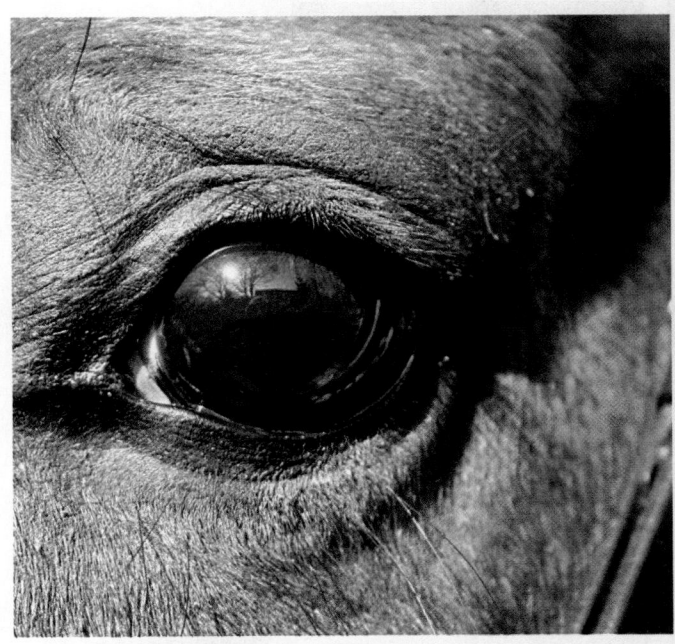

PHOTORECEPTORS

Photoreceptor cells became the primary sensing system of primates. Vision is important for most animals in obtaining food, avoiding predators, and getting around. But there are gradations to sight. The photoreceptors in the flatworm form eyespots. An eyespot has no lens, cannot focus, and cannot form an image. About all it can do is distinguish light from dark and possibly detect direction and intensity.

Compound eyes evolved in trilobites, crustaceans, and insects. The compound eye is made up of thousands of closely packed optical units called ommatidia (small eyes) that see independently, each focused on a particular spot. The resulting image is a mosaic made up of thousands of dots, something like the grainy picture formed on poor television screens. If the overall picture is crude, the individual ommatidium enables the extraordinarily quick detection of movement. A dragonfly with 30,000 ommatidia per eye can scoop its prey out of the air with unerring accuracy.

Other Receptors. The photoreceptors that can see parts of the electromagnetic spectrum labeled visible light and infrared are included in a broader category called radioreceptors—receptors that detect electromagnetic energy. While mammals cannot see infrared, they can feel it as heat through radioreceptors in the skin.

In addition to radioreceptors and chemoreceptors, animals have several other kinds of receptors, not all shared by human beings, to orient them to their world.

- Mechanoreceptors detect mechanical stimuli, such as sound, touch, pressure, tension, vibration, acceleration and deceleration, gravity, and cold, as a reduction in kinetic energy.

- Magnetoreceptors detect magnetic fields. Birds can use this ability to take advantage of the fact that Earth is a giant magnet to aid their navigation in migrations.

- Galvanoreceptors detect weak electrical fields and are possessed by sharks, rays, jellyfish, some bony fish, and the duckbill platypus, the only mammal with such a sense.

Migratory birds such as this arctic tern are believed to use magnetoreceptors to navigate through long migrations.

ANIMAL LIFE SPANS

Individuals within a species can live for different lengths of time because of individual experiences that might bring about a premature death. However, the range of life spans within a species is determined primarily by factors such as size, metabolism, and genetic makeup.

Domesticated animals may experience different life spans than wild populations of the same species. There are a variety of reasons for this: domesticated populations have been bred to emphasize characteristics that will lengthen or shorten life span; animals are protected from predators; and they may have a distinctly different diet than wild animals.

How Long Do They Live?

Mammals	
Buffalo, American	20
Cat	14 *
Chimpanzee	30–40
Deer (fallow)	20
Dog	12–20 *
Elephant	50–70
Goat (mountain)	14–18
Grizzly bear	25
Hippopotamus	41
Horse	20–30 *
Lion	13
Monkey (rhesus)	27–28
Mouse (field)	1
Sheep	10–20
Squirrel	7
Tiger	20
Wolf (gray)	12–16
Zebra	22

Cat

Chimpanzee

Elephant

*Domesticated animal; life span in captivity
Note: Figures are average life spans in years for animals in the wild, unless otherwise noted.

Fish	
Dogfish (lesser spotted)	8
Goldfish	10
Halibut	25
Lamprey	7
Lungfish (African)	18
Perch	3–10
Pike	60–70
Salmon (Pacific)	4–5
Seahorse	$4^1/_2$
Sturgeon	50
Trout (rainbow)	11

Seahorse

Birds	
Blue jay	6–9
Canada goose	12–23
Canary	6–8
Cardinal	13
Chickadee	6–8
Condor	35–40
Heron	10–20
Macaw	64
Ostrich (African)	40
Owl (snowy)	10
Penguin (emperor)	20
Pigeon	6
Raven	5
Robin, American	17
Sky lark	9
Sparrow	$2^1/_2$–7
Starling	9–16

Blue-throated macaw

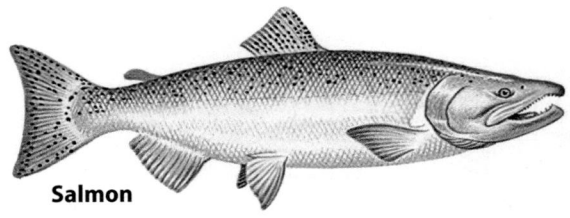

Salmon

Chameleon

Reptiles and Amphibians	
Bullfrog	5
Chameleon	4–5
Cottonmouth	18–20
Crocodile (Nile)	25–50
Garter snake	3–4
King snake	3
Puff adder	14
Rattlesnake (diamondback)	14–15
Salamander (spotted)	20
Turtle (box)	80
Water snake	11

Spotted salamander

Ostrich

ANIMAL BEHAVIOR

The biological goal of animal behavior, like the physiological goal, is survival of the individual until maturity so the animal can reproduce. Animal behaviors involve such pursuits as finding a place to live; securing food; avoiding predators and guarding against danger in general; finding a mate; and caring for one's young. Behavior has genetic roots. It is specific to each species and is governed by each animal's structural, hormonal, and nervous system. Behavior enhances what the body can do or compensates for what it is unable to do.

Some fiddler crabs change in color from light to dark during the day. This change occurs because of the movement of pigment (coloring matter) within special cells in the skin. ▶

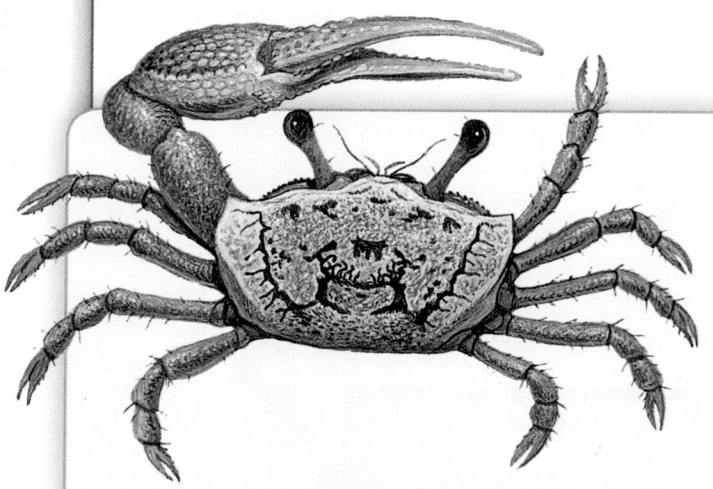

Varieties of Rhythms

Periodicities

Biological rhythms could be discussed under hormonal or nervous systems or animal ecology, as well as under behavior, because all are important aspects of this phenomenon. Rhythmic biological behaviors have physiological elements under the direction of brain centers and are largely carried out through hormonal influences.

Most biological rhythms are cued to daily, monthly, seasonal, and yearly time frames. Daily regularities are known as circadian rhythms, from the Latin *circa*, meaning "about," and *dies*, meaning "day." Earth rotates once in exactly 24 hours, so the sun is in virtually the same position 24 hours later; it takes 24 hours and 50 minutes for the moon to be back in its same position in the sky.

Pull of the Moon. While the position of the sun in the sky determines the periods of light and darkness, which are extremely important environmental cues, the moon exerts a much stronger influence than the sun (more than double) on the ocean's tides. The pull of the moon is strongest, and high tides occur, whenever the moon is directly overhead or directly opposite on the other side of the planet. Since life began in the oceans with single-celled microorganisms, the tidal regularity and lunar day are significant influences for multicellular animals. (See page 575.)

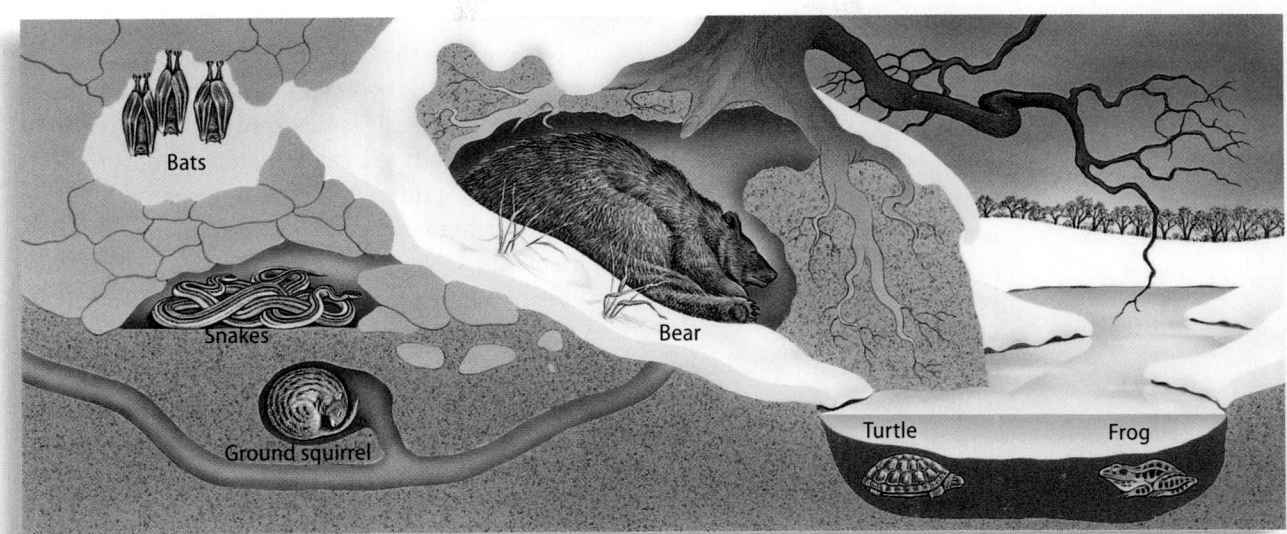

▲ **Hibernation** is an inactive, sleeplike state that some animals enter during the winter to protect themselves from cold and hunger. This illustration shows a number of animals hibernating. Bats hibernate in caves, hanging from the ceiling. Ground squirrels burrow underground to hibernate. Hibernating reptiles and amphibians—such as the snake, turtle, and frog in this illustration—often occupy crevices in rocks or bury themselves underground. Many bears experience a state of dormancy during the winter as their heart rate and metabolism fall greatly. Some scientists call this state incomplete hibernation.

Circadian Rhythms. Prominent circadian rhythms are involved with light and darkness. *Diurnal* animals, such as songbirds, hawks, lizards, butterflies, bees, and wasps, are active during the daytime. *Nocturnal* animals, such as mice, moths, owls, bats, skunks, raccoons, and cockroaches, are active at night. All sorts of physiological variations recur on a daily basis to prepare an animal for periods of activity and rest. Human beings are diurnal. A great many people who work at night have difficulty sleeping during the day and feel out of sorts much of the time because their schedule does not fit the normal circadian rhythm.

Synodic Rhythms. A synodic month, measuring one orbit by the moon, appears to have imprinted its timing on the reproductive cycles of many marine animals. These rhythms can be predicted according to the phase of the moon and season of the year. Reproductive swarming of mayflies has been related to moon phase. So has the menstrual cycle in some primates, with initiation of menstruation linked to the new moon.

Annual Rhythms. Annual rhythms also are commonly observed in reproductive cycles, timed so that the young can take maximum advantage of good weather. Sheep that gestate for 6 months conceive in the fall; songbirds with a 1-month period for pregnancy mate in early spring. Bird migrations are another annual rhythm. Of course, as in all biological rhythms, there are good reasons for migrations. Species that migrate could not survive winter in the north but would suffer from overpopulation if they remained and bred in their southern habitats.

Hibernation by mammals and pupation in insects are biological rhythms that accomplish winter survival. Desert rodents and some other mammals, lungfish, and some insects employ estivation—a kind of torpor—to live through the hot, dry months. Dormancy in reptiles can exhibit either circadian or seasonal rhythms, or both.

Innate Behaviors

This bird, the masked northern weaver, builds a complicated hanging nest out of long, thin leaves and other materials. Weavers never learn how to build such nests—instead, the basic pattern of activity is built into their nervous systems. ▼

Instinct

Instinctive behaviors are acts that an animal of the proper age performs without experience or learning the first time it meets the proper environmental stimulus. These behaviors are genetically stamped to be performed in the same way by animals in a species generation after generation.

Animals with simple nervous systems may not be capable of learning behaviors important to their survival. The simpler the organism, the more it must rely on inborn behavior patterns. An animal that freezes at the sight of a predator has to do it right the first time because it may not get a second chance.

The term *instinct* also has been applied to what is called *drive*. A drive is an inner push or motivation caused by some disturbance of an animal's homeostasis. For example, an animal that has not eaten for a long time will be driven by hunger to seek food. Presumably, a lowering of blood sugar rather than some external trigger elicits the behavior. Thirst, sexual desire, and curiosity are other animal drives.

Kinesis. Kinesis is the change in the speed of movement brought about by an environmental stimulus. Even though the changes in speed are nondirectional, and the movements are random, the effect is to bring an organism to a more favorable environment. For instance, certain insects are more active in dry areas. Their activities eventually take them away from the dry area to a moist area that is more congenial. They stop moving and settle down; they have found a home. In a hostile environment, movements are speeded up. Organisms want to get away.

ETHOLOGY

Ethology is the branch of zoology that deals with animal instincts and animal behavior under natural or near-natural conditions. Ethologists study such instinctive behavior as courtship, mating, and care of young. They also study how animals communicate and how they establish and defend their territories. Ethologists seek to determine what causes instinctive behavior, how such behavior developed over millions of years, and how it helps a species survive. For each kind of animal studied, ethologists prepare an ethogram, which is a list that describes the known behavior patterns of the species. In the ethogram, they also try to specify the conditions under which each instinctive act occurs. Ethologists have developed ethograms for various species of insects, fishes, birds, and mammals.

Taxis. A taxis is a directed movement toward or away from a stimulus. Moths and other insects are irresistibly attracted to light. One of the ways a fish orients itself in the water is by keeping its dorsal side toward the light, which normally comes from the surface. If the light comes from the side of a fish tank, the animal becomes disoriented. Many organisms that die quickly from desiccation show a negative taxis to sunlight and avoid it. Mosquitoes show a positive taxis to the warmth of their prey.

Reflex. A reflex is an involuntary movement in response to a stimulus that involves only a part of an organism. Reflexes, such as blinking, are rapid because the conscious brain is not involved. People pull their hands away from a hot stove long before they make a conscious decision to do so. Sensory nerves tell motor neurons to act via the spinal cord, bypassing the brain for the immediate action.

Fixed Action Patterns. The discovery of fixed action patterns was one of the first breakthroughs by ethologists. They found that the repertoire of an animal's behavior is composed of certain unvarying patterns. Each of these patterns—a fixed action pattern—is a behaviorally rigid response to some specific feature in the environmental situation. The feature is called a sign stimulus or, when it comes from members of the same species, a *releaser*.

Stuffing food into the mouths of chicks is a fixed action pattern. Young nestlings of several species of birds have distinctive markings inside their mouths. When they open their mouths, the markings serve as releasers that cause feeding movements in the parents.

Instinctive behaviors are those that an animal performs without having to be taught, for instance, a newborn animal's suckling. ▼

How Animals Learn

Learning

Innate behaviors have their limitations. An animal has a better chance to survive if it can modify its behavior based on experience. In general, the more complete an animal's nervous system, the more flexible it is and the more adaptable. This is called learning. There are four types:

- imprinting.
- habituation.
- operant conditioning.
- insight.

Habituation. This modification of behavior is simply learning to ignore stimuli that are unimportant or irrelevant. A sea anemone will contract if touched. But after repeated touching, it will disregard the provocation and go about its business. This ability to learn the difference through experience between harmless distractions and legitimate threats cuts down the waste of an animal's time and energy.

Imprinting. Imprinting is a welding of innate and learned behavior. It takes place at a critical time of receptivity in an animal's development. Konrad Lorenz was the first to discover this phenomenon when he separated a group of goslings from their mother right after they hatched and then imitated goose calls. The goslings identified him as the parent and thereafter followed him around. The relationship was permanently imprinted on their nervous systems.

It has been established since then that parental identification (almost always with the mother) occurs with domestic fowl, ducks, ungulates, and guinea pigs, in addition to geese, immediately after birth. For mallard ducks, the critical time period is 13 to 16 hours after hatching. The chicks are learning a releaser for a fixed action pattern.

The young in these imprinting species are at a more advanced stage of development. They are able to walk soon after birth and thus are capable of wandering away from the mother even when they still need her for nourishment and protection. In contrast, the newborn of songbirds, dogs, cats, rats, and primates are helpless at birth and require constant attention. Song acquisition in birds also involves a receptive period when the learner is exposed to a model at the right time.

Sexual imprinting also occurs during early associations. The animal learns to recognize appropriate individuals for future mating. In this case, imprinting is a matter of species identification to help avoid mating that would prove to be infertile.

◀ **Imprinting** occurs in species where the young are quickly able to move about on their own.

CONDITIONING

In this more complex form of learning, an animal responds to a stimulus substituted for the normal trigger. Russian physiologist Ivan Pavlov won the 1904 Nobel Prize in Physiology or Medicine for his research on digestion. He showed how the vagus nerve controls the flow of digestive juices of the stomach and pancreas. He found that, by repeated association, an artificial stimulus (such as a bell) could be substituted for a natural stimulus (food) to cause a physiological reaction (salivation). In his most famous experiment, he found that if a bell were rung each time a dog was given meat, the dog could eventually be conditioned—taught—to salivate at the sound of the bell. This kind of response is widespread in the animal kingdom. A flatworm given an electric shock at the same time a light is flashed soon learns to contract to the light alone. Pavlov called this a conditioned reflex. He

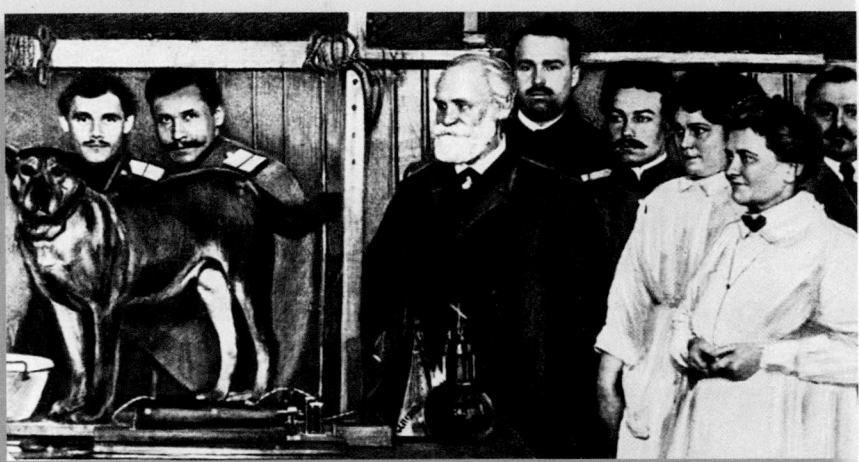

Ivan Pavlov, *center,* and his staff gather around a dog undergoing a typical conditioning reflex experiment. ▼

believed that all acquired habits, and even higher mental activity, depend on chains of conditioned reflexes.

The value of this kind of learned behavior is that it expands an animal's response to a variety of environmental indicators.

Operant Conditioning. In an experiment, Harvard psychologist B. F. Skinner taught pigeons and white rats certain behaviors in what came to be known as *operant conditioning.* They learned to press levers or peck at buttons in order to gain some reward or avoid punishment. The animal was allowed to make its own discoveries and in effect train itself. Operant conditioning is a form of trial-and-error learning under controlled conditions, such as a rat's ability to run through a maze.

In the wild, animals are confronted naturally with rewards and punishments. To a toad, any flying insect is a sign stimulus, meaning food. But a toad that strikes and encloses a bee in its mouth learns its error in one painful trial. Experimenters have presented such a toad with a smorgasbord of flying insects. It would not bite at anything resembling a bee, but it would bite a dragonfly.

Insight. The most complex form of learning might be described as trial and error that takes place entirely in the mind: solving a problem never confronted before without any training. Human beings call this form of learning insight or reason. In 1917, William Kohler showed in a famous experiment that a chimpanzee was able to figure out how to reach a bunch of bananas suspended from the ceiling of its cage. Boxes of different sizes had been placed in the cage. After a while the chimp moved the largest box to a point beneath the bananas, piled the other boxes on top, and climbed up to its objective. More recent studies of primates in the wild have provided more indications of animal intelligence.

SOCIAL BEHAVIOR

Animal lifestyles range from that of a lone hunter, such as the leopard, to that of group hunters, such as wolves or hyenas; from solitaries, like some crickets, to the elaborate societies of ants, bees, and termites. But even loners like foxes get together annually to mate, and so all animals must be able to communicate.

How Animals Interact

Communication

Some animal communication takes place with members of other species. The odoriferous communication of a skunk will affect the behavior of any intruder. We can tell fairly easily whether a dog is threatening or friendly, and behave accordingly.

However, most animal communication is with members of the same species. Communication is essential to any kind of social behavior and is the cement of social organization. The means by which animals communicate are highly varied and use all the senses.

Pheromones. The use of pheromones is a common form of insect communication. The female odor serves as a releaser for the male's fixed action pattern. The reason that insects cannot avoid traps with simulated pheromone attractants is that their directional movement is a positive chemotaxis, as automatic as a reflex. But pheromones can send all sorts of signals, marking territory, for instance. A tiger urinates along its path to let other tigers know the trail is taken.

▲ **A pheromone** secreted by the queen bee of a hive prevents all the other females in the group from becoming sexually mature. The queen then becomes the only bee in the hive that can mate and lay eggs.

Humpback whale

214

Wolf behavior involves tactile, visual, and auditory signals. ▶

Tactile signaling is particularly important among creatures with poor eyesight or no vision. Many deep-sea animals living in perpetual darkness have elaborate feelers to detect prey and sexual partners. Physical contact is especially important among primates and some other mammals in cementing social relationships. Wolves conduct a greeting ceremony of mutual licking, sniffing, and gentle nipping around the mouth. Monkeys deprived of the cuddling contact of their mothers grow up to be neurotic.

Visual signals can be sent only to animals with good vision. The receiver, of course, must be within line of sight, not a requirement for chemical or auditory communication. Visual signals have the advantage of being instantaneous, with the capacity of sending varied information. Gradations of intensity can be conveyed. A wolf changes its appearance, and shows increasing aggression, by gradually lowering its head, ruffling the fur on its neck and along its back, staring directly at its adversary, and finally baring its fangs. Disadvantages to visual communication are that it can take place only within a relatively short distance, has the danger of exposing the signaler to a predator, and usually cannot take place in the dark.

Sound. Sound is virtually instantaneous and can be projected over much greater distances than any other form of communication. Sound also can be sent through darkness and water. The howls of wolves can be heard for miles, and it is believed the low signal of a humpback whale can be detected by other whales hundreds of miles away. (See pages 802–805.)

- Sound production is limited to certain insects, such as crickets and locusts, to frogs, some reptiles, birds, and mammals.

- Signals can be so varied by changes in amplitude, frequency, rate, and sequencing that the amount of information that can be conveyed is almost infinite. Western and eastern meadowlarks, for instance, look alike, but their distinctive songs prevent inter-breeding where their ranges overlap in the American Southwest.

Conflict and Courtship

Competition

There is far more competition among members of the same species than between individuals of different species. Members of the same species require the same resources: the same kind of food, the best place to live, and a fit mate. There may not be enough of these to go around. Disputes arise, leading to fights. But nature has provided a solution to avoid serious injury. Confrontations between members of the same species are innate rituals that have been worked out over millions of years. These confrontations take place only when there is a challenge. But animal societies have found two main ways to hold these socially disruptive actions to a minimum.

Threat Display. The first stage of a confrontation over a mate or territory or social status is a threat display. The adversaries display their most threatening behaviors. This may be enough to discourage some contestants because the square-off is intended to decide which is the stronger, more vigorous, and motivated animal.

▲ **Competition** between members of the same species is usually settled without violence, although there may be a battle.

Fighting. If threat does not settle matters between animals, fighting takes place. But they are rarely lethal fights. Venomous snakes do not use their fangs; they wrestle. Male tortoises do not attack with their beaks or claws but instead try to overturn their opponent, rendering it helpless.

At some point, one of the animals concedes it is the weaker and adopts a submissive posture. This ritual action is a releaser that inhibits the victor from taking further aggressive action.

The bald-headed uakari is known for its hairless, bright red face. Like other monkeys, groups of uakaris studied in captivity display well-defined dominance hierarchies, social rankings determined by the ability of individuals to win conflicts.

Dominance Hierarchies

One outcome of fights is to establish social dominance. Many animal groups form dominance hierarchies with or without fighting. Social ranking may be decided by size—in the case of bighorn sheep, it is the size of the horns that determines dominance—or bluff. Chickens, after some squabbling that could include pecks with bills that inflict nondisabling wounds, sort themselves into a peck order. In a peck order, there is an absolute ranking. Number one is superior to all others. Number two is submissive to number one, but dominant over the others, and so on. This social order comes at the expense of the individuals at the lower end, which may not have a chance to mate, may suffer deprivation of food, and may have to live with the debilitating stress that goes with being an underling.

Territoriality

Territoriality is practiced by worms, arthropods, fish, birds, and mammals. Usually, an adult male will defend an area that has important resources. It could be a dead tree guarded by a woodpecker or a section of forest that provides food for a squirrel. Once a territory has been established, an animal will defend it and often will outfight stronger invaders. Choice territories attract would-be mates. Female red-winged blackbirds may virtually ignore a posturing resident male, but will closely inspect his territory for quality of food resources and nesting.

Courtship Behavior

Females may choose to mate with holders of territories and winners of battles for a very good reason—they are the most vigorous males and most likely to contribute to reproductive success.

In order to mate, animals must identify each other as belonging to the same species, as a member of the opposite sex, and as sexually receptive. In addition, many animals must overcome a natural resistance to the close approach of another animal.

For all these reasons, animals have developed a variety of courtship rituals. These rituals are innate behaviors that prevent the waste of energy and reproductive potential by the mating of inappropriate individuals.

Adult male peacocks have elaborate plumage, which they display for females during courtship. The plumage is heavy and slows down the males when they need to take sudden flight. The ability to survive with such an elaborate plumage signals to the female that this particular male is strong and healthy. ▼

- Male grasshoppers and crickets announce their species and sex by their chirps.

- The male peacock displays its gorgeous tail feathers. Females often have an unpretentious appearance since they do the choosing, and drabness protects them and their young from predators.

- The bowerbird is a drab male that overcomes this deficiency by dressing its nest with brightly colored objects, including some that humans discard.

- A courting drake acts mad. While swimming it may teeter-totter like a rocking horse, stand up straight in the water with its wings spread, dunk its beak in the water, bury it in its shoulder feathers, and then go on to other antics.

▲ **Courtship behavior,** which can sometimes involve quite an elaborate ritual, has developed in order to help animals identify appropriate mates.

The encounters of ungregarious animals can be tense, so that submissive signals are given.

Among spiders with poor vision, the male approaches the female in her web, but very gingerly. Vibrations on the web usually signal the presence of prey, so the male has developed an elaborate plucking ritual to signal that a suitor is on the way.

Social Interactions

Cooperation

Mating is a crucial act of cooperation in the extension of life. Parenting behavior is seen in some fish—where sometimes it is the male that builds a nest—and in amphibians, reptiles, birds, and mammals.

Cooperation in mammals is influenced by the fact that the mother has a built-in food supply that nurtures the newborn. While many mammals live in social groups, few mammals pair-bond, and few fathers participate in parenting. Exceptions are foxes, wolves, marmoset monkeys, and human beings.

The most conspicuous pair-bonding, with both mates sharing parental duties, is seen in birds. Many birds, such as ducks, mate for the season while some, such as eagles, geese, and swans, mate for life.

Another form of cooperation is communal parenting. All female ostriches in a harem lay eggs in a single nest to be incubated by the male and dominant female. In another form of communal nesting, a nest is shared by two mated couples of Mexican jays who are assisted by unmated individuals.

▲ **Ducks,** such as this pair of pochards, will usually mate just for one season.

Hunting. Social hunters include the wolves, hyenas, wild or hunting dogs, and lions. While fierce but solitary predators like leopards almost always kill prey smaller than themselves, group hunters often take animals larger than themselves. Group defense involves various strategies.

- Musk oxen will form a ring with horns outward around juveniles.

- Young penguins huddle together to give protection to one another from the cold and from attacks by gulls.

- Prairie dogs may trade off the role of sentry. These outlying scouts in the field have been known to sacrifice their lives in giving warning to their fellows.

ALTRUISM

Altruistic social behavior is often found among animals. Altruism is the expenditure of energy by one animal to help another without direct benefit to itself. All cases of parental behavior would come under this heading, and most—but not all—cases of altruistic behavior involve closely related animals. An exception would be a bird giving an alarm call for a predator that serves as a warning to all birds in the vicinity, including members of other species. Vervet monkeys have three different alarm calls to alert members of their troop against eagles, leopards, and snakes. Wolves in a pack other than the parents will regurgitate meat for cubs that beg, but usually members of a pack are related in some way. Whales and porpoises are

well known for coming to the help of one another. Whales have refused to leave a wounded animal or will actually support a sick whale, even one of another species.

Animal Societies

Some animals live in complex social groups and have clearly defined roles within those animal societies. Some of the most remarkable of these are the insect societies.

▲ **Ant colonies** differ enormously in size. A colony may have a dozen, hundreds, thousands, or in rare cases, even millions of members.

Complex insect societies are made possible because insect behavior is almost entirely instinctive. Any show of individuality would bring the collapse of the society. Social insects are born into one of several castes in the society. A caste is composed of individuals, each genetically programmed to perform a specific function.

Honeybees. Honeybees have three castes.

1. **The queen.** Its job is to produce about a thousand eggs each day in a lifetime of up to 10 years, and to regulate the lives of the workers. The queen does this with its sex pheromone, which both keeps females sterile and attracts males.

2. **Male bees,** called *drones*, mate with the queen during the first week of the queen's life, supplying enough sperm to fertilize more than 3 million eggs over the queen's lifetime. Their job done, the drones eventually are driven out of the hive or killed.

3. **Sterile female workers** do all the tasks necessary in the hive, including tending the queen and her eggs, guarding the hive against intruders, and foraging for food.

LIONS

Probably because vertebrates have greater freedom from innate behavior than insects, their societies are not so rigidly organized. Lions, unlike almost all other cats, which are solitary animals, live in a group called a pride. The pride can range in size from an adult male with a few females and cubs up to a total of 30 animals. The larger prides can at times be tense irritable assemblages, but the advantages of the group arrangement outweigh its disadvantages. The cubs can be reared communally—by the females— and the food from a kill shared with little waste.

Most cats are nocturnal, but lions will hunt during the day and at dusk as well as at night. The male is a larger animal than the female, but the male often leaves the hunting to the lioness. Lionesses frequently hunt in pairs, and group hunting is also practiced. The male's powerful roar is used sometimes to drive prey toward lionesses waiting in ambush.

ANIMAL INTELLIGENCE

The grandest achievement of nervous systems has been the development of brains and intelligence. The subject involves a relatively new understanding that intelligence is not the exclusive property of human beings.

Sponges do not have nervous systems. Radially symmetrical coelenterates such as jellyfish and hydras have nerve nets. Since these animals do not have a front end, there is no reason for nerves to group in one spot, and in general they do not. In a few places are clusters of neurons called *ganglia*, the beginning of brains. Nerve signals can be flashed in any direction.

From Ganglia to Brains

Brains

The centralized nervous system starts with animals that have bilateral symmetry, with a front end and a tail end giving the animal direction. Since the front end first encounters new environments, danger, food, and potential mates, sense organs were concentrated there.

A flatworm, in possessing a head ganglion, has a central nervous system—a brain prototype with longitudinal nerve cords. A flatworm can regenerate a complete body, including the head ganglion, from a severed tail end. A severed flatworm that has been reconstituted will remember previous conditioning as long as its neural RNA is intact, indicating that its memory is stored throughout the central nervous system.

Arthropods also have a pair of central nerve trunks and ganglia in their segments, as well as a central ganglion with connective cords ringing the digestive tract. In insects, eight ganglia in the abdominal segment are fused, taking on the dimensions of a brain. But space is a limiting factor for brain size.

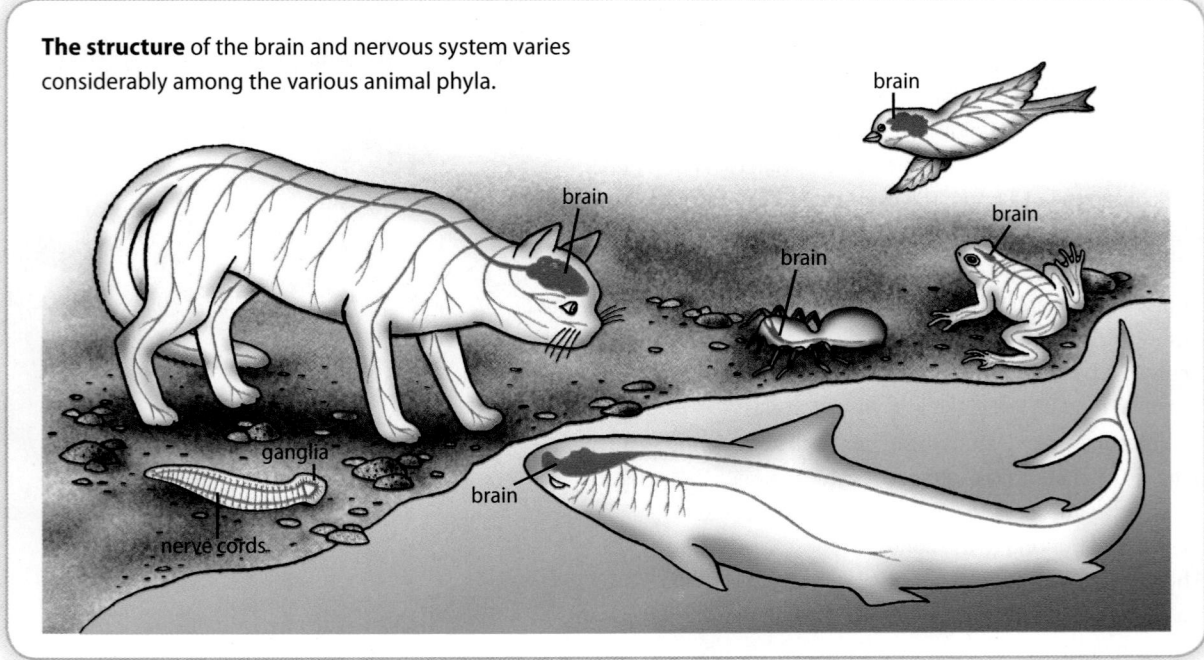

The structure of the brain and nervous system varies considerably among the various animal phyla.

Mollusks. Marine snails with sufficient neurons bunched in the head to form a well-developed ganglion crawl rapidly or even swim. The cephalopods, particularly the octopus, have developed a large, complex brain to rival the capabilities of some mammals. Octopuses in captivity have shown considerable learning ability in two-choice operant conditioning tests. They can discriminate between shapes and between colors; one animal even pulled a cork out of a bottle to reach a crab inside.

The Vertebrate Brain. With fish, a true brain has a chamber of its own in the head. What one sees is a steady enlargement of the cerebral hemispheres from the fish brain to the amphibian to the reptilian to the mammalian brain. This progression is further emphasized in mammals. Not only does brain size increase from rat to cat to monkey to chimpanzee to human being, so does the size of the cerebral cortex, the outer layer that constitutes the thinking part of the brain.

There is another progression. The cerebral cortex of a rat is almost entirely filled with areas that direct the animal's sensory and motor functions and instinctual behavior. Very little of the rat's cortex is left unassigned at birth. This open or association area increases from rat to human being.

There is no structural difference between human and other mammalian brains. The difference is in size and proportion. With a much greater cortex and association area, the human brain has up to 100 billion neurons. The complexity of the brain is measured by the fact that each neuron is connected to 1,000 to 100,000 other neurons—a network of up to 10 quadrillion interconnections. (See pages 230–231.)

The power of this mental instrument has made it self-evident to human beings throughout history that their species is distinct from all other animals. But recent field research has raised the question of whether intelligence—insight and reasoning—may extend further into the animal world.

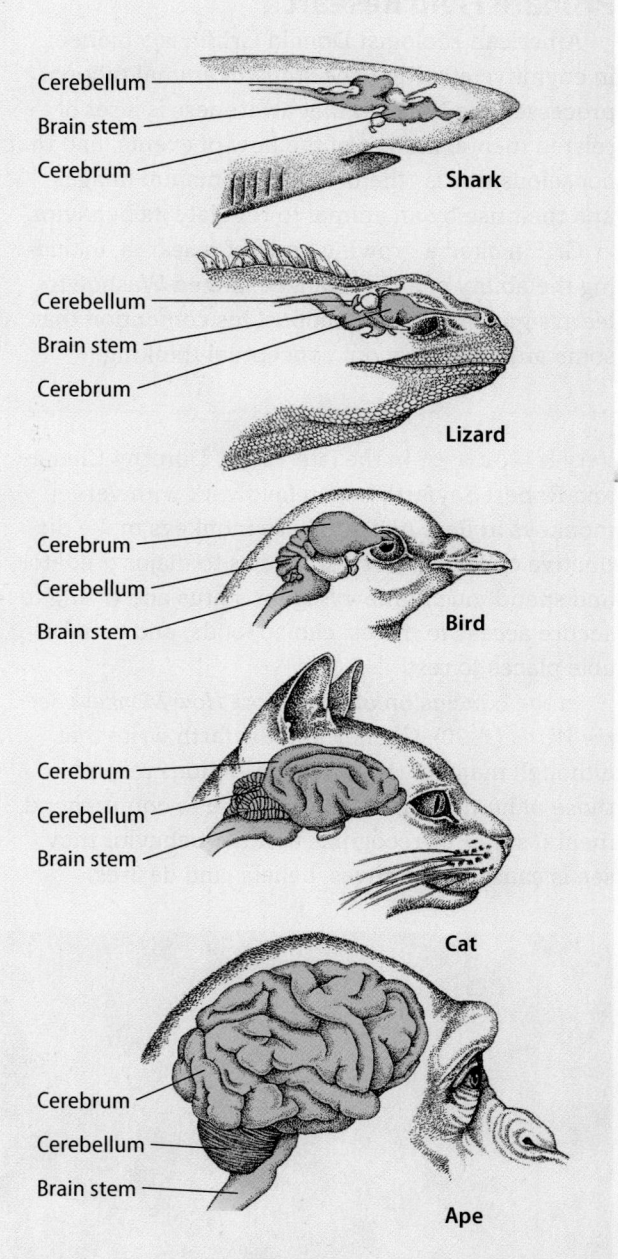

▲ **Brains of some vertebrates** show the progression of brain development as animals evolved over millions of years. Sharks and other fish have a relatively simple brain with a small, smooth cerebrum. The cerebrum is larger but still quite smooth in reptiles and birds. The most advanced mammals, such as cats and apes, have a large, wrinkled cerebrum with billions of neurons.

Intelligence in the Great Apes

Primate Field Research

American zoologist Donald Griffin is a pioneer in cognitive ethology, the study of animal thought processes. He has said that awareness is a set of related mental images of the flow of events, and that consciousness is "the presence of mental images, and their use by an animal to regulate its behavior."

Griffin cited a growing body of research, including the ability of a chimpanzee named Washoe to learn sign language, to support his contention that some animals carry out conceptual thinking.

Vervet Monkeys. In the late 1970s, Dorothy Cheney and Robert Seyfarth began fieldwork with vervet monkeys in East Africa. These monkeys make distinctive calls to alert their fellows to major predators and spend much time vying for status and trying to secure access to mates, choice foods, and comfortable places to rest.

In the conclusion of the report *How Monkeys See the World* (1990), Cheney and Seyfarth write that although many of the monkeys' actions resemble those of humans, they seem unable to comprehend mental states or recognize that the behavior they see is caused by motives, beliefs, and desires.

▲ **Vervet monkeys** were the subject of pioneering research in the field of primate field research.

Great Apes. Field studies of the great apes were made by Birute Galdikas with orangutans, Dian Fossey with mountain gorillas, Jane Goodall with groups of chimpanzees, and Frans de Waal with bonobos, generally known as pygmy chimps. In comparing social behavior in the wild with that in captivity, investigators were able to verify that there are no great differences in the behavior exhibited by the animals living in the two different environments.

Gordon Gallup in 1979 and 1980 showed that chimpanzees can use mirrors to recognize themselves and to remove spots of paint from their brows that could be seen only in a mirror. Although monkeys have used mirrors to look around corners and can recognize the reflections of other monkeys, they cannot learn to recognize themselves. But chimps could recognize themselves on video monitors as they were being televised live. The television screen, of course, showed them smaller than life size. The chimpanzees also quickly distinguished live from recorded scenes and lost interest in the recorded ones.

Chimpanzee Intelligence. Primatologist Alison Jolly cites various examples of social awareness—deception and concealment, distraction and lying, planning ahead, and creating an image. To illustrate the last two abilities, Jolly took an example from Jane Goodall's field observations. Mike, a socially inferior male, was being ignored and ostracized by a group of males. Finally, Mike came into Goodall's tent, took two empty kerosene cans, and carried them back to his former place. Mike began to rock from side to side and issue hoots. The other males paid no attention, whereupon Mike charged them, banging the cans ahead of him. Startled, the superior males fled. Mike waited until his rivals had resumed grooming, then scattered them again with another charge. He did this four times, enhancing his social status in the process.

▲ **Dr. Jane Goodall** devoted her life to extensive work with groups of chimpanzees, including these at Gombe Stream National Park, studying their behavior and social structure.

Years later, Goodall came upon a young chimp named Figan alone in the forest "practicing" his charging technique, even using the kerosene cans that by this time had catapulted Mike to the position of dominant male.

Jolly and other scientists believe that social behavior in primates is far more complicated in its demands on intelligence than other environmental problems. Indeed, the growth of human language and intelligence is attributed to the skills that were required to master such difficult social arrangements.

Spotlight on... JANE GOODALL

1934–

Jane Goodall is an English zoologist who studies the behavior of animals. She became known for her studies of chimpanzees. She has also worked to ensure that chimps survive in the wild. Goodall began her research in 1960 at what is now Gombe Stream National Park in northwestern Tanzania. She won the trust of many chimpanzees through daily contact with them. She observed them at close range and wrote detailed reports.

Before Goodall's research, scientists believed that chimpanzees ate chiefly fruits and vegetables. But Goodall found that chimpanzees also hunt and eat larger animals. Their prey includes young monkeys and pigs. She also discovered that they make and use tools more than any other animal except human beings. Goodall observed them stripping tree twigs and using the twigs as tools for catching termites. She also observed one group of chimpanzees kill off another group for no obvious survival reason. Goodall's research surprised most naturalists because it suggests that hunting, tool use, and "warfare" are not unique to human beings.

Valerie Jane Goodall was born on April 3, 1934, in London. She earned a Ph.D. from Cambridge University. Her writings include *My Friends, the Wild Chimpanzees* (1967), *In the Shadow of Man* (1971), *The Chimpanzees of Gombe* (1986), and *Through a Window* (1990). She has also produced numerous films on the Gombe chimpanzees.

HUMAN ANATOMY

includes the study of the structure of the skeleton, muscles, nerves, and the various organs of the human body. Knowledge of the structure of the body is essential for an understanding of its function in health and disease.

The human body is highly adaptable. It has few specialized features that could limit its activities. People can walk, run, swim, and climb. Human adaptability enables people to live in an extremely wide variety of environments—from the tropics to the Arctic.

A human being starts out as one cell. In time, this tiny cell develops into a newborn and eventually an entire adult body consisting of trillions of cells that make up the many parts of the human anatomy.

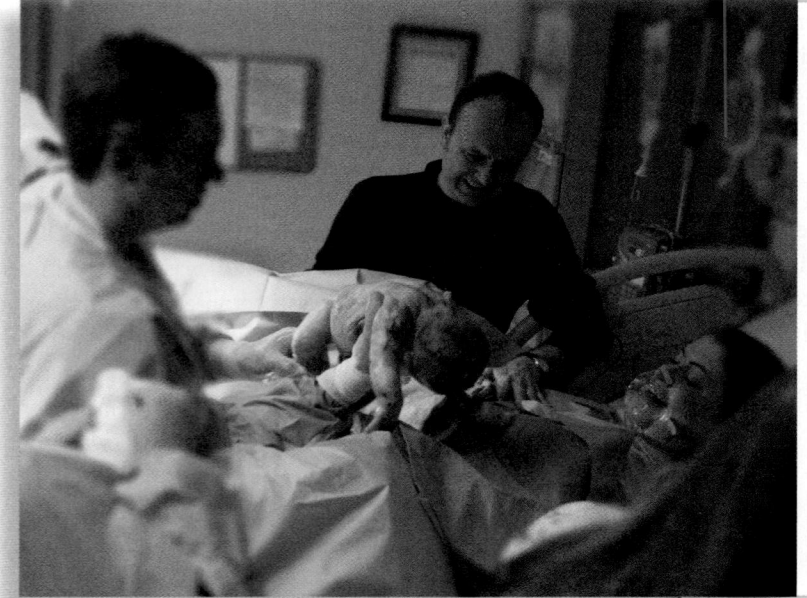

The Human Body

In many ways, the human body can be compared to a machine. Like a machine, the body is made up of many parts. Each part of the body, like each part of a machine, does special jobs. But all the parts work together to make the body or the machine run smoothly. Also like a machine, the body needs energy to work. This energy is produced by the cellular breakdown of food in the presence of oxygen.

HARD-WORKING ORGANS

Many body parts, such as the heart and kidneys, work continuously throughout a person's life.

- The heart of a 70-year-old person has pumped about 208 million liters (55 million gallons) of blood during that person's life.
- The kidneys of a 70-year-old have removed wastes from more than 3.8 million liters (1 million gallons) of blood.

Amazing Anatomy

Although it can be compared to a machine, the human body can do things that no machine can do.

Growth. The human body can grow. The body starts out as one cell. In time, this tiny cell develops into a body consisting of trillions of cells.

Repair. The human body can also replace certain worn-out parts. Each day, several billion cells in the body die and are replaced through the process of cell division. Thus, the body is always rebuilding itself. Every 35 to 45 days, for instance, the human body replaces the outermost layer of skin.

The human body can defend itself against hundreds of diseases. The body can also repair itself after most small injuries.

Sensing the Environment

By using its senses, the body can detect changes in its surroundings, such as changes in temperature, light, or sounds. It can adjust to these changes quickly. The body's senses are truly incredible. For instance, people can learn to identify thousands of odors, yet our sense of smell is not as highly developed as in other members of the animal kingdom.

Detecting Changes

The human body can also detect changes that occur within itself, such as changes in body temperature. The various parts of the body continuously adjust their activities to keep the "inside" environment normal.

Such adjustments rely on a system of nerves that carries messages from one part of the body to another. The messages travel at speeds of up to 400 to 425 feet (120 to 130 meters) per second.

THE basics

HUMAN ANATOMY

✔ **The skeletal system** consists of the axial skeleton (the bones of the head, neck and trunk) and the appendicular skeleton (the bones of the arms and legs).

✔ **The muscular system,** with more than 600 muscles, moves the human body. The two main types of muscle are skeletal muscle and smooth muscle.

✔ **The nervous system** controls bodily functions and consists of the central nervous system and the peripheral nervous system.

✔ **The circulatory system** carries blood throughout the body, supplying the cells with food and oxygen and carrying carbon dioxide and other wastes away from the cells.

✔ **The respiratory system** consists of the organs of breathing. It delivers oxygen to the blood and rids the body of carbon dioxide.

✔ **The digestive system** breaks down food into simple substances that the cells can use and absorbs the substances into the bloodstream.

✔ **The reproductive system** consists of the sex glands and organs that enable men and women to produce children.

✔ **The endocrine system** produces hormones, substances that regulate various body functions.

✔ **The urinary system** removes various wastes from the blood and flushes them from the body.

✔ **The integumentary system** consists of the skin, which is the largest organ of the body, as well as the hair, nails, and sweat glands.

✔ **The sense organs** provide people with information about their environment. The five main sense organs are the eyes, ears, nose, tongue, and skin. There are also internal senses that give the body information about itself.

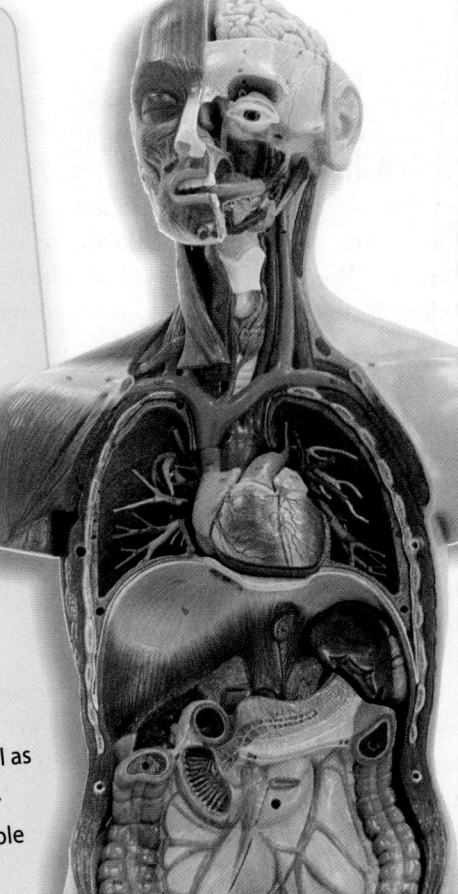

The human body consists of many parts working together. The parts are divided into systems based on their functions.

Skeletal System

The *skeleton* is a bony, flexible framework that gives shape to the bodies of humans and other vertebrates. It serves as a scaffolding to protect vital organs and, activated by the muscles, aids in body movement.

There are about 206 bones in the adult body, of varying shapes and sizes. These 206 bones are divided into two main parts.

- the axial skeleton
- the appendicular skeleton

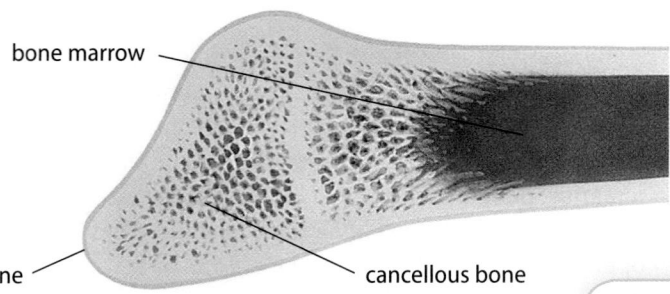

Parts of a Bone. There are two forms of bone, hard *compact bone* and spongy *cancellous bone.* The bone's center, called the *medullary cavity,* is filled with marrow.

The Axial Skeleton

The axial skeleton is made up of the bones of the head, neck, and trunk. Cranial bones of the skull form the dome-shaped casing for the brain. The facial bones form the features and protect the eyes and the oral and nasal passages.

The spine, or *spinal column*, with its flexible vertebrae supports the head and trunk of the body and shields the spinal cord. The spine consists of separate bones, called *vertebrae*, with fibrous disks between them. Seven bones make up the *cervical vertebrae* (neck bones). The 12 *thoracic vertebrae* are at the back of the chest.

The ribs are attached to the thoracic vertebrae. The cylinder-like rib cage shelters the heart, lungs, liver, and spleen. There are usually 12 ribs on each side of the body. The upper ribs fasten in front to the *sternum* (breastbone). The ribs protect the heart and lungs and act as a bellows box for the breathing process.

Lower Vertebrae and Pelvis. The five *lumbar* vertebrae lie in the lower part of the back. Below the last lumbar vertebra is the *sacrum*. The pelvis is attached to the sacrum. The pelvic bones protect internal organs. The *coccyx* is at the bottom of the spine.

The Appendicular Skeleton

The appendicular skeleton is made up of the bones of the arms and legs and their supports.

Arms. The *shoulder girdle* consists of the *scapula* (shoulder blade) and the *clavicle* (collarbone). The skeleton of the arm is divided into the

- *humerus* (upper arm)
- *radius* and *ulna* (forearm)
- *carpus* (wrist bones)
- *metacarpus* (palm)
- *phalanges* (fingers)

Legs. The leg is attached to the trunk by a pelvic girdle made up of two hipbones. Each hipbone consists of three bones:

- the *ilium*
- the *ischium*
- the *pubis*

The bones of the leg consist of the

- *femur* (thigh)
- *tibia* and *fibula* (lower leg)
- *tarsus* (back of the foot)
- *metatarsus* (forefoot)
- *phalanges* (toes)

Bones

Bones are thought of as hard and dry, but in fact, water makes up about one-quarter of the weight of human bone. Another quarter consists of organic matter: *collagen* (connective tissue, a type of protein) fibers. The remaining half consists of inorganic compounds: calcium, phosphorus, and other minerals.

Composition. Bones are covered on the outside by a fibrous membrane, the *periosteum,* and lined inside by the *endosteum.* The center of a bone—the medullary cavity—is filled with either red or yellow *bone marrow.* Yellow bone marrow consists mostly of fat. Red bone marrow is a network of blood vessels, connective tissue, and blood-forming cells. Red bone marrow makes red blood cells. All bones have blood vessels and nerves.

Specialized Cells. Bone tissue contains three kinds of specialized cells.

1. **Osteoblasts** form bone matrix by laying down collagen fibers and other proteins and depositing hard mineral material.

2. **Osteocytes** are osteoblasts that have become trapped in the bone matrix they manufactured and live embedded there for years. Osteocytes help to control the mineral balance of the body and also respond to the stresses created by physical activity.

3. **Osteoclasts** erode the matrix during normal bone turnover, during growth, and during the healing of fractures.

Joints

Bones are attached to each other by a series of tissues known as *joints.* Joints are made up of

- *cartilages* (smooth tissues that reduce friction)
- *ligaments* (strands of elastic, fibrous tissue), which hold together the ends of bone, keeping them properly aligned

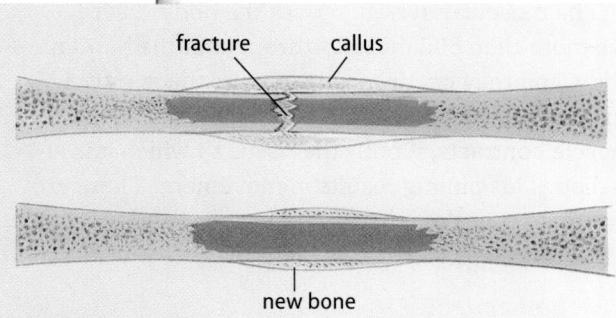

fracture   callus

new bone

BROKEN BONES

When a bone breaks, a doctor should set it as soon as possible and put it in a plaster cast if necessary. The cast holds the bone securely in place. When a bone breaks into several pieces, doctors may wire or pin the pieces together for proper healing.

In most cases, the body forms a *fracture callus,* a mass of new cartilage and bone, to hold the broken ends together. New bone gradually replaces the callus to finally heal the fracture. This process takes from 4 weeks to a year, depending on the size of the bone, the location of the fracture, and the patient's age and health.

In some cases, the break does not heal by itself. Doctors treat such *nonunion fractures* with bone grafts or with electrical current to stimulate bone growth.

X-RAYS

During an experiment with electric current in 1895, German physicist Wilhelm Conrad Roentgen discovered an unknown form of radiation that he called X-rays.

Roentgen found that these rays passed easily through some substances, such as flesh, but were largely stopped by others, such as metal or bone. Roentgen was able to use the rays to photograph the bones of his wife's hand.

The use of X-rays revolutionized medical and surgical techniques, and eventually provided scientists with new insights into the nature of radiation and the structure of the atom.

Muscular System

The muscular system moves the body. There are more than 600 muscles throughout the human body, and they occur mostly in pairs. Each muscle consists of special fibers that can contract. When a muscle contracts, it pulls the tissue to which it is attached. This pulling results in movement. There are two main types of muscles.

- skeletal muscles
- smooth muscles

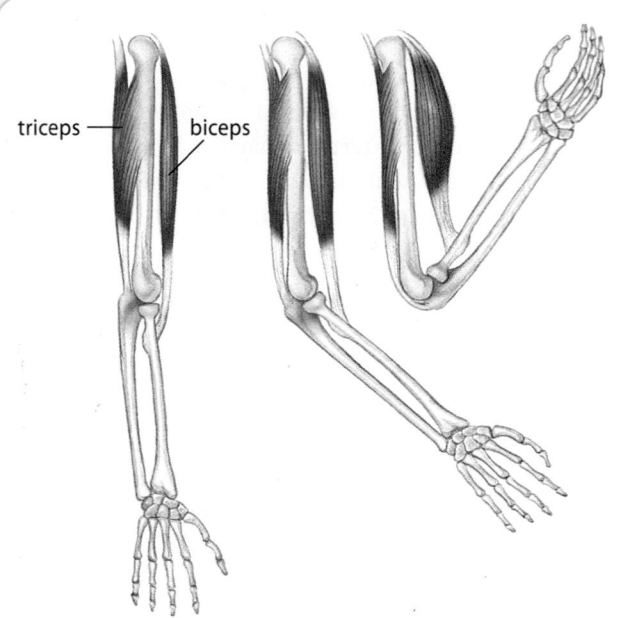

Skeletal Muscles

- the consciously controlled muscles; known as *voluntary muscles*
- attached to the bones
- move the bones of the arms, legs, fingers, and other parts of the skeleton
- made up of fibers called striations that have alternate light and dark crossbands

Attachments. One end of each skeletal muscle is attached to a bone that does not move when the muscle contracts. In most cases, the other end of the muscle is attached to another bone, either directly or by means of cordlike bundles of connective tissue called *tendons*. This second bone moves when the muscle contracts.

PULLING IN PAIRS

Muscles move the body only by pulling. They cannot push the tissues to which they are attached. Two sets of muscles therefore control most skeletal movements, such as the raising and then lowering of the forearm. One set pulls the bones in one direction, and the other set pulls the bones in the opposite direction. Such pairs of muscles are known as antagonistic muscles.

For example, one set of muscles pulls the forearm up, but it cannot push the forearm down. To lower the forearm, a second set of muscles must contract and pull it down.

Some Important Skeletal Muscles		
Part of Body	Muscle	Action
face	several different muscles	work together to help express emotion—to smile, frown, or raise an eyebrow; make it possible to bite, chew, or speak
shoulder	deltoids	raise the arms
shoulder	trapezius	raises the shoulder; pulls back the head
upper arm	biceps	bend the elbow
upper arm	triceps	straighten the elbow
torso	diaphragm	main muscle involved with breathing; laughing, coughing, sneezing
buttocks	gluteus medius and gluteus maximus	move the body from sitting to standing; help the body to run or walk up stairs
thigh	sartorius and quadriceps	bend knees, move legs, balance when standing
thigh	hamstrings (biceps femoris; semitendinous and membranous tendons)	bend the knee joint; straighten the hip joint

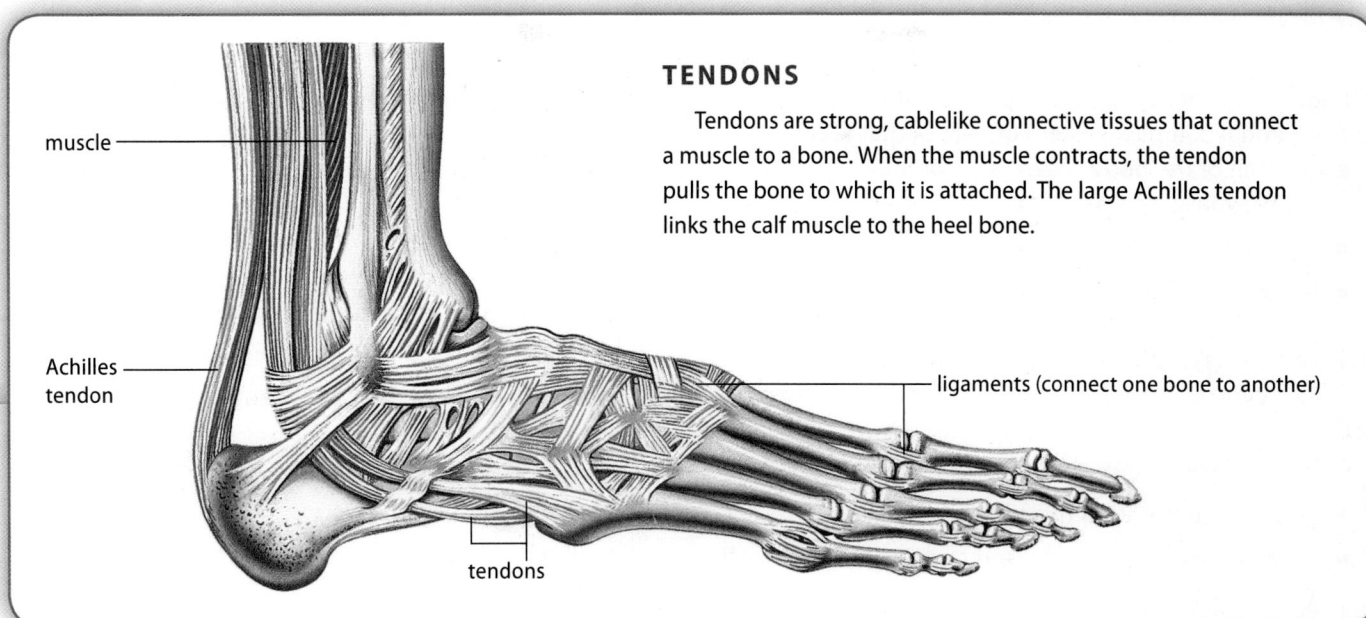

TENDONS

Tendons are strong, cablelike connective tissues that connect a muscle to a bone. When the muscle contracts, the tendon pulls the bone to which it is attached. The large Achilles tendon links the calf muscle to the heel bone.

muscle

Achilles tendon

ligaments (connect one bone to another)

tendons

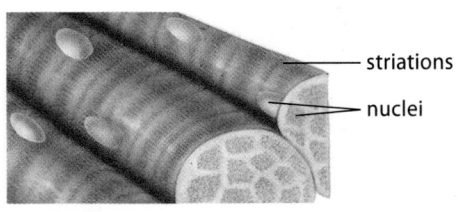

striations

nuclei

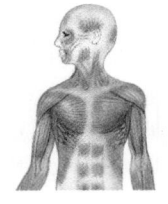

Skeletal Muscles

Smooth Muscles

- the *involuntary muscles;* contract and relax automatically—a person has no direct control over them
- found in most of the body's internal organs
- do not have striations
- cannot contract as rapidly as skeletal muscles
- can contract more completely than skeletal muscles and do not tire as quickly
- can produce powerful, rhythmic contractions over long periods

Vital Functions. Smooth muscles in the walls of the stomach and intestines move food through the digestive system. Smooth muscles also control the diameter of the blood vessels and the size of the breathing passages.

intestine

nucleus

Smooth Muscles

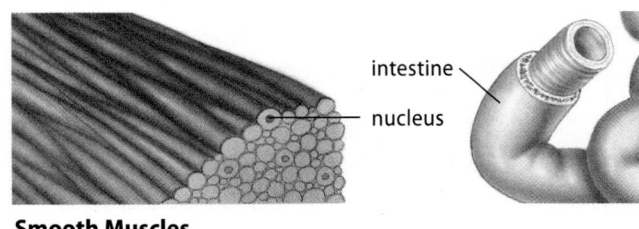

striations

nucleus

Cardiac Muscles

Cardiac Muscle

There is a third kind of muscle that is found only in the heart. Called *cardiac muscle,* it has features of both skeletal muscle and smooth muscle. Cardiac muscle has striations like skeletal muscle, but contracts automatically and rhythmically like smooth muscle.

Cardiac muscle enables the heart to beat an average of 70 times a minute without rest throughout a person's lifetime.

Nervous System

The nervous system controls and coordinates all bodily functions. It is made up of the brain, the spinal cord, and a complex system of nerves that reaches every inch of the body. There are two main divisions of the nervous system.

- the central nervous system
- the peripheral nervous system

The Central Nervous System

The central nervous system (CNS), which consists of the brain and spinal cord, functions as the control center of the nervous system. The central nervous system

- receives information from the senses.
- analyzes this information and decides how the body should respond.
- sends instructions that trigger the required actions.

How the CNS Decides. The central nervous system makes some simple decisions within the spinal cord, such as directing the hand to pull away from a hot object. Such simple decisions are called *spinal reflexes.*

Most decisions, however, involve the brain. Much brain activity occurs at the conscious level. We are aware of decisions made at this level and can voluntarily control them. Other activity occurs at the subconscious level. This activity regulates the smooth muscles and is beyond voluntary control.

The Peripheral Nervous System

The peripheral nervous system is made up of the nerves that connect the central nervous system with every part of the body. These nerves include both *sensory neurons,* which carry information to the central nervous system, and *motor neurons,* which relay instructions from the central nervous system.

The body has many kinds of sense *receptors.*

- Vision receptors in the eyes change light waves into nerve impulses.
- Hearing receptors in the ears convert sound waves into nerve impulses.
- Smell receptors in the nose convert chemical information into nerve impulses.
- Taste receptors on the tongue convert chemical information into nerve impulses.
- Receptors in the skin respond to heat, cold, pressure, touch, and pain.
- Receptors deep within the body provide information on the chemical and physical conditions of inner body tissues.

The autonomic nervous system is part of the peripheral nervous system. It carries messages from the subconscious level of the brain to the internal organs. The autonomic nervous system regulates such automatic functions of the body as the beating of the heart.

HOW MESSAGES ARE SENT

Neurons serve as local headquarters for the nerve unit. Each neuron has one or more nerve fibers extending from its center. These fibers vary in length from a fraction of an inch or centimeter to 3 feet or more (about 1 meter), depending on their function. *Axons,* the longer fibers, carry nerve impulses away from the cell body. *Dendrites,* the shorter fibers, carry nerve impulses toward the cell body.

Nerve impulses travel by a kind of chain reaction, one neuron triggering the next along the nerve pathway. When the nerve impulse reaches a nerve junction, or *synapse,* it causes the release of a chemical substance at the nerve endings. This substance enables the impulse to bridge the gap between nerve endings and go on to the next neuron.

Sensory neurons carry messages from various parts of the body through the spinal cord or directly to the brain. Motor neurons carry messages from the brain or spinal cord to tissues and muscles in fingers, toes, heart, and elsewhere.

The fibers of the motor neurons terminate in *motor end plates,* which are small flat structures coming in close contact with individual muscle fibers. When the nerve impulse arrives at the motor end plate, the nerve ending releases *acetylcholine,* a chemical substance that acts as a neurotransmitter to trigger muscle cell activity. As the muscle contracts, an enzyme called *cholinesterase* breaks down and clears away the acetylcholine, making way for the next chemical cycle.

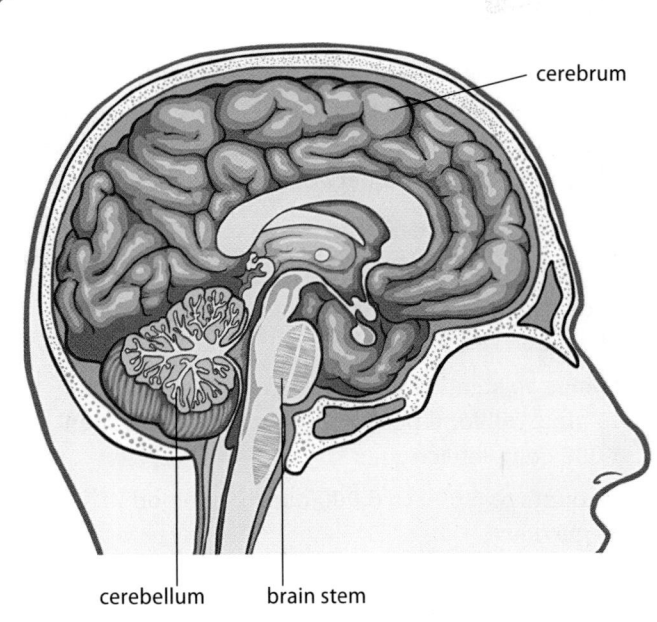

cerebrum

cerebellum　brain stem

The brain is an enormously complicated collection of billions of neurons. These neurons are linked together in precise patterns that enable the brain to think and remember.

The Brain

The key organ of the nervous system is the brain. (See also pages 220–221.) It consists of three main sections.

- cerebrum
- cerebellum
- brain stem

The cerebrum is the largest section of the brain. The outer layer of the cerebrum is called the *cerebral cortex*. It is about 1/8-inch (0.4 cm) thick and is convoluted into many folds. The cortex contains billions of neurons, or nerve cells. These cells extend into an area below the cerebral hemispheres, the two halves of the cerebrum, which control conscious mental activity.

The cerebellum aids in maintaining body balance and coordination of muscle movement.

The brain stem contains vital reflex centers that help to control heart rate, blood pressure, and respiration.

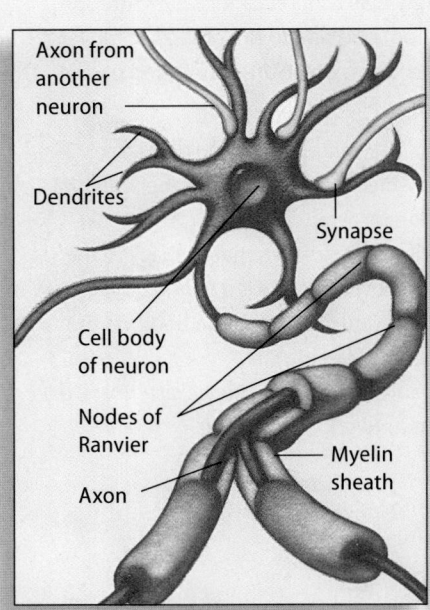

Axon from another neuron

Dendrites

Synapse

Cell body of neuron

Nodes of Ranvier

Axon

Myelin sheath

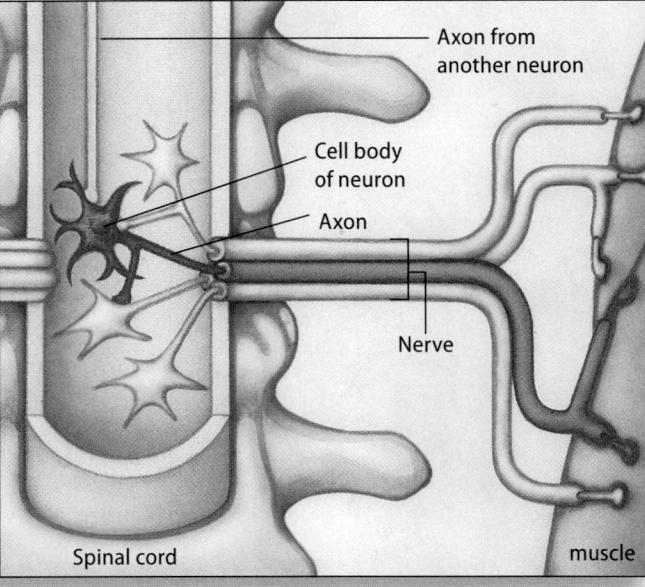

Axon from another neuron

Cell body of neuron

Axon

Nerve

Spinal cord

muscle

A neuron has three basic parts. The *cell body* serves as the control center for the cell's activities. The *axon* is a tubelike extension that carries messages. The *dendrites* are shorter extensions specialized to receive messages. A nerve consists of a cordlike bundle of axons from several neurons. The nerve shown runs from the spinal cord to a muscle.

Circulatory System

The circulatory system carries blood throughout the body. Blood circulates continuously—in and out of the heart, throughout the body, and back to the heart again to start another cycle. The circulatory system consists of three main parts.

- the heart
- the blood vessels
  (*arteries, arterioles, capillaries, venules,* and *veins*)
- the blood

Functions of the Circulatory System

- supplies the cells of the body with food and oxygen
- carries carbon dioxide and other wastes away from the cells
- helps regulate body temperature
- carries substances that protect the body from disease
- transports chemical substances called *hormones,* which help regulate the activities of various parts of the body

The Heart

The heart is a bundle of muscles, about the size of a fist and weighing less than a pound. It beats continuously throughout a person's lifetime; its only pause is the fraction of a second between heartbeats.

- contracts and dilates at an average rate of 72 beats a minute, each cardiac cycle lasting about 0.85 second
- adds up to about 100,000 times a day, or nearly 40 million times a year
- pumps so steadily and powerfully that it forces 10 pints of blood per minute through more than 1,000 complete circuits
- amounts to 5,000 to 6,000 quarts of blood in a single day

Structure of the Heart. The heart has four chambers: the upper left and right *atria* are the receiving chambers, while the lower left and right *ventricles* are the pumping chambers.

Each atrium is separated from the ventricle beneath it by a valve. A wall of muscle, called a *septum,* separates the left and right side of the heart.

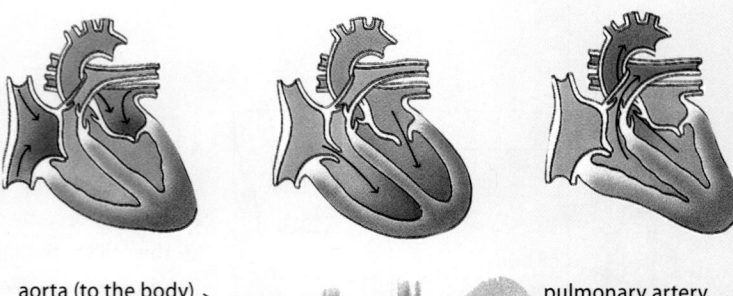

THE FLOW OF BLOOD

In a healthy heart, blood cannot pass through the system from one side to the other, but moves by way of the lungs, which are considered part of the respiratory system. Blood flows

- from the right atrium down into the right ventricle, which forces blood into the lungs via the pulmonary artery.
- from the lungs (now oxygenated) back to the left atrium, down into the left ventricle.
- from the left ventricle out to the body via the aorta, or great artery.
- from the aorta out to the arteries, arterioles, and a vast network of capillaries.

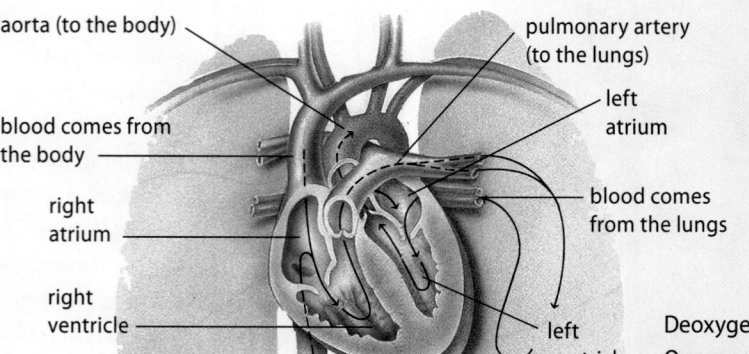

aorta (to the body)

pulmonary artery (to the lungs)

left atrium

blood comes from the body

blood comes from the lungs

right atrium

right ventricle

left ventricle

Deoxygenated blood is shown in blue.
Oxygenated blood is shown in red.

The Blood

The blood has four main components:

- plasma
- red blood cells (erythrocytes)
- white blood cells (leukocytes)
- platelets (thrombocytes)

Plasma makes up 55 percent of a person's blood. It is a straw-colored liquid that consists of 92 percent water. The remaining 8 percent contains nutrients, special inorganic materials, proteins, antibodies, and hormones.

Red blood cells are shaped like disks and outnumber white blood cells 700 to one. They carry oxygen from the lungs to all parts of the body, and carry off waste carbon dioxide. Red blood cells live for about 3 to 4 months, being replaced by new recruits sent into the bloodstream from bone marrow, where they are manufactured.

White blood cells protect the body against the invasion of toxic organisms by engulfing and destroying them.

Platelets, which are tiny, flat fragments of cells, are vital in producing coagulation, or blood clotting.

The Blood Vessels

The blood vessels form a complicated system of connecting tubes throughout the body. There are three major types of these vessels.

- *Arteries* carry blood from the heart.
- *Veins* return blood to the heart.
- *Capillaries* are extremely narrow vessels that connect the arteries and the veins. Capillaries are smaller in diameter than a hair.

Lymphatic System

The lymphatic system is sometimes considered a part of the circulatory system. It consists of a network of small vessels that return fluid from body tissue to the bloodstream. The lymphatic system consists of: *lymph capillaries, lacteals, lymph nodes, lymph vessels,* and the main lymphatic ducts *(thoracic and right lymphatic ducts).*

Lymph is a pale, watery fluid that helps oxygen, nutrients, and waste pass between the capillaries and the body cells. The body contains about 2 gallons (7.5 liters) of lymph.

The lymph nodes, scattered along the lymph route, are cell-manufacturing factories that produce *lymphocytes.* Lymphocytes act as filters to keep bacteria from entering the bloodstream. Lymphocytes normally number from 20 to 50 percent of all white cells.

The lymphatic system includes all the structures that carry lymph from the tissues to the blood. ▼

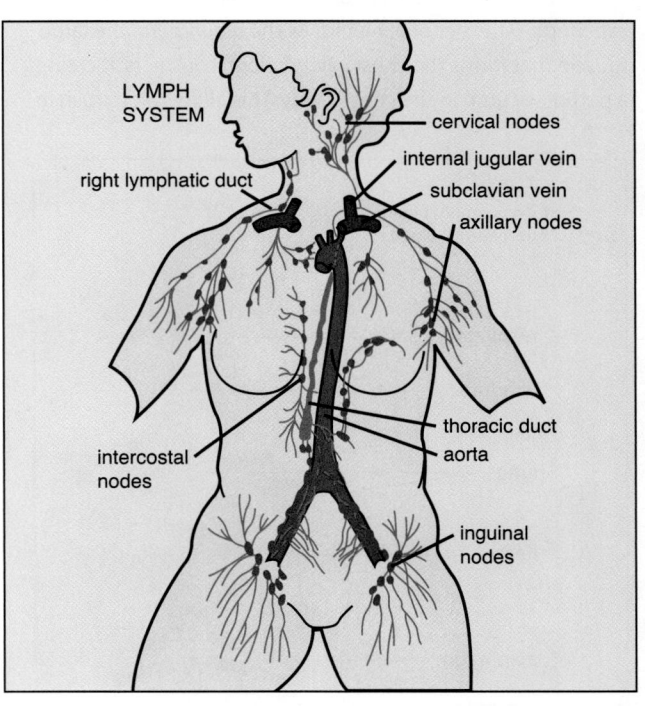

Respiratory System

The respiratory system consists of the organs of breathing. These include the nose, the *pharynx* (the cavity behind the nose and mouth), the *trachea* (windpipe), the *larynx* (voice box), and the lungs. The respiratory system performs two main functions.

- delivering oxygen to the blood (through inspiration)
- ridding the body of carbon dioxide (through expiration)

The cells of the body need oxygen to break down and release the energy in food. During this process, carbon dioxide forms as a waste product.

Upper Respiratory Tract

Oxygen enters the body when a person inhales. Air entering the respiratory system goes first to the upper respiratory tract—the nose, pharynx, and larynx—where it is filtered, warmed, and moistened.

Lower Respiratory Tract

The lower respiratory tract begins with the trachea, at the end of which it divides into two *bronchi,* one entering the left lung and the other the right lung. Inside the lung, these bronchi continue to subdivide into smaller bronchi, then into *bronchioles,* and finally into tiny thin-walled, balloonlike air sacs, the *alveoli.*

The alveoli constitute the bulk of lung tissue. There are an estimated 300 million of these air sacs in an average adult. It is these alveoli, rather than the chest, that actually expand or contract during breathing, and provide the vital surface needed for intake of oxygen into the blood.

The pleura is an airtight membranous sac that covers the lungs as well as the inner walls of the chest. The pleura secretes a lubricating fluid that prevents the pleural layers from rubbing against the chest wall.

BREATHE IN, BREATHE OUT

Breathing involves *inspiration*—the act of inhaling—and *expiration*—the act of exhaling. As the *diaphragm,* the large muscle that forms the chest cavity's floor, contracts, it creates a partial vacuum in the chest cavity. This allows air to rush in and fill the trachea, bronchi, and alveoli. With the drawing in of air, the alveoli expand. Relaxation of the diaphragm muscles forces the air out again. With the expulsion of air, the alveoli contract.

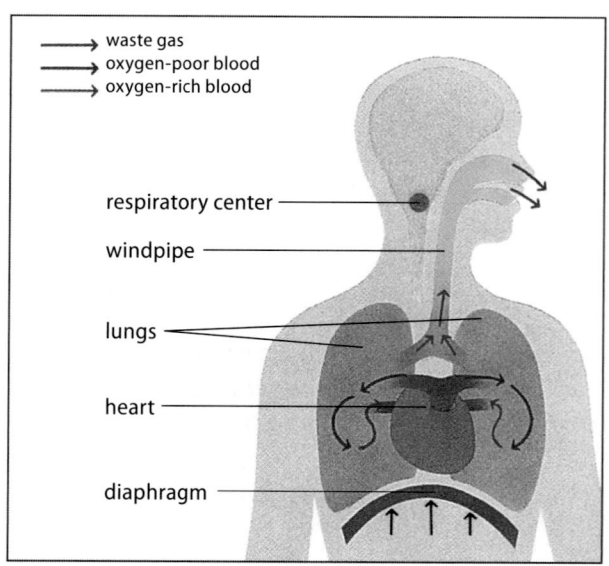

Inspiration

Expiration

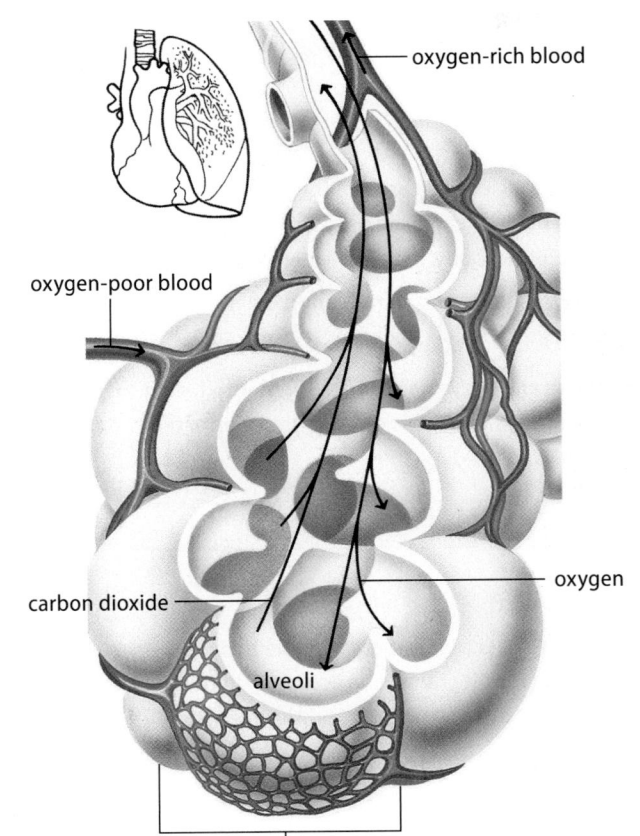

exchange of carbon dioxide and oxygen

The lungs weigh about 2½ pounds (1.1 kilograms). They can hold from 3 to 5 quarts (2.8–4.8 liters) of air. The right lung consists of three lobes (sections). The left lung consists of two lobes. A lung has a spongy texture and may be thought of as an elastic bag filled with millions of tiny air chambers (the alveoli).

The Brain's Role

The rate and depth of breathing are controlled by respiratory centers in the brain, one located in the medulla oblongata. These centers are sensitive to the blood's chemical content, especially to carbon dioxide.

During sleep, the amount of carbon dioxide in the blood is low, and the respiratory centers slow down the breathing rate.

During waking hours, with more vigorous exertion, there is an increased amount of carbon dioxide in the blood; this automatically stimulates deep and rapid breathing.

CARBON DIOXIDE/OXYGEN EXCHANGE

The circulatory system carries oxygen to the body tissues and carries carbon dioxide away from them in the blood.

Carbon dioxide and oxygen are exchanged in the lungs, which lie close to the heart. Each lung contains millions of *alveoli,* or air sacs. Blood vessels, shown here only on the bottom sac, surround each alveolus. As blood flows through these vessels, it releases carbon dioxide, a waste picked up from the body tissues, into the alveoli. It then receives fresh oxygen from the alveoli.

TINY HAIRS AND MUCUS

The nasal passages are lined with tiny hairlike structures called *cilia* and a sticky substance called *mucus.* When we inhale, air enters the body through the nose (or the mouth). The cilia and mucus filter dust and dirt from the air, keeping foreign bodies from entering the lungs.

Exercise. As the body exerts itself during exercise, the muscles need more oxygen. The body responds by taking more frequent breaths to ensure that the right amount of oxygen is taken in and the right amount of carbon dioxide is let out.

Digestive System

The digestive system breaks down food into simple substances that the cells can use. It then absorbs these substances into the bloodstream and eliminates any leftover waste matter.

The main part of the digestive system is a long tube called the *alimentary canal.* This tube consists of two main sections:

- the mouth, esophagus, and stomach
- the small intestine and large intestine

Other parts of the digestive system include the gall-bladder, liver, pancreas, salivary glands, and teeth.

The Mouth, Esophagus, and Stomach

Food digestion begins in the mouth.

- Food is crushed by the teeth and mixed with saliva.
- Enzymes secreted by the salivary glands immediately begin to break down carbohydrates into simple sugars.
- The swallowed food moves from the pharynx into the esophagus and on to the stomach.

In the Stomach

- Millions of tiny glands manufacture about 3 quarts (2.8 liters) of gastric juice a day, including *hydrochloric acid* and the enzymes *pepsin* and *rennin.*
- Food remains in the stomach for about 2 to 5 hours and is changed into a semifluid called *chyme.*
- Stomach muscle contractions and digestive juices readily digest carbohydrates and convert them into the blood sugar glucose.
- It takes more time for proteins to be digested, and even longer for fats.

ULCERS

A peptic ulcer is a break in the mucous membrane of the esophagus, stomach, or duodenum. A large percentage of ulcers are caused by a bacterium, *H. pylori,* which can disrupt the mucous layer, thus inflaming tissue lining. Specific medications and pain relievers such as ibuprofen and aspirin can also cause ulcers. Ulcers can cause pain, nausea, fatigue, weight loss, and bleeding.

HOW DOES THAT WORK

FOOD DIGESTION

Digestion is the process of breaking down food into smaller particles that can pass through the intestinal wall into the bloodstream. The particles are distributed to nourish all parts of the body. In the digestive tract

- food is squeezed or pushed by muscles.
- food is dissolved by digestive juices and enzymes.
- juices and enzymes act as catalysts, producing chemical changes in food but not becoming part of the chemical produced.

THE LIVER

The liver is the largest gland in the body. It weighs about 4 pounds (1.8 kilograms) and acts as an important chemical plant. Among its many functions, the liver

- manufactures bile, numerous enzymes, and blood proteins.
- stores fat products and makes them available as fuel.
- neutralizes some of the poisons entering the bloodstream.
- processes iron for the blood system.
- delivers glycogen to the body tissues on demand, providing needed fuel or energy to carry out their many activities.

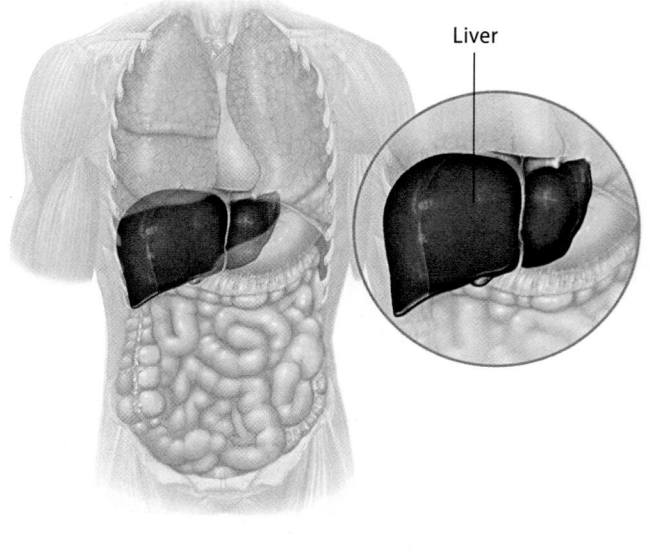

Liver

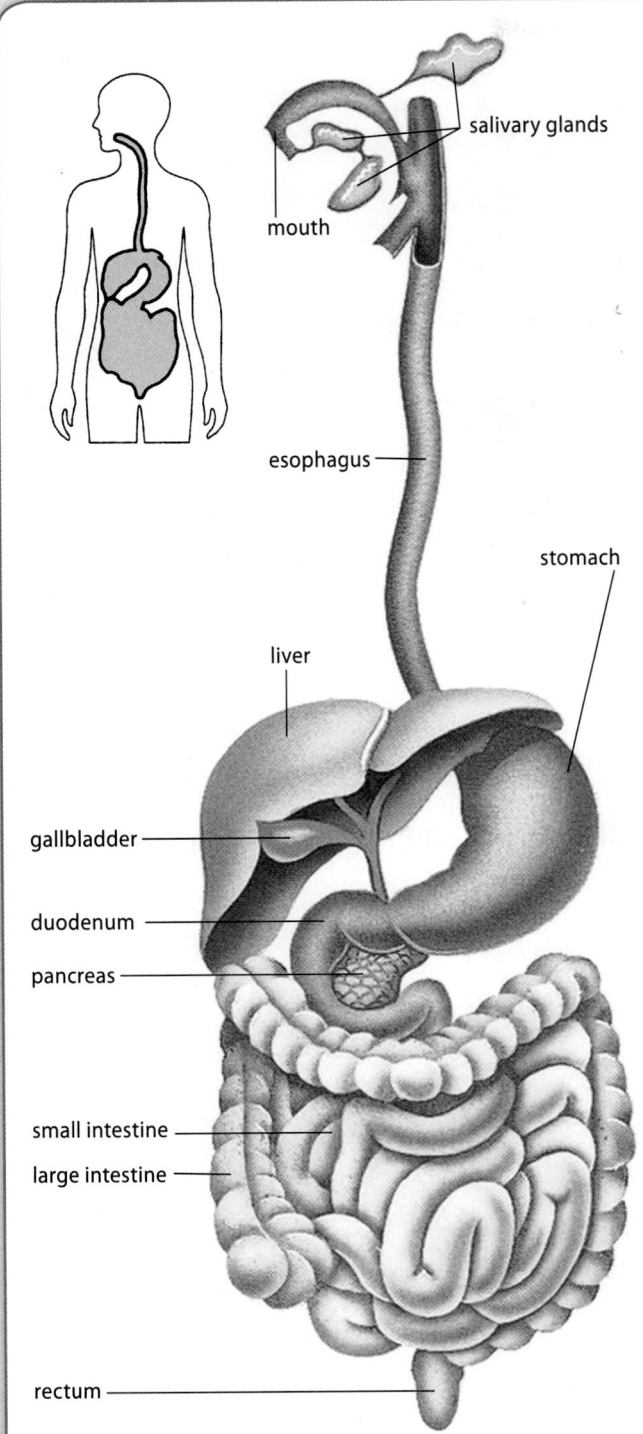

The digestive system consists of a flexible mucus-lined muscular tube from 7 to 11 meters (20 to 36 feet) long, beginning at the mouth and ending at the anus.

The Small Intestine and Large Intestine

After it leaves the stomach, the chyme enters the *duodenum,* which is the first part of the small intestine. The small intestine is a coiled tube about 6 meters (18 feet) long.

In the Small Intestine

- More digestive juices are added to the chyme.
- Fluids from the pancreas and bile from the liver help to further digest the chyme.
- Bile does not contain any enzymes, but its salts aid in the physical digestion of fats.
- Pancreatic juices contain a number of enzymes that act on a variety of foods.
- Proteins are broken down into amino acids.
- Complex sugar molecules are broken down into simple sugars.
- Fats are reduced to fatty acids prior to absorption into the blood or lymph vessels.

Absorbing Food Particles. Projecting from the inner lining of the small intestine are thousands of microscopic, fingerlike projections called *villi.* These absorb the broken-down food particles, conveying them to the bloodstream for distribution to the rest of the body.

By the time food has traveled from the mouth along what can be thought of as a conveyor belt in a chemical refinery to the end of the small intestine, the process of digestion has been completed. All that remains of ingested food are water and waste products, which pass into the large intestine, where much of the water is absorbed. In the meantime, food products are transported by blood vessels from the walls of the small intestine to the liver.

Reproductive System

The organs of the reproductive system enable men and women to produce children. Human beings reproduce sexually. Sexual reproduction involves the union of sex cells. A new human being begins to develop after a sex cell produced by the father unites with a sex cell produced by the mother. The union of a sperm, a male sex cell, and an egg, a female sex cell, results in *fertilization*. (See also page 55.)

In both males and females, the reproductive system comprises the *gonads,* a general term referring to the sex glands forming the cells necessary for human reproduction.

- the *testes,* or male sex glands
- the *ovaries,* or female sex glands

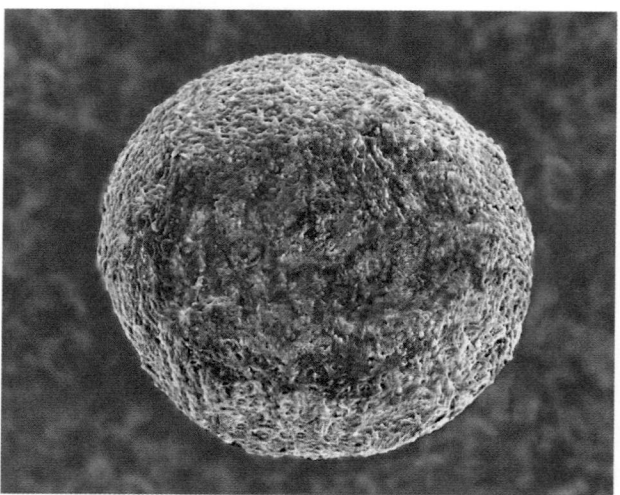

One ovum, or egg cell, is released from an ovary about every 28 days during a woman's childbearing years. A covering surrounds the egg. If a sperm cell penetrates the covering and unites with the egg, a new human being begins to develop.

In Males

- *Spermatozoa,* or sperm cells, form in the testes.
- *Testosterone,* the male sex hormone, is produced in the testes.
- Sperm cells, produced in the billions during the lifetime of an average man, are stored in the *epididymis,* a coiled tube alongside each testicle.
- The sperm travels into the *vas deferens,* a straight muscular tube that joins with the urethra, the passageway through the penis for semen and urine.
- Semen consists of a mixture of sperm and secretions derived from the seminal vesicles, prostate gland, and Cowper's glands.

The average adult male produces about 200 million sperm per day.

THE HUMAN REPRODUCTIVE SYSTEM

vas deferens

bladder

prostate gland

seminal vesicle

urethra

penis

epididymis

testicle

scrotum

Male Reproductive System

In Females

- The ovaries produce *ova,* or egg cells.
- The ovaries produce *estrogen* and *progesterone,* the female sex hormones.
- These hormones prepare the uterus to receive and sustain a fertilized ovum.
- One ovum, released from one of the two ovaries, merges with just one sperm cell, usually in the *fallopian tube*.
- The fertilized ovum travels through the fallopian tube, descending to the wall of the uterus, where it is implanted for development into an embryo.
- If an ovum is not fertilized, as happens with most of the 400 or so ova released during the lifetime of an average woman, it is expelled from the uterus during menstruation.
- The vagina, serving as the passageway through which sperm cells are supplied, also acts as the birth canal.

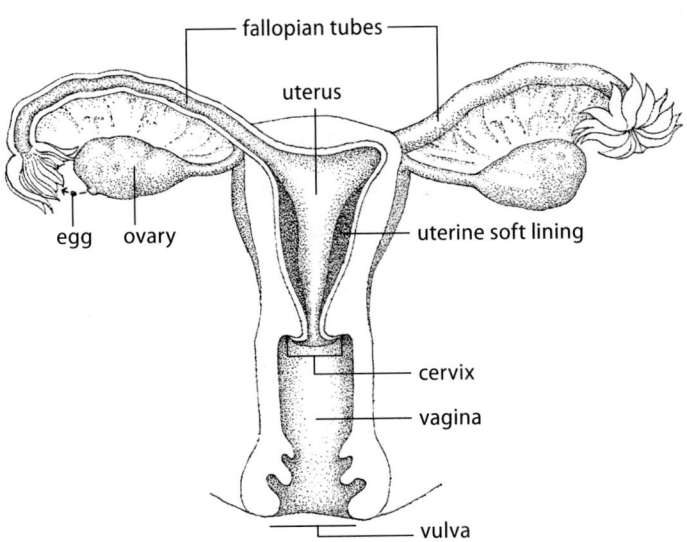

Female Reproductive System

Special organs are involved in human reproduction. In the male, sperm travel through the vas deferens, are mixed with semen, and are released through the urethra. In the female, eggs from the ovaries pass through the fallopian tubes to the uterus.

Fertilization

When fertilization takes place, tissues from the mother and the embryo form the *placenta*, the spongy organ through which the embryo is nourished and through which waste products are eliminated.

Cells Multiply. In the fertilized ovum, within a period of 12 hours, 23 chromosomes from the spermatozoa of the father merge with 23 chromosomes from the nucleus of the ovum of the mother. About 36 hours later, the new nucleus divides into two cells and continues to multiply, through the process of cleavage, at a more rapid rate into four, eight, and 16 cells. A week or so after fertilization, the fertilized ovum enters the uterus with 64 to 128 cells, almost the start of an embryo.

Developing Traits. The bodily characteristics of the new individual are determined by both the paternal and maternal chromosomes within each cell. Each chromosome has many genes responsible for the development of a variety of physical features, such as the color of eyes and hair, body size and shape of limbs, form of the skull, and bone length. Sex is determined by the constitution of the chromosomes.

Pregnancy

During the first trimester (3 months) of pregnancy, the embryo, even though little more than a tiny piece of grayish-white tissue, has the beginnings of a brain, heart, nervous system, and eyes. By the second month, features, including ears, begin to form. At 3 months, fingers and toes are fully formed, and sex can be determined.

The fourth month marks the start of the second trimester. By this time, the mother can feel movement, and heartbeats can be detected.

In the third trimester, at the end of 8 months, the fetus is nearly fully developed. At term (9 months), the average newborn infant weighs 7 pounds 5 ounces and is about 20 inches long.

Endocrine System

The endocrine system consists of glands that regulate various body functions. The system plays a major role in regulating growth, the reproductive process, and the way the body uses food. It also helps prepare the body to deal with stress and emergencies.

The endocrine glands control body functions by producing *hormones*.

Hormones are molecules that are released into the blood, which carries them throughout the body. Hormones act as chemical messengers. After a hormone reaches the organs or tissues it affects, it triggers certain actions.

Many hormones have widespread effects. For example, the hormone *insulin* causes cells throughout the body to take in and use sugar from the bloodstream.

Endocrine glands regulate and integrate separate body functions. The endocrine glands of the human body include the *adrenals, gonads, islets of Langerhans, parathyroids, pituitary,* and *thymus*.

OTHER GLANDS

The body also has glands that do not produce hormones. These *exocrine glands,* such as the sweat glands and salivary glands, make substances that perform specific jobs in the area where they are released. Major exocrine products include

- digestive juices
- mucus
- sweat
- tears

Some Important Endocrine Glands			
Gland	**Location**	**Hormones Secreted**	**Function**
pituitary	base of the skull	secretes a series of hormones	sometimes called the "master gland"; spurs hormone production in other endocrine glands, and influences metabolic processes throughout the body
thyroid	In the neck	thyroxin and triiodothyronine	regulate metabolism, the rate at which food is converted into heat and energy in body cells
parathyroids	in the neck	parathormone	regulates the level of calcium and phosphorus in the blood
islets of Langerhans	within the pancreas	insulin	decreases the amount of sugar in the blood
		glucagon	increases the amount of sugar in the blood
adrenals	one on top of each kidney	from the *medulla,* the inner part of the adrenal: epinephrine, or adrenaline	the "fight or flight" hormone; prepares the body to deal with stress
		from the medulla, the inner part of the adrenal: norepinephrine	constricts blood vessels; helps coordinate the body's response to stress
		from the *cortex,* the outer part of the adrenal: adrenocorticosteroids, often called corticoids	help the kidneys regulate salt and water balance; aid in protein metabolism; and form antibodies against bacteria and viruses

Urinary System

The urinary system removes various wastes from the blood and flushes them from the body. The chief organs of this system are the two kidneys.

The kidneys function as a filtering system for the blood. The kidneys

- lie at the back of the abdominal cavity on each side of the spinal column.

- help regulate the body's internal environment: fluid volume, blood composition, and blood pressure.

- dispose of the body's metabolic wastes and excess water as urine.

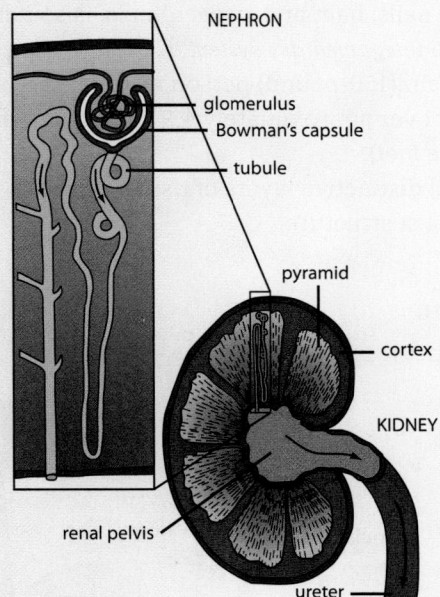

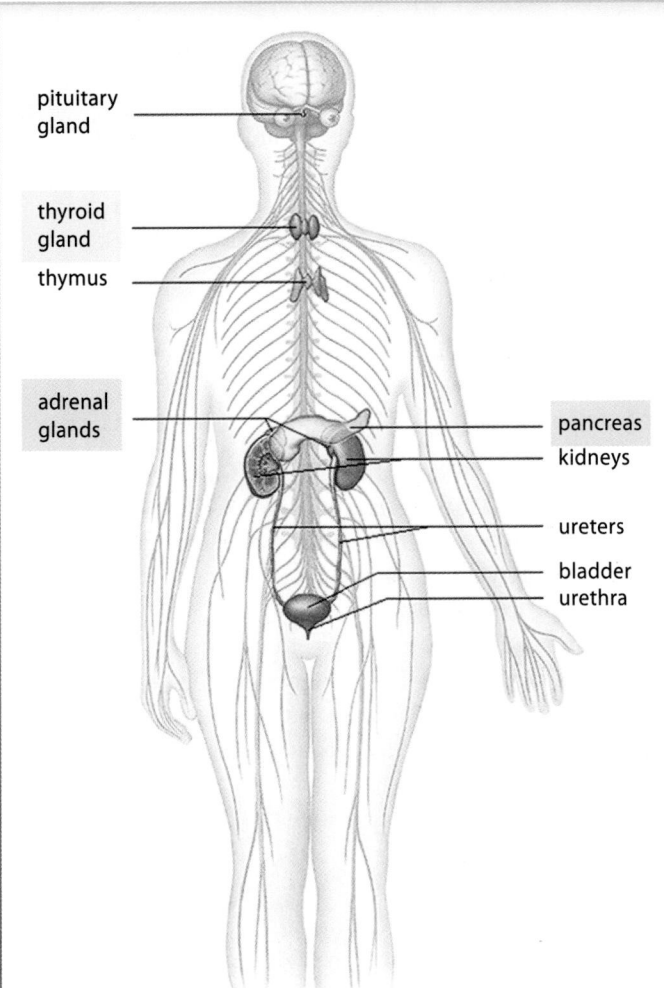

THE ENDOCRINE AND URINARY SYSTEMS

FILTERING OUT THE WASTE

Formation of urine is a continuous process. The rate of filtration depends on fluid intake and on blood pressure in the *glomeruli,* clusters of blood capillaries within the kidneys. Each glomerulus marks the beginning of a *nephron,* the absorbing, filtering, and secreting unit. There are a million or so of these miniscule nephrons in each kidney.

As blood courses through the glomeruli, a considerable amount of its fluid filters out through the membranes and into the tubules. The tubules extract and return to the bloodstream a variety of useful substances, such as glucose, amino acids, ions, minerals, and water. Dissolved waste materials, such as *urea* (a constituent of urine), are kept from returning to the bloodstream.

About 42 gallons (160 liters) of water per day soak into the tubules from the glomeruli to dissolve waste products. However, the body cannot afford to lose so much fluid. Nearly 99 percent of water filtering out through the nephrons is reabsorbed into the bloodstream via the tubules. The remaining 1 percent, together with the wastes, is converted into urine.

The urine is then drained from the nephrons into collecting ducts, transported to the *renal pelvis* (center of the kidney), into the ureters to the bladder, and finally into the urethra for elimination.

Integumentary System

The skin is the largest organ of the body. The skin, including nails, hair, and sweat glands, is sometimes called the *integumentary system*. If the skin of a 68-kilogram (150-pound) person were spread out flat, it would cover approximately 1.9 square meters (20 square feet).

Several distinctive layers of tissue make up this complex structure.

- the epidermis
- the dermis
- the subcutaneous tissues

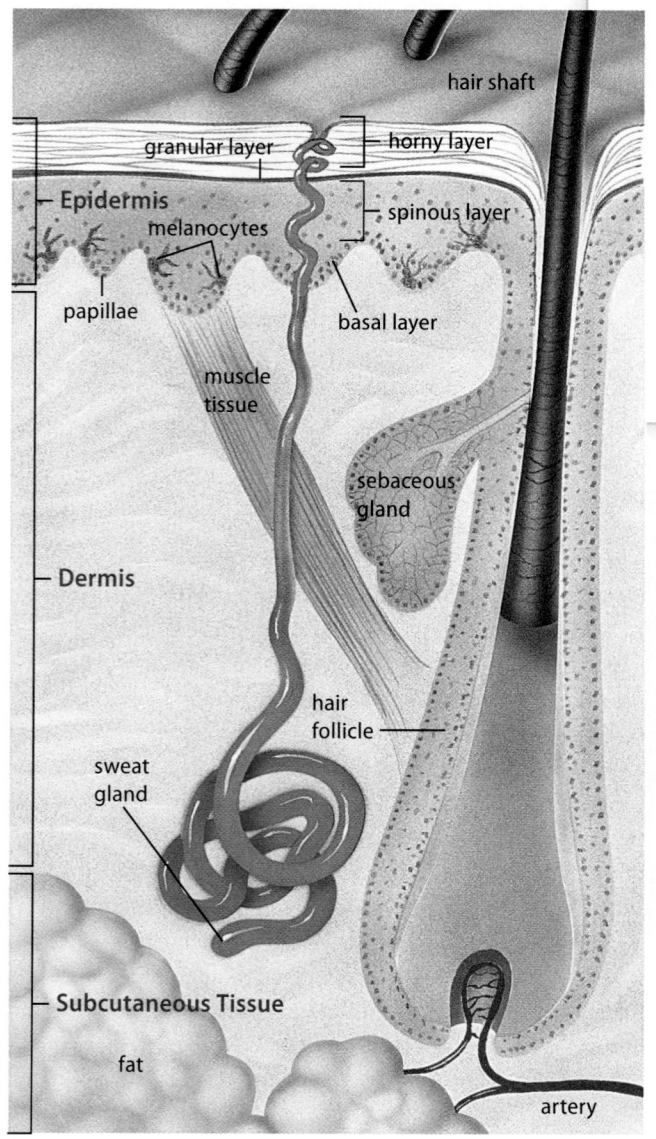

The Outer Layer

The epidermis, or outer surface, is the portion of the skin we actually see. It is composed of four layers of cells. From the outermost to the innermost, they are the *horny, granular, spinous,* and *basal layers.*

The horny layer consists of between about 15 and 40 rows of dying cells. These cells are filled with a tough, waterproof protein called *keratin.*

The granular layer consists of one or two rows of dying cells that contain small grains of a substance called *keratohyaline.*

The spinous layer is composed of between about four and 10 rows of living cells that have spinelike projections where the cells touch one another.

The basal layer is also made up of living cells. It consists mainly of a single row of tall, narrow basal cells. The basal layer also includes cells called *melanocytes.* These cells produce a brown-black pigment called *melanin.*

TOUGH SKIN

Cells in the basal layer of the epidermis called keratinocytes produce a substance called keratin. Keratin is found only in the epidermis, hair, and nails. Keratin makes the skin tough. It also prevents fluids and certain substances from passing through the skin.

As the keratinocytes move upward through the epidermis, they become filled with more and more keratin. By the time they reach the surface of the skin, they have died and become flat and dry. Eventually, they are shed as thin flakes.

◄ **Human skin** is no more than 3/16 of an inch (0.6 cm) thick at any point in the body. The skin receives one-third of the blood circulating throughout the body.

True Skin

The dermis, or true skin, lies beneath the epidermis. It also consists of several layers. This living tissue is tough and fibrous, and is rich in nerve endings, blood vessels, and glands.

It has undulating surfaces that penetrate into the epidermis above and the subcutaneous tissue below. These undulations form ridges, especially on the hands or feet, which create the pattern that makes each individual's fingerprints unique.

Beneath the Skin

Subcutaneous tissues lie directly beneath the skin. They provide extra fuel for the body. The fuel is stored in fat cells. Subcutaneous tissues also help retain body heat and cushion the inner tissues against blows to the body.

Functions of the Skin

- protects the body against invasion by harmful bacteria
- houses nerve endings that receive sensory stimuli from the external environment
- regulates body temperature, providing the mechanism by which heat is retained or dissipated
- is a practically waterproof enclosure; prevents the body contents from drying out

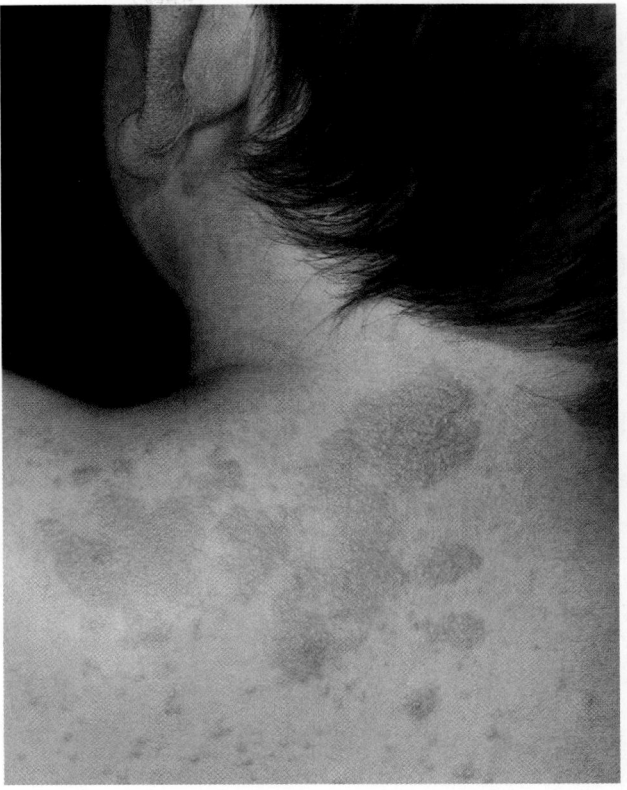

Inflammation of the skin is called *dermatitis. Contact dermatitis* is an allergic reaction to certain substances that a person touches. For example, many people develop itchy blisters after touching poison ivy.

Sweat helps to keep the body from overheating.

HOT AND COLD

The skin helps keep the internal temperature of the body within normal levels. Glands in the skin release sweat when a person becomes overheated. There are about 2 million sweat glands over the body surface, with the largest number found on the palms of the hands and the soles of the feet.

The moisture secreted by the sweat glands is controlled by a heat regulator in the brain. The sweat evaporates and so cools the body.

When a person becomes too cool, the body retains heat by narrowing the blood vessels in the skin. As a result, the flow of blood near the surface of the body decreases, and the body gives off less heat.

SENSE ORGANS provide people—and other multicelled animals—with information about what is happening in their environment.

The five main sense organs are the eyes, ears, nose, tongue, and skin. However, there are other, *internal senses* that also give information about the position and movement of the body and about the body's needs.

Each sensory system responds to a particular kind of stimulus. Cells called *sensory receptors* alter electrical impulses along their membranes. The brain handles the information provided by the senses. Pathways inside and outside the brain move sensory information throughout the body.

Eye

The eye is the organ of sight. It is our most important organ for finding out about the world around us. The eye is able to see objects by capturing light that either reflects from or is emitted by the objects.

The eye can see in bright light and in dim light, but it cannot see in no light at all. Light rays enter the eye through transparent tissues. The eye changes the rays into electrical signals. The signals are then sent to the brain, which interprets them as visual images.

Parts of the Eye

Each eyeball is set in a *socket* in the skull. Its ridges form the brow and the cheekbone. Fatty tissue inside the socket nearly surrounds the eyeball and cushions it. Six muscles move the eyeball in much the same way that strings move the parts of a puppet.

Within the Socket

- The visible parts of the eyeball are the white *sclera* and the colored *iris*.
- A clear membrane called the *conjunctiva* covers the sclera.
- The transparent *cornea* lies in front of the iris.
- The *lens* is connected to the *ciliary body*.
- Inside the eyeball is a clear jellylike substance called *vitreous humor*.
- The *retina*, which underlies the *choroid*, changes light rays into electrical signals.
- The *optic nerve* carries the signals to the brain.
- The *fovea centralis*, a pit in the macula lutea, is the area of sharpest vision.

Rods and cones are named for their distinct shapes. The retina has about 120 million rods and about 6 million cones. ▼

to optic nerve — nerve fibers

optic nerve
retina
rods
fovea centralis
macula
cones

SEEING IN COLOR

The retina has two types of light-sensitive cells: *rods* and *cones*. These cells absorb light rays and change them into electrical signals. Pigment (colored material) in the cells absorbs particles of light.

- **Rods:** The pigment in the rods enables the eye to see shades of gray and to see in dim light.
- **Cones:** The three types of pigment in the cones enable the eye to see colors. The pigments absorb blue, green, or red light, and allow humans to distinguish more than 200 colors.

How We See

The eyes direct the light rays reflected off objects to a single point on the retina to form a focused image.

Images that form on the retina are upside down, reversed left to right, and flat. Depth perception allows the brain to interpret the image correctly.

Depth perception is the ability to judge distance and to tell the thickness of objects. Because the eyes are set slightly apart, each one sees objects from a slightly different angle. As a result, each eye sends a slightly different message to the brain.

Some of the nerve fibers from each eye cross over at the optic chiasm. Each side of the brain thus receives visual messages from both eyes. The brain puts the images together and so provides depth perception.

PARTS OF THE EYE

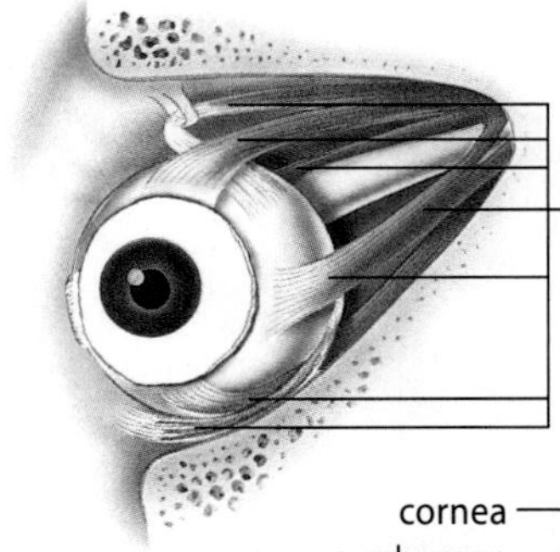

Eye muscles rotate the eyeball within its socket. The eye has six of these muscles.

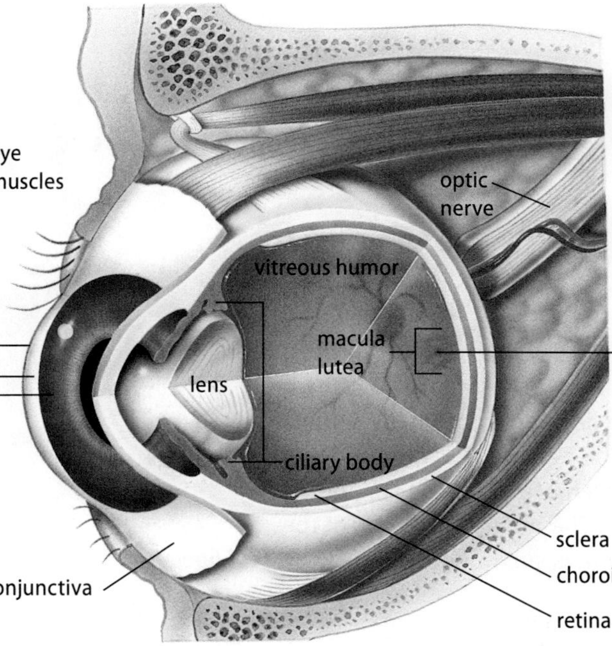

eye muscles

optic nerve

vitreous humor

macula lutea

fovea centralis

cornea

aqueous humor

iris

lens

ciliary body

sclera

choroid

retina

conjunctiva

Focusing. The cornea and lens are the focusing parts of the eye. They direct the light rays to a point on the retina, allowing a clear visual image to form. The cornea provides most of the *refracting* (bending) power of the eye.

After light rays pass through the cornea, they travel through the *aqueous humor* and the pupil to the lens. The lens bends the rays even closer together before they go through the vitreous humor and strike the retina.

The eye shifts focus from between nearby objects and distant ones through *accommodation*. When the eye looks at close objects, the muscles around the lens contract. The lens becomes rounder and thicker and thus more powerful. When the eye looks at distant objects, the muscles relax and the lens becomes flatter.

Light and Dark. The eye adjusts to changing levels of light through a process called *adaptation*. In bright light, muscles in the iris contract. The pupil gets smaller so that less light is allowed in. In dim light, the pupil gets larger to let in more light.

Ear and Skin

The Ear

The ear is the organ that allows us to hear. Hearing enables us to communicate with one another through speech. Hearing can also alert us to danger.

Hearing is a complicated process. Sound consists of vibrations that travel in waves. Sound waves enter the ear and are changed into nerve signals that are sent to the brain. The brain interprets the signals as sounds.

The human ear consists of three main parts.

- the outer ear
- the middle ear
- the inner ear

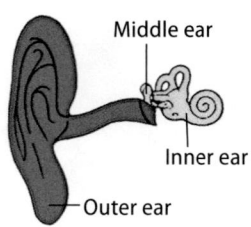

The **outer ear** consists of the *auricle,* which is the fleshy part of the ear on the side of the head; a passageway called the *external auditory canal;* and the *eardrum.* The inner two-thirds of the auditory canal is surrounded by the *temporal bone.*

The **middle ear** has three bones—the *malleus* (hammer), *incus* (anvil), and *stapes* (stirrup). They link the eardrum to the *oval window,* a membrane of the inner ear. The *eustachian tube* leads from the middle ear to the back of the throat.

The **inner ear** consists of the *vestibule, semicircular canals,* and *cochlea.* The vestibule includes the *utricle* and *saccule,* which with the semicircular canals form the ear's organs of balance. The cochlea has three fluid-filled ducts. One wall of the central *cochlear duct* consists of the *basilar membrane.* This membrane supports the *organ of Corti,* which has over 15,000 hair cells and is the actual organ of hearing. The *tectorial membrane* lies above the hair cells.

HOW DOES THAT WORK ?

BALANCE

Our ears also help us keep our balance. Organs in the inner ear—the semicircular canals, the utricle, and the saccule—are filled with fluid that flows in response to movement.

These organs inform the brain about any changes in the position of the head. The brain then sends messages to various muscles that keep our head and body steady as we move.

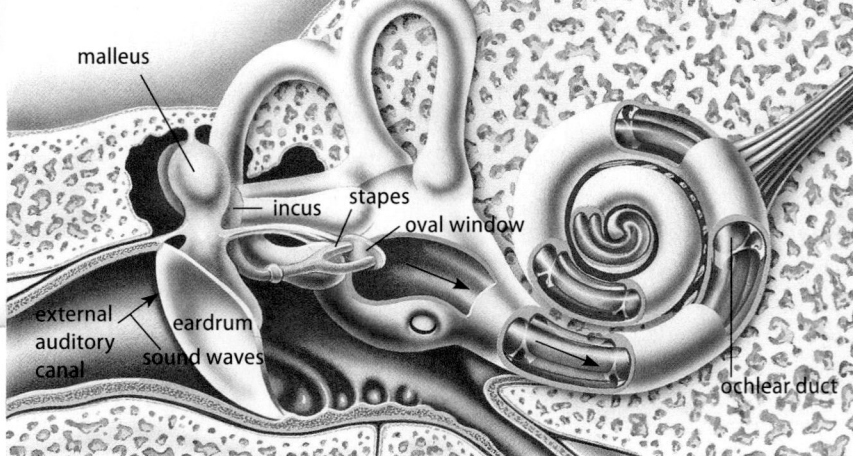

How We Hear

- Sound waves enter the ear through the external auditory canal.
- They strike the eardrum, causing it to vibrate.
- The vibrations flow across the malleus, incus, and stapes, which amplify the sound some 22 times.
- The footplate of the stapes vibrates within the oval window, creating waves in the fluid that fills the ducts of the cochlea.
- The waves push against the basilar membrane.
- The hair cells of the organ of Corti on the basilar membrane slide against the overhanging tectorial membrane.
- The hairs bend and so create impulses in the cochlear nerve fibers attached to the hairs.
- The cochlear nerve transmits the impulses to the brain.

The Skin

The skin and the mucous membranes contain the receptors responsible for the sense of touch. Touch is the sense that makes someone aware of contact with an object. It also is called the *tactile sense*.

We learn the shape and hardness of objects through this sense. Touching an object can give rise to feelings of warmth, cold, pain, and pressure. Free nerve endings in the tissue give the sense of pain. Touch, warmth, cold, and pain also are called *cutaneous senses*.

Organs of Touch

There are several kinds of touch organs, called *tactile corpuscles*, in the skin and the mucous membranes. One kind of touch organ is found near hairs, another kind in hairless areas, and still another kind in deeper tissues.

The sensation of touch occurs when an object comes in contact with the sense organs and presses them out of shape, or touches a nearby hair. Nerves from the organs then carry nerve impulses to the brain.

Sensitivity. Touch is more sensitive in some parts of the body than in others. This difference is due to the fact that the end organs for touch are not scattered evenly over the body but are arranged in clusters.

The feeling of pressure is keenest where there are the greatest number of end organs. It is most highly developed on the tip of the tongue and is poorest on the back of the shoulders. The tips of the fingers and the end of the nose are other sensitive areas.

Hot and Cold. The organs that sense warmth and cold also are distributed unevenly. This can be discovered by running a pointed metal instrument over the skin. The instrument is colder than the skin, but it feels cold only at some points. At other points, the instrument is felt simply as pressure.

Pain causes people to automatically pull their hands away from a hot object, helping them avoid burns.

PAIN

Though it hurts, pain helps in survival. It alerts the body to danger or injury. Pain begins in specialized nerves called nociceptors, which convert a hurtful stimulus into electrical energy. This energy triggers a pain signal that passes through a sequence of nerve structures called a pain pathway. The signal travels along pain nerves to the spinal cord and, finally, to the brain. When the signal reaches the brain, the person becomes aware of pain. (See pages 230–231.)

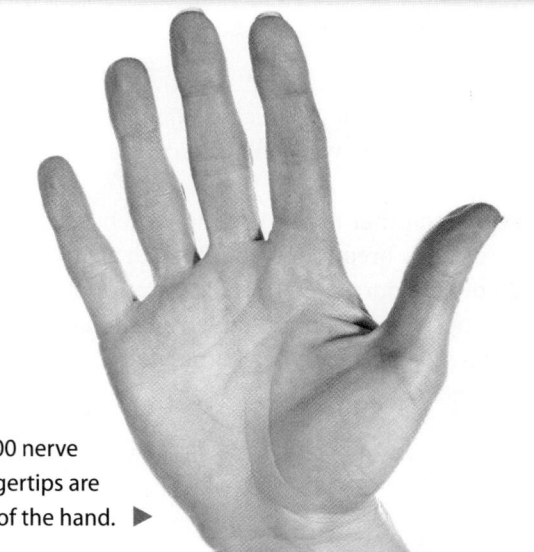

The human hand has up to 1,300 nerve endings per square inch. The fingertips are twice as sensitive as other parts of the hand. ▶

Nose and Tongue

The Nose

The nose is the organ used for breathing and smelling. It forms part of the face, just above the mouth. Outwardly, it seems simple, but it is complicated inside.

Breathing

- Air enters the nose through two openings called *nostrils.*
- Nostrils are separated by the *septum,* a thin wall of cartilage (tough tissue) and bones.
- Air passes from the nostrils into two tunnels called the *nasal passages,* which lead back to the upper part of the throat.
- From the nasal passages, air passes through the pharynx and trachea into the lungs.

The nasal passages have a lining of soft, moist mucous membrane covered with microscopic, hairlike projections called *cilia.* The cilia move in coordination, passing dust, bacteria, and fluids from the nose to the throat for swallowing.

Each nasal passage also has three large, shelf-like bones that are called *conchae* or *turbinates.* The conchae warm the air before it enters the lungs. These bones also stir up the air so that dust in the air sticks to the mucous membrane of the conchae and does not pass into the lungs.

How We Smell

The scientific term for smell is *olfaction,* and the system by which we smell is known as the *olfactory system.*

People (and other land-dwelling vertebrates) detect smells by breathing or sniffing air that carries odors. Odors come from molecules of gas that have been released into the air from many different substances. These molecules stimulate receptor cells deep inside the nose.

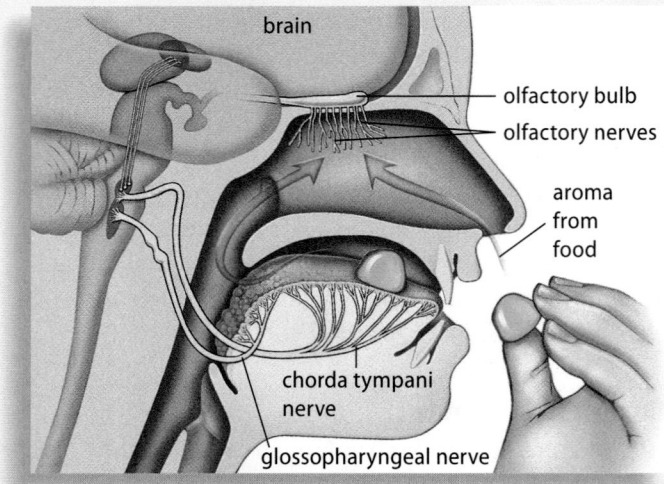

Taste and Smell. Taste is sent to the brain through nerves located in the tongue. Aromas from food also stimulate the sense of smell through nerves in the nasal cavity. Many complex taste sensations are possible through the combination of different flavors and aromas detected through taste and smell.

Perception of Smell

- The perception of smell occurs in the highest part of the nasal cavity, where *olfactory nerve receptors* lie in a small, flat piece of mucous membrane about the size of a thumbnail.
- The olfactory nerve receptors generate nerve impulses in response to chemicals in the air.
- Olfactory nerve fibers then carry the impulses to a part of the brain called the *olfactory bulb.*
- One olfactory bulb lies just above each nasal passage.
- From the olfactory bulb, the impulses are carried to other parts of the brain, where they are translated into sensations of odor.

TASTE AND SMELL

Generally, we taste and smell food at about the same time. Thus, we have come to think of the two senses as being related. But in fact, they are separate. Only at some point in the brain are the separate senses combined.

The smell-stimulus parts in food can be separated from the taste-stimulus parts. When smell stimuli are separated from taste stimuli, people cannot identify some foods and beverages—for example, cherries, chocolate, and coffee—though they still taste them.

Some experts believe that many of our taste sensations are really sensations of odor that we have associated with certain tastes.

For example, we really smell apples and potatoes more than we taste them. If a person is blindfolded and the nose stopped up so that the person cannot smell, the person has great difficulty telling apples from potatoes by taste.

The Tongue

The tongue is the chief organ of taste. It also helps in chewing and swallowing and plays an important part in forming the sounds of words.

Tongue Muscles. The tongue is made up of groups of muscles that a person can consciously control.

- The tongue muscles are a type of muscle called skeletal muscle.
- They run in many different directions.
- They arise from the hyoid bone and the inner surfaces of the *mandible* (jawbone) and temporal bones.

Movement. A person can move the front part of the tongue many different ways. The tongue can move food about, push it between the teeth, and roll it into small masses. It helps clean the mouth by removing food from between the cheeks and teeth. In swallowing, the tongue pushes the food back into the *pharynx* (throat).

How We Taste

The tongue is covered with a mucous membrane. The undersurface of the tongue is smooth. But many *papillae* (small projections) give the tongue a rough surface on the top. Four types of *taste buds*, found in the papillae, enable us to distinguish between sweet, sour, salty, and bitter tastes.

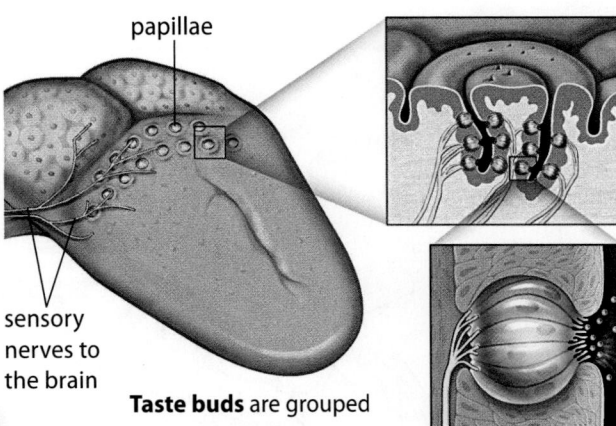

papillae

sensory nerves to the brain

Taste buds are grouped on the tongue into small mounds called papillae.

taste bud

Taste sensation begins when taste receptor cells in taste buds are stimulated by chemicals from food or other substances dissolved in saliva.

- The taste receptor cells are connected to branches of three *cranial nerves* connected directly to the brain.
- When stimulated, they transmit sensory signals to the *medulla*, the lower part of the brain stem.
- Here, some taste signals are separated and travel to the *thalamus*, the area at the front of the brain stem.
- From the thalamus, the signals move to the *cerebral cortex*, the part of the brain that controls higher brain functions.
- At the cerebral cortex, the brain interprets the nerve signals it has received, and we become aware of taste.

A FIFTH TASTE

Some scientists think a fifth distinct taste, called *umami*, can be detected. This taste is described as "savory" or "meaty."

The sensation of umami is caused by a chemical called *glutamate*, which is found in many protein-rich foods. However, not all scientists agree that umami constitutes a fifth taste category.

Brain and Skeletal System

Human Anatomy

This section on human anatomy is designed to show the various structures of the body and their exact location in relation to each other.

Many of the labels in these illustrations not only identify a structure but give additional information about the structure and its function.

The illustrations are based on the famous wall charts by Professors Franz Frohse of the University of Berlin and Max Brödel of Johns Hopkins Medical School.

The Brain

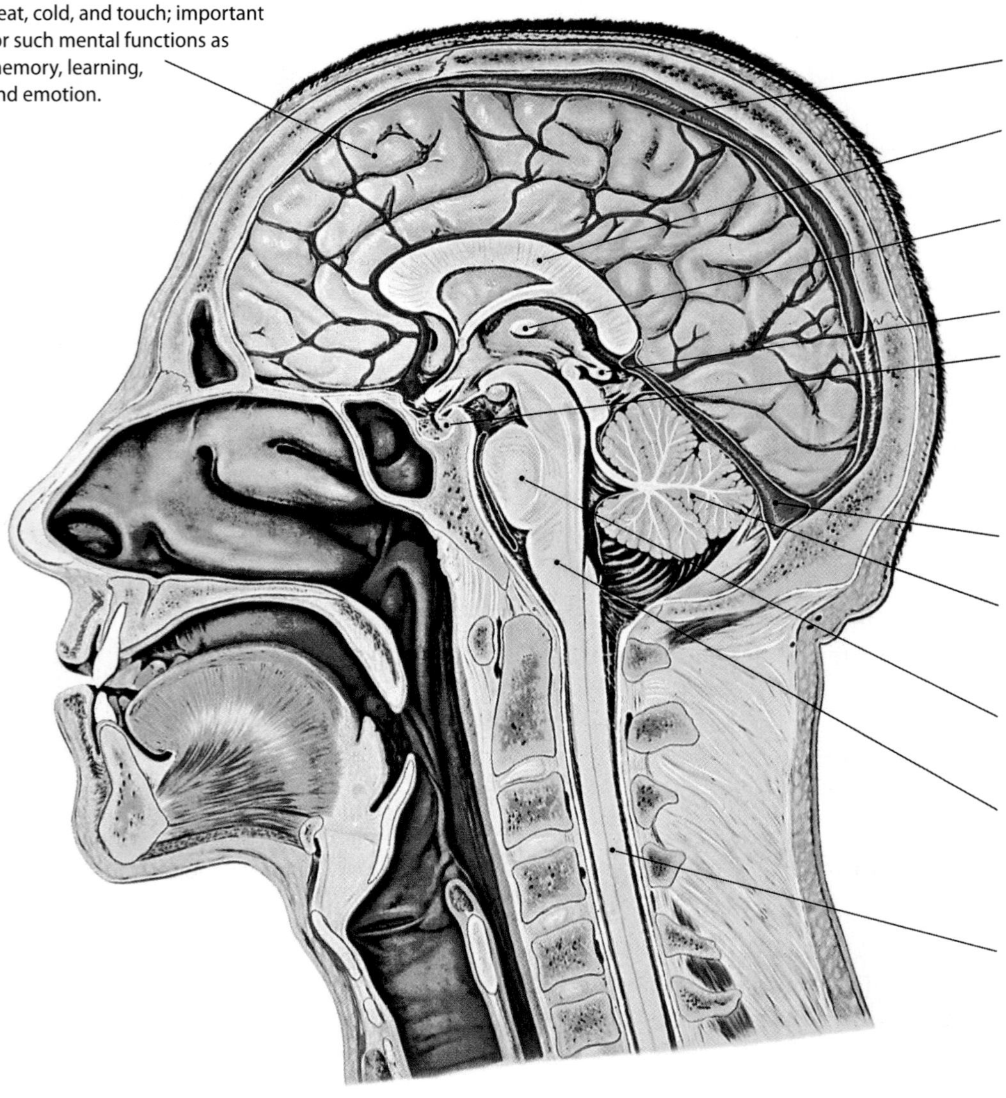

Cerebrum: divided into two halves called cerebral hemispheres; controls such sensations as pain, heat, cold, and touch; important for such mental functions as memory, learning, and emotion.

Superior Sagittal Sinus: receives blood from the brain.

Corpus Callosum: made up of nerve fibers that connect the cerebral hemispheres.

Thalamus: acts as a pathway for almost all nerve impulses to the cerebrum.

Pineal Body

Pituitary Gland: secretes at least seven hormones whose actions include regulation of skeletal growth, development of gonads, activation of thyroid, and regulation of insulin and adrenaline.

Straight Sinus: receives blood from the brain.

Cerebellum: coordinates voluntary muscle movement, helps maintain muscle tone, posture, and equilibrium.

Pons: contains fibers connecting the medulla oblongata with higher brain centers.

Medulla Oblongata: regulates heartbeat, swallowing, and breathing; acts as a pathway for nerves from the spinal cord to other areas of the brain.

Brain Stem

The Skeletal System

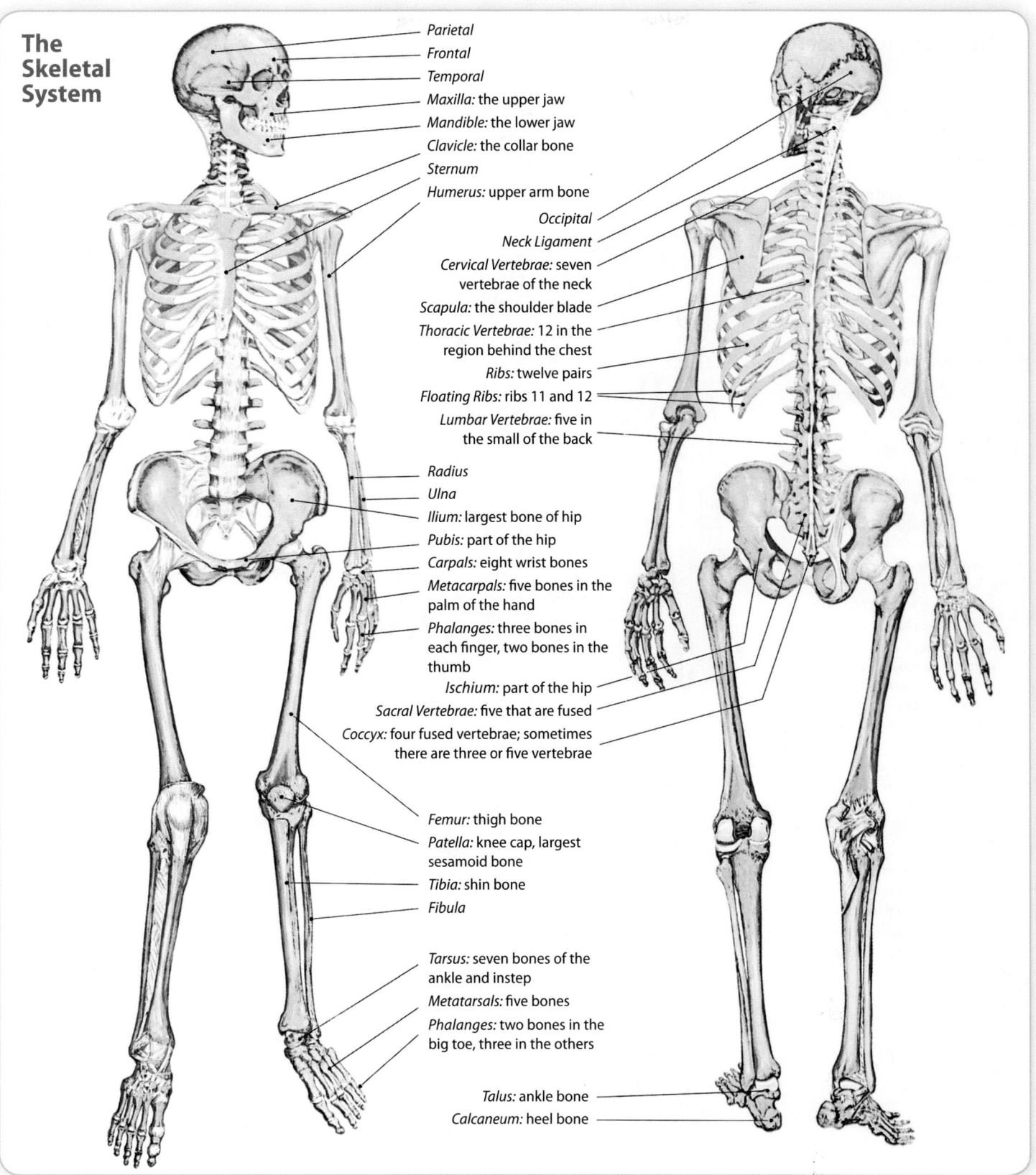

Parietal

Frontal

Temporal

Maxilla: the upper jaw

Mandible: the lower jaw

Clavicle: the collar bone

Sternum

Humerus: upper arm bone

Occipital

Neck Ligament

Cervical Vertebrae: seven vertebrae of the neck

Scapula: the shoulder blade

Thoracic Vertebrae: 12 in the region behind the chest

Ribs: twelve pairs

Floating Ribs: ribs 11 and 12

Lumbar Vertebrae: five in the small of the back

Radius

Ulna

Ilium: largest bone of hip

Pubis: part of the hip

Carpals: eight wrist bones

Metacarpals: five bones in the palm of the hand

Phalanges: three bones in each finger, two bones in the thumb

Ischium: part of the hip

Sacral Vertebrae: five that are fused

Coccyx: four fused vertebrae; sometimes there are three or five vertebrae

Femur: thigh bone

Patella: knee cap, largest sesamoid bone

Tibia: shin bone

Fibula

Tarsus: seven bones of the ankle and instep

Metatarsals: five bones

Phalanges: two bones in the big toe, three in the others

Talus: ankle bone

Calcaneum: heel bone

The Nervous System

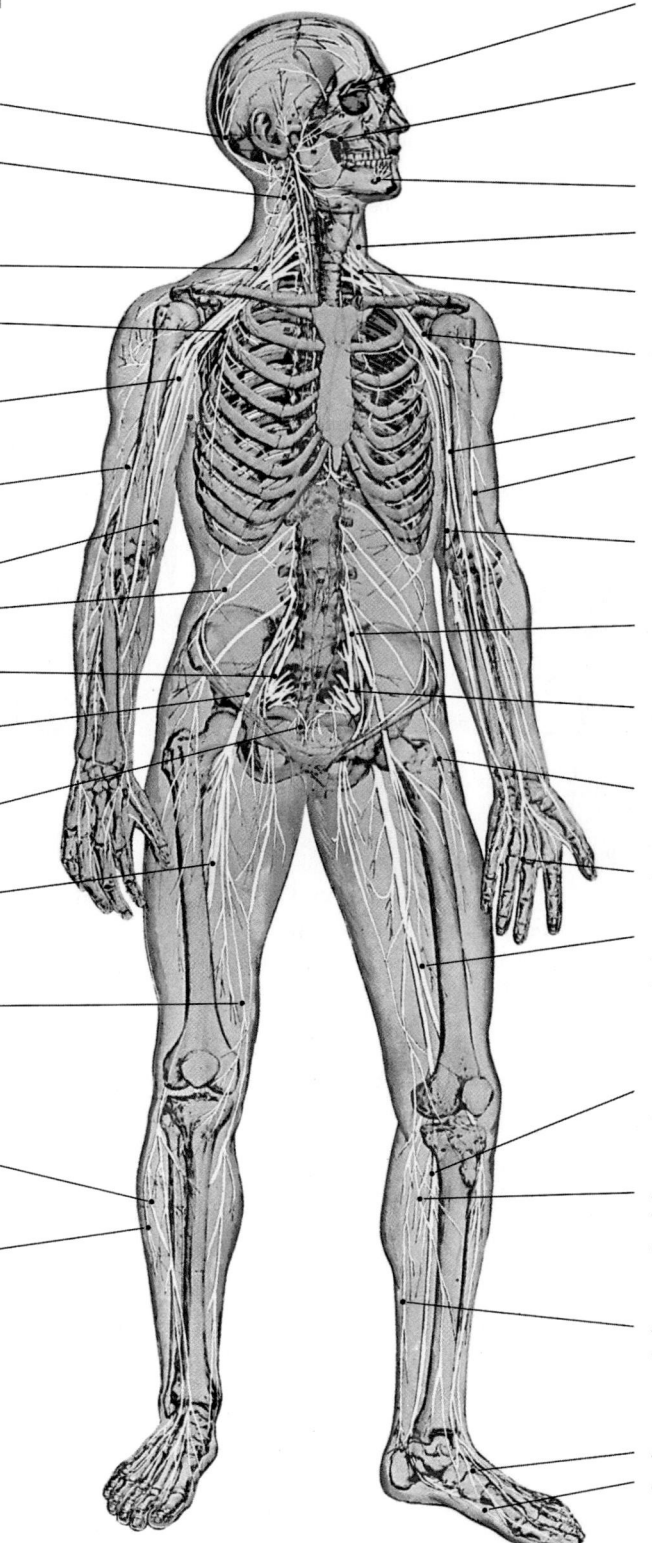

Occipital: goes to the skin at the back of the head.

Cervical Plexus: source of nerves to muscles and skin of head, neck, and shoulders; one nerve goes to diaphragm.

Supraclavicular

Subscapular: goes to the subscapularis, latissimus dorsi, and teres major muscles.

Musculocutaneous: goes to the coracobrachialis, biceps brachii, and brachialis muscles.

Posterior Cutaneous

Middle Cutaneous

Iliohypogastric: goes to the skin in the area of the buttocks.

Superior Gluteal: goes to the gluteal muscles.

Femoral: source of nerves to the muscles and skin on anterior and medial sides of the thigh.

Coccygeal Plexus: source of nerves to the skin and muscles in the region of the coccyx.

Sciatic: largest nerve in the body; divides into the tibial and common peroneal nerves.

Saphenous: branches extend to the foot where the nerves are mainly sensory; branches also go to the thigh.

Deep Peroneal: goes to foot and toe muscles and to joints of ankle and foot.

Superficial Peroneal: goes to muscles and skin of foot.

Supraorbital: goes to the skin of the upper part of face and front of scalp.

Infraorbital: goes to upper gums and teeth, mucous membrane of nose, skin below eyes, and part of upper lip.

Mental

Phrenic: part of the cervical plexus, goes to the diaphragm.

Brachial Plexus: source of nerves to the upper extremities.

Axillary: largest branch of the brachial plexus.

Median

Radial: goes to the muscles and skin at the back of arm, hand, and elbow.

Ulnar: goes to the joints of the wrist, hand, and elbow; to the muscles of the forearm and hand.

Lumbar Plexus: source of nerves to muscles and skin of lower abdomen and lower extremities.

Sacral Plexus: source of sciatic nerve and nerves to thigh, leg, and groin.

Lateral Femoral Cutaneous: source of nerves to the skin of the thigh and leg.

Proper Volar Digital

Common Peroneal: gives off branches to the muscles and skin of the leg and flexes the knee joint.

Tibeal: gives off branches to the muscles and skin of the leg.

Medial Cutaneous: a branch of the femoral; goes to the skin of the thigh and leg.

Suralis: goes to muscles and skin of the calf and lower leg.

Medial Plantar

Lateral Plantar

The Circulatory System

Superficial Temporal Artery and Vein: take blood to and from the side of the head.

Vertebral Artery: one of two main branches arising from the subclavian artery.

External Jugular Vein: drains the surface areas of the head, scalp, and face.

Internal Jugular Vein: receives blood from all parts of the head and neck.

Axillary Artery and Vein: form many branches that take blood to and from the arm.

Cephalic Artery and Vein

Brachial Artery and Vein: branch from the axillary; divide into the ulnar and radial arteries and veins.

Basilic Vein

Ulnar Artery and Vein: take blood to and from the lower arm.

Radial Artery and Vein: take blood to and from the lower arm.

Common Iliac Artery and Vein: the two arteries merge to form the abdominal aorta; the two veins form the inferior vena cava.

Deep Femoral Artery and Vein

Femoral Artery and Vein: pass through the thigh as an extension of the external iliac.

Posterior Tibial Artery and Vein: deep vessels of the lower leg.

Plantar Arterial and Venous Arch: main vessels of the foot.

The blue vessels represent veins; the red vessels represent arteries.

Facial Artery and Vein: take blood to and from the face.

External Carotid Artery: supplies muscles, skin, and other structures of the face and scalp.

Internal Carotid Artery: extends through the neck, ending at the base of the brain.

Common Carotid Artery: divides into the external carotid and internal carotid arteries.

Subclavian Artery and Vein: pass into the arm.

Heart

Portal Vein: takes blood from the spleen, gallbladder, and digestive organs to the liver.

Renal Arteries and Veins: take blood to and from the kidneys.

Superior Mesenteric Artery and Vein: parts of the portal system.

Internal Iliac Artery and Vein: unite with the external iliac to form the common iliac.

External Iliac Artery and Vein: take blood to and from the upper leg; continue as the femoral vein and artery.

Great Saphenous Vein: originates at the foot and extends the entire length of the leg; longest vein in the body.

Small Saphenous Vein

Popliteal Artery and Vein: extension of the femoral artery and vein.

Peroneal Artery and Vein

Anterior Tibial Artery and Vein: deep vessels of the lower leg.

The Muscular System

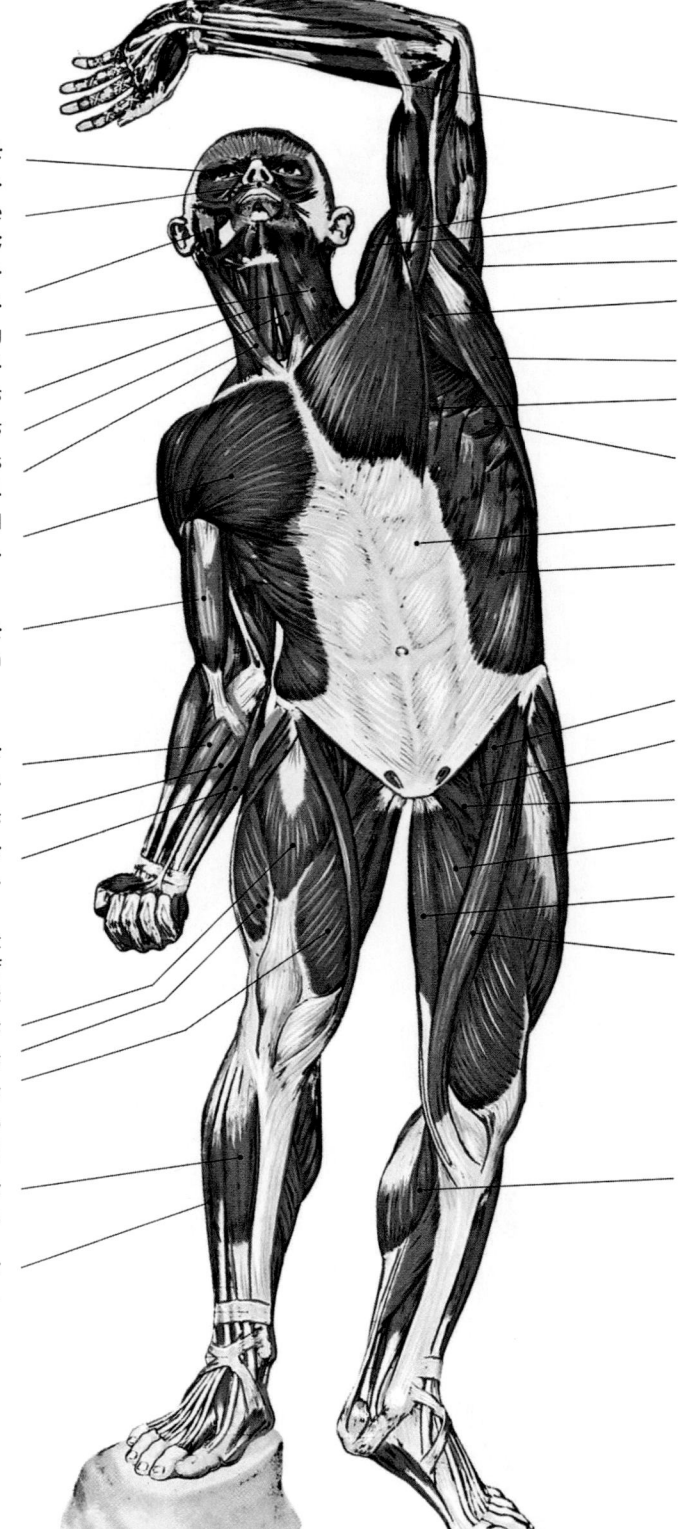

Orbicularis oculi: circles the eye.

Orbicularis oris: forms the fleshy portion of the lips; circles the mouth.

Masseter: moves the lower jaw up.

Platysma: aids in lowering the lower jaw.

Omohyoideus

Sternohyoideus

Sternocleidomastoideus: stands out when the head is rotated.

Pectoralis major: flexes and rotates the arm.

Biceps brachii: flexes the forearm

Flexor carpi radialis: flexes the hand at the wrist.

Palmaris longus

Flexor carpi ulnaris: flexes the hand and forearm.

Quadriceps femoris: largest and most powerful muscle of the body, made up of:

Rectus femoris

Vastus lateralis

Vastus medialis

Vastus intermedius (lies next to femur under rectus femoris)

Tibialis anterior: flexes the foot.

Peroneus longus: flexes the foot.

Brachioradialis: flexes the forearm.

Coracobrachialis

Deltoid

Teres Major

Subscapularis: rotates the humerus.

Latissimus dorsi

Pectoralis minor: lies under pectoralis major.

Serratus anterior: aids in elevating the ribs.

Rectus abdominis

External oblique: aids in rotating the vertebral column.

Iliacus

Pectineus: adducts and flexes the femur.

Psoas major

Adductor longus: adducts and flexes the femur.

Gracilis: flexes and rotates the thigh.

Sartorius: flexes the leg at the knee; flexes the thigh at the hip.

Gastrocnemius: flexes the leg at the knee.

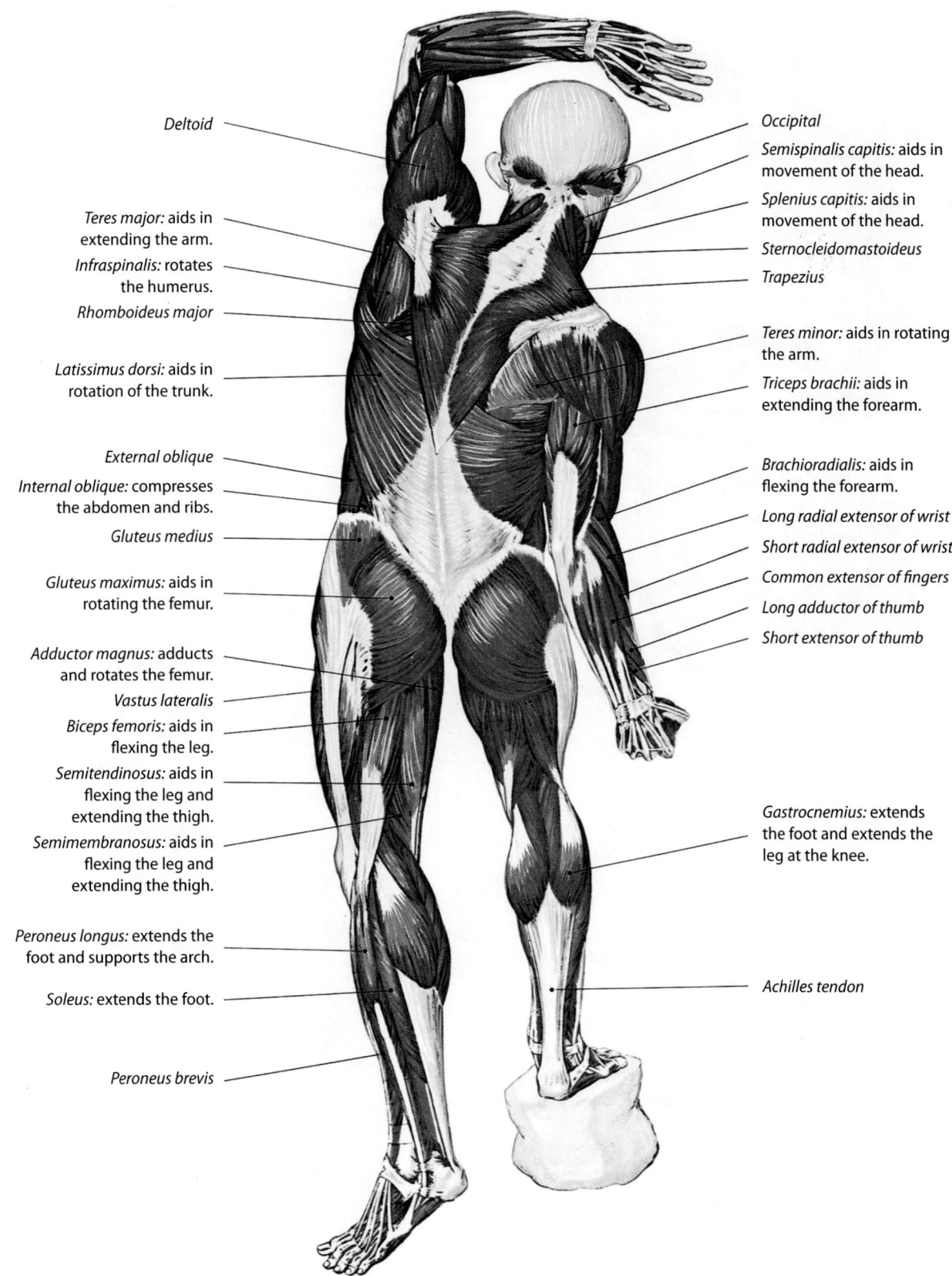

Deltoid

Teres major: aids in
extending the arm.

Infraspinalis: rotates
the humerus.

Rhomboideus major

Latissimus dorsi: aids in
rotation of the trunk.

External oblique

Internal oblique: compresses
the abdomen and ribs.

Gluteus medius

Gluteus maximus: aids in
rotating the femur.

Adductor magnus: adducts
and rotates the femur.

Vastus lateralis

Biceps femoris: aids in
flexing the leg.

Semitendinosus: aids in
flexing the leg and
extending the thigh.

Semimembranosus: aids in
flexing the leg and
extending the thigh.

Peroneus longus: extends the
foot and supports the arch.

Soleus: extends the foot.

Peroneus brevis

Occipital

Semispinalis capitis: aids in
movement of the head.

Splenius capitis: aids in
movement of the head.

Sternocleidomastoideus

Trapezius

Teres minor: aids in rotating
the arm.

Triceps brachii: aids in
extending the forearm.

Brachioradialis: aids in
flexing the forearm.

Long radial extensor of wrist

Short radial extensor of wrist

Common extensor of fingers

Long adductor of thumb

Short extensor of thumb

Gastrocnemius: extends
the foot and extends the
leg at the knee.

Achilles tendon

Organs

The Organs

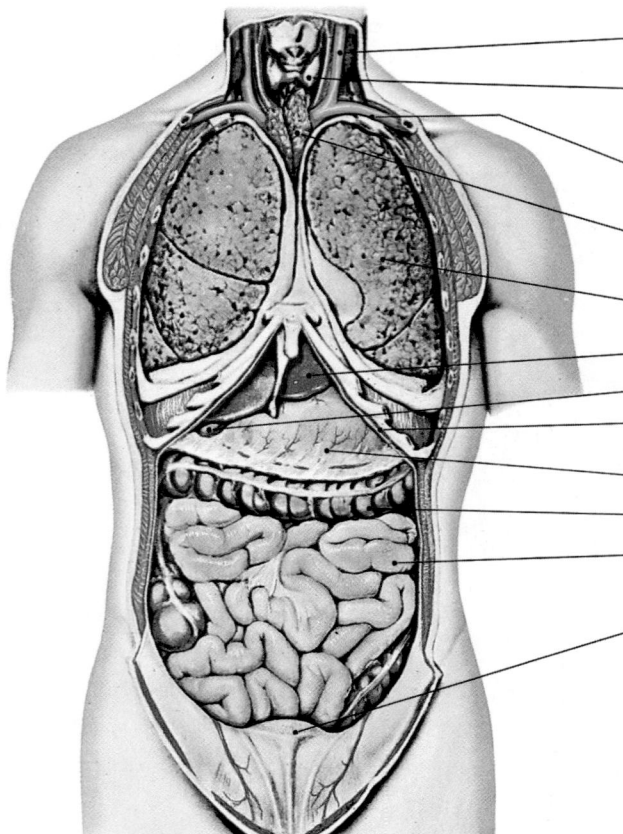

Internal Jugular Vein: receives blood from head and neck.

Thyroid Gland: endocrine; influences body growth, basal metabolism, development of teeth, muscle tone, body temperature, and function of gonads and adrenal glands.

Subclavian Vein: receives blood from the arm and hand.

Thymus Gland: lymphoid organ that produces lymphocytes.

Lung: main site of respiration.

Liver: see below.

Gallbladder: stores bile secreted by the liver.

Diaphragm: aids in expanding and contracting the lungs.

Stomach: see below.

Transverse Colon

Small Intestine: contains pancreatic and intestinal juice and bile that aid in digestion.

Bladder: collects and stores urine from the kidneys.

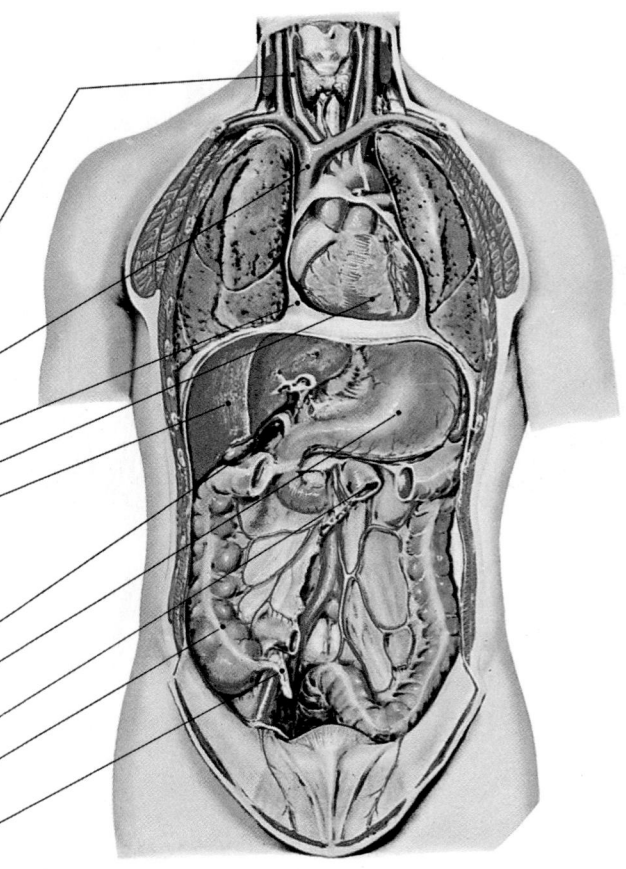

Common Carotid Artery: supplies blood to the head and neck.

Superior Vena Cava: returns blood to the heart from head, neck, thorax, and upper extremities.

Pericardium: sac that encloses the heart.

Heart

Liver: largest gland in the body; secretes bile; forms blood cells; regulates blood volume; metabolizes carbohydrates, fats, and proteins; stores iron, copper, and vitamins A, D, and B_{12}; forms vitamin A; detoxifies some poisons; activates some hormones.

Gallbladder: see above.

Stomach: contains hydrochloric acid, pepsin, mucin, and inorganic salts that aid in digestion.

Duodenum: passage from stomach to small intestine.

Colon or Large Intestine: absorbs water from digested food and eliminates waste.

Appendix

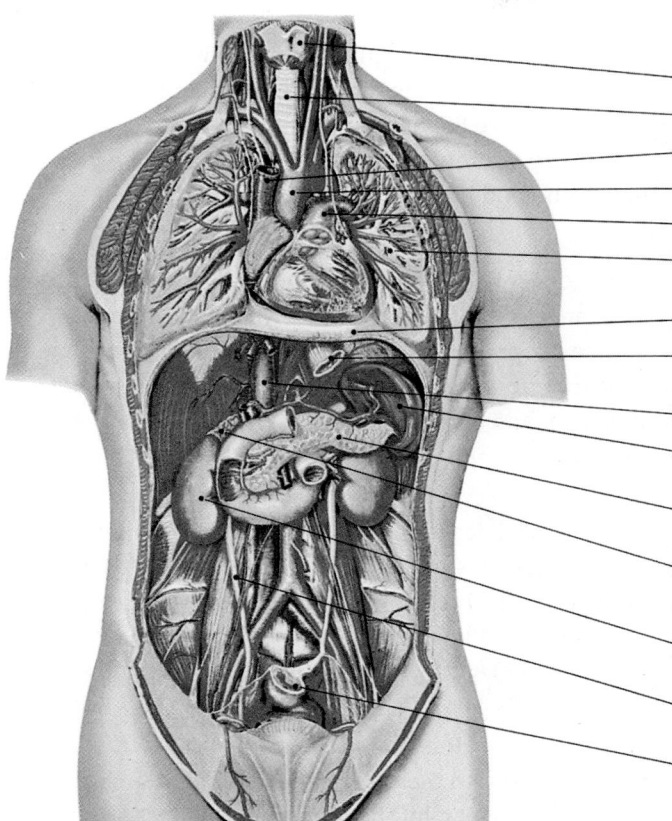

Thyroid Cartilage: main cartilage of the larynx.

Trachea or Windpipe: air passage to the lungs.

Superior Vena Cava

Aortic Arch

Pulmonary Artery

Pulmonary Vessels and Bronchi: extend into the lungs to carry out respiration.

Pleura: separates thoracic from abdominal cavity.

Cardiac End of Stomach: leads from the esophagus, which lies behind the trachea.

Inferior Vena Cava

Spleen: lymphatic organ; produces blood cells and antibodies, and stores blood and iron.

Pancreas: produces the hormones insulin and glucagon, and secretes enzymes into the stomach.

Adrenal Gland: endocrine gland; regulates salt metabolism, kidney function, muscular activity, carbohydrate metabolism, and

Kidney: excretes the waste products of metabolism (urine) and toxic substances; maintains proper water balance and salt concentration.

Ureter: carries urine from kidneys to bladder.

Rectum

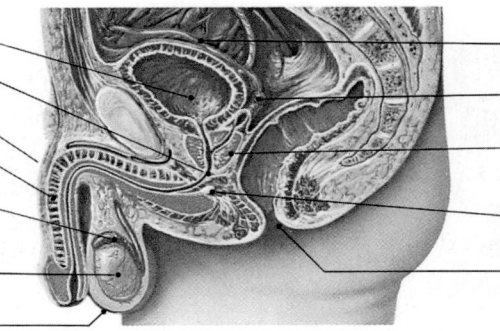

Bladder

Urethra: leads from the bladder to the penis.

Penis

Spongy Body: spongylike tissue that fills with blood to produce erection.

Epididymus: collection of tubes that carry sperm from testes to the vas deferens.

Testicle: produces sperm and some hormones.

Scrotum: encloses the testicles.

Vas Deferens or Ductus Deferens: carries sperm from the testes to the urethra.

Seminal Vesicle: produces viscid fluid that is added to the sperm.

Prostate Gland: secretes alkaline fluid that alkalinizes the urethra and activates the sperm.

Cowper's Gland: secretes a mucuslike substance that acts as a lubricant.

Anus

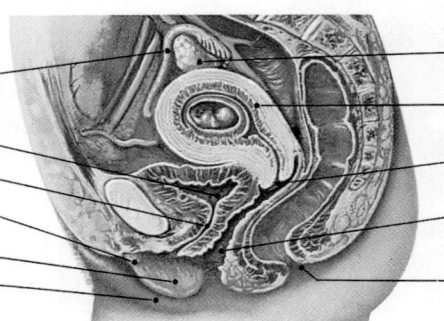

Fallopian Tube: carries the ovum to the uterus.

Bladder

Urethra

Clitoris: sensitive structure homologous to the male penis.

Labia Minor

Labia Major

Ovary: site of ova production, also produces some hormones.

Uterus: where fertilization occurs and fetus develops.

Cervix of the Uterus: leads from the uterus to the vagina.

Vagina: passage from the uterus to the outside of the body; the birth canal for the fetus.

Anus

HEALTH AND NUTRITION

In 1900, life expectancy in the United States was about 50 years. Today, many people reach the age of 80 and beyond. Scientists and health professionals continue to make progress in the fields of nutrition and health.

Nutrition is the science that deals with food and how the body uses it. Food supplies the energy for everything we do. It also provides the substances the body needs to regulate its organs and systems.

Health is a state of physical, mental, and social well-being. It involves more than just the absence of disease. A truly healthy person not only feels well physically but also has a realistic outlook on life and gets along well with other people.

Physical Health

All parts of the body must work together properly to maintain physical health. A person who is in good physical condition has the strength and energy to enjoy an active life and withstand the stresses of daily life. There are several practices that can help a person maintain good health.

Nutrition. A balanced diet provides all the food substances needed by the body for healthy growth and development. Nutritionists classify nutrients into six main groups: water, carbohydrates, fats, proteins, vitamins, and minerals. Dietary fiber is also important to health.

Exercise. Physical activity helps keep the body healthy and fit. Vigorous exercise strengthens muscles and improves the function of the circulatory and respiratory systems. Physical fitness benefits both physical and mental health and helps the body withstand stress.

Rest and Sleep. Rest helps overcome fatigue and restore energy to the body. Most adults sleep from 7 to 8½ hours a night, though some need less sleep and others need more. Young children may need more sleep at night plus a daytime nap.

Cleanliness. Good hygiene controls the growth of bacteria and other germs that can cause disease. A regular bath or shower keeps the body free from dirt and odor. Regular hair-washing and daily dental care are other important parts of personal cleanliness.

Medical and Dental Care. Regular checkups by a physician and dentist play an important role in safeguarding health. Early care in the case of sickness or injury can result in quicker recovery and lower medical costs. Prevention of disease is an important part of medical care.

◀ **Regular exercise** can help a person build strong muscles and maintain a healthy heart.

ChooseMyPlate

The United States Department of Agriculture (USDA) developed ChooseMyPlate to illustrate the five major food groups and identify the general proportion from each group that is needed daily to provide a healthful, well-balanced diet. It should be noted that no single food group is more important than another—all are needed to guarantee a balanced diet.

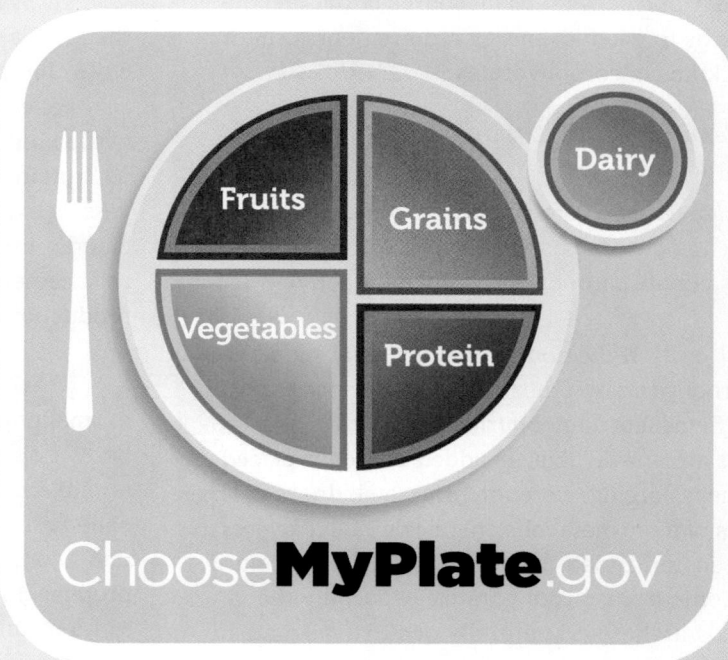

Make half your plate fruits and vegetables.

- Eat red, orange, and dark-green vegetables, such as tomatoes, sweet potatoes, and broccoli, in main and side dishes.
- Eat fruit, vegetables, or unsalted nuts as snacks—they are nature's original fast foods.

Switch to skim or 1% milk.

- They have the same amount of calcium and other essential nutrients as whole milk, but less fat and calories.
- Try calcium-fortified soy products as an alternative to dairy foods.

Make at least half your grains whole.

- Choose 100% whole-grain cereals, breads, crackers, rice, and pasta.
- Check the ingredients list on food packages to find whole-grain foods.

Vary your protein food choices.

- Twice a week, make seafood the protein on your plate.
- Eat beans, which are a *natural* source of fiber and protein.
- Keep meat and poultry portions small and lean.

Choose foods and drinks with little or no added sugars.

- Drink water instead of sugary drinks. There are about 10 packets of sugar in a 12-ounce can of soda.
- Select fruit for dessert. Eat sugary desserts less often.
- Choose 100% fruit juice instead of fruit-flavored drinks.

Look out for salt (sodium) in foods you buy—it all adds up.

- Compare sodium in foods like soup, bread, and frozen meals—and choose the foods with lower numbers.
- Add spices or herbs to season food without adding salt.

Eat fewer foods that are high in solid fats.

- Make major sources of saturated fats—such as cakes, cookies, ice cream, pizza, cheese, sausages, and hot dogs—occasional choices, not everyday foods.
- Select lean cuts of meats or poultry and fat-free or low-fat milk, yogurt, and cheese.
- Switch from solid fats to oils when preparing food.

Nutrition

Carbohydrates

Carbohydrates are the main source of the fuel the body burns to meet its energy requirements. There are two kinds of carbohydrates.

- *simple carbohydrates:* sugars; have a simple molecular structure
- *complex carbohydrates:* include starches; have a more complex molecular structure that consists of many simple carbohydrates linked together

Energy Needs. If the body is inadequately supplied with carbohydrates, it must utilize fats and proteins for energy. Since fats do not burn efficiently when carbohydrates are unavailable, an added burden is placed on the kidneys, forcing excretion from the kidneys of large amounts of toxic metabolic chemicals called *ketones*.

It is recommended that 60 percent of daily calorie intake come from carbohydrates, especially the complex starches and naturally occurring sugars in fruits and vegetables.

Proteins

Proteins are a vast family of complex molecules that play a major role in body chemistry. (See pages 66–67.) Proteins come in a variety of forms, including *enzymes, hormones,* and *antibodies,* and are a main part of the human cell.

Proteins help muscles to contract, and blood vessels expand and contract in maintaining normal blood pressure. They are needed for growth and tissue replacement, for the regulation of water, and for the production of antibodies.

Amino Acids. Large protein molecules are made up of smaller molecules called *amino acids.* The human body is able to produce all but nine of the 22 different amino acids that are found in nature. The nine, called *essential amino acids,* must be obtained in the diet in order for the body to make the hundreds of proteins it needs.

Most animal proteins contain all the essential amino acids, while most vegetable proteins lack one or another of them. This fact makes it desirable to combine several different vegetables in one meal, or to add animal protein to a vegetable diet.

Selecting Carbohydrates	
Bread	Whole grain (unrefined); whole wheat
Cereal	Hot, whole-grain (farina-enriched) oatmeal; cold, whole-grain (shredded) wheat
Fruits and vegetables	Fruits and many vegetables contain simple carbohydrates, but since they are good sources of vitamins and minerals and are relatively low in calories, they are not considered to be "empty calories."
Legumes and seeds	Dried peas, beans, seeds, and nuts are rich sources of protein, vitamins, and minerals. Seeds and nuts contain fairly large amounts of fat (polyunsaturated vegetable oils), which add to their calorie content.
Milk products	Simple carbohydrates provide the bulk of calories in skim milk, buttermilk, and low-fat yogurt. These foods are excellent sources of protein.
Pasta	Enriched spaghetti and noodles can be bought in various forms. Many are high-protein varieties, and spinach pasta contains more vitamins and minerals than white enriched pasta.
Rice	Brown rice contains almost all nutrients found in the original rice grain. Polishing removes the brown coat as well as the germ containing most of the B vitamins and minerals. Still, parboiled or white rice has more nutritional value than instant or minute rice.

EMPTY CALORIES

Foods that are high in sugar, salt, and fat but have little protein and few vitamins or minerals are called *junk food.* Junk food is said to have "empty calories" because it is high in calories and low in nutrition.

Eating a lot of junk food—such as soft drinks and other sugary drinks, candy, and salty foods—can lead to poor health and obesity.

Fiber

Fibers are the chemical substances in cell walls that give plants their structure. The types of dietary fibers are *cellulose, hemicellulose, lignin, pectins,* and *gums.*

Cellulose, hemicellulose, and lignin possess a remarkable ability to absorb water, which eases the passage of food through the intestine. This leaves less time for harmful substances to breed. It also speeds up the transit of toxins, which may help prevent the development of colon cancer. Lignin helps the digestion of all other fibers and helps reduce blood cholesterol levels.

Pectins and gums help to lower blood cholesterol and influence the conversion rate of carbohydrates to sugar in the blood.

More Fiber. The average American diet is low in fiber, mainly because of the consumption of processed foods. Forty grams of fiber a day is recommended.

Two servings of fresh vegetables and two servings of whole grains daily will usually provide enough fiber for the average person.

Selecting Fiber-Rich Foods		
	Serving Size	Fiber (grams)
Breads and Cereals		
100% bran	1 cup	23.0
Cornflakes	1 3/4 cups	2.75
whole-wheat bread	1 slice	1.9
Fruit		
pear (unpeeled)	1 medium	5.5
raisins	1/2 cup	5.0
apple (unpeeled)	1 small	3.1
orange	1 medium	3.1
grapefruit	1/2 medium	2.6
strawberries, fresh	1/2 cup	2.6
tangerine	1 medium	2.1
figs (dried)	2	1.8
grapes (green)	20	1.0
plums, raw	2 small	1.6
peach, raw	1 medium	1.3
Vegetables		
beans, (baked)	1 cup	10.4
peas, frozen, raw	1/2 cup	5.5
corn (canned)	1/2 cup	4.75
beans, kidney, cooked	1/2 cup	4.5
spinach	1 cup	3.5
potatoes, cooked	2/3 cup	3.1
tomatoes	1 medium	3.0
beans, green	1 cup	2.4
carrots, cooked, raw	1/2 cup	2.2
cabbage, cooked	3/4 cup	2.2
cabbage, raw	3/4 cup	2.1
beets, cooked	2/3 cup	2.1
broccoli, cooked	3/4 cup	1.6
Nuts		
Brazil nuts	10	5.5
peanut butter	2 tbsp.	2.0
peanuts	10	1.0
almonds (shelled)	10	1.0

Eat Your Veggies! The USDA recommends people eat 2½ cups of vegetables and 2 cups of fruits every day, and cut down on foods high in fat, salt, and added sugar.

Fat

Fat is one of three main classes of nutrients that provide energy to the body (the other two are carbohydrates and proteins). Fats are found in animals and plants. An animal fat or plant fat that is liquid at room temperature is called an *oil*. A processed type of beef fat called *tallow* and some other fats are hard at room temperature.

Fat's Importance

- Fat is a concentrated source of food energy for animals and plants.

- Fat is stored under the surface of the skin of many kinds of animals, including human beings.

- These fat deposits provide energy reserves and act as insulation against heat loss.

- Most of the fat in plants is stored in seeds, where it provides the first food for young seedlings as they grow.

Fat's Structure

Fats consist primarily of compounds called *triglycerides*. Triglycerides contain one molecule of an alcohol called *glycerol* or *glycerin*.

- Glycerol consists of atoms of carbon, hydrogen, and oxygen.

- Glycerol combines with three molecules of substances called *fatty acids*.

- Each of these fatty acids consists of a long chain of carbon atoms that have hydrogen atoms attached.

- The fatty acid chains are linked to the glycerol molecule to form a molecule of triglyceride.

ESSENTIAL FATTY ACIDS

Certain fatty acids, called *essential fatty acids,* are needed for growth and maintenance of the body. The body cannot make essential fatty acids, so they must be obtained from the diet.

Essential fatty acids are building blocks for the membranes around cells. They also help form many of the complicated structures inside cells. All essential fatty acids are polyunsaturated.

FAT'S MANY USES

Fats from a wide variety of plants and animals supply many of the raw materials used in manufacturing. Linseed oil is used in making paint. Manufacturers use coconut oil in making such products as hydraulic brake fluid, lipstick, soap, and chocolate coating for ice cream bars. Tallow is an important ingredient in soaps, cosmetics, and lubricants.

Fat's Two Forms

Fatty acids occur in two forms.

- saturated
- unsaturated

A saturated fatty acid has a chemical structure in which as many hydrogen atoms as possible are linked to its carbon chain. When all three of the fatty acids in a triglyceride are saturated, it is called a saturated fat. Most fats from animal sources contain a large proportion of saturated fats.

An unsaturated fatty acid contains at least two fewer hydrogen atoms than a saturated fatty acid containing the same number of carbons. A triglyceride that contains one or more unsaturated fatty acids is known as an unsaturated fat.

A fat with one unsaturated fatty acid is called a *monounsaturated fat*. A fat that contains more than one is called *polyunsaturated*. Most—but not all—fats from vegetable sources are unsaturated.

Fat's Efficiency

Fats and oils do not dissolve in water, which enables them to form membranes that surround all the body's cells. These membranes help cells maintain an environment within their borders that differs from the environment outside them. Some of the body's most important processes occur in this environment inside cells.

Fat is a more efficient fuel than either carbohydrates or proteins.

- Fat can produce about 9 calories of energy per gram (4,000 calories per pound).
- Carbohydrates and proteins can each produce about 4 calories per gram (1,800 calories per pound), less than half the energy produced by fat.
- The body converts carbohydrates and proteins into fat for storage and draws on this fat when extra fuel is needed.

Fats and Disease

Many scientists believe that limiting the amount and types of fats eaten can help reduce the risk of developing certain diseases, including coronary artery disease and certain types of cancer.

Eating a high-fat diet can contribute to excess consumption of calories, which can lead to obesity. People with obesity have an increased likelihood of many health problems, including diabetes, coronary artery disease, and a liver disorder called *cirrhosis*. (See pages 276–279.)

Types of Fats	
Saturated Avoid use of (tend to raise blood cholesterol)	
butter	meat
cheese	milk chocolate
coconut	palm oil
coconut oil	vegetable shortening
egg yolks	whole milk
lard	
Monounsaturated Good to use (may help lower blood cholesterol)	
avocados	peanut butter
cashews	peanut oil
olives	peanuts
olive oil	
Polyunsaturated Use occasionally (may help lower blood cholesterol)	
almonds	sunflower oil
corn oil	safflower oil
cottonseed oil	salad dressing
filberts	soybean oil
fish	walnuts

Cholesterol

Cholesterol is a fatty, waxy, yellowish substance found in tissues in the human body (and other animals). It belongs to the *sterol* group of fats, a different type from saturated and unsaturated fats.

An Essential Component

Cholesterol is a normal and essential component of cells throughout the body. It plays a vital part in the production of nerve tissue, digestive bile, and sex hormones.

In the average person, about 80 percent of cholesterol is produced in the liver. Typically, the liver manufactures the 1,000 mg of cholesterol required by the body daily.

Cholesterol Carriers

Cholesterol is not *soluble,* meaning it doesn't dissolve in liquid. Therefore, it must be carried through the bloodstream in packets of fat and protein called *lipoproteins.* There are two types of lipoproteins.

- low-density lipoprotein (LDL)

Bad Cholesterol. LDLs transport cholesterol to the cells. The cholesterol carried by LDLs is sometimes called the bad cholesterol because it is linked to heart disease.

When there is more cholesterol circulating through the bloodstream than can be used by the cells, the LDL carriers deposit the excess on the artery walls. High levels of LDL have been linked to atherosclerosis.

- high-density lipoprotein (HDL)

Good Cholesterol. HDLs carry excess cholesterol in the bloodstream back to the liver for disposal. The cholesterol carried by HDLs is sometimes called the good cholesterol. Low levels of HDL in the bloodstream increase the risk of a heart attack.

An easy way to remember which cholesterol is good and which is bad: keep in mind that you will be healthiest with *high* levels of *H*DL and *low* levels of *L*DL.

FAT IN THE BLOOD

Cholesterol and another lipid, *triglycerides,* are two of the major fatty substances in the blood. Triglycerides may be used by cells for energy, or they may be stored for later use. Doctors often measure the amount of cholesterol and triglycerides in blood to help determine a patient's overall health. High levels of both lipids increase the risk of heart disease.

Several factors lead to elevated triglyceride levels. They include alcohol consumption, stress, weight gain, certain medications, and a diet high in carbohydrates. People can lower their triglyceride levels by reducing the amount of calories and fat in their diet and by exercising regularly.

ATHEROSCLEROSIS

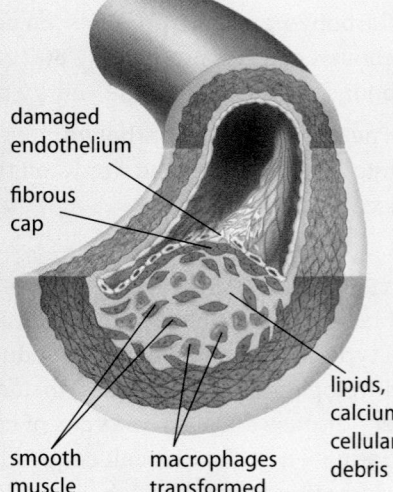

Normal human artery

Artery narrowed by atherosclerotic plaque

damaged endothelium

fibrous cap

lipids, calcium, cellular debris

smooth muscle   endothelium

smooth muscle   macrophages transformed into foam cells

Cholesterol is carried to the cells by LDL and to the liver by HDL. Too much LDL and not enough HDL in the bloodstream is a sign that there is too much cholesterol present, and it is being deposited in the arteries, clogging them up.

High Doses

If a diet is too rich in cholesterol, which is found in egg yolks, butter, and fats, the liver cuts back production, but not always enough to avoid an increase in cholesterol level in the blood.

An excessive amount of cholesterol circulating in the blood can be dangerous.

- Excessive cholesterol can leave deposits, or plaque, on the lining of the artery walls.
- Continued accumulation of these deposits can result in *atherosclerosis,* impeding blood flow and eventually shutting it off in an artery.
- If the artery is one leading to the heart, a heart attack will occur.
- If plaque causes a blockage of the carotid arteries in the head and neck, a stroke will occur.
- A stroke is the equivalent in the brain of a heart attack.

Lowering Cholesterol

According to the National Heart, Lung, and Blood Institute, over 65 million Americans have cholesterol levels that are too high. The best way to lower cholesterol is to adjust the diet.

- Reduce saturated fats, especially animal fats and dairy products.
- Restrict the amount of fatty meats, liver, and shellfish.
- Lean meats, fish, and poultry are better choices.

According to the American Heart Association, there would eventually be a 50 percent lower incidence of heart disease if Americans reduced their blood cholesterol levels by 25 percent.

Cholesterol Content of Common Foods		
Type of Food	Serving Size	Approx. Content
Meat (cooked)		
bacon	2 slices	115 mg
beef, lean	3 oz.	107 mg
lamb	3 oz.	112 mg
pork, ham	3 oz.	100 mg
pork sausages	3 oz.	80 mg
Fish (cooked)		
haddock	3 oz.	68 mg
mackerel	3 oz.	108 mg
salmon	3 oz.	53 mg
trout	3 oz.	62 mg
tuna	3 oz.	62 mg
Shellfish (cooked)		
oysters	3 oz.	57 mg
scallops	3 oz.	45 mg
shrimp	3 oz.	170 mg
Poultry (cooked)		
chicken	3 oz.	65 mg
egg white	any amount	0 mg
egg yolk	1 egg	240 mg
turkey	3 oz.	68 mg
Milk Products		
American cheese	1 oz.	30 mg
butter	1/2 oz. (1 tbsp.)	30 mg
cottage cheese	8 oz. (1 cup)	16 mg
Parmesan cheese	1 oz.	25 mg
ricotta cheese	1 oz.	14 mg
skim milk	8 oz. (1 cup)	5 mg
Swiss cheese	1 oz.	28 mg
whole milk	8 oz. (1 cup)	32 mg
Cooking Oils		
lard	1/2 oz. (1 tbsp.)	12 mg
margarine	any amount	0 mg
vegetable oils	any amount	0 mg

Diet and Health

A diet that consists of proper food and careful regulation of how much one eats can be the basis of good health and general well-being.

Good nutrition becomes an achievable goal when one observes this simple rule: Plan healthful, well-balanced meals to include servings from each of five basic food groups represented in the USDA's *MyPyramid*. Diet should be varied because no single type of food contains all the nutrients (proteins, carbohydrates, fats, vitamins, and minerals) needed for good health.

A Balanced Diet

What we eat directly affects our health. Eating a balanced diet is the best way to ensure that the body receives all the food substances it needs.

Nutrition experts recommend that the daily diet include a certain number of servings from each of the five major food groups.

1. breads, cereals, rice, and pasta
2. vegetables
3. fruits
4. milk, yogurt, and cheese
5. meat, poultry, fish, dried beans and peas, eggs, and nuts

(Fats are also essential but, like sweets, should be eaten in small quantities.)

GENERAL DIETARY GUIDELINES

Consume less	Consume more
• fat and cholesterol	• complex carbohydrates
• refined sugar	• fiber
• salt	• fruits and vegetables
• alcohol	• whole grains
• calories	• unrefined foods
• processed foods	• fresh foods

Diet and Heart Attacks

A proper diet helps prevent certain illnesses and aids in recovery from others. An improper or inadequate diet increases the risk of various diseases.

For instance, in the opinion of the American Heart Association, reduction of fat intake is one of the most important steps to take to lower the risk of heart disease. No more than 30 percent of total daily calories should come from fat. In general, fats are made up of three types of fatty oils:

- saturated fats, which tend to increase cholesterol and aid formation of fatty plaques that clog arteries
- polyunsaturated fats and monounsaturated fats which may both help lower cholesterol

Dividing Fats. It is recommended that less than 10 percent of daily calories come from saturated fats, while 10 to 15 percent should come from monounsaturated fats, which have some advantages over polyunsaturated fats.

It is further recommended by the American Heart Association that fats in the diet be equally divided among the three types of fats. All natural fats contain a mixture of the three fats. For example, butter is about 64 percent saturated fat; soybean oil is about 60 percent polyunsaturated fat. (See page 263.)

A MEATLESS DIET

A vegetarian diet is one that does not include meat. There are four basic types of vegetarian diets.

1. *Vegetarian (strict or pure vegetarian):* Restricted to foods of plant origin, seeds, grains, nuts, fruits, and vegetables
2. *Lacto-vegetarian:* Includes all foods of plant origin; also foods made of milk, such as cheese, cream, and yogurt
3. *Ovo-vegetarian:* Includes all foods of plant origin; also eggs
4. *Lacto-ovo-vegetarian:* Includes all foods of plant origin; also dairy foods and eggs

Vegetarians must add legumes and nuts to their diets to obtain sufficient iron, calcium, and B vitamins.

Diet and Cancer: Guidelines		
Foods that studies show can REDUCE the risk of cancer, according to the American Cancer Society		
Food	**Nutrient**	**Effect**
Fresh dark green, orange, and yellow vegetables (broccoli, carrots, squash, spinach)	Beta-carotene, a substance that is converted by the body into vitamin A (high doses of beta-carotene should be avoided)	Appears to be of value in reducing the risk of lung, bladder, and breast cancers
Cabbage-family vegetables (brussels sprouts, cauliflower, kale)	Several chemicals are responsible for reduced cancer risk	Associated with reduced risk of certain cancers, especially cancer of the colon
Citrus fruits (oranges, grapefruits, tangerines, lemons), red fruits (strawberries, watermelon), and dark green vegetables (broccoli, collard greens)	Vitamin C	According to studies of persons at high risk of cancer, vitamin C reduces the incidence of stomach or esophageal cancer.
Whole grains, fresh fruits, and vegetables	Fiber (40 grams or more per day)	Appears to protect against colon and rectal cancer
Foods that studies show can INCREASE the risk of cancer, according to the American Cancer Society		
Food	**Substance**	**Effect**
Red meat and other fatty meats, butter fat, palm oil, and coconut oil	Saturated fat	Increases risk of certain types of cancer, particularly of the breast and colon
Cured, pickled, and smoked foods (cured meats, smoked fish and ham, pickles, olives, sauerkraut)	Nitrosamines (chemicals that are potent carcinogens, or agents known to cause cancer)	Populations consuming large amounts show a high incidence of esophageal and stomach cancer
Beer, wine, or liquor	Alcohol	Increases risk of cancer of the mouth, pharynx, larynx, esophagus, liver, and breast

Complementary Vegetable Proteins

For complete protein from plant foods, combine any mature legume, such as

- lentils
- peanuts
- garbanzos (chickpeas)
- navy beans
- soybeans or soy products
- lima beans
- pinto beans
- kidney beans

with any of the following

- barley
- corn
- oats
- rice (white or brown)
- seeds (sesame, pumpkin, sunflower)
- wheat (bread, pasta, cereal, grains)

(or combine rice or corn with wheat germ or seeds)

A vegetarian diet can be a healthful one as long as it includes necessary proteins and amino acids.

Vitamins and Minerals

Vitamins and *minerals* are substances that are essential for good health. They make up two of the major groups of *nutrients,* food substances necessary for growth and health.

Vitamins are organic chemical compounds that the body needs in small amounts. They regulate chemical reactions by which the body converts food into energy and living tissues.

Minerals are *inorganic compounds*—they do not come from living things. They are needed for the growth and maintenance of body structures. They are also needed to maintain the composition of the digestive juices and the fluids that are found in and around the cells. People need only small amounts of minerals each day.

DEFICIENT DISCOVERY

Over time, continued lack of one vitamin can result in a *vitamin deficiency disease.* Such diseases include beriberi, pellagra, rickets, and scurvy. Investigators first discovered vitamins while searching for the causes of such diseases.

Vitamins

Vitamins act as regulators in helping to process other vital nutrients: proteins, fats, and carbohydrates. Thirteen compounds are considered to be vitamins. They can be divided into two types.

- fat soluble
- water soluble

The fat-soluble vitamins dissolve in and are stored in body fat. There are four of them—A, D, E, and K. The fat-soluble vitamins are not readily excreted. They can be stored in the liver and fatty tissues and do not necessarily have to be consumed every day.

The water-soluble vitamins dissolve more easily in water and other fluids, including blood and urine. There are nine water-soluble vitamins—the eight B vitamins and vitamin C. The body does not store these vitamins, so the B vitamins and vitamin C must be included in the daily diet in adequate amounts to fulfill bodily demands.

Minerals

Unlike vitamins, carbohydrates, fats, and proteins, minerals are inorganic compounds. Plants obtain minerals from the water or soil, and animals get minerals by eating plants or plant-eating animals. Unlike other nutrients, minerals are not broken down by the body.

Functions

- Minerals carry out some functions similar to those performed by vitamins—assisting in bringing about biochemical reactions.

- They serve as structural components in tissues, for example, calcium and phosphorus in bone.

- They serve as raw materials in chemical reactions. For example, sodium is needed to pump water in and out of cells, and iron is the constituent of hemoglobin carrying oxygen to the cells.

Macrominerals are minerals that are required in large amounts for proper body function. They include calcium, chlorine, magnesium, phosphorus, potassium, sodium, and sulfur.

Calcium, magnesium, and phosphorus are essential parts of the bones and teeth. Calcium is also necessary for blood clotting. Milk and milk products are the richest sources of calcium. Cereals and meats provide phosphorus. Whole-grain cereals, nuts, legumes, and green leafy vegetables are sources of magnesium.

Dietary deficiencies of major minerals are rare, but dietary shortages of trace minerals do occur. A shortage of iron, for example, represents the most widespread nutritional deficiency seen in the United States.

Percent Daily Value. The Food and Nutrition Board of the National Academy of Sciences' Institute of Medicine has established a *percent daily value* for each vitamin and mineral. This is the average daily amount of each nutrient that a person needs to remain healthy.

The percent daily value of each vitamin is based on the amount needed to avoid signs of a deficiency in the average person. At the same time, the recommended amount allows for varying individual needs and for the capability of the body to absorb the consumed vitamins.

Vitamins and Diet. The most effective way for the body to absorb vitamins is through a balanced diet. Anyone who eats a variety of foods based on the five food groups should not need additional vitamins.

However, many people do not eat a balanced diet. Many people eat a lot of fast foods, processed foods, and canned foods. In such instances, a physician may advise that a multivitamin supplement be taken.

Megadose Vitamins. When vitamins are taken in *megadoses*—amounts much greater than the percent daily value—harmful effects may occur. Vitamins in these doses should not be taken without medical approval. The chart on pages 270–271 summarizes the functions of each vitamin, good food sources for them, and possible effects of excessive use.

Microminerals, or *trace elements,* are needed only in extremely tiny amounts. They include chromium, copper, fluorine, iodine, iron, manganese, molybdenum, selenium, and zinc.

Iron is an important part of hemoglobin, the oxygen-carrying molecule in red blood cells. Copper helps the body make use of iron to build hemoglobin. Manganese and zinc are required for the normal action of various enzymes. Green leafy vegetables, whole-grain breads and cereals, seafood, and liver are good sources of trace elements.

The iron used to make the steel in this skyscraper is the same as the iron found in your red blood cells in a substance called *hemoglobin.* ▶

Vitamins

Vitamins			
Fat-Soluble	**Good Food Sources**	**Primary Functions**	**Effects of Excessive Amounts**
Vitamin A **Retinol**	Yellow, orange, and dark green vegetables; liver; cheese; milk; eggs; butter.	Known as the "growth vitamin." Essential in maintaining healthy skin, hair, mucous membranes, and bone. Provides visual pigments that aid vision in dim light.	May cause headache, poor appetite, nausea, vomiting, damage to the liver and blood cells, skin rashes, hair loss, injury to brain and nervous system.
Vitamin D **Calciferol**	Egg yolks; butter; fortified milk; liver; fish liver oils; tuna; salmon; herring; sardines; oysters.	Known as the "sunshine vitamin." Aids normal growth of bones and teeth. Important in intestinal absorption of calcium and phosphorus. Protects against rickets.	May cause excessive calcium deposits in the blood; kidney stones, nausea, fragile bones, loss of appetite, high blood pressure, high blood cholesterol.
Vitamin E **Alphatocopherol**	Lettuce and other leafy green vegetables; seed oils; whole grains; dried beans; liver.	Helps in production of red cells and in strengthening of muscle tissue. Protects vitamin A and fats from reacting with oxygen (oxidation causes cell damage).	May cause blood clotting problems; may destroy some vitamin K in the intestines. May interfere with conversion of beta-carotene into vitamin A.
Vitamin K	Liver; potatoes; green leafy vegetables; cabbage; cauliflower; peas; cereals.	Aids in synthesis of substances needed for blood clotting; helps maintain normal bone metabolism. Made by bacteria in human intestine, except in newborns.	May cause blood clotting problems. May cause jaundice in infants.

SCURVY

Scurvy is a disease caused by lack of ascorbic acid (vitamin C) in the diet. It causes wounds to heal poorly and bruises to form easily. The walls of the capillaries (small blood vessels) become so weak that slight pressure may cause them to break. The mouth and gums become sore. The gums bleed, and the teeth may become loose. Patients lose their appetite, their joints become sore, and they become restless. Anemia may also develop.

Scurvy has been known since ancient times. During long voyages, sailors rarely had fresh fruits and vegetables that contain vitamin C. They lived on salt beef and hardtack (dry biscuits) for weeks at a time.

Foods especially rich in vitamin C include citrus fruits, tomatoes, lettuce, celery, onions, carrots, and potatoes. Including such foods in the diet will prevent or cure scurvy.

◀ **Scurvy.** Portuguese navigator Vasco da Gama once lost about 100 of 170 men due to scurvy.

Vitamins			
Water-Soluble	**Good Food Sources**	**Primary Functions**	**Effects of Excessive Amounts**
Vitamin B$_1$ Thiamin	Whole wheat grains; wheat germ; liver; kidney; pork; peas; beans; peanuts; oranges; various fruits and vegetables.	(All B vitamins play a similar role in the body; they help enzymes do their work.) Assists in function of 24 enzymes, helping cells to utilize carbohydrates. Assists in proper function of nervous system and digestive tract.	Not known; it is known that B vitamins are interdependent, so an excess of one may produce a deficiency of another.
Vitamin B$_2$ Riboflavin	Liver; kidney; lamb; beef; veal; eggs; whole wheat products; yeast; asparagus; beets; peas; dark green vegetables.	Cofactor in enzymes helping cells to use carbohydrates, proteins, and fats, and to produce energy. Promotes growth, healthy skin, and healthy mucous membranes.	None known.
Vitamin B$_3$ Niacin Nicotinamide Nicotinic acid	Lean meat; fish; liver; yeast; eggs; whole-grain breads; cereals; peas; beans; nuts.	Essential component of enzymes that contribute to production of energy in cells. Assists in the breakdown of fats.	Sweating, palpitations, circulatory problems, inability to digest carbohydrates, duodenal ulcer, abnormal liver function, excessive uric acid in blood.
Vitamin B$_6$ Pyridoxine Pyridoxal	Poultry; fish; liver; whole grains; cereals; breads; tomatoes; yellow corn; spinach; green beans; bananas; yogurt.	An enzyme activator; aids in breakdown of protein and carbohydrates, and in forming hormones such as adrenalin and insulin. Also helps regenerate red blood cells and produce antibodies.	Liver dysfunction; dependency on high dose can lead to deficiency symptoms on return to normal amounts.
Vitamin B$_{12}$ Cobalamin	Liver; kidney; fish; dairy products; brewer's yeast; wheat germ.	Assists in production of red blood cells, functioning of the nervous system, and building of genetic material.	None known.
Folic acid (a B vitamin)	Liver; kidney; green leafy vegetables; dried legumes.	Needed for formation of red and white blood cells. Aids in protein metabolism and in creating some components of DNA molecule.	None known; however, because it is stored in the body, it is potentially dangerous and can mask a B$_{12}$ deficiency.
Vitamin C Ascorbic acid	Abundant in most fruits and vegetables, especially citrus fruits, tomatoes, potatoes, green peppers, and dark green vegetables.	Enhances activity of certain enzymes. Aids body in use of iron and in blood clotting. Helps formation of teeth, gums, and bones. Aids in healing of bone fractures and wounds.	Diarrhea, formation of kidney and bladder stones, increased tendency for blood to clot, urinary tract irritation; may induce a B12 deficiency.

Minerals

Minerals		
Macrominerals	**Chief Food Sources**	**Chief Body Functions**
Calcium	Milk; dairy products; yogurt; hard cheeses; sardines; green leafy vegetables; collard and dandelion greens.	Supports growth of bones and teeth; helps maintain cell membranes; essential for proper blood clotting; helps regulate ions in and out of cells; aids muscle contraction and relaxation; essential for functioning of several important enzymes.
Phosphorus	Meat; fish; poultry; milk; nuts; legumes; whole grain breads; cereals.	Important in formation of bones and teeth, and the functioning of several B vitamins; transports fats throughout the body; necessary for release of energy from carbohydrates; present in every cell as part of nucleic acids.
Magnesium	Meat; fish; milk; whole grains; salad greens; nuts (especially almonds and cashews).	Essential for release of energy from glycogen, production of proteins, regulation of body temperature, and proper functioning of nerves and muscles.
Potassium	Bananas; orange juice; dried fruits; meat; peanut butter; potatoes; coffee.	Aids in transmission of nerve impulses; buffers body fluids; catalyzes release of energy from carbohydrates, proteins, and fats; regulates amount of water in cells and so aids proper cell function.

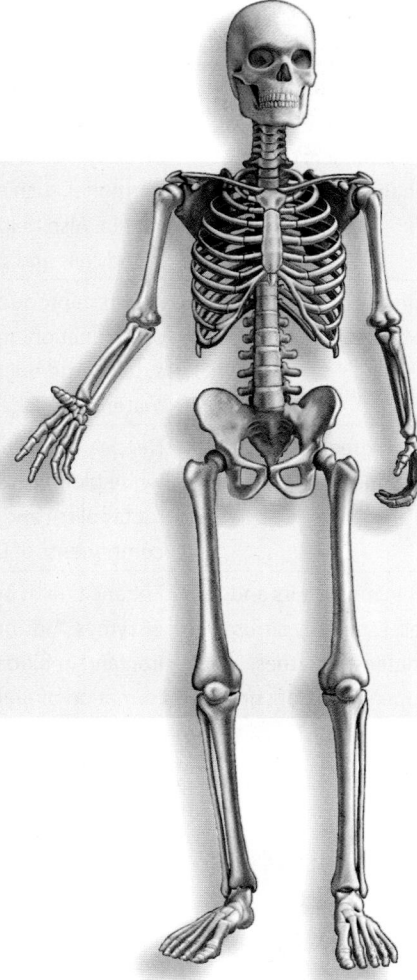

METAL IN THE BODY

Several of the minerals essential for a healthy human body are actually metal. Calcium is one of the most abundant metals on Earth. It makes up about 3.5 percent of Earth's crust. Calcium is also the most abundant metal in the human body.

Calcium is essential to all living things. It is vital for the growth and maintenance of the bones and teeth, and it helps the blood to clot and the muscles to contract. A daily diet that includes green vegetables, milk, and milk products supplies enough calcium for the human body's normal needs.

The Elements of Bone. About two-thirds of the weight of bone tissue consists of minerals, mostly calcium, phosphate, and carbonate.

Minerals		
Microminerals (Trace minerals)	**Chief Food Sources**	**Chief Body Functions**
Chromium	Liver; beef; dried beans; cheese; whole-grain breads and cereals; peanuts; brewer's yeast; molasses; beets.	Aids the body, together with insulin, in deriving energy from blood sugar; plays an important role in the synthesis of fatty acids and cholesterol in the liver.
Copper	Oysters; fish; nuts; dried peas; beans, beef and pork liver; organ meats; eggs; spinach; asparagus; corn oil margarine.	Aids in the manufacture of red blood cells, and helps body store iron. A component of several respiratory enzymes, copper is also part of the enzyme that helps make melanin (skin pigment).
Fluorine (fluoride)	Fish; tea; most animal foods; fluoridated water; foods grown with or cooked in fluoridated water.	Helps form strong teeth and resistance to decay, aids in maintaining bone strength.
Iodine	Seafood; saltwater fish; seaweed; sea salt; iodized salt.	A component of thyroid hormones, which control metabolism. Aids in development and functioning of the thyroid gland, and in the prevention of goiter (enlarged thyroid gland).
Iron	Liver (especially pork, then calf, beef, and chicken); kidney; red meat; egg yolks; green leafy vegetables; raisins; apricots; prunes; dried beans, peas; potatoes; blackstrap molasses; enriched and whole-grain cereals.	Helps form red blood cells and myoglobin in muscles that supply oxygen in cells. Found in enzyme systems, including one that works to produce energy in the body.
Manganese	Nuts; whole grains; fruits; vegetables; tea; instant coffee; cocoa powder.	Aids in proper functioning of the nervous system, normal bone structure, and reproduction; extremely important in many vital enzyme systems in the body; needed for utilization of iron.
Molybdenum	Legumes; cereal grains; liver; kidney; some dark green vegetables.	Required by three important enzymes. May aid in prevention of tooth decay; associated with carbohydrate metabolism.
Selenium	Seafood; whole-grain cereals; meat; egg yolks; chicken; milk.	Prevents breakdown of fats and other body chemicals; interacts with vitamin E in protecting cell membranes.
Zinc	Beef; liver; eggs; poultry; seafood, especially oysters; peas; carrots; whole grains; pure maple syrup.	A component of as many as 100 enzymes in the body. Involved in wound healing; needed for growth and development.

The Nutrition Labeling and Education Act of 1990 requires that all packaged and processed food sold in the United States carry labels with nutritional information. The labels help people compare their daily dietary needs with the nutritional content of the foods they eat. Food labeling in Canada is regulated by Health Canada, a department similar to the U.S. Food and Drug Administration (FDA).

The following pointers may help you make more informed decisions about the foods you purchase. For more information, go to www.fda.gov.

Ingredient Lists and Nutrition Facts

Ingredient Listings. For foods containing more than one ingredient, companies must list each ingredient. They are listed in descending order by weight. For example, if sugar is the first ingredient listed, the product contains more sugar than any other ingredient.

Artificial Colors. The FDA regulates all color additives used in the U.S. Certified colors are man-made. Each batch is tested for safety, quality, consistency, and strength by the manufacturer and the FDA. Pigments derived from natural sources (such as vegetables or minerals) and their man-made counterparts do not have to be certified. They are listed as "artificial color," "artificial coloring," or by their common names.

In Canada, color additives are listed in the ingredients list by their common name or simply as "colours."

Spices, Natural Flavors, and Artificial Flavors. In the U.S., these can be listed by their common names or as "spices," "flavor" or "natural flavor," or "artificial flavor." Spices that are also colorings must be denoted as "spice and coloring" or by their common names, such as "paprika."

In Canada, all food additives are regulated by Health Canada.

Alternative Fats and Oils. If a food contains a small quantity of added fat or oil, and the manufacturer cannot predict which fat or oil will be used, then the alternatives must be listed. For example, a label might say: "vegetable oil (contains one or more of the following: corn oil, soybean oil, or safflower oil)."

Juice Percentages. Beverages claiming to contain juice must list the total percentage of juice in the product.

Nutrition Panels. If a food or product is required to contain a *nutrition panel* (sample shown at right), data on the following nutrients must be included in that panel: total calories; calories from fat; total fat; saturated fat; cholesterol; sodium; total carbohydrate; dietary fiber; sugars; protein; vitamin A; vitamin C; calcium; and iron.

Similar nutrition labels are used in Canada.

Serving Size. The serving size is the basis for reporting a food's nutrient content and is based on the amounts of food people actually eat. In the U.S. serving sizes must be given in both common household measures (such as cup, tablespoon, or slice) and in metric measures (such as grams and milliliters).

Calories and Calories from Fat. The number of calories listed shows how much energy we get from one serving of a food. In the U.S. sample shown here, approximately one-third of this food's calories come from fat.

Indicating calories from fat is not mandatory in Canada.

Nutrient Listings. The nutrients listed first on the U.S. panel (fats, cholesterol, and sodium) are the ones Americans generally eat in adequate amounts, or even in too large an amount. Dietary fiber, vitamin A, vitamin C, calcium, and iron are nutrients that Americans frequently don't consume enough of.

Percent Daily Values. For labeling purposes, both the FDA and Health Canada set 2,000 calories as the reference amount for calculating the percent of daily values. Most nutrients are listed as percentages of these daily values. This information helps you see how a food fits into an overall daily diet. Even if you don't

HISTORICAL REGULATION

The first effective, enforceable pure food law in the United States was the Meat Inspection Act, passed in 1906 after Upton Sinclair's novel *The Jungle* exposed the wretched, unsanitary working conditions in the meat-packing industry.

know how many calories you consume in a day's time, you can use this information to tell whether the food is high or low in a given nutrient. As a general rule, a %DV of 5% or less is low; 20% or more is high.

Footnote. The information at the bottom of the panel contains general dietary advice about how much or how little of certain nutrients you should consume in a day. For example, if your daily diet is 2,000 calories, you should consume less than 65 grams of total fat.

Nutrient Content Claims. The following are some uniform definitions for terms that denote specific nutrient claims. (This is a partial list.)

- *Free.* Use of the word "free" (such as "fat-free") means a product contains no amount—or only an inconsequential amount—of that ingredient.
- *Low.* "Low-fat" means a food contains 3 grams of fat or less per serving; "low-sodium" means 140 milligrams or less per serving; "low-calorie" means 40 calories or less per serving.
- *Reduced.* The product contains at least 25 percent less of a nutrient or of calories than the "regular" product. The label should include a comparison to the "regular" product.

Health Claims. Only a few claims of a relationship between a nutrient or a food and the risk of a disease or health-related condition are allowed. Only claims that are supported by scientific evidence can be used. Such claims must also state that other factors play a part. An allowable claim might be: "While many factors affect heart disease, diets low in saturated fat and cholesterol may reduce the risk of this disease."

Nutrition Facts

Serving Size 1/2 cup (114g)
Servings Per Container 4

Amount Per Serving

Calories 90   Calories from Fat 30

	% Daily Value*
Total Fat 3g	**5%**
Saturated Fat 0g	**0%**
Cholesterol 0mg	**0%**
Sodium 300mg	**13%**
Total Carbohydrate 13g	**4%**
Dietary Fiber 3g	**12%**
Sugars 3g	
Protein 3g	

Vitamin A	80%
Vitamin C	60%
Calcium	4%
Iron	4%

*Percent Daily Values are based on a 2,000 calorie diet. Your Daily Values may be higher or lower depending on your calorie needs:

	Calories:	2,000	2,500
Total Fat	Less than	65g	80g
Sat Fat	Less than	20g	25g
Cholesterol	Less than	300mg	300mg
Sodium	Less than	2,400mg	2,400mg
Total Carbohydrate		300g	375g
Dietary Fiber		25g	30g

Calories and Fat

Food	Calories	Grams
Meats		
Bacon, pan-fried, 3 strips	109	9
Bacon, meatless, pan-fried, 3 strips	47	4
Chuck roast, braised, 3 ounces	282	20
Chuck roast, braised, 100g	332	24
Ground beef, lean, pan-fried, 3 ounces	235	15
Ground beef, lean, pan-fried, 100g	275	19
Kidneys, beef, cooked, 3 ounces	122	3
Kidneys, beef, cooked, 100g	144	3
Pork roast, loin, roasted, 3 ounces	275	21
Pork roast, loin, roasted, 100g	248	15
Sausage, fresh, cooked, 1 link	48	4
Steak, T-bone, broiled, 3 ounces	263	20
Steak, T-bone, broiled, 100g	309	23
Beverages		
Apple juice, from concentrate, 1 cup (8 ounces)	117	0
Chocolate milk, whole milk, 1 cup (8 ounces)	208	8
Chocolate milk, low-fat, 1 cup (8 ounces)	158	3
Milk, whole, 1 cup (8 ounces)	150	8
Milk, 2%, 1 cup (8 ounces)	121	5
Milk, 1%, 1 cup (8 ounces)	102	3
Lemonade, from concentrate, 1 cup (8 ounces)	99	0
Orange juice, from concentrate, 1 cup (8 ounces)	112	0
Tomato juice, 1 cup (8 ounces)	41	0

Food	Calories	Grams
Fish and Seafood		
Cod, cooked, 1 fillet	189	2
Crab, blue, canned, drained, 6.5 ounces	124	2
Crab, blue, canned, drained, 100g	99	1
Grouper, cooked, 1 fillet	238	3
Ocean perch, cooked, 1 fillet	61	1
Salmon, pink, canned, 3 ounces	118	5
Salmon, pink, canned, 100g	139	6
Shrimp, breaded, fried, 4 large	73	4
Tuna, canned in water, 3 ounces	99	1
Tuna, canned in water, 100g	116	1
Poultry		
Chicken, 1/4 broiler/fryer, with skin, battered, fried	673	40
Chicken, 1/4 broiler/fryer, without skin, battered, fried	283	12
Chicken, 1/2 breast, with skin, roasted	193	8
Chicken, 1/2 breast, no skin, roasted	142	3
Chicken, 1 drumstick, with skin, roasted	112	6
Chicken, 1 drumstick, no skin, roasted	76	2
Chicken, livers, 1 cup, simmered	220	8
Chicken livers, simmered, 100g	157	5
Chicken, canned, 5 ounces	234	11
Chicken, canned, 100g	165	8
Turkey, 1 cup chopped, roasted, with skin	291	14
Turkey, 1 cup chopped, roasted, without skin	238	7
Turkey, 1/2 breast, no skin, roasted	413	2
Turkey sausage, smoked, 2 ounces	90	5
Turkey sausage, smoked, 100g	160	10

Food	Calories	Grams
Eggs		
Hard-boiled, 1 large	78	5
Scrambled with milk, 1 large	101	7
Substitute, frozen, 1/4 cup	96	7
Substitute, frozen, 100g	160	11
Cheese		
American, 1 ounce	106	9
American, 100g	375	31
Brie, 1 ounce	95	8
Brie, 100g	334	28
Cheddar, 1 ounce	114	9
Cheddar, 100g	403	33
Cottage, 4 ounces	117	5
Cottage, 100g	103	5
Cream, 1 ounce	99	10
Cream, 100g	349	35
Feta, 1 ounce	75	6
Feta, 100g	264	21
Mozzarella, whole milk, 1 ounce	80	6
Mozzarella, whole milk, 100g	281	22
Mozzarella, part skim milk, 1 ounce	72	5
Mozzarella, part skim milk, 100g	254	16
Ricotta, whole milk, 1/2 cup	216	16
Ricotta, whole milk, 100g	174	13
Ricotta, part skim milk, 1/2 cup	171	10
Ricotta, part skim milk, 100g	138	8

Food	Calories	Grams
Fruit		
Apple, 1 medium, with peel	81	0
Applesauce, unsweetened, 1/2 cup	52	0
Applesauce, unsweetened, 100g	43	0
Banana, 1 medium	109	1
Blackberries, 1/2 cup	37	0
Blackberries, 100g	52	0
Grapefruit, 1/2 medium	41	0
Orange, 1 medium	62	0
Peach, 1 medium	42	0
Pineapple, 1/2 cup	38	0
Pineapple, 100g	49	0
Plantain, 1/2 cup, cooked	89	0
Plantain, cooked, 100g	116	0
Raisins, seedless, 1/2 cup	248	0
Raisins, seedless, 100g	300	3
Raspberries, 1/2 cup	30	0
Raspberries, 100g	49	1
Strawberries, 1/2 cup	25	0
Strawberries, 100g	30	0
Watermelon, 1/2 cup	24	0
Watermelon, 100g	32	0

Calories and Fat

Food	Calories	Grams
Vegetables		
Asparagus, fresh, boiled, 4 spears	16	0
Beans, black, boiled, 1/2 cup	114	0
Beans, black, boiled, 100g	132	1
Beans, green, canned, 1/2 cup	14	0
Beans, green, canned, 100g	20	0
Beets, boiled, 1/2 cup	37	0
Beets, boiled, 100g	44	0
Broccoli, raw, 1/2 cup	12	0
Broccoli, raw, 100g	28	0
Cabbage, boiled, 1/2 cup	17	0
Cabbage, boiled, 100g	22	0
Carrots, boiled, 1/2 cup	35	0
Carrots, boiled, 100g	45	0
Chickpeas, boiled, 1/2 cup	134	2
Chickpeas, boiled, 100g	164	3
Corn, cream-style, canned, 1/2 cup	92	1
Corn, cream-style, canned, 100g	72	0
Eggplant, boiled, 1/2 cup	14	0
Eggplant, boiled, 100g	28	0
Lentils, boiled, 1/2 cup	115	0
Lentils, boiled, 100g	116	0
Mushrooms, boiled, 1/2 cup pieces	21	0
Mushrooms, boiled, 100g	27	0
Peas, green, boiled, 1/2 cup	67	0
Peas, green, boiled, 100g	84	0
Potato, baked with skin, 1	220	0

Food	Calories	Grams
Vegetables		
Radishes, 1/2 cup	12	0
Radishes, 100g	20	1
Sauerkraut, canned, 1/2 cup	22	0
Sauerkraut, canned, 100g	19	0
Spinach, boiled, 1/2 cup	21	0
Spinach, boiled, 100g	23	0
Squash, winter, baked, 1/2 cup	57	0
Squash, winter, baked, 100g	56	0
Sweet potato, baked with skin, 1	117	0
Turnips, boiled, 1/2 cup	16	0
Turnips, boiled, 100g	21	0
Breads and Grains		
Bagel, egg, 1 medium	197	1
Brown rice, cooked, 1/2 cup	108	1
Brown rice, cooked, 100g	111	1
Egg noodles, cooked, 1/2 cup	106	1
Egg noodles, cooked, 100g	133	1
Flour tortilla, 1 medium	104	2
Italian bread, 1 medium slice	69	1
Saltine crackers, 1	13	1
Spaghetti, cooked, 1/2 cup	99	1
Spaghetti, cooked, 100g	141	1
White rice, cooked, 1/2 cup	103	0
White rice, cooked, 100g	130	0
Whole wheat bread, 1 medium slice	69	1

Food	Calories	Grams
Cereals		
Cornflakes, 1 cup	102	0
Cornflakes, 100g	365	1
Couscous, cooked, 1 cup	176	0
Couscous, cooked, 100g	112	0
Cream of wheat, cooked, 1 cup	133	1
Cream of wheat, cooked, 100g	53	0
Oats, cooked, 1 cup	145	2
Oats, cooked, 100g	62	1
Raisin bran, 1 cup	186	1
Raisin bran, 100g	305	2

Food	Calories	Grams
Desserts and Snacks		
Angel food cake, 1 slice (1/12 of 12-ounce cake)	73	0
Banana chips, 1 ounce	147	10
Banana chips, 100g	519	34
Chocolate chip cookies, 1 medium	48	2
Chocolate ice cream, 1/2 cup	143	7
Chocolate ice cream, 100g	216	4
Chocolate pudding, prepared from mix with 2% milk, 1/2 cup	150	3
Chocolate pudding, prepared from mix with 2% milk, 100g	102	2
Corn chips, 1 ounce	153	9
Corn chips, 100g	539	33
Frozen yogurt, soft-serve, 1/2 cup	115	4
Frozen yogurt, soft-serve, 100g	159	6
Orange sherbet, 1/2 cup	102	1
Orange sherbet, 100g	138	2
Popcorn, plain, air-popped, 1 cup	31	0
Popcorn, plain, air-popped, 100g	382	4
Potato chips, plain, 1 ounce	152	10
Potato chips, plain, 100g	536	35
Pretzels, 1 ounce	108	1
Pretzels, 100g	381	4
Tortilla chips, 1 ounce	142	7
Tortilla chips, 100g	501	26

Source: U.S. Department of Agriculture, Agricultural Research Service. 2002. Nutrient Data Laboratory Home Page, www.ars.usda.gov/nutrientdata

FITNESS is the ability to meet the physical demands of daily life and to resist diseases associated with inactivity. Physical fitness enables people to perform well in sports and other activities, and to look and feel their best.

The requirements for health-related fitness are similar for all people. Everyone must maintain certain aspects of health-related fitness to feel good and to resist disease. To achieve and maintain physical fitness, people should exercise regularly, eat a balanced diet, and maintain a healthy weight.

Exercise

Exercise helps keep the body healthy and fit. Vigorous exercise strengthens muscles and improves the function of the circulatory and respiratory systems. Physical fitness benefits both physical and mental health and helps the body withstand stress.

Moderate and Regular

Moderate and regular exercise offers benefits: a feeling of well-being, with increased self-confidence and reduced irritability and fatigue. Above all, research studies have shown that a person who exercises becomes noticeably healthier.

Activity	Calories per Hour
Bicycling, 5 1/2 mph	210
Bicycling, 13 mph	660
Bowling	270
Driving an automobile	120
Gardening	220
Golf	250
Housework	180
Lawn mowing	250
Roller skating	350
Running, 10 mph	900
Sitting	100
Skiing, 10 mph	600
Sleeping	80
Square dancing	350
Squash and handball	600
Standing	140
Swimming (moderate speed)	300
Tennis	420
Volleyball	350
Walking, 2 1/2 mph	210
Walking, 3 3/4 mph	300
Wood chopping or sawing	400

EXERCISE: ENERGY EXPENDITURES

This table gives approximate energy expenditures by a 150-pound person in performing various activities.

If You Eat...	You Add...	To Lose, You Must Walk
2 strips of bacon	100 calories	20 minutes
10 potato chips	100 calories	20 minutes
1 doughnut	150 calories	29 minutes
1 piece of cake	358 calories	68 minutes
1 slice of apple pie	375 calories	73 minutes
1 milkshake	500 calories	97 minutes

- The more physically active a person is, the lower the risk of suffering a heart attack. (See page 232.)
- Continued physical activity throughout life helps ward off osteoporosis, a leading cause of disability in people past 50.
- Exercise can also help relieve anxiety and tension found in high-pressure work or in difficult life circumstances.

Weight Control

Exercise helps a person maintain a healthy weight in two ways.

- It burns calories directly.
- The body continues to burn extra calories up to 15 hours after exercise.

Any type of exercise, including the doing of house chores or a repair job, or weeding in the garden, can help control weight. The more activity, the greater the number of calories expended. In general, exercise decreases appetite, helping the body to readjust food intake to energy expenditure.

Types of Exercise

Choice of exercise depends on a number of factors: age, physical condition, body build, capabilities, and manner of living. Before plunging into physical activity, it is wise to make certain that one's body is in condition to undertake the contemplated exercise program. It is advisable for anyone with a chronic health problem, or anyone over 35 and long inactive, to have medical advice before launching an exercise program.

Aerobic Exercises. Walking, cross-country skiing, swimming, running, and bicycling are *aerobic exercises,* meaning they increase the demand for oxygen for prolonged periods. Such physical activity strengthens the heart and lungs, and increases muscular endurance.

It has been determined that aerobic exercise, when combined with a healthful diet, is probably the most effective way to lose weight. Calisthenics and gymnastics improve strength, agility, and muscle tone.

Stretching Exercises. Stretching exercises improve flexibility. Ten to 15 minutes a day of stretches can benefit both body and mind, reduce muscle tension, improve coordination, and promote circulation.

After exercising for a while, there is a tendency for muscles to shorten. For this reason, such activity should be followed by gentle exercises that relax and stretch the muscles. If this is not done, the shortened muscles are more likely to go into muscle spasm, a common cause of post-exercise stiffness. (See pages 228–229.)

WALK IT OFF

Walking is considered by many health authorities to be the best overall nonstrenuous activity for the heart and legs. A brisk walk lasting 20 to 30 minutes each day can help take weight off and keep it off.

ROLL IT OFF

Exercise can help you stay happy and healthy. One of the key factors to gaining the benefits of exercise is consistency. People are more likely to do something regularly if they enjoy it.

Skateboarding burns about 340 calories per hour, about the same amount as playing volleyball or square dancing.

Weight Control

A healthy weight is important for overall good health. *Obesity*—the condition of having an excessive amount of body fat—increases a person's risk for many conditions and diseases, including:

- diabetes
- heart disease
- hypertension (high blood pressure)
- arthritis
- cancer

Height and Weight Tables

Ideal body weight may be determined by checking a table of suggested desirable weights. Such tables give no absolute answers on what constitutes ideal weight, but they can be helpful in determining an advisable weight range.

The height and weight tables shown here apply to people ages 25 to 59. Weight is stated in pounds, according to body frame size, and including the wearing of indoor clothing (5 pounds for men and 3 pounds for women in shoes with 1-inch heels).

Body Mass Index

Some experts at the National Institutes of Health consider debatable the value of charts of desirable weights, preferring a *body mass index* (BMI) instead as an indicator of body fitness. The BMI represents the proportion between a person's weight and height.

Body Math. To obtain a BMI, body weight (in pounds) is multiplied by 703, and the product is divided by height (in inches). The quotient is then divided by body height once again, yielding the body mass index.

A final answer showing a value of 20 to 25 is considered normal. Between 26 and 30, many experts advise losing weight. A value over 30 is usually regarded as an indication of medically significant obesity that requires treatment in some fashion.

HEIGHT/WEIGHT TABLES

© 2006 Metropolitan Life Insurance Company. Source of basic data: 1979 Build Study, Society of Actuaries and Association of Life Insurance Medical Directors of America, 1980.

Women				Men			
Height	Weight (in pounds)			Height	Weight (in pounds)		
	Small Frame	Medium Frame	Large Frame		Small Frame	Medium Frame	Large Frame
4'10"	102–111	109–121	118–131	5'2"	128–134	131–141	138–150
4'11"	103–113	111–123	120–134	5'3"	130–136	133–143	140–153
5'0"	104–115	113–126	122–137	5'4"	132–138	135–145	142–156
5'1"	106–118	115–129	125–140	5'5"	134–140	137–148	144–160
5'2"	108–121	118–132	128–143	5'6"	136–142	139–151	146–164
5'3"	111–124	121–135	131–147	5'7"	138–145	142–154	149–168
5'4"	114–127	124–138	134–151	5'8"	140–148	145–157	152–172
5'5"	117–130	127–141	137–155	5'9"	142–151	148–160	155–176
5'6"	120–133	130–144	140–159	5'10"	144–154	151–163	158–180
5'7"	123–136	133–147	143–163	5'11"	146–157	154–166	161–184
5'8"	126–139	136–150	146–167	6'0"	149–160	157–170	164–188
5'9"	129–142	139–153	149–170	6'1"	152–164	160–174	168–192
5'10"	132–145	142–156	152–173	6'2"	155–168	164–178	172–197
5'11"	135–148	145–159	155–176	6'3"	158–172	167–182	176–202
6'0"	138–151	148–162	158–179	6'4"	162–176	171–187	181–207

Height (in.)	120	130	140	150	160	170	180	190	200	210	220	230	240	250	260	270	280	290	300	320	340	360	380	400
60	23	25	27	29	31	33	35	37	39	41	43	45	47	49	51	53	55	57	59	63	66	70	74	78
62	22	24	26	27	29	31	33	35	37	38	40	42	44	46	48	49	51	53	55	59	62	66	70	73
64	21	22	24	26	28	29	31	33	34	36	38	40	41	43	45	46	48	50	52	55	58	62	65	68
66	19	21	23	24	26	27	29	31	32	34	36	37	39	40	42	44	45	47	49	52	55	58	61	65
68	16	20	21	23	24	26	27	29	30	32	34	35	37	38	40	41	43	44	46	48	52	55	58	61
70	17	19	20	22	23	24	26	27	28	30	32	33	35	36	37	38	40	42	43	46	48	52	55	57
72	16	18	19	20	22	23	24	26	27	29	30	31	33	34	35	37	38	39	41	43	46	49	52	54
74	15	17	18	19	21	22	23	24	26	27	28	30	31	32	33	35	36	37	39	41	44	48	49	51
76	15	16	17	18	20	21	22	23	24	26	27	28	29	30	32	33	34	35	37	40	41	44	48	49

Legend: Underweight — Normal weight — Overweight — Obese — Very obese

Weight (lb.)

Body Mass Index. To find your BMI on this chart, locate your weight in pounds along the bottom and your height in inches along the left. The number where these two values intersect is your BMI.

Losing Weight

On the whole, commercial diet plans are nutritionally unbalanced and seldom result in permanent weight loss. Some health professionals consider repeated cycles of weight loss and gain to have a more damaging effect upon health than being consistently and moderately overweight.

Reduce Calories. In sensible weight loss, calorie intake should be reduced, but without a cutback on the nutrients needed for proper body function.

To gain 10 pounds in 1 year, for example, takes no more than an extra 100 calories a day. This amount is easily obtained with one extra tablespoonful of butter, one pear, a plain muffin, or a biscuit of shredded wheat.

In a day during which a total of 2,000 or so calories may be consumed, an extra spoonful of cereal at breakfast, several more bites of cheese at lunch, a sweet snack in the afternoon, and an extra helping of meat at dinner will add up to many extra calories.

Gaining Weight

In general, a person who desires to gain weight needs to eat more nutritious foods and to increase the total number of calories in the daily diet. Proper living habits also are important: regular meals, moderate exercise, sufficient sleep and rest, and avoidance of unnecessary tension.

In some cases, medical problems such as hyperthyroidism or diabetes must be corrected before considering any program to gain weight. A physical checkup may be indicated to determine the underlying cause of being underweight or of having continued weight loss.

CREEPING OBESITY

Physiologists state that about 3,500 calories equal 1 pound of fat. That is, 100 unburned calories per day for 35 days will add 1 pound of fat. At this rate, weight gain at the end of a year would amount to 10 pounds.

Often, added pounds go unnoticed in what has been called "creeping obesity." Many Americans average between 15 and 30 pounds of excess weight.

Eating Issues

An *eating disorder* is an illness characterized by a disturbance in attitudes and behaviors relating to eating, body weight, and body image.

Types of Eating Disorders

- anorexia nervosa
- bulimia nervosa (*commonly referred to as bulimia*)
- eating disorder not otherwise specified (*EDNOS*)

Anorexia Nervosa. People who suffer from anorexia nervosa are underweight and usually restrict their eating. Many suffer severe weight loss.

The disease typically affects adolescent girls and young women, but can also occur in older women and men. A person suffering from anorexia nervosa may restrict food intake to as little as 300 to 600 calories a day and lose more than 25 percent of body weight. Other symptoms include low blood pressure, slow heartbeat, and growth of fine hair on the body. In adolescents, the start of puberty may be delayed. Females with anorexia may not begin to menstruate, or their menstrual periods may stop.

Physicians disagree about the cause of anorexia nervosa. Some psychiatrists believe that sufferers try to starve themselves in order to avoid growing into adults. Other experts suggest that sufferers may want to gain attention and a sense of being special.

Anorexia nervosa can be fatal in some cases. Individualized treatment, including psychotherapy, and hospitalization may be ordered if a person is extremely malnourished.

A PSYCHOLOGICAL ISSUE

Health professionals consider eating disorders to be mental illnesses. A first step in treatment usually is psychotherapy, especially group therapy, which offers support from peers at a crucial time.

Some hospitals offer treatment programs for eating disorders. They use a team that may include a psychiatrist, psychologist, nurses, and social workers, as well as including the patient's family.

Bulimia nervosa is a disorder in which individuals have frequent and uncontrollable periods of overeating. These periods are called binges.

After bingeing, most bulimics purge (eliminate) the food. They may do so by making themselves vomit. Or they may take large doses of laxatives to help empty the bowels. Some bulimics try to burn off the calories consumed during a binge by exercising excessively. Others temporarily starve themselves. Thus, most bulimics do not gain weight.

EDNOS refers to any eating disorder that has prominent eating or body image symptoms that are different from the usual symptoms of anorexia nervosa or bulimia or that has most, but not all, of their defining symptoms.

SIGNS OF ANOREXIA NERVOSA

Various behavioral and physical changes may signal a developing anorexia.

- Extreme weight loss: Loss of at least 25 percent of body weight. Weight loss may be 15 to 20 percent in some women.
- Obsession with body weight: Fear of becoming obese; often, this exists even though the anorexic appears emaciated. A feeling of security as long as weight loss continues.
- Excessive exercise: Exercises compulsively to burn off calories.
- Dieting and calorie counting: The anorexic refuses to maintain normal, healthy body weight. Counts calories, may only eat certain foods.
- Other symptoms: Insomnia, constipation, dry skin, hair loss, brittle nails, and a feeling of always being cold. May be continuing withdrawal from social contacts, especially situations involving eating.

Fast Foods

Fast food and processed or convenience foods have had a profound effect on the eating habits of millions of Americans. Many of these foods can be thought of as junk foods—soft drinks, snack foods, candies—which contain nothing more than "empty calories," offering high sugar content with no nutritional value.

Food Values of Fast Foods					
Fast Food	Calories	Protein (grams)	Carbohydrates (grams)	Fats (grams)	Sodium (mg.)
Burger King French Fries – salted (medium)	440	5	56	22	670
Burger King Vanilla Shake (medium)	520	12	84	16	420
Burger King Original Chicken Sandwich	630	24	46	39	1,390
Burger King Whopper	670	28	51	40	980
Dairy Queen Banana Split	520	9	94	13	160
Dairy Queen Chocolate Xtreme Blizzard (medium)	970	17	130	45	600
Dairy Queen Chili Cheese Dog	380	16	23	24	980
Dairy Queen Onion Rings	360	6	47	16	840
Kentucky Fried Chicken, Grilled Chicken (breast)	210	34	0	8	460
Kentucky Fried Chicken, Original Recipe (breast)	320	42	4	15	710
McDonald's Big Mac	540	25	45	29	1,040
McDonald's Triple Thick Chocolate Shake (small)	440	10	76	10	190
McDonald's Egg McMuffin	300	18	30	12	820
McDonald's Filet-o-Fish	380	15	38	18	640
Pizza Hut Meat Lover's Pizza (hand-tossed crust, 1 medium slice)	330	14	27	18	830
Pizza Hut Personal Pan Pizza (pepperoni)	610	26	67	26	1,410
Taco Bell Taco	170	8	12	10	330
Source: Data obtained from corporate Web sites, 2010.					

Protein Power. While meals of such foods can hardly be considered balanced, a number of experts think they are better than one might be led to believe. Fast foods contain ample amounts of protein; for example, a burger, fries, and a shake supply 42 percent of the recommended daily allowance for protein.

Sweet Sweets. Except for drinks and desserts, fast-food meals contain little sugar. However, it would be well to choose milk or fruit juice rather than the typical fast-food shake, which may have from 8 to 14 teaspoons of sugar in it.

Calorie Considerations. For the nutritional value they offer, fast foods are laden with too many calories. A Kentucky Fried Chicken Dinner, for example, with a 12-ounce soft drink, may amount to about 1,100 calories, or more than half the daily caloric needs for many individuals.

Filled with Fat. Fast foods on the whole contain too much fat, mostly in the cheese, the sauce added to burgers—the meat is generally rather lean—the deep-fried potatoes, and the shakes, which are made with vegetable oils. (See pages 262–263.)

So Much Sodium. Most fast foods are extremely high in sodium: a typical meal may contain as much as three-fourths of the daily recommended intake (about 2,200 milligrams a day). Those on a restricted salt diet had best eat burgers plain, without pickles, and use no salt on French fries.

Find Other Fiber. Fast foods are lacking in fiber and in vitamins A and C. It is a good idea, therefore, to include fruit, salad, a green or yellow vegetable, and whole or enriched grains in other meals on days when a fast-food meal has been eaten.

MENTAL HEALTH plays an important role in both the way people behave and the way they feel. It is closely connected to physical health.

Emotionally healthy individuals accept themselves as they are—with all their weaknesses as well as their strengths. They remain in contact with reality and can deal with stress and frustration. They also act independently of outside influences and show genuine concern for others.

Mentally healthy people are able to handle stress in a healthy manner and maintain positive personal relationships.

Stress

Stress is the body's emergency response to real or imagined danger. A stress reaction prepares the body for a burst of action to fight or flee a threat. The heart races, the hands get cold and sweaty, the muscles tense, and the stomach feels jittery.

Causes of Stress

- Severe stress results from such serious events as the death of a loved one, a divorce, or loss of a job.
- Day-to-day problems, such as taking tests or driving in traffic jams, may also be stressful.
- Physical stressors include natural disasters, illnesses, and noise.
- The demands of jobs, school, and other activities are stressors for children and their overworked parents.
- Television, radio, newspapers, and the Internet flood people with information about crime, disasters, terrorism, and other upsetting occurrences throughout the world.

HANS SELYE

1907–1982

The Canadian scientist Hans Selye pioneered studies of stress in the 1930s. His study of endocrine glands helped him develop new understandings of the nature and effects of disease and the body's reactions to problems or events in a person's life. After retiring in 1976, Selye founded the International Institute of Stress at the University of Montreal.

Effects of Stress

- Stress reactions may appear initially as heart palpitations, a headache, a cough, a rash, irritability, or tightness in the chest, neck, or shoulders.
- Other early symptoms may include difficulty in falling asleep, back pain, upset stomach, loss of appetite, lack of concentration, or general fatigue.
- With increased stress, the reactions intensify. A person may find it impossible to relax, become impatient or depressed, spend sleepless nights, or have frequent headaches and stomach disturbances.
- If negatively channeled stress continues for a long time, the accumulated effects may contribute to such serious ailments as asthma, heart disease, migraine headaches, high blood pressure, stomach ulcers, alcoholism, and drug addiction.

POST-TRAUMATIC STRESS DISORDER

When it is particularly intense, stress can have lasting effects, even after the cause of stress is removed.

Post-traumatic stress disorder (PTSD) is a psychological illness in which people repeatedly remember, relive, or dream about a terrible experience. The disorder may result from experiencing or witnessing a natural disaster, warfare, or any other violent or life-threatening incident.

PTSD may persist for many years. Treatment of PTSD involves psychotherapy and, often, medication. Prompt treatment following the trauma may help prevent PTSD or lessen its severity.

PTSD. Many soldiers returning from the wars in Iraq and Afghanistan experience post-traumatic stress disorder.

Handling Stress

No one can avoid stress, but a person can do certain things to help lessen the danger of becoming ill from it.

Relaxation techniques are a useful means of managing stress. These techniques include breathing deeply and slowly, tensing and then relaxing each muscle in the body, and imagining a calm, peaceful place. More formal relaxation techniques include meditation, yoga, hypnosis, recorded relaxation programs, and biofeedback training.

Stay Fit. Regular, well-balanced meals with plenty of high-energy foods such as whole grains, fruits, and vegetables are part of sensible living. People can also manage stress by exercising regularly.

Social Support. Close personal relationships with friends and relatives provide opportunities for communication, sharing, and emotional growth. Such relationships also can provide strength and support for dealing with challenging situations or personal problems.

Better Sleep. Millions of Americans suffer from insomnia, or sleeplessness. Insomnia can be caused by too much stress, but it can also contribute to stress.

People differ greatly in the amount of sleep they need. Some people feel fine on only 4 to 5 hours a night, while others may need more than 8 hours a night. The average sleep need for a human adult is approximately $8\frac{1}{2}$ hours. Teenagers often need more sleep than adults.

For a healthy, stress-reducing night's sleep,

- Follow a pattern: The body functions best when it establishes rhythms. It is best to go to sleep and wake up at the same times each day.

- Think happy thoughts: Using relaxation techniques just before bed can help a person fall asleep.

- Exercise: Studies have shown that exercising in the late afternoon seems to improve sleep more than exercising in the morning. Exercise appears to increase the depth of sleep, if not necessarily the amount.

Emotional Health

Being emotionally healthy does not mean that a person is always happy. People who are emotionally healthy are able to deal with the situations that occur in their life in a positive manner. This means accepting both the good times and the hard times as challenges and opportunities.

Emotional Development

Experiences during childhood strongly influence a person's mental health throughout life.

Children are dependent on their parents for many years, but they slowly mature and learn to do things for themselves. They make many mistakes during this long period of growth and maturation. Through these errors, they learn certain guidelines for relating to other people. Thus, children develop the knowledge necessary to deal with difficult situations in life. This knowledge helps them maintain good mental health throughout life.

Emotional development does not end when a person reaches adulthood. Similarly, an individual's mental health continues to change from time to time. These changes result from daily circumstances that cause either pleasure or pain for the person.

MENTAL ILLNESS

A mental illness is any disease of the mind that seriously affects a person's thoughts, emotions, personality, or behavior. A mentally ill person has severe symptoms that damage the person's ability to function effectively in everyday activities and situations.

Mental health professionals sometimes use different terms to describe the severity of various mental illnesses.

- A *neurosis* is a mild disorder that causes distress but does not interfere greatly with a person's everyday activities.

- A *psychosis* is a severe mental disorder that prevents an individual from functioning in a normal manner.

Causes
- physical changes in the brain resulting from illness or injury
- chemical imbalances in the brain
- genetic factors
- psychological and social factors

Most researchers believe that the majority of mental disorders result from a combination of two or more causes.

Social relationships have an important influence on mental health.

Friends and Family

Close personal relationships with friends and relatives provide opportunities for communication, sharing, and emotional growth. Such relationships also can provide strength and support for dealing with challenging situations or personal problems.

Social Situation

An individual's entire social environment also affects his or her mental health. Such social problems as poverty, racism, and overcrowding contribute to situations that influence emotional health. As a result, social and economic changes are needed to help reduce the rate of some types of mental illness.

Adolescence is the time when an individual grows from a child into an adult. During middle adolescence, individuals begin to act the way they think is right, rather than trying to impress their friends or please their parents.

ADOLESCENCE

Between childhood and adulthood lies a period of change and growth called adolescence. It involves changes in the individual's body, thinking abilities, and place in society. Adolescence is a time of great psychological and intellectual development.

Identity and Self-Esteem. As individuals mature, they come to see themselves in more sophisticated, complicated ways. Adolescents can provide complex, abstract psychological descriptions of themselves. As a result, they become more interested in understanding their own personalities and why they behave the way they do.

Teenagers' feelings about themselves may fluctuate, especially during early adolescence. However, self-esteem increases over the course of middle and late adolescence, as individuals gain more confidence.

Independence and Responsibility. Adolescents gradually grow more independent. Older adolescents generally do not rush to their parents whenever they are upset or need assistance. They solve many problems on their own.

In addition, most adolescents have a great deal of emotional energy wrapped up in relationships outside the family. They may feel just as attached to their friends as to their parents. By late adolescence, children see their parents, and interact with them, as people—not just as a mother and father.

Being independent also means being able to make one's own decisions and behave responsibly. In general, decision-making abilities improve over the course of the adolescent years, with gains in being able to handle responsibility continuing into the late years of high school.

HEALTH ISSUES

Staying fit and eating right can lessen the chances that a person will get sick. But injuries and exposure to illness can threaten even the healthiest of people.

It is important to see a doctor, both for a regular checkup and when illness or injury strikes. A doctor will provide basic medical treatment, including checking the things that are difficult or impossible for patients to monitor on their own.

In addition, individuals should make choices that lessen their risk of disease, such as getting vaccinated and learning the dangers of unhealthy behavior.

Healthy Decisions

It is important to take responsibility for one's own health. This means not only knowing the preventive measures to be taken in maintaining health, but also the steps to be taken when serious illness strikes, or an accident or other emergency arises.

Regular Checkups

Regular checkups by a physician and dentist play an important role in safeguarding health. Doctors recommend that people seek medical care at the first sign of illness. Early care can result in a quicker cure and lower medical costs. A physician or medical clinic has the knowledge and special equipment to provide accurate diagnosis and treatment.

Prevention of disease is an important part of medical care. Children should visit a doctor or clinic to receive immunization against chickenpox, diphtheria, measles, mumps, polio, rubella, tetanus, whooping cough, meningitis caused by the bacterium *Haemophilus influenzae* type b, and hepatitis B.

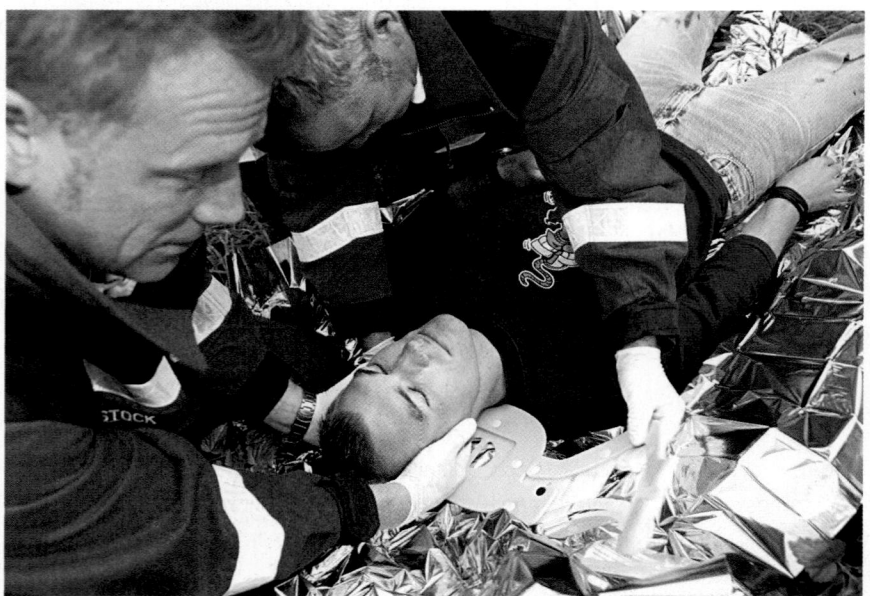

▲ **First aid** is immediate medical attention given to a victim of an accident, sudden illness, or other emergency. Knowing what to do in an emergency—being trained in CPR, for instance—can mean the difference between life and death.

BE PREPARED!

Despite every effort to prevent emergencies, they can and do happen. It is wise to be prepared to deal with an emergency situation.

Being prepared begins before the emergency arises: A wise first step is to select a family doctor and other health professionals while in good health. A list of names can be obtained by calling the nearest hospital or medical school, or by checking with a local pharmacist or reliable friends or neighbors. Keep a list of phone numbers handy that includes

- 911 (emergency)
- family doctor
- poison control center
- hospital
- other emergency services

Visiting the Doctor

A doctor's receptionist or office nurse can give information about the doctor's credentials, as well as describe such practical matters as office hours, routine appointments, and fee schedules. All these things should influence one's final selection of a doctor.

To obtain the desired quality of medical care, it is wise to consider the benefits and costs of each service before making a final decision. Regardless of choice, it is important to realize that a satisfactory association between an individual and a doctor depends on clear communication.

- Before a visit, it is useful to write down questions to ask.

- During examinations, be specific about symptoms.

- Do not withhold any information that will help the doctor make a proper diagnosis.

- If asked, the doctor will give a full explanation of any medical question that needs clarification.

▲ **Regular checkups** are important for maintaining good health. Yearly physicals, in which a primary care physician does a complete evaluation of the patient, are recommended.

IMMUNIZATION

Immunization is the process of protecting the body against disease by means of *vaccines*. Vaccines provide immunity by causing the body to manufacture disease-fighting substances called *antibodies*. (See pages 302–303.)

Vaccines contain substances that are powerful enough to trigger antibody production but that do not actually cause disease. Many vaccines consist of disease-causing bacteria or viruses that have been killed. Others consist of the live germs, but in a weakened form that does not cause the disease.

More than 95 percent of children in the United States receive all the recommended immunizations by the time they enter school. Disease has been greatly reduced by the recommended childhood immunizations.

- In 1952, more than 21,000 cases of paralytic polio were reported in the United States.

- By the end of the 1900s, fewer than 10 cases per year were reported.

Important Health Care Providers	
Health Care Provider	**Role**
Primary Care Physician	Provides basic medical treatment such as checkups; refers patients to correct specialist when necessary
Internist	A primary care physician who focuses on internal medicine, the general medical needs of adults
Pediatrician	A primary care physician who focuses on treating children
Osteopath	Doctors who place particular emphasis on the body's bones, muscles, ligaments, and tendons
Chiropractor	Considers proper alignment of the spine to be of critical importance to health. Treats disorders through a system of manual manipulation; cannot prescribe medicine or perform surgery
Dentist	Corrects and helps prevent problems of the teeth and gums

Disease

A *disease* is a disorder of the body or the mind. Diseases may occur as sudden illnesses, as long-term disabilities, or as an unavoidable result of aging.

Infectious Disease

Infectious diseases occur when an organism or other agent gains entry to the body and reproduces itself. Infectious agents are also called *pathogens* or *germs*.

Some pathogens damage or destroy the cells or tissues in which they reproduce. Others produce toxic chemicals that harm the body. Infectious diseases can be grouped according to the type of agent that causes them. The most common pathogens are

- bacteria
- viruses

Bacteria are microscopic, one-celled organisms that rank among the most widespread of all living things. Most bacteria do not cause disease. Many kinds live harmlessly on the skin or in the mouth and intestines. (See page 93.)

Most bacterial diseases result when bacteria multiply rapidly in living tissue. As they multiply, the bacteria release substances called *enzymes* that cause inflammation and damage or destroy living tissue. The body's response to invading bacteria also contributes to inflammation. This inflammation causes many of the familiar symptoms of disease, including cough, diarrhea, discharge, and pain.

Some bacteria cause disease by producing poisonous substances called *toxins*.

SPREAD OF INFECTIOUS DISEASES

- *Epidemic:* An unusually contagious illness that sweeps through a community or an entire continent.
- *Pandemic:* An epidemic that travels rapidly from one continent to another.
- *Endemic:* Describes infectious diseases that are always present in a particular region. For example, malaria is endemic to the jungles of Asia and Africa.

Some Ways Infectious Diseases Are Spread
by people
by animals
by water
by food
by nonliving sources

Viruses are even smaller than bacteria—scientists can see them only with powerful electron microscopes. Viruses cannot multiply except within the cells of other living things. Once viruses gain entry to living cells, they take over the cells' own reproductive machinery to produce more viruses.

As viruses multiply, they damage or destroy cells. The dying cells release greater numbers of viruses, which then move on to infect other cells. If the body's defenses cannot stop this viral multiplication, disease results.

Some of the most familiar diseases—including influenza and the common cold—are caused by viruses. Viruses also cause chickenpox, measles, mumps, and rubella (also called German measles). Most cases of diarrhea and vomiting result from viral infections.

MALARIA

Malaria is a disease spread through the saliva of mosquitoes. It is neither a bacterial nor a viral disease, but is instead caused by a type of one-celled organism called *protozoans*. Malaria ranks among the greatest worldwide causes of death and suffering. According to UNICEF, malaria kills one child every 30 seconds and causes one-fifth of all childhood deaths in Africa.

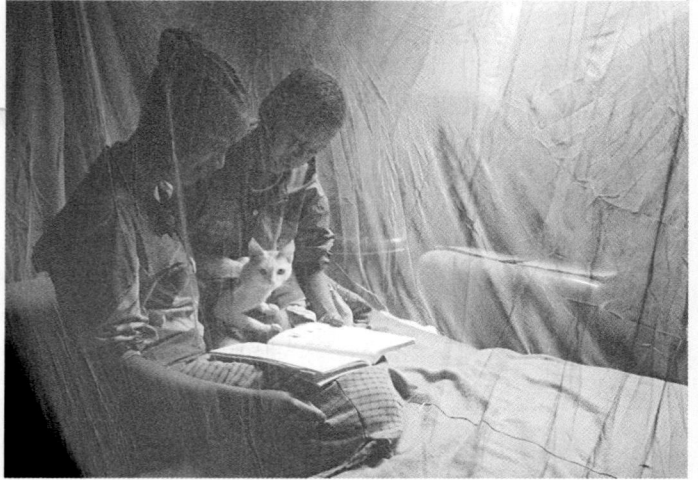

◀ **Malaria rates** have been lowered in Africa in recent years through the use of insecticide-treated nets for children and pregnant women to sleep under.

Noninfectious Diseases

Noninfectious diseases are an extremely broad group of illnesses that are not caused by pathogens. Six important categories of noninfectious diseases can be found in the table below.

DEVELOPMENTAL DISEASE

The habits of pregnant women affect not only themselves but also their unborn babies. A mother's smoking can hinder her baby's ability to gain weight and can cause other health problems. Exposure to drugs or alcohol before birth can also interfere with normal development.

Noninfectious Diseases		
Type	**Description**	**Example(s)**
Inherited diseases	Involve defects in genes that can be passed from one generation to another. In some cases the role of such genes is well understood. Other inherited diseases run in families, but there is no set pattern to how they occur. Scientists suspect that many such conditions involve inherited genes, but the particular defective genes have not yet been identified.	Huntington's, sickle cell anemia, heart disease
Cancer	One of the most common and feared diseases throughout the world. Occurs when cells in the body multiply without control. Can begin in almost any type of cell. Cancer cells invade and eventually destroy surrounding normal tissue. In addition, cells from the original cancer can spread and form more cancers in distant parts of the body. If left untreated, most types of cancer are fatal.	Common cancers include cancer of the breast, colon, lungs, and prostate
Metabolic diseases	Result from disturbances in the metabolism, the complex system of chemical processes by which the body nourishes, maintains, and regulates itself. Metabolic diseases may arise chiefly as a result of poor nutrition or endocrine disorders.	Diabetes, osteoporosis
Immune system disorders	Occur because of flaws in the immune system's ability to recognize harmful substances. Most common are allergies, including asthma, hay fever, and hives. Autoimmune diseases are another common immune disorder. In these diseases, the immune system attacks the body's own tissues as if they were foreign invaders. Autoimmune diseases can affect tissues and organs throughout the body.	Lupus, allergies
Environmental/ Occupational	Result from substances in the air, water, or other surroundings. Such disorders are called occupational diseases when they are caused by factors associated with a particular workplace. Air pollution is a common environmental cause of disease.	Asthma, lung infection, cancer, heart disease, birth defects
Diseases associated with aging	Involve gradual breakdown of cells, tissues, and organs as people grow older. No one can avoid all diseases forever—some disorder eventually causes everyone's body to fail and die. But several factors influence how soon people's bodies begin to show signs of age. Genes have some effect on which diseases people get and at what age. People can delay or avoid development of some diseases through a balanced diet, exercise, and other healthy habits.	Atherosclerosis, hypertension (high blood pressure), heart attack, stroke, arthritis, Alzheimer's

Heart Disease

Heart Disease

More than 64 million Americans, or about 23 percent of the population, have some form of heart damage or disease. There are three major types of heart disease.

- atherosclerosis
- cardiomyopathy
- damaged heart valves

Atherosclerosis

- It is the most common form of heart disease.
- It is believed to begin early in life and is found present at death in about half of all Americans.
- It leads to heart attack.
- It is a progressive hardening of the arteries, including the coronary arteries (the blood vessels that surround and nourish the heart).
- Plaque, composed of fatty substances, builds up in a blood vessel and causes artery walls to harden and thicken.

HOW DOES THAT WORK

ATHEROSCLEROSIS

When plaque builds up in blood vessels, the artery walls harden and thicken. The passage gradually narrows, restricting—and, in time, completely blocking—blood flow to the heart.

This blockage is known as *myocardial infarction,* commonly referred to as a heart attack. When this happens, a part of the heart muscle loses its nourishing supply of blood and dies. If enough muscle dies, the output of the heart is greatly reduced and, unless prompt medical attention is given, the patient dies.

Even when small areas of the muscle die, there may be serious consequences. The electrical signals that ensure normal pumping become alerted. The heart may begin to fibrillate (twitch uncontrollably). If this happens in the ventricles, the heart no longer pumps enough blood to sustain life.

Cardiomyopathy

- It is a disease of the heart muscle itself.
- The heart tries to compensate for its impaired pumping action by growing larger and larger.
- Damage to the heart increases.
- Danger increases of clotting and *cardiac arrhythmia,* a disturbance in the function of the heart's electrical system.
- Patients with cardiomyopathy are often candidates for a heart transplant.

Damaged Heart Valves

- Damage to the heart valves results from infection or a *congenital defect* (birth defect).
- Strep throat, untreated or improperly treated, can lead to rheumatic fever, which may result in damage to the heart valves.
- Rheumatic fever is well controlled in the United States, but the disease was responsible for more than 3,500 deaths in 1999.
- Congenital heart defects claim an equal number of victims.
- 25,000 babies are born yearly with heart defects (only some of them have damaged valves).
- One known cause for abnormal heart development in a child is rubella (German measles) incurred by the mother early in pregnancy.

HEART ATTACKS

A heart attack occurs suddenly, but the factors that cause it take years to build up. Deposits in the coronary arteries begin early in life and eventually block the artery. These diagrams show one possible sequence of events leading to a heart attack.

- At age 21, the patient's coronary arteries are in good condition. The first plaque deposit is shown in yellow.

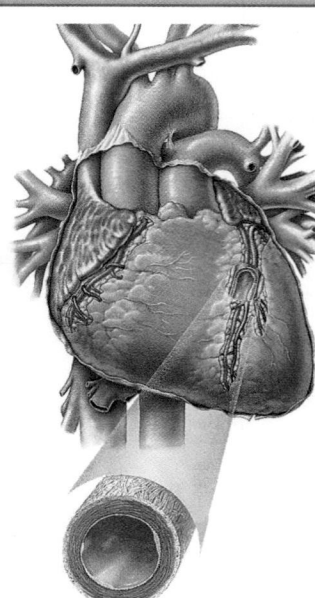

Hypertension

Hypertension, or high blood pressure, affects an estimated 50 million Americans. In the early stages of the disease, most people are able to go about their daily duties as usual. Because there is no pain or discomfort, hypertension has been called the silent killer.

- About 30 percent of sufferers are unaware of their condition.
- It is a prime factor in the 1.2 million heart attacks that occur each year.
- It is the major cause of stroke, which annually claims more than 160,000 lives.

How It Works

- The *arterioles,* or small arteries, become constricted, slowing down blood flow and making the heart work harder.
- This increases the pressure of blood against artery walls.
- Pressure damages blood vessels, leading to atherosclerosis or enlargement of the heart.
- Kidneys are unable to function under the increased pressure and cease to filter out waste products from the blood, creating potential for serious renal impairment.
- Visual disturbances can develop as tiny retinal arteries swell and hemorrhage.

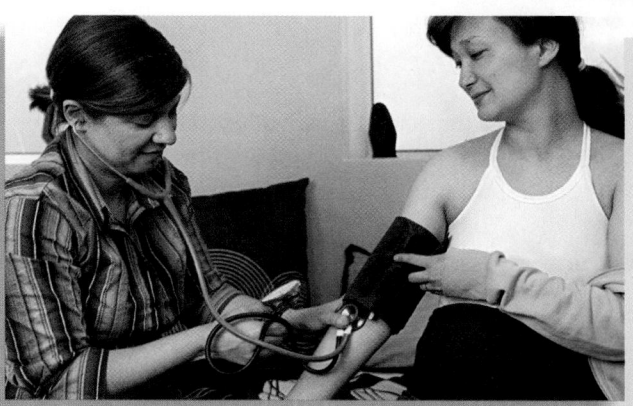

▲ **Blood pressure** is the pressure that blood pumped by the heart exerts against the walls of the arteries. It is measured with an instrument called a *sphygmomanometer.*

Risk Factors

- The cause of hypertension is determinable in about 10 percent of cases (for example, kidney abnormalities and brain tumor).
- Of the other 90 percent, more than half have a family history of high blood pressure.
- Other risk factors are age (more common after 65) and race (black Americans are more susceptible than white Americans).
- Smoking increases blood pressure; smokers have a 70 percent greater chance of having a heart attack than nonsmokers.
- Obesity and high sodium intake increase the risk of high blood pressure.

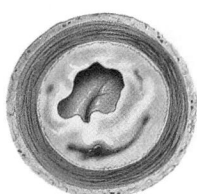

- At age 51, the coronary arteries are dangerously narrowed. Fatty deposits have reduced the artery opening to about one-fourth its original area.

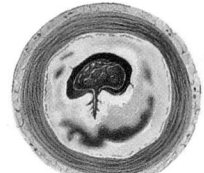

- At age 58, the artery is almost closed. A *thrombus* (blood clot) forms and blocks the artery, causing a heart attack.

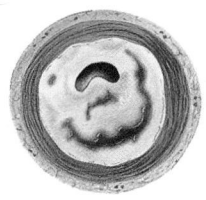

- At age 60, the patient has recovered. The artery has reopened after the heart attack, but the channel is much smaller.

CONTROLLING HYPERTENSION

There is no cure for high blood pressure, but in a majority of cases it can be controlled through reduction of risk factors. Periodic medical checkups may provide early detection of hypertension.

Living with high blood pressure

1. Stop smoking, especially cigarette smoking.
2. Be sure to get regular exercise and keep weight under control.
3. Do not use salt and stimulants excessively.
4. Avoid undue stress and overexertion as much as possible.
5. Be sure to get regular rest and relaxation.

Cancer and Diabetes

Cancer

Cancer is a disease in which cells multiply wildly, destroy healthy tissue, and endanger life.

The Facts

- Current statistics indicate one in four Americans will have some form of cancer during his or her lifetime.

- It strikes people of all ages but is most common in the middle-aged and the elderly.

- Cancer is not considered to be a single disease with a single cause, curable or preventable by a specific vaccine, drug, or diet.

- It may be as many as 120 different diseases, each with its own complex causes—from radiation to toxic chemicals in the food chain.

How It Works. In cancer, certain cells begin a process of uncontrollable growth and spread. These abnormal cells divide and redivide until they grow into masses of tissue called *tumors*.

Tumors that are said to be *malignant* (cancerous) invade and destroy normal tissue. They may also *metastasize,* or spread to other parts of the body via the blood or lymph systems, where they form new growths.

Causes

Many experts believe that most cancers have a genetic cause or develop through repeated and prolonged contact with *carcinogens* (cancer-causing agents), such as sunlight, X-rays, tobacco smoke, and chemicals found in air, water, food, and the workplace.

Radiation therapy, drug therapy (*chemotherapy*), hormones, immunotherapy, and surgery are the currently available cancer treatments.

HOW LUNG CANCER DEVELOPS

Most cases of lung cancer start in the tissue that lines the *bronchi,* the tubes that supply the lungs with air. (See pages 234–235.)

1. The lining of a normal bronchus is composed of various kinds of cells with different functions, such as to eliminate mucus.
2. Cancer begins to develop when certain cells in the lining

start to reproduce at a rate faster than normal. As these cells accumulate, they interfere with the elimination of mucus.

3. Some of the rapidly multiplying cells turn into cancer cells. Mucus becomes trapped in the lung.
4. The cancer cells form a tumor that partly blocks the bronchus. Unless surgeons can remove the tumor completely, cancer cells will spread to other sites in the body.

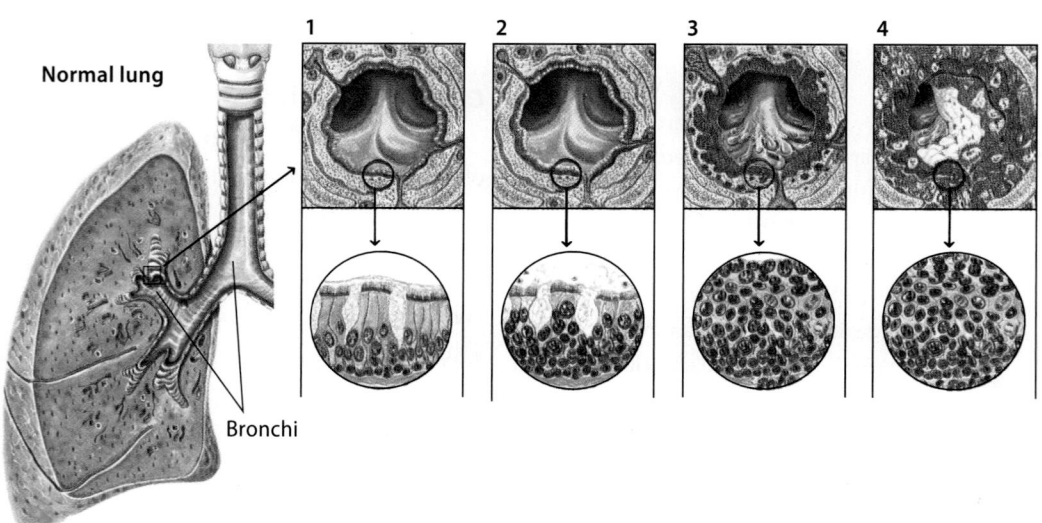

Normal lung

Bronchi

▲ **Glucose Levels.** People with diabetes must check their blood glucose levels several times a day.

Diabetes

Diabetes is a long-term disease that disrupts the body's ability to use a sugar called *glucose*. Glucose is a product of carbohydrate digestion. It circulates in the blood to the body's cells, where it serves as one of the chief sources of energy.

The Facts

- Diabetes leads to a high concentration of glucose in the blood, a condition called *hyperglycemia*.
- Over time, hyperglycemia injures small blood vessels in the eye, kidneys, and nervous system.
- It can lead to blindness, kidney failure, and nerve damage.
- Diabetes leads to greater risk of heart attack, stroke, heart failure, and development of Alzheimer's.
- There are two main types of diabetes: Type 1 and Type 2.

Risk Factors

- A family history of diabetes
- Obesity (80 to 90 percent of diabetics are overweight)
- Being 40 or older (40 percent of diabetic Americans are over 65)
- Sex (females develop diabetes twice as often as males)

Type 1 diabetes, the insulin-dependent or juvenile type, may start at any age, although it is generally first noted during childhood or early adolescence. In this type, the body stops producing *insulin,* the hormone produced in the pancreas that enables body cells to take up and use glucose for energy.

Type 1 diabetics need insulin injections several times a day to maintain normal glucose levels and prevent the effects of hyperglycemia.

Type 2 Diabetes. In this type, the noninsulin-dependent or adult-onset type, the body still produces some insulin, which may even be present in above normal levels. However, body tissues may not be able to utilize the insulin properly, a condition termed insulin resistance.

In general, Type 2 diabetics can control their disease by diet alone or with the addition of oral drugs.

HIDDEN DISEASE

It has been estimated that 5 million Americans have diabetes and do not know it. Undiagnosed, they remain untreated. Heeding the warning signs given below can lead to early detection and appropriate medical treatment.

The four most important symptoms.

1. Frequent, copious urination

2. Abnormal thirst

3. Rapid weight loss

4. Weakness and tiredness

Other symptoms include

5. Drowsiness and fatigue

6. Increased appetite; craving for sweets

7. Itching of the skin, particularly in the genital area

8. Disturbances of vision (for example, blurring)

9. Irritability, nervousness, or nausea

10. Skin disorders such as boils, carbuncles, and infections

Alcoholism and Drug Abuse

Alcoholism

Alcoholism is a serious disease in which people have an overwhelming desire for the mental and physical effects of drinking alcoholic beverages. People with alcoholism, called *alcoholics,* feel a strong, continuing urge to drink. Alcoholism has four main symptoms.

1. craving
2. lack of control
3. physical tolerance
4. physical dependence

Craving is a strong need to drink in spite of harmful consequences, such as drinking-related illnesses or job problems.

Lack of control is the inability to stop drinking once a drinking episode starts.

Physical tolerance is the need to consume increasing amounts of alcohol to feel its effects.

Physical dependence occurs when people's bodies become accustomed to alcohol. Such people have withdrawal symptoms after they stop drinking. Symptoms of withdrawal include shakiness, rapid heartbeat, nausea, sweating, and anxiety. Physical dependence does not occur in all alcoholics.

Alcohol Abuse. People who are not alcoholics may also have problems caused by excessive drinking. These problems include difficulties at work or school, neglect of family responsibilities, and strains in personal relationships. Drinking that causes problems but does not meet the formal definition for alcoholism is called *alcohol abuse.*

Causes

- Scientists do not fully understand what causes alcoholism.
- Researchers are beginning to identify ways the brains of alcoholics differ from the brains of nonalcoholics.
- Tests show different patterns of electrical activity in the brain.
- Research shows that heredity plays a key role.
- The pattern of brain electrical activity associated with alcoholism appears to be inherited.
- People with an alcoholic parent are at greater risk than children of nonalcoholics.
- Most experts think that many genes are involved and that environment also plays a role.

Effects

- damage to the brain, stomach, intestines, and heart
- liver problems especially common, including a disorder called *cirrhosis*
- drinking also a factor in many vehicle crashes, falls, and other accidents

---

WARNING SIGNS

The following are some of the problems associated with a drinking problem. They may be signs of alcoholism or alcohol abuse.

1. Drinking increasing amounts of alcohol and becoming intoxicated often
2. Being preoccupied with drinking, to the exclusion of other activities
3. Making promises to quit but breaking them
4. Being unable to remember what was said or done while drinking
5. Experiencing personality changes
6. Denying, hiding, or making excuses for drinking
7. Beginning to drink alone, in the morning, or before a party
8. Refusing to admit excessive drinking and becoming angry if the subject is raised
9. Beginning to have trouble at work. Arriving late or missing work altogether
10. Changing jobs frequently, usually a demotion rather than a promotion
11. Losing interest in personal appearance or hygiene
12. Suffering from poor health, with loss of appetite, respiratory infections, or nervousness
13. Suffering marital and economic hardships

Drug Abuse

Drug abuse is the nonmedical use of a drug that interferes with a healthy and productive life. Drug abuse occurs at all economic levels of society, from the wealthy to the impoverished, and among young people as well as adults. Any drug may be abused, including illegal drugs and legal drugs like alcohol, tobacco, and medications.

Many young people begin to use drugs or alcohol to experiment with the pleasurable effects of drugs, to fit in with peers, or to try on adult roles and behaviors.

Addiction

- Physiological and psychological dependence on a drug is known as *addiction*.
- The reaction of the body when regular drug use is stopped is *withdrawal*.
- In addiction, a drug becomes so rewarding that the user may continue taking it despite harmful medical or social consequences.
- Addiction leads to poor motivation, impaired judgment and memory, personality changes, and disrupted family relationships.
- Drug abusers often develop health problems such as hepatitis, AIDS, and other serious medical consequences, including death.

Some Commonly Abused Illegal Drugs			
Drug	**What It Does**	**Short-term Effects**	**Long-term Effects**
Marijuana	Relaxes the mind and body, distorts perceptions, alters mood, impairs coordination	Faster heartbeat and pulse, impaired perception and reactions, possible hallucinations, panic attacks, decreased motivation	Impaired memory and coordination, bronchitis. If used in pregnancy, babies may have lower birth weight and slower growth rate.
Cocaine	Speeds up physical and mental processes, creates sense of heightened energy and confidence	Rapid heartbeat, depression, sleeplessness, muscle spasms, convulsions, loss of sexual desire, impaired judgment, extreme suspiciousness, violence	Damage to nasal lining, heart attack, stroke, hepatitis or AIDS (if injected). Risk of fatal overdose. If used in pregnancy, danger of miscarriage and risk of birth defects.
Methamphetamine	Increases alertness, physical activity, heart rate, and body temperature	Can increase anxiety, tremors (shaking), seizures, insomnia, paranoia, and aggression	Highly addictive, can cause malnutrition, depression, memory impairment, mental illness, stroke, heart failure
Heroin	Relaxes central nervous system, relieves pain, produces sense of well-being	Restlessness, nausea, vomiting, slowed breathing, lethargy, mood swings, sweating	Physical dependence, malnutrition, lower immunity, infections of the heart lining and valves, liver disease, hepatitis or AIDS (from contaminated needles), and fatal overdoses
Ecstasy	Speeds up physical and mental processes, boosts energy, creates sense of excitement, may produce hallucinations	Increased heart rate, distorted perception and sensation, confusion, depression, sleep problems	Mood disorders, aggression, and learning problems

Sexually Transmitted Diseases

Sexually Transmitted Diseases

Sexually transmitted diseases, also called STDs, are any diseases spread primarily through intimate sexual activity. Many bacteria, viruses, and other kinds of germs cause STDs. In the United States, the four leading sexually transmitted diseases (STDs) are

- chlamydia
- gonorrhea
- genital herpes
- syphilis

Chlamydia

- the leading STD in the United States
- four times more common than gonorrhea; six times more common than herpes
- more than 1 million Americans contract the disease each year
- majority of people infected are under 25
- detection of symptoms may be difficult: may be mild in men, may produce no symptoms in women
- unchecked chlamydia in men may not have permanent ill effects
- can be easily and unknowingly transmitted to women
- in women, can lead to sterility, tubal pregnancy, and premature births or stillbirths
- treated with antibiotics

PREVENTION AND CONTROL

The most effective strategies for staying free of STDs are to abstain from sexual intercourse altogether or to limit such contact to one uninfected partner who, in turn, has no other sexual partners.

People can significantly reduce the chance of infection by using condoms or other protective measures during sex, by avoiding sex with prostitutes and other high-risk individuals, and by not using illegal drugs.

Individuals who believe they may have a sexually transmitted disease should see a physician immediately. They should also stop all sexual activity until told by a physician that they are not at risk of infecting others.

Gonorrhea

- most women have no symptoms
- men generally experience a puslike urethral discharge, painful urination
- both gonorrhea and chlamydia often exist in a person at the same time
- treated with antibiotics

Genital Herpes

- an infection of the genital skin and mucous membranes
- marked by blisterlike lesions that erode and produce painful ulcers
- no cure; symptoms can return periodically throughout life

Syphilis

- has three phases: primary, secondary, and tertiary
- primary phase characterized by a painless genital *chancre* (sore)
- in secondary phase, the chancre disappears, and a rash generally develops
- in tertiary phase, years after the primary and secondary phases, untreated syphilis can cause brain or heart damage, or both, and may end in death
- treated with antibiotics

Spread of STDs. An individual's chances of becoming infected with an STD depend on a variety of factors. STDs can affect people from all social and economic backgrounds. People with the greatest amount of risk are those who begin sexual activity at an early age, have many sex partners, or engage in sexual intercourse with high-risk individuals, such as prostitutes.

Diagnosis. For a person who shows few or no symptoms, doctors will often perform an STD test if the person reported a risky behavior or a sexual encounter. If a person shows obvious symptoms, doctors may order a variety of laboratory tests to confirm the presence of the infecting organisms. The most important factor after the diagnosis of an STD is obtaining appropriate medical care.

HIV/AIDS

AIDS is the final, life-threatening stage of infection with *human immunodeficiency virus* (HIV). AIDS stands for "acquired immune deficiency syndrome." The name refers to the fact that HIV damages the immune system, the body's most important defense against disease.

Cases of AIDS were first identified in 1981 in the United States. Researchers have detected HIV in a specimen collected in 1959 in central Africa. Millions of AIDS cases have been diagnosed worldwide.

How HIV Is Transmitted. Researchers have identified three ways in which HIV is transmitted.

1. sexual intercourse
2. direct contact with infected blood, such as through the sharing of hypodermic needles with an infected person
3. transmission from an infected mother to her baby

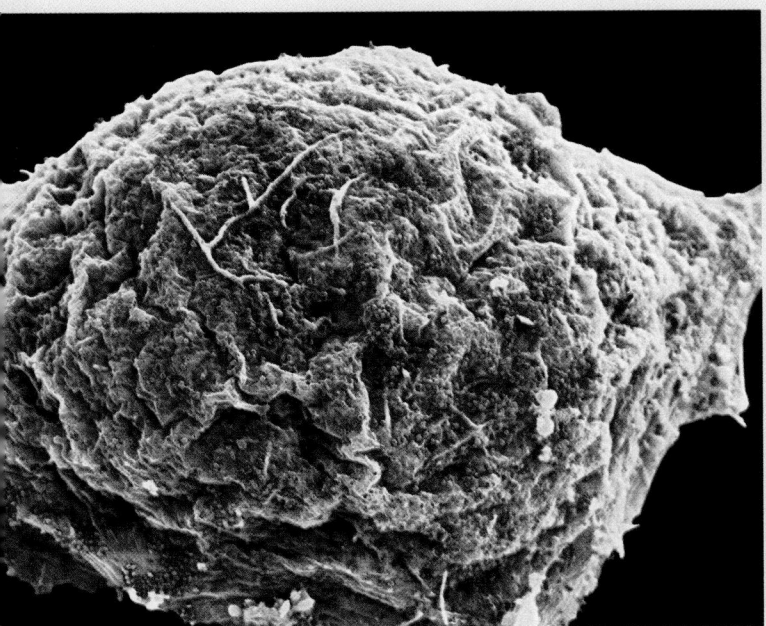

AIDS viruses reproduce in *CD4 cells* and circulate in the blood. In this electron micrograph of a white blood cell, AIDS viruses can be seen as the small white dots covering the cell's surface.

Treatment for HIV infection or AIDS has been developed, but no cure has yet been found. Scientists have developed a class of antiviral drugs that are used in combinations that can decrease HIV in the blood to undetectable levels.

The drugs must be taken in large quantities for a long time. In addition, HIV may develop resistance to the drugs. Doctors need to determine which combinations of drugs are safest and most effective over the long term.

STAGES OF INFECTION

People infected with HIV go through three stages of infection. The length of time any person stays in each stage varies greatly and depends on many factors, including medical treatment. HIV can be transmitted during all stages of infection, even when no symptoms occur. The three stages are

1. acute retroviral syndrome and asymptomatic period.
2. symptomatic HIV infection.
3. AIDS.

Acute Retroviral Syndrome and Asymptomatic Period. Most people get a flulike or mononucleosis-like illness within 12 weeks after becoming infected with HIV. This illness usually goes away without treatment. From this point on, the infected person's blood tests positive for HIV antibodies even though symptoms usually do not develop for 2 to 15 years or more. During this early stage of infection, the patient maintains a near normal number of CD4 cells. CD4 cells are the white blood cells that are infected by HIV.

Symptomatic HIV Infection. In this stage, a wide variety of mild or severe symptoms may appear. Common symptoms include tiredness, enlarged lymph glands, yeast infections, skin rashes, and dental disease. This stage of the infection may last from a few months to many years. During this time, the patient's CD4-cell count gradually declines.

AIDS is characterized by severe damage to the immune system and such opportunistic infections as *Pneumocystis carinii* pneumonia and Kaposi's sarcoma. The progressive breakdown of the immune system eventually leads to death, usually within a few years.

Immunity to Disease

Within the last few decades, scientists have begun to understand the body's ingenious network of defense against infection and disease. The *immune system,* as presently understood, is a collection of organs, vessels, and circulating white blood cells.

For all its complexity and elaborate interconnections, the human immune system consists of relatively few basic components: a number of specialized cells and substances produced by cells.

Lymphocytes are the principal agents in immune defense. They are special types of white blood cells. The majority of these specialized cells are scavengers that devour foreign particles. Every second of the day, more than 200,000 lymphocytes are produced in the bone marrow, and an equal number grow old and are eliminated.

Phagocytes (cell eaters), another type of white blood cells, are constantly on the alert for foreign cells. Phagocytes have the ability to engulf and destroy invading viruses, bacteria, fungi, protozoa, and helminths.

T Cells. When pathogens—disease-causing organisms—are attacking in great numbers very quickly, phagocytes may be unable to keep up with the rapid cell destruction. They are then aided by more powerful white blood cells, called T lymphocytes or T cells, which are capable of identifying specific antigens (antibody producers) by their shape.

B lymphocytes, also called B cells, are formed in the bone marrow. B cells produce chemical weapons called antibodies. These complex proteins are constructed of amino acids and can neutralize and destroy a wide range of disease-producing microbes.

THE IMMUNE RESPONSE

There are two forms of the immune response. They differ mainly in the parts of the immune system that are involved. Many antigens trigger both forms of the immune response.

1. **the humoral immune response**
2. **the cell-mediated immune response**

The humoral immune response begins with the detection of an antigen by a B lymphocyte. Each B lymphocyte responds to a particular antigen. After it attaches to an antigen, the B cells divide into many identical cells. Some mature into plasma cells.

Plasma cells produce antibodies, also known as *immuno-globulins,* which protect the body from infection and from the toxins (poisons) secreted by some bacteria.

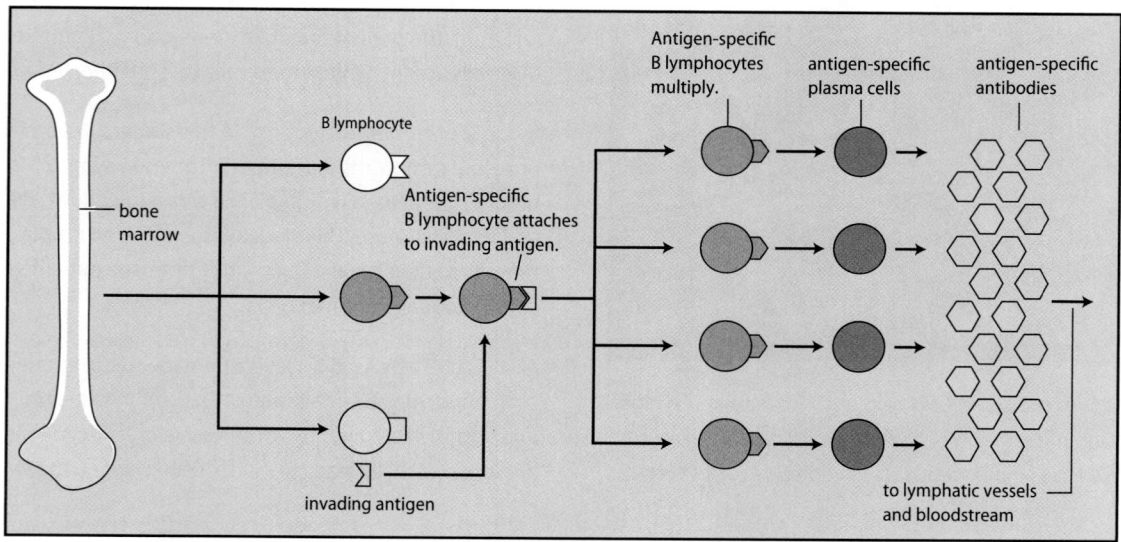

Natural Killer Cells. Killer T cells and antibodies are joined in the body's defense by yet another type of cell, the *natural killer cell,* which does not require T cell receptors to be activated. Natural killer cells kill cells containing foreign substances on their own.

Natural killer cells, killer T cells, and phagocytes constitute the body's major strategy of defense against disease: the cell-mediated immune response. In this form of immune response, immune cells are pitted against invading microorganisms in direct combat.

IMPERFECT IMMUNITY

Allergies are mistaken and harmful responses of the body's immune system to substances that are harmless to most people.

The substances that provoke an allergic reaction are called *allergens.* They include pollen, dust, mold, and feathers. Among the common allergic diseases are asthma, eczema (itchy red swellings of the skin), hay fever, and hives.

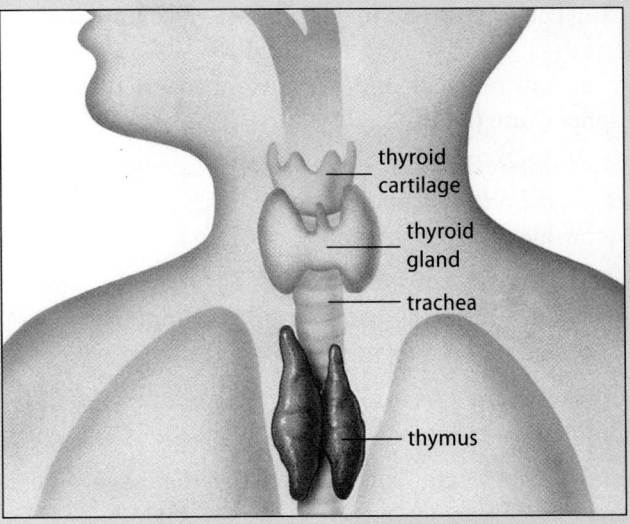

▲ **The thymus** is an important part of the immune system. It helps to develop lymphocytes by producing a substance called *thymosin*. Thymosin helps change lymphocytes into T cells.

The cell-mediated immune response involves T lymphocytes, which originate in bone marrow but mature in the thymus.

First, an antigen-presenting cell digests an antigen into smaller antigen peptides. The peptides attach to *major histo-compatibility complex* (MHC) proteins to form *peptide-MHC complexes.* Binding of a peptide-MHC complex to a T cell receptor begins T cell activation.

The kind of T cell that participates in a cell-mediated immune response depends on the type of antigen involved. Antigens in virus-infected cells often activate *cytotoxic T cells,* also called *killer T cells,* which kill the infected cell. Other antigens activate T helper lymphocytes, which secrete chemicals called *lymphokines.*

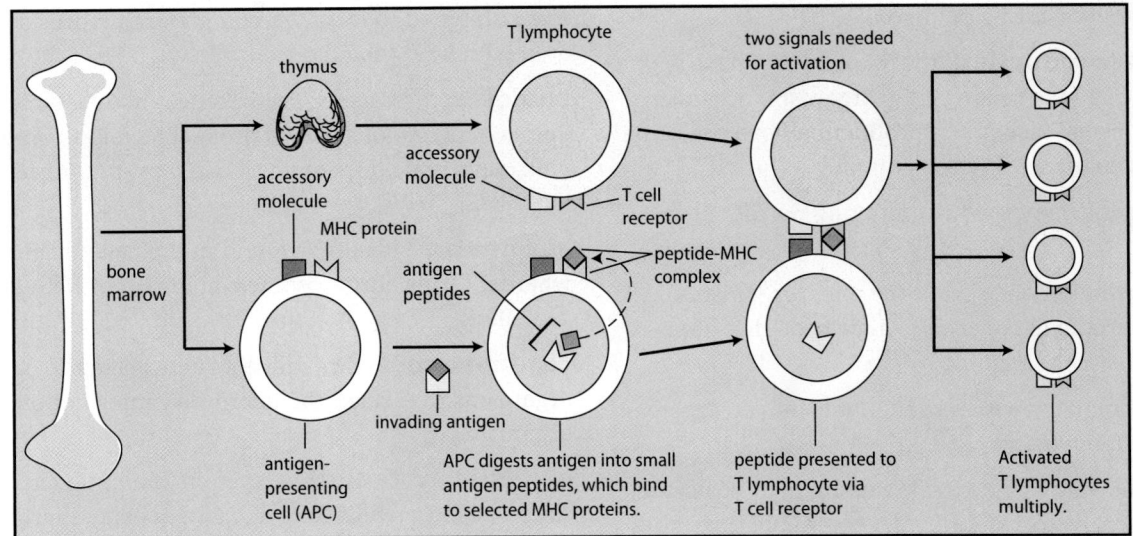

Biology Glossary

adenine one of two major purines (nitrogen-containing bases) found in both RNA and DNA. Also found in various free nucleotides, for example, adenosine triphosphate (ATP).

adenosine diphosphate (ADP) a compound of adenosine and two phosphate groups, formed from adenosine triphosphate in the muscles.

adenosine triphosphate (ATP) an enzyme found in all cells, especially muscle cells; a compound of adenosine and three phosphate groups.

allele different forms of the same gene; may be dominant or recessive.

analogous features of living things that have similar functions but do not share a common origin.

angiosperm the flowering plants; seed-bearing plants that are the dominant and most varied division of plants on Earth today.

antibiotics substances produced by some molds that weaken or destroy bacteria and other organisms that cause disease.

antibodies protein substances produced by white blood cells that specifically bind to a single foreign antigen, neutralizing or destroying the invading microorganisms in the bloodstream.

archaea a group of single-celled organisms that make up one of the three basic divisions of life; rank among the oldest forms of life on Earth.

asexual reproduction the formation of new organisms from parts of a single organism; organisms that form through asexual reproduction have the same exact DNA structure as their parent.

auxins the prime growth-promoting hormones in plants.

bacteria single-celled plantlike microorganisms lacking chlorophyll; consist of single cells that are rod-shaped, spherical, or spiral.

bivalve a mollusk with a shell that is hinged together so that it can open and close.

botany the study of plants, including their structure, life processes, historical origins, geographic distribution, economic uses, and roles in the ecosystem.

brain stem the part of the brain that contains vital reflex centers that help to control heart rate, blood pressure, and respiration; connects the spinal cord to the forebrain.

calyx the outermost portion of the flower; consists of leaflike sepals, which are usually green and closely resemble small leaves.

carbohydrates water-soluble sugars; provide the main source of energy for the body.

carpels or pistils, make up the female reproductive structure of a plant; develop the egg and ultimately a fertile seed.

cell the basic unit of all life; cells are self-reproducing, with new cells arising by cell division.

centrioles a pair of small, rodlike bodies in a cell that assist in the distribution of the chromosomes during the process of cell reproduction.

cerebellum the part of the brain that aids in maintaining body balance and coordination of muscle movement; located below the back part of the cerebrum.

cerebrum the largest portion of the brain; consists of two large lobes, on the right and left sides of the brain.

chemical evolution theory that simple organic compounds formed naturally early in Earth's history and combined to form the complex structures associated with living things.

cholesterol a sterol; fatlike substance found in animal fats and oils, nerve tissue, bile, blood, and egg yolk; a normal constituent of bile, also produced in the liver.

chromatin substance found in the cell nucleus, where it forms chromosomes; made up of DNA and proteins.

chromosomes threadlike structures in the cells of organisms that carry the hereditary information of the organism.

cladistic systematics system of animal classification based on how long ago two species shared a common ancestor.

collagen an insoluble protein that accounts for about 30 percent of total body protein; found in the white fibers of connective tissue, cartilage, and bone.

corolla organ of a flower; consists of the flower's petals, which are often the most ornamental part of the flower; may secrete nectar.

cortex botany, plant tissue that forms the bulk of stems, roots, leaves, and fruits; biology, the outer layer of an internal organ.

creationism a set of beliefs based on the idea that a Supreme Being brought into existence Earth and all its life through a direct act of creation.

cytokinesis division of the cytoplasm of a cell which begins during telophase and leads to cell division.

cytoplasm the cell material between the outer membrane and the nucleus; contains the organelles that perform many of the vital functions of the cell.

cytosine a pyrimidine base found in nucleic acids; an essential constituent of both RNA and DNA.

decomposer an organism, such as bacteria or fungi, that feeds on the dead remains of organisms and organic waste.

deoxyribonucleic acid (DNA) the substance of which genes are made; a double-stranded macromolecule, located in the nucleus of eukaryotic (plant and animal) cells and in the organelles, mitochondria, and chloroplasts; often referred to as the genetic code.

diatoms single-celled algae; among the living things that comprise plankton.

dicot group of flowering plants containing two cotyledons, or seed leaves; includes oaks, maples, beeches, willows, mustards, roses, poppies, and mints.

diffusion the movement of a substance from an area of high concentration to an area of low concentration.

digestion the process by which food is broken down, mechanically and chemically, and is converted into absorbable forms, in the gastrointestinal tract.

diploid having a homologous pair of chromosomes for each characteristic except sex, the total number of chromosomes being twice that of a gamete.

dominant a gene which expresses itself when paired with either a recessive or another dominant allele.

dormancy a control mechanism in seed plants that keeps the seed in a state of suspended animation until the time of the year in which its chances for survival are best.

egg a female gamete.

embryo a stage in prenatal development; in humans, it includes the period from the second through the eighth week.

endemic describes infectious diseases that are always present in a particular region.

enzymes proteins that act as biochemical catalysts; speed up the chemical reactions of life; they help digest food, produce energy, and assist in building other proteins.

epidemic an unusually contagious illness that sweeps through a community or an entire continent.

epidermis cuticle, or outer layer, of the skin; consists of four layers of skin, the stratum corneum being the outermost.

eudicot group of flowering plants containing two cotyledons, or seed leaves.

eukaryotic means having a true nucleus. All multicellular animals and plants consist of eukaryotic cells, as do the fungi and some unicellular organisms.

evolution scientific theory that states that all living things developed naturally from simple organisms over millions of years.

fertilization the process by which sperm and egg unite during reproduction.

fixed action patterns unvarying patterns of behavior exhibited by some animals in response to specific environmental conditions.

flavonoids substances in plants that are the basic building blocks of many pigments; play a role in coloring flowers and in attracting insects that carry out pollination.

flower the part of a plant that produces the seeds.

Biology Glossary

fossil the hardened remains or traces of an animal or plant of a former age.

fruit the part of a flowering plant that contains the seeds.

fungi organisms, such as mildews, molds, mushrooms, rusts, and smuts, that obtain food by absorbing it from other living organisms or from parts of formerly living things.

gamete a reproductive cell capable of uniting with another gamete to form a fertilized cell during sexual reproduction.

gene a functional hereditary unit that occupies a fixed location in a chromosome, has a specific influence on phenotype, and is capable of mutation to various alleles.

genome a set of all the genes a species has in its chromosomes.

genotype the underlying genetic makeup of a trait of an organism.

geotropism response by plants to the action of gravity.

germination the sprouting of a plant; a beginning of growth or development.

glucose an important carbohydrate in body metabolism, formed during digestion and absorbed from the intestines into the blood.

Golgi complex a stacked arrangement of small, flattened membrane-bound sacs in a cell that synthesize carbohydrates and package proteins.

guanine one of two major purines (nitrogen-containing bases) found in both RNA and DNA.

gymnosperm a naked seed plant; one of two large groups of seed-bearing plants; gymnosperms do not produce flowers.

habituation the modification of behavior through learning to ignore stimuli that are unimportant or irrelevant.

haploid having half as many chromosomes as somatic cells, such as in a gamete or germ cell.

heredity the passing on of biological characteristics from one generation to the next.

heterozygous having two different alleles on paired chromosomes; that is, one is dominant and the other recessive.

hibernation an inactive, sleeplike state that some animals enter during the winter to protect themselves from cold and hunger.

homeostasis the tendency of an organism to maintain an internal state of balance, or temperature and fluid content, and by the regulation of body processes.

hominid any one of a family of primates that is bipedal and walks upright; includes humans.

Homo erectus species of hominid that existed from about 1.6 million years ago until 250,000 years ago.

Homo habilis earliest known hominid; distinguished by its use of tools.

Homo sapiens the species of primate made up of all existing races of humans.

homologous features of living things that developed from a common ancestor; have a similar structure but not necessarily similar function. In genetics, having the same genes arranged in the same order.

homozygous having two identical alleles on paired chromosomes; that is, they are both dominant or both recessive.

hormone a chemical substance that begins in an organ, gland, or body part and is conveyed by the blood to some other part of the body where its activity and secretion are stimulated.

insight the solving of a problem that has never been encountered before, without any training.

instinct behavior that an animal performs without learning or experience under certain environmental conditions.

intelligent design the idea that, because of the complexity of certain features of nature, an "intelligent designer" must have played a role in the development of life.

invertebrate an animal that does not have a backbone.

kinesis a change in the speed of movement brought about by an environmental stimulus. **larynx** the upper end of the trachea; the voice box.

leaves the plant structures that are specialized primarily for the manufacture of food through photosynthesis.

lipid any of a group of fats or fatlike substances that are insoluble in water.

locus the position of a gene on the chromosome.

lymph a pale, watery fluid that helps oxygen, nutrients, and waste pass between the capillaries and the body cells.

lymph nodes glandlike bodies of the immune system in which specific antigens activate T cells and B cells.

lysosomes small membranous sacs of varying size and shape containing powerful digestive enzymes that break down carbohydrate, protein, and fat molecules into simpler substances.

mammal any one of a class of animals that are warm-blooded, have a backbone, usually have hair, and feed their young with milk from the mother's breasts.

meiosis the process by which the number of chromosomes in reproductive cells of sexually reproducing organisms is reduced to half the original number, resulting in the production of gametes.

mesophyll in the leaf of a tree, the multilayered region between the upper and lower epidermis.

metabolism the sum of the chemical processes by which cells produce the materials and energy necessary for life.

mitochondria the relatively large, sausage-shaped, fluid-filled sacs scattered throughout the cytoplasm of a cell; the power plants of the cell.

mitosis cell division; the process by which a cell divides to form two new cells, each containing the same number of chromosomes as the original cell.

monocot group of flowering plants containing one cotyledon, or seed leaf; includes grasses, lilies, orchids, palms, and cattails.

moss rudimentary plants that lack true leaves, stems, and roots.

multicellular consisting of many cells.

mutation a permanent change in the hereditary material of an organism; produces random variation in the biological makeup of a species or a population.

mycologist scientist who studies fungi.

nastic movements in plants, physiological responses to specific stimuli; nondirectional and involve no plant growth.

natural selection the process by which individual organisms better suited to their environment are more likely to survive and therefore tend to leave more descendants.

neuron a nerve cell; the structural and functioning unit of the nervous system, consisting of the nerve cell body, the dendrites, and the axon.

neurosis a mild disorder that causes distress but does not interfere greatly with a person's everyday activities.

nonvascular plants plants that do not possess a system of specialized cells for carrying water and food through the plants.

nucleotides compounds of sugar, phosphoric acid, and a purine or pyrimidine base that make up DNA.

nucleus a structure within a cell, which contains the cell's genetic program, the master plan that controls almost everything the cell does.

organ a part of a plant or animal made up of various tissues to perform a specific function, such as the eyes, stomach, and heart.

osmosis a form of diffusion in which water or another solvent moves through a semipermeable membrane such as a cell wall.

ovary gland in the female that produces the reproductive cell, the ovum, and the hormones estrogen and progesterone.

ovum the germ cell produced in the ovary of the female; egg.

pandemic an epidemic that travels rapidly from one continent to another.

panspermia theory that life began somewhere other than on Earth and was carried to Earth from elsewhere in the solar system or universe, perhaps by a comet or meteorite.

parenchyma tissue in higher plants that acts as the site of chloroplasts (for photosynthesis) and of storage.

phagocyte a cell, either a macrophage (an immune cell) or granulocyte (a granular white blood cell), primarily involved in engulfing pathogenic organisms.

pharynx the cavity behind the nose and mouth; serves as the passageway for air from the nasal cavity to the larynx, and for food from the mouth to the esophagus.

phenetic systematics system of animal classification that compares as many traits as possible and groups them according to the number of similarities.

phenotype the way the trait of an organism is expressed—the actual appearance of the trait; as opposed to the genotype, which is the underlying genetic makeup of a trait.

pheromones a substance secreted externally by certain animal species, especially insects, to affect the behavior or development of other members of the species.

phloem the tissue that carries food throughout a vascular plant.

photosynthesis the process by which plants harness sunlight to synthesize food molecules.

phototropism tendency of plants to turn toward or grow toward light.

pinocytosis a cellular process in which the cell engulfs and ingests a fluid or very small particle.

pistils or carpels, make up the female reproductive structure of a plant; develop the egg and ultimately a fertile seed.

plankton tiny organisms that float along the water's surface; plankton serves as food for many marine animals. **plasma** the liquid part of the lymph and of the blood; makes up 55 percent of a person's blood; a straw-colored liquid that consists of 92 percent water and 8 percent nutrients, inorganic material, proteins, antibodies, and hormones.

pollination one of two main steps in the sexual reproduction of flowers; the transfer of pollen from a stamen to a pistil.

prokaryotic meaning before the nucleus. Prokaryotic cells are unicellular organisms like bacteria. They do not have a nucleus.

protein a complex substance, containing nitrogen, carbon, hydrogen, and oxygen, that is a necessary part of the cells of animals and plants.

psychosis a severe mental disorder that prevents an individual from functioning in a normal manner.

recapitulation the retaining by some animals of developmental features of their evolutionary ancestors.

recessive a gene which, in the presence of its dominant allele, does not express itself.

recombinant DNA DNA fragments which, under proper conditions, can find each other and recombine at random. This permits DNA from two different sources to be treated with the same enzyme, and then to be recombined with some of the resulting fragments consisting of DNA from both sources.

reflex an involuntary movement in response to a stimulus that involves only a part of an organism.

respiration in plants, the process that breaks down food made through photosynthesis and releases energy for the plant; in animals, the act of inhaling and exhaling—breathing.

ribonucleic acid (RNA) a substance found in all living cells, important in making proteins and in genetic transmission; similar to DNA except that the sugar in RNA is ribose, and RNA contains uracil instead of thymine.

ribosome a spherical cytoplasmic RNA-containing particle that is active in protein synthesis.

root the part of a plant that grows downward into the ground and absorbs water and nutrients from the soil.

seed the part of a plant from which a flower, vegetable, or other plant grows; consists of a protective outer coat enclosing the embryo that will become the new plant and a supply of food for its growth.

sexual reproduction the formation of new organisms through the joining of gametes from two separate organisms; organisms that form through sexual reproduction receive DNA from two separate parents.

speciation the evolution of a new species.

species a group of animals or plants that have certain permanent characteristics in common and are able to interbreed.

sperm a male gamete.

spermatozoa a male reproductive cell; a sperm cell; formed within the tubules of the testes.

spore a reproductive cell, usually unicellular and asexual, produced by nonflowering plants such as fungi, mosses, or ferns.

stamens the essential male reproductive structures of a flower; contained within the enfolding circle of sepals and petals.

stem the part of a plant that produces and supports the buds, leaves, flowers, and fruit; transports materials to and from the roots.

subcutaneous under the skin.

tannins astringent, aromatic compounds found in the leaves, bark, wood, and fruit of many plants.

taxis a directed movement toward or away from a stimulus.

taxonomy the scientific discipline that deals with the identification, naming, and classification of organisms.

thymine a constituent of thymidylic acid, and a nitrogen-containing base in DNA; it is always paired with adenine.

tissue a collection of similar cells which perform a particular function.

trachea the tube that leads from the larynx to the bronchi, through which air is carried to and from the lungs; the windpipe.

transpiration the act of exhaling water, gas, or vapor through skin or a membrane.

triglycerides glycerol that is combined with three fatty acids (stearic, oleic, and palmitic); found in most animal and vegetable fats.

tropism a movement toward or away from the direction of a stimulus; most involve true plant growth and once expressed become a permanent part of the plant's physical size and shape.

unicellular consisting of a single cell.

variation a difference in the traits of individuals of a single species.

vascular plant plants that have conducting tissue that carries water, minerals, and other nutrients throughout the plant body.

vertebrae the 33 bony segments of the spinal column comprised of 7 cerebral, 12 thoracic, 5 lumbar, 5 sacral, and 4 coccygeal vertebrae.

vertebrate an animal that has a backbone.

vestigial organ the useless remains of organs that were once useful in an evolutionary ancestor.

viruses minute organisms responsible for a wide variety of diseases.

vitamins organic chemical compounds that the body needs in small amounts; regulate chemical reactions in the body.

xylem the tissue that carries water throughout a vascular plant.

zygote a fertilized egg.

General Chemistry. **312**

Organic Chemistry. **408**

Practice Problems and Glossary **426**

MATERIAL OF THE UNIVERSE

Chemistry is the study of the composition, structure, and properties of substances, the transformations of these substances, and the energy changes that accompany these transformations.

Matter is the physical material of the universe. All objects consist of matter. The solid objects that we use in everyday life consist of molecules and crystals. These structures, in turn, consist of atoms that are linked together. Atoms are made up of smaller units called subatomic particles.

Energy

When physical or chemical changes occur, *energy*—the ability to do work or to transfer heat—is either absorbed or released.

- *Endothermic reactions* are changes in which energy is absorbed.
- *Exothermic reactions* are changes in which energy is released.

Classification of Energy. Energy has many forms. You use *mechanical energy* to toss a ball, *heat energy* warms a room, *electric energy* makes a light bulb glow, and *solar energy* (energy from the sun) warms and illuminates Earth and its atmosphere.

Two general classifications of energy are fundamental—any other form of energy consists of one or both of these two forms. These are kinetic energy and potential energy.

- *Kinetic energy* is the energy of an object due to its motion.
- *Potential energy* is the energy of an object due to its position. It can be thought of as "stored" energy.

Matter and Energy

Matter is the material of the universe—any substance that occupies space and takes up mass. *Energy* is the ability to do work or transfer heat.

Chemistry deals with the properties of matter and the energy that is released or absorbed when matter undergoes change. (See pages 778–783.)

Matter

Matter exists in three main physical states.

- *Gas* has no fixed volume or shape—it takes the volume and shape of its container.
- *Liquid* has a definite volume but no specific shape.
- *Solid* has both a fixed volume and a fixed shape.

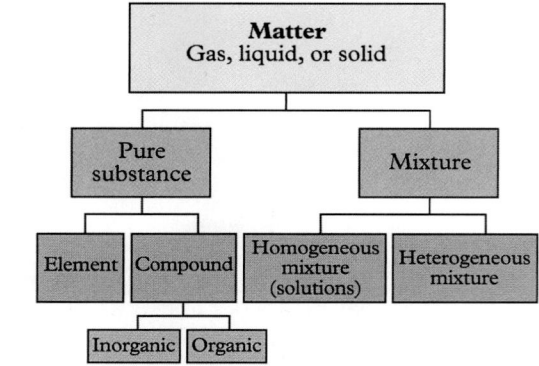

LAW OF CONSERVATION OF ENERGY

Energy appears in a variety of forms—light, sound, heat, mechanical energy, electrical energy, and chemical energy. One form of energy can be converted to another form, but energy itself can be neither created nor destroyed. This principle is called the *law of conservation of energy.*

LAW OF CONSERVATION OF MASS

During a chemical change, the total mass of the original substance always equals the total mass of the new substance. This principle, called the *law of conservation of mass,* is often stated as follows: In a chemical change, mass is conserved; it is neither created nor destroyed.

Classification of Matter. There are several other ways in which matter can be classified. If a sample of matter consists of only one kind of matter, the sample is a *pure substance*. If a sample of matter consists of two or more kinds of matter, the sample is a *mixture*.

Properties of Matter. Each substance has a unique set of properties, or characteristics, that distinguishes it from other substances. *Physical properties,* such as color and density, can be measured without changing the basic identity of the substance. *Chemical properties* describe the way a substance may change to form other substances.

Changes in Matter. When matter undergoes a change, the change may be either a *physical change,* in which a substance changes in its physical appearance but not its basic identity, or a *chemical change,* in which one substance is converted to another.

Classification of Matter		
Matter	**Type**	**Properties**
Pure substance		consists of only one kind of matter
	element	made of only one type of matter
	compound	consists of two or more elements combined in a definite ratio
Mixture		consists of two or more kinds of matter
	homogeneous	has uniform appearance and composition throughout
	heterogeneous	does not have uniform appearance and composition

Potential Energy

Kinetic Energy

◀ **Potential Energy and Kinetic Energy.** When the car is raised off the floor onto the track, its potential energy increases with respect to the floor. If the car is pushed down the track, its potential energy is converted into kinetic energy as it rolls.

Atoms

All matter is made up of *atoms*. An atom is the smallest particle of an element that can exhibit the properties of that element. An atom is incredibly tiny—more than a million times smaller than the thickness of a human hair.

Parts of an Atom

Atoms consist of *subatomic particles*.

- *protons*
- *neutrons*
- *electrons*

Protons and neutrons have approximately the same mass and constitute the *nucleus* of the atom. Electrons have almost no mass and move around the outside of the nucleus.

The subatomic particles also carry electrical charges: the proton has a single positive charge, the electron has a single negative charge, and the neutron is electrically neutral.

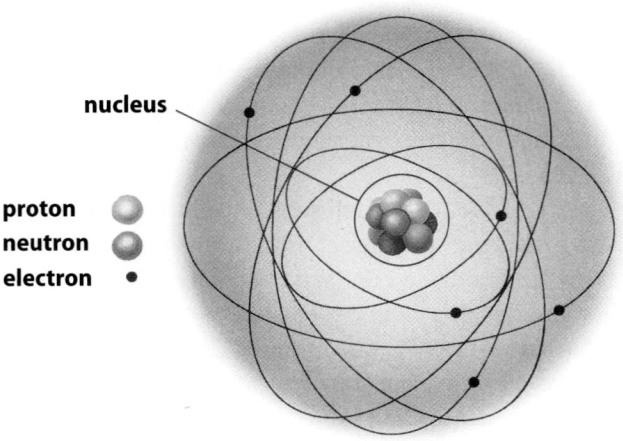

▲ **An Atom.** The protons and neutrons are clustered in the nucleus, a tiny region near the center of the atom. The electrons whirl at fantastic speeds through the empty space outside the atom's nucleus.

Properties of Atoms

All atoms of a given element have the same number of protons. This number is called the *atomic number*. The atomic number determines an element's place in the *periodic table*. This table organizes the elements into groups with similar chemical properties.

The *mass number* of an atom is equal to the number of protons and neutrons in the nucleus. In most lighter elements, the nucleus of each atom contains about an equal number of protons and neutrons. Most heavier elements, however, have more neutrons than protons.

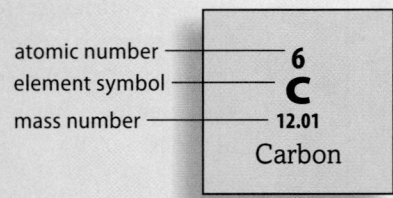

THE NUCLEUS

The protons and neutrons are crowded into the nucleus, which is an exceedingly tiny region at the center of the atom. If a hydrogen atom were 6.5 kilometers (about 4 miles) in diameter, its nucleus would be no bigger than a tennis ball. The rest of an atom outside the nucleus is mostly empty space.

The nucleus makes up nearly all the *mass* of an atom. Mass is the quantity of matter in an atom. Each proton has a mass roughly equal to that of 1,836 electrons. It would take 1,839 electrons to equal a neutron's mass.

Each proton carries one unit of positive electric charge. Each electron carries one unit of negative charge. Neutrons have no charge. Under most conditions, an atom has the same number of protons and electrons, and so the atom is electrically neutral.

Subatomic Particles					
Particle	**Symbol**	**Charge**	**Mass**	**Location**	**Discovered**
Electron	e–	–1	0.00055 u*	Outside nucleus	1897 by Joseph J. Thomson
Proton	p or p+	+1	1.0073 u	Inside nucleus	1919 by Ernest Rutherford
Neutron	n or n0	0	1.0087 u	Inside nucleus	1932 by Sir James Chadwick
* u = unified atomic mass unit					

Isotopes

Sometimes the number of neutrons in atoms of the same element may vary. Consequently, these atoms have different masses. Atoms of the same element that differ in mass are known as *isotopes*.

The isotope of an element is identified by its nuclear symbol, which shows the symbol for an element and the mass number of the element. For example, carbon has a few important isotopes. The most common one has a mass number of 12; another isotope has mass number 13. They are written ^{12}C (or carbon 12) and ^{13}C (or carbon 13).

Molecules and Ions

Atoms can combine to form *molecules*. (See pages 346–347.) Both atoms and molecules can gain or lose electrons, resulting in electrically charged particles called *ions*.

The loss of electrons forms positively charged particles called *cations*. The gain of electrons forms negatively charged particles called *anions*.

Diatomic Molecules. The simplest type of molecule is called a *diatomic molecule* and contains two atoms—either two of the same type or two different types. Seven elements exist as diatomic molecules—hydrogen, oxygen, nitrogen, fluorine, chlorine, bromine, and iodine.

Polyatomic Molecules. Molecules with more than two atoms are called *polyatomic molecules*. Sulfur (S_8) and phosphorus (P_4) are examples of polyatomic elements.

HOW SMALL IS IT?

An atom is so small that the smallest speck you can view under an ordinary microscope contains more than 10 billion atoms!

The diameter of an atom ranges from about 0.1 to 0.5 nanometer. A nanometer is a billionth of a meter, or about 1/25,400,000 inch.

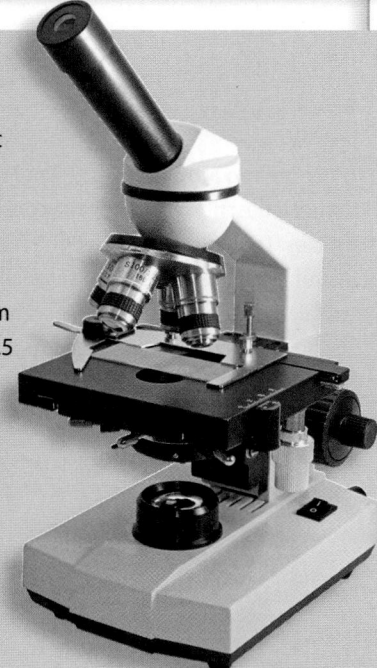

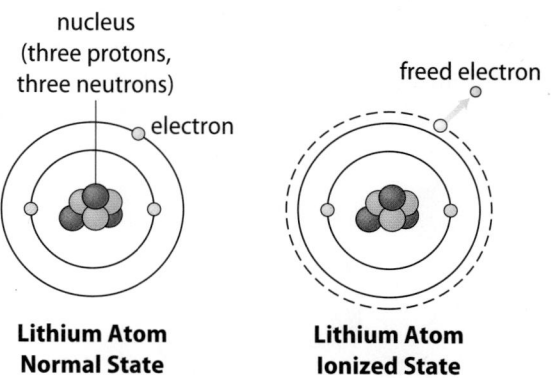

nucleus
(three protons,
three neutrons)

electron

freed electron

**Lithium Atom
Normal State**

**Lithium Atom
Ionized State**

▲ **An atom becomes an ion** when it gains or loses an electron and so acquires an electric charge. A normal atom has an equal number of positive protons and negative electrons. If it loses an electron, it becomes a positively charged ion.

Atomic Structure

The idea that matter can be divided down to the level of an atom, which cannot be divided any further, was first proposed by Greek philosophers about 400 BC. More than 2,000 years later, the idea became the basis for modern chemistry.

Theories of Atomic Structure

In 1803, the English chemist John Dalton reformulated the atomic theory and showed that it explains a great deal about the chemical properties of substances. Subsequently, John Dalton's atomic theory of matter became a basic theory of modern chemistry.

A Developing Theory. Since Dalton's time, further research and insight have brought scientists closer to a true model of the structure and behavior of atoms. Joseph J. Thomson discovered the electron in 1904. Seven years later, Ernest Rutherford declared correctly that nearly all the mass of an atom is concentrated in a tiny nucleus, and that the electrons travel at tremendous speeds around the nucleus.

The modern theory of atomic structure was developed from studies of light. When electrons strike the atoms of a gas, the atoms emit electromagnetic waves, such as light, X-rays, and radio waves. These emissions can be observed as discrete lines (called line spectra) using a device known as a *spectrometer*. Each atom produces its own unique spectrum.

In 1913, Danish physicist Niels Bohr created a model of the hydrogen atom that explained the observed line spectra of hydrogen. Bohr based his model on the assumption that the energy possessed by an electron was *quantized:* at any instant an electron may have one of several possible energy values, but at no time may it have an energy that falls in between those values.

Orbits. Bohr proposed that electrons move around the nucleus in circular paths, called *orbits,* and that these orbits are restricted to certain energy levels. Each orbit was assigned an integer, *n,* known as the *principal quantum number*. Higher quantum numbers were associated with higher orbital energies.

MODELS OF ATOMIC STRUCTURE

The Dalton Model. In 1803, English chemist John Dalton described atoms as small, spherical, indivisible particles. His theory states that each element is composed of its own kind of atoms, all with the same relative weight. This theory explained why a fixed weight of one substance always combines with a fixed weight of another substance in forming a compound.

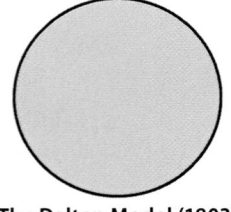

The Dalton Model (1803)

The Thomson Model. In 1897, English physicist Joseph J. Thomson described the atom as consisting of smaller subatomic particles. Thomson discovered the first subatomic particle: the electron. He determined that since all atoms are electrically neutral, the atoms must contain as many positive charges as they do negatively charged electrons.

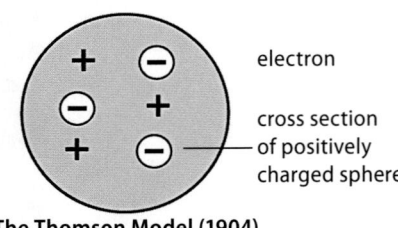

electron

cross section of positively charged sphere

The Thomson Model (1904)

Bohr stated that the electron of hydrogen was normally in the lowest energy level, known as the *ground state*. By absorbing energy, the electron could be raised to an unstable *excited state*. When the electron dropped back to its ground state, it emitted energy that appeared as a line in the atom's line spectrum.

Quantum Mechanics. Later experiments showed that electrons could not move in the well-defined orbits Bohr suggested, but Bohr's theory was expanded by other scientists into a new field of physics, *quantum mechanics*, which explains the structure of atoms, the way they give off light, and other related matters.

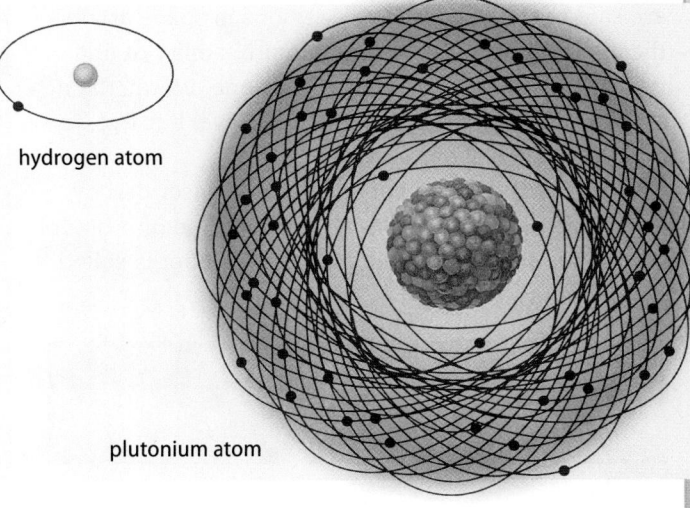

hydrogen atom

plutonium atom

ATOMIC WEIGHT AND SIZE

Atoms vary greatly in weight, but they are all about the same size. The smallest and lightest atom is the hydrogen atom. It consists of 1 proton and 1 electron. The largest and heaviest atom found in nature is the plutonium atom. It has 94 protons, 150 neutrons, and 94 electrons. An atom of plutonium weighs more than 200 times as much as an atom of hydrogen. However, a plutonium atom is only about three times as large in diameter as a hydrogen atom.

The Rutherford Model. Ernest Rutherford, another English physicist, stated that the atom is mostly empty space. In 1911, he proposed the theory that the atom consists of a nucleus with a positive charge with enough electrons rotating around it to balance the charge. These electrons were kept within the atom by the attraction of the positively charged nucleus.

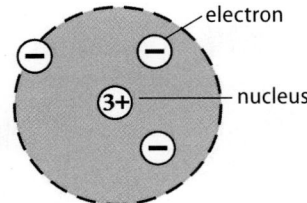

The Rutherford Model (1911)

The Bohr Model. In 1913, Danish physicist Niels Bohr proposed that an atom's electrons could travel only in certain successively larger orbits around the nucleus. He thought the outer orbits could hold more electrons than the inner ones. Bohr also suggested that the electrons in the outermost orbit determined the atom's chemical properties.

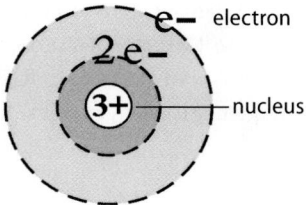

The Bohr Model (1913)

Electron Cloud Model

In 1913, Danish physicist Niels Bohr proposed that an atom's electrons could travel only in a certain set of successively larger orbits around the nucleus. This model has proven to be inadequate, but many of the ideas behind it proved correct.

Bohr's model of atomic structure has been replaced with a model called the *electron cloud model,* or the *quantum-mechanical model.*

Matter in Motion

In 1924, French physicist Louis de Broglie suggested that matter in motion has properties normally associated with waves. In 1926, Erwin Schrödinger took this concept a step further and developed the *Schrödinger equation,* which describes the motions and energies of particles. From this equation, the quantum-mechanical model of the atom was developed. This model describes electron behavior in terms of wave mechanics.

Principal Energy Levels. The fixed energy levels in the quantum-mechanical model are called *principal energy levels.* Each energy level is identified by a principal quantum number, n. Within each principal level are one or more *sublevels* designated by the letters s, p, d, and f.

The total number of sublevels within a given principal energy level is equal to the principal quantum number. A sublevel is identified by both the principal energy level number and the sublevel letter, for example, 1s, 2s, 2p, 3s, and so on.

Orbitals. Instead of clearly defined orbits, electrons are said to travel in *orbitals*—regions in space around the nucleus where there is a high probability of finding the electron. The s sublevel has one orbital, the p sublevel has three orbitals, the d sublevel has five, and the f sublevel has seven.

The size and energy of an orbital is described by its principal quantum number. A collection of orbitals having the same principal quantum number is called an *electron shell.*

Sublevels and Orbitals			
Energy Level	Number of Sublevels	Sublevel Designations	Orbitals per Sublevel
n = 1	1	1s	1
n = 2	2	2s 2p	1 3
n = 3	3	3s 3p 3d	1 3 5
n = 4	4	4s 4p 4d 4f	1 3 5 7

THOSE ACCURATE ATOMS

The most accurate clocks in the world will not lose or gain more than a second in tens of millions of years. Why? Because they're atomic.

An atomic clock keeps time by counting the energy changes of atoms. When an atom of a certain element gains or loses energy, it vibrates at a certain frequency. This frequency is identical from atom to atom. Thus, timekeeping based on the frequency is nearly perfect.

Atomic Clock. In 1967, atomic clocks became the basis for world timekeeping. The second is defined as the amount of time a cesium atom takes to make 9,192,631,770 energy transitions. ▶

Electrons

Opposite electric charges attract. The positively charged nucleus therefore exerts a force on the negatively charged electrons that keeps them within the atom. However, each electron has energy and so is able to resist the attraction of the nucleus.

The more energy an electron has, the farther from the nucleus it will be. Thus, electrons are arranged in shells at various distances from the nucleus according to how much energy they have. Electrons with the least energy are in inner shells, and those with more energy are in outer shells.

Electrons have almost no mass. The mass of an electron in grams is written with a decimal point followed by 27 zeros and a nine.

Electron Configurations. The electron configuration of an atom describes the distribution of electrons among the atom's orbitals. Electrons occupy the orbitals in order of increasing energy. All orbitals that are equal in energy are filled with electrons before the next level of energy begins to fill up.

The electrons in the electron shell with the largest principal quantum number are called the outer shell, or *valence shell,* electrons. These valence shell electrons take part in chemical bonding. Most bonded atoms tend to share a total of eight valence electrons. This observation is called the *octet rule.*

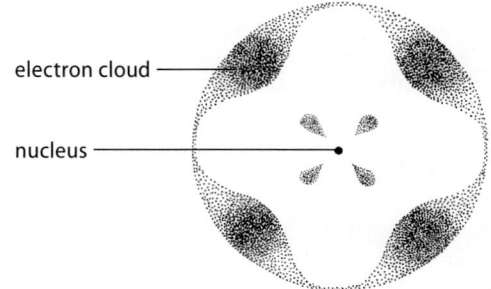

▲ **The electron cloud model** indicates the regions within the atom where electrons may be found. Electrons are most likely to be where a cloud is darkest.

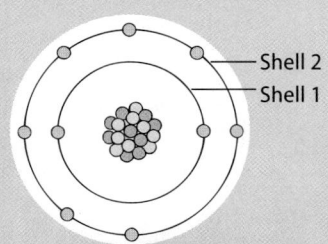

Fluorine Atom

The valence shell of a fluorine atom has seven electrons. In a chemical reaction, the atom fills the shell by accepting one electron from another atom.

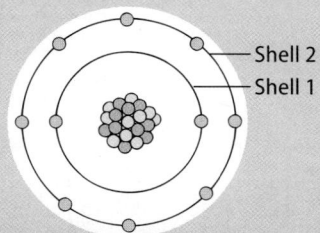

Neon Atom

The valence shell of a neon atom is filled. As a result, neon generally does not enter into chemical reactions with other atoms.

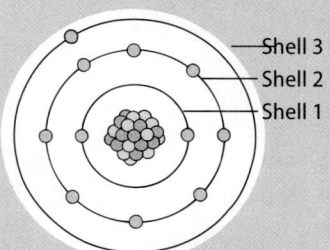

Sodium Atom

A sodium atom tends to lose the single electron in its valence shell during a chemical reaction. The filled shell 2 then becomes the valence shell.

ELEMENTAL ORGANIZATION

A *chemical element* is any substance that contains only one kind of atom. All chemical substances are elements or *compounds* (combinations of elements). There are 93 elements that naturally occur on Earth. Scientists have produced 19 more elements, most in machines called *particle accelerators*.

The elements are the fundamental units of chemistry (and, in fact, of the universe). In 1869, Russian chemist Dmitri Medeleev organized the known elements based on their properties into a chart that came to be known as the *periodic table*.

Periodic Table

The periodic table ranks as one of the most useful tools in chemistry and perhaps in all of science. The chart organizes the chemical elements into rows and columns. Elements in the same column share certain chemical properties. These properties repeat row by row in a regular or periodic fashion, giving the table its name. (See pages 322–323.)

Structure of the Table

Elements on the periodic table are arranged in order of increasing *atomic number*. The atomic number is the number of protons an atom has. All atoms of the same element have the same number of protons.

Groups. Elements that have similar chemical properties and the same number of *valence electrons*—the electrons in the outer shell—are placed in vertical columns that are referred to as *groups* or *families*. The groups are usually numbered across the top of the table. The individual columns are numbered 1 through 18, from left to right.

Some groups have been given names. Group 1 is known as the *alkali metals*. Group 2 is the *alkaline earth metals*. The elements of group 17 are the *halogens*, and the elements of group 18 are the *noble gases*.

$$2^+$$
12
Mg
24.31
Magnesium

- ion charge
- atomic number
- chemical symbol
- atomic mass
- name of element

Each element occupies a separate square and is represented by its symbol, its atomic number, and its atomic mass.

Periodic Table of Elements

1+
6
C
12.01
Carbon

- ion charge
- atomic number
- chemical symbol
- atomic mass
- name of element

- ☐ Alkali Metals
- ☐ Alkali Earth Metals
- ☐ Transition Metals
- ■ Lanthanide Metals
- ☐ Actinide Metals
- ☐ Other Metals
- ☐ Nonmetals
- ☐ Noble Gases
- ☢ radioactive

| Period 3 | | 12 2+ Mg 24.31 Magnesium | | | | | | | | | | 13 3+ Al 26.98 Aluminum | 14 Si 28.09 Silicon | 15 3- P 30.97 Phosphorus | 16 2- S 32.06 Sulfur | 17 1- Cl 35.45 Chlorine | 18 Ar 39.95 Argon |

(Periodic table columns: III B, IV B, V B, VI B, VII B, VIII, I B, II B; transition metals; groups 3–12)

Period 4: 19 1+ K 39.10 Potassium · 20 2+ Ca 40.08 Calcium · 21 3+ Sc 44.96 Scandium · 22 4+ Ti 47.90 Titanium · 23 5+ V 50.94 Vanadium · 24 3+ Cr 52.00 Chromium · 25 2+ Mn 54.94 Manganese · 26 3+ Fe 55.85 Iron · 27 3+ Co 58.93 Cobalt · 28 2+ Ni 58.71 Nickel · 29 2+ Cu 63.55 Copper · 30 2+ Zn 65.37 Zinc · 31 3+ Ga 69.72 Gallium · 32 4+ Ge 72.59 Germanium · 33 3- As 74.92 Arsenic · 34 2- Se 78.96 Selenium · 35 1- Br 79.90 Bromine · 36 Kr 83.80 Krypton

Period 5: 37 1+ Rb 85.47 Rubidium · 38 2+ Sr 87.62 Strontium · 39 3+ Y 88.91 Yttrium · 40 4+ Zr 91.22 Zirconium · 41 5+ Nb 92.91 Niobium · 42 6+ Mo 95.94 Molybdenum · 43 7+ Tc 98.91 Technetium · 44 4+ Ru 101.07 Ruthenium · 45 3+ Rh 102.91 Rhodium · 46 2+ Pd 106.4 Palladium · 47 1+ Ag 107.87 Silver · 48 2+ Cd 112.40 Cadmium · 49 3+ In 114.82 Indium · 50 4+ Sn 118.69 Tin · 51 3+ Sb 121.75 Antimony · 52 2- Te 127.60 Tellurium · 53 1- I 126.90 Iodine · 54 Xe 131.30 Xenon

Period 6: 55 1+ Cs 132.91 Cesium · 56 2+ Ba 137.34 Barium · 72 4+ Hf 178.49 Hafnium · 73 5+ Ta 180.95 Tantalum · 74 6+ W 183.85 Tungsten · 75 7+ Re 186.2 Rhenium · 76 4+ Os 190.2 Osmium · 77 4+ Ir 192.2 Iridium · 78 4+ Pt 195.09 Platinum · 79 3+ Au 196.97 Gold · 80 2+ Hg 200.59 Mercury · 81 1+ Tl 204.37 Thallium · 82 2+ Pb 207.2 Lead · 83 3+ Bi 208.98 Bismuth · 84 2+ Po (209) Polonium · 85 1- At (210) Astatine · 86 Rn (222) Radon

Period 7: 87 1+ Fr (223) Francium · 88 2+ Ra (226) Radium · 104 Rf (261) Rutherfordium · 105 Db (262) Dubnium · 106 Sg (263) Seaborgium · 107 Bh (262) Bohrium · 108 Hs (265) Hassium · 109 Mt (266) Meitnerium · 110 Ds (269) Darmstadtium · 111 Rg (272) Roentgenium · 112 Cn (277) Copernicium · 114 Uuq* (285) · 116 Uuh* (289)

other metals

Lanthanide series / rare earth elements: 57 3+ La 138.9 Lanthanum · 58 3+ Ce 140.12 Cerium · 59 3+ Pr 140.91 Praseodymium · 60 3+ Nd 144.24 Neodymium · 61 3+ Pm (145) Promethium · 62 3+ Sm 150.4 Samarium · 63 3+ Eu 151.96 Europium · 64 3+ Gd 157.25 Gadolinium · 65 3+ Tb 158.93 Terbium · 66 3+ Dy 162.50 Dysprosium · 67 3+ Ho 164.93 Holmium · 68 3+ Er 167.26 Erbium · 69 3+ Tm 168.93 Thulium · 70 2+ Yb 173.04 Ytterbium · 71 3+ Lu 174.97 Lutetium

Actinide series: 89 3+ Ac (227) Actinium · 90 4+ Th 232.04 Thorium · 91 5+ Pa 231.04 Protactinium · 92 6+ U 238.03 Uranium · 93 5+ Np 237.05 Neptunium · 94 6+ Pu (244) Plutonium · 95 4+ Am (243) Americium · 96 3+ Cm (247) Curium · 97 3+ Bk (247) Berkelium · 98 3+ Cf (251) Californium · 99 3+ Es (254) Einsteinium · 100 3+ Fm (257) Fermium · 101 3+ Md (258) Mendelevium · 102 2+ No (259) Nobelium · 103 3+ Lr (260) Lawrencium

18 noble gases O — 2 He 4.00 Helium

13 — III A — 5 B 10.81 Boron
14 — IV A — 6 C 12.01 Carbon
15 — V A — 7 3- N 14.01 Nitrogen · 8 2- O 16.00 Oxygen
16 — VI A — 9 1- F 19.00 Fluorine
17 — VII A — 10 Ne 20.18 Neon

nonmetals

 **DMITRI MENDELEEV**

1834–1907

In 1869, a Russian chemist named Dmitri Mendeleev created what scholars widely consider to be the first modern periodic table. Mendeleev based the table on the observation that when elements are arranged according to their relative atomic masses, elements with similar properties appear at regular intervals, or periods, in the table.

Mendeleev left gaps in his table where no known elements seemed to fit, predicting that elements with certain properties would be discovered to fill the gaps. Mendeleev was proven correct—and his periodic table proven accurate—when several new elements were discovered with properties matching Mendeleev's predictions.

Periods. The horizontal rows of the table are called *periods* or *rows*. The periods correspond to the sequential filling of the electron shells. Each row terminates with an element that has a complete valence shell.

Other Regions. There are three distinct regions of the periodic table: Groups 1A through 8A, taken together, comprise the *representative elements*. Groups 3B to 2B comprise the *transition metals*.

The elements in the two 14-member rows that are placed below the main portion of the table are the *inner transition metals*. The inner transition metals of the first row are called the *lanthanides*, and those of the second row are called the *actinides*.

Other Divisions. Elements can also be divided into metals, nonmetals, and semimetals, also known as *metalloids*. Generally, metallic character increases from top to bottom of the periodic table and decreases from left to right.

Metals. Chemically, an element is known as a *metal* if it can lose one or more electrons and become a positively charged ion. Metals comprise roughly 70 percent of the known elements and are situated on the left side of the table. For the most part, metals have a metallic luster, exhibit good electrical and thermal conductivity, and can be flattened or drawn into wire as solids.

Nonmetals—elements that do not lose electrons—are located in the upper-right corner of the periodic table. These elements vary greatly in appearance and are generally poor conductors of heat and electricity.

Metalloids. Between the metals and the nonmetals are the semimetals, which have properties characteristic of both metals and nonmetals.

Atomic Property Trends. Many atomic properties are *periodic*—the properties of elements are basically repeated through each family. For example, the size of an atom varies for each element. However, within each group, the atomic radius tends to increase going from top to bottom; and within each period, the atomic radius tends to decrease moving from left to right.

Other trends include such things as reactivity, metallic character, and ionization energy.

Periodic Table

SOUTHWESTERN

Key	
1^+	ion charge
6	atomic number
C	chemical symbol
12.01	atomic mass
Carbon	name of element

- Alkali metals
- Alkaline earth metals
- Transition metals
- Lanthanide metals
- Actinide metals
- Other metals
- Nonmetals
- Noble gases
- ☢ Radioactive

	1 alkali metals I A	2 alkaline earth metals II A	3 III B	4 IV B	5 V B	6 VI B	7 VII B	8	9 VIII
			transition metals						
Period 1	1^+ 1^- 1 **H** 1.01 Hydrogen								
Period 2	1^+ 3 **Li** 6.94 Lithium	2^+ 4 **Be** 9.01 Beryllium							
Period 3	1^+ 11 **Na** 23.00 Sodium	2^+ 12 **Mg** 24.31 Magnesium							
Period 4	1^+ 19 **K** 39.10 Potassium	2^+ 20 **Ca** 40.08 Calcium	3^+ 21 **Sc** 44.96 Scandium	4^+ 3^+ 22 **Ti** 47.90 Titanium	5^+ 4^+ 23 **V** 50.94 Vanadium	3^+ 2^+ 24 **Cr** 52.00 Chromium	2^+ 4^+ 25 **Mn** 54.94 Manganese	3^+ 2^+ 26 **Fe** 55.85 Iron	2^+ 3^+ 27 **Co** 58.93 Cobalt
Period 5	1^+ 37 **Rb** 85.47 Rubidium	2^+ 38 **Sr** 87.62 Strontium	3^+ 39 **Y** 88.91 Yttrium	4^+ 40 **Zr** 91.22 Zirconium	5^+ 3^+ 41 **Nb** 92.91 Niobium	6^+ 42 **Mo** 95.94 Molybdenum	7^+ 43 **Tc** 98.91 ☢ Technetium	3^+ 4^+ 44 **Ru** 101.07 Ruthenium	3^+ 45 **Rh** 102.91 Rhodium
Period 6	1^+ 55 **Cs** 132.91 Cesium	2^+ 56 **Ba** 137.34 Barium		4^+ 72 **Hf** 178.49 Hafnium	5^+ 73 **Ta** 180.95 Tantalum	6^+ 74 **W** 183.85 Tungsten	7^+ 75 **Re** 186.2 Rhenium	4^+ 76 **Os** 190.2 Osmium	4^+ 77 **Ir** 192.2 Iridium
Period 7	1^+ 87 **Fr** (223) ☢ Francium	2^+ 88 **Ra** (226) ☢ Radium		104 **Rf** (261) ☢ Rutherfordium	105 **Db** (262) ☢ Dubnium	106 **Sg** (263) ☢ Seaborgium	107 **Bh** (262) ☢ Bohrium	108 **Hs** (265) ☢ Hassium	109 **Mt** (266) ☢ Meitnerium

rare earth elements

Lanthanide series	3^+ 57 **La** 138.9 Lanthanum	3^+ 58 **Ce** 140.12 Cerium	3^+ 59 **Pr** 140.91 Praseodymium	3^+ 60 **Nd** 144.24 Neodymium	3^+ 61 **Pm** (145) ☢ Promethium	3^+ 2^+ 62 **Sm** 150.4 Samarium	3^+ 2^+ 63 **Eu** 151.96 Europium
Actinide series	3^+ 89 **Ac** (227) ☢ Actinium	4^+ 90 **Th** 232.04 ☢ Thorium	5^+ 4^+ 91 **Pa** 231.04 ☢ Protactinium	6^+ 4^+ 92 **U** 238.03 ☢ Uranium	5^+ 93 **Np** 237.05 ☢ Neptunium	4^+ 6^+ 94 **Pu** (244) ☢ Plutonium	3^+ 4^+ 95 **Am** (243) ☢ Americium

A figure in parentheses is the isotope of longest known half-life. No stable isotope is known.

Polyatomic ions—theoretical summary

1^- Ions

• acetate	CH_3COO^-	• hydrogen carbonate (bicarbonate)	HCO_3^-	• hypochlorite	CLO^-; OCl^-
benzoate	$C_6H_5COO^-$	hydrogen oxalate	$HOOCCOO^-$	• nitrate	NO_3^-
chlorate*	ClO_3^-	• hydrogen sulfate (bisulfate)	HSO_4^-	nitrite	NO_2^-
chlorite	ClO_2^-	hydrogen sulfide (bisulfide)	HS^-	perchlorate*	CLO_4^-
cyanide	CN^-	hydrogen sulfite (bisulfite)	HSO_3^-	• permanganate	MnO_4^-
dihydrogen phosphate	$H_2PO_4^-$	• hydroxide	OH^-	stearate	$C_{12}H_{35}COO^-$
glutamate	$C_5H_8NO_4^-$			thiocyanate	SCN^-

*** There are also corresponding ions containing Br and I instead of Cl.** **• Frequently used ions**

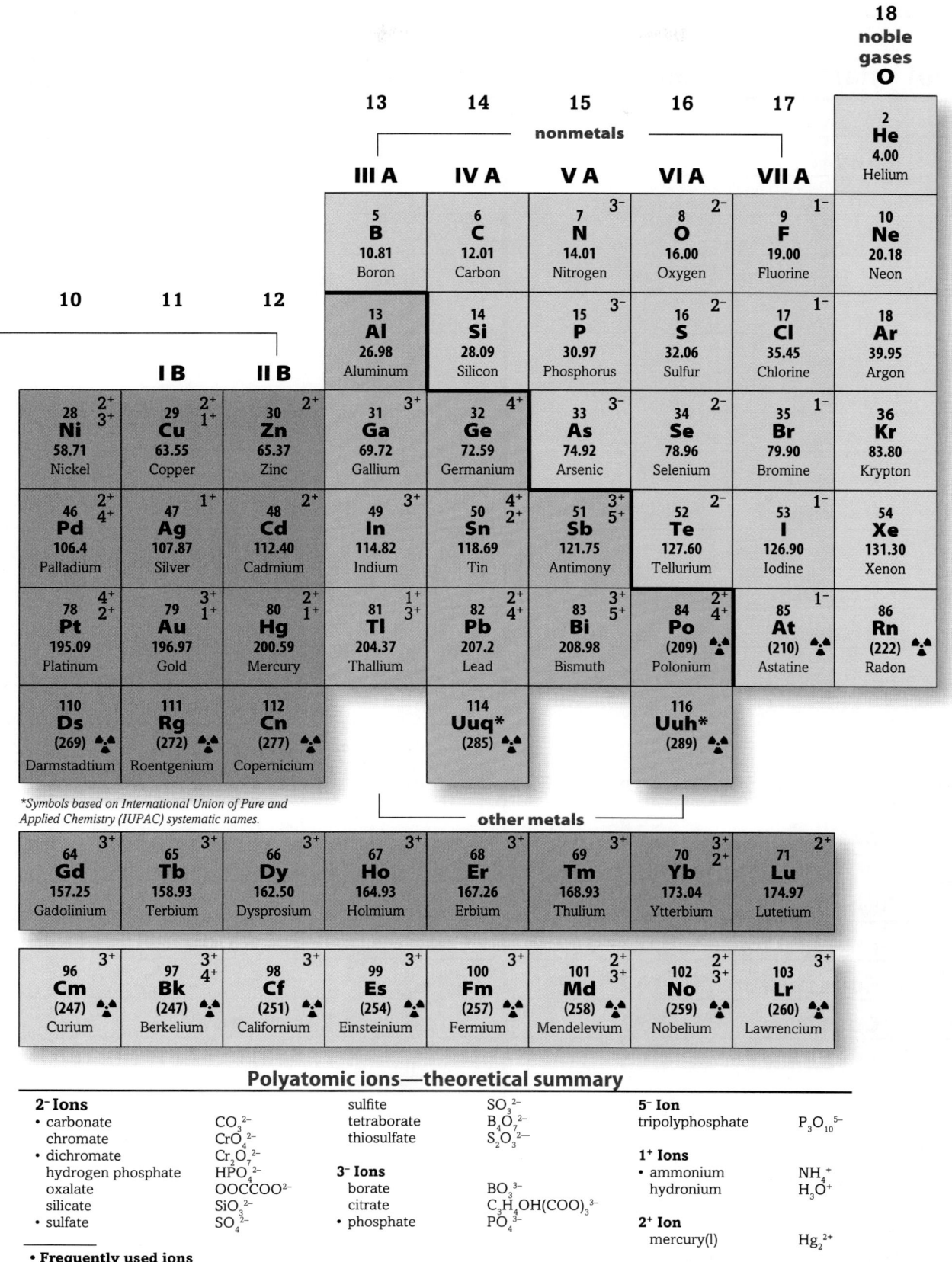

18
noble gases
O

	13	14	15	16	17	
			nonmetals			
	III A	**IV A**	**V A**	**VI A**	**VII A**	

2 **He** 4.00 Helium

10 11 12		
I B	**II B**	

Periodic table elements:

- 5 **B** 10.81 Boron
- 6 **C** 12.01 Carbon
- 7 **N** $3-$ 14.01 Nitrogen
- 8 **O** $2-$ 16.00 Oxygen
- 9 **F** $1-$ 19.00 Fluorine
- 10 **Ne** 20.18 Neon

- 13 **Al** $3+$ 26.98 Aluminum
- 14 **Si** $4+$ 28.09 Silicon
- 15 **P** $3-$ 30.97 Phosphorus
- 16 **S** $2-$ 32.06 Sulfur
- 17 **Cl** $1-$ 35.45 Chlorine
- 18 **Ar** 39.95 Argon

- 28 **Ni** $2+$ $3+$ 58.71 Nickel
- 29 **Cu** $2+$ $1+$ 63.55 Copper
- 30 **Zn** $2+$ 65.37 Zinc
- 31 **Ga** $3+$ 69.72 Gallium
- 32 **Ge** $4+$ 72.59 Germanium
- 33 **As** $3-$ 74.92 Arsenic
- 34 **Se** $2-$ 78.96 Selenium
- 35 **Br** $1-$ 79.90 Bromine
- 36 **Kr** 83.80 Krypton

- 46 **Pd** $2+$ $4+$ 106.4 Palladium
- 47 **Ag** $1+$ 107.87 Silver
- 48 **Cd** $2+$ 112.40 Cadmium
- 49 **In** $3+$ 114.82 Indium
- 50 **Sn** $4+$ $2+$ 118.69 Tin
- 51 **Sb** $3+$ $5+$ 121.75 Antimony
- 52 **Te** $2-$ 127.60 Tellurium
- 53 **I** $1-$ 126.90 Iodine
- 54 **Xe** 131.30 Xenon

- 78 **Pt** $4+$ $2+$ 195.09 Platinum
- 79 **Au** $3+$ $1+$ 196.97 Gold
- 80 **Hg** $2+$ $1+$ 200.59 Mercury
- 81 **Tl** $1+$ $3+$ 204.37 Thallium
- 82 **Pb** $2+$ $4+$ 207.2 Lead
- 83 **Bi** $3+$ $5+$ 208.98 Bismuth
- 84 **Po** $2+$ $4+$ (209) Polonium
- 85 **At** $1-$ (210) Astatine
- 86 **Rn** (222) Radon

- 110 **Ds** (269) Darmstadtium
- 111 **Rg** (272) Roentgenium
- 112 **Cn** (277) Copernicium
- 114 **Uuq*** (285)
- 116 **Uuh*** (289)

*Symbols based on International Union of Pure and Applied Chemistry (IUPAC) systematic names.

other metals

- 64 **Gd** $3+$ 157.25 Gadolinium
- 65 **Tb** $3+$ 158.93 Terbium
- 66 **Dy** $3+$ 162.50 Dysprosium
- 67 **Ho** $3+$ 164.93 Holmium
- 68 **Er** $3+$ 167.26 Erbium
- 69 **Tm** $3+$ 168.93 Thulium
- 70 **Yb** $3+$ $2+$ 173.04 Ytterbium
- 71 **Lu** $2+$ 174.97 Lutetium

- 96 **Cm** $3+$ (247) Curium
- 97 **Bk** $3+$ $4+$ (247) Berkelium
- 98 **Cf** $3+$ (251) Californium
- 99 **Es** $3+$ (254) Einsteinium
- 100 **Fm** $3+$ (257) Fermium
- 101 **Md** $2+$ $3+$ (258) Mendelevium
- 102 **No** $2+$ $3+$ (259) Nobelium
- 103 **Lr** $3+$ (260) Lawrencium

Polyatomic ions—theoretical summary

2⁻ Ions

- carbonate CO_3^{2-}
  chromate CrO_4^{2-}
- dichromate $Cr_2O_7^{2-}$
  hydrogen phosphate HPO_4^{2-}
  oxalate $OOCCOO^{2-}$
  silicate SiO_3^{2-}
- sulfate SO_4^{2-}

sulfite SO_3^{2-}
tetraborate $B_4O_7^{2-}$
thiosulfate $S_2O_3^{2-}$

3⁻ Ions
borate BO_3^{3-}
citrate $C_3H_4OH(COO)_3^{3-}$
- phosphate PO_4^{3-}

5⁻ Ion
tripolyphosphate $P_3O_{10}^{5-}$

1⁺ Ions
- ammonium NH_4^+
  hydronium H_3O^+

2⁺ Ion
mercury(l) Hg_2^{2+}

- **Frequently used ions**

Chemical Elements

Symbol	Name	Atomic Number
Ac	Actinium	89
Ag	Silver	47
Al	Aluminum	13
Am	Americium	95
Ar	Argon	18
As	Arsenic	33
At	Astatine	85
Au	Gold	79
B	Boron	5
Ba	Barium	56
Be	Beryllium	4
Bk	Berkelium	97
Bh	Bohrium	107
Bi	Bismuth	83
Br	Bromine	35
C	Carbon	6
Ca	Calcium	20
Cd	Cadmium	48
Ce	Cerium	58
Cf	Californium	98
Cl	Chlorine	17
Cm	Curium	96
Cn	Copernicium	112
Co	Cobalt	27
Cr	Chromium	24
Cs	Cesium (Caesium)	55
Cu	Copper	29
Db	Dubnium	105

Symbol	Name	Atomic Number
Ds	Darmstadtium	110
Dy	Dysprosium	66
Er	Erbium	68
Es	Einsteinium	99
Eu	Europium	63
F	Fluorine	9
Fe	Iron	26
Fm	Fermium	100
Fr	Francium	87
Ga	Gallium	31
Gd	Gadolinium	64
Ge	Germanium	32
H	Hydrogen	1
He	Helium	2
Hf	Hafnium	72
Hg	Mercury	80
Ho	Holmium	67
Hs	Hassium	108
I	Iodine	53
In	Indium	49
Ir	Iridium	77
K	Potassium	19
Kr	Krypton	36
La	Lanthanum	57
Li	Lithium	3
Lr	Lawrencium	103
Lu	Lutetium	71
Md	Mendelevium	101

Symbol	Name	Atomic Number	Symbol	Name	Atomic Number
Mg	Magnesium	12	Rh	Rhodium	45
Mn	Manganese	25	Rn	Radon	86
Mo	Molybdenum	42	Ru	Ruthenium	44
Mt	Meitnerium	109	S	Sulfur	16
N	Nitrogen	7	Sb	Antimony	51
Na	Sodium	11	Sc	Scandium	21
Nb	Niobium	41	Se	Selenium	34
Nd	Neodymium	60	Sg	Seaborgium	106
Ne	Neon	10	Si	Silicon	14
Ni	Nickel	28	Sm	Samarium	62
No	Nobelium	102	Sn	Tin	50
Np	Neptunium	93	Sr	Strontium	38
O	Oxygen	8	Ta	Tantalum	73
Os	Osmium	76	Tb	Terbium	65
P	Phosphorus	15	Tc	Technetium	43
Pa	Protactinium	91	Te	Tellurium	52
Pb	Lead	82	Th	Thorium	90
Pd	Palladium	46	Ti	Titanium	22
Pm	Promethium	61	Tl	Thallium	81
Po	Polonium	84	Tm	Thulium	69
Pr	Praseodymium	59	U	Uranium	92
Pt	Platinum	78	V	Vanadium	23
Pu	Plutonium	94	W	Tungsten	74
Ra	Radium	88	Xe	Xenon	54
Rb	Rubidium	37	Y	Yttrium	39
Re	Rhenium	75	Yb	Ytterbium	70
Rf	Rutherfordium	104	Zn	Zinc	30
Rg	Roentgenium	111	Zr	Zirconium	40

AN ALPHABETICAL GUIDE TO THE ELEMENTS

Unlike the periodic table of elements, which groups elements according to properties, this is an alphabetical listing of all currently known elements, including general information about the element: when and by whom it was discovered, practical uses (if any), chief compounds built from the element, and a description of the element's properties. Use this table in conjunction with the periodic table on pages 322 and 323.

Table of Elements

Alkali metals

Alkaline earth metals

Transition metals

Lanthanide metals

Actinide metals

Other metals

Nonmetals

Noble gases

At. wt., atomic weight (C=12)
At. no., atomic number
Sp. gr., specific gravity
V., valence
M.P., melting point °C
B.P., boiling point °C
All temperatures in the text are in degrees Celsius (°C.).
C.S., crystal structure
C = cubic, whether body- or face-centered unknown
Cb = cubic, body-centered
Cf = cubic, face-centered
H = hexagonal
T = tetragonal

Element		Occurrence, Preparation, Date of Discovery, and Discoverer	Properties	Chief Compounds and Uses
Actinium **Ac**	At. wt. 227 (?) At. no. 89 V. 3 Sp. gr. 10.1 M.P. 1,050° B.P. 3,200°	In uranium ores, resulting from radioactive decay of uranium. Bombardment of bismuth. 1899; Debierne.	Radioactive; half-life ranges from 20 years to 3.7 seconds. It is chemically quite similar to lanthanum.	Used in research.
Aluminum **Al**	At. wt. 26.9815 At. no. 13 V. 3 Sp. gr. 2.7 M.P. 660.2° B.P. 2,327° C.S. Cf	Cryolite, bauxite, impure emery, ruby, sapphire (Al_2O_3). Commercially, by electrolysis of Al_2O_3 from bauxite, dissolved in cryolite; water power usual source of electrical energy. 1825; Oersted.	Silver-white, ductile metal; malleable at 120°; tensile strength (wrought) 16 tons per square inch. Better conductor of electricity, weight for weight, than copper. Acted upon by dilute hydrochloric acid, slowly by sulfuric acid, but not by nitric acid or the acids in foods. Soluble in alkaline hydroxides.	Used for cooking utensils, boatbuilding, airplanes, small articles requiring lightness and strength, and electric leads. The powdered metal is used as a body for paint; its mixture with ferric oxide, called thermite, is used for producing very high temperatures (up to 2,700°).
Americium **Am**	At. wt. 243.13 At. no. 95 V. 3, 4, 5, 6 Sp. gr. 13.67 M.P. 995°	Does not occur naturally. Bombardment of uranium-238 with very high energy electrons. 1944; Seaborg, James, Morgan, Ghiorso.	Radioactive, transuranium element. Alpha activity amounts to 70 billion alpha disintegrations per minute per milligram.	Its short half-life restricts use of this element to nuclear research.
Antimony **Sb**	At. wt. 121.75 At. no. 51 V. 3, 5 Sp. gr. 6,684 M.P. 630.5° B.P. 1,640° C.S. H	Free and as stibnite (Sb_2S_3). Roasting stibnite gives Sb_2O_4, which is then reduced by heating with carbon. 1450; Valentine.	White, brittle, crystalline metal. Its alloys expand on solidification, give very sharp castings for type. Does not tarnish, but may be burned in air; unites directly with the halogens.	Constituent of type metal, Britannia metal, Babbitt metal (used for bearings), and other alloys. Oxide (Sb_2O_3) is both basic and acidic. Trichloride, butter of antimony ($SbCl_3$), is easily hydrolyzed. Tartar emetic is used in medicine and dyeing.
Argon **Ar**	At. wt. 39.948 At. no. 18 V. 0 M.P. −189.2° B.P. −185.7°	Present in the air 0.94 percent by volume. To isolate from air, carbon dioxide is removed by soda lime, water by phosphorus pentaoxide, oxygen by red-hot copper, nitrogen by magnesium and calcium; fractional distillation of residue yields argon. 1894; Rayleigh, Ramsay.	Monatomic gas, identified by its characteristic spectrum seen by examining light emitted when the gas is placed in a vacuum tube at low pressure and sparked. More soluble than nitrogen in water; 100 volumes of water dissolves 4 volumes of argon under ordinary conditions.	Forms no compounds, hence its name, argon, meaning "inert."
Arsenic **As**	At. wt. 74.9216 At. no. 33 V. 3, 5 Sp. gr. 5.7 M.P. 817° (under pressure) B.P. 613° (sublimes)	Free as arsenical pyrites ($FeSAs$), or pigment (As_2S_3), and realgar (As_2S_2). By heating arsenical pyrites to change as follows: ($FeSAs \rightarrow FeS + As$). 1649; Schröder.	Steel-gray, dull metallic, crystalline element classed as a metalloid because it is between metals and nonmetals. Vapor density corresponds to As_4 at 644°, and to As_2 at 1,700°. Burns in air and unites directly with the halogens, sulfur, and many metals.	Used for hardening lead shot. All compounds are poisonous. White arsenic (As_2O_3) is partly basic, forming a chloride, and partly acidic, forming arsenites. Scheele's green is a dangerous pigment used in wallpaper. Traces of arsenic may be detected by Marsh's test, in which intensely poisonous arsine (AsH_3) is formed.
Astatine **At**	At. wt. 210 (?) At. no. 85 V. 1, 3, 5, 7	Does not occur naturally. By bombardment of bismuth with a stream of alpha particles. 1940; Segré, Corson, MacKenzie.	Synthetic element similar to polonium. All the known isotopes are short-lived, the longest-lived isotope having a half-life of 8.3 hours.	Its limited stability restricts its use to nuclear research.

Element	Occurrence, Preparation, Date of Discovery, and Discoverer	Properties	Chief Compounds and Uses
Barium **Ba** At. wt. 137.34 At. no. 56 V. 2 Sp. gr. 3.5 M.P. 729° B.P. 1,637° C.S. Cb	As barite, or heavy spar, ($BaSo_4$) and witherite ($BaCO_3$). By electrolysis of the fused chloride ($BaCl_2$). 1808; Davy.	Silver-white, lustrous, malleable metal harder than lead. Like calcium, it reacts slowly with water to give barium hydroxide and hydrogen. The vapors of its compounds impart green color to the Bunsen flame.	Peroxide (BaO_2) is used in manufacture of oxygen and hydrogen peroxide; nitrate and chlorate in pyrotechnics to produce green fires; sulfate as the body for permanent white paint and for filling glazed paper. All its soluble compounds are poisonous.
Berkelium **Bk** At. wt. 248 (?) At. no. 97 V. 3, 4 M.P. 1,278°	Does not occur naturally. By bombardment of americium-241 with alpha particles. 1949; Seaborg, Ghiorso, Thompson.	Radioactive, transuranium element. The longest-lived isotope has a half-life of several thousand years.	Expensive to make; restricted to radioactive research.
Beryllium **Be** At. wt. 9.0122 At. no. 4 V. 2 Sp. gr. 1.8 M.P. 1,284° B.P. 2,970° C.S. H	In beryl [$Be_3Al_2(SiO_3)_6$]. By electrolysis of the fused double fluoride ($BeF_2 \cdot 2KF$). 1797; Vauquelin.	Hard, white metal that tarnishes when heated in air; soluble in dilute acids when powdered.	Hydroxide [$Be(OH)_2$] is feebly acidic as well as basic, thus resembling the hydroxide of zinc. Emerald is beryl colored green by chromium oxide. Used as nuclear reactor fuel-rod casing.
Bismuth **Bi** At. wt. 208.980 At. no. 83 V. 3, 5 Sp. gr. 9.8 M.P. 271.3° B.P. 1,560° C.S. H	Free and as trioxide (Bi_2O_3) and trisulfide (Bi_2S_3). Ore is roasted, then heated with charcoal and metallic iron to remove traces of sulfur. 1450; Valentine.	Exceedingly brittle, crystalline, shiny metal, white with tinge of pink. Expands on solidification. Does not tarnish, and can be burned in air. Dissolves in oxygen acids. Most diamagnetic substance known.	Used for making fusible alloys such as Wood's metal (melting point 60.5°), used in plugs of fire sprinklers, boiler safety valves, and for taking casts. The oxynitrate is used in medicine and as a cosmetic.
Bohrium **Bh** At. wt. 262 (?) At. no. 107	Does not occur naturally. By bombardment of bismuth-209 with chromium-54 ions. 1981; Armbruster, Münzenberg et al.	Radioactive, transuranium element.	No commercial applications; of research interest only.
Boron **B** At. wt. 10.811 At. no. 5 V. 3 Sp. gr. amorphous 2.4 crystalline 2.5 M.P. 2,300° B.P. 2,550°	Occurs as follows: boric acid (H_3BO_3), borax ($Na_2B_4O_7 \cdot 10H_2O$), and colemanite ($Ca_2B_6O_{11} \cdot 5H_2O$). Amorphous, by reducing B_2O_3 with magnesium; impure crystalline, by reducing B_2O_3 with excess aluminum. 1808; Gay-Lussac, Thénard, Davy	Amorphous form is a greenish-black powder that burns in air at 700°, forming B_2O_3 and BN. Boron is oxidized by adding hot concentrated nitric acid or sulfuric acid to boric acid.	Compounds are analogous to those of silicon. Borax is used as a flux and, in solution, as a mild alkali because of its hydrolysis. Boric acid is used as a weak antiseptic and preservative.
Bromine **Br** At. wt. 79.909 At. no. 35 V. −1, 5 Sp. gr. 3.12 M.P. −7.2° B.P. 58.78°	In seawater, as alkali bromide; in layers of salt deposits, as sodium and magnesium bromide. By treatment of brine with sulfuric acid and manganese dioxide, or with chlorine. 1826; Balard.	Dark red liquid; smells like chlorine; vapor irritates eyes, throat, and nose. Dissolves in 30 parts of water (bromine water). Combines with most other elements, but less vigorously than chlorine.	Potassium bromide is used in pharmacy; silver bromide, in photography. Bromine is used in preparation of organic dyes and as a disinfectant and a bleach.

Element		Occurrence, Preparation, Date of Discovery, and Discoverer	Properties	Chief Compounds and Uses
Cadmium **Cd**	At. wt. 112.40 At. no. 48 V. 2 Sp. gr. 8.6 M.P. 320.7° B.P. 765°	With zinc ores, as carbonate and sulfide. Comes over in first portions in distillation of impure zinc. 1817; Stromeyer.	Silver-white metal, more ductile and more malleable than zinc. Burns in air; is attacked by dilute acids.	All compounds are poisonous, little ionized. Sulfide is basis of cadmium yellow; iodide is used in pharmacy; metal as protective plating.
Calcium **Ca**	At. wt. 40.08 At. no. 20 V. 2 Sp. gr. 1.55 M.P. 850° B.P. 1,420° C.S. C	As carbonate (Iceland spar, calcite, aragonite, marble, chalk, limestone), sulfate, phosphate (apatite), fluoride (fluorspar), complex silicates (feldspars, pyroxines, amphiboles). By electrolysis of the fused chloride, or heating the iodide with sodium. 1808; Davy.	White crystalline metal, harder than lead. Can be cut, drawn, rolled, and turned. Reacts with water and burns in air at red heat, forming the oxide (CaO) and the nitride (Ca_3N_2). Unites with hydrogen to form CaH_2, whose reaction with water is source of hydrogen for balloons. Salts color test flame yellowish-red.	Oxide (quicklime) is used for mortar and to remove hair from hides. Hydroxide mixed with sand forms mortar; solution is limewater. Plaster of Paris is less hydrated sulfate; takes up water on setting to form gypsum. Phosphates are fertilizers.
Californium **Cf**	At. wt. 251 (?) At. no. 98 V. 3	Does not occur naturally. By bombardment of curium-242 with alpha particles. 1950; Seaborg, Thompson, Ghiorso, Street.	Radioactive; transuranium element.	Expensive to make; restricted to radioactive research.
Carbon **C**	At. wt. 12.01115 At. no. 6 V. 4, 6 Sp. gr. diamond 3.5 graphite 2.3 amorphous 1.9 M.P. not realized: volatilizes at 3,652° B.P. 4,827°	Free as diamond and graphite; in combination with hydrogen as petroleum; with oxygen as carbon dioxide; with these and other elements as coal; and in plant and animal tissues as many carbonates. By dry distillation of wood or coal, yielding charcoal and coke, respectively. Known in antiquity.	Diamond is crystalline, and is the hardest of minerals; dark-colored bort used for cutting and grinding. Graphite has black metallic luster, is crystalline, and may be scratched by the fingernail. Charcoal is amorphous and can absorb gases and coloring matters. All three forms burn in oxygen to form carbon dioxide.	The carbon compounds form the substance of organic chemistry. Carbon dioxide results from burning coal, coke, wood, oil, or illuminating gases, from fermentation and decay (slow burning), and from exhalation. Carbon monoxide is a deadly gas. Graphite is a popular lubricant; diamond is a precious gem; coal, coke, and petroleum are fuels.
Cerium **Ce**	At. wt. 140.12 At. no. 58 V. 3, 4, 6 Sp. gr. 6.90 M.P. 804° B.P. 3,468° C.S. C	As silicate in cerite, along with neodymium, praseodymium, and lanthanum; also in monazite sand. By electrolysis of the fused chloride. 1803; Berzelius, Klaproth, Hisinger.	Rare earth metal with the color and luster of iron; like tin in hardness; very ductile and malleable. Burns in air more easily and more brightly than magnesium. Emits sparks when scratched with steel.	Welsbach incandescent gas mantles contain 1 percent cerium dioxide (CeO_2). Alloys are used for gas and cigar lighters.
Cesium **Cs**	At. wt. 132.905 At. no. 55 V. 1 Sp. gr. 1.9 M.P. 28.5° B.P. 670° C.S. Cb	In certain micas, mineral waters, and the ashes of certain plants. By heating the hydroxide (CsOH) with magnesium or by electrolysis. 1860; Bunsen, Kirchhoff.	Silver-white metal resembling rubidium and potassium. The softest of all solid metals; one of the most active metals and the most electropositive. Reacts violently with water. Cesium gives two bright lines in the blue of the spectrum; its name comes from *caesius*, meaning "sky-blue."	Used in certain photoelectric cells; in vacuum tubes to eliminate traces of gases. One of its radioactive isotopes is used in medical radiation therapy.

Table of Elements

Element		Occurrence, Preparation, Date of Discovery, and Discoverer	Properties	Chief Compounds and Uses
Chlorine **Cl**	At. wt. 35.453 At. no. 17 V. –1, 5, 7 Sp. gr. (liquid) 1.5 M.P. –103° B.P. –34.6°	In sea water as chlorides of the alkalis and alkaline earths; in salt deposits as like compounds. By electrolysis of alkali chloride, fused or in solution; by the action of manganese dioxide (MnO_2) on hydrochloric acid (HCl). 1774; Scheele.	Greenish-yellow gas with characteristic odor. Acts violently on respiratory tract. Unites directly with all elements except oxygen, nitrogen, and the argon family. Displaces bromine and iodine from their compounds; substitutes for hydrogen in organic compounds.	Gas is used in extracting gold and in preparing bleaching and disinfecting agents. In presence of water, it bleaches many coloring matters. Forms chlorides, such as NaCl, KCl, $CaCl_2$; hypochlorites, as solution of $Ca(OCl)_2$; chlorates, as $KClO_3$, used for matches and in pyrotechnics; and perchlorates, as $KClO_4$. Common table salt is NaCl.
Chromium **Cr**	At. wt. 51.996 At. no. 24 V. 2, 3, 6 Sp. gr. 7.2 M.P. 1,890° B.P. 2,480° C.S. Cb	As chromite [$Fe(CrO_2)_2$]. By reducing the oxide of chromic acetate (Cr_2O_3) with aluminum filings. 1797; Vauquelin.	Steel-gray, lustrous, brittle, very hard metal. At high temperatures, it burns in air to form green Cr_2O_3. Attacked by dilute sulfuric acid or hydrochloric acid, but not by nitric acid.	Used in alloys of steel and nickel. Chrome green (Cr_2O_3) and chrome yellow ($PbCrO_4$) are pigments. Bichromates (such as $K_2Cr_2O_7$) are used in photo processes, tanning and dyeing, and as oxidizing agents, as in batteries. The metal, like nickel, is used as a protective and decorative plating.
Cobalt **Co**	At. wt. 58.9332 At. no. 27 V. 2, 3 Sp. gr. 8.71 M.P. 1,495° B.P. 2,900° C.S. H (?)	As smaltite ($CoAs_2$) and cobaltite (CoAsS) found with iron and nickel. By igniting the oxide in hydrogen. 1735; Brandt.	White, malleable metal, less tenacious than iron. Turns pinkish on exposure to air. Less active chemically than iron.	Intensely blue silicates are used in coloring porcelain and constitute the pigment smalt. Used in commercial dyes; also used in medical radiation therapy.
Copernicium **Cn**	At. wt. 285(?) At. no. 112	Does not occur naturally. By bombardment of lead with zinc ions. 1996; Hofmann, Ninov et al.	Radioactive	No commercial applications; of research interest only.
Copper **Cu**	At. wt. 63.54 At. no. 29 V. 1, 2 Sp. gr. 8.93 M.P. 1,083° B.P. 2,336° C.S. Cf	Free as cuprite (Cu_2O), copper glance, chalcopyrite ($CuFeS_2$), and malachite [$Cu_2(OH)_2CO_3$]. After removal of iron and sulfur, the oxide is reduced by heating with carbon. It is refined electrolytically. Known in antiquity.	Red, lustrous, very ductile and malleable metal; high tensile strength (14 tons per square inch); second only to silver in electrical conductivity. In ordinary air it gradually becomes coated with basic carbonate. In absence of air, nitric acid alone among the dilute acids attacks it; in the presence of air, even acids in foodstuffs can dissolve it.	Used for coins, ornaments, electrical leads, electroplating, roofing, cooking vessels, and for making such alloys as brass, bell and gun metals, German silver, and the bronzes. The soluble compounds are poisonous and are used as agricultural germicides. Blue vitriol is $CuSO_4 \cdot 5H_2O$; the basic acetate is verdigris.
Curium **Cm**	At. wt. 247 (?) At. no. 96 V. 3 Sp. gr. 13.51	Does not occur naturally. By bombardment of plutonium-239 with alpha particles. 1944; Seaborg, James, Ghiorso, Morgan.	Radioactive, transuranium element. The longest-lived isotope has a half-life of a half-million years.	Expensive to make; restricted to nuclear and radioactive research.
Darmstadtium **Ds**	At. wt. 269 (?) At. no. 110	Does not occur naturally. By bombardment of lead-208 with nickel-62 ions. 1994; Armbruster, Hofmann et al.	Radioactive.	No commercial applications, of research interest only.

Element		Occurrence, Preparation, Date of Discovery, and Discoverer	Properties	Chief Compounds and Uses
Dubnium **Db**	At. wt. 262 (?) At. no. 105 V. 5	Does not occur naturally. By bombardment of californium-249 with nitrogen-15 ions. 1968; Flerov et al.; 1970; Ghiorso et al. (shared credit)	Radioactive, transuranium element. It is chemically similar to niobium and tantalum.	No commercial applications, of research interest only.
Dysprosium **Dy**	At. wt. 162.50 At. no. 66 V. 3 Sp. gr. 8.56 M.P. 1,407° B.P. 2,564°	In monazite, in gadolinite, and in other rare minerals. By fractional crystallization of bromates. 1886; Boisbaudran.	Rare earth. The oxide, dysprosia (Dy_2O_3), is found with three other rare earths.	Salts are green or yellow and show characteristic absorption bands. They are the most magnetic of all salts.
Einsteinium **Es**	At. wt. 252 (?) At. no. 99 V. 3	Does not occur naturally. Prepared by intensive neutron irradiation of plutonium-239. 1952; Thompson, Harvey, Choppin, Seaborg, Ghiorso.	Radioactive, transuranium element. Half-life of longest-lived isotope is 280 days.	Expensive to make; limited to nuclear research.
Erbium **Er**	At. wt. 167.28 At. no. 68 V. 3 Sp. gr. 9.16 M.P. 1,497° B.P. 2,900°	In gadolinite and other rare minerals. 1843; Mosander.	Rare earth. The oxide erbia (Er_2O_3) is found with holmia, thulia, and dysprosia	Salts are rose-colored and show characteristic absorption spectra.
Europium **Eu**	At. wt. 151.96 At. no. 63 V. 2, 3 Sp. gr. 5.24 M.P. 826° B.P. 1,439°	In monazite and other rare minerals. By electrolysis of the chloride. 1896; Demarçay.	Rare earth. This element so closely resembles samarium that the two elements are difficult to separate analytically.	Salts are pinkish and show a faint absorption spectrum. Sometimes used in control rods of nuclear reactors.
Fermium **Fm**	At. wt. 257 (?) At. no. 100 V. 3 M.P. 1,527°	Does not occur naturally. Prepared by intensive neutron irradiation of plutonium-239. 1953; Thompson, Harvey, Choppin, Seaborg, Ghiorso.	Radioactive, transuranium element.	Expensive to make; limited to nuclear research.
Fluorine **F**	At. wt. 18.9984 At. no. 9 V. 1 Sp. gr. (liquid) 1.1 at −187° M.P. −223° B.P. −188.14°	As cryolite (Na_3AlF_6), fluorspar (CaF_2), and very widely elsewhere in small quantities. By electrolysis of dry hydrogen fluoride at −23°. 1886; Moissan.	Pale yellowish-green gas that unites with every element except oxygen. Rapidly displaces oxygen from water, and displaces chlorine from hydrogen chloride.	Hydrogen fluoride is used for etching glass and in silicate analysis. Silver fluoride is soluble and calcium fluoride is insoluble, in contrast with the other halides of these metals.
Francium **Fr**	At. wt. 223 (?) At. no. 87 V. 1	Does not occur naturally. Disintegrates so rapidly that it is almost impossible to obtain in sufficient quantity to enable weighing. 1939; Perey.	Synthetic radioactive element; heaviest of the alkali metals.	Expensive to make; limited to radioactive and nuclear research.

Element		Occurrence, Preparation, Date of Discovery, and Discoverer	Properties	Chief Compounds and Uses
Gadolinium **Gd**	At. wt. 157.25 At. no. 64 V. 3 Sp. gr. 7.94 M.P. 1,312° B.P. 2,800°	In gadolinite and samarskite. By electrolysis of the chloride. 1886; Marignac.	Rare earth. Closely resembles terbium in its compounds.	Salts are colorless and show absorption bands only in the ultraviolet.
Gallium **Ga**	At. wt. 69.72 At. no. 31 V. 2, 3 Sp. gr. 6.095 M.P. 30.150° B.P. 1,983°	In iron ores, zinc blende (ZnS), and bauxite (Al_2O_3). By electrolysis of an alkaline solution of its salts secured from zinc. 1875; Boisbaudran.	Bluish-white, tough metal that can be cut with a knife. Like aluminum, it is soluble in hydrochloric acid and caustic soda, but not in nitric acid.	Forms two chlorides, $GaCl_3$ and $GaCl_2$, that yield very characteristic spark spectra. Alloys with aluminum and cadmium are used for optical mirrors and cathodes.
Germanium **Ge**	At. wt. 72.59 At. no. 32 V. 2, 4 Sp. gr. 5.35 M.P. 947° B.P. 2,700°	In the rare mineral argyrodite. By the reduction of the dioxide (GeO_2) by the element carbon. 1886; Winkler.	Grayish-white, brittle, lustrous metal, insoluble in hydrochloric acid. Combines directly with the halogens.	Close relation of this element to carbon and silicon is shown in the compound germanium chloroform. Mendeleev described it before its discovery, calling it ekasilicon. The oxide is used to treat pernicious anemia.
Gold **Au**	At. wt. 196.967 At. no. 79 V. 1, 3 Sp. gr. 19.4 M.P. 1,063° B.P. 2,600°	Chiefly free, but also a telluride; many specimens of iron pyrites are auriferous. From gold-bearing sands by washing away the lighter materials and dissolving the gold from the residue in mercury, which is subsequently separated from the gold by distillation. Known in antiquity.	Soft, bright-yellow metal, easily scratched by a knife; most ductile and malleable of the metals; excellent conductor of heat and electricity. Chemically, gold is rather inert and is not attacked by the oxygen of the air, by hydrogen sulfide, or by any single acid.	Pure gold is 24-carat gold. Jewelry is made in 18-, 14-, and 9-carat gold because alloying it with copper increases hardness and rigidity. Sodium chloraurate is used for toning in photography, and potassium auricyanide is used in electrogilding.
Hafnium **Hf**	At. wt. 178.49 At. no. 72 V. 4 Sp. gr. 13.3 M.P. 2,230° B.P. 3,200°	Associated with zirconium. By decomposing the tetraiodide. 1922; Coster, Hevesy.	Analogous to zirconium.	Similar to zirconium compounds, from which it is separated by fractional crystallization.
Hassium **Hs**	At. wt. 265 (?) At. no. 108	Does not occur naturally. By bombardment of lead-208 with iron-58 ions. 1984; Armbruster, Münzenberg et al.	Radioactive, transuranium element.	No commercial applications; of research interest only.
Helium **He**	At. wt. 4.0026 At. no. 2 V. 0 Sp. gr. (liquid) 0.15 M.P. −272.2° (at 26 atmospheres) B.P. −268.9°	In the air to the extent of 1 to 2 volumes per million; also occluded in certain minerals. First observed in sun's spectrum (1868; Lockyer, Jannsen). Neon and helium are boiled off crude argon, and the neon, when cooled, solidifies. 1895; Ramsay.	Lightest gas except hydrogen; transparent, odorless, and colorless.	Forms no compounds. Used for balloons; not flammable.

Element		Occurrence, Preparation, Date of Discovery, and Discoverer	Properties	Chief Compounds and Uses
Holmium **Ho**	At. wt. 164.930 At. no. 67 V. 3 Sp. gr. 8.803 M.P. 1,461° B.P. 2,600°	Occurs with, and is separated from, the erbium subgroup of the rare earths. Has never been isolated. 1879; Cleve.	Rare earth. Salts are orange-yellow and similar to those of dysprosium.	Used in glass to transmit radiant energy for wavelength-calibration instruments.
Hydrogen **H**	At. wt. 1.00797 At. no. 1 V. 1 Sp. gr. (liquid) 0.09 M.P. –259.1° B.P. –252.7°	In the air to the extent of 1 volume per 20,000 volumes of air; combined, in water (11.19 percent by weight), natural gas, petroleum, and animal and vegetable bodies. By treating zinc with hydrochloric or sulfuric acid; by electrolysis. 1766; Cavendish.	Lightest gas, transparent, odorless, and colorless. Soluble in water (2 volumes in 100 volumes of water under average conditions), in platinum, in palladium (502 volumes in 1 volume of palladium). Burns in air and in chlorine and unites with many other elements.	Its two oxides are water and hydrogen peroxide, the latter used in solution as a bleaching agent. Every acid contains hydrogen as an essential constituent. Its compounds with carbon and other elements number over 100,000.
Indium **In**	At. wt. 114.82 At. no. 49 V. 1, 3 Sp. gr. 7.3 M.P. 156° B.P. 2,000°	In zinc blende (ZnS) in small quantities. Electrolytically from solutions of its salts. 1863; Reich, Richter.	White, malleable metal, softer than lead; about as heavy as tin.	Compounds color the nonluminous gas flame blue and show a characteristic indigo blue line in the spectrum—hence its name. Sometimes used as a coating on bearings.
Iodine **I**	At. wt. 126.9044 At. no. 53 V. 1, 3, 5, 7 Sp. gr. 4.93 M.P. 113.7° B.P. 184.35°	In the ocean and certain seaweeds; always in the combined state. From iodides by displacement of their iodine by chlorine. 1811; Courtois.	Dark gray, brittle solid with a metallic luster. Vapor is violet, as are its solutions in chloroform and carbon bisulfide. Requires more than 5,000 parts of water for solution. Combines directly with many elements, but is much less active than chlorine or bromine.	Used in pharmacy as an antiseptic and in prescriptions for treatment of goiter. Potassium iodide and iodoform likewise find application in medicine. The alkyl iodides are much used in synthetic organic chemistry.
Iridium **Ir**	At. wt. 192.2 At. no. 77 V. 3, 4 Sp. gr. 22.42 M.P. 2,454° B.P. 4,800° C.S. Cf	With platinum and osmium. Obtained from platinum ores by a complex series of operations. 1804; Tennant.	White metal, brittle when cold, very hard, and one of the densest substances known. Attacked by fused alkalis, but not by aqua regia.	Used for pointing gold pens. Its alloy with 9 parts of platinum is used for standard meter bars because of its unalterability. Used as a black color in china decorations.

Iron
Fe
	At. wt. 55.847
	At. no. 26
	V. 2, 3
	Sp. gr. 7.86
	   pig 7.03 – 7.73
	M.P. 1,535°
	   wrought 1,600°
	   steel 1,375°
	   gray pig 1,275°
	   white pig 1,075°
	B.P. 3,000°
	C.S. Cf, Cb
		As magnetite (Fe_3O_4), hematite (Fe_2O_3), limonite ($2Fe_2O_3 \cdot 3H_2O$), siderite ($FeCO_3$), which are important ores; iron pyrites (FeS_2); in rocks as complex silicates; in plants and animals.
		Pig iron is prepared in blast furnace by reduction of the ore by means of carbon monoxide in presence of suitable flux. From pig iron, wrought iron is obtained by puddling, and steel by the Bessemer, or by open-hearth or other processes.
		Known in antiquity.
			Malleable, ductile, magnetic metal, that is unchanged in dry air, but rusts in water and moist air. Easily attacked by dilute acids, but not by fused alkalis. Cast iron contains 2 to 5 percent carbon and other impurities, and is hard and brittle. Wrought iron contains less than 0.2 percent carbon and is softer and tougher, with tensile strength of 22 to 25 tons per square inch. Steel contains from 0.2 to 1.5 percent carbon, and is permanently magnetic.	The metal is used as a structural material for rails, machinery, tools, etc. Jeweler's rouge and Venetian red consist of the oxide (Fe_2O_3). Rust is chiefly hydrated oxide. Hammer scale and lodestone have the composition Fe_3O_4. Ferric chloride ($FeCl_3$), ferrous iodide (FeI_2), and other iron compounds are used in medicine. Green vitriol ($FeSO_4 \cdot 7H_2O$) is used in making ink and in dyeing.

Table of Elements

Element		Occurrence, Preparation, Date of Discovery, and Discoverer	Properties	Chief Compounds and Uses
Krypton **Kr**	At. wt. 83.80 At. no. 36 V. 0, 2, 4 M.P. −156.6° B.P. −152.3°	In minute quantities in the air. From crude argon by fractional distillation. 1898; Ramsay, Travers.	Inert, colorless, and odorless gas resembling, but denser than, argon.	Once thought to be chemically inert; forms series of fluoride compounds, such as KrF_2 and KrF_4.
Lanthanum **La**	At. wt. 138.91 At. no. 57 V. 3 Sp. gr. 6.15	As lanthanite [$La_2(CO_3)_3$•$8H_2O$]. By electrolysis of the fused chloride ($LaCl_3$). 1839; Mosander.	Rare earth; iron-gray metal; tarnishes in air to steel-blue; malleable and ductile. Attacked slowly even by cold water.	When heated in air, it forms a strongly basic oxide (La_2O_3) that is diamagnetic, and a nitride (LaN).
Lawrencium **Lr**	At. wt. 256 (?) At. no. 103 V. 3	Does not occur naturally. By bombardment of californium-252 with boron ions. 1961; Ghiorso, Sikkeland, Larsh, Latimer.	Radioactive, transuranium element.	Expensive to make; used in nuclear research.
Lead **Pb**	At. wt. 207.19 At. no. 82 V. 2, 4 Sp. gr. 11.34 M.P. 327.43° B.P. 1,515° C.S. Cf	End product of certain radioactive decompositions. As galena (PbS) and in silver ores. By calcination of partially roasted galena. Purification is affected by Parkes process. Known in antiquity.	Soft, gray metal; malleable and of low tensile strength, relatively impermeable to X-rays and atomic radiation. In presence of air, water acts on lead to produce the hydroxide which, being slightly soluble, may cause lead poisoning. When heated in air, lead is oxidized to litharge and, under suitable conditions, to minium.	Used for water pipes, roofs and gutters, and storage batteries. For shot, it is alloyed with 0.4 percent arsenic. Type metal contains 80 percent lead. Babbitt metal, for bearings, contains over 70 percent lead. Solder and pewter are alloys of lead and tin. The basic carbonate, white lead, is the basis of most oil paints.
Lithium **Li**	At. wt. 6,939 At. no. 3 V. 1 Sp. gr. 0.53 M.P. 179° B.P. 1,317° C.S. C	In amblygonite [$Li(AlF)PO_4$]. By electrolysis of the fused chloride (LiCl). 1817; Arfwedson.	Lightest metal; silver-white, softer than lead, tarnishes quickly in air, and easily reacts with water. When heated, it unites vigorously with nitrogen.	The carbonate (Li_2CO_3) is used in medicine as a solvent for uric acid, lithium urate being soluble. The salts give a carmine flame coloration.
Lutetium **Lu**	At. wt. 174.97 At. no. 71 V. 3 Sp. gr. 9.84 M.P. 1,652° B.P. 3,330°	In euxenite. By electrolysis of the chloride. 1907; Urbain, Welsbach	Rare earth. Like ytterbium but has lower magnetic susceptibility.	Its compounds resemble those of ytterbium. It was once known as Casseopium.
Magnesium **Mg**	At. wt. 24.312 At. no. 12 V. 2 Sp. gr. 1.74 M.P. 651° B.P. 1,107° C.S. H	Occurs as magnesite ($MgCO_3$), dolomite ($MgCO_3$•$CaCO_3$), carnallite ($MgCl_2$•KCl•$6H_2O$), and in very many complex silicates. By electrolysis of dried, fused carnallite. 1808; Davy.	Silver-white, very lightweight metal, ductile when hot, and malleable. It tarnishes in air and reacts slowly with water, rapidly with steam. Burns in air to the oxide (MgO), emitting a very bright light. Unites directly with nitrogen.	Used as a reducing agent. Sulfate, known as Epsom salts, is used in medicine, as are the oxide (magnesia), the carbonates, and the citrate. The bright light emitted when the metal is burned in air is used in photography.

Element		Occurrence, Preparation, Date of Discovery, and Discoverer	Properties	Chief Compounds and Uses
Manganese **Mn**	At. wt. 54.9380 At. no. 25 V. 2, 3, 4, 6, 7 Sp. gr. 7.2 M.P. 1,220° B.P. 2,152° C.S. CT	As pyrolusite (MnO_2), braunite (Mn_2O_3), hausmannite (Mn_3O_4), and manganese spar ($MnCO_3$). By heating Mn_3O_4 with aluminum filings. 1774; Gahn.	Steel-gray, hard, brittle metal with a pinkish tinge. Rusts in moist air and is attacked by dilute acids.	Ferromanganese and spiegeleisen are alloys with iron, used in making steel tougher. With copper, it forms the tough, hard manganese bronzes, with tensile strength up to 30 tons per square inch.
Meitnerium **Mt**	At. wt. 266 (?) At. no. 109	Does not occur naturally. By bombardment of bismuth-209 with iron-58 ions. 1982; Armbruster, Münzenberg et al.	Radioactive, transuranium element.	No commercial applications, of research interest only.
Mendelevium **Md**	At. wt. 258 (?) At. no. 101 V. 3	Does not occur naturally. By bombardment of einsteinium-253 with alpha particles. 1955; Thompson, Harvey, Choppin, Ghiorso, Seaborg.	Radioactive, transuranium element.	Expensive to make; limited to nuclear and radioactive research.
Mercury **Hg**	At. wt. 200.59 At. no. 80 V. 1, 2 Sp. gr. 13.6 M.P. −38.87° B.P. 356.58° C.S. H	Free and as cinnabar (HgS). By roasting cinnabar: $HgS + O_2 \rightarrow Hg + SO_2$. Known in antiquity.	Silver-white, mobile liquid, 20 percent heavier than lead. Has vapor pressure of 0.0002 millimeter at 0°. Tarnishes slowly in air and is attacked only by nitric among the dilute acids. Vapor is monatomic.	Used in thermometers and barometers. Alloys, some of which are used in dentistry, are called amalgams. Calomel (HgCl) is administered internally in medicine; corrosive sublimate ($HgCl_2$) forms a solution with very powerful germicidal properties.
Molybdenum **Mo**	At. wt. 95.94 At. no. 42 V. 3, 4, 5, 6 Sp. gr. 10.2 M.P. 2,620° B.P. 4,507° C.S. Cb	As molybdenite (MoS_2) and wulfenite ($PbMoO_4$). By reducing the oxides with aluminum powder. 1778; Scheele.	White metal as malleable as iron; will not scratch glass. Insoluble in hydrochloric or dilute sulfuric acid.	Ferromolybdenum alloys are used in the manufacture of special steels.
Neodymium **Nd**	At. wt. 144.24 At. no. 60 V. 3, 4 Sp. gr. 6.9 M.P. 1,024° B.P. 3,027°	With cerium and lanthanum. By electrolysis of the fused chloride. 1885; Welsbach.	Rare earth; yellowish metal; tarnishes in air.	Salts are rose-violet; solutions show characteristic spectra.
Neon **Ne**	At. wt. 20.183 At. no. 10 V. 0 M.P. −248.67° B.P. −245.92°	Minute quantities in atmosphere. Neon and helium are boiled out of crude argon and the neon separated from helium by cooling with liquid hydrogen. 1898; Ramsay, Travers.	Colorless, odorless, transparent, monatomic, inert gas.	Forms no compounds; is recognized by its characteristic spectrum. Used in glow tubes for display signs.
Neptunium **Np**	At. wt. 237 At. no. 93 V. 3, 4, 5, 6 Sp. gr. 20.45 M.P. 640°	Does not occur naturally. By bombardment of uranium with neutrons. 1940; McMillan, Abelson.	Radioactive element. First transuranium element to be synthesized. Emits alpha particles. Half-life of longest-lived isotope is 2,200,000 years.	Oxide is dark brown; costly to make; limited to nuclear and radioactive research.

Table of Elements

Element		Occurrence, Preparation, Date of Discovery, and Discoverer	Properties	Chief Compounds and Uses
Nickel **Ni**	At. wt. 58.71 At. no. 28 V. 2, 3 Sp. gr. 8.9 M.P. 1,455° B.P. 2,730° C.S. Cf	As nicollite (NiAs) and nickel glance (NiAsS). By igniting the oxalate in hydrogen. 1751; Cronstedt.	White, very hard, lustrous metal; malleable, ductile, and tenacious. Rusts slowly in air and is easily attacked only by nitric acid.	Metal furnishes protective coating when plated on iron. German silver is an alloy of nickel, copper, and zinc. Nickel chromium steel is used for armor. Manganin, containing nickel, copper, and manganese, is used for electrical resistors. It is a catalyst, especially in hydrogenation.
Niobium **Nb**	At. wt. 92.906 At. no. 41 V. 1, 2, 4, 5 Sp. gr. 8.57 M.P. 2,415° B.P. c. 3,300°	In the mineral columbite ($FeCb_2O_6$). By reduction of the dioxide (NbO_2) by paraffin. 1801; Hatchett	Light gray, malleable, ductile metal, as hard as wrought iron; not affected by acids, even aqua regia. The hydride (NbH) burns in air.	Compounds occur with those of tantalum, which they closely resemble. It was originally called Columbium.
Nitrogen **N**	At. wt. 14.0067 At. no. 7 V. 3, 5 Sp. gr. (liquid) 0.808 M.P. −209.86° B.P. −195.8°	Free nitrogen forms about 79 percent of the air by volume. Also in Bengal saltpeter (KNO_3). Chile saltpeter ($NaNO_3$). By fractional distillation of liquid air. 1772; Rutherford.	Colorless, odorless, transparent gas, rather inactive chemically. At ordinary temperature and pressure, 100 volumes of water dissolve 1.5 volumes of nitrogen.	Nitrous oxide, or laughing gas, is used by dentists. Nitric acid has many applications in analytic and industrial chemistry. Ammonia is a very soluble gas. Many nitrogen compounds are used as fertilizers, explosives, dyes, and drugs.
Nobelium **No**	At. wt. 255 (?) At. no. 102 V. 2	Does not occur naturally. By bombardment of curium-246 with carbon-12 ions. 1958; Ghiorso, Sikkeland, Walton, Seaborg.	Radioactive, transuranium element.	Costly to make; limited to nuclear and radioactive research.
Osmium **Os**	At. wt. 190.2 At. no. 76 V. 2, 3, 4, 6, 8 Sp. gr. 22.48 M.P. 2,700° B.P. 530°	With platinum and iridium. By reducing the tetroxide (OsO_4). 1804; Tennant.	Gray metal, harder than glass; densest of the known elements.	Its alloy with iridium is used in tipping gold pens. Osmium tetroxide is used as a microscope stain for fat.
Oxygen **O**	At. wt. 15.9994 At. no. 8 V. 2 Sp. gr. (liquid) 1.13 M.P. −218.4° B.P. −183°	Free oxygen forms about 20 percent of air by volume. Water contains 88.88 percent oxygen. Rocks of Earth's crust contain about 46 percent in combination, chiefly as silicates. In the laboratory, by heating potassium chlorate ($KClO_3$). Commercially, by fractional distillation of air. 1774; Priestley, Scheele.	Colorless, odorless, tasteless, transparent gas, slightly heavier than air. At ordinary temperature and pressure, 100 volumes of water dissolve 3 volumes of oxygen. Very active chemically, combining directly with all but a few elements to form oxides. Most substances burn more vigorously in oxygen than in air. Liquid oxygen is magnetic.	Gas is sold compressed in mild steel cylinders, and is used for the oxyhydrogen blowpipe, in medicine, and for chemical purposes. Necessary to support animal respiration and ordinary combustion. Enters as a constituent into all oxides, most salts, and many organic compounds. Liquid oxygen (LOX) is an important propellant for rockets.

Element		Occurrence, Preparation, Date of Discovery, and Discoverer	Properties	Chief Compounds and Uses
Palladium **Pd**	At. wt. 106.4 At. no. 46 V. 2, 4, 6 Sp. gr. 11.97 M.P. 1,549° B.P. c. 2,200° C.S. Cf	With platinum and gold in nickel ores. By a complex series of processes from platinum ores. 1803; Wollaston.	Silvery, malleable, ductile metal, related to platinum, unlike which, however, it may be attacked by nitric acid. Under suitable conditions, it can absorb over 900 volumes of hydrogen.	Since it does not tarnish, it is used for coating silver goods, and by dentists as a substitute for gold. Like platinum, it is used as a catalyst.
Phosphorus **P**	At. wt. 30.9738 At. no. 15 V. 3, 5 Sp. gr. white 1.82 red 2.2 M.P. (white) 44° B.P. (white) 280°	As phosphates, such as apatite [$Ca_5F(PO_4)_3$]; in bones, teeth, and brain; and in seeds of plants. By reduction of calcium phosphate by carbon with a suitable flux in an electric furnace. 1669; Brand.	Exists in two allotropic modifications: white phosphorus, which is waxy in consistency, soluble in carbon bisulfide, foul-smelling, and poisonous; and red phosphorus, which is a solid, insoluble in carbon bisulfide, odorless, and not poisonous. White phosphorus has a low ignition temperature.	Red phosphorus is used in the manufacture of matches, as is the compound P_4S_3. In the form of superphosphate of lime, phosphorus is an important artificial fertilizer. The chlorides, PCl_5 and PCl_3, are much used in organic chemistry. Compounds are used in medicine. Phosphine, PH_3, is a poison gas.
Platinum **Pt**	At. wt. 195.09 At. no. 78 V. 2, 4 Sp. gr. 21.45 M.P. 1,773° B.P. 4,300° C.S. Cf	Free, alloyed with iridium and osmium, as nuggets in alluvial sands. Freed from the metals with which it is alloyed by a complex series of processes. 1557; Scaliger.	Silvery, tenacious, very heavy, ductile, malleable metal, unaltered in moist air and not attacked by any single common acid. Aqua regia, fused alkalis, alkali nitrates, and cyanides, however, do attack it. Platinum sponge and platinum black are finely divided forms.	Because of its resistance to acids, platinum is used for chemical vessels and electrodes. Since its coefficient of expansion is close to that of glass, platinum wires can be fused through glass without danger of breakage on cooling. The salts are used in photography. The metal is used in jewelry.
Plutonium **Pu**	At. wt. 239.05 At. no. 94 V. 3, 4, 5, 6 Sp. gr. 19.84 M.P. 640°	Present to a small extent in uranium ores. Produced in nuclear reactors starting with natural uranium. 1940; Seaborg, McMillan, Wahl, Kennedy.	Radioactive transuranium element. Emits alpha particles. Half-life of longest-lived isotope is 24,300 years.	Used as a pure nuclear fuel in reactors and weapons. It may be alloyed with carbon, iron, and aluminum, which are also used as nuclear fuels.
Polonium **Po**	At. wt. 210.05 At. no. 84 V. 2, 4 Sp. gr. 9.3 M.P. 254° B.P. 962°	With bismuth in uranium minerals. Metal has been isolated only in minute quantities because almost 13 tons of pitchblende ore yields only about 1 gram of the element. 1898; the Curies	Radioactive element. Half-life is 138.7 days.	Compounds resemble those of tellurium.
Potassium **K**	At. wt. 39.102 At. no. 19 V. 1 Sp. gr. 0.86 M.P. 62.3° B.P. 760° C.S. Cb	As sylvite (KCl), carnallite ($KCl \cdot MgCl_2 \cdot 6H_2O$); in plant and animal ashes, and in many complex silicates. By reduction or electrolysis of fused potassium hydroxide (KOH). 1807; Davy.	Silver-white, lustrous, very light-weight metal, as soft as wax; tarnishes instantly in moist air. Chemically very active, decomposing in the cold and uniting violently with the halogens, sulfur, and oxygen.	Alloy (with sodium) is used in high-temperature thermometers. Bengal saltpeter is the nitrate and is used in pyrotechnics, for gun-powders, and as a preservative. Iodide, KI, is used in pharmacy. It is one of the three basic fertilizer elements, nitrogen and phos-phorus being the others.

Table of Elements

Element		Occurrence, Preparation, Date of Discovery, and Discoverer	Properties	Chief Compounds and Uses
Praseodymium **Pr**	At. wt. 140.907 At. no. 59 V. 3, 4 Sp. gr. 6.78 M.P. 935° B.P. 3,127°	With cerium and lanthanum. By electrolysis of the fused chloride. 1885; Welsbach.	Rare earth; yellowish metal; remains untarnished in air.	Salts are leek-green, and their solutions have characteristic absorption spectra.
Promethium **Pm**	At. wt. 145 (?) At. no. 61 V. 3	Does not occur naturally. 1947; Marinsky, Glendenin, Coryell.	Rare earth metal, produced artificially. Recognized by its X-ray spectrum and optical absorption spectrum. Radioisotopes identified.	Compounds are similar to those of samarium and neodymium.
Protactinium **Pa**	At. wt. 231.10 At. no. 91 V. 5 Sp. gr. 15.37 M.P. 1,230°	In uranium ores. Metal has been isolated; about 70 milligrams may be secured from 1,000 kilograms of pitchblende. 1917; Hahn, Meitner, Soddy, Cranston.	Radioactive element, emitting alpha particles. Its half-life is 12,000 years.	Compounds resemble those of tantalum.
Radium **Ra**	At. wt. 226 At. no. 88 V. 2 Sp. gr. 5 (?) M.P. c. 960° B.P. 1,140°	In minute quantities in pitchblende and other uranium ores. Metal has been isolated; bromide is separated from the barium bromide prepared from pitchblende by fractional crystallization. 1898; the Curies; Bémont.	In all of its compounds, the metal has the power of emitting certain radiations. These can pass through materials that are opaque to light, render air a conductor, affect a photographic plate, and cause a zinc-sulfide screen to fluoresce visibly.	Rays from radium compounds (such as $RaBr_2$, $RaCl_2$, $RaCO_3$) during medical treatment act destructively on living tissues.
Radon **Rn**	At. wt. 222 At. no. 86 V. 0, 2, 4 Sp. gr. (liquid) 4.4 M.P. −71° B.P. −68°	Admixed with air. By passing air through solutions of radium salts. 1900; Dorn.	Inert gas of the helium family; radioactive, emitting alpha particles; half-life of longest-lived isotope is 3.83 days.	Forms fluoride salts. Used in treatment of cancer; enclosed in minute glass vessels the size of a small match head, it is inserted into the tumor.
Rhenium **Re**	At. wt. 186.2 At. no. 75 V. 1, 4, 6, 7 Sp. gr. 20.53 M.P. 3,167° B.P. c. 5,900°	In molybdenum and platinum ores. Hydrogen reduction of NH_4ReO_4. 1925; Noddack, Tacke, Berg.	Silver-white, hard metal, heavier than gold. Only tungsten is less fusible. Chemical properties are similar to those of manganese.	Used in electronics.
Rhodium **Rh**	At. wt. 102.905 At. no. 45 V. 2, 3, 4 Sp. gr. 12.4 M.P. 1,966° B.P. 2,500° C.S. Cf	In the ores of platinum. By a complex series of processes from platinum ores. 1803; Wollaston.	Silvery, malleable, ductile metal; does not tarnish in air; not attacked by aqua regia.	The red chloride ($RhCl_2$) is formed by the action of chlorine on the metal. Rhodium-platinum alloy is used for thermocouples to measure high temperatures.
Roentgenium **Rg**	At. wt. 272 (?) At. no. 111	Does not occur naturally. By bombardment of bismuth-209 with nickel-64. 1994; GSI et al.	Radioactive.	No commercial applications; of research interest only.

Element		Occurrence, Preparation, Date of Discovery, and Discoverer	Properties	Chief Compounds and Uses
Rubidium **Rb**	At. wt. 85.47 At. no. 37 V. 1, 3, 5 Sp. gr. 1.53 M.P. 38.5° B.P. 700° C.S. Cb	Found with cesium. Salts are associated with those of potassium. By heating the hydroxides with magnesium or by electrolysis of cyanides or hydroxides. 1860; Bunsen, Kirchhoff.	Silver-white metal resembling potassium; reacts vigorously with water.	Compounds show characteristic flame spectra with two red lines. Used in photocells and in pharmaceuticals.
Ruthenium **Ru**	At. wt. 101.07 At. no. 44 V. 3, 4, 6, 7, 8 Sp. gr. 12.3 M.P. 2,450° B.P. 4,150°	In the ores of platinum. By a complex series of processes from platinum ores. 1844; Klaus.	Hard, white, brittle metal, oxidized when heated in air. Scarcely attacked by aqua regia; very infusible. Chemical properties resemble those of osmium.	The following oxides are known: Ru_2O_3, RuO_2, RuO_4, as well as salts corresponding to RuO_3 and Ru_2O_7. Ruthenium red, an ammoniacal compound, dyes silk a beautiful yellow, but its high price limits its usefulness.
Rutherfordium **Rf**	At. wt. 261 (?) At. no. 104 V. 4	Does not occur naturally. By bombardment of californium-249 with carbon-12 and carbon-13 ions. 1964; Flerov et al.; 1969; Ghiorso et al. (shared credit).	Radioactive, transuranium element. It is chemically similar to hafnium and zirconium.	No commercial applications; of research interest only.
Samarium **Sm**	At. wt. 150.35 At. no. 62 V. 2, 3 Sp. gr. 7.536 M.P. 1,072° B.P. 1,900°	In monazite and samarskite. By electrolysis of the chloride. 1879; Boisbaudran.	Rare earth; whitish-gray metal; tarnishes in air.	Salts are topaz-yellow and are similar to those of lanthanum.
Scandium **Sc**	At. wt. 44.956 At. no. 21 V. 3 Sp. gr. 2.992 M.P. 1,539° B.P. 2,727°	In the minerals euxenite and gadolinite. Existence of this element was predicted by Mendeleev in 1869; he called it ekaboron. Leached from ores with sulfuric acid. 1879; Nilson.	Forms an oxide and a number of colorless salts.	An alloying element for nickel and nickel steels.
Seaborgium **Sg**	At. wt. 263 (?) At. no. 106	Does not occur naturally. By bombardment of californium-249 with oxygen-18 ions. 1974; Flerov et al.; Ghiorso et al. (shared credit).	Radioactive. Resembles tungsten.	No commercial applications; of research interest only.

Element	Occurrence, Preparation, Date of Discovery, and Discoverer	Properties	Chief Compounds and Uses
Selenium **Se** At. wt. 78.96 At. no. 34 V. 2, 4, 6 Sp. gr. amorphous 4.26 monoclinic 4.28 hexagonal 4.8 M.P. amorphous 50° monoclinic 170° hexagonal 217° B.P. 684.9° C.S. THC	Free in some specimens of sulfur and in combination with lead, iron, and other metals, as in pyrites. Amorphous, by reducing selenious acid (H_2SeO_3) with sulfur dioxide. With tellurium, it is obtained from the anode slime occurring in copper refineries. 1817; Berzelius.	Three varieties are known: (1) red amorphous, soluble in carbon bisulfide from which it is deposited as (2) red translucent monoclinic crystals, soluble in carbon bisulfide; (3) blue-gray metallic selenium, insoluble in carbon bisulfide. This last form conducts electricity much better when exposed to light; conductivity increases with light intensity.	Selenium cells are used as indicators of intensity of illumination. The compounds strongly resemble those of sulfur. Hydrogen selenide is a foul-smelling, flammable gas. Selenic acid (H_2SeO_4) is a more powerful oxidizer than sulfuric acid and dissolves gold. The oxychloride is a valuable solvent for resins, fish oils, etc. Selenium is used in the manufacture of colorless and red-tinted glass, and in electronic rectifiers.
Silicon **Si** At. wt. 28.086 At. no. 14 V. 4 Sp. gr. amorphous 2.35 crystalline 2.4 M.P. 1,410° B.P. 2,355°	Silicon dioxide (SiO_2) occurs as flint, quartz, quartz sand, etc. Igneous rocks are composed largely of silicates, and silicon constitutes more than 27 percent of the earth's crust—more than any other element except oxygen. By reducing sand with coke in a furnace. 1823; Berzelius.	Amorphous silicon is a brown powder that burns when heated in air. Crystalline silicon forms black needles. It is less active than the amorphous variety and is attacked only slowly by a mixture of hydrofluoric acid and nitric acid. It unites with fluorine, however, at ordinary temperatures.	Silicon is used in steelmaking. Silicon steel is more magnetic than iron. Ornamental varieties of quartz find uses as gems, as do several natural silicates. Silicon carbide, or carborundum (SiC), is used as an abrasive. Sodium silicate solution is water glass, used to protect sandstone and to preserve eggs. Common glass is a mixture of sodium and calcium silicates.
Silver **Ag** At. wt. 107.868 At. no. 47 V. 1 Sp. gr. 10.53 M.P. 960.8° B.P. 1,950° C.S. Cf	Native, as sulfide (AgS_2) often associated with galena; as chloride (AgCl). From lead alloys by the Pattinson process or the Parkes process; from the ores by the Mexican and other processes. Known in antiquity.	White, highly lustrous, tough, very ductile, malleable metal; best conductor of heat and electricity known. Liquid silver dissolves oxygen. It is unaffected by the oxygen of moist air; its tarnishing is caused by the action of hydrogen sulfide. It dissolves in dilute nitric acid and in hot concentrated sulfuric acid.	Used for tableware, ornaments, coins, etc. U.S. sterling silver contains 90 percent silver, 10 percent copper. Lunar caustic is silver nitrate. This salt and the halides of silver are used extensively in photography. For electroplating, a bath of potassium argenticyanide is used.
Sodium **Na** At. wt. 22.9898 At. no. 11 V. 1 Sp. gr. 0.97 M.P. 97.5° B.P. 883° C.S. Cb	In the sea, as chloride (NaCl); in salt deposits, as chloride, borate, and nitrate; in many complex silicates in rocks. By electrolysis of fused sodium hydroxide (NaOH). 1807; Davy.	Silver-white metal, soft as wax. Immediately tarnishes at ordinary temperatures. Like potassium, it is very active, uniting directly with many other elements and vigorously reacting with cold water.	Used in manufacture of chemicals. Sodium chloride is a necessity of life for most animals, and is used in manufacture of hydrochloric acid, chlorine, and sodium compounds. Sodium carbonate and sodium hydroxide are used for cleaning and for manufacture of soap and chemicals. Sodium bicarbonate is baking soda. The sulfate is known as Glauber's salt; the thiosulfate, by photographers, as "hypo."

Element	Occurrence, Preparation, Date of Discovery, and Discoverer	Properties	Chief Compounds and Uses
Strontium **Sr** At. wt. 87.62 At. no. 38 V. 2 Sp. gr. 2.6 M.P. 774° B.P. 1,366° C.S. C	As strontianite ($SrCO_3$) and celestite ($SrSO_4$). By electrolysis of the chloride. 1790; Crawford.	White metal; harder than sodium, softer than calcium; tarnishes to a yellow tint. Like calcium, it is active enough to react vigorously with cold water.	The nitrate and chlorate are used in fireworks for red color. All volatile compounds color the Bunsen flame red.

Sulfur
S
At. wt. 32.064
At. no. 16
V. 2, 3, 4, 6
Sp. gr.
  rhombic 2.07
  monoclinic 1.96
M.P.
  rhombic 112.8°
  monoclinic 119°
B.P. 444.6°
	Native, in combination with most metals as sulfides, and with some metals as sulfates.
	By melting the free sulfur away from the rocky matrix (Frasch process), and subsequent purification by distillation.
	Known in antiquity.
		Natural sulfur is rhombic in crystalline form, yellow, brittle, and of vitreous luster. It is a poor conductor of heat and electricity. This and the monoclinic variety are soluble in carbon bisulfide, while amorphous sulfur is not. When heated, sulfur unites directly with most other elements.	Used to prepare sulfur dioxide (SO_2), which is used in making sulfuric acid and sulfites and for bleaching; also for vulcanizing rubber and in manufacture of black gunpowder. Sulfuric acid (H_2SO_4) is to the chemical industry what iron is to engineering. Thiosulfuric acid and its salts are important in the processing of film.

Tantalum **Ta** At. wt. 180.948 At. no. 73 V. 2, 4, 5 Sp. gr. 16.6 M.P. 2,996° B.P. 5,425°	In tantalite and many other rare minerals. By the action of sodium tantalofluoride (Na_2TaF_7). 1802; Ekeberg.	Hard, silver-white metal; ductile and malleable when hot; of very high tensile strength. The hot metal can absorb 740 volumes of hydrogen. Not attacked by aqua regia.	Used for filaments for electric lamps until tungsten replaced it; in surgical instruments and in rectifiers; and as a substitute for platinum.
Technetium **Tc** At. wt. 97 (?) At. no. 43 V. 6, 7 Sp. gr. 11.50 M.P. 2,200°	Does not occur naturally. By bombardment of molybdenum with a stream of deuterons. 1937; Perrier, Segré.	The first artificially produced element. Resembles rhenium and manganese.	Used experimentally and for making technetium carbonyl $Tc_2(CO)_{10}$, which is stable, is soluble in organic compounds, and is reactive with halogens.

Tellurium
Te
At. wt. 127.60
At. no. 52
V. 2, 4, 6
Sp. gr.
  rhombic 5.93
  monoclinic 6.3
M.P. 449.5°
B.P. 989.8°
	Free and as tellurides.
	By reducing tellurous acid (H_2TeO_3) by means of sulfur dioxide.
	1782; Müller von Reichenstein.
		Crystalline variety is white, has metallic luster, and conducts heat and electricity. Precipitated variety is black and of lower density. Element is related to sulfur, but is more metallic.	Compounds find few applications; in coloring glass, gives silver a platinum finish. Telluric acid (H_6TeO_6) has basic as well as acidic characteristics, in keeping with the position of the element between the metals and nonmetals.

Terbium **Tb** At. wt. 158.924 At. no. 65 V. 3 Sp. gr. 8.27 M.P. 1,356° B.P. 2,800°	In gadolinite, in samarskite, and in other rare minerals. By electrolysis of the chloride. 1843; Mosander.	Rare earth element. Closely resembles the element gadolinium.	Salts are almost colorless; oxide is almost black.
Thallium **Tl** At. wt. 204.37 At. no. 81 V. 1, 3 Sp. gr. 11.86 M.P. 303.5° B.P. 1,457° C.S. T	In crookesite and in small quantities in many samples of iron pyrites. Precipitated by zinc from solution obtained by suitable treatment of flue dust from sulfuric acid works. 1861; Crookes.	Bluish-white, leadlike metal; rather soft and malleable, but of low tensile strength. Decomposes water rapidly at red heat and dissolves in dilute acids.	Forms two sets of salts: thallous and thallic. The salts, used in making optical glass, are poisonous. All the compounds show a characteristic green line in the spectrum.

Table of Elements

Element		Occurrence, Preparation, Date of Discovery, and Discoverer	Properties	Chief Compounds and Uses
Thorium **Th**	At. wt. 232.038 At. no. 90 V. 4 Sp. gr. 11.7 M.P. 1,845° B.P. 4,230° C.S. C	In monazite sand. By reducing potassium thorium chloride with sodium, or by electrolysis of fused potassium and sodium chlorides. 1828; Berzelius.	Metal has the color of nickel; can be burned in air. Hydrochloric acid attacks it slowly. Most isotopes are radioactive.	The nitrate $Th(NO_3)_4 \cdot 6H_2O$ is used in making Welsbach incandescent mantles, which consist of 99 percent thorium dioxide. Alloyed with magnesium for special purposes.
Thulium **Tm**	At. wt. 168.934 At. no. 69 V. 3 Sp. gr. 9.33 M.P. 1,545° B.P. 1,727°	In gadolinite and other yttrium minerals. 1879; Cleve.	Rare earth metal; has never been isolated.	Salts are a pale green that is destroyed very easily by minute quantities of erbium.
Tin **Sn**	At. wt. 118.69 At. no. 50 V. 2, 4 Sp. gr. 7.3 M.P. 231.89° B.P. 2,260° C.S. TC	As cassiterite (SnO_2). After roasting, the ore is reduced by heating with carbon. Known in antiquity.	Silver-white, rather soft, very malleable, ductile metal; practically unchanged in air. When heated, it may be burned in air. Dilute nitric acid is the only dilute acid that attacks it rapidly. When kept long at temperatures below 0°, ordinary tin changes to a brittle, gray, powdery form.	Much tin is used in coating iron as tinplate. A constituent of Britannia metal, pewter, solder, bronze, etc. Forms two sets of salts: stannous and stannic. Pink salt is used in dyeing. Mosaic gold is essentially stannic sulfide.
Titanium **Ti**	At. wt. 47.90 At. no. 22 V. 2, 3, 4 Sp. gr. 4.5 M.P. 1,675° B.P. 3,260° C.S. C	As rutile (TiO_2) and ilmenite ($FeTiO_3$). By reducing the chloride ($TiCl_4$) by means of sodium. 1791; Gregor.	Hard, brittle metal, resembling polished steel. May be forged at low red heat. Dissolves in dilute sulfuric acid and decomposes in steam at 800°. Unites easily with nitrogen.	Used in alloys, as a white pigment (paint and paper), and as a coloring for ceramics. Used as structural material in supersonic aircraft.
Tungsten **W**	At. wt. 183.85 At. no. 74 V. 2, 4, 5, 6 Sp. gr. 19.3 M.P. 3,410° B.P. 5,927° C.S. Cb	As wolframite ($FeWO_4$) and as scheelite ($CaWO_4$). By reducing tungstic acid (H_2WO_4) with carbon at high temperatures. 1783; the De Elhuyars.	Hard, brittle, gray metal, attacked by chlorine only at 250°, although it can be caused to burn in air. Slowly acted upon by dilute acids and even by water.	Used for filaments of incandescent electric lamps, giving an efficiency of 1.3 watts per candlepower. Tungsten steel has 5 percent tungsten. Sodium tungstates are used as mordants in dyeing processes. Was originally known as wolfram.
Uranium **U**	At. wt. 238.03 At. no. 92 V. 2, 3, 4, 5, 6 Sp. gr. 19.05 M.P. 1,132.3° B.P. 3,818°	As pitchblende, which contains U_3O_8. By reducing the oxides with aluminum. 1789; Klaproth.	White, lustrous metal; tarnishes in air and reacts slowly with cold water. Combines directly with many other elements.	All compounds are radioactive in proportion to their radium content. Glass to which uranium compounds have been added shows a greenish-yellow fluorescence. Used in nuclear weapons. Chief fuel for nuclear reactors.

Element		Occurrence, Preparation, Date of Discovery, and Discoverer	Properties	Chief Compounds and Uses
Vanadium **V**	At. wt. 50.942 At. no. 23 V. 2, 3, 4, 5 Sp. gr. 5.96 M.P. 1,890° B.P. 3,000° C.S. Cb	In a few rather rare minerals. By reducing the dichloride (VCl_2) in hydrogen. 1830; Sefström.	Silver-white lustrous metal, harder than quartz. Does not tarnish or react with water at ordinary temperatures, but can be burned in oxygen.	Added to steel even in small quantities (0.2 percent), it increases the tenacity and elastic limit without reducing ductility.
Xenon **Xe**	At. wt. 131.30 At. no. 54 V. 0, 2, 4 Sp. gr. (liquid) 3.52 M.P. −111.9° B.P. −107.1°	In minute quantities in the air, 1 volume in 170 million. By fractionation of liquid argon. 1898; Ramsay, Travers.	Transparent, colorless, odorless gas. Densest member of the noble gases.	Once thought to be chemically inert; forms fluorides (XeF_2, XeF_4, XeF_6), oxide (XeO_3), and hexafluoroplatinate (Xe_2PtF_6) compounds.
Ytterbium **Yb**	At. wt. 173.04 At. no. 70 V. 3 Sp gr. 7.01 M.P. 824° B.P. 1,427°	In gadolinite, euxenite, and other rare minerals. By electrolysis of the chloride. 1878; Marignac.	Rare earth. Forms colorless salts	Compounds exhibit a characteristic spark spectrum.
Yttrium **Y**	At. wt. 88.905 At. no. 39 V. 3 Sp. gr. 4.34 M.P. 1,495° B.P. 2,927°	In gadolinite, euxenite, and other rare minerals. By electrolysis of sodium yttrium chloride. 1794; Gadolin.	Gray, lustrous metal.	Chloride yields a characteristic, though complex, spectrum.
Zinc **Zn**	At. wt. 65.37 At. no. 30 V. 2 Sp. gr. 7.14 M.P. 419.4° B.P. 907° C.S. H	As zinc blende (ZnS), calamine ($ZnCO_3$), zincite (ZnO), etc. After roasting, the ore is reduced by coal, the metal distilling off. Known in antiquity.	Bluish-white, lustrous, brittle metal; malleable and ductile at 120°; tarnishes in moist air. Reacts slowly with cold water, and rapidly when heated in steam. Dissolves in dilute acids and sodium hydroxide solution.	Used for roofs, gutters, galvanic batteries. Iron galvanized with zinc, preventing rust. Zinc alloyed with copper to make brass. In paint, zinc oxide is less toxic than lead oxide. Salts used in medicine, chloride and sulfate used in anti septic solutions.
Zirconium **Zr**	At. wt. 91.22 At. no. 40 V. 4 Sp. gr. 6.4 M.P. 1,852° B.P. 3,578°	As zircon ($ZrSiO_4$). By reducing the oxide (ZrO_2) with carbon in an electric furnace. 1789; Klaproth.	Hard, gray metal remaining bright in air; oxidizes slowly at white heat. Dissolves in aqua regia and caustic potash solution.	Oxide is contained in some incandescent gas mantles; is used for furnace linings and as a cleansing agent in metallurgy. Increases tensile strength of armor plate. Carbide is an abrasive.

CHEMICAL BONDS

Atoms with incomplete valence shells will interact with certain other atoms in such a way that each partner completes its valence shell. Atoms do this by either sharing or completely transferring valence electrons. These interactions usually result in atoms staying close together, held by attractions called *chemical bonds*.

A chemical bond is the attraction that holds atoms together in groups of two or more. Bonds hold together every substance in the universe that is made of atoms. Bonds arise from the activity of electrons, negatively charged particles that whirl about the positively charged nucleus of an atom.

2
He
4.00
Helium

10
Ne
20.18
Neon

18
Ar
39.95
Argon

36
Kr
83.80
Krypton

54
Xe
131.30
Xenon

86
Rn
(222)
Radon

NONBINDING GASES

The *octet rule* states that electrons will be transferred or shared between atoms until an atom has eight electrons in its valence shell.

The elements in the far right column of the periodic table all have full valence shells, and therefore do not bond with other elements under normal circumstances. They are called the *noble gases*. All the noble gases except helium have eight electrons in their valence shells. Helium has only two electrons that fill the element's single electron shell.

◀ **The Noble Gases**

Attracted Atoms

A bond forms when an electron that belongs to one atom forms a pair with an electron that belongs to another atom. (See Electrons, page 319.) There are two main types of bonds.

- *covalent*
- *ionic*

A group of atoms held together by covalent bonding is called a *molecule.* Ionic bonds hold together *ionic compounds.* The type of chemical bond formed depends on differences in *electronegativity*—the ability of an atom to attract electrons—between the atoms of the molecule.

LEWIS DIAGRAMS

Lewis diagrams are used to represent covalent bonds in molecules. Usually each electron pair shared between atoms is shown as a line. Unshared electron pairs are shown as dots.

When drawing Lewis diagrams, it is a good idea to follow a regular procedure. Each step will be illustrated by drawing the diagram for nitric acid (HNO_3).

1. *Draw a tentative diagram for the molecule.* A hydrogen atom always forms a bond at the end position. If the molecule has two or more oxygen atoms and a nonmetal atom, the oxygen atoms usually are placed around the central nonmetal atom.

   O   N   O   H

   O

2. *Count the total number of valence electrons in the molecule or ion.* If necessary, adjust the number of electrons for charge: add one for each negative charge and subtract one for each positive charge.

   In HNO_3, there is one valence electron from hydrogen, five from nitrogen, and six from each oxygen: $1 + 5 + (3 \times 6) = 24$. There are no ions, so it is not necessary to adjust for charge.

Covalent Bonds

A covalent bond forms when two atoms share a pair of electrons. The sharing of one pair of electrons produces a *single bond.* The sharing of two or three pairs of electrons produces *double bonds* and *triple bonds,* respectively. *Lewis diagrams* are often used to show the bonding arrangement between the atoms.

Bond Energy. The strength of a covalent bond is measured by its *bond energy.* The strengths of covalent bonds increase with the number of electron pairs shared between two atoms. In single bonds, the bond strengths are generally higher between atoms of smaller size.

If both atoms are equally electronegative, a *nonpolar covalent bond* is formed. Hydrogen—H_2—and oxygen—O_2—are both diatomic elements that form nonpolar covalent bonds.

3. *Draw a single bond between each atom. Then distribute the remaining electrons around each symbol until each atom is surrounded by eight electrons. Remember that each single bond counts as two electrons for each element.*

$$\ddot{\text{O}}\text{—N—}\ddot{\text{O}}\text{—H}$$
$$|$$
$$\ddot{\text{O}}$$

4. *If there are not enough electrons to give the central atom an octet, use one or more of the unshared pairs of electrons to form double or triple bonds.*

$$\ddot{\text{O}}\text{=N—}\ddot{\text{O}}\text{—H}$$
$$|$$
$$\ddot{\text{O}}$$

Polar Covalent Bonds. If one atom is somewhat more electronegative, a *polar covalent bond* results. In polar covalent bonds, the electron pair is pulled closer to one atomic nucleus than to the other.

Water—H_2O—is a polar covalent molecule. The oxygen atom is partially negative, while the hydrogen atoms carry a slightly positive charge. This is a result of oxygen having a stronger pull or affinity for electrons than the hydrogen atoms.

Ionic Bonds

An ionic bond forms when two atoms differ so much in electronegativity that one or more electrons are actually transferred from one atom to the other. The recipient atom becomes negatively charged. The donor atom becomes positively charged. The attraction between the two atoms holds them together.

Ionic bonds generally form between a metal and a nonmetal. For example, sodium (Na), in group I, has one electron in its outer shell. This electron is held loosely and will easily be given up if the sodium atom comes in contact with a chlorine atom that needs but one electron in order to fill its outer shell. In this way, recipient atoms and donor atoms complete their valence shells yet stay mutually attracted to each other because of their opposite charges.

Ionic compounds are compounds made up of ions held together by ionic bonds. For an ionic compound to form, the sum of the positive charges must equal the sum of the negative charges. Thus, the total charge of cations is exactly balanced by the total charge of the anions.

Most ionic compounds, such as table salt—sodium chloride (NaCl)—are solids in which the positive and negative ions pack together to form a crystal.

Molecules

Molecules are made up of atoms held together in certain arrangements. A molecule's size and shape depends on the size and number of its atoms.

The shape of a molecule depends upon two factors.

1. The atoms tend to take up positions relative to one another such that the bonds formed are the strongest of all the bonds that this particular group of atoms could form.

2. Atoms that are not bonded to each other tend to move far apart.

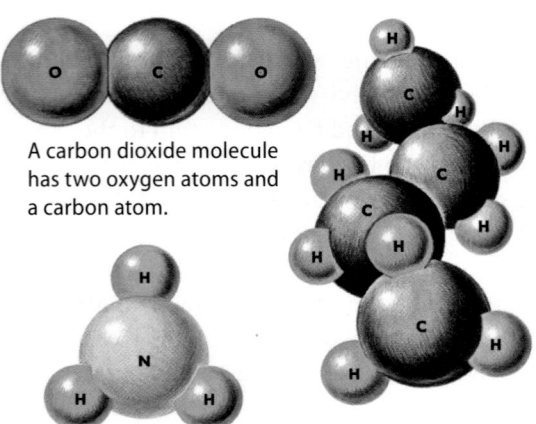

A carbon dioxide molecule has two oxygen atoms and a carbon atom.

An ammonia molecule has three hydrogen atoms and a nitrogen atom.

A butane molecule is a chain of carbon atoms with hydrogen atoms.

Molecular Geometry

The shape and size of a molecule play an important role in determining the physical and chemical properties of a substance.

Shape. The overall shape of a molecule, its *molecular geometry,* is determined by the bond angles in the molecule. A *bond angle* is the angle between any two bonds formed by the same atom.

For example, CO_2, or carbon dioxide, is a linear molecule with the carbon atom at the center and a double-bonded oxygen on each side. Carbon has no lone pairs of electrons to alter its linear shape (O=C=O).

On the other hand, water has two lone pairs of electrons above the central oxygen atom which cause the molecule to be bent in a v-shape.

The number of different ways that bonds can be arranged in space is rather limited. For example, a molecule consisting of two atoms can be arranged only in a linear fashion. A molecule of three atoms can be a linear molecule or a v-shaped molecule.

Intermolecular Forces

The forces that act between molecules or between molecules and ions are called *intermolecular forces.* Generally these forces are much weaker than bonding forces. Three important intermolecular forces are forms of electrostatic attraction.

- *dipole forces*
- *hydrogen bonds*
- *dispersion forces*

Dipole forces occur when the positive region of one polar molecule is attracted to the negative region of another polar molecule.

Dipole Forces

positive pole

negative pole

Hydrogen Bonds

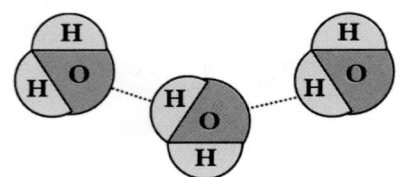

Size. The actual size of a molecule is determined by its *bond lengths,* the distances between the nuclei of bonded atoms.

Polar and Nonpolar Molecules. The shape of a molecule helps determine the distribution of charge in the molecule. A *polar molecule,* or *dipole,* is a molecule in which there is a nonsymmetrical distribution of electrical charge, even though the molecule as a whole is electrically neutral. One region of a dipole has a negative charge (the negative pole), while another region has a positive charge (the positive pole).

A *nonpolar molecule* has a symmetrical charge distribution. Molecules that have no polar covalent bonds are nonpolar. Molecules that have polar covalent bonds may still be nonpolar molecules if the polar covalent bonds are perfectly symmetrical (for example, CO_2).

Molecular Geometry

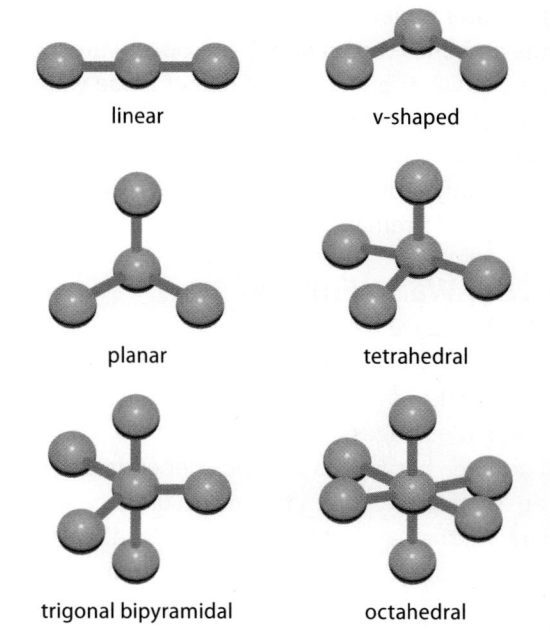

linear   v-shaped

planar   tetrahedral

trigonal bipyramidal   octahedral

Hydrogen bonds are another form of dipole force. These bonds form when the partially positive hydrogen atom of a polar covalent bond in one molecule is attracted to the partially negative atom of a polar covalent bond in another molecule. This type of bonding generally occurs between molecules in which a hydrogen atom is bonded to an atom of nitrogen, oxygen, or fluorine.

Dispersion forces, or *London forces,* are attractive forces between nonpolar molecules that have been distorted, or polarized, to create temporary dipoles. Even the simplest molecules have some dispersion attraction.

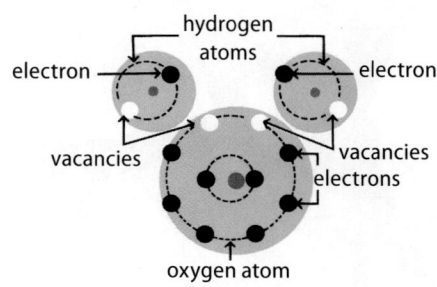

Water molecule

▲ **A water molecule** forms when two atoms of hydrogen and one of oxygen join together in sharing their electrons. The electrons fill the vacancies in all the atoms.

Molecules and Matter

Molecules come together to form substances. A single water molecule is made up of two hydrogen atoms and one oxygen atom. A drop of water contains billions of water molecules. If one of those water molecules were separated from the rest, it would still behave as water. But if that water molecule were divided, only atoms of the elements hydrogen and oxygen would remain.

Van der Waals Forces

Molecules are held together in a group by electrical forces called *van der Waals forces*. These forces are usually weaker than those that hold a molecule itself together. (See pages 346–347.)

The force between molecules depends on how far apart they are. When two molecules are widely separated, they attract each other. When they come very close together, they repel each other.

Solids

In a solid, the molecules are so arranged that the forces that attract and repel are balanced. The molecules vibrate about these positions of balance, but they do not have enough energy to move to different parts of the solid.

As the temperature of a solid is raised, the molecules vibrate more strongly. When the van der Waals forces can no longer hold the molecules in place, the solid melts.

Liquids

In a liquid, the molecules move about easily, but they still have some attractive force on one another. These forces are strong enough to keep the liquid together.

LIQUID CRYSTALS

Certain organic compounds called *liquid crystals* have properties of both liquids and solids. Within a particular temperature range, such a compound flows like a liquid, but has a more ordered molecular arrangement. Its molecules line up side-by-side and form tiny groups or clusters that slide past one another in certain directions.

A unique property of liquid crystals enables scientists and engineers to make use of their molecular alignment: The alignment can be disrupted electrically, magnetically, or by a temperature change. A crystal that is normally clear becomes murky. A colored crystal changes color.

▲ **Liquid crystals** are used in liquid crystal displays (LCDs), displays for electronics as wide-ranging as watches, calculators, cellular telephones, personal digital assistants, automobile dashboards, computer screens, and television sets.

Gases

In a gas, the molecules move about so fast that the attractive forces have little effect on them. When two molecules in a gas collide, the repelling force sends them apart again. Therefore, gas molecules fill a container completely, because they move freely through all the space available.

Changing Matter

Most substances can be changed into solids, liquids, or gases by either raising or lowering their temperatures. The temperature at which these changes occur—and also other characteristics of a substance—depends on the size, shape, and mass of the molecules and also on the strength of the van der Waals forces between them. (See pages 784–785.)

STUDYING MOLECULES

Scientists can study some molecules directly with an electron microscope or a scanning tunneling microscope.

Scientists also study molecules indirectly. For example, they study the way molecules absorb or give off light. Each kind of molecule absorbs or gives off certain colors of light that make up the molecule's spectrum.

By studying the spectrum of a substance, scientists can find the sizes and shapes of its molecules, the strength of the forces that hold the atoms together in the molecules, and the way the electrons move about in the molecules.

▲ **Scanning tunneling microscopes** produce images of some individual atoms in a solid substance.

Polymerization

Under certain conditions, two molecules may collide with enough energy to react and form one or more new molecules. The process by which many small molecules combine chemically to produce a large molecule is called *polymerization*.

Molecules can also break down into smaller molecules. Causes of molecular disintegration include ultraviolet light, fast-moving electrons, and nuclear radiation.

Important Dates in Chemistry	
1770s	Carl Scheele and Joseph Priestley discover oxygen.
Late 1700s	Antoine Lavoisier states the law of the conservation of mass and proposes the oxygen theory of combustion.
1803	John Dalton proposes his atomic theory.
1811	Amedeo Avogadro suggests that equal volumes of all gases at the same temperature and pressure contain equal numbers of particles.
Early 1800s	Jons J. Berzelius calculates the masses of a number of elements.
1828	Friedrich Wohler makes the first synthetic organic substance from inorganic compounds.
1856	Sir William H. Perkin makes the first synthetic dye.
1869	Dmitri Mendeleev develops the first modern periodic table. Julius Lothar Meyer independently creates a similar table the following year.
1910	Fritz Haber patents a process to produce synthetic ammonia.
1913	Niels Bohr proposes his model of the atom.
1916	Gilbert N. Lewis describes electron bonding between atoms.
1950s	Biochemists begin to discover how such chemicals as deoxyribonucleic acid (DNA) and ribonucleic acid (RNA) affect heredity.
Early 1980s	Chemists begin working to develop a solar-powered device that produces hydrogen fuel by means of the chemical breakdown of water.
1985	Richard E. Smalley, Robert F. Curl, Jr., and Harold W. Kroto discover buckminsterfullerene, a ball-shaped molecule consisting only of carbon.

STATES OF MATTER

The physical properties of a substance often depend on the state of the substance. The three main states of matter are *solid, liquid,* and *gas.*

The state that a particular substance appears in depends on temperature, pressure, and the characteristics of the substance. Aluminum, for instance, is a solid at room temperature, while water is a liquid and oxygen is a gas.

Substances can exist in more than one state of matter. A solid can change into a liquid or gas, a liquid can change into a solid or gas, and a gas can change into a liquid or solid. The change of matter from one state to another is called a *phase change.*

▲ **In a gas,** the molecules can move essentially independently of one another.

▲ **In a liquid,** the packing of the molecules is looser than in a solid. The molecules can move past one another but not totally break loose. Thus, liquids flow.

Solids

Solids exist in the most ordered state of matter. The particles of a solid are generally fixed in a definite position and maintain a definite shape. (See also pages 780–781.)

Types of Solids

Most solids are *crystalline solids,* which means their atoms are arranged in an orderly geometric pattern that repeats itself. Each particle occupies a fixed position in the crystal. Although the particle can vibrate, it cannot move past its neighbors. Most nonliving substances are made up of crystals. Metals and rocks consist of crystals, as do snowflakes, salt, and sugar.

Noncrystalline solids are called *amorphous solids.* In an amorphous solid, the particles lack a well-defined arrangement. Glass, rubber, gels, and plastics are all amorphous solids.

Crystalline Solids

The structure and properties of crystalline solids are determined by the kinds of forces that hold the particles together. Crystals can be classified as one of four types.

- *ionic*
- *molecular*
- *covalent*
- *metallic*

▲ **In a solid,** the molecules are packed tightly together so there is little freedom of movement.

Ionic Crystals

- held together by electrostatic attraction
- in an ideal ionic lattice, or geometrical pattern of ions, each positive ion surrounded by several negative ions
- each negative ion surrounded by several positive ions
- tight packing ensures that the ions are not free to move, and therefore do not conduct electricity

Covalent Crystals

- held together by covalent bonds
- have chemical bonds that interlock all the atoms into one giant molecule
- can be very hard and durable, like a diamond
- other covalent crystals can be quite soft, like graphite
- electrons in most covalent networks are held tightly in chemical bonds, and they give no electrical conductivity

Molecular Crystals

- held together by intermolecular forces called van der Waals forces
- solids with clearly defined molecules in their structures
- most organic solids are molecular solids
- van der Waals forces are weak and very short range
- molecules only attracted by their nearest neighbors
- strong enough to produce molecular solids at low temperatures and liquids at higher temperatures

Metallic Crystals

- held together by metallic bonds—electrostatic attractions between positive metal ions and electrons
- metallic bonds make metals strong and durable
- electrons are shared among a very large number of atoms
- a lattice of ions surrounded by a sea of relatively free electrons
- only two electrons can go into one energy level
- electrons can conduct heat and electricity, but when a metal is heated, the last electrons have such a high energy that they do not contribute to the heat capacity

IONIC CRYSTAL

The ions of a sodium chloride (NaCl) crystal are packed tightly together. The negatively charged ions (light green) are larger than the positively charged ions (dark green).

The critical factor is the number of the large negative ions that can be grouped around a positive ion before the negative ions touch each other and move away from the positive ions. The forces between ions are strong but must include many ions. As a result, when force is applied, groups of ions can slip and cause the crystals to fracture easily.

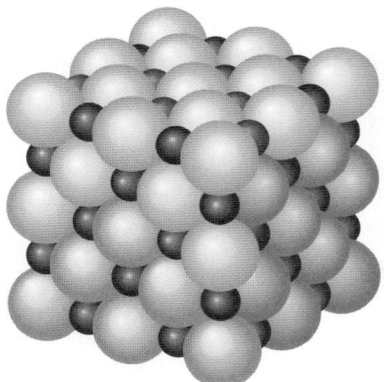

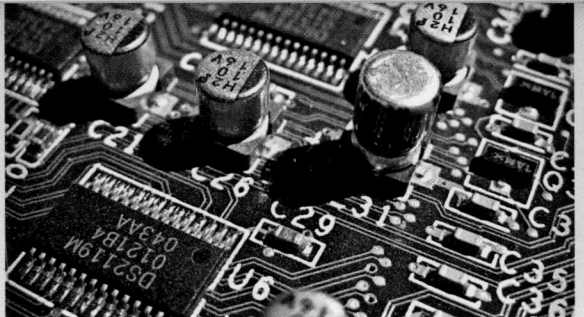

SEMICONDUCTORS

If small amounts of aluminum or phosphorous are incorporated into a crystal of silicon, they generate either positive or negative charges in the silicon. This results in a material whose conductivity rises with temperature. It is called a *semiconductor*. The electronics industry is now based on devices fabricated from these materials.

Liquids

A liquid is a substance that is *fluid,* meaning it can flow to fit the shape of the container in which it is poured. (See also page 782.) A liquid

- has no shape of its own—it takes on the shape of its container.
- always occupies a fixed volume.
- is unlike a gas and similar to a solid because it has a definite volume, and its molecules are only slightly compressible.
- has intermolecular forces that are stronger than those of a gas, so that a liquid's molecules are packed more tightly.
- has a larger density and is less compressible than a gas.
- has *surface tension* and *viscosity.*

Surface tension occurs because molecules at a liquid's surface experience different forces than molecules in the interior. Surface tension enables the water's surface to support this insect. ▶

Surface Tension

At the surface of a liquid, the intermolecular forces pull the surface molecules into a sort of tight "skin" over the liquid or around a drop. The surface tension of a liquid is the amount of energy needed to stretch or increase the surface "skin."

Liquids with strong intermolecular attractions have higher surface tension than liquids with weak intermolecular forces.

WATER AND HYDROGEN BONDS

Water is the only common substance that exists in its liquid state at temperatures found in most places on Earth. Water is liquid above 0°C (32°F) and does not boil until it reaches 100°C (212°F).

Substances with similar molecular structures, such as H_2S or H_2Se, are gases at room temperature. They do not become liquid until the temperature is brought down to between −100°C (−148°F) and −90°C (−130°F).

Hydrogen Bonds. The unique forces that hold water molecules together are called *hydrogen bonds.* The hydrogen end of the water molecule has a positive electric charge. At the opposite, oxygen end, the molecule has a negative charge. Water molecules link together because the positive and negative charges attract. The positive ends of water molecules attach to the negative ends of other water molecules, whose positive ends attach to the negative ends of still other water molecules.

Hydrogen Bonds in Ice. In ice, each oxygen atom is surrounded by a tetrahedral arrangement with two hydrogen atoms in conventional bonds and two others with hydrogen bonds. The bonding can be shifted from one hydrogen atom to another.

This tetrahedral arrangement leaves a great deal of open space. As a result, solid ice is less dense than liquid water. As a result, ice floats in water. This is an unusual relationship between solids and their liquids.

If ice sank, Earth would become a lifeless Arctic desert. Each winter, more and more ice would pile up on the bottom of lakes, rivers, and oceans. In summer, the sun's heat could not reach deep enough to melt the ice. Water life would die. The water cycle would slow down. In time, all of the water would turn to solid ice, except perhaps for a thin layer of water over the ice during the summer.

Viscosity

Within a liquid, the liquid molecules are free to move past one another. This freedom to move is what allows liquids to flow.

Viscosity may be thought of as an internal resistance to flow. Liquids that have strong intermolecular forces are generally more viscous than liquids with weak intermolecular forces.

CAPILLARITY

The molecules of a liquid often have a greater attraction for other substances than they have for each other. If the walls of a *capillary,* or narrow tube, attract the molecules of a liquid's surface more strongly than the molecules of the liquid itself, the molecules will rise into the capillary. This action is called *capillarity.*

Capillarity has many benefits. It draws water through soil to the roots of plants. The capillarity of clothing keeps people comfortable by absorbing moisture. Capillaries in rainwear repel water yet let in air for greater comfort.

Liquid always seeks its own level. If a liquid is put in a container with several arms of equal diameters, it will rise to the same level in all the arms.

CHANGES OF STATE

Any substance may exist in more than one state of matter. The change of matter from one state to another is called a *phase change.* Conversions of a solid to a liquid (melting), a liquid to a gas (vaporization), or a solid to a gas (sublimation) are *endothermic processes.* The reverse processes—conversion of a liquid to a solid (freezing), a gas to a liquid (condensation), or a gas to a solid (deposition)— are *exothermic processes.*

There is a continuous transfer of particles from one phase to another, and the state of a substance at any given time depends on temperature and pressure. The temperatures and pressures at which the various phases of a substance can exist can be summarized in a *phase diagram.*

Each region in a phase diagram represents a pure phase— that is, a phase in which the substance is entirely a gas, liquid, or solid. The boundaries between the regions show the temperatures and pressures at which the substances are in equilibrium between two states. The point where all three boundaries intersect is known as the *triple point.* Phase diagrams are used to anticipate transitions in phase brought about by changes in temperature and pressure.

Phase Diagram

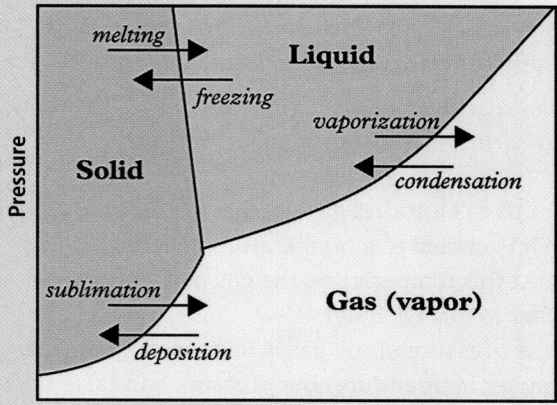

Gases

Gases have certain characteristics that differentiate them from solids and liquids. (See also page 783.)

- They have low density.
- Gases can be compressed—that is, a fixed quantity of gas may be made to occupy a smaller volume by applying pressure.
- They expand to fill the containers uniformly.
- Gases exert constant pressure on the walls of their containers uniformly in all directions.

Hydrogen is the most abundant element—about 90 percent of all atoms in the universe are hydrogen atoms.

How Gases Behave

The behavior of gases is explained by what scientists call the *kinetic theory*. According to the kinetic theory, all matter—including gases—is made up of particles—atoms or molecules—that are in constant motion.

Speed of Gas

- Gas particles fly around in all directions at about the speed of sound.
- The exact speed of particles is determined by their weight and by the temperature of the gas.
- Gas particles move faster when the gas is hot than when it is cold.
- Lighter gas particles move faster than heavier ones at all temperatures.
- Each moving gas particle crashes into billions of other particles each second.
- Gas particles crashing into the walls of their container produce an effect called *pressure*.

From Gas to Liquid. A gas *liquefies* (changes to a liquid) when it is cooled to a temperature called its *boiling point*. At this temperature, the gas particles gather together to form a liquid.

If the pressure of the gas is increased, it liquefies at a higher temperature. But pressure can raise the liquefying temperature only to a limiting value called the *critical temperature*.

For example, oxygen under normal atmospheric pressure liquefies at its boiling point, −183°C. But under a pressure of 5,171 kilopascals, oxygen liquefies at −119°C, its critical temperature.

History of the Study of Gases

Scientists first described gas in the 1600s, when they realized that some matter can exist in a form that is similar to air.

Belgian chemist and physician Jan Baptista van Helmont invented the word *gas* to describe this special kind of matter. He altered the Greek word *chaos*, meaning *space*, to form the word *gas*. In this way, the word describes the ability of a gas to fill any amount of space.

Discovery. Many gases were discovered and studied during the 1600s and 1700s. These gases include hydrogen, oxygen, and nitrogen.

The English scientist Henry Cavendish first described hydrogen as an individual substance in 1766. Under normal conditions on Earth, pure hydrogen exists in the form of bound pairs of atoms. This type of hydrogen, called molecular hydrogen or H_2, is a tasteless, odorless, colorless gas.

Oxygen is a life-supporting gas and a chemical element. Nearly all living things need oxygen to stay alive. It was discovered in the 1770s by two chemists working independently, Carl Scheele of Sweden and Joseph Priestley of England. Oxygen combines with other chemicals in plant and animal cells to produce energy needed for life processes.

Nitrogen is a nonmetallic chemical element. It occurs in nature as a colorless, odorless, and tasteless gas. This gas makes up about 78 percent of the earth's atmosphere by volume. Daniel Rutherford, a Scottish physician, discovered nitrogen in 1772.

BY THE NUMBERS

The number of atoms or molecules of gas in a container the size of a pinhead is many millions of times as large as the number of people on Earth! But these gas particles are so small that they occupy only about one-thousandth of the space inside the container. The remaining space between the particles is empty.

Gas Mixtures

Gases may be mixed together by adding one gas to another gas already occupying a rigid container of fixed volume. The partial pressure of one component of the mixture is the pressure that the component would exert if it were present alone at the same volume and temperature.

According to *Dalton's law of partial pressure*, the total pressure exerted by a mixture of gases is the sum of the partial pressures of the gases in the mixture.

KINETIC THEORY OF GASES

According to the kinetic theory of gases, gas molecules are in constant motion. They collide with each other and with the walls of the container. The molecules of gas are spaced widely apart, which causes the strength of interparticle attractions to be very weak in most gases. A gas that conforms perfectly to this model of gas behavior is known as an *ideal gas*.

A FOURTH STATE OF MATTER

Under special conditions, gases change into a fourth state of matter called a *plasma*. Plasmas are formed by heating a gas to an extremely high temperature or by passing an electric current through it.

THE basics

PRESSURE

Pressure is defined as force per unit area. The greater the force, the greater the pressure. In the metric system, the standard unit of pressure is the pascal. Pressure is measured in pounds per square inch in the inch-pound system customarily used in the United States.

Atmospheric pressure is produced by the weight of the air from the top of the atmosphere as it presses down upon the layers of air below it. At sea level, the average atmospheric pressure is 101.3 kilopascals (14.7 pounds per square inch). This decreases with altitude because of less air pressing from above.

The greater the pressure in a gas, the smaller its volume. This decrease in volume occurs because the molecules are pushed closer together. Under ordinary conditions, the volume of a gas decreases by half when the pressure doubles.

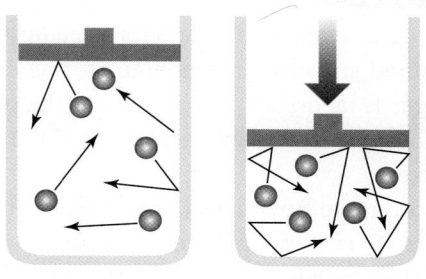

▲ **Pressure** in a gas increases the smaller the volume of its container. The pressure increases because the molecules of gas are pushed closer together.

The sun and the other stars, and most of the other objects in space, consist of plasma. Lightning bolts also consist of plasma, but few other plasmas occur naturally on Earth.

Gas Laws

Experiments with a large number of gases reveal that the state, or condition, of many gaseous substances can be defined using four variables: temperature (T), pressure (P), volume (V), and the quantity of gas measured in a unit called a *mole* (n). Three laws explain the relationships between these variables.

- *Boyle's law*
- *Charles's law*
- *Avogadro's law*

The three gas laws have been combined into a single statement known as the *ideal gas law*.

MOLE

A mole is a unit used to measure the amount of a substance. One mole of any substance contains about 6.022×10^{23} (602.2 billion trillion) of the elementary entities that make up the substance. These entities can be molecules, atoms, ions, electrons or other subatomic particles, or groups of particles.

The number is known as *Avogadro's constant*. For example, a mole of water contains 6.022×10^{23} molecules of H_2O.

In addition, one mole of a substance has a mass in grams that is numerically equal to its weight in *atomic mass units* (amu's). The term *molar mass* is used to describe the mass in grams of one mole of a substance. The molar mass of water is determined by adding the amu's of each atom in the molecule.

H_2O
$2\,H = 2 \times 1.01\ \text{amu} = 2.02$
$1\,O = 1 \times 16.00\ \text{amu} = 16.00$
Molar mass of water: 18.02 g/mol (grams per mole)

Boyle's Law

Boyle's law states that for a fixed quantity of gas maintained at constant temperature, the volume of the gas is inversely proportional to the pressure. Therefore, pressure increases as the volume of gas decreases.

According to Boyle's law, the product of the pressure (P) multiplied by the volume (V) remains constant if there is no change in the temperature or in the number of particles inside the container. The law is written this way.

$$PV = \text{constant}$$

Boyle's law says that the pressure doubles when a gas is compressed to half its volume at constant temperature.

Robert Boyle first published Boyle's law in 1662. Boyle (1627–1691) was an Irish scientist who is considered one of the first modern chemists. He helped establish the experimental method in chemistry and physics.

Charles's Law

Charles's law states that for a fixed quantity of gas at constant pressure, the volume of the gas is directly proportional to its temperature. Therefore, a gas expands by the same fraction of its original volume with each degree that its temperature rises.

According to Charles's law, the ratio between the volume (V) of a gas and its temperature (T) remains constant if the pressure does not change. The law is written this way.

$$V/T = \text{constant}$$

In this equation, T is the *absolute temperature* of the gas. It is usually measured in *kelvins* (Celsius degrees plus 273.15). Kelvin is abbreviated K.

For example, when a gas is heated from 300 K (room temperature) to 600 K, its absolute temperature doubles. Doubling the temperature doubles the gas's volume if the pressure does not change.

Jacques Alexandre Cesar Charles, a French chemist, stated Charles's law in 1787.

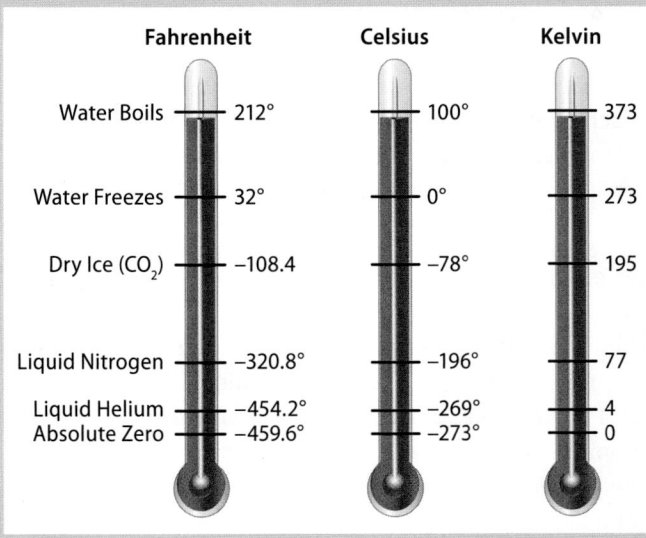

Fahrenheit	Celsius	Kelvin
Water Boils — 212°	— 100°	— 373
Water Freezes — 32°	— 0°	— 273
Dry Ice (CO_2) — −108.4	— −78°	— 195
Liquid Nitrogen — −320.8°	— −196°	— 77
Liquid Helium — −454.2°	— −269°	— 4
Absolute Zero — −459.6°	— −273°	— 0

ABSOLUTE TEMPERATURE SCALE

Temperature in gas law equations is measured in kelvins, on the *absolute temperature* scale. The unit size of one kelvin is the same as one °C, but no degree symbol is used for kelvins. The Kelvin scale is defined in terms of two points: 1. *absolute zero* and 2. the *triple point* temperature of water.

Absolute zero is the lowest possible temperature. It is assigned a value of 0 K. The triple point of a substance is the one temperature and pressure at which its solid, liquid, and gas phases can coexist in equilibrium. The triple point of water occurs at a temperature of 273.16 K.

Avogadro's Law

Avogadro's law states that at constant temperature and pressure, the volume of the gas is directly proportional to the moles of gas. It says that equal volumes of different gases all contain the same number of particles if they all have the same pressure and temperature.

Amedeo Avogadro, an Italian scientist and philosopher, proposed Avogadro's law in 1811. It was later discovered that a volume of 22.4 liters of gas at 0°C and atmospheric pressure contains about 602 billion trillion particles. This number is called Avogadro's constant. (See Mole, on the facing page.) This number of particles of any substance is called one mole of the substance.

Atomic Mass. Avogadro distinguished between gases composed of complex units (molecules) and gases made up of simple units (atoms). He was able to use gas densities to calculate the amount of matter in atoms and molecules.

Ideal Gas Law

The three laws have been combined together in one equation, known as the ideal gas law. The law is written:

$$PV = nRT$$

In this equation, *P* represents the pressure of the gas, *V* represents its volume, *n* represents the number of moles of gas, and *T* represents its absolute temperature. *R* is a constant called the *universal gas constant*. Its value is 8.314 *joules* per kelvin per mole.

A joule is a unit used to measure work or energy. One joule is the amount of work done when a force of one newton acts on an object that moves 1 meter in the direction of the force. (See pages 770–771.)

According to the ideal gas law, the pressure of a gas can be doubled in three ways.

1. The gas can be squeezed into one-half its original volume.

2. Twice as much gas can be forced into the original volume.

3. The absolute temperature can be doubled.

COMPOUNDS are substances

that contain more than one kind of atom. Every compound has a definite composition that can be described by a chemical formula. For example, water is a compound that contains two kinds of atoms, hydrogen and oxygen.

Atoms of chemical elements combine in many ways to form millions of compounds. In some cases, atoms of the same elements combine in different proportions to produce a large number of compounds. For example, there are thousands of compounds that contain only the elements carbon and hydrogen.

COMMON COMPOUNDS

There is a small group of molecular compounds that have what are called common or trivial names. For example, H_2O is water, not dihydrogen monoxide.

Common Molecular Compounds	
IUPAC* Name	**Molecular Formula**
water	H_2O or HOH
hydrogen peroxide	H_2O_2
ammonia	NH_3
glucose	$C_6H_{12}O_6$
sucrose	$C_{12}H_{22}O_{11}$
methane	CH_4
propane	C_3H_8
octane	C_8H_{18}
methanol	CH_3OH
ethanol	C_2H_5OH
hydrogen sulfide	H_2S

*International Union of Pure and Applied Chemistry

Formulas and Reactions

Chemical Formulas

A chemical formula expresses the composition of a compound using the symbols of the elements involved. Subscripts are used to show the number of atoms of each element in the compound. If only one atom of an element is present, the number is not shown as a subscript. Two important types of chemical formulas are

- molecular formulas
- empirical formulas

Molecular formulas show the exact number and type of atoms combined in each molecule of a compound.

For example, CH_4 is the molecular formula for the compound methane, a common hydrocarbon. The formula tells us that in each molecule of methane there is one carbon atom and four hydrogen atoms.

Empirical formulas show the simplest ratios of the *ions*—atoms or molecules that have an electric charge—present in an ionic compound.

For example, the empirical formula for sodium chloride, or common table salt, is NaCl while that of barium fluoride is BaF_2.

Ionic compounds do not form individual, discrete molecules but instead are arranged in a crystal lattice. For this reason, their empirical formula must reflect an overall net charge of zero.

The compound sodium chloride, or table salt, is a hard, white, crystalline solid formed of the elements sodium and chlorine. Separately, sodium is a soft metal and chlorine is a poisonous yellowish gas.

Chemical Reactions

Although tens of millions of chemical reactions can occur, many of these can be classified into six general types of reactions. Understanding the characteristics of each helps chemists predict what type of reaction will occur when different reactants are combined.

There are six general types of reactions.

Combination Reactions. Two or more substances combine to form a single product.

Decomposition Reactions. The opposite of a combination reaction—one reactant breaks down into two or more substances.

Combustion Reactions. Almost always contain molecular oxygen as a reactant, and produce a flame. The products of complete combustion are carbon dioxide (CO_2) and water.

Single Replacement Reactions. A type of oxidation-reduction reaction. In these reactions, an atom or ion in a compound is replaced by an atom or ion of another element.

Precipitation Reactions. The reactants are solutions and the products include a solid, known as a precipitate, that separates from the solution.

Neutralization Reactions. Involve acids (compounds whose solution contains hydrogen ions, or H^+) and bases (compounds whose solutions contain hydroxide ions, or OH^-). The products of neutralization reactions include water and a salt.

Both precipitation reactions and neutralization reactions are types of double-replacement reactions.

▲ **Lighting a match** demonstrates a chemical reaction between potassium chlorate on the head of the match and red phosphorous on the scratchy side of the matchbox.

THE basics

CHEMICAL REACTIONS

A chemical reaction is a process by which one or more substances are converted into one or more different substances.

✔ The original substances are called *reactants*.

✔ The resulting substances are called *products*.

In a simple chemical reaction, the reactants may be two atoms that bond together to form a product molecule. Another simple reaction might involve a reactant molecule breaking apart into two or more product atoms.

In more complex reactions, some or all of the bonds of reactant molecules break and the new bonds of product molecules form. Many enduring substances, such as rock and water, are highly stable (resistant to chemical reaction). However, all substances can react chemically under certain conditions.

Sodium

Chlorine

Naming Compounds

Currently there are about 10 million known chemical substances. Naming them all would be a difficult task at best if each had a special name independent of all the others.

Instead, a set of rules has been developed that allow chemical substances to be named in an informative and systematic way. The following are some of the rules used to name inorganic compounds.

TWO KINDS OF COMPOUNDS

Compounds can be divided into two groups. *Organic compounds* contain carbon atoms. Proteins, fats, carbohydrates, nucleic acids, and many other compounds in living things are organic compounds. All other compounds are called *inorganic compounds.*

Naming Inorganic Compounds

Binary Covalent Compound (two elements). Name of the first element, followed by the name of the second element, which includes a prefix indicating the number of atoms and ends in *ide*—carbon *dioxide.*

▲ **Iron (III) oxide,** or rust, consists of an iron ion with a +3 charge and oxygen.

Monoatomic Cation (one positive ion). Name of the element, followed by the word *ion*—sodium *ion.* If the element can form more than one positive ion (see transition metals, period 4 of the periodic table, pages 322–323), the positive charge of the ion is indicated by a Roman numeral in parentheses following the name of the element—iron *(II)* ion.

Monoatomic Anion (one negative ion). Drop the ending of the element name and add the ending *ide*—a chlorine ion is named chlor*ide.*

Ionic Compounds (two ions). Name of the cation followed by name of the anion—lithium bromide.

Binary Acids (H and anion). For compounds containing hydrogen and an anion, add the prefix *hydro* and change the ending of the nonmetal element to *ic*—*hydro*chlor*ic* acid or *hydro*sulfur*ic* acid.

Oxyanions (anion containing oxygen). Depends on the relative number of oxygen atoms in the anion. If the element forms only two oxyanions, the oxyanion that contains more oxygens ends in *ate,* and the name of the one with less oxygen ends in *ite*—1 nitrogen and 2 oxygens is nit*rite* ion while 1 nitrogen and 3 oxygens is nit*rate* ion.

If three or four oxyanions are formed, the oxyanion with less oxygen than the *ite* oxyanion has the prefix *hypo* attached to the name of the *ite* oxyanion—*hypo*chlor*ite* has less oxygen than chlorite. The oxyanion with more oxygen than the *ate* oxyanion has the prefix *per* attached to the name of the *ate* oxyanion—*per*chlor*ate* has more oxygen than chlorate.

Carbon compounds make up the living tissues of all plants and animals. ▶

ON YOUR OWN

Using the ionic charges from the periodic table as well as the table of polyatomic ions, name or give the formula to fill in the blanks in the table below.

Name	Formula	Answer
carbon dioxide		CO_2
nitrogen monoxide		NO
	NH_3	ammonia
barium fluoride		BaF_2
	Na_2S	sodium sulfide
	$Fe(OH)_2$	iron (II) hydroxide
ammonium sulfide		$(NH_4)_2S$
calcium acetate		$Ca(CH_3COO)_2$
	Li_3PO_4	lithium phosphate
iron (III) carbonate		$Fe_2(CO_3)_3$
	H_2O_2	hydrogen peroxide
hydrochloric acid		HCl
	HBr	hydrobromic acid
sulfuric acid		H_2SO_4
	HNO_2	nitrous acid

Oxyacids (H and oxyanion). Names are usually derived from the corresponding oxyanion. If the oxyanion has an *ate* ending, the corresponding acid is given an *ic* ending. If the oxyanion ends in *ite*, then the corresponding acid name ends in *ous.* Prefixes in the name of the oxyanion are kept in the name of the oxyacid—if oxyanion = chlorate, then oxyacid = chlor*ic* acid; if oxyanion = hypochlorite, then oxyacid = hypochlor*ous* acid.

Equations and Energy

A *chemical reaction* is the process by which one or more substances are converted into one or more different substances. The *law of conservation of mass* states that mass is neither created nor destroyed during a chemical reaction. The *law of conservation of energy* states that one form of energy can be converted to another form, but energy itself can be neither created nor destroyed.

Chemists summarize chemical reactions using formulas called *chemical equations*.

Chemical Equations

Chemical reactions can be represented in a concise way using chemical equations. For example, when molecular hydrogen (H_2) burns, it reacts with molecular oxygen (O_2) to form water (H_2O). The chemical equation for this reaction is:

$$2H_2 \rightarrow O_2 + 2H_2O$$

▲ **Spontaneous combustion** occurs most readily in large piles of coal, heaps of oily rags, and damp hay.

COMBUSTION

One of the most familiar reactions is *combustion*. Combustion is the process by which a material burns in air, giving off light and heat.

In most cases, combustion involves the rapid combination of oxygen with a fuel to produce burning. The fuel may be a solid, liquid, or gas. Combustion occurs, for example, when oxygen in the air reacts with charcoal in a barbecue grill.

When oxygen combines slowly with another substance, the reaction is usually called *oxidation*. The rusting of iron is an example of oxidation.

The following chemical equation describes the combustion of methane, the main ingredient in natural gas.

$$CH_4 + 2O_2 \rightarrow CO_2 + 2H_2O$$

One molecule of methane and two molecules of oxygen yield one molecule of carbon dioxide and two molecules of water.

How Combustion Occurs

- In most cases, combustion occurs between a gaseous fuel and the oxygen in the air.
- The fuel may begin as a solid or liquid, but it must be vaporized (changed to a gas, or vapor) before it can burn.
- Substances vaporize at their surface.
- The molecules on the surface are attracted to one another and the molecules underneath.
- Heat can energize surface molecules of liquids and some solids enough to overcome this attraction.
- These molecules then escape into the air.

Spontaneous Combustion. Sometimes, a substance suddenly ignites without having contact with a spark or flame. This is called *spontaneous combustion*. It occurs when chemical reactions within the substance produce heat that cannot escape.

The Elements of Equations

- The plus sign in a chemical equation means "reacts with" and the arrow means "produces."
- The chemical formulas to the left of the arrow represent the *reactants,* or starting substances.
- The formulas to the right of the arrow show the *products,* or substances produced.
- The numbers in front of the formulas are called *coefficients*.
- Coeffecients indicate how many units of the substances are used and produced in the reaction.

Physical States. When writing chemical equations, chemists also often indicate the physical states of the reactant and products by using the abbreviations *g, l, s,* and *aq* in parentheses to denote gas, liquid, solid, and the aqueous (water) environment, respectively. So the equation for the creation of water might look like this:

$$2H_{2(g)} + O_{2(g)} = 2H_2O_{(l)}$$

Equal Atoms. Because atoms are neither created nor destroyed in a reaction, an equation must have an equal number of atoms of each element on each side of the arrow. This creates a *balanced equation*. When balancing equations, be sure to keep the following in mind.

- Formulas of substances must be written correctly.
- The number of atoms of each type of element must be the same on both sides of the equation.
- Only coefficients in front of substances may be changed to change the number of atoms on the reactant or product side. Subscripts in chemical formulas must not be changed.
- The sum of charges of ions on the left side of the arrow must be the same as the sum of charges of ions on the right side.

ENTHALPY

Enthalpy, designated by the letter *H,* may be thought of as the amount of heat possessed by the chemical involved in a reaction at a given temperature and pressure.

THE basics

ENDOTHERMIC AND EXOTHERMIC REACTIONS

During a chemical reaction, energy is either absorbed or released.

✔ Reactions in which energy is absorbed are called *endothermic reactions.*

✔ Reactions in which energy is released are called *exothermic reactions.*

Energy and Reactions

Nearly all chemical changes involve an energy transfer, usually in the form of heat. (See pages 756–757.) This heat flow is referred to as the *heat of reaction* or the *enthalpy of reaction*.

Change in Enthalpy. The absolute enthalpy of a substance cannot be measured directly. Instead, chemists measure the change in enthalpy, ΔH, which is the heat change during a reaction.

This change in enthalpy can be calculated using the formula

$$\Delta H = \sum H_{final} - \sum H_{initial}$$

where $\sum H_{final}$ is the sum of the final enthalpies and $\sum H_{initial}$ is the sum of the initial enthalpies.

In exothermic reactions, the products of the reaction have a smaller heat content than the reactants, so ΔH is a negative quantity. In endothermic reactions, the products of the reaction have a greater heat content than the reactants, so ΔH is a positive quantity.

Balancing Equations

Chemists balance chemical equations according to a fundamental principle of chemistry known as the *law of conservation of mass.* (See page 312.) To satisfy the law, a chemical equation must have the same number and types of atoms in both the reactants and the products.

Consider the reaction that occurs when hydrochloric acid is added to solid calcium carbonate. It produces carbon dioxide. A skeletal description of this reaction is

$$HCl + CaCO_3 \rightarrow CO_2 + CaCl_2$$

Represent All Atoms. The equation at left may properly identify the important reactants and products, but it is not a balanced chemical equation. To balance the equation, we must see that all the atoms that are on the left side are properly represented on the right side and vice versa.

To make $CaCl_2$, we must use two molecules of HCl. In addition, the hydrogen from the HCl must go somewhere. We note that CO_2 accounts for only two oxygen atoms, and so the solution to the two extra hydrogens and the one extra oxygen is the formation of water, H_2O. These considerations give the following balanced chemical equation:

$$2HCl + CaCO_3 \rightarrow CO_2 + CaCl_2 + H_2O$$

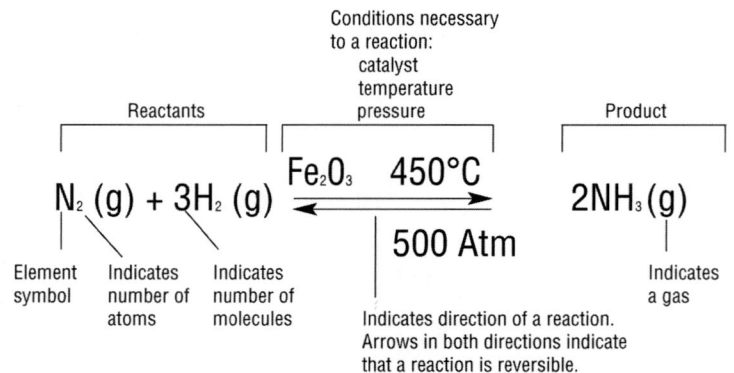

The coefficient values in an equation do not indicate amounts in any particular system of measure. The coefficients in an equation indicate a proportion of one reactant to another. For example, if the following values were assigned to the above equation, differing amounts of the same product would result.

1 molecule N_2 + 3 molecules H_2 → 2 molecules NH_3

1 mole N_2 + 3 moles H_2 → 2 moles NH_3

28 metric tons N_2 + 6 metric tons H_2 → 34 metric tons NH_3

Indicating Phases. We can also indicate the state of the reactants and products by writing:

$$2HCl_{(aq)} + CaCO_{3(s)} \rightarrow CO_{2(g)} + CaCl_{2(aq)} + H_2O$$

where the (aq) indicates an aqueous solution and the (s) and (g) refer to solid and gas phases.

For many purposes, this equation is still not the best description of the reaction. The acid HCl is fully ionized, as is the salt $CaCl_2$. As a result, the chloride ion, Cl^-, is present on both sides of the equation and is not really a reactant. It is called a spectator ion. The net ionic reaction is

$$2H^+ + CaCO_{3(s)} \rightarrow CO_{2(g)} + Ca^{2+} + H_2O$$

◄ **Adding hydrochloric acid to calcium carbonate** causes a chemical reaction that yields carbon dioxide, calcium chloride, and water.

How to Balance Equations	
1. Write down the unbalanced equation.	$N_2 + H_2 \leftrightarrows NH_2$ Unbalanced
2. Balance the partial equation involving only the hydrogen, oxygen, or atom whose valence combining state has been assumed.	Assume that each H has a positive valence, H^{+1}, but $3H^{+1}$ protons exist for each nitrogen (N) atom. Therefore, the latter should have three negative charges, N^{-3}. Now balance the hydrogens on the left with those on the right. $[H_2]$ Unbal. $\rightarrow$ $[3H^{+1} + 3e-]$ $3[H_2]$ Trial $\rightarrow$ $2[3H^{+1} + 3e-]$ $3H_2$ Balanced $\rightarrow$ $6H^+ + 6e-$
3. Assign the countervalence state that the other combined atom should have with H^{+1} or O^{-2}.	N in combined NH_3 is assigned a valence state of −3 and represented as N^{-3}.
4. Balance the partial equation for the other combined atom.	$[N_2]$ Unbal. $\rightarrow$ $[N^{-3} - 3e-]$ $[N_2]$ Trial $\rightarrow$ $2[N^{-3} - 3e-]$ N_2 Balanced $\rightarrow$ $2N^{-3} - 6e-$
5. Add up the positive and negative charges and see if they cancel each other out, as illustrated at the right.	Add up the partially balanced equations. $N_2 \rightarrow 2N^{-3} - 6e-$ $3H_2 \rightarrow 6H^{+1} - 6e-$ $N_2 + 3H_2 = 2N^{-3} - 6H+1$ The valences cancel out. $N_2 + 3H_2 \rightarrow 2NH_3$ The total number of atoms on the left equals the total on the right. Nitrogen is reduced (gains electrons); hydrogen is oxidized (loses electrons to nitrogen).

Balancing Equations

ON YOUR OWN

Practice balancing the following reactions:

1. During electrolysis, water is decomposed into hydrogen and oxygen gas.

___ $H_2O_{(l)}$ → ___ $H_{2(g)}$ + ___ $O_{2(g)}$

2. Ammonia breaks down readily into nitrogen and hydrogen gas.

___ $NH_{3(g)}$ → ___ $N_{2(g)}$ + ___ $H_{2(g)}$

3. Hydrochloric acid reacts with sodium hydroxide in a neutralization reaction to form sodium chloride and water.

___ $HCl_{(aq)}$ + ___ $NaOH_{(s)}$ → ___ $NaCl_{(aq)}$ + ___ $HOH_{(l)}$

Note: HOH may also be used to represent water or H_2O.

4. Methane burns in the presence of oxygen to form carbon dioxide and water and is an example of a combustion reaction.

___ $CH_{4(g)}$ + ___ $O_{2(g)}$ → ___ $CO_{2(g)}$ + ___ $H_2O_{(g)}$

5. In a double replacement reaction, lead nitrate reacts with potassium iodide to form lead iodide and potassium nitrate.

___ $Pb(NO_3)_{2(aq)}$ + ___ $KI_{(aq)}$ → ___ $PbI_{2(s)}$ + ___ $KNO_{3(aq)}$

Note: In most reactions, the bonds within the polyatomic ion (NO_3) will not be broken.

6. Butane from a lighter and oxygen combine to form carbon dioxide and water.

___ $C_4H_{10(l)}$ + ___ $O_{2(g)}$ → ___ $CO_{2(g)}$ + ___ $H_2O_{(g)}$

Note: When balancing hydrocarbon combustion reactions, first balance the C atoms on each side of the equation followed by H and then O. If an odd number of O atoms results, go back and double the Cs and Hs respectively.

7. In a single replacement reaction, aluminum reacts with nickel bromide to form aluminum bromide and solid nickel.

___ $Al_{(s)}$ + ___ $NiBr_{2(aq)}$ → ___ $AlBr_{3(aq)}$ + ___ $Ni_{(s)}$

Note: Balance bromide ions first.

8. Rust or iron (III) oxide forms when iron combines with oxygen in the air.

___ $Fe_{(s)}$ + ___ $O_{2(g)}$ → ___ $Fe_2O_{3(s)}$

	Answers	Explanation*
1.	2, 2, 1	Since there are two atoms of oxygen in oxygen gas, there must be two atoms of oxygen in the reactant. Therefore, you need to add a two in front of H_2O. This leaves two molecules of hydrogen gas and one molecule of oxygen gas in the products.
2.	2, 1, 3	Ammonia has three hydrogen atoms. The chemical reaction must occur with an even number of ammonia molecules in order to yield hydrogen gas, H_2.
3.	1, 1, 1, 1	Since each element needs only one atom to yield the molecules in the reactants, the coefficient is one for each molecule. On the products side, the coefficient remains one since there are two hydrogen atoms available to form the water molecule.
4.	1, 2, 1, 2	There are four atoms of hydrogen in a methane molecule, which means that H_2O in the products needs a coefficient of two. That gives you four oxygen atoms in the products, so you need to give O_2 in the reactants a coefficient of two as well.
5.	1, 2, 1, 2	Two molecules of potassium iodide in the reactants give you enough atoms to balance out the products. You are left with one molecule of lead iodide (PbI_2) and two molecules of potassium nitrate (KNO_3).
6.	2, 13, 8, 10	You need at least four carbon atoms on the products side to balance the equation. But that leaves you with five water molecules and an uneven number of oxygen atoms. Doubling the coefficient for butane allows you to balance the oxygen atoms, giving you eight molecules of carbon dioxide and 10 molecules of water.
7.	1, 3, 2, 3	Since there are three atoms of bromine in an aluminum bromide molecule, you need at least two $AlBr_3$ molecules to balance out the bromine in the reactants. Balancing the rest of the equation, you are left with three atoms of solid nickel.
8.	4, 3, 2	Start by balancing the oxygen, since there are three atoms in the products. You are left with four iron atoms and three oxygen molecules, which gives you two molecules of Fe_2O_3, or rust.

To ease understanding in the explanations above, the units used will be individual molecules and atoms. Remember, however, that in reality the coefficients indicate only a proportion of one reactant to another; they do not indicate amounts in any particular system of measure.

REACTIONS AND EQUILIBRIUM

Beyond predicting whether or not a chemical reaction will take place, it is also important to calculate how fast a reaction occurs and how far the reaction will go before it is finished. The area of chemistry concerned with the speeds, or rates, at which a chemical reaction occurs is called *chemical kinetics*.

Most chemical reactions are reversible. When the rate of the forward reaction is equal to the rate of the reverse reaction, the two reactions have reached a state of balance called *chemical equilibrium*.

Reaction Rates

According to the *kinetic theory of chemical reactions*, reactions occur as a result of collisions between molecules. Not all collisions result in reactions—a reaction occurs only when molecules collide with enough energy to break the bonds and initiate the reaction. The minimum energy required for a reaction is called the *activation energy*.

Change Over Time

When a reaction occurs, the rate of the reaction describes how the concentration of reactant or product changes over time. The rate of a reaction can be calculated using the ratio of the change in concentration of a reactant or product to the time interval required for the observed concentration change.

Factors Affecting Rates

Three factors can influence the rate of a reaction.

- temperature
- catalysts
- concentration

▲ The *Hindenburg* **airship** exploded on May 6, 1937, when the hydrogen gas that kept the ship aloft ignited. One theory states that the spark that set off the explosion was caused by the buildup of static electricity on the airship.

HYDROGEN + OXYGEN + HEAT

The chemical reaction between hydrogen and oxygen is very slow at 25°C (77°F), but if a small source of heat such as a spark is introduced, the mixture will explode in a very fast reaction. This is the result of hydrogen atoms starting a chain reaction, forming oxygen and hydrogen molecules, resulting in water and heat.

This heat finally raises the temperature enough until H_2 molecules break apart and form H-atoms. These atoms then react with oxygen, generating more heat and a thermal explosion.

Temperature. Chemical reactions occur more quickly at higher temperatures. This is primarily because an increase in temperature increases the number of particles with sufficient kinetic energy to overcome the activation energy barrier. (See page 756.)

Most chemical reactions increase their rates by at least a factor of two for a temperature rise of 10°C. On the other side, lower temperature will often prevent chemical reactions from taking place. The household refrigerator is designed to delay the spoilage of foods from both oxidation and bacterial attack.

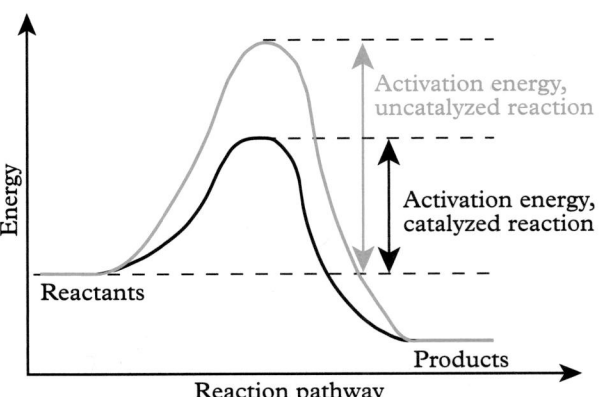

A **catalyst** lowers the activation energy for a reaction.

Catalysts. A *catalyst* is a substance that increases the rate of a chemical reaction by lowering the activation energy for the reaction. Catalysts exist in several different forms—some are mixed in with the reacting chemicals, while others seem to provide a surface upon which the reaction may occur.

Regardless of its form, a catalyst is not permanently affected by the reaction. Unless the catalyst is poisoned or drastically altered due to heat, it can be used again and again for the production of product.

The enzymes found in living things are catalysts. They direct the complex chemistries involved in metabolism and other processes that are so important to life. One enzyme in our blood speeds up the equilibrium between HCO_3^-, a bicarbonate in the blood, and dissolved carbon dioxide (CO_2). Without it we would have to breathe very slowly to get rid of the CO_2 in our blood. Many diseases are caused by the genetic absence or mutation of certain enzymes.

Concentration. The initial concentration of the reactants can also influence a reaction rate. Generally, it can be stated that the higher the concentration, the faster the reaction.

CHEMISTRY IN THE GARAGE

A *catalytic converter* is a device in the exhaust system of a car that uses catalysts—the substances that speed chemical reactions—to reduce the amount of pollution produced by the vehicle.

A catalytic converter consists of tiny honeycomb-like passages that are coated with noble metals such as platinum and rhodium. As the exhaust gases run through the catalytic converter, the metals cause a chemical reaction called *oxidation*. Oxygen is added to the hydrocarbons and carbon monoxide, converting them to water vapor and carbon dioxide.

The nitrogen oxides in the exhaust undergo a *reducing* reaction separating the oxygen atoms from the nitrogen oxide, producing nitrogen and oxygen.

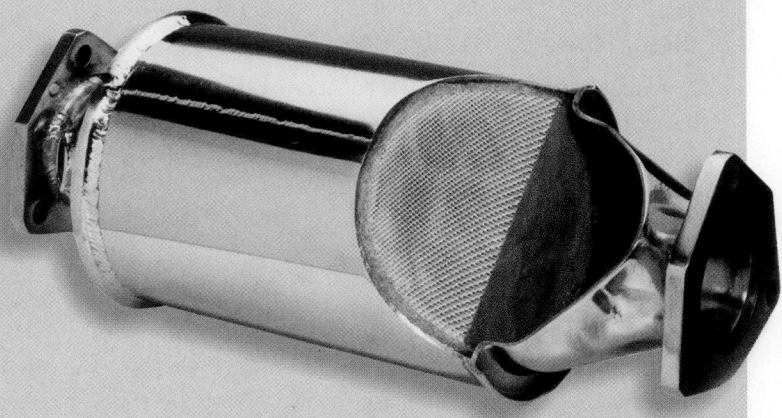

▲ A **catalytic converter** is a device in automobiles that uses catalysts to convert harmful exhaust pollutants to harmless substances.

Equilibrium

Few chemical reactions proceed in only one direction. Instead, most are reversible. The state of balance achieved when the rate of the forward reaction is equal to the rate of the reverse reaction is called *chemical equilibrium*.

How Equilibrium Is Achieved

- At the start of a reversible reaction, the reaction proceeds toward the formation of products.

- Then, as soon as some product molecules are formed, the formation of reactant molecules from product molecules begins to take place.

- When the rates of the forward and reverse reactions are equal, a state of chemical equilibrium exists.

Stable Concentrations. In a system at equilibrium, the concentrations of reactants and products no longer change with time. The relative concentrations of reactants and products at equilibrium can be expressed in terms of a quantity called the *equilibrium constant* (K).

REMEMBER THIS. . .BOYLE'S LAW

Boyle's law states that for a fixed quantity of gas maintained at constant temperature, the volume of the gas is inversely proportional to the pressure. Therefore, pressure increases as the volume of gas decreases.

CHEMICAL EQUILIBRIUM

A double arrow in a chemical equation, such as the one below, indicates equilibrium. At equilibrium, the rate of the forward reaction (left to right in the equation) is equal to the rate of the reverse reaction (right to left).

$$N_2 + 3H_2 \rightleftarrows 2NH_3$$

In the forward reaction, N_2 (nitrogen) is combining with H_2 (hydrogen) to form NH_3 (ammonia). In the reverse reaction, ammonia is breaking up into nitrogen and hydrogen. At equilibrium, the concentrations of the various substances do not change.

Factors Affecting Equilibrium

Chemical equilibrium represents a balance between forward and reverse reactions. In most cases, this balance is quite delicate and can be easily disturbed by change.

Le Châtelier's Principle. A rule, known as *Le Châtelier's principle,* makes it possible to predict how a system in equilibrium will react if a change is introduced. The rule states that the equilibrium will shift if the change causes the forward and reverse reactions to become unequal, and a new equilibrium will be reached. Le Châtelier's principle takes into account changes in

- concentration
- temperature
- pressure
- volume

▲ **Henry Louis Le Châtelier (1850–1936)** was a French chemist who began his career as a mining engineer. He later turned to chemistry and became known for his principle describing chemical equilibrium.

Concentration Changes

For a System at Equilibrium	
Concentration of a reactant or product is increased	**Concentration of a reactant or product is decreased**
The reaction will shift in the direction that *uses* more of that substance, so that equilibrium is reestablished.	The reaction will shift in the direction that *forms* more of that substance, so that equilibrium is reestablished.

Temperature Changes. A change in temperature not only changes both forward and reverse reaction rates, but also changes the value of the equilibrium constant.

For a System at Equilibrium	
When heat is added	**When heat is removed**
The reaction will shift in the direction that *absorbs* heat.	The reaction will shift in the direction that *gives* off heat.

Pressure and Volume Changes. Changes in pressure and volume ordinarily do not affect the concentrations of liquids and solids. However, a change in pressure or volume will affect a system that includes one or more gases.

For a System at Equilibrium	
When pressure is increased (or volume decreased)	**When pressure is decreased (or volume increased)**
The reaction will shift in the direction that *decreases* the total number of gas molecules.	The reaction will shift in the direction that *increases* the total number of gas molecules.

INDUSTRIAL CHEMISTRY

Ammonia is a colorless gas made up of one part nitrogen and three parts hydrogen. It is used as a fertilizer, to make TNT and other explosives, and in the manufacture of many chemicals, plastics, vitamins, and drugs.

The commercial production of ammonia was developed by German chemist Fritz Haber in 1909. He used Le Châtelier's principle to produce ammonia from nitrogen and hydrogen.

Haber's process takes place at about 550°C (1022°F) and at 200 to 250 times atmospheric pressure. It uses an iron catalyst to speed up the reaction that combines the two separate gases into NH_3.

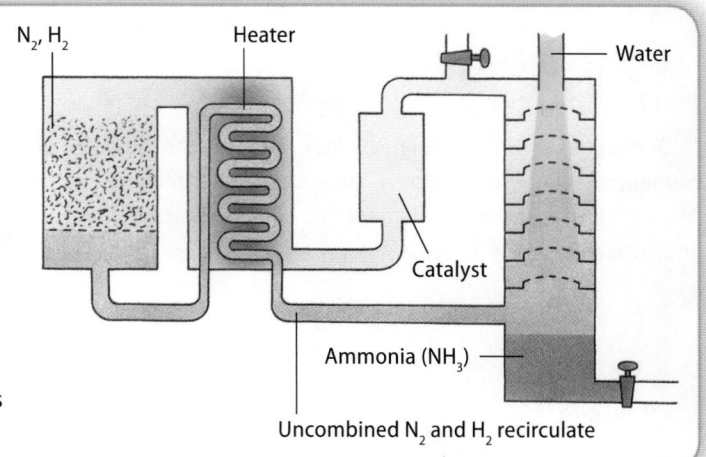

MATTERS OF SCALE

Molecules, atoms, ions, and subatomic particles are unimaginably small. An atom is more than a million times smaller than the width of a human hair. Scientists have had to develop techniques in order to make calculations and measurements involving these tiny bits of matter.

These techniques utilize the properties of elements found on the periodic table, as well as properties of molecules and ions, to determine such measurements as *relative atomic mass,* *relative molecular mass,* and *formula weight.*

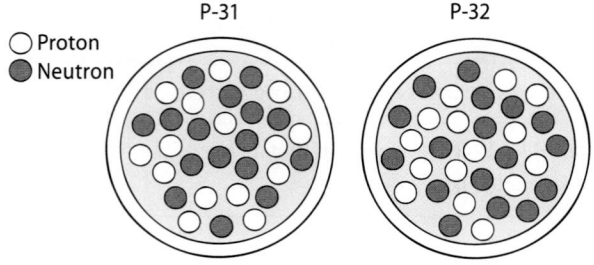

○ Proton
● Neutron

▲ **The isotopes of an element** contain a different number of neutrons. For example, ordinary phosphorus, P-31, has 16 neutrons, but its radioactive form, P-32, contains 17.

ISOTOPES

Sometimes the number of neutrons in atoms of the same element may vary. Consequently, these atoms have different masses. Atoms of the same element that differ in mass are known as *isotopes.*

Types of Measurements

Chemists do not ordinarily work with single molecules or atoms, but rather with trillions upon trillions of them. Therefore, instead of trying to count individual atoms or molecules, chemists usually determine the number of atoms or molecules indirectly from their masses.

Relative Atomic Mass

The mass of a single atom is much too small to be measured on a balance. (See pages 314–315.) So instead, chemists use a method of ratios to calculate relative atomic mass based on the mass of an atom of carbon-12, the most abundant isotope of carbon.

Relative atomic mass is a measure of how heavy an isotope or an element is. It is expressed as a number without a mass unit. For example, the relative atomic mass of the copper 63 isotope, rounded to four digits, is simply "62.93."

Unified Atomic Mass Units. The number that represents a relative atomic mass is based on a measurement that consists of a number followed by a unit of mass known as the *unified atomic mass unit* (u). In fact, the two numbers are identical. Thus, if you know the mass of an isotope or an element in unified atomic mass units, you can express the relative atomic mass by dropping the "u."

For example, the mass of the copper 65 isotope is 64.93 u, and so the relative atomic mass of that isotope is 64.93.

What Is a u? By definition, one u equals 1/12 of the mass of an atom of carbon-12. Unified atomic mass units are so tiny that one kilogram equals about 6.02×10^{26} u. That number would be written out as 602 followed by 24 zeros.

IONIC COMPOUNDS

A group of atoms held together by an ionic bond is called an *ionic compound*. An ionic bond results when one atom loses an electron to form a positive ion, and another atom accepts the electron to form a negative ion. The attraction between the two atoms holds them together.

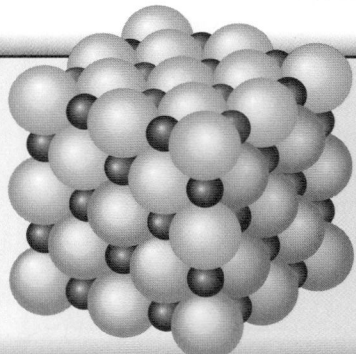

◀ **Sodium chloride** (NaCl), or table salt, is an important ionic compound.

Relative Molecular Mass

The mass of a molecule is indicated by its *relative molecular mass*. You can find the relative molecular mass of a molecule by adding the relative atomic masses of all the atoms in the molecule.

Suppose, for example, you wished to calculate the relative molecular mass of a molecule of carbon dioxide (CO_2) that consists of one atom of carbon-12 and two atoms of the most abundant form of oxygen. The relative atomic mass of the carbon atom would be exactly 12, and the relative atomic mass of each of the oxygen atoms, rounded to five figures, would be 15.995.

Your calculation would be:

$$12.000 + 15.995 + 15.995 = 43.990$$

A molecule's mass can also be measured with an instrument called a mass spectrometer. Carbon dioxide has a molecular mass of about 44.

Formula Weight

The formula weight of a substance is the sum of the atomic mass of each atom in its chemical formula. It is useful for determining the weight of substances that do not consist of individual atoms or molecules, such as ionic compounds.

For example, table salt—sodium chloride (NaCl)—is an ionic compound. Its formula weight can be determined by adding the atomic mass of sodium (Na) and chlorine (Cl). Looking at the periodic table, sodium's atomic mass is 23.00 and chlorine's is 35.45. So, the formula weight of sodium chloride would be

$$23 + 35.45 = 58.45$$

THE basics

CHEMISTRY MEASUREMENTS

✔ **Relative atomic mass** is a measure of how heavy an isotope or an element is. It is based on the element's weight in relation to the weight of carbon-12 and is expressed without a mass unit.

✔ **Relative molecular mass** indicates the mass of a molecule. It can be found by adding the relative atomic masses of all the atoms in the molecule.

✔ **Formula weight** of a substance is the sum of the atomic mass of each atom in its chemical formula.

✔ **A mole** is a unit used to measure the amount of a substance. One mole of any substance contains about 6.022×10^{23} of the elementary entities that make up the substance.

✔ **Molar volume** can be calculated from molecular weight and density. Many solids and liquids have a molar volume in mL that is close to their molecular weight. For metals and other dense solids, molar volume is much smaller than molecular weight.

✔ **Avogadro's number** is the number of atoms, molecules, ions, electrons, or other subatomic particles that make up one mole of a substance. It is equal to 6.022×10^{23}.

✔ **Stoichiometry** is the branch of chemistry that allows chemists to determine what quantities of the reactants in a chemical reaction are needed to produce a specific amount of product.

Molar Mass and Volume

To facilitate the counting and weighing of large samples of a substance, chemists have created a quantity called the *mole*. Molecules, atoms, ions, electrons, and other subatomic particles are so small that a standard unit had to be devised for scientists to be able to measure substances practically.

The Mole

One mole of any substance contains 6.022×10^{23} (602.2 billion trillion) of the elementary entities that make up the substance. This number is also called *Avogadro's number*. It is equal to the number of atoms found in 12 grams of the isotope carbon-12. Scientists chose the number as a standard reference number for the International System of Units.

- Thus, one mole of any substance contains Avogadro's number of atoms, molecules, or ions. For example, a mole of water contains 6.022×10^{23} molecules of water.

- In addition, one mole of a substance has a mass in grams that is numerically equal to its formula weight in atomic mass units.

- The term *molar mass* is used to describe the mass in grams of one mole of a substance.

- The molar mass of water (H_2O) would be equal to 18.02 g/mol (grams per mole).

- Molar mass is different from relative molecular mass because molar mass is a substance's mass per amount, expressed in grams per mole, while relative molecular mass is the mass of a single molecule, expressed in unified atomic mass units.

One Mole:
602,213,700,000,000,000,000,000
elementary entities!

Calculating Molar Mass

Molar mass is calculated by adding together the atomic mass of each atom in a chemical formula.

1. Chlorine gas (Cl_2)
   2 Cl = 2 × 35.45 = 70.90 g/mol (grams per mole)

2. Water (H_2O)
   2 H = 2 × 1.01 = 2.02
   1 O = 1 × 16.00 = $\dfrac{16.00}{18.02 \text{ g/mol}}$

3. Ammonia (NH_3)
   1 N = 1 × 14.01 = 14.01
   3 H = 3 × 1.01 = $\dfrac{3.03}{17.04 \text{ g/mol}}$

4. Sugar ($C_{12}H_{22}O_{11}$)
   12 C = 12 × 12.01 = 144.12
   22 H = 22 × 1.01 = 22.22
   11 O = 11 × 16.00 = $\dfrac{176.00}{342.34 \text{ g/mol}}$

INTERNATIONAL SYSTEM OF UNITS

The *metric system* is a group of units used to make measurements in science and engineering. The modern version of the metric system is called the *International System of Units*, abbreviated *SI*, which stands for its name in French.

SI allows scientists around the world to share information clearly and consistently. There are seven base units in SI. Each measurement is the same throughout the world.

1. the meter, which is the unit for length
2. the kilogram, for mass (amount of matter)
3. the second, for time
4. the ampere, for electric current
5. the kelvin, for temperature
6. the candela, for the brightness of light
7. the mole, for amount of substance

Mass of a Substance. In addition, total mass of a substance can be calculated if you know how many moles are present.

m (mass) = n (number of moles)
  × M (molar mass of substance)

5. If a reaction requires 3 moles of chlorine gas, then the relationship is

   number of moles = 3

   molar mass of chlorine gas (Cl_2) = 70.90 g/mol

   m = 3 mol × 70.90 g/mol = 212.70 g of Cl_2

Number of Moles. Given the total mass of a substance, the number of moles can be calculated.

$$n \text{ (number of moles)} = \frac{m \text{ (mass of sugar)}}{M \text{ (molar mass of sugar)}}$$

6. How many moles are present in 1,000 grams of sugar?

   mass of sugar = 1,000 g

   molar mass of sugar ($C_{12}H_{22}O_{11}$) = 342.34

   $$n = \frac{1,000 \text{ g}}{342.34 \text{ g/mol}}$$

   n = 2.921 mol

Calculating Molar Volume

The volume of one mole of any substance can be calculated from the molecular weight and the density. Volume is the amount of space something takes up.

Solids and Liquids. Many solids and liquids have densities close to 1 g/mL. One milliliter is equal to 1 cubic centimeter. For these solids and liquids, the molar volume in mL is close to the molecular weight.

Metals. Because of the high density of metals and other dense solids, the molar volume is much smaller than the molecular weight.

Ideal Gas. The molar volume of an ideal gas is often used in calculations. At 1 atm of pressure and 0°C, the molar volume of an ideal gas is 22.4 liters (L).

Ideal Gas Molar Volume Calculation

We will calculate the molar volume of an ideal gas at 1 atm and 25.0°C.

On the Kelvin scale:

0°C = 273.15K
25.0°C = 298.15K

Charles's law states that for a fixed quantity of gas at constant pressure, the volume of the gas is directly proportional to its temperature. Therefore, a gas expands by the same fraction of its original volume with each degree that its temperature rises.

So, according to Charles's law:

$$V_2/V_1 = T_2/T_1$$

and:

$$V_2 = V_1(T_2/T_1)$$

$$V_2 = 22.4 \text{ L} \left(\frac{298.15K}{273.15K}\right) = 24.5 \text{ L}$$

The molar volume of an ideal gas at 25°C is 24.5 L.

In addition to proposing Charles's law, French chemist Jacques Alexandre Cesar Charles was also the inventor of the hydrogen balloon.

Charles and a partner made the first hydrogen balloon flight on December 1, 1783, rising about 600 meters (2,000 feet) and drifting more than 40 kilometers (25 miles).

Stoichiometry

When working with chemical reactions, it is important for chemists to know what measured quantities of the reactants are needed to produce a specific amount of product. *Stoichiometry* is the branch of chemistry that allows chemists to determine these quantities.

Relationships and Ratios

Stoichiometry deals with the relationships between the elements making up substances and the properties of the substances. The mole concept is important in making stoichiometric calculations. (See page 374.)

For example, look at the following reaction.

$$2H_{2(g)} + 1O_{2(g)} \rightarrow 2H_2O_{(l)}$$

Two hydrogen molecules react with one oxygen molecule to form two water molecules. To yield any significant amount of water, this reaction will involve trillions of hydrogen and oxygen molecules. We can use the coefficients of the balanced reaction to provide us with a *mole ratio*.

Mole ratio for the above reaction forming water:

2 : 1 : 2

So, if 3.5 mol of H_2O are produced from this reaction, how many moles of hydrogen and oxygen gas were consumed during the reaction?

$2H_2 : 2H_2O = 1 : 1 = 3.5$ mol of H_2

$1O_2 : 2H_2O = 1 : 2 = 1.75$ mol of O_2

The mole ratio can then be used to determine the mass of the reactants needed to produce a specific amount of a substance.

$$3.5 \text{ mol of } H_2 = 3.5 \text{ mol} \times 2.02 \text{ g/mol}$$
$$= 7.04 \text{ g of } H_2$$

$$1.75 \text{ mol of } O_2 = 1.75 \text{ mol} \times 32.00 \text{ g/mol}$$
$$= 56.00 \text{ g of } O_2$$

Utilizing all of the above information, you can solve for the various unknowns in a reaction.

LAWS OF PROPORTION

There are two laws that form the basis for stoichiometry. They allow chemists to accurately calculate the relationships between the reactants and products in chemical reactions.

- the law of definite proportions
- the law of multiple proportions

The law of definite proportions deals with chemical *compounds,* or substances that consist of two or more elements. The law states that the elements of every pure compound exist in the same ratio by mass.

The law of multiple proportions states that when chemical elements combine in a chemical reaction to form a compound, they combine in a ratio of small whole numbers.

▲ **John Dalton,** an English chemist, discovered the law of multiple proportions in 1804. The law helped support Dalton's theory that matter is made up of atoms.

Stoichiometry Problems

1. How many moles of hydrogen gas are needed to react with 12.1 g chlorine gas to produce hydrogen chloride gas?

   Balanced equation:
   $$H_2 + Cl_2 \rightarrow 2HCl$$
   ? mol   12.1 g

2. How many grams of oxygen gas are needed to react completely with 17.5 g of hydrogen gas to produce water?

   Balanced equation:
   $$O_2 + 2H_2 \rightarrow 2H_2O$$
   ? g   17.5g

3. How many grams of aluminum are required to produce 515 g of aluminum oxide in a reaction with oxygen gas?

   Balanced equation:
   $$4Al + 3O_2 \rightarrow 2Al_2O_3$$
   ? g   515g

4. How many grams of zinc chloride will be produced in a reaction between zinc and 61 g of hydrochloric acid?

   Balanced equation:
   $$Zn + 2HCl \rightarrow ZnCl_2 + H_2$$
   61 g   ? g

Solutions

1. a) Determine number of moles in 12.1 grams of Cl_2.

   $$\frac{12.1 \text{ g}}{70.90 \text{ g/mol}} = 0.171 \text{ mol } Cl_2$$

   b) Convert number of moles of Cl_2 into moles of H_2.

   $$0.171 \text{ mol } Cl_2 \times \frac{1 \text{ mol } H_2}{1 \text{ mol } Cl_2} = 0.171 \text{ mol } H_2$$

2. a) Determine number of moles of H_2 in 17.5 g of H_2.

   $$\frac{17.5g \ H_2}{2.02 \text{ g/mol}} = 8.66 \text{ mol } H_2$$

   b) Convert moles of H_2 into moles of O_2.

   $$8.66 \text{ mol } H_2 \times \frac{1 \text{ mol } O_2}{2 \text{ mol } H_2} = 4.33 \text{ mol } O_2$$

   c) Convert moles of O_2 into grams of O_2.

   $$4.33 \text{ mol } O_2 \times 32.00 \text{ g/mol } O_2 = 138g \text{ of } O_2$$

3. a) Determine number of moles of Al_2O_3 in 515 g of Al_2O_3.

   $$\frac{515 \text{ g } Al_2O_3}{101.96 \text{ g/mol}} = 5.05 \text{ mol } Al_2O_3$$

   b) Convert moles of Al_2O_3 into moles of Al.

   $$5.05 \text{ mol } Al_2O_3 \times \frac{4 \text{ mol Al}}{2 \text{ mol } Al_2O_3} = 10.1 \text{ mol Al}$$

   c) Convert moles of Al into grams of Al.

   $$10.1 \text{ mol Al} \times 26.98 \text{ g/mol} = 273 \text{ g of Al}$$

4. a) Determine number of moles of HCl in 61 g of HCl.

   $$\frac{61 \text{ g HCl}}{36.5 \text{ g/mol}} = 1.67 \text{ mol HCl}$$

   b) Convert moles of HCl into moles of $ZnCl_2$.

   $$1.67 \text{ mol HCl} \times \frac{1 \text{ mol } ZnCl_2}{2 \text{ mol HCl}} = 0.84 \text{ mol } ZnCl_2$$

   c) Convert moles of $ZnCl_2$ into grams of $ZnCl_2$.

   $$0.84 \text{ mol } ZnCl_2 \times 135.4 \text{ g/mol} =$$
   $$114.58 \text{ g of } ZnCl_2$$

THERMOCHEMISTRY

In a chemical reaction, when the energy stored in the chemical bonds of the products is less than that which was stored in the bonds of the reactants, energy will be released as heat. *Thermochemistry* is the study of the ways in which heat is given off during a chemical reaction.

Bond-dissociation energy measures how much energy is needed to break a molecular bond.

Thermodynamics is the study of forms of energy, such as heat and work, and of the conversion of energy from one form into another.

▲ **Measuring Heat.** Scientists measure the amount of heat produced in a chemical reaction with an instrument called a calorimeter.

Heat

Heat is the excess energy released during a chemical reaction. It is stored in the products mainly as vibrational energy of the molecules or also as the rotational and translational energy of gaseous molecules.

Stored Energy

Molecules have structures well defined by the chemical bonds, but these bonds are elastic and they can bend and stretch. These motions are called *vibrations,* and they can store energy.

The molecules of a gas have kinetic energy and fly back and forth striking each other or the walls of their container. In addition, the molecules can rotate. This excess energy is expressed as an increase in the temperature of the products and their immediate surroundings.

Heat Capacity

When a substance absorbs heat energy, the temperature of the substance rises. The amount of heat energy required to raise the temperature of an object by 1° is called its *heat capacity*.

Heat energy can be measured either in *calories* (cal) or in *joules* (J). The relation between the two is defined as 1 cal = 4.184 J.

- *Specific heat capacity* refers to the heat capacity of 1 gram of a particular substance.

- *Molar heat capacity* refers to the heat capacity of 1 mole of the substance being heated.

COUNTING CALORIES

The calorie is a useful unit of measure because the specific heat capacity of liquid water near room temperature is 1 calorie per degree.

One of the most important uses of the calorimeter is to measure the amount of heat given off by different foods when they burn. This measurement tells how much energy a certain food yields when it is completely used by the body. Food scientists measure the heat produced in the calorimeter in kilogram calories, but they report the measurements as calories.

The law of conservation of energy states that energy is never created or destroyed. It can change form or be transferred from one object to another, however. (See Thermodynamics, page 381.)

The effects of this law can be seen in the transfer of heat. When a hotter object transfers heat to a cooler object, the amount of heat lost by the hotter object is equal to the amount of heat taken up by the cooler one.

State Change

The heat needed to change a material from a solid to a liquid or from a liquid to a gas is called *latent heat*. It must be removed to change a gas back to a liquid or a liquid back to a solid.

- 540 calories of heat must be removed from each gram of steam at 100°C to produce water.

- 80 calories must be removed from each gram of water at 0°C to produce ice.

The boiling and condensation points of a substance are at the same temperature, as are the melting and freezing points. The amount of heat that has entered or left a substance determines the substance's state.

SAMPLE PROBLEM: MELT ICE WITH WATER

Suppose that you have 10.0 g of ice at 0°C. The specific heat capacity of water is 1 calorie per degree. How much liquid water starting at 20°C would have to be added to melt this ice if all the water ended at 0°C? How much total water would remain?

Melting Point. If heat is added to a block of ice that is colder than 0°C, the temperature of the ice will increase until it reaches 0°C, its *melting point*. Then the temperature will stop increasing for a time, even though more heat flows into the ice. The additional heat will increase the disorder of the molecules in the ice and cause the ice to melt.

Heat of Fusion. Until all the ice has melted, the water will remain at 0°C. The latent heat needed to change ice to water is called the *heat of fusion*. The heat of fusion for ice at 0°C is 1,440 cal/mol (80 cal/g). This amount of energy will melt the ice to water at 0°C.

The temperature does not change when a well-crystallized solid is melted because heat is required to break up the structure of the solid and this structure comes apart only all at one time. This is called a *phase transition*.

Heat of Evaporation. The concept of a phase transition also applies to a liquid changing into a gas. The *heat of evaporation* for liquid water going to gaseous water at 100°C is 9,730 cal/mol (540 cal/g).

This is so much larger than the heat of fusion because all the forces holding the liquid together have to be overcome to free the water molecules, while the melting of a solid only has to break up a few of these forces.

Solution:

1. *Convert to moles.* The molar mass of water is 18.02 g/mol. The number of moles in 10.0 g of ice is 10.0 g/18.0 g/mol = 0.555 mol.

2. *Calculate calories.* Since the heat of fusion is 1,440 cal/mol, it will require 1,440 cal/mol × 0.555 mol = 800 cal to melt this ice.

3. *Factor in specific heat capacity.* Each gram of liquid water at 20°C adds 20 calories to the ice as its temperature lowers to 0°C.

4. *Divide the two.* Since it will take 800 cal of energy to melt 10.0 g of ice, divide 800 cal by 20 cal/g to get a total of 40.0 g of water to melt the ice.

5. *Add the total.* Once the 40.0 g of water has melted the 10.0 g of ice, the final amount of water at 0°C is 50.0 g.

Bond Energy and Thermodynamics

Bond-Dissociation Energy

Bond-dissociation energy is a measure of the strength of a chemical bond. It measures how much energy is needed to break a molecular bond.

- From the table to the right it can be seen that single bonds often require about 400 kJ/mol (about 100 kcal/mol) to break.

- The double bonds in oxygen and carbon dioxide are a little stronger.

- The triple bonds in dinitrogen and carbon monoxide are even stronger.

- It is generally true that bonds between unlike atoms are stronger than bonds between atoms of the same kind.

- American chemist Linus Pauling ascribed this to differences in the electronegativity of the unlike atoms.

Electronegativity measures how strongly an atom attracts the shared pair of electrons in a covalent bond. In any such bond, the more electronegative atom will pull on the shared electrons more strongly than the less electronegative atom.

BOND-DISSOCIATION ENERGIES

The bond that is broken is indicated by the bond dashes. The rest of the molecule (to the left of the dashes) is left intact.

Bond-Dissociation Energies (in kilojoules per mole)	
Bond	**Energy**
C-H	335
CH-H	418
CH2-H	469
CH3-H	426
H-H	432
O-H	424
HO-H	495
O=O	494
N≡N	942
C≡O	1070
OC=O	528
H-Cl	428
Cl-Cl	239
F-F	155

Spotlight on... LINUS PAULING

Linus Pauling (1901–1994) was an American chemist who won two Nobel Prizes, the 1954 Nobel Prize in Chemistry and the 1962 Nobel Peace Prize.

Pauling won the chemistry prize for his research on the nature of chemical bonds. He showed that a knowledge of the way atoms are linked helps explain the structure of complex molecules.

Pauling combined theories of quantum mechanics and the ways in which atoms share and exchange electrons to calculate the energies that bind atoms, the distances between the atoms, and the angles at which the bonds form.

Bond-Dissociation Calculation

Carbon monoxide (CO) is a stable molecule with a high bond-dissociation energy of 528 kJ/mol. It reacts with oxygen gas (O_2) to produce carbon dioxide. How much energy is released by the formation of CO_2 from CO and O_2?

The chemical equation for the reaction is:

$$2CO + O_2 \rightarrow 2CO_2$$

The addition of an oxygen atom to CO to produce CO_2 will release 528 kJ/mol of energy as shown in the table. It requires 494 kJ/mol of energy to separate O_2 into individual oxygen atoms.

(2 mol x 528 kJ/mol) − (1 mol x 494 kJ/mol) = 562 kJ

562 kJ of energy would be released by the formation of two moles of CO_2 from two moles of CO and one mole of O_2.

LAWS OF THERMODYNAMICS

There are four laws of thermodynamics, two of which can be considered the main principles.

First Law of Thermodynamics. The law of conservation of energy states that energy is never created or destroyed. Energy may change form, for example, from internal energy to mechanical motion. But the total quantity of energy in any system, or set of parts forming a whole, remains the same.

Second Law of Thermodynamics. All natural events act to increase the entropy within a system. Entropy is a measure of the amount of disorder or randomness in a system. Until a system reaches its maximum entropy, it can do useful work. But as a system does work, its entropy increases until the system can no longer perform work.

Thermodynamics

Thermodynamics is the study of forms of energy, such as heat and work, and of the conversion of energy from one form into another. (See also pages 790–791.)

- Engineers and physicists use the principles of thermodynamics in understanding events in nature and in such activities as designing machines.
- Chemists can use thermodynamics to calculate the loss or gain of energy in chemical reactions.

Exothermic reactions are chemical reactions in which heat is released.

Endothermic reactions are chemical reactions in which heat is absorbed. The property that allows an endothermic reaction to take place is *entropy*, which is a measure of the amount of disorder or randomness in a system.

Heat and Entropy. Most chemical reactions have a balance of heat and entropy. Sometimes they work together and sometimes they oppose each other in determining how far a reaction can proceed.

For example, when sodium chloride (NaCl) is dissolved in water, little or no heat is given off, but the chemical reaction still takes place. This is because the solvent—the water—offers the NaCl freedom to move around, increasing the entropy in the reaction. When sufficient NaCl has dissolved that the entropy is no longer increasing, the reaction will stop.

SOLUTIONS

A *solution* is a homogeneous mixture of two or more individual substances that cannot be separated by a mechanical means, such as through a filter. A homogenous substance is one that is uniform throughout.

Solutions are found throughout nature: air is a solution; the oceans are solutions; even rain is a solution. Most chemical reactions take place in solution. Many processes necessary for life rely on solutions, such as circulation, which carries oxygen in the blood to all parts of the body.

▲ **Crystallization,** the process by which matter forms crystals, can occur once a solution has passed the saturation point.

Dissolving Substances

A solution occurs when one substance *dissolves* in another, such as when sugar dissolves in coffee. Solutions consist of *solvents* and *solutes*.

- A solvent is the substance that causes another substance to dissolve.
- A solute is the substance that is dissolved.

Generally, the solute is the substance present in a relatively small amount, and the solvent is the medium in which the solute is dissolved. In the above example, coffee is the solvent and sugar is the solute.

The two or more substances that make up a solution may be gases, liquids, or solids. When solids or gases are dissolved in liquids, the solid or gas is said to be the solute and the liquid is the solvent.

Concentration

Solutions contain differing amounts of solutes and solvents. A solution's *concentration* is the amount of solute present in a given amount of solution.

- A *concentrated* solution has a relatively large quantity of solute per unit amount of solution.
- A *dilute* solution has a relatively small quantity of solute per unit amount of solution.
- *Solubility* is the measure of how much solute dissolves in a given amount of solvent at a given temperature.

SOLUTIONS AND OTHER MIXTURES

A *mixture* is two or more substances mixed together, but not chemically combined. For instance, water is not a mixture, because even though it consists of hydrogen and oxygen, the two elements are combined chemically. Seawater is a mixture, because even though salt and other substances dissolve in water, they do not combine chemically.

A mixture can be *homogeneous* or *heterogeneous*. A homogeneous mixture is uniform throughout, like a solution. A heterogeneous mixture is one that consists of two or more easily identifiable substances.

- sugar dissolved in water is a homogeneous mixture
- sand mixed in water is a heterogeneous mixture

Forming Solutions

A solution is formed when one substance disperses uniformly throughout another substance. This process involves three distinct steps.

1. the separation of solute molecules

2. the separation of solvent particles

3. the mixing of solvent and solute molecules so that the solute particles occupy positions that are normally taken by solvent molecules

Solubility. The ease with which a solute particle may replace a solvent molecule depends on the relative strengths of the interactive forces between the solute and solute, the solute and solvent, and the solvent and solvent.

- If the solute-solvent attraction is stronger than the solvent-solvent attraction, then the solute will dissolve readily.

- If the solute-solvent forces are weaker than the other forces, then only a relatively small amount of the solute will dissolve.

Temperature and pressure also have an effect on solubility.

As temperature increases . . .	Solubility
For most solids	increases
For most gases	decreases
As pressure increases . . .	**Solubility**
For gases	increases

SATURATION

Once a solution has reached a point where no more solute can be dissolved in it at the same temperature and pressure, it is *saturated*. For instance, if you add more salt to a saturated solution of water and salt, it will not dissolve. Instead the extra salt will settle on the bottom of the container as a solid.

CONCENTRATION UNITS

Quantitative study of a solution requires knowing the solution's concentration. Chemists use several different concentration units. The choice of concentration unit is generally based on the kind of measurement made of the solution.

Percent by weight is the percentage of mass of a component of a solute in a given mass of the solution.

$$\% \text{ by weight of solute} = \frac{\text{grams solute}}{\text{grams solution}} \times 100$$

Mole fraction (X) is the ratio of the number of moles of a component to the total number of moles of all the components.

$$X = \frac{\text{moles component}}{\text{moles all components}}$$

Molarity (M) is the number of moles of solute in a liter of solution.

$$M = \frac{\text{moles solute}}{\text{liters solution}}$$

Molality (m) of a solution is the number of moles of solute in a kilogram of solvent.

$$m = \frac{\text{moles solute}}{\text{kilograms solvent}}$$

Solution Calculations

Molality and Molarity

The two most common ways to express the concentration of a solution are

- *molal*
- *molar*

The molal unit is the number of moles of solute dissolved in a kilogram of solvent. If two moles of solute are dissolved in 0.5 kilograms of solvent, then the solution is four molal, or 4 m. This value does not change with temperature.

The molar unit is the number of moles of solute in a liter of solution. If two moles of solute are dissolved in enough solvent to make the final volume of the solution 0.5 liters, then the solution is four molar, or 4 M.

Since the density of water is close to 1 kg/L, these two concentrations have about the same amount of solute present in aqueous solutions, but the molarity value does change with temperature, and at high concentrations these two values may differ considerably.

SVANTE ARRHENIUS

In 1884, Swedish chemist Svante Arrhenius presented the theory of *electrolytic dissociation* as his doctoral thesis at Uppsala University.

Electrolytic dissociation states that sodium chloride and similar salts form ions when they are dissolved in water. Arrhenius's work won him the Nobel Prize in Chemistry in 1903.

Electrolytic Dissociation

Svante Arrhenius's theory of electrolytic dissociation, or *ionization,* explains why some solutions conduct electricity. The theory states that sodium chloride and similar salts form ions when they are dissolved in water.

Conductivity. The ability of a solution to conduct electric current depends on the concentration of ions in the solution. For example, drinking water drawn from a typical municipal treatment plant in the United States contains few ions and therefore is a poor conductor of current. But seawater, with significant amounts of dissolved ionic compounds, is a good conductor.

Freezing Point Depression. When an aqueous solution freezes, the ice that is formed consists of pure ice and is free of the ions dissolved in the solution. For example, the large icebergs found in the sea near the North and South poles are pure water.

When a substance dissolves in water, it lowers the *vapor pressure,* or escaping tendency, of the water in solution. At 0°C, the vapor pressures of pure liquid water and ice are equal.

In order to form ice from a solution, the temperature must be lowered below 0°C to make the vapor pressures equal again. The number of degrees that the temperature must be lowered depends on the concentration of the ions in the solution. This drop in temperature is called the *freezing point depression*.

IONS

Ions are atoms or molecules that have an electric charge from gaining or losing electrons. (See page 315.)

- If the number of electrons around an atom's nucleus equals the number of protons inside the nucleus, the atom is neutral.
- The process of removing electrons from atoms or molecules to produce positive ions is called ionization.
- The electrons removed may then join other atoms or groups of atoms, causing them to become negative ions.
- The number of electrons gained or lost by the atom or molecule determines the amount of electric charge of an ion.

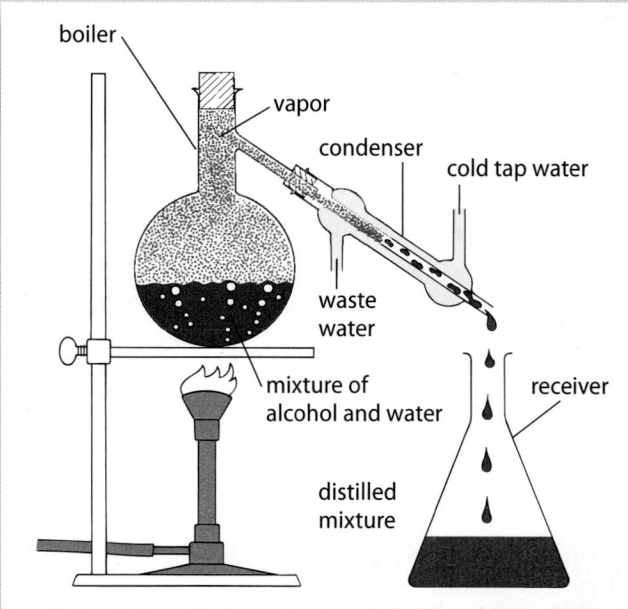

boiler

vapor

condenser

cold tap water

waste water

mixture of alcohol and water

receiver

distilled mixture

DISTILLATION

Distillation is a process that separates a substance or a mixture of substances from a solution through vaporization. Distillation usually involves boiling a liquid and condensing the vapor that forms.

Distillation is carried out in an apparatus called a *still.* The mixture to be vaporized is heated in a *boiler.* Whichever substance in the mixture boils at the lowest temperature will be the first to turn into vapor. The vapor enters the *condenser,* where it cools and becomes liquid again. The distilled liquid, called the distillate, then collects in the *receiver.*

◀ **A still** consists of a boiler, a condenser, and a receiver.

Calculating Concentration and Freezing Point Depression

1. **Molality and Molarity.** A chemist dissolved 1.11 g of $CaCl_2$ in 50.0 g of water. The density of this solution was determined to be 1.016 g/mL at about 20°C. What are the molality and molarity of this solution? The molecular weight of $CaCl_2$ is 111 g/mol.

Molality:
$moles\ of\ CaCl_2 = 1.11\ g/111\ g/mol = 1.00 \times 10^{-2}\ mol$
$kg\ of\ water = 50.0\ g/1000\ g/kg = 5.00 \times 10^{-2}\ kg$
$molality\ of\ CaCl_2\ solution = 1.00 \times 10^{-2}\ mol/5.00 \times$
$10^{-2}\ kg = 0.200\ m$

Molarity:
$volume\ of\ the\ solution = (50.0\ g\ H_2O +$
$1.11\ g\ CaCl_2)/1.016\ g/mL = 50.3\ mL = 5.03 \times 10^{-2}\ L$
$molarity\ of\ CaCl_2\ solution = 1.00 \times 10^{-2}\ mol/5.03 \times$
$10^{-2}\ L = 0.199\ M$

2. **Freezing Point Depression.** Chemists have shown through theory and experiment that the freezing point of water is depressed by 1.86° when the solution contains 1 m of a species in solution. A 1-m solution of NaCl contains 1 m of Na^+ and 1 m of Cl^-. As a result of ionization, a 1-m NaCl solution will depress the freezing point of water by 2 × 1.86° = 3.72°. What will be the freezing point depression of the $CaCl_2$ solution from the previous problem?

The $CaCl_2$ solution has a molality of 0.200 m. Because of ionization the total concentration of all the species in solution is 3 × 0.200 m = 0.600 m. The resulting freezing point depression will be:

freezing point depression = 0.600 m × 1.86°/m = 1.12°

ACIDS AND BASES are

two types of chemical compounds characterized by their opposite effects in certain physical and chemical properties and their ability to neutralize each other in a chemical reaction.

Many acids occur naturally and some are essential for life. For example, hydrochloric acid (HCl) is produced in the stomach of most people and helps digestion. But many acids are poisonous, and strong acids can cause severe burns.

Bases have many practical uses. For example, magnesium hydroxide ($Mg(OH)_2$) is often used as an ingredient in antacids.

▲ **Carbonic acid** (H_2CO_3) is an acid that forms when rainwater absorbs carbon dioxide in the soil. Over long periods of time, the acid removes calcium carbonate from limestone underground, forming magnificent caves.

Over the years, scientists have tried to explain the fact that all acids and bases show certain characteristic properties. Two important theories that explain these properties are

- the Arrhenius theory
- the Brønsted-Lowry theory

The Arrhenius Theory

In 1884, the Swedish chemist Svante Arrhenius observed that all substances classified as acids contain hydrogen ions, H^+, and that all substances known as bases contain the hydroxide ion, OH^-.

An *Arrhenius acid* was thus identified as a substance whose water solution contains a high concentration of hydrogen ions.

An *Arrhenius base* was identified as a substance whose water solution contains a high concentration of hydroxide ions.

Properties of:	
Acid	**Base**
have a sour taste and produce a prickling or burning sensation if they come into contact with the skin	react with an acid to decrease or neutralize its acidic properties
dissolve many metals	are also called *alkalis*
turn blue litmus paper red	turn red litmus paper blue
are neutralized by bases	feel slippery and taste bitter when dissolved in water

USEFUL AND CORROSIVE

One of the most important commercial chemicals is sulfuric acid (H_2SO_4). It is a colorless, dense, oily liquid that is extremely corrosive.

Sulfuric acid is one of the strongest acids. It can burn the skin and irritate the lining of the nose, trachea, and lungs.

The Brønsted-Lowry Theory

In 1923, chemists Johannes Brønsted and Thomas Lowry independently announced a new acid-base theory. They theorized that an acid-base reaction is a proton-transfer reaction in which a proton (a hydrogen ion) is transferred from the acid to the base.

Receivers and Donors. According to this theory, a *Brønsted acid* can be defined as a proton donor, and a *Brønsted base* is a proton acceptor. The general equation for a Brønsted-Lowry reaction is

$$B + HA < \rightleftharpoons > HB^+ + A^-$$

- In this equation, B is the base proton receiver and HA is the acid proton donor.
- Notice that if this reaction is reversed, then A^- is the base and HB^+ is the acid.
- Combinations such as the acid HA and the base A^- that result from an acid losing a proton or a base gaining one are called *conjugate acid-base pairs*.

Common Acids and Their Conjugate Bases	
Acid	**Base**
Hydrochloric acid (HCl)	Chloride ion (CL–)
Nitric acid (HNO_3)	Nitrate ion (NO_3–)
Hydrocyanic acid (HCN)	Cyanide ion (CN–)
Perchloric acid ($HClO_4$)	Perchlorate ion (ClO_4–)
Sulfuric acid (H_2SO_4)	Hydrogen sulfate ion (HSO_4–)

Sulfuric acid is used

- in the manufacture of fertilizer.
- in the refining of petroleum.
- in the production of such items as automobile batteries, explosives, pigments, iron and other metals, and paper pulp.
- to make alcohol from ethylene.
- to make sulfonates, which are used in powerful detergents.
- in making some dyes and medicines.

Strengths of Acids and Bases

According to the Brønsted-Lowry theory, the strength or weakness of different acids and bases is a measure of their tendency to lose or gain protons.

Acid Strength

- A strong acid donates protons easily.
- A weak acid clings to its protons.

Base Strength

- A strong base has a strong attraction for protons.
- A weak base has a weak attraction for protons.

Conjugate Base Strength. In addition, the strengths of conjugate acid-base pairs are related.

- the stronger the acid, the weaker its conjugate base
- the weaker the acid, the stronger its conjugate base

SALT FORMATION

Salts are formed from the reaction of acids and bases. At one time, salts were considered to be neither acidic nor basic, but it turns out salts formed from weak acids are actually weak bases. An example is Na_3PO_4, or *trisodium phosphate* (TSP), which is so basic that its solutions are used to clean floors.

▲ **Trisodium Phosphate.** Poultry processors dunk chickens into water containing TSP to lessen the risk of salmonella.

The pH Scale

Chemists use a scale called the pH scale to measure the acidity and alkalinity (quality of being a base) of a substance. Knowing the pH measurement of a substance is important in many fields, such as farming. It is essential for farmers to know the pH value of the soil and what can be done to control or modify that value. It determines the type of crops that can be grown.

Equilibrium Constant and pH

Water spontaneously ionizes into H^+ and OH^- ions. The product of the concentrations of these ions is called the *equilibrium constant* for the ionization of water. This constant is given the symbol K_w. At 25°C:

$$K_w = [H^+][OH^-] = 1.0 \times 10^{-14}$$

In this formula, the $[H^+]$ and $[OH^-]$ are the concentrations of the hydrogen ion and the hydroxide ion, respectively.

- Theoretically, the concentrations of H^+ and OH^- are equal in pure water.
- If the concentrations are equal, the water or aqueous solution is said to be *neutral*.
- If $[H^+]$ is greater than $[OH^-]$, the solution is *acidic*.
- If $[H^+]$ is less than $[OH^-]$, the solution is *basic*.

CALCULATING pH

If enough base is added to a solution to make the concentration of the hydroxide ion equal 0.020 M, what would be the pH of this solution?

Using the equilbrium constant:

$$K_w = [H^+][OH^-] = 1.0 \times 10^{-14}$$

then, substitute 0.020 M for $[OH^-]$:

$$[H^+] = 10^{-14}/0.020\ M = 5.0 \times 10^{-1}$$
$$pH = -\log[H^+] = -\log(5.0 \times 10^{-13}) = 12.3$$

From the pH scale, you can see that this solution is highly basic.

The pH of a solution is equal to the negative logarithm of the hydrogen ion concentration:

$$pH = -\log[H^+]$$

- Most solutions have a pH range of 0 to 14.
- Solutions with pH less than 7 are acidic.
- Solutions with pH greater than 7 are basic.
- Solutions with pH equal to 7 are neutral.

THE pH SCALE

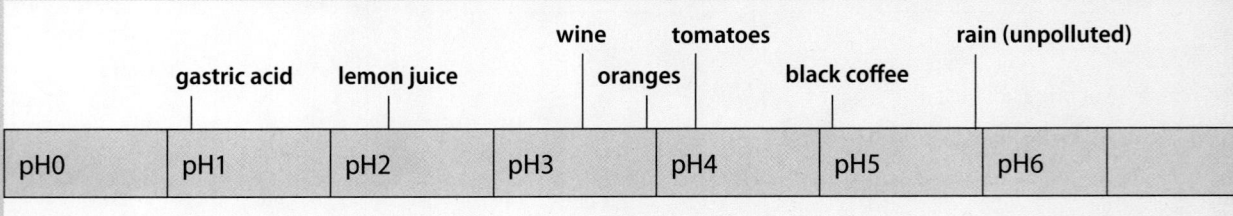

	gastric acid	lemon juice		wine	oranges	tomatoes	black coffee		rain (unpolluted)	
pH0	pH1	pH2	pH3		pH4		pH5	pH6		

ACID

Acid Dissociation Constant

Each acid has its own constant, called the *acid dissociation constant,* which is a measure of the acid's strength. This constant is given the symbol K_a. For acid *HA,* made up of the ions H^+ and A^-, you can determine the strength using the following equilibrium constant expression:

$$K_a = \frac{[H^+][A^-]}{[HA]}$$

The values for these dissociation constants can vary a great deal, but for sulfuric acid (HSO_4^-), it is close to 10^{-2}; for a very weak acid such as HPO_4^{2-} it is 10^{-12}. For the common organic acid, acetic acid (CH_3COOH), $K_a = 1.8 \times 10^{-5}$.

Weak Acids and Buffers. In many cases, it is important to keep the pH independent of dilution or small additions of acids or bases. This is done by using a *buffer* to keep the $[H^+]$ nearly constant. A buffer is a solution with similar amounts of a weak acid, HA, and its conjugate base, A^-, both present in solution. The hydrogen ion concentration can be solved using the following equation:

$$[H^+] = K_a \frac{[HA]}{[A^-]} = K_a \frac{[\text{weak acid}]}{[\text{conjugate base}]}$$

PH OF BLOOD

The weak acid that determines the pH of blood is carbonic acid (H_2CO_3), formed by dissolved CO_2 gas. The conjugate base of the CO_2 in blood plasma is a hydrogen carbonate ion (HCO_3^-) that comes from the kidneys.

Direct chemical analysis determined that the concentrations in the blood plasma of a person at rest were:

$$[H_2CO_3] = 1.3 \times 10^{-3} \text{ M}$$
$$[HCO_3^-] = 26 \times 10^{-3} \text{ M}$$

If $K_a = 8.1 \times 10^{-7}$ for carbonic acid in blood plasma at 37°C, what is the normal pH of blood?

$$[H^+] = 8.1 \times 10^{-7} \times 1.3 \times 10^{-3}/26 \times 10^{-3} = 4.1 \times 10^{-8}$$
$$pH = -\log[H^+] = -\log[4.1 \times 10^{-8}] = 7.4$$

If a person hyperventilates (that is, quickly breathes too hard while at rest), too much CO_2 gas is removed, and before the kidneys can respond, the pH may increase by 0.2 units. This results in fainting.

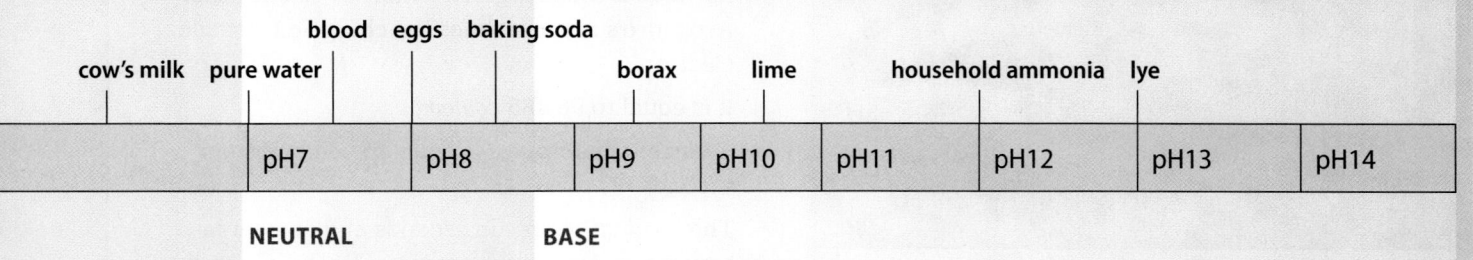

ELECTROCHEMISTRY

is a science that deals with chemical reactions that involve electricity.

Scientists can use electrochemical reactions to do useful work, such as running a motor with a battery. In addition to batteries, electrochemistry produces chemicals that are otherwise very difficult to prepare. Electrochemistry is also used to protect the surface of metals.

Additionally, electrochemistry is a branch of thermodynamics that allows us to characterize elements and compounds as to their stability and ability to react with other compounds.

Electrochemical Reactions

Most electrochemical reactions take place in a vessel that has two electrodes surrounded by an *electrolyte*. An electrolyte is a substance that conducts electricity.

Some electrochemical processes produce electricity from chemical changes, and others use electricity to produce chemical changes. Electrochemical processes are used

- to produce chemicals and electricity.
- to refinish and plate metals.
- to conduct research.

Electrochemical Cells

Any device that produces electricity from chemical reactions or produces chemical reactions using electricity is called an *electrochemical cell*. An electrochemical cell is formed by placing two *electrodes,* which are conductors of electricity, into a solution that has dissolved ions.

▲ **The corrosion of metals** in the presence of moisture is a naturally occurring electrolytic process. Electrochemists study corrosion to develop ways to protect metals.

Faraday Constant

Michael Faraday (1791–1867) was an English chemist and physicist who discovered the relationship between electricity and the combining power of an element. The *Faraday constant* is named after him. The Faraday constant allows one to determine the amount of electricity required to accomplish a certain amount of electrolysis.

- Its value is the charge on a mole of electrons, or Avogadro's number times the charge on a single electron
- It is equal to 96,485 *coulombs*
- A current in amperes is equal to coulombs per second
- The product of time in seconds and current in amperes gives the charge in coulombs, which has passed through an electrode.

Types of Cells. There are several types of electrochemical cells. A few of them are

- electrolysis cells
- galvanic (or voltaic) cells
- batteries
- fuel cells

Anodes and Cathodes. In electrochemical cells, one electrode, called the *anode,* has a chemical reaction at its surface where a chemical is oxidized and gives electrons to the electrode. The other electrode, the *cathode,* gives electrons to a chemical, which is reduced.

The functioning of an electrochemical cell can be illustrated through the process of *electrolysis,* in which an electric current passes through a liquid, causing chemical reactions to occur.

Electrolysis Calculation

Consider the electroplating of silver from the illustration at right. If the current produced by the battery through the cell is 0.100 amperes, how long would it take to electroplate 1.00 g of silver?

Moles of silver = 1.00 g/107.9 g/mol = 9.27
× 10^{-3} mol

Since the electroplating of one silver atom requires one electron, this value is also equal to the moles of electrons to pass through the cell.

Next, multiply moles by the Faraday constant:

9.27 × 10^{-3} mol × 96,485 coulombs/mol =
94 coulombs

The time required for 0.100 amperes to produce this charge is:

894/0.100 = 8,940 seconds (or 2 hours and 29 minutes)

HOW DOES THAT WORK ?

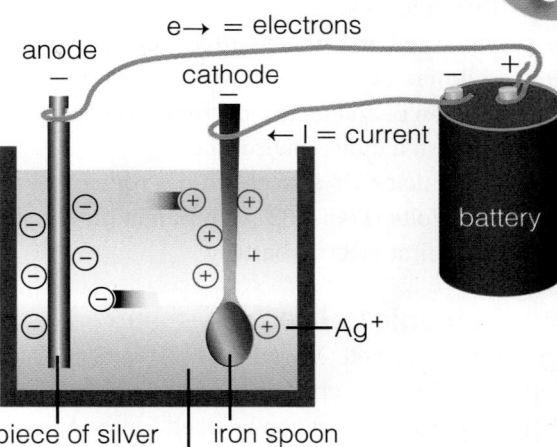

piece of silver | iron spoon
electrolyte of silver cyanide (AgCN)

ELECTROLYSIS

The above illustration shows how electrolysis is used to electroplate, or put a metallic coat on, an iron spoon. The spoon will be coated with silver.

- The electrodes are placed in a solution of silver cyanide (AgCN) and water.
- They are connected by wires to a direct current, in this case a battery.
- The cathode transfers electrons, which are negatively charged, from the battery into the electrolysis cell.
- The anode transfers electrons from the electrolysis cell back to the battery.
- This movement of electrons produces an electric current.
- Two chemical reactions take place, one at the anode and one at the cathode.
- At the anode, electrons are transferred from the ions in the AgCN solution and join the current flowing to the battery.
- At the cathode, electrons are transferred to the ions in the solution. This is called *reduction,* and it causes a chemical reaction that removes silver from the solution and causes it to form a thin layer of the metal on the cathode.
- The two chemical reactions are:

    anode $Ag \rightarrow Ag^+ + e^-$
    cathode $Ag^+ + e^- \rightarrow Ag$

Galvanic Cells

A *galvanic cell* is a type of electrochemical cell that converts chemical energy directly into electrical energy. The galvanic cell was named after Luigi Galvani (1737–1798), an Italian doctor. Galvani discovered *galvanism,* the production of an electric current from two metals in contact with a moist environment.

The galvanic cell is also called the *voltaic cell,* after Alessandro Volta (1745–1827), an Italian physicist who invented the first electric battery.

How Galvanic Cells Work

For a galvanic cell to produce a voltage, two solutions and two electrodes are needed. For a small voltage, the same metal can be used for the two electrodes and solutions can simply be of a different concentration.

To obtain more than about 0.1 volts, however, electrodes of different metals and solutions with different compositions must be used.

Zinc and Copper. For example, a galvanic cell could use zinc and copper as electrodes. Each galvanic cell has two half-reactions and a net cell reaction. A cell based on zinc and copper involves the two half-reactions:

$$\text{anode} \quad Zn \rightarrow Zn^{2+} + 2e^-$$

$$\text{cathode} \quad Cu^{2+} + 2e^- \rightarrow Cu$$

and the net cell reaction:

$$Cu^{2+} + Zn \rightarrow Cu + Zn^{2+}$$

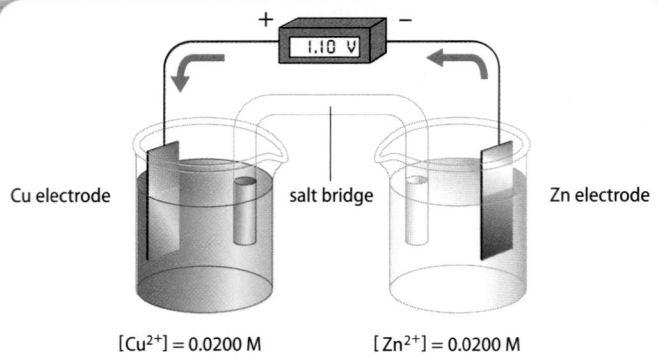

$[Cu^{2+}] = 0.0200 \text{ M}$ $\qquad$ $[Zn^{2+}] = 0.0200 \text{ M}$

▲ **A galvanic cell** with a salt bridge. The arrows indicate the flow of electrons.

Salt Bridge. The two halves of a galvanic cell are connected by a *salt bridge.* A salt bridge is usually a glass tube that is filled with a solution containing an *electrolyte,* or substance that conducts electricity.

In the above example, since Cu^{2+} is consumed, the solution at the cathode must contain a salt such as copper sulfate ($CuSO_4$). To obtain a stable voltage, the anode solution should be zinc sulfate ($ZnSO_4$).

The two solutions must be connected by a conductive solution in the salt bridge so that charge can flow between the two solutions, but the two solutions should not be allowed to easily mix. One can even use filter paper dampened with an inert salt instead of the fancy salt bridge.

The reason that the solution should not be allowed to mix is that the net cell reaction will spontaneously take place if the zinc electrode is exposed to Cu^{2+} ions.

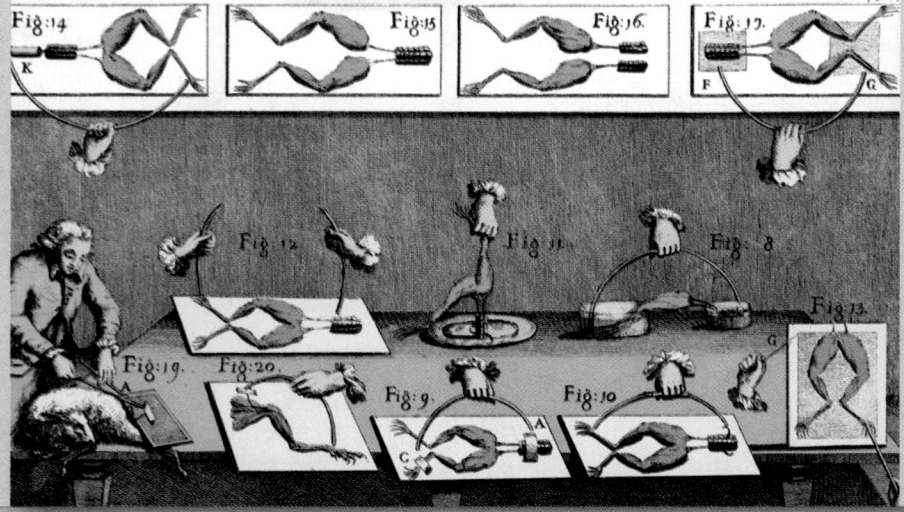

DISCOVERING GALVANISM

In 1771, Luigi Galvani found that the leg of a recently killed frog would twitch when touched with two different metals at the same time. He would insert brass hooks in the spinal cords of frogs (see left) and attach the hooks to an iron railing.

In the late 1790s, Alessandro Volta showed that chemical action occurs in a moist material in contact with two different metals. The chemical action results in an electric current. This current made Galvani's frog twitch.

Standard Reduction Potentials

If the solutions containing Cu^{2+} and Zn^{2+} have equal concentrations, the voltage measured has special significance:

$$\text{voltage} = \varepsilon°(Cu^{2+}/Cu) - \varepsilon°(Zn^{2+}/Zn)$$

The symbol $\varepsilon°$ designates the *standard reduction potentials* of the indicated half-reactions. The standard reduction potential is a quantitative measure of the relative ease of reduction in the half-reactions.

Determining the Difference. Measured voltages can only determine the difference between any pair of reduction potentials. Therefore, one reduction potential is taken as reference and its potential set as equal to zero. By custom, scientists use the (H^+/H_2) reduction potential as the zero reference.

Standard potentials are those potentials that would be measured for ideal 1-m solutions and with gases at 1 atm.

REDUCTION AND POTENTIAL

Reduction is a chemical reaction in which an atom or group of atoms gains one or more electrons. *Reduction potential* is a measure of the ease with which a given solution will gain electrons.

Reduction Potentials	$\varepsilon°$(volts)
$F_{2(g)} + 2e^- = 2F^-$	2.89
$MnO_4^- + 8H^+ + 5e^- = Mn^{2+} + 4H_2O$	1.51
$Cl_{2(g)} + 2e^- = 2Cl^-$	1.36
$O_{2(g)} + 4H^+ + 4e^- = 2H_2O$	1.23
$Fe^{3+} + e^- = Fe^{2+}$	0.77
$Cu^{2+} + 2e^- = Cu$	0.34
$2H^+ + 2e^- = H_{2(g)}$	0.00
$Ni^{2+} + 2e^- = Ni$	−0.24
$Zn^{2+} + 2e^- = Zn$	−0.76
$Mg^{2+} + 2e^- = Mg$	−2.36

Gibbs Free Energy

The voltage for the copper-zinc galvanic cell is a direct measurement of the tendency of the net reaction to take place at 25°C.

The thermodynamic term that describes this tendency is called *Gibbs free energy*. Gibbs free energy is a measurement that reflects both the heat involved in the reaction and the entropy change. Cell voltage is just another way to measure, and often to tabulate, this free energy change.

Oxidizing and Reducing Agents

In the table of reduction potentials below left, the oxidizing agents appear on the left side of the equations. The best oxidizing agents are at the top of the list.

Metals as reducing agents are on the right side of the equations. The most reactive are at the bottom of the list.

A positive voltage indicates that reduction is easy, at least compared to the hydrogen ion. Chemists have determined hundreds of reduction potentials. They can be used to predict the results of thousands of chemical reactions.

Reduction Potential Calculation

A cell was constructed from a Cu electrode in a 0.01-M $CuSO_4$ and an $\varepsilon°$ Fe electrode in a 0.01-M $FeSO_4$ with both solutions connected by a salt bridge.

The measured voltage was 0.78 V, and the Fe electrode was the negative one. What can be concluded about $\varepsilon°(Fe^{2+}/Fe)$?

Since the Fe electrode was negative, it must be generating electrons by making Fe^{2+} ions in solution.

- *Its half-reaction is $Fe = Fe^{2+} + 2e^-$*
- *The net cell reaction is: $Cu2+ + Fe = Cu + Fe2+$*
- *$0.78\ v = \varepsilon°(Cu2+/Cu) - \varepsilon°(Fe2+/Fe)$*

Since $\varepsilon°(Cu2+/Cu) = 0.34$ V, then:

$$\varepsilon°(Fe2+/Fe) = 0.34 - 0.78 = -0.44\ V$$

Batteries

A *battery* is an electrochemical cell that is similar to a galvanic cell. (See pages 392–393.) In fact, the term *battery* refers to a group of galvanic cells that convert chemical energy directly into electrical energy.

The First Batteries

Italian physicist Alessandro Volta (1745–1827) invented the battery in 1799. He stacked together alternating plates of silver and zinc separated by a material soaked in salt solution. The salted material acted as the salt bridge that allows an electric current to flow through a galvanic cell. Volta's invention was called the *voltaic pile*.

Gravity Cells. Voltaic piles were replaced by cells that used active solutions and metal electrodes. One of these was the *gravity cell*.

- Gravity cells consisted of a large glass container called a *battery jar*, a copper electrode on the bottom, and a zinc electrode mounted near the top.
- It had copper sulfate crystals on the bottom, and water was added to half fill the jar.
- A dilute solution of zinc sulfate was used to carefully fill the jar without mixing into the concentrated copper sulfate.
- The gravity cell could produce electricity until some of the lower copper sulfate diffused to the top to react with the zinc electrode.
- Such wet cell batteries were used to power the early telegraph system.

Dry Cells

The glass jar and acid in wet cell batteries made them inconvenient. In the 1860s, George Leclanché invented the *dry cell battery*, which made portable electrical devices practical.

Dry cells use a paste rather than a liquid as the electrolyte. They are commonly prepared with a metal electrode as an anode and a cathode formed by a conductive oxidizing agent supported on an inert conductor.

Advantages. Dry cell batteries have many advantages over wet cells.

- good shelf life
- no salt bridge
- work at any angle since the paste electrolyte will not pour
- truly portable

The voltaic pile, seen here demonstrated by Alessandro Volta, had a small current capacity since there was very little oxidizing agent present at the silver cathode, but it was the first practical means of generating electricity. ▼

HISTORICAL BATTERIES

1799 Alessandro Volta invents the voltaic pile.

1836 John F. Daniell, an English chemist, introduces a more efficient primary cell. The Daniell cell has two liquid electrolytes and produces a steadier current than Volta's device.

1859 French physicist Gaston Plante invents the first secondary, or rechargeable, battery, a lead-acid storage battery.

1860s French scientist Georges Leclanché invents an early carbon-zinc primary battery.

The **Leclanché dry cell** has a cylindrical zinc case for the negative electrode. The positive electrode is a carbon rod surrounded by the oxidizing agent—powdered manganese dioxide (MnO_2). The electrolyte is a paste of ammonium chloride (NH_4Cl).

This battery had several sizes called D, C, AA, and AAA. (The designations A and B were reserved for other types of cells.) Each cell produces 1.5 V. The cell reaction is:

$$Zn + 2NH_{4+} + 2MnO_2 \rightarrow Zn(NH_3)_2^{2+} + 2MnOOH$$

Alkaline Dry Cell. In the 1950s, an improved version of this cell was developed—the *alkaline dry cell*. Alkaline dry cells use potassium hydroxide (KOH)—an *alkaline,* or base—as an electrolyte instead of an acid. The alkaline dry cell

- is much better for high current usage than the ordinary dry cell.
- is described as an "inside out" dry cell, since powdered zinc is at the center and the manganese dioxide (MnO_2) is on the outer edges.

FUEL CELLS

A *fuel cell* is similar to a battery in that it converts chemical energy to electrical energy. However, a battery contains all of the parts required to produce electric power. A fuel cell must constantly be fed a fuel and an *oxidizer* to produce power. An oxidizer is a substance that removes electrons in a chemical reaction.

The ideal fuel cell would use a liquid fuel such as gasoline for a reducing agent and oxygen from air as the oxidizing agent. After a considerable amount of research, the only fuel cell that is currently used is based on hydrogen and oxygen.

Fuel cells are used in the space program, and scientists are working to make fuel cells that can be used in automobiles.

Rechargeable Cells

Another type of battery is a *rechargeable cell battery.* The oldest rechargeable battery is the *lead-acid battery,* which is the common storage battery used in automobiles. Lead-acid automobile batteries have

- six cells, each of which produces 2.2 V.
- 6 to 9 M sulfuric acid (H_2SO_4) for an electrolyte.
- lead electrodes: both electrodes are lead, but the cathode is coated in lead dioxide (PbO_2).
- electrodes turn into lead sulfate ($PbSO_4$) on discharge.

The lead-acid battery cell reaction:

$$Pb + PbO_2 + 2H_2SO_4 = 2PbSO_4 + H_2O$$

Danger of Explosion. Charging a lead-acid battery often produces hydrogen and the cathode and oxygen at the anode. This creates a risk of explosion when any rechargeable battery is being recharged.

Preventing Explosion. The nickel-cadmium cell is rechargeable and is popular because it uses lower current. Explosion is prevented with an extra large cathode so that hydrogen is not produced during recharging.

Lead-Acid Storage Battery

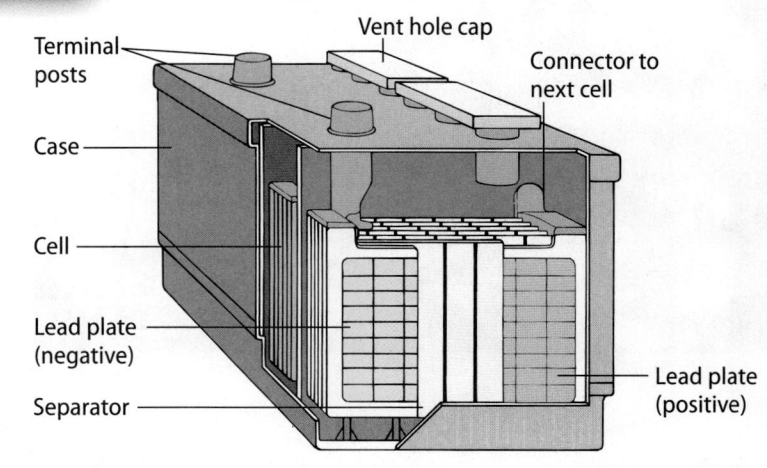

INORGANIC CHEMISTRY is the study of

the chemical elements and their compounds except for most carbon compounds. The compounds that contain carbon are called *organic compounds*.

Inorganic chemists make new compounds, determine the arrangement of atoms in inorganic compounds, and study how these compounds react with each other. There are more than 100 elements, and their reactions with each other can produce millions of compounds.

Oxidation. The sulfur dioxide that pollutes the air over an oil refinery forms from the oxidation half-reaction of the redox reaction. ▼

Oxidation and Reduction

Many of the reactions of inorganic chemistry are known as *oxidation-reduction reactions*. Oxidation-reduction reactions, or *redox reactions*, involve two processes: oxidation and reduction—the loss and gain of electrons.

The Redox Process

These two processes always go on simultaneously. When one substance is oxidized, another must be reduced. All reactions of the types known as direct combination, decomposition, and single replacement are oxidation-reduction reactions.

Half-Reactions. When metallic and nonmetallic elements join together to form ionic compounds, the overall reactions can be considered as two separate steps—the loss of an electron by the metal, and the gain of an electron by the nonmetal.

Each of these reactions is called a *half-reaction*. Redox reactions involve two separate half-reactions.

- *oxidation reaction,* a chemical reaction in which a substance loses electrons
- *reduction reaction,* a chemical reaction in which a substance gains electrons

When the two half-reactions are combined, the result is an oxidation-reduction reaction.

Equal Loss. The total number of electrons lost by the reducing agent must equal the number of electrons gained by the oxidizing agent. For example, during the formation of magnesium oxide (MgO), there are two half-reactions: Mg loses two electrons to become Mg^{2+} and O gains two electrons to become O^{2-}.

In this case, Mg is oxidized and is the *reducing agent* because it loses two electrons. O is reduced and is the *oxidizing agent* because it accepts two electrons.

Oxidation Numbers

In some redox reactions, it is very easy to determine which substance has gained electrons and which has lost electrons. But many redox reactions are not so readily analyzed.

For this reason, chemists have created a form of "electron bookkeeping" to keep track of electrons in chemical reactions. This "bookkeeping" is accomplished by using *oxidation numbers,* which are numbers assigned to each element in a compound, ion, or elemental species based on the following rules:

- When using oxidation numbers, oxidation is an increase in oxidation number, and reduction is a decrease in oxidation number.

- The oxidation number of any uncombined element is 0.

- The oxidation number of a monoatomic ion is the same as the charge on the ion.

- The oxidation number of combined oxygen is -2, except in peroxide (-1), and superoxides ($-1/2$).

- The oxidation number of combined hydrogen is $+1$, except in hydrides (-1).

- The oxidation number of combined fluorine is -1.

- In any molecular or ionic species, the sum of the oxidation numbers of all atoms in the formula unit is equal to the charge on the species.

BALANCING REDOX REACTIONS

There are two main ways to balance redox reactions: the *oxidation-number method* and the *half-reaction method.*

Oxidation-Number Method. This method of balancing redox reactions is based on identifying and following changes in oxidation numbers. The procedure involves the following steps.	**Half-Reaction Method.** In this method, the overall equation is divided into two reactions—one for oxidation and one for reduction. The equations for the two half-reactions are balanced separately and then added to give the overall balanced equation. The steps for this method are as follows.
1. Write the overall unbalanced equation.	1. Write the overall unbalanced equation, then divide the overall reaction into two equations, one for oxidation and the other for reduction.
2. Assign oxidation numbers to the atoms in each element on both sides of the equation and determine which elements have been oxidized and which have been reduced.	2. Balance the atoms in each half-reaction that undergo oxidation or reduction, then balance the elements other than H and O.
3. Assign coefficients to make the total gain in oxidation numbers for the substances being oxidized equal to the total decrease in oxidation numbers for the substances being reduced.	3. Balance the O atoms by adding H_2O and balance the H atoms by adding H+. If the reaction is in a basic solution, then also add an OH− ion for every H+ ion. If H+ and OH− appear on the same side, combine the ion to form H_2O.
4. Balance the remaining atoms by inspection. For reactions in acidic solutions, add H+ or H_2O or both to the equation as needed. For reactions in basic solutions, add OH− or H_2O or both to the equation as needed.	4. Balance the charge on each side of the equation by adding e− to the side with the greater positive charge. If necessary, equalize the number of electrons by multiplying one or both half-reactions by the appropriate coefficients.
	5. Add the two half-reactions together and balance the final equation by inspection.

Inorganic Compounds

There are more than 100 elements, and their reactions with each other can produce millions of compounds. The organization of the periodic table can simplify any discussion of inorganic chemistry. (See pages 322–323.)

Main Group Elements

The elements in groups 1, 2, 13, 14, 15, 16, and 17 can be called the *main group elements*. The main group elements display a fairly predictable progression of chemical properties. They include:

- metals such as sodium (Na), calcium (Ca), and aluminum (Al).
- semimetals such as boron (B) and germanium (Ge).
- nonmetals such as sulfur (S) and chlorine (Cl).

Hydrogen is unique. Although it appears among the metals on the periodic table, chemists typically group it with the nonmetals.

Beryllium oxide is a white crystalline solid used as a heat-conducting electrical insulator in electronic devices and lasers. ▶

Group 1 Metals

The group 1 metals react vigorously with water, releasing H_2 and the metal hydroxide as products. Often, the H_2 is heated enough by the exothermic reaction to explode. Of the group 2 metals, only calcium and the elements below it react directly with water at room temperature.

Beryllium is unique in group 2. Its chemistry is often as close to that of aluminum (in group 13) as it is to magnesium, directly below it. This unique chemistry is due to the small size of the Be^{2+} ion.

Beryllium metal and its oxides are carcinogens and must be handled with great care.

Metal Oxides. When the group 1 metals are exposed to oxygen gas, they can form metal oxides such as sodium oxide (Na_2O), sodium peroxide (Na_2O_2), and sodium superoxide (NaO_2).

Ionic Compounds and Hydrides. Metals and nonmetals can directly react and form ionic bonds, yielding compounds such as sodium sulfide (Na_2S), calcium bromide ($CaBr_2$), and aluminum oxide (Al_2O_3).

Metals can also react with hydrogen and form compounds called *hydrides,* such as lithium hydride (LiH), which contain the hydride ion, H^-. The most popular hydrides for reducing-agent purposes are lithium aluminum hydride ($LiAlH_4$) and sodium borohydride ($NaBH_4$). They contain Li^+ and Na^+ ions, but the AlH_4^- and BH_4^- ions are covalently bonded.

This chemical reaction with oxygen gas is used in the commercial production of sodium peroxide and its acid—hydrogen peroxide (H_2O_2). The acid is most commonly available in a 3 percent H_2O_2 solution, which contains a stabilizing agent. Since H_2O_2 is −1 oxygen, it can either be oxidized to O_2 or reduced to H_2O. It has to be stabilized, for it can react with itself in an auto-oxidation-reduction reaction:

$$2H_2O_2 \rightarrow O_2 + 2H_2O$$

A number of things catalyze this reaction, such as hydrogen bromide (HBr), manganese dioxide (MnO_2), and blood. The 3 percent solution is a common antiseptic.

OXYACIDS AND OXYANIONS

Some of the most common forms of the nonmetals are their *oxyacids* and *oxyanions*. An oxyacid is simply an acid that contains oxygen. An oxyanion is an *anion*—a negatively charged ion of an element—that contains oxygen.

The acidity of oxyacids and oxyanions is related to the number of oxygens in the formula. Perchloric acid ($HClO_4$) is quite strong. Hypochlorous acid ($HClO$) is very weak. Sulfurous acid (H_2SO_3) has intermediate acid strength.

Some Oxyacids and Their Anions

Acid	Formula	Anion	Formula
Nitric	HNO_3	Nitrite	NO^{3-}
Nitrous	HNO_2	Nitrite	NO^{2-}
Sulfuric	H_2SO_4	Sulfate	SO_4^{2-}
Sulfurous	H_2SO_3	Sulfite	SO_3^{2-}
Thiosulfuric (unstable)	$H_2S_2O_3$	Thiosulfate	$S_2O_3^{2-}$
Perchloric	$HClO_4$	Perchlorate	ClO^{4-}
Chloric	$HClO_3$	Chlorate	ClO^{3-}
Chlorous	$HClO_2$	Chlorite	ClO^{2-}
Hypochlorous (unstable)	$HClO$	Hypochlorite	ClO^-

Nonmetals

The most important compounds formed by the nonmetals are their hydrides. All but water are gases.

- ammonia (NH_3)
- phosphine (PH_3)
- water (H_2O)
- hydrogen sulfide (H_2S)
- hydrogen fluoride (HF)
- hydrogen chloride (HCl)

Ammonia is a weak acid but a fairly good base. Hydrogen chloride is a strong acid and a very weak base. Water's intermediate position makes it both a weak acid and a weak base, which is important for its solvent properties.

Noble Gases

The first six elements in group 18 of the periodic table are called the *noble gases*. These elements are argon (Ar), helium (He), krypton (Kr), neon (Ne), radon (Rn), and xenon (Xe). They occur naturally and can be found in the atmosphere.

They are called *noble* or *inert* gases because they do not readily react with other elements. Unlike most gaseous elements, the noble gases are *monoatomic*—that is, they occur as single atoms instead of as molecules of two or more atoms.

The atoms have stable configurations (arrangements) of electrons. Therefore, under normal conditions, the atoms do not gain or lose electrons or share them with other elements. But most of the noble gases form certain compounds under specialized conditions.

Group 18 Compounds. In 1962, Neil Bartlett (1932–2008), a British chemist, prepared the first xenon compound. Since that time, more than 10 compounds formed between xenon and fluorine or oxygen have been prepared.

If a glass bulb is filled with F_2 and Xe and exposed to sunlight, in a few days white deposits of XeF_2 will appear on the walls. At low temperatures, krypton (Kr) compounds can also be prepared, but the relatively low ionization energy of xenon makes it unique for forming compounds.

XENON COMPOUNDS

Unstable xenon compounds
- xenon trioxide (XeO_3)
- xenon tetroxide (XeO_4)

Stable xenon compounds
- xenon difluoride (XeF_2)
- xenon tetrafluoride (XeF_4)
- xenon hexafluoride (XeF_6)

Transition and Lanthanide Metals

Transition Metals

The metallic chemical elements found in the center of the periodic table are called *transition metals*. (See pages 322–323.) These elements form a connection—or a transition—between the alkali metals and what are known as the *other metals*.

The transition metals include many commonly recognized metals, such as copper, gold, iron, nickel, and silver. They are generally considered to be the metals found in rows 4–7, groups 3–12 of the periodic table.

Orbital Filling. In groups 3 through 12, electrons are being added to fill the metals' d-orbitals. This produces a variety of oxidation states, but the 2+ and 3+ ions are the most common.

Starting with Ti^{3+}, the 4s orbitals are empty and only the 3d is being filled. This ends with Zn^{2+} where the 3d orbitals are filled with 10 electrons and the 4s is still empty.

This means that the order of the 4s and 3d orbitals is changed in transition metal ions over the order at potassium (K) and calcium (Ca). The filling of the 3d orbitals produces as many similar chemistries between adjacent transition metals as between those in the same group.

Molecular Compounds. The unique chemistry of the transition metals is that they can form complexes historically called *molecular compounds*. These complexes are transition metals or ions with coordinated molecules called *ligands*.

Examples of ligands are Cl^-, NH_3, CN^-, H_2O, and CO. They have lone pair electrons that can act as *Lewis bases*—or electron donors—to empty orbitals on the transition metal. Some of these complexes are

- $CuCl_4^{3-}$
- $Co(NH_3)_6^{3+}$
- $Fe(CN)_6^{4-}$
- $Cu(H_2O)_4^{2+}$
- $Fe(CO)_5$

Many follow the 18-electron rule to fill the 4s, 3d, and 4p orbitals.

Eighteen-Electron Rule. If we sum the number of valence electrons on the central atom or ion with 2 electrons donated from each ligand, it often equals 18. How does this check with the examples?

Cu^+ has 10 valence electrons, and if we add 8 from the four ligands, we obtain 18.

For the others, in order, we obtain 6 + 12 = 18, 6 + 12 = 18, 9 + 8 = 17, and 8 + 10 = 18.

FOLLOWING THE RULES

Ferrocene, $(C_5H_5)_2Fe$, is the most famous transition metal complex to follow the 18-electron rule. It can be considered as an Fe^{2+} between two $C_5H_5^-$ five-membered rings with the final complex looking like a sandwich. Ferrocene is used to improve the burning qualities of petroleum fuels.

Ferrocene

Fe^{2+}

Lanthanide Metals

The *lanthanides* are the 15 elements that follow the element barium in the periodic table. They are formed from filling the 4f orbitals.

In forming compounds, lanthanides tend to lose three electrons, gaining a 3+ charge. The exceptions are Ce^{4+} and Gd^{2+}, whose stability can be explained from the filling of the 4f orbitals.

Unlike the 3d orbitals, the 4f orbitals are somewhat obscured by the other electrons and participate little in bonding. Except for the ions with the unusual 2+ and 4+ charges, all the lanthanides have similar chemistry. They do have some unusual excited electronic states that are used in optical devices such as lasers.

Periodic Table of Elements

▲ **The lanthanides** and a group called the actinides are shown separate from the rest of the elements in the periodic table. If the rows were shown in place, the table would be too wide for easy display.

Coordination Compounds

One important class of inorganic compounds, called *coordination compounds,* contains a central metal atom surrounded by nonmetal atoms.

Hemoglobin, vitamin B_{12}, and chlorophyll are examples of coordination compounds. The central metal atom in hemoglobin is iron; in vitamin B_{12} it is cobalt; and in chlorophyll it is magnesium.

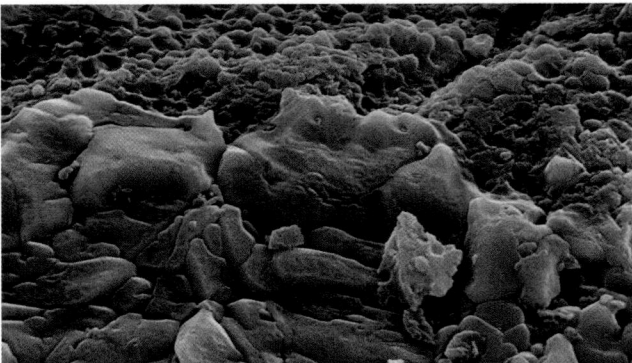

▲ **Hemoglobin,** the large, red molecule that carries oxygen in the blood, contains iron atoms, each of which is surrounded by nitrogen and oxygen atoms.

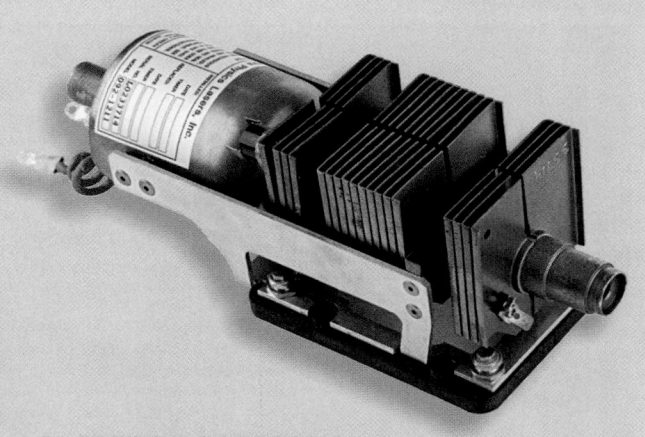

ELECTRON PATTERNS

The electrons in a lanthanide atom can exist in a complex pattern, enabling lanthanides to give off or absorb light in particular ways. For this reason, they appear in lasers and lenses. Other uses for them include magnets, pigments, lighters, and X-ray screens.

NUCLEAR CHEMISTRY

The reactions of both inorganic and organic chemistry involve changes that take place outside the nuclei of atoms. However, the nuclei of certain isotopes of many elements are unstable and break down; that is, they undergo *radioactive decay*.

Isotopes whose nuclei break down in this process are called *radioactive isotopes,* or *radio-isotopes*. When nuclei break down spontaneously, the process is called *natural radioactivity*. However, some nuclei can be made radioactive artificially, and they exhibit *induced radioactivity*.

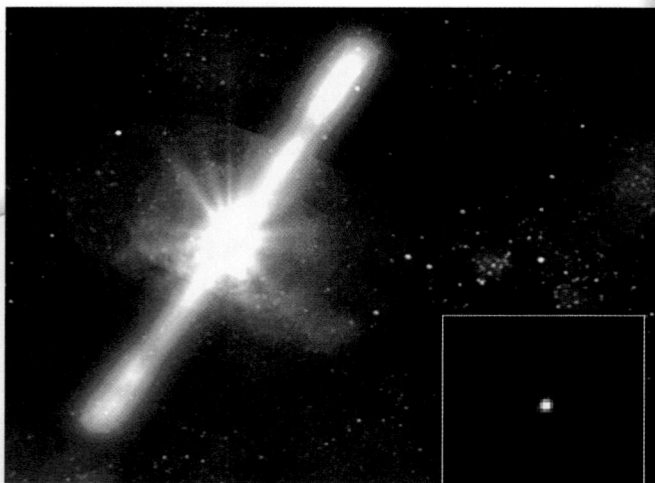

▲ **Gamma ray bursts** are huge explosions of gamma rays and X-rays in space. Even though they might take place billions of light years away, they are bright enough to be seen by telescopes.

Radioactivity

Radioactivity is the property of certain elements of giving off radiation through the breakdown of their nuclei. Radioactive atoms emit three types of radiation.

- *alpha particles*
- *beta particles*
- *gamma rays*

An alpha particle is made up of two protons and two neutrons and is therefore identical to the nucleus of a helium atom. As such, its symbol is ^4_2He, in which the four indicates the mass and the two indicates the atomic number.

Symbols used for isotopes of other elements are written in the same system for the purpose of representing nuclear reactions.

A beta particle is a high-speed electron given off by the nucleus of an atom. However, an atom's nucleus does not contain electrons, only protons and neutrons. (See pages 314–315.) Beta particles come from the breakdown of neutrons, each of which forms a proton and an electron in the process.

- A beta particle is very tiny—it has only about 1/1,840 the mass of a proton.
- Its high energy enables it to travel far in air and to pass through solid matter several millimeters thick.
- Scientists gauge a beta particle's energy by measuring how far it can penetrate certain substances.

Gamma rays, which often accompany the emission of alpha or beta particles, are a very penetrating form of radiant energy similar to X-rays. Gamma rays have a higher energy and a shorter wavelength than X-rays do, but the dividing line between the two forms of radiation is not clearly defined.

Uranium and other radioactive elements emit alpha particles or beta particles from their nuclei when they transform into new elements. An instant later, these nuclei may give off gamma rays.

REMEMBER THIS...

ISOTOPES

Sometimes the number of neutrons in atoms of the same element may vary. Consequently, these atoms have different masses. Atoms of the same element that differ in mass are known as *isotopes*.

Radioactive Elements

All the isotopes of every naturally occurring element with an atomic number above 83 are radioactive.

Transmutations. Radioactive elements undergo decay, usually in a series of reactions, some with the emission of an alpha particle and some with the emission of a beta particle, ending with the formation of a stable isotope of lead.

For example, uranium-238, that is, the isotope of uranium that has an atomic mass of 238, emits an alpha particle to form thorium-234, which, in turn, emits a beta particle to form protactinium-234. After a number of additional steps, the series ends with the formation of lead-206. Changes such as these, in which atoms of one element are converted into atoms of another element, are called *transmutations*.

The artificial transmutation of elements takes place as the result of the bombardment, in the laboratory, of certain atoms by particles such as alpha particles, protons, or neutrons. Ernest Rutherford, in 1919, carried out the first artificial transmutation, from stable nitrogen-14 to stable oxygen-17. (See page 855.)

Irène and Frédéric Joliot-Curie, in 1934, were the first scientists to produce, artificially, a radioactive isotope, starting with stable aluminum-27 and obtaining radioactive phosphorus-30. The phosphorus-30, having a half-life of only 3.55 minutes, was soon converted to stable silicon-30.

Neutron Bombardment. Today many radioisotopes are produced by bombardment of the same element with neutrons. These reactions occur without transmutation, since the atomic number, and thus the identity of the element, remains the same. Only the atomic mass changes.

Radioisotopes produced artificially exhibit induced radioactivity. They are used as tracers in chemical reactions, in medical diagnoses, and in industrial processes.

MARIE CURIE

1867–1934

Marie Curie was a French physicist and chemist who won two Nobel Prizes—one in the study of radiation and one for discovering new radioactive elements. She was the first woman to win a Nobel Prize and the first person to win two.

Curie and her husband, Pierre, worked together in the late 1890s. They studied the radiation given off by such chemical elements as uranium and thorium. In 1898, they announced their discovery of radium and polonium, two previously unknown highly radioactive elements.

Curie theorized that radioactivity was a property linked to individual atoms rather than one that depended on the arrangements of atoms in molecules. Previously, scientists had not known that atoms could change in any way.

Curie was the mother of Irène Joliot-Curie, discussed above.

RADIOCARBON DATING

Another example of a transmutation is the decay of carbon-14, which emits a beta particle, into nitrogen-14, which is stable. This nuclear reaction occurs naturally and is the basis for *radiocarbon dating,* a valuable technique for finding the age of objects containing carbon, such as wood, cloth, or paper.

- Organic objects, such as wood, cloth, or paper, start out with a certain proportion of radioactive carbon-14.

- By determining the proportion of carbon-14 to the total carbon content of an object, scientists can calculate the age of that object.

- In carrying out this calculation, the half-life of carbon-14 is used. The half-life is the period of time that it takes for half of the radioactive atoms in a substance to decay.

- The period of time it takes varies among different radioisotopes; for carbon-14, it is 5,730 years.

Nuclear Energy

Nuclear energy, also called *atomic energy,* is the powerful energy released by changes in the nuclei of atoms.

Nuclear Reactions

In a nuclear reaction, the total mass of the nuclei of the reactants is greater than the total mass of the nuclei of the products. Some mass appears to be lost, but in reality, the missing mass is converted into energy, according to Einstein's equation for the equivalence of mass and energy.

In this equation, $E = mc^2$, *m* stands for mass and *c* represents the velocity of light, a very large number. Thus, the amount of energy that is produced from the conversion of a small amount of mass is tremendous.

Nuclear reactions in atomic or *fission bombs,* in thermonuclear or *fusion bombs,* and in *thermonuclear fusion reactions* in the sun and other stars are remarkable for the spectacular amounts of energy that is released.

Two types of nuclear reactions that result in the release of enormous amounts of energy are

- *nuclear fission*
- *nuclear fusion*

Nuclear fission is the splitting of a heavy nucleus to produce lighter nuclei. (See page 860.)

Both the atomic fission bomb and the nuclear reactor use a fissionable isotope, such as uranium-235, as fuel. The uranium-235 captures a neutron, splits, and releases two or three neutrons, which can enter other uranium-235 nuclei, creating a chain reaction.

When materials are used to absorb some of the extra neutrons, the chain reaction is controlled, and energy is produced at a steady, slow rate. This takes place in a nuclear reactor that produces energy for conversion into electricity.

But when a critical mass of a fissionable isotope is present, the reaction is uncontrolled, and an explosion occurs. This takes place in a fission bomb.

Since the supply of naturally occurring fissionable isotopes is limited, a *breeder reactor* is used to produce fissionable materials. These reactors can produce new elements, such as plutonium, that do not exist in nature.

Particle Emission and Half-Lives

When a radioisotope decays, it may emit an alpha particle, a beta particle, or a positron. The half-lives of radioisotopes vary from very brief to very long periods of time. Some examples are listed here.

Radioisotope	Particle Emission	Half-Life
carbon-14	beta	5,730 years
cobalt-60	beta	5.3 years
iodine-131	beta	8.07 days
uranium-238	alpha	4.51×10^9 years
radium-226	alpha	1,620 years
potassium-42	beta	12.4 hours
francium-229	alpha	27.5 seconds
bismuth-212	alpha	60.5 minutes
silver-106	positron	24.5 minutes
yttrium-88	positron	2.0 hours
plutonium-239	alpha	24,000 years
lithium-8	beta	0.88 seconds
nitrogen-13	positron	9.93 minutes

Nuclear Chemistry Particles and Symbols

Particle	Symbol	Charge	Mass in Atomic Mass Units
beta particle (electron)	$_{-1}^{0}e$	negative	0 u
positron	$_{+1}^{0}e$	positive	0 u
proton (hydrogen-1 nucleus)	$_{1}^{1}H$	positive	1 u
alpha particle (helium-4 nucleus)	$_{2}^{4}He$	positive	4 u
neutron	$_{0}^{1}n$	neutral	1 u

Nuclear fusion is the combining of light nuclei to produce a heavier nucleus. (See page 861.)

Nuclear fusion has been carried out in the laboratory but not yet developed for the production of energy in a controlled reaction.

Fusion bombs have, however, been made with deuterium, or hydrogen-2, and tritium, or hydrogen-3, as the reactants. Because of the use of hydrogen isotopes in the fusion bomb, it has also been called the hydrogen bomb.

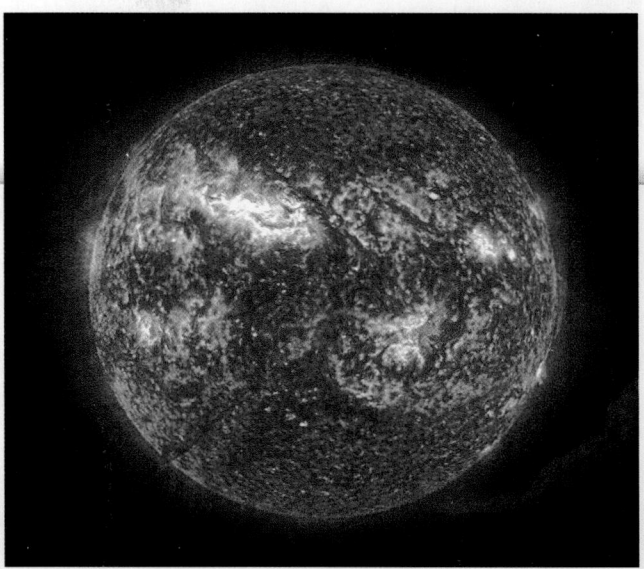

▲ **Fusion reactions,** or thermonuclear reactions, produce the energy of both the sun and the hydrogen bomb.

NUCLEAR FISSION AND CHAIN REACTION

- When a neutron traveling at the right speed strikes a uranium-235 nucleus at the right place, the nucleus splits into two smaller nuclei, krypton-92 and barium-141.

- Two or three neutrons and energy are also released in the reaction.

- Neutrons released when an atom of uranium-235 is split can strike other uranium-235 nuclei, which split and produce additional neutrons, and so on.

- The chain reaction is controlled if the mass of uranium-235 is below the critical mass.

EQUATION: $^{1}_{0}n + ^{235}_{92}U \rightarrow ^{92}_{36}Kr + ^{141}_{56}Ba + 3^{1}_{0}n + \text{energy}$

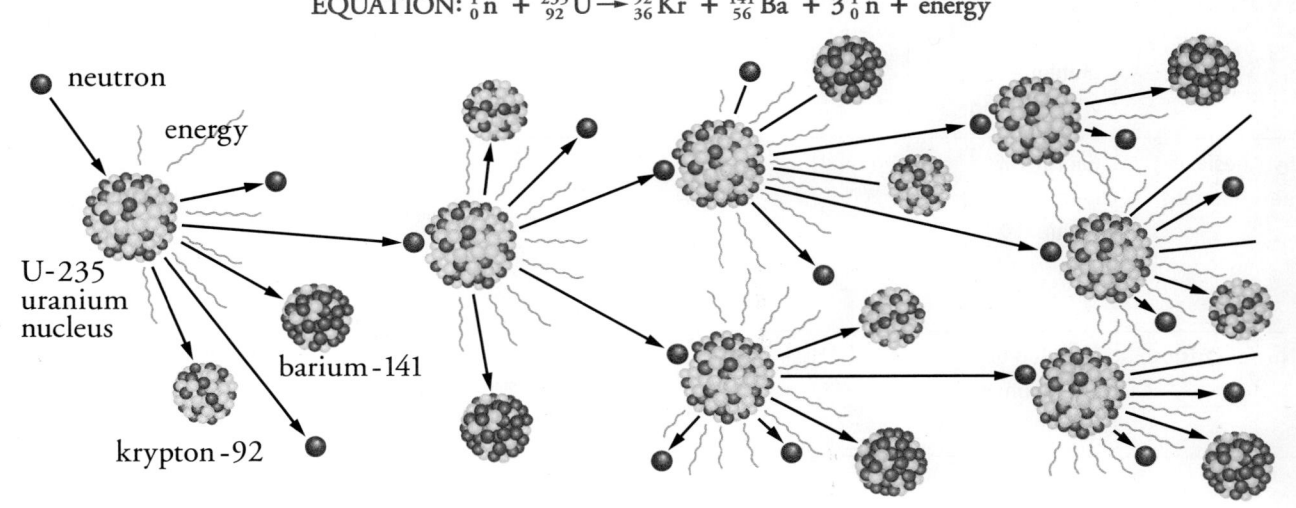

neutron

energy

U-235
uranium
nucleus

barium-141

krypton-92

Types of Nuclear Reactions

SOUTHWESTERN

		Some Types of Nuclear Reactions		
Type	**Example**	**Equation**		**Occurrence or Use**
Alpha decay	Emission of alpha particle by uranium-238	$^{238}_{92}\text{U}$ (uranium-238, radioactive) $\rightarrow$ $^{234}_{90}\text{Th}$ (thorium-234, radioactive) $+$ $^{4}_{2}\text{He}$ (alpha particle, helium-4)		Natural radioactivity
Beta decay	Emission of beta particles by thorium-234	$^{234}_{90}\text{Th}$ (thorium-234, radioactive) $\rightarrow$ $^{234}_{91}\text{Pa}$ (protactinium-234, radioactive) $+$ $^{0}_{1}-\text{e}$ (beta particle, electron)		Natural radioactivity
Beta decay	Emission of beta particle by carbon-14	$^{14}_{6}\text{C}$ (carbon-14, radioactive) $\rightarrow$ $^{14}_{7}\text{N}$ (nitrogen-14, stable) $+$ $^{0}_{1}-\text{e}$ (beta particle, electron)		Radiocarbon dating
Artificial transmutation	Bombardment of nitrogen-14 with alpha particle	$^{14}_{7}\text{N}$ (nitrogen-14, stable) $+$ $^{4}_{2}\text{He}$ (alpha particle, helium-4) $\rightarrow$ $^{17}_{8}\text{O}$ (oxygen-17, stable) $+$ $^{1}_{1}\text{H}$ (proton, hydrogen-1)		Rutherford experiment
Artificial transmutation	Bombardment of aluminum-27 with alpha particle	$^{27}_{13}\text{Al}$ (aluminum-27, stable) $+$ $^{4}_{2}\text{He}$ (alpha particle, helium-4) $\rightarrow$ $^{30}_{15}\text{P}$ (phosphorous-30, radioactive) $+$ $^{1}_{0}\text{n}$ (neutron)		Joliot-Curie experiment (step 1)
Decay of synthetic radioisotope	Emission of positron by phosphorous-30	$^{30}_{15}\text{P}$ (phosphorous-30, radioactive) $\rightarrow$ $^{30}_{14}\text{Si}$ (silicon-30, stable) $+$ $^{0}_{1}+\text{e}$ (positron)		Joliot-Curie experiment (step 2)
Production of radioisotope of same element	Bombardment of sodium-23 with neutron	$^{23}_{11}\text{Na}$ (sodium-23, stable) $+$ $^{1}_{0}\text{n}$ (neutron) $\rightarrow$ $^{24}_{11}\text{Na}$ (sodium-24, radioactive) $+$		Nuclear reactor
Nuclear fission	Capture of neutron by uranium-235, with splitting	$^{235}_{92}\text{U}$ (uranium-235, radioactive) $+$ $^{1}_{0}\text{n}$ (neutron) $\rightarrow$ $^{141}_{56}\text{Ba}$ (barium-141, radioactive) $+$ $^{92}_{36}\text{Kr}$ (krypton-92) $+$ $3\,^{1}_{0}\text{n}$ + energy (neutrons, radioactive)		Nuclear reactor (controlled) or atomic fission bomb (uncontrolled)
Synthesis of new element	Capture of neutron by uranium-238, with synthesis of plutonium-239	$^{238}_{92}\text{U}$ (uranium-238, radioactive) $+$ $^{1}_{0}\text{n}$ (neutron) $\rightarrow$ $^{239}_{94}\text{Pu}$ (plutonium-239, radioactive) $+$ $2\,^{0}_{1}-\text{e}$ (beta particles, electrons)		Breeder reactor for production of nuclear fuels
Nuclear fusion	Reaction of deuterium with tritium	$^{2}_{1}\text{H}$ (deuterium, hydrogen-2) $+$ $^{3}_{1}\text{H}$ (tritium, hydrogen-3) $\rightarrow$ $^{4}_{2}\text{He}$ (proton, helium-4) $^{1}_{0}\text{n}$ + energy (neutron)		Thermonuclear or hydrogen-bomb reaction

Mushroom Cloud. When a nuclear weapon explodes, it releases a fireball of dust and extremely hot gases. The fireball releases neutrons and gamma rays. More gamma rays are released by the huge mushroom-shaped cloud that forms from the explosion. ▶

NUCLEAR WEAPONS

The first nuclear weapons were two fission bombs dropped by the United States on the Japanese cities of Hiroshima and Nagasaki in 1945, during World War II. The bombs killed from 110,000 to 140,000 people and destroyed large areas of both cities. The bombs are the only two nuclear weapons that have ever been used.

Hiroshima, Japan, was largely destroyed by a gun-type fission bomb called the Little Boy bomb on August 6, 1945. The bomb was dropped from a B-29 bomber. When the bomb reached 564 meters (1,850 feet), a radar echo set off an explosive inside. This explosive drove a wedge of U-235 into a larger piece of U-235, setting off the nuclear blast.

Nagasaki, Japan, was struck by an implosion-type fission bomb called the Fat Man bomb on August 9, 1945. In this bomb, an explosive crushed a hollow sphere of plutonium into a core made up of the chemical elements beryllium and polonium. This core then released neutrons, which triggered a fission chain reaction in the plutonium.

Gun-Type Fission Bomb (Little Boy)

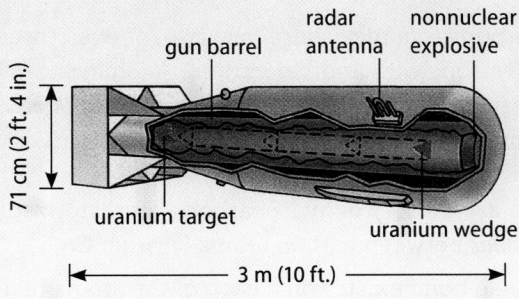

Implosion-Type Fission Bomb (Fat Man)

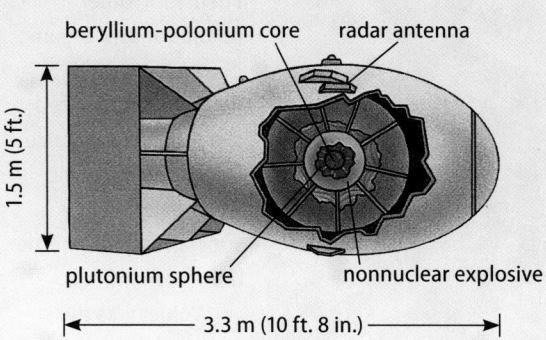

ORGANIC CHEMISTRY

is the study of compounds that contain carbon atoms. It is considered a separate branch of chemistry because of the unique ways in which carbon atoms can link to form long molecular chains.

It is called organic because until 1828 chemists believed that familiar carbon compounds, such as ethyl alcohol, acetic acid, and sugars, could only be produced by living things. In 1828, however, the German chemist Friedrich Wöhler succeeded in making urea, a typical organic compound, from ammonium chloride and silver cyanate, typical inorganic compounds.

Spotlight on...

FRIEDRICH WÖHLER

1800–1882

German chemist Friedrich Wöhler revolutionized organic chemistry in 1828 when he synthesized the organic substance urea from inorganic substances. Urea is a substance found in the urine of mammals.

Wöhler was the first person to make an organic substance from inorganic chemicals. His experiments helped disprove the belief that organic substances could be formed only in the living bodies of animals or plants.

Hydrocarbons

Carbon is unique because its atoms have the ability to link together to form chains of great size and complexity. Carbon has four electrons in its outer shell, and these are available for covalent sharing with other elements but especially with other carbon atoms.

The most important class of organic compounds consists solely of the elements carbon and hydrogen. They are called *hydrocarbons*. The number and variety of compounds that carbon forms with hydrogen is quite large.

Hydrocarbons can be divided into three classes.

- *aliphatics*
- *alicyclics*
- *aromatics*

Aliphatics

Aliphatics consist of compounds with their carbon atoms arranged in an open-chain structure. The simplest of these compounds, methane (CH_4), can be represented by a structural formula in which each dash represents a pair of shared electrons between the atoms indicated by their symbols.

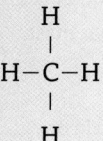

A carbon atom may share one, two, or even three of its electrons with another carbon. Aliphatics can be further subdivided into *alkanes, alkenes,* and *alkynes,* based on the bonds between their carbon atoms.

Alkanes are a series of hydrocarbons characterized by *single bonds* between carbon atoms (written $C-C$).

- A single bond exists when each of the atoms that share electrons contributes only one electron to the bond.
- Methane, the main component of natural gas, is the simplest of the alkanes. (See pages 670–671.)
- The alkanes are *saturated* hydrocarbons. This means that they contain only single bonds.
- The *–ane* in *methane* indicates that it is an alkane.

408

Alkenes are a series of hydrocarbons that have a double bond between carbon atoms (written C = C).

- The first member of the alkenes is ethylene.
- Alkenes and alkynes are *unsaturated* hydrocarbons—they may undergo reactions in which hydrogen atoms are added at the double or triple bond.

Alkynes are a series of hydrocarbons that have a triple bond in their structure (written C ≡ C).

- Acetylene is the first member of the alkynes.
- Alkynes have reactions similar to the alkenes.

Alicyclics

Alicyclics are hydrocarbons that have their carbon atoms arranged in a ring. These atoms may have single or double bonds between them. Triple bonds in alicyclics are rare, but they can occur in sufficiently large rings. Many naturally occurring organic compounds fall into this class.

Aromatics

Aromatics are highly unsaturated ring compounds. They are so named because many members have a distinctive odor. Each of the aromatics has a ring of six carbons that contains three double bonds.

Aromatics are extremely stable compared with ordinary unsaturated compounds. The most common of the aromatics is benzene.

Structures of Some Hydrocarbons			
Series	**Hydro-carbon**	**Molecular Formula**	**Structural Formula**
Alkane	Methane	CH_4	H — C — H (with H above and below)
	Ethane	C_2H_6	H — C — C — H (with H's)
Alkene	Ethene	C_2H_4	$H_2C=CH_2$
	Propene	C_3H_6	H — C = C — C — H
Alkyne	Ethyne	C_2H_2	H — C ≡ C — H
	Propyne	C_3H_4	H — C ≡ C — C — H
Aromatic	Benzene	C_6H_6	benzene ring
	Toluene	C_7H_8	toluene ring with CH₃

◄ **Hydrocarbons.** Petrochemical companies use hydrocarbons from crude oil and natural gas to manufacture solvents, plastics, and synthetic fibers and rubber.

Hydrocarbon Structure and Names

The simplest organic molecule is methane (CH_4). The four hydrogens are arranged three-dimensionally to form a regular tetrahedron with the carbon using sp3 hybrid orbitals. This is a major geometry that determines the structures of organic molecules. Each C−H bond is covalent and made by the sharing of two electrons between the atoms. In total, the carbon atom donates four electrons, its valence electrons, one to each of the four bonds.

Naming Aliphatics

After methane, the next largest alkane is the two-carbon ethane, represented by C_2H_6 or, better yet, by CH_3CH_3. This second representation better reflects ethane's structure. An even better representation is given by the structural formula

```
    H   H
    |   |
H − C − C − H
    |   |
    H   H
```

Chemical Formulas. The next larger alkane is propane (C_3H_8), followed by butane (C_4H_{10}), pentane (C_5H_{12}), and hexane (C_6H_{14}). In general, the chemical formula for an alkane is given by the expression C_nH_{2n+2}, where n is the number of carbons in the compound.

Other alkanes include heptane (C_7H_{16}), octane (C_8H_{18}), nonane (C_9H_{20}), and decane ($C_{10}H_{22}$), which finishes the list of the first 10 alkanes.

Alkane Structure. Although there is only one possible structure for ethane or propane, an alkane with four or more carbon atoms will have more than one possible structural isomer. For instance, there are two possible isomers of butane, n-butane (n for normal), which is linear, and isobutane, which is depicted below.

```
        CH_3
        |
H_3C − C − CH_3
        |
        H
     isobutane
```

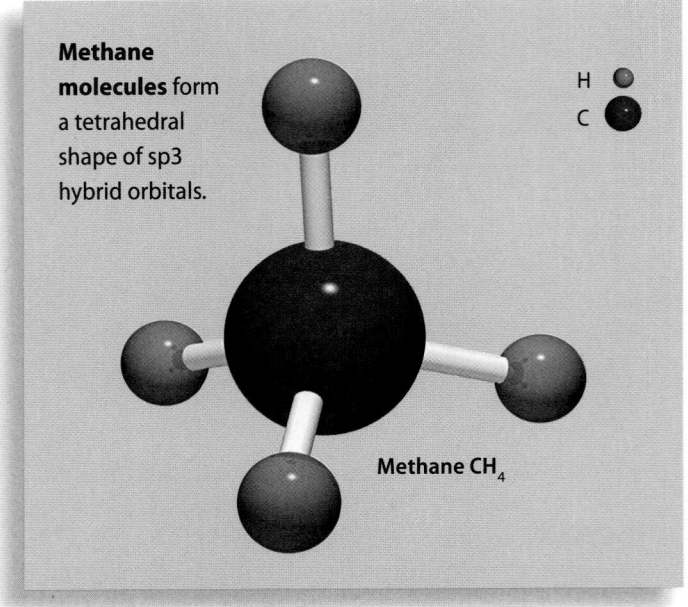

Methane molecules form a tetrahedral shape of sp3 hybrid orbitals.

H
C

Methane CH_4

Pentane has three isomers, including the linear form called normal pentane. The other two forms are listed below.

```
     H   CH_3                    CH_3
     |   |                       |
H_3C − C − C − CH_3       H_3C − C − CH_3
     |   |                       |
     H   H                       CH_3
   isopentane                  neopentane
```

As the number of carbons in an alkane increases, so does the number of possible isomers. For instance, hexane, which has six carbons, has five possible structural isomers. Octane, which has eight carbons, has 18 possible structural isomers. As the number of carbons gets quite large, the number of isomers increases significantly.

Naming Alkenes. The smallest alkene is ethylene, or ethene (C_2H_4). The next in size is propene (C_3H_6), followed by butene (C_4H_8), pentene (C_5H_{10}), and hexene (C_6H_{12}). In general, the chemical formula for an open-chain monounsaturated (that is, having one double bond) molecule is C_nH_{2n}, where n is the number of carbons.

BUCKYBALLS

In 1985, three chemists produced a molecule consisting of 60 carbon atoms. The *buckminsterfullerene* molecule is shaped like a geodesic dome and named after R. Buckminster Fuller, the engineer who designed the geodesic dome.

Buckminsterfullerenes, nicknamed "buckyballs," can be chemically modified to block a key step in the reproduction of the human immunodeficiency virus (HIV), which causes AIDS. Similar molecules can be filled with metal atoms to form the smallest wire imaginable, or made into superconductors, which conduct electric current with no resistance at extremely low temperatures.

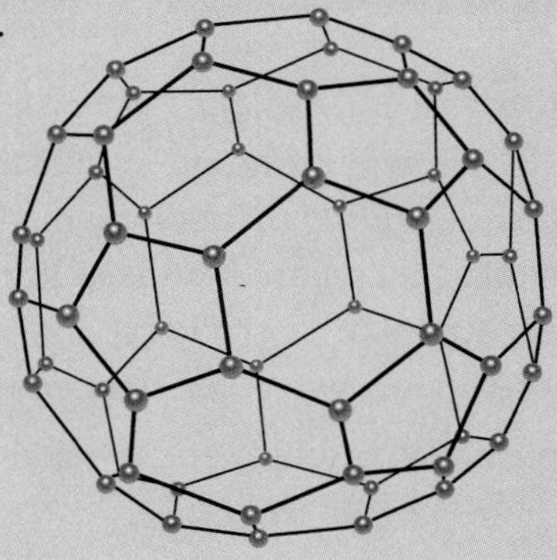

> **Multiple Double-Bonds.** There is the possibility of multiple double-bonds in alkenes having four or more carbons. The simplest example is butadiene (C_2H_6), but its proper name is 1,3-butadiene to indicate the location of the double bonds.
>
> The *di* in *butadiene* indicates that there are two double bonds in the structure. In the same manner, *triene* indicates there are three double bonds present.

Alkynes containing a single triple bond have the general formula of C_nH_{2n-2}, where n is again the number of carbons. The simplest and most common of these compounds is ethyne, better known as acetylene (C_2H_2).

The next in size is propyne (C_3H_4), followed by butyne (C_4H_6), pentyne (C_5H_8), and hexyne (C_6H_{10}). Alkynes are not as common as other aliphatics except for acetylene, which is used as a fuel for torches in welding.

Naming Alicyclics

A good example of an unsaturated alicyclic is cyclohexane (C_6H_{12}). The *cyclo* indicates it is a ring system, and *hexane* indicates it contains six carbons and has no double bonds, as discussed in the alkane section. Of course, as with the open-chained compounds, there is the possibility of having a double bond, as in the case of cyclohexene (C_6H_{10}).

As one can now see, the naming of alicyclics is analogous to the naming of aliphatic compounds except for the addition of the prefix *cyclo-*.

SIMPLIFYING MOLECULAR STRUCTURE DIAGRAMS

The naming and drawing of organic molecules becomes very complex as the size of the molecule becomes larger.

- One method of simplifying the drawing of organic structures is to omit the hydrogen atoms from the drawing. For example, figure 4 depicts benzene without showing the hydrogens.

- We can take this simplification even further by removing the C–H bonds and the letter C (figure 5). In the same way, cyclohexene may be represented as in figure 6.

- These structural formulas are easier to draw and are commonly used.

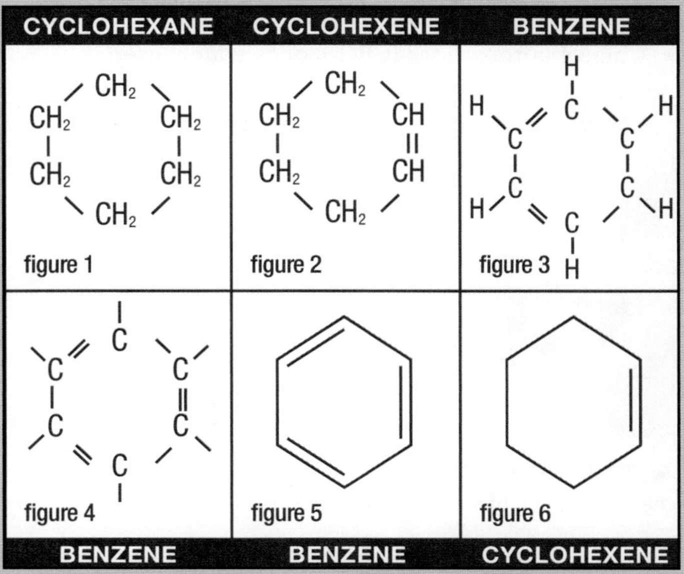

figure 1 — CYCLOHEXANE

figure 2 — CYCLOHEXENE

figure 3 — BENZENE

figure 4 — BENZENE

figure 5 — BENZENE

figure 6 — CYCLOHEXENE

Organic Reactions

The simpler hydrocarbons—methane, ethane, propane, butane, ethene, propene, and acetylene—are all gases at 25°C (77°F). Hydrocarbons having 5 to 16 carbon atoms are typically liquids, as is benzene. Larger molecules exist as molecular solids.

Oxidation

All hydrocarbons will burn and oxidize to water and carbon dioxide, giving up heat. (See pages 396–397.) Gasoline and fuel oil are blends of purified liquid hydrocarbons isolated from crude oil. Fuel oil contains longer and more linear molecules than does gasoline.

- Methane, propane, and butane are used as fuel gases.
- Other useful hydrocarbons are also produced from petroleum, such as alkanes, alkenes, and aromatics.
- The majority of industrial chemicals and plastics are derived from petroleum.
- The alkenes are the most reactive, followed by the alkynes, aromatics, and alkanes.
- All of these can be *halogenated* (the addition of a halogen atom to a hydrocarbon molecule; the halogen elements are fluorine, chlorine, bromine, iodine, and astatine).
- Chlorinated products are used as cleaning compounds or to make other organic compounds.
- Fluorinated hydrocarbons are used in the making of Teflon, as well as in refrigeration.
- Chlorofluorocarbons (CFCs), once widely used in refrigeration, are now rarely used because of their harmful effects on atmospheric ozone.

▲ **Plastics** are polymers, large linear molecules formed by the chemical linking of many smaller molecules into a long chain.

Major Reactive Groups	
Reactive Group	**Name of Group**
$R-Cl$	R Chloride
$Cl-R-Cl$	R Dichloride
$CH_2=CH_2$	Ethylene
$CH\equiv CH$	Acetylene
$R-O-R$	R Ether
$R-ONa$	Sodium R Oxide
$R-OH$	R Alcohol
$OH-R-OH$	R Dialcohol
$R-CH=O$	R Aldehyde
$\begin{matrix} O \\ \parallel \\ R-C-R \end{matrix}$	R Ketone
$R-CN$	R Cyanide
$R-COOH$	R Acid
$R-C=O-O-C=O-R$	R Anhydride
$R-C=O-OR$	R Acetate
$HOOC-R-COOH$	R Diacid
$R-COONa$	Sodium Rtate
$R-COCl$	Rnyl Chloride
$R-CONH_2$	R Amide
$OH-R-CO-NH_2$	R Amino Acid
$R-NH_2$	R Amine
NH_2-R-NH_2	R Diamine
$R-NCO$	R Isocyanate

MAJOR REACTIVE GROUPS

Hydrocarbons can be modified by the addition of many different reactive groups to the carbon backbone. The capital letter *R* is used to represent any *alkyl group*. An *alkyl* is an alkane that has had one of its hydrogens removed, leaving an opening for another atom to attach to the molecule.

The table lists the major groups as attached to some alkyl group. Groups are added to produce organic molecules with specific physical and chemical properties to serve as useful industrial or consumer products, or as intermediates for the synthesis of other organic molecules.

Examples of Reactions

The table below lists some typical reactions involving simple organic molecules.

Addition reactions occur when an alkene or an alkyne is added to with the loss of the multiple bond. Typically, there are no by-products.

- Ethylene, $CH_2=CH_2$, is reacted with HCl to yield CH_3CH_2Cl, ethylchloride.

Substitution Reactions. In a substitution reaction, one chemical group is replaced by another.

- Acetamide (CH_3CONH_2) is formed from acetyl chloride (CH_3COCl) with the release of HCl.

Catalysts. Some reactions require a *catalyst*, a material that speeds a chemical reaction. In the table, catalysts or other required conditions are contained in brackets.

- Ethyl alcohol (CH_3CH_2OH) is more easily oxidized to acetaldehyde (CH_3CHO) in the presence of copper.

Polymers

Polymers are a very important class of organic molecules. A polymer is typically a very large linear molecule that was made by linking together many small molecules, called *monomers*.

Plastics are polymers. As an example, polyethylene, which is used in the manufacture of bottles and packaging, consists of a very large chain of added ethylene monomers ($CH_2=CH_2$) to yield $-[CH_2CH_2CH_2CH_2]n-$, where n is the repeat of the sequence in the chain.

Another plastic is polyvinyl chloride (PVC), a chain of linked vinyl chloride molecules ($CH_2=CHCl$), which is used in the production of water pipes.

Biological Polymers. Polymers also play a very large role in biological chemistry. *Proteins* (building blocks and catalysts of life), *nucleic acids* (blueprints of life), and *starches* (fuel for life) are all polymers.

Examples of Organic Reactions	
Reaction	**Equation**
Ethylene is oxidized to ethyl alcohol.	$CH_2=CH_2$ [H_2SO_4/H_2O] $\rightarrow CH_3CH_2OH$
Ethyl alcohol is oxidized to acetaldehyde.	CH_3CH_2OH [Cu] $\rightarrow CH_3CHO$
Acetaldehyde is oxidized to acetic acid.	$CH_3CHO + 1/2O_2 \rightarrow CH_3COOH$
Acetic acid is reduced to acetyl chloride.	CH_3COOH [PCl_3] $\rightarrow CH_3COCl$
Acetyl chloride is converted into acetamide by substitution.	$CH_3COCl + NH_3 \rightarrow CH_3CONH_2 + HCl$
Acetic acid is reacted with ethyl alcohol to make ethyl acetate by a condensation reaction (forms water).	$CH_3COOH + CH_3CH_2OH \rightarrow CH_3COOCH_2CH_3 + H_2O$
Ethyl alcohol is condensed to diethyl ether.	CH_3CH_2OH [H_2SO_4 @ 130°C]. $CH_3CH_2-O-CH_2CH_3 + H_2O$
Ethyl alcohol is dehydrated back to ethylene.	CH_3CH_2OH [H_2SO_4 @ 190ºC] $\rightarrow CH_2CH_2$
Acetic acid is chlorinated and forms chloroacetic acid by substitution.	$CH_3COOH + Cl \rightarrow ClCH_2COOH + HCl$
Chloroacetic acid is ammoniated and yields aminoacetic acid by substitution.	$ClCH_2COOH + NH_3 \rightarrow NH_2CH_2COOH + HCl$

BIOLOGICAL POLYMERS

DNA, RNA, and proteins—the molecules that provide the blueprints and the building blocks of life—are all polymers, large linear molecules made by linking together many small molecules.

DNA and RNA are nucleic acids made up of monomers consisting of a sugar, a phosphate, and four or five bases. Proteins are long-chained polymers made up of monomers called amino acids. Lipids are another type of organic polymer essential for good health.

Nucleic Acid

Nucleic acid is a complex polymer found in all cells. The two types of nucleic acids are *deoxyribonucleic acid (DNA)* and *ribonucleic acid (RNA)*. DNA is mainly found in the nucleus of a cell. But RNA may be found throughout the cell. Even bacterial cells, which do not have a nucleus, contain DNA and RNA. Certain viruses contain only RNA while some viruses contain only DNA. (See pages 64–67.)

DNA

Deoxyribonucleic acid, the molecule that contains the genetic code of all organisms, is a very large polymer. A single monomer consists of sugar (deoxyribose), a phosphate group, and one of four bases. These four bases are aromatic molecules.

- *adenine*
- *thymine*
- *guanine*
- *cytosine*

The bases are more simply referred to by the letters *A, T, G,* and *C*.

The Double Helix. James Watson and Francis Crick discovered in 1953 that DNA was typically found as a double-stranded form, known as the *double helix*. The strands in the helix are held together not by covalent bonds but by hydrogen bonds between specific bases.

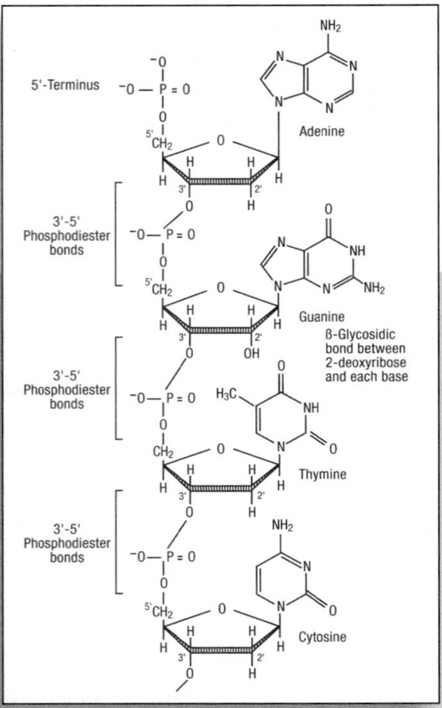

A SINGLE STRAND

This diagram illustrates a short portion of a single strand of the complex DNA molecule. A strand consists of segments of deoxyribose ($C_5H_{10}O_4$) connected by segments of phosphate (PO_4^{3-}). The four bases are bonded to the segments of deoxyribose. Their chemical formulas are

- adenine ($C_5H_5N_5$)
- guanine ($C_5H_5N_5O$)
- thymine ($C_5H_6N_2O_2$)
- cytosine ($C_4H_5N_3O$)

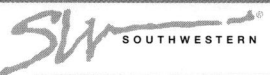
Base Bonding. Guanine and cytosine are bonded together by three hydrogen bonds, and adenine to thymine by two. These base pairs can be found at the center of the helix, and in the most common form aligned perpendicularly to the main axis of the helix.

Watson and Crick also discovered that, since the two strands are held together relatively weakly by hydrogen bonding, they can be separated, allowing the bases to be read as if reading a book. This is the blueprint for life, written in a simple language of four letters, A, T, G, and C.

Base Sequence. The genetic coding for humans consists of a total of about 3 billion bases. Each is one of the four—A, T, G, and C—combined in a specific order to carry out the genetic instructions.

The bases cluster together in about 25,000 genes, which are arranged on 23 pairs of rod-shaped structures called chromosomes.

Although bases can occur in any order, they exist in almost the same order in all human beings or all the members of any other species. In any two human genomes, only about 1 base in 1,000 differs.

RNA

Ribonucleic acid is another class of polymers very similar in structure to DNA, but a fifth base—*uracil (U)*—closely related to thymine, is also utilized in RNA. It plays important roles in the expression of the genetic code and in the production of proteins.

REMEMBER THIS...

HYDROGEN BONDS

A hydrogen bond is different from the covalent bonds holding molecules together or the ionic bonds that bind ionic compounds. A hydrogen bond is a weak intermolecular force between a hydrogen atom in one molecule and an electron pair associated with an oxygen, nitrogen, or fluorine atom in another molecule.

An intermolecular force results when the negative charge associated with a polar bond in one molecule interacts with the positive charge of another molecule.

BASE PAIRING

The bases of a DNA molecule are paired in a specific way to form combinations known as *base pairs*. There are A-T and G-C base pairs.

Wherever there is adenine in one strand, there is thymine in the opposite strand. The adenine-thymine (A-T) base pair has two hydrogen bonds.

Wherever there is guanine in one strand, there is cytosine in the other. The guanine-cytosine (G-C) base pair has three hydrogen bonds.

Because of this specific pairing of the bases, the two DNA strands are said to be *complementary*. The sequence of bases in one strand determines the sequence of bases in the other.

Adenine :::::: Thymine
(two hydrogen bonds)

—11Å—

Guanine :::::: Cytosine
(three hydrogen bonds)

—11Å—

Lipids and Fatty Acids

Lipids are a large group of oily or fatty substances essential for good health. Lipids, carbohydrates, and proteins are the classes of compounds in all living things. (See pages 260–263.)

Animal fats and plant oils are lipids. So are animal sex hormones and vitamins A, D, E, and K. Egg yolks, liver, and embryos of grains are rich in lipids. According to their structure, lipids are classified as simple lipids or complex lipids.

Simple Lipids

- Simple lipids contain only carbon, hydrogen, and oxygen.
- They consist of an alcohol in combination with certain organic acids containing a variable number of carbon atoms.
- The most common type of simple lipid, a molecule of *triglyceride* (fat), contains one molecule of an alcohol called glycerol and three molecules of *fatty acid* (a kind of organic acid).
- Fats include butter, lard (pig fat), tallow (beef or mutton fat), blubber (whale fat), castor oil, coconut oil, and olive oil.
- Waxes, another common group of simple lipids, contain an alcohol molecule that is larger than the glycerol molecule.

Complex Lipids

- Complex lipids have a more complicated structure than simple lipids.
- They include *phospholipids* (lipids that contain phosphorus), *steroids* (lipids made up of four rings of carbon atoms joined together), and other compounds such as *glycolipids* (lipids with one or more sugar molecules), fat-soluble vitamins (vitamins A, D, E, and K), and *terpenes* (yellow pigments like carotene).
- Phospholipids are found in all bacteria, and in the cells of all plants and animals; most plentiful in sperm, eggs, embryos, and brain cells.
- A molecule of phospholipid contains a molecule of glycerol, a phosphate ion, and two molecules of fatty acid.
- Most phospholipids also have a nitrogen compound.
- Some contain *inositol,* a substance found in vitamin B complex.

A triglyceride molecule consists of a glycerol molecule—which is made up of atoms of carbon, hydrogen, and oxygen—and three fatty acid molecules—each of which consists of a long chain of carbon atoms with hydrogen atoms attached. ▶

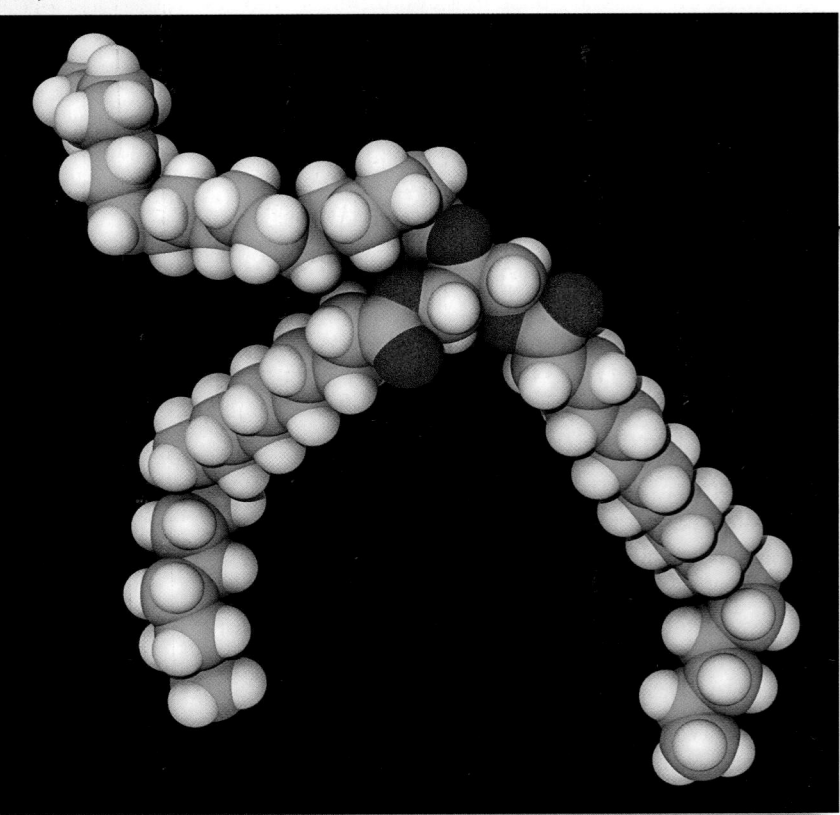

Fatty Acids

Fats consist primarily of compounds called triglycerides. Triglycerides contain one molecule of an alcohol called glycerol, which is made up of atoms of carbon, hydrogen, and oxygen. The glycerol combines with three molecules of substances called fatty acids.

Each of these fatty acids consists of a long chain of carbon atoms that have hydrogen atoms attached. The fatty acid chains are linked to the glycerol molecule to form a triglyceride molecule. Fatty acids occur in two forms: *saturated* and *unsaturated*.

Saturated fatty acid has a chemical structure in which as many hydrogen atoms as possible are linked to its carbon chain. When all three of the fatty acids in a triglyceride are saturated, it is called a saturated fat. A compound is *saturated* when it contains only single bonds between atoms.

Most fats from animal sources contain a large proportion of saturated fats and are said to be *highly saturated.* For example, butter contains about 60 percent saturated fat.

Unsaturated fatty acid contains at least two fewer hydrogen atoms than a saturated fatty acid containing the same number of carbons. An *unsaturated* compound is one that may form a double or triple bond between two carbon atoms.

A triglyceride that contains one or more unsaturated fatty acids is known as an unsaturated fat. A fat with one unsaturated fatty acid is called a monounsaturated fat. A fat that contains more than one is called polyunsaturated. Most—but not all—fats from vegetable sources are unsaturated.

PRODUCING ENERGY

Fatty acids and *amino acids,* another group of organic compounds, play an important role in providing the human body with energy. Most energy is produced in tiny structures called mitochondria and is stored in a compound called ATP.

To produce ATP, the digestive system first breaks down food into amino acids, fatty acids, and simple sugars. The amino, fatty, and pyruvic acids enter the mitochondria.

There, in a series of chemical reactions, ATP is produced, and carbon dioxide and water are released as waste products.

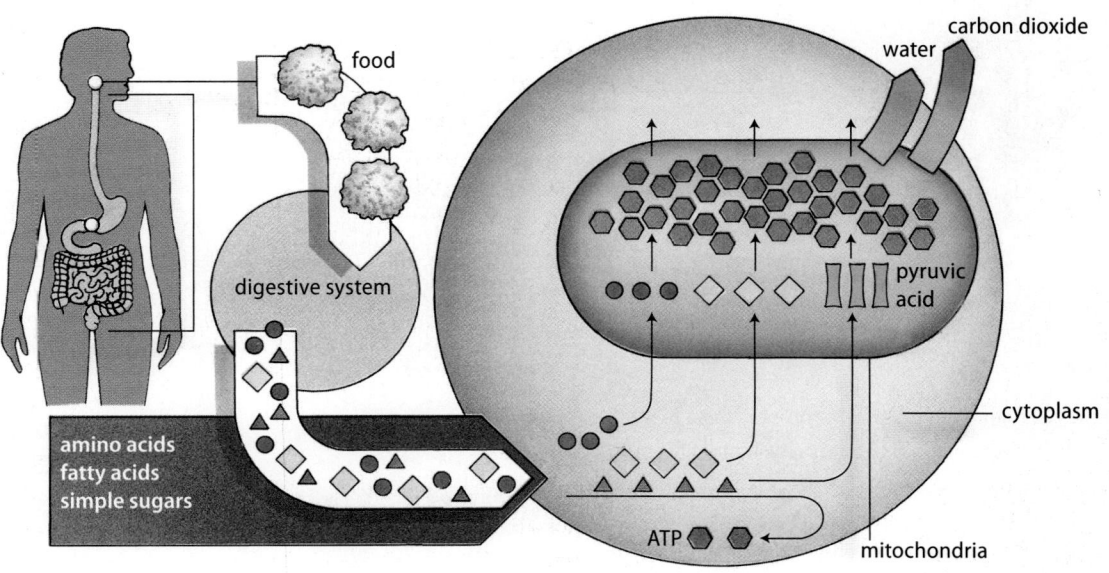

Amino Acids

DNA contains the genetic instructions for the construction of the polymers known as *proteins*. Proteins serve both as building blocks in the construction of living organisms and as catalysts that drive the chemical reactions that support them.

Proteins are long-chained polymers consisting of monomers known as *amino acids*. (See page 260.)

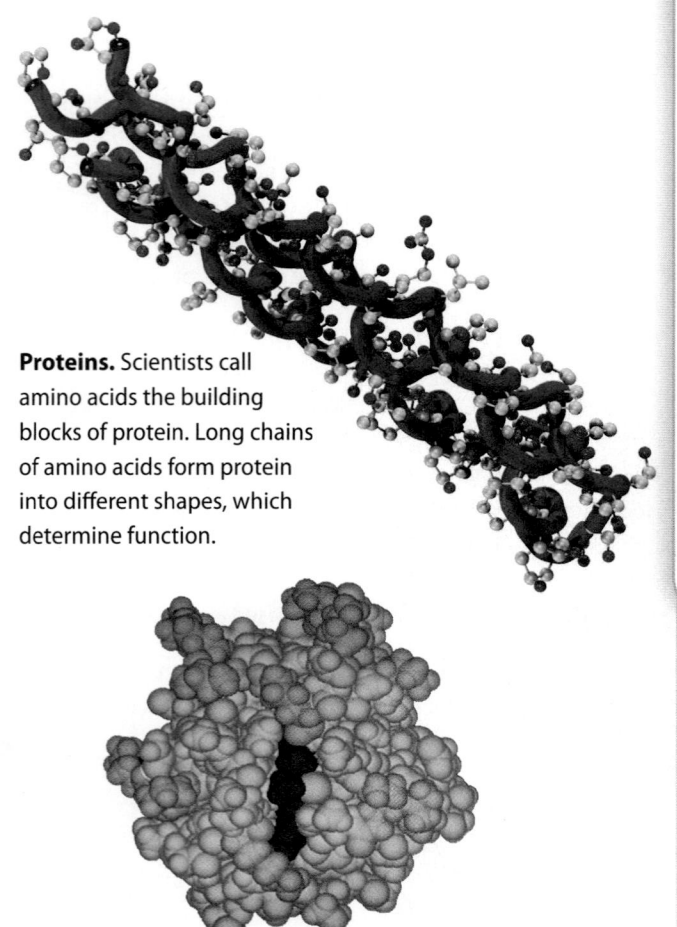

Proteins. Scientists call amino acids the building blocks of protein. Long chains of amino acids form protein into different shapes, which determine function.

Chemical Makeup

All amino acids contain carbon, hydrogen, oxygen, and nitrogen. They have at least two functional groups attached to a central carbon, called the *α-carbon*. The two groups are

- the *amine group*, $-NH_2$
- the *carboxylic acid group*, $-COOH$

At *physiological pH* (the pH of blood, which is 7.4), these groups are typically ionized, although there is no net charge.

$$\begin{array}{c} H \\ | \\ H_3N^+ - C - COO^- \\ | \\ R \end{array}$$

In addition to these two groups, a hydrogen atom and additional functional group is bonded to the α-carbon. This additional group is represented by *R-*, indicating that it is an *alkyl group*. An *alkyl* is an alkane that has had one of its hydrogens removed, leaving an opening for another atom to attach to the molecule.

Polypeptides

Molecules consisting of several linked amino acid residues are called *polypeptides*. Proteins are naturally occurring polypeptides.

Proteins do not form double helices like DNA, but they do fold into many and varied shapes. All these conformations are held together by many hydrogen bonds, often over 100.

PEPTIDE BONDS

The bond between amino acid monomers (also known as *residues*) is found between the carboxylic acid carbon and the nitrogen on the amine. This bond is called the *peptide bond*. In the reaction shown, a peptide bond forms between two amino acids with release of a water molecule.

Peptide Bond

$$H_3N^+ - \overset{\overset{\displaystyle H}{|}}{\underset{\underset{\displaystyle R_1}{|}}{C}} - COO^- + H_3N^+ - \overset{\overset{\displaystyle H}{|}}{\underset{\underset{\displaystyle R_2}{|}}{C}} - COO^- \rightarrow H_3N^+ - \overset{\overset{\displaystyle H}{|}}{\underset{\underset{\displaystyle R_1}{|}}{C}} - \overset{\overset{\displaystyle O}{\|}}{C} - \overset{\overset{\displaystyle O}{}}{\underset{\underset{\displaystyle H}{|}}{N}} - \overset{}{\underset{\underset{\displaystyle R_2}{|}}{C}} - COO^- + H_2O$$

Protein Shape

- The shapes proteins form are dependent on the sequence of the amino acids in the chain. This sequence is known as the *primary structure*.
- *Secondary structures* are relatively short stretches of local structure.
- Some stretches of chain will form single helices known as the α-*helix*.
- Other stretches might form loops or parallel strands known as β *sheets*.
- Finally, the entire chain will fold up into its final shape, a complex form known as the *tertiary structure*.

Protein Function

The sequence of amino acids finally leads to the tertiary structure of a protein, which determines its function.

- *Structural proteins*, such as collagen and keratin, are large constructs of many protein molecules, laid out in a repeating fashion, and are insoluble.
- *Enzymes*, the biological catalysts, are often single-chained, water soluble, and globular in shape.

Amino Acids from Food

There are 20 amino acids that serve as monomers in the formation of a protein, ranging from another H- to aromatics, which are highly unsaturated ring compounds.

Human beings and other higher animals cannot make all of the 20 amino acids their bodies need to build tissues. Humans must get at least nine amino acids from their food. Protein foods, such as eggs, meat, milk products, and some vegetables, provide amino acids. The body breaks down these foods into amino acids. It then links the amino acids to form new proteins.

The Common Amino Acids		
Amino Acid	Three- and One-Letter Symbols, Molecular Weight	Side Chain R $(RCH(NH+3)CO-2)$
Glycine	Gly, G, 75	H–
Alanine	Ala, A, 89	CH_3–
Valine	Val, V, 117	CH_3-CH-CH_3
Leucine	Leu, L, 131	CH_3-$CHCH_2$-CH_3
Isoleucine	Ile, I, 131	CH_3CH_2-CH-CH_3
Phenylalanine	Phe, F, 165	⬡–CH_2–
Tyrosine	Tyr, Y, 181	HO–⬡–CH_2–
Tryptophan	Trp, W, 204	–CH_2– (indole ring)
Serine	Ser, S, 105	$HOCH_2$–
Threonine	Thr, T, 119	HO-CH-CH_3
Cysteine	Cys, C, 121	$HSCH_2$–
Methionine	Met, M, 149	$CH_3SCH_2CH_2$–
Asparagine	Asn, N, 132	$H_2NC(=O)CH_2$–
Glutamine	Gin, Q, 146	$H_2NC(=O)CH_2CH_2$–
Aspartic Acid	Asp, D, 133	$^-O_2CCH_2$–
Glutamic Acid	Glu, E, 147	$^-O_2CCH_2CH_2$–
Lysine	Lys, K, 146	$H_3N^+(CH_2)_4$
Arginine	Arg, R, 174	H_2N^+-C-$NH(CH_2)_3$-, H_2N
Histidine	His, H, 155	CH_2 (imidazole ring)
Proline	Pro, P, 115	(pyrrolidine ring) CO_2, H, N, H_2

Enzymes

Enzymes are molecules that speed up chemical reactions in all living things. Without enzymes, these reactions would occur too slowly or not at all, and no life would be possible.

What They Are

All living cells make enzymes, but enzymes are not alive. Most enzymes are proteins. A small number of RNA (ribonucleic acid) molecules also function as enzymes.

The human body has thousands of kinds of enzymes. Each kind does one specific job. Without enzymes, a person could not breathe, see, move, or digest food. Photosynthesis in plants also depends on enzymes.

What They Do

- Many enzymes break down complex substances into simpler ones.
- Others build complex compounds from simple ones.

Where They Do It

- Most enzymes remain in the cells where they were formed.
- Some enzymes work elsewhere. For example, the pancreas secretes the enzyme lipase, which travels to the small intestine to break down fats.

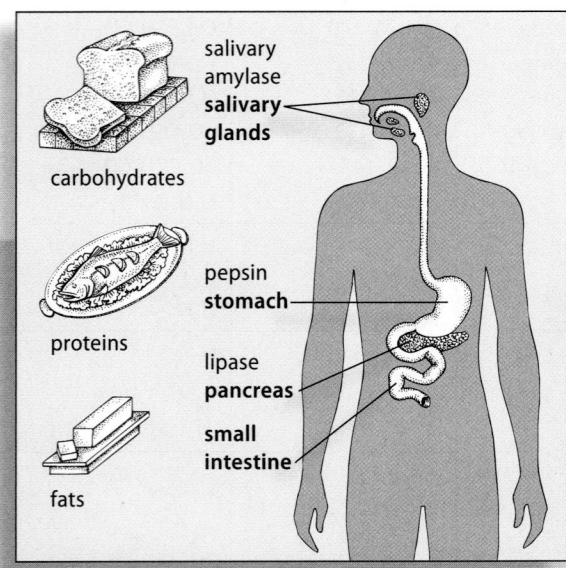

salivary amylase
salivary glands

carbohydrates

pepsin
stomach

proteins

lipase
pancreas

small intestine

fats

HOW DOES THAT WORK ?

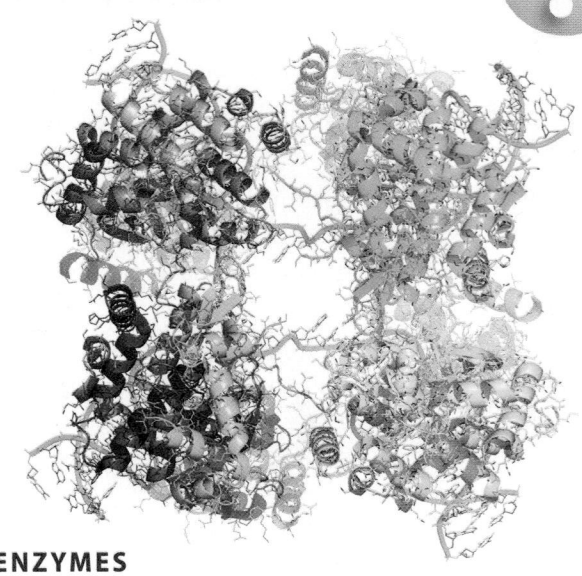

ENZYMES

- Enzyme molecules function by altering other molecules.
- Enzymes combine with the altered molecules to form a complex molecular structure in which chemical reactions take place.
- The enzyme, which remains unchanged, then separates from the product of the reaction.
- Enzymes thus serve as *catalysts,* substances that increase the rate of a chemical reaction by lowering the activation energy for the reaction.
- A single enzyme molecule can perform its entire function a million times a minute.
- The chemical reactions occur thousands or even millions of times faster with enzymes than without them.

ENZYMES AT WORK

Enzymes in the digestive system break down food for use in the body. Each enzyme performs a specific job. (See page 236.)

For example, *salivary amylase,* an enzyme produced by the salivary glands, splits carbohydrates into simpler chemicals. *Pepsin,* secreted by the walls of the stomach, acts on proteins. *Lipase* is secreted by the pancreas into the small intestine, where it breaks down fats.

Enzyme Structure

Enzymes are too tiny to be seen even with the most powerful light microscopes. However, scientists know through various research techniques that enzymes occur in a number of shapes and sizes. Although enzymes of different plants and animals have different protein structures, they function in similar ways. The structure of any particular enzyme enables it to cause chemical reactions in other molecules.

Destruction and Deficiency. An enzyme's structure can easily be destroyed by heat, acids, or alkalis. Many deadly poisons act by damaging important enzymes.

Hereditary diseases may occur in people born without certain enzymes. In many cases, tests can detect these enzyme deficiencies. Physicians can sometimes treat them with diet and drugs to prevent deformities, intellectual disability, and even death.

ENZYME TIME LINE

1926 American biochemist James B. Sumner becomes the first person to isolate a pure enzyme in the form of crystals. He extracts the enzyme urease from beans and proves that enzymes are protein molecules.

1969 Scientists first chemically synthesize an enzyme, ribonuclease, from amino acids. This enzyme breaks down ribonucleic acid into molecules of other amino acids.

Today Scientists are trying to make new synthetic enzymes that carry out reactions not found in nature.

Enzyme Uses

Enzymes have many uses in addition to their natural functions in the body.

Manufacturers use enzymes in making a wide variety of products. For example, some detergents contain enzymes that break down protein or fats that cause stains. Enzymes are also used in the manufacture of antibiotics, beer, bread, cheese, coffee, sugars, vinegar, vitamins, and many other products.

Physicians use medicines containing enzymes to help clean wounds, dissolve blood clots, relieve certain

Trace Elements. Although most enzymes are proteins, some must be attached to certain nonprotein molecules in order to function. Many of these nonprotein molecules are metals, such as copper, iron, or magnesium. They occur within the body as trace elements.

Coenzymes. Some enzymes attach to organic compounds called *coenzymes*. If a coenzyme is tightly attached to the protein part of the enzyme, the unit is called a *prosthetic group*. Neither the coenzyme nor the protein part of a prosthetic group can function alone.

Many coenzymes consist of vitamins, especially B vitamins. If a person's diet lacks adequate amounts of these vitamins, the enzymes cannot function properly, and various body disorders may develop.

Biochemist James B. Sumner

forms of leukemia, and check allergic reactions to penicillin. Doctors also diagnose some diseases by measuring the amount of various enzymes in blood and other body fluids. Such diseases include anemia, cancer, leukemia, and heart and liver ailments.

In the future, enzymes may be widely used to change raw sewage into useful products. Enzymes also may be used to help get rid of spilled oil that harms lakes and oceans. The enzymes would turn the oil into food for sea plants.

CHEMISTRY TOOLS

Chemists use a wide variety of tools and techniques, specialized instruments, and computers.

A device called a *mass spectrometer,* for example, enables chemists to determine the mass and atomic composition of molecules. Chemists use *spectroscopy* to identify how atoms are arranged in molecules.

A technique called *magnetic resonance imaging* (MRI) is used in medicine and research for producing images of tissues inside the body. MRI enables physicians to identify abnormal tissue without opening the body through surgery.

Mass Spectrometry

Mass spectrometry is a method of separating and analyzing the atoms and molecules in a chemical sample. In mass spectrometry, scientists *ionize* the atoms and molecules in a sample—that is, convert them into electrically charged particles called ions. (See page 315.)

Mass Spectrometers

Once a sample of atoms and molecules has been ionized, a device called a *mass spectrometer,* or a *mass spectrograph,* separates the various ions according to their mass and electric charge. People sometimes refer to mass spectrometry as *mass spectroscopy,* but many scientists reserve the term spectroscopy to describe methods of analysis that rely on light.

Techniques

To carry out mass spectrometry, scientists use several techniques to ionize chemical samples.

- *Electron bombardment* involves shooting a beam of electrons at the sample.
- *Electrospray ionization* ionizes a sample by forcing it through a charged needle.

After ionization, the sample is fed into a mass spectrometer.

Mass spectrometers work on the principle that neutral molecules can be ionized as a gas. These ions can arise by direct ionization of the original molecule as a gas by striking them with energetic electrons or by a number of other methods. ▶

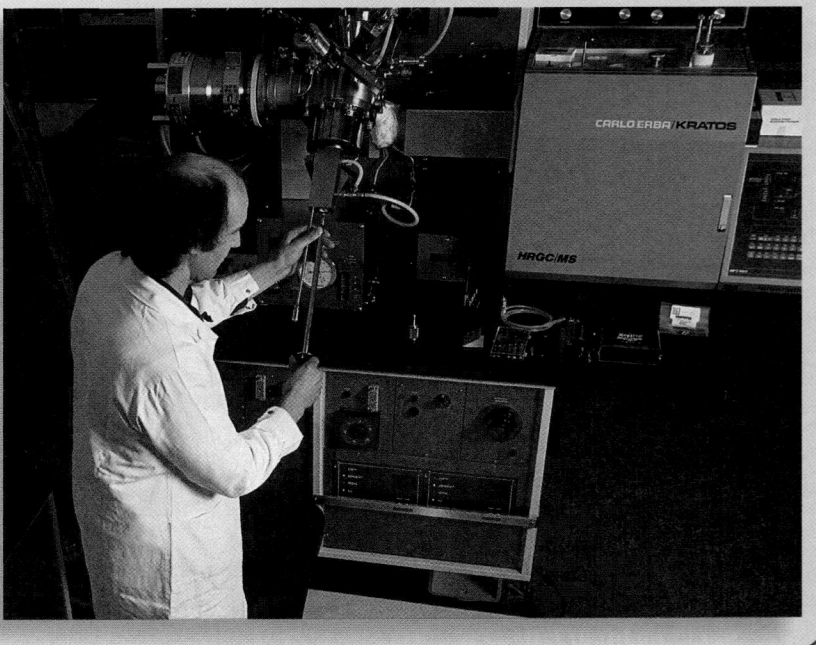

Uses

Mass spectrometry has many important uses in chemistry and biology.

- Chemists use it to determine the molecular weights of elements, isotopes (different forms of the same element), and compounds.

- Chemists use it to analyze the composition and structure of complex molecules.

- Environmental scientists use mass spectrometry to detect and measure the amounts of pollutants in water and soil.

- Biologists and medical researchers use mass spectrometry to analyze proteins and other biological substances isolated from bacteria, viruses, and bodily fluids.

At one time high-resolution mass spectrographs used photographic plates to detect the ion beam and present the mass spectrum.

Developments

New methods can produce ion beams from very large nonvolatile molecules. Instruments are able to resolve molecular weights as high as 15,000 to 20,000. This has made mass spectroscopy a valuable tool for molecular biology, where molecular weights can be very large.

The sensitivity of mass spectroscopy can also be very high. A typical mass spectrum is obtained by starting with 10^{-9} moles, but some instruments require only 10^{-12} moles of sample or 10^{-8} grams for a molecule with a molecular weight of 10,000.

HOW DOES THAT WORK ?

MASS SPECTROMETERS

Mass spectrometers use *electric fields* and *magnetic fields* (areas of electric charge and magnetic force) to separate ions.

A magnetic sector mass spectrometer, the most basic kind, uses an electric field to accelerate the ions and a magnetic field to deflect them onto a detector.

The amount that an ion is deflected depends on how heavy it is—that is, on the ratio of its mass to its charge. By varying the intensity of the magnetic field, the device causes different ions to hit the detector at different times.

This results in a graph called a *mass spectrum* that shows the relative numbers of ions with different ratios of mass to charge. Most mass spectrometers send this information to a computer that can store, manipulate, and interpret the data.

Mass Spectrum. The result of electron impact ionization of cyclohexane (C_6H_{12}, MW=84). The parent peak is fairly prominent at 84, but the most abundant ions are fragments. The small signal at 85 is due to 6 percent abundant carbon-13 molecules from 1 percent carbon-13 for each of the six carbons. The weak 83 signal must be due to the loss of a hydrogen in the parent ion. ▶

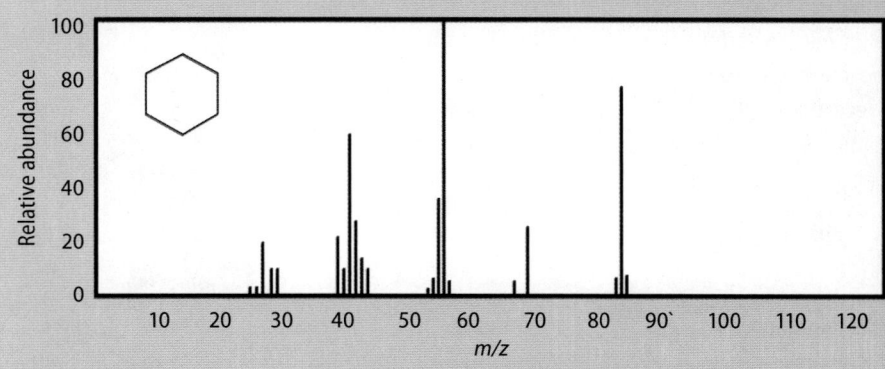

Magnetic Resonance Imaging

Magnetic resonance imaging (MRI) produces images of tissues inside the body. It enables physicians to identify abnormal tissue without opening the body through surgery, and it does so without exposing the patient to radiation, unlike tests that use X-rays.

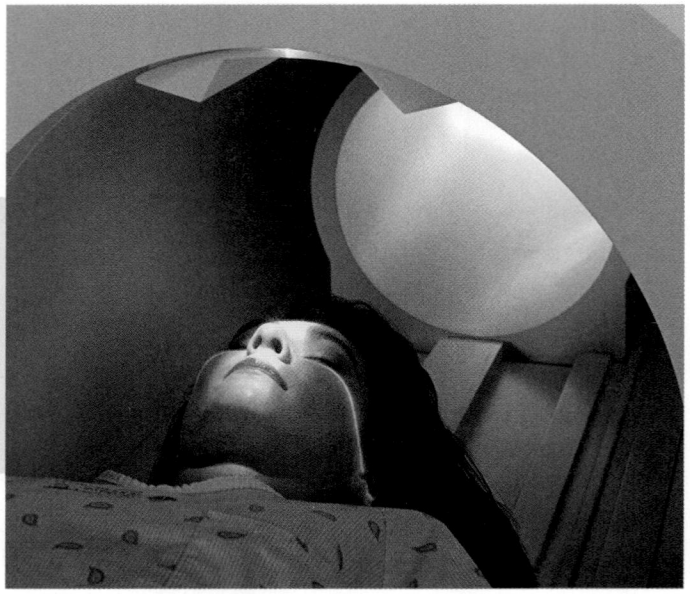

Medical Uses

In medicine, MRI is used for diagnosing diseases, disorders, and injuries, and helps physicians determine treatment. MRI is used to view the structures of the head and spine and to detect tumors and other abnormalities in the chest, abdomen, joints, and other parts of the body.

Other Uses

MRI technology is used outside medicine in various areas of science and research, particularly chemistry.

Nuclear Magnetic Resonance. A specialized form of this technology called *nuclear magnetic resonance* (NMR) spectroscopy helps scientists determine the chemical makeup and molecular structure of substances. NMR spectroscopy is often used in the pharmaceutical industry to analyze new chemical compounds.

MAGNETIC POWERHOUSES

Most MRI devices are so large and have such a strong magnetic field that they need to be housed in special facilities, such as clinics, medical centers, and research institutes. However, smaller, less powerful, and portable MRI units can be used for some imaging procedures.

Nevertheless, the strength of the magnetic field is so great that MRI cannot be used on people with metal implants, such as pacemakers or certain artificial joints.

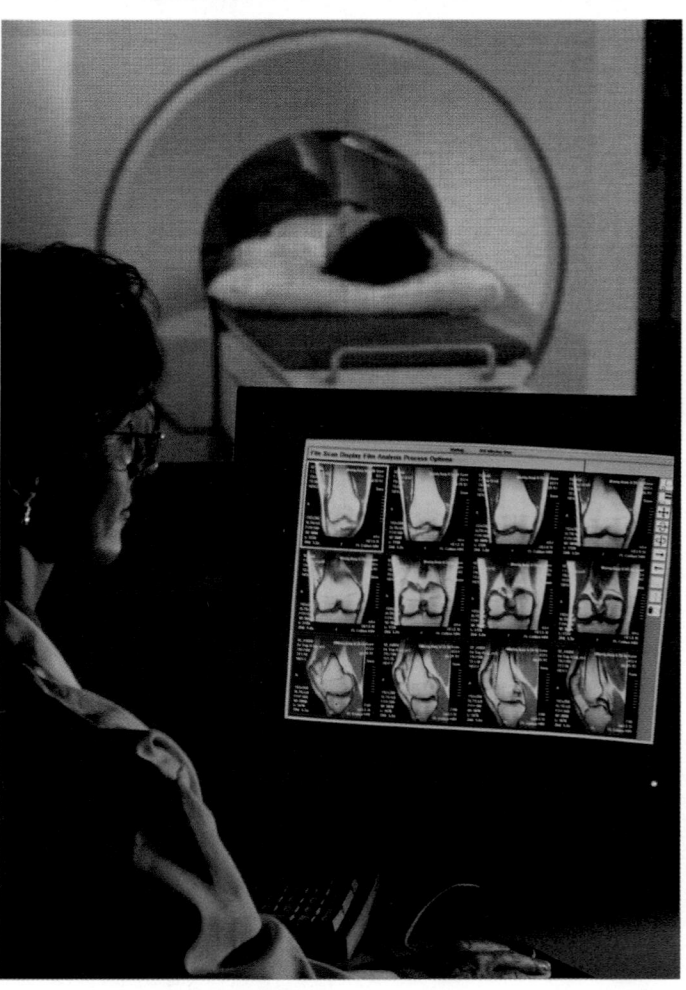

An MRI examination or scan is supervised by a *radiologist*— a physician trained in using images for medical diagnosis. ▶

How It Works

An MRI system is made up of one or more large magnets as well as computers and devices for transmitting and receiving radio waves.

- During the MRI scan, a magnetic field is applied to the person's body. (See pages 818–819.)
- The magnetic field causes nuclei in certain atoms in the body, mainly atoms of water, to line up.
- Radio waves are then directed at the nuclei.
- If the frequency of the radio waves equals that of the atom, a *resonance condition* results.
- This condition enables the nuclei to absorb the energy of the radio waves.
- When the radio-wave stimulation stops, the nuclei return to their original state and emit energy in the form of weak radio signals.

Translating the Signals. The strength and length of these signals—and therefore the kind of image produced—depends on the properties of the tissue. For example, the signal generated in portions of the body containing fluid is different from the signal generated by portions composed of fat.

Computers translate the signals into detailed images. In some imaging procedures, patients may receive an injection of a *contrast agent,* a chemical that enhances the resulting image.

MRI can measure the diffusion of water molecules in the body. This information is used to construct images that indicate the connections and directions of nerve fibers in the brain.

Reading the Images. With these images, scientists can study the structure of the healthy brain and the diseases that damage nerve tissue, such as multiple sclerosis. They can also identify areas of restricted diffusion in brain tissue, which occurs in a type of stroke called ischemic stroke, where a blood vessel in the brain becomes blocked.

Quantifying Magnetism

MRI devices have a strong magnetic field, the strength of which is measured in units called *gauss* or *tesla*.

- One tesla equals 10,000 gauss.
- Earth's magnetic field at its surface is about 1/2 gauss.
- Fields of magnets used in industry may measure more than 2 tesla (20,000 gauss).
- Hospitals use MRI systems of 0.5 to 3 tesla (5,000 to 30,000 gauss).
- Medical scientists use systems of about 1.5 to 9.0 tesla (15,000 to 90,000 gauss) for research.

MAPPING BRAIN FUNCTION

A more specialized form of MRI called *functional MRI* (fMRI) can provide information about brain function as opposed to conventional MRI techniques, which only image brain anatomy. Functional MRI is used to detect and view areas of increased blood flow and blood volume in the brain.

Scientists know that blood flow increases in regions of the brain where brain cells are active. Increases in blood flow in a particular region of the brain observed with fMRI suggest activity there. Research scientists use fMRI to reveal which regions of the brain are active during particular mental operations.

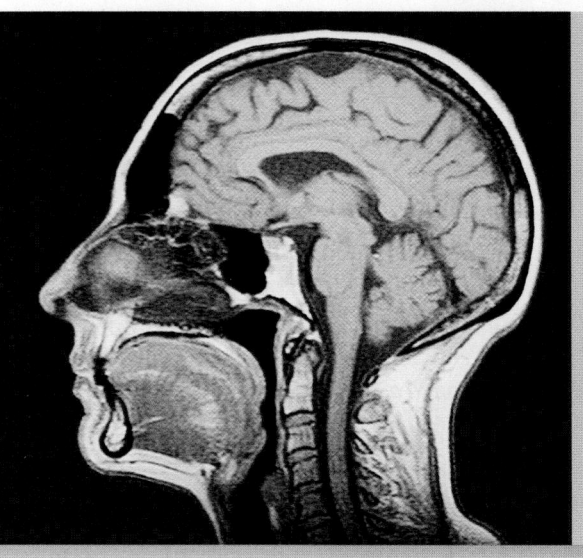

CHEMISTRY PRACTICE

In solving these problems, we will show the units with modern scientific abbreviations. We will also try to keep the same number of figures in the final answers as are in the original data. The solutions have been separated from the problems. Solutions begin on page 430.

Moles, Molecules, Gases, and Stoichiometry

1. **a)** Suppose that you have 25.0 g of SeO_2, how many moles and molecules would you have?

   b) If it was treated to make H_2Se and this gas was collected in a 2.00 L bulb, what would be its pressure in atmospheres at 25°C?

2. Assume that the chemical reaction, $3H_2(g) + N_2(g) \rightarrow 2NH_3(g)$, goes to completion.

   a) If the gases were measured by volume, all at the same temperature and pressure, what would be the final volume if 3 volumes of H_2 were allowed to react with 1 volume of N_2?

   b) To make 1.00 mol of NH_3, how many moles of H_2 and N_2 would have to be mixed?

   c) If 2.00 mol of H_2 were mixed with 1.00 mol of N_2, how many moles of NH_3 would be produced?

Molecular and Electronic Structures

3. Write valence and electron dot diagrams for: Cl_2, HCl, CH_4, C_2H_2, and C_2H_2O.

4. Molecules with a central atom which is surrounded by four atoms and has a closed octet are found to have perfect tetrahedral structures. Examples are CH_4, NH_4^+, BH_4^-, ClO_4^-, and many organic molecules. The molecule SF_4 does not have a perfect tetrahedral structure. Give a logical reason why this might be true.

5. What is the simplest electron configuration for the carbon atom which has four unpaired electrons suitable to form four single bonds? Is this the normal configuration for carbon?

Bond Energy, Spectroscopy, and Thermochemistry

6. Use bonding arguments to explain why the bond-dissociation energy for the first oxygen from CO_2 giving CO and an O-atom is much less than the bond-dissociation energy of CO.

7. When the atomic weights of the elements were first being established, an important tool was the law of Dulong and Petit. It stated that the heat capacity of metals was equal to 6.0 cal/mol, and it was used to establish approximate atomic weights. They had no idea why this might be true, but later simple theory has explained why this can be true. As an example, use the following data to determine an approximate atomic weight for a metal and identify it in the periodic table. A 278 g sample of shiny metal was heated to 98.7°C in a dry beaker immersed in boiling water. The heated metal was dropped into 200 g of water, previously cooled to 8.7°C, in an insulated cup and the final temperature reached was 29.5°C.

8. An important chemical question about the interaction of light and matter is whether ordinary visible light can break chemical bonds and so take molecules apart. Its energy is high enough to make excited electronic states in many molecules, but is it large enough to break chemical bonds? We have not given you Planck's constant, but from it one can calculate that the energy of a photon of visible light, and at 500 nm wavelength it is very close to $4.0 \cdot 10^{-19}$ J. This seems a small number, but when we talk about molecules, chemists use moles. Compare this photon energy to the bond-dissociation energies of typical molecules. If it can break bonds, what kind of bonds could it break?

Acids, Bases, and Chemical Equilibrium

9. Every acid has a conjugate base. The stronger the acid, the weaker its conjugate base. The weaker the acid, the stronger the base. For each of the following acids, identify their conjugate base.

H_2S, HS^-, H_3PO_4, $H_2PO_4^-$, HPO_4^{2-}, NH_4^+, H_2SO_4, HSO_4^-

10. Ammonium ion is a typical weak acid, and its acid dissociation constant, $K_a = 5.7 \cdot 10^{-10}$. Assume that one started with a solution which had $[NH_4^+] = 0.10$ M and initially had the $[NH_3] = 0$. Calculate the equilibrium $[H^+]$ and pH.

11. Balance the following chemical equations using the principle that the same number of atoms of each type must be present on both sides of the equation. Some may involve oxidation and reduction, but they can be easily balanced using atoms alone. For aqueous reactions omit spectator ions.

a) $H_{2(g)} + Fe_2O_{3(s)} \rightarrow Fe_{(s)} + H_2O_{(g)}$

b) $HCl_{(aq)} + Fe_2O_{3(s)} \rightarrow Fe^{3+}_{(aq)} + H_2O$

c) $NaOH_{(aq)} + H_2S_{(g)} \rightarrow$ two possible products $+ H_2O$

Problems

Oxidation-Reduction and Electrochemistry

12. Balance the following oxidation-reduction reactions. These reactions are sufficiently complex that the gain and loss of electrons are best accounted for in your balancing method. In aqueous solution, it is often not known if water is consumed or produced. This is part of the balancing, but assume these reactions take place in a solution with excess H^+.

a) $Cr_2O_7^{2-} + Fe^{2+} \rightarrow Cr^{3+} + Fe^{3+}$

b) $Cu^+ \rightarrow Cu^{2+} + Cu_{(s)}$

c) $Cu_{(s)} + NO^{3-} \rightarrow NO_{2(g)} + Cu^{2+}$

13. Look at the table of reduction potentials. Which species listed is the best reducing agent? Which is the best oxidizing agent? If you bubbled $O_{2(g)}$ into an acidic solution of $FeCl_2$ what chemistry should take place?

14. The lead-acid storage batteries used in automobiles are quite large and heavy. They are often rated by the number of amperes of current that could be delivered over an hour. Calculate the number of moles of electrons produced by a 100-ampere-hour battery drain. Also calculate the number of grams of lead per cell which would be converted into lead sulfate because of this current drain.

Inorganic Chemistry, the Periodic Table, and Table of Elements

15. One of the interesting properties of the elements which was found shortly after the periodic table was first proposed was called the "apparent atomic volume." It was calculated by dividing the atomic weight of each element by its measured density. Use the density for solid argon of 1.83 g/cm³ that we previously used to calculate a true atomic volume and radius, and the specific gravity for potassium and calcium given in the table of elements, to calculate these three elements' "apparent atomic volume." Specific gravity uses the density of water as reference, but they are close in value to the actual densities in g/cm³. What can you conclude about this property at the start of a new group 1 element? Can you think of a reason based on orbitals, which of course were unknown at that time?

16. Most properties of elements and their compounds vary uniformly with their position in the periodic table. The boiling temperatures of the noble gases, for example, increase uniformly from He at 4K to Ne at 27K and down to Xe at 166K. The same uniform trend is followed by the group 14 compounds with hydrogen where CH_4 boils at 112K and SiH_4, for example, boils at 161K. On the other hand, when we consider the similar group 15 compounds, NH_3 boils at 240K while PH_3 boils lower at 186K. This deviation is most extreme in group 16 where H_2O boils at 373K while H_2S boils at 211K, and when we go down to H_2Se, the normal trend resumes since it boils at 231K. What causes the uniform increase, and why is the uniform increase in group 14 but in groups 15 and 16?

Organic Molecules and Organic Chemistry

17. The carbonyl group is one of the most important ones in organic chemistry. It is an oxygen which is double bonded to a carbon and the simplest example, formaldehyde, $H_2C=O$, has the same number of electrons as ethylene, $H_2C=CH_2$. Discuss the bonding in formaldehyde including the lone pairs and bonding orbitals.

18. The compound called allene has a central carbon with two double bonds, and its structural formula can be written as $H_2C=C=CH_2$. It is found that the planes formed by the two CH_2 groups are at right angles to each other. Use the orbital description of the bonding in ethylene, $H_2C=CH_2$, to explain why the two CH_2 groups in ethylene are in the same plane while in allene they are at right angles.

19. Alcohols are a simple example of the systematic IUPAC naming of chemical compounds. One puts a designation of "ol" after the name of the longest chain of hydrocarbons in the molecule. A lowest possible number is added to designate the location of the $-OH$ group. Similar numbers are also added to indicate any branching of the hydrocarbon chain. The rules are quite complex, but try to write structures for the following alcohols.

a) Ethanol

b) 2-Propanol

c) 2-Methyl-2-propanol

d) 1-Butanol

Solutions

Moles, Molecules, Gases, and Stoichiometry

1. a) The symbol Se represents Selenium. Its atomic weight is 78.96, or 78.96 g-mol^{-1} with units, and the molecular weight of the compound is

$$78.96 + 2(15.999) \, 5 = 110.96 \text{ g-mol}^{-1}$$

Then for the moles,

$$\frac{25.0 \text{ g}}{110.96 \text{ g-mol}^{-1}} = 0.225 \text{ mol of } SeO_2.$$

For molecules, 0.225 mol $\times 6.02 \cdot 10^{23}$ molecules/mol $= 1.35 \times 10^{23}$ molecules.

b) Since SeO_2 and H_2Se both contain one Se atom, we can conclude that the moles of gaseous H_2Se would also be 0.225 mol. To solve for the pressure, we need to use the ideal gas relations. At 1 atm and 0°C, it would occupy

$$0.225 \text{ mol} \cdot 22.4 \text{ L-mol}^{-1} = 5.04 \text{ L}$$

with

$$\frac{P_1 V_1}{T_1} = \frac{P_2 V_2}{T_2}$$

$$P_1 = P_2 \left(\frac{V_1}{V_2}\right)\left(\frac{T_1}{T_2}\right)$$

$$= 1 \text{ atm} \, \frac{5.04 \text{ L}}{2.00 \text{ L}} \cdot \frac{273 \text{ deg} + 25 \text{ deg}}{273 \text{ deg}}$$

$$= 2.75 \text{ atm}$$

2. a) Since the number of moles is proportional to the volume, we can see that these volumes follow the balanced chemical reaction. As a result, the reaction will produce 2 volumes of NH_3.

b) If we divide all the coefficients in the equation by 2, the equation will then produce 1.00 mole of NH_3. It will then show that 3/2 moles of H_2 and 1/2 moles of N_2 will give 1.00 mole of NH_3.

c) This is known as a limiting reagent problem. One of the two reactants is too small compared with the other to follow the balanced equation. This means that one reactant will be used up completely, the limiting reagent, and some of the other will be left over after the reaction takes place. Since the reaction requires three times more moles of H_2 than of N_2, and we only start with twice as much, it is clear that the H_2 would be the limiting reagent.

To determine how much NH_3 is produced, we need to determine how many moles of NH_3 can be produced by 2.00 moles of H_2. We can multiply all the coefficients in the equation by 2/3 or we can use a conversion factor. From the equation, we have

$$3 \text{ mol of } H_2 = 2 \text{ mol of } NH_3$$

Using this as an algebraic formula, we obtain

$$\frac{(2 \text{ mol of } NH_3)}{(3 \text{ mol of } H_2)} = 1$$

This is a conversion factor. So if we start with

$$2.00 \text{ mol of } H_2 \cdot 1$$

$$= 2.00 \cdot (2/3) \text{ mol of } NH_3$$

$$= 1.33 \text{ mol of } NH_3$$

This is the same result as multiplying all the coefficients by 2/3. One can also see that 2/3 moles of N_2 will be turned into NH_3, and 1/3 moles of N_2 will be left unreacted.

Molecular and Electronic Structures

3. For Cl_2, its valence diagram is $Cl-Cl$, and its electron dot diagram is

$$:\overset{..}{\underset{..}{Cl}}:\overset{..}{\underset{..}{Cl}}:$$

For HCl, the covalent valence diagram is $H-Cl$, and its ionic diagram is H^+ and Cl^-. The two corresponding electron dot diagrams are

$$\text{ionic } H^+:\overset{..}{\underset{..}{Cl}}:^-, \text{ covalent } H:\overset{..}{\underset{..}{Cl}}:$$

For CH_4, they are

$$H:\overset{H}{\underset{H}{C}}:H, \quad H-\overset{\displaystyle H}{\underset{\displaystyle H}{C}}-H$$

For C_2H_2, they are

$$H-C\equiv C-H, \quad H:C:::C:H$$

For C_2H_2O, there are three possible valence diagrams, but the one with an O–H bond and the one with a three-membered ring are not stable molecules. The only stable molecule with the formula of C_2H_2O is called ketene and its diagrams are

$$\overset{\displaystyle H}{\underset{\displaystyle H}{\diagdown\diagup}}C=C=O, \quad \overset{\displaystyle H}{\underset{\displaystyle H}{C}}:\overset{..}{\underset{..}{C}}::\overset{..}{\underset{..}{O}}$$

4. The sulfur atom has 6 valence electrons and each fluorine has 7 valence electrons. This is a total of 34 valence electrons. If we assume that each fluorine has a closed octet, this will require 32 electrons, and if four single bonds are formed to the sulfur that would complete its octet, we have a pair of electrons left over. The simplest reasoning is that the sulfur keeps this extra pair and is surrounded by five pairs of electrons. This is called an expanded octet. A similar expanded octet is found in PF_5, with the phosphorous surrounded by five pairs of electrons. The structure of PF_5 is that of a trigonal bipyramid, that is, two three-sided pyramids back to back with shared bases. The two 180° bonds along the axis of the pyramids are longer, and weaker than, the three 120° bonds along the base. The structure found for SF_4 looks a little like two 180° bonds and two 120° bonds, and the extra electron pair is assumed to take up the space of the missing 120° bond. This is explained by the repulsion of the electron pairs, both bonding and lone pair, by a very useful method called valence shell electron pair repulsion (VSEPR) theory.

5. Carbon has six electrons with the first two filling the 1s. For the remaining four electrons to be unpaired, they would occupy the next four orbitals which are the 2s, $2p_x$, $2p_y$, and $2p_z$. This electron configuration would be $(1s)^2(2s)^1(2p_x)^1(2p_y)^1(2p_z)^1$. The lowest energy configuration has the 2s orbital filled with paired electrons, and the last two electrons in any two of the 2p orbitals. As a result, in forming its four chemical bonds, carbon utilizes an excited electronic configuration, but this extra energy is more than made up by the extra energy released in forming four bonds instead of just two.

Solutions

Bond Energy, Spectroscopy, and Thermochemistry

6. The bond-dissociation energy for the first oxygen in CO_2 is the difference between the energy stored in the CO_2 molecule and that stored in CO plus an O-atom. Chemical bonds decrease the energy stored in a molecule compared to the separated parts. Starting with CO, which has a triple bond, it has a high bond-dissociation energy equal to 1,070 kJ/mol. This is because triple bonds are very stable and are hard to break. For CO_2, while it is a stable molecule with two double bonds, one of the products from bond-dissociation is CO with its triple bond. As a result, the value of 528 kJ/mol for the bond-dissociation energy of one oxygen from CO_2 is the energy required to break a double bond in CO_2 minus the energy released by changing the remaining double bond into a triple bond. Carbon dioxide is almost unique in this regard. For H_2O one can see that breaking the bond in OH requires even less energy than the bond-dissociation energy of the first H-atom in H_2O.

7. We assume that the heat lost by the metal is equal to the heat gained by the water.

$$\text{heat gained by water} =$$
$$1.00 \text{ (cal/g-deg)} \cdot 200 \text{ g} \cdot (29.5 - 8.7)$$
$$\text{deg} = 4{,}160 \text{ cal, and}$$

$$\text{heat lost by metal} = 4{,}160 \text{ cal} =$$
$$C \text{ (cal/g-deg)} \cdot 278 \text{ g} \cdot (98.7 - 29.5) \text{ deg}$$

Then, solving for C:

$$C = 0.216 \text{ cal/g-deg}$$

With Dulong and Petit,

$$C = 0.216 \text{ (cal/g-deg)}$$
$$= \frac{6.0 \text{ (cal/mol-deg)}}{\text{Atomic Weight (g/mol)}}$$

Solving, we obtain atomic weight = 27.7 g/mol. The metal must be aluminum since silicon is not a metal. But with this approximate atomic weight one could determine its valence as a check.

Acids, Bases, and Chemical Equilibrium

9. Each acid loses one proton to make its conjugate base. We will write them as acid/base pairs.

$$\frac{H_2S}{HS^-}, \frac{HS^-}{S^{2-}}, \frac{H_3PO_4}{H_2PO_4^-}, \frac{H_2PO_4^-}{HPO_4^{2-}},$$

$$\frac{HPO_4^{2-}}{PO_4^{3-}}, \frac{NH_4}{NH_3}, \frac{H_2SO_4}{HSO_4^-}, \frac{HSO_4^-}{SO_4^{2-}}$$

In the case of NH_3, it was, in the past, written as NH_4OH and called ammonium hydroxide, but this confuses its relation to NH_4^+. We now call it aqueous ammonia and it is simply gaseous NH_3 dissolved in water. The weakest acid on the list is HS^-, and the strongest is H_2SO_4.

10. The acid-base equilibrium for NH_4^+ is

$$NH^{4+} = H^+ + NH_3, \text{ and}$$

$$\frac{[H^+][NH_3]}{NH4^+} = 5.7 \cdot 10^{-10}$$

Since there was no initial NH_3 in the solution, both H^+ and NH_3 should be produced equally, and

$$[H^+] = [NH_3] = x$$

So the equilibrium equation should be

$$\frac{x^2}{0.10} = 5.7 \cdot 10^{-10} \text{ or } x^2 = 5.7 \cdot 10^{-11}$$

This gives $[H^+] = x = 7.5 \cdot 10^{-6}$ M, and pH = 5.1. This is a slightly acid solution. We assumed that the $[NH^{4+}]$ is not decreased much by the ion-ization and we set it equal to 0.10 M. Since $(0.10 - 7.5 = 10^{-6}) = 0.10$ to two figure accuracy, this was a correct assumption.

8. If we multiply this photon energy by Avogadro's number, we obtain

$$4.0 \cdot 10^{-19} \text{ J/particle} \cdot 6.0 \cdot 10^{23} \text{ particles/mol}$$
$$= 2.4 \cdot 10^5 \text{ J/mol}$$
$$= 240 \text{ kJ/mol}$$

If we look at the table of bond-dissociation energies, we see that only F_2 and Cl_2 can be dissociated by such a small energy, and for Cl_2 it is very close. Most chemical bonds require almost twice this much energy. Twice the photon energy goes into the ultraviolet, and it has one-half the wavelength or about 250 nm. On the surface of the earth, the ozone in the upper atmosphere keeps such short wavelengths from reaching us, but in the upper atmosphere short wavelength light from the sun can do lots of photochemistry. We can conclude that only weak single bonds could be directly broken by visible light.

11. a) For every oxygen turned into water, we must have one H_2 molecule, so

$$3H_{2(g)} + Fe_2O_{3(s)} \rightarrow 2Fe_{(s)} + 3H_2O_{(g)}$$

b) HCl dissolved in water produces H^+ and Cl^- ions. In this case, Cl^- is a spectator ion.

$$6H^+ + Fe_2O_{3(s)} \rightarrow 2Fe^{3+}_{(aq)} + 3H_2O$$

Note that the charges are also balanced.

c) NaOH dissolved in water produces Na^+ and OH^- ions, and the Na^+ is a spectator ion. Either one or two hydrogens can be removed from the dissolved H_2S, giving two different products.

$$OH^- + H_2S_{(g)} \rightarrow HS^- + H_2O, \text{ or}$$
$$2OH^- + H_2S_{(g)} \rightarrow S^{2-} + 2H_2O$$

Oxidation-Reduction and Electrochemistry

12. a) The way to calculate the oxidation state of the Cr in $Cr_2O_7^{2-}$ is explained in the text, and so

$$Cr_2O_7^{2-} + 6e^- \rightarrow 2Cr^{3+} + 7O^{2-}$$

as reduction and

$$Fe^{2+} \rightarrow Fe^{3+} + e^-$$

as oxidation. The oxide ion, O^{2-}, is a very strong base, and in an acid solution it is turned into H_2O. If we balance the electrons by using $6Fe^{2+}$ for every $Cr_2O_7^{2-}$ and turn the oxide ions into water, we have

$$Cr_2O_7^{2-} + 6Fe^{2+} + 14H^+ \rightarrow$$
$$2Cr^{3+} + 6Fe^{3+} + 7H_2O$$

We can check the balancing by seeing that the charges are equal on both sides so that

$$-2 + 6(+2) + 14(+1) = -2 + 12 + 14 = 24$$

on the left, and

$$2(+3) + 6(+3) = 6 + 18 = 24$$

on the right. They have the same charge, and so the equation must be balanced.

b) In this case, the species, Cu^+, is not stable and it is both oxidized and reduced. These two changes are

$$Cu^+ + e^- \rightarrow Cu_{(s)}, \text{ reduction, and}$$
$$Cu^+ \rightarrow Cu^{2+} + e^-, \text{ oxidation.}$$

Balancing these gives

$$2Cu^+ \rightarrow Cu_{(s)} + Cu^{2+}$$

c) In strong acid, NO_3^- is an oxidizing agent. The nitrogen in NO_3^- is +5 and in NO_2 it is reduced to +4. The electron changes are

$$NO_3^- + e^- \rightarrow NO_{2(g)} + O^{2-}, \text{ and}$$
$$Cu_{(s)} \rightarrow 2e^- + Cu^{2+}$$

Balancing

$$2NO^{3-} + Cu_{(s)} + 4H^+ \rightarrow$$
$$2NO_{2(g)} + Cu^{2+} + 2H_2O$$

for an acid solution.

Solutions

13. The more negative the reduction potential the more difficult it is to reduce the oxidizing agent on the left side of the reaction, and the stronger is the reducing agent on the right side. So Li metal is the best reducing agent in this table, and $F_{2(g)}$ is the best oxidizing agent.

In the table, $O_{2(g)}$ in acid is a better oxidizing agent than is Fe^{3+}, going to Fe^{2+}, and a poorer oxidizing agent than $Cl_{2(g)}$, going to Cl^-. As a result, when $O_{2(g)}$ is bubbled into a $FeCl_2$ solution, the Fe^{2+} should be oxidized to Fe^{3+}, but the Cl^- will not be oxidized to $Cl_{2(g)}$.

14. An ampere is equal to a flow of a coulomb of charge per second. The total charge is given by

$$\text{charge} = 100\ (\text{coulomb/sec}) \cdot 1\ \text{hr} \cdot$$
$$60\ (\text{min/hr}) \cdot 60\ (\text{sec/min})$$
$$= 3.60 \cdot 10^5\ \text{coulomb}$$

Using the Faraday, we can calculate the moles of electrons to give this charge,

$$\text{moles of electrons} = 3.60 \cdot \frac{10^5\ \text{coulomb}}{(96{,}500\ \text{coulomb/mol})}$$
$$= 3.73\ \text{mol}$$

To convert 1 mol of Pb into 1 mol of Pb^{2+} requires 2 mol of electrons, as a result

$$\text{grams of lead} = 3.73\ \text{mol} \cdot 1/2 \cdot 207\ \text{g/mol}$$
$$= 386\ \text{g}$$

Inorganic Chemistry, the Periodic Table, and Table of Elements

15. If we use densities of 1.83, 0.86, and 1.55 g/cm³ for Ar, K, and Ca, we obtain 45.5, and 25.9 cm³/mol for their apparent atomic volumes. Using potassium as an example, apparent atomic volume of potassium =

$$\frac{39.1\ (\text{g/mol})}{0.86\ (\text{g/cm}^3)} = 45.5\ \text{cm}^3/\text{mol}$$

It is clear that this volume passes through a maximum for this group 1 element. Further calculations show that this volume jumps up in value at Na, K, Rb, and Cs. Since this jump in volume must be due to a marked increase in the atomic radius, we can conclude that the new electron in the $(ns)^1$ orbital has a large radius. When one goes to the group 2 element with a filled $(ns)^2$ orbital, the increased nuclear charge brings this ns orbital back to more normal size.

16. One has to remember that turning a substance into its gas breaks all the intermolecular forces present in its liquid. The van der Waals forces, which hold most liquids together, are stronger in the heavier elements with more electrons, and this establishes the normal trend. The unusual intermolecular forces in NH_3 and H_2O, which raise their boiling points, are clearly their very strong hydrogen bonds. The group 14 compounds have no lone pair electrons and no hydrogen bonds, and so they follow the normal trend. At the same time, we must conclude that the hydrogen bonds are much weaker in H_2S than in H_2O, but this is expected since oxygen is more electronegative than is sulfur.

Organic Molecules and Organic Chemistry

17. Ethylene has σ bonds between the carbons and the hydrogens and a σ bond between the two carbons which is part of the double bond. The double bond is completed by a π bond between the carbons. The electron dot diagram for formaldehyde looks very similar to that for ethylene except that there are two lone pairs on the oxygen instead of shared pairs between a carbon and two hydrogens. So we would expect the same bonding orbitals as in ethylene except that two lone pairs on the oxygen take the place of two σ bonds to hydrogens. The C=O bond is much more polar than the C=C bond and this has a great effect upon the hydrogens or other groups substituted on the carbon.

19. a) This is often called ethyl alcohol, and it is $CH_3CH_2\_OH$. The number 1 is not necessary.

b) This is often called isopropyl alcohol, and it is

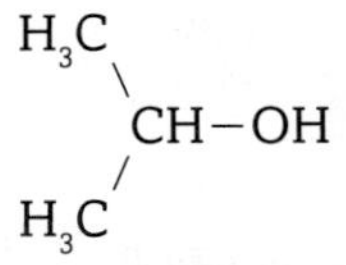

$$H_3C$$
$$\diagdown$$
$$CH-OH$$
$$\diagup$$
$$H_3C$$

c) This is often called tert-butyl alcohol, where tert means tertiary, and it is

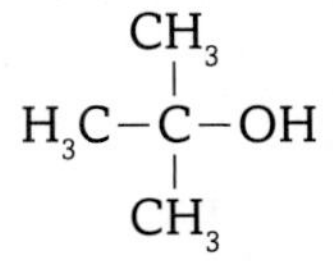

$$CH_3$$
$$|$$
$$H_3C-C-OH$$
$$|$$
$$CH_3$$

d) This is often called n-butyl alcohol, and it is $CH_3CH_2CH_2CH_2\_OH$. The number 1 is not necessary.

18. The double bond in ethylene is formed by the p_z orbitals on each carbon overlapping to form a π molecular orbital. The second component of the double bond is a σ molecular orbital which forms the x-y plane along with the σ bonds of the CH_2 groups. The central carbon in allene has a problem. If it uses its p_z orbital to form one of its π bonds, it cannot use this same orbital to form the other π bond. As a result, the second π bond has to be formed using either its p_x or p_y orbitals. Since this must be true, one of the two end carbons must be using its p_z orbitals in its double bond and the other end carbon is using either a p_x or p_y orbital for its double bond. This leaves the planes formed by the two CH_2 groups at right angles to each other.

Chemistry Glossary

SOUTHWESTERN

acid compound that produces hydrogen ions in water and that is able to donate hydrogen ions to other compounds.

addition reaction in organic chemistry, a reaction in which one substance is added on to the structure of another, producing a single compound.

alcohol class of organic compounds in which the hydroxyl group (−OH) is added on to a hydrocarbon group.

alicyclics hydrocarbons that have their carbon atoms arranged in a ring.

aliphatics hydrocarbon consisting of compounds with their carbon atoms arranged in an open-chain structure.

alkali metal metallic element that belongs to Group IA of the periodic table and that forms a strong base when combined with the hydroxide group.

alkane hydrocarbon in which there are only single bonds between carbon atoms.

alkene hydrocarbon in which there is one double bond between two carbon atoms, and the rest of the carbon bonds are single.

alkyne hydrocarbon in which there is one triple bond between two carbon atoms, and the rest of the carbon-carbon bonds are single.

alpha particle particle consisting of two protons and two neutrons; a helium nucleus.

anion a negatively charged molecule (radical) or atom that collects at the anode (positive electrode) of an electrolytic cell and gives up its excess electrons to that anode. Positively charged ions migrate to the cathode (negative electrode), where they accept electrons and are designated as cations.

aromatic hydrocarbon in which the benzene ring structure is present. They are so named because many members have a distinctive odor.

atmospheric pressure the pressure produced by the weight of the air from the top of the atmosphere as it presses down upon the layers of air below it.

atom the smallest particle of an element that can exhibit the properties of that element.

atomic mass the mass of an atom compared with carbon-12, which has been assigned a mass of 12 atomic mass units.

atomic number number of protons that are in the nucleus of an atom, or the number of electrons.

Avogadro's number 6.022×10^{23} (602.2 billion trillion), or the number of elementary entities that make up 1 mole of any substance. It is equal to the number of atoms found in 12 grams of the isotope carbon-12. Scientists chose the number as a standard reference number for the International System of Units.

balanced equation an equation that has an equal number of atoms of each element on each side of the arrow.

base compound that produces hydroxide ions in water, or that is capable of receiving a hydrogen ion from an acid.

beta particle electron that is emitted by the nucleus of a radioactive atom.

breeder reactor nuclear reactor used to produce nuclear fuel (often in the form of synthetic elements) as well as nuclear energy.

catalyst a substance that increases the rate of a chemical reaction by lowering the activation energy for the reaction.

chain reaction process in which the splitting of one atomic nucleus gives off neutrons that cause the splitting of other atomic nuclei.

chemical change a change in which one substance is converted to another.

chemical element any substance that contains only one kind of atom.

chemical equation a statement, consisting of symbols and formulas, that summarizes the changes that occur in a chemical reaction.

chemical equilibrium the state of balance achieved when the rate of the forward reaction is equal to the rate of the reverse reaction.

chemical properties properties that describe the way a substance may change to form other substances.

chemical reaction the process by which one or more substances are converted into one or more different substances.

coefficients the numbers in front of the formulas. Coeffecients indicate how many units of the substances are used and produced in the reaction.

compound substance consisting of two or more elements joined by chemical bonds.

covalent bond chemical bond between two atoms in which electrons are shared.

crystalline solids solids whose atoms are arranged in an orderly geometric pattern that repeats itself. Most solids are crystalline solids.

distillation a separation process in which a liquid's components are separately converted to a vapor by applying heat (a vacuum may be applied simultaneously to lower the boiling points of the components involved), then drawn off, cooled or condensed, and collected.

electrolyte a substance that conducts electricity.

electron fundamental negatively charged particle of matter.

electronegativity the ability of an atom to attract electrons—between the atoms of the molecule.

element substance that cannot be broken down into simpler substances by ordinary chemical means.

endothermic process the conversion of a solid to a liquid (melting), a liquid to a gas (vaporization), or a solid to a gas (sublimation).

endothermic reactions changes in which energy is absorbed.

energy the ability to do work or transfer heat.

enzymes molecules (usually proteins) that speed up chemical reactions in all living things.

exothermic process the conversion of a liquid to a solid (freezing), a gas to a liquid (condensation), or a gas to a solid (deposition).

exothermic reactions changes in which energy is released.

gamma rays high-frequency radiation, similar to X-rays, emitted by substances that are radioactive.

gas matter that has no fixed volume or shape—it takes the volume and shape of its container.

half-life period of time it takes for half the radioactive atoms in a given mass to decay.

heat the energy that results from the vibrations, motions, reactions, and collisions of nuclear particles, atoms, and molecules.

heat capacity the amount of heat (calories) necessary to raise the temperature of 1 gram of a given substance by 1°C. The heat of fusion is the amount of heat needed to convert 1 gram of a solid into a liquid at its melting point. The heat of vaporization is the amount of heat required to convert 1 gram of a liquid into a vapor at its boiling point.

hydrocarbon compound consisting only of hydrogen and carbon.

inorganic chemistry this is the branch of chemistry that deals with the reactions of elements other than carbon.

ion atom or group of atoms bearing an electric charge.

ionic bond chemical bond formed by the transfer of electrons from one atom to another.

isotope form of an element differing from other forms in atomic mass but not in atomic number.

ketone class of organic compounds in which the carbonyl group ($-CO-$) is contained.

metal element that loses electrons easily, has a high luster, and is a good conductor of heat and electricity.

kinetic energy the energy of an object due to its motion.

kinetic theory the theory that states that all matter—including gases—is made up of particles—atoms or molecules—that are in constant motion.

Chemistry Glossary

law of conservation of energy principle stating that one form of energy can be converted to another form, but energy itself can be neither created nor destroyed.

law of conservation of mass during a chemical change the total mass of the original substance always equals the total mass of the new substance. In a chemical change, mass is conserved; it is neither created nor destroyed.

liquid matter that has a definite volume but no specific shape.

mass the quantity of matter in an atom.

mass number the number of protons and neutrons in the nucleus of an atom.

mass spectrometry a method of separating and analyzing the atoms and molecules in a chemical sample by converting them into electrically charged particles called ions.

matter the material of the universe—any substance that occupies space and takes up mass.

mixture matter that consists of two or more kinds of matter.

molar mass the mass (in grams) of one mole of a substance.

mole a standard unit devised to take practical measurements of molecules, atoms, ions, electrons, and other subatomic particles.

molecule the smallest particle of a substance that can exist free and retain the properties of that substance.

neutron nuclear particle having the same mass as a proton but zero electric charge.

noble gases the first six elements in group 18 of the periodic table: argon (Ar), helium (He), krypton (Kr), neon (Ne), radon (Rn), and xenon (Xe). They occur naturally and can be found in the atmosphere. They are called noble, or inert, gases because they do not readily react with other elements.

nuclear fission a nuclear reaction in which a large nucleus is split into smaller nuclei.

nuclear fusion nuclear reaction in which small atomic nuclei join to form a larger nucleus.

nuclear reactor device in which a nuclear reaction is controlled to produce energy.

nucleic acid a complex polymer found in all cells. The two types of nucleic acids are deoxyribonucleic acid (DNA), mainly found in the nucleus of a cell, and ribonucleic acid (RNA), which can be found throughout the cell.

organic acid class of organic compounds in which the carboxyl group ($-COOH$) is contained.

organic chemistry chemistry of carbon compounds.

oxidation reaction a chemical reaction in which a substance loses electrons.

oxidation-reduction a chemical reaction in which one or more electrons are transferred from one atom or molecule to another.

periodic table of the elements a chart that organizes the known elements based on their properties.

phase change the change of matter from one state to another.

physical change a change in which a substance changes in its physical appearance but not its basic identity.

physical properties properties, such as color and density, which can be measured without changing the basic identity of the substance.

polyatomic ion group of atoms carrying an electric charge that usually react as a unit in chemical reactions.

polymerization the process by which many small molecules combine chemically to produce a large molecule.

polymers class of organic, typically very large, linear molecules, made by linking together many small molecules, called monomers. Plastics are examples of polymers, as are proteins and nucleic acids.

potential energy the energy of an object due to its position. It can be thought of as "stored" energy.

products in a chemical formula, the substances to the right of the arrow—the substances produced.

proton nuclear particle with the same mass as a neutron, but with a positive electric charge.

pure substance a sample of matter consisting of only one kind of matter.

quantum mechanics a field of physics that explains the structure of atoms, the way they give off light, and other related matters.

radioactivity spontaneous breakdown, or decay, of unstable atoms, during which alpha, beta, or gamma radiation is emitted.

reactants in a chemical formula, the substances to the left of the arrow—the starting substances.

reduction reaction a chemical reaction in which a substance gains electrons.

salt the product, other than water, of the reaction between an acid and a base.

solid matter that has both a fixed volume and a fixed shape.

solute the substance in a solution that is dissolved.

solution a homogeneous mixture of two or more individual substances that cannot be separated by a mechanical means (such as through a filter).

solvent the substance in a solution that causes another substance to dissolve.

spectrometer a device used to observe the electromagnetic waves, such as light, X-rays, and radio waves, that atoms of a gas emit when electrons strike them. These emissions can be observed as discrete lines (called line spectra).

surface tension the amount of energy needed to stretch or increase the surface "skin" of a liquid.

thermonuclear reaction atomic fusion reaction, such as the one that occurs in the fusion or hydrogen bomb.

transmutation nuclear change in which one element is converted into another.

unsaturated hydrocarbon organic compound in which some of the carbon atoms are joined by double or triple bonds.

valence electrons electrons in the outermost shell of an atom, which take part in the formation of chemical bonds.

viscosity the internal resistance to flow in a fluid that has strong intermolecular forces.

Geology 442

Physical Geography 502

Glossary 582

PHYSICAL GEOLOGY

is the study of the interior and exterior structure of Earth. It is concerned with the processes that result in the formation of rocks and minerals as well as Earth's large-scale features, such as mountains and ocean basins.

Physical geology includes the fields of geophysics, mineralogy, and petrology, which is the study of rocks. Physical geologists hold a variety of jobs, from exploring for oil, gas, coal, and uranium, to creating maps and interpreting aerial photographs of regions of land.

Seismographs, which measure seismic waves, have taught geologists much about Earth's interior.

Earth's Interior

The inside of Earth is mostly unexplored territory. To date, no drilling project has been able to drill deeper than 15 kilometers (9.3 miles). Considering Earth's average radius of 6,370 kilometers (3,949 miles), less than 1 percent of the interior has been explored directly.

However, seismologists—scientists who study earthquakes—have learned a great deal about Earth's interior by studying shock waves generated by earthquakes. They have determined probable composition, density, pressure, gravity, and temperature deep inside Earth.

P-Waves and S-Waves

Geologists make inferences about the structure and composition of Earth's interior by measuring the behavior and velocity of seismic waves, waves generated by earthquakes. Seismic waves penetrate Earth's interior. The two types of seismic waves are *primary waves (P-waves)* and *secondary waves (S-waves).*

P-waves are compressional waves generated by the expansion and contraction of material. As P-waves travel through Earth, they push and pull the rock. P-waves can travel through solids, liquids, or gases, but they travel fastest through solids. This is because solids are denser (their atoms are more tightly packed together) than liquids or gases.

S-waves are transverse seismic waves. They are generated by shearing, or side-to-side movement of a material. S-waves can only pass through solids. They travel more slowly than P-waves and vibrate in a direction that is perpendicular to P-waves.

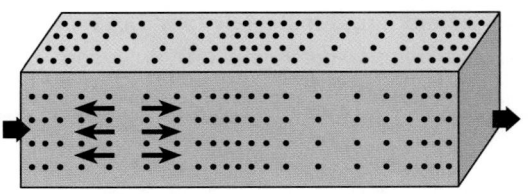

P-waves can be illustrated by a push on one end of a stretched spring. The particles in the spring vibrate parallel to the direction the wave travels.

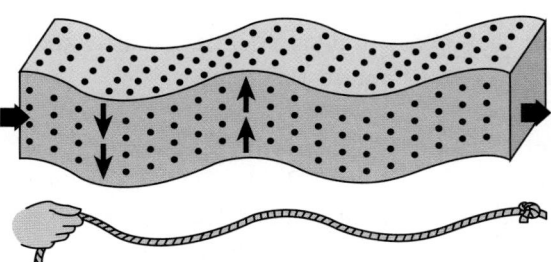

S-waves can be illustrated by flicking a stretched rope up and down or side to side. The particles vibrate perpendicular to the wave movement.

P-WAVES AND S-WAVES

P-waves

- travel through solids, liquids, and gases
- move through rock at 4–7 kilometers (2.5–4 miles) per second
- move faster through solids than through less dense liquids or gases
- travel faster deep inside Earth, where pressure is greater and rock more dense, than near the surface

S-waves

- only travel through solids
- move through rock at 2–5 kilometers (1–3 miles) per second
- are generated by side-to-side movement of material such as rock
- travel more slowly than P-waves
- vibrate perpendicular to P-waves

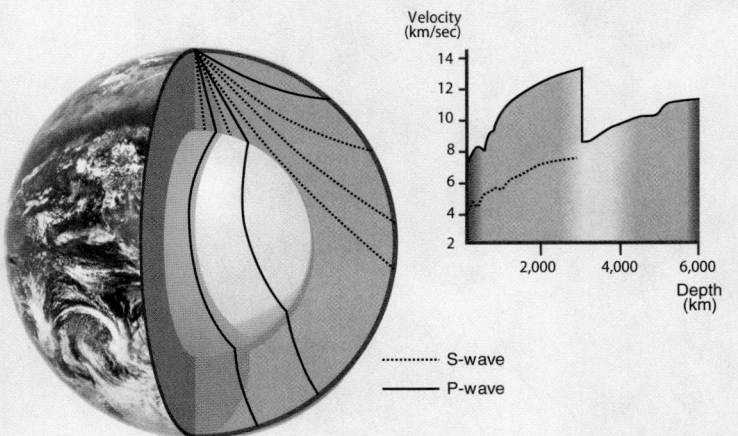

Seismic Waves. P-waves travel through both the solid and *molten,* or liquid, rock in Earth's core. S-waves stop when they hit molten rock.

EARTH'S LAYERS

Crust

- 5–10 kilometers (3–6 miles) thick under oceans
- 40–60 kilometers (24–36 miles) thick under continents

Mantle

- consists of the upper mantle, the asthenosphere, and the mesosphere
- upper mantle and the crust form the lithosphere
- the asthenosphere consists of partially melted rocks and minerals
- the mesosphere makes up 82 percent of Earth's volume and consists of solid rock

Outer Core

- consists of a dense liquid, believed to be mostly iron

Inner Core

- solid, about 2,600 kilometers (1,600 miles) in diameter

Earth's Layers

Since the early 1900s, geologists have been accumulating data showing that Earth's interior is not uniformly solid. Based on the study of seismic waves, Earth's interior is now thought to consist of solid, semisolid, and liquid materials found in four main layers: *crust, mantle, outer core,* and *inner core.*

Crust

Earth's crust is the relatively thin, brittle outer layer of Earth. The crust varies in thickness. It is thinner under the oceans than under the continents. On average, the crust extends downward through the ocean floor for 5 to 10 kilometers (3 to 6 miles). The oceanic crust is thin because of the separation of crustal plates. (See Plate Tectonics, pages 448–459.)

Continental Crust. Under continents, the crust is much thicker. The continental crust reaches an average depth of 40 to 60 kilometers (24 to 36 miles). Earth's crust is so much thicker under the continents because crustal plates collide and push upward at their boundaries.

Despite Earth's towering mountain ranges, the crust makes up only 0.6 percent of Earth's volume and only 0.4 percent of its mass.

Oceanic Crust. P-waves travel faster through oceanic crust than through continental crust. This tells geologists that the oceanic crust is denser than the continental crust. Oceanic crust samples show a greater percentage of iron and magnesium than samples of continental crust. Iron and magnesium are denser than quartz and feldspar, two minerals that are found in most rocks of the continental crust.

M-Discontinuity. Separating Earth's crust from its mantle is a region in which rocks are denser. This density boundary is called the Mohorovicic discontinuity, or M-discontinuity. The M-discontinuity was named after a Yugoslav seismologist, Andrija Mohorovicic, who discovered its presence in 1909.

The Himalaya Mountains were built up at the collision of the Asian and Indian crustal plates. Earth's crust there is over 90 kilometers (56 miles) thick.

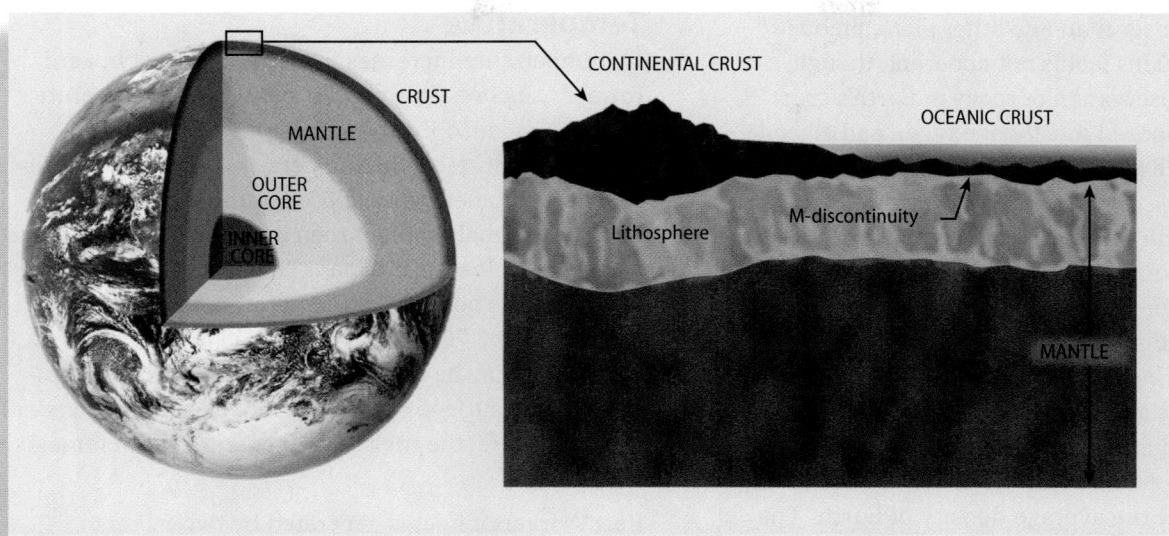

▲ **Earth's layers** consist of solid rock in the crust, upper mantle, mesosphere, and inner core. The outer core consists of a dense liquid, and the asthenosphere consists of a thick slush.

Mantle

The crust and upper mantle are together called the lithosphere (rock sphere). The upper part of the mantle, from 50 kilometers (30 miles) to a depth of about 100 kilometers (60 miles), is similar to the crust. Because of the increased velocity of P-waves, however, it is believed the material here is composed of denser, more durable rock containing a large percentage of iron and magnesium.

Zone of Weakness. From depths of about 100 kilometers (60 miles) to 250 kilometers (140 miles), P-waves slow down. Therefore, geologists think that this part of the mantle, called the *asthenosphere* (zone of weakness), is probably not solid rock. But since S-waves can travel through the asthenosphere, the asthenosphere cannot be a liquid. Geologists think that the asthenosphere is made up of a thick slush consisting of partially melted rocks and minerals.

The mesosphere, the enormously thick lower part of the mantle, is composed of solid rock. The mesosphere extends downward to a depth of 2,780 kilometers (1,724 miles). It makes up 82 percent of Earth's volume and 67 percent of its mass.

Outer Core

Earth's core is about the size of Mars. Based on the behavior of P- and S-waves, geologists think the outer core must be a dense liquid. They believe the outer core is composed mostly of iron with some nickel and trace elements, such as sulfur, carbon, and silicon. Some geologists believe that the movement of liquid iron in the outer core explains the origin of Earth's magnetic field.

Inner Core

Deeper than 5,155 kilometers (3,196 miles), P-waves speed up and S-waves reappear. Based on this and additional seismic data, geologists believe the innermost part of the core, about 2,600 kilometers (1,600 miles) in diameter, is made of a similar material as the outer core, but it is solid. The inner core is about four-fifths as big as Earth's moon.

Earth's Density

Earth is denser than any other planet in our solar system. This fact is not apparent, though, from direct observation of rocks in Earth's crust. They are composed mostly of oxygen and silicon, elements much too light to account for Earth's high density.

During Earth's formation, heavier elements, such as iron and nickel, descended to the center of the planet. The lighter elements (oxygen and silicon) were displaced and forced upward. Seismic data verify that rocks near the center of Earth are about twice as dense as rocks in the mantle and four to five times as dense as crustal rocks near the surface.

The average density of the crust and the mantle are well below the average density of Earth. The core, therefore, must be extremely dense. In fact, density readings indicate that Earth's center has a density of 12 to 13 grams per cubic centimeter (6.9 to 7.5 ounces per cubic inch). By comparison, silver has a density of about 11.5 grams per cubic centimeter.

Temperature

Temperature increases from Earth's crust inward toward the core. This regular pattern of temperature increase is called Earth's *geothermal gradient*.

Near the surface, the temperature rises 25° Celsius for every kilometer (about 85° Fahrenheit per mile). The geothermal gradient then drops sharply within the mantle to as low as 1° C per kilometer.

Geologists believe the temperature of Earth's outer core is about 3,700 to 4,300°C (6,700 to 7,800°F). The inner core may be as hot as 7,000°C (12,600°F)—hotter than the surface of the sun. But, because it is under great pressure, the rock in the center of Earth remains solid.

Earth's interior heat is generated by two factors:

- initial heat from the planet's formation, which radiates from the metallic core outward toward Earth's surface

- the decay of radioactive elements—radium, uranium, thorium, and potassium—within Earth's interior

DENSITY

Density is a physical quality that reflects how tightly the atoms in a substance are packed. Solids are denser than liquids, and liquids are denser than gases. In addition, certain solids are denser than other solids, liquids than other liquids, and gases than other gases. Earth scientists can identify minerals and other solids by measuring their density.

Earth's Density. The average density of the planet is 5.5 grams per cubic centimeter (32 ounces per cubic inch). This is about the same density as that of iron ore, shown here.

Gravity

Gravity is the force by which objects are attracted to one another. Objects feel heavy because of that force and when dropped appear to fall to earth due to Earth's greater mass, although the object is exerting attraction also. (See pages 766–767.)

The force of gravity decreases rapidly toward Earth's core. After descending past the halfway point inside Earth, more of Earth's mass is above than below. Once this point is reached, the force of gravity gradually decreases. Thus, gravitational conditions at Earth's center must be similar to the weightless state of outer space.

Pressure

In Earth's interior, pressure increases steadily from the surface to the inner core. Deep in Earth, pressures are so great that minerals can be compressed into dense forms not found on the surface.

▲ **Zero Gravity Inside Earth?** It's strange to think about, but there is very little gravity at the center of Earth's core. This is because all of Earth's mass is above the center point.

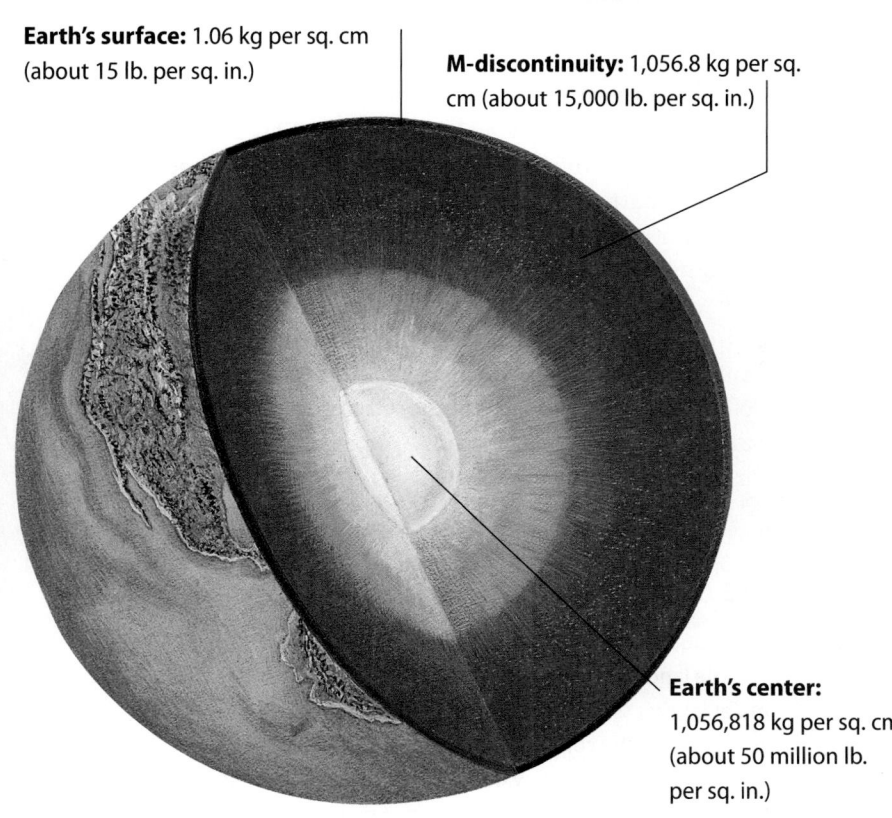

Earth's surface: 1.06 kg per sq. cm (about 15 lb. per sq. in.)

M-discontinuity: 1,056.8 kg per sq. cm (about 15,000 lb. per sq. in.)

Earth's center: 1,056,818 kg per sq. cm (about 50 million lb. per sq. in.)

Chemical Composition of Earth's Crust		
Element	**Continental Crust (%)**	**Oceanic Crust (%)**
Oxygen	46.6	45.4
Silicon	27.2	22.8
Aluminum	8.1	8.7
Iron	5.0	6.4
Calcium	3.6	8.8
Sodium	2.8	1.9
Potassium	2.6	0.3
Magnesium	2.1	4.1
Titanium	0.4	0.8
Hydrogen	0.1	0.1

PLATE TECTONICS

is a theory that explains the origin of most of the major features of Earth's surface. According to the theory, the outer layer of Earth is composed of approximately 10 major *lithospheric plates* and about 20 minor plates. The plates spread apart and collide into one another, forming trenches, ridges, mountains, and volcanoes. The theory of plate tectonics incorporates the theories of *continental drift,* which describes the global movement of landmasses, and *seafloor spreading,* which is the formation of new crust along plate boundaries on the ocean floor.

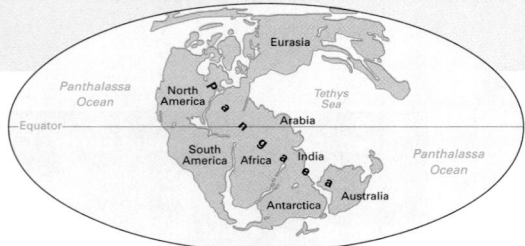

200 million years ago

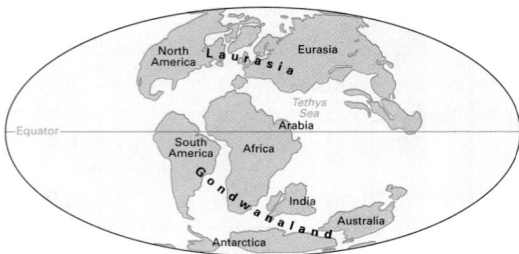

100 million years ago

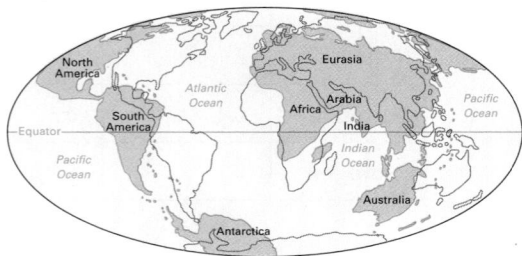

Present day to 50 million years from now

Continental Drift

In 1912, a German scientist named Alfred Wegener proposed the theory of continental drift. According to Wegener, about 200 million years ago all the land on Earth was one large continent that he called Pangaea. Approximately 180 million years ago, Pangaea began to break apart to form three separate continents. The large block to the north (which later became Europe, Asia, North America, and Greenland) is called Laurasia. It broke away from the other two landmasses, which together are called Gondwanaland.

◀ **Alfred Wegener** proposed the theory of continental drift in 1912, after noticing that the coastlines of the continents seemed to fit together like the pieces of a giant jigsaw puzzle.

The northern block of Gondwanaland eventually became South America and Africa. The southern block formed Antarctica, Australia, and New Zealand. A small piece broke away between the northern and southern parts of Gondwanaland. It moved northward and eventually formed India.

About 65 million years ago, the continents began to look as they do today. South America and Africa had drifted apart, and soon North America and Greenland would break away from Laurasia. India was close to colliding with Asia. The southern block of Gondwanaland would soon break apart into separate pieces, forming Antarctica, Australia, and New Zealand.

◀ **THE DRIFTING CONTINENTS**

About 200 million years ago, most of Earth's land formed a single landmass called Pangaea, *top.* Pangaea split into two major landmasses, Laurasia and Gondwanaland, that later broke apart to form the continents, *middle.* The bottom map shows where the continents may drift during the next 50 million years. The black outlines indicate their current positions.

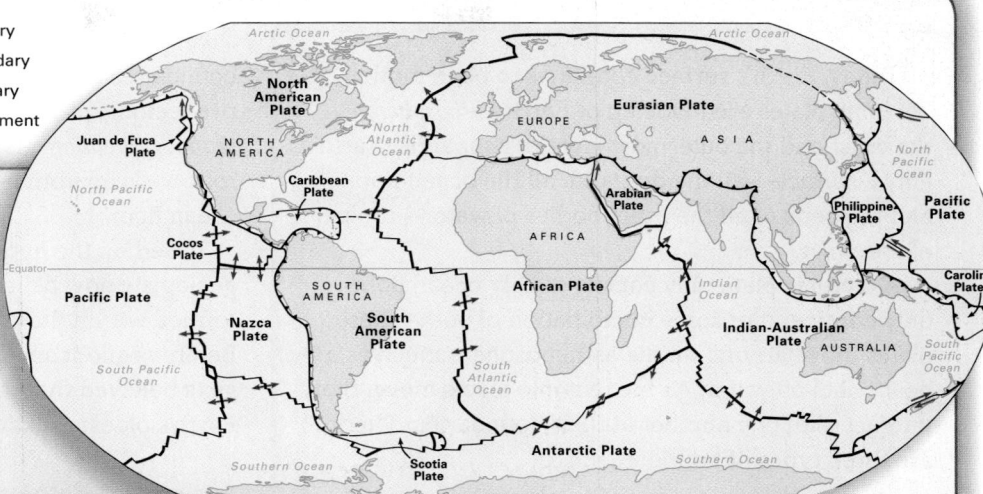

—◣— Divergent plate boundary
▲▲▲ Convergent plate boundary
—— Transform plate boundary
—→ Direction of plate movement

▲ EARTH'S TECTONIC PLATES

Many of Earth's tectonic plates include both ocean floor and dry land. The plates move, spreading apart from, colliding with, or grinding past one another. The areas where plates meet experience intense seismic and volcanic activity.

Evidence. Many scientists doubted Wegener's theory of continental drift at first, even though geologists found geological, fossil, and magnetic evidence that the continents once formed a single landmass.

- **India, Australia, Africa, South America:** rock deposits from ancient glaciers found; indicates continents were once in a very cold climate, probably near the South Pole.

- **South America, Africa:** similarities found in volcanic activity, erosion, flooding, sedimentation, and coal formation; indicates that the two continents were once joined.

- **North America:** fossils of tree ferns and other tropical features found; indicates that it was once at the equator.

New Discoveries. By the late 1920s, seismic researchers had discovered the asthenosphere, the thick layer of Earth's mantle that lies under the lithosphere. The asthenosphere is made of rock so hot that it flows, even though it remains partially solid. In 1929, geologist Arthur Holmes claimed that mountains are formed by the collision of slowly moving continents floating on the flowing asthenosphere.

By the 1950s, most geologists accepted the continental drift theory. Research indicated that the continents were still drifting apart, although the driving force for this movement had yet to be discovered. Then came the International Geophysical Year of 1957–1958, when two discoveries provided evidence of seafloor spreading, helping to explain the mechanics behind continental drift. (See next page.)

INTERNATIONAL GEOPHYSICAL YEAR OF 1957–1958

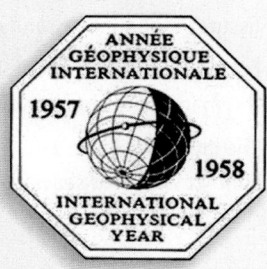

The international scientific community held a series of events and expeditions to make progress in the field of Earth science. Oceanographers studying the ocean floor made two startling discoveries:

- a mid-ocean ridge snakes around Earth's ocean floor like seams on a baseball

- rocks on the ocean floor are millions of years younger than expected

The youngest rocks were found closest to the mid-ocean ridge. The meaning was clear: new oceanic crust was being continually produced from vents in the mid-ocean ridge.

Plate Movement

Today, Earth's surface continues to be in motion. Tectonic plates are made up of Earth's *lithosphere*—the crust and the outermost layer of its mantle. Earth's entire surface—all the dry land, all the ocean floors, and the beds of all the other bodies of water—are part of the crust.

A tectonic plate may consist of only ocean floor, only continent, or some combination of both. These plates move around on the asthenosphere much as a boat floats on water. As the tectonic plates move, they interact with one another at their boundaries. There are three types of boundaries:

Divergent Plate Boundaries. Divergent plate boundaries occur mostly on ocean floors, where two tectonic plates move apart in a process called *seafloor spreading*. As the plates move apart, molten rock wells up from beneath the surface to form new ocean floor.

Based on the hypothesis of seafloor spreading, geologists now believe that the entire seafloor has formed within the past 100 to 200 million years. Before seafloor spreading was discovered, geologists believed that the ocean floor was the site of Earth's oldest rocks, billions of years old.

Convergent Plate Boundaries. In some parts of the world, tectonic plates converge, or collide with one another. When two plates collide, *subduction* occurs, or one plate slides beneath the other. During subduction, crust is destroyed. This offsets the new crust being formed by seafloor spreading. Otherwise, Earth's surface would be getting larger each year.

Transform Plate Boundaries. Instead of separating or coming together, two plates may simply slide against each other. These boundaries are called transform plate boundaries, or transform faults. Crust is neither created nor destroyed along transform faults, but powerful earthquakes can occur there. Devastating earthquakes have occurred in California along parts of a transform plate boundary known as the San Andreas Fault.

SEAFLOOR SPREADING originates in the long undersea mountain system often called the mid-ocean ridge. The process, repeated for millions of years, widens the ocean basins and carries along the continental plates like luggage on a conveyor belt.

1. The spines of the mid-ocean ridge contain active fissures that are constantly pulled apart.

2. Each time a fissure opens, lava from the upper part of the mantle rises to fill the gap.

3. The lava quickly hardens into rock after coming into contact with cold seawater.

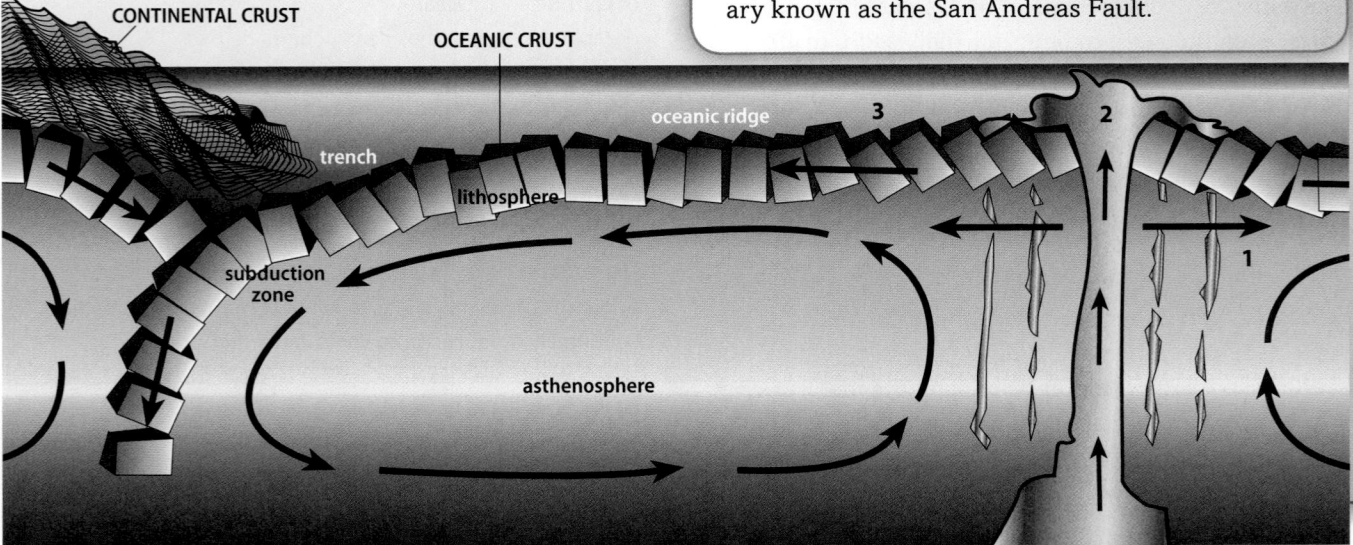

The Big Picture. The overall pattern of movement of the tectonic plates is a widening of the Atlantic Ocean and a shrinkage of the Pacific Ocean. The Atlantic is widening because seafloor spreading at the mid-Atlantic ridge continues to create lithosphere. The Pacific is shrinking because much of it is ringed by convergent plate boundaries that are consuming its lithosphere.

WHEN PLATES COLLIDE!

Oceanic Plate Collides with a Continental Plate
- the heavier seafloor sinks beneath the continent
- forms a deep ocean trench
- volcanoes common in these areas

Two Oceanic Plates Collide
- one forced beneath the other
- forms an ocean trench
- undersea volcanic activity and earthquakes

Two Continental Plates Collide
- neither plate subducts
- layers of rock in the overriding plate crumple and fold
- creates a mountain range

The Aleutian Islands —a volcanic island chain off the tip of Alaska—formed when an oceanic plate collided with a continental plate. ▼

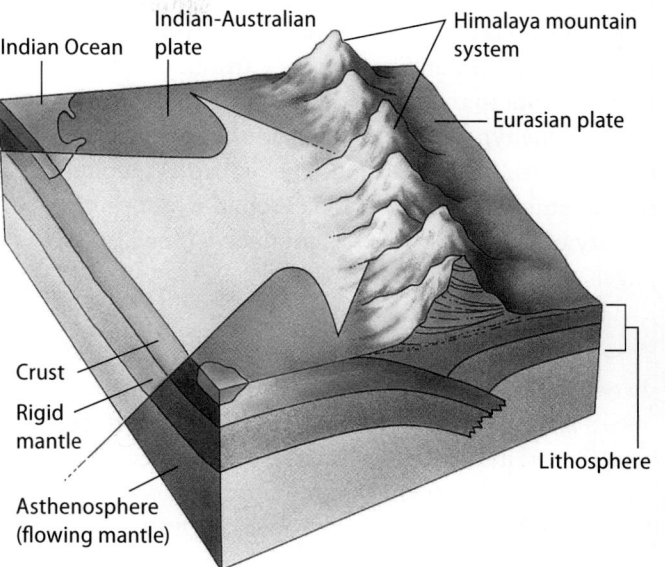

▲ **The Himalayas,** the world's highest mountain system, formed when the Indian-Australian plate collided with the Eurasian plate about 50 million years ago.

HOW DOES THAT WORK

SEAFLOOR SPREADING

During World War II, a geologist named Harry Hess commanded a submarine for the Navy. He used instruments on the sub to map the ocean floor. Hess's findings led him to develop the hypothesis of seafloor spreading.

In 1968, a research vessel gathered samples of oceanic crust from the mid-Atlantic ridge. They found that the rocks nearest the ridge were the youngest, indicating that they had been pushed up through the ridge.

Photographs taken from a deep-sea diving vessel in 1974 showed newly erupted lava flows from the mid-ocean ridge, providing the first visual evidence of seafloor spreading.

Harry Hess

Volcanoes

A volcano is a fissure, or vent, in Earth's crust where ash, gases, and molten rock from deep underground erupt to the surface. The word volcano also refers to the type of mountain that forms as the erupted rock and ash build up around the fissure. As molten rock accumulates and hardens around a fissure, a variety of volcanic cones are produced. (See also pages 526–527.)

Where Volcanoes Form. There are about 500 active volcanoes on Earth. Volcanoes form above regions where *magma*, molten rock beneath Earth's surface, is produced in the mantle, the rocky layer beneath Earth's crust. Nearly all volcanoes form along the tectonic plate boundaries. Some appear above locations called hot spots that can be far from plate boundaries.

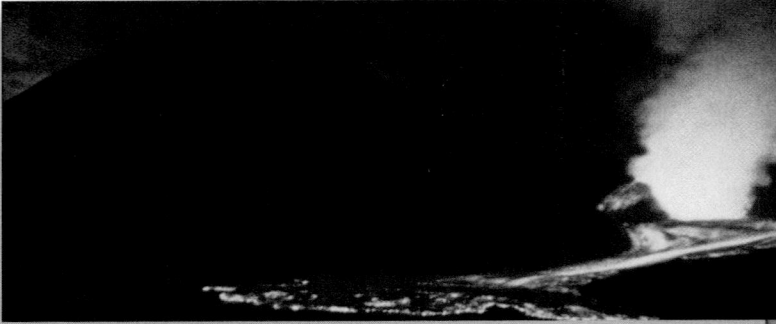

▲ **Surtsey,** an island off the coast of Iceland, appeared in 1963 when a volcanic cone built up over the mid-ocean ridge and broke the water's surface.

Eruptions. A volcanic eruption takes place when magma rises through a vent leading from a magma chamber deep within Earth's crust. The main products of an erupting volcano are lava (molten rock), gases (steam, carbon dioxide, nitrogen, sulfur dioxide, and other gases), and pyroclastic material. Pyroclastic fragments include pumice, rock, cinders, and ash propelled into the air by superheated volcanic gases and ejected by the force of the eruption.

The violence of an eruption is determined by the magma's chemical composition and the quantity and content of the gases.

KRAKATOA ERUPTS!

In 1883, Mount Krakatoa in Indonesia erupted with tremendous force, killing 36,000 people. The eruption caused abnormal sea waves, weather phenomena, and extraordinary sunsets throughout the world. It was also notable as the first large volcanic eruption that occurred after the invention of the telegraph. Consequently, the news of Krakatoa's eruption was sent around the world within hours, enabling its worldwide effects to be related to a single cause.

Magma Composition			
	Silica	**Gases and Fluid**	**Eruption**
Molten rhyolite	High percentage of silica results in high viscosity (thickness)	Large quantity of dissolved gases and fluids	Violent
Molten basalt	Lower percentage of silica; magma is thinner	Lower quantity of dissolved gases	Gentler

Violent Eruptions. The most violent eruptions occur at convergent plate boundaries. When two plates collide, subduction occurs (one plate slides beneath the other). The melting of one of the plates often results in molten rock being forced violently upward through cracks in the ocean floor or on land.

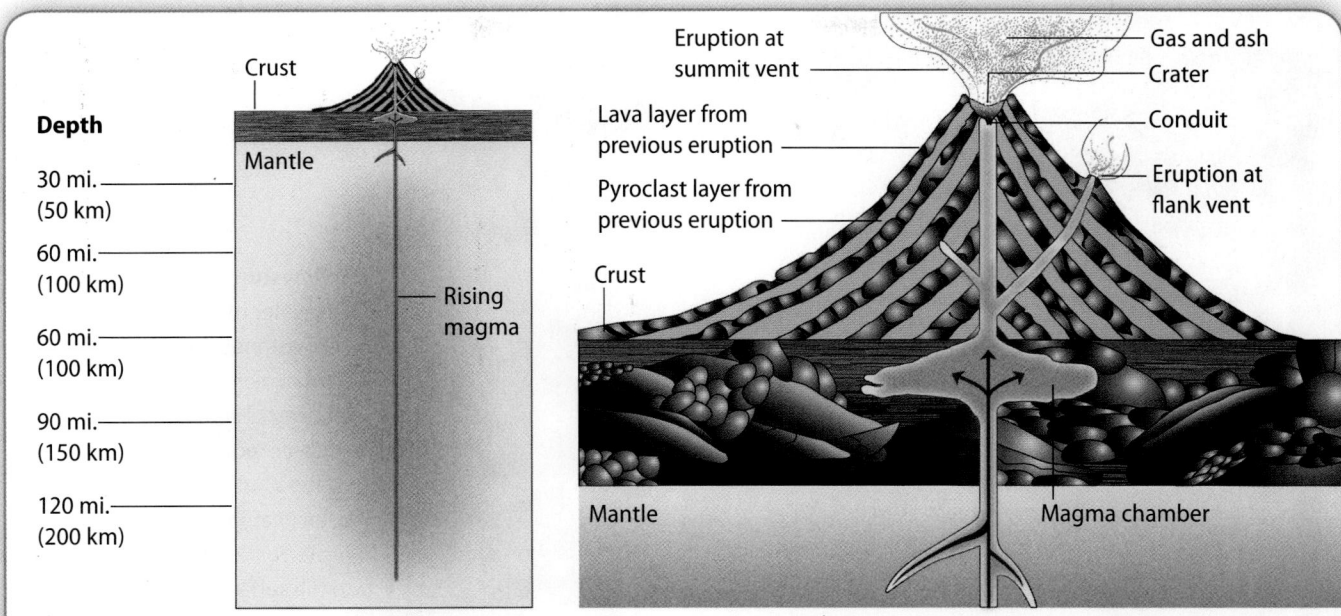

Depth

30 mi. (50 km)

60 mi. (100 km)

60 mi. (100 km)

90 mi. (150 km)

120 mi. (200 km)

Crust

Mantle

Rising magma

Eruption at summit vent

Lava layer from previous eruption

Pyroclast layer from previous eruption

Crust

Mantle

Gas and ash

Crater

Conduit

Eruption at flank vent

Magma chamber

How a Volcano Erupts. Magma forms deep underground and rises toward the surface, *left*, collecting in a magma chamber. As pressure builds, the chamber breaks open and magma rises through a conduit, *right*. At openings called vents, the magma erupts as gas, lava, and pyroclasts (rock and ash).

VOLCANOES OCCUR AT …

- **convergent boundaries,** where tectonic plates collide. The most powerful eruptions occur at these boundaries. The Pacific Rim is often called the "Ring of Fire" because of the many active volcanoes around the Pacific plate.

- **divergent boundaries,** where tectonic plates separate, such as at the mid-ocean ridge. As the lava pours out through openings, it forms new seafloor and may build up into huge cones. Sometimes a cone above the mid-ocean ridge breaks the water's surface, thereby forming an island.

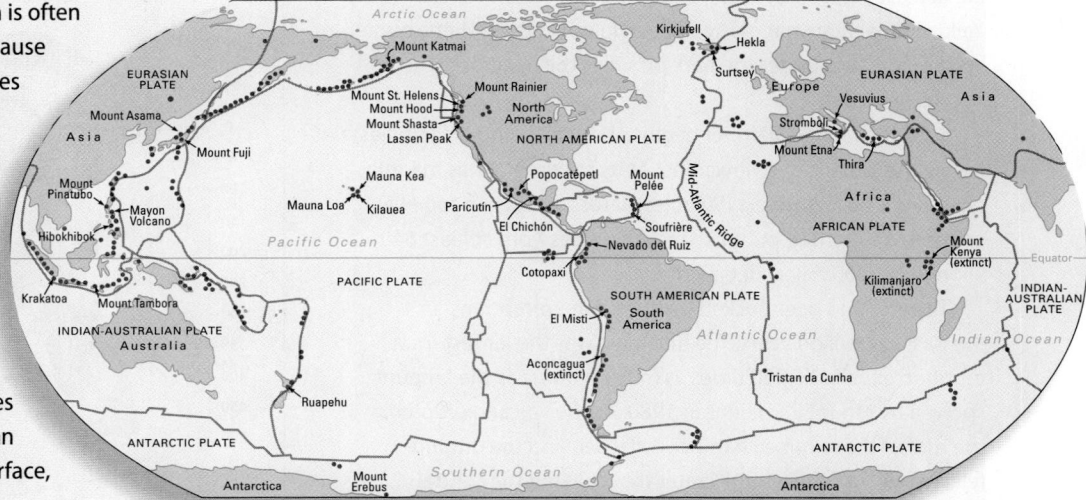

- **hot spots,** which are located in the middle of a tectonic plate. Perhaps the most famous examples are the volcanoes in the Pacific plate that form the Hawaiian Islands.

▲ **Volcanoes** occur where plates collide, where plates separate, and at hot spots in the middle of a plate.

Yellowstone's Geysers.
The water that gushes from Yellowstone's geysers comes from rain or snow. It seeps into cracks and fissures in the volcanic rock where it is heated by the solid rock that has, in turn, been heated by magma. The heated water then rises back up to the surface.

SUPER VOLCANO

Yellowstone National Park is famous for its geysers, springs that erupt columns of water into the air at certain times. There are at least 10,000 geysers, hot springs, and steam vents in Yellowstone. But what many people do not know is that a huge volcano that lies under the park provides the heat for these natural wonders.

A huge magma chamber begins about 8 kilometers (5 miles) below the surface of Yellowstone. At its maximum, this magma chamber is 80 kilometers (50 miles) across. It rests on top of a column of superhot, puttylike rock that rises from at least 640 kilometers (400 miles) deep in the mantle.

The area has been rocked by three "supereruptions" in the past 2.5 million years. The first blast was the largest. That eruption expelled 6,000 times as much magma as the amount spewed by Mount St. Helens in 1980. As the volcano erupted, the roof of the magma chamber collapsed and the ground fell inward, forming a huge crater that covered the central and southwestern parts of the park. Yellowstone's last major eruption was about 70,000 years ago.

The Yellowstone volcano is fueled by a gigantic, relatively stationary plume of magma, called a hot spot, that acts like a blowtorch on the crust above.

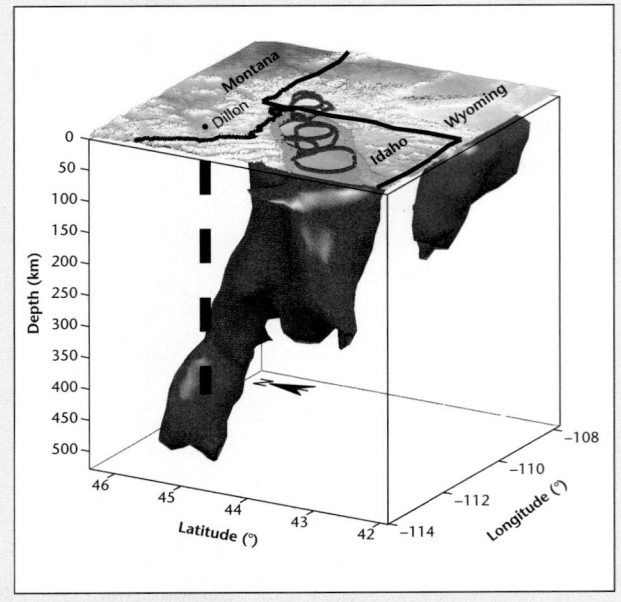

The Hawaiian Islands— the eight main islands and 124 smaller islands—are made up of volcanoes that formed on the ocean floor and were built up by repeated eruptions until they broke the surface.

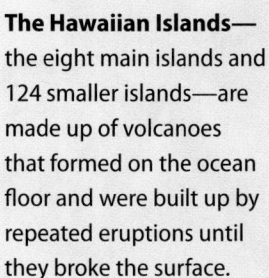

HAWAIIAN HOT SPOT

Most volcanoes form along the edges of tectonic plates, at convergent and divergent boundaries. But like Yellowstone, the Hawaiian Islands formed over a hot spot, which is an area of Earth's mantle that erupts through the crust.

The intense heat in a hot spot melts rock in the mantle. The melted rock, called magma, rises to the surface, where it erupts as lava. The lava builds up until eventually the volcano rises above the surface of the water, forming an island.

Hot spots provide visual evidence of tectonic plate movement. As the Pacific plate moves slowly over the hot spot, volcanic islands have formed over millions of years. The oldest islands are those to the northwest. They formed as the plate passed over the hot spot, and have been moving northwest ever since.

◀ **A hot spot** beneath the Pacific Ocean created the Hawaiian Islands. Magma rose through several mantle layers and the tectonic plate and erupted on the surface as lava. The lava hardened to form the islands. Magma continues to rise from the hot spot, building an undersea volcano that will one day become an island.

Earthquakes

An earthquake is a sudden, strong trembling, or shaking, of the ground. Earthquakes generally occur as a result of the movement of tectonic plates. The crust cracks along a line called a *fault,* which is at the boundary between two plates. As the crust moves apart, rocks on either side bend until they finally break, causing the ground to shake.

What Causes Earthquakes? If crustal plates moved at a constant rate, earthquakes would not occur. However, plate movement is not uniform. Sections of the moving plates sometimes lock and resist the overall movement. As the plates continue to move, the rocks bend until they break. As the rock breaks, it snaps into a new position, causing the shaking of an earthquake. Once an earthquake releases the strain on a rock mass, it takes a long time—about 50 to 100 years—for the strain to become great enough to cause another earthquake.

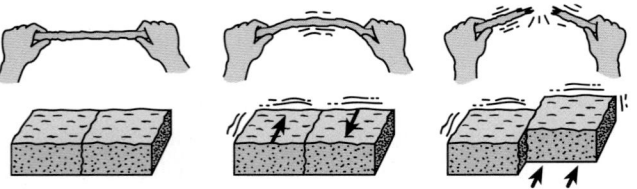

Earthquakes occur when tension builds up along a fault until the rock masses snap. The tension is released similarly to the way tension is released when a stick is broken.

▲ **Central Chile.** In February 2010, an earthquake that measured 8.8 on the Richter scale struck central Chile. It was one of the most powerful earthquakes on record.

Shock Waves. The spot under Earth's surface where an earthquake originates is called the *focus,* or the *hypocenter.* The *epicenter* is the point on the surface directly above the focus. When an earthquake occurs, vibrations from the snapping of rock masses generate shock waves that radiate out from the focus. These earthquake-generated waves are called *seismic waves.* Seismic waves cause the ground shaking and trembling associated with earthquakes.

EARTHQUAKES generate three types of seismic waves (see pages 442–445):

- Primary waves (P-waves) are like springs that are compressed and released. They cause particles of matter to vibrate back and forth along the direction of travel.

- Secondary waves (S-waves) cause particles of matter to vibrate side-to-side, perpendicular to the direction of travel.

- Surface waves travel only along the ground, causing vertical and horizontal vibrations.

P-waves and **S-waves** move faster than **surface waves** and cause more damage. Surface waves are long, slow waves that cause little to no damage to buildings.

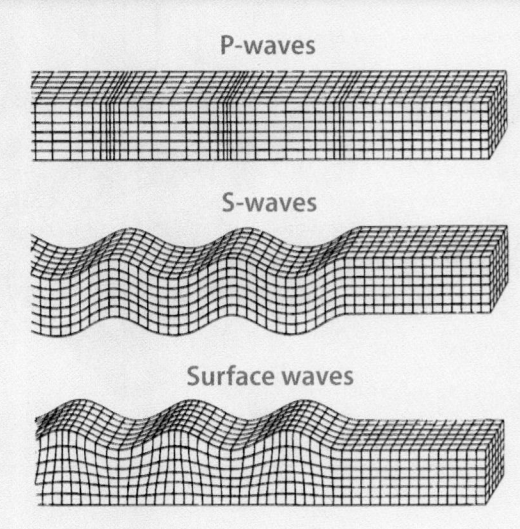

P-waves

S-waves

Surface waves

Measuring Earthquakes. To determine the strength and location of earthquakes, scientists use a recording instrument known as a *seismograph*. A seismograph is equipped with sensors called *seismometers* that can detect ground motions caused by seismic waves from both near and distant earthquakes. Some seismometers are capable of detecting ground motion as small as 0.1 nanometer. One nanometer is one billionth of a meter or about 39 billionths of an inch.

A network of seismograph stations is maintained worldwide to record and study earthquakes (as well as explosions of nuclear bombs). These seismographs begin to pick up seismic waves within minutes after an earthquake occurs. By analyzing seismograms, geologists can learn a great deal about earthquakes, including their size and location.

Earthquake Strength. The strength of an earthquake is indicated on a scale called the *Richter scale*, which is based on the magnitude of the waves recorded by a seismograph. On this scale, a tenfold increase in the amplitude of the wave corresponds to an increase of one on the magnitude scale. In addition, each unit of magnitude increase is equal to roughly a thirtyfold increase in the energy released. Therefore, an earthquake of 5.0 has vibrations 10 times larger than an earthquake of 4.0, but it will release 31.5 times more energy. A 3.0 quake is scarcely noticeable, a 6.0 quake

Most Powerful Recent Earthquakes		
Year	**Location**	**Magnitude**
2010	Central Chile	8.8
2007	Indian Ocean floor, near Sumatra	8.4
2005	Indian Ocean floor, near Sumatra	8.6
2004	Indian Ocean floor, near Sumatra	9.1
2003	Hokkaido, Japan	8.3
2001	Western Peru	8.4
2000	Papua New Guinea	8.0

is considered moderate, and a 7.5 is a large quake that can cause a great deal of destruction.

Most earthquakes occur without people noticing. About 30,000 earthquakes occur globally each year that can be detected by seismographs. Only a small percentage of these is serious enough to cause damage. Some factors that affect total damage are the location of the epicenter in reference to urban areas, the density and type of underlying rock and soil, the general terrain, and the materials and methods used to construct buildings.

An earthquake that struck the Indian Ocean in 2004 registered at least 9.1 on the Richter scale. It created a tsunami, or giant wave, that caused the deaths of more than 225,000 people.

RICHTER SCALE

Magnitude	Category	Effects	Frequency (per year)
less than 1.0 to 2.9	micro	Generally not felt, but can be recorded by local instruments	more than 100,000
3.0–3.9	minor	Felt by many people; causes little to no damage	12,000–100,000
4.0–4.9	light	Can cause local damage	2,000–12,000
5.0–5.9	moderate	Some damage to weak structures	200–2,000
6.0–6.9	strong	Can be destructive	20–200
7.0–7.9	major	Major earthquake, serious damage over large areas	3–20
8.0 and higher	great	Major earthquake, serious destruction and loss of life over large areas	fewer than 3

Seismographs measure the vertical motion of the ground during an earthquake. On the Richter scale, each increase of one indicates a tenfold increase in earthquake strength.

Earthquakes

Earthquake Zones. Earthquakes usually occur along faults, at the boundary between two tectonic plates. More than 80 percent of the world's earthquakes occur in a narrow zone, or belt, which encircles the rim of the Pacific Ocean. This belt is sometimes called the Ring of Fire because it has many volcanoes, earthquakes, and other geologic activity.

Another major earthquake zone, the Mediterranean-Himalayan zone, cuts across the Mediterranean Sea, crosses the Mideast and the Himalayas, and passes through the East Indies before meeting the Ring of Fire north of Australia.

Japan experiences frequent earthquakes because of its location near two colliding plates. In fact, Tokyo has experienced at least one earthquake each century for the past 2,000 years. In China, severe earthquakes occur as the Asian plate is pushed upward by the descending Indian plate. In the United States, earthquakes occur in California, along the San Andreas Fault. However, earthquakes also occur along the Eastern seaboard and in the Midwest.

HOW TO RESIST AN EARTHQUAKE
Quakeproof Buildings

An earthquake-resistant building includes such structures as *shear walls*, a *shear core*, and *cross-bracing*. *Base isolators* act as shock absorbers. A *moat* allows the building to sway.

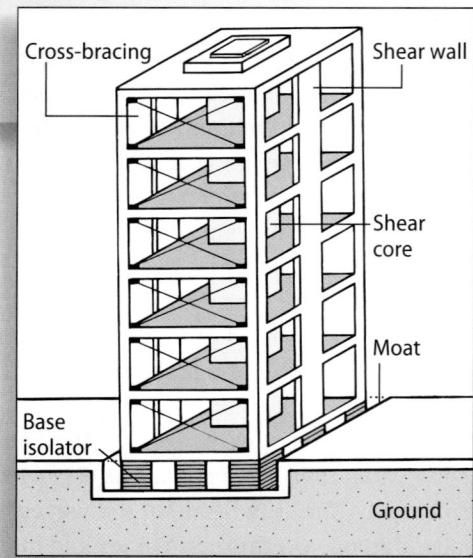

TYPES OF FAULTS

There are three main types of faults.

- **normal fault:** the upper block of crust is displaced downward along the dip of the fault plane. Movement along a normal fault broadens the area of crust.

- **reverse fault:** the block of crust above the fault is displaced upward. Movement along a reverse fault shortens the crustal area.

- **strike-slip fault:** also called a transform fault, movement along a strike-slip fault is lateral rather than vertical.

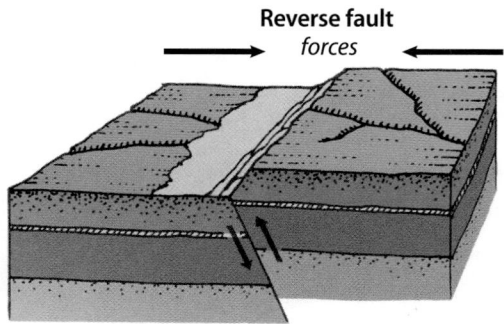

Reverse fault
forces

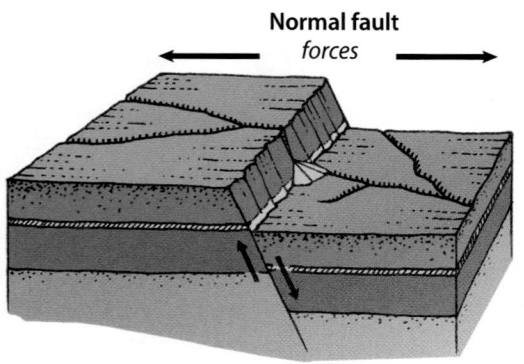

Normal fault
forces

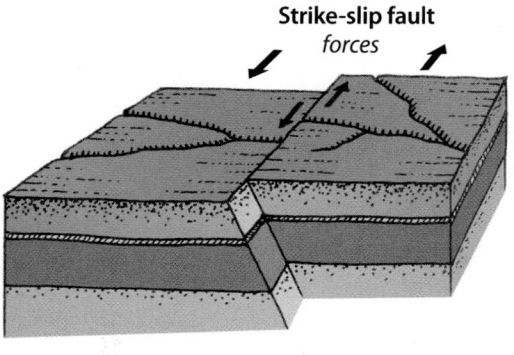

Strike-slip fault
forces

Predicting Earthquakes. Seismologists still cannot predict precisely when an earthquake will occur. By studying the incidence of earthquakes in a given area over thousands of years (paleoseismology), however, predictions can be made regarding the general area where an earthquake is most likely to occur. Seismologists also can predict where the chances are greatest for a large earthquake to occur soon, but those predictions cannot be accurately pinpointed.

Where Earthquakes Occur. This map shows where many major earthquakes have occurred. Each dot on the map represents a major earthquake. Most earthquakes occur near and along the boundaries of the rocky plates that cover Earth's surface. ▼

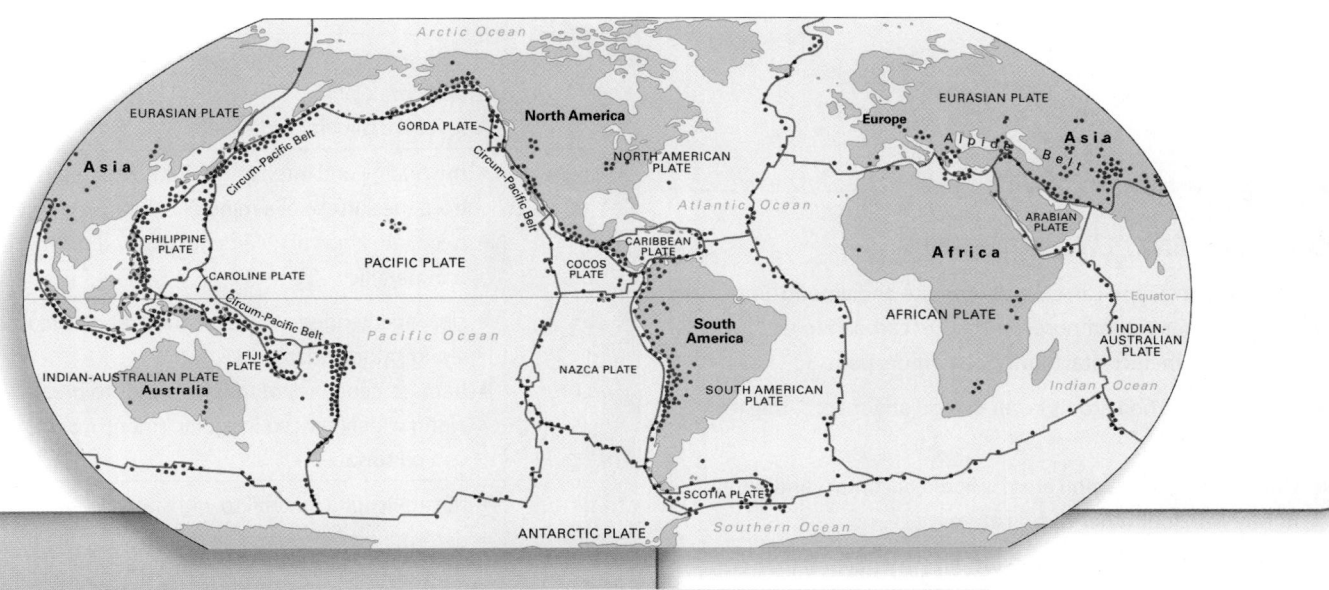

WILL CALIFORNIA FALL INTO THE OCEAN?

It is a popular misconception that someday a powerful earthquake—the "big one"—will strike southern California and it will fall into the Pacific Ocean. In reality, southern California is not moving west. In fact, the southern half of California, which is part of the Pacific plate, is actually moving northward at a rate of 4 to 5 centimeters (about 2 inches) a year. At this rate, in about 15 million years, Los Angeles could become a suburb of San Francisco.

◄ **The Southern California coast** is moving slowly northward, but it will probably not fall into the ocean from an earthquake.

MINERALS are solid, inorganic elements and compounds that occur naturally in rocks. They have a distinctive crystal form and usually have a definite chemical composition. Mineralogists, geologists who study minerals, have described and named about 3,000 different minerals.

Mineral Facets

Without exception, every mineral has a chemical composition and an arrangement of atoms that give it unique properties. These properties can be useful in identifying a mineral.

Mineral Properties	
Color	• some minerals can be reliably identified by their color • color alone may not be a dependable identifier, as the same mineral may have different colors
Streak	• determined by grinding a mineral into a fine powder • reveals a mineral's true color
Luster	• the quality and intensity of light reflected from the surface of a mineral • two main kinds of luster: metallic and nonmetallic
Cleavage and Fracture	• cleavage: tendency of some minerals to break along smooth, flat planes • fracture: tendency of most minerals to break along widely spaced irregular, smooth, or curved surfaces
Hardness	• the ability of a mineral to withstand scratching • determined mostly by the atomic structure of the mineral
Specific Gravity	• describes the density of a mineral compared to the density of water

ONE ELEMENT, TWO MINERALS

The element carbon can exist as graphite or diamond. Both are minerals that are composed entirely of carbon atoms. The difference is in their crystal form. (See Carbon, page 329.)

- **graphite:** carbon atoms occur in regularly spaced, thin parallel sheets
- **diamond:** each carbon atom is in direct contact and bound tightly with four other carbon atoms

The result? Graphite is a very soft, slippery mineral that splits easily, while diamonds are the hardest naturally occurring substance.

Graphite

Diamond

460

Crystal Form

The distinctive geometric form of a mineral is known as its *crystal form*. The crystal form of a mineral is caused by the atomic structure, or the way that the atoms of its elements are bound together. All minerals are classified into six crystal systems. ▶

CRYSTAL STRUCTURES

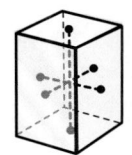

tetragonal
one axis longer than the other two, all at right angles. *example:* zircon

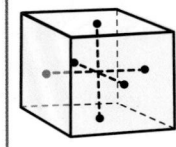

cubic
all axes of equal length at right angles. *example:* halite

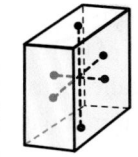

orthorhombic
three axes of unequal length, all at right angles. *example:* barite

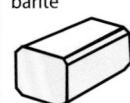

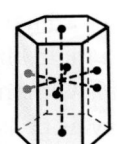

triclinic
three axes of unequal length, none at right angle to the others. *example:* rhodonite

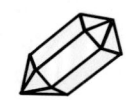

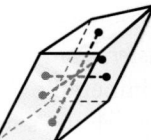

hexagonal
three axes of equal length forming angles of 120°, one axis of variable length at right angles to the rest. *example:* apatite

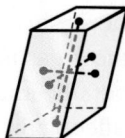

monoclinic
three axes of unequal length, two at right angles, the third at some other angle. *example:* gypsum

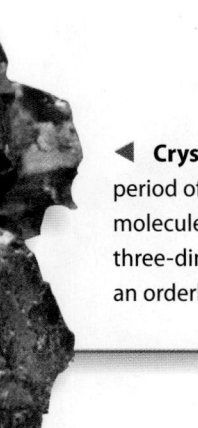

◀ **Crystals** grow over a period of time as atoms and molecules form complex three-dimensional shapes in an orderly manner.

Color

Some minerals can be reliably identified by their color. For example, *native metals*, metallic minerals of only one element, such as gold and copper, can be identified by color.

In most cases, though, color alone is not a dependable way to identify minerals. This is because the same mineral may have different colors. For example, pure quartz is a glasslike, colorless mineral, but there are some varieties of quartz that are dark gray, milky white, or pink owing to the impurities of other minerals.

Streak

A more accurate way to identify minerals by color is to grind the minerals into fine powder. When a mineral has been powdered, the true color, or *streak*, of the mineral shows. The colors of the impurities do not appear. The streak of a mineral usually is more reliable than its external color. For example, the external color of pyrite (fool's gold) is brassy yellow, but its streak is black. Real gold, on the other hand, does leave a golden streak.

Mineral Facets

Luster

The quality and intensity of light reflected from the surface of a mineral viewed in ordinary light is known as its *luster*. There are two main kinds of luster: metallic and nonmetallic. Minerals with metallic luster reflect light in much the same way as polished metals such as iron, copper, or chrome.

Most minerals exhibit nonmetallic luster. A mineral with a vitreous luster reflects light in the manner of glass or porcelain. Other nonmetallic lusters include earthy, greasy, waxy, dull, resinous, pearly, and silky.

Cleavage and Fracture

Cleavage is the ability of some minerals to break along smooth, flat planes. It results from the ordering of atoms inside a mineral. Cleavage occurs in places where atoms are weakly bound inside a mineral.

Most minerals do not have cleavage. They break, or *fracture*, along widely spaced irregular, smooth, or curved surfaces.

Cleavage and Fracture. Fluorite (*top*) demonstrates cleavage, with breaks in regular, flat surfaces. Obsidian (*bottom*) demonstrates fracture.

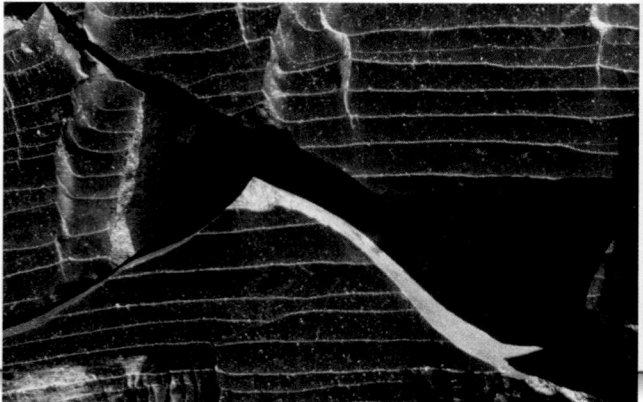

GEMS

Most precious stones are minerals. Diamonds, emeralds, rubies, and sapphires are all minerals prized for being beautiful, rare, durable, and valuable. They are cut and polished by expert gem cutters to bring out their luster.

Hardness

The ability of a mineral to withstand scratching is called its *hardness*. Hardness is determined mostly by the atomic structure of the mineral. Diamond and graphite are made of pure carbon. Yet diamond is the hardest known natural substance, while graphite is one of the softest minerals.

The relative hardness of a mineral is a physical property that is easily determined: A harder mineral will scratch a softer one.

Quartz is a relatively hard mineral, rated number 7 on the Mohs' hardness scale. It cannot be scratched by a steel file.

PANNING FOR GOLD

Gold has a very high specific gravity (19.2) and can therefore be collected by panning. In panning, the lighter minerals, such as quartz and feldspar, found in gravel, sand, and clay, are washed out of the pan. The heavy gold particles, or nuggets, remain behind.

MOHS' HARDNESS SCALE

At the beginning of the 18th century, an Austrian mineralogist, Friedrich Mohs (1773–1839), devised a scale for judging the hardness of minerals. Mohs picked 10 common minerals, covering the range of hardness, and arranged them in numerical order from 1 to 10. The softest mineral in the scale, talc, was rated 1. The hardest mineral, diamond, was rated 10.

To determine the hardness of an unknown mineral, a mineralogist finds out which of the minerals in the hardness scale the unknown mineral can scratch and which ones resist scratching.

Scale	Mineral	Common Materials
(softest)		
1	Talc	fingernail
2	Gypsum	penny
3	Calcite	
4	Fluorite	knife blade, glass
5	Apatite	steel file
6	Orthoclase	
7	Quartz	
8	Topaz	
9	Corundum	
10	Diamond	
(hardest)		

Specific Gravity

Specific gravity shows how much more dense a mineral is than an equal volume of water. If a mineral has a specific gravity of 5, the mineral is five times denser than an equal volume of water. The weight of a given volume of a mineral divided by the weight of an equal volume of water at 4°C (39°F) is the specific gravity of the mineral.

The specific gravity of a mineral is determined by the atomic arrangement of the elements that make up the compound. Specific gravity is an indication of how densely the atoms are packed in the crystal form of the mineral. Minerals with a specific gravity less than that of quartz (2.6) have loosely packed atoms. Minerals with a specific gravity of more than 2.6 have densely packed atoms.

Special Properties

There are special properties in addition to the properties common to most minerals. These special properties are useful in identifying particular minerals. Special properties include flavor and odor. For example, the mineral halite has a salty taste and the mineral kaolinite has an earthy odor.

The mineral magnetite, as its name suggests, is attracted to a magnet. Large concentrations of magnetite in the crust of Earth cause compass needles to point to the body of magnetite rather than to magnetic north. In fact, airplane pilots navigating by compass have become lost because of the influence of large bodies of magnetite.

More About Minerals

The rocks on Earth's surface are made up of minerals. Rock-forming minerals fall into two main groups: silicates and nonsilicates. The silicates contain the two most abundant elements—oxygen and silicon—and are the most plentiful minerals in the crust. Besides silicon and oxygen, silicates also may contain one or more different metals and small amounts of hydrogen. The nonsilicate minerals are those that lack silicon. They are much rarer than the silicates.

Silicates

About 95 percent of Earth's crust is made up of silicates. Soil consists chiefly of silicates, as do most rocks. The most common silicate mineral is quartz. It has a glassy luster, a hardness of 7 on the Mohs' scale, and a six-sided crystal form. In most rock, quartz occurs as tiny sparkling grains.

About 60 percent of surface rocks are made up of a group of silicates called *feldspars*. Feldspars have a steplike cleavage and a hardness of 6 on the Mohs' scale. Two common varieties of feldspar are pink-colored orthoclase feldspar (rich in potassium) and pale gray-colored plagioclase feldspar (rich in sodium and calcium).

Micas are soft silicates with a hardness of about 2.5 and characterized by basal cleavage, or cleavage in one direction. Because of their basal cleavage, mica crystals form in thin layers, or parallel sheets—like the pages in a book.

SILICATE STRUCTURE

Silicate minerals are formed from the basic building block of the silicon-oxygen tetrahedron—one silicon atom and four oxygen atoms. Each oxygen atom can be shared between two tetrahedrons in order to form more complex structures. For example, a single chain is formed when one oxygen atom from each tetrahedron is shared with another tetrahedron. In the most complex combination, each oxygen atom is shared between two tetrahedrons to form a three-dimensional framework structure.

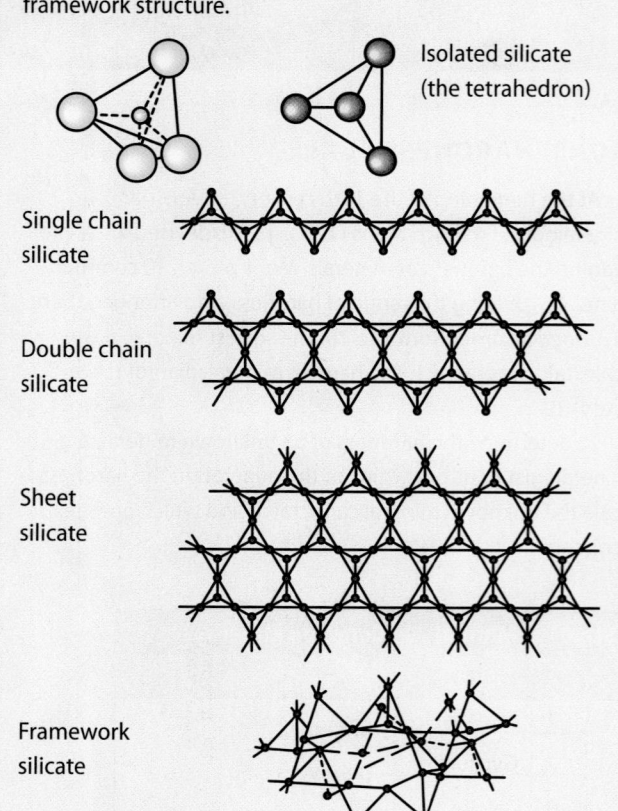

Isolated silicate (the tetrahedron)

Single chain silicate

Double chain silicate

Sheet silicate

Framework silicate

Muscovite, a common type of mica, breaks so cleanly into sheets that it was once used as window glass in Russia.

Nonsilicates

Nonsilicates include the native (uncombined) elements, oxides, halides, carbonates, sulfides, and sulfates. Native element nonsilicates occuring in the crust are rare, and include platinum, gold, silver, copper, and graphite.

Oxides: minerals in which one or more metallic elements combine with oxygen.

- two common iron oxides: hematite and magnetite
- hematite: reddish brown mineral; earthy luster; hardness of 5 to 6
- magnetite: dark gray to black; metallic luster; hardness of about 6

Magnetite

Halides: compounds of elements, such as sodium and calcium, combined with the halogen elements: chlorine, bromine, fluorine, and iodine.

- two most common halides: halite (sodium chloride) and fluorite (calcium fluoride)
- halite, or table salt: salty taste; cubic cleavage; hardness of about 2.5; transparent to translucent appearance
- fluorite: glassy luster; hardness of 4; light green to yellow-green; some varieties of fluorite have fluorescence (glow under ultraviolet light)

Halite

Carbonates: form when carbon combines chemically with three atoms of oxygen.

- often join with metals, such as calcium, magnesium, and iron
- two important carbonates: calcite and dolomite
- calcite: vitreous luster; a hardness of 3; diamond-shaped cleavage; white or light color
- dolomite: looks like calcite but is heavier; pearly luster; a hardness of 3.5

Sulfides: compounds of sulfur in combination with one or more metals, including copper, iron, lead, zinc, mercury, nickel, and molybdenum.

- have bright colors; high specific gravity; metallic luster
- common sulfide minerals include pyrite (iron sulfide), galena (lead sulfide), sphalerite (zinc sulfide), and cinnabar (mercury sulfide)

Copper

Sulfates: form when sulfur combines chemically with four atoms of oxygen.

- most abundant sulfate minerals are anhydrite (calcium sulfate) and gypsum (calcium sulfate combined with a molecule of water)
- gypsum: vitreous to pearly luster; a hardness of 2; colorless to white
- anhydrite: distinguished from gypsum by its greater hardness (3) and cubic cleavage

ROCKS are the hard mineral substances that form the solid part of Earth's crust. The study of rocks is called *petrology*. Petrologists have classified rocks into three broad groups based on how they formed. The three groups are *igneous, sedimentary,* and *metamorphic rock*.

Igneous rocks form when minerals in a molten state, called magma, harden. Sedimentary rocks form when particles of other rocks (sediment) accumulate and harden into layered rock. Metamorphic rocks form when other rocks are changed by heat and/or pressure at great depths inside the crust.

Extrusive igneous rock forms from lava, molten rock that pours out of volcanoes or from cracks in Earth's surface. ▼

Igneous Rocks

Igneous rocks form from magma, or molten minerals, deep inside the crust or on the surface. Geologists divide igneous rocks into two types:

- **intrusive rocks:** igneous rocks that form inside the crust
- **extrusive rocks:** igneous rocks that form when magma erupts from a volcano or spreads over the surface from a lava flow

Composition. The bulk of igneous rocks are made up of only a few minerals. These minerals are all silicates. (See page 464.) Some are light colored, such as the white and pink feldspars, transparent and milky varieties of quartz, and muscovite mica. The light-colored igneous rocks often contain a high percentage of calcium, sodium, or potassium in combination with silicon and oxygen.

Other silicates are dark colored, such as the dark green to black pyroxenes and amphiboles, as well as olivine and biotite mica. These darker-colored minerals are heavier—have a higher specific gravity—than the light-colored minerals. Their higher specific gravity results from a greater content of iron and magnesium. Because they contain iron and magnesium, the dark-colored minerals are known as ferromagnesian minerals (ferro- means "iron").

▲ **Basalt** is a fine-grained igneous rock composed of dark minerals. The presence of microscopic mineral crystals indicates that basalt—like that found in the columns of Svartifoss waterfall in Skaftefell National Park in Iceland—forms from a lava flow.

IGNEOUS ROCK TEXTURES

Coarse-grained
- mineral crystals can be seen without the aid of a microscope
- most crystals are about the same size, resulting from slow cooling deep in the crust

Fine-grained
- mineral crystals can be seen only under a microscope, signifying rapid cooling of magma
- form near Earth's surface or inside lava flows

Glassy
- do not show crystal forms even when viewed under a microscope
- form so rapidly that the atoms of each element do not have time to combine into crystal form
- form on the surface of a lava flow or where lava enters water

Porphyritic
- two-textured igneous rocks
- large crystals in a porphyritic rock result from slow cooling
- small crystals signify rapid cooling

Fragmental
- different from other kinds of igneous rocks in that they lack mineral crystals
- form when bits of broken rock fragments and magma are blown out of the top of an erupting volcano

Texture. Igneous rocks are also classified by their texture. Texture refers to the size of mineral grains or crystals within an igneous rock. Texture is directly related to the cooling history and location of magma from which particular igneous rocks form.

For example, granite and rhyolite are igneous rocks composed of the same minerals. Granite has large crystals of quartz, feldspar, and biotite mica. In contrast, rhyolite has microscopic crystals of these three minerals. Large mineral crystals take longer to form than small crystals. Thus, petrologists know that granite forms slowly deep inside the crust. Rhyolite forms rapidly at or near the surface.

Geologists classify igneous rocks into five main kinds of texture. Four are based on the size of mineral crystals. They are coarse-grained, fine-grained, glassy, and porphyritic. The fifth texture, fragmental, is a special type related solely to volcanic eruptions.

▲ **Granite** is a coarse-grained igneous rock that varies in color from white to dark gray to pink and red. It is an intrusive rock that forms from magma 25 to 40 kilometers (16 to 25 miles) below the surface of the continents.

Sedimentary Rocks

Sedimentary rock forms from loose materials called *sediments*. Sediments can include fragments of older rocks and the remains of plants and animals. Geologists classify sedimentary rocks into three types, based on how they were formed:

- **clastic rocks:** the most common type; the result of a natural process that begins when rocks are broken into sediments by water, ice, and wind
- **chemical rocks:** form when minerals precipitate, or settle, out of chemical solutions or bodies of water; evaporation plays a major role
- **organic rocks:** form from the accumulation and hardening of organic remains of either plants or animals

TYPES OF CLASTIC ROCKS

Conglomerates
- coarse-grained; formed from the cementing of gravel-sized sediment (greater than 2 millimeters, or 0.08 inch)
- formed from cementation of rounded gravel
- often forms in streambeds at high elevations
- rounded gravel indicates that the sediment was carried by water; degree of roundness indicates how far the gravel was transported

Breccia
- coarse-grained; formed from the cementing of gravel-sized sediment
- formed from cementation of angular pieces of gravel
- made up of angular gravel, indicating rapid burial with little or no transport by water

Sandstone
- medium-grained; formed by the cementation of sand-sized grains
- formed when sand grains accumulate on beaches, on the seafloor, in river channels, at the base of cliffs, or as dunes on a desert
- three main types of sandstone are quartz, arkose, and greywacke

Shale
- fine-grained; composed of clay and mud-sized sediment
- hardens from clay and mud that accumulate on lakebeds, in deltas, and on the ocean floor
- surface usually smooth due to fine grains

▲ **Arkose sandstone,** containing at least 25 percent feldspar, indicates that the sediment did not travel far from its source. It often is formed from landslides at the base of a rocky cliff.

Clastic Rocks. Clastic sedimentary rocks form from grains of sediment that have been pressed and cemented together. Sediments are carried by rivers or wind currents to lakes and oceans, where they settle on the lakebed or ocean bottom in layers. Larger, heavier sediments (gravel and sand) settle first. Layers of smaller, less heavy sediments (mud and clay) cover the heavier sediments. Over thousands of years, the weight of the upper layers presses down heavily on older layers. The increased pressure forces air and water out of the spaces in between individual particles, and the older, bottom layers of sediment harden and cement into sedimentary rock. There are several kinds of clastic sedimentary rock, based on the size of sediment.

Floating rock. *Pumice is a rock that floats on water. It was once volcanic lava filled with gases. When the gases escaped, they left millions of tiny holes that filled with air.*

Chemical Rocks. Minerals left behind after water evaporates form chemical rocks. When water evaporates from salty lakes and shallow bodies of seawater, salts are left behind. The precipitated salts form a mineral called halite. Rock salt is a chemical rock composed almost entirely of halite. Limestone, another chemical rock, forms when water heavy with calcite evaporates.

Limestone often forms along the edges of geysers and hot springs, as well as on the floors and ceilings of some caves from the dripping of calcite-bearing water. ▶

Organic Rocks. The remains of plants and animals form organic rocks. Many sea organisms, especially clams and snails, use calcium carbonate from seawater to build up protective shells. When the shellfish die, their shells accumulate on the seafloor. If there are many shellfish in a certain part of the seafloor, a great accumulation of shell material will be deposited in layers. When the layers are pressed together and cemented by minerals in the seawater, coquina, which is an organic variety of limestone, is produced.

Coal is another organic sedimentary rock that forms when the remains of prehistoric plants are compressed and hardened over millions of years.

◀ **The White Cliffs of Dover,** in southeastern England, were formed from accumulation of the calcite shells of single-celled organisms.

Metamorphic Rocks

When existing igneous or sedimentary rock is exposed to extreme heat or pressure, the mineral composition or texture of the rock may be altered. This process, known as *metamorphism*, takes place deep in the earth's crust. The resulting metamorphic rock can be distinguished from the original rock type by composition and texture.

Metamorphism does not involve melting. All changes occur in the rock's solid state. New minerals form, but elements are not added or removed.

The heat of metamorphism comes from a combination of three sources:

- magma
- Earth's core and the decay of radioactive elements
- frictional movement caused by the lateral shifting of continental plates

Petrologists classify metamorphic rocks primarily as to whether they exhibit a property called *foliation*. Foliation is a parallel arrangement of flaky and needlelike minerals.

NONFOLIATED ROCKS

Marble
- coarse-grained
- sparkling appearance caused by the recrystallization of calcite
- usually light colored, but any color between white and black is possible
- impurities form stripes or blotches (a marbling effect)
- develops from the alteration of limestone

Hornfels
- fine-grained
- gray-black, heavy; resembles basalt
- usually develops from the alteration of shale; sometimes from basalt

Serpentinite
- composed mostly of serpentine
- usually green, but can range from yellow to black
- develops from the alteration of igneous rocks, especially peridotite

FOLIATED ROCKS

Slate
- fine-grained
- splits readily into thin sheets
- usually black or gray, but can be purple, red, brown, or yellow, depending on impurities
- develops primarily from the alteration of shale

Schist
- medium- to coarse-grained
- mineral grains are easily visible
- varieties named after the most abundant mineral in the rock: talc schists, graphite schists, mica schists, and chlorite schists
- develop from a variety of rocks, including shale, sandstone, and basalt

Slate is a fine-grained, foliated rock.

Gneiss
- coarse-grained
- poorly developed foliation
- minerals—mostly quartz and feldspar, with some biotite mica—form light and dark bands
- colored bands tend to be folded where gneiss is exposed at the surface
- develops from the alteration of granite, shale, and sandstone

Kinds of Metamorphism. There are two main kinds of metamorphism: *thermal*, or contact, *metamorphism* and *regional metamorphism*.

- **thermal metamorphism** is the cooking of rocks that come in contact with magma. (See page 452.) A body of magma rises and comes in contact with surrounding rocks. The intense heat from the magma bakes the surrounding rocks within a narrow region of about 1 to 10 meters (3 to 30 feet). Nonfoliated rocks, such as marble, are produced by thermal metamorphism.

- **regional metamorphism** produces the greatest volume of metamorphic rocks. It involves the alteration of rocks in an area of at least several thousand square kilometers. Great pressure, rather than heat, is mostly responsible for the alteration of rocks. As crustal plates move, rock layers are squeezed together and downward, subjecting the layers to great pressure while they are heated by a combination of friction and increasing temperatures found deeper in the crust. Regional metamorphism results in the formation of foliated rocks, such as gneiss, schist, and slate.

Marble is a nonfoliated metamorphic rock. Impurities account for differences in color. ▼

METAMORPHIC ROCK

The main agents of metamorphism are heat and pressure. As these increase, density increases. Minerals may recrystallize, and mineral grains may become reoriented, leaving the rock with a banded appearance.

Layers of Metamorphic Rock

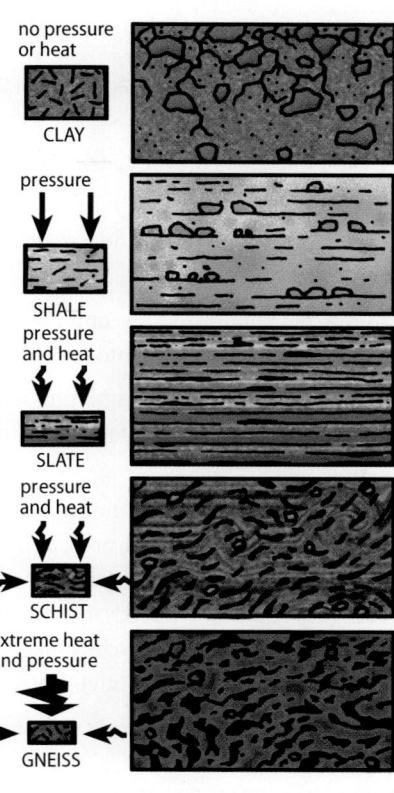

no pressure or heat — CLAY

pressure — SHALE

pressure and heat — SLATE

pressure and heat — SCHIST

extreme heat and pressure — GNEISS

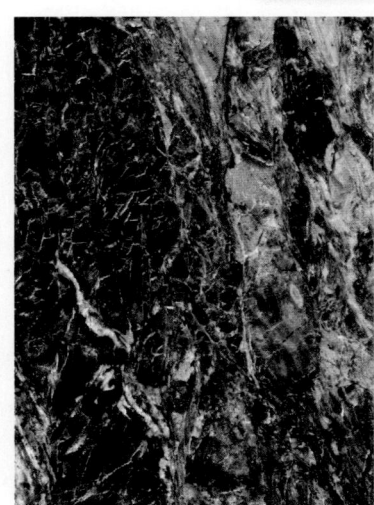

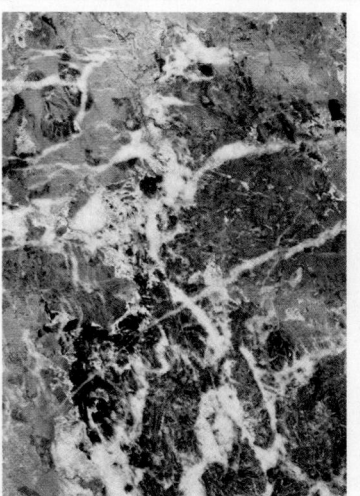

The Rock Cycle

HOW ROCKS FORM

Each type of rock develops from other types of rock. Geologists use the rock cycle to explain how rocks form.

1. Igneous rock created by magma flows to Earth's surface.

2. Weathering alters the rock chemically and breaks it into particles.

3. The particles accumulate and harden to form sedimentary rock.

4. As the sedimentary rock becomes buried, heat and pressure transform it into metamorphic rock.

5. With enough heating, metamorphic rocks melt into magma that can form igneous rock, completing the cycle.

Rock rarely proceeds through the entire rock cycle. The cycle may be halted, or steps can be skipped, repeated, or reversed. For example, some igneous rocks transform directly into metamorphic rock, and sedimentary rock can be broken down by weathering and then form other kinds of sedimentary rock.

▲ **Balanced Rock,** in the Garden of the Gods near Colorado Springs, Colorado, is an enormous block of sandstone delicately balanced on a small base.

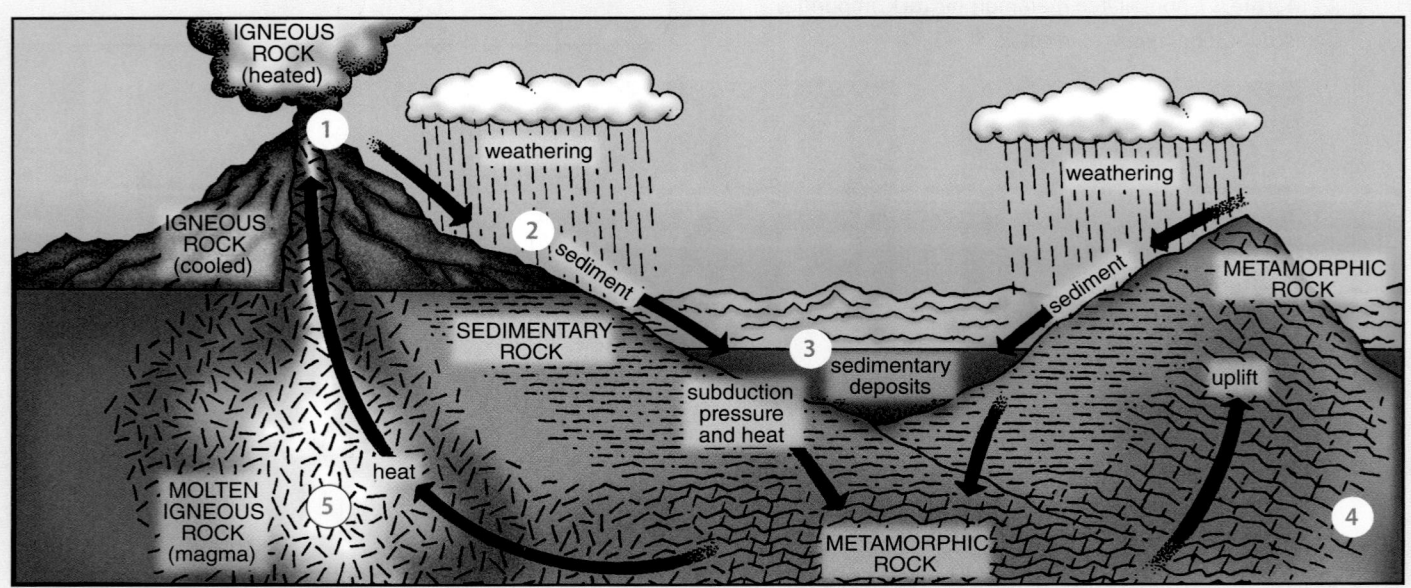

ROCKS OF NORTH AMERICA

This map shows the types of rock found at or near the surface in different areas of North America. Sedimentary rock underlies most of North America. Pockets of igneous and metamorphic rock appear in the Allegheny Mountains in the east and in the Rocky Mountains and other regions along the continent's west coast. A vast region of igneous and metamorphic rock called the Canadian Shield covers the eastern half of Canada.

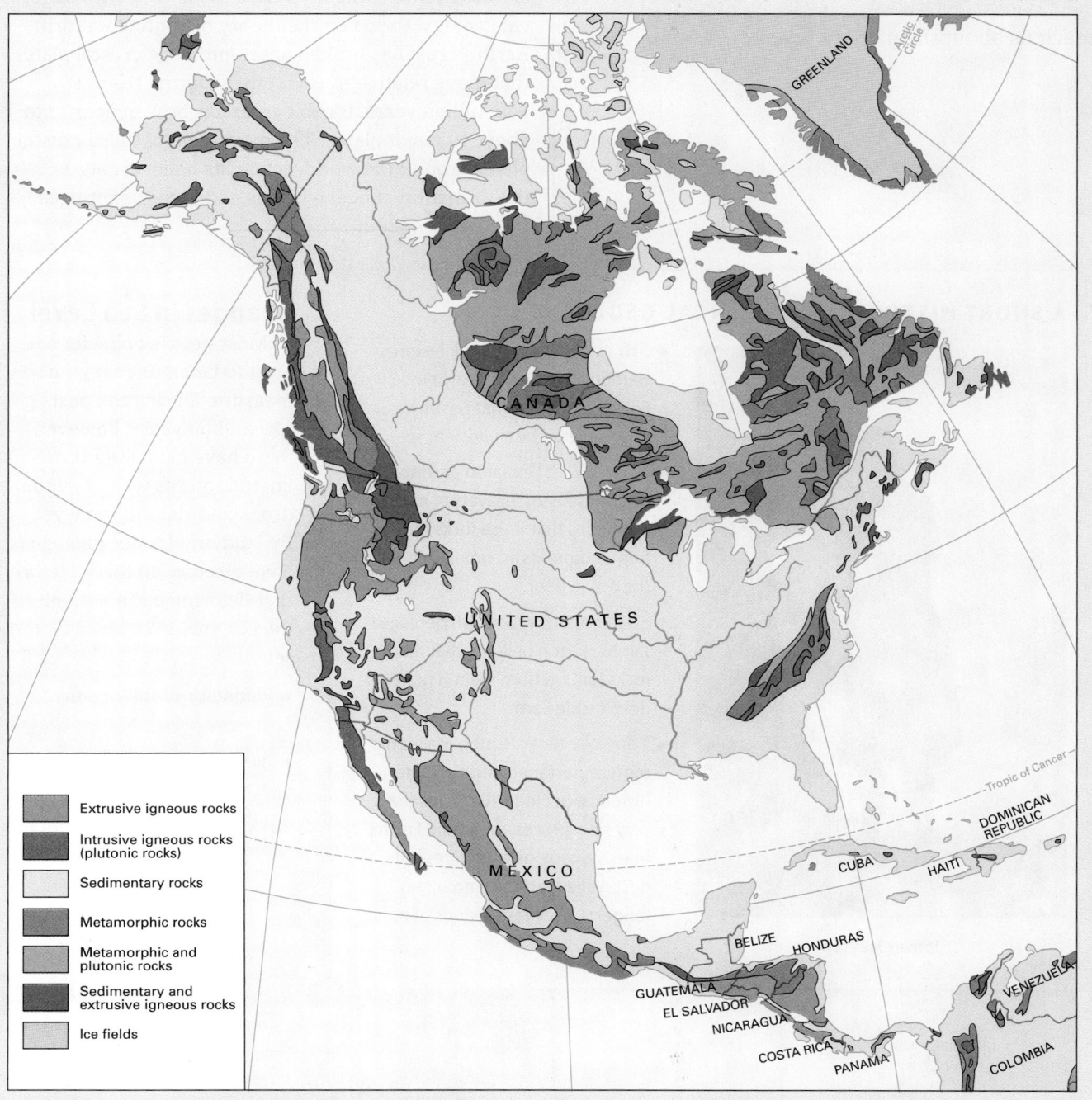

Legend:
- Extrusive igneous rocks
- Intrusive igneous rocks (plutonic rocks)
- Sedimentary rocks
- Metamorphic rocks
- Metamorphic and plutonic rocks
- Sedimentary and extrusive igneous rocks
- Ice fields

HISTORICAL GEOLOGY

HISTORICAL GEOLOGY is the study of changes that have occurred in Earth's structure and appearance. It is concerned with different forms of life that existed in each stage of Earth's history, as well as with what the evidence of early life on Earth—fossils, for example—can teach us about the planet's history.

Earth's Changing Surface

Early historical geologists were baffled by some of the evidence they found in Earth's crust. For example, how could nearly identical fossils be found in both South America and Africa? How did nonswimming organisms travel across an ocean?

The relatively recent theory of plate tectonics has clarified some of the mysteries associated with historical geology. Based on the theory of continental drift, Earth's crust has broken apart into huge crustal plates that move relative to each other. During the past 200 million years, Earth's crust has broken apart into about 10 major plates. The movement of these crustal plates around the world, scientists believe, causes the formation of ocean basins and mountain ranges. (See pages 448–451.)

A SHORT HISTORY OF HISTORICAL GEOLOGY

James Hutton

- **5th century BC:** Greek historian Herodotus observes seashells in Egypt; concludes that Egypt was once covered by an ancient sea.

- **circa 1500:** Leonardo da Vinci observes fossils in layers of rock; concludes that these rocks formed from sediments accumulating on the ocean floor.

- **18th century:** Scottish geologist James Hutton believes that many rocks formed from molten material deep inside Earth.

- **18th century:** Hutton makes his most important contribution to historical geology: he claims that very slow processes formed Earth's massive geological features—its deep valleys and tall mountain ranges—over vast periods of time.

Changes in Sea Level

Most people consider sea level to be an unchanging measure. During the past 570 million years, however, there have been long-term fluctuations as well as sudden drops and rises in sea level. By studying fossils, geologists have discovered three factors that determine the amount of the continents covered by the seas:

- capacity of the ocean basins

- volume of water in the ocean basins

- height of the continents

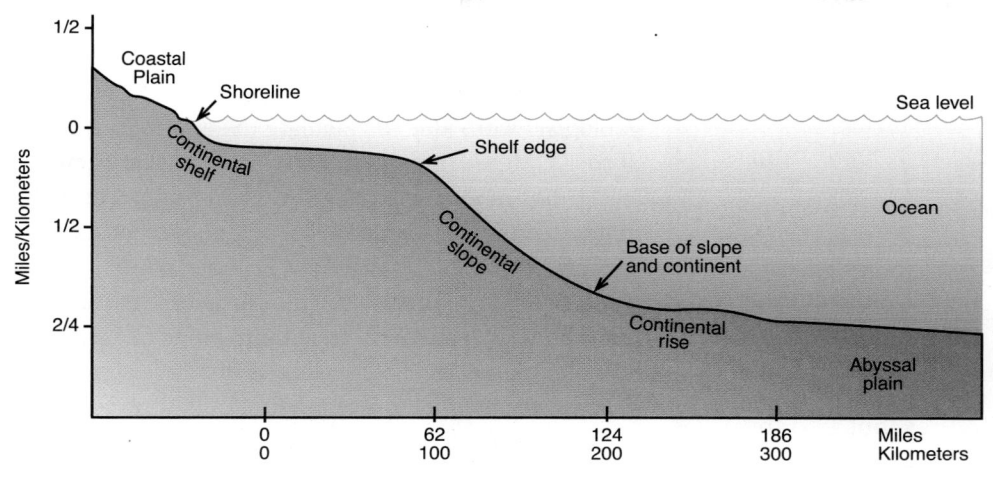

The continental shelf that forms the shallow underwater plain offshore can be as wide as several hundred miles.

Factors Affecting Sea Level

Capacity of the Ocean Basins

- most important factor influencing capacity is height of mid-ocean ridges

- when mid-ocean ridges are high, oceans hold less water

- high mid-ocean ridges also believed to be responsible for flooding of low-lying regions of continents

- when mid-ocean ridges are low, water drains off continents

- height of mid-ocean ridges controlled by rate at which crustal plates are separating

- the faster two plates are moving apart, the higher the mid-ocean ridge

Volume of Water in the Ocean Basins

- changes in volume believed to be related to the development of glaciers, huge sheets of ice that have covered entire continents

- continental glaciers store huge volumes of water previously held in the oceans

- during the last Ice Age—between 20,000 and 30,000 years ago—sea level fluctuated by about 150 meters (500 feet) over a 10,000-year period

- a similar sea level drop today would transform the offshore continental shelf zone into dry land

- appears sea level is relatively high today, based on the submergence of the continental shelf off the east coast of the United States

Height of the Continents

- changes in the height of continents due to plate collisions can affect sea level

- convergence of two crustal plates creates a tall coastal mountain range

- tall coastal mountains cause moisture-laden air from the ocean to rise

- air cools and condenses into clouds as it rises; results in rain and snow (See pages 538–541.)

- precipitation falls on continents instead of oceans; sea level drops

- however, over several million years, mountain range may be worn down to sea level; precipitation will fall into oceans again, causing sea level to rise

GEOLOGIC TIME

refers to the passage of enormous units of time involved in the formation of geologic features, such as deep valleys, mountain ranges, and shorelines.

Based on recent information gathered from the dating of meteorites and lunar rocks, many geologists think that Earth's history spans about 4.6 billion years. These scientists believe this huge chunk of time has made possible not only the formation of geologic features, but also the development of Earth's varied life forms.

THE basics

RADIOMETRIC DATING

✔ Radioactive elements decay at a continuous rate.

✔ For example, the *half-life* of the element carbon-14 is 5,730 years. Half-life is the amount of time it takes for half the atoms of an element to decay.

✔ To find out how old a certain rock is, geologists measure the amount of radioactive material found in the minerals of the rock. They compare that amount to the amount present when that mineral first forms, and this tells them the age of the rock.

Dating Rocks

Rock Dating

With the discovery of natural radioactivity in 1896, the vastness of geologic time became clear. By 1900, geologists were able to calculate the approximate ages of rocks. Measuring the rate of decay that characterizes radioactive elements, geologists assigned approximate ages to large outcrops of rock on or near Earth's surface.

Radioactive elements, such as uranium, thorium, potassium-40, rubidium, strontium, and carbon-14, are found in many kinds of matter. Radioactive elements possess a special property. Their atoms continuously decay, or give off neutrons. The radioactivity in these elements has a constant and measurable rate of decay. In addition, the high pressures and high temperatures of Earth's interior do not affect the rate at which radioactive elements decay.

Igneous Rocks

Inside igneous rocks, radioactive elements begin to decay as soon as the rocks crystallize from magma. (See pages 466–467.) Three values must be known for scientists to date igneous rocks:

- amount of radioactivity present in the mineral when crystals first form
- rate of radioactive decay
- amount of radioactivity currently inside the rock

The first two values are known for all radioactive elements. Once the third is measured, a geologist can calculate the approximate age of the igneous rock.

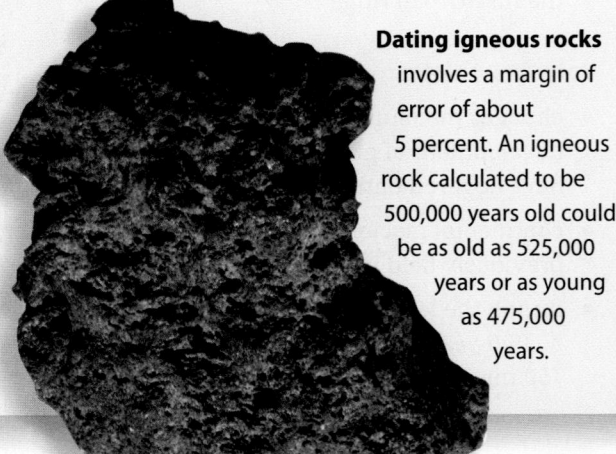

Dating igneous rocks involves a margin of error of about 5 percent. An igneous rock calculated to be 500,000 years old could be as old as 525,000 years or as young as 475,000 years.

Metamorphic Rocks

The same procedure used for dating igneous rocks can be used to date the formation of metamorphic rocks. (See pages 470–471.) The crystallization of new minerals, which often takes place when a rock undergoes intense heat and great pressure, forms a baseline for determining the amount of time that has elapsed since the rock was subjected to metamorphism. By measuring the amount of radioactivity contained in a mineral found inside a metamorphic rock, a geologist can determine when the rock was altered.

▲ **Dating Metamorphic Rocks.** Scientists date metamorphic rocks using the same procedure as igneous rocks.

Sedimentary Rocks

Rocks formed from sediments cannot be dated in the same way as igneous or metamorphic rocks. (See pages 468–469.) The minerals in sedimentary rocks were brought from distant locations by natural forces like streams, glaciers, and winds. Consequently, a large part of a mineral's radioactive decay may have taken place before the mineral became part of a sedimentary rock.

In order to date sedimentary rocks, geologists use their location in respect to bodies of igneous rocks whose ages are known. After an age has been determined for a body of igneous rock, that age can be used to find the approximate age of the adjacent layer of sedimentary rock. Ages assigned to sedimentary rocks are not as accurate as those assigned to igneous and metamorphic rocks.

▲ **Dating Sedimentary Rocks.** Geologists approximate the age of sedimentary rocks by measuring the age of igneous rock found in contact with or near the layer of sedimentary rock.

Fossils

Fossils are the remains or traces of prehistoric plants and animals. Most fossils are found embedded in layers of sedimentary rock that formed on the ocean floor or at the bottom of lakes and ponds. The history of Earth is recorded in the life forms that died and left fossils.

Formation. The most common fossils are those made from the hard parts—skeletons, shells, and other hard materials—of animals. These hard parts may form either molds or casts. A *fossil mold* is a rock cavity that has the same shape as the buried organism. A *fossil cast* is formed when a mold fills in with sediments that subsequently harden.

Petrified logs in the Petrified Forest National Park are probably about 225 million years old. ▼

RARE REMAINS

Fossils have been found that formed in other, less common ways.

- entire insects preserved in *amber*, or hardened tree sap
- elephant-like animals called mammoths preserved in the frigid soil of the Arctic
- the bones of thousands of animals that lived between 15,000 and 20,000 years ago preserved in tar pits, such as the famous La Brea Tar Pits of southern California

Amber can contain entire insects preserved for millions of years. ▼

The La Brea Tar Pits are one of the world's richest known sources of ice age fossils.

An *imprint* is another kind of fossil. It is a cast of a footprint or a part of a plant or animal—not the entire organism. Most of the imprints that have been found were left by dinosaurs. Many dinosaurs lived in swamps and marshes where the ground is soft and moist. These dinosaurs left wide, deep footprints in the mud. If the mud hardened and was quickly buried by sediments, footprints could be preserved as imprints. Leaves and stems of plants have also been found preserved as fossil imprints.

Petrification is another form of fossilization. During this slow process, water carries off the organic materials from the remains of the dead organism. Minerals dissolved in the water then replace the organic materials. This process formed the petrified logs of coniferous trees in the Petrified Forest National Park in Arizona.

HOW DOES THAT WORK

HOW FOSSILS FORM

Three events must take place before a fossil can form within a sedimentary rock.

1. Soon after an organism dies, it must be buried by sediments. The rapid burial slows the organism's decay by heat, precipitation, and decomposers, such as bacteria and fungi.

2. The soft parts of the buried plant or animal must decay, leaving behind only the skeleton, shell, or other hard parts.

3. Layers of sediment must accumulate around the organism and harden into sedimentary rock. (See pages 468–469.)

If all three of these events occur, the organism, or part of it, is then preserved as a fossil in a layer of sedimentary rock.

Fossils

Age of Fossils. Geologists determine the absolute, or specific, age of fossils by measuring the age of radioactive material. In 1947, an American geologist named W. F. Libby discovered that both radioactive carbon (carbon-14) and the more plentiful, nonradioactive carbon-12 occur naturally in the air.

When plants take in carbon dioxide during photosynthesis, or animals eat those plants, they take in both forms of carbon. When a plant or animal dies, the carbon-14 in its tissues begins to decay. All organisms lose carbon-14 at the same rate. As carbon-14 decays, it changes into the element nitrogen. The length of time required for half of the carbon-14 in a dead organism to decay into nitrogen is about 5,700 years.

Suppose a geologist determines that half of the carbon-14 in a particular fossil has changed into nitrogen. The geologist can then infer that the fossil is about 5,700 years old. If 75 percent of the carbon-14 has changed into nitrogen, the fossil would be 11,400 years old.

DATING ISSUES

Carbon-14 dating allowed geologists to accurately date fossils for the first time. But the process is not without its issues. The process assumes that

- an organism ceases taking up carbon-14 from its environment when it dies.

  However, if the organism being dated is buried in soil, circulating groundwater that contains carbon-14 might contaminate it.

- the amount of carbon-14 has remained relatively constant over the last 40,000 years.

  However, recent research has shown that carbon-14 levels in the air vary over time. Variations in the production of carbon-14 over several hundred or thousand years have led to errors in the ages calculated for organisms living during those times.

Because of these issues, geologists are now using another technique—measuring the radioactive decay of uranium into thorium. This form of radioactive dating is especially used to find the age of relatively recent marine fossils. All marine organisms contain traces of uranium in their bodies. It is currently believed that the amount of uranium in seawater has not changed throughout geologic history.

COUNTING RINGS

In the early days of carbon-14 dating, there was no way to check the accuracy of the data. In the 1950s, *dendrochronology,* or tree-ring dating, provided a way to compare carbon-14 dates with actual calendar dates.

Counting the growth rings of very old, fossilized trees provides a reliable way of dating fossils found buried in the same location. By using carbon-14 dating on growth rings, geologists can determine systematic variations in the radiocarbon dates. (See page 125.)

Growth rings form in the trunks of trees—one for each year the tree lives.

Relative Age of Fossils. The relative age of a fossil can be determined by observing the fossil's position in a sequence of sedimentary rock layers. Some fossils, called *index fossils,* are always found in rock layers of a particular age. Index fossils are valuable to geologists because they occur in great numbers in rocks of the same age throughout the world. Index fossils are organisms that lived only during a relatively brief period of Earth's history. An example of an index fossil is the trilobite, believed to have lived mostly between 450 and 500 million years ago.

Index fossils help geologists determine the relative age of the sedimentary rocks in which the fossils have been preserved. Suppose geologists uncover identical trilobite fossils in two rock formations, one in China and the other in the United States. Because trilobites lived only during a particular period, the geologists can infer that the two widely separated rock layers were deposited about the same time.

THE LAW OF SUPERPOSITION

Geologists have discovered that layers of sedimentary rock are deposited one at a time. The oldest layers are on the bottom, and the youngest layers are on the top. This geological phenomenon is known as the Law of Superposition.

INTERPRETING FOSSILS

Geologists interpret fossils in order to learn about Earth's history. Fossils provide physical indicators about ancient landscapes, prehistoric climates, continental drift, and biological evolution.

- **ancient landscapes:** Fossils of marine organisms discovered stacked in sedimentary rock in North America reveal that the continent has been covered in seas several times during the past 600 million years.

- **prehistoric climates and continental drift:** 400-million-year-old coral reefs discovered in the east-central United States reveal that this region had a tropical climate. From this, geologists infer that the continent was once much closer to the equator.

- **biological evolution:** Based on the fossil record, organisms are thought to have progressed from simple to complex throughout Earth's history. For example, fossils reveal that horse size has increased dramatically during the past 60 million years. The first horse was the size of a small dog. Today, some horses are more than 2 meters (6 feet) tall.

Permian

Carboniferous

Devonian

Silurian

Ordovician

Cambrian

Index fossils are fossils of organisms known to have existed only during a particular period of time. Thus, if they are found in a particular layer of sediment, they can be dated reliably.

Geologic Time Scale

As geologists accumulated knowledge of sedimentary rock layers in different parts of the world, they were able to make age comparisons based on fossil content. (See pages 468–469.) First, it was necessary to determine the order in which the sediments were deposited in one region. The sequence of rock deposition could then be compared with a different sequence from another region, even another continent. The comparison was not based on the type of sedimentary rock, but on the presence of index fossils.

Applying the Law of Superposition, geologists were able to figure out which fossils were older. As more and more layers of fossil-bearing rock were correlated, it became possible to establish a chronological order called the geologic time scale.

The development of the geologic time scale was a giant step forward in historical geology, enabling geologists from around the world to compare the timing of geologic processes and events.

The geologic time scale consists of two major time periods, separated on the basis of age and fossil content.

- **Precambrian time:** divided into three separate eons; characterized by very old rocks with few or no fossils present.

- **Phanerozoic eon:** characterized by younger rocks in which fossils are commonly found.

The Cretaceous period, which lasted from 145 million to 65 million years ago, witnessed the rise of the Rocky Mountains in the western United States. ▼

The Geologic Time Scale Theory						
Time	Eon	Era	Period	Epoch	Years Ago	Duration	Conditions
Precambrian	Hadean				4.6 billion	700 million	conditions uncertain; probably intense volcanic activity, not suitable for life
	Archean				3.9 billion	1.4 billion	conditions uncertain; probably intense volcanic activity, not suitable for life
	Proterozoic				2.5 billion	2 billion	conditions uncertain; first glaciers; plant and multicellular animal life
	Phanerozoic	Paleozoic	Cambrian		540 million	40 million	mild; lowlands and inland seas
			Ordovician		500 million	60 million	mild; warm in the Arctic, most of the land submerged; vertebrate animals exist
			Silurian		440 million	25 million	mild; inland seas
			Devonian		415 million	55 million	land rises; shallow sea and marshes and some arid areas; amphibians first appear
			Carboniferous	Mississippian (Early Carboniferous)	360 million	40 million	warm, humid; shallow inland seas; coal age begins
				Pennsylvanian (Late Carboniferous)	320 million	20 million	warm, humid; widespread swamps and forests; coal age
			Permian		300 million	50 million	hot, dry; mountains rising
		Mesozoic	Triassic		250 million	50 million	warm, dry; extensive deserts; dinosaurs and small mammals first appear
			Jurassic		200 million	55 million	warm; lowlands and continental seas; peak development of dinosaurs
			Cretaceous		145 million	80 million	warm; swamps dry out; Rocky Mountains rise up; dinosaurs become extinct
		Cenozoic	Paleogene	Paleocene	65 million	10 million	very warm; large mammals dominate the land and sea; Europe and North America are still joined in the north
				Eocene	55 million	21 million	very warm; sea level gradually falls; flowering plants appear
				Oligocene	34 million	11 million	warm; major crustal movements; worldwide volcanic activity
			Neogene	Miocene	23 million	17.7 million	temperate; horses first appear
				Pliocene	5.3 million	2.7 million	cold; snow builds up; link between Europe and North America is broken
			Quaternary	Pleistocene	2.6 million	2.59 million	warm and cold climates; four stages of glaciation; people appear
				Holocene	11.5 thousand	to present	moderate; receding glaciers

Precambrian Time

Precambrian Time

The Precambrian time is, by far, the longest segment of Earth's history. It represents about 88 percent, or close to 4 billion years, of history. The Precambrian time begins with Earth's formation, considered by geologists to have occurred about 4.6 billion years ago, and lasts until fossils become numerous at the start of the Cambrian period.

Earth's Formation

- about 4.6 billion years ago Earth is a swirling cloud of dust and gases

- over the next several hundred million years, particles of dust and gas unite into a molten mass; the mass separates according to the density of each substance within it

- eventually Earth cools to form a sphere with an unbroken solid surface, or crust

Precambrian time included roughly Earth's first 4 billion years. The crust, the atmosphere, and the oceans were formed, and the simplest kinds of life appeared. ▼

Late Precambrian rocks are usually found as sedimentary or metamorphic rock. This peak in the Marble Hills of Antarctica was originally deposited as limestone, but changed into marble at the end of the Precambrian time. ▶

Earth Develops

- at first, Earth is too small to hold an atmosphere

- once Earth accumulates matter equal to about 40 percent of its present mass, gaseous elements given off from the crust are held around Earth like an envelope; these gases probably include water vapor, carbon monoxide, nitrogen, and methane

- about 40 million years ago the primitive atmosphere rains water down into the depressions in Earth's crust, forming the first oceans and seas

- the higher elevations become the first continents, or landmasses

- intense volcanic activity and frequent earthquakes likely widespread during Earth's early geologic history

Setting the Stage for Life

- during the early Precambrian time, Earth is not suitable for the support of life as we know it

- over time, gradual changes occur: air and water temperatures cool and chemical changes produce the carbon dioxide required for green plants to make food and oxygen (photosynthesis)

- finally, organic compounds form, setting the stage for the many forms of life that have appeared on Earth over the past several billion years

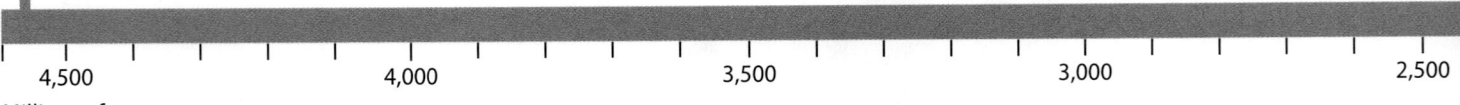

| 4,500 | 4,000 | 3,500 | 3,000 | 2,500 |

Millions of years ago

Precambrian Rocks

- oldest rocks on Earth form during the early part of the Precambrian time

- most Precambrian rock has been broken down and dispersed by erosion

- consequently, geologists have not yet found any evidence of the original crust of Earth

- oldest Precambrian rocks to be found are 3.8 billion years old, based on potassium-40–argon radioactive dating

- meteorites and rock samples brought back from the moon have been dated between 4.5 and 4.7 billion years old.

- astronomers currently think all planets in our solar system formed simultaneously; for this reason, the present scientific estimate of Earth's age is 4.6 billion years

Precambrian Fossils

- first fossil evidence of life on Earth comes from a rock formation in southern Africa called the Fig Tree Formation; rocks from this formation have been dated at 3.4 billion years

- Fig Tree Formation fossils are microscopic and resemble varieties of living bacteria

- about 3 billion years ago blue-green algae appear, the first organisms that geologists are certain carried out photosynthesis

- earliest evidence of plants and multicellular animal life to be found in rocks is 1 to 1.5 billion years old

- 570 million years ago, shelled fossils appear in large numbers, marking the start of the Cambrian period (See page 154.)

EDIACARAN PERIOD

Life began to flourish throughout the world in the last period of Precambrian time. Geologists have named this period the Ediacaran period, after the Ediacara Hills of southern Australia. In these hills, a rich assemblage of fossil animals has been discovered in rocks dated at 680 million years. These fossils were made strictly by soft-bodied animals. They contain more than 30 species from four phyla, including jellyfish, worms, sea pens, sponges, and coral-like animals. In addition, unidentified forms of life left an assortment of tracks and trails.

Ediacaran fossils, found in the Ediacara Hills and other parts of the world, are molds and casts formed when soft-bodied organisms died and were rapidly buried on the seafloor. ▶

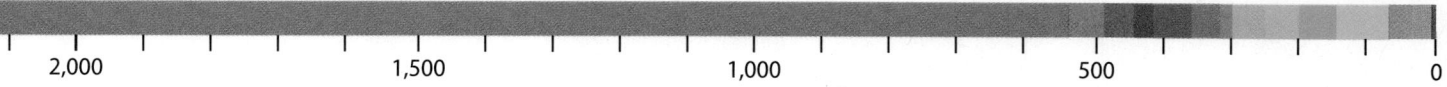

2,000   1,500   1,000   500   0

Cambrian and Ordovician

Cambrian Period

The Phanerozoic eon begins with the Paleozoic era and its first subdivision, the Cambrian period. The Cambrian period lasted for 40 million years—from about 540 to 500 million years ago.

Earth During the Cambrian Period

During the Cambrian period, most of Earth's land lay in the Southern Hemisphere. The land consisted mainly of several large continents formed earlier in the breakup of a giant landmass. These continents continued to spread apart, and what is now North America drifted northward, crossing the equator in parts. Global sea levels rose through the Cambrian period until most of the land was covered by oceans. The climate was generally warm, and ice probably did not cover Earth's poles as it does today.

Cambrian Explosion. Many major types of animals first appear in fossils from the early Cambrian period. Scientists often call this dramatic increase in the variety of animal fossils the *Cambrian Explosion*. During the Cambrian Explosion:

- animals began interacting with one another and their environment in more complex ways
- animals began eating other animals, growing skeletons for protection, and burrowing into seafloor sediments for food and shelter
- the first reefs formed, built by early sponges and bacteria

Marine life dominated during the Cambrian period. No fossil evidence indicates that plants or animals lived outside of the oceans at this time. Genetic studies, however, have suggested that certain plants and fungi lived on land.

THE OZONE LAYER

Once the *ozone layer* was thick enough to act as a solar screen, organisms moved out of the oceans. The ozone layer shields Earth from *ultraviolet radiation*—a form of sunlight deadly to living things. (See pages 680–681.)

In fact, there is evidence that living things began to move onto land during the Ordovician period. Spores and bits of what look like vascular plant tissue have been found fossilized in Ordovician-age rocks. However, no well-preserved land plants occur in the fossil record until the Silurian period.

Trilobites are well preserved in a variety of different sedimentary rocks from the Cambrian period. ▶

Cambrian Fossils

- **trilobites,** sea animals related to modern crabs, lobsters, and insects, are the most abundant Cambrian fossil
- **stromatolites,** mounds of rock formed by algae, are plentiful, building up large reefs in many places
- toward the end of the Cambrian period, small **cephalopods,** squidlike animals, first appear
- **bivalves**—clamlike animals—and echinoderms—sea stars, sea urchins, and sand dollars—are found in Early Cambrian rocks, but they are rare

Ordovician Period

Like the Cambrian period, the Ordovician period was a long period of geologic time, lasting about 60 million years. At the beginning of this period—500 million years ago—most life forms were still primitive compared with modern organisms. However, by the end of the period, all of the common *invertebrates,* or animals without backbones, had appeared, as well as some *vertebrates,* or animals with backbones.

▲ **The Appalachian Mountains** in the eastern United States formed during the Ordovician period as the Eurasian plate collided with the North American plate.

Earth During the Ordovician Period

- the continents are moving together
- thick beds of limestone and shale indicate that as much as 70 percent of North America is underwater during the latter part of the Ordovician period
- parts of Australia, central South America, and much of Europe and Asia are also submerged
- at the end of the Ordovician period, the continents begin to rise and mountain building causes the seas to retreat from many land areas

Ordovician Fossils

- Ordovician rocks have many fossils, especially brachiopods, which are marine invertebrate animals
- few trilobite *families,* or groupings of animal types, from the Cambrian period remain; however, several new trilobite families appear during the Ordovician period

▲ **Ostracoderms,** the first vertebrates, appeared during the Middle Ordovician period. The ostracoderms are considered to be the ancestors of all vertebrate animals.

- in the Early Ordovician period, colonies of coral and *bryozoans* (moss animals) first appear; by the Middle Ordovician period, some rocks were almost completely composed of bryozoans
- sea stars, brittle stars, sea urchins, and *crinoids* (sea lilies) are also abundant, as well as *gastropods* (snail-like animals) in the shallow seas
- bivalves, such as clams and oysters, first appear during the Cambrian period; during the Ordovician period they become larger, more abundant, and more varied in appearance
- *cephalopods,* or squidlike creatures, increase in size and diversity

Mass Extinction

- about 430 million years ago a mass extinction marks the end of the Ordovician period
- about 25 percent of all families perish during this extinction
- trilobites suffer most, losing more than 50 percent of their families
- the extinction also decimates sponges, brachiopods, and echinoderms

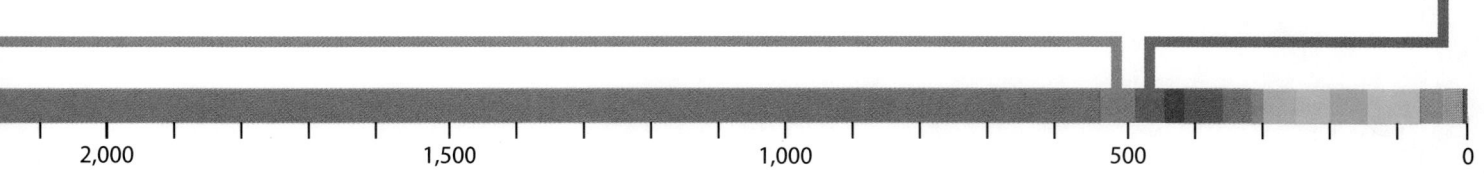

2,000   1,500   1,000   500   0

Silurian and Devonian

Silurian Period

The Silurian period lasted about 25 million years. During this period, which began about 440 million years ago, the northern continents were joined into a supercontinent known as Laurasia. (See pages 448–449.) The southern continents also were joined into a supercontinent; it was known as Gondwanaland. Both supercontinents moved closer together during the Silurian period.

Earth During the Silurian Period

- most of North America is part of Laurasia; Mexico and southeastern United States are part of Gondwanaland, which is moving steadily toward Laurasia
- Europe had collided with the northeastern coast of North America during the Ordovician period; now this region experiences a great deal of tectonic activity
- with the exception of the northeastern coast, most of North America is submerged beneath a warm, shallow sea
- coral reefs form in what are today the states of Michigan, Indiana, and Illinois
- in Siberia, mountain building occurs that is so intense that the region has remained above water for the rest of geologic time—almost 400 million years

SILURIAN SWAMP LIFE

Land organisms remained scarce during the Silurian period. However, some well-preserved fossils of vascular plants have been found in Wales. It is believed that these plants, called *psilophytes,* were transitional plants—part marine algae, part land plants. Millipede-like fossils have also been recovered from Silurian-age rocks. Both the psilophytes and millipede-like animals probably lived in a very moist environment, similar to that of a marsh or swamp.

▲ **Vertebrates** were still rare during the Silurian period. However, spines and scales discovered in Late Silurian rocks may have belonged to acanthodians—the first fish with jaws. Acanthodians became numerous during the Devonian period.

Eurypterids, sea scorpions that flourished during the Silurian period, could grow as large as 3 meters (9 feet) long. ▶

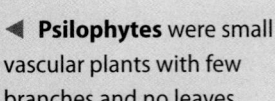

◀ **Psilophytes** were small vascular plants with few branches and no leaves.

Silurian Fossils

- no new major groups of organisms appear in the fossil record
- most of the previously established groups flourish
- however, trilobites become less numerous, but still locally abundant
- the most prominent creatures are the eurypterids (sea scorpions)

Devonian Period

During the 55-million-year-long Devonian period, which began about 415 million years ago, plants and animals spread onto land. Most of Earth's land remained part of the supercontinents of Laurasia and Gondwanaland.

Earth During the Devonian Period

- Europe and North America continue to drift together; the northern part of the Appalachian Mountains nears completion
- North America has either a tropical or subtropical climate; the equator runs through Canada from northern British Columbia to Newfoundland
- shallow seas cover most of the continents
- most of northern Europe, Russia, southern Siberia, and south China are submerged
- seas cover parts of central and western South America
- in North America, the sea covers the Mississippi Valley region and much of what is now the western United States and Canada

▲ **The first tetrapods** resembled modern amphibians in some features, like their need to return to water to lay eggs. In others, they closely resembled crocodiles, like the one pictured here.

Devonian Life

- plants and animals continue to spread onto land
- the first land colonizers are plant-eaters, but spider fossils indicate that predators soon follow
- first tree-sized plants appear, forming forests that house the first insects and *tetrapods* (four-legged animals) that resemble today's amphibians
- these plants and animals probably cannot survive far from the damp conditions found along riverbanks and in swamps; away from such areas, the land most likely remains barren
- fish become the dominant life form in the Devonian seas; sea creatures evolve (develop gradually) into many new forms (See page 156.)
- the first *ammonites,* distant relatives of the squid, appear; fossil collectors prize ammonites' tightly coiled shells for their beauty
- many new types of fish also evolve, including modern-looking sharks and giant predatory fish with bone-armored skulls

▲ **The Acadian Mountains** were a range that formed during the Devonian period. The White Mountains of New Hampshire (pictured here) formed from Acadian Mountain granite.

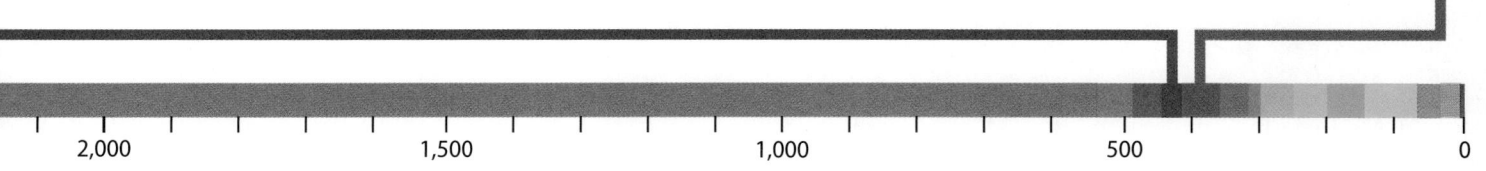

| 2,000 | 1,500 | 1,000 | 500 | 0 |

Carboniferous

The Carboniferous period began 360 million years ago and lasted for 60 million years. *Carboniferous* is Latin for "coal-bearing." Rocks of this age contain abundant coal deposits. Carboniferous rocks remain an important source of energy because many petroleum deposits formed in them. Geologists divide the Carboniferous period into two epochs, the *Mississippian epoch* and the *Pennsylvanian epoch*.

Mississippian Epoch

The Mississippian epoch lasted about 40 million years. The fossils discovered from this epoch are almost entirely of marine organisms that lived in the clear, shallow, warm seas that covered most of North America. The Mississippian epoch derives its name from the thick limestone deposited in the Mississippi Valley at that time.

Earth During the Mississippian Epoch

- most of England, Belgium, and northern France are underwater
- rocks of Mississippian epoch are not widespread in Africa, South America, or Australia; geologists think these continents are above water

The Age of Crinoids. Geologists sometimes refer to the Mississippian epoch as the Age of Crinoids because of the large number of fossils found in Mississippian limestone.

▲ **Indiana limestone,** deposited in the Mississippi Valley during this epoch, was used in the construction of many U.S. government buildings, including the National Archives, pictured here.

- glaciers form on all the southern continents
- extensive mountain building takes place in Europe at the end of the epoch
- mountain building and the growth of glaciers on the southern continents cause the seas to withdraw from North America

Mississippian Fossils

- large numbers of *crinoid* and *blastoid* fossils found in limestone; crinoids and blastoids are a related group of stemmed marine creature that first appear during the Silurian period
- microscopic, single-celled marine animals called *foraminiferans* are so numerous that whole beds of limestone are composed of their calcium-rich skeletons
- land plants and terrestrial animals noticeably absent from the fossil record of the Mississippian epoch, perhaps because conditions in North America were unfavorable for life on land or unsuitable for the preservation of fossils

4,500   4,000   3,500   3,000   2,500

Millions of years ago

Pennsylvanian Epoch

The 20-million-year-long Pennsylvanian epoch began about 320 million years ago. Life flourished in a vast expanse of swamps that stretched for great distances along the equator, and all the continents had begun to form the vast supercontinent called Pangaea.

North America During the Pennsylvanian Epoch

- extensive mountain building in North America
- Gondwanaland pushes Mexico and the southeastern United States against North America
- mountains rise in Colorado, Wyoming, and Utah, precursors to present-day Rocky Mountains
- the southern Appalachian Mountains begin to rise
- the shallow sea withdraws from the interior of the North American continent, leaving long, narrow troughs along the southern Appalachian Mountains
- volcanic eruptions and erosion of the rising mountains fill these troughs with enormous amounts of sediment

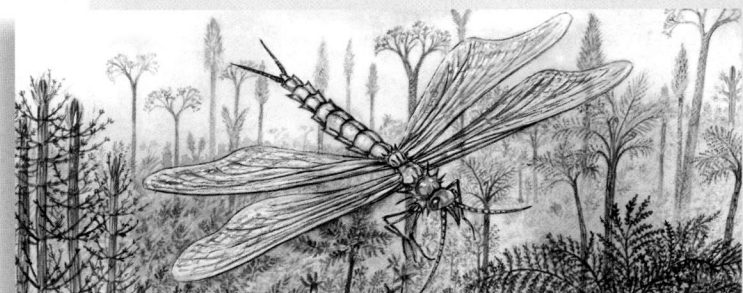

Dragonflies with a wingspan of 74 centimeters (29 inches) lived in the forests and swamps during the Pennsylvanian epoch.

CARBONIFEROUS FORESTS

During most of the Pennsylvanian epoch, large areas of North America supported lush swamps and forests. Of these plants, the lycopods were the tallest—reaching heights of 30 meters (100 feet). Ferns grew to 15 meters (50 feet).

When plants of the swamp forests died, they fell into the mud and water that covered the forest floor. The mud and water did not contain enough oxygen to support decomposers. As a result, the plants did not decay but became buried under layer after layer of mud. Over millions of years, the weight and pressure on the plants turned them into great coal deposits.

Pennsylvanian Fossils

- some marine animals are affected dramatically by the loss of the clear, warm, shallow sea
- the crinoids decline permanently, and the immobile brachiopods smother within the sediment-filled troughs bordering the southern Appalachian Mountains
- mobile organisms, such as the bivalves and the gastropods, flourish
- invertebrates during the Pennsylvanian epoch include the largest insects that ever lived
- cockroaches that measure 100 millimeters (4 inches) and foot-long centipedes scurry on the forest floor
- spiders and scorpions also inhabit the drier forests during the Pennsylvanian epoch
- amphibians are common; more than 90 species of giant salamanders have been found in swampy deposits of the Pennsylvanian epoch (See Age of Amphibians, page 157.)
- earliest known reptile fossils are discovered in Early Pennsylvanian rock; the fossils are fragmentary, but they appear to have resembled alligators

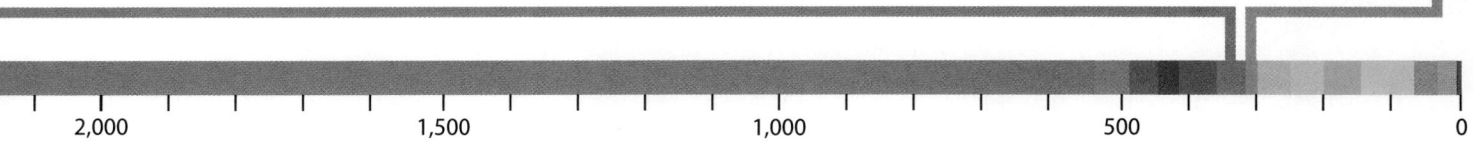

2,000   1,500   1,000   500   0

Permian and Triassic

Permian Period

The Permian period began about 300 million years ago and lasted for 50 million years. The Permian period was the last period of the Paleozoic era, a time in which early living things left behind an abundance of fossils. Throughout the period, most of Earth's land formed the supercontinent called Pangaea.

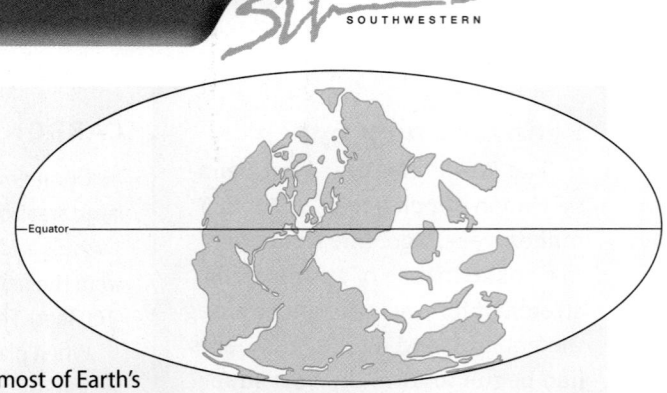

Pangaea contained most of Earth's land during the Permian period. ▲

PERMIAN EXTINCTION

The most devastating event in Earth's history marked the end of the Permian period. A mass extinction wiped out more than 95 percent of all species, in the water and on land. There is no generally accepted explanation for this mass extinction. Some geologists point to a sudden, dramatic fall in sea level, which may have dried up all of the shallow marine environments on Earth. Other geologists claim that the impact of a huge meteorite on Earth may have caused the mass extinction at the end of the Permian period. There is some indirect evidence of a meteorite-Earth collision, but no direct proof. (See End of an Era, page 157.)

ANCESTOR OF MAMMALS

Therapsids became numerous during the Late Permian period, colonizing environments that had never been inhabited by any other land vertebrates. Some of these areas were so near the poles that therapsids probably were warm-blooded. They may also have developed fur that provided insulation against cold air temperatures. They were similar to pelycosaurs in size and were also meat eaters.

Earth During the Permian Period

- a very dry stage of Earth's history
- western interior of the United States is hot and dry
- salt deposits form in Kansas, New Mexico, and Texas as seawater evaporates from the intense heat
- sand dunes are widespread throughout North America
- the Permian seas in North America are much more confined than at any other time during the entire Paleozoic era

Pelycosaur

Permian Fossils

- large amphibians and reptiles of various sizes are found in Permian rocks in the southwest United States
- *pelycosaurs*, cold-blooded reptiles with tall, sail-like fins on their backs develop; fins are probably used to regulate body heat
- during the Late Permian period, *therapsids*, the ancestors of all mammals, develop; descendants of pelycosaurs

Therapsid

4,500	4,000	3,500	3,000	2,500

Millions of years ago

Triassic Period

The first period of the Mesozoic era is called the Triassic period. The Triassic period began about 250 million years ago and lasted for about 50 million years. It followed the Permian extinction, which changed life on Earth so dramatically that it marked the end of the Paleozoic era, the earliest era of life on Earth.

Earth During the Triassic Period

- a seaway extends southward from western Canada into the western part of the United States
- the equator passes through central Mexico
- most of North America is located in the northern horse latitudes, a climate zone about 30° north of the equator where little rain falls
- consequently, scientists assume the Triassic period is one in which land plants and animals adapted to conditions that were more arid
- Pangaea breaks up at the end of the Triassic period; rift valleys (areas where crustal plates separate) develop in eastern North America, from Nova Scotia to Florida

Triassic Fossils

- life-forms are scarce at the beginning of the Triassic period due to Permian extinction
- reptiles become the dominant animals on land and in the sea, including the first dinosaurs and early large marine reptiles
- present-day lizards and turtles, as well as ancestral crocodiles called phytosaurs, first appear
- early ancestors of modern mammals appear
- plant life includes some of the earliest *conifers* (cone-bearing plants), the primitive ancestors of modern pine and spruce trees

Ichthyosaurs were among the most successful of reptiles during the Triassic period. Shaped like sharks, ichthyosaurs were the largest animals of the period, as much as 9 meters (30 feet) long, with jaws full of long stabbing teeth.

Triassic-age cycads and ferns have been fossilized along with entire conifer tree trunks in the Petrified Forest National Park in Arizona.

A MYSTERIOUS GLACIER

At the end of the Triassic period there was a sudden, worldwide drop in sea level. Such a drop is usually caused by the growth of a continental glacier. However, evidence of glaciation has not been found.

One explanation offered is that a huge meteorite or group of meteorites bombarded Earth. If there was a collision, dust from the impact could have blocked incoming solar radiation. The subsequent cooling would have allowed thick glaciers to form in the northern latitudes, drawing water from the Triassic seas and thus causing sea levels to drop.

2,000   1,500   1,000   500   0

Jurassic

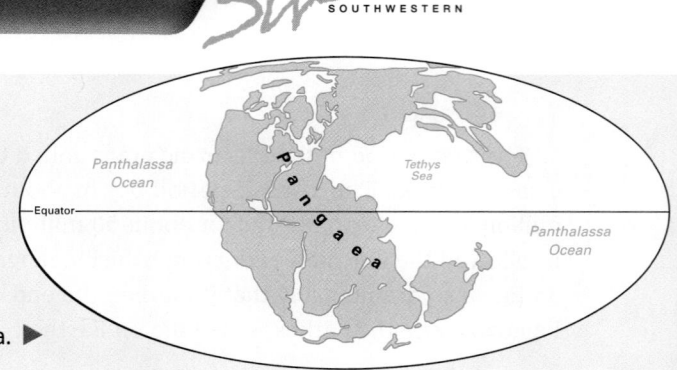

Jurassic Period

The Jurassic period began about 200 million years ago and lasted for 55 million years. During this period, dinosaurs were at their peak of development and Pangaea again split into the separate continents of Laurasia and Gondwanaland. (See pages 158–161.)

Laurasia and Gondwanaland formed in the breakup of Pangaea. A vast ocean called Panthalassa surrounded Pangaea. ▶

Panthalassa Ocean
Tethys Sea
Panthalassa Ocean
Equator
Pangaea

Seismosaurus, *top,* was one of the largest of all dinosaurs. It may have weighed 77 metric tons (85 short tons), more than 10 times as much as a full-grown elephant.

Dinosaurs and birds, *center,* are closely related. Many dinosaurs looked much like modern birds. For example, the dinosaur Ornithomimus, *below,* resembled the modern ostrich, *above.*

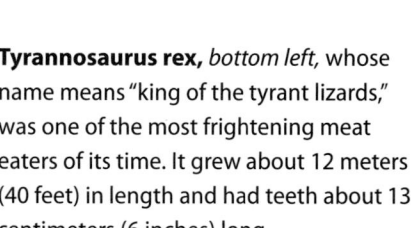

Tyrannosaurus rex, *bottom left,* whose name means "king of the tyrant lizards," was one of the most frightening meat eaters of its time. It grew about 12 meters (40 feet) in length and had teeth about 13 centimeters (6 inches) long.

Earth During the Jurassic Period

- about 200 million years ago, Africa and North America begin to drift apart; this divergence of continental plates causes fault lines to develop along the east coast of North America and northwestern Africa
- Gondwanaland starts to pull away from the southern border of North America
- the west coast of North America is geologically active, with many live volcanoes, because the Pacific plate is sliding underneath the North American plate
- most of Germany, France, and England, as well as parts of western Russia, are submerged under the sea
- in North America, Jurassic seas occur only in the western part of the continent
- thick deposits of sandstone and shale are laid down to the north and east of the Grand Canyon
- the shale deposits are famous for their many dinosaur fossils
- during the Late Jurassic period, Africa begins to separate from South America, and Greenland begins to separate from North America
- crustal movements in the western United States result in the creation of the Sierra Nevada range

4,500   4,000   3,500   3,000   2,500

Millions of years ago

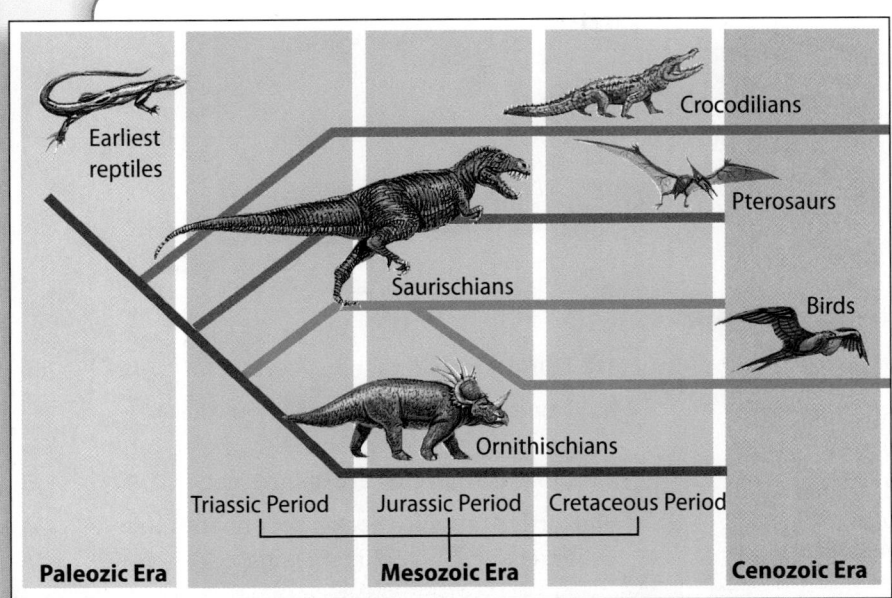

The Mesozoic era contained the two major kinds of dinosaurs—ornithischians and saurischians.

THE AGE OF DINOSAURS

The Mesozoic era, which includes the Triassic, Jurassic, and Cretaceous periods, is often called the Age of Dinosaurs. This is because during the 185 million years that make up the era, reptiles became so diverse and numerous that they dominated the land, the sea, and even the air.

In the Jurassic period, giant dinosaurs such as stegosaurus ruled the land, while plesiosaurs and ichthyosaurs were the dominant form of marine life. By the mid-Jurassic period, about 160 million years ago, some ichthyosaurs were 15 meters (50 feet) long.

The Jurassic period featured flying dinosaurs (pterosaurs) as well as the first bird, archaeopteryx. Pterosaurs differed from birds in that they lacked feathers and walked on all fours when on the ground. Archaeopteryx had feathers but may not have been able to fly because its breastbone was not properly shaped to support flight muscles. Instead of flying, these first birds probably glided from tree to tree.

Jurassic Fossils

* oysters, crabs, lobsters, and shrimplike crustaceans appear
* reefs of many different kinds of organisms are widespread
* abundant and diverse marine life thrive throughout the world
* many coal deposits form: in North America major coal deposits form in British Columbia; the forests that produce this coal are composed mainly of conifers, ginkgos, and tree ferns
* no fossil evidence of flowering plants has been discovered from the Jurassic period
* reptiles remain the dominant land and sea creatures
* the dinosaurs are at their peak of development

Archaeopteryx, the first bird, had feathers but probably could not fly.

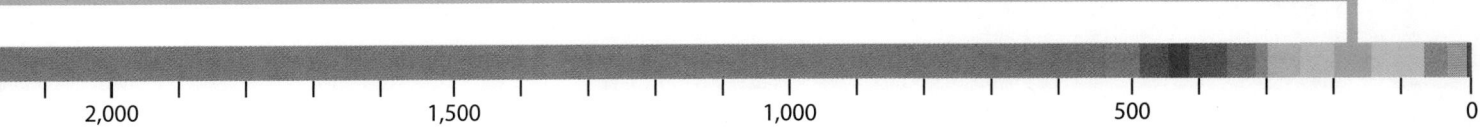

Cretaceous

Cretaceous Period

The Cretaceous period began about 145 million years ago and lasted for 80 million years. Among the most significant geologic events during the long Cretaceous period were the rapid breakup of Pangaea, widening of the Atlantic Ocean, and formation of the Rocky Mountains.

Laurasia and Gondwanaland as they appeared about 120 million years ago ▶

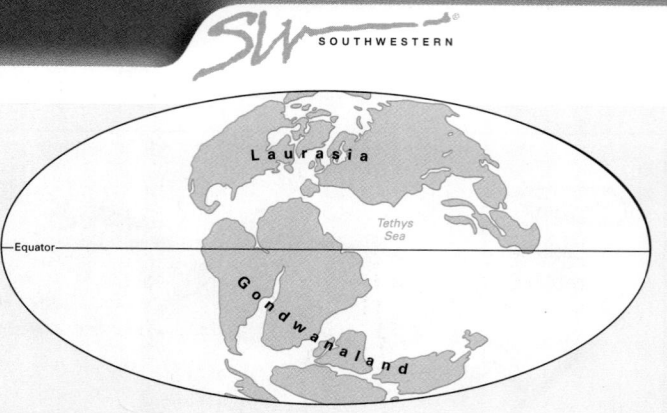

DINOSAURS WIPED OUT!

Many hypotheses have been presented to explain the Cretaceous mass extinction. Some geologists have suggested that the cause of the Cretaceous extinction was a huge asteroid, about 10 kilometers (5 miles) in diameter, that struck Earth about 65 million years ago. The impact produced a large crater and vast clouds of dust. According to this explanation:

- the dust entered the upper atmosphere and spread around the world, forming a barrier against incoming sunlight
- lack of sunlight prevented plants from carrying out photosynthesis for several years
- without plants to eat, the herbivores died from starvation
- without herbivores to eat, the carnivores also died from starvation

hence, the mass extinctions.

Earth During the Cretaceous Period

- mid-ocean ridges rise throughout the Cretaceous period; most of Earth's continental margins are submerged
- in North America, the sea covers both the Atlantic and Gulf coastal plains
- another sea submerges the west coast, extending inward through California to the relatively new Sierra Nevada range
- the most widespread invasion of the sea occurs in the west-central part of North America
- extensive mountain building occurs at the close of the period in North America, South America, and eastern Asia
- in South America, the sediment that has been accumulating in the Andean *geosyncline*, or elongated, downward curve of Earth's crust, folds and compresses to form the Andes Mountains

◀ **Dinosaurs of the Cretaceous period** included hadrosaurs, *center*, which had wide, ducklike bills. Other dinosaurs included the fierce, meat-eating Tyrannosaurus rex and the horned Triceratops, *both upper left.*

| 4,500 | 4,000 | 3,500 | 3,000 | 2,500 |

Millions of years ago

THE ROCKIES

During the Cretaceous period, the Rocky Mountain geosyncline developed in west-central North America when a large sea stretched from the Gulf of Mexico northward through western Canada. This sea covered the area where the Great Plains and the Rocky Mountains now stand. Thick deposits of sandstone, shale, and limestone were laid down on the seabed. Crustal movement then compressed and folded the Rocky Mountain geosyncline to form the Rocky Mountains.

DID AN ASTEROID STRIKE EARTH?

The evidence for the supposed asteroid–Earth collision comes from sediment deposited at the boundary between the Cretaceous and Tertiary periods. (See pages 934–935.)

- At many locations around the world, the sediment contains the element iridium.
- High concentrations of iridium occur only in meteorites.

These iridium-rich sediments do not prove that an asteroid impact actually occurred. To date, however, there is no other way to explain this phenomenon. ▼

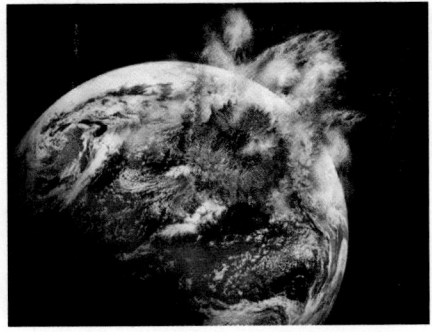

Cretaceous Fossils

- flowering plants appear for the first time
- by the Middle Cretaceous period, they constitute about 90 percent of all plants
- along with the rise of flowering plants comes a corresponding increase in the numbers and kinds of insects
- marine algae and shelled sea organisms reach their peak due to the presence of submerged continental margins; their great abundance is responsible for the massive chalk deposits that give the Cretaceous period its name
- on land, huge reptiles are the dominant form of life
- the carnivorous Tyrannosaurus rex (king of the dinosaurs) reaches 12 meters (40 feet)
- in the sea, plesiosaurs grow to lengths of more than 10 meters (30 feet)
- some turtles grow up to 4 meters (12 feet) long and pterosaurs have wingspans of 10 meters (30 feet)
- opossums, snakes, and lizards are common
- the end of the Cretaceous period is marked by yet another mass extinction; all of the dinosaurs, as well as most of the other Cretaceous organisms, become extinct

2,000   1,500   1,000   500   0

Paleogene and Neogene

Paleogene Period and Neogene Period

Traditionally, the Paleogene and Neogene periods were grouped together and called the Tertiary period. Recently, however, geologists have divided the Tertiary into two separate periods. The Paleogene period began about 65 million years ago and ended about 23 million years ago. The Neogene period began about 23 million years ago and ended 2.6 million years ago.

Earth During the Paleogene and Neogene Periods

- at the beginning of the Paleogene period, Europe and North America are still joined in the far north, and Australia still has not separated from Antarctica

- the Indian plate is moving rapidly toward Asia

- the South Atlantic Ocean is only about 75 percent of its current width, but the North Atlantic Ocean is just slightly less than its present width

- in the early Paleogene period, many parts of Europe, Asia, and northern Africa are submerged

- sea level falls gradually during the Paleogene and Neogene periods; on average, sea level is low, with only 3 percent of the continents covered by seas

- in the Neogene period, Europe and Africa collide, closing off what is now the Mediterranean Sea

- between two and three million years ago, India collides with the Asian plate, causing the Himalayan Mountains to rise

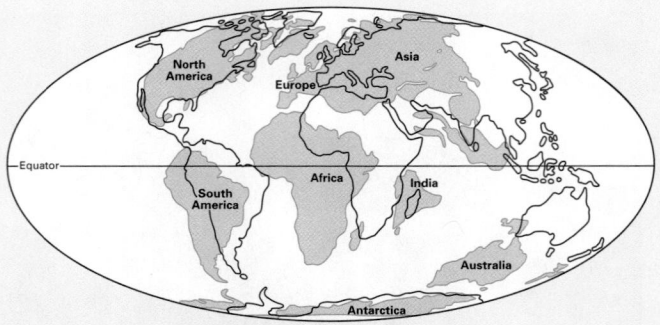

Sixty million years ago, early in the Paleogene period, the continents were approaching their present positions, shown here in black outline. (See pages 448–449.)

Age of Mammals. Mammals dominated the land during the Cenozoic era. This illustration shows mammals that lived during the Neogene period. ▶

| 4,500 | 4,000 | 3,500 | 3,000 | 2,500 |

Millions of years ago

Paleogene and Neogene Fossils

- mammals dominate the land with the extinction of the giant reptiles at the end of the Cretaceous period

- the Cenozoic era is often called the Age of Mammals

- at the beginning of the Paleogene period, mammals are still small insect eaters, similar to present-day moles and shrews

- new larger mammals, including camels, elephants, whales, and a variety of hoofed species, appear

- mammals reach the peak of their diversity during the Neogene period (See also pages 162–163.)

- a large variety of apes appear in Africa and Asia

NOW YOU "SEA" IT...

About 6 million years ago, the collision of Africa and Europe completely closed off what is now the Mediterranean Sea. This area became a desert basin. Many scientists think it went through several cycles of drying and flooding during this time. Eventually, massive flooding from the Atlantic Ocean created the Mediterranean Sea.

PALEOGENE LIMESTONE

During the Paleogene period, the Tethys Sea covered most of the Near East. The sea deposited thick beds of limestone over most of northern Egypt. Blocks of this limestone, called nummulitic limestone, were used in building the pyramids.

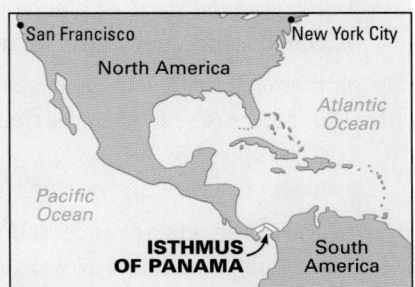

▲ **The Isthmus of Panama** formed as North and South America collided about 3 to 4 million years ago. The formation of the narrow strip of land separated the Atlantic and Pacific oceans. The isthmus also enabled land animals to pass between North and South America.

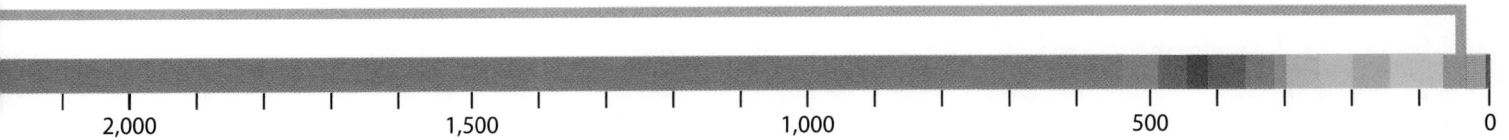

Quaternary

Quaternary Period

The Quaternary period is divided into the Pleistocene epoch and the Holocene epoch. The Pleistocene epoch began about 2.6 million years ago. It eventually resulted in the four stages of continental glaciation, or ice ages. The Pleistocene epoch ended, and the Holocene epoch began, about 11,500 years ago. This date corresponds with the retreat of the last continental ice sheet.

Earth During the Pleistocene Epoch

- glaciers advance and retreat four times across North America, Europe, and Asia
- as much as 30 percent of each of these continents is covered by a thick ice sheet 3,000 to 4,000 meters (10,000 to 13,000 feet) thick
- between each stage of glaciation, the climate is warmer than it is at the present time
- at the peak of each ice age, sea level is about 130 meters (430 feet) lower than it is at present

Life During the Pleistocene and Holocene Epochs

- as the ice sheets advance and retreat, mammals—including *Homo sapiens*—migrate south and north
- during the frigid glacial stages, North America is inhabited by large, hairy mammals, such as mastodons, wooly mammoths, and wooly rhinoceroses
- during the warm interglacial periods, the continent is inhabited by giant ground sloths, saber-toothed cats, wolves, lions, bison, cattle, camels, and one-toed horses
- at the end of the final Ice Age, between 5,000 and 10,000 years ago, more than 30 genera of North American mammals become extinct

The wooly mammoth was a huge, lumbering, elephant-like beast with long hair and a long trunk and tusks.

WHAT CAUSED THE ICE AGES?

Plate movements may have been responsible for the four ice ages during the Pleistocene epoch. These movements closed the Arctic Ocean off from the Pacific Ocean in the Neogene period and caused Antarctica to migrate to the South Pole. Since warm ocean water could not flow over the poles, heat was distributed less evenly over the globe. As a result, the Arctic Ocean froze permanently and at the same time a thick ice sheet grew over Antarctica. (See pages 514–517.)

Glaciers, like this one in Patagonia, covered much of Earth's land during the Pleistocene ice ages.

4,500   4,000   3,500   3,000   2,500

Millions of years ago

DEMISE OF THE LARGE MAMMALS

The extinction of large mammals, such as the mastodons and wooly mammoths, is still a mystery. Many of these extinct mammals had survived the other three glacial and interglacial periods that took place during the Pleistocene epoch. One possible explanation is that human hunters had become so efficient that they had exterminated all of the large plant-eating mammals. As a result, such predators as the saber-toothed cats and the prehistoric wolves became extinct because their food supply had been exhausted.

The giant ground sloth was a plant-eating mammal that was nearly as tall as a house, standing 4.4 meters (14.5 feet) tall on its hind legs.

Holocene Epoch. Based on the size of the ice caps at the North and South poles, as well as the ice sheet that covers most of Greenland, it is likely that Earth's Holocene epoch is an ice age. Geologists are not sure, however, whether Earth is now in an interglacial period or beginning to enter another glacial period. An interglacial period would mean that the ice caps would melt. Another glacial period would mean that continental glaciers would move over the continents.

NORTH AMERICAN MAMMOTH HUNTERS

The earliest known humans in the Americas lived from about 13,500 years ago to 8,000 years ago, from the end of the Pleistocene epoch into the Holocene epoch. During the Pleistocene epoch, they hunted giant animals such as mammoths, mastodons, ground sloths, and giant bison. Hunters launched stone-tipped spears using a shaft with a spur at one end to hold the butt of the spear. This device increased the range and force of their spears.

Earth's Future

- seafloor spreading and the subduction of crustal plates will cause some ocean basins to grow and others to shrink
- in 30 million years, the Atlantic Ocean will be much wider and the Pacific will be narrower
- as Africa moves north, Europe's Alps may grow taller as a result of the collision of these two crustal plates
- the Himalaya Mountains will continue to grow taller
- Australia will move northward and may override the island chain of Indonesia
- in 25 million years, a north-south sea may split Africa in two at the site of the present-day Great Rift Valley
- in 50 million years, Los Angeles may move north to unite with Alaska

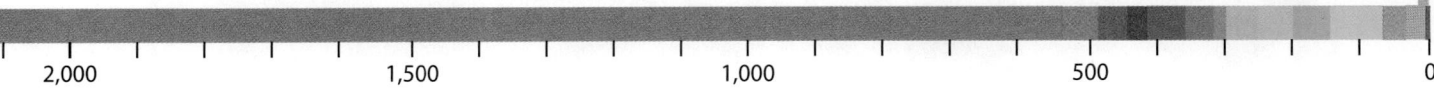

2,000	1,500	1,000	500	0

EARTH IN SPACE

Earth is a spinning, magnetized sphere of solid and molten rock. Although Earth is spherical, it is not a perfect sphere. Earth's spin causes it to bulge slightly at its middle, the equator. The difference is too tiny to be easily seen in pictures of Earth from space, so the planet appears round. Analyses of measurements taken from orbiting satellites show that the equatorial bulge is not exactly at the equator, but slightly to the south. For this reason, some earth scientists consider Earth to be slightly pear-shaped.

Earth's Magnetic Field

Earth is a huge natural magnet. Research has proven the existence of Earth's magnetic field, whose force extends far out into space, forming an invisible *magnetosphere*. (See pages 818–819.) The magnetosphere protects Earth from the *solar wind*, a flow of charged radioactive particles from the sun.

The Spinning Earth

Like all planets, Earth spins around a central axis with imaginary ends at the north and south poles. This spinning causes the sun to appear to rise and set each day, although the sun actually remains in the center of the solar system.

- Each complete rotation of Earth lasts about 24 hours, producing day and night.

- Earth rotates toward the east, so the sun seems to rise in the east and travel across the sky, setting in the west.

- During summer in the Northern Hemisphere, the North Pole is tilted toward the sun; sunlight falls on much more than half of the Northern Hemisphere.

- This causes the sun to appear to take longer to cross the sky, so the days are longer than the nights.

- During winter in the Northern Hemisphere, the South Pole is tilted toward the sun, so the nights are longer than the days in the Northern Hemisphere.

Earth on Its Axis. The diagram below shows how the tilt of Earth's axis affects where the sun's rays strike Earth at particular times of the year.

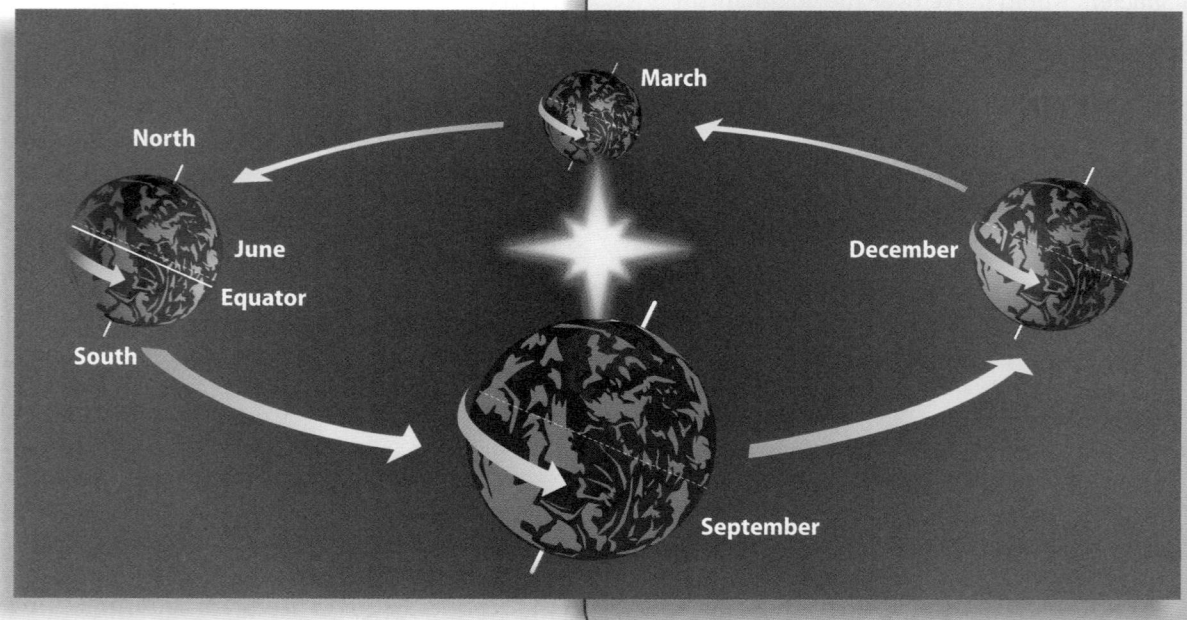

North
June
Equator
South
March
December
September

The magnetized needle of a compass aligns itself with Earth's magnetic field and points toward the magnetic north pole. ▶

Drifting Westward

Earth's magnetic field has *magnetic north* and *south poles*. It is the magnetic north pole that exerts a force on a compass needle, causing it to point north. Earth's magnetic north and south poles are not located at the same places as the geographic North and South poles. The north pole that attracts a magnetic compass is located near Prince of Wales Island in Canada—about 1,600 kilometers (1,000 miles) from the true North Pole. The magnetic south pole is about 2,500 kilometers (1,500 miles) from the true South Pole.

Earth's magnetic field appears to be drifting westward each year. It has been suggested that this westerly drift occurs because the core is rotating eastward a little slower than the outer, more solid parts of Earth.

Magnetic Field Reversal

The theory of plate tectonics has provided evidence that Earth's magnetic field has reversed its polarity many times in the past. The last reversal occurred about a million years ago.

During a time of normal polarity, magnetic lines of force leave Earth near the geographic South Pole and reenter near the geographic North Pole. When a magnetic reversal takes place, the magnetic lines of force move in the opposite direction, leaving Earth near the North Pole and entering near the South Pole. In effect, the north magnetic pole and south magnetic pole exchange positions.

Many rocks contain an internal record showing the direction of Earth's magnetic field at the time that the rocks were formed. For example, when the mineral magnetite forms from molten rock, atoms within its crystals respond to Earth's magnetic field by pointing toward the north magnetic pole. As magnetite cools and hardens into rock, this magnetic record then becomes a permanent feature.

HOW DOES THAT WORK

EARTH'S MAGNETIC FIELD

1. Inside Earth the heat generated by the decay of radioactive elements keeps streams of molten iron flowing through the outer core.

2. The flow of molten iron generates electric currents that result in the formation of a magnetic field—similar to the way that electricity flowing through a coil of copper wire creates a magnetic field around the wire.

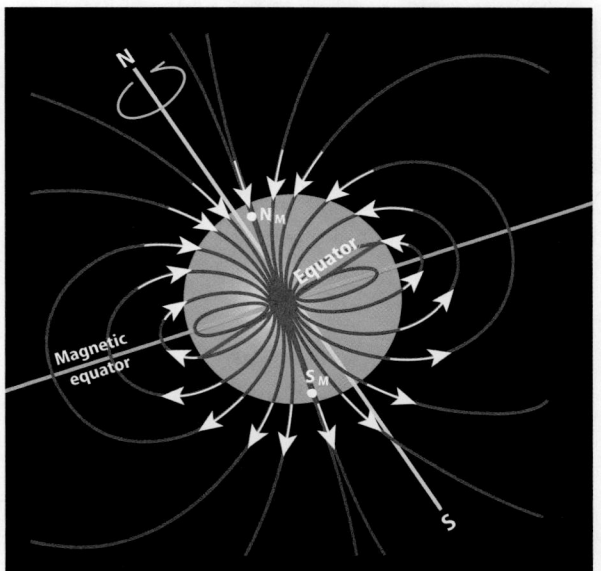

Earth, the Magnet. The magnetic lines of force are vertical at Earth's magnetic poles. Near the equator, the magnetic lines of force are nearly horizontal.

Mapping Earth

An important task of geographers is to identify and record the location of places, of Earth features, and of human populations and activities. To do this, geographers have marked off Earth's surface with *parallels* and *meridians*. Parallels are imaginary lines that run east and west. They measure *latitude* (position north or south of the equator). Meridians are imaginary lines that run north and south. They measure *longitude* (position east or west of the prime meridian).

GPS

The *Global Positioning System,* or GPS, is a worldwide navigation system that uses radio signals broadcast by satellites. The GPS has at least 24 satellites, and often more than 30. Computerized GPS receivers use signals from four or more satellites to calculate their latitude and longitude. They can provide directions for people in airplanes, ships, cars, or on foot. The United States Air Force operates the satellites, but the system has both military and civilian users.

GPS users can normally determine their location within 10 meters (33 feet). A technique called *carrier phase GPS* can be accurate to within 1 centimeter (0.4 inch).

LATITUDE

Changes in location in a north-south direction are described by a system of imaginary lines that are parallel with the equator. These lines are called *parallels of latitude*. The north-south location of any place on Earth is referred to as the latitude of that place.

- The equator is located at 0° latitude; the location of any parallel of latitude can be described as a particular number of degrees from the equator.
- The distance from the equator to either the North or the South Pole is one-quarter (90°) of the full circle (360°) around Earth.
- A point midway between the equator and one of the poles has a latitude of 45°.
- Parallels of latitude are described as either north latitude—north of the equator—or south latitude—south of the equator.
- To be more precise, each degree of latitude is divided into 60 equal parts called minutes.
- Even greater exactness is obtained by dividing minutes into 60 equal parts, called seconds.
- In actual distance over Earth's surface, a degree of latitude is equal to about 117 kilometers (70 miles); a minute of latitude is almost 2 kilometers (1.1 miles); a second of latitude is about 30 meters (100 feet).

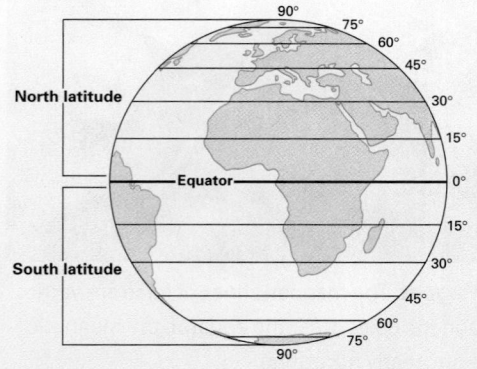

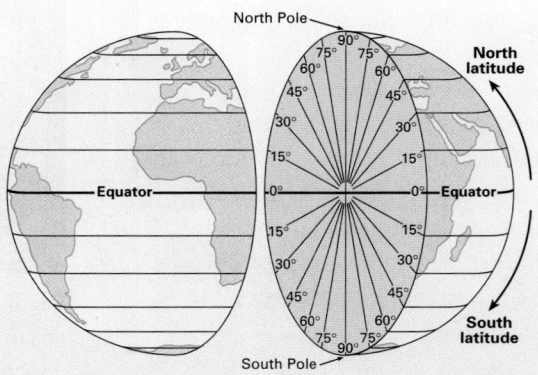

Parallels of latitude are imaginary lines running parallel to the equator that are used to measure north-south location.

The time zone of Chicago, Illinois, is 6 hours behind Greenwich, England. At 15° per hour, you can estimate that Chicago's longitude is about 90° west. The exact calculation is 87° 68'W (87 degrees, 68 minutes west).

LONGITUDE

To find the east-west position of a particular place, its longitude—another set of imaginary lines—is drawn from the North Pole to the South Pole. These *meridians of longitude* form imaginary half circles around Earth.

- Longitude for a given place is established by determining where it lies in relation to the meridians, which are divided into degrees, minutes, and seconds.
- Places that lie to the east of the prime meridian are referred to as having east longitude, and places to the west have west longitude.
- East and west longitude can extend only halfway around Earth; the 180° meridian, directly opposite Earth from the prime meridian, separates east longitude and west longitude.
- Longitude can be determined by sightings made on celestial bodies such as the sun and stars.
- However, longitude is frequently found by measuring the passage of time.

DETERMINING LONGITUDE WITH A CLOCK

In 24 hours, Earth rotates through 360° of a full circle, or 15° each hour. Since Earth rotates to the east, each hour changes the longitude of a particular location by 15° to the west. Local time for that location can be used to determine longitude. Each hour's difference between the local time and the time at the prime meridian (Greenwich time) is equal to 15° of longitude. Local time later than Greenwich time is east longitude. Earlier local time is west longitude.

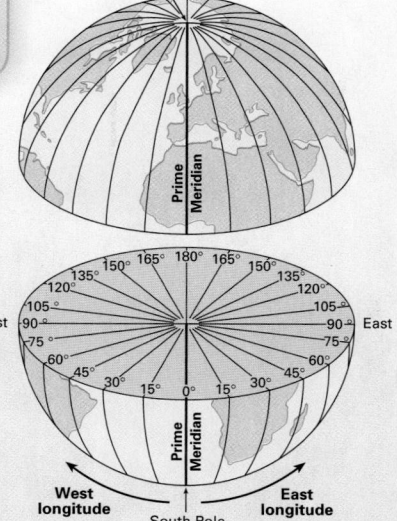

Meridians of longitude measure east-west location. For longitude, there was no natural starting point like the equator for latitude, so the meridian that passes through Greenwich, England—called the prime meridian—was chosen as the 0° line of longitude.

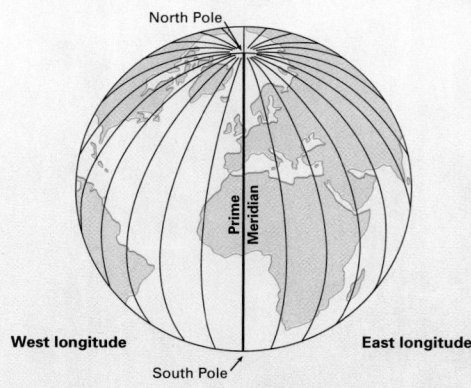

LITHOSPHERE

The *lithosphere* is made up of Earth's crust and upper mantle. It is subjected to mechanical, chemical, and biological changes. For example, the lithosphere is characterized by mountain ranges and ocean basins, which are continually being created by the movement of tectonic plates. The lithosphere is subjected to constant attack by water, ice, wind, and organisms.

Weathering and Erosion

Rocks found in the top 2 meters (6 feet) of Earth's crust usually are subjected to physical, biological, and chemical processes. Because of the interaction of these processes over long periods of time, rocks change and are eroded, or carried away, from their source areas. Erosion is the physical removal of rock by agents such as running water, ice, or wind. (See pages 510–511.)

The slow change that rocks undergo in the upper part of Earth's crust is known as *weathering*. Weathering is the disintegration of rocks and minerals exposed at Earth's surface. The two main types of weathering are *mechanical weathering* and *chemical weathering*. In most areas, both types are taking place at the same time.

- **mechanical weathering:** rocks break up into fragments of different sizes
- **chemical weathering:** rocks decay and decompose, and are eventually changed into substances with different chemical compositions and physical properties

Block fields are usually found on gently rolling landscapes in high latitudes or high altitudes. Block fields found in temperate or tropical climates are proof that the region was subjected to the effects of a polar climate some time in the past. ▶

Weathering and erosion break down and redistribute rock and soil, both forming and wearing away the features of Earth's landscape. ▼

Mechanical Weathering

Most rocks have small or large *joints,* or *cracks,* that allow water and the roots of different kinds of plants to penetrate the rocks. These joints leave the rocks vulnerable to the forces of mechanical weathering.

Frost Wedging

- the volume of water increases by about 9 percent when it freezes
- when water freezes in a confined space, it exerts tremendous pressure against the containing walls
- water freezing in the joint of a rock acts like a wedge prying the rock apart; this rock-splitting process is called *frost wedging*
- frost wedging is a major factor in the breakup of rock material in temperate and cold climates
- over time, frost wedging creates large fields of broken rock (block fields)

Plants and Animals

- as the roots of large trees mature and grow, they enlarge cracks and joints in rocks; eventually the rocks split apart
- burrowing animals, such as moles and earthworms, break up rock material into small fragments

Salt Crystals

- after a rainfall, water in soil and in rock joints often contains dissolved salts
- as the water evaporates, the concentration of salts increases
- eventually the concentration reaches the point at which salt crystals form
- the pressure accompanying formation of salt crystals can dislodge rock fragments
- when rain falls on salt crystals, *hydration* occurs— the process by which mineral salts expand when water is added
- hydration can break up rocks
- mechanical weathering from salt crystals occurs predominantly in areas of hot, dry climates

Rock Expansion

- most rocks are formed deep in the crust
- at great depths, rocks are under high pressure that is equal to the weight of the overlying mass
- when overlying rocks are removed by weathering and erosion, the underlying rocks expand
- the expansion produces *rock exfoliation,* which is when rock joints parallel the surface of Earth, giving the rocks an onionskin appearance

Rock exfoliation involves separation of successive layers of rock.

Weathering and Erosion

Chemical Weathering

Chemical weathering occurs in all environments, but it is most active in regions where temperatures are high, large amounts of water are available, and vegetation is abundant.

Chemical weathering is speeded up by the presence of acids like carbonic acid. This relatively weak acid is produced when water and carbon dioxide molecules unite. The water comes from the air and soil. Carbon dioxide is partly obtained from the air, but a great deal comes from the decay of organic material and the respiration of plant roots.

Three main processes occur during chemical weathering of rocks. These processes—*solution, hydrolysis,* and *oxidation*—involve the influence of chemical and biological agents.

Solution is responsible for the formation of many caverns, underground streams, and disappearing rivers in regions underlain by limestone. ▼

Solution

- during solution, a rock dissolves like a sugar cube in a cup of coffee, but at a much slower rate
- for example, when carbonic acid reacts with calcite, which is found in limestone, the acid frees the calcium atoms from the calcite
- the calcium is then washed away by water or blown away by wind

Hydrolysis

- the common rock-forming minerals are weathered mostly by hydrolysis (See pages 464–465.)
- a mineral reacts with water and is changed into one or more other substances
- for example, exposure to rainwater causes feldspar, an aluminum-silicate mineral, to break down, freeing potassium and some silica while leaving a clay mineral as the end product

Oxidation

- *oxidation* is the term for the process of rusting
- occurs when oxygen combines chemically with objects made of iron
- in most climates, all unprotected objects made of iron will eventually oxidize, or rust away
- in rainy tropical climates near the equator, rust quickly attacks objects made of iron and steel
- most rocks start out gray and contain some iron-bearing minerals
- when exposed to warm, humid air, the rocks oxidize and change color from gray to red, yellow, orange, or reddish brown

AT THE BEACH

Most beach sand is made up mainly of grains of quartz. This is because quartz is resistant to weathering by air and water. As a rock is continually weathered and transported, only the resistant quartz grains remain unchanged. The other grains often form clay minerals.

Rate of Weathering. Minerals and rocks weather at different rates. Rocks weather more rapidly after erosion removes them from their source area. Low areas and slopes occur where the underlying rock types are less resistant to weathering. Prominent ledges and cliffs occur where the rocks are more resistant to weathering.

When a mineral is broken into small particles, weathering occurs more rapidly than when a mineral appears in a large chunk. This is because the large chunk of mineral has less surface area exposed to the air or the dissolving acids in rainwater than the small particles.

GOT TO KNOW

EARTH'S SPHERES

- **lithosphere:** the crust and upper mantle of Earth from the surface to about 100 kilometers (60 miles)

- **atmosphere:** the envelope of gases that surrounds Earth; three gases—oxygen, nitrogen, and carbon dioxide—make up 99 percent of the atmosphere and are essential for the survival of all life forms on Earth

- **hydrosphere:** the water of Earth, made up mainly of the oceans and seas, but also consisting of the lakes, streams, and water that flows beneath Earth's surface

Running Water

The most important geologic agent in eroding and depositing sediment is running water. It breaks weathered rock fragments into smaller and smaller pieces. As particles of gravel, sand, and other sediments are carried by water, they continually bump into each other, resulting in rock disintegration. The disintegration of rock by running water and other kinds of sediment is called stream erosion. Most landscapes display the results of stream erosion.

Streams cut deeper channels in mountain areas where water moves swiftly. Where the land levels off, streams move slower and deposit more sediment, cutting shallower, wider channels.

Stream Erosion

Over long periods of time, streams carry away weathered sediment and cut valleys into the landscape. The rock particles and sediments that a mountain stream picks up are carried along and eventually deposited at lower elevations. Streams erode rock and sediment through *hydraulic action, solution,* and *abrasion*.

Hydraulic Action

- the ability of running water to lift and move rock and sediment
- the force of swirling water in a rock crevice may eventually crack the rock and break rock fragments loose
- the fragments are carried downstream
- a swirling eddy of water often exerts enough force to lift a rock fragment above the streambed into the main body of flowing water
- loose sediment on a streambed may tumble along the stream bottom, pushed by the pressure of flowing water

Solution

- normally considered a process of chemical weathering
- however, a stream flowing over limestone is an agent of both chemical weathering and erosion; as the carbonic acid in the stream dissolves the calcite in limestone, the stream channel deepens and widens

Abrasion

- a stream's channel is deepened and widened by the friction and impact of sediment
- it is the most effective form of erosion on streambeds
- sand and gravel tumbling along near the bottom of a stream erode the streambed like sandpaper on wood
- the more sediment in a stream, the faster it will erode its bed
- coarse sediments like gravel and sand cause rapid erosion

◀ **The Colorado River** eroded layers of rock over a period of about 6 million years to form the Grand Canyon.

Stream Transport

The sediments in a stream are transported by either suspension or solution. (See page 468.) The load, or mass of sediments, of a stream is divided into three types: the *bed load, suspended load,* and *dissolved load.*

Bed Load

- the heavy sediment that travels on or near the bottom of a stream
- sediments move by either *traction* or *saltation*

Suspended Load

- the sediments that are light enough to remain indefinitely above the streambed because of water turbulence
- causes the muddy appearance of a stream during a flood or after a heavy rain
- achieves less erosion than the bed load, but an enormous amount of sediment is transported by suspension

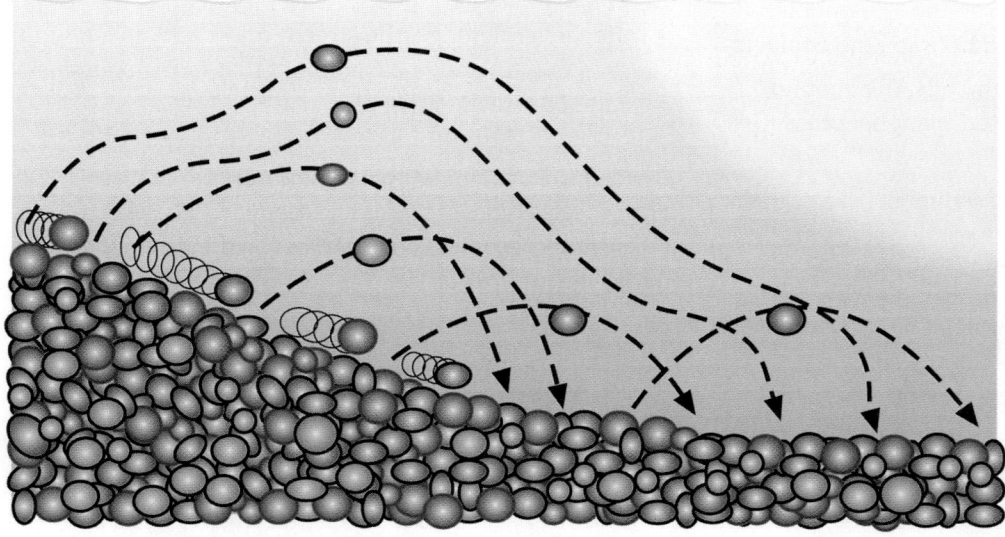

Traction and Saltation. Running water can drag the sediments in a bed load across the streambed (traction), or send the sediments bouncing over the streambed (saltation).

- *traction:* boulders, pebbles, and other large rock particles move along the streambed by rolling, sliding, or dragging; moving rock fragments erode the streambed by abrasion
- *saltation:* sand grains are lifted off the streambed by eddies, or turbulent water flow, and carried downstream in a series of short leaps or bounces

Dissolved Load

- mineral particles that dissolve within the water of a stream
- most streams contain dissolved sodium, calcium, and potassium, as well as ions of bicarbonate, chloride, and sulfate
- much of the dissolved load of a stream empties into the ocean
- if a stream dries up, the ions may become visible as they unite to form *evaporates,* minerals or salt deposits formed by evaporation

Running Water

Stream Deposition

Along the course of a stream, sediments are temporarily deposited either as *bars* or *floodplains*. Through repeated cycles of erosion and deposition, the sediments move downstream. At or near the mouth (end) of a stream, more permanent deposits like *deltas* and *alluvial fans* are formed.

Bars

- a visible ridge of sand or gravel deposited in the middle or along the banks of a stream

- after a flood, a decrease in stream velocity causes large boulders to drop down on the streambed; gravel and sand are deposited between the boulders

- if the water level in the stream falls, this mound of coarse- and fine-grained sediment becomes exposed as a bar

- a stream with a heavy load of sediment may deposit numerous bars in its channel; as more bars are deposited, the stream widens

Floodplains

- broad strips of land built up by sediment deposited on both sides of a stream channel

- most form when *meanders,* snakelike curves in a stream, shift laterally back and forth over a valley floor, leaving a series of ridges on the insides of their curves

- others form when streams overflow their banks; fine-grained sediment is deposited in horizontal layers, left by successive floods

- during a flood, a stream slows down suddenly as it moves over a floodplain, causing most of the sediment to be deposited near the main channel

- after several floods, the stream may build up a natural *levee,* or a low ridge of sediment that forms on either side of a stream channel

Braided streams form when a stream loses its main channel after repeated cycles of erosion and deposition. Masses of sediment are deposited, forming bars of sand and gravel and forcing the stream to divide. ▼

Deltas

- bodies of accumulating sediment that form at the mouth of a stream or river, where it flows into a lake or ocean
- caused by a decrease in the stream's velocity
- many deltas, such as the Nile River delta, are triangular (named for the triangular Greek letter *delta*)
- other deltas resemble long toes extending out into the ocean or sea; these form when large quantities of sediment are deposited in quiet waters

Alluvial Fans

- fan-shaped accumulations of sediment that form where a stream emerges from a narrow mountain canyon onto a flat plain
- occur in dry climate, do not reach the ocean or any other body of water
- fan shape built up gradually as the result of infrequent rainstorms
- when the rain comes, fast-flowing streams emerge from mountain canyons loaded with sediment
- when the rain ends, the stream dries up, leaving muddy sediment over the alluvial fan

MIGHTY MISSISSIPPI'S ALLUVIAL PLAIN

Covering parts of Missouri, Tennessee, Arkansas, Louisiana, and Mississippi, the Alluvial Plain of the Mississippi River is a region of fertile land covering 90,600 square kilometers (35,000 square miles). Floodwaters from the Mississippi and other rivers have enriched the soil of the alluvial plain with deposits of silt. A wide variety of crops are grown in the plain's fertile soil. *Alluvial plain* is another term for *floodplain*.

FALLING WATER

In wearing down its channel, a river uncovers certain layers of rock that are softer than others. If the hard rock is farther upstream than the soft, the channel below is worn more rapidly, and a waterfall results. Sometimes the hard ledge forms the edge of a vertical cliff, over which the water plunges.

Glaciers

Glaciers are huge masses of ice that flow due to gravity. They cover about 10 percent of Earth's total land area—15 million square kilometers (5.8 million square miles). Most of the ice is found in two *continental glaciers*, or ice sheets: Antarctica, which accounts for about 79 percent of Earth's ice, and Greenland, which accounts for about 12 percent. The rest of the ice is scattered around the world as *alpine glaciers* in mountainous areas.

Glacier Formation. Glaciers develop in parts of the world where snow remains on the ground throughout the year. Year by year, the snow builds up. It is eventually converted to ice and begins to move.

Glaciers form in high mountains as well as in polar regions of the Northern and Southern hemispheres. In polar regions, glaciers can occur at sea level, but near the equator, mountains must be at least 5,000 meters (16,400 feet) to have glaciers form at cold temperatures.

FROM SNOW TO ICE

Snow changes to ice to form glaciers in much the same way that metamorphic rocks form. (See pages 470–471.) As snow falls on the ground, it builds up sedimentary layers. With increased temperature and pressure, the bottom layers of snow crystals *metamorphose,* or change, into ice. When the bottom layers of ice reach a depth of 40 to 50 meters (about 120 to 150 feet), the entire frozen mass begins to move downslope. Because of this movement, many glaciers exhibit folding—a characteristic of deformed sedimentary rock layers as well as some metamorphic rocks.

TYPES OF GLACIERS

Alpine glaciers form on mountain slopes and summits that rise above the snow line. Gravity moves them downslope; they often follow an existing stream valley. Erosion by alpine glaciers causes mountain peaks to become more jagged and canyons to become steeper.

Continental glaciers cover a large land area. They usually do not follow the underlying landscape features, such as river valleys or steep canyons. Continental glaciers are called *ice sheets* if they cover more than 50,000 square kilometers (19,300 square miles) and ice caps if they cover less than that. Ice sheets cover most of Antarctica and Greenland.

The Great Lakes are an excellent example of erosion by a continental ice sheet. They were gouged out of the landscape by a continental ice sheet. ▶

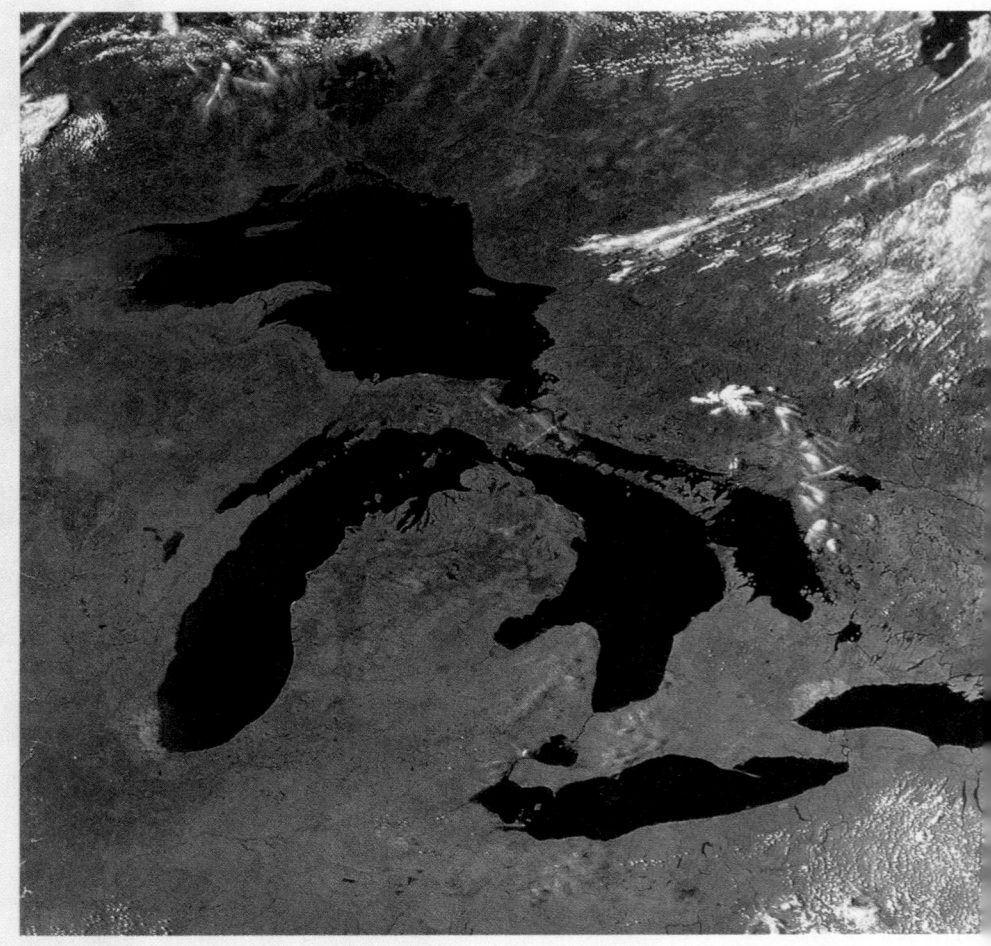

Fjords, narrow, steep-walled valleys, like this one in Norway, are the result of glacial erosion.

Svalvard, Norway, a group of islands in the North Atlantic Ocean, has glaciers that surge regularly, at least 86 times since the end of the 19th century.

GLACIAL SURGES

Sometimes a glacier moves at speeds approaching 6,000 meters (19,680 feet) a year. These rapid movements of glaciers are known as *glacial surges*. Some geologists think that earthquakes trigger glacial surges. Others believe that an increase in the amount of water dripping down through a glacier speeds its movement. More recently, geologists have theorized that a huge block of stagnant ice at the lower end of a glacier can act as a dam until the pressure of the flowing ice above forces it to give way suddenly, causing the surge.

Glaciers

Movement of Glaciers. The speed of ice movement in glaciers is similar to that of water in a stream. The ice moves fastest in the center, slowest on the sides and bottom. The slower velocity along the sides and bottom of a glacier is due to friction between the ice and the bedrock. The average speed of glaciers varies from place to place. However, most glaciers move at a speed of between 3 and 300 meters (10 and 984 feet) a year.

How Glaciers Shape the Land. The impact of prehistoric glaciers can be seen in many modern landscapes. Advancing glaciers create a variety of landforms by eroding, transporting, and depositing rock debris.

For instance, glacial erosion deepens valley floors and results in steep valley walls. The part of an alpine valley occupied by a glacier resembles a river channel but is much wider.

A glacier that fills a mountain valley shoves loose material ahead and plucks rocks from the valley sides. The loosened rocks embedded in the glacier rasp more rock material from the sides of the valley than does the water in a stream. Thus, glaciers in mountainous areas produce U-shaped valleys in cross section while rivers produce V-shaped valleys.

Glacier National Park in northwestern Montana was named for the large number of glaciers found there. ▼

GLACIAL EROSION

There are two main ways that glaciers erode rocks:

- **Quarrying** involves the prying out of boulders from underlying bedrock. *Crevasses,* or large cracks in glaciers, provide a route for melting snow and ice to stream down into a glacier. If this meltwater reaches the bottom, it invades joints in the bedrock. As the meltwater freezes, it expands and applies tremendous pressure on the enclosing rock, which may then be pried loose from the bedrock. These rock fragments—ranging in size from huge boulders to grains of sand—then become embedded in the ice of the glacier.

- **Abrasion** occurs when glaciers scour bedrock containing rock fragments. The rocky debris is carried along with the glacier and acts as an abrasive as it moves downslope. Large rock fragments embedded in a glacier may gouge out *glacial striations,* long grooves and scratches in the underlying bedrock. Where the embedded rock fragments are small, abrasion may polish the surface of bedrock like sandpaper on a wooden surface.

FEATURES CARVED BY GLACIERS

- **drumlins:** low, rounded hills formed by glacial deposits; always aligned parallel to the direction of the glacier's movement

- **eskers:** long, snakelike ridges with rounded crests and steep lateral slopes, deposited by streams flowing through ice tunnels in a glacier

- **kettles:** rounded depressions formed when blocks of ice become trapped in the till and then melt; many of the northern states, such as Minnesota, have many kettle lakes

- **outwash plains:** wide floodplains of fine-grained sediment deposited by streams that emerge from the front of a glacier

- **tarns:** mountain lakes that form when rocks are pried out of the bedrock by glacial scouring

- **cirques:** horseshoe-shaped basins enclosed by steep, high walls

- **horns:** saw-toothed peaks left behind after an alpine glacier continues to erode the ends of a cirque

- **arete:** thin razor-sharp ridge formed when two alpine glaciers erode the divide between the valleys they occupy

Glacial Deposition. A moving glacier transports and deposits *till,* rock fragments that range in size from gravel to boulders. As the glacier melts or retreats, the till is heaped into ridges called *moraines.* Ridges of rock debris that accumulate along the sides of a glacier form *lateral moraines.* If two alpine glaciers join, the lateral moraines that meet at the intersection unite to form a band of rocky debris called a *medial moraine.* The moraines that loop around the lower limit of a glacier are called *terminal,* or end, *moraines.*

The Matterhorn, in Switzerland, is the most famous example of a horn.

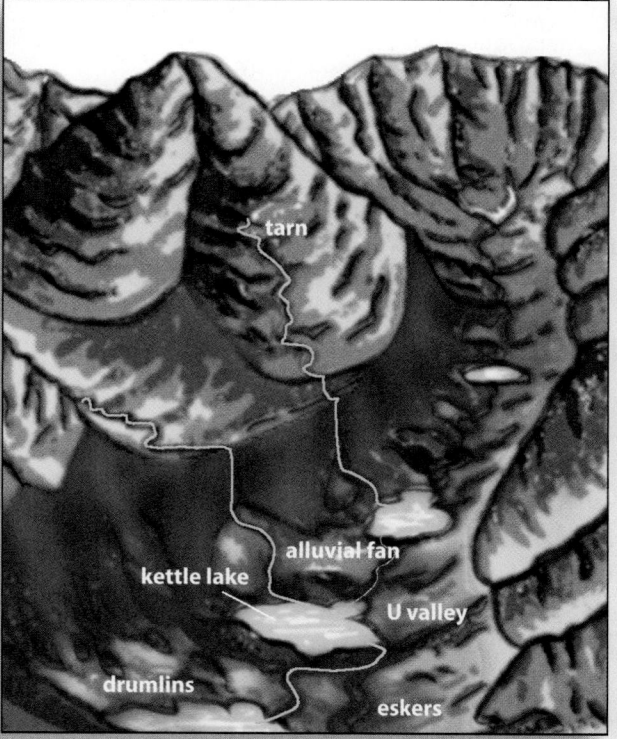

Wind

Wind causes erosion in any climate where particles of sediment are loose and dry, especially in desert regions. Wind erosion differs in two main ways from erosion by running water:

- air is less dense than water, so wind can only erode fine-grained sediment like silt and clay
- wind is not confined to channels, so it can cause widespread erosion over large areas

Strong winds cause the most intense erosion. Because winds are caused mainly by extremes in air temperature, deserts have stronger winds than humid, temperate climates. In fact, desert winds often exceed 100 kilometers (60 miles) an hour.

Wind erosion helped create the unique features of Bryce Canyon in Utah. ▶

Types of Particles

Dust Storms

- loose silt and clay is picked up by the wind from cultivated fields, and these fine-grained sediments can remain suspended in turbulent air for a long time
- a strong wind may carry a cloud of dust hundreds of meters upward, as well as hundreds of kilometers horizontally

Sediment at Sea

- strong winds can carry sediment eroded from land areas far out to sea on strong wind currents
- much of the fine-grained sediment covering the seafloor has been eroded and transported from land areas by the wind
- sometimes very fine-grained sediments cross entire oceans

Volcanic Ash

- strong winds also blow the ash from erupting volcanoes for great distances
- when a volcano erupts, ash may be sent more than 15 kilometers (9 miles) upward into the air
- volcanic ash may then be carried for hundreds or even thousands of kilometers by high-altitude jet streams (See page 537.)

Sand

- windblown sand travels close to the ground
- like some of the sediment in streams, windblown sand grains travel by saltation, that is, in a leaping pattern
- sandstorms occur when strong winds cause clouds of sand to move rapidly near the surface
- sandstorms can sandblast smooth surfaces on rock outcrops

Types of Dunes

Barchan dunes

wind

Transverse dunes

wind

Parabolic dunes

wind

Seif dunes

wind

Sand dunes develop characteristic shapes based on three main factors: wind velocity and direction; supply of sand; and vegetation cover.

Wind Deposition. The most familiar windblown deposits are *sand dunes*. These mounds of sand grains usually develop in regions characterized by strong winds that blow in the same direction. Most of the world's major deserts contain sand dunes.

Sand dunes also form just landward of lake and ocean beaches. Here, sand is continually blown inland. Consequently, sand dunes are common along the shores of the Great Lakes as well as along beaches that fringe the Atlantic and Pacific oceans.

The gentle slope of a sand dune faces the wind and its steep slope is on the downwind side. The downwind slope of a sand dune is known as the *slip face*. The steep slip face forms from loose, flowing sand and generally maintains an angle of about 34°. Sand grains blow up the gentle slope and over the top of the dune, tumbling down the slip face.

Sand dunes are characterized by rounded grains of sand that are uniform in size. This is because the fine-grained sediments (silt and clay) are carried much farther by the wind than sand is carried. In contrast, coarse-grained sediments (gravel and pebbles) are pulled to Earth by the force of gravity as the sand moves. The result is sand dunes made up entirely of nearly identical sand grains.

THE DUST BOWL

During the Great Depression, the Great Plains of the United States were hit hard by extreme drought and soil erosion. For several years, dust storms called "black blizzards" covered towns, filled rivers, and damaged people's lungs. The area was called the "Dust Bowl" because of the frequency and severity of the dust storms.

Mass Movement

Mass movement, also known as mass wasting, is the process by which large masses of weathered rock material and soil move downhill due to the pull of gravity.

Rapid Mass Movement

Rapid mass movement usually results from earthquakes, heavy rains, or mining operations characterized by frequent explosions.

- *Rock falls* and *rock slides:* large slabs or masses of bedrock suddenly fall or slide downslope
- *Earth flow* and *mudflow:* heavy rains carry *regolith*—weathered rock fragments mixed with soil—down a slope

Powerful mudflows can be triggered by volcanoes. This abandoned house was swept away by a mudflow triggered by the 1980 eruption of Mount St. Helens. ▶

Rock fall is when a mass of rock falls freely or bounces down the side of a cliff. Large fissures are cut into cliffs by frost wedging, a type of mechanical weathering. *Slabs*—large blocks of rock—tend to break off cliffs at these fissures. Because of periodic rock falls, most cliffs have a mound of fallen rocks, called *talus,* at their base.

Rock slide is a rapid sliding of a large slab of bedrock down a fractured slope. As with rock falls, frost wedging is responsible for causing fractures in the bedrock. As a slab of rock dislodges and slides downhill during a rock slide, it breaks apart into several smaller rock masses.

Earth flow is the downhill movement of a large mass of regolith. Earth flow can be either a rapid or a slow type of mass movement—lasting several hours, days, or even months. Saturated hillsides exposed to several days of steady rain often are the sites of earth flows. Large chunks of a hillside may slump downward at various rates of speed. Earth flows can also be caused by erosion of ocean waves along a shoreline or by a stream eroding and steepening its banks. In fact, along coastlines, mass movement by earth flows frequently destroys beachfront homes.

Mudflow is a mixture of flowing water and regolith—usually moving within a channel. A mudflow may begin after a heavy rainfall if regolith and water start to flow downhill. A mudflow frequently resembles a stream of melted chocolate ice cream. Because of its heavy load of soil and rock fragments, a mudflow moves more slowly than a stream. Because of its high viscosity, or thick texture, a mudflow has enormous power, being capable of carrying huge boulders, cars, houses, and even railroad trains.

◄ **Avalanche.** A powerful, rapid rock slide is called a rock avalanche. Large, angular boulders slide down a mountainside at great speed.

Slow Mass Movement

Slow mass movement occurs over many years as soil or regolith moves downslope by slow movements.

- *Soil creep:* slow, continuous movement of soil or regolith down the side of a mountain or hill
- *Solifluction:* flow of water-saturated regolith over impermeable material

Soil creep is a very slow, continuous movement of soil or regolith down the side of a mountain or hill. Because soil and rock particles move downhill only about a centimeter a year, creep cannot be noticed by the casual observer. The occurrence of creep in an area can be detected only by careful long-term observations made over several months or years. Creep occurs when the soil experiences daily cycles of thawing and freezing or when the soil is alternately soaked by rain and dried out. The presence of water in the ground is necessary for the particles of soil to move downward.

Solifluction is the flow of water-saturated regolith over impermeable material (material that does not allow water to enter). Solifluction is a variety of earth flow that occurs mostly in cold climates, where deep layers of soil remain frozen throughout the year. This permanently frozen impermeable soil is aptly called permafrost and is commonly found in northern Canada and Alaska.

On May 31, 1970, an earthquake struck Peru, triggering an avalanche that crashed down from the north peak of Huascaran, Peru's highest mountain. About 80 million cubic feet of rocks and debris roared down the steep mountainside, reaching speeds of about 400 kilometers per hour (250 miles per hour). The city of Yungay was almost completely obliterated, and 20,000 people were killed.

EARTH'S SHIFTING CRUST

The movement of the lithosphere affects large bodies of rock. When tectonic plates are subjected to stress, they eventually buckle and break. Plate movements often cause horizontal layers of sedimentary rock to undergo *deformation*—the rocks become tilted, folded, or cracked.

The Broken Crust

Folds

Folds are wavelike features in rock layers that may be compared to waves on the ocean. Each fold has a *crest*, or upfold, and a *trough*, or downfold. The two main kinds of folds are *anticlines* (upfolds) and *synclines* (downfolds).

- anticlines: folds that resemble wave crests
- synclines: folds that resemble wave troughs
- the sides of either anticlines or synclines are called *limbs* or *flanks*
- if it were possible to see an uneroded region that had recently been folded, the anticlines would be the ridges and the synclines would be the valleys

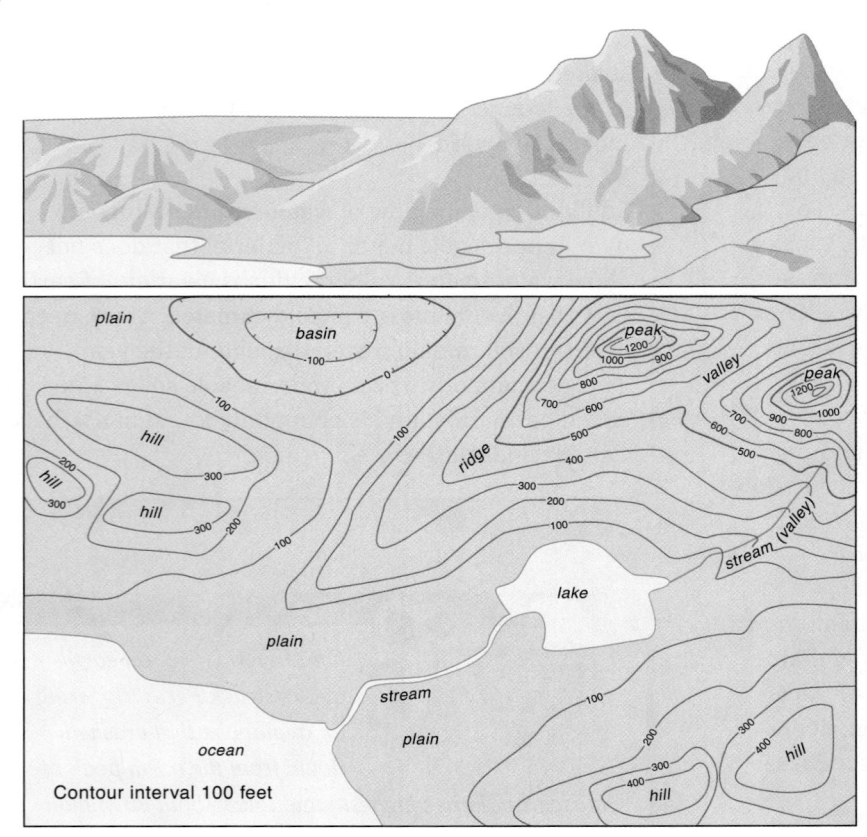

Contour interval 100 feet

TOPOGRAPHIC MAPS

Topographic maps are general reference maps that show the details and heights of land features in a small area. Basically, a topographic map is a two-dimensional representation of three-dimensional landscape features, such as mountains and valleys on Earth's surface. On topographic maps, *contour lines* show areas that are the same height—providing the third dimension otherwise missing on a map.

Topographic maps also indicate the *elevation* (altitude) of a particular place, as well as the *relief* of a given area. Elevation is the vertical distance between sea level and a particular place. Relief is the difference in elevation between the highest and lowest points of a particular region. An area of high relief would be mountainous, with considerable distances between valley floors and mountain peaks. An area of low relief would be much flatter, or would consist of low hills, with hilltops not far above valley floors.

Folds, Joints, and Faults. The movement of land on either side of a fault line can slip to cause vast damage or collide and fold to uplift land.

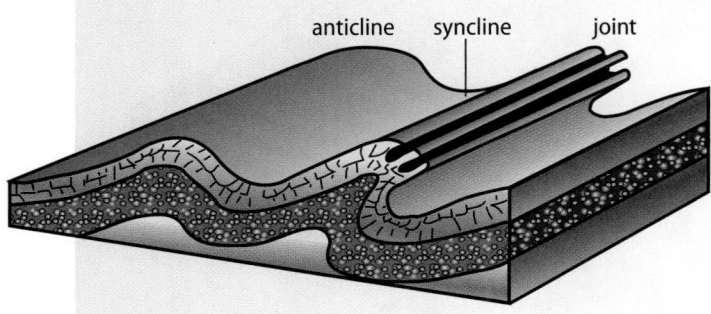

Folding results from the deformation of solid rock. Deep within the crust, great pressure caused by the weight of the overlying rock material compresses the lower layers. Thus, any crack or fissure that develops is quickly filled in with flowing rock material. Near the surface, however, the confining pressure is much lower. This causes the rocks to fracture instead of flow. As a result, cracks form at or near the surface.

Joints

As a result of lithospheric movement, most rocks at or close to Earth's surface have cracks or fractures in them, called *joints*.

- most result from the deformation of preexisting rocks
- some—called *columnar joints*—result from the cracking of thin sheets of igneous rock during cooling
- during tremors and earthquakes, joints widen and physical weathering of the rock occurs

Faults

Like joints, *faults* are fractures in the rock of Earth's crust. Faults, however, occur where plate movement has taken place, while joints result from fractures along which there has been little or no movement of the rock on either side. Faults are characterized by vertical or horizontal displacement of rock masses at a site called the *fault line*. There are two main kinds of faults:

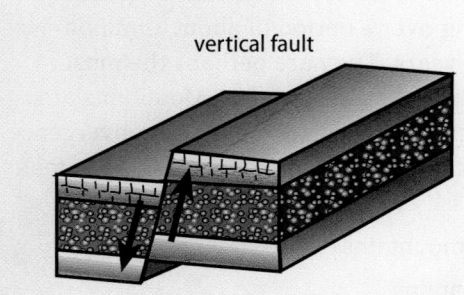

vertical fault

Vertical Faults

- occur when an entire block of rock material is raised evenly so that the rock layers remain in their original horizontal position
- the rock layers on one side of the fault are displaced, or offset, so that they are no longer continuous; when this happens, a cliff called a *fault scarp* will form at the surface
- may cause a displacement of 1,000 meters (3,000 feet) or more

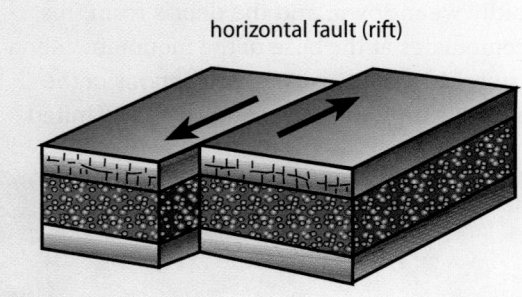

horizontal fault (rift)

Horizontal Faults

- can be observed at the surface, where streams and other landscape features are offset
- do not displace the rock layers vertically along the fault
- movement along a horizontal fault is usually not very great
- amount of offset at a horizontal fault line may be as small as several centimeters (about an inch); in time, however, the offset may amount to hundreds of kilometers (See pages 450–457.)

Mountain Building

Mountains are created by tremendous forces in Earth operating over a period of about 1 million to 100 million years. They are perhaps the most dramatic product of plate tectonics. Mountains are formed through volcanic activity, by the convergence of tectonic plates, and through movement along faults. Geologists classify mountains into distinct types.

- fault-block mountains
- folded mountains
- volcanic mountains

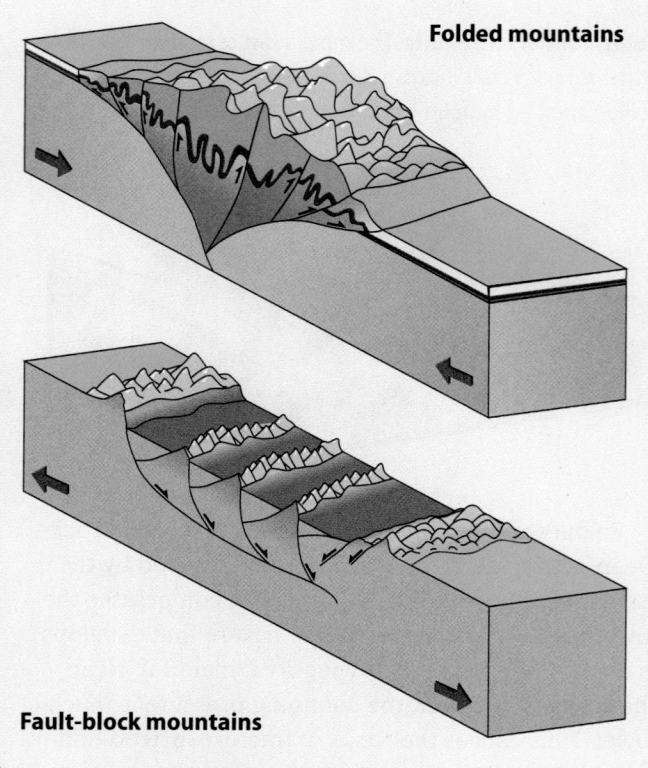

Folded mountains

Fault-block mountains

Fault-Block Mountains

Fault-block mountains form when huge blocks of crust become tilted or pushed up along faults. This type of mountain can form along *normal faults* or *strike-slip faults*. (See pages 458–459.)

Along normal faults, huge blocks of crust are pushed up while neighboring regions drop down to form basins. Most such mountains occur where a block is tilted up along one side of a single fault, but some blocks are pushed up between two separate faults. The uplifted blocks rapidly wear down, and the debris from this erosion accumulates at the base of the mountain, filling nearby basins. Most of the isolated mountains of the Basin and Range region, in the southwestern United States and northern Mexico, are fault-block mountains separated by broad plains filled with such debris.

Along strike-slip faults, blocks of rock slide past each other horizontally, often producing earthquakes. Fault-block mountains such as the Peninsular Ranges in southern California and Baja California developed along strike-slip faults.

◄ **The Basin and Range region** in the western United States provides a picturesque example of fault-block mountains. The region is covered with hundreds of elongated mountains alternating with broad basins covered with gravel.

▲ **The Alps** are the largest mountain range in Europe. They are so sharply folded that a person climbing them may cross the same layer of rock several times during a single ascent.

Folded Mountains

Folded mountains form when two plates collide head-on. During the collision, the plates' edges fold or crumple, and some layers of rock may be thrust over other layers.

- consist mainly of sedimentary rocks, such as limestone and shale (See pages 468–469.)
- thickest deposits of sedimentary rock generally accumulate along the edges of continents
- one plate subducts beneath another and any continents riding on the two plates collide
- accumulated layers of rock—and any previously formed volcanic mountains—crumple together
- rock layers wrinkle up like a tablecloth pushed across a table
- resulting folds range in character from gentle, wavelike patterns to sharp, complex folds
- compression may also produce extensive *thrust faults*, fractures in the rock layers in which one layer is pushed up and over another

THE WORLD'S LONGEST MOUNTAIN RANGE

There is a mountain range that stretches for somewhere between 50,000 and 80,000 kilometers (30,000 and 50,000 miles), and nearly all of it is invisible. That is because it lies almost completely hidden beneath the ocean's surface. *Oceanic ridges* and *rises* form a nearly continuous mountain system throughout the world's ocean basins.

The oceanic ridges and rises are located at the zone of the lithosphere where two plates are moving apart. Many volcanic eruptions occur directly beneath the ridges, emitting lava. Ridges develop from the upward flow of hot mantle material pushing the lithosphere up, as well as from accumulation and hardening of lava flows between the separating plates.

Most mountains of the mid-ocean ridges stand about 1,500 meters (5,000 feet) above the seafloor. Some peaks rise above the surface and form islands, such as the Azores and Iceland in the Atlantic Ocean.

Mountain Building

Volcanic Mountains

Volcanic mountains are built up from accumulations of igneous rock material. This material, such as ash and lava flow, originates deep within the crust and piles up on the surface. Consequently, volcanoes rise as cone-shaped or dome-shaped mountains. (See pages 452–453.)

Most of Earth's active or recently active volcanoes occur where tectonic plates converge. Here, blocks of rock material push and slide past one another. The frictional energy released during such movement melts rocks and produces hot magma, which rises to the surface. There are three main types of volcanoes: *cinder cone*, *shield*, and *composite*.

CINDER CONE VOLCANOES

- formed by explosive eruptions triggered by heavy concentrations of gas in magma
- constructed of loose rock fragments ejected from a central vent
- most of the rock lands near the vent during an eruption, builds the cone up to a peak
- have fairly narrow bases and steep, symmetrical slopes of interlocking cinders
- life span of an active cinder cone tends to be relatively short since the gas is exhausted quickly during periods of eruption
- erode away relatively quickly because they are composed of loose material

Cinder Cone Volcano

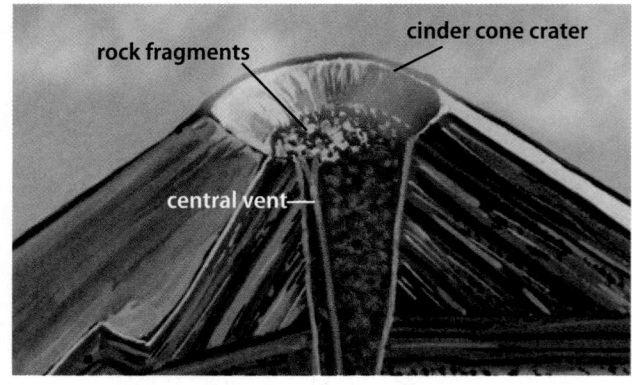

VOLCANIC CRATERS

A *volcanic crater* is the funnel-shaped pit at the top of a volcanic cone. By definition, a crater is less than 1 kilometer (0.6 mile) in diameter. A crater widens as periods of erupting magma gradually melt and break down its walls.

A *caldera,* or crater larger than 1 kilometer in diameter, is produced when a violent volcanic eruption completely destroys the upper part of a cone.

Mount St. Helens, in Washington state, erupted violently on May 18, 1980, blasting away more than 300 meters (1,000 feet) from the peak and creating a huge crater.

SHIELD VOLCANOES

- in the shape of a flattened dome, or shield
- broad at the base with gentle slopes made of solidified lava flow
- during eruptions the lava, which is watery in texture, spreads widely and thinly
- lava flows from a central vent, without much accumulation
- result from quiet volcanic eruptions
- two types of lava flow with Hawaiian names: *pahoehoe* and *aa*
- *pahoehoe*: fast-flowing lava with a ropy surface formed by the rapid cooling and hardening from the surface downward of a lava pool that was completely liquid
- *aa*: flowing lava that is cool enough to have partially solidified; moves as a slow, pasty mass

Shield Volcano

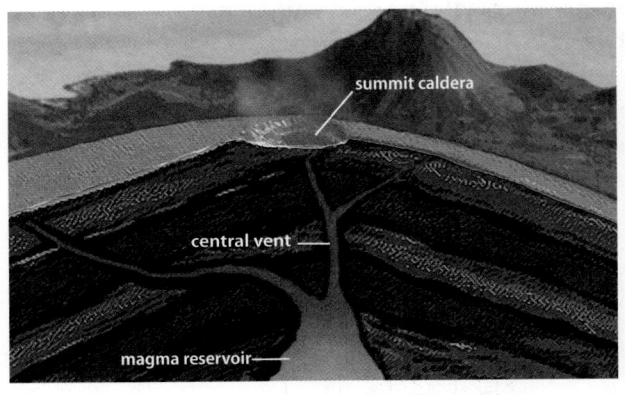

COMPOSITE VOLCANOES

- formed by a combination of alternating layers of rock fragments from explosive volcanic eruptions (cinder cones) and hardened lava from relatively quiet eruptions (shield volcanoes)
- intermediate in steepness between shield and cinder cone volcanoes
- steep slopes are built up as debris collects near the vent, just as in cinder cones
- subsequent lava flows partially flatten the profile of the cone
- hardened lava covers the loose rock fragments, making composite volcanoes much less vulnerable to erosion than cinder cones
- built up over long spans of time; can reach great heights

Composite Volcano

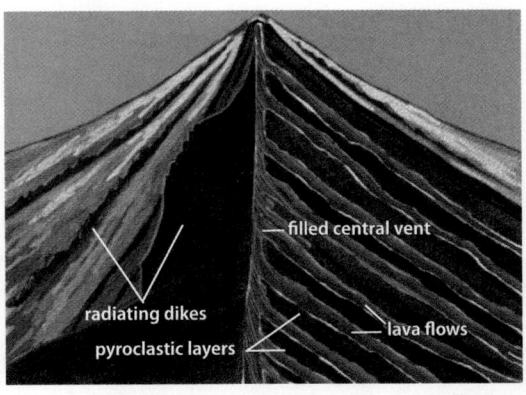

Mount Fuji, in Japan, is a composite volcano that resulted from the collision between the Asian and Pacific tectonic plates.

NATURAL RESOURCES

NATURAL RESOURCES are those products and features of the earth that permit it to support life and satisfy people's needs. Minerals, land, and water are natural resources, as are such biological resources as plants, trees, wild animals, and fish. Mineral resources include oil, coal, metals, stone, and sand. Other natural resources are air, sunshine, and climate. Natural resources are used to make food, fuel, and raw materials for the production of finished goods.

Mining is the process of extracting natural resources from the ground. Most iron ore is extracted by surface mining, as seen here.

Metal Ores

An *ore* is a naturally occurring material that can be mined profitably. Most ores contain metal. The search for metals depends on finding rocks with a high content of metal-bearing minerals. In addition, the metal-bearing minerals must be able to be extracted without too much difficulty or expense.

For example, the mineral hematite is a valued iron ore because it contains about 70 percent iron by weight. Limonite is another iron-bearing mineral. It is ignored as an ore of iron because it contains much less iron by weight than does hematite. Consequently, limonite is not mined extensively.

Many ores form in or near a mass of molten magma. For this reason, igneous rock and the rock adjacent to igneous rock formations often are fruitful sources of valuable ores. In magma that cools slowly, among the first minerals to harden, or crystallize, are apatite, magnetite, and chromite, the sources of phosphorus, iron, and chromium, respectively.

Ores also form where a large body of molten rock injects hot, mineral-rich fluids under pressure into nearby rock. As the fluids cool, the minerals in them crystallize in fissures—producing veins of ore minerals known as *lodes*. Hot mineral-rich solutions that filter out of cooling granite replace nearby rock with tin, copper, lead, zinc, iron, gold, and mercury.

Common Metal Ores			
Ore	Minerals in Which Ore Is Found	Major Deposits in North America	Major Uses
Iron	Hematite and magnetite	Southern Canada and the United States, from the region around Lake Superior	Manufacture of steel for use in construction, automobile parts, and machine parts; cookware, cutlery, kitchen appliances
Copper	Found in sulfides; chalcopyrite is the most important copper ore mineral	Arizona and Utah	Electrical wire and equipment; manufacture of brass
Aluminum	Bauxite, a rock that forms in hot, humid climates	Largest bauxite mine in U.S. is in Arkansas; more than 90 percent of aluminum ore imported to U.S. from tropical countries	One of the most widely used metals: beverage cans, airplanes, electrical cable, many household appliances
Lead	Galena	Missouri, Idaho, Utah, Colorado	Batteries
Zinc	Sphalerite	Missouri, Idaho, Utah, Colorado (usually found in lead mines)	Galvanizing (providing a rust-resistant cover) iron; used in the manufacture of brass and other alloys
Silver	Found as a native metal in veins; also found in sulfide ores	Lead and zinc mines of Idaho are the largest U.S. silver producers	Many products, including coins, tableware, jewelry, photographic film
Gold	Found as a native metal in the form of nuggets and individual grains	Largest U.S. gold mine is in South Dakota; gold mixed with limestone is mined in Nevada	Jewelry, coins, dentistry, electronics; bars of gold are stored to back up national currencies

Types of Ores

There are two types of ores—*native metals* and *compound ores.*

Native metals: the valuable mineral occurs as a pure metal. It is not chemically combined with other substances. Gold, silver, platinum, and copper often occur as native metals.

Compound ores: the valuable metal is joined to other substances such as oxygen, sulfur, carbon, or silicon to form various chemical compounds. The ores of iron, aluminum, and tin are usually found joined with oxygen in compounds called *oxides.* Copper, lead, zinc, silver, nickel, and mercury are found joined with sulfur in compounds called *sulfides.*

METAL FROM ORE

Once ore has been mined from the ground, the valuable metal must be separated from the waste material. This complicated process is called *extractive metallurgy.* In the case of iron, the metal is separated from the ore through *smelting.* The ore is placed in a huge brick-lined furnace called a blast furnace and subjected to high heat. The ore melts, the impurities rise to the top, and the iron is left behind.

The molten iron is still not completely free of impurities. But almost all the iron has been taken from the ore. The metal must now be refined further, usually by causing it to react with oxygen in a furnace.

Rocks and Fuels

Nonmetal Resources

With the exception of gemstones such as diamonds, rubies, and emeralds, nonmetal resources are not as valuable as metals or energy resources. Nonmetal resources are generally needed in very large quantities and are usually inexpensive.

Construction Materials. Mortar, cement, concrete, and stone are valuable nonmetal resources used in constructing buildings and highways.

- **Mortar** is a mixture of sand and finely crushed limestone, or calcium carbonate. It is used to hold together bricks and stones or as plaster.
- **Cement** is a substance made from heated, crushed limestone, clay, sand, and water. It is used to make mortar.
- **Concrete** is formed when gravel is added to cement.
- **Stone** is used as a construction material in buildings and streets and is crushed to form roadbeds.

Fertilizers. Compounds of phosphate, nitrate, and potassium are used in the manufacture of fertilizers, an indispensable ingredient in modern agriculture.

- **Phosphate** is derived from the remains of marine organisms. The major phosphate deposits in the United States are in Florida, Wyoming, and Idaho.
- **Potassium** compounds are extracted from underground sites in New Mexico and other southwestern states.
- **Nitrates** are not mined any longer, since these compounds can now be synthesized in laboratories directly from nitrogen gas.

Evaporites. Minerals that are deposited when water evaporates are called *evaporites*. The fertilizers potassium and nitrates are both evaporites. Rock salt is an evaporite composed of the mineral halite. Rock salt is used to deice roads in winter, preserve food, and manufacture baking soda and soap. Gypsum is a valuable evaporite used in the construction of homes. It is the main ingredient in plaster and wallboard.

BUILDING WITH STONE

Many building stones are composed of granite or limestone. Most crushed stones in roadbeds are also made of limestone. Pulverized limestone is used as a principal ingredient in many chemical products, including fertilizers and soil conditioners. Slate is a kind of stone used primarily to cover roofs. Stone is usually dug from large open pits called *quarries*.

◀ **Limestone** is a type of rock made up mostly of calcite, a mineral form of calcium carbonate. It is often used to make mortar and cement, and in the roadbeds of many highways.

Fossil fuels like coal are burned to generate the vast majority of electricity in the United States.

Subgrade **Base** **Surface** **Shoulders**

Fossil Fuels

Fossil fuels such as coal, oil, and natural gas come from the remains of plants and animals that lived hundreds of millions of years ago. The solar energy stored in these fossil fuels is released when they are burned as fuel. Today, fossil fuels are used to generate more than 90 percent of the electricity in the United States.

Coal

- black or brown rock that can be ignited and burned; produces useful energy in the form of heat
- formed through metamorphism (See pages 470–471.)
- heat and pressure from overlying rock layers change the remains of prehistoric plants; leave varying amounts of carbon
- the several types, or grades, of coal are related to the degree of metamorphism
- low-grade coals, such as peat and lignite, contain less carbon than the high-grade
- high-grade coals, bituminous and anthracite, are subjected to more pressure and heat (more intense metamorphism); thus, higher-grade coals contain more carbon

Oil and Natural Gas

- sedimentary rocks formed from marine sediments are the most common sources
- a large volume of microscopic plants and animals became trapped in particles of sediment
- most geologists believe oil and natural gas formed when marine sediments compacted into shales and limestones
- resulting heat and pressure, combined with bacterial processes, helped transform the organic remains into *hydrocarbons* (compounds made mainly of hydrogen and carbon)
- over time the hydrocarbons were chemically changed into oil and gas
- origins of oil and natural gas, however, are still a controversial topic among earth scientists
- sedimentary rocks that contain oil and gas are known as *reservoir rocks*
- reservoir rocks in an area develop oil pools to produce oil fields
- about 50 percent of the world's oil and gas is found in carbonate rocks (See page 465.)

Soil

Soil is an important natural resource that covers much of the earth's land surface. Most life on Earth depends upon the soil as a direct or indirect source of food. Soil contains mineral and organic particles, other plant and animal matter, and air and water. Soil forms when rocks and plant and animal remains exposed at the surface are weathered into a mixture of layered materials.

Formation of Soil

- rock material undergoes weathering and erosion (See pages 506–509.)

- air temperature, water, ice, and wind hasten the breakup of rocks and minerals

- living things and biological processes are also important

- roots of large shrubs and trees grow downward into sediments or through cracks in rock outcrops; called *root wedging*

- root wedging opens surface layers, allowing water, air, and soil animals to enter; also lets decomposing plant remains mix with rock and mineral fragments

SOIL PROFILE

Most soils consist of four main layers, or horizons. These are the A, B, C, and D horizons. Collectively, these horizons are known as the soil profile.

A Horizon. The dark-colored layer on and just beneath the surface, which consists of decomposed and decaying organic matter (humus), mainly from the leaves, stems, and roots of plants. Also called topsoil.

B Horizon. Layer formed by the accumulation of weathering products—such as clay, iron and aluminum, and calcite (calcium carbonate)—and humus that have been deposited by rainwater. The region of the B horizon with high concentrations of clay, iron, and aluminum is characterized by brown- to red-colored soil.

C Horizon. Layer characterized by large fragments of underlying bedrock. Little or no organic materials are found in the C horizon.

D Horizon. Region of unweathered bedrock (parent material) below the C horizon. Together, the C and D horizons make up the subsoil.

In some soil profiles, B horizon is absent and C horizon lies directly below A horizon. These soils are called immature. A mature soil contains all four horizons. In time, weathering changes immature soils into mature soils.

SOIL EROSION

Soil is continually being removed from land areas by running water and wind. Modern agriculture has speeded up the loss of soil worldwide. Earth loses an estimated 24.5 billion tons of topsoil each year from croplands. As soil loss continues, fewer crops can be produced on the same amount of land. As the world population grows, it is believed that soil conservation techniques will have to be implemented worldwide to prevent mass starvation.

Drought, farming methods, and high winds can erode topsoil quickly. In this picture, taken in Oklahoma in 1935, a great cloud of topsoil engulfs a ranch.

Age of Soil

- climate is the major influence affecting soil thickness and type

- A horizon forms fastest: from several hundred years in humid environments up to several thousand years in arctic and mountainous regions

- B horizon takes much longer to form because minerals weather slowly

- noticeable color changes from the weathering of iron-bearing minerals in the B horizon take about 1,000 years; the deep red of strongly oxidized iron-bearing minerals requires at least 100,000 years

- clay minerals require from 10,000 to 100,000 years to develop

- in arid regions, the caliche, or rocklike layer of calcium carbonate, layer may take from 100,000 to 500,000 years to form

- deep-seated tropical soils take the longest time to form; some tropical soils in the Amazon rain forest may be as much as a million years old

Soil differs from place to place, based on the climate. Pedalfers, and lateritic and pedocal soils are all found in the United States.

Types of Soil			
Soil Type	**Climate**	**Profile**	**Properties**
Pedalfer	Humid, temperate	Consists of A, B, and C horizons as deep as 3 meters (9 feet)	High content of organic material in the A horizon
Podzol	Cooler climates (such as northern Canada and Russia)	Characterized by a white layer between the A and B horizons resulting from the removal of iron oxides by rainwater	High content of iron rather than clay in the B horizon
Lateritic soil	Warm, humid	Consists mainly of iron oxides derived from weathering of iron-bearing minerals	Reddish brown, produced by extreme weathering; the elements calcium, sodium, and potassium are leached, or washed out, of the soil by tropical rain
Pedocal soil	Semiarid to arid	Very thin A horizon with a minimum amount of organic matter due to little rainfall and scarce vegetation; B horizon contains the clay mineral montmorillonite; underneath the B horizon is the caliche	Gets its name from the caliche, the accumulation of calcium carbonate that underlies the B horizon

ATMOSPHERE

The *atmosphere* is an envelope of gases that surrounds Earth. Three of the gases—oxygen, nitrogen, and carbon dioxide—are essential for the survival of all life forms on our planet.

The atmosphere contains the oxygen required in respiration by animals and humans as well as the nitrogen and carbon dioxide necessary in plant growth. These three gases make up about 99 percent of the atmosphere.

With increasing altitude, the atmosphere changes in temperature, pressure, and composition. Research balloons and satellites have shown that the atmosphere consists of a series of distinct layers.

WHY IS THE SKY BLUE?

The colors of the sky result from the scattering of sunlight by the gas molecules and dust particles in the atmosphere. Sunlight consists of light waves of varying wavelengths, each of which is seen as a different color. When the sky is clear, the waves of blue light are scattered much more than those of any other color. As a result, the sky appears blue. When the sky is full of dense clouds or smoke, the light waves of all colors are scattered, causing the sky to turn gray. At sunrise or sunset, sunlight must travel farther through the atmosphere than when the sun is overhead. Light waves of most colors are scattered. However, red light waves are undisturbed and give the sun and sky near the horizon a red or orange appearance.

Layers of Air

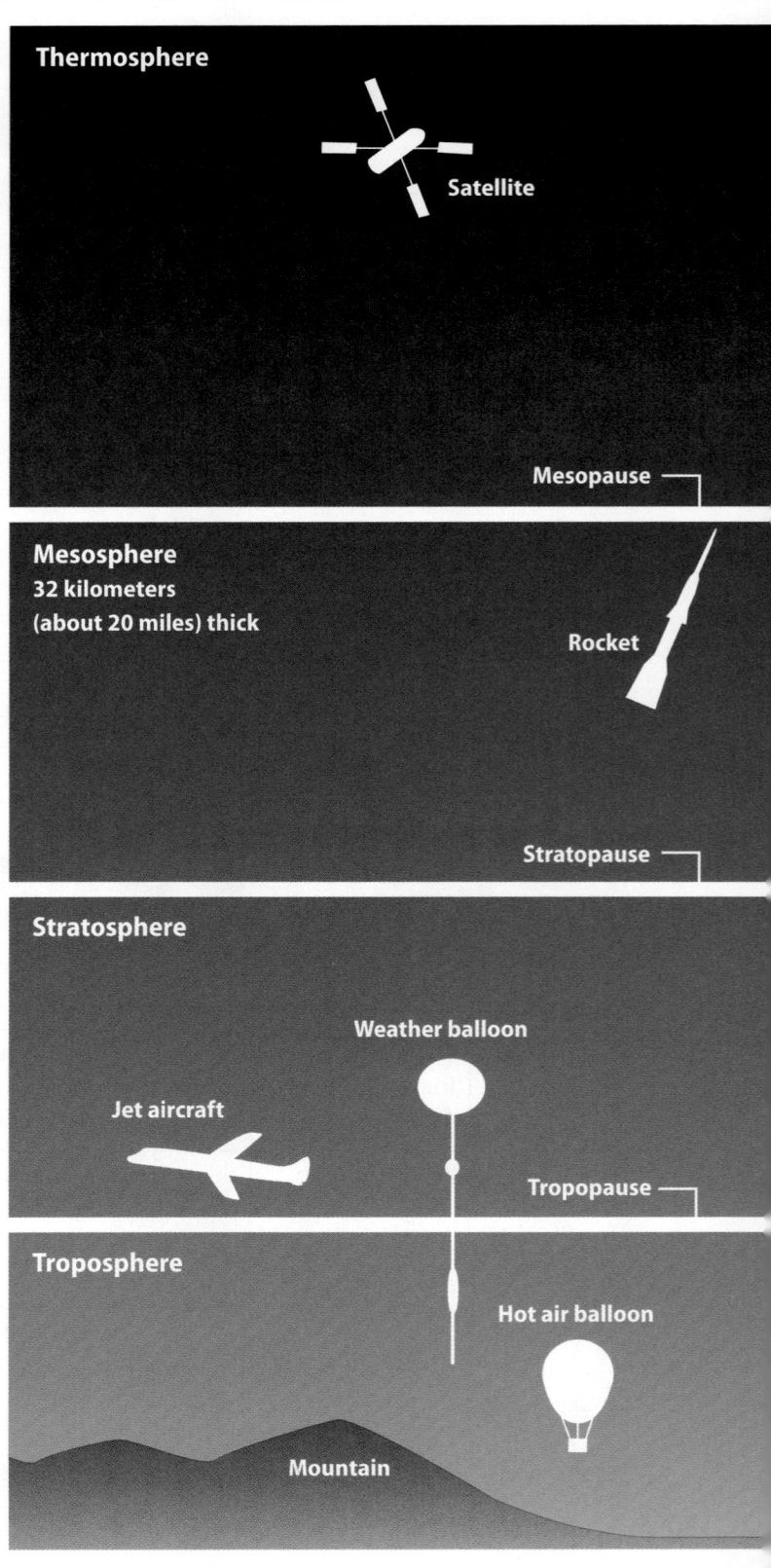

Thermosphere

Satellite

Mesopause

Mesosphere
32 kilometers
(about 20 miles) thick

Rocket

Stratopause

Stratosphere

Weather balloon

Jet aircraft

Tropopause

Troposphere

Hot air balloon

Mountain

LAYERS OF THE ATMOSPHERE

Thermosphere

- uppermost layer of Earth's atmosphere; begins at an average altitude of about 80 kilometers (50 miles) and extends into space.
- air is extremely thin; nitrogen and oxygen make up most of the lower parts
- above about 1,000 kilometers (620 miles), contains mainly hydrogen and helium
- temperature rises from about –90°C (–130°F) at an altitude of 80 kilometers (50 miles) to more than 1,200°C (2,200°F) at about 350 kilometers (220 miles)
- solar radiation and cosmic rays ionize (electrically charge) atoms in the upper atmosphere
- region of ionized particles, known as the ionosphere, extends through parts of the upper mesosphere and lower thermosphere
- atoms in the outermost region of the thermosphere, called the exosphere, can gain enough speed to escape the atmosphere

Mesosphere

- from an altitude of about 48 kilometers (30 miles) to about 80 to 100 kilometers (50 to 60 miles)
- temperature drops with rising altitude due to a falling concentration of ozone
- averages 0°C (32°F) at the base of the mesosphere and –85°C (–120°F) at the mesopause, the upper limit of the mesosphere
- lowest temperatures in Earth's atmosphere occur at the mesopause; can drop below –130°C (–200°F)
- too high for weather balloons and airplanes; scientists can only directly measure the layer by rocket

Stratosphere

- from an altitude of about 10 kilometers (6 miles) to about 48 kilometers (30 miles)
- air temperature fairly uniform and very cold; average temperature of about –55°C (–67°F)
- in upper reaches, ultraviolet rays from the sun split molecules of oxygen
- oxygen molecules then recombine to form ozone
- ozone makes life possible on Earth by absorbing much of the ultraviolet radiation that strikes the upper atmosphere

Troposphere

- contains water vapor, dust particles from wind erosion, and smoke
- altitude varies, averages about 19 kilometers (12 miles) above the equator and 10 kilometers (6 miles) above the poles
- contains most of the atmosphere's mass
- all weather phenomena occur in the troposphere
- air temperature decreases with increasing altitude; between sea level and top of troposphere, drops a total of 28° to 56°C (98° to 196°F)

EARTH'S GREENHOUSE

The atmosphere functions like a giant greenhouse. (See pages 670–671.) By trapping the heat from solar energy in its lowest layer, the atmosphere keeps the temperature in most places on Earth within the narrow range necessary for life. The lower part of Earth's atmosphere contains sufficient oxygen, water vapor, and carbon dioxide to support a wide variety of plants and animals. Most living things inhabit the relatively narrow region where the atmosphere blends with the lithosphere and the hydrosphere.

EARTH'S SHIELD

Earth's atmosphere also acts as a shield. It protects the planet from certain forms of solar radiation and from impact by meteorites. For example, the atmosphere blocks most of the harmful X-rays and ultraviolet radiation from the sun.

Small rocky meteors continually plummet toward Earth. Most of these meteors disintegrate before reaching the ground because of the heat generated by friction as they pass through the atmosphere. When a meteor survives passage through the atmosphere and actually strikes Earth, it is called a meteorite.

WEATHER is the condition of the atmosphere at a particular time and place. Factors that influence weather include air temperature, air pressure, and moisture. The combined effect of these factors produces a wide variety of weather phenomena, including winds, clouds, storms, and various forms of precipitation. The science of the atmosphere, especially the study of weather phenomena and weather forecasting, is called *meteorology*.

WHY DOES HOT AIR RISE?

Air consists of molecules in motion. When air is warmed, the average speed of the molecules increases, increasing the space between the molecules. The air is less dense, and therefore lighter, and it rises as the heavier cool air falls.

Wind Systems

Wind is the movement of air from one place to another in response to a change in temperature and pressure. Wind is produced whenever cooler air replaces warmer air in an area. Initially, wind is created by the upward movement of air that has been heated by Earth's surface and the downward movement of cool air.

All weather begins with the sun's radiant energy falling on Earth's atmosphere. Because Earth is spherical, this radiant energy falls unevenly, most of it near the equator. Progressively less falls as it approaches the North and South poles. In response to this uneven heating, global wind systems develop at the equator. These wind systems redistribute the sun's energy to Earth's Northern and Southern hemispheres.

The movement of air, or circulation of winds in the atmosphere, is initially due to convection, the movement of air from areas of high pressure to areas of low pressure. At the equator, air pressure tends to be low because of the greater heating influence of the sun. Thus, Earth is characterized by low pressure at the equator. At the poles, colder, denser air creates regions of high pressure. As a result, there is a surface flow of cold air from the poles toward the equator and a return flow of warmed air from the equator to the poles.

WIND BELTS

Wind belts encircle Earth. Winds in these areas tend to blow in the same direction. Wind belts are separated by areas of little to no wind.

Wind direction is described by its source area, or the direction from which it blows. For example, a northerly wind blows from the north to the south. A westerly wind blows from the west to the east. ▶

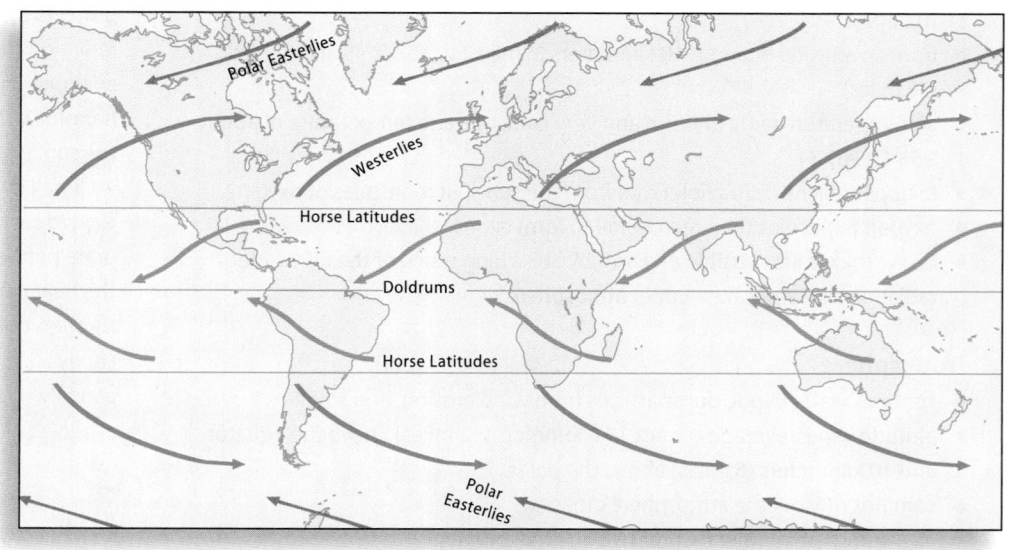

THE JET STREAM

The jet stream is a narrow band of high-altitude wind near the tropopause, or the upper limit of the troposphere, that circles Earth in a wavy pattern. As its name implies, the jet stream is a rapidly moving current of air blowing through the atmosphere at speeds often greater than 60 meters a second (130 miles an hour). The jet stream spans the North American continent, guiding storms from west to east. The movement of the jet stream often determines the temperature range and weather in a given area for 2 weeks or longer.

World War II bomber pilots discovered the jet stream when their high-altitude bombers were hampered by the strong wind between 6 and 12 kilometers (20,000 to 40,000 feet). ▶

In response to solar heating and Earth's rotation, other horizontal wind systems develop. For example, along the equator there is a belt of light winds known as the *doldrums*. They cover a region slightly north and south of the equator. The warm, moist air rising from the equatorial low-pressure region is affected by Earth's west-to-east rotation, causing a deflection in these winds.

Beginning at about 30° north latitude (central Florida) and extending northward to about 60° north latitude (southern Alaska) is the belt of the *westerlies*. The westerlies control the sequence of weather in the middle latitudes. These winds follow the rotation of Earth and mark the boundary zones between cold polar air and warm tropical air masses. Owing to the extreme contrast in air masses, this region, comprising the United States and Canada, is the stormiest on Earth.

Blowing wind makes already low temperatures feel even colder, and the threat of frostbite increases. ▼

Wind Chill					
Wind Speed	**Air Temperature (F°)**				
0	30°	25°	20°	0°	−10°
5 mph	27°	22°	16°	−5°	−15°
10 mph	16°	10°	3°	−22°	−34°
20 mph	4°	−3°	−10°	−39°	−53°
30 mph	−2°	−10°	−18°	−49°	−64°

Water Cycle

Water on Earth moves constantly, from the oceans to the air, from the air to the land, and then back to the seas again, changing from liquid, to gas, to solid, and back again. This continuous cycle is called the *hydrologic cycle,* or the water cycle.

Evaporation and Transpiration

Evaporation is the changing of water from a liquid state to a gaseous state. The sun's heat evaporates water from land, lakes, rivers, and oceans. About 85 percent of the vapor in the air comes from the oceans.

Plants also add moisture. After plants have drawn water from the ground through their roots, they pass it out through their leaves as vapor in a process called *transpiration*. (See page 133.)

Condensation

Condensation is the process in which water changes from a vapor to a liquid or a solid. Water condenses to form clouds, dew, fog, rain, and snow. When air cools to its saturation or dew point (the lowest temperature at which it can hold water vapor), it condenses, or contracts, into visible clouds or water droplets. When air temperatures are below freezing, snow forms.

Humidity

Humidity is the amount of water vapor, or moisture, that is present in the air. Because the molecules of gases in warm air are spread farther apart than the molecules in cool air, warm air can hold much more moisture than cool air.

Measurements of humidity are normally stated in terms of relative humidity. Relative humidity is a ratio of the amount of water vapor in the air to the greatest amount of water vapor the air can hold at a given air temperature. Relative humidity is usually converted into a percent; it is 100 percent when the air is saturated with water vapor.

THE HYDROLOGIC CYCLE

- The sun's heat evaporates water from the oceans.
- The water rises as invisible vapor and falls back to Earth as rain, snow, or some other form of moisture.
- This moisture is called precipitation. Most precipitation drops back directly into the oceans.
- The remainder falls on the rest of Earth. In time, this water also returns to the sea, and the cycle starts again.

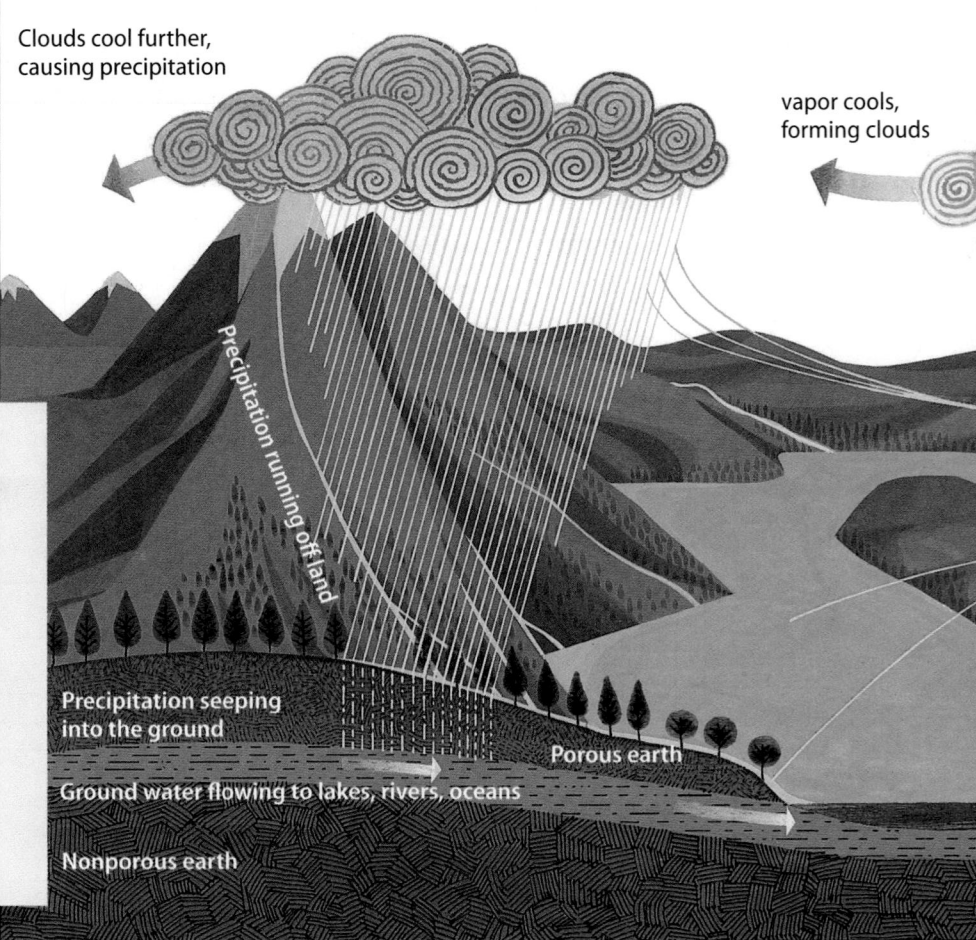

Clouds cool further, causing precipitation

vapor cools, forming clouds

Precipitation running off land

Precipitation seeping into the ground

Ground water flowing to lakes, rivers, oceans

Porous earth

Nonporous earth

ANCIENT WATERS

Because of nature's water cycle, there is as much water on Earth today as there ever was, or ever will be—1.4 billion cubic kilometers (326 million cubic miles) to be exact. Water changes only from one form to another, and moves from one place to another. The water you drank last night might have flowed in Russia's Volga River last year. Or perhaps Alexander the Great bathed in it more than 2,000 years ago.

The same water that flowed through this ancient Roman aqueduct still exists somewhere on Earth today.

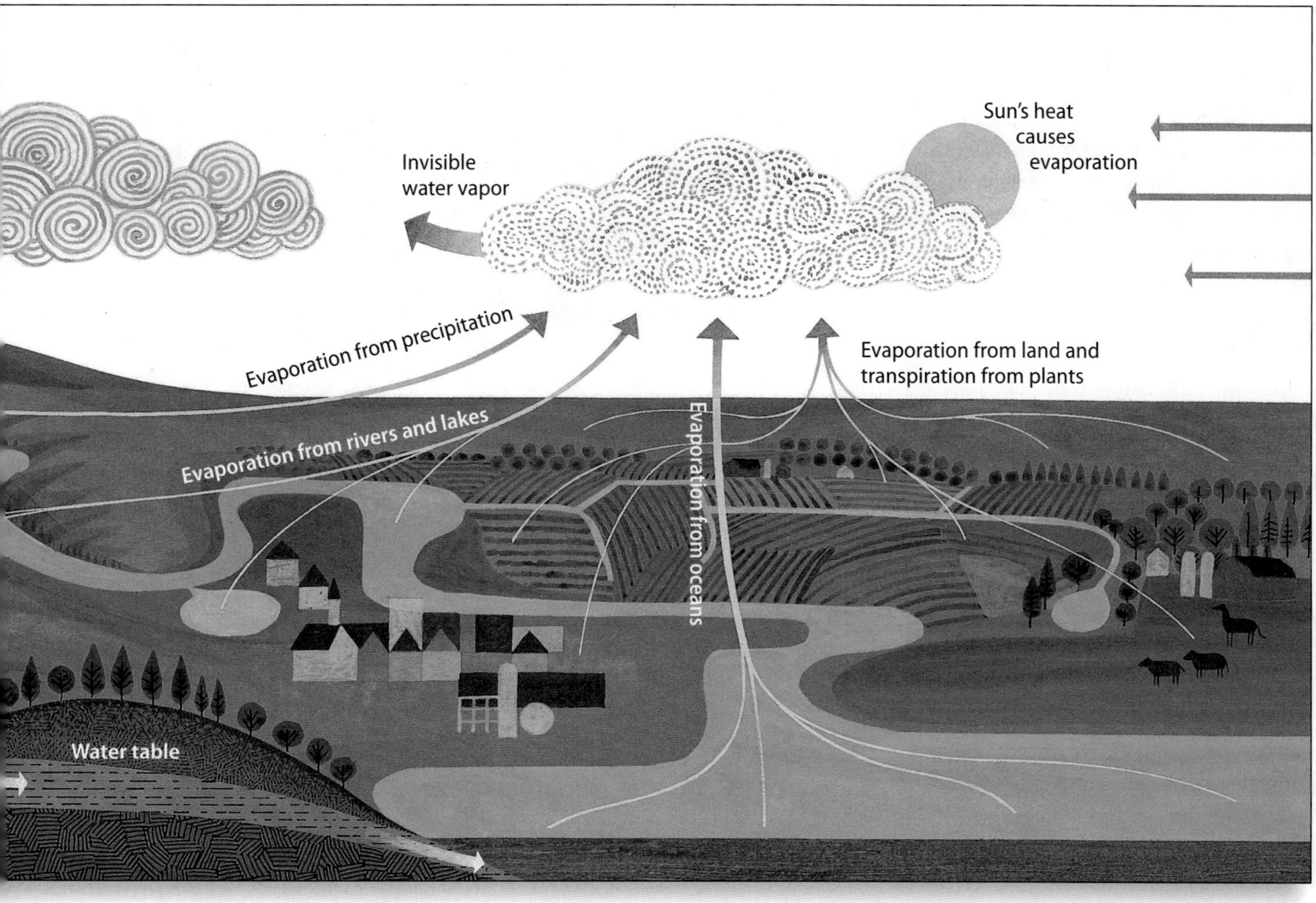

Invisible water vapor

Sun's heat causes evaporation

Evaporation from precipitation

Evaporation from rivers and lakes

Evaporation from oceans

Evaporation from land and transpiration from plants

Water table

Water Cycle

SOUTHWESTERN

Cloud Formation

Clouds form when a moisture-laden column of air rises through the atmosphere. As the air rises, the atmospheric pressure decreases, causing the air to expand. The energy required for this expansion comes from within the rising air in the form of heat. If the moist air continues to rise, it will eventually reach the *dew point*, or the air temperature at which water condenses from vapor into liquid. Water vapor will condense around particles of dust or salt, called *condensation nuclei*, to form clouds. The dust is from windblown soil and volcanic eruptions, while the salt is from the waves breaking at sea or crashing along shorelines.

Precipitation

Precipitation—water that falls from clouds—can take several forms, both liquid and solid. The water starts as tiny cloud droplets that form clouds. Clouds that rise to great heights often contain both ice crystals and water droplets that have been supercooled below the freezing point. These supercooled droplets remain unfrozen if they do not contain condensation nuclei (dust or salt). However, the air usually contains an abundance of condensation nuclei, which cause water droplets to freeze at or near 0°C (32°F). The ice crystals grow as the droplets freeze.

KINDS OF CLOUDS

The prefix *strato-* means layerlike or sheetlike; *stratus* clouds appear as layers or sheets. The prefix *cumulo-* means pile or heap; *cumulus* clouds are piled-up masses of white clouds. The prefix *cirro-* means curl; cirrus clouds are curly white clouds.

Low clouds: Stratus and stratocumulus clouds are usually seen near the earth; the bases are usually less than 1,800 meters (6,000 feet) above the earth.

Middle clouds: Altostratus, altocumulus, and nimbostratus clouds usually lie from 1,800 to 6,100 meters (6,000 to 20,000 feet) above the earth.

High clouds: Cirrus, cirrostratus, and cirrocumulus clouds form entirely of ice crystals; other clouds are mainly water droplets; cirrus clouds are delicate wispy clouds that appear high in the sky, sometimes higher than 10,700 meters (35,000 feet).

Clouds that grow vertically: Cumulus and cumulonimbus clouds may grow to great heights while their bases are near the ground.

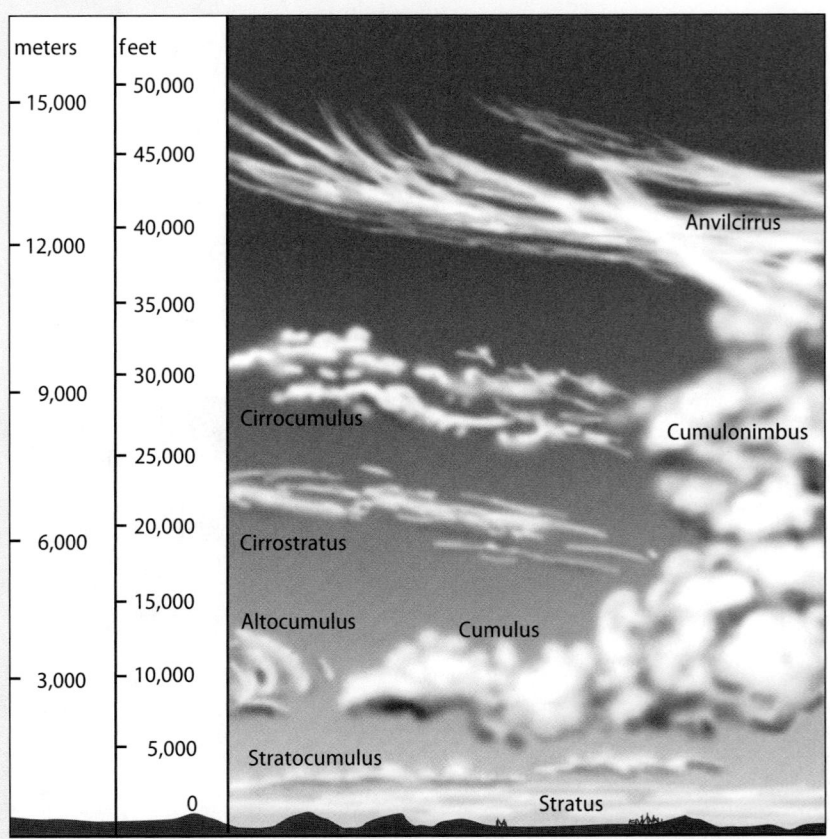

FORMS OF PRECIPITATION

Rain: Once the ice crystals in a cloud have grown heavy enough, they fall toward Earth. Upon reaching the warmer level of the troposphere, the ice crystals melt to form rain.

Tropical rain: In tropical areas, clouds are rarely cold enough to permit formation of ice crystals, so rain forms differently. Some of the water droplets start out much larger than others. These larger droplets form by the condensation of water vapor around nuclei composed of large particles of salt from the ocean. When they become heavy enough, the large droplets fall. On their way down, they collide and unite with smaller droplets, then fall out of a cloud as rain.

Freezing rain: One of the most dangerous forms of precipitation is freezing rain. When temperatures near the ground are at or near freezing, the falling raindrops freeze on contact with cold surfaces such as power lines, tree branches, and pavement. As the rain freezes, it leaves a thin layer of ice on walkways and roads, creating treacherous conditions for pedestrians and motorists.

Hail: Hailstones form when ice crystals remain aloft in a cloud of supercooled water droplets long enough to grow thousands of times larger than normal. Hailstones usually form during severe thunderstorms, when heat causes strong and continual updrafts that keep ice pellets suspended long enough to acquire several coatings of ice.

Snow: In winter, when the air close to the ground may not be warm enough to melt the ice crystals, the precipitation falls in the form of snow.

STORM CLOUDS

A cumulonimbus cloud may reach heights as great as 18,000 meters (60,000 feet) from its base. Its top, which contains ice crystals, spreads out in the shape of an anvil. This kind of cloud is often called a *thunderhead* because it frequently produces thunder. Cumulonimbus clouds also produce heavy rain and lightning. Sometimes hail or, on rare occasions, a deadly tornado comes from a cumulonimbus cloud.

Air Masses

Air masses are large bodies of air with uniform temperature and humidity. Air masses form in the lower level of the troposphere and develop by remaining stationary over land or ocean waters for several days or weeks. As a result, the temperature and humidity of an air mass become similar to the temperature and humidity of the land area or body of water beneath it.

Lows

In the United States, air masses often meet along a boundary known as the *polar front*. This front extends worldwide in the middle latitudes. Typically, tropical air from the south meets polar air from the north, with the wind in each air mass blowing in a different direction.

Eventually, a wave may develop along the front. Cold air begins pushing into warm air, creating a cold front. The warm air mass tries to displace the cold air mass, producing a warm front. As the warm air rises, it creates an area of low pressure. This gives the entire weather system its name—a *low*.

Cyclones. When a low enters a region, weather conditions change rapidly. A storm will begin with the rainy weather generally associated with a warm front. Clear skies and higher temperatures will follow. Soon a cold front will arrive, bringing more rain. Then skies will clear.

As moist air ascends along the fronts and water condenses to form precipitation, large amounts of heat are released. This deepens the low-pressure area. The winds flowing into this area increase, and the storm grows in intensity. A satellite photo of the storm system would show that the winds form a spiral. For this reason, the low is called a *cyclone*. A cyclone is a very large body of air, sometimes as great as 2,500 kilometers (1,500 miles) in diameter. The winds from a cyclone blow in circular paths around the low-pressure region at the center. (See also pages 544–545.)

TYPES OF AIR MASSES

Air masses form in regions where the air temperature and moisture content are fairly uniform, as in arctic regions or the open ocean. Four types of air masses influence weather conditions in North America. They are classified according to their source regions.

- **Continental polar** (labeled **cP** on weather maps) air masses form over the frigid landscape of Canada. This cool, dry air mass is carried southward by the polar easterly winds. It brings clear, crisp weather to the eastern United States in winter, and relief from hot spells in summer.

- **Continental tropical (cT)** air masses originate in Mexico. They are blown by the westerlies into the southwestern United States, creating hot, dry weather conditions.

- **Maritime polar (mP)** air masses form over the northern Pacific Ocean and the icy north Atlantic. A maritime polar air mass may be blown inland by the easterlies, creating a heavy storm called a *northeaster*.

- **Maritime tropical (mT)** air masses form over the Caribbean Sea and the Atlantic Ocean. They absorb moisture from the sea and carry it to the southeastern United States. Maritime tropical air brings humid weather and precipitation to the South, the Atlantic coastal states, and farther inland.

As an air mass travels away from its source region, it gradually changes. For example, cold, dry air becomes warmer and moister as it moves from land over warm ocean waters.

Fronts

A *front* is the boundary that forms when a warm air mass and a cool air mass meet. Because the air of a cool air mass is denser than the air of a warm air mass, the two air masses remain separate, and a front forms between them. Most fronts are about 100 kilometers (60 miles) long. Weather changes usually occur along the various kinds of fronts. The kind of front that forms depends on how the air masses are moving. A weather front is named for the temperature of the inflowing air. Thus, when cold air replaces warm air in a region, a cold front has moved into the area.

Cold Fronts. A *cold front* forms when a mass of cold air overtakes a mass of warm air. As the cold air mass collides with the warm air mass, warm air rises. If the warm air is moist, clouds form. Large cumulus and cumulonimbus clouds typically form along a fast-moving cold front.

Storms are usually brief but violent and are accompanied by strong, gusty winds and a short period (less than a couple of hours) of heavy rain. A slow-moving cold front produces small cumulus clouds and only scattered precipitation.

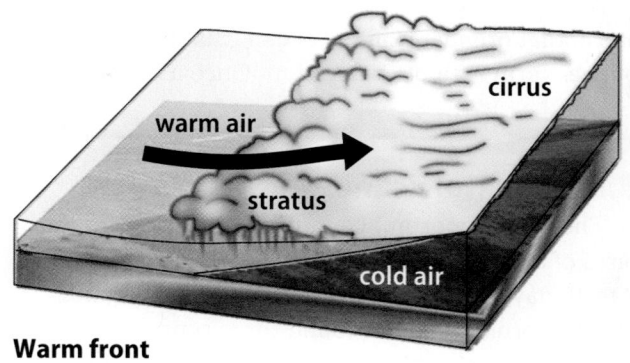

Warm front

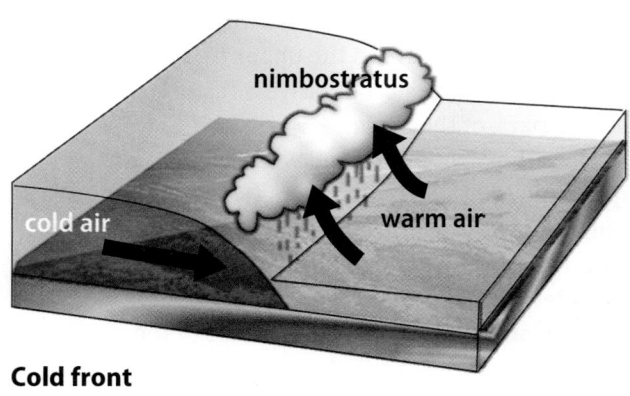

Cold front

Warm Fronts. A *warm front* forms when a warm air mass overtakes a cooler air mass. A warm front is characterized by less dense warm air rising over cooler air. Because the slope at the boundary of a warm front is gradual, clouds often form far ahead of the base of a warm front.

The first clouds to be seen are high-altitude cirrus clouds. Following the cirrus clouds are cirrostratus clouds, followed by altostratus, then by nimbostratus. Finally, stratus clouds form at the base of the warm front. A warm front generally produces steady rain over a large area lasting from 12 to 24 hours or longer.

Occluded Fronts. Cold fronts move faster than warm fronts. An *occluded front* forms when a cold front overtakes a warm front and lifts it off the ground. As the warm air rises, more heat is released. Winds can be especially strong, and intense storms can form.

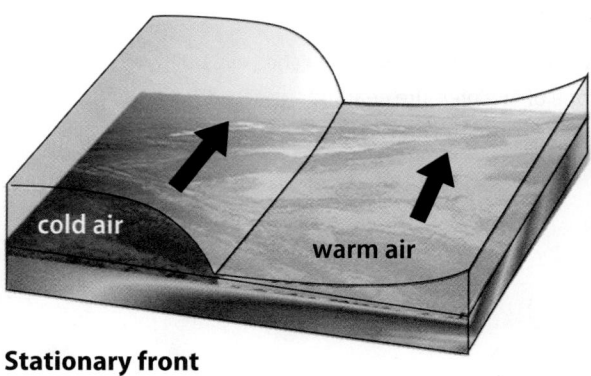

Stationary front

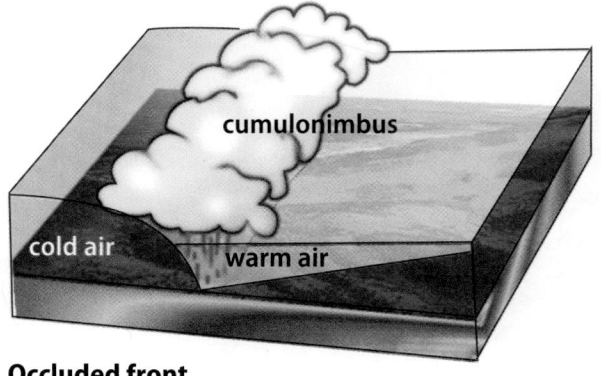

Occluded front

Stationary Fronts. Sometimes when two air masses meet, neither is displaced. In this event, the two air masses move parallel to the front that separates them. When the front separating the two air masses does not move, it is called a *stationary front*. The weather conditions in the vicinity of a stationary front are similar to those produced by a warm front.

Hurricanes

A *hurricane,* or a tropical cyclone, is a large tropical storm that originates in the ocean. Hurricanes form over a warm area of open ocean. Once a hurricane has formed it moves westward and often toward the poles. It can affect a huge area, covering thousands of square kilometers.

Birth of a Hurricane

The most important conditions necessary for the birth of a hurricane are warm seawater, heated by 7 to 10 days of direct tropical sunlight, and humid air. Meteorologists have found three separate conditions that are capable of causing the hot, humid air to develop into a moving hurricane:

- **easterly wave:** A trough of low pressure that accompanies the easterly winds to the south of the subtropical high-pressure areas. An easterly wave moves from east to west.

- **intertropical convergence zone:** A region near the equator where opposing trade winds of the Northern and Southern hemispheres converge.

- **polar trough:** A polar trough can be visualized as the reverse of an easterly wave. It is a region of low pressure that accompanies the prevailing westerly winds of the middle latitudes.

One of these three conditions may cause the hot, moist air of a newly formed hurricane to concentrate and rise higher into the troposphere. (See pages 534–535.) As the air rises, water vapor begins to condense, heat is released, and clouds form as a result of the lower air temperature in the upper troposphere. The rising hot air moves progressively faster in the *eye,* or central part, of the storm.

Near the hurricane's eye, wind speeds can approach 290 to 335 kilometers (175 to 200 miles) an hour. Suddenly, as the eye passes over a particular area, the wind speed may drop to about 15 kilometers (10 miles) an hour, the rain stops, and patches of blue sky appear. However, the appearance of the eye means that the hurricane is only half over. For this reason, the eye is often considered the most dangerous and deceptive feature of a hurricane, because within minutes the violent winds and rains will return to batter the area.

A core of warm air in a hurricane's eye builds a zone of low pressure near the surface, drawing more air into the hurricane. ▼

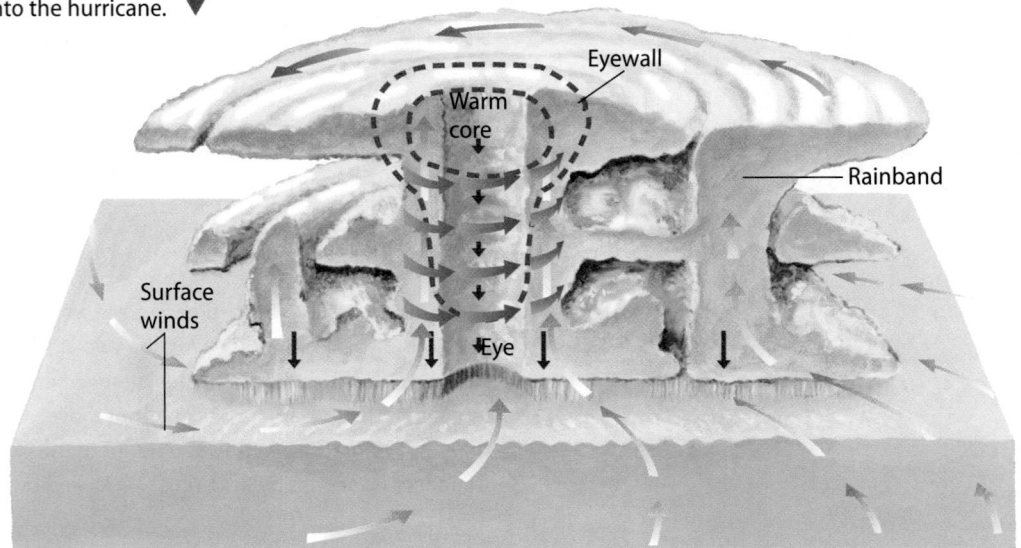

THE EYE OF THE STORM

The eye of a hurricane is one of meteorology's most interesting phenomena. It is the region of lowest air pressure, because rapidly rising hot air is lighter than the colder, denser, slower-moving air that surrounds the storm. As the hurricane grows, its eye can range in diameter from about 14 kilometers (25 miles) to as much as 500 kilometers (300 miles).

ATOMIC STORM

An average hurricane contains total energy equal to about 500,000 atomic bombs of the kind dropped on Hiroshima and Nagasaki during World War II. Fortunately, a hurricane is spread out over an area of about 500 to 650 kilometers (300 to 400 miles). Moreover, a hurricane often travels more than 2,000 kilometers (1,200 miles) during its life cycle.

The eye of a hurricane is a calm, clear region surrounded by extremely strong winds.

LIFE OF A HURRICANE

Meteorologists describe the life of a hurricane as having four stages: *tropical disturbance, tropical depression, tropical storm,* and *hurricane.*

Tropical disturbance is an area where rain clouds are building. The clouds form when moist air rises and becomes cooler. Cool air cannot hold as much water vapor as warm air can, and the excess water changes into tiny droplets of water that form clouds. The clouds in a tropical disturbance may rise to great heights, forming the towering thunderclouds that meteorologists call cumulonimbus clouds.

Tropical depression is a low-pressure area surrounded by winds that have begun to blow in a circular pattern. The low pressure near the ocean creates wind, which evaporates seawater and so feeds more thunderclouds. The winds swirl slowly around the low-pressure area at first. As the pressure becomes even lower, the winds blow faster, and more ocean water evaporates.

Tropical storm. When the winds exceed 61 kilometers (38 miles) per hour, a tropical storm has developed. Viewed from above, the storm clouds now have a well-defined circular shape. The seas have become so rough that ships must steer clear of the area. The strong winds near the surface of the ocean draw more and more heat and water vapor from the sea. The increased warmth and moisture in the air feed the storm.

Hurricane. A storm achieves the status of hurricane—or the equivalent name used in another region—when its winds exceed 119 kilometers (74 miles) per hour. By the time a storm reaches hurricane intensity, it usually has a well-developed eye at its center. Surface pressure drops to its lowest in the eye.

Hurricanes

Destruction

The three destructive agents of a hurricane are wind, ocean waves, and rain. Any one can cause serious damage to a given area. For example, a poorly constructed home on a hilltop may be blown apart by hurricane winds. A home or bridge built near the shoreline may be toppled by powerful hurricane-generated ocean waves. In low-lying regions, large amounts of rainfall may result in severe flooding conditions.

Wind: Wind speeds greater than 330 kilometers (200 miles) an hour have been recorded by hurricane reconnaissance aircraft. However, the maximum wind speed of an average hurricane usually exceeds 205 kilometers (125 miles) an hour. (See pages 536–537.)

Ocean Waves: Waves thrown ashore by advancing hurricanes are often more feared by people living on or near the coast than are the winds. In the open ocean, large ships can usually withstand 13-meter (40-foot)-tall hurricane waves. Once these waves reach shallow coastal waters, however, they behave like enormous battering rams. Hurricane waves erode seawalls, undermine roads, and sweep away houses.

Rain: Most hurricanes drop about 15 centimeters (6 inches) of rainfall. The rain from hurricanes can cause streams to spill over their banks, dams to break under pressure, and storm sewers to fill past capacity. City streets can be turned into turbulent rivers in minutes.

Wind, ocean waves, and rain are the three destructive agents of a hurricane. Any one can cause serious damage to a given area.

Wind Speed and Location

The maximum wind speed of an average hurricane usually exceeds 205 kilometers (125 miles) an hour, and winds have been recorded traveling at speeds greater than 330 kilometers (200 miles) an hour. Engineers who studied the damage caused by a hurricane that struck the Florida Keys in 1935 concluded that wind gusts of about 415 kilometers (250 miles) an hour must have accompanied that storm.

Hurricanes mainly form in the north Atlantic Ocean, off Africa, as well as in the Caribbean Sea and the Gulf of Mexico. Most hurricanes develop from June through October. To date, for reasons unknown, there is no record of a hurricane forming in either the southeastern Pacific or the south Atlantic Ocean.

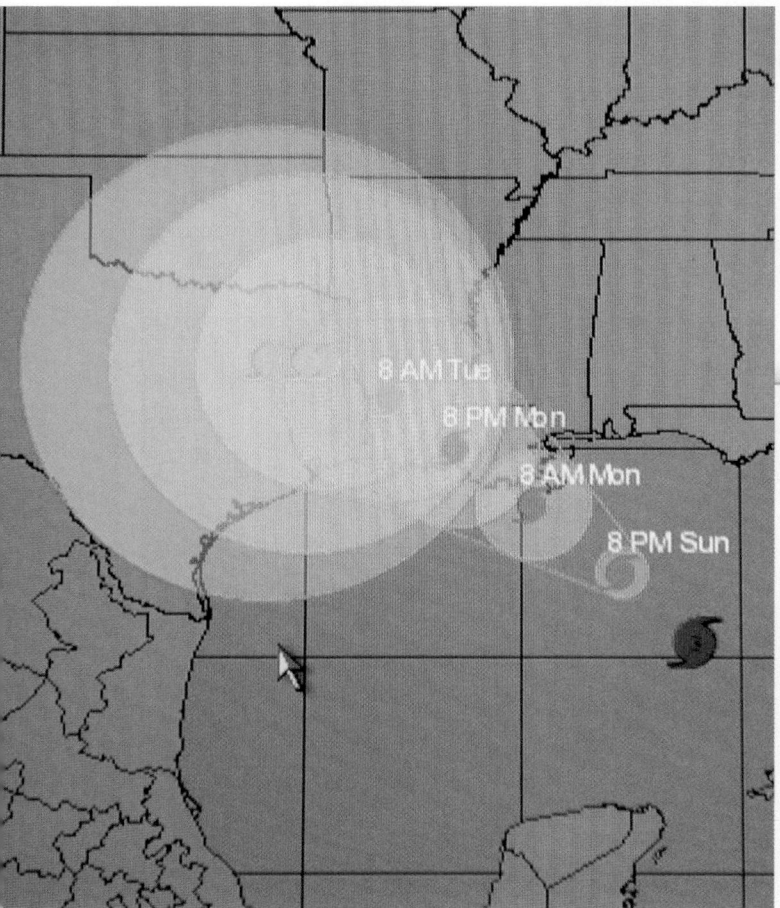

Hurricane Gustav formed on August 25, 2008, southeast of Haiti. After causing serious damage in Haiti, Jamaica, and Cuba, Gustav struck the Louisiana coast on September 1.

NAME THAT HURRICANE

Every tropical storm is given a name. The name helps meteorologists avoid confusion when tracking storms. During World War II, pilots began naming hurricanes after their wives and girlfriends, beginning the tradition of giving hurricanes female names. By the late 1960s, the tradition had become controversial because of protests from women's rights groups, so in 1978 the World Meteorological Organization formulated a list of 105 male and female names for tropical storms and hurricanes. The list is repeated every 5 years. The names of hurricanes that are extremely destructive are "retired" with new names replacing them.

THE CORIOLIS EFFECT

The devastating wind of a hurricane is caused by the *Coriolis effect*. This force, first described by the French scientist G. G. Coriolis in 1835, is related to Earth's rotation. Coriolis observed that winds in the Northern Hemisphere are deflected to the right. In the Southern Hemisphere, winds are deflected to the left because of Earth's rotation. Thus, in the Northern Hemisphere, the Coriolis effect causes a hurricane to spin rapidly, and its direction will be counterclockwise.

The Path of a Hurricane

Hurricanes last an average of 3 to 14 days. In the Northern Hemisphere, hurricanes usually begin by traveling from east to west. As the storms approach the coast of North America or Asia, however, they shift to a more northerly direction. Most hurricanes turn gradually northwest, north, and finally northeast. In the Southern Hemisphere, the storms may travel westward at first and then turn southwest, south, and finally southeast. The path of an individual storm is irregular and often difficult to predict.

All hurricanes eventually move toward higher latitudes where there is colder ocean water, less moisture, and greater wind shear. These conditions cause the storm to weaken and die out. The end comes quickly if a hurricane moves over land, because it no longer receives heat energy and moisture from warm tropical water.

Thunderstorms and Twisters

Thunderstorms

A *thunderstorm* is a storm that produces lightning and thunder and sometimes hail, violent winds, and tornadoes. About 1,800 thunderstorms occur daily around the world. Like a hurricane, a thunderstorm is caused by the evaporation of huge amounts of water, condensation into clouds, and release of heavy rain.

The Approaching Storm. Thunderstorms form mostly in late spring and in summer. The main requirement for development of a thunderstorm is an unstable atmosphere.

- Warm, moist air rises from near Earth's surface.

- As the air rises, it cools.

- Cool air can hold less water, causing the excess moisture to condense into clouds and eventually fall as precipitation.

- Inside the storm, clouds develop a buildup of electric charge, probably from collisions among ice and water particles.

- This static electricity is discharged as lightning.

Thunder and Lightning. A thunderstorm can be compared to a giant storage battery. The negative charges are located in the lower half of the cloud. Positively charged particles exist in the upper half of the cloud, where temperatures are below freezing. When the positive charges and negative charges become very large, about a million volts per meter, lightning strikes. Visible electricity is discharged by the interaction of these electrical charges within a particular cloud, from one cloud to another, or from a cloud to Earth.

The thunder that follows a bolt of lightning is the sound of electricity being discharged. It has been calculated that a bolt of lightning produces a temperature in the vicinity of 10,000°C (50,000°F). At this great heat, the air along the path of the lightning bolt expands with a great explosion. Thunder is the sound of the explosion.

Lightning can be formed only in clouds where temperatures are below freezing. As a result, thunderstorms form when convection currents are strong enough to lift moist air up into the frigid upper regions of the troposphere.

Tornadoes

A *tornado* is a rapidly rotating column of air that can develop under a large, anvil-shaped thundercloud. Tornado winds swirl at speeds that may exceed 480 kilometers (300 miles) per hour. Tornadoes are serious, violent storms. They are sometimes powerful enough to pick up heavy trucks and locomotives and carry people and livestock for long distances. Loose objects in a tornado become potentially deadly high-speed missiles.

When to Expect a Tornado. Like the development of a tropical cyclone, the formation of a tornado requires specific atmospheric conditions:

- a southerly flow of warm, moist air
- a high-level westerly flow of cool, dry air
- the combination produces an unstable atmosphere capable of strong updrafts and heavy precipitation

TORNADO ALLEY

The United States is the world's hot spot for tornadoes, recording between 700 and 1,000 twisters each year. And while tornadoes have occurred in all 50 states, they strike most often in a region called Tornado Alley. Tornado Alley stretches across the southern and midwestern states, including Texas, Oklahoma, Kansas, Nebraska, Iowa, and Missouri.

A tornado funnel can vary in shape from a ropelike form dangling from the base of a cumulonimbus cloud to a massive black column of whirling debris a mile in diameter.

Twisting Funnel. The characteristic funnel cloud of a tornado forms a tight circle in which winds blow at speeds greater than 480 kilometers (300 miles) an hour. Most tornadoes travel about 10 kilometers (6 miles) from the time they form until they dissipate. The forward ground speed of a tornado ranges from 50 to 100 kilometers (30 to 60 miles) an hour.

Over the brief lifetime of a tornado—usually a few hours—the size, shape, and color of the funnel cloud can change dramatically. The color varies from a dirty white to a blue gray when the funnel cloud primarily contains water droplets. Most of a funnel cloud is composed of water vapor from the parent cloud and dust and debris picked up when the tornado makes contact with the ground.

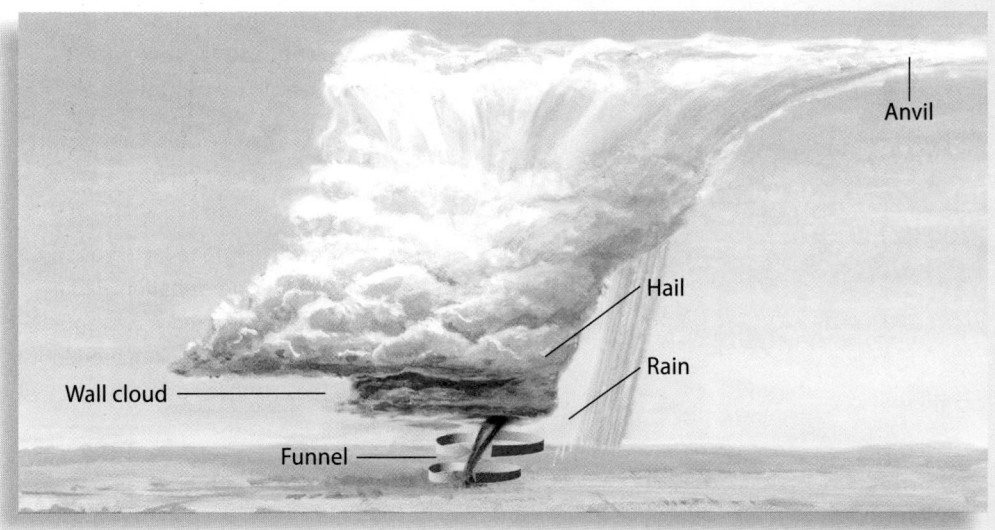

Anvil

Hail

Rain

Wall cloud

Funnel

A tornado forms when the air in the updraft of a severe thunderstorm begins to rotate owing to the formation of a low-pressure center. Once rotation begins, the tornado builds toward the ground. If a tornado makes contact with the ground, its funnel cloud sucks up air at its lower end like the hose of a vacuum cleaner.

PREDICTING WEATHER

Meteorology is the study of the variations in atmospheric conditions that produce weather. Meteorologists measure precipitation and such conditions as wind, temperature, and humidity. They can predict the weather as far ahead as a few days. Their forecasts include ranges of temperature and the chances of rain or snow as well as warnings of strong winds, floods, hail, or severe air pollution. Meteorologists use a variety of tools to make their predictions.

Radar

Radar is an instrument for determining distance, direction, and speed of unseen objects by the reflection of radio waves. Meteorologists in the United States have used radar to predict the weather since the 1950s. Primarily, radar has been employed to detect precipitation associated with severe storms and fronts. Radar projects radio waves, which are immediately reflected off water vapor, raindrops, snow crystals, or hail.

New Advances. Recent modifications in radar imaging have enabled meteorologists to scan the images sent back for precipitation intensity. The radar image is received as a patchwork of colors covering the spectrum. The reds and violets indicate areas receiving the heaviest precipitation. Thus, by tracing the path of a storm, meteorologists can now predict where the heaviest precipitation is likely to occur.

Limitations. One of the limitations of radar is its range, less than 161 kilometers (100 miles). Nevertheless, the applications and importance of radar in the field of meteorology are increasing. For example, meteorologists now can see threatening weather conditions on the radar screen as well as the development of a storm from beginning to end. This enables them to issue weather advisories to the public on a timely basis.

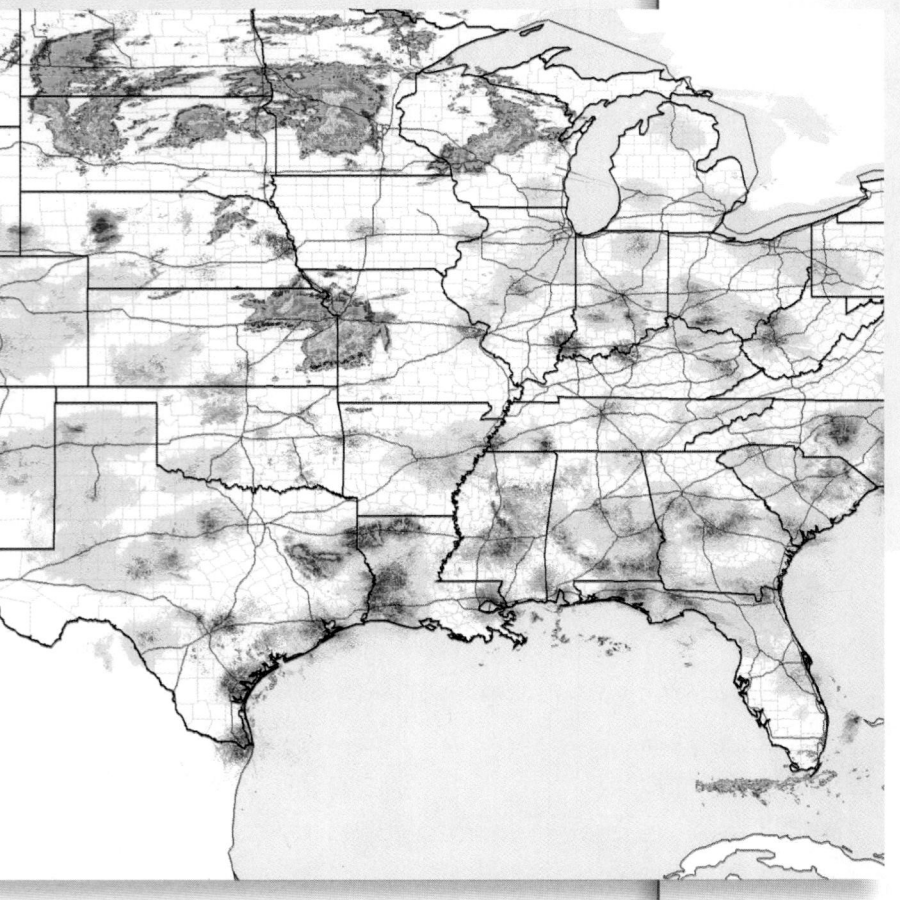

◀ **Radio waves** are reflected off various forms of precipitation. Radar sets collect the reflected waves and display them on a screen. Meteorologists analyze the images to make their forecasts.

DOPPLER RADAR

One of the more recent advances in radar technology was the development of *Doppler radar*. Doppler radar measures the speed of an object, either toward or away from the observation station. (See Doppler Effect, page 805.) The most important meteorological application of Doppler radar is the early detection of tornadoes. Doppler radar can be used to scan the motion inside severe thunderstorms for signs of the funnel cloud formation that precedes a tornado. Once a tornado funnel drops from the bottom of a cumulonimbus cloud, the image is quickly detected on the Doppler screen. This gives meteorologists—and their audience—increased warning time before the actual formation of a full-fledged tornado.

Doppler radar domes detect changes in wind speed and direction. They are an effective tool for forecasting severe storms.

CHANGING THE WEATHER

Meteorologists have devoted much time and effort to finding ways of changing the weather. Probably the single most researched technique of weather modification has been a method to increase rain and snowfall.

This illustration shows three methods of cloud seeding, a process that attempts to cause clouds to produce rain. In the first method, an airplane flies above the clouds and drops dry ice pellets into the clouds' updraft, *top*. The pellets chill water droplets inside the clouds, producing rain. In the second method, an airplane below the clouds releases salt particles into the updraft, *middle*. The particles attract water, forming large droplets that can fall as rain. The third method uses a ground-based generator that distributes vapor containing silver iodide crystals, *bottom*. The crystals stimulate the formation of rain-producing ice crystals.

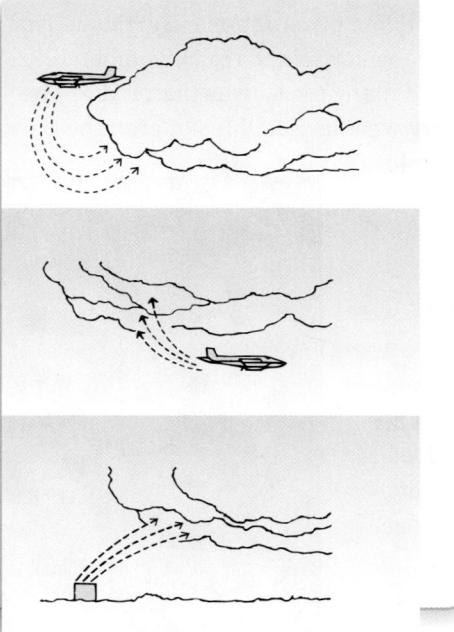

Satellites and Computers

Satellites

Weather satellites orbit Earth, collecting and sending back data that help meteorologists study and forecast the weather and climate. They measure several forms of *electromagnetic radiation* (energy moving through space), including ultraviolet and visible light, infrared radiation, and microwave radiation. They provide scientists with information on atmospheric properties, such as temperature, humidity, precipitation, ozone concentration, and wind speed and direction.

Presently, 120 nations take advantage of the network of orbiting and geostationary weather satellites that the United States has launched into space. A geostationary weather satellite is one that orbits at the precise speed of Earth's rotation, so it is always positioned over the same point on Earth. Today, thanks to weather satellites, television viewers can observe the entire country's weather system on news programs.

Tracking Hurricanes. One of the most important uses of satellite pictures by meteorologists is in tracking tropical cyclones and hurricanes. (See pages 544–547.) In many remote parts of the world, where land observations are not made, people must rely on satellite images. Without satellite observations, Hurricane Iwa, which struck the Hawaiian Islands in November 1982, would have claimed many more lives than it did. The images provided by weather satellites offered the only warning to meteorologists that Hurricane Iwa had made an abrupt turn directly toward the islands.

Satellite images help meteorologists predict the path that a hurricane will take, giving residents of an endangered area more time to prepare. ▶

APRIL 1960: U.S. LAUNCHES FIRST EXPERIMENTAL WEATHER SATELLITE

With the launching and operation of TIROS 1 (an acronym for *television infrared observation satellite*), meteorologists were finally able to obtain a world perspective on weather phenomena. Soon after it was launched, TIROS relayed the first photographs of cloud structures from the Pacific to the Atlantic Ocean.

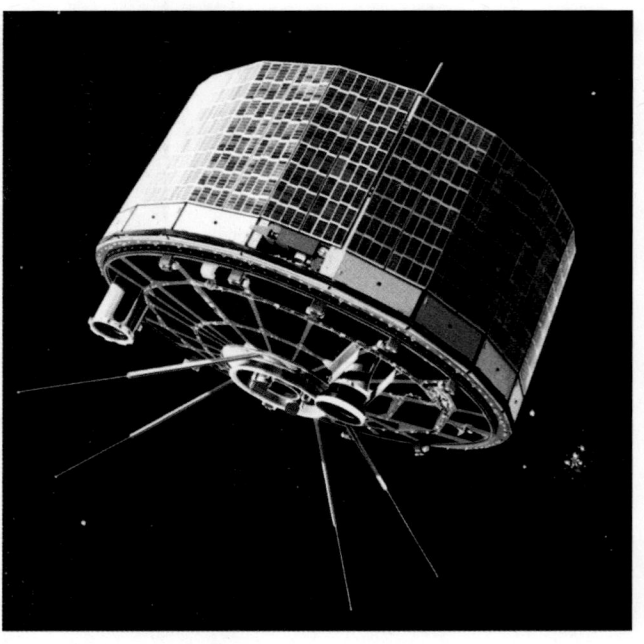

Computers

The most significant improvement in weather forecasting has been the use of computers. Computer processing speed has revolutionized the modern weather forecast.

Before the Computer. Prior to the 1950s, a battery of methods had to be used to analyze conditions in the atmosphere. Thousands of meteorologists compiled, analyzed, and interpreted data collected by weather balloons. The main problem these meteorologists faced was the amount of time it took to do an analysis. Weather forecasting was based on information that was between 12 and 24 hours old. By the time all the data were considered, the forecast usually did not accurately reflect the rapidly changing conditions in the atmosphere.

Weather computers have greatly increased the speed and accuracy of weather forecasts.

MARGIN OF ERROR

The output from a weather computer is not in a precise language. It shows squiggly lines indicating temperature and pressure for several levels of the atmosphere, patterns of precipitation, and wind-flow charts. Meteorologists must interpret the data, and just as different people will give varying accounts of what they witnessed at a crime scene, meteorologists will differ in their assessment of computer data. Therefore, different weather forecasts for the same location can sometimes vary dramatically.

Weather forecasts are usually accurate a day or two in advance, but not far beyond that.

Crunching the Numbers. Early in the 20th century, meteorologists teamed up with mathematicians to create a model to forecast the weather. They viewed weather phenomena as the end result of a three-dimensional interaction in Earth's troposphere. They developed formulas and equations to predict what would happen in the atmosphere based on known quantities such as wind speeds, temperatures, dew points, and barometric pressures.

Today advanced computers make calculations based on meteorologists' formulas and equations. But the laws governing the atmosphere are still not completely understood, and the use of calculus does not perfectly represent conditions in the atmosphere.

Despite the drawbacks, numerical forecasting is currently the common method of predicting the weather. While computer projections using formulas and equations have yet to forecast weather conditions accurately more than 3 days in advance, they are relatively accurate on a short-term basis (24 to 36 hours).

CLIMATE is the average weather in a specific place over a long period of time. Climate results from many different factors. Weather variables such as heat, moisture, and wind are some of the factors that govern the climate of an area. In addition, temperature and moisture-bearing winds are sometimes affected by local conditions, resulting in a wide variety of climates. Climate also changes with time. For example, a thousand years ago, northern latitudes were milder than they are today.

Factors Affecting Climate

Climates vary from place to place because of five main factors:

- **latitude** (distance from the equator)
- **altitude** (height above sea level)
- **topography** (surface features)
- **distance** from oceans and large lakes
- **atmospheric circulation**

Latitude

Energy from the sun reaches Earth in the form of solar radiation. The total energy that Earth receives as solar radiation is called *insolation*. The amount of insolation that a particular location receives is determined by the angle at which the sun's rays strike Earth, and the amount of daylight during each day. Each factor is governed by the location's latitude. (See page 504.)

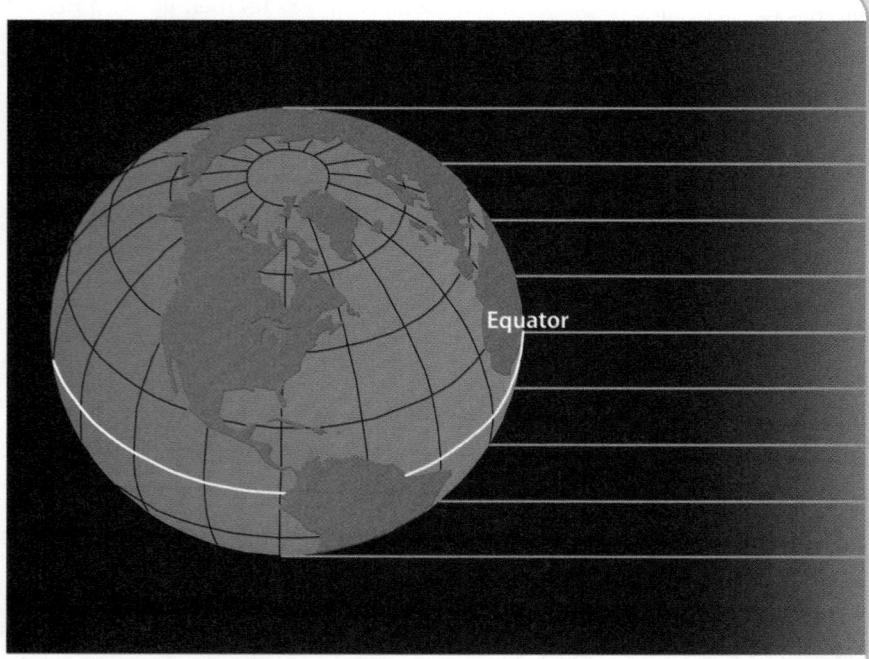

Latitude. The energy in the sun's rays spreads out over a greater surface area the farther the rays are from the equator, producing cooler climates.

Near the Equator:

- the sun's rays are almost always vertical
- the period of daylight does not change much throughout the year
- regions receive more insolation than any other part of the world

In the Higher Latitudes:

- near the poles, solar rays are more slanted when they strike Earth
- temperatures are lower
- during winter, nights are long and days are short
- during summer, high latitudes have very long periods of daylight
- summer temperatures are much higher than winter temperatures

Topography affects climate. Mountains, for instance, cause warm, moist air to rise and release moisture. The land behind the mountains is often dry because the air has lost most of its moisture by that point.

warm, moist air

Sea

rain shadow

Altitude

Altitude—height above sea level—affects climate in a simple way: the higher you go, the colder it gets.

- in the troposphere, air temperature decreases at an average rate of 1°C per 300 meters (3.5°F per 1,000 feet)

- high-altitude locations have lower average temperatures than locations at sea level, even along the same parallel of latitude

- the summits of some tall mountains along the equator are covered with snow and ice

 *Air pressure decreases with altitude. At altitudes over 2,100 meters (7,000 feet), many people experience altitude sickness. Altitude sickness is caused by a lack of oxygen in the blood and body tissues. It can result in nausea, headaches, fluid in the lungs, and even death.*

Topography

The surface features of a region—its *topography*—affect temperature and the development of clouds and precipitation.

- changes in temperature occur when large air masses move across mountains

- the air mass cools as it rises on the *windward* side of a mountain—the side facing the wind

- the water in the air condenses as it cools, forming clouds

- some of the rainiest, snowiest places on Earth are on windward slopes

- when an air mass descends on the *leeward* side of the mountain—the side away from the wind—it is drier and becomes warmer

- clouds thin out or vanish

- on the leeward side, dry warm winds develop, called *foehn* or *chinook* winds

Factors Affecting Climate

Distance from Water

Oceans and large lakes make the air temperature less extreme in places downwind of them. This is because bodies of water heat up and cool off more slowly than land.

- Warm surface waters are mixed by waves and currents and are continuously replaced by cooler water below.

- When surface water is cool, convection currents force the cool water to sink, replacing it with warmer water from below.

- Water retains heat for a longer period of time, so it cools off more slowly than land.

- Water temperature strongly influences the temperature of the air above it.

- Places that are immediately downwind of large bodies of water have milder winters and cooler summers than inland places at the same latitude.

Distance from Water. Water has a higher *specific heat* than land, meaning water requires more heat than land does to increase its temperature the same number of degrees. ▶

OCEAN CURRENTS

For its latitude, the temperatures of northwestern Europe are unusually high. The reason? Ocean currents. A warm ocean current called the North Atlantic Drift, along with prevailing westerly winds, directs warm air toward European coastal regions. The southwestern coast of Alaska has a mild climate for the same reason. In contrast, the Gulf Stream, another warm ocean current, has little effect on the climate of the east coast of North America. In this case, the prevailing westerly winds blow warm air away from the coast.

◀ **The Gulf Stream** originates in the western Caribbean Sea and flows northeast along the North American coast. But because of westerly winds, the Gulf Stream does not significantly affect the climate of the coast.

MONSOONS

Monsoons are powerful seasonal winds caused by the uneven heating and cooling of oceans and continents. In summer, the land heats up faster and to a greater extent than the ocean. As a result, a low-pressure center forms over the continent with winds blowing from the ocean toward the land.

During the winter, the continent becomes much colder than the ocean. The wind direction then reverses—with air moving from the land to the ocean. Monsoons are most commonly found where large continents and oceans are situated close together near the equator.

Summer monsoons hit India hard, carrying huge amounts of moisture from their trip over the ocean and bringing extremely heavy rainfall. ▶

Atmospheric Circulation

Six belts of wind encircle Earth, influencing climate by distributing heat and moisture. (See page 536.)

Trade Winds

1. that blow between the equator and 30° north

2. that blow between the equator and 30° south

Westerlies (winds from the west)

3. that blow between 30° and 60° north of the equator

4. that blow between 30° and 60° south of the equator

Polar Winds

5. north of 60° north latitude

6. south of 60° south latitude

As the seasons change, the global wind belts shift north and south. In the spring, they move toward the poles. In the fall, they shift toward the equator. These shifts help explain why some areas have distinct rainy seasons and dry seasons.

Trade winds north of the equator blow from the northeast. South of the equator, they blow from the southeast. The trade winds of the two hemispheres meet near the equator, causing air to rise. As the rising air cools, clouds and rain develop. The resulting band of cloudy and rainy weather near the equator is called the *doldrums.*

Westerlies blow from the southwest in the Northern Hemisphere and from the northwest in the Southern Hemisphere. Over broad regions centered at 30° latitude, surface winds are light or calm. The air is warm and dry. Tropical deserts, such as the Sahara of Africa, occur under these regions of descending air.

Polar winds blow from the northeast in the Arctic and from the southeast in the Antarctic. In the Northern Hemisphere, the polar front forms at the boundary between the cold polar easterly winds and the mild westerly winds. Where the air masses overlap, storms can develop and move along the polar front, bringing cloudy weather, rain, or snow.

CLIMATE ZONES divide

Earth into three distinct regions based on temperature and average annual precipitation: the *tropical zone, middle latitude zone,* and *polar zone*. The tropical zone is the warm zone near the equator. The middle latitude zone is located between the tropical zone and the polar regions. The polar zone is located near the North and South poles. Various climate types are found within each of the climate zones. The climate types are distinguished mainly by differences in the amount of precipitation.

Tropical Climates

The tropical climates are the warmest on Earth. They lie on either side of the equator, within about 30 degrees of latitude. Earth receives the maximum amount of *insolation,* or solar radiation, in this zone, where the sun always is directly or nearly directly overhead at noon. To be classified as tropical, a region must have a yearly average temperature above 19°C (68°F).

On the equator and directly around it is the belt of the doldrums. The doldrums receive abundant rainfall and are warm and humid throughout the year. In the belts of the trade winds—farther north and south of the equator—the climate becomes drier.

Tropical Climates			
Climate	**Rainfall and Temperature**	**Features**	**Regions of the World**
Tropical Rain Forest	• warm, humid • averages 250 cm (100 in.) rainfall per year	• dense growth of tall trees • greater amounts of rain on the windward sides of mountain slopes	• central Africa • the Amazon basin • parts of Central America • Indonesia • the Malay peninsula • the southern tip of Florida
Savanna	• relatively dry • during wet season, 13 to 25 cm (5 to 10 in.) rainfall per month • during dry season, months may pass with no rain	• distinct wet and dry seasons • caused by seasonal movement of the doldrums	• Sudan of North Africa • southern Africa • northern Australia
Tropical Desert	• little rainfall • daytime temperatures frequently exceed 35°C (100°F) • Earth's highest temperature—more than 50°C (136.4°F)—was recorded in a North African desert • night temperatures in the tropical desert may frequently dip below 10°C (50°F)	• Earth's driest climates • located between 20° and 25° latitude, within the belt of the trade winds • usually are found in the western half of a continent or on the west side of a mountain range	Largest deserts: • the Sahara of North Africa • the Kalahari of southern Africa • the Arabian of the Middle East • the tropical desert located in central Australia Smaller tropical and subtropical deserts: • along the coast of Peru • northern Mexico • parts of the southwest United States
Tropical Steppe	• rainfall slightly higher than in the tropical deserts	• often completely surround tropical deserts • many kinds of drought-resistant vegetation	• regions bordering the tropical deserts and extending into the middle latitude zone

The tropical rain forest on the Hawaiian island of Kauai receives about 1,150 centimeters (450 inches) of rainfall each year.

Middle Latitudes

The middle latitude climate zone experiences a wide variety of weather. This is because the middle latitudes are located where wave cyclones develop—at the boundary between polar and equatorial air masses. The two most distinctive features of the middle latitude climates are the daily weather changes and the changing seasons. The middle latitudes also face extreme temperature and precipitation differences among its climate types.

One major factor producing the variety of climate types in this zone is the prevalence of continents. Most of the world's continents are in the middle latitudes, particularly in the Northern Hemisphere. The largest part of Asia, North America, and Europe are about halfway between the equator and the North Pole.

Because the prevailing winds in the middle latitudes are westerlies, the western coastal sections of the continents are usually wet. Westerlies bring in moisture from the ocean and release most of their precipitation before traveling far inland. As a result, the interiors of continents are relatively dry in the middle latitudes. The eastern parts of continents in the middle latitude climate zone tend to have an alternating wet and dry season, often produced by monsoons.

Sunshine is the rule in Mediterranean climates. Even during the rainy winter, it is rarely cloudy for more than 24 hours. The Mediterranean climate is found all along the shores of the Mediterranean Sea. This image shows the beautiful coast of Greece.

Middle Latitude Climates

Climate	Rainfall and Temperature	Features	Regions of the World
Mediterranean	• warm, dry summers • temperatures average about 23°C (75°F) • mild winters, coldest month averages about 8°C (45°F) • 40 to 60 cm (15 to 25 in.) of rain per year, mostly in winter	• lots of sunshine common • found along the west coasts of continents, between 30° and 40° latitude • summers are warm and dry • variable winter weather	• shores of the Mediterranean Sea • southernmost part of South Africa • central Chile • southern Australia • southern and central coastal California
Humid Subtropical	• temperature similar to Mediterranean • twice as much rainfall as Mediterranean • rains throughout the year	• occurs along the eastern sides of continents in middle latitudes • humid summers	• eastern and southern regions of Asia • northern Argentina • Uruguay • southern Brazil • southeastern United States
Marine West Coast	• heavy precipitation—about 75 cm (30 in.) per year • very heavy rainfall—255 to 380 cm (100 to 150 in.)—where mountain ranges block westerlies	• occurs from about 40° latitude to the south edge of the polar regions • continuous flow of cool, moist air blown inland by the prevailing westerlies	• southern Chile • northwestern Europe • western Australia • coastal Oregon and Washington • British Columbia
Middle Latitude Desert	• hot summers • extremely cold winters • little annual precipitation, less than 25 cm (10 in.)	• middle latitude deserts merge into the semiarid steppe climate, which has more abundant vegetation	• China • Mongolia • Nevada and Utah • Argentina
Humid Continental	• average annual rainfall of at least 75 cm (30 in.) • summer temperatures average more than 25°C (80 °F) • average January temperature down to −1°C (30°F) or less	• occurs along the eastern margins of continents • climate influenced by the west-to-east movement of storms • rainfall produced mostly by winter storms and summer thunderstorms	• found only on the large continents of the Northern Hemisphere • eastern Europe • eastern Asia • eastern half of North America
Subarctic	• short, warm summer • extremely cold winter; coldest month averages about −34°C (−30°F) • dry, receives less than 30 cm (15 in.) precipitation per year, mainly as snow and ice	• between 50° and 65° latitude • very warm summers due to long periods of summer daylight	• found in a band across Europe and Asia, from Sweden and Finland east through northern Siberia to the Pacific Ocean • in North America, extends from Alaska across Canada and on to Labrador

Polar Climates

The polar climates have no summer as we know it. During summer months at these latitudes, the sun's rays strike Earth too indirectly to provide much heat. The frigid polar winter can last for up to 6 months; it is characterized by perpetual night. Polar climates also are very dry because the air is too cold at these extreme latitudes to be able to hold much moisture.

An ice cap covers most of Greenland—the remains of the last continental ice sheet that blanketed North America about 25,000 years ago. ▼

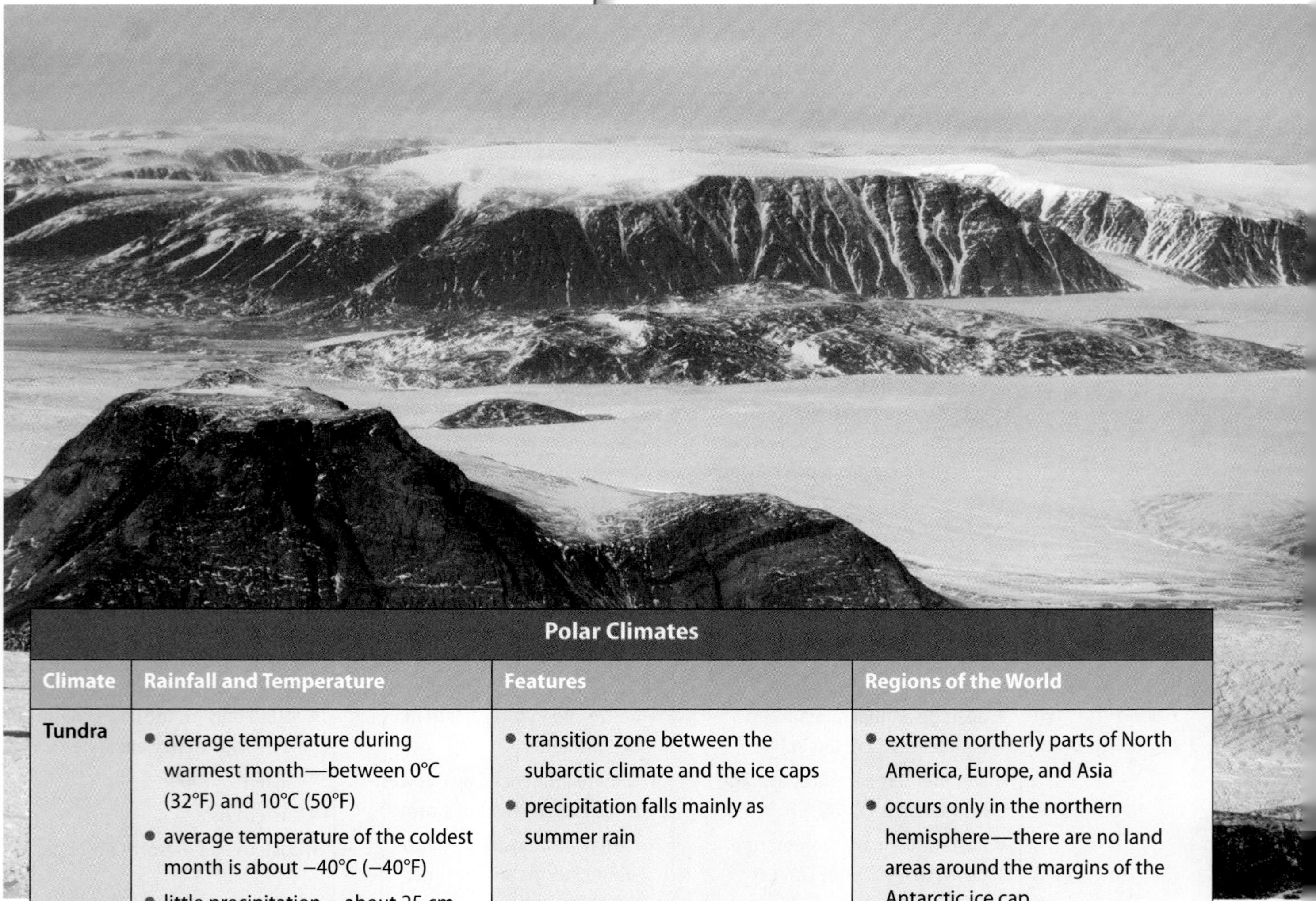

Polar Climates			
Climate	**Rainfall and Temperature**	**Features**	**Regions of the World**
Tundra	• average temperature during warmest month—between 0°C (32°F) and 10°C (50°F) • average temperature of the coldest month is about −40°C (−40°F) • little precipitation—about 25 cm (10 in.) a year	• transition zone between the subarctic climate and the ice caps • precipitation falls mainly as summer rain	• extreme northerly parts of North America, Europe, and Asia • occurs only in the northern hemisphere—there are no land areas around the margins of the Antarctic ice cap
Ice Cap	• air temperature never rises above 0°C (32°F) • any precipitation that falls accumulates on the surface of the ice cap	• in the immediate vicinity of the North and South poles • consists of polar ice and snow fields • lowest temperature ever recorded on Earth, −87°C (−125°F), occurred on the Antarctic ice cap	• found over most of Greenland • Antarctica • the Arctic

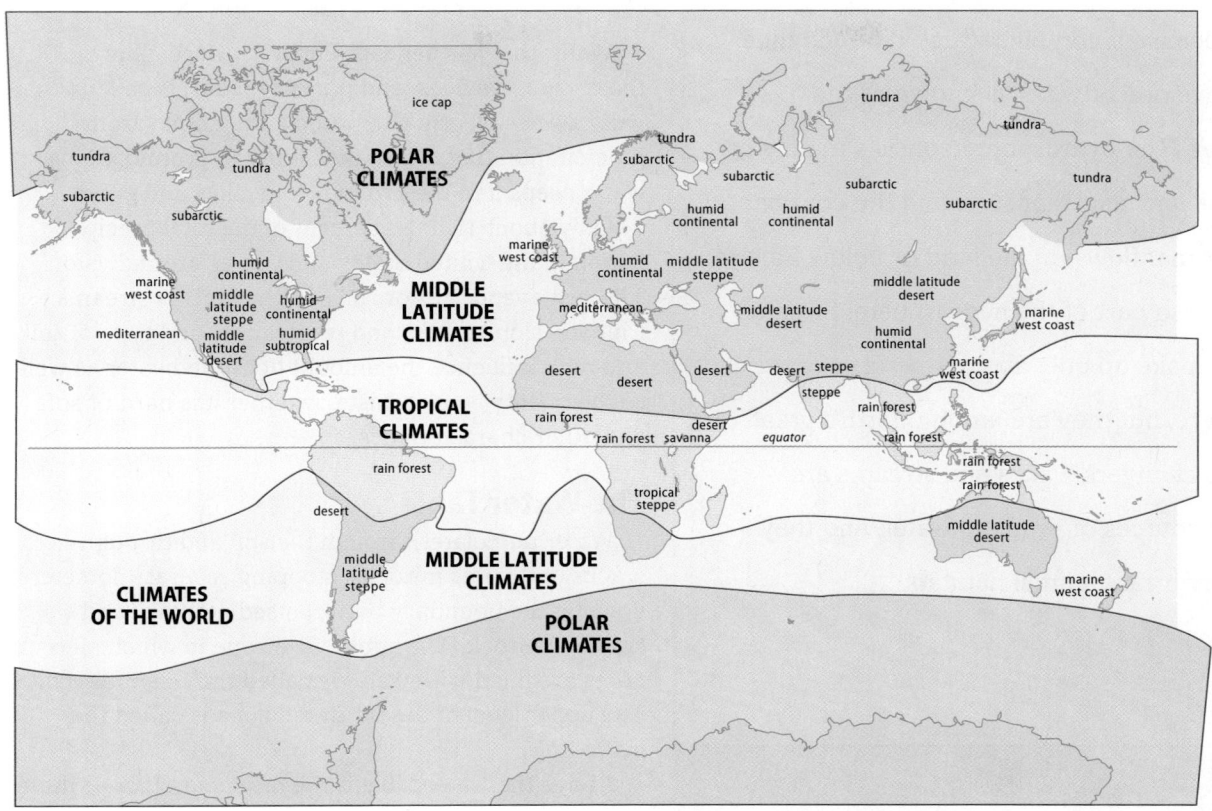

Climates of the World. Polar climates dominate the areas around the North and South poles. Middle latitude climates occur between about 30° north and 30° south of the equator and the polar climates. Tropical climates occur in regions near the equator.

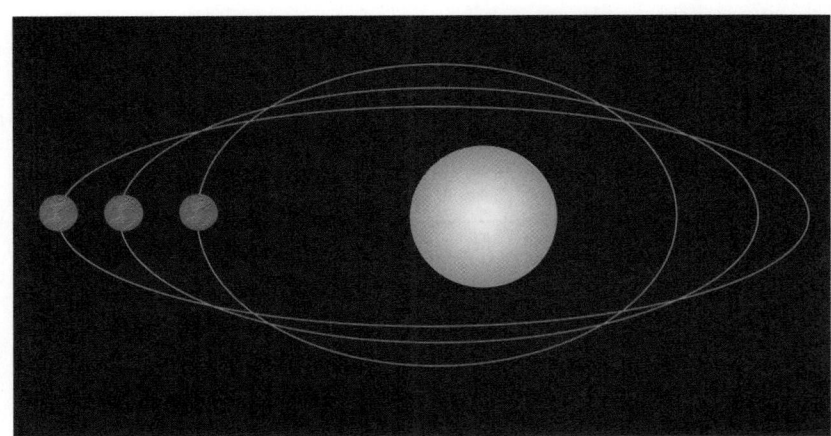

▲ **Earth's orbit** follows a path that changes over a period of 100,000 years. This change in orbit alters the distance from the earth to the sun at different times of year, varying the amount of sunlight hitting the earth. (Diagram not to scale.)

CLIMATE AND EARTH'S ORBIT

Earth's orbit is always *elliptical,* or shaped like a flattened circle. But during the 100,000-year cycle, the amount of flatness changes from a maximum to a minimum, then back to the maximum. Changes in Earth's orbit about the sun may cause climate changes over tens of thousands to hundreds of thousands of years.

Climatologists believe that these cycles may have caused major fluctuations in the planet's glacial ice cover during the Pleistocene Epoch, the period from about 2.6 million years ago to 11,500 years ago. The three cycles probably produced temperature changes that caused the ice cover to expand and contract at regular intervals. (See pages 514–517.)

HYDROSPHERE

Earth is unique among the planets in our solar system because it contains water in abundance. Earth's envelope of water is known as the *hydrosphere*. The hydrosphere consists mainly of the oceans and seas that surround the continents. The water that flows on the land or below Earth's surface is also part of the hydrosphere. Streams and lakes make up only about 1 percent of the hydrosphere, but they are among Earth's great landscape changers. Lakes and streams are important sources of drinking water, and they provide important animal habitats.

Groundwater

Water that lies beneath Earth's surface, filling the cracks, crevices, and pores of rocks, is called *groundwater*. Nearly all groundwater comes from precipitation that has soaked into the ground. Some water seeps into the ground from lakes and ponds.

Only about 15 to 20 percent of the total precipitation in the United States ends up as groundwater. The rest evaporates or runs off the land as streams. Climate, slope of the land, vegetation, and type of soil and rock influence the amount of groundwater as well as the quality—color, taste, whether it is hard or soft, and other characteristics.

The Water Table

Water percolates through the soil and through cracks and pores in rocks, stopping several kilometers down at the boundary between sedimentary and crystalline rock. The subsurface zone in which all rock pores are filled with water is called the *saturated zone*. The upper level of the saturated zone is called the *water table*.

Above the water table is the *unsaturated zone*, where rock openings are filled partly with air and partly with water. The roots of plants usually get their water from the soil near the top of the unsaturated zone, where fine-grained clay minerals hold moisture.

The Water Table. Groundwater flows slowly through underground rock, but faster if the water table slopes. ▼

Wells. Groundwater is an important source of water for humans. A *well* is a deep hole dug or drilled into the ground to penetrate an aquifer below the saturated zone. Water tapped by a well is generally lifted or pumped to the surface.

Artesian Wells. When a well is drilled into a sloping aquifer, the water pressure forces water up the well. If the water rises above the level of the aquifer without pumping, the well is called an *artesian well*. In some artesian wells, the water is under such pressure that it spouts continuously into the air.

The Well Runs Dry. During dry seasons, the water table falls as water flows out of the saturated zone into springs and rivers. Thus, shallow wells run dry during these seasons, but they are replenished as new water is added to the saturated zone.

SPRINGS AND AQUIFERS

A **spring** is a place where water flows naturally from rock onto the land surface. Most springs discharge water where the water table intersects the land surface. Springs also are found where water flows out from caverns or along fractures or faults that come to the surface.

An **aquifer** is a body of saturated rock or sediment through which water can move easily. Aquifers are porous and permeable, so wells are frequently drilled into aquifers to reach substantial sources of water.

HOT SPRINGS

If a spring's water is warmer than human body temperature, it is called a *hot spring*. Groundwater can gain heat in two ways.

1. Most commonly, groundwater circulates near a body of hot magma or cooling igneous rock. In the U.S., most hot springs are found in western regions associated with recent volcanic activity, such as Yellowstone National Park. (See page 454.)

2. Groundwater can also gain heat if it circulates deeply underground along a major fault. For example, water circulating at a depth of 2 or 3 kilometers (about 1.5 to 2 miles) is warmed substantially above normal surface water temperatures. Because warm water is lighter than cold water, it readily rises to the surface.

A geyser is a hot spring that periodically erupts hot water and steam. ▶

Streams and Lakes

Earth has a tremendous amount of water, but almost all of it is in the oceans. Only about 3 percent of the water on Earth is fresh water, and most of that is locked in icecaps and other glaciers or is under Earth's surface. Streams and lakes contain only about one-fiftieth of one percent of Earth's water.

Streams

A body of running water that is confined in a channel and pulled downhill by gravity is called a *stream*. In common terminology, rivers are large, streams are somewhat smaller, and creeks are even smaller. To Earth scientists, however, they are all streams.

A stream fills its *channel*, which is a long, narrow depression shaped by the stream. The channel may be cut into solid rock or into loose sediment. The banks of a stream are the sides of the channels, and the bed of the stream is the bottom of the channel. Only during a flood will a stream spill over its banks.

A stream—according to Earth scientists—is any body of running water, whether it's a small trickle or a large river like the Colorado River pictured here. ▼

Lakes

A lake is a body of water surrounded by land. Lakes may be found in all parts of the world. Almost any depression on the surface of Earth may become a lake or pond during wet periods. Most lakes are relatively temporary features of the landscape. Even the largest lake generally exists for a much shorter period of geologic time than other landscape features, such as mountains or deep canyons.

SALT LAKES

Salt lakes, like the Great Salt Lake in Utah, usually start out as freshwater lakes. When a freshwater lake has no outlet, all the water it loses is through evaporation. As water evaporates, it leaves behind dissolved salts and minerals. The higher concentration of salts makes the remaining water saltier. The total salt content of the Great Salt Lake is about 25 percent.

How Lakes Form.

The greatest number of lakes were formed by glaciers. As glaciers traveled downslope, they carved basins that then filled with water to form lakes. Lake basins also form as a result of movements in Earth's crust known as *faulting*. When a river deposits enough silt to close the natural outlet to the sea, the water backs up and a lake forms. Dam construction creates great artificial lakes that are called *reservoirs*.

How Lakes Disappear.

Many lakes disappear when their basins fill with sediment. Streams carry sediments into lakes, forming deltas that eventually fill in entire lake basins.

The growth of vegetation around lake borders frequently destroys lakes. The plants advance into the lake, accumulating sediment around the borders. The lake becomes a bog or marsh, then fills in completely and disappears.

In addition, a drought or a change in climate can cause a lake to dry up.

▲ **The Great Lakes,** a group of five lakes in the United States and Canada, are the largest group of lakes in the world. They contain 18 percent of the world's fresh water.

VOLCANIC LAKES

Lakes can develop out of the violent eruptions of volcanoes. A lake basin can be produced when lava flows from an erupting volcano and builds a dam across an existing valley. The basin is then filled by streams or with rainwater. Extinct volcanoes may also be the site of lake basins when a *caldera*, or large crater, fills in with water. (See pages 452–453.)

◄ **Crater Lake** in Oregon, located in a gigantic caldera, is a well-known example of a lake formed in the crater of an extinct volcano.

OCEANS

OCEANS and seas cover more than 70 percent of Earth's surface. Usually the oceans are considered to be separate bodies of water, but all of Earth's oceans are actually sections of one great sea that covers most of the planet. There are no natural divisions of the seafloor to separate one ocean from another.

Oceanography is a field of study that employs all of the sciences in order to understand the world's oceans. It is generally divided into four separate fields: chemical oceanography, physical oceanography, geological oceanography, and biological oceanography.

Salty Seas

Chemical oceanography is the study of seawater, its composition, and the chemical reactions it undergoes with marine plants and animals.

Seawater Composition

The ocean likely contains every natural chemical element, but seawater is best known for its salts. Every 45 kilograms (100 pounds) of seawater yields about 1.5 kilograms (3.5 pounds) of dissolved minerals. This means that the *salinity,* or average salt content, of seawater is about 3.5 percent.

The most abundant mineral salts in the ocean are those that are most soluble in water, especially sodium chloride. Other dissolved compounds in seawater in their order of abundance are magnesium chloride, magnesium sulfate, calcium sulfate, potassium sulfate, calcium carbonate, and magnesium bromide.

Earth's oceans are usually thought of as separate bodies of water, but they are actually all sections of one great sea that covers most of the planet. There are no natural divisions of the seafloor to separate one ocean from another. ▼

Factors Affecting Salinity

Evaporation. Evaporation removes fresh water from the ocean surface, leaving behind the salts. Evaporation in subtropical areas is greater than precipitation, so these areas have especially salty surface waters.

Precipitation. Precipitation returns fresh water to the ocean. Closer to the equator, precipitation is greater than evaporation, making surface waters less salty there.

Rivers. Rivers bring fresh water to the ocean, which lowers the salinity of seawater near river mouths.

Rock. Many minerals in the ocean come chiefly from the dissolving of rocks on land. As rocks break down, rivers carry the resulting minerals to the ocean.

ANCIENT SEAWATER

The composition of seawater today is much different than it was in the first ocean, which formed about 4 billion years ago. Scientists believe this first ocean was filled by water vapor released from volcanic eruptions. The water vapor was not salty. Ocean water became salty only after millions of years of streams and runoff flowed over the land into the ocean basins. As running water eroded the land, elements such as sodium, chlorine, and magnesium were dissolved and carried into the ocean.

Composition of Seawater	
Elements and Compounds	Parts per Million
Hydrogen H_2O* Oxygen	108,000 857,000
Chlorine Cl	19,000
Sodium Na	10,500
Magnesium Mg	1,350
Sulfates SO_4	885
Calcium Ca	400
Potassium K	380
Bromine Br	65
Carbon C	28
Strontium St	8
Boron B	4.6
Silica SiO_2	3.0
Fluorine Fl	1.0
Nitrogen N	0.5
Lithium Li	0.17
Rubidium Ru	0.12
Phosphorus P	0.07
Iodine I	0.06
Iron Fe	0.01

*96.5 percent of seawater is freshwater—a compound of hydrogen and oxygen (H_2O).

◄ **Creatures of the ocean,** like this blue whale, can only survive in saltwater.

Physical Oceanography

Physical oceanography is the study of the physical characteristics of the ocean, including the motion of seawater, as well as the interaction of the ocean with the atmosphere. Among the important properties of seawater are its salinity, temperature, and density. Variations in any of these properties result in horizontal and vertical water movements. Physical oceanographers also study water movements, such as currents, waves, and tides. (See pages 574–575.)

Temperature. The most commonly measured physical property of oceans is their temperature. The ocean's surface temperature is closely related to latitude and seasonal change.

For example, more heat per square kilometer or square mile is received at the equator than at the poles, and more heat is received during summer than in winter.

The surface of the ocean is heated in three ways.

- radiation from the sun
- conduction of heat from the atmosphere
- condensation of water vapor

In the open ocean, there are three main temperature layers.	
Surface layer	warm and well-mixed, with a thickness of 150 to 300 meters (500 to 1,000 feet)
Thermocline	a transition layer with a thickness of between 300 and 900 meters (1,000 to 3,000 feet); water temperature decreases quickly, at a rate of 1°C per meter
Lowest layer	a cold layer of seawater several kilometers thick; becomes slowly colder the closer it lies to the ocean bottom; ocean temperature ranges between 1° and 4°C (34° and 39°F) near the bottom

HOW SALT CHANGES WATER

Some of the properties of seawater are like those of freshwater, such as the capacity it has to either absorb or give off heat energy. However, four important changes take place in the properties of water with the addition of salt.

1. The *specific heat* of water decreases as salinity increases. Consequently, the boiling point of seawater rises with increasing salinity. When seawater evaporates, most of the salts stay behind, increasing the salinity of the remaining solution.

2. The *density* of water increases with the addition of salts. Pure water is most dense at 4°C (39°F). The addition of salt lowers the temperature of maximum density. The maximum density of seawater occurs at −3.5°C (26°F).

3. The *freezing point* of water is lowered with the addition of salt. The effect of salinity and temperature on water density results in water with the greatest density in the ocean being the coldest and saltiest.

4. The *vapor pressure*—a measure of how easily water molecules escape from the liquid phase into the gaseous—is lowered with increasing salinity. This is because the salts make it more difficult for water molecules to evaporate, and freshwater evaporates much more quickly than seawater.

Water depth

0	
656 ft (200 m)	
1,640 ft (500 m)	
4,921 ft (1,500 m)	
9,843 ft (3,000 m)	
16,404 ft (5,000 m)	
22,966 ft (7,000 m)	
29,528 ft (9,000 m)	
36,089 ft (11,000 m)	

Density increases as	
salinity increases	↑
temperature decreases	↓
pressure increases	↑

Temperature and Density. The densest water sinks to the bottom of the ocean floor. The coldest, densest, saltiest water is found where the ocean is the deepest.

Density. Another important physical property of water is its density. Density is important to physical ocean-ographers because it affects the movement of ocean currents.

The density of seawater is slightly greater than the density of freshwater. Density of seawater is controlled by three variables: salinity, temperature, and pressure. Colder, deeper, and saltier water is usually the densest water.

Because of gravity and buoyancy, dense seawater sinks and less dense seawater rises to the ocean's surface. This movement results in a kind of density layering in the ocean.

Winds and waves keep the upper 100 meters (300 feet) of the ocean well mixed. Therefore, these surface waters have a fairly uniform density.

Below this surface layer of seawater, large changes in temperature and salinity produce a rapid increase in density. Consequently, from this point downward, seawater becomes progressively denser until it reaches the ocean floor.

Water in Motion

The water of the ocean is in constant motion. Vast currents move across the oceans of the world in complex parts. Some of the factors that cause ocean currents are

- wind.
- Earth's rotation.
- seawater density and temperature.

Wind. Currents close to the ocean's surface are caused almost entirely by the wind. The wind pushes water into currents that flow parallel to Earth's surface.

Earth's Rotation. The spinning of the planet causes the path of a moving object to veer from a straight line. (See page 547.) Ocean currents shift to the right in the Northern Hemisphere and to the left in the Southern Hemisphere.

TRAVELING TURTLES

The Gulf Stream is a major ocean current that flows from the Caribbean Sea, through the Gulf of Mexico, then northeast along the North American coast. Loggerhead sea turtles, like the one at right, use the Gulf Stream to guide them on a migration that eventually takes them across the Atlantic Ocean.

Density and Temperature. Heating of the oceans in the warmer climates near the equator, combined with cooling near the poles, also produces ocean currents. Since water becomes slightly heavier when cooled, the cold water from the polar regions tends to sink.

Conversely, the warmer water near the equator tends to remain near the surface of the sea, so there is a slow but steady movement of very cold water along the seafloor toward the equator. Water near the seafloor is always near freezing, even in tropical climates.

Gyres flow clockwise in the subtropics of the Northern Hemisphere and counterclockwise in the subtropics of the Southern Hemisphere. ▼

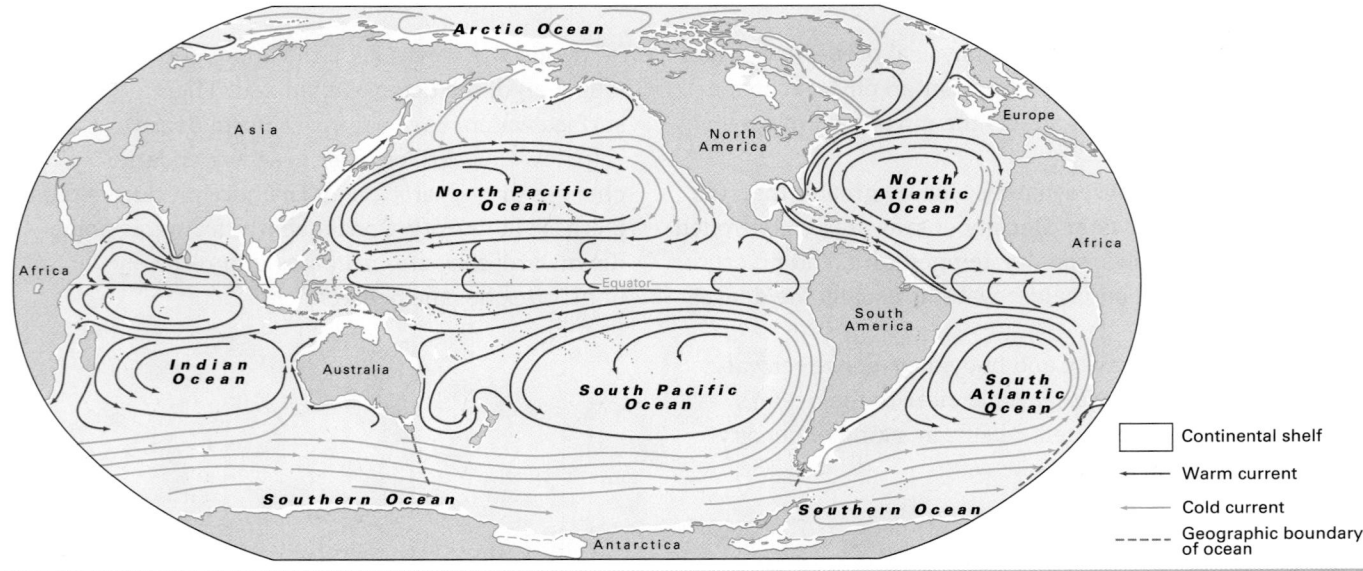

Surface Currents

Earth's wind systems produce the surface currents of the ocean. The force of the wind mainly affects the water within the upper 300 meters (1,000 feet) of the ocean.

Gyres. Wind-driven currents move in enormous circular patterns called *gyres*. Several conditions influence the direction of wind-driven currents and make them form gyres. Earth's wind systems drive the currents in an easterly or westerly direction. Continents direct the flow toward the north or south.

Upwelling. In some areas, *upwelling* occurs when winds cause surface waters near the coast to move offshore. Colder, deeper waters, which are rich in nutrients, then rise to the surface near the coast. The upwelling of deeper waters provides nutrients for the growth of phytoplankton, which fish and other sea animals eat.

Upwelling areas have great numbers of fish and, in fact, yield half of the world's fish catch. Important upwelling regions include the coasts of Peru and northwestern Africa, as well as along the equator and around Antarctica.

El Niño. The east-to-west winds and currents over the tropical Pacific weaken or even reverse when an El Niño is present, and the pattern of heavy rainfall shifts eastward.

EL NIÑO

One of the best examples of how an ocean current can affect the global climate and the environment can be seen in *El Niño*, a phenomenon caused by a warm ocean current flowing off the coast of western South America.

During an El Niño, winds cause a current of warm water to flow south from Ecuador down the coastlines of Peru and Chile. An El Niño occurs about every 2 to 7 years and lasts about 18 months.

The warm waters result in a dramatic decline of the amount of plankton—small floating plants and animals—as well as of the fish that eat plankton, and, in turn, of the sea birds that eat the fish.

An El Niño is caused by a buildup of westward trade winds. The buildup results in an increase in the amount of warm water carried westward. When the winds weaken, the warm water sloshes back eastward toward the western coast of South America, producing an El Niño.

Currents, Tides, and Waves

In addition to the wind-driven surface currents, strong currents also flow deep beneath the ocean surface. The most powerful deep currents, known as *density currents*, are caused by the sinking of water as it becomes denser from cooling or from an increase in salt content.

The world ocean would rise about 60 meters (200 feet) if the Greenland and Antarctic ice sheets should suddenly melt. New York City would be submerged, with only the tops of the tallest buildings above water.

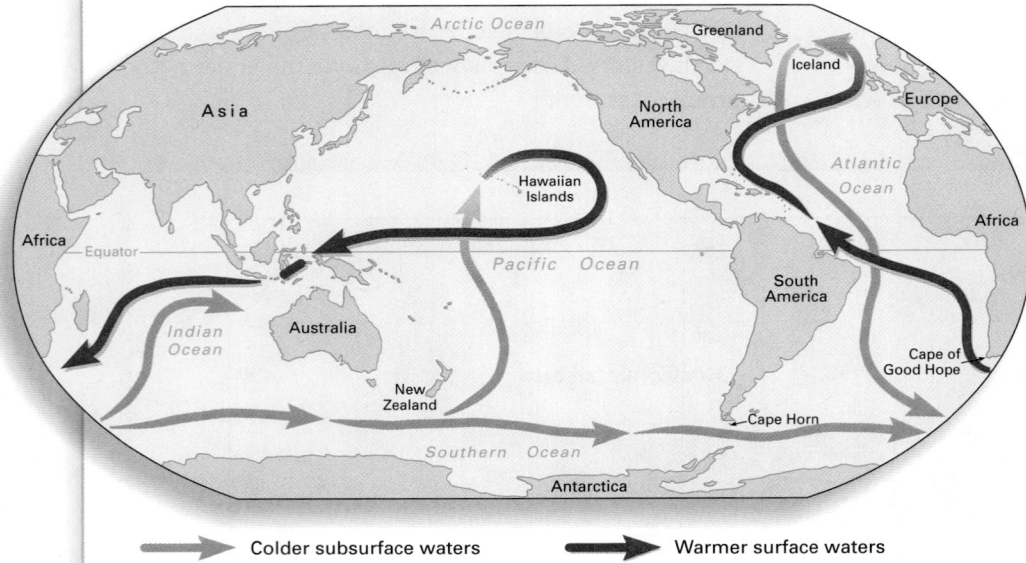

Colder subsurface waters   Warmer surface waters

◀ **Thermohaline circulation** occurs when cold, dense water in the polar regions sinks and spreads toward the equator. There, the water warms up and rises to the surface, then spreads back toward the polar regions. Water in thermohaline circulation takes about 1,000 years to complete a global circuit.

Deep Currents

One type of density current is called *thermohaline circulation*. Thermohaline circulation is a convection process in which dense cold water from high latitudes sinks and flows slowly toward the equator. As the water moves toward the equator, it warms, rises, and flows back again toward the poles. In this way, the ocean water of the entire world is mixed.

Thermohaline circulation occurs primarily in two places: the North Atlantic Ocean and the Antarctic.

In the North Atlantic, cold, heavy water sinks and moves southward across the equator.

In the Antarctic region, cold, heavy water sinks and moves northward across the equator.

Tides and Waves

In addition to the circulation of ocean water by surface and deep-sea currents, there are other, more familiar, motions of seawater, such as the periodic movements of the sea called tides and waves.

Tides are the daily rising and falling of sea level. They are related to the gravitational pull of the moon and sun on Earth.

Waves are produced by the action of winds on the surface of the ocean. (See pages 576–577.)

HOW DOES THAT WORK

OCEAN TIDES

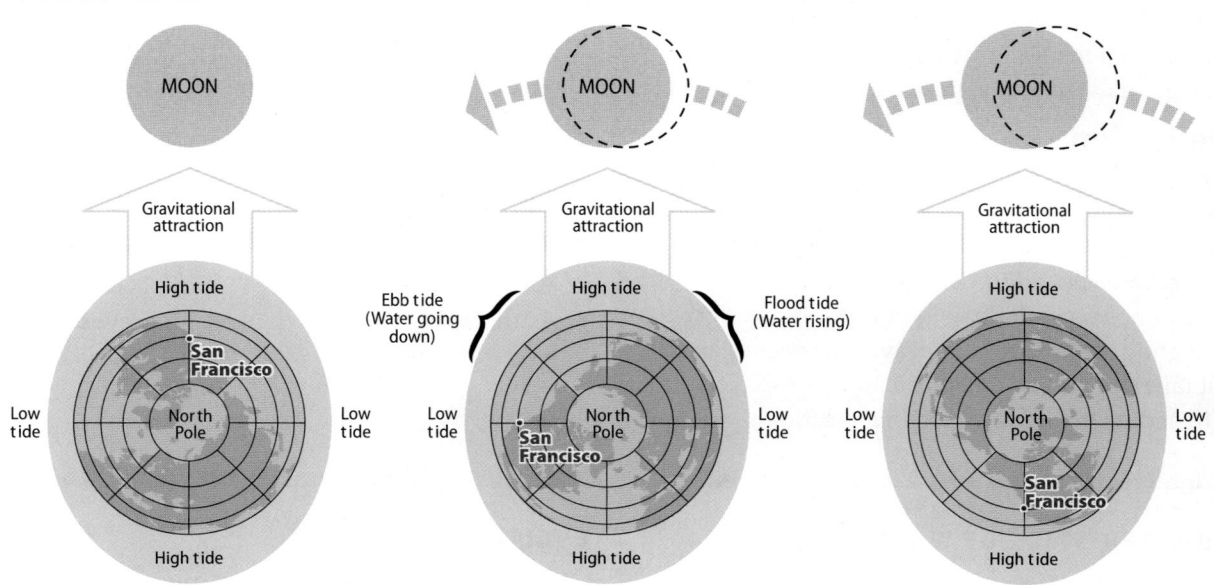

High tide occurs directly below the moon and on the opposite side of Earth. When Earth is in the position above, San Francisco has a high tide.

As Earth turns, the tides rise and fall at each place on the ocean. About 6 hours and 13 minutes after high tide, San Francisco has a low tide, above.

The next high tide at San Francisco occurs about 12 hours and 25 minutes after the first. Earth has turned 186° in this time. The moon has moved 6°.

Tides

Tides are primarily caused by the gravitational pull of the moon on Earth. The moon's gravitation causes the oceans to bulge (high tide) on one side of Earth and depress (low tide) on the other.

Earth's spin results in every meridian of longitude having two high tides and two low tides each day. The time interval between high tides is about 12 hours and 25 minutes, or half of a lunar day. Therefore, high tide occurs about 50 minutes later each day.

Twice each month, there are unusually high and low tides, called *spring tides* and *neap tides*.

Spring tides, which are very high tides, occur at the times of the new and full moons. The term "spring" has no seasonal significance. It is used to denote the extreme range of the tide.

Neap tides, which are very gentle low tides, occur twice monthly, near the times of the first- and the last-quarter phases of the moon.

Ocean Waves

Ocean waves are mainly created by the wind. A wave on the surface of the ocean has two main parts. The *crest* is the ridge that is elevated above the surrounding water surface. On either side of the crest at sea level is a *trough,* or depression.

How Waves Form

- As wind blows over the water, small waves form from the air friction moving against the water.
- At first, only small wavelets are produced.
- Soon, the wavelets make the surface of the water rougher.
- Then, the wind is able to pile up the rough water into bigger waves.
- As the waves increase in size, it is easier for the wind to push on the water.
- As the wind continues to blow, the waves grow larger and larger.

Wave Motion

Waves do not actually move water forward even though they appear to do so. Floating objects are not carried along as waves pass by. The objects rise and fall and rock back and forth as the waves pass.

For example, a cork floating in water moves forward slightly as the crest of a wave approaches, but then it falls back a short distance as it passes into the trough, ending in nearly its original position.

CHARACTERISTICS OF WAVES

All waves can be described by three characteristics.

- **Height:** the distance from the bottom of the trough to the top of the next crest
- **Wavelength:** the distance between crests
- **Period:** the time it takes for two successive crests to pass a given point

Ocean waves can be described by their height, wavelength, and period. As a wave moves over the water, the water molecules move in an orbit with a diameter that equals the height of the wave.

CYCLING MOLECULES

Waves are produced when individual water molecules move in orbits, or circular paths. (See Molecules, pages 346–347.)

- As a wave passes a given point, each water particle makes a complete circuit, tracing a circle whose diameter is equal to the height of the wave, ending up almost exactly where it started.
- Only the wave moves over the surface of the water. The water remains in place, merely transmitting the wave motion by the circular movements of the individual water particles.

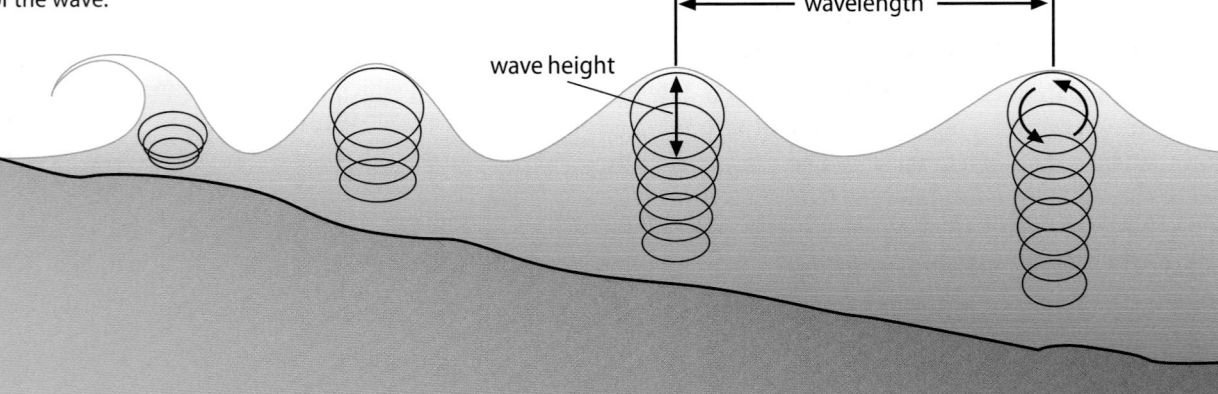

▲ **The crest** of a wave gets progressively higher as it moves closer to shore. Finally, the crest tumbles forward into the trough, and the wave becomes a breaker, or surf wave.

fyi! Tsunamis—*powerful waves usually caused by an earthquake or under-water landslide—can reach speeds of 970 kilometers (600 miles) per hour and travel across an entire ocean.*

Wave Size. The eventual height of a wave depends mainly on the force of the wind and how far the wind moves across the ocean. Strong, steady winds can produce very large waves. Such conditions are most likely to occur during a storm. Waves over 30 meters (100 feet) tall have been recorded during hurricanes at sea.

Whitecaps. In most regions, winds are not steady. Consequently, most ocean waves do not grow very large. If the wind blows very hard, the force may push water off the tops of the waves. This produces *whitecaps*, water with foamy white tops.

Swells. Waves with the longest wavelengths tend to last longer because they receive the greatest push from the wind. For this reason, the most common waves on the open ocean are long, rolling ones known as *swells*. Swells travel great distances from their areas of origin. For example, swells that wash up on the Atlantic seashore may have formed in the windy regions of the mid-Atlantic a thousand or more miles from shore.

Hitting Shore. An ocean wave changes direction as it heads toward the shoreline because of the circular motion of the water molecules. When a wave reaches water that is shallower than its height, the ocean bottom affects the movement of the water particles.

- First, the water molecules rub the ocean floor as they move in circular orbits, and the wave slows down.
- If the wave approaches the shoreline at an angle, this slowing down of water molecules causes *refraction*, or bending, of the wave.
- One end of the wave strikes the shallow water first.
- Refraction occurs because this end is slowed down more than the rest of the advancing wave.
- Refraction lines up incoming waves parallel with the shore, and ocean waves usually approach the shore head-on, regardless of their original direction.
- This is the reason why waves tend to straighten shorelines.

The Seafloor

Geological oceanography is mainly concerned with the study of the seafloor—the *continental margins* and *ocean basins*—especially the sediment and rock that underlie seawater. Studies of ocean sediment are used to determine the history of ocean basins and the ocean currents that deposited the sediment.

Continental Margins

The continental margins are the portions of the ocean that border the continents. They include the *coastal regions*, *continental shelves*, *continental slopes*, and *continental rises*. For most people, the continental margins are the most valuable parts of the ocean. Yet, these near-shore regions make up only a little more than 20 percent of the seafloor.

▲ **The continental margins** contain most of the world's major fisheries.

Coastal Regions

- the parts of the continental margins just landward of the ocean or intermittently covered by seawater
- include beaches, estuaries, lagoons, marshes, and deltas
- occupy only a small portion of the continental margins
- more than half of the U.S. population lives within 80 kilometers (50 miles) of the ocean
- most of the world's large cities are near the ocean, many on *estuaries,* where rivers empty into the sea

Continental Shelves

- relatively smooth, gently sloping platforms that end abruptly at the continental slope; this abrupt end of the shelf is called the *shelf break*
- the shallow parts of the continental margins, less than 60 meters (65.6 yards) deep, just seaward of the coastal regions
- consist of sedimentary rock and loose sediment, which cover about one-sixth of Earth's seafloor
- two main kinds are *glaciated* and *unglaciated*
- glaciated shelves show the visible effects of glacial erosion
- average width is 75 kilometers (40 miles)
- the shelf may be very narrow or even absent off coasts where there are strong ocean currents

Continental Slopes

- located just landward of the ocean basin
- considered to be the actual margin of a continent
- subsurface geology of the continental slope relatively unresearched
- believed that the slope is a transitional zone between continental and oceanic crust
- extends down to the seafloor from the seaward portion of the continental shelf
- average angle of inclination is a gentle 4°
- off mountainous coastlines, the continental slope can have an inclination of more than 20°

Continental Rises

- an accumulation of sediments at the base of the continental slope
- angle of inclination of a continental rise is very gentle, about half a degree
- width of the rise can be considerable, from about 100 to 1,000 kilometers (62 to 620 miles)
- may contain layers of sediments as much as 10 kilometers (about 6 miles) thick; these layers of sedimentary rock and sediment may eventually be uplifted by plate movement to form coastal mountain ranges

Ocean Basins

Research done by oceanographers has shown that ocean basins are generally even more rugged than continental landscapes. There are huge volcanic mountains, deep trenches, and submarine canyons that extend from the continental slope into the ocean basins.

Mid-Ocean Ridges. Perhaps the most outstanding feature of the ocean basins is the system of *mid-ocean ridges* that stretches for 50,000 to 80,000 kilometers (30,000 to 50,000 miles), like one interconnected mountain range throughout the world's oceans. (See pages 450–451.) Most mountains of the mid-ocean ridges stand about 5,000 feet (1,500 meters) above the seafloor. Some peaks rise above the surface and form islands. Some mid-ocean ridges have valleys down through the center of them. Frequent volcanic eruptions and earthquakes occur along such valleys.

Abyssal Plains. The sides of the mid-ocean ridges slope down to the *abyssal plains*. These flat parts of the ocean basin cover about 10 percent of the world's ocean basins. Sediment-filled currents flowing down the continental slope created the plains. The chief sources of deep-sea sediment are the land itself and marine life. Rivers carry land sediment to the ocean. Wind carries dust and volcanic ash to the ocean. Marine life sediment consists mainly of tiny shells and the remains of dead planktonic organisms.

Seamounts. Scattered in large numbers over the seafloor are volcanic peaks, called *seamounts*. Deep gashes called *trenches* stretch along the base of seamounts, forming the deepest part of the ocean. Some seamounts rise up to 16,665 kilometers (10,000 feet) above the seafloor. Some have flat tops, called *guyots*. These guyots indicate that the seamounts probably were islands whose tops were eroded by wave action.

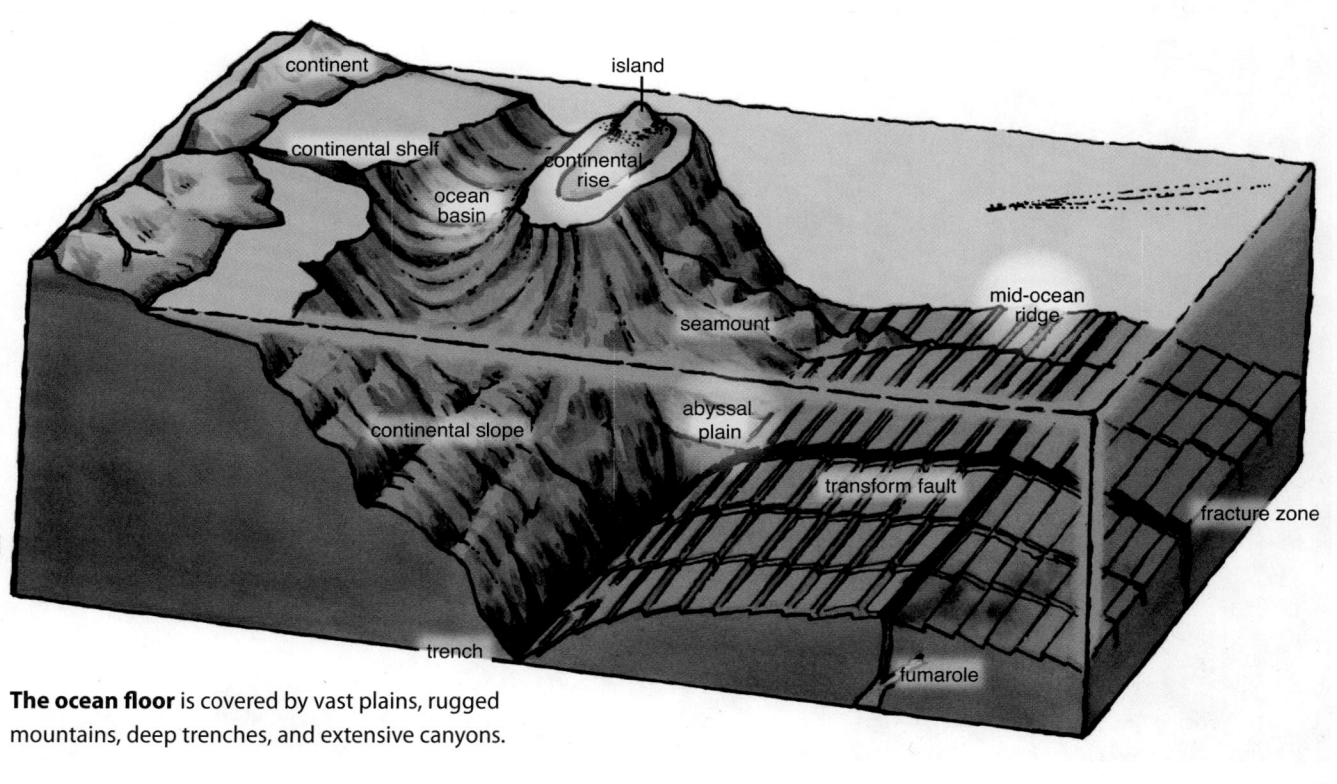

The ocean floor is covered by vast plains, rugged mountains, deep trenches, and extensive canyons.

Ocean Life

Biological oceanography is the study of marine plants and animals and their distribution in the world's oceans. Biological oceanographers study organisms that live in shallow coastal areas as well as along the deep ocean trenches.

Biological oceanography deals with two main environments: the *pelagic* and the *benthic*. Pelagic organisms are marine organisms that live in the open ocean. Benthic organisms live on the seafloor, either near the shore or at great depths.

Pelagic Environment

The pelagic environment refers to the water column, or vertical layers, above the floor of the world's oceans. The water column of the oceans is divided into the *neritic zone*, or near-shore region, and the *oceanic zone*, or offshore region. The boundary between these two regions is arbitrarily set at the edge of the continental shelf.

The neritic zone contains many kinds of *habitats*, or living conditions, especially where freshwater from a river mixes with seawater. Organisms living in the neritic zone must be able to tolerate a wide range of salinity.

Nutrients supplied by river water and upwellings of ocean water support an abundant growth of small, free-floating marine organisms called *plankton*. Plankton is the basic food source in oceans. It attracts many forms of marine life. In fact, the neritic zone is where most fish and shellfish live. It is the most biologically productive zone in the ocean.

The oceanic zone can be divided into light and dark regions, with the boundary between the two at a depth of about 200 meters (650 feet). The oceanic zone has a more constant salinity than the neritic zone. In the oceanic zone, water temperature decreases with depth. The temperature of surface waters is usually influenced most by latitude.

The neritic zone has the most abundant life in the ocean. Most fish and shellfish live in this zone.

Benthic Environment

The benthic environment, or ocean bottom, covers a wide range of oceanographic conditions, stretching horizontally from the *supralittoral zone* of beaches to the *hadal zone*, or seafloor. The benthic environment usually is divided into two zones: the *littoral zone*, the seafloor out to a depth of 200 meters (650 feet); and the *deep-sea zone*, at depths greater than 200 meters.

The littoral zone of the benthic environment has been classified by oceanographers into three regions: the *supralittoral*, *eulittoral*, and *sublittoral*.

Supralittoral Region

- consists of beach areas that are submerged periodically
- an extremely harsh environment for marine animals and plants; must tolerate exposure to the air for long periods
- covered by seawater only during the highest tides, severe storms, and spraying provided by breaking waves
- plants and animals of this region are similar throughout the world; consist of snails and lichens on rocky shores and crabs and small-shelled creatures called *amphipods* on sandy beaches

Eulittoral Region

- also known as the intertidal zone
- periodically exposed at low tide
- extends out to a depth of 40 to 60 meters (130 to 200 feet)
- supports the greatest number and variety of marine organisms
- animals living here must adapt to both the crashing of waves and exposure to direct rays of the sun
- region's outer boundary is near the depth limit at which most attached plants can grow on the bottom because of the amount of sunlight required for photosynthesis

Sublittoral Region

- extends to a depth of 200 meters (650 feet) or more
- noticeable decrease in plant life and increase in animal life, especially fish, from eulittoral outward to sublittoral region
- outer part, the edge of the continental shelf, is extensively fished by commercial fishermen

▲ **Biological oceanographers** directly observe and even experiment on organisms living at great depths in the ocean.

The deep-sea zone of the benthic environment is less well understood than regions closer to ocean shores. Because light cannot penetrate the water column in this zone, it is devoid of higher plants, but it is known to contain various kinds of bacteria.

Deep-Sea Conditions

- conditions relatively uniform
- salinity constant
- temperature decreases slowly with depth
- pressure increases rapidly with depth
- food scarce; deep-sea organisms thought to get most of their food from organic material that descends from above

Deep-Sea Creatures

- remain largely mysterious to marine biologists
- most information provided by underwater photography, deep-sea dredging, and submersible oceanographic vessels
- most animals are strange in appearance and relatively small
- because of the great amount of water pressure, most animals are composed mainly of water, with very little air in their bodies

aa flowing lava that is cool enough to have partially solidified; and moves as a slow, pasty mass.

air mass a large body of air with uniform temperature and humidity.

alluvial fan fan-shaped accumulation of sediment that forms where a stream emerges from a narrow mountain canyon onto a flat plain.

anticline a fold or folds of rock layers that slope upward to form a crest.

aquifer a body of saturated rock or sediment through which water can move easily.

asthenosphere the thick layer of Earth's mantle that lies under the lithosphere, thought to consist of a thick slush of partially melted rocks and minerals.

atmosphere the envelope of gases that surrounds Earth; three gases essential to life on Earth—oxygen, nitrogen, and carbon dioxide—make up 99 percent of the atmosphere.

avalanche a powerful, rapid rock slide.

bar a visible ridge of sand or gravel deposited in the middle or along the banks of a stream.

bed load the heavy sediment that travels on or near the bottom of a stream.

caldera a volcanic crater larger than 0.6 kilometers (about 0.4 miles) in diameter, produced when a violent volcanic eruption completely destroys the upper part of a volcanic cone.

caliche a layer of calcium carbonate that forms in soil in dry regions over 100,000 to 500,000 years.

Cambrian Explosion the dramatic increase in the variety of life found on Earth during the Cambrian period.

chemical weathering the process by which rocks decay and decompose, and are eventually changed into substances with different chemical compositions and physical properties.

clastic rock sedimentary rock formed from grains of sediment that have been pressed and cemented together.

cleavage the ability of some minerals to break along smooth, flat planes.

climate the average weather in a specific place over a long period of time.

condensation the process in which water changes from a vapor to a liquid or a solid.

conifer any of a group of trees and shrubs that bear cones.

continental drift the slow movement of large landmasses over Earth's surface, caused by pressure that shifts them over the asthenosphere.

convection the movement of air from areas of high pressure to areas of low pressure.

crest the highest part of a wave.

crust the relatively thin, brittle outer layer of Earth.

crystal form the distinctive geometric form of a mineral.

cyclone a storm or winds that blow around in a spiral toward a calm center of low pressure, which also moves.

deformation the process by which plate movements cause horizontal layers of sedimentary rock to become tilted, folded, or cracked.

delta body of accumulating sediment that forms at the mouth of a stream or river, where it flows into a lake or ocean.

dendrochronology the study of tree rings to establish the ages of fossils and environmental conditions in the past.

density a physical quality that reflects how tightly the atoms in a substance are packed.

dew point the air temperature at which water condenses from vapor into liquid.

dissolved load mineral particles that dissolve within the water of a stream.

doldrums the belt of light winds around the equator characterized by frequent thunderstorms or squalls. The doldrums are located between the trade winds of the Northern and Southern hemispheres.

earthquake a sudden, strong trembling, or shaking, of the ground, usually occurring as a result of the movement of tectonic plates.

electromagnetic radiation energy from space that consists of waves of electricity and magnetism.

elevation height above sea level.

El Niño a periodic ocean current of warm water that flows south from Ecuador down the coasts of Peru and Chile, causing a decline in plankton, fish, and birds.

equator an imaginary circle around the center of Earth, halfway between the North Pole and the South Pole.

erosion the removal of rock particles from exposed bedrock or topsoil by the impact of water, wind, or ice. Erosion is also the result of the impact on the landscape of rock particles carried by water, wind, or ice.

evaporation the process by which water changes from a liquid into a vapor.

evaporite a mineral that is deposited when water evaporates.

fault a crack in Earth's crust that occurs at the boundary between two lithospheric plates.

floodplain a broad strip of land built up by sediment deposited on both sides of a stream channel.

folds wavelike features in rock layers that resemble ocean waves.

foliation a parallel arrangement of flaky and needlelike minerals characteristic of some metamorphic rock.

fossil the remains or traces of prehistoric plants and animals, usually preserved in sedimentary rock.

front the boundary that forms when a warm air mass and a cool air mass meet.

frost wedging the process by which a rock splits after water freezes and expands in a joint, prying the rock apart.

fumarole a vent in Earth's continental or oceanic crust emitting volcanic gases and steam at high temperatures.

geology the study of Earth's structure, composition, and history.

geosyncline an elongated, downward curve of Earth's crust.

geothermal gradient the regular pattern of temperature increase from Earth's crust inward toward the core.

geyser spring that erupts columns of water into the air at certain times.

glaciers huge masses of ice that flow due to gravity and currently cover about 10 percent of Earth's total land area.

GPS the Global Positioning System, a worldwide navigation system that uses radio signals broadcast by satellites to pinpoint locations.

gravity the force by which objects are attracted to one another.

groundwater water that lies beneath Earth's surface, filling the cracks, crevices, and pores of rocks.

gyres enormous circular patterns made by wind-driven ocean currents.

half-life the amount of time it takes for half the atoms of an element to decay.

historical geology the study of changes that have occurred in Earth's structure and appearance.

hot spot an underground concentration of magma, located in the middle of a lithospheric plate, that creates volcanoes.

humidity the amount of water vapor, or moisture, that is present in the air.

humus decomposed and decaying organic matter.

hurricane a large tropical storm that originates in the ocean.

hydrologic cycle the water cycle, the continuous cycle by which water on Earth moves constantly, from the oceans to the air, from the air to the land, and then back to the seas again, changing from liquid, to gas, to solid, and back again.

hydrosphere the water of Earth, made up mainly of the oceans and seas, but also consisting of the lakes, streams, and water that flows beneath Earth's surface.

ice age a period of geologic time in which glaciers cover much of Earth's land areas.

ice cap a continental glacier that covers less than 50,000 square kilometers (19,300 square miles).

ice sheet a continental glacier that covers more than 50,000 square kilometers (19,300 square miles).

igneous rock rock formed when minerals in a molten state, called magma, harden.

inner core the solid inner portion of Earth's core, about 2,600 kilometers (1,600 miles) in diameter, thought to consist of solid iron and nickel.

insolation the amount of solar radiation absorbed by a particular place over a period of time.

invertebrate an animal without a backbone.

jet stream a narrow band of strong, high-altitude wind near the tropopause, or the upper limit of the troposphere, that circles Earth in a wavy pattern.

joint a crack in a rock. Joints leave rocks vulnerable to mechanical weathering.

lake a body of water surrounded by land.

lateral moraine a ridge of rock debris that accumulates along the sides of a glacier.

latitude position north or south of the equator.

Law of Superposition the law that forms the basis for relative dating of rocks. The law states that in any sequence of undisturbed sedimentary rocks, the underlying beds will be older than the beds above.

levee a low ridge of sediment that forms on either side of a stream channel.

lithosphere the portion of Earth consisting of the crust and the outermost layer of the mantle.

lithospheric plates large pieces of Earth's lithosphere that float on top of the asthenosphere, spreading apart and colliding into one another, according to plate tectonics.

longitude position east or west of the prime meridian.

luster the quality and intensity of light reflected from the surface of a mineral viewed in ordinary light.

magma molten rock beneath Earth's surface.

magnetic pole one of the two poles on Earth toward which a compass needle points.

magnetosphere a zone of strong magnetic forces created by Earth and extending far out into space.

mantle the part of Earth's interior beneath the crust and above the outer core.

mass movement also known as mass wasting, the process by which large masses of weathered rock material and soil move downhill due to the pull of gravity.

M-discontinuity or the Mohorovicic discontinuity, a region of dense rocks separating Earth's crust from its mantle.

meander a winding turn in a stream.

mechanical weathering the process by which rocks are broken up into fragments of different sizes.

medial moraine a band of rocky debris formed at the intersection of two lateral moraines, where two alpine glaciers join.

meridians of longitude imaginary lines running around Earth through the North and South poles, used to measure east-west location.

mesosphere 1. the enormously thick lower part of Earth's mantle, composed of solid rock. 2. the layer of Earth's atmosphere between the stratosphere and the thermosphere.

metamorphic rock rock formed when other rocks are changed by heat and/or pressure at great depths inside the crust.

meteorology the science of the atmosphere, especially the study of weather phenomena and weather forecasting.

mid-ocean ridges a system of ridges and mountain ranges on the ocean floor that stretches for 50,000 to 80,000 kilometers (30,000 to 50,000 miles).

mineral a solid, inorganic element and compound that occurs naturally in rocks.

monsoon powerful seasonal winds caused by the uneven heating and cooling of oceans and continents.

moraine a ridge that forms as a glacier melts or retreats, piling up rock, dirt, and other debris.

native metal a metallic mineral of only one element.

natural resource a product or feature of Earth that is useful or necessary to support life and satisfy people's needs.

neap tide a very gentle tide that occurs twice monthly, near the times of the first- and last-quarter phases of the moon.

nonsilicates rare minerals that do not contain silicon.

oceanography the scientific study of Earth's oceans, usually divided into four separate fields: chemical oceanography, physical oceanography, geological oceanography, and biological oceanography.

ore a naturally occurring material that can be mined profitably.

outer core the outer portion of Earth's core, thought to consist of dense liquid iron, nickel, and trace elements such as sulfur, carbon, and silicon.

oxidation the process of rusting.

ozone layer the layer of the upper atmosphere that shields Earth from ultraviolet radiation.

pahoehoe fast-flowing lava with a ropy surface formed by the rapid cooling and hardening of a liquid lava pool from the surface downward.

parallels of latitude imaginary lines running parallel to the equator that are used to measure north-south location.

petrification a form of fossilization in which water carries off organic materials from the remains of a dead organism and minerals dissolved in the water replace the organic materials.

petrology the study of rocks.

physical geography the study of Earth's physical features and attributes, including its size, shape, magnetism, and movements.

physical geology the study of the interior and exterior structure of Earth.

plate tectonics a theory that the outer layer of Earth is composed of a series of large plates that spread apart and collide into one another, forming the major features of Earth's surface.

precipitation water that falls from the clouds to Earth, as rain, snow, or hail.

primary waves (P-waves) compressional seismic waves generated by the expansion and contraction of material.

prime meridian the meridian line that is used as the starting point for measuring longitude. It runs through Greenwich, England, and its longitude is 0°.

radar an instrument for determining distance, direction, and speed of unseen objects by the reflection of radio waves.

regolith weathered rock fragments mixed with soil.

relative humidity a ratio of the amount of water vapor in the air to the greatest amount of water vapor the air can hold at a given air temperature.

relief the difference in elevation between the highest and lowest points of a particular region.

Richter scale a system for measuring the strength of an earthquake based on the magnitude of the waves recorded by a seismograph.

rift valley a valley with steep parallel sides formed at the boundary of two separating lithospheric plates.

rock hard mineral substance that forms the solid part of Earth's crust.

root wedging the process by which roots of large shrubs and trees grow downward into sediments or through cracks in rock outcrops.

salinity the concentration of salt in a substance.

sand dune a mound of sand heaped up by strong winds.

seafloor spreading the formation of new crust along plate boundaries on the ocean floor.

secondary waves (S-waves) transverse seismic waves generated by shearing, or side-to-side movement, of a material.

sediment loose material on Earth's surface, including fragments of rocks, soil, and the remains of plants and animals.

sedimentary rock rock formed when particles of other rocks (sediment) accumulate and harden into layered rock.

seismic waves waves generated by earthquakes that penetrate Earth's interior.

seismograph an instrument for recording the direction, intensity, and duration of earthquakes and other movements of Earth's crust.

seismometers sensors in a seismograph that can detect ground motions caused by seismic waves from both near and distant earthquakes.

silicates minerals that contain the two most abundant elements—oxygen and silicon. Silicates are the most plentiful minerals in the crust.

slip face the steep, downwind side of a sand dune.

soil the top layer of Earth's surface, composed of rock and mineral particles mixed with animal and vegetable matter.

soil creep slow, continuous movement of soil or regolith down the side of a mountain or hill.

solifluction flow of water-saturated regolith over impermeable material.

specific gravity a measurement that shows how much more dense a mineral is than an equal volume of water.

specific heat the number of calories of heat needed to raise the temperature of 1 gram of a substance 1 degree centigrade.

spring a place where water flows naturally from rock onto the land surface.

spring tide a very high tide that occurs at the times of the new and full moons.

stratosphere the layer of Earth's atmosphere between the troposphere and the mesosphere, from an altitude of about 10 kilometers (6 miles) to about 48 kilometers (30 miles).

streak the true color of a mineral, shown when the mineral has been ground into a powder.

stream a body of running water that is confined in a channel and pulled downhill by gravity.

subduction the process by which one lithospheric plate slides beneath another, destroying portions of Earth's crust.

surface waves seismic waves that travel only along the ground, causing vertical and horizontal vibrations.

suspended load the light sediments that remain suspended by water turbulence above a streambed.

syncline a fold or folds of rock layers that slope downward to form a trough.

terminal moraine a moraine that loops around the lower limit of a glacier.

thermohaline circulation an ocean current in which dense, cold water from high latitudes sinks and flows toward the equator where it warms, rises, and flows back toward the poles, eventually mixing the ocean water of the entire world.

thermosphere the uppermost layer of Earth's atmosphere; begins at an average altitude of about 80 kilometers (50 miles) and extends into space.

thunderstorm a storm that produces lightning and thunder and sometimes hail, violent winds, and tornadoes.

tides the daily rising and falling of sea level, caused by the gravitational pull of the moon on Earth.

till rock fragments that range in size from gravel to boulders.

topographic map a reference map that shows the details and heights of land features in a small area.

topography the surface features of a region.

tornado a rapidly rotating column of air that can develop under a large, anvil-shaped thundercloud.

Tornado Alley an area in the southern and midwestern United States that is struck by a large number of tornadoes every year.

troposphere the layer of Earth's atmosphere closest to the surface, where all of Earth's weather occurs.

trough the lowest part of a wave.

tsunami a powerful wave, usually caused by an earthquake or underwater landslide, that can reach speeds of 970 kilometers (600 miles) per hour and travel across an entire ocean.

upwelling the rising of cold, deep, nutrient-rich waters near coastlines. Upwelling provides nutrients for the growth of phytoplankton.

vapor pressure a measure of how easily water molecules change from a liquid into a gas.

vertebrate an animal that has a backbone.

volcano a fissure, or vent, in Earth's crust where ash, gases, and molten rock from deep underground erupt to the surface. Also refers to the type of mountain that forms as the erupted rock and ash build up around the fissure.

water table the level under Earth's surface below which the ground is saturated with water.

wave a moving ridge over the surface of water, caused mainly by the wind.

wavelength the distance between two wave crests.

weather the condition of the atmosphere at a particular time and place.

well a deep hole dug or drilled into the ground to penetrate an aquifer below the saturated zone.

wind the movement of air from one place to another in response to a change in temperature and pressure.

Ecology

General Ecology **590**

The Environment **630**

Energy and Glossary **734**

INTRODUCTION TO ECOLOGY

In nature, every living thing exists as part of an intricate structure composed of other living organisms and the physical environment that encompasses them. The study of organisms in relation to each other and to their environment is known as ecology.

Ecology has been arbitrarily divided into plant ecology and animal ecology. In studying the ecology of plants, however, an involvement with animals is inevitable, and vice versa. There is fundamentally just one ecology, embracing three different concepts: population, community, and ecosystem.

An Intricate Structure

No Organism Lives Alone

The world includes a tremendous variety of living things, from complex plants and animals to simpler organisms, such as fungi, amoebae, and bacteria. But whether large or small, simple or complex, no organism lives alone. Each depends in some way upon other living and nonliving things in its surroundings. For example, a moose must have certain plants for food. If the plants in its environment were destroyed, the moose would have to move to another area or starve to death. In turn, plants depend upon such animals as moose for the *nutrients* (nourishing substances) they need to live. Animal wastes and the decay of dead animals and plants provide many of the nutrients plants need.

The study of ecology is important because our survival and well-being depend on ecological relationships around the world. Even changes in distant parts of the world and its atmosphere affect us and our own environment.

▲ **The savanna,** or grasslands, of eastern Africa supports large herds of grazing animals, like the giraffe, as well as their predators.

A Multidisciplinary Approach

Although ecology usually is considered a branch of biology, ecologists must employ such disciplines as chemistry, physics, and computer science. They also rely on such fields as geology, meteorology, and oceanography to study land, air, and water environments. This multidisciplinary approach helps ecologists understand how physical environments affect living things. It also helps them assess the impact of environmental problems such as acid rain.

Ecologists study the organization of the natural world on three main levels.

1. Populations

2. Communities

3. Ecosystems

They analyze the structures, activities, and changes that take place within and among these levels. Ecologists normally work out of doors, studying the operations of the natural world. They often conduct field work in isolated areas, such as islands, where the relationships among the plants and animals may be simpler and easier to understand.

▲ **The ecology of Isle Royale,** an island in Lake Superior, has been studied extensively. Many ecological studies focus on solving practical problems. For example, ecologists search for ways to curb the harmful effects of air and water pollution on living things.

Populations

A population is the number of inhabitants occupying an area. The main factors that affect the size of a population are the rate of birth, or natality, and the rate of death, or mortality. Immigration (individuals who migrate in) also can be an influence along with emigration (individuals who move out).

Biotic Potential. Imagine that there is a bacterium that can reproduce under ideal conditions every 20 minutes. That would mean eight cells after 1 hour, 64 after 2 hours, and so on. After 36 hours, the entire Earth would be covered 1-foot deep in the bacteria. One hour after that, the bacteria would be over our heads.

Counterweight. Fortunately, there is a counterweight to biotic potential. Limits are set by the living and/or nonliving environment. Most codfish eggs are eaten by other animals or they fail to reproduce into new fish for a variety of reasons. A human female could conceivably give birth to a child a year for her reproductive lifetime of 35 or more years, but most women choose not to do so. Some animal populations, like a plague of locusts, do grow exponentially. This means that at some point they use up and run out of critical resources, and the population falls dramatically, or crashes.

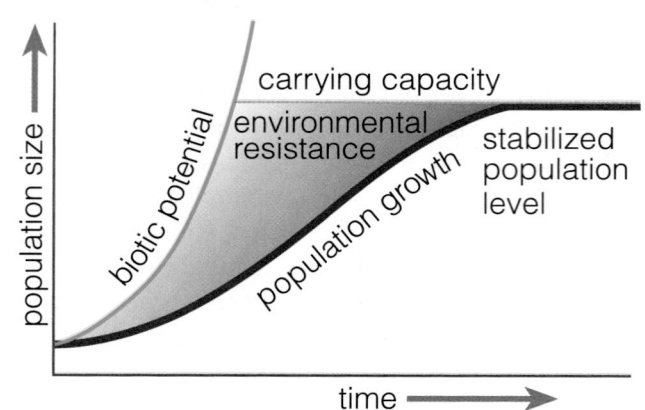

▲ **Environmental resistance** will limit an animal population from growing at its full biotic potential rate.

Carrying Capacity. Animal populations do not grow forever. But most animal populations accommodate gradually to environmental limitations. Usually, when the size of a population pushes past a certain point, the population declines, then recovers, and finally stabilizes, hovering at some maximum level. This level is known as the *carrying capacity* of the ecosystem.

Carrying capacity equals all the resources available that can be used by each particular species in conjunction with the existing hazards that put a brake on the population size.

GOT TO KNOW

GROWTH RATES

Population size depends upon two factors.

- *Biotic potential*, the inherent capacity or maximum rate at which a population could increase under the best of conditions. This in turn depends on the birth potential or maximum birthrate of a species under ideal conditions. A female codfish lays up to 6 million eggs per spawning; a chicken, 300 eggs a year; but female elephants give birth only once every 7 or more years.

- The number of reproductive females in the population. Even if the birthrate—the number of births per thousand individuals per year—remains steady, as the size of a population expands, the growth rate balloons because of ever-growing numbers of reproductive females.

Limiting Factors. In order to live, grow, and reproduce, all organisms have to fulfill certain basic requirements, such as sufficient space, air, food, and water. Below a certain minimum, they will suffer and die. This implies there is a maximum limit as well: Too much heat or water or salt or toxic chemicals can be equally limiting. According to this *law of tolerance,* some species may have a wide range of tolerance for one factor and a narrow range for another. A species with wide ranges of tolerance for all factors is likely to be large and widespread. Close to the borderlines of tolerance, an animal suffers physiological stress that affects its ability to reproduce. Limiting factors on an animal population are imposed from the outside—by the physical environment or by other species—and from within the population itself.

Some key limiters are

- **lack of food,** not only because of starvation but also because of its negative effect on reproductive ability.

- **loss of habitat:** the destruction of natural ecosystems in favor of agriculture, wood supplies, settlements, highways, and other needs of the growing human population.

PARASITES

Another limitation to population growth takes the form of parasitism, in which members of one population feed on members of another. Parasites like flukes, tapeworms, fleas (*above*), and ticks live inside or on their hosts. A distinguishing feature of parasites is that it is in the parasite's self-interest not to kill its host. Nevertheless, parasitism weakens host populations, increasing their vulnerability to disease and predators. (See page 597.)

PREDATORS

It may seem obvious that predators will hold down the prey population, but the relationship is not so simple.

In 1907, the U.S. government and the state of Arizona decided to protect a herd of 4,000 deer on the Kaibab Plateau near the Grand Canyon in Arizona. A bounty was established on the predators of the deer—cougars, wolves, and coyotes. The campaign went well; 600 mountain lions were killed in the first 10 years. By 1918, the deer population had increased tenfold to 40,000; in 1924, to 100,000. During the next two winters, 60,000 deer died from starvation and disease. The decline continued until 1939, when the deer population leveled off at 10,000. (See page 597.)

Population Controls

Overpopulation and Population Density

The main limiting factor coming from within a population is overpopulation. Overpopulation takes an inevitable toll on many animal populations because of its twin: intolerable population density.

When it comes to animals of the same species, two major kinds of spacing patterns can be seen.

Contact Species. In some species, members want to live close together in groups, and for good reason. The clustering of bees enables the massed individuals to generate enough heat to survive the low temperatures that would kill isolated individuals. When a group of pronghorns numbers 16 or more members, the herd will stand its ground against a wolf attack. These animals, along with other herd animals, such as pigs, some penguins, brown bats, walruses, hippos, and others, are contact creatures. They need to touch and have close contact.

Social animals have a social distance, the outer limits of which are loss of contact with the group. There are obvious reasons for this—for one thing, the stray is vulnerable to attack by a predator. But there also seems to be a psychological boundary beyond which the contact animal feels anxiety. Social distance varies with species. It is only a few yards with flamingos, but much farther among other birds. And it can vary with the situation. For a young ape who does not obey his mother's vocal commands, social distance may be only as far as her arms' reach.

Noncontact Species. Other animals belong to noncontact species. Felines, rats, mice, muskrats and other rodents, hawks, dogs, and horses in general avoid touching. They have a personal distance that they keep between themselves and fellow members of their species. Their personal distance serves as an invisible bubble around them, reducing intimate contact.

Animals within a population suffer stress when their natural spacing is violated—too many squeezed together—as explained below.

POPULATION DENSITY

Population density—overcrowding—produces stress in animals forced to live in unbearable closeness with their fellows. When a rabbit population reaches a certain density, there is a large die-off from what is called shock disease. Stress by itself can break down organs, causing death. Stress also causes bizarre and neurotic behavior. Even when food and other resources remain plentiful, a population can die off from its own toxic wastes. Animal populations usually will move to another site when their wastes accumulate to an intolerable level, but if they cannot, they become the victims of their own metabolic processes.

Regulating Factors

Many wild animal populations have ways of limiting their numbers without the suffering of starvation and disease. Dominance hierarchies accomplish this limiting. (See also page 216.)

- Reproduction often is restricted to socially dominant members. Insects, whose powers of reproduction are prodigious, limit eggs to a queen and sterilize the other females.

- *Territoriality* promotes a condition that is the opposite of crowding. Individuals will defend their space. Nonterritorial members cannot breed. Their choice is to emigrate.

- *Dispersal* effectively maintains the numbers of a stable population. Young woodchucks often move away from the domineering adults. In dispersal, the venturers are leaving an established habitat for the unknown with unforeseeable risks.

- Reducing birthrate in areas of overcrowding controls the rate at which animals reproduce and the timing of the maturation process in individual animals. The delayed beginning of reproduction and longer spacing cut the total number of offspring over the course of a female's lifetime. In some situations of intense overcrowding, nature will shut off reproduction completely.

▲ **Each species of animal** in an ecosystem fills a different niche, so animals do not compete directly with each other for food or space. If two species compete for the same niche, the end result will be elimination of one of the species.

But there is another possible outcome to this scenario. Members of one species may alter their habits. Such a change can even take place among members of the same species forced to compete for a limited resource.

BIRTHRATE REDUCTION AMONG ELEPHANTS

In an African sanctuary that averaged two elephants per square mile, the young were weaned at age eight. A female would give birth for the first time at age twelve, then reproduce every 7 years for a total number of six offspring in her lifetime. In another overcrowded preserve with a density of 10 elephants per square mile, the young were not weaned until age ten. Females did not begin reproducing until age twenty and only bred once every 12 years.

COMMUNITIES

In addition to studying populations of individual species, ecologists study the interactions between species living together in communities. *Competition* is one kind of interaction among different animal species. When competition exists where niches are not identical, direct competition is reduced or avoided. For example, hawks and owls both feed on small rodents, but hawks hunt during the day and owls are nocturnal.

There also can be behavioral modifications. A study of 11 similar freshwater fish in Panama found that when food was plentiful, they all used the same resource. When food became scarce, each species switched to its own specialized diet. They competed only when competition did them no harm.

THE FEEDING LADDER

Each step in the feeding ladder is known as a trophic (nutrition) level. An enormous amount of usable chemical energy, ordinarily about 90 percent, is lost with each step up the ladder. This has been determined by studying the total biomass of all members of different species in an ecosystem.

For example, in a study conducted on Isle Royale, an island on Lake Superior, ecologists found that it takes 762 pounds (346 kilograms) of plant food to support 59 pounds (27 kilograms) of moose. This is the amount of moose needed to support one pound (0.45 kilogram) of wolf. This explains why there are so few animals, such as eagles and panthers, at the top of food chains, and why they are not nearly as numerous as herbivores. Many animals, including bears, red foxes, skunks, snapping turtles, deer mice, and mockingbirds, are omnivores. A greater choice of food resources contributes greatly to their survival.

Forms of Interaction

Mutualism

In mutualism, both organisms benefit from the relationship, which is, in fact, a partnership. The microorganisms that make it possible for termites to digest wood cannot live outside the termite's body. Similarly, the microbes that help cows digest cellulose get a place to live in return. Some small fish are allowed to approach larger fish in order to eat parasites infecting their bodies. So one fish gets a meal; the other fish gets a cleaning.

Remora and shark

Yellow lady's slippers

Predation

A major animal interaction is called *predation*. In order to live, animals must eat plants and/or other animals. *Herbivores,* animals that eat plants, are the most plentiful because the plants they need are even more plentiful. The ecological term for plants is *producers;* for herbivores, it is *primary consumers.*

Animals that eat other animals are known as *carnivores* and *secondary consumers*. Animals that eat animals that eat animals are known as tertiary carnivores. The seal, which eats the squid that eats the fish that lives off tiny animals, is known as a quaternary carnivore.

Bald eagle

Parasitism

In parasitism, like predation, one species feeds on another. One species benefits; one is harmed. Parasites are smaller than their hosts and many, such as fleas, are far more numerous than their hosts. While parasites may limit their prey population, they usually do not eliminate it. The parasite may consume nutrients from the host's body or steal them from the host's diet, but unlike predators, parasites consume relatively small amounts of the host's resources at a time.

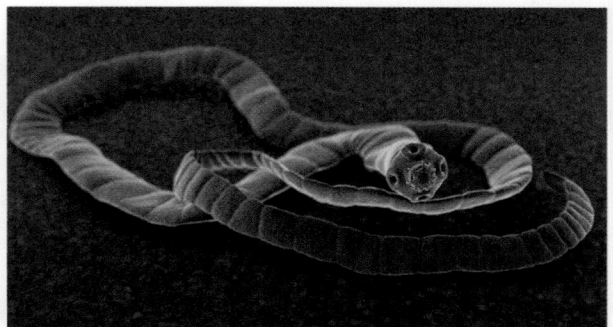

Tapeworm

Moose

Wolves

Invasions from Other Ecosystems

Invasive Species

Invasive species are animals, plants, and other living things that spread rapidly in new environments where there are few or no natural controls on their growth. People transport large numbers of species from one region to another. Only a small portion of these *introduced species* become invasive, but invasive pests can cause great environmental damage. They crowd out native species, putting them at risk of extinction. They also cause billions of dollars in damage each year to agriculture, fisheries, forestry, and public health.

▲ **In parts of the Great Lakes,** millions of zebra mussels clog pipes that provide water for drinking, irrigation, and industrial uses. They also cover boat bottoms, piers, fish traps and nets, and marker and navigation buoys.

How Species Invade. People have carried species from one environment to another for thousands of years. But increases in travel since 1800 have greatly expanded the number and variety of introduced species. Travelers and cargo on ships, airplanes, or other vessels carry some creatures accidentally.

Some invasive pests spread quickly after they arrive in new environments. The zebra mussel, a kind of shellfish, arrived in North America from Russia in the late 1980s, carried in ballast water in the deep holds of ships. It quickly spread out of control in North American lakes, threatening native aquatic life.

Invasive species have several destructive effects.

- They prey on native species.
- They compete with native species for resources.
- They alter native species through mating.
- Some pests may change an entire habitat and endanger a wide array of native life.

Habitat Alteration. An invasive pest can alter an entire habitat in ways that threaten many native species. Here's an example.

- In parts of Florida, Australian paperbark trees with highly flammable leaves and twigs have increased the number and intensity of forest fires.
- This environmental change has driven out native plants not adapted to frequent or intense fires.
- The loss of native vegetation has, in turn, harmed native animals that relied on the old plants for food and shelter.

◄ **The American chestnut** was once the most important forest tree in the eastern United States. From 1905 to 1940, a fungal disease called chestnut blight killed most of these trees in North America. This die-off affected untold numbers of moths, birds, and mammals that relied on these trees.

MANAGING INVASIVE SPECIES

The most effective way to manage invasive species is to keep them out. Many nations restrict the importation of species that might become damaging or of products that can carry them—such as untreated wooden packing material.

To combat invasive species after they arrive, people can use one or more of four basic approaches. These approaches are mechanical control, chemical control, biological control, and ecosystem management.

▲ **Mechanical control** includes trapping animals and uprooting plants. People in the United Kingdom completely eliminated the nutria, an invasive South American rodent, through trapping. But mechanical control usually involves intensive human labor. The United States has combated the Asian long-horned beetle, a pest imported from China, by cutting down and burning hundreds of beetle-infested trees.

◄ **Chemical Control.** People employ chemical pesticides to manage many introduced species. Pesticides have helped control such pests as the *Anopheles* mosquito, which spreads the disease malaria. But chemicals can prove expensive, particularly if used over large areas. Moreover, many pesticides become ineffective if species develop resistance to them.

◄ **Biological control** involves introducing a natural enemy of an introduced pest to reduce the pest's numbers. However, biological control agents can also cause harmful side effects.

The Russian wheat aphid, a native of southeastern Europe and southwestern Asia, reached the United States in 1986. It quickly spread through western North America and nearly eliminated wheat and barley crops in certain areas. To combat the aphid, farmers distributed the Eurasian seven-spotted lady beetle. But this beetle competed fiercely with native ladybugs for natural resources, threatening native populations.

◄ **Ecosystem Management.** Management of an entire ecosystem—that is, all living and nonliving things in a particular place—is one of the newest methods of controlling invaders. For instance, many North American farmers and ranchers prevent livestock from overgrazing on native grasses. This policy helps keep an invasive plant called the Eurasian musk thistle from becoming a damaging weed. If native grasses remain plentiful, they can successfully compete with the thistle and keep its numbers low.

ECOSYSTEMS: BASIC INTERACTING ECOLOGICAL UNITS

No biotic community exists apart from its physical, or abiotic, environment. Each community depends on sunlight to provide energy, soil minerals, water, and atmospheric gases, and each is influenced by all the physical and chemical forces that characterize the area in which it is found. The living portion of an ecological community and its virtually inseparable abiotic environment together form an ecosystem, the fundamental unit of study for the ecologist. Ecosystems, like the communities within them, can be simple or complex. However, even the simplest often reveals complexities that require detailed study.

The Biotic and Abiotic

Components of Ecosystems

Any ecosystem has three components.

- *Energy,* usually derived from sunlight, but rarely and in small quantities derived from other sources. This energy then moves through the ecosystem, going along pathways known as food chains. (See pages 602–603.)

- *Abiotic factors,* including water, soil minerals, and atmospheric gases. The abiotic environment is made up of many objects and forces that influence one another and influence the surrounding community of living things.

- *Biotic factors,* including producer organisms, consumer organisms, and reducer organisms. An organism's survival and well-being depend largely on getting the foods it requires and on associations with other living things.

The nutrients required by all forms of life circulate continually between abiotic and biotic factors. Both energy and nutrients are the vital components sustaining all living organisms in all ecosystems.

Herds on the savanna depend on the seasonal appearance of vast quantities of water, an abiotic factor, to stimulate the growth of plant life, which absorbs energy from the sun. ▼

Producer organisms, usually green plants, are capable of capturing sunlight energy through the process of photosynthesis. They utilize the energy to construct the organic chemical compounds that form the plant body, or they store the energy in energy bonds and link the various atoms or molecules in these organic compounds. (See pages 134–135.)

Consumer organisms include some plants and all animals in the community. Consumers do not obtain their energy directly, but acquire it secondhand from the sunlight energy originally stored in green plants. All animals are completely dependent on the producers for energy and for the chemicals they require for nutrition. Consumers are subdivided into two categories: primary consumers, or herbivores, which feed directly on plants; and secondary consumers, or carnivores, which feed mainly on other animals and thus receive their energy or food chemicals after they have been processed through two other kinds of organisms.

Reducer organisms are mainly bacteria and fungi that decay and decompose the bodies of dead plants and animals. These organisms feed on the complex chemical compounds of the dead organisms and in turn release simple compounds. Through this process, mineral materials that can be picked up and used once more by the roots of growing plants are eventually returned to the soil or water. Without such organisms, an entire community would stagnate, choked by its own debris, and the fertility of the soil would be drained without being restored.

Energy's One-Way Path

Initial Energy Flow

In ecosystems, the source of almost all energy is sunlight, and only green plants, algae, and certain microscopic organisms are equipped to utilize it.

Photosynthesis. The mechanism by which green plants use solar energy is known as photosynthesis. The presence of the green pigment chlorophyll permits capture of energy from the sun and storage of that energy in the chemical bonds of glucose. Through further use of sunlight energy, molecules of glucose are broken down and linked with other chemicals. This results in the formation of the various carbohydrates, proteins, vitamins, and other substances that constitute the body of a plant. (See also pages 134–135.)

PHOTOSYNTHESIS

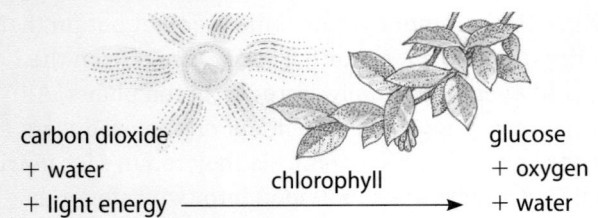

carbon dioxide
+ water
+ light energy ——— chlorophyll ———→
glucose
+ oxygen
+ water

▲ **In herbivores,** some energy remains in the undigested plant residue, some is lost as heat generated in the process of digestion, and some is lost during various other metabolic processes.

Oxygen Restoration. During photosynthesis, two chemical compounds—carbon dioxide from the air and water from the soil—are combined into simple sugars. In the process, oxygen is released back into the atmosphere. Without green plants or some other means of restoring atmospheric oxygen, the continued respiration by animals would eventually exhaust the supply of oxygen.

GOT TO KNOW

ONE-WAY ENERGY FLOW

Energy follows a one-way path through the ecosystem, with the initial supply rapidly decreasing as it passes from one organism to the next. In order for the system to function, energy must be supplied continually at the green plant end of the chain.

Energy Storage

Green plants are capable of storing large amounts of solar energy. However, only about 1 percent of the total solar energy reaching Earth is actually fixed and stored by plants. The rest is lost because it is in unusable wavelengths of light, because it is reflected away, or because it is dissipated in the form of heat. Nevertheless, the 1 percent remaining is more than adequate to maintain life on Earth.

The energy stored within plant bodies cannot be transferred to animal tissues without further loss. At most, 20 percent of the energy is stored in the body tissues of herbivores. A diminished amount of energy is thus available to carnivores. Further energy is lost in eating, digesting, and metabolizing the energy stored in the body of the herbivore, resulting in only a quarter or less of that energy being stored in the body of a carnivore. Further energy is also lost when one carnivore feeds on another.

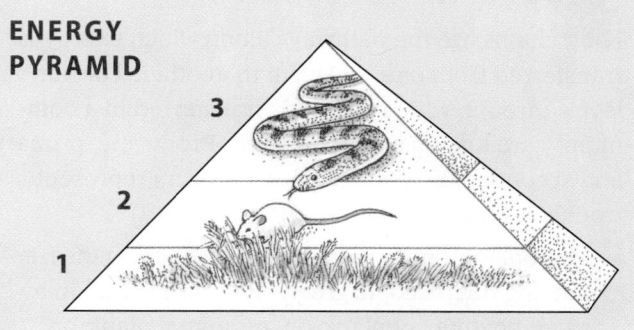

ENERGY PYRAMID

1. energy stored and used by green plants
2. energy available to herbivores
3. energy available to primary carnivores

The sun's energy flows to the producer organisms, which are then eaten by primary consumers. As the food chain lengthens, from primary to secondary to tertiary consumers, energy is lost. Reducer organisms can break down chemical compounds and return them to the soil, but they cannot return energy to the system. Energy needs to be constantly fed into an ecosystem via the producer organisms (plants). ▶

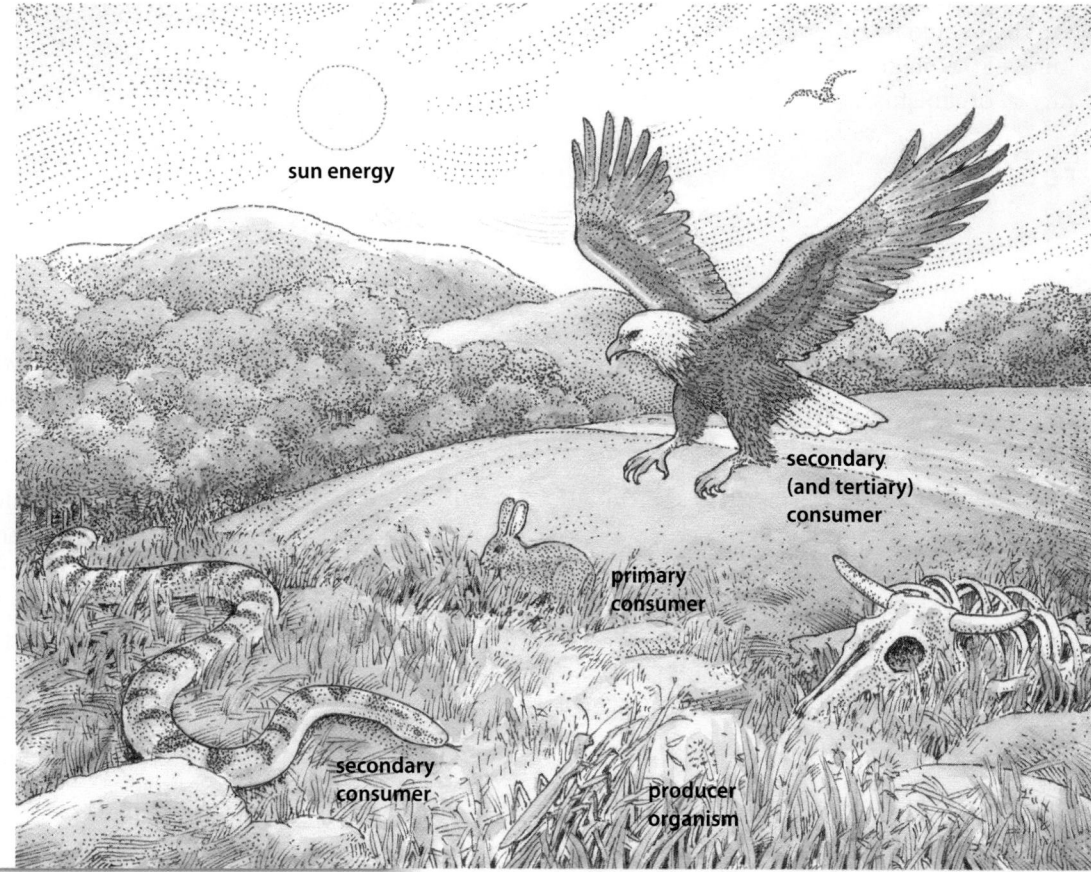

sun energy

secondary (and tertiary) consumer

primary consumer

secondary consumer

producer organism

Trophic Levels

Food Chains and Food Webs

Food chains are the pathways along which energy is transferred from one organism to another. The various levels through which energy is transferred in a community are known as *trophic levels*. Producers, primary and secondary consumers, and reducers represent trophic levels. Consider a pond.

- Phytoplankton, or plant plankton, such as the free-floating microscopic green algae, are fed upon by small floating zooplankton, or animal plankton.

- Zooplankton are eaten by aquatic insects that supply food for small carnivorous fish.

- These small fish may in turn support a population of large fish, for example, bass or pike.

Food Webs. Food chains are difficult to isolate in natural ecosystems because they are usually intertwined into complex food webs. Besides feeding a steer, a green plant may also furnish food for a variety of small animals, including insects and microorganisms, which are then eaten by other species. Hence, it is difficult to unravel the chains and webs in any complex community of organisms.

Ecological Pyramids

The necessary loss of energy between links in each food chain directly affects the number of organisms that can be supported at any trophic level. Thus, the number of green plants upon which deer will feed is always greater than the number of deer that will be supported by the plants. The number of deer, in turn, is always greater than the number of mountain lions that may feed on them.

These relationships can be diagrammed in the form of ecological pyramids, which may illustrate the number of organisms, the total biomass of organisms, or kJ (kilojoules) of energy stored in each layer of organisms.

- In a numbers pyramid, there will be more green plants than herbivores supported by them, and more herbivores than carnivores. The pyramid will show a broad base of plants and a narrow apex of carnivores.

- In a biomass pyramid, it would take about 12,000 pounds (5,455 kilograms) of range forage to support a 1,000-pound (455 kilogram) steer for a year, and the steer could be converted into beef to support a human weighing 170 pounds (77 kilograms).

FOOD CHAIN

plant → mouse → snake → fox

FOOD WEB

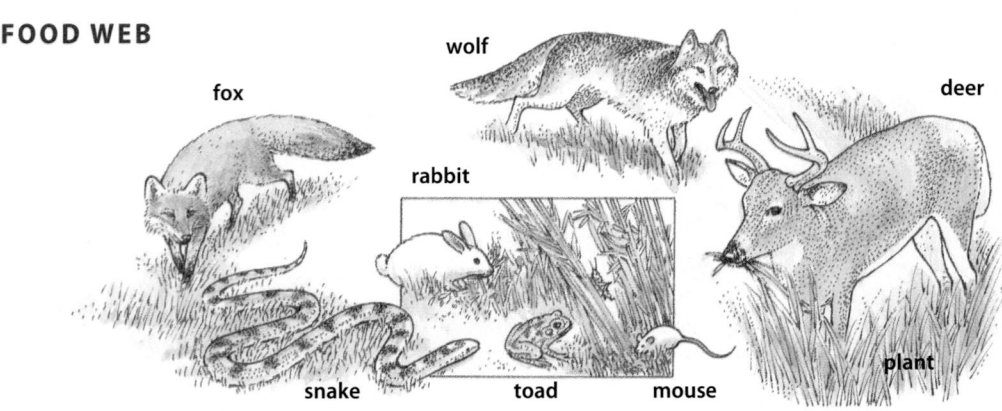

◄ **Chains vs. Webs.** A food chain is linear, whereas a food web involves intertwined food dependencies. Omnivores—creatures that eat plants and animals—complicate linear food chains.

OCEAN'S CYCLE OF LIFE

The creatures of the ocean make up a complex web of life. For most marine life, the food cycle begins with tiny organisms called plankton. Plantlike phytoplankton use sunlight, carbon dioxide, water, and nutrients in the water to make food. Zooplankton, which are animals, eat phytoplankton or other zooplankton. These organisms, in turn, serve as food for fish, whales, and other animals that swim, called the nekton. Many larger creatures of the nekton eat smaller nektonic animals. Animals of the benthos (seafloor), such as sponges and sea lilies, depend on organic debris falling from the upper ocean. Finally, upwellings (deep waters that rise to the surface) carry waste products and other organic debris back to the surface, where they serve as nutrients for the phytoplankton.

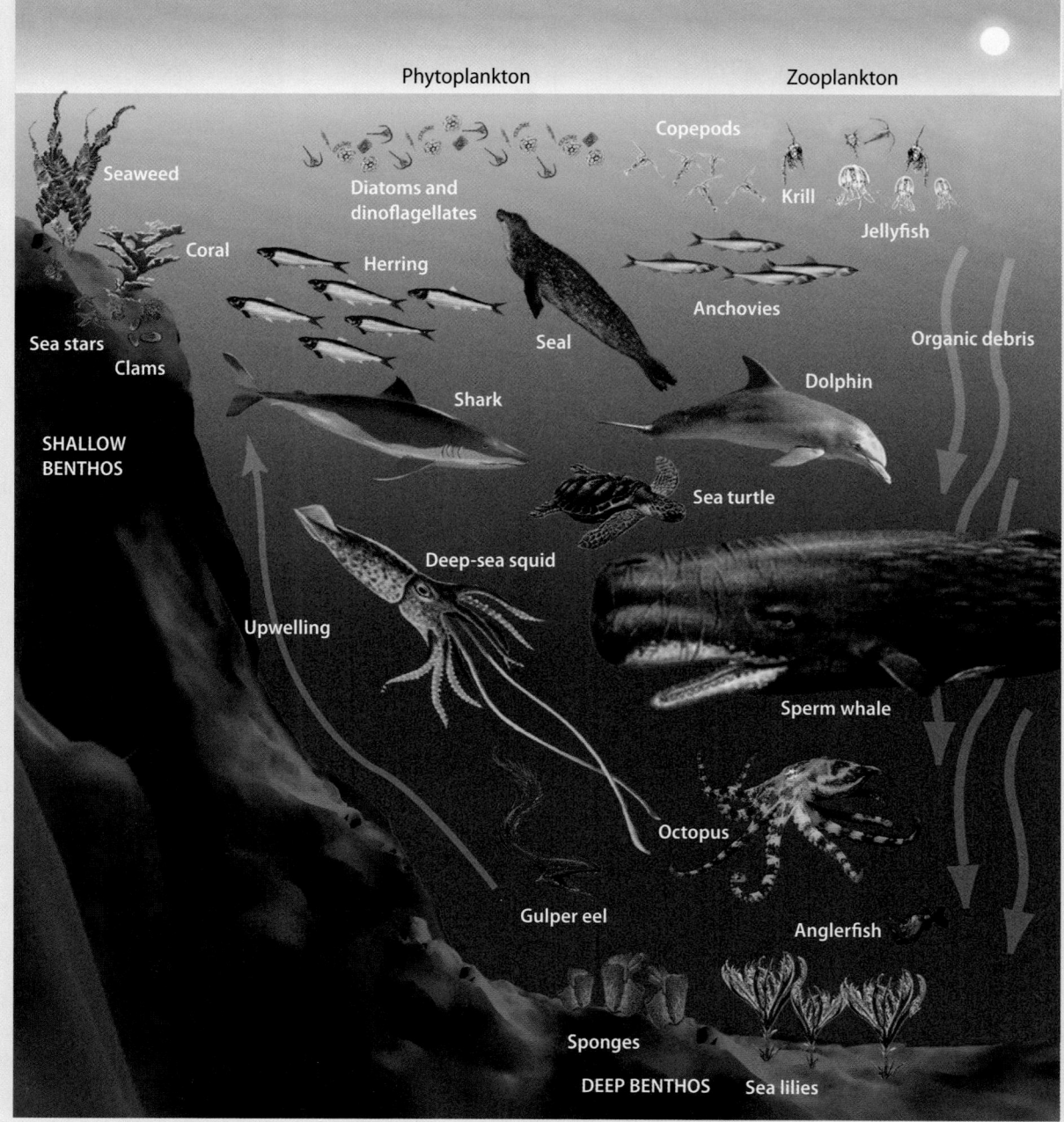

Water, Carbon, and Nitrogen

THE CARBON CYCLE

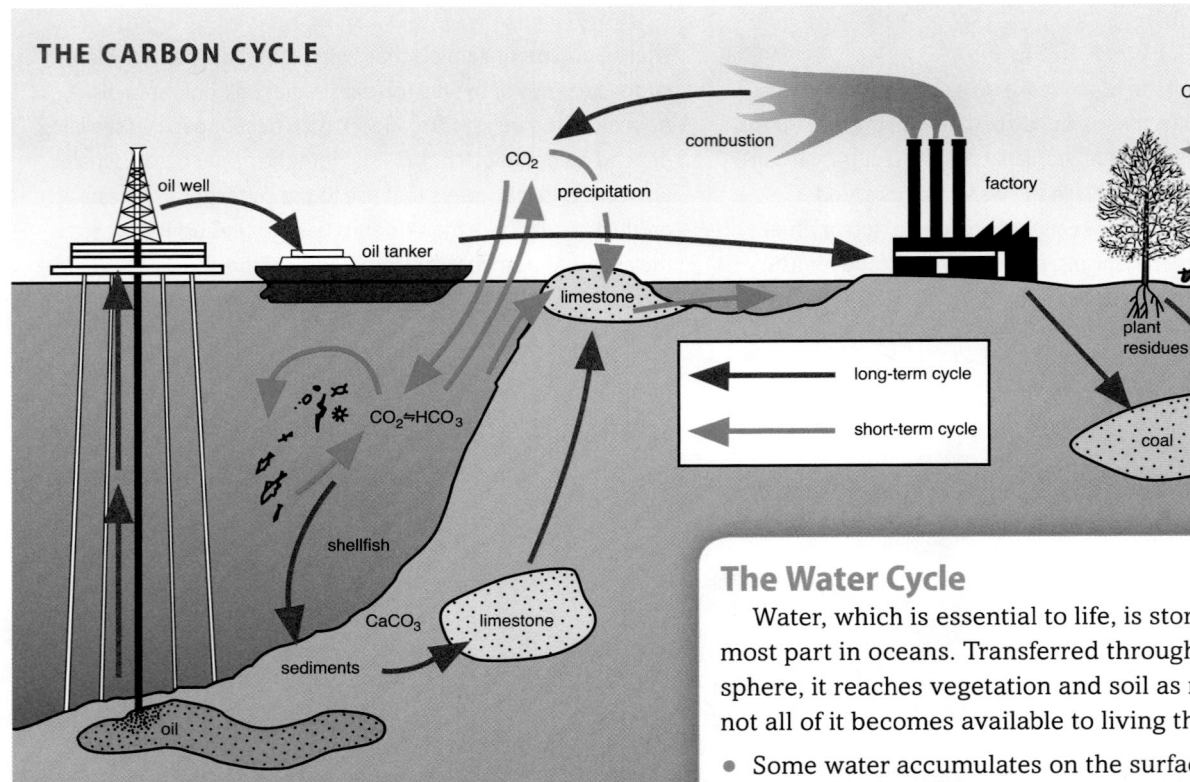

oil well

oil tanker

combustion

CO_2

precipitation

factory

CO_2

tree

cow

limestone

long-term cycle

short-term cycle

plant residues

coal

$CO_2 \rightleftharpoons HCO_3$

shellfish

$CaCO_3$

limestone

sediments

oil

▲ **The flow of certain nutrients,** such as water and carbon, is circular, the nutrients being used again and again. ▼

THE WATER CYCLE

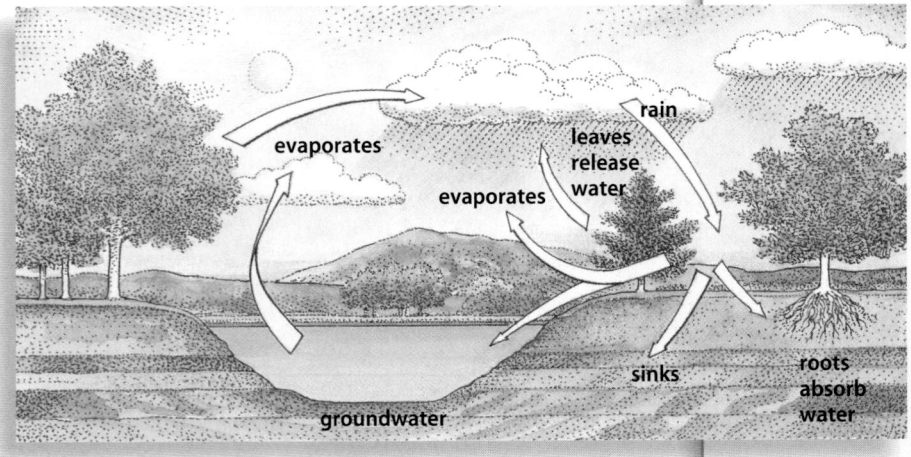

evaporates

evaporates

rain

leaves release water

sinks

roots absorb water

groundwater

The Water Cycle

Water, which is essential to life, is stored for the most part in oceans. Transferred through the atmosphere, it reaches vegetation and soil as rainwater, but not all of it becomes available to living things.

- Some water accumulates on the surface of the ground and returns to the atmosphere through evaporation.

- Much water moves through the soil and runs into underground channels.

- In heavy rains, or when the soil is soaked, water may run off the surface and again be lost.

- Some water that enters the soil becomes bound to soil compounds and unavailable to plants.

The water held in the soil provides not only the water but also the dissolved chemicals necessary for plant life. Only part of the solution that enters the plant roots is taken into the plant cells. The rest is lost through the leaves in the process of transpiration. From plants, the water is transferred to animals. Eventually, all of the water used by plants and animals returns to the soil or goes directly into the atmosphere to begin another cycle. (See also pages 538–539.)

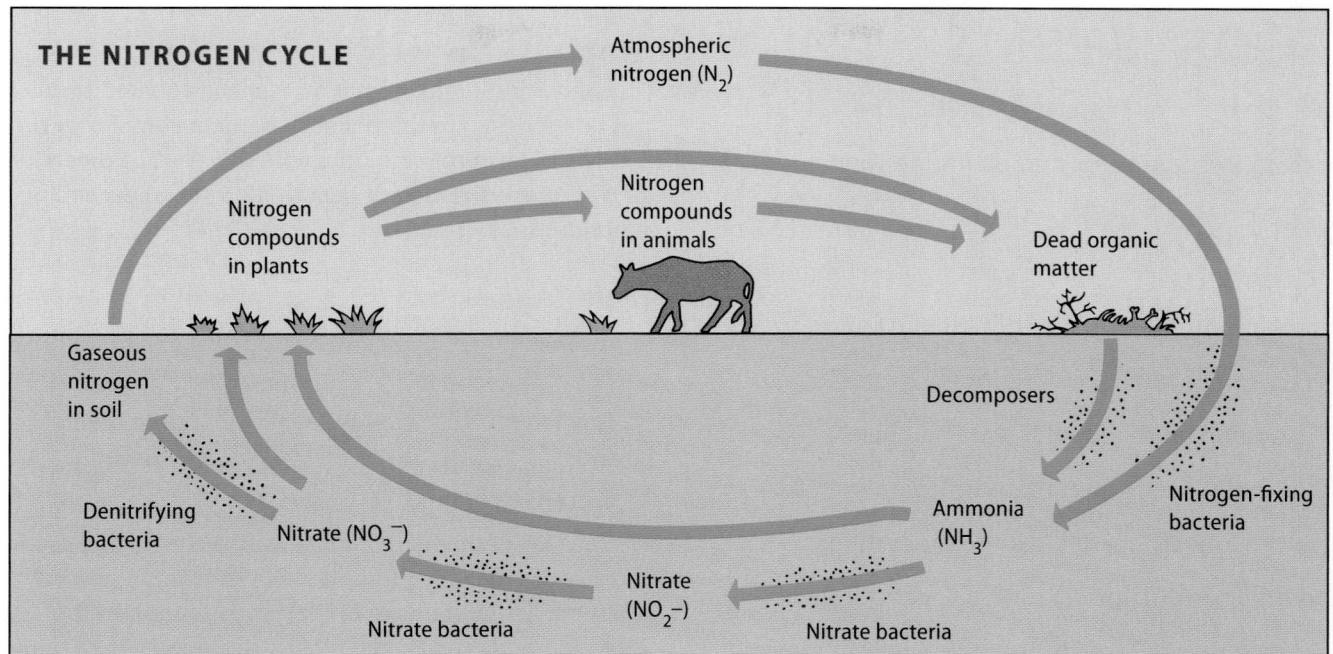

THE NITROGEN CYCLE

Atmospheric nitrogen (N$_2$)

Nitrogen compounds in plants

Nitrogen compounds in animals

Dead organic matter

Gaseous nitrogen in soil

Decomposers

Nitrogen-fixing bacteria

Denitrifying bacteria

Nitrate (NO$_3^-$)

Nitrate bacteria

Nitrate (NO$_2^-$)

Nitrate bacteria

Ammonia (NH$_3$)

Mineral Nutrient Cycle

Food chains provide pathways for mineral nutrients. From soil, fresh water, or saltwater, minerals can be taken up by green plants and introduced into food chains. Mineral nutrient flow is cyclical; the same atom or molecule may move from plant to animal, from animal to microorganism, and from microbe back to plant. When returned to the soil, it is taken up once again by some other plant.

The supply of mineral nutrients in the soil is not limitless. There must be a continuing turnover of these materials if an area is to continue to support life. When soil nutrients are scarce, new growth depends on the decay of dead plants and animals. Organisms such as earthworms process great amounts of plant litter through their bodies. Their actions accelerate decomposition and make available the materials required for new growth. When the cycle is interrupted for any reason, the soil may become infertile.

▲ **Nitrogen** makes up about 78 percent of Earth's atmosphere, but most organisms cannot use nitrogen in its gaseous form. Nitrogen-fixing bacteria convert atmospheric nitrogen into a form that other living things can use. After nitrogen has been fixed by the bacteria, it circulates repeatedly between organisms and the soil. Denitrifying bacteria help regulate the amount of nitrogen in biological circulation by changing some fixed nitrogen back into a gas.

IMPORTANT MINERAL NUTRIENTS

The following elements are commonly found in fertile soil.

- nitrogen
- sulfur
- phosphorus
- calcium
- carbon
- oxygen
- hydrogen
- magnesium
- potassium
- boron
- chlorine
- copper
- iron
- manganese
- molybdenum
- zinc

CLASSIFICATION OF MAJOR ECOSYSTEMS

Life of many kinds is found on land; within the soil; in fresh, marine, and estuarine waters; and in the atmosphere. Because the distribution of ecosystems is determined largely by climate and topography, the kinds of ecosystems vary greatly from one part of the world to another. Climate, vegetation, and animal life are so closely related that in the past, when meteorological records were relatively scarce, geographers mapped the boundaries of climatic regions according to a scheme that reflected the occurrence of major changes in vegetation.

GOT TO KNOW

BIOMES

Ecologists divide the world into a few major ecosystems that share common characteristics but are scattered worldwide. They term these ecosystems *biomes*. Seven is the number of biomes most commonly recognized. Starting at the equator and moving toward the colder poles, these are

- tropical rain forests
- savannas
- deserts
- grasslands
- temperate deciduous forests
- coniferous forests
- tundra

Aquatic biomes, freshwater and saltwater, existing at virtually all latitudes, are an eighth type.

Types of Ecosystems

Tropical Rain Forests

Found predominantly at or near the equator, tropical rain forests are the richest and most complex of the biomes in terms of plant life, with the average diversity of tree species alone per hectare (2.5 acres) exceeding a hundred.

Characteristics

- Consistently high mean (average) daily temperatures of about 30°C (86°F)
- Day lengths that vary little from month to month
- Annual rainfalls of between 200 and 500 centimeters (78 to 195 inches)

Because of the high rainfall, soils are highly leached, usually of red clay or laterite, with little in the way of plant nutrients available in their subsurface. On the other hand, there is much rapidly decomposing organic litter atop the soil. *Mycorrhizal associations,* in which the roots of the plants receive nutrients through the intercession of soil fungi, are a major means of guaranteeing to nutrient-hungry plants all the materials needed to grow in the otherwise poor soil.

LOCATIONS OF TROPICAL RAIN FORESTS

The three largest tropical rain forests are those of

- the Amazon River basin in Brazil and surrounding nations
- the Congo basin in central Africa
- Southeast Asia

Tropical rain forests can also be found in

- Australia
- Mexico
- the Philippines
- many Pacific islands

Vegetation is dominated by very tall, broad-leafed evergreen trees that branch near the crown to weave a solid layer, or canopy, of leaves, typically about 45 meters (146 feet) high. Giant trees often poke through to rise as high as 60 meters (200 feet) or more.

- Plants living below the canopy must compete vigorously for the filtered light that finds its way through. This results in the vertical stratification of species, with earth-rooted lianas, or woody vines, finding their way to the forest canopy, and epiphytes occupying many levels below.

- Epiphytes are plants that rely wholly on other plants for their aerial site but do not obtain nutrients from them; they include orchids, mosses, bromeliads, and ferns.

- The relatively dark floor of the rain forest attracts plants such as ferns, which are capable of surviving in light of low intensity.

Deciduous Rain Forest. A variant on the tropical rain forest biome is the deciduous rain forest that occurs in regions where precipitation is more seasonal. Here, the trees drop their leaves during dry spells as a form of self-protection. Examples are

- monsoon forests, such as those found in India.

- the rain forest of the Pacific coast of Washington State. Warmed by the Japan Current, the Olympic Peninsula forest receives constant precipitation and supports many plant species of rain forest character.

The Sepik River winds through dense rain forest in Papua New Guinea on the island of New Guinea. Many rain forest peoples and animals live along rivers. ▼

Savannas and Deserts

Savannas

Savannas are transitional areas usually found between tropical rain forests and deserts. They can be considered tropical grasslands, though they may support scattered clumps of trees as well.

Characteristics

- Changing seasonal temperature and day length patterns
- Marked variation in the amount of rainfall available, depending on their proximity to other biomes. The range is between 80 centimeters (31 inches) and 160 centimeters (62 inches) of rain annually, most of it coming during the hot season, followed by a relatively dry cooler season.

LOCATIONS OF SAVANNAS

The best-known savannas are those found in a broad band across central Africa (including the savannas of the East African Rift Valley).

Other savannas are found in

- northern Australia
- India
- Brazil
- Central America

Vegetation

The difficulty plants have in obtaining and conserving water has made rapid-growing, tufted perennial grasses with dense root systems the dominant vegetation. The grasses are adapted to die above-ground during the dry season, but they rebound quickly during the rainy period. This resilience is also important in surviving the natural and man-made fires that frequently sweep the savanna. The fires actually serve to maintain the integrity of the biome, controlling weeds and speeding decomposition of organic matter.

Trees, typically acacias, can weather ordinary dry seasons and grass fires, but they are less able to do so in prolonged droughts and have a less certain survival rate. In savanna areas that border a desert biome, tree species are often smaller, denser, and thorny, giving rise to the term *thorn forest*.

A wide variety of animals live on savannas. Lush grasses provide abundant food for many species of grazing animals such as gazelles and zebras. Giraffes eat leaves, twigs, and fruit from widely scattered trees. Such meat-eaters as lions and leopards prey on grazing animals. Many kinds of birds, insects, and other small animals also inhabit savannas. ▼

Deserts

Deserts are defined as regions where evaporation exceeds rainfall. These climatic conditions are often found in lands lying between 20° to 30° north and south of the equator.

Characteristics

- Most deserts receive 15 centimeters (6 inches) to 25 centimeters (10 inches) of rainfall annually, enough to support scattered low-growing vegetation atop arid, grayish soils containing little organic matter.

- Because of the dryness and lack of moderating vegetation, days tend to be very hot and nights quite cold, sometimes with freezing winter temperatures in continental deserts.

LOCATIONS OF MAJOR DESERTS

Some of the world's largest and driest deserts are

- the Sahara (parts of which are lifeless)
- the Gobi of Mongolia
- the Sonoran of North America
- the Arabian of the Middle East
- the Atacama of northern Chile

Vegetation

Desert plants, or *xerophytes,* can be categorized according to their adaptations to drought conditions.

- *Succulents* are perennial plants that store water in thickened leaves or stems and protect it with spines and thorns. Agave, sedum, and yucca are leaf succulents; plants of the cactus family are stem succulents.

- *Resinous shrubs* conserve water in woody stems and protect it with spines and thorns or with foul-tasting compounds, such as creosote or tar. Acacia and mesquite are examples of the former group; creosote bush, tar bush, and camphorous sagebrush are typical of the latter group.

- *Ephemerals* are named for the long periods their seeds remain dormant and the short life cycles in which they mature and reproduce. Ephemerals are not true xerophytes because they need precipitation to flourish, but they make do with brief periods of rain, such as occur even in the desert. Following rain, ephemerals can burst into bloom and then disappear almost as quickly, having completed their reproductive cycle.

- *Halophytes,* or salt plants, are succulents especially adapted to growing in the sometimes *saline,* or salty, soils of the desert.

◄ **Many kinds of plants and animals** live in desert regions. The photo at left shows some plant life of the Sahara. These organisms have developed various ways to survive the extremely hot, dry climate of the desert. One way animals survive is by staying underground or otherwise out of the sun during the day, which is why you don't see them in this picture.

Grasslands and Forests

Temperate Deciduous Forests

Temperate deciduous forests appear in continental areas where seasonal changes are moderate.

Characteristics

- Moderate precipitation of 75 centimeters (29 inches) to 225 centimeters (88 inches) annually
- A mild growing season alternating with a colder season of little or no plant growth

Soil in the temperate forest is often very rich, owing to the annual leaf fall and the humus it generates.

Vegetation. Deciduous trees dominate. In more northerly and upland regions, birch, beech, and maple are prominent. In more southerly and lowland regions, oak and hickory tend to be dominant. Forest floor plants take advantage of early spring or autumn growth, when the thin forest canopy allows generous quantities of light to reach the floor.

Location. Temperate forests are located in the Northern Hemisphere, in broad bands across the northeast of North America, across England and northern Europe, in parts of coastal China and Korea, and throughout the islands of Japan. Smaller examples are found on the east coasts of Brazil, on Madagascar, and on the east coast of Australia.

▲ **Deciduous trees** lose their leaves every autumn, sometimes in a spectacular display of varied colors. These trees erupt in an autumnal blaze on the side of Elmore Mountain, in Vermont.

SCRUB FORESTS

A variant on the temperate deciduous forest biome is the so-called scrub forest, found in the drier Mediterranean parts of the biome, where summers are dry and the cyclonic rainy season comes in the cool winter months. The vegetation of the scrub forest includes many broad-leaved evergreens with tough, waxy, water-conserving leaves. Beneath the scrub forest, a collection of undergrowth typically appears in spring. In California, the scrub forest is known as *chaparral,* from the Indian word for scrub oak; along the French coast it is the *maquis;* and in Chile it is the *matorral.* Scrub forests also occur in portions of South Africa and along coastal portions of Australia.

Grasslands

Grasslands typically occur in temperate regions north and south of 30° latitude, usually in the drier interiors of continents.

Characteristics

- Seasonal drought periods
- Average rainfall ranging annually from 30 centimeters (12 inches) to 150 centimeters (60 inches), depending on proximity to desert or temperate forest

Vegetation. Plants tend to be sod-forming perennial grasses whose roots are best adapted to making their way in the matted turf. Tallgrass prairie plants are characteristic of the areas of higher precipitation, shortgrass prairie plants of the regions of less rainfall and high winds.

Location. The North American grasslands have largely disappeared. Other important grasslands are the steppes of eastern Europe and Russia, the pampas of Argentina, and the veldt of South Africa. Grasslands are also found in eastern Australia and New Zealand.

▲ **Argentine grasslands**

Coniferous Forests

Coniferous forests appear along the northern boundary of deciduous forest biomes at the point where summers become too short and the winters too long for deciduous trees to propagate.

Characteristics

- Average annual rainfall of 38 to 100 centimeters (15 to 40 inches), most of it in summer
- Plant growth is confined to a few summer months.

Vegetation. Coniferous forests are made up of cone-bearing evergreens with small, needlelike leaves and shallow roots. Montane coniferous forests grow at high elevations. Boreal forests, known as taiga, are snow forests typically growing in glaciated regions dotted with bogs, lakes, and rivers.

Location. Coniferous forests are strictly reserved to the Northern Hemisphere and cover much of Canada, Alaska, Scandinavia, and Siberia. They also are found in the higher elevations of the Rocky Mountains, the Cascades, the Sierra Nevadas, and the Alps.

▲ **Coniferous forest** covers the foothills of the Alps in southern Germany.

Tundra

Tundra represents the farthest limit of plant growth in either hemisphere. Here, the climate is too harsh to support even conifers. The tundra is a type of Arctic grassland that is also found at elevations above timberline, the limit of altitude in the high mountain ranges beyond which trees do not normally grow.

Characteristics

- Extreme temperatures (subzero for many months)
- Extremely long winter nights and extremely long summer days
- Less than 25 centimeters (10 inches) of precipitation per year

The inhospitable soil is known as *permafrost*, a layer of permanently frozen subsoil atop which lies a thin layer of active soil of about 23 centimeters (9 inches). This upper soil thaws and heaves briefly in summer to become wet, soggy, and often very acidic.

Vegetation. The herbaceous plants that grow here tend to be small and stunted; they include species of grasses, sedges, rushes, and heather, together with a ground layer of mosses and lichens. All the flowering plants are perennials. Trees are virtually unknown. The growing season is often less than 2 months.

Many living things inhabit the Arctic tundra. Mosses, bright flowers, and plantlike organisms called lichens cover the ground in summer. Each fall, Arctic hares, ermines, willow ptarmigans, and other tundra animals grow white winter coats. These winter coats blend with the snow and help protect the animals from such enemies as wolves and foxes. ▼

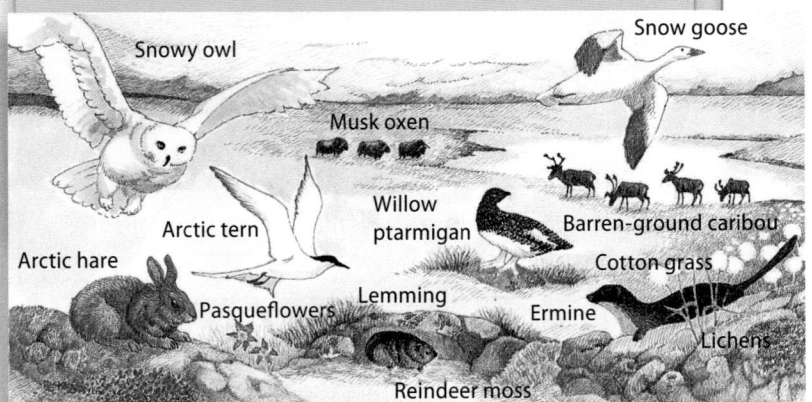

Snowy owl · Snow goose · Musk oxen · Willow ptarmigan · Barren-ground caribou · Arctic tern · Cotton grass · Arctic hare · Lemming · Pasqueflowers · Ermine · Lichens · Reindeer moss

Aquatic Environments

Water covers just over 70 percent of Earth's surface. While there are no major aquatic biomes as such, aquatic environments, where life on Earth is most abundant, are usually considered to be either freshwater or marine.

In both environments, little sunlight reaches any great depth. Therefore, photosynthetic algae and plants occupy only the upper surface region, called the *euphotic zone*, which is lighted from above.

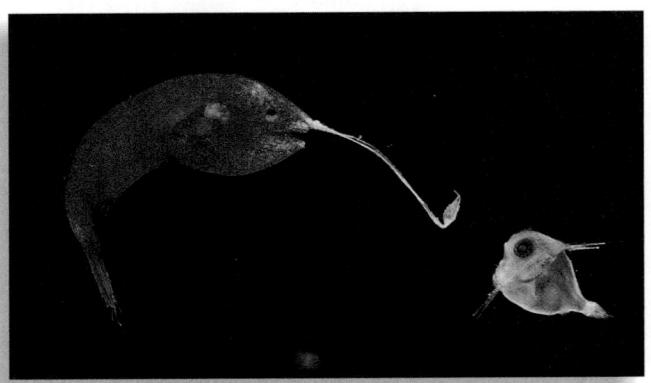

▲ **A deep-sea anglerfish** lures prey with a special light-producing organ at the end of a long, flexible spine. The spine looks like a fishing pole.

Marine (Saltwater) Environments. In the oceans, the euphotic zone produces almost all the food and supports the greatest mass of life. However, great layers of animal life have been located at depths well below the level of light penetration. Squid move to the surface to feed at night and submerge into the darkness during daylight. A great variety of other fish feed either on other organisms that move between the surface and the depths or on materials that sink from above. In the great ocean depths, animals scavenge organic material that filters down through the upper layers of life. In the open ocean, the zone below the euphotic zone, extending down to about 6,500 feet (1,981 meters), is called the bathyl region. Still deeper lies the abyssal region. Most plants and animals in the open ocean are pelagic, leading a free-swimming or free-floating existence, independent of contact with land.

The Neritic Zone. Around the edges of the oceans are the continental shelves, the submerged portions of the continents. Although narrow by comparison with the great breadth of the oceans, the productive neritic zone occupies a considerable area. It is found

Piranha

Knifefish

- following the edges of all the continents.
- surrounding all the islands.

Clown loach

- occurring wherever submerged banks or reefs are near the surface.

Life here is more plentiful than in the open oceans beyond. Light penetrates to support plants on the ocean floor as well as a great variety of attached or bottom-dwelling animal life.

On the upper edge of the shelf is the intertidal zone. Here are found plants and animals that can withstand exposure to the air during low tide. (See also page 580.)

Freshwater Environments. A common classification of freshwater environments separates the low nutrient waters from the high nutrient waters. At one extreme is the glacial lake of the high mountains, fed by melting ice or snow, resting on a sterile substrate of granite, and supporting few plants and animals; at the other, the farm pond in an area of rich soil, green with algae and teeming with animal life.

But life can become precarious in a farm pond. Dissolved oxygen becomes limited in freshwater more often than in the ocean. When photosynthesis occurs uninterruptedly, shallow lakes are rich in oxygen.

However, in the winter, light is screened out by ice and snow, and animal populations may exhaust the available oxygen supply. In freshwater ponds, the environment changes rapidly, and plants and animals must adapt or die. Life in a pond is more complicated but not more complex than in the ocean.

▲ **Brightly colored reef fish** occupy the neritic zone.

Tropical regions of Africa, Asia, and South America have a tremendous variety of freshwater fish. Many of the smaller species are popular aquarium fish. These fish include the guppies, mollies, and swordtails of North and South America and the Siamese fighting fish of Asia. Large tropical freshwater fish include the giant arapaima, which lives in jungle rivers of South America. The arapaima is one of the largest freshwater fish in the world. Some arapaimas weigh more than 200 pounds (91 kilograms). ▶

Elephant-nose mormyrid

Arapaima

ANIMALS AND HUMANS

For almost the entire prehistoric period of human existence, the relationship between humans and animals in their ecological community was that of the hunter and the hunted. The move to supplement a diet of roots, berries, fruits, and nuts by killing animals in order to eat meat profoundly altered the human species.

It ordained a division of labor not found in the animal world. Hunting had to be carried out by the physically stronger males, while gathering was left to women and children. The diet enriched with protein helped lead to the success and ultimate dominance of the species.

When Animals Were Domesticated			
Dog	9000 BC	Camel	3000 BC
Sheep	8500 BC	Honeybee	3000 BC
Goat	7500 BC	Chicken	2000 BC
Pig	7000 BC	Cat	1600 BC
Cattle	6500 BC	Guinea pig	1000 BC
Silk moth	3500 BC	Reindeer	1000 BC
Horse	3000 BC		

Taming the Wild

Domestication

The dog is believed to be the first animal to be domesticated—at least 10,000 years ago but probably longer ago than that. There is even a possibility that the credit of being the first should go to the dog's ancestor, the wolf. Dogs probably descended from wolves, foxes, and jackals, with whom they are grouped. Taming probably came about as dogs ventured into human encampments to eat leftovers. Thus, an association between the two species developed. Prehistoric North American Indians tolerated dogs as scavengers and encouraged them to chase away wild animals. In time, dogs became useful companions in hunting and herding.

Between 8500 and 1000 BC, more than 20 species of animals were domesticated. By 1000 BC, human beings had domesticated the species they needed for shepherding and animal husbandry. Farming was thousands of years old, and the first cities were beginning to form.

THE SIZES OF DOGS

The chihuahua is the smallest breed of dog. The St. Bernard is one of the heaviest breeds, and the Irish wolfhound is one of the tallest. Other breeds range in size between these extremes. The measurements for each dog pictured below are the average weight and shoulder height for the breed.

St. Bernard
165–200 lb.
(75–90 kg);
25½–30 in.
(65–76 cm)

Irish wolfhound
126–145 lb.
(57–66 kg);
32–39 in.
(81–99 cm)

Cocker spaniel
22–28 lb.
(10–13 kg);
14–15 in.
(36–38 cm)

Collie
50–75 lb.
(23–34 kg);
22–26 in.
(56–66 cm)

Chihuahua
1–6 lb.
(0.5–3 kg);
5 in. (13 cm)

Ethics

A burgeoning awareness of the plight of animals has led to a relatively new phenomenon: human beings who militantly defend the rights of animals. These animal rights activists have targeted the fur industry and also research that inflicts painful methods on animals.

The Three R's. The agitation led in 1985 to an amendment to the federal Animal Welfare Act, which requires the three R's.

- Reduction in the number of animals sacrificed
- Refinement of techniques that cause suffering
- Replacement of primates and mammals with other more primitive species wherever possible

Up to 22 million animals are used each year in biomedical research. About 90 percent of them are rats, mice, and other rodents. Dogs and cats account for less than 1 percent, and primates 0.5 percent. Many scientists oppose the aims and tactics of animal rights activists, but primatologist Alison Jolly points out that there are only about 100,000 chimpanzees left in the world. "We shall never forgive ourselves," she says, "if we let the wild populations of our nearest relation dwindle and die."

BREEDING

Breeds began with the small groups of domesticated animals in certain localities that gained reputations for being superior in some way to other members of their species. Humans, seeking improved animals, began isolating such groups. Breeding was conducted to meet human purposes. For example, two common types of sheep are raised for mutton and wool, and two main types of cattle are raised for milk and beef. Animals are bred for food, fur, sport, pleasure, and research. Breeding of dogs, cats, and horses, especially racehorses, is big business.

The Limousin, shown above, is a breed of cattle with a muscular body. Breeders often use Limousins in crossbreeding programs to enhance the muscle development of other cattle. Farmers raise this breed for its meat.

◀ **Activists** join hands to demonstrate for animal rights.

PLANTS AND THE WORLD

Plants play a major role in any ecosystem. Since they are the organisms that collect the sun's energy through photosynthesis, plants are considered to be primary producers, starting the flow of energy through the food chain by providing nutrients for animals—the consumers.

To be a true ecosystem, all the parts must work together in a state of relative balance, so that the ecosystem continues to perpetuate itself and have permanence over long periods of time.

Habitat and Niche

In order to fully understand why any plant species succeeds or fails, it is essential to look beyond the plant's structure and physiology and consider the entire ecosystem in which the species lives. This includes

- habitat
- niche
- community
- population
- carrying capacity

DOMINANCE AMONG TREES

A common example of *competitive exclusion* (see below) can be seen in the dominance of tall-growing trees with dense leaf canopies over shorter trees growing next to them. The taller trees shade the lower trees and cut off their supply of sunlight, thereby either stunting or killing them.

▲ **Tropical rain forests** contain a majority of the world's plant species. These forests have tremendous carrying capacity for both plant and animal species, but competition is intense, which exerts pressure on the numerical limits of any species.

Competition

Competition strongly influences evolutionary change, as each species develops, over many generations, a variety of adaptive improvements. (See page 36.)

Wrestling for Resources. In theory, any two species can occupy the same niche so long as resources are abundant. But usually there is not enough of something—light, water, nutrients, or space—to allow both to prosper.

The species with even a slight advantage will succeed. The less-favored one will be driven out. This phenomenon is known as competitive exclusion.

Many Species, Many Niches. The existence of many species within a given habitat is an index of the habitat's ability to provide many different niches.

Competition for a niche occurs as each plant and animal attempts to preempt the environmental conditions needed for its survival.

Plant Ecosystems	
Habitat	• the local place within a plant's biome in which it is best suited to carry on its way of life • provides a plant with its favored range of temperature, soil, nutrients, humidity, altitude, and sun exposure
Niche	• the functional role of a plant in its ecosystem • includes all the factors of the physical habitat plus the plant's interactions with all other living organisms in the habitat
Community	• describes all the organisms that share a habitat and occupy separate but complementary niches within it
Population	• a group of individual organisms of the same species occupying a given habitat at a given time
Carrying capacity	• the number of organisms of a particular species that a habitat can support • regulated by competition between individuals for survival, both within their community and within their own population

Chemical Warfare

Some plants wage chemical warfare to discourage competition from other plants, a capacity termed *alleopathy*. The chemicals produced by these plants include antibiotics, lactones, terpenes, and phenolic compounds.

Some of these chemicals inhibit the growth of competitive plants. Other chemicals function as chemical shields, discouraging predators—including humans—by making the plant bad-tasting or poisonous.

Aggressive Plants

• The guayule of the Mexican desert excretes cinnamonic acid from its roots, creating a zone around itself that other plants cannot live in.

• The leaves and fruits of citrus plants produce sticky, acrid-smelling volatiles that discourage many insects.

• Nightshade, foxglove, yew, and many weeds are poisonous or unpleasant to taste.

Structural Adaptations

Still other plants protect themselves from animal predators through structural adaptations that make them unpalatable.

• the spines on cacti

• irritant-filled hairs on stinging nettles

• thorns on rose bushes

• sharp-toothed leaves on holly

Paying for Protection

Finally, certain plants gain protection from animal enemies through a relationship called *mutualism*.

In mutualism, the plant provides a special type of food for a particular insect species in return for protection from a larger animal.

One such mutual arrangement is found between the ants living in hollow thorns of acacia trees. The acacia provides a sugar solution attractive to the ants, and the ants attack creatures that threaten the acacia.

Geography and Succession

Further complicating the issues of biome, habitat, and niche are geographic barriers and ecological succession, which modify a plant's ability to become established and multiply.

Physical Barriers. The range of a species is often limited by physical barriers beyond which its seeds cannot cross through natural means. The barriers may be mountain ranges, oceans, an intervening desert, or even a local obstruction. Thus, a rocky outcrop in the way of animal migration routes will influence the dispersal of seeds that depend on animals for transport.

Fireweed recolonizes the slopes of Mount St. Helens, 4 years after the 1980 eruption devastated the blast area. This plant has established a pioneer community. ▼

Succession. Descriptions of classic biomes presume a large degree of permanence and stability in vegetation. Such stable communities of plants are said to be *climax communities,* in that the environment has the optimum assemblage of species that it is equipped to support, and the species are reproducing themselves at a rate equivalent to the rate at which mature and senescent plants are dying.

But it is also true that ecosystems are dynamic. That is, they are subject to changes due to several factors.

- Shifts in regional temperature patterns
- Natural catastrophes, such as volcanoes and floods
- Biological processes such as disease

The sequence of plant communities that occupy an area or a biome undergoing environmental change is called *succession.* Succession usually follows a predictable pattern.

fyi! *Ecological succession can be a relatively rapid event, as when a forest is cleared and certain herbaceous plants spring up within the year. It can also be a matter of thousands of years, as when glacial lakes dry up and become bogs and then woodlands.*

Succession Patterns

Pioneer Communities. The first organisms to occupy an area constitute its *pioneer community*. Pioneer species tend to be small in size and to have growth characteristics that give them advantages in a somewhat inhospitable environment.

- Rapid development
- Early and prolific reproduction

The pioneer community, by its very existence, changes the growing conditions.

- It adds some nutrients to the soil and depletes others.

- It also alters the soil's alkalinity or acidity, called its pH index, through the addition of decayed vegetable matter as plants die and regenerate.

- The first plants may also change the soil's texture and water-holding capacities.

These alterations set the stage for another, more complex, plant community to move in.

▲ **Bogs** are a kind of wetland with soil that is acidic and low in oxygen and minerals. Many bogs are all that remain of great glacial lakes. As they continue to dry, bogs will eventually (over thousands of years) become woodlands.

Progressive Stages. After the pioneer stage, community after community continues to succeed, with the number and diversity of plant species often rising with each new stage. The progressive stages of succession typically bring three general changes.

- Increased shade, as the plant community includes larger and taller plants and decreases air movement near the ground
- Changes in soil composition and chemistry
- Changes in animal life

The last stage, the climax community, arrives when equilibrium is achieved, and the biome as we know it is created.

With the exception of savanna, the United States and Canada offer examples of all of Earth's biomes, though intensive human settlement over the last 400 years has altered some of the biomes considerably.

Prairie of south-central Wisconsin

North American Grasslands. The natural grasslands of North America lie east of the Continental Divide. Tallgrass prairie is more or less coincident with the North American wheat belt and is found where rainfall averages 64 centimeters (25 inches) in the north and 100 centimeters (40 inches) in the south. On its western fringes, the prairie merges into more arid short-grass lands, including grama and buffalo grass. Here, rainfall averages less than 50 centimeters (20 inches).

Tundra of northern Yukon, Canada

North American Tundra. North of the coniferous forests, and reaching up to the Arctic ice cap, is tundra country, with thin-soiled glacial land dotted with bogs known as muskegs. Here, the dominant vegetation is sphagnum moss and lichens such as reindeer moss, although brilliantly colored flowers make a brief showing during the short summer growing season. (See pages 110–111.)

North American Deserts. To the east of the Pacific Forest, desert or near-desert conditions prevail in much of the region, which includes the Great Basin deserts to the north, the Mojave Desert in the center, the Sonoran Desert in the south, and the Chihuahuan Desert along the Texas-Mexico border. Marked differences in vegetation occur throughout, with forests of western yellow pine and Douglas fir in the higher elevations, and piñon and juniper in some particularly dry mountainous areas. Mesquite grass and other grasses occupy the highlands of southeastern Arizona, New Mexico, and the Columbia River basin east of the Cascade Mountains.

Desert areas of the Southwest are populated with xerophytic plants, most of them of dwarf size, with small leaves and water storage adaptations. Sagebrush occupies areas where the soil is relatively free of alkaline salts, while shadscale favors soils with alkaline salts. Creosote bush, greasewood, mesquite grass, cactus, and yucca are also found here, each in a rather narrowly defined habitat and niche.

Chihuahuan Desert in Texas

Maple trees in Vermont

North American Deciduous Forests. South of the coniferous forests, in the eastern half of the continent, is an area once covered with virgin deciduous forests and now largely populated by secondary deciduous forests. Broadleafed oak, maple, ash, and hickory dominate the forests. Farther south, in an area bounded roughly by southern New England on the east, Pennsylvania and Ohio on the north, and Arkansas and Oklahoma on the west and south, is the so-called Central Forest. Here, the tree species are principally oak, hickory, yellow poplar, yellow pine, and red cedar.

Mangroves in Florida

The Southern Forest, stretching from Virginia to Louisiana, comprises several species of yellow pines, including loblolly, slash, and longleaf, mixed with such hardwoods as sweet gums, tupelos, and oaks. The southern tip of Florida is naturally a tropical evergreen forest, as is a small section of southeastern Texas. Mangroves and mahogany are native trees here.

North American Scrub and Pacific Forest. California west of the Sierra Nevada range and south of roughly the 38th parallel supports Mediterranean scrub forest. A thin strip of land running some 4,800 kilometers (3,000 miles) from Kodiak, Alaska, to the Santa Cruz Mountains near San Francisco gives rise to the Pacific Forest, which includes stands of giant sequoias and coast redwoods, and to the Olympic rain forest of Washington State, with its dense tracts of western hemlock, red cedar, Sitka spruce, and Pacific silver fir.

Giant redwoods in California

North American Coniferous Forests. In continental North America, coniferous forests occupy a 6,400-kilometer-(4,000-mile-) wide, horseshoe-shaped region stretching from Alaska across the Canadian Shield to Newfoundland and down the higher peaks of the Appalachian mountain range. The soil here is generally poor, and the most characteristic tree life is a mix of spruce, balsam, fir, hemlock, northern white cedar, and white pine. Scattered paper birch and aspen are found in clearings.

Rocky Mountain forest in British Columbia, Canada

PLANTS AND HUMANS

At the moment in human history when food gatherers became farmers, many useful species of plants and animals began to undergo change as well. What had been wild species over which people had no control became *domesticated,* or tamed, species, over which people were gradually exercising control to suit their needs. Historians describe this transition to formal agriculture as the most important event in human cultural development, for it provided the basis for settled communities, increased population, the accumulation of material goods, the specialization of labor, and ultimately civilization itself.

When and Where Plants Were Domesticated		
Wheat	9000 BC	Fertile Crescent
Barley	9000 BC	Fertile Crescent
Peas	9000 BC	Fertile Crescent
Rice	8000 BC	China
Millet	8000 BC	China
Squash	8000 BC	Andes of South America
Beans	7000 BC	Mexico and Thailand
Maize	7000 BC	Mexico and Central America
Gourds	7000 BC	Thailand
Water chestnuts	7000 BC	Thailand
Potatoes	4000 BC	Andes of South America
Avocados	4000 BC	Mexico and Central America

Domesticating Plants

The Birth of Agriculture

Tracing how and why the agricultural revolution occurred, and assigning it a time in human history, is a fascinating problem. Did it happen among one group of people and spread by example to all others, or was it invented over and over again in many isolated places as different groups of hunter-gatherers arrived at the same stage of intellectual and technical development? And which crops did these first farmers grow?

Gradual Transition. Historians now believe that the process of gathering food in the wild, repeated over many millennia, created the conditions that led naturally to farming. They also believe that it happened repeatedly in many places, in response to similar conditions.

- In most cases, the first crops were wild cereal grasses whose dry single-seeded fruits (grains) could be stored for long periods of time without deterioration and which are high in calories and protein. (The stalks of cereal plants also were useful as bedding, basket straw, or thatching for shelters.)

- In some instances, as in the Peruvian highlands, root crops were probably the first crops tried. (See pages 122–123.)

EARLY AGRICULTURE

Richard MacNeish is an American archaeologist specializing in early agriculture among the Indians of the Americas. He believes that as the great *herbivores,* or grazing animals, that had once been major suppliers of human nutrition gradually disappeared, humans had to shift more and more of their attention to plant foods. Increasingly, human foragers tended to return yearly to the same places of abundant food.

Some of the seeds of these favored plants were inevitably scattered around camp during the eating, and over time the camps came to have their own populations of food crops. The semi-wild camp crops tended to be as good as, or even better than, the plants at the gathering site, because they grew from carefully selected parent plants.

When people noticed that drooping plants always perked up after a rainfall, they may have added watering to their routines. If some plants grew extra vigorously around the camp's garbage dump, they might try putting some of their refuse directly on their gardens. And surely some in the group observed that seeds seemed to germinate better in loose soil than in hard-crusted earth, and so they took to scratching the earth with a digging stick. Thus, says MacNeish, the gatherers and their wild seeds were gradually transformed into farmers and their domesticated crops.

▲ **These seeds** come from ancient varieties of vegetable plants. Today, such varieties are preserved in seed banks around the world. The plants themselves are no longer cultivated.

Origins in the Middle East. The best evidence for the first attempts at farming has been found in the Middle East, in the hilly, semidesert region between modern-day Turkey, Iran, and Iraq. This area, an arc-shaped region, is often referred to as the Fertile Crescent. Gatherers there may have been under particular pressure to find a more reliable way to ensure an annual food supply, given the short supply of meat animals following global climatic changes. Evidence of small farming settlements dating from perhaps 10,000 BC has been found there.

The first crops were almost certainly the indigenous wild grasses—species of Eurasian wheat known as emmer and einkorn, and wild barley—and they were probably first domesticated in the region that is today the border between Iraq and Iran.

▲ **Wheat** is believed to have become domesticated more than 9,000 years ago in the Middle East. It is derived from one of the wild grasses common to the region, perhaps einkorn (pictured above) or emmer.

Controlling Plants

Early Technology

To speed the work, early farmers developed simple tools, beginning with primitive digging sticks, spades, hoes, and sickles, followed by hand plows and later the traction plow, drawn by a domesticated beast. Other early practices that improved yields were

- *irrigation,* the delivery of water to planted fields by hand pump and canal.
- the use of organic *fertilizers,* such as fish and animal wastes.

Crop rotation grew out of the astute observation that plants seem to do less well after a few seasons of growing in the same plot. Farmers did not at first understand that the soil was becoming depleted by the plants' uptake of specific nutrients, but the fact that leaving a field fallow, or planting another crop there for a year, brought better yields was reason enough to alter the planting pattern.

Plant improvement was also practiced as a matter of trial and error. When farmers wanted better crops, they generally selected the seeds or roots of the fattest, largest, tastiest plants and discarded the weaker, less satisfactory plants. In time, many ancestral plants, or races, disappeared.

ZEA MAYS

Wild corn, or Zea mays, the ancestor of today's hybrid sweet corn and cattle corn, is a classic example of plant improvement. Researchers believe that the first domesticated corn plants produced inch-long cobs of a popcornlike hard-kernel corn, and that they were perennials, capable of bursting open their husks and reseeding themselves. By contrast, modern corn cobs measure 15 to 20 centimeters (6 to 8 inches) in length, carry relatively soft kernels, and are enclosed tightly in husks that render the plants dependent on people for seed dispersal and plant regeneration.

◀ **Agriculture** has reshaped many of Earth's natural environments. Farmers in China have carved flat terraces into the slopes of hills and mountains. The terraces allow the farmers to grow rice in flooded sections, called *paddies,* without the water running down the slope.

Powered farm machines, such as this gasoline-powered tractor, helped lead to industrialized agriculture. Machines proved much more effective than draft animals for pulling farm equipment. ▶

Modern Science and Plants

The drive to increase agricultural production has been in the forefront of much scientific progress over the centuries and continues so today. Worldwide, at least 90 percent of all human caloric intake is provided by commercially grown plants, of which wheat, corn, and rice are the leading staples.

The Industrial Revolution of the 19th century mechanized much of Western agriculture, greatly increasing the productivity of the farmer, but it was only in the 20th century, with the dawn of scientific plant breeding, tissue culture, and plant management practices, that the crop yields themselves underwent vast changes.

Plant Breeding. The improvement of the quality of plants to suit human needs or preferences began in earnest after the rediscovery of Gregor Mendel's laws of heredity in 1900. Since that time, the rapidly expanding knowledge of genetics has made it possible to modify plant populations to achieve specific goals. Much of the work of scientific plant breeding was carried out in the 20th century by government research stations, such as those run by the U.S. Department of Agriculture and the Research Branch of Agriculture in Canada, as well as by state and provincial agencies and agricultural colleges.

Plant breeding techniques have generally been based entirely on the idea of creating new *genotypes* (genetic combinations). This is done by crossing, or joining artificially, the genetic materials of closely related but different plants selected for some desirable trait or traits. The offspring of these various new combinations, known as *hybrids,* are then evaluated and tested, and perhaps crossbred again, until the sought-after improvement is achieved.

GOT TO KNOW

WHAT ARE THEY LOOKING FOR?

Some of the many desirable traits that plant geneticists aim for are

- disease resistance
- drought resistance
- better taste
- faster and larger growth
- (or, conversely) dwarfism
- hardiness (resistance to temperature extremes)
- cooking characteristics
- shipping durability
- specific flower colors (for horticultural crops)

Reshaping Plants

Genetic Engineering. In more recent years, thanks to advances in molecular biology, *genetic engineering,* also known as *gene splicing,* has also become a significant high-technology tool in breeding programs. Genetic engineering is the process of inserting portions of the genetic instructions of one organism into the genetic instructions of another for the purpose of adding a desirable trait. Unlike hybridizing, which requires a degree of affinity between parent plants, genetic engineering can sometimes transfer material between wholly unrelated plants. The first successful example of the latter is the so-called sunbean, which was engineered in 1981 using a sunflower and a French bean. The French bean's gene for protein production was inserted into the genetic code of a sunflower. (See also page 80.)

Genetic Diversity. Hybridization and genetic engineering depend to a major extent on the genetic diversity of the plant kingdom. However, as the plants become more and more uniform in their desirable characteristics, they also become more and more vulnerable.

In recent years, high-yield strains of wheat and rice have doubled and tripled yields in vast regions of the developing world. However, the new grains are highly dependent on chemical fertilizers, which may themselves become difficult to obtain in the future. Further, they are so uniform in type that any insect, fungus, bacterium, virus, or climatic change that proves disastrous to wheat or rice could quickly sweep the world before scientists could find a way to stop it. Meanwhile, the older, less vulnerable strains of wheat and rice have all but disappeared.

BLIGHTED HARVEST

In 1970, much of the corn crop in the United States was attacked by a particularly virulent form of the fungus *Helminthosporium maydis,* which causes corn-leaf blight. With a nearly uniform host of corn plants—80 percent had one parent in common—a substantial part of the nation's 1970 harvest was lost to disease.

To prevent a recurrence, breeders of many commercial crops now offer greater diversity in seed choices. To do this, they return frequently to the plant species' gene pool for material from which to construct new hybrids. The traditional and best source of much of this genetic raw material is contained in primitive varieties of domesticated plants and in their still hardier wild ancestors. These plants hold unique genetic material, developed naturally as adaptations to specific, often harsh, local conditions. Genetically, they have remained untouched, often for millennia. Their traits hold the promise of being useful if and when plants are farmed in lands now considered marginal, such as deserts.

◄ **Hydroponic gardening** is a system of growing plants in a controlled environment without any soil and using water to which nutrients have been added.

Science and Technology: Changing Farming in Many Ways	
Method	**Definition**
Conservation tillage	The preparation of soil in ways that greatly reduce soil erosion and depletion
Controlled environment agriculture (CEA)	The raising of crops in sheltered environments, such as greenhouses, where light, temperature, humidity, and water are effectively controlled for optimum plant production
Hydroponics	The growing of plants without soil, using instead water that is enriched with necessary nutrients
Integrated pest management (IPM)	A system of controlling rather than eliminating plant pests, whether insects, weeds, or *pathogens* (bacteria, viruses, or fungi)
Intercropping	A technique for growing two or more crops side by side in alternating rows in combinations that increase soil fertility and crop yields
Plant growth regulators	Artificially produced chemical equivalents of plant hormones used to produce more desirable performance in plants
Satellite monitoring	A system offering farmers, scientists, and government economists detailed data on crop and harvest conditions, as well as on the long-term health of major biomes, using information derived from remote sensors and computerized scanning devices

THE ENVIRONMENT

"Teach your children what we have taught our children, that the Earth is our mother. Whatever befalls the Earth befalls the sons of the Earth."

Chief Seattle of the Suquamish tribe spoke these words to U.S. president Franklin Pierce in 1854. But many decades passed before Chief Seattle's wisdom penetrated the consciousness of large numbers of people. Even today, it is often difficult for people to comprehend the multitude of effects that their actions can have on other people, animals, plants, and environments.

Hairy woodpeckers require trees in their habitat. The insects they eat live in the bark. Trees provide nesting opportunities. The bird is built to climb trees, not alight and move around on the ground. ▼

The Biosphere

The part of the world where organisms live is called the biosphere. The biosphere includes the entire surface of Earth—both land and water—as well as the atmosphere. Each species, or type of organism, has its own habitat—that is, its own natural home within the biosphere. The polar bear's habitat is the coastal areas of the North American Arctic region. The mule cactus grows in deserts. The hairy woodpecker lives in woods and orchards.

Habitat Extents. Some species have broad habitats. Humans have made almost the entire biosphere their habitat. House mice are found on every continent except Antarctica and on many ships at sea. Cattails are found in marshlands throughout temperate North America, Europe, and Asia. Other species have very limited habitats. Koalas are restricted to several areas in eastern Australia. The nene, a relative of the Canada goose, is found on only two islands in Hawaii. The Tiburon mariposa lily lives only on a small peninsula north of San Francisco.

▲ **Polar bears** require solid ice pack in their habitat because they hunt their main food source, seals, through holes in the ice. If the seals can surface for air anywhere in open water, the bears have much less chance of killing them.

The Balance of Nature. An organism does not exist by itself. It constantly interacts with its physical environment and with other organisms in that environment. (See pages 596–597.) It is affected by temperature, rainfall, oxygen levels, germs, predators, and so on. If the environment changes, the organism is affected, sometimes drastically.

- Harvesting bamboo forests decreases the food supply of pandas.
- Falling oxygen levels in a lake cause fish to suffocate.
- An exploding volcano topples millions of nearby trees.

People sometimes speak of the balance of nature. This concept holds that there is a stability in nature—that as one change occurs, it causes a response that balances the effects of that change.

Thought Experiment: Rabbits. For example, if the rabbit population increases, there will be more food for foxes, so the fox population will increase. This will limit the rabbit population, which will limit the fox population, and so on. Generally, a balance is established between the populations of the prey and the predator. But this is just one relationship that an organism has with its world. Many forces operate within the rabbits' habitat to affect the size of their population. The system of checks and balances maintains stability only to a degree. Nature is much more complex than that.

▲ **Giant pandas** feed exclusively upon bamboo shoots, stems, and leaves, which renders them especially vulnerable because they cannot eat something else if bamboo forests disappear.

A pond is a typical ecosystem; it can serve to illustrate how all parts of an ecosystem interact. Sunlight provides the energy needed for biological processes. The climate determines how much rain falls on the pond and on the surrounding watershed; how long the growing season lasts; and whether the pond will be covered with ice in winter. The soil affects the water's chemistry, which helps determine which species can live in the water.

The life of a pond changes as the water level changes. In a pond with high water, *left,* plants are less dense and animals that live best in open areas are abundant. When water is low, *right,* plants cover more of the pond surface and animals that thrive in dense plant growth are more common.

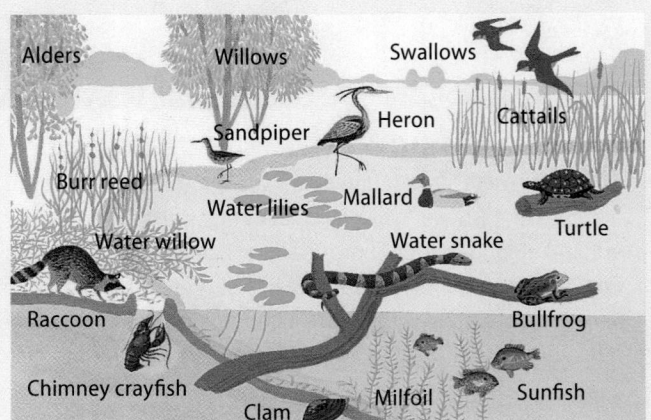

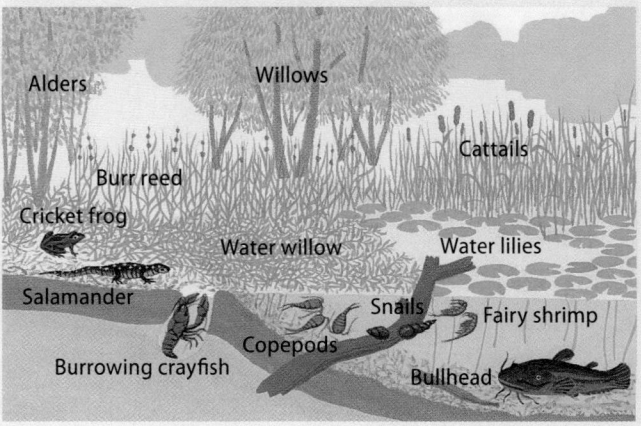

Changing the Environment

People and Ecosystems. The activities of humans have a major effect on every kind of ecosystem, regardless of its location or size. Some activities have immediate, often dramatic, consequences; for example, construction of a new house beside a pond may fill half the pond with bulldozed debris. Other activities have gradual, hard-to-measure effects, but they can be as deadly as the more dramatic events. For example, at first, acid rain falling on a pond may be neutralized by chemicals naturally present in the pond. Only when the neutralizing agents are used up will the pond begin to become acidic. Thereafter, each polluted rainfall will further increase the acidity. Before long, one species after another will be harmed by its changed environment.

Such problems ultimately affect every form of life, including people. Pollution damages crops, reduces forest yields, corrodes buildings and bridges, endangers travelers by limiting visibility, increases the cost of purifying water supplies, and causes illness and premature death.

Environmental Boomerangs

People have often purposely changed ecosystems. Prairies have been turned into wheat fields, pesticides have been sprayed to kill mosquitoes, and wetlands have been drained to build houses. In the case of many of these activities, attempts to solve one problem have inadvertently created new and worse problems.

DDT. Shortly before World War II, scientists discovered that DDT (dichlorodiphenyltrichloroethane) was an effective insecticide. Over the next few decades, the use of DDT to control agricultural, garden, and household pests became widespread. Unfortunately, it takes a long time for DDT to break down into harmless substances. When birds ate insects sprayed with DDT, the DDT accumulated in their bodies, killing them or interfering with their reproduction. American bald eagles, brown pelicans, and peregrine falcons were among the species whose futures were seriously threatened by DDT.

▲ **Fertilizer runoff,** sewage, industrial waste, and radioactive emissions are some of the human activities that can have an adverse impact on plant and animal life.

RABBIT INVASION

One of the more famous and damaging boomerang effects occurred in Australia. When Europeans first settled there, they brought along rabbits out of a desire to have familiar animals from their homelands. The rabbits, in a new environment free of natural predators, multiplied at a phenomenal rate and became serious pests, causing extensive environmental and economic damage. (See pages 598–599.)

Wetlands. In another boomerang effect, more than 80 percent of the freshwater wetlands that existed in the United States in colonial times have since been drained, many for farmland or housing. But loss of the water-holding capacity of the wetlands has resulted in flash flooding.

Smokestacks. Even attempts to solve pollution problems can boomerang. In the 1970s, tall smokestacks were built to reduce local pollution in industrialized areas. Some of these stacks were more than a thousand feet tall. Pollutants emitted at these heights are less likely to settle over surrounding communities, thus preventing or greatly reducing local pollution problems. Unfortunately, the tall stacks turned a local problem into a national or even an international one. Prevailing winds carry the pollutants over hundreds or even thousands of miles, depositing them as acid rain in distant states or countries.

▲ **These spruce trees** in the Czech Republic were killed by acid rain.

BIOSPHERE 2

Biosphere 2 is a 3.15-acre glass-enclosed habitat near Oracle, Arizona. It contains living quarters, an agricultural area, and five different ecosystems (desert, marsh, ocean, savanna, and rain forest). Its original purpose was to explore the interaction between different environments as well as test the potential of building self-sufficient ecosystems for use in space exploration. Mission I took place with eight inhabitants from 1991 until 1993 and is generally looked at as a failure. Oxygen was pumped in from the outside when inside levels continually fell, and food could not be produced at an adequate rate. Mission II took place in 1994 and experienced multiple crew changes and sabotage. It ended 4 months short of its 10-month run.

Columbia University took over management in 1995 and ran Biosphere 2 as a research site until 2003. In June 2007, it became a research project for the University of Arizona, and their experiments began 2 months later. Biosphere 2 has been open to the public as a tourist attraction since 2001.

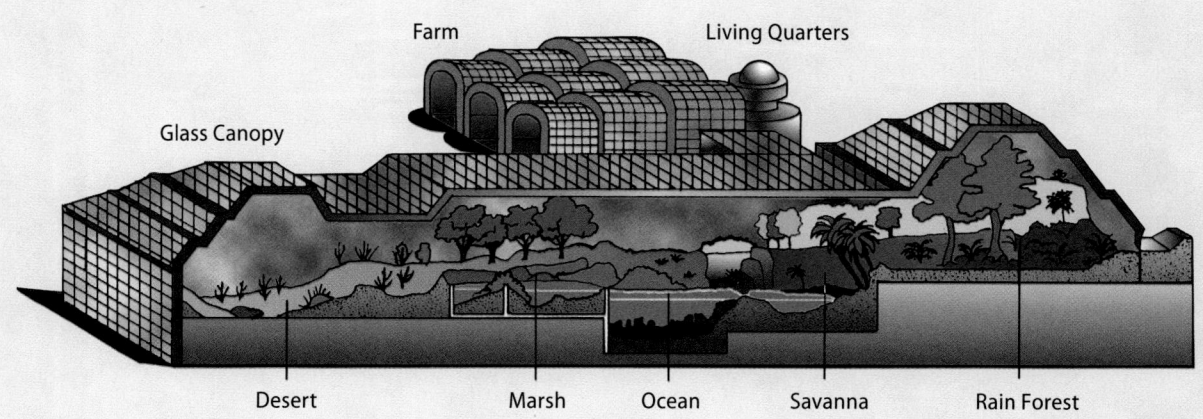

THE GROWING POPULATION

The rate at which a population grows reflects the difference between the birthrate and the death rate. Despite disease, famines, wars, and accidents, people have produced babies faster than people have died, and so the world's human population has grown.

During people's first 2 million years on Earth, their total population probably never exceeded 10 million.

Growing populations result in increased demands on food supplies and other resources. More people also means more wastes, which pollute the air, soil, and water. ▼

Population Explosion

From the Margins to Dominance

It was not until the Stone Age, when people domesticated animals and developed agriculture, that numbers increased more rapidly. But as recently as AD 1, there were only 250 million people on Earth. It took until 1650 for the population to grow to 500 million.

Since then, the human population has increased at an ever faster rate. Around the year 1830, the population reached 1 billion. It reached 2 billion in 1930, 3 billion in 1960, and 4 billion around 1975.

In 1999, there were an estimated 6 billion people living on Earth. Every second, three more babies are born. Every day, there are a quarter of a million new people. Every year, there are an additional 90 to 100 million people to feed, clothe, and house.

SOLID WASTE GENERATED EACH DAY IN THE UNITED STATES

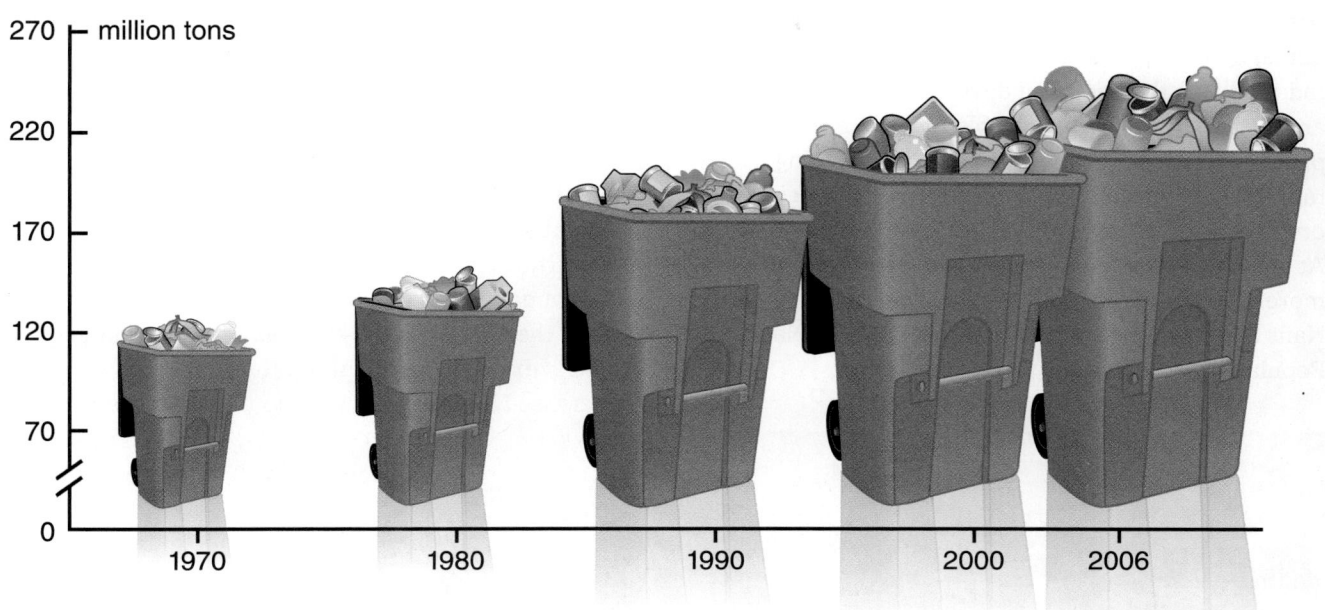

DEVELOPING COUNTRIES

Most current population growth is occurring in developing countries, particularly in southern Asia and in Africa. Southern Asia, which had almost a quarter of the current total of the world's population in 1990, was to account for 31 percent of the total increase during the 1990s. Africa, with 12 percent of the world's population, was to account for 23 percent of the increase.

Dr. Nafis Sadik, executive director of the United Nations Population Fund, points out that these increases are occurring in the nations that are least equipped to meet the needs of the new arrivals and least able to invest in the future. "These increasing numbers are eating away at the Earth itself," said Sadik. "The combination of fast population growth in poor countries has begun to make permanent changes to the environment. These changes include continued urban growth; degradation of land and water resources; massive deforestation; and buildup of greenhouse gases. Many of these changes are now inevitable because they were not foreseen early enough, or because action was not taken to forestall them. Our options in the present generation are narrow because of the decisions of our predecessors. Our range of choice, as individuals or as nations, is narrower and the choices are harder."

More People, Less Space

Dangers for Both Rich and Poor

While more and more people in developing countries are causing increasingly extensive environmental damage in such areas as deforestation and land degradation, it is the people in developed countries who are overwhelmingly responsible for environmental problems such as the inevitable global warming, acid rain, and destruction of the ozone layer. "Developed or developing, the more people the more pollution: At any level of development, larger numbers consume more resources and produce more waste," notes Dr. Nafis Sadik, executive director of the United Nations Population Fund.

Food Production. The United Nations predicted that the world's population would reach 8.47 billion by 2025, with 95 percent of the growth occurring in the developing countries of Africa, Asia, and Latin America. With the world's population increasing about 1.2 percent a year, food production must grow at about the same rate to feed the increasing number of people. Many experts believe food production will fail to keep up with population growth unless the birthrate falls sharply. So far, these needs have been met by food surpluses in other nations, especially the United States and Canada. But what happens if extended drought or other problems should decrease North America's crop yields?

◄ **Environmental Damage from Chickens.** Factory farms, such as this chicken operation, pollute local water tables when liquid sewage is released untreated. But raising chickens tens of thousands at a time is required to feed vast numbers of people.

WORLD POPULATION AND YEARLY GROWTH

Major area	Population (current estimate)	Yearly Growth (current estimate)
World	6,895,542,000	1.19%
Africa	1,027,783,000	2.33%
Asia	4,186,414,000	1.17%
Australia	21,865,000	0.86%
Europe	706,966,000	−0.01%
North America	538,417,000	1.00%
Pacific Islands (including New Zealand)	17,839,000	1.62%
South America	396,258,000	1.33%

Fighting over limited resources has already occurred in some areas, and disputes are expected to grow, threatening the security of governments and nations. In 1969, El Salvador went to war with neighboring Honduras, primarily in an effort to obtain more land for its growing population. In 1983, widespread ethnic violence in northeastern India claimed thousands of lives as native Assamese demanded the deportation of Bengalis who had fled to India because they could not obtain enough food or other basic necessities in their native Bangladesh.

Wealthy nations, such as the United States, are unlikely to remain immune to conflict. Court battles between developers and farmers over water rights and between loggers and preservationists over ancient forests are dangerous omens of the future, as are plans to attempt to restrict immigration.

Slowing Population Growth. Many environmentalists, demographers, and other experts stress the need to slow population growth. In developing nations, the birthrate averages 3.9 per woman. This is a major improvement since 1960, when the rate was 6.0, but it is still considered too high because it is significantly higher than the death rate. In industrialized nations, the birthrate averages 1.9 children per woman. This is below the death rate. However, the population of most of the industrialized nations continues to grow because of immigration.

This map shows how the world's population is distributed. About three-fourths of all people live in Asia and Europe. Regions with severe climates, such as desert areas, are thinly populated. The map also shows the location of some of the world's largest metropolitan areas. ▼

WORLD POPULATION DENSITY

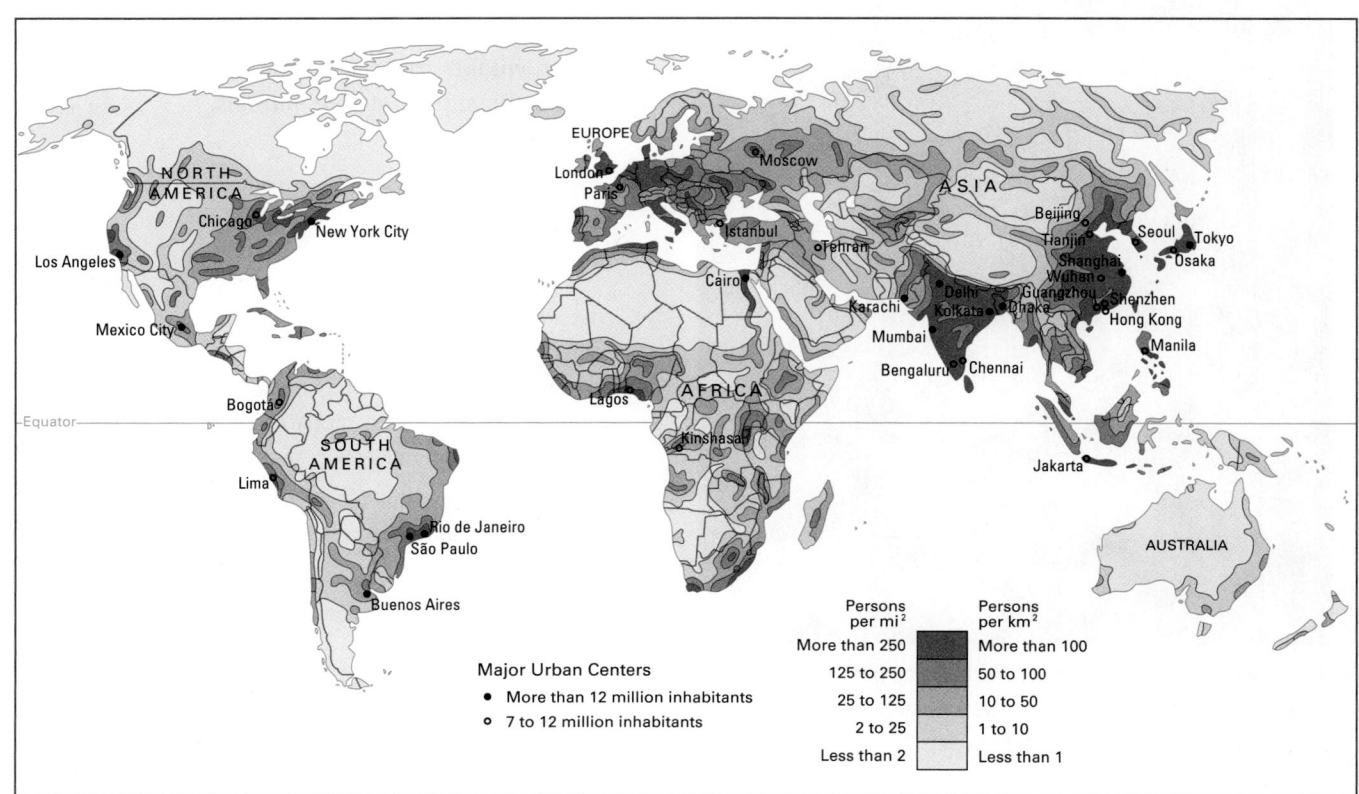

Major Urban Centers	
●	More than 12 million inhabitants
○	7 to 12 million inhabitants

Persons per mi²	Persons per km²
More than 250	More than 100
125 to 250	50 to 100
25 to 125	10 to 50
2 to 25	1 to 10
Less than 2	Less than 1

CONSERVATION

is the management, protection, and wise use of natural resources. Natural resources include all the things that help support life, such as sunlight, water, soil, plants, animals, and minerals. Some resources, such as forests, are renewable; that is, they can replace themselves. Other resources are nonrenewable. Once these are used up, they cannot be replaced. A rising population, coupled with rising consumption, has greatly increased the demands on natural resources. Conservationists work to ensure that the environment can continue to provide for human needs.

▲ **The Disappearing Parrot.** The imperial parrot, shown here, is endangered by the loss of its natural habitat and by people who trap the birds illegally as pets.
  According to the International Council for Bird Preservation, more than 1,000 of the 9,000 species of birds in the world are at risk of extinction—three times more than in the late 1970s.

Plants and Animals

Plants and animals are natural resources, and they are essential to human life.

- Plants provide us with the oxygen we need in order to live.
- The foods we eat come from plants themselves, or from animals that eat plants in order to survive.
- Many of our most valuable medicines are derived from plants and animals.
- Many of the items we use in daily life—buildings, furniture, cloth—are made from plants and animals.

Endangered Species

Technically, plants and animals are renewable natural resources. They can replace themselves through reproduction. Sometimes, however, all the members of a species die. This is called *extinction*. Once a species becomes extinct, it is gone forever; neither it nor its genes can ever be replicated. A species that is at risk of extinction is called *endangered*.

Species mainly become endangered because of loss of habitat, wildlife trade, overhunting, and competition with domestic and nonnative animals.

RATES OF EXTINCTION

Since life began on Earth, millions of species have become extinct. Mass extinctions—events in which large numbers of species suddenly become extinct—have occurred several times, mostly due to environmental changes, volcanic eruptions, and other catastrophic changes. Today, most species are endangered by human activity.

- Scientists believe that during most of the past 600 million years, extinctions occurred at the rate of one species a year.
- Now, as the human population has grown and spread, the rate has accelerated.
- The noted biologist E. O. Wilson has calculated that we may currently be losing as many as 17,500 species annually.
- Some scientists predict that several hundred extinctions per day may occur during the early 21st century.

How Species Become Endangered		
	Causes	**Examples**
Loss of habitat	Habitats are destroyed to provide houses, roads, energy, farms, and timber for human populations. Pesticides, industrial wastes, and other chemicals contaminate the habitats.	• The forests of Central America are being replaced by cattle ranches.
Wildlife trade	Species are captured and/or killed for commercial use or as trophies. Still other species are captured and sold alive to zoos or as exotic pets.	• Elephants are killed for their ivory tusks, whales for their meat, and leopards for their fur. • Species such as the polar bear are hunted because their heads or skins are desirable trophies.
Overhunting	Some species are hunted as food; many species are killed by people who believe that the animals threaten their livelihoods.	• Livestock owners may shoot, trap, or poison wild animals that they consider a danger to their herds. • Farmers and ranchers in North America have nearly eliminated the red wolf and many species of prairie dogs.
Competition	Introduction of a new species into an area leads to competition for food and other resources. A new species might also prey upon the other species living in an area.	• On many islands, native birds, mammals, and reptiles have become endangered after people introduced domestic animals. • In mainland areas, stocking of game fish threatens native fish. • Nonnative plants and animals crowd out many native species.

A Lethal Chain Reaction

The decline of one species can create a chain reaction that adversely affects other species in the ecosystem. For example, the prairie dog is a burrowing rodent that digs extensive tunnels in the grasslands of the American prairie.

Ranchers who raised cattle on the prairies wished to do away with the prairie dog. Their cattle and horses would break their legs when they stepped into prairie dog holes. Even worse, the prairie dogs ate the grass, depriving the cattle of food. In the early 1900s, federal and state governments began programs to poison the prairie dogs.

As the poisoning took effect and the prairie dogs began to disappear, so did the black-footed ferret,

which depended on the prairie dogs for food. By 1986, too few ferrets remained to ensure their survival in the wild. Researchers captured 18 ferrets and brought them into captivity to help save the species.

The prairie dog was considered a threat to the cattle industry. ▶

Species in Trouble

Tracking Endangered Species

Various organizations publish lists of endangered species to improve public awareness. Some species have qualified for legal protections.

- The United States Fish and Wildlife Service tracks endangered plant and animal species.
- The IUCN (International Union for the Conservation of Nature and Natural Resources) compiles lists that include thousands of animal and plant species that are threatened or endangered.

By the Numbers. As of 1990, more than 560 native American plants and animals had been listed by the U.S. Department of the Interior as endangered. Their populations or habitats were so small that scientists feared they would soon become extinct, unless serious efforts were made to protect them.

In addition, Interior's list now includes more than 500 endangered species that live not in the United States but elsewhere in the world. Environmentalists believe that unknown numbers of additional species are doomed, many of them not yet known to us.

▲ **Certain tiger varieties** have already died out completely, and scientists consider all tigers to be in great danger. Wild tigers are found only in Asia.

▲ **The green pitcher plant** is an example of endangered plant life. Its habitat has been degraded by construction and agriculture. The wild population has also been reduced by commercial and private collectors.

GETTING ON THE LIST

The IUCN's lists sort species according to levels of population reduction or habitat loss, as well as the number of remaining individuals. The lists are divided into nine categories.

- **Extinct** (all individuals of the species have died)
- **Extinct in the wild** (the only living individuals are in captivity, such as zoos)
- **Critically endangered** (at extremely high risk of extinction)
- **Endangered** (at very high risk of extinction)
- **Vulnerable** (at high risk of extinction)
- **Near threatened** (likely to be at risk of extinction in the near future)
- **Least concern** (does not qualify as "at risk")
- **Data deficient** (not enough information to determine the risk)
- **Not evaluated** (scientists have not attempted to determine the risk of extinction)

SOME ENDANGERED SPECIES

The following chart lists some species that have been determined to be at high risk of extinction, and what kinds of threats they face. Protection programs have improved the outlook for some of these species, such as the black-footed ferret and the California condor.

Common Name	Scientific Name	Distribution	Survival Problems
Asian elephant	*Elephas maximus*	South-central and southeast Asia	Habitat destruction; illegal killing for ivory
Asiatic lion	*Panthera leo persica*	India	Habitat destruction; overhunted for sport
Black-footed ferret	*Mustela nigripes*	Wyoming	Poisoning of prairie dogs, its chief prey
Black rhinoceros	*Diceros bicornis*	South of Sahara in Africa	Habitat destruction; overhunted for its horn
Blue whale	*Balaenoptera musculus*	All oceans	Overhunted for blubber, food, and whale oil
California condor	*Gymnogyps californianus*	Southern California, Arizona	Habitat destruction; hunted for sport; poisoned from lead shot and predator-control programs
Cheetah	*Acinonyx jubatus*	Africa, Iran	Habitat destruction; overhunted for sport and fur
Giant panda	*Ailuropoda melanoleuca*	China	Habitat destruction; illegal killing for fur; illegal capture for zoos
Imperial parrot	*Amazona imperialis*	West Indies, Dominica	Habitat destruction; illegal capture for pets
Kemp's (or Atlantic) ridley sea turtle	*Lepidochelys kempii*	Tropical and temperate parts of the Atlantic	Overhunted for its leather; overcollection of eggs
Orangutan	*Pongo pygmaeus*	Borneo, Sumatra	Habitat destruction; illegal killing of mothers to obtain young for zoos and for pets
Red wolf	*Canis rufus*	Southeastern United States	Habitat destruction; killed in predator-control programs
Snow leopard	*Uncia uncia*	Central Asia	Overhunted for its fur; killed in predator-control programs
Tiger	*Panthera tigris*	Southern Asia, China, Eastern Russia	Habitat destruction; illegal killing for sport and body parts
Floating sorrel	*Oxalis natans*	South Africa	Habitat destruction
Green pitcher plant	*Sarracenia oreophila*	Alabama, Georgia	Overcollection; habitat destruction
Running buffalo clover	*Trifolium stoloniferum*	Central United States	Unknown
Snakeroot	*Eryngium cuneifolium*	Florida	Habitat destruction

Wildlife Conservation

Environmentalists are among those who believe people have a moral obligation to share Earth with other species and to help those species survive, whether they be sleek tigers, showy orchids, or tiny, dull-looking worms. Wildlife conservation is the wise management of natural environments for the protection and benefit of plants and animals.

Methods of Conservation

The method used to protect wildlife depends on the source of the danger to the species. Much wildlife can be helped by ensuring that their environment provides enough food, water, and shelter. This method, habitat management, involves such action as soil conservation, good forestry practices, and water management.

Wildlife refuges like this one are essential for protecting species that are threatened by the destruction or pollution of their natural habitats. ▼

Legal Protections. Both international and national laws protect endangered species.

- In the United States, the secretary of the Interior, acting through the U.S. Fish and Wildlife Service, has broad powers to protect and conserve wildlife and plants.

- The secretary of Commerce, acting through the National Marine Fisheries Service, has similar authority for protecting and conserving most marine life.

- The U.S. Endangered Species Act of 1973 calls for the conservation of critical habitats—the areas of land, water, and air space that endangered species need for survival.

- Hunting and fishing laws have been passed to conserve wildlife by limiting the capture of various animals.

Wildlife refuges, parks, and preserves have been established in all parts of the world to help protect endangered species.

- More than 37,000 protected areas exist worldwide. The majority of them are less than 4 square miles (10 square kilometers) in size.

- The U.S. National Park System has about 200 protected areas with significant wildlife habitats.

- The U.S. National Wildlife Refuge System includes more than 500 refuges.

Zoos also play a critical role in conserving and protecting certain species.

- Many zoos have sophisticated breeding programs that may save some endangered species.

- More than 100 animal species are now part of formal breeding programs in North American, European, and Australian zoos.

- Species helped by breeding programs include the snow leopard, black rhinoceros, orangutan, gorilla, Bali myna bird, and Puerto Rican toad.

It is debatable, however, whether all zoo-reared animals can be successfully reintroduced to the wild.

Obstacles to Conservation

Conservationists face a number of obstacles in their mission to protect threatened species and habitats. Two major obstacles are law enforcement and human economic needs.

Law Enforcement. Often, endangered species live in remote areas, making it difficult for law enforcement officers to spot poachers (people who hunt protected species illegally). To help counteract this, many countries prohibit the importation of species protected by law, thereby restricting the market for them.

Economic Needs. Another problem is the need to balance habitat preservation with economic growth. In many developing countries, critical habitats are being destroyed by people desperate for food, firewood, and other necessities.

In developed countries, economic growth is often cited to justify habitat destruction, too, though in these cases the validity of the argument is generally hotly contested by environmentalists.

STOPPING POACHERS

Bans on importing protected species—or products made from them—can help restore endangered populations.

In 1989, the Convention of International Trade in Endangered Species banned trade in elephant ivory. Poaching had reduced Africa's elephant population by more than half in only 10 years, from 1.3 million in 1979 to 625,000 in 1989. The ban has helped elephant populations to increase once again.

SUCCESS STORIES

Some species—such as the Santa Barbara song sparrow—have received protection too late to save them, and they have become extinct. Still, conservationists have been successful in some cases.

- Protective laws plus the banning of the pesticide DDT helped the bald eagle make a comeback. In 2007, the species was removed from the endangered species list.

- Breeding programs succeeded so well in raising black-footed ferrets that by 1990 their population totaled 118. Game officials were hopeful that some could soon be released into the wild.

- While they are still on the endangered list, whooping cranes have made a comeback thanks to an elaborate breeding and migration program. In 1993, after slowly increasing the birds' population, biologists began releasing young whooping cranes into the wild.

▲ **Whooping Crane Rescue.** Because whooping cranes learn migration routes from their parents, scientists in whooping crane suits used a specially designed small aircraft to lead captive-born birds in an experimental migration.

FOSSIL FUELS—coal, oil, and natural gas—are formed from the remains of plants and animals that lived millions of years ago. They are our main sources of energy, supplying about 88 percent of the world's needs. Unfortunately, they are non-renewable resources, and their use causes other environmental problems. The major consumers are industrialized nations; they use over 70 percent of the world's energy. Developing nations currently use only a small portion of fossil fuel energy, but that is expected to change as they industrialize and try to improve living standards for their rapidly growing populations.

THE TROUBLE WITH CARS

In addition to using fossil fuels, cars create a number of environmental problems as they burn gasoline (which is refined from oil, or petroleum).

- They are the major source of carbon dioxide and other pollutants that threaten to raise temperatures worldwide.

- Even a clean-burning car emits 20 pounds of carbon dioxide for every gallon of gas it burns. (This carbon dioxide is formed from the carbon in the gasoline and the oxygen in air.)

- The gases emitted by cars also deplete the ozone layer, contribute to acid rain, and harm human health. (See pages 678–681.)

Conserving Fossil Fuels

Four major sectors of the economy account for almost all energy use.

- transportation
- electrical generation utilities
- industry
- home and commercial facilities

All of these sectors are expected to grow. For example, markets for automobiles are growing rapidly in many developing countries.

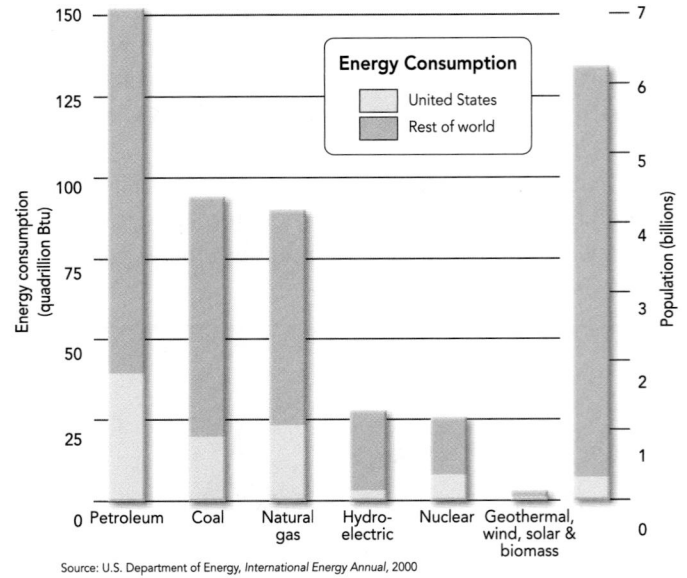

Source: U.S. Department of Energy, *International Energy Annual, 2000*

▲ **Energy Consumption.** This graph shows the amount of energy consumed by the United States relative to the rest of the world. It also illustrates the relative size of the population of the U.S. as compared to the overall world population. Large, industrialized nations such as the U.S. and Canada use far more energy than other nations.

Meeting the Demand

The enormous demand for fossil fuels is rapidly depleting known reserves of these resources. Despite increasingly sophisticated technology, we do not expect to find major new reserves.

Assuming that our levels of use never increase, the world's oil and gas resources may last only into the mid-2000s; coal reserves may last another 200 years. If consumption increases, which seems probable, the reserves will be depleted sooner. Making these limited reserves last longer requires

- more efficient use of fossil fuels.
- vastly expanded conservation measures.
- development of alternative energy sources.

Among the important benefits realized from these actions would be economic savings and an improved environment.

Riding a bicycle instead of driving short distances saves energy and helps to reduce pollution, as well. ▼

Efficiency. Better insulation and other technologies have already improved the energy efficiency of some appliances. For example, some refrigerators and electric water heaters use 50 to 60 percent less energy than other models of similar capabilities.

One study has shown that applying available energy-efficient improvements to seven basic types of home appliances would provide net energy savings of more than $50 billion over 20 years.

Cogeneration, a process that simultaneously produces heat and electricity, can improve energy efficiency in industry and communities. Typically, fuel is burned in a boiler to make steam that powers an electric generator. After being used for generation, however, the steam still has a lot of energy. Rather than discarding the steam into the atmosphere, it could be used to provide heat or to power machines.

A power plant that produces only electricity is about 32 percent efficient. A cogeneration plant using the same amount of fuel has an efficiency of almost 80 percent.

Energy conservation is safe, inexpensive, and applicable to a broad range of processes and activities. Individuals can save energy by making small changes in their daily lives.

Impressive energy savings can be realized through conservation measures in industry, too. For example, substituting recycled scrap for virgin materials in the manufacture of aluminum leads to a 95 percent energy savings.

WHAT YOU CAN DO

There are several things you can do to use energy more efficiently at home and at school.

- Reduce drafts around windows and doors.
- Lower thermostats at night during cold months.
- Add insulation around water heaters.
- Turn off lights in unused rooms.
- When traveling, walk or bicycle short distances.
- Use car pools and mass transit for longer distances, and for commuting to and from school or work.

Alternative Energy

If people are to maintain or improve living standards while decreasing their dependency on fossil fuels, alternative energy sources must be developed and used. No one source is likely to replace fossil fuels completely. Some depend on limited resources; others are limited to certain geographical or topographical locations.

▲ **Nuclear power** is extremely efficient, but it is also dangerous. Nobody has yet developed an ideal way of storing or disposing of the radioactive waste nuclear power plants produce.

STILL IN THE WORKS

Scientists are working to develop even more alternative energy sources. Some of these sources remain too expensive, or have technical obstacles. One day, however, sources like these could change the way we think of energy.

- Hydrogen could someday replace both gas and oil as a fuel.
- Magnetohydrodynamic (MHD) generators convert fuel directly into electric energy.
- Nuclear fusion produces the heat and light of the sun and other stars. Scientists and engineers are working on ways to control nuclear fusion reactions. ▶

Nuclear Energy

Nuclear power reactors generate electricity in at least 26 nations. Worldwide, they produce about 6 percent of commercial energy. In the United States, they supply about 8 percent of electricity. In a nuclear reactor, uranium atoms are split into smaller atoms during a process called *fission*. (See pages 736–737.)

Pro: Fission releases huge amounts of heat energy from very small amounts of fuel.

Con: There are three main objections to nuclear power plants.

- Uranium, like fossil fuels, is a nonrenewable resource.
- An accident at a nuclear power plant can expose large numbers of people and other organisms to deadly radiation.
- Wastes from nuclear power plants are toxic; some remain radioactive for hundreds of thousands of years.

Hydroelectricity

Hydroelectricity is electricity produced by harnessing the power of moving water. It accounts for about six percent of the world's commercial electricity.

Pro: This renewable energy source does not produce polluting gases.

Con: It creates other environmental damage. The massive dams built to harness falling water destroy forests and other ecosystems, spread waterborne diseases, and degrade downstream fisheries and farmland.

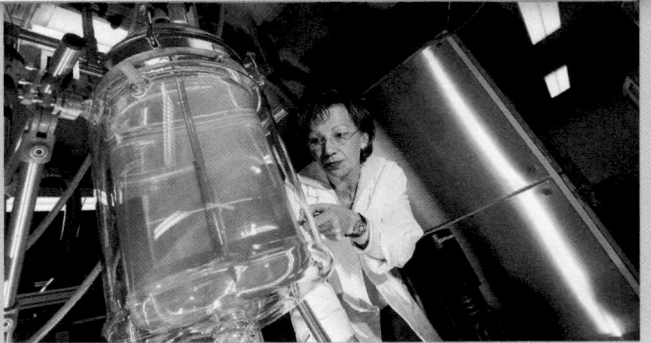

Wind Power

Giant turbines harness the wind's energy and use it to generate electricity.

Pro: Like solar energy, wind power is a renewable, nonpolluting resource with important potential.

Con: The giant turbines used to harness the wind's energy must be placed on hilltops or other areas exposed to winds, which means they can't be used everywhere.

▲ **Wind turbines,** like the ones shown here, produce clean energy. Unfortunately, their size poses problems, as does their need for available open land.

People are also using agricultural crop residues to produce ethanol (ethyl alcohol), which can be used as a gasoline substitute or blended with gasoline to produce gasohol. One advantage is that alcohol fuel emits less pollution than gasoline when burned. In some places, farmers are growing crops specifically for conversion to alcohol.

Geothermal Energy

Geothermal energy is heat created deep within Earth, apparently by the decay of radioactive material. This energy can be tapped at hot spots within Earth's crust where the heat turns water into steam.

Pro: Geothermal energy is virtually inexhaustible and nonpolluting.

Con: Can only be used where hot spots are accessible beneath the Earth's surface.

Wood and Other Sources

Billions of people depend on the burning of wood, crop residue, manure, and other plant and animal materials to meet their energy needs.

Pro: In theory, these are renewable resources.

Con: In practice, they are used up faster than they can be replaced. Another problem is the air pollution created during combustion.

Solar Energy

Solar collectors, such as those seen on the roofs of many newer buildings, convert the energy of the sun into heat energy. Photovoltaic cells change light energy into electric energy. Solar reflector systems with giant mirrors produce heat that can be used in industrial processes or converted to electricity.

Pro: Solar power can provide a clean and almost unlimited source of energy.

Con: It is thinly distributed over a wide area and must be collected and concentrated to produce energy. In addition, darkness and bad weather interrupt the supply of sunlight.

HEALTH AND THE ENVIRONMENT

When the environment suffers, people and animals suffer too. One major effect of pollution is ill health. Pollution-related illness costs billions of dollars annually. Air pollution, for example, contributes to lung disease, heart disease, and other fatal illnesses. The effects of different *pollutants*, or agents that cause pollution, on the human body are complicated. Still, scientists and environmentalists are working to reduce pollution-related suffering through awareness, regulation, and efforts to prevent large-scale environmental disasters.

HOW GENOTOXINS WORK

Genotoxins damage cells, affecting the way they work or the way they reproduce (form new cells).

- Exposure to radioactivity, for example, is known to damage chromosomes, the structures in cells that contain genes and that transmit characteristics from one generation to the next.
- If chromosomes in reproductive cells (eggs in females, sperm in males) are damaged, the person with the damaged chromosomes is not harmed.
- A child formed from those reproductive cells, however, may be severely deformed or disabled.

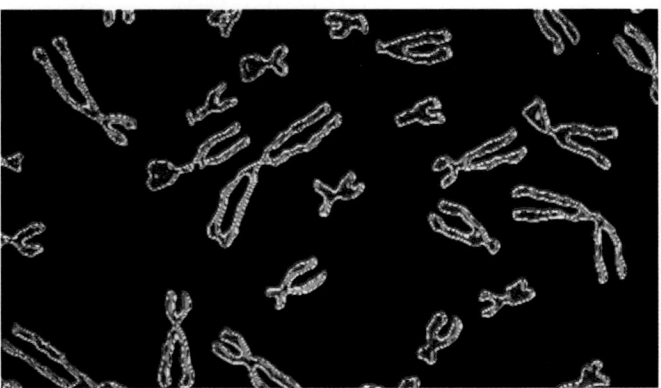

The Human Cost

Pollutants can harm many parts of the body. Different pollutants affect different body functions and systems. Some pollutants may also have what is called a *synergistic effect*. Synergism is a situation in which a combination of pollutants may have a greater effect than expected from either pollutant alone.

Pollutants and the Body

Some pollutants affect the body by causing illness or stopping important life functions. For example, carbon monoxide is a poisonous gas that comes mainly from engine exhausts. It interferes with the blood's ability to carry oxygen, thereby limiting the amount of oxygen that reaches the brain, heart, and other tissues.

Genotoxins are pollutants that interfere with cell reproduction. These pollutants can cause infertility, cancer, and birth defects. Known genotoxins include:

- pesticides.
- herbicides.
- many common industrial chemicals.

Some pollutants can cause genetic damage to children born to people who are exposed to the pollutants.

Obstacles to Prevention. Various factors make it difficult to assess the health effects of pollutants.

- There is no way to keep track of the amount of each specific chemical a particular person ingests as he or she breathes air, drinks water, eats food, touches contaminated objects, and so on.
- Many problems do not appear until decades after exposure; by this time, people may have forgotten that they were exposed to dangerous pollutants.

◄ **Chromosomes** are one kind of cell affected by pollutants. Damage to a person's chromosomes can cause infertility or cause birth defects in the children who are born to that person.

Environmental Disasters

History is filled with instances in which large amounts of pollution have caused widespread illness and death. Sometimes natural events combine with human activities to create deadly situations.

"Killer Smogs." These can develop when cool surface air is trapped by a layer of warmer air above it. The cool air cannot rise, and pollutants in the air cannot disperse.

London, England: In 1952, a 5-day smog took an estimated 4,000 lives. (See pages 664–665.)

Industrial Accidents. Accidents can release harmful pollutants into the environment.

Bhopal, India: In 1984, a Union Carbide pesticide plant's storage tank developed a leak. A toxic gas called methyl isocyanate was released into the air. Within a few hours, 2,800 people were dead. Another 150,000 were injured.

Toxic Waste. Inappropriate disposal or use of harmful products can destroy communities and land.

Times Beach, Missouri: In the early 1970s, this community of 2,000 people had been contaminated by dioxin in landfills and by dioxin-containing oil sprayed on streets to control dust. A decade later, after officials began to measure the levels of dioxin, residents were warned to evacuate immediately. In 1983, the U.S. Environmental Protection Agency (EPA) bought the residents' property for a total of $33 million.

▲ **Burning coal** created the killer smog that brought London to a halt in 1952.

THE CHERNOBYL DISASTER

In 1986, a nuclear reactor at the Chernobyl nuclear power plant in Ukraine exploded and caught fire. The result was the worst accident in reactor history.

- A cloud of radioactive gas killed 31 people, injured 200, and may eventually cause thousands of cancer deaths in the former Soviet Union.

- Lingering radioactive fallout forced the evacuation of an estimated 116,000 people from the region adjacent to the plant in the months after the accident.

- In 1990, the Soviet government resettled an additional 200,000 people; some scientists claimed that a total of 4 million people were living on contaminated land.

- Cases of anemia and thyroid cancer were already reported to be on the rise.

Fallout from Chernobyl covered large parts of Ukraine, Belarus, and Russia. This map shows ground contamination by cesium-137, a radioactive form of the chemical element cesium. ▶

Less than 5 curies per km²

5 to 40 curies per km²

More than 40 curies per km²

0   200 Miles
0   200 Kilometers

Indoor Pollution

The air in homes, schools, offices, and other buildings often contains pollutants that can cause or aggravate illnesses. People exposed to these pollutants may suffer from such problems as irritation of the eyes, nose, and throat; headaches; dizziness; and fatigue. This is sometimes called "sick-building syndrome."

Other health effects might not show up until years after exposure has occurred, or only after long or repeated periods of exposure. These include emphysema and other respiratory diseases, heart disease, and cancer.

Who Is at Risk?

Research indicates that people spend approximately 90 percent of their time indoors. Thus, for many people, indoor air pollution may cause greater risks than outdoor pollution. Also, the people who are exposed to indoor air pollutants for the longest periods of time are frequently those who are most susceptible to the adverse effects of such pollution. They include

- young children.
- the elderly.
- people who are chronically ill, particularly those with respiratory or cardiovascular diseases.

THE USUAL SUSPECTS

The many potential sources of indoor air pollution can be grouped into six major categories.

- combustion sources, such as oil and kerosene burners
- central heating and cooling systems and humidification devices
- building materials and furnishings, including insulation, carpeting, furniture, and cabinets made of certain pressed wood products
- products used for cleaning, personal care, and hobbies
- tobacco smoke from cigarettes, pipes, and cigars
- outside sources, including air pollution, pesticides, and radon

Many of these pollutants are present in minute quantities. This makes it difficult to prove that they are threats to health. It can also be difficult to determine the effects caused by interactions among the various pollutants.

◀ **Chemicals** in household cleaning products can pose health risks.

◀ **Indoor pollution** is not limited solely to homes. Many office buildings have significant sources of air pollution, often made worse because they lack ventilation.

In addition to the indoor pollutants found in homes, offices can also contain chemicals from certain carpeting and cleaning materials, rest room air fresheners, adhesives, and copy machines. They may also contain biological pollutants from dirty ventilation systems.

Solutions

It can be difficult to remove indoor air pollution. Some pollutants are trapped by carpets, drapes, and other surfaces. These particles remain in the home and are gradually rereleased into the air.

Reduction. The best way to improve indoor air quality is to eliminate sources of pollution or reduce their emissions. For example, converting gas appliances from pilot lights to spark ignitions reduces carbon monoxide emissions.

Ventilation. Another approach is to improve ventilation. Ventilation gradually lowers the offending substances' concentration indoors. Circulate fresh air by opening windows and doors and by using fans or heat-recovery ventilators (also known as air-to-air heat exchangers).

Plants. Another method of reducing pollution is to keep indoor plants. Many houseplants absorb carbon monoxide, nitrogen dioxide, and formaldehyde.

Common Indoor Pollutants		
Pollutant	**Sources**	**Effects**
Biological (bacteria, fungi, pollen, viruses, animal dander)	Wet or moist walls, ceiling, and carpets; air conditioners; humidifiers; bedding; household pets	Allergies, asthma, Legionnaire's disease, digestive problems, humidifier fever, dizziness, lethargy
Tobacco smoke	Cigarettes, pipes, cigars	Respiratory diseases, including lung cancer
Carbon monoxide, nitrogen oxides, sulfur dioxide	Stoves, heating systems, clothes dryers, water heaters	Headaches, drowsiness, nausea, chronic bronchitis, death (in high concentrations of carbon monoxide)
Benzene	Solvent cleaners, cigarette smoke	Cancer
Formaldehyde	Foam insulation, particleboard, plywood, draperies, carpets, tobacco, smoke, fire	Irritation of eyes, skin, lungs; flulike symptoms; shortness of breath; fatigue; cancer
Asbestos	Insulation, ceiling and floor tiles	Lung disease, cancer
Lead	Sanding or burning of lead paint, soldering	Impaired mental and physical development of children; damage to kidneys, nervous system, red blood cells
Pesticides	Products used to kill household pests; outdoor products that drift or are tracked inside	Eye, nose, and throat irritation; damage to nervous system and kidneys; cancer
Styrene	Carpets, plastics	Kidney and liver damage
Radon	Uranium in soil	Lung cancer

Occupational Hazards

An *occupational hazard* is a danger that a person encounters in the course of doing his or her job. Many occupational hazards are the result of industrial pollutants. Poisonous chemicals, radiation, noise, and other pollutants in the workplace are a major cause of illness and death.

Often, workers are exposed to much higher levels of these pollutants than the general public and are therefore at much greater risk. For example, the National Cancer Institute has estimated that about 20 percent of all cancer in the United States results from occupational exposure.

TYPES OF HAZARDS

Some environmental health problems are closely associated with certain occupations.

- Workers in uranium mines, nuclear power plants, fuel reprocessing plants, and shipyards where nuclear-powered ships are built are exposed to radioactive substances that increase their risk of developing cancer.

- Machine shop workers are exposed to a variety of chemical hazards, including cancer-causing nitrosamines in cutting fluids and lubricating oils, skin irritants in dyes and disinfectants that contain phenolic amines, and respiratory threats from chromic acid in corrosion inhibitors.

- Potters inhale carbon monoxide, sulfur dioxide, chlorine, and other toxic fumes and gases produced during the firing process.

- Workers in most dry-cleaning plants are exposed to trichloroethylene, a spot-removing solvent that irritates the skin and respiratory passages. Exposure to very high levels can cause intoxication, vomiting, and even death; long-term exposure can cause damage to the nervous system, heart, kidneys, liver, and other organs.

Industrial workers, like the mill workers shown here, are often at risk for exposure to harmful pollutants. Masks and filters can help reduce some dangers.

Exposure to radiation in large doses can cause radiation sickness. Repeated exposure in small amounts can increase the risk of cancer. Protective clothing, like the suits shown here, is one precaution taken by workers who encounter radiation.

Protecting Workers

Many steps have been taken to make potentially dangerous workplaces safer and reduce the incidence of disease.

Workplace Changes. Respirators and protective clothing can be used to limit exposure to pollutants in the workplace. Companies can install proper ventilation so that air pollutants do not build up. Other equipment can be used to limit harmful emissions.

Education of workers and managers about workplace health hazards is essential in preventing occupational illnesses.

Monitoring. Another important safeguard against long-term illness is annual medical exams. Workers should make their physicians aware of the type of work they do and the substances to which they are exposed.

OSHA

In 1970, the U.S. Congress passed a law that established the Occupational Safety and Health Administration (OSHA), a division of the U.S. Department of Labor.

- OSHA's job is "to assure so far as possible every working man and woman in the nation safe and healthful working conditions."
- It establishes basic health and safety standards, carries out surprise inspections of workplaces, and sets penalties for violators of these standards.
- Among OSHA's regulations are standards on worker exposure to toxic chemicals, pesticides, asbestos, and cotton dust.

Long-term coal miners are at such high risk of black lung that it is also called *coal workers' pneumoconiosis*. There is no cure for black lung, but the disease can be prevented by minimizing dust inhalation. ▶

DUST DISEASES

Diseases related to harmful dust pollutants are a potential hazard for hundreds of thousands of workers. Among these diseases are black lung disease, brown lung disease, and silicosis.

Black Lung. This lung disease is caused by long-term inhalation of coal dust. It is an occupational disease of coal miners and coal loaders. The dust scars and eventually destroys the alveoli (air sacs) in the lungs, through which oxygen passes into the bloodstream. People suffering from black lung often develop emphysema and are at increased risk for other respiratory infections.

Brown Lung. Also known as byssinosis, this chronic, irreversible respiratory ailment develops as small particles of dust and thick mucus accumulate in the respiratory system. This causes a constriction of the air passages and destroys the alveoli. Workers in textile mills who are exposed to cotton dust are particularly susceptible to the disease.

Silicosis. This respiratory disease afflicts miners, tunnel workers, potters, and others who work near silica dust. The silica particles damage the lungs, causing a slowing in the flow of blood through the alveoli. This can result in cor pulmonale, a heart disease in which the right side of the heart enlarges and pumps harder in an effort to compensate for the inefficient circulation in the lungs. (See page 464.)

PROTECTING THE EARTH

Widespread concern for the world's environment is a relatively new development. It has grown from two major realizations: that natural resources are not limitless and that the activities of growing human populations severely impact all aspects of the environment. Initially, the focus was on the protection of the wilderness and preservation of natural resources. In the second half of the 20th century, however, the movement expanded to include global concerns, such as climate, pollution, and energy development.

History of Environmentalism

The Industrial Revolution, which began in England in about 1760, resulted in the growth of urban centers, the rise of machines and factories, and the beginning of widespread burning of fossil fuels. It also led to the first major environmental problems.

- Black lung disease became common among coal miners.
- Chimney sweeps developed cancer caused by chemicals in chimney soot.
- Railroads began crisscrossing continents, destroying natural habitats.
- Hunters, carried by the new railroads, ventured into the wilderness, where they slaughtered thousands upon thousands of animals for fun.

PRESERVING YELLOWSTONE

In 1872, the United States established the world's first national park, Yellowstone National Park in Wyoming. In 1891, America's first national forest was formed in the area surrounding Yellowstone.

Today, national parks, grasslands, forests, and wildlife refuges are important preserves in almost every nation of the world. State and local preserves have also been established. In some places, private organizations have also been extremely active in protecting habitats. (See also page 454.)

Yellowstone is also one of the largest wildlife preserves in the United States. It has a greater concentration of large and small animals than any other area in the United States except Alaska. ▶

The Conservationists

Conservation was the focus of almost all environmental actions taken during the first half of the 20th century. Nations took actions primarily to preserve and coordinate the development of natural resources.

- Writers like American naturalist Henry David Thoreau stressed the importance of nature above materialism and urged that wilderness areas be set aside.

- Artists, particularly the painter John J. Audubon, aroused popular interest in the beauty of wildlife.

- U.S. president Theodore Roosevelt contributed to the early conservation movement by increasing the nation's forest reserves and protecting them from development.

The Environmentalists

In the early 1960s, the environmental movement began to expand. In 1962, the American biologist Rachel Carson wrote a book called *Silent Spring* about the dangers of the indiscriminate use of pesticides.

Other influential environmentalist books included *Canada North* by Canadian author Farley Mowat (1967) and *The Population Bomb* by American ecologist Paul Ehrlich (1968). Lawyer and writer Ralph Nader also touched on the need for the government to consider environmental concerns.

▲ **The Cuyahoga River** became a longtime joke among Ohio residents, who called it a fire hazard. The polluted river had caught fire nine separate times since the 1800s.

ENERGIZING THE MOVEMENT

In 1969, a series of ecological catastrophes brought a sense of urgency to the new environmentalist movement.

- In January, the blowout of an oil well off Santa Barbara, California, fouled miles of beaches and killed sea lions, seals, and countless birds.

- In June, a pesticide spill from a chemical plant in Frankfurt, West Germany, killed 40 million fish in the Rhine River and also imperiled drinking water supplies along much of the 840-mile (1,354-kilometer) waterway.

- Also in June, an oil slick on the sludge-filled Cuyahoga River that flows through Cleveland ignited. Flames spread along the river, causing two bridges to catch fire.

Earth Day and After

After the ecological crises of the late 1960s, Americans were galvanized for Earth Day on April 22, 1970. This program, the first national environmental teach-in, was the brainchild of Gaylord Nelson, then U.S. senator from Wisconsin, and environmentalist Denis Hayes. Hundreds of thousands of people participated, and the event is still held annually on April 22.

New Legislation. The success of Earth Day served as a catalyst for the passage of many important pieces of legislation in the United States.

- the Clean Air Act (1970)
- the Noise Control Act (1972)
- the Endangered Species Act (1973)
- the Safe Drinking Water Act (1974)

Developing Nations. In the developing nations of the world, immense social and economic problems have generally overshadowed environmental concerns. In the 1980s, however, some of these nations began to raise awareness of the high cost of pollution and degradation of their lands.

Often with the support of foreign governments and international organizations, these nations are taking steps to safeguard their resources. Among the most encouraging developments have been moves by Brazil to protect its rain forest and efforts by African nations to save rapidly shrinking wildlife populations.

◄ **The Endangered Species Act** has helped to protect many species, such as the sea otter, from extinction.

MILESTONES

1864 George Perkins Marsh publishes *Man and Nature,* the first textbook on conservation and the first detailed study of the extent of human influence on the environment.

1872 The first national park in the world, Yellowstone National Park in Wyoming, is established.

1887 Canada establishes its first national park around Banff, Alberta.

1891 The first national forest in the United States is formed in the area surrounding Yellowstone National Park.

1908 U.S. president Theodore Roosevelt appoints the National Conservation Commission, headed by Gifford Pinchot, to make the first inventory of the nation's natural resources.

1916 The U.S. National Park Service is established.

1924 The Soviet Union establishes its first natural reserve.

1929 Arizona passes its Native Plant Law, the first of its kind in the United States.

1962 *Silent Spring* by Rachel Carson is published; it describes the potential dangers of the indiscriminate use of pesticides.

1965 The U.S. Congress passes the Solid Waste Disposal Act, its first major solid waste legislation.

1968 *The Population Bomb* by Paul Ehrlich, which stresses the significance of human population growth as an environmental issue, is published.

1970 Earth Day, a landmark in awakening the general public to the need to clean up the environment, is held on April 22; the U.S. Environmental Protection Agency is established.

1972 The UN Conference on the Human Environment, the first worldwide meeting on environmental quality, is held in Stockholm, Sweden; the use of DDT is banned in the United States.

1973 The U.S. Congress passes the Endangered Species Act to provide federal protection for plants and animals threatened with extinction.

1979 The first broad international agreement covering acid rain, the Convention on Long Range Transboundary Air Pollution, is signed by 34 member nations of the UN Economic Commission for Europe.

Environmentalism Today. Numerous environmental problems continue to plague the world. As in the past, solving these problems involves efforts on two major fronts.

- solving the problems themselves
- convincing the often-powerful human forces who do not believe the problems are serious

Those forces can be very effective in preventing the passage of much-needed environmental legislation and in weakening and preventing adequate enforcement of existing environmental standards. But today, unlike many times in the past, these forces must contend with well-organized environmental organizations.

Rain Forest Protection. The expansion of industry and agriculture in Latin America has resulted in destruction of forests and wildlife habitats. Many countries have established national parks to conserve forests and wildlife. But in other cases, the parks are not well protected. ▶

INTERNATIONAL MOVEMENTS

The United States was not the only nation to begin focusing on the environment in the late 20th century. Other governments were also taking steps to control pollution.

- In 1972, major North Sea nations signed the Oslo Convention, which forbids the dumping of wastes from ships and aircraft into the North Sea and the northeastern Atlantic.
- That same year, the United Nations (UN) Conference on the Human Environment was held in Stockholm, Sweden.
- The UN Conference led to the formation of the UN Environment Program and spurred the creation of national environmental agencies.
- In the decade following the conference, the number of countries with such agencies grew from less than a dozen to more than a hundred.

1980	Congress passes the Alaska National Interest Lands Conservation Act, the most massive public land legislation ever adopted in the United States, designating 56,577,000 acres in national parks, forests, and wildlife refuges.
1982	The International Whaling Commission votes to phase out commercial whaling by 1985.
1988	In response to growing concerns about global warming, Sweden becomes the first nation to enact legislation to freeze its levels of carbon dioxide emissions.
1990	Ninety-three nations agree to cease production of chlorofluorocarbons (CFCs) and several other ozone-destroying chemicals by the end of the century.
1992	The Convention on Protecting Species and Habitats is signed by 167 countries at the Earth Summit in Rio de Janeiro, Brazil.
1994	The Convention on Desertification, a plan to halt the growth of deserts, is signed by some 100 nations in Paris, France.
1997	The Kyoto accord, a treaty to limit emissions of greenhouse gases, is ratified.
2004	The European Union releases its landmark pollution register, which contains information on industrial emissions.
2007	A 3-year study by the Intergovernmental Panel on Climate Change (IPCC) confirms that human activity is very likely causing global warming.

A Role for Everyone

Environmentalism is an attitude as well as a movement. It begins with individuals and involves every level of social organization: towns, states, nations, the international community. Each has important responsibilities in protecting the environment.

What You Can Do

Turning on the lights, driving your car, even taking out the garbage—all the things you do during your day have an effect on the environment. The Environmental Protection Agency, or EPA, has identified multiple ways people can decrease their harmful impact.

At Home. The changes you can make in your home range from simple to complex.

- Change lightbulbs in your home from conventional bulbs to compact fluorescent bulbs, which use less energy.
- When buying new appliances, look for products with ENERGY STAR qualifications.
- Clean or change your air filters regularly.
- Seal and insulate your house for better heating and air conditioning performance.

At Work. You can decrease greenhouse gas emissions by making changes at your workplace.

- Activate the power-saving feature on office equipment such as computers.
- Turn off lights and connect printers, routers, computers, etc., to power strips, which can be turned off at the end of the day.
- You can also use less energy on your way to work—take public transportation, carpool, or ride a bicycle instead of single-driver commuting.

Everywhere. People everywhere can always try to remember the three R's: reduce, reuse, and recycle.

- Reduce the amount of waste you produce and energy you use.
- Repair and reuse old items around your house instead of discarding them and purchasing new.
- Recycle everything from soda cans to old ink cartridges. Find a facility near your home or look into curbside recycling pickup.

Most importantly, don't think what you do doesn't matter. Participating in even one of these activities makes a difference.

▲ **Environmental activists** work to raise public awareness of ecological problems. They also lobby the government for new, environmentally friendly policies and funding.

ENFORCING THE LAW

Suppose there is a pollution problem in your community. What can you do to stop it? First, says the U.S. Environmental Protection Agency (EPA), make careful observations of the problem. Then report your observations to the proper authorities.

Record. The EPA stresses the importance of complete, written records.

- Write down the date and time when you observed the problem, where you observed it, and how you came to notice it.

- If the problem occurs more than once or is a continuing problem, write that down.

- Try to identify the person or source responsible. If, for example, it is a truck dumping wastes, note the license plate, the type of truck, and any signs or emblems on the truck.

- If you notice a particular smell, write down a description of the odor.

- If the pollution is visible and you have a camera, take a picture.

- If friends, neighbors, or family members also observe the problem, have them confirm your observations.

Report. Once you have written down this information, the EPA recommends that you telephone the appropriate local or state authorities. Typically, such agencies are listed in the government pages in your local telephone book or online. Give the official all the information on what you observed and ask him or her to look into the problem.

Follow Up. If the problem persists, your next step is to contact the EPA. You may also consider contacting an attorney or a public interest environmental group.

If you are told that the pollution problem you observed is legal but you believe it should not be legal, suggest changes in the law by writing to your state governor, state legislators, and U.S. senators and representatives.

▲ **Going Green.** The cost of making environmentally friendly changes is often balanced by other benefits. For example, hybrid cars, which use more than one source of energy for fuel, generally cost more than regular cars. Their fuel efficiency, however, means their owners save money on gas.

Costs and Benefits

The responsibilities of industries and individuals toward the environment sometimes involve considerable financial costs. Unfortunately, the high costs of environmental action are often used as an excuse to do nothing—when the costs in many cases turn out to be much lower than predicted. In fact, industries frequently realize significant savings from environmental measures.

For example, in recent years, some in the United States have argued that restrictions of greenhouse gas emissions will ruin the economy. Yet Germany, which already uses only half as much energy per unit of gross national product as the United States, planned a further 25 percent cut in its carbon dioxide emissions and expects these efforts to result in a net savings to its economy.

POLLUTION

One definition of pollution is the introduction of something into the environment that negatively affects the environment. For example, when a factory discharges large quantities of hot water into a cold stream, fish and other organisms in the stream cannot survive such a drastic change in their habitat. When toxic wastes seep into groundwater, the groundwater can no longer be used as drinking water. Problems such as air pollution, acid rain, and groundwater pollution affect everyone on Earth. Environmentalists are working to decrease or reverse the effects of these problems.

Nearly 150 million Americans live in areas where the air contains unhealthy levels of pollutants. In addition to such local and regional problems, such as smog, there are also global problems created by pollutants that spread far from the places they are emitted. For instance, the thinning ozone layer and increasing concentrations of carbon dioxide are global problems. ▶

Air Pollution

Air pollution occurs when wastes dirty the air. Pollutants can be in the form of gases or particulates (particles of solid or liquid matter). These substances result chiefly from burning fuel to power motor vehicles and to heat buildings. Industrial processes and the burning of garbage also contribute to air pollution.

THE AIR WE BREATHE

People can live for days without food or water. But they can live for only a few minutes without air. Air contains oxygen, an element needed by the body's cells to turn food into energy in a process called respiration. During respiration, carbon dioxide is produced as a waste gas.

"Pure" air consists mostly of nitrogen and oxygen. All the other gases combined usually make up less than 1 percent. Air is never entirely pure, however. It always contains at least some pollutants. When air contains large amounts of these materials, we say that it is polluted.

Composition of "Pure" Air	
Nitrogen	78 percent
Oxygen	21 percent
Argon	0.94 percent
Carbon dioxide	0.03 percent
Water vapor	0 to 4 percent
Other gases (helium, ozone, neon, methane, krypton, hydrogen, and xenon)	Trace amounts

Natural Pollution

While most pollutants that are causing today's serious problems are produced by human activities, some air pollutants do result from natural processes.

Volcanoes. A volcano may spew vast amounts of ash and other particles into the atmosphere. When Mount St. Helens in Washington erupted in 1980, two columns of ash-laden gas and steam were ejected more than 12 miles (19 kilometers) into the air.

Fires. Smoke from forest fires can be a significant source of air pollution, although, generally, only areas near the fires are affected. For instance, so much smoke is produced by fires in the Amazon River basin that measurable amounts have been carried and detected all over the world.

Dust and Salt. As it moves over Earth's surface, wind can pick up huge amounts of soil, sand, and other particles. These particles can then fall to the ground along with rain and snow.

Wind also lifts up water droplets as it moves over oceans and lakes. Large droplets quickly fall back to Earth, but smaller droplets remain aloft and evaporate, leaving tiny salt particles in the air. People who live near the sea are familiar with the damage done to paint and automobiles by this salt pollution.

Outer Space. As Earth orbits around the sun, it passes through large clouds of cosmic dust. As much as 3,000 tons of this dust enter Earth's atmosphere every day. The particles may remain in the atmosphere for a long time before they are deposited on Earth's surface.

Radiation is another type of pollution present in the atmosphere.

- Cosmic rays coming from outer space are a source of radiation.
- Another source is the breakdown of uranium and other radioactive elements naturally present in the ground.

Volcanic Pollution. In 2010, a volcano erupted under the Eyjafjallajokull glacier, creating a gigantic ash cloud that disrupted air travel across Europe. ▼

fyi! *Each day a person breathes about 30 pounds of air into his or her lungs. Oxygen in the air passes through the walls of the lungs into the blood, which carries it to all the cells. Carbon dioxide is carried from the cells to the lungs and breathed out into the atmosphere. (See also pages 234–235.)*

Air Pollution

Pollution from Human Activities

Millions of tons of air pollutants are emitted by human activities each year. The major source of pollutants is transportation: the burning of fossil fuels to operate cars, trucks, buses, trains, ships, airplanes, and other vehicles. Other significant sources include:

- industrial processes.
- solid waste disposal.
- fossil fuel combustion in power plants and heating furnaces.

Industrial processes produce a wide range of pollutants. Oil refineries discharge ammonia, hydrocarbons, organic acids, and sulfur oxides. Metal smelting plants give off large amounts of sulfur oxides and particulates containing lead and other metals. Plants that make aluminum expel fluoride dust. ▼

MAJOR AIR POLLUTANTS

There are many different substances that can become harmful when they are in the air in large quantities. Some of the major pollutants are carbon dioxide, carbon monoxide, sulfur dioxide, nitric oxide, hydrocarbons, and lead.

Carbon dioxide (CO_2) is a natural component of air, but it is also a pollutant. It is a product of combustion. The burning of fossil fuels releases an estimated 5.6 billion tons of carbon dioxide into the air every year—an amount that is expected to increase during the coming decades, possibly to as much as 30 billion tons per year.

Effects: Carbon dioxide is a major cause of global warming.

Carbon monoxide (CO) is a product of incomplete combustion, primarily in motor vehicles. It contributes to the formation of smog.

Effects: Carbon monoxide is an extremely dangerous and poisonous gas, causing impaired vision, poor coordination, headaches, angina, and, if sufficient quantities are inhaled, death.

Sulfur dioxide (SO_2) is primarily generated by the burning of fossil fuels, particularly coal, to generate electricity. Other sources include ore smelters, chemical plants, and trash-burning facilities.

Effects: Sulfur dioxide in the atmosphere limits visibility. It causes harm to human respiratory systems and yellows plant leaves. It also combines easily with water vapor to form sulfuric acid (H_2SO_4), which is a corrosive substance that damages lungs, eats away iron and steel, and is a major component of acid rain.

Nitric oxide (NO) is yet another pollutant produced during the burning of fossil fuels. In the atmosphere, it quickly changes to nitrogen dioxide (NO_2), and the two gases are generally referred to as nitrogen oxides (NO_x).

Motor vehicles are responsible for about half of the nitrogen oxides emitted by human activities. About one-third comes from power plants. Most of the remainder comes from industrial plants.

Effects: Nitrogen dioxide is a major component of smog. When it reacts with water vapor, nitric acid (HNO_3) is formed. This acid corrodes metals and is present in acid rain.

Hydrocarbons are compounds that contain hydrogen and carbon in various combinations. There are more than a thousand hydrocarbon compounds; they include such major pollutants as methane and benzene. (See also pages 408–411.)

Hydrocarbons are present in fossil fuels and are released into the atmosphere during combustion. Motor vehicles and coal-burning power plants are major sources.

Effects: Many hydrocarbons are harmful to human health. They are important in smog formation and some, methane in particular, contribute to global warming.

Lead (Pb) is a metallic element emitted during the burning of leaded gasoline. The federally mandated switch from leaded to unleaded gasoline has resulted in a substantial decline in lead emissions.

Effects: Lead tends to accumulate in the body, where it is believed to cause mental retardation, kidney disease, anemia, and various other ailments.

There are many additional air pollutants: agricultural pesticides and herbicides; arsenic from metal melting; toxic by-products from the incineration of plastics and other wastes; and radioactive material from nuclear weapons, fuels, and radioisotopes used in medicine and scientific research.

Reducing Pollution

Removing pollutants from the atmosphere once they have been emitted is not possible. Still, we can reduce pollution by preventing pollutants from entering the atmosphere in the first place.

In the United States. Efforts to control air pollution in the United States have been generally successful. All levels of government—federal, state, and local—have passed laws designed to control pollution. The Clean Air Act of 1970, and its amendments, have set strict standards for air quality and emissions.

New standards will remove most sulfur from fuels and reduce emissions of particulates. However, industry groups have repeatedly opposed stricter standards.

In Other Countries. The lack of controls on automobile emissions in Western Europe has contributed to extensive damage to forests there. Countries in Eastern Europe have lacked pollution controls altogether and, as a result, have suffered enormous environmental damage.

▲ **Many forms of transportation,** such as automobiles, airplanes, ships, and trains, are the leading source of air pollution in most industrial nations. The major pollutants produced by these sources are carbon monoxide, carbon dioxide, hydrocarbons (compounds of carbon and hydrogen), and nitrogen oxides (compounds of nitrogen and oxygen).

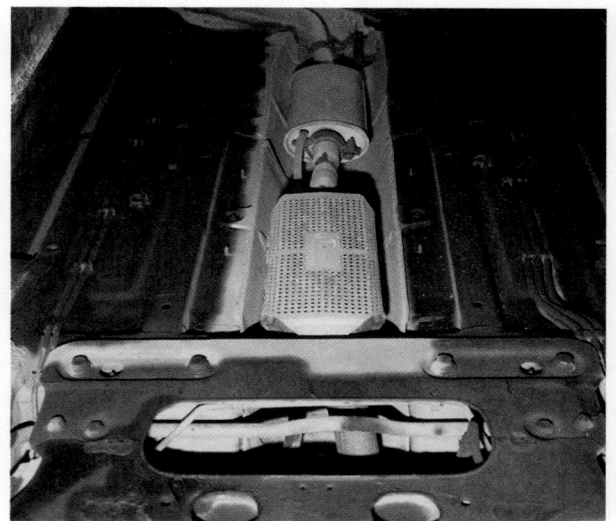

▲ **Catalytic Converters.** The Clean Air Act of 1970 requires automobile manufacturers to equip all new vehicles with pollution-control devices called *catalytic converters*. These devices convert harmful exhaust substances into harmless ones.

Smog

▲ **Smog forms** when a layer of warm air rests above a layer of cold air. Some cities, such as Los Angeles (*right*), have managed significant improvement in air quality.

INVERSION

The problem of smog is made worse by a phenomenon called *atmospheric inversion*.

How It Works. Typically, air near the ground is warmed by heat radiated from the ground. Since warm air is lighter than cool air, the heated air rises, carrying the pollutants upward, to be dissipated by winds in the upper atmosphere.

But in river valleys, along bays, and on level areas next to mountains, atmospheric inversions often occur. A layer of warm air lies above a layer of cold air, trapping the cold air, as well as any pollutants that are in it.

When an inversion occurs over an urban or industrialized area, ever-increasing amounts of pollutants accumulate in the cold air.

The term "smog" was first used in 1905 to describe the combination of smoke and thick fog that at times hung over London and other cities in the United Kingdom. Today the meaning of smog has been broadened to include a more severe phenomenon.

Called *photochemical smog*, this substance consists of chemicals formed as sunlight acts on various pollutants, especially components of motor vehicle exhausts. Photochemical smog is now common in urban areas around the world, including many cities that previously had eliminated the more traditional form of smog.

Creating Smog

Smog is formed through a series of chemical reactions.

- Nitrogen oxides and hydrocarbons enter the air from automobiles and industrial processes.
- Nitrogen dioxide, in the presence of hydrocarbons, absorbs solar energy.
- This change is speeded by the presence of carbon monoxide.
- In a series of reactions, ozone is formed.
- Continuing reactions form other undesirable compounds, including formaldehyde and peroxyacetyl nitrate (PAN).

Photochemical smog is an example of how combinations of pollutants react to produce additional pollutants and end up aggravating the original problem.

Moving on from Autos. Automobile congestion is one contributor to air pollution. To help reduce congestion, Los Angeles has improved its bus service and begun a mass-transit rail system. Convenient public transportation, special bicycle paths, and lower bridge tolls for drivers of car pools help reduce automobile use.

REDUCING SMOG

Because motor vehicle emissions are the main contributors to photochemical smog, restrictions on them are essential if smog formation is to be reduced. Several different approaches to motor vehicle emissions have already been taken.

- Improved fuel economy—cars that run more efficiently use less fossil fuel and produce fewer harmful emissions.

- Alternative fuels, such as methanol, ethanol, natural gas, and electricity, would reduce certain emissions, but at a cost.

- Discouraging the use of cars and encouraging alternative transportation is an option that is both effective and comparatively inexpensive.

- Some cities have banned motor traffic in downtown areas. For example, in Mexico City, one-fifth of all vehicles are banned each weekday, based on license plate numbers.

Effects of Smog. Smog can cause severe health problems, as well as environmental damage.

Humans

- Repeated exposure to the ozone in smog causes scarring and premature aging of the lungs, permanently decreasing lung capacity.

- Elderly people, children, and people who already suffer from such diseases as emphysema, asthma, and chronic bronchitis often cannot tolerate this additional stress on their respiratory systems.

- Eye irritation, headaches, fatigue, and chest pains are other reactions to smog.

- Children's growth and development may be stunted and they may become more susceptible to eczema.

Animals and Plants

- Experiments with mice indicate that long-term exposure to smog reduces fertility and the survival rate of newborns; these findings may apply to other species, including humans.

- Various components of photochemical smog, such as ozone and nitrogen oxide, can cause severe damage to crops and other plants.

Environmental Damage

- The chemicals in smog increase the rate of corrosion of steel, iron, zinc, brass, tin, and other metals.

- Stone also corrodes; smog eats away the surface of buildings and monuments.

- Rubber products dry and crack, fabrics decay, and paint is discolored.

Some 23 million tons of ozone-producing chemicals are released each year in the United States. About 75 percent of this is produced by motor vehicles and industry. Thousands of smaller sources include gasoline-powered lawn mowers, starter fluids for backyard barbecues, cleaning solvents, and even vapors from bakeries.

ACID RAIN is precipitation that has become acidic. It is caused by pollution in the air. (The term also includes acidic sleet and snow.) Acid rain harms thousands of lakes, rivers, and streams worldwide. It kills fish and other wildlife. It also damages buildings, bridges, and statues. High concentrations of acid rain can harm forests and soil. Today, problems caused by acid rain have been documented in many parts of the world. Even ancient Mayan ruins in southern Mexico are being destroyed; their colorful murals are being etched away by acid rain attributed to pollutants from oil refineries and tourist buses.

Causes of Acid Rain

Normal rainfall is slightly acidic for two main reasons.

- Some carbon dioxide in the air combines with water droplets in clouds to form weak carbonic acid.
- Volcanoes spew acidic compounds into the atmosphere, thereby increasing the acidity of precipitation.

This acidity is balanced to some degree by natural sources of alkaline compounds, such as windblown soil, that raise the pH of rainfall (see The Basics of Acids and Bases, *below*).

Acid rain usually is defined as precipitation with a pH below 5.6. In many parts of the world today, the annual average pH of precipitation is about 4.5 to 4.0—a level lethal to many aquatic species. Much stronger acidic rain has been recorded, as well. Among the record holders is Wheeling, West Virginia, which has had rainfall measuring 1.5—a pH more acidic than lemon juice.

THE BASICS OF ACIDS AND BASES

Acidity is expressed in terms of pH—a numerical value based on the concentration of hydrogen ions (H+). The pH scale ranges from 0 to 14. (See pages 386–389.)

- A neutral substance, such as distilled water, has a pH of 7.
- An alkaline, or basic, substance has a pH of more than 7.
- An acid substance has a pH of less than 7.

The lower the pH, the stronger the acid. The pH scale is logarithmic, so that each increase or decrease of one pH represents a tenfold change in acidity or alkalinity. Thus, rain with a pH of 5 is ten times more acidic than rain with a pH of 6.

Comparing pH. This diagram shows the pH levels of several common substances, and the levels at which different types of animals can no longer survive. It also shows the pH level of the Adirondack lakes at two separate times; over 40 years, the lakes' acidity rose sharply, from just below a pH of 7 to a pH under 5. ▼

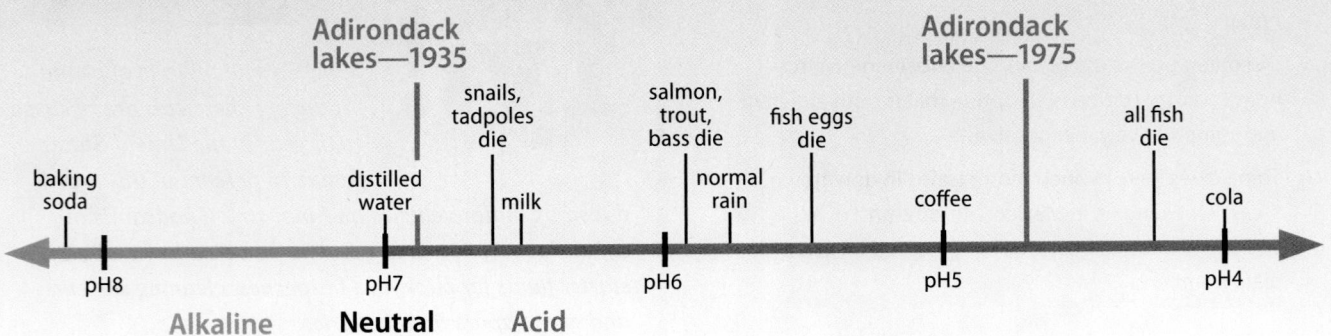

Adirondack lakes—1935

Adirondack lakes—1975

snails, tadpoles die

salmon, trout, bass die

fish eggs die

all fish die

baking soda

distilled water

milk

normal rain

coffee

cola

pH8   pH7   pH6   pH5   pH4

Alkaline   Neutral   Acid

Acid Rain in Action. This diagram shows the formation of acid rain. Prevailing winds can carry sulfur dioxide and nitrogen oxide for hundreds or even thousands of miles before the chemicals are dissolved and carried to Earth's surface. ▼

The acid rain that has destroyed this spruce forest in North Carolina is believed to have originated in the Ohio and Tennessee river valleys. ▶

HOW DOES THAT WORK

HOW ACID RAIN FORMS

The principal causes of acid rain are the gases sulfur dioxide and nitrogen oxides.

Sulfur dioxide is emitted primarily from stationary sources that burn coal as a fuel, including ore smelters, power plants, and other industrial facilities. A single smokestack may emit 500 tons of sulfur dioxide a day.

Nitrogen oxides are produced by utilities and by transportation-related sources, such as automobiles and trucks. In a year, millions upon millions of tons of the gases are discharged into the atmosphere.

Other acids and acid precursors produced by human activities contribute to the acid rain problem.

The Process

1. Industrial processes and transportation sources emit pollutants into the air.

2. In the atmosphere, sulfur dioxide and nitrogen oxides undergo a series of changes.

3. Eventually, they react with moisture to form sulfuric acid and nitric acid, which then falls to Earth.

(Remember that any form of precipitation may be acidic—not only rain but also snow, sleet, mist, or fog.)

Effects of Acid Rain

The extent of damage caused by acid rain depends on two factors.

- the total amount of acid deposited in an area
- the sensitivity of that area to acids (see Acids and the Soil, *right*)

Acids and Living Things

Acids affect living things both directly and indirectly.

Plants. As acids seep into the ground, they affect plant life in several different ways.

- They may deplete the soil of calcium and magnesium, which are needed by plants for the formation of chlorophyll and wood. This process of dissolving soil chemicals is called leaching.
- Acids also promote the release of several toxic metals from soil and lake beds. For example, aluminum is released from soils at a pH of approximately 4.5. This aluminum can kill plant roots and decrease the ability of trees to absorb necessary calcium and magnesium.

Animals. Fish and many other water creatures cannot reproduce once the pH of their environment falls below 5.5. As lake water becomes even more acidic, animals begin to die off.

Like plant cells, animal cells are very sensitive to aluminum. The metal kills the eggs of many fish species as well as the embryos of salamanders and other amphibians.

Bodies of Water. Acid rain is most closely associated with damage to lakes. These bodies are affected not only by the acid rain that falls directly on them but also by the far larger quantities that enter via rivers and land runoff. Rivers have also experienced increasing acidity.

The Adirondack Mountains in New York are one example of an area that is sensitive to acid damage.

ACIDS AND THE SOIL

An area's sensitivity to acid depends upon its contents, and how those contents react to acidity. (See Soil, pages 532–533.)

- Areas with acid-neutralizing compounds in their soil have a buffer against acid damage.
- Alkaline substances such as calcium carbonate and magnesium carbonate react with and neutralize the acids, bringing the pH closer to 7.
- Where soils are thin and lack alkaline substances, such as in mountainous and glaciated areas, acids are not neutralized. These places are more sensitive to damage from acid rain.

▲ **Erosion caused by acid rain** has put thousands of treasured historical buildings and statues at risk.

MORE EFFECTS OF ACID RAIN

Billions of dollars worth of damage is believed to occur annually as acid rain damages buildings, monuments, and other structures.

- Acid accelerates erosion of such stones as marble and limestone, the basic building materials used in many cities.

- Acid rain also corrodes galvanized steel and may damage paint finishes, such as those on homes and automobiles.

- Mercury and other heavy metals leached from rocks by acid rain can seep into reservoirs and groundwater, polluting municipal and home water systems.

- As acids flow through the water systems, they dissolve toxic metals from the conduits and pipes, further polluting the water we drink and bathe in.

Combating Acid Rain

To reduce acid rain, it is essential to reduce the gaseous emissions of sulfur dioxide and nitrogen oxides.

Individuals can play a role by conserving energy.

- By purchasing fuel-efficient automobiles that travel farther on a given amount of gasoline, and by driving less, people lower the amount of nitrogen oxides they produce.

- By using energy-efficient appliances and avoiding wasteful uses of electricity, they reduce the demand for electrical production at power plants.

- Individuals can also bring pressure on government agencies and officials to toughen emission regulations for industries and automobiles.

Industries can also take several different steps to lower harmful emissions.

- Removing problem substances from fuel before the fuel is burned.

- Removing the pollutants from smoke before the smoke enters the atmosphere by using "scrubbers," which use a spray of water and chemicals to remove, or scrub out, sulfur dioxide.

- Developing new ways of burning fuels that reduce production of harmful emissions.

- Switching from high-sulfur fuels to low-sulfur fuels.

◀ **Dead Lakes.** Hundreds of lakes in the northeastern United States and in eastern Canada are beautifully blue, crystal clear . . . and lifeless. Though they teemed with fish only a few decades ago, they are now so acidic that nothing can survive in them. When the damage caused by acid rain is not too severe, lakes may be able to recover if acid input stops.

THE GREENHOUSE EFFECT

For tens of thousands of years, atmospheric carbon dioxide has kept Earth at an average temperature of about 60°F (16°C), helping create an environment suitable for living things. It does this through a natural phenomenon called the *greenhouse effect*. Now, however, increased levels of carbon dioxide and other greenhouse gases threaten to raise Earth's average temperatures.

Greenhouse Gases	Source
Carbon dioxide	• burning of fossil fuels • destruction of forests
Methane	• decomposition in rice paddies, swamps, marshes • released from digestive systems of plant-eating animals such as cows
Nitrous oxide	• nitrogen-based fertilizers • deforestation, burning of wood and plant matter • burning of fossil fuels
CFCs	• coolants in refrigerators and air conditioners • aerosol propellants, medical sterilizers, cleaning solvents, and raw materials for making plastic foam

Greenhouse Gases

Carbon dioxide, which comprises only 0.03 percent of the gases in Earth's atmosphere, behaves much like the glass in a greenhouse. It allows light rays from the sun to reach and warm Earth's surface. Earth then reradiates the heat as infrared radiation. But the carbon dioxide traps some of this heat, preventing it from escaping into space.

Other gases also behave this way in the atmosphere. Together, they are referred to as the greenhouse gases.

Where They Come From

The primary greenhouse gases are carbon dioxide, methane, nitrous oxide, and chlorofluorocarbons, or CFCs. The concentrations of all of these gases have been increasing at large annual rates since the mid-1800s, mostly due to human activities.

To compound the problem, some of these gases linger in the atmosphere for many decades. Nitrous oxide and some chlorofluorocarbons remain 75 to 150 years; carbon dioxide remains even longer.

METHANE ON THE RISE

Methane is actually a more powerful greenhouse gas than carbon dioxide—it traps 20 to 30 times as much heat. It decays more rapidly than CO_2, however, since it has an atmospheric lifetime of only about 10 years.

Although much of the atmosphere's methane comes from natural sources—such as wetlands, oceans, and wild animals—people are responsible for increased methane levels in several ways.

- Rice cultivation, which produces methane, has increased along with the population.

- People are raising more cows, which produce methane as a by-product of digestion. The increase in the number of cattle leads to an increase in manure, which also releases methane.

- Landfills contribute to methane levels as the waste material inside them decays.

- Sewage treatment plants release methane during certain treatment processes.

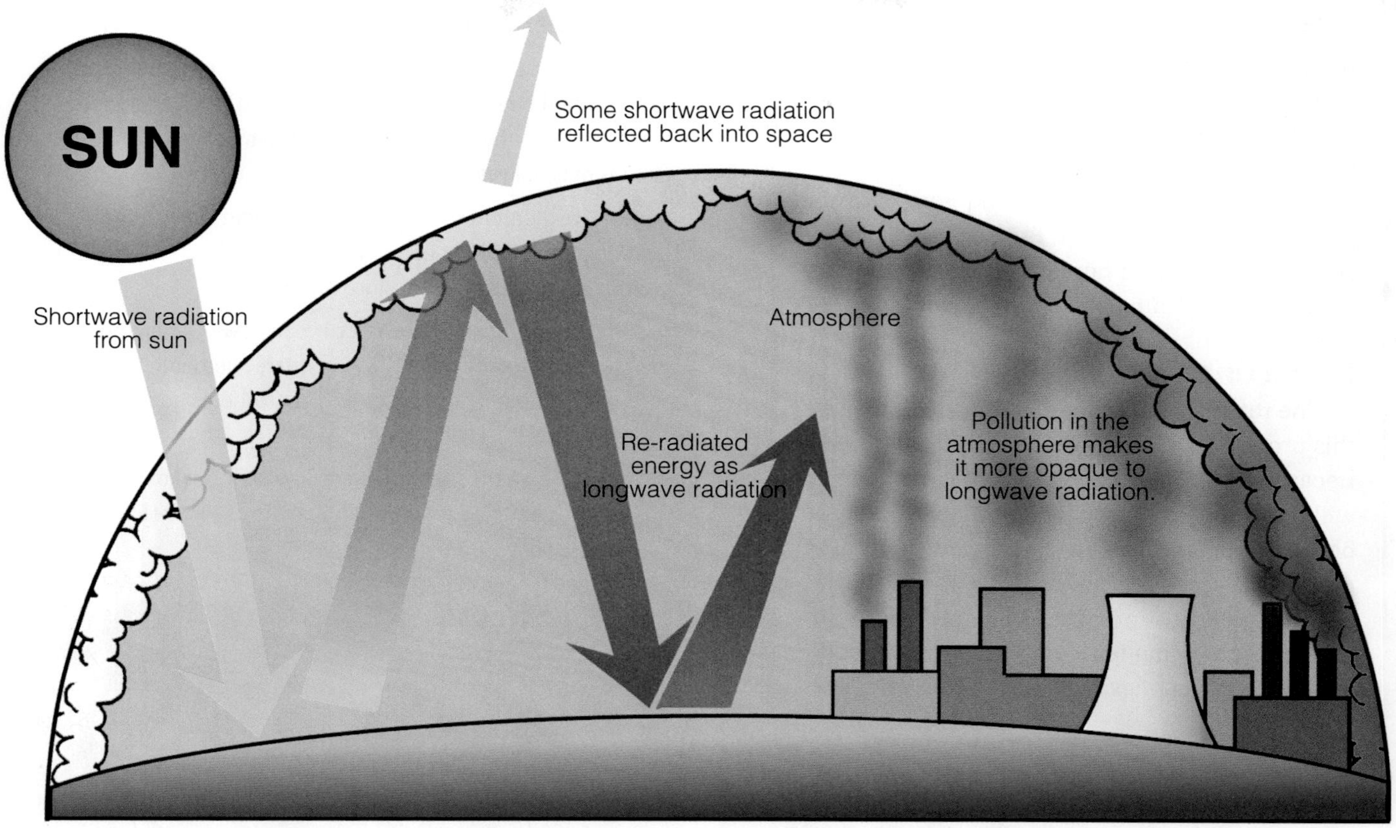

SUN

Some shortwave radiation
reflected back into space

Shortwave radiation
from sun

Atmosphere

Re-radiated
energy as
longwave radiation

Pollution in the
atmosphere makes
it more opaque to
longwave radiation.

THE GREENHOUSE EFFECT

This diagram illustrates the processes that lead to the greenhouse effect. (See Atmosphere, pages 534–535.)

1. Shortwave radiation reaches the Earth through the atmosphere.

2. Some of this radiation is reflected back into space; the rest is trapped by carbon dioxide.

3. Increased pollution in the atmosphere means that more of the heat radiation is trapped, leading to a rise in temperatures.

More Methane. There are about 1.2 billion large ruminants—cattle, sheep, buffalo, and goats—in the world. These animals produce 80 million metric tons of methane each year.

Climate Change

Increasing concentrations of greenhouse gases in the atmosphere are expected to alter the global climate, increasing temperatures and changing rainfall and other weather patterns. Some people refer to this process as global climate change.

Natural processes have caused Earth's climate to change in the distant past. But scientists have found strong evidence that human activities have caused most of the warming since the mid-1900s.

Predicting Changes

The rate and magnitude of changes caused by this process cannot be predicted with total certainty. Because all of Earth's systems are connected, changes will depend on an astonishing number of interactions between the atmosphere, the oceans, vegetation, soil, and so on.

Still, scientists can make some predictions about the effects of rising temperatures on precipitation, sea levels, water supplies, plants, animals, and humans.

▲ **Droughts** are a result of decreased rainfall over a long time. In areas without irrigation, droughts result in dead or stunted crops. This in turn can lead to food shortages.

THE MELTING POLAR ICE CAPS

The ice cap that covers Antarctica holds 91 percent of Earth's ice. Most of the remainder is over Greenland. Smaller amounts are found in northern Canada, Scandinavia, Iceland, and mountainous river valleys. (See pages 514–517.)

- Satellite monitoring has shown that Antarctica has shed more than 11,000 of its 5 million square miles (12,953,000 square kilometers) of ice since the 1970s.

- A major portion of this loss occurred in 1986, when more than 8,800 square miles (22,798 square kilometers) of ice broke off, floating out to sea as giant icebergs hundreds of feet thick.

- In Greenland, the world's fastest flowing ice, Jakobshavn Glacier, is entering into the sea at a rate of 113 feet (34.5 meters) a day.

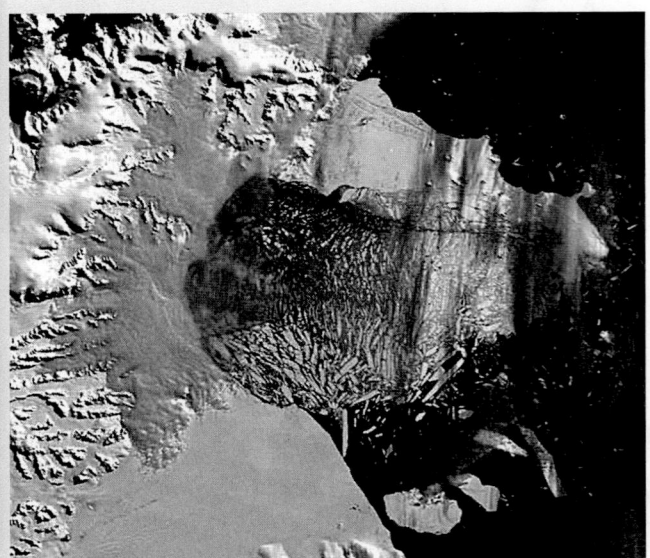

PRECIPITATION

In general, scientists believe that rising temperatures will lead to increased evaporation and, therefore, to more precipitation. But while some regions will experience increased rainfall, others will become drier. For example, several of the complex computer models used to predict changes indicate that rainfall in the American Midwest will decrease, harming agriculture in the region.

SEA LEVELS

Average sea level rose about 7 inches (17 centimeters) over the 1900s. Global warming contributed to the rise.

- Part of the increase occurred because water expands as it warms.
- Rising temperatures also melt ice on land, which then flows into the oceans.
- Rising sea levels have already contributed to coastal flooding, erosion, and the loss of wetlands.

Researchers project that further warming could cause sea levels to rise another 7 to 23 inches (18 to 59 centimeters) by 2100. However, the projections do not include possible contributions from the melting of major ice sheets in Greenland and Antarctica. Increases in the rates at which the sheets are melting could lead to an additional rise in sea levels.

▲ **Low-lying coastal regions,** such as Bangladesh, are especially at risk due to rising sea levels. A study by researchers at Woods Hole Oceanographic Institution indicates that the sea level rise in the delta area of Bangladesh may exceed 6.5 feet (1.9 meters) by 2050. This would cause

- heavy loss of agricultural lands .
- widespread displacement of people.
- catastrophic damage from storm surges (sudden onrushes of massive amounts of water).

HOW WILL TEMPERATURES CHANGE?

Scientists predict that Earth's average surface temperature will rise an additional 2.0 to 11.5 Fahrenheit degrees (1.1 to 6.4 Celsius degrees) by 2100. This will mean different things for different regions.

- Some places may experience greater extremes between summer and winter temperatures.

Example: New York is expected to see summer temperatures rising above 90°F (32.2°C), while in winter brutal storms will sweep down from the north.

- Places that already experience high temperatures may experience more of them.

Example: Washington, D.C., which now averages 36 days a year with temperatures above 90°F (32.2°C), is expected to have 87 days of such temperatures.

According to the United Nations, the 10 nations most vulnerable to rising sea levels are Bangladesh, Egypt, The Gambia, Indonesia, the Maldives, Mozambique, Pakistan, Senegal, Suriname, and Thailand. Much of the land area in these nations is between 0 and 16 feet (4.9 meters) above mean sea level. In addition, these nations are densely populated and poor.

WATER SUPPLIES

Changes in precipitation and sea levels are expected to affect the world's supply of usable and drinkable water. In some places, decreased water supplies coupled with increased demand will intensify conflicts between users, communities, and even nations.

Scarcity. One example of the risk for increasingly scarce water supplies is the state of California. This region is already experiencing water supply difficulties, and they are likely to get worse as the climate changes.

- Higher temperatures are expected to increase water needs.
- At the same time, those temperatures will begin to shrink the snowpack in the mountains that supplies much of the state's water.
- The result would be decreased availability of water.

Salinity. A rise in sea level is expected to increase the *salinity* (salt content) of estuaries. As seawater migrates up rivers and into aquifers, it will also contaminate water supplies. (See pages 568–569.)

▲ **A reduced water supply** would have tremendous impact on California's farming industry. Most of the state's farms lie in dry regions and already must be irrigated.

◄ **The Delaware River** provides Philadelphia with water. A 2-foot (0.6-meter) rise of sea levels would inundate Philadelphia's water intakes, making the water too salty to drink. Many other coastal communities would also experience salinity increases in their surface water and groundwater supplies.

▲ **Global warming** can reduce the ice on which polar bears live and hunt, threatening their survival.

PLANTS AND ANIMALS

Climate is a critical factor in determining which plants and animals live in an area. Palm trees and oak trees, lizards and polar bears, orchids and marigolds—where each lives is dependent, to a great extent, on climate. If the climate changes, then these organisms must either adapt to the changes or move to a more suitable place. If neither is possible, the species faces extinction.

- Changes in temperature and sea level may shrink or destroy natural habitats, forcing many species to migrate.

- Scientists are concerned that the faster our climate changes, the more difficult it will be for species to adapt.

- They project that 20 to 30 percent of species would face a higher risk of extinction if the average temperature rose more than 2.7 to 4.5 Fahrenheit degrees (1.5 to 2.5 Celsius degrees).

HUMAN LIFE

Climate changes could significantly affect human society on many levels. While there may be some benefits—a reduction in cold-related deaths, for example—researchers predict that those benefits will be outweighed by harm.

- How and where we farm: higher temperatures in particular would result in reduced U.S. yields of corn, wheat, and soybeans. (In northern areas such as Minnesota, however, the frost-free growing season may be extended.)

- If the climate becomes drier, limited availability of water to irrigate crops would worsen agricultural problems due to temperature.

- Diseases that thrive in warmer climates may become common in new regions.

- More frequent and intense hot days and heat waves can contribute to heat-related death and illness.

- Warmer weather is also likely to increase air pollution, exacerbating respiratory diseases such as asthma and emphysema.

- Scientists also project more deaths and diseases caused by storms, floods, droughts, and fires.

▲ **Increased flooding** is just one of many possible outcomes of climate change that pose a hazard to humans.

Slowing Climate Change

The potential impact of global changes in climate is far too disastrous to ignore. Researchers have developed a number of ways to limit global warming. But because the warming is a global problem, many strategies require the cooperation of a diversity of nations, each with its own interests.

Nevertheless, many countries are taking action individually and by international agreement to limit future warming.

Limiting Future Warming

Two areas of action are considered to be particularly important in the fight to reduce global warming: fuel conservation and reforestation.

Fuel Conservation. Decreasing consumption of fossil fuels is essential if global warming is to be slowed. One conservation method is improved efficiency.

- Increasing the average fuel efficiency of automobiles has already slowed carbon dioxide emissions—and helped extend diminishing oil reserves.
- Buildings can be made more fuel efficient by adding extra insulation, installing storm or thermal windows and heat pumps, caulking around windows and doors, and so on.
- Appliances can be improved with better heat-transfer techniques and more efficient motors.

Fossil fuels can also be conserved by switching to alternate energy sources and technologies. For example, solar energy—used to produce heat and electricity—is nonpolluting and inexhaustible.

▲ **After the Fire.** In 1999, a forest fire destroyed a pine plantation in Florida's Apalachicola National Forest. The area has since been replanted with slash pine.

Reforestation. A fast-growing tree absorbs 48 pounds of carbon dioxide per year. An acre of trees uses 10 tons per year! Increased tree planting in large areas of once-forested land, as well as the planting of trees in urban areas, would significantly reduce carbon dioxide buildup.

- Trees placed around buildings offer the added benefit of reduced energy needs for winter heating and summer cooling.
- Three trees placed around a house can cut home air conditioning energy needs by as much as 10 to 50 percent—a significant savings.
- Studies show that each tree that provides summer shade and cooling indirectly causes reductions in carbon dioxide emissions equivalent to 15 times the amount of carbon dioxide the tree alone can absorb.

At the same time, it is important to halt the rapid destruction of many of the world's forests. Consumers can contribute to this effort by recycling paper. If Americans recycled all their Sunday newspapers, they would save more than 500,000 trees a week!

◄ **Solar plants,** like the ones in California's Mojave Desert, have played an important role in meeting the electrical needs of Los Angeles.

◄ **Genetically modified plants** may be one way that humans will adapt to the changes resulting from global warming; however, the use of such crops remains controversial.

THE KYOTO PROTOCOL

The Kyoto Protocol entered into force in 2005.

- The protocol restricts emissions of carbon dioxide (CO_2), methane (CH_4), nitrous oxide (N_2O), and three other greenhouse gases.

- Each nation's, or party's, target is a certain percentage of its emission levels in 1990. As a whole, the developed parties (wealthier nations) must cut their emissions to an average of 5 percent below 1990 levels.

- Most of the world's countries have agreed to the protocol. But a few nations, including the United States, have refused.

- In late 2005, delegates from the parties agreed to extend the Kyoto Protocol beyond 2012.

ADAPTING

Even if immediate action is taken to severely limit greenhouse gas emissions, some warming will still occur because of the great volume of gases already emitted into the atmosphere by human activities. A variety of steps may enable people to prepare for the changes ahead.

- building bulkheads and levees to protect buildings and roads in coastal areas

- restricting building in coastal areas to enable wetlands and beaches to migrate inland as sea levels rise

- growing more heat- and drought-resistant crops, such as semitropical crops

- genetically engineering new varieties of crops and plants

HOW DO WE KNOW THAT

GLOBAL WARMING

Climatologists (scientists who study climate) use information from many sources to analyze global warming. Since the late 1800s, the most reliable climate information has come from standardized measurements using weather instruments. To look further back, climatologists analyze other types of evidence. Such evidence includes:

- growth rings in trees.

- cores (cylindrical samples) of ice drilled from Antarctica and Greenland.

- cores of sediment from ocean or lake beds.

THE OZONE LAYER

Ozone (O_3) comprises 0.005 percent of the atmosphere. The greatest concentration of ozone is in a layer of air called the stratosphere, some 10 to 30 miles (16 to 48 kilometers) above Earth's surface. Also present in the stratosphere are atomic oxygen (O) and ordinary oxygen (O_2). At ground level, ozone, a form of oxygen, is a pollutant, a menace to living things. High in the atmosphere, it is a lifesaver, for it absorbs deadly ultraviolet radiation emitted by the sun. Without this high-altitude ozone, Earth's ecosystems and all its organisms would be in peril.

▲ **Ozone on Earth** is a toxic pollutant that causes damage to plants, animal tissue, rubber, and plastic. Pure ozone is a blue gas with a sharp odor.

The Ozone Hole

Until comparatively recently, the concentrations of ozone, atomic oxygen, and ordinary oxygen in the stratosphere were relatively stable. Then, in the 1970s, scientists began to record decreases in the amount of ozone.

Discovering the Ozone Hole

The first indication of problems developed in Antarctica, where British scientists have been measuring atmospheric ozone levels since 1957. In 1985, the British scientists published their data, reporting that since the 1960s a 40 percent loss in ozone had occurred over Antarctica during the spring months. American and Japanese scientists soon confirmed this finding.

The phenomenon became known as the ozone hole, though in reality it is a thinning, not a complete disappearance, of the ozone.

- Each spring, ozone levels over Antarctica decline.
- In some years, the decline is more severe than in other years.
- In 1988, ozone concentrations fell only 15 percent. In 1989, however, they fell 45 percent.

Worldwide Depletion. By 1988, it became apparent that atmospheric ozone levels had also declined over most other parts of the world, though not as severely as over Antarctica. According to Ivar S. A. Siaksen of Norway's Institute of Geophysics, concentrations have decreased 10 percent since 1967 over the middle latitudes of North America and Europe.

 *CFCs are also a troublesome contributor to the greenhouse effect. A single CFC molecule may absorb 10,000 times as much heat as a carbon dioxide molecule.*

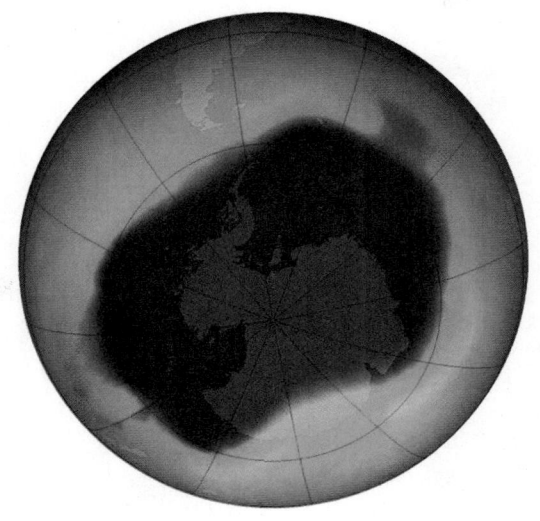

◀ **The ozone hole** is a region over Antarctica where ozone becomes less concentrated every spring. This image shows the extent of the hole in 2006.

OTHER OZONE DESTROYERS

Halons. Like CFCs, halons are stable at ground level but are dissociated by ultraviolet light in the stratosphere. Developed during World War II for fighting fires in tanks, the primary use of halons today is in handheld fire extinguishers.

Nitrous oxide (N_2O), produced by many industrial activities, is another ozone destroyer.

Carbon tetrachloride and methyl chloroform. These compounds are widely used solvents; in addition, carbon tetrachloride is used to make CFCs.

Causes

Thinning of the ozone layer has been caused by a variety of ozone-destroying chemicals released by human activities. More than half the damage has been caused by chlorofluorocarbons; the remainder has been due to halons, nitrous oxide, carbon tetrachloride, and other gases.

Chlorofluorocarbons (CFCs). These synthetic compounds consist of a combination of chlorine, fluorine, and carbon atoms.

- First marketed in the 1930s, they are nontoxic, nonflammable, stable, and relatively easy to manufacture.
- They are used as coolants in refrigerators, freezers, and air conditioners.
- They are also used as cleaning solvents in the manufacture of electronic circuits; as aerosol spray propellants (a use generally banned in the United States since 1978); as foaming agents in the manufacture of Styrofoam and other plastics; and in the manufacture of foam insulation.

Filling the Air with CFCs. Some 2 billion pounds of CFCs are manufactured each year. About one-third of that amount is made in the United States. The U.S. has the world's highest per capita use of CFCs—six times the global average.

It typically takes 7 to 10 years for CFC molecules to rise through the lower atmosphere and reach the stratosphere. Even without further emissions of CFCs, their level in the stratosphere is expected to rise. But further emissions will occur—today, tomorrow, next year—adding to, and prolonging, destruction of Earth's protective ozone layer.

The Ozone Hole

Effects of Ozone Depletion

The effects of ozone depletion add up quickly. For example, for each 1 percent decrease in stratospheric ozone, there is a 2 percent increase in the amount of ultraviolet radiation that reaches the ground. This, in turn, is estimated to increase the rate of skin cancer by 4 to 6 percent.

According to Environmental Protection Agency estimates, if ozone destruction continues at its present rate, there will be an additional 155 million cases of skin cancer and an additional 3.2 million cancer deaths in the United States during the next 100 years.

▲ **Ultraviolet radiation** can interfere with the lives of many species of animals by affecting just one part of an ecosystem's food chain.

▲ **Reduced ozone** in the atmosphere will make exposure to the sun more dangerous, as more ultraviolet radiation reaches Earth.

Health Problems. Increased levels of ultraviolet (UV) radiation would lead to a number of health problems in human beings.

- People exposed to high UV levels become sunburned faster and more severely. Their skin ages more rapidly, undergoing such changes as patchy pigmentation, widening of small blood vessels, loss of elasticity, and the formation of furrows.

- Ultraviolet radiation seems to be a cause of or factor in certain eye problems, such as cataracts, benign tumors of the conjunctivas and cornea, and corneal disease.

- The body's immune system, which is responsible for fighting disease, is harmed by ultraviolet radiation, making people more vulnerable to infections.

Effects on the Ecosystem. The potential impact of increased ultraviolet radiation on the world's ecosystems is also a concern.

- Ultraviolet radiation can damage crops, resulting in decreased yields.

- The radiation causes mutations in animals; kills fish eggs, larvae, and microorganisms; and interferes with the photosynthesis and metabolism of phytoplankton, the microscopic plants that form the basis of the ocean food chain.

- Without phytoplankton, the tiny animals (zooplankton) that feed on them would disappear. In turn, there would be no food for whales, seals, fish, penguins, and many other marine animals.

Combating Ozone Depletion

In 1990, 93 nations agreed to halt production of CFCs by the year 2000. A 10-year grace period was provided for developing nations, although some nations and many environmentalists had hoped for a more rapid phase-out. One analysis has indicated that ozone-destroying chlorine will not start to decline until approximately 2050.

Finding Substitutes. Industries that use CFCs and other ozone-destroying chemicals affected by the 1990 treaty, including carbon tetrachloride and methyl chloroform, are working to develop replacement chemicals and improved equipment, but there are risks and costs involved.

Substitute	Pros	Cons
Hydrochloro-fluorocarbons (HCFCs)	Less chlorine than CFCs	Still present a risk of ozone depletion
Ammonia	Reliable; used as a refrigerant before the development of CFCs	Toxic
Propane	Good refrigerant	Explosive and contributes to global warming

New Developments. New product designs and revised procedures can eliminate or reduce the need for ozone-destroying chemicals. For example:

- Glazings can reduce the absorption of solar radiation through automobile windows, thereby reducing the need for air conditioning.

- Since more than 50 percent of halon emissions come from the testing of fire extinguishers, rather than their emergency use, new testing procedures that do not involve the release of gas could curb halon emissions.

HOW DOES THAT WORK ?

DESTROYING OZONE

Pollutants in the atmosphere destroy ozone through a series of chemical reactions.

1. Once in the stratosphere, CFC molecules are exposed to intense ultraviolet radiation, which splits them, releasing chlorine (Cl) atoms.

2. The chlorine atoms react with ozone, forming chlorine monoxide (ClO) and oxygen (O_2).

3. Ultraviolet radiation soon splits the chlorine monoxide molecule, releasing the chlorine atom, which is then able to attack another ozone molecule.

4. This happens over and over again. A single chlorine atom may be able to destroy as many as 100,000 ozone molecules!

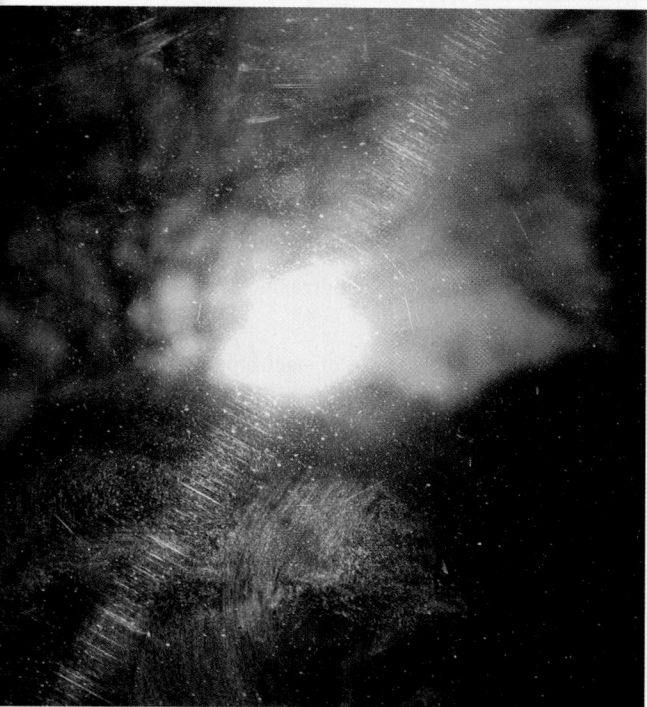

▲ **California** has proposed that windshields must reflect 30 percent of the total solar spectrum, beginning in the 2012 model year.

RADIATION is energy given off in the form of waves or particles. Light and heat are well-known forms of radiation. X-rays, ultraviolet and infrared radiation, and radio waves are other examples. Another form of radiation is produced during the disintegration of the nucleus of an atom of a radioactive substance such as uranium, radium, or radon. Called *radioactivity*, this disintegration emits three types of radiation: gamma radiation, in the form of waves, and alpha and beta radiations, which are streams of particles. Several forms of radiation have aroused concern among environmentalists and health experts.

Harmful Radiation

The types of radiation that are of most concern to environmentalists and health experts are ultraviolet radiation, nuclear radiation, and electromagnetic radiation.

- Ultraviolet radiation is reaching Earth in increasing amounts because of ozone thinning. (See pages 678–679.)
- Nuclear radiation is released from atomic weapons, uranium mining, and accidents occurring at nuclear power plants and weapons facilities.
- Some electromagnetic radiation is believed to be given off by electrical equipment.

With all types of radiation, the degree of injury to people and other organisms will depend on many factors, including total radiation dose and length of exposure.

PARTICLES GIVEN OFF BY RADIOACTIVE ATOMS

1. **Alpha particles** consist of two protons and two neutrons that act as one particle. When the nucleus of a radioactive atom emits an alpha particle, it thus loses two protons and two neutrons.

2. **Beta particles** are high-speed electrons emitted from the nuclei of certain radioactive elements. Beta particles can be either negative or positive. When a nucleus emits a negatively charged beta particle, it also gives off an antineutrino. When a nucleus emits a positively charged beta particle, called a positron, it also gives off a neutrino.

3. **Gamma rays** are particles of electromagnetic energy called photons. Gamma rays are released when a nucleus, after radioactive decay, is in a high-energy state. The rays travel at the speed of light.

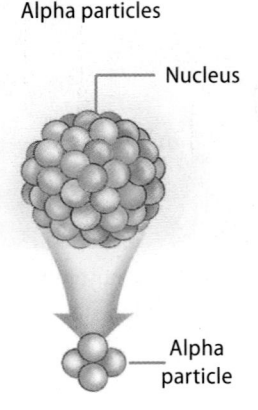

Alpha particles

Nucleus

Alpha particle

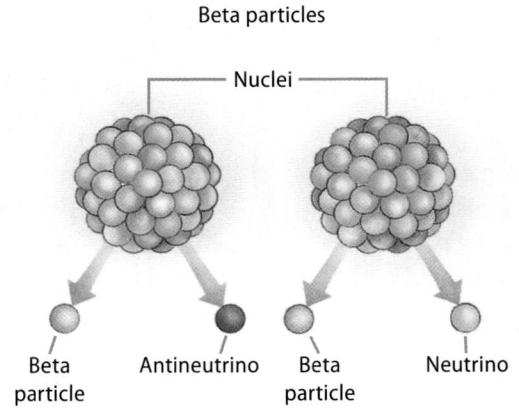

Beta particles

Nuclei

Beta particle — Antineutrino   Beta particle — Neutrino

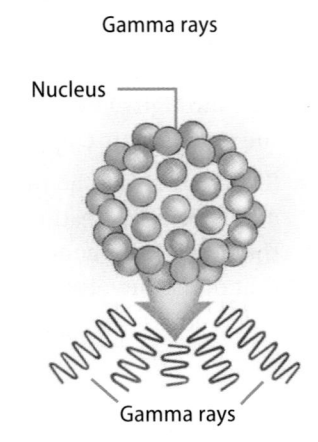

Gamma rays

Nucleus

Gamma rays

682

Nuclear Radiation

When nuclear power was introduced in the 1950s, it was presented as the energy of the future: cheap, almost inexhaustible, easy to produce, nonpolluting, and safe. The reality has been much more complicated, due in large part to the health and environmental concerns over nuclear radiation.

Concerns. Polluting radiation is produced during all stages of the nuclear power production process. Similar pollution is a by-product of nuclear weapons production.

Effects. Radiation produced during the decay of uranium and other radioactive elements can damage and kill living cells and cause cancer, anemia, and sterility.

Assuming the doses are not lethal to a person, these effects usually do not occur until some time after exposure; in cases such as the development of cancer, they may not appear for many years. If the genetic material in an egg or sperm cell is damaged, mutations causing such abnormalities as Down syndrome can be passed on to offspring.

HOW MUCH IS TOO MUCH?

Radiation doses are usually expressed in *rem*, which stands for "roentgen equivalent, man," or *millirem*, which equals one-thousandth of a rem. A chest X-ray, for example, exposes a person to 10 millirems, or 10 one-thousandths of a rem.

- The average American receives approximately 360 millirems of radiation annually.
- Exposure to 700 rems or more in a short period of time is immediately fatal.
- Exposure to 200 to 700 rems results in a 50 percent likelihood of death within a few months.
- Exposures of 100 to 200 rems increase the long-term risk of cancer.
- Exposure to lesser amounts of radiation may have a long-term impact on health, but this is difficult to measure.

Electromagnetic Radiation

Wherever electricity flows through wires, two types of invisible fields—electric and magnetic—are generated; together these are called electromagnetic (EM) fields, or radiation. Power lines, cell phones, and industrial and office equipment all produce EM fields.

Concerns. In modern society, EM fields are everywhere, so public health consequences of even a slight danger could be significant. Studies have yielded conflicting results. Some researchers found strong evidence that EM fields are dangerous, though they could not establish a direct link between the radiation and health problems. Other researchers have found no proof of adverse effects.

Effects. Because research is not entirely conclusive, the exact effects of EM radiation are not completely known. Still, some correlations have been studied.

- People with jobs that involve high exposure to EM fields, such as power line workers, have a higher incidence of cancer than other workers.
- A study of women who spent more than 20 hours a week working on video display terminals (VDTs) during the first 3 months of pregnancy found that these women experienced twice as many miscarriages as did pregnant women who did not use VDTs.
- Animal studies also indicate a link between EM fields and some neurological problems.

▲ **Electromagnetic radiation** emitted by power lines, cell phones, and other electronics may be harmful. Several steps have been taken by industries to reduce exposure.

NOISE POLLUTION

The word *noise* generally means "unwanted or excessive sound." Noise pollution comes from such machines as airplanes, motor vehicles, construction machinery, and industrial equipment. Noise does not dirty the air, water, or land, but it can cause discomfort, anxiety, and hearing loss in human beings and other animals.

From Sound to Noise

Noise pollution is a composite of many different sounds generated by human activities. *Audiologists*, scientists who study sound and its effects, report that industrialized nations are noisier than ever before.

Part of this growing noise pollution results from population growth. Homes and workplaces must be built, and food has to be raised for a growing population. People need transportation to travel between home and work. All these needs and activities are further sources of noise.

Sources of Noise

The major sources of noise in the modern world are airplanes, automobiles, heavy machinery, work equipment, and household appliances and devices.

Automobiles. Engine noise and exhaust sounds, squealing tires, honking horns—all are pollutants. The tens of millions of trucks, buses, motorcycles, and other motorized vehicles also produce large amounts of noise.

Airplanes are the biggest offenders, and their numbers also have increased; busy airports have aircraft arriving and departing every few minutes during peak periods. A jet airplane on takeoff has a loudness of about 140 dB.

▲ **A growing population** also means more urbanization. City streets become more crowded and noisier. A street in a quiet residential neighborhood may have a daytime noise level of 40 dB. On the main street of a small city, this jumps to around 80 dB. On an avenue in New York City, the level is 90 dB or higher.

In addition to the noise they make at takeoff, jet planes can also create a disturbance as they fly over residential areas. ▶

Heavy machinery and other equipment used in factories are other major sources of noise pollution. Farmers, construction workers, transport workers, and even some office workers may also be exposed to dangerous levels of environmental noise.

Homes and neighborhoods have become noisier for several reasons.

- More people are living in condominiums and town houses that share walls with neighboring units.

- Construction methods, including such practices as erecting thinner walls between apartments, allow more sounds to filter from one home to another.

- People own more and more noise-generating equipment. Television sets, radios, garbage disposal units, electric mixers, dishwashers, hair dryers, and other appliances fill our homes with noise.

MEASURING SOUNDS

The human ear can detect a huge range of sounds, from soft whispers to sounds that are millions of times louder. To measure perceived loudness, scientists use the decibel (dB) scale. This is a logarithmic rather than a linear scale. (See pages 802–803.)

- Every 10-dB difference is perceived as a loudness difference of a factor of two. For example, a sound measuring 80 dB is twice as loud as a sound measuring 70 dB.

- Sound from multiple sources does not add up the way you might think: two appliances may each emit 60 dB of sound, but when they are next to one another, the total sound will be about 63 dB, not 120 dB.

- One decibel is the faintest sound that can be detected by a young person with good hearing. A whisper may have a loudness of 20 dB, a refrigerator 40 dB, a vacuum cleaner 70 dB, and a Saturn rocket on takeoff 200 dB.

Household items such as lawn mowers, snow blowers, leaf blowers, and electric hedge clippers make outdoor chores easier . . . but noisier. ▶

Effects of Noise Pollution

In the early 1980s, when the Swedish navy wanted to track a suspected Soviet submarine, it ran into a problem. Officers had difficulty finding sailors who could hear well enough to operate the listening devices. The hearing of many sailors and other young Swedes had been permanently damaged. The cause? Years of listening to loud music.

Damage to hearing is the most obvious and most easily measured effect of noise pollution, but there are other effects as well. Among them are sleep disturbance and other stress symptoms.

HOW LOUD IS TOO LOUD?

At a certain point, generally around 120 dB, sounds become painful. Your ears actually hurt! Even before reaching this level, however, sounds are loud and capable of having significant physical and psychological effects.

- If noise causes ringing in your ears or forces you to shout in order to be heard, then it is probably loud enough to damage your hearing.
- Another rule of thumb: The fewer decibels, the better.

Hearing Damage

When sound waves enter the ear, they cause the eardrum to vibrate. The vibrations are passed through three small bones of the middle ear to the inner ear, which contains a structure called the *cochlea*. (See page 246.) There, excessive vibrations can destroy the delicate hair cells that are responsible for picking up the vibrations and transmitting them to nerve cells, which in turn carry the vibrations to the brain.

Hearing Loss. Hearing loss may be either temporary or permanent, depending on how badly the cochlea has been damaged. In its early stages, hearing loss may not be obvious. By the time a person notices difficulty in understanding other people's speech, quite a bit of loss may have occurred.

Who Is at Risk? In general, frequent or continuous noise at levels of 85 to 90 dB will cause permanent hearing loss. If the noise at these or higher levels is intermittent or infrequent, though, a person's ears may be able to recover between attacks and the rate of loss will be slowed.

Audiologists believe that more than 20 million Americans are exposed in their daily lives to persistent noises loud enough to cause hearing loss. Even noises a person does not notice can cause deterioration of the inner ear's hair cells.

Hearing damage depends upon both the level and frequency of noise. Thus, a person who operates a vacuum cleaner once a week for 10 or 15 minutes will not be at great risk. But a professional maid who regularly operates a noisy vacuum cleaner may be in real danger of becoming partially deaf. ▼

Other Risks

In addition to damaging the ear, noise stresses other parts of the body, increasing the potential of a very broad range of health problems.

Circulatory Problems. Noise has been associated with such stress-related circulatory problems as increased heart rate, higher blood pressure, and constricted blood vessels.

Stress Symptoms. Noise is also believed to increase the incidence of ulcers, migraine headaches, and allergic responses. It disturbs sleep and can cause blurred vision and nausea.

Mental and emotional effects can be as significant as physical effects.

- Even low-level noise can make people irritable. Experiments suggest that noise increases aggressive tendencies, making people more willing to fight or harm others.
- In noisy working environments, people find it difficult to think and to concentrate. They become less efficient, working more slowly, making more mistakes, and suffering more accidents.

Reducing Noise

Noise abatement consists of reducing the amount of sound to acceptable levels or, preferably, even lower. Though the U.S. government had active noise abatement programs during the 1970s, in recent years abatement efforts have received little or no financial support from government agencies.

It is therefore up to individuals and industry to take steps to reduce and protect against noise. Fortunately, a variety of steps are possible. These include:

- playing music and TV at reasonable levels.
- using sound suppressors on aircraft jets.
- installing soundproofing and barrier walls in homes and offices.
- wearing earmuffs or earplugs.

ANTINOISE

One of the latest techniques for fighting noise is antinoise. This technology blocks noise but does not affect acceptable sounds.

- In an antinoise system, sound waves are converted into data that can be read by a computer.
- The frequency and amplitude of unwanted sounds are calculated and a mirror-image sound wave is generated and played through a speaker.
- The characteristics of this sound wave are the reverse of those of the unwanted sounds—this cancels out the noise wave.

▲ **Sound barriers** along highways, such as the one shown here, help reduce the level of sound that reaches nearby homes and businesses.

Typical Environmental Sounds	
Sound	**Average Decibels***
whisper	20
refrigerator	40
normal conversation	60
vacuum cleaner	75
motorcycle	85
subway train	90
jackhammer	100
jet flyover	100
rock music (amplified)	120

*Average decibels depend on the distance between the noise source and the point of measurement. Figures presented here are typical levels at common distances.

POLLUTED LAND

The biosphere can be divided into three major segments: land, water, and air. The land portion contains many of the natural resources essential for human life—and lifestyles. We depend on soil to grow most of our food and to grow the forests for our timber and other products. We also depend on underground mineral reserves for fuels, metals, and gems. The soil is home to ecosystems that support millions of species. But human activities are depleting these resources. Environmentalists and ecologists are working on ways to lessen our harmful impact on the soil.

The average American produces about 9 pounds of solid wastes daily. Most of these wastes are dumped in sanitary landfills. The wastes are compacted and then covered with soil. ▼

Waste: Where It Comes From

Every day, the United States generates about 1 million tons (907,000 metric tons) of solid waste—the equivalent of about 9 pounds (4.1 kilograms) of waste per person. In addition, more than 80 billion gallons (303 billion liters) of wastewater are poured into sewers and septic tanks.

The natural processes that can break down wastes are unable to handle such huge amounts. Also, many of the wastes are not biodegradable; that is, they cannot be decomposed into harmless substances.

The Waste Crisis

As a result, the United States—along with most other nations—faces a waste disposal crisis.

- Communities are running out of habitats to be covered over with trash.
- Disposal fees are escalating.
- Incidences of illegal dumping are increasing.
- Mismanaged wastes are creating pollution.
- The export of garbage from industrialized nations to developing countries is rightly viewed as scandalous.

9 Lbs. Per Day Per Person

The Disposable World. Americans spend billions of dollars each year on disposable plates, cups, tableware, lighters, flashlights, and paint rollers. Every year, they discard

- 2 billion pens.
- 2.5 billion batteries.
- 2 billion razors and blades.
- 18 billion diapers.

Once they are thrown away, these items do not disappear. They must somehow be disposed of, which cannot be done without polluting the biosphere.

Avoiding Waste. One of the best ways to avoid waste is to reuse materials for their original purpose. Materials that are durable and repairable save resources and money while reducing pollution and solid wastes.

Reducing Waste. Better packaging would reduce the waste stream. A large portion of paper, glass, metal, and plastic is used solely to wrap and decorate consumer products. Often, hard-to-dispose-of materials, such as plastic foam, are used instead of such biodegradable materials as cardboard. However, replacing one disposable for another seldom reduces the total amount of waste produced.

SOURCES OF WASTES

Solid municipal waste generally refers to residential and commercial waste. These wastes include garbage, newspapers, and other items commonly disposed of by homes and businesses. In the United States, this waste stream consists of the following items:

Plastics are resins synthesized from petroleum or natural gases with various additives to modify or enhance the properties of these resins. Most plastics are not degradable, either by bacteria or by solar radiation.

Medical wastes from hospitals, such as intravenous bags, syringes, and needles, have also received a great deal of attention. The U.S. Environmental Protection Agency (EPA) estimates that 10 to 15 percent of hospital waste is potentially infectious, presenting a health hazard.

Automotive wastes include not only the millions of cars, trucks, and buses that are scrapped each year, but also oil filters, batteries, tires, and other items. More than 200 million tires are discarded annually in the United States alone.

Industrial wastes are materials discarded from industrial operations and manufacturing processes. They include toxic chemicals, radioactive materials, and other hazardous wastes.

Waste Material	Percentage by Weight
paper	33.9
yard debris	12.9
food	12.4
plastics	11.7
metals	7.6
rubber, leather, textiles	7.3
wood	5.5
glass	5.3
other	3.3

Medical wastes washing up on beaches led to new, stricter disposal regulations. ▶

Taking Out the Trash

The three most common methods for solid waste disposal are dumping, incineration (burning), and recycling. Each has advantages and limitations, and each has an impact on the environment as a whole.

Dumping

Traditionally, people simply dumped their wastes on open ground or in pits. In addition to being smelly and unsightly, these were breeding grounds for rats and other pests. Sometimes the wastes in dumps were burned, either deliberately or accidentally, but in either case the burning created air pollution.

Process:

- Municipal wastes and certain industrial and agricultural wastes are spread in layers and compacted to reduce their volume.

- At least once a day, a layer of soil is placed on top of the compacted wastes.

- It, too, is compacted before more wastes are added.

- When the site is full, a final thick layer of soil is added and vegetation is planted. In some cases, the land can be used for recreational, commercial, and other purposes.

Drawbacks:

- As organic materials in the landfill slowly decompose, there is a gradual settling of the ground.

- Another problem is runoff or leaching of contents into aquifers.

- Although sanitary landfills are supposed to be sited to minimize such water pollution, contamination does occur.

Landfills. In the United States and many other nations, most solid wastes are now dumped on prepared sites called sanitary landfills. These are built on open land and in strip mines, gravel pits, and abandoned quarries.

▲ **A methane tower** in the middle of the McCullough's Emerald Links golf course is the only clue to its having once been a landfill.

A secure sanitary landfill is lined with materials that prevent water from carrying *leachates* (dissolved substances) from the refuse into underground water supplies. Pipes collect the water for transfer to a treatment plant that removes the leachates. Wells drilled nearby allow landfill operators to check for leachates in the groundwater. ▼

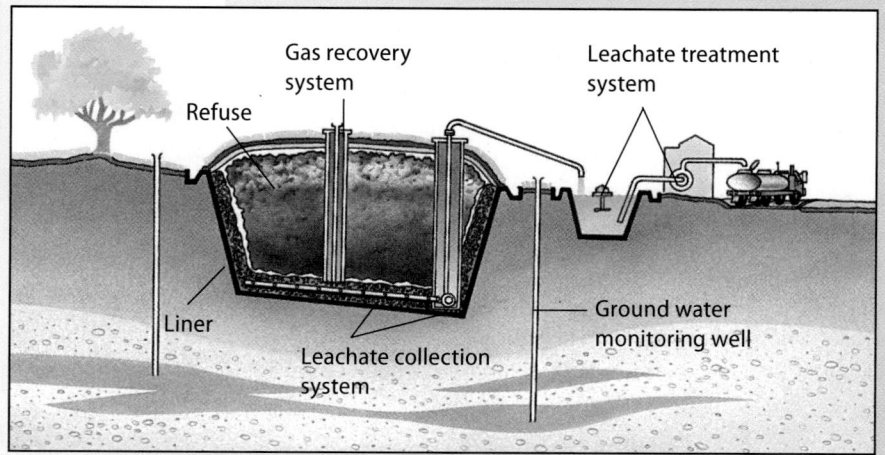

Incineration

Incineration, or burning, of residential and commercial solid wastes has grown in popularity because it reduces the volume of wastes and limits the amount of space needed for landfills.

Process:

- Large incinerators heat waste to up to 2000°F (1100°C), hot enough to break down toxic organic (carbon-containing) chemicals into less harmful gases and water.
- The heat also sterilizes infectious waste.
- Waste-to-energy incinerators use the heat generated during combustion of wastes to produce steam, which in turn is used to generate electricity.

Drawbacks:

- The ash produced during incineration can contain hazardous materials, including metals and extremely toxic chemicals called dioxins.
- Lead is the most common hazardous substance found in ash. Sources of lead include batteries, electronic products (television sets, radios, etc.), glass containers, ceramic tableware, plastics, soldered cans, and paint pigments.

Ocean incineration has been employed since 1969 as an alternative to dumping toxic wastes directly into the sea. The wastes are burned in incinerators mounted on ships.

However, wastes produced during ocean incineration create havoc in marine ecosystems. And the incinerator ships frequently spew black smoke, indicating an incomplete burning of the hazardous wastes. The deadly chemicals can then easily be carried toward land by winds.

◀ **Many incinerators** prohibit items such as glass and appliances, in order to limit the amount of harmful lead and other chemicals released by incineration.

OCEAN DUMPING

The dumping of wastes in the ocean is practiced in many parts of the world, causing great concern about the long-term threat of contamination of the ocean environment and its impact on sea organisms, including those eaten by people Plastic products pose more immediate problems.

- Ingestion of plastic wastes is particularly serious among seabirds and turtles, which mistake plastic items for food.
- The animals suffer injury to the digestive tract, intestinal blockage, and starvation.
- In addition, there is damage and its related economic costs to beach and other coastal recreational areas.

▲ **Wastes dumped in the ocean** can harm marine life. They can also wash ashore, polluting beaches and coastlines.

Recycling

Wastes usually include large amounts of reclaimable metals, glass, and other materials. Salvaging these materials reduces waste-disposal problems, conserves resources, and frequently saves money.

What Gets Recycled?

Recycling is not possible for all materials, but it can handle a significant percentage of the solid wastes produced by homes and businesses. In Japan, where recycling is well established, effective programs recycle 50 percent of trash.

Commonly recycled items include paper, glass, metal, automobile wastes, plastic, and organic wastes.

RECYCLING PROGRAMS

Several kinds of collection programs are currently in effect.

- Curbside collection programs offer scheduled pickups of separated, recyclable products.
- Drop-off centers are sites where people can leave materials for recycling.
- Buy-back centers pay consumers for such recyclable materials as glass bottles and aluminum cans.
- Waste companies buy and pick up trash from offices, businesses, institutions, schools, and industries in some communities.

Recyclable materials can be recovered from municipal waste streams and used to produce new products. ▼

Paper. Use of recycled fiber as opposed to virgin pulpwood in paper and paperboard manufacturing results in energy savings ranging from 60 to 70 percent. (In fact, Southwestern Advantage books are printed on recycled paper.)

- Old newspapers and cardboard are important sources of waste paper for recycling.
- Office papers, such as white copy paper, printouts, note pads, and index cards, are considered high-quality waste papers. They can be readily used as a direct substitute for pulpwood in making paper.

Automotive Wastes. Several car components are recyclable or reusable and offer large potential savings. For example, if Americans recycled all their used motor oil, the nation would save 1.3 million barrels of oil per day!

- Worn tires in decent condition can be retreaded or recapped for reuse.
- Tires can also be chopped, shredded, or ground and reused in such smaller items as rubber mats and molded objects.
- Car batteries are also being recycled in large quantities.

Organic Wastes. Grass cuttings, leaves, brush, and other yard wastes can be recycled through composting. In this process, the wastes decompose, forming a dark brown substance that can be used to lighten and enrich the soil. In addition to backyard composting, there are centralized composting facilities operated by municipalities and private companies.

Another technique is being used to tap energy from animal wastes at dairy farms and cattle feedlots.

- Manure flows into an insulated trench, where it gives off a mixture of gases consisting almost entirely of methane and carbon dioxide.
- This gas, called *biogas*, burns as cleanly as does natural gas (methane).

Percentage of Total Waste Recycled Each Year

= 10%

1970   1980   1990   2000   2006

Glass. Glass is one of the most commonly and easily recycled materials. Often, it is separated by color to be reprocessed. The glass is crushed to form a material called cullet, which is mixed with sand, soda ash, and limestone to form new glass containers.

Plastics. About 1 percent of plastic waste is currently recycled. Most efforts have focused on recycling drink bottles made of polyethylene terephthalate (PET). About 20 percent of these bottles are being recycled. However, drink bottles represent only about 3 percent of plastic wastes. According to the Environmental Protection Agency, the heterogeneity, or different compositions, of plastics poses a major technical hurdle to widespread plastics recycling.

▲ **The rubber from car tires** has many uses. Whole tires can even be used for playground equipment and in reef construction.

Metals. Some of the most successful recycling efforts have involved metals, such as aluminum and steel.

- Recycling aluminum requires about 5 percent of the energy needed to produce aluminum from virgin materials.

- Aluminum cans, window frames, storm doors, gutters, and other aluminum items can be recycled.

- Producing steel from scrap uses about 26 percent of the energy needed to make steel from iron ore.

- Worn or broken appliances, such as stoves and refrigerators, can be shredded to recover steel components for reuse in mills and foundries.

- Cans, cars, and other steel items are also being recycled.

Separating recyclable materials keeps them uncontaminated, which increases their value. When this process is done at a waste-processing plant, such special equipment as conveyor belts, screens, and magnets is used to separate large quantities of waste mechanically. ▶

Hazardous Wastes

Wastes that are toxic, corrosive, flammable, ignitable, or reactive are considered to be hazardous wastes. The Environmental Protection Agency (EPA) classified 60,000 of the 66,000 chemicals currently in use as being hazardous or potentially hazardous.

Unless properly managed and disposed of, these chemicals pose short- and long-term dangers to health and the environment. Unfortunately, people have often carelessly disposed of hazardous wastes.

DISASTER AT LOVE CANAL

One of the most infamous hazardous waste sites in the United States was the Love Canal neighborhood of Niagara Falls, New York. In the summer of 1978, people in the neighborhood learned that they were living on top of or near some of the most poisonous chemicals in existence.

The Beginnings. Love Canal had been used as a dump site since the 1920s. Between 1947 and 1953, Hooker Chemical and Plastics Corporation dumped an estimated 21,800 tons (19,777 metric tons) of toxic chemicals into the canal.

They covered the canal with dirt and sold the land to Niagara Falls for a token $1. The city built an elementary school, playground, and residences on the rest of the land. Soon, Love Canal was a bustling community.

Disaster. In the 1970s, however, several years of unusually heavy precipitation apparently corroded the buried waste drums. The poisonous contents leaked into the ground.

Black ooze bubbled in pools on the playground and seeped through basement walls. Putrid fumes filled the air. Trees and ground cover died. People became ill, experiencing abnormally high rates of miscarriages, birth defects, epilepsy, nervous disorders, liver diseases, and other ailments.

Evacuation. When government agencies investigated, they found 82 chemicals in the ground, air, and water, including 11 known carcinogens and six known mutagens. Love Canal was declared an emergency area.

What Are the Risks?

Among the most familiar hazardous wastes are such heavy metals as cadmium, arsenic, manganese, chromium, mercury, and lead. Used in a broad range of manufacturing processes, they cause birth defects, cancer, neurological problems, and other damage to people and animals.

Other hazardous wastes include:

- dioxins and polychlorinated biphenyls (PCBs), which are carcinogenic (cancer-causing).
- strong acids and other corrosive liquids.
- pesticides containing chlorinated hydrocarbons.
- solvents such as trichloroethylene and benzene.
- hospital wastes.

▲ **Love Canal** before cleanup operations.

Residents were advised to move, and the state bought up their homes. Eventually, some 200 homes nearest the canal were razed. The toxic wastes in the canal were covered with layers of clay and plastic and fenced off.

By 1990, the state and federal government agreed that much of the Love Canal area was safe enough to permit people to move back in. They gave it a new name—Black Creek Village—and put the first homes up for sale.

Disposal

State-of-the-art facilities for the disposal of hazardous wastes have two liners in containers, a leak detection system, groundwater monitoring wells, and a collection system to catch leaks. Most experts believe that such methods are only temporary solutions; eventually, liners will develop cracks and the corrosive action of chemicals will eat away containers.

Deep-Well Injection. An alternative disposal method is deep-well injection; the wastes are pumped into porous sandstone and limestone formations hundreds of feet below Earth's surface. Lack of appropriate sites plus the potential contamination of groundwater limits the suitability of this approach.

Treatment prior to disposal can reduce both the volume and toxicity of hazardous wastes, thereby reducing the potential for harm.

- Currently, the preferred treatment is incineration, which destroys organic components of the waste. PCBs, dioxin, organic solvents, and some other toxins are broken down completely when burned at temperatures over 2400°F (1315°C).
- Incineration at lower temperatures, however, may release the hazardous wastes into the atmosphere.

Cleanup

Thousands of sites used for the careless or illegal disposal of hazardous wastes pose serious threats to public health and the environment. The costs of cleaning them up are staggering.

- Generally, cleanup involves removal of contaminated soil and transportation of it to an approved landfill site.
- Contaminated groundwater is pumped into wells lined with double cement walls.
- A government cleanup project called Superfund, run by the EPA, works to eliminate unsafe toxic waste dumps in the United States.

MINIMIZING HAZARDOUS WASTE

The most preferable solution to disposing hazardous waste is to minimize the creation of the waste from the start.

- One way to do this is to substitute less hazardous substances in manufacturing processes.
- Another method is to segregate the waste disposal stream so that some materials can be reused or recycled.
- For example, a toxic fluid used in the manufacture of semiconductors is now used to refine old crankcase oil, thereby eliminating two disposal problems at once.

◀ **Hazardous wastes** must be carefully handled during both use and exposure. Disposal workers wear protective suits, sometimes called hazmat suits (after *haz*ardous *mat*erials), masks, and gloves.

Radioactive Wastes

Wastes that are radioactive create special disposal problems because they emit radiation that is harmful to humans and other organisms. Even in small amounts, radioactive materials such as plutonium can cause cancer or genetic damage in human beings. Larger amounts can cause radiation sickness and death. (See pages 402–403.)

Types of Radioactive Waste

Five major types of radioactive wastes are produced by the nuclear power and weapons industries. They differ significantly in their physical form and in the intensity of the radiation they emit. Some decay in 10 to 100 years. Others remain radioactive for thousands of years. There is no known technology for changing any of these radioactive materials into nonradioactive forms.

HALF-LIVES

Wastes produced by commercial nuclear power plants contain levels of radioactivity that will be harmful to people for at least 250,000 years. One of these wastes is plutonium-239, which has a half-life of 24,000 years. This means that it takes 24,000 years for 50 percent of the radioactivity to be dissipated as plutonium decays into stable elements.

In other words, if you start with a pound of plutonium-239,

- after 24,000 years, there will still be 0.5 pound (0.22 kilogram) of plutonium-239.

- after another 24,000 years, there will be 0.25 pound (0.11 kilogram); and so on.

- Scientists believe it takes 10 to 20 half-lives for a radioactive substance to become safe.

To protect people and environments, radioactive wastes must be carefully transported and then isolated until they are no longer radioactive. ▼

Types of Radioactive Wastes		
Type	**Source**	**Characteristics**
Tailings	Uranium mines and their processing operations	• Sandy wastes containing several radioactive elements, including thorium, radium, and radon • Emit low levels of radiation
Fuel rods	Nuclear reactors	• Enriched uranium shaped into long cylindrical rods • Highly radioactive and generate a lot of heat • Contain unused uranium as well as plutonium-239 created during the nuclear reaction • Also contain waste products, including such highly radioactive elements as cesium-137 and strontium-90
High-level wastes	Reprocessing of spent fuel rods	• Wastes in liquid form • Can be chemically treated to form a mixture of liquid and sludge or a dry granular substance called calcine
Transuranic wastes	Nuclear weapons programs and testing activities; a small amount from nuclear power plants	• Contain plutonium or any of the other 10 radioactive transuranic elements (artificial elements having atomic numbers greater than that of uranium) • Less intensely radioactive than other high-level wastes, but take an extremely long time to decay
Low-level wastes	Nuclear power plants, industrial firms, defense facilities, research laboratories, hospitals	• Include all items that come into unprotected contact with radioactive material and become contaminated • Examples: gloves, tools, cleaning rags, medical isotopes, and so on

◄ **Hospitals and research facilities** are a source of many low-level radioactive wastes. Radiation plays an important part in many cancer treatments and diagnostic procedures.

Radioactive Cleanup

If humans and other organisms are to be protected, radioactive wastes must be isolated until they have lost their radioactivity. This has been no easy task.

Disposal Methods

In the United States, the federal government is working on guidelines for the safe and permanent disposal of nuclear wastes. The current U.S. plan calls for isolating long-lived radioactive waste from the environment in underground storage sites.

Tailings. These represent the largest volume of radioactive wastes. The best solution is to bury piles of tailings, but this has generally been considered to be too expensive. The next best option is to cover them with thick layers of soil. In many cases, however, tailings simply lie in huge mounds, exposed to the air and subject to erosion by wind and leaching by rainwater.

Fuel Rods. Spent fuel contains both high-level wastes and transuranic wastes. Some countries reprocess these wastes, recovering usable uranium and plutonium. In general, however, the spent fuel rods have been stored in pools of water at nuclear power plants. The water cools the rods and acts as a shield against the radiation.

High-level Wastes. When spent fuel is reprocessed, the wastes that remain require extremely careful handling.

- They must be converted to a form that is not expected to leak, dissolve, or otherwise enter the biosphere for at least a thousand years.
- Then a safe disposal place must be found.

Some high-level wastes are disposed of through a process called *vitrification*.

1. High-level wastes are changed into glass.
2. The hot, radioactive glass can then be embedded in concrete or stainless steel tanks and buried.
3. In theory, the glass and its containers would not break down until the radiation had fallen to a level comparable to that of the original uranium ore.
4. In France, vitrified wastes are being stored in air-conditioned underground vaults.

Wastes also are sometimes converted into a ceramic material or a substance called Syn-Roc, an artificial rocklike material.

▲ **Airtight containers** of steel and concrete can be used to store nuclear wastes. Fuel rods are stored and cooled in large concrete pools filled with water (shown at left). Some spent rods have been stored in this manner for more than 20 years, awaiting permanent disposal.

Transuranic Wastes. These wastes must be isolated from the environment for 250,000 years or longer. Although proponents say this can be done safely using special stainless steel drums, opponents doubt that any kind of containment will be safe for so long a period of time. At present, transuranic wastes are stored in a way similar to that of high-level wastes.

Low-level Wastes. Clothing that has been contaminated and other low-level wastes do not require cooling, but they must be stored and buried in containers that will not leak for at least a century. Storage methods have improved and monitoring equipment detects any escaping radiation. Still, leaks have occurred, releasing radiation into the environment.

Some current disposal sites are rapidly reaching their capacity. Attempts to construct storage sites, however, still face a great deal of opposition from communities. ▼

OTHER PROBLEMS

The problem of disposal is a complicated one, but it is not the only problem posed by radioactive wastes. Other concerns include transport, future security, and cleanup.

Transport. If and when a permanent repository is built for high-level wastes, the wastes will have to be transported from nuclear power plants and other temporary storage places to the repository.

- Truck and train transportation of nuclear materials already creates the risk that accidents will release radiation into the atmosphere.
- Transporting vast amounts of spent fuel rods and other materials will increase this risk.

Future Security. Another concern is how high-level waste disposal sites will be identified to ensure that people living hundreds or thousands of years in the future will understand the danger they pose. Currently, the oldest known structures built by people are less than 4,000 years old, yet we are uncertain about the intended uses of many of these structures.

Site Cleanup. Another major nuclear waste problem facing society is the cleanup of decommissioned nuclear power plants and weapons facilities. When a reactor is decommissioned, it must either be dismantled (with the removal of all radioactive parts to a waste disposal facility), or entombed in concrete or steel. Both methods are enormously costly.

HABITATS IN PERIL

Numerous human activities threaten and destroy the habitats of plants and animals. Urban sprawl has displaced wildlife from huge areas. So, too, have strip mining and the construction of dams and airports. Habitats are also harmed by the pollutants of human activities. Toxic substances may kill organisms directly, or become concentrated in food chains, eventually causing problems throughout the chain. But habitat destruction doesn't only threaten plants and animals. Eventually, it also threatens humans.

Wetland plants and animals have evolved to thrive in damp conditions. ▼

Wetlands

Wetlands are among the world's most productive habitats. These include swamps, marshes, estuaries, and other areas that are regularly saturated by water, and whose vegetation is adapted for life in saturated soil conditions. Some wetlands form inland and contain fresh water; others are along the seacoast and contain salty or brackish water.

Threats

Unfortunately, the value of wetlands was not fully appreciated until comparatively recently. Wetlands were considered wastelands because they are breeding grounds for mosquitoes and other pests, and because they are unsuitable for building and farming.

Causes of Destruction. The major cause of wetland destruction in the United States has been agricultural practices. Today, less than half of the original wetlands in the continental United States remain.

- Additional wetlands have been drained for housing developments and other construction.
- Some wetlands have been dredged to make channels for ships.
- Some have been destroyed or damaged because people have used them as dumps for sewage and other wastes.

WHAT GOES ON IN A WETLAND?

Wetlands are homes for water birds, fish, and a variety of other wildlife.

- In the United States, wetlands are critical to the survival of 35 percent of the plants and animals listed as endangered or threatened.
- Wetlands absorb excess runoff from rivers and streams, thereby helping to prevent flooding downstream.
- They also help to maintain and improve water quality by acting as natural filters—removing and retaining nutrients, and processing chemical and organic wastes.
- In coastal areas, they act as buffers against the destructive force of ocean waves and currents.

Preservation

In recent years, national and local governments have enacted laws to limit construction projects that destroy wetlands.

- Wetlands are being purchased and preserved by governments and environmental organizations.
- Management plans have been developed to maintain wetlands and to restore damaged areas.
- Courts are handing down increasingly stiff sentences and fines to people who violate wetland protection laws.

Urban wetlands are now recognized as being as important as those in rural areas.

- New York City's large Gateway National Recreation Area—the only known wetland that has a subway running through it—is an important bird breeding ground and a resting place for migratory birds.
- Portland, Oregon, has a network of wetlands that cover more than 4,000 acres. These wetlands are home to bald eagles, coyotes, bobcats, salmon, peregrine falcons, minks, and many other wild creatures.

New Wetlands. In some places, people are building new wetlands. The city of Arcata, California, created 175 acres of wetland. Treated wastewater from the city's sewage treatment facilities flows into the wetlands and is naturally cleansed.

Wildlife has settled in the area, thousands of people visit each year, and the $700,000 spent to create the wetlands was much less than would have been needed to build mechanical facilities to treat the wastewater effluent.

Once crystal clear, Lake Okeechobee, the Everglades' chief source of water, is polluted with runoff from dairy farms and filled with algae. ▶

SAVING THE EVERGLADES

The ecologically unique Everglades, a vast wetland of southern Florida, once covered 4 million acres. Today the Everglades region has shrunk to 2 million acres, about one-fifth of which is protected as a national park. The future of these wetlands and their inhabitants is seriously threatened because of years of mismanagement coupled with extensive agricultural and urban development.

- By the end of the 20th century, species of wading birds had dropped by 90 to 95 percent. As of 2003, the Everglades hosted only 366 species of birds.
- Less than 50 Florida panthers are believed to remain.
- Bass and catfish are contaminated with mercury that leached into the water from dried soil.

To the Rescue. Many groups have joined the fight to save the Everglades. The state of Florida has bought land around Lake Okeechobee to create new marshes that will store water and filter out toxic chemicals before releasing the additional water into the wetlands to the south.

In 1999, the U.S. Army Corps of Engineers also introduced a 20-year plan to reconnect the various parts of the Everglades that have been fragmented by the building of artificial barriers and drainage canals.

Forests

A forest is a large area of land covered with trees. But a forest is much more than just trees. In addition to providing food and shelter for myriad species, forests play other essential roles in the world's environment.

- Their trees efficiently trap carbon dioxide and also produce oxygen.
- Forest soils are like giant sponges, soaking up precipitation. This limits runoff and prevents flooding.
- The large root systems hold the soil together, preventing soil erosion.
- Forests make soil, too. Decaying leaves, branches, and trunks, together with the remains of animals, form a rich humus on the forest floor.

The Many Facets of Forests

People obtain many products from forests. Wood from trees is used to build homes and furniture, make paper and paperboard, and manufacture hundreds of chemical products. Fruits, nuts, and other foods are obtained from forest plants, as are rubber and medicines. People also use forests for such recreational activities as hiking, picnicking, fishing, and camping.

Types of Forests. There are four major kinds of forests: evergreen coniferous, deciduous, tropical deciduous, and tropical rain forests. Each has its own complex mix of living and nonliving components. Other types of forests occur in various parts of the world. (See pages 612–613.)

Major Kinds of Forests	Where They Are Found	Characteristics
Evergreen coniferous	• Higher latitudes of the Northern Hemisphere, where the climate is generally cold • Also found in parts of Brazil, Chile, southeastern Asia, the Philippines, and New Zealand	Spruce and fir predominate in many of these forests.
Deciduous, or broadleaf	In more temperate regions of the Northern Hemisphere	Trees that shed their leaves annually. Oak, maple, and hickory trees are common.
Tropical deciduous forests, or dry forests	Parts of Central and South America, southeastern Asia, Indonesia, and southern and western Africa	• Alternating dry and wet seasons characterize these areas. • The trees generally shed their leaves during the dry season.
Tropical rain forests	Equatorial regions that receive a lot of rain, such as the Amazon River basin of South America, Central America, and the Congo River basin in Africa	• Most of the trees have broad leaves but are evergreen. • Vines and epiphytes (plants that grow attached to larger plants without deriving nourishment from the hosts) are common.

Deforestation

Human activities have had tremendous impact on modern forests. For at least 10,000 years, people have cut down forests to clear areas for farmland. Beginning in the 1800s, great expanses of forest have also been eliminated because of logging and industrial pollution. The destruction and degrading of forests is called deforestation.

Causes of Deforestation. Forests are cleared for lumber and firewood and to make way for agriculture, ranches, mining projects, transmission lines, and urban development. In addition, pollution created by industry and motor vehicles is killing some forests, particularly in the Northern Hemisphere.

Much deforestation in tropical areas results from social and economic factors. Rapidly growing populations need firewood and farmland to survive. But there is also a rapidly growing global demand for paper, lumber, and a wide range of other forest products. As forests are destroyed, the long-term possibility of meeting these demands declines.

Effects of Deforestation. Deforestation has serious and widespread effects on the environment.

Loss of Habitats. Forest loss has led to serious depletion of numerous species. Many scientists fear that tropical forests will be gone in another 60 years. When they disappear, so will half the species on Earth.

Global Climate. As forests dwindle, less and less carbon dioxide is removed from the atmosphere. This results in rising atmospheric temperatures because of the greenhouse effect. (See pages 670–677.)

Erosion. As hillsides are deforested, erosion increases. Without large tree roots to hold the soil, water quickly runs off the land, eventually leading to flooding.

Loss of Resources. When trees are cut down faster than they can be replaced, the economic value forests can provide decreases. The nutrient-poor forest soil becomes exhausted in a few years. People must then abandon the ruined land and clear more forest to support themselves.

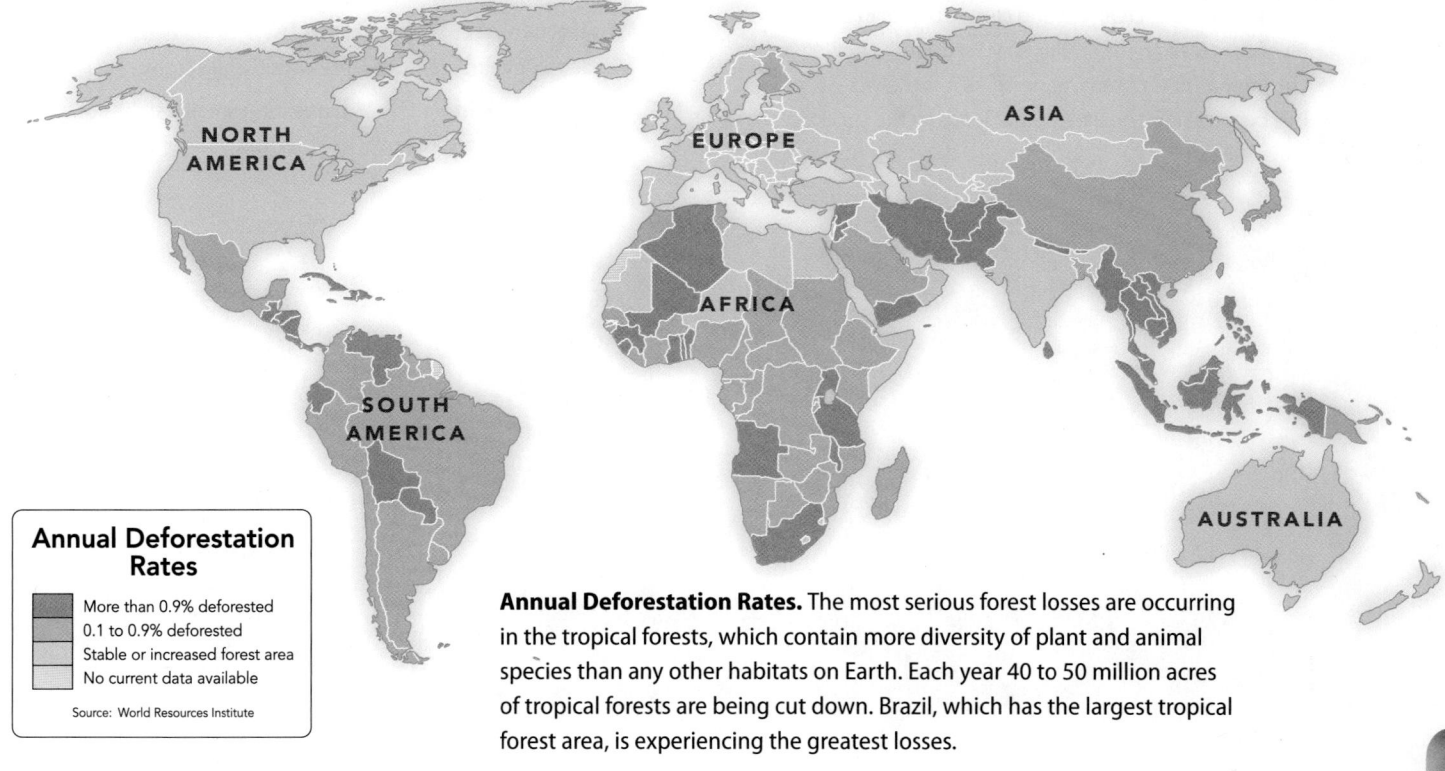

Annual Deforestation Rates

- More than 0.9% deforested
- 0.1 to 0.9% deforested
- Stable or increased forest area
- No current data available

Source: World Resources Institute

Annual Deforestation Rates. The most serious forest losses are occurring in the tropical forests, which contain more diversity of plant and animal species than any other habitats on Earth. Each year 40 to 50 million acres of tropical forests are being cut down. Brazil, which has the largest tropical forest area, is experiencing the greatest losses.

Conserving Forests

Protecting the world's remaining forests involves wiser management practices, changed government policies, and better use of lumber and other forest products.

Forest Management

A primary purpose of forest management, or forestry, is to make certain that there is continuous production of lumber.

- Foresters make inventories to determine the number of trees and the volume of timber in a forest.
- They evaluate watersheds, measure wildlife populations, and prepare plans for protection against fire, insects, and disease.
- They also establish how many trees can be cut annually in the forest to ensure a sustained yield.

Parks and Preserves. Large tracts of forest can be set aside for national parks and preserves. For example, in 1989, the Brazilian government, which has long offered subsidies and incentives for clearing land in the Amazon rain forest, began to develop a conservation program.

By mid-1990, the country had established four reserves covering 8,351 square miles (21,635 square kilometers) in which logging is forbidden. Long-term harvesting of rubber and other products is allowed.

Legislation. Lawmaking bodies and government agencies play a central role in how a country treats its forests. Governmental programs that provide incentives for conserving forests rather than for cutting them down are needed.

SUSTAINED YIELD MANAGEMENT

In sustained yield management, the amount of timber harvested equals the growth rate of the forest. Different harvesting techniques can be used, depending on the type of forest and its composition.

For example, clear-cutting can be useful in areas where all of the trees are of similar age. Frequently, however, clear cutting has been used not because it is the wisest course, but because it is the easiest and leads to the quickest profits.

1. **Clear-cutting** removes all the trees in a large area. It provides full sunlight in which new seedlings can develop.

2. **Seed tree cutting** leaves a few scattered trees in the area to provide a source of seeds for a new crop.

3. **Shelter-wood cutting,** which is used for trees that require shade to develop, removes trees in several stages.

4. **Selection cutting** involves harvesting small patches of mature trees to make room for new and younger trees.

1
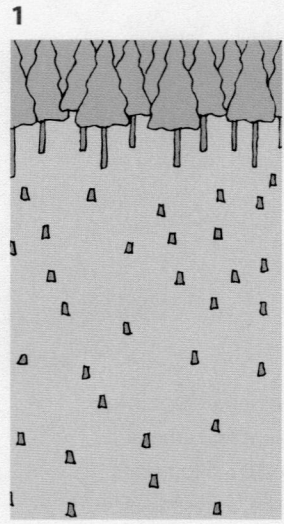

2
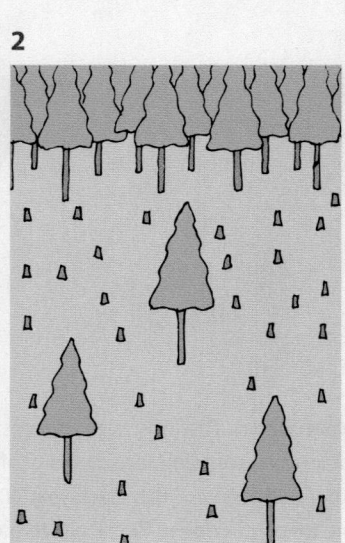

3
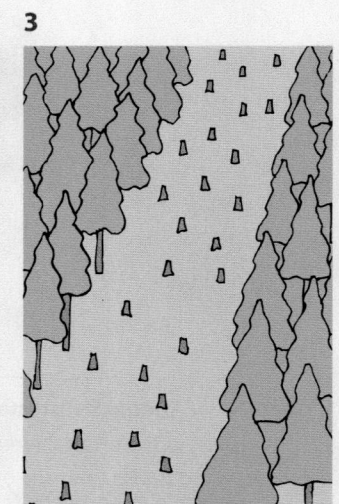

4

Debt-for-Nature Swap. In these transactions, an organization such as The Nature Conservancy acquires part of a developing country's debt that is held by a bank in the United States, Canada, or another developed country.

- This debt is either donated by the bank to the conservation organization or purchased at a discounted price.

- The organization converts the debt into the developing country's currency to use in funding conservation projects in that country.

- Each dollar used to purchase the debt buys several dollars' worth of local currency for conservation activities.

Reducing Demand. Reducing the demand for timber would aid in the conservation of forests. Helpful steps include:

- increased recycling of paper.
- more efficient use of lumber.
- better utilization of lumber remnants.

To help conserve tropical forests, consumers can avoid buying furniture and other timber products that contain teak, mahogany, and other tropical hardwoods. More efficient wood stoves and the development of alternative energy sources would also help conserve forests.

REFORESTING

In addition to conserving present forests, environmentalists are stressing the need to reforest areas once covered with trees. Such projects are under way in both industrialized and developing nations.

The new forests protect watersheds, prevent erosion, absorb carbon dioxide, and provide future wood products. Unfortunately, new forests seldom resemble the original forests. Trees are usually planted in orderly rows, with no bushes, ferns, and smaller trees to form an undergrowth attractive to wildlife.

Restoration Ecology. To attempt to return a denuded forest to its original state, including its undergrowth, requires the long-term efforts of restoration ecologists. A group of these scientists is trying to revive the once-expansive dry forest of Central America, which is only 2 percent of its original size.

The ecologists' efforts are centered in Costa Rica, which is one of the world's most ecologically conscious nations. But restoration is a slow process.

- At least 200 years of care will be needed to make the forest look like the original dry forest.

- A thousand years may be needed before the habitat actually reproduces all the original forest's interrelationships.

◄ **In Costa Rica,** where ecologists are working to restore dry forests, there are some signs of success: For the first time in 400 years, the forest's boundaries are expanding rather than shrinking. The restoration of this forest would increase the habitats of animals such as ocelots, scarlet macaws, and white-faced monkeys.

Protecting Habitats

To safeguard wild plants and animals, it is necessary to protect their habitats. Governments and private organizations have established nature preserves, refuges, and sanctuaries. The number of these areas has increased rapidly.

- In 1950, there were about 600 such areas worldwide, covering less than 250 million acres.
- By the mid-1980s, there were about 3,500 areas containing some 1 billion acres.

Nature Reserves

Protected areas cover every type of ecosystem.

- Australia has reserves that protect important areas of the Great Barrier Reef, a conglomeration of atolls, cays, and islands that constitutes the largest coral formation in the world.
- Russia is maintaining a national park that protects Lake Baikal, the deepest freshwater lake in the world, and its watershed.

▲ **The Great Barrier Reef** is one of the seven natural wonders of the world. The main threat to the reef today is bleaching caused by global warming. In 2004, the Australian parliament passed a law that prohibits all commercial activities, except tourism, in one-third of the reef's area.

▲ **Geologists estimate** that Lake Baikal was formed about 25 million years ago, making it the world's oldest lake.

- Several Russian national parks and nature reserves surround the lake.
- In 1996, the United Nations Educational, Scientific and Cultural Organization (UNESCO) named Lake Baikal a World Heritage Site as an area of unique natural importance.

▲ **The world's largest nature reserve** is the continent of Antarctica. In 1961, nations with an interest in this continent signed the Antarctic Treaty. The treaty stated that Antarctica would be used for peaceful purposes only. It also prohibited the exploitation of living resources as well as any activities that would harm those resources.

Managing Nature Reserves. Many protected areas are managed on a policy of multiple use.

- A national forest can be used for timber, wildlife habitats, fishing, hiking, and camping.

- Protected wetlands can serve as breeding grounds for commercial fish, homes for endangered birds, and recreational areas for kayakers and hikers.

Conflicts among the various users may arise, however. For example, removing timber from a national forest may require the construction of logging roads and other facilities. These restrict the area's value as a wildlife habitat and recreational site.

Protective Laws. In addition to establishing protected areas, governments need to pass protective laws.

- These may control the number of animals that can be hunted or fished to ensure that no species becomes severely depleted.

- The laws may limit timber operations, require restoration of areas that have been damaged by pollutants, prohibit campfires, and so on.

International Cooperation. In addition to local and national laws, international treaties—such as the one that protects Antarctica—and organizations are important.

The International Union for the Conservation of Nature and Natural Resources (IUCN) gathers information on the world's endangered species. It publishes this data in its Red Data Book. In 1961, the IUCN helped set up the World Wildlife Fund (now also called World Wide Fund for Nature). This fund raises money for conservation.

The Convention on International Trade in Endangered Species of Wild Fauna and Flora (CITES) is an international agreement administered by the United Nations to protect wildlife. It prohibits the trade of many nongame animals and their body parts.

▲ **One of the oldest international agreements** is the International Migratory Bird Treaty, signed by the United States and Canada in 1918 and later extended to include Mexico. It limits hunting of migratory water birds and provides for protection of the birds in their natural breeding grounds and in their natural wintering areas.

Nature preserves sometimes preserve more than just nature: Kakadu National Park in Australia protects evidence of human life from about 30,000 years ago. This evidence includes one of the world's greatest collections of prehistoric cave paintings.

AGRICULTURE

More than 90 percent of the world's food comes from the land. During the 20th century, improved technologies expanded the amount of food that could be produced per unit area of land. Each year, despite these advances, an estimated 40 to 60 million people die from hunger and hunger-related diseases. As world population continues to increase, food production must also increase. Meeting food needs requires expanding the amount of land devoted to agriculture and improving agricultural efficiency.

Threatened Soils

According to the Food and Agriculture Organization (FAO), an agency of the United Nations, only about 11 percent of Earth's land area is suitable for agriculture. Each year, however, millions of acres of agricultural land become unproductive because of erosion, water-logging, salinization, development, and other changes.

Preserving farmland and discouraging its conversion are essential if sustainable agriculture is to be achieved. Improved efficiency involves a broad range of measures, including more efficient irrigation systems, integrated pest management, and development of new high-yield crops.

Soil

There are hundreds of thousands of kinds of soil. Each kind has its own mix of substances, depending on the type of rock that is weathered, the size of the particles, the amount of organic material, the nature of the climate, and other factors. (See pages 532–533.)

Soils with high amounts of clay and humus (organic material in various stages of decay) are most suitable for agriculture. Such soils hold water in the ground and are rich in the nutrients needed for plant growth.

HOW SOIL WORKS

Mature soil has three distinct layers, or horizons: topsoil, or A horizon; subsoil, or B horizon; and C horizon:

1. Topsoil contains a high percentage of organic matter and is the most fertile part of the soil. As water percolates downward, it deposits minerals leached from the topsoil into the next layer.

2. The subsoil layer consists almost entirely of clay. Little humus is present in the B layer.

3. The third layer, the C horizon, consists of partly weathered rock. It extends downward to the unweathered parent rock below.

The depth of the layers varies greatly. For example, tropical regions tend to have soils that are rich in clays but that have low levels of nutrients because of excessive leaching. Grassland and prairie soils in temperate regions, by contrast, contain comparatively large amounts of humus and are very fertile.

800 Years to Build
1 Inch of Topsoil

1 Inch

▲ **Soil** is a renewable resource, but it forms very slowly. It takes about 800 years to form an inch (2.5 centimeters) of topsoil! Good farming practices are needed to conserve the fertile soil that currently exists.

Erosion

In many parts of the world, including most of the major agricultural regions, soil erosion is a serious problem. Soil erosion is most severe in developing countries, particularly in tropical regions and along the edges of deserts. But it is also a problem in industrialized lands.

Causes of Erosion. Soil erosion has a few primary causes, some of which are human-caused and some of which are natural. Among them are

- improper agricultural practices, such as leaving the land bare during the winter months in places where heavy rains and winds are common.
- overgrazing by cattle and other livestock, which destroys the plant cover, leaving the ground barren and susceptible to wear by wind, water, and other weathering forces.
- droughts, which worsen the problem by turning the soil into dust.

Effects of Erosion. Erosion limits agricultural productivity by wearing away the most fertile layer of soil, but that is not its only negative effect.

- Soil erosion shortens the life of dams and irrigation projects, as huge amounts of sediment collect behind them.
- Sediment washed from fields also fills in irrigation projects and canals.
- Worldwide, rivers carry an estimated 20.3 billion tons (18.4 billion metric tons) of topsoil to the seas each year, harming wetlands, coral reefs, and other habitats.

In arid and semiarid areas, erosion can lead to desertification. This is occurring in Africa, especially south of the Sahara; it is also a growing problem in parts of northern China. ▼

Soil Conservation

Fighting Erosion

Among the farming practices that help to minimize water runoff and soil erosion are contour plowing, strip-cropping, terracing, cover-cropping, and windbreaking. (See pages 506–509.)

Minimizing Erosion	
Method	**Details**
Contour plowing	• Land is plowed parallel to the contours of sloping land. • Each furrow acts as a miniature terrace, slowing water and giving it time to soak into the soil.
Strip-cropping	• Often used together with contour plowing • Alternating strips of different crops are planted, so the roots can slow water runoff.
Terracing	• Bench terraces are constructed on steep, otherwise untillable slopes. • This slows water falling on the land, giving it more time to penetrate the soil.
Cover-cropping	• The practice of growing non-crop plants on fields rather than allowing the fields to lie fallow (without crops) • The plants may then be plowed under to enrich the soil.
Windbreaking	• Farmers often plant windbreaks, or shelter belts of trees, at the edges of fields. • The windbreaks break the force of winds, thereby limiting soil erosion.

Terraces constructed on hillsides allow for farming in areas that could otherwise not be tilled for crops. This process also helps to slow erosion. ▶

Other Methods. In places where the soil is too poor to enable farmers to grow crops, it is still important to combat erosion and desertification.

- Vetiver grass can be used to reduce erosion in tropical areas. Its deep, dense roots hold the soil firmly in place. If grown between encroaching deserts and farmland, it will act as a barrier to erosion.

- Overgrazing can be prevented by determining the carrying capacity of the grassland—that is, the number of animals that can be raised while allowing the grass to renew itself. Then the herds must be maintained within this number.

Irrigation

Some fertile lands do not receive adequate precipitation for crop growth. Irrigation is the practice of artificially supplying water to these lands.

Approximately 15 percent of the world's farmland is irrigated. In some places, all the water needs are met by irrigation; in other places, irrigation is used to supplement precipitation. Worldwide, crop irrigation accounts for about 70 percent of all water use.

Irrigation enables farmers to grow crops in places that receive little precipitation; however, the process can cause problems—such as salinization of poorly drained land. ▼

How It Works. Water for irrigating land is obtained either from groundwater or from surface water. A variety of application methods are used.

- Surface irrigation systems apply water either by flooding the entire field or by diverting water down narrow ditches, called furrows, between rows of crops.

- Closed-conduit systems use pipes to distribute water. One such system is sprinkler irrigation, in which a fine mist of tiny droplets is sprayed over the land; this is particularly suitable for crops that require frequent light watering.

- In drip, or trickle, irrigation, pipes with tiny holes or valves are used to carry water at a very slow rate to the soil around the crop roots.

Efficiency. As competition for limited water resources increases, greater irrigation efficiency becomes essential. For instance, drip irrigation is much more efficient than other irrigation methods because it can supply the precise amount of water needed by the plants directly to their roots. Recycling excess water through the use of pumps and ponds is another conservation method.

SALINIZATION

In irrigated lands with inadequate drainage, the soil may become salty. The buildup of salt is called salinization.

- As excessive water evaporates, it leaves behind salts that were dissolved in the water.

- Over a period of years, enough salts may accumulate to make the soil unsuitable for crops.

- Worldwide, an estimated 2.5 million acres of farmland become salty each year.

The problem can be solved by regulating the application of water, thereby limiting waterlogging and evaporation. Another solution is to build drainage canals to remove excess water. However, this method simply carries the salts—plus soil nutrients and excess fertilizers and pesticides—to other parts of the environment, creating such problems as polluted drinking water supplies.

Fertilizers and Pesticides

As plants grow, they remove nutrients from the soil. When the plants die and decay, these nutrients are returned to the soil, to be used by future plants. But if the plants are harvested and used by people, the nutrients are not returned to the soil and the soil gradually becomes less fertile.

Fertilizers

Chemicals called *fertilizers* can restore the fertility of soil. Fertilizers contain essential elements needed for plant growth.

- Six elements, called macronutrients, are needed in large quantities: nitrogen, phosphorus, sulfur, potassium, magnesium, and calcium.
- Seven additional elements, called micronutrients, are needed in trace amounts: iron, zinc, copper, manganese, molybdenum, chlorine, and boron.

The use of fertilizers is particularly important on soils that are naturally low in nutrients and on soils that are farmed intensively.

Negative Effects. Excessive use of fertilizers can be harmful, injuring or even killing plants. Also, excess nutrients may run off into rivers and lakes, accelerating an aging process known as eutrophication, in which the body of water is overtaken by algae, evolves into a marsh, and eventually disappears.

Methods of Fertilization

The earliest fertilizers were natural materials. In ancient Greece, farmers mixed manure from cattle and other domesticated animals into the soil. In North America, Indians are known to have placed dead fish in the soil before sowing corn. Today, most farmers use synthetic fertilizers.

Synthetic Fertilizers. These fertilizers have greatly increased food production during the past 30 years. As energy costs have risen, however, synthetic fertilizers have become increasingly expensive.

Limiting Use. Crop rotation helps to limit soil depletion. By planting different crops—with different nutritional needs—each year, the farmer helps ensure that nutrients will not be exhausted.

Green manuring is another technique that enriches the soil. A crop is raised and then plowed under. (Usually, the green-manure crop is a legume, such as soybeans or peanuts.) The crops are harvested, and the legumes provide soil cover through the winter. In the spring, they are plowed under and the ground is seeded with the next cash crop.

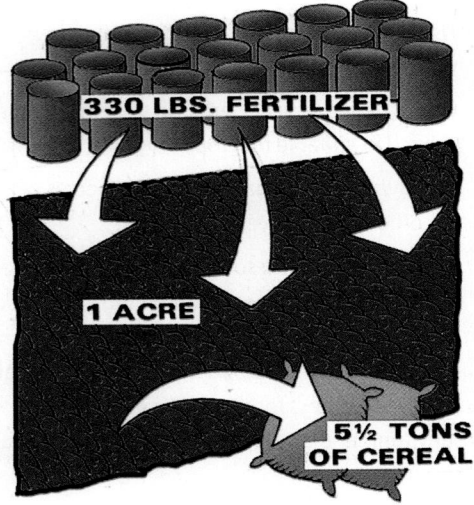

330 LBS. FERTILIZER

1 ACRE

5½ TONS OF CEREAL

ORGANIC FARMING

Organic farming is the growing of crops without the use of synthetic fertilizers and pesticides. Nutrients are obtained primarily from compost, bone meal, wood ash, manure, green manure, seaweed, sewage sludge, and legume-based crop rotation.

◀ **Fertilizer** can increase crop sizes, but it does not always bring a proportional increase—large amounts of fertilizer may result in only a small increase.

Pesticides

Pesticides are chemicals used to control pests by either killing them or rendering them harmless. Pesticides are used on crops, lawns, forests, roadsides, golf courses, ponds and lakes, forests, city parks, and animal herds. They are also used to control pests that infest stored grains and other harvested foods.

Types and Classes. There are two major classes of synthetic pesticides.

- Chlorinated hydrocarbons include well-known pesticides such as DDT.
- Organic phosphorus compounds include nerve gases.

Other types of pesticides include arsenic compounds, dinitro compounds, and methyl carbamates.

Types of Pesticides	Used to Control
insecticides	insects
acaricides	mites and ticks
rodenticides	mice and other rodents
fungicides	molds, mildews, rusts, and other fungi
herbicides	plants

Risks of Pesticides. The use of synthetic pesticides has greatly improved crop yields and reduced labor costs, resulting in lower food costs for consumers. Opposition to synthetic pesticides is due to their effects on the environment and human health.

- Some chemical pesticides kill off benign and useful organisms as well as pests.
- Many pesticides currently in use are not biodegradable. The metals they contain accumulate in the soil, building to toxic levels after repeated applications
- Pesticides often leach through the soil, increasing the possibility that they will reach groundwater and contaminate drinking water supplies.

Who Is at Risk? The people most at risk are farm workers, because they frequently face exposure to pesticides. People who work in food-processing operations also face increased health risks. Finally, people in general may be at some risk, due to pesticides in the food supply (though pesticide manufacturers claim that there is little if any conclusive scientific evidence of this).

Regulation. In the United States, all pesticides must be registered with the EPA. This does not guarantee the safety of the pesticides. The majority of pesticides that were on the market prior to 1972 have not been fully tested for health hazards. Federal agencies also regulate the amount of pesticides used on produce.

DDT

From the mid-1940s to the 1970s, the pesticide DDT was important in controlling numerous pests, including malaria-carrying mosquitoes. As DDT built up in the soil and in food chains, however, it harmed wildlife, particularly birds.

Extensive use of DDT was banned in the United States in 1972, yet traces of this pesticide are still found in the milk and body fat of mammals, in fish, and in lake and river sediments.

◄ **DDT** was also used to control agricultural pests and carriers of animal diseases.

Alternatives to Pesticides

Because of the risks posed by synthetic pesticides, some farmers have begun using—or returned to using—alternative methods of pest control. Biological pest control, genetic engineering, and integrated pest management are all ways of protecting crops and preventing disease without full reliance on dangerous pesticides.

▲ **Biological Pest Control.** In California, the use of European white moths to control tumbleweed—a plant considered by many farmers to be a pest—saves at least $1 million annually in pesticide costs.

Biological Pest Control

One form of biological pest control uses pests' natural enemies to limit pest populations. For example, in China, parasitic wasps control sugarcane stem borers at one-third the cost of using chemical pesticides.

Irradiation. One modern technique is to irradiate male insect pests to cause sterility.

1) Large numbers of the sterile males are released in areas where the species is a pest.

2) Females breed with the males, but because the males are sterile, the females' eggs fail to hatch and no offspring are produced.

Irradiation was used to solve a serious pest problem in Florida, where the screwworm fly once was common. The female screwworm flies would deposit their eggs in open sores or wounds of cattle. When the eggs hatched, the larvae fed on the cattle's flesh, causing considerable economic losses to ranchers.

Pheromones are chemicals produced by female insects to lure males. Farmers have controlled the pink cotton bollworm by applying to cotton fields a synthetic compound identical to a female bollworm moth's pheromones. The compound attracts male moths, which then find no females with whom to mate. As a result, the moth population dwindles.

Natural pesticides are manufactured using everything from crab shells to grasshoppers. The crab shell pesticide is used to control the population of nematodes—pests that feed on plant roots.

- Crab shells, which contain a substance called chitin, are ground up into granules and spread onto fields.

- Fungi and other organisms in the soil convert the chitin in the granules to enzymes that destroy nematodes.

◄ **Grasshopper populations,** which can destroy crops, can be controlled by treating fields with a fungus that is lethal only to grasshoppers.

Integrated Pest Management

Using all suitable methods of pest control in an integrated, systematic manner is called integrated pest management (IPM). The approach focuses on natural methods, with chemical pesticides used minimally at the appropriate time.

Both biological controls and natural pesticides are important in IPM. For example:

- Farmers are encouraged to shift to pest-resistant crop strains.

- They also use strains whose growing seasons are not synchronized with pests' life cycles.

IPM programs have been successful in many countries and against a variety of pests. In Brazil, for example, IPM strategies on soybean crops led to an 80 to 90 percent decrease in pesticide use over 7 years.

ENGINEERING A NATURAL PESTICIDE

Genetic engineers offer the promise of natural vaccines to protect plants. One such product that has proven safe during 2 years of field tests involves the use of organisms called endophytes.

1. The gene that produces a protein that kills insects is inserted into the endophyte.

2. The endophytes are then put into plant seeds.

3. As the plants grow, the endophytes spread the protein throughout the plants.

This process has been used to protect corn against the European corn borer, a tiny caterpillar that destroys $500 million worth of corn each year in the United States.

▲ **Integrated pest management** focuses on using pesticides effectively and sparingly, in combination with other, more natural methods. The aim is to protect crops and increase crop yields, while minimizing the harmful effects of many synthetic pesticides.

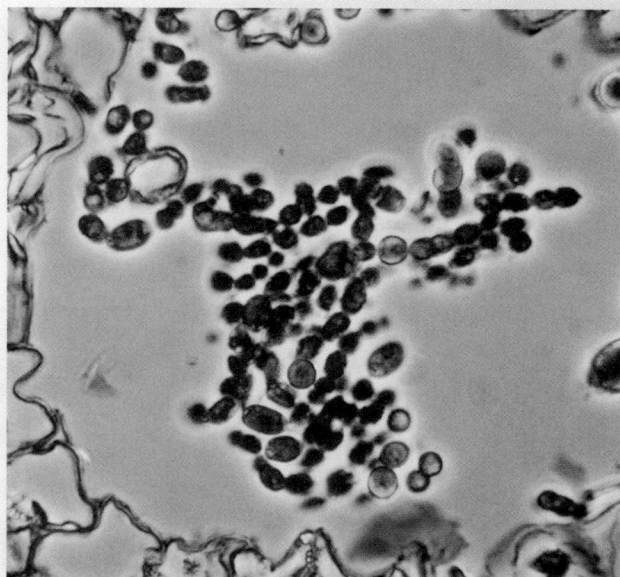

▲ **Endophytes,** which can live inside a plant without harming the plant, are often fungi or microorganisms, such as bacteria.

Genetic Diversity

To achieve the highest productivity and the best economic returns for their labors, farmers and ranchers have concentrated on a limited group of plant strains and animal breeds.

The Need for Diversity

A widespread dependence on a restricted group of organisms can have devastating consequences. Crops and animal populations full of genetically identical organisms mean that a disease can wipe out the entire group. Plus, if the genetic variety of a species becomes lost, farmers and scientists cannot breed new varieties to replace those that fail.

The most infamous example of what can happen took place in the 1840s, when a fungal blight struck the vast potato crop of Ireland. The resulting famine caused the deaths of a million people. In the late 20th century, blight destroyed nearly 15 percent of America's corn crop. Since then, scientists have increased efforts to collect and save the genetic material of as many species as possible.

The Texas longhorn is one example of an animal breed brought back into popular use for the sake of genetic diversity. At one time, millions of these cattle grazed in the American southwest. In the early 1900s, however, ranchers began replacing them with British cattle breeds. ▼

Seed development plays an important role in establishing diversity—during the corn blight, distribution of blight-resistant seeds helped to minimize the damage to America's corn supply. One technique is the establishment of seed banks. (See pages 130–131.)

- These are repositories of seeds of endangered species, crop strains that are seldom planted, and other plants that are rare.

- In most cases, seeds are cleaned, bottled, and placed in a desiccator for several weeks to remove any water. Then they are chilled.

- Periodically, some seeds are tested to determine germination rates.

Animal Diversity. Animal breeders have worked to locate and protect rare breeds of domestic animals. Frequently it is discovered that these breeds have valuable characteristics that had been overlooked. Such is the case with the famed Texas longhorn.

By the 1960s, the numbers of these cattle had dwindled. Ranchers began to recognize that the longhorns' hardiness and longevity made them well suited for grazing on marginal, semiarid lands. Fortunately, a few longhorns still remained. Breeding programs have since expanded their population to close to 100,000.

THE GREEN REVOLUTION

In 1944, geneticists began plant breeding programs to create new high-yield varieties of wheat, corn, and rice that could be grown in developing countries.

During the next two decades, their work produced dramatic increases in crop yields in Mexico, India, and elsewhere. The term "Green Revolution" was coined to describe this possible cure for world hunger.

Setbacks. The new varieties required large amounts of fertilizer and water to grow well. Unfortunately, fertilizers are expensive and, in many places, water resources are limited.

The Green Revolution Today. The Bill and Melinda Gates Foundation supports a similar initiative, Alliance for a Green Revolution in Africa (AGRA). AGRA helps small-scale farmers in Africa overcome poverty and hunger by providing the means needed to increase crop production—better seeds, fertilizers, and water management systems.

▲ **The Green Revolution** brought improved varieties of several crops. This picture shows three varieties of grain used in plant research—long-stemmed wheat, high-yielding dwarf wheat, and triticale, a cross between wheat and rye.

Genetic Engineering

This still-developing technique expands the genetic diversity of organisms, including those of agricultural importance. It involves the manipulation of genetic material—either transferring genes from one organism to another or creating new genes. In this manner, plants, animals, and microbes can be altered to create new varieties and species.

Genetic Vaccines. One product of genetic engineering is the genetic vaccine. This involves the manipulation of genetic material in order to protect a certain organism or to destroy a threat.

- One early vaccine was a vaccine for scours, a bacterial disease that strikes cattle and pigs.
- Another product is genetically altered "ice-minus" bacteria that can be sprayed on crops to reduce frost damage.
- Yet another product is a genetically altered virus that infects and kills the cabbage looper, a caterpillar that destroys cabbage and several other vegetables.

Future possibilities for improved crops apparently are limited only by people's imaginations. Researchers foresee crops with higher nutritional value and plants that take advantage of more efficient photosynthesis; plants that can grow in salty water; more flavorful popcorn; potatoes that resist bruising; chickens that lay more eggs; and so on.

Potential Risks. Genetic engineering can have unexpected results, however. For example, when the gene for human growth hormone was inserted into mouse embryos, the mice grew to be twice as large as normal—the result that was expected. Critics of genetic engineering fear that introducing new organisms may inadvertently harm the environment, beneficial organisms, or people.

WATER POLLUTION

is one of the world's most serious environmental problems. Polluted water may appear clean or dirty, but it contains bacteria, viruses, chemicals, or other materials that may cause illness or death. These impurities must be removed before water can be used safely for drinking, cooking, or laundering.

The Water Supply

Water is the most common substance on Earth. It covers more than 70 percent of Earth's surface. Without water, there can be no life. Your body is about two-thirds water. A chicken is about three-fourths water, and a pineapple is about four-fifths water. Most scientists believe that life itself began in water—in the salty water of the sea.

Fresh Water

About 97 percent of our water is found in the salty oceans. The rest is called fresh water. (See pages 538–539.)

- 77 percent of fresh water is frozen in ice caps and glaciers.
- About 1 percent of fresh water is found in moving water (like rivers) and standing water (like lakes).
- 22 percent of fresh water is underground.

Groundwater

Water that exists in openings in soil and rock below the land's surface is called groundwater. A small percentage of this water, called juvenile water, is formed chemically from molten rock deep within Earth. Most groundwater comes from precipitation and surface water. Acted on by gravity, this water moves downward through the soil.

How much water is on the earth? There are about 326 million cubic miles of water. That's over a million million gallons of water per cubic mile.

How much water does a person take in over a lifetime? On the average, a person takes in about 16,000 gallons of water during his or her life.

How much water does a person use every day? On the average, each person in the United States uses more than 100 gallons of water a day in the home.

What is the largest single use of water? The largest single use of water is by industry. It takes about 80 gallons of water to make the paper for one Sunday newspaper, and about 20 gallons of water per pound of steel produced.

Two thousand gallons of water are needed to produce a single pound of rice.

The Water Table

Groundwater moves downward until it reaches the water table. Below this, all the spaces in the soil are filled with water. The water table is not level; it varies in height depending on the contour of the land surface. In valleys, the water table is generally near the surface. In mountains, it's generally far below the surface. At places where the water intersects with the surface of the land, a lake, stream, swamp, or other body of water is found.

During periods of heavy precipitation, the water table rises. During droughts, it falls. This is often easily visible in swamps. A short spell of dry weather will cause the water table to fall enough to let the swamp dry up, while a heavy rain will turn the swamp into a shallow lake.

Very little of Earth's water is fresh (about 3 percent). The remainder is salty ocean water.

HOW WE USE WATER

- All living things need water to build tissue, regulate body temperature, lubricate joints, remove wastes, and perform other essential processes.

- Thousands of species live in water. They range from microscopic plankton to giant whales.

- A human being needs to take in more than 2 quarts of water each day to remain healthy. About 70 percent of a person's body weight is water. If this amount falls by 5 percent, a person has difficulty moving and thinking clearly. If it falls by more than 10 percent, a person dies.

- Water power is used to turn waterwheels, to produce electricity, and to turn turbines.

- People travel from place to place via water. Millions of tons of oil, food, and other cargo are carried each year across oceans and lakes and up and down rivers.

- Bodies of water are important recreational sites. Swimming, fishing, boating, and waterskiing are popular pastimes.

Water Pollution

Pollution occurs when people contaminate water with wastes, toxic chemicals, metals, and oils.

Healthy Systems

Rivers, lakes, and other bodies of water have a remarkable ability to cleanse themselves. Special alkaline substances in the water neutralize acid from acid rain. Bacteria in the water break down, or oxidize, organic wastes. Sunlight breaks down other compounds. (See pages 564–567.)

Unhealthy Systems

But there are limits to a water system's purifying ability. If too many wastes are dumped into the water, the natural systems become overloaded. They cannot break down the wastes fast enough.

Oxygen Levels. As bacteria multiply to feed on increasing amounts of organic wastes, they consume more and more oxygen. Oxygen levels fall. This makes breathing difficult or impossible for fish and other organisms in the water.

If the water loses all its oxygen, it becomes "dead," which means it contains few (if any) living things.

Accumulation. Another problem is that many of the pollutants produced by modern industries are not biodegradable. They cannot be broken down by natural systems. For example, plastics dumped into water will remain unchanged for hundreds of years. Other pollutants, such as pesticides, become concentrated in the bodies of organisms. This buildup poses a threat not only to the organisms, but also to those who eat them.

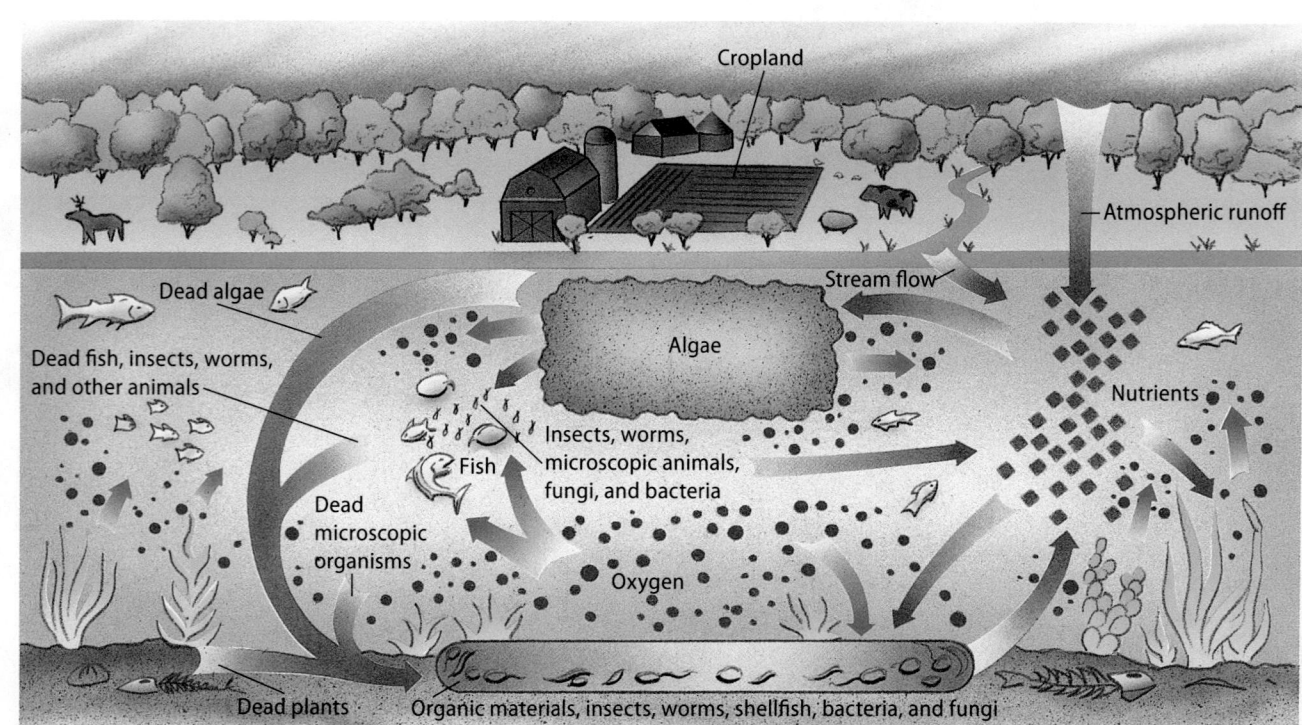

A healthy water system relies on a cycle of natural processes that turns waste into useful substances. Aerobic (oxygen-using) bacteria break down dead plants and animals and animal wastes, releasing nitrates, phosphates, and other nutrients (chemicals needed for growth). Nutrients also enter the water from streams. Algae absorb the nutrients. Aquatic plants release oxygen. Microscopic animals called zooplankton eat the algae, and fish eat the zooplankton. The fish produce wastes and eventually die. Bacteria break down the wastes and dead fish, and the cycle continues.

POINT AND NONPOINT SOURCES

Point-source pollutants come directly from identifiable sources. For example, wastes carried from a factory or sewage treatment plant into a waterway by discharge pipes are a point-source pollutant.

Nonpoint-source pollutants cannot be traced easily to a single source. They include pollutants that are washed into waterways or seep into groundwater from fields, streets, landfills, mine tailings, and building sites. Acid rain and other forms of polluted precipitation that fall on waterways are also nonpoint-source pollutants.

- Nonpoint sources are difficult to locate and control because they have no single source. Therefore, no individual or organization can be held responsible.

- To date, most water cleanup efforts have focused on regulating point-source pollutants. With the exception of toxic chemicals, these pollution sources have been controlled to a large extent in industrialized countries.

- Until recently, there has been a lax attitude toward pollution from nonpoint sources, largely because such contamination has not been recognized or well understood by the general public.

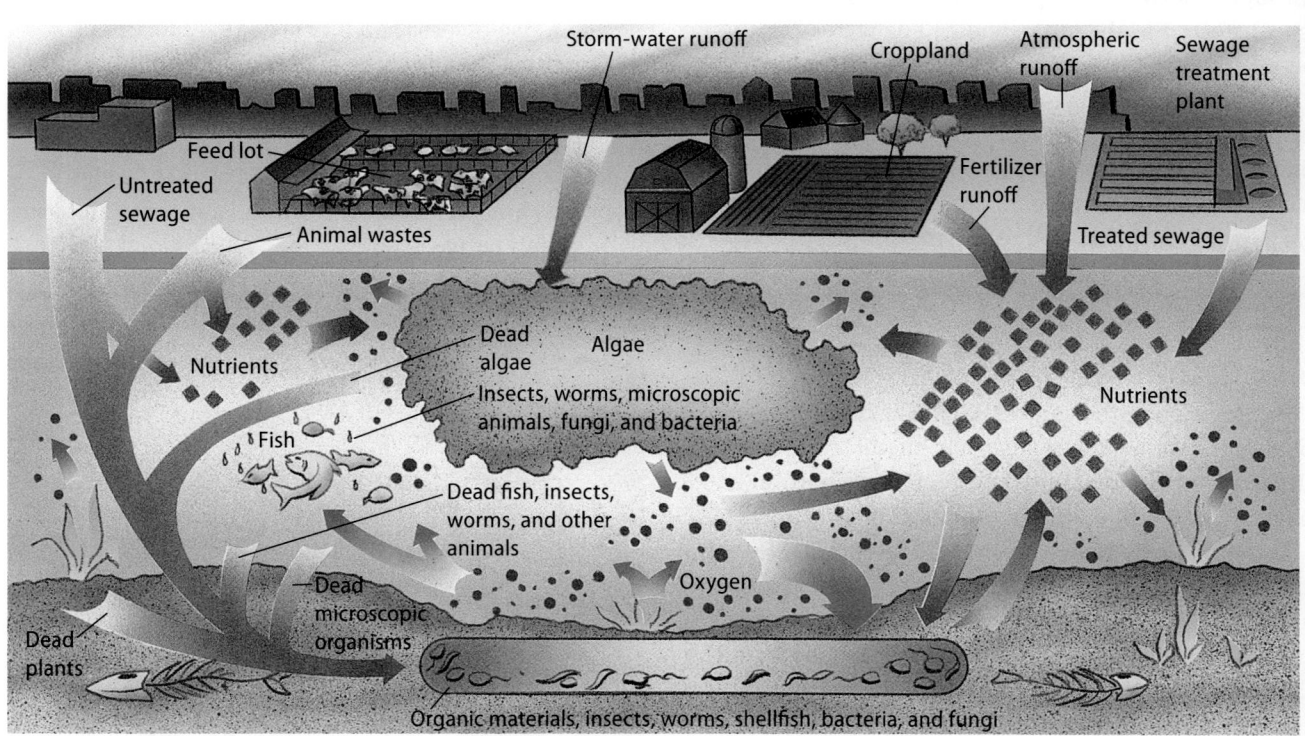

Water pollution occurs when human activities upset the balance, often by introducing excess nutrients from fertilizers and untreated sewage. The algae grow faster than the fish can eat them. As more algae grow, more die and block light needed by aquatic plants to make oxygen. Bacteria use up much oxygen while consuming the excess dead algae. As the oxygen levels drop, many aquatic plants and animals die and decay, using more oxygen. Without oxygen, the aerobic bacteria work at a slower rate. Dead fish and other wastes sink to the bottom.

Types of Water Pollution

Thermal Pollution

Thermal pollution occurs when people release hot water into bodies of water such as rivers, lakes, and oceans.

Cause. Factories and power plants that use water to cool equipment or heat water to produce steam rank as the major sources of thermal pollution. Some electric power plants and other industries use tremendous amounts of water as a coolant to absorb heat created during various processes. The heated water is frequently returned to the waterways from which it was originally withdrawn.

Solutions. One way to reduce thermal pollution is to construct high cooling towers. After the water has been used in a power plant or factory, it is circulated through a network of pipes in the towers and its heat is transferred to the atmosphere. The water can then be returned to the waterway.

Another method is to dig a large pond near the factory. Hot water is pumped to the pond and held there until it cools off. In some places, these ponds have been used for recreation or for fattening fish like carp, which respond well to warmth.

Effects. Thermal pollution presents a particular set of challenges that differ from those caused by other types of pollution.

- Warm water can hurt fish by interfering with their health, food supply, reproduction, and growth.
- The heated water reduces the solubility of oxygen in water, limiting the amount of dissolved oxygen that the water can hold. This makes it hard for native fish and other aquatic organisms to breathe. It also reduces the ability of microorganisms to decompose wastes.
- Some fish, such as lake trout, become less active as water temperatures increase. This decreases their ability to catch food.
- Higher water temperatures often interfere with reproduction. For example, scientists have reported that a rise of less than 6 degrees Celsius in the Columbia River causes excessive mortality of eggs from chinook salmon.
- In some cases, the sudden rise in temperature can kill fish. Warmer water may also attract foreign plants, animals, and other organisms that can harm an area's native species.

Industrial Wastes

Factories and other industrial facilities discharge pollutants that include many toxic chemicals. They release much chemical waste directly into natural bodies of water. In addition, the burning of coal, oil, and other fuels by power plants and factories releases sulfur and nitrogen oxides into the air. These pollutants, also given off by motor vehicles, cause acid rain that can enter streams and lakes. Acid rain is rainfall that contains such acids as sulfuric acid and nitric acid. (See also pages 666–669.)

The toxic metal mercury ranks as a widespread water pollutant. Scientists have found high levels of mercury in fish far from industrial areas. This mercury appears to originate primarily in airborne emissions from coal-fired boilers, municipal incinerators, and smelters.

Millions of fish have been killed by chemical spills and other forms of water pollution.

Other Wastes

People have long used lakes, rivers, and other bodies of water as places to dump wastes. Rain and other water percolating through garbage dumps, landfills, and other waste sites can pick up dangerous contaminants and seep into groundwater.

Residential. Raw sewage and partially treated sewage is created wherever people live. Raw sewage is everything that is flushed from sinks, bathtubs, toilets, and washing machines. It contains human waste, soap, and kitchen waste. Rainwater and snow that run off streets, carrying soil particles, leaves, and other litter, are also a form of sewage.

Other contaminants from underground storage tanks, pipelines, wells, holding ponds, and graveyards also contribute to water pollution.

Agricultural. Farm activities are sources of animal wastes, silt, fertilizers, and pesticides.

Other Sources. Surface and underground mining operations produce heavy metals and other pollutants. Uranium mines, weapons factories, and nuclear power plants are sources of radioactive pollutants. Ships release oil into waterways either accidentally or when flushing their holds. They also discharge raw sewage and other wastes into estuaries and harbors as well as into the open ocean. Passenger trains that discharge sewage and garbage onto railroad right-of-ways contribute to water pollution as the wastes move into the surface and underground water supplies.

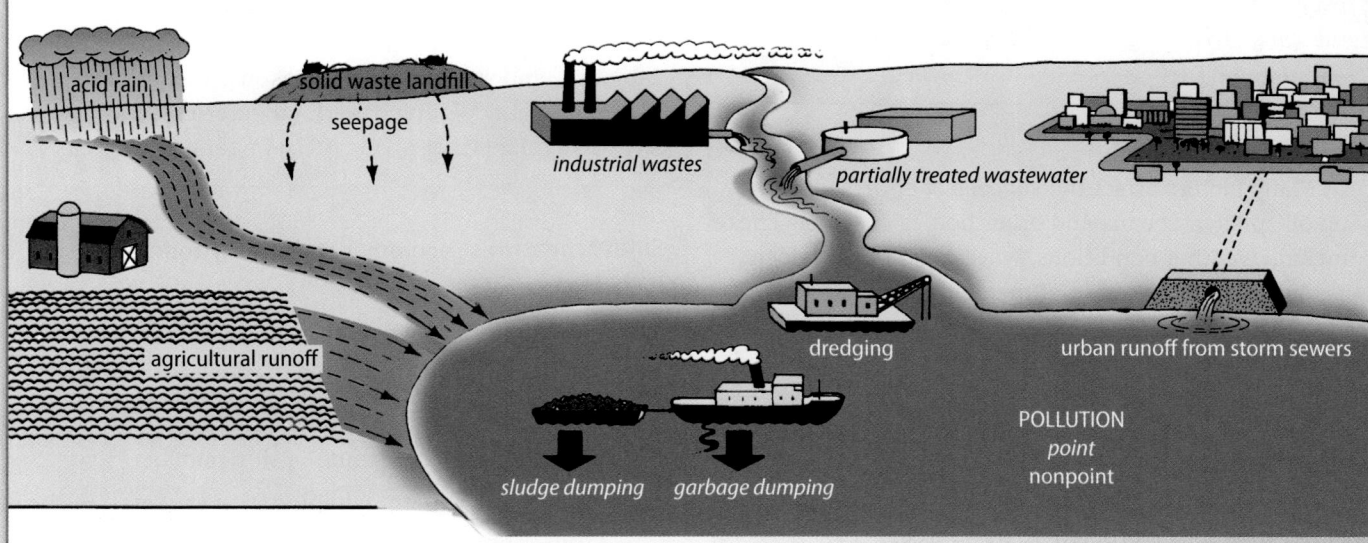

acid rain

solid waste landfill

seepage

industrial wastes

partially treated wastewater

agricultural runoff

dredging

urban runoff from storm sewers

POLLUTION
point
nonpoint

sludge dumping   garbage dumping

Pollutants that come straight from a source are called point-source pollutants. Pollutants from difficult-to-trace sources are called nonpoint-source pollutants. Most water cleanup efforts have focused on controlling point-source pollutants. This diagram illustrates the distinction between point and nonpoint pollutants described on page 721 and the sources discussed in the section "Other Wastes," *above.*

Oil Pollution

Oil pollution enters the ocean from oil spills on land or in rivers. Oil also seeps into the ocean naturally from cracks in the seafloor. Oil tanker and oil well accidents at sea account for only a small portion of ocean oil pollution, but their effects may be disastrous.

Oil Spills

One of the largest accidental oil spills in history occurred in 2010, when an explosion on an offshore oil rig caused about 206 million gallons (780 million liters) of oil to spill into the Gulf of Mexico. The world's largest deliberate oil spill occurred when Iraq released between 240 million and 465 million gallons (910 million and 1,760 million liters) of oil into the Persian Gulf during the Persian Gulf War of 1991.

For each of these oil spills, there are tens of thousands of smaller ones—in oceans, bays, rivers, and other waterways. The exact total is unknown because there is no international agreement for reporting them. In the U.S. alone, more than 13,000 oil spills of varying magnitudes are reported annually.

Cleanup Efforts

Many factors affect the success of efforts to clean up oil spills in oceans and other bodies of water. These include weather conditions, wave height and velocity, distance from the shore of the spill, and speed of cleanup efforts. The three most commonly used methods of cleanup are mechanical containment and collection, chemical dispersion, and burning.

Prevention

Cleaning up oil contamination is difficult, so it's better to stop the problem at its source.

Laws. Some regulations have been passed by governments in efforts to prevent oil spills, speed cleanup of spills that do occur, and make people who cause spills take financial responsibility for the damage. Law enforcement can be problematic, though. Also, many proposed regulations have been killed or weakened because of highly effective lobbying efforts by oil industry representatives.

Waste Oil

Some people thoughtlessly dump waste oil into septic systems, storm drains, or roadside ditches when changing the oil in their car engines. This oil also harms habitats and finds its way into water supplies. It is estimated that Americans incorrectly dispose of more than 400 million gallons of used oil each year.

Effects

Oil-polluted waters cause severe damage to the environment and to the economy.

Wildlife. Oil coats fish, birds, mammals, and other organisms. For many, death comes almost immediately. Others die slowly or suffer from long-term problems, such as respiratory and kidney ailments, reproductive problems, and genetic damage.

Economy. Oil spills often cause substantial economic losses. For instance, Alaskan fishermen were idled after the *Exxon Valdez* spill. Officials canceled the herring, sablefish, and shrimp fishing seasons. When oil from an underground spill in Brooklyn entered a sewage treatment plant, that plant had to be temporarily closed.

Safety measures recommended by environmentalists include:

- double hulls on tankers and barges.
- better traffic control systems to guide tankers.
- improved training of navigators.
- drug and alcohol screening of ship pilots.
- more oil-containment equipment on tankers.

Contingency Plans. Improved contingency plans are needed to deal with oil spills. Prior to the *Exxon Valdez* spill, the oil industry consortium that operates Valdez, Alaska, harbor consistently maintained that they could handle a huge spill in Prince William Sound, boasting that cleanup equipment would be at the scene within 5 hours. Subsequent events disproved this claim.

THE GULF OF MEXICO OIL SPILL

In April 2010, there was an explosion on the Deepwater Horizon oil rig in the Gulf of Mexico, off the coast of Louisiana. The explosion killed 11 people and blew out an underwater well pipe. For nearly 3 months afterward, about 206 million gallons (780 million liters) of oil poured from the well into the Gulf of Mexico. BP p.l.c., a major international oil company, was the well's principal owner.

Prior to the explosion, Deepwater Horizon was about 50 miles off the Louisiana coast. BP had hired Transocean Ltd., the rig's owner and operator, to drill a well beneath the Gulf's surface. On April 20, gases building up in the well pipe ignited on the rig, causing the explosion and oil spill. The rig sank 2 days later.

Both BP and the U.S. Coast Guard attempted a number of measures to stop the flow of oil, but the leakage continued for months. Oil coated coastal lands and harmed birds, fish, and other wildlife. The spill also devastated fisheries and tourism-based businesses along the Gulf Coast.

After a series of failed attempts, on July 15, BP succeeded in capping the well. On September 19, BP engineers sealed the well using a relief well. The relief well intercepted the damaged well about 2.5 miles (4 kilometers) beneath the seafloor. Engineers then pumped cement through the relief well, permanently sealing the damaged well.

The Gulf oil spill of 2010 was one of the worst environmental disasters in United States history. The full extent of environmental damage is not yet known.

A Massive Cleanup Task. Nearly 3 months after the Deepwater Horizon rig sank, these ships can be seen circling the source of the spill. On July 18, 2010, when this photograph was taken, an oil sheen still coated the water, and scientists were still concerned about well leakage despite the well having been capped 3 days earlier.

Costs of Water Pollution

Scientists have estimated that more than a million different chemicals have entered water supplies. Each of these has a unique effect on the environment. Some may have beneficial effects. Others are harmful even in tiny amounts.

Often, materials have been dumped into water without people knowing their potential effect on the environment and the health of living things. This has been true with many fertilizers and pesticides.

The effects of water pollution can be divided into three categories: human illness, diminished natural resources, and economic costs.

Human Illness

Polluted water can make people very ill. People get sick by

- drinking contaminated water.
- inhaling disease-causing organisms that live in the water.
- inhaling disease-causing organisms that live in moisture that collects in ventilation systems.
- being exposed to contaminants at beaches and pools.
- eating contaminated fish or shellfish.

Waterborne illnesses are most common where living conditions are bad and where sanitation facilities are minimal. Problems include:

- cholera.
- typhoid fever.
- hepatitis A.
- gastroenteritis.
- giardiasis.

Chemical contaminants can also cause a broad range of health problems. Cadmium causes liver damage and high blood pressure. Lead causes nerve problems, birth defects, and learning disabilities. Chlorinated solvents cause cancer. Nitrates have also been linked to cancer and can interfere with the blood's ability to carry oxygen.

Diminished Natural Resources

Water pollution can disrupt natural processes that turn wastes into useful or harmless substances. This disruption harms living things primarily by lowering the amount of oxygen dissolved in the water.

Natural Waters. Water pollution can prevent people and wildlife from enjoying the full use of natural waters. For example, odors and floating debris may make boating and swimming unpleasant, and the risk of disease can make them unsafe.

Animals. Any aquatic species can be injured or killed by toxic pollutants. At times, huge numbers of organisms are affected. Oil spilled from ships or offshore wells may float to shore, where it can kill water birds, shellfish, and other wildlife.

Plastic objects in the oceans are very dangerous to marine animals. Turtles and seabirds often eat bags and other plastic trash, mistaking them for prey. The animals then starve because the plastic prevents them from digesting real food. Animals also die after becoming entangled in discarded or broken plastic fishing net and lines.

Organisms. Sometimes organisms are harmed even though they live far from the site where pollutants were discharged. At one time, the U.S. government's plutonium factory at Hanford Reservation near Richland, Washington, regularly dumped radioactive water into the Columbia River. Radioactive zinc and phosphorus from this wastewater poisoned oysters living in the sea 360 miles (580 kilometers) from the factory.

Economic Price

The financial effects of water pollution are enormous.

- Water treatment costs rise.
- Ships, bridges, and dams require costly repairs.
- Fishermen, resort owners, and other people suffer when their business is reduced.
- Medical care for people sickened by pollutants raises insurance rates, governments' budgets, and victims' direct expenses.

LEAD IN YOUR DRINKING WATER

- Too much lead in the human body can cause serious damage to the brain, kidneys, nervous system, and red blood cells. People are exposed to lead via air, soil, dust, food, and drinking water. The degree of harm depends on the level of exposure from all sources.

- According to the Environmental Protection Agency (EPA), young children, infants, and fetuses appear to be particularly vulnerable to lead poisoning. A dose of lead that would have little effect on an adult can have a big effect on a small body. Also, growing children will more rapidly absorb any lead they consume. A child's mental and physical development can be irreversibly stunted by overexposure to lead.

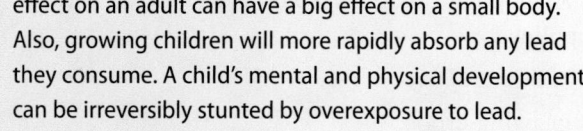

- Typically, the lead in a home's water comes from its plumbing. Up through the early 1900s, it was common practice in some places to use lead pipes for internal plumbing. Later, copper pipes replaced lead, but the use of lead solder to join the pipes is still common. As water flows through the pipes and past the solder, it reacts with the lead, causing corrosion.

- The only way to learn how much lead is in your household water is to have the water tested by a laboratory. Contact your local water utility or your local health department for information and assistance.

Lakes, rivers, and other bodies of water have long been used by people as places to dispose of wastes. Often the wastes have been dumped into water without an understanding of their effect on the environment and on the health of living things.

As populations grow, so do demands on water supplies for

- residential use.
- growing crops.
- industry.

Water supplies are already limited in many parts of the world.

According to the World Health Organization, 1.2 billion people—about one-fifth of the world's population—are without safe water. Millions more receive water only sporadically or for only a few hours a day. And more than 1.7 billion people in the developing world have no sanitation facilities.

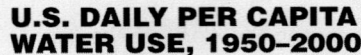

U.S. DAILY PER CAPITA WATER USE, 1950–2000

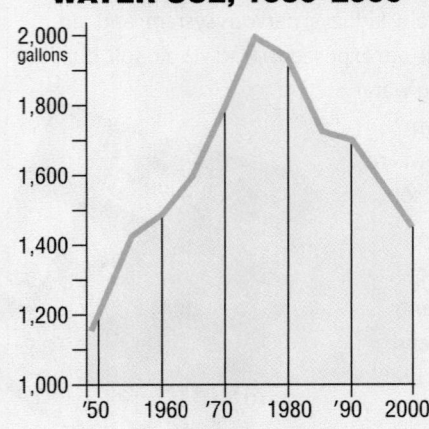

CLEANING SURFACE WATERS

Rivers, lakes, bays, and other surface waters all over the world are polluted, often to the point where they have been called dying or dead. Efforts to counteract this pollution have often been remarkably successful.

Case Study 1. In the 1950s, life was virtually extinct in the Thames River, which flows through London, England. Wastes from sewers, mills, breweries, chemical plants, and other sources made the Thames unsuitable for most species.

In the 1960s, the government began cleaning up the river. Sewage treatment plants were improved so that the water became almost free of pollutants; strict pollution controls were set on industry.

These measures soon showed results. By the early 1980s, some 91 fish species were found in the Thames. As the fish returned, so did the fish-eating birds. Large flocks of other birds also returned.

Case Study 2. Lake Erie is another body of water that became so polluted that it was declared dead. Massive amounts of nitrates and phosphates, mostly in fertilizers and sewage, had caused explosive growths of algae. As the algae decayed, the lake's oxygen content was used up. Once again, stricter sewage treatment and industrial pollution controls were successful in improving conditions. Today there is less algae in Lake Erie, and fish populations are rebounding.

Shortages. In some places, shortages result from natural factors like limited rainfall. There just isn't enough water for the region's population. Elsewhere, shortages result from heavy demand or inefficient use.

Pollution is another factor that limits water supplies, for it can render water useless. The world's waterways receive enormous amounts of municipal sewage, agricultural runoff, and industrial waste. Such substances also poison groundwater.

Cleanup efforts can restore waterways, but they are generally costly and difficult. Many costly cleanup projects might have been avoided by preventive measures. Exxon spent $2 billion in 1989 to clean up oil spilled in the *Exxon Valdez* accident, and an additional $200 million in 1990, yet significant amounts of oil still pollute Alaskan beaches and the sea bottom.

Local and national governments have increasingly taken action to protect and clean up waterways. Strong laws concerning sewage treatment, industrial discharge, water conservation, and other pollution problems have been passed. Unfortunately, legislators often failed to include sufficient funding for enforcement of the laws.

Aquifers

Aquifers are underground formations filled with groundwater. (See pages 564–565.) Much of the water in aquifers has been stored there for hundreds of thousands of years.

Importance. Aquifers supply a significant portion of people's water needs. According to the Environmental Protection Agency (EPA), half of all Americans and more than 95 percent of rural Americans obtain their household water supplies from groundwater. Groundwater is also used for about half of the nation's agricultural irrigation. Nearly one-third of U.S. industrial water needs are met by groundwater.

Problems. Aquifers are naturally replenished by precipitation seeping into the ground or by the surface waters with which they are interconnected. But if underground supplies are depleted faster than they are recharged, the water table falls. Wells can run dry and have to be dug deeper to reach water.

Dams and Reservoirs

A dam is a barrier placed across a river to stop the flow of the water. A reservoir is a place where large quantities of water are stored to be used for irrigation, power generation, water supply, and recreation.

Importance. Large rivers all over the world have been dammed to retain water for irrigation, drinking supplies, flood control, power generation, and other uses.

Problems. While dams and reservoirs provide many benefits, they often have adverse effects on the environment, including

- displaced residents.
- evaporation of water.
- blocked passages for fish.
- unsuitable thermal environments for organisms.
- salts flushed from farmlands.
- natural nourishment of crops prevented.

AMERICA'S LARGEST AQUIFER

A vast underground lake sprawls from Wyoming and South Dakota into Nebraska, Kansas, Colorado, Oklahoma, New Mexico, and Texas. Called the Ogallala Aquifer, it covers about 170,000 square miles and contains about 3.3 billion acre-feet of water. That's about as much water as in Lake Huron plus one-fifth of Lake Ontario—enough to cover all 50 U.S. states with water about 1.5 feet deep.

The Ogallala provides irrigation water for millions of acres of America's most productive farmland and rangeland. Up to 40 percent of the nation's beef and 25 percent of its food and fiber crops are produced on land irrigated with water from the Ogallala. The annual value of this output is worth more than $20 billion.

Much of the water taken from the Ogallala is absorbed by plants or drunk by cattle. Some evaporates. Some runs off the land. Little of the water finds its way back to the aquifer. Since water is being withdrawn much faster than

it is being replaced by nature, the Ogalllala is being rapidly drained.

Another problem is pollution of the Ogallala's water. In 1987, for example, farmers and ranchers in Nebraska used 775,000 tons of fertilizer, plus uncounted tons of pesticide. Their cows and hogs produced 235,000 tons of manure. Gradually, these substances are leaching downward toward the water.

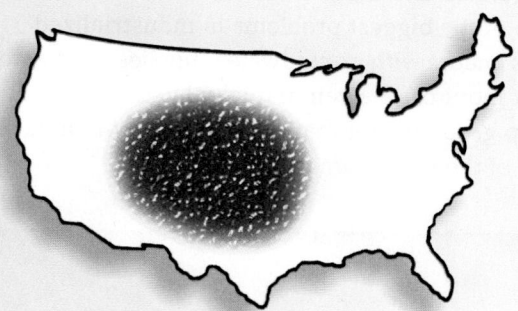

Water Treatment

Some water is pure enough for human use as it comes from a river, reservoir, or well. But usually water must be treated to remove undesirable pollutants. For example, most disease-causing bacteria must be removed so people don't become ill after drinking the water. (See page 292.) Algae must be removed because it gives water a bad taste.

In some cases, the degree of treatment required depends on the use to which the water will be put.

- Water used by the pharmaceutical and food industries must be very pure.
- Laundries and some chemical processes require water that is free of iron.
- Water used as a coolant doesn't have to be particularly pure.

Water and wastewater plants use physical and chemical processes to remove pollutants. Aeration mixes the water with air and speeds oxidation. ▶

Municipal facilities. Because so many different types of pollutants are present in water, various processes are used at water treatment plants. These processes comprise two categories.

- Physical treatment may include screening, sedimentation, flocculation, aeration, and filtration.
- Chemical treatment may include water softening, disinfection, coagulation, oxidation, and adsorption.

Standards. Water consumed by people varies greatly in quality, even in industrialized nations with comparatively high safety standards. One problem is that not all pollutants are removed in municipal water treatment facilities. Some serious contaminants are not regulated and monitored.

One of the biggest problems in industrialized nations occurs with groundwater supplies. Many wells are not monitored. Even municipal water systems that tap groundwater may contain contaminants in excess of the maximum permitted by law.

Water Hardness. Depending on the amount of dissolved minerals, water is either hard or soft. Hard water contains large amounts of dissolved minerals. Soft water does not contain significant amounts of these minerals.

Septic Tanks

Septic tank systems are a major source of groundwater contamination. Many rural areas are not served by public sewers. In such areas, most homeowners use septic tanks to treat their sewage. These tanks are concrete or steel containers buried underground at homes and buildings.

Sewage flows through a pipe from the home into the tank. A liquid effluent gradually passes out of the tank and into the surrounding soil. Solid matter settles to the bottom of the tank.

Sewage Treatment

In order to avoid health hazards and environmental damage caused by sewage, most communities pipe sewage from homes, businesses, and industries through large conduits to wastewater treatment plants. There, the sewage undergoes a series of treatments designed to remove pollutants.

There are three primary standard treatment stages: primary, secondary, and tertiary.

Primary treatment removes about 30 percent of pollutants. A series of screens, grit-settling chambers, and sedimentation tanks are used to remove undissolved solids, including trash, leaves, excreta, sand, and small stones. The water may then be disinfected, usually with chlorine. This destroys disease-causing bacteria and reduces odors. In many places, the wastes are then discharged into a lake or another waterway.

Secondary treatment removes from 85 to 90 percent of the solids and oxygen-consuming wastes remaining in sewage after it has undergone primary treatment. The most common methods of secondary treatment are the activated sludge process and the trickling filtration process.

Tertiary treatment methods include biological nutrient removal, chemical treatment, microscopic screening, radiation treatment, and the discharge of the effluent into lagoons. Tertiary treatment systems are usually very expensive to build and operate. Few treatment plants in the United States use all three methods of treatment—primary, secondary, and tertiary.

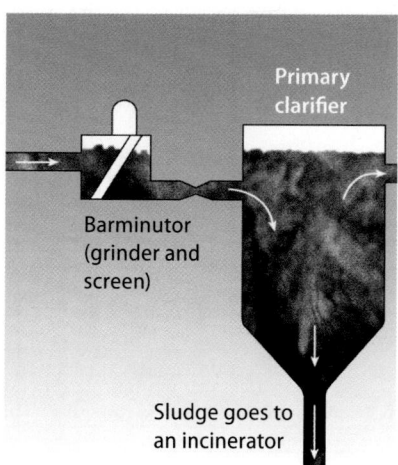

Primary treatment at a modern treatment plant removes 50 to 60 percent of the waste in sewage. The largest solids are ground up and settle in a clarifier.

Primary clarifier

Barminutor (grinder and screen)

Sludge goes to an incinerator

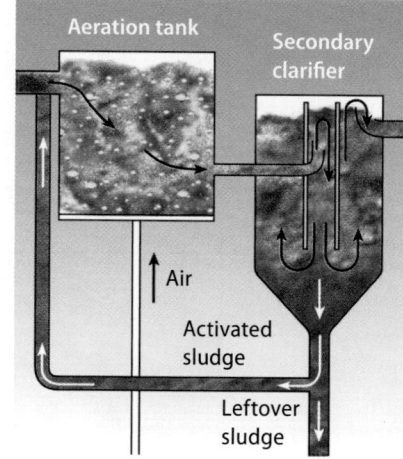

Secondary treatment uses bacteria to further purify the effluent in an aeration tank after primary treatment. Sludge is removed in another tank. Primary and secondary treatment together remove about 95 percent of the waste from sewage.

Aeration tank

Secondary clarifier

Air

Activated sludge

Leftover sludge

Tertiary treatment removes even more impurities from the effluent after primary and secondary treatment. Few plants provide tertiary treatment.

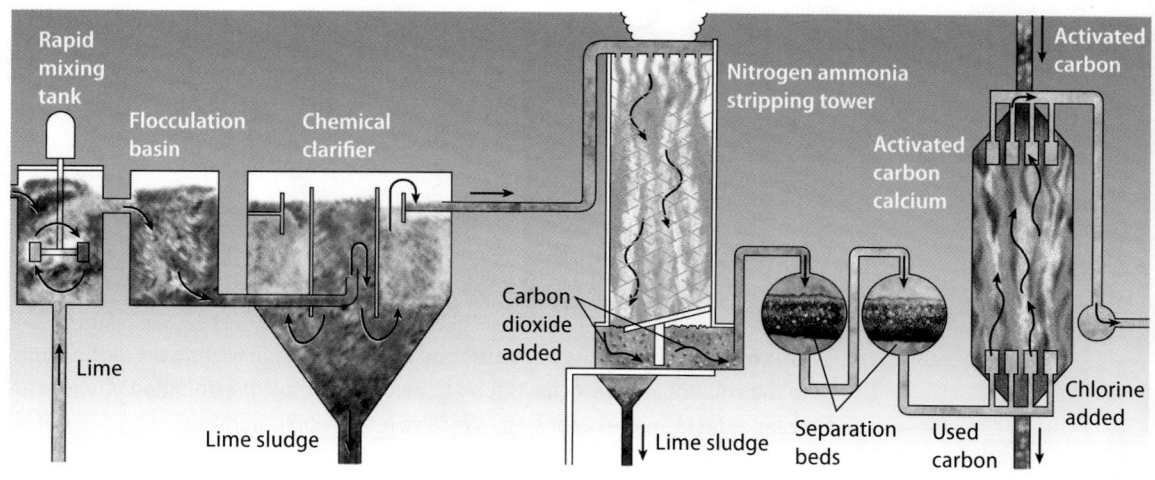

Rapid mixing tank

Flocculation basin

Chemical clarifier

Nitrogen ammonia stripping tower

Activated carbon

Activated carbon calcium

Carbon dioxide added

Lime

Lime sludge

Lime sludge

Separation beds

Used carbon

Chlorine added

Water Conservation

The demand for water is constantly increasing as a result of population growth and the expansion of agriculture and industry. Earth has an abundant supply of water, but that water is unevenly distributed. Some areas do not receive enough rainfall, while others get more than they need.

Many dry regions of the world, such as the Middle East, North Africa, and parts of western and central North America, face serious water shortages.

Solutions to the difficulties depend largely on conservation efforts by users, plus legislative changes.

Legislation

In many places, people have taken cheap water for granted. They have not felt the need to conserve. As a result, lawmakers have crafted regulations that discourage water waste. These include:

- building codes that demand more efficient plumbing.
- lawn-watering limits.
- seasonal rates.

Residential Customers

There are many simple actions people can take to conserve water at home. Although savings from each act may seem small, they can add up to make a significant difference.

Agriculture

Growing crops consume huge quantities of water. Farms can conserve water by

- switching to more efficient irrigation methods, such as drip irrigation.
- damming and recirculating irrigation runoff.
- lining irrigation ditches with plastic or concrete.

Industry

Due in part to tougher pollution-discharge regulations, industries have developed a broad range of new techniques that require less water or allow for the reuse of water. For instance, many power plants and factories now recycle water used for cooling purposes.

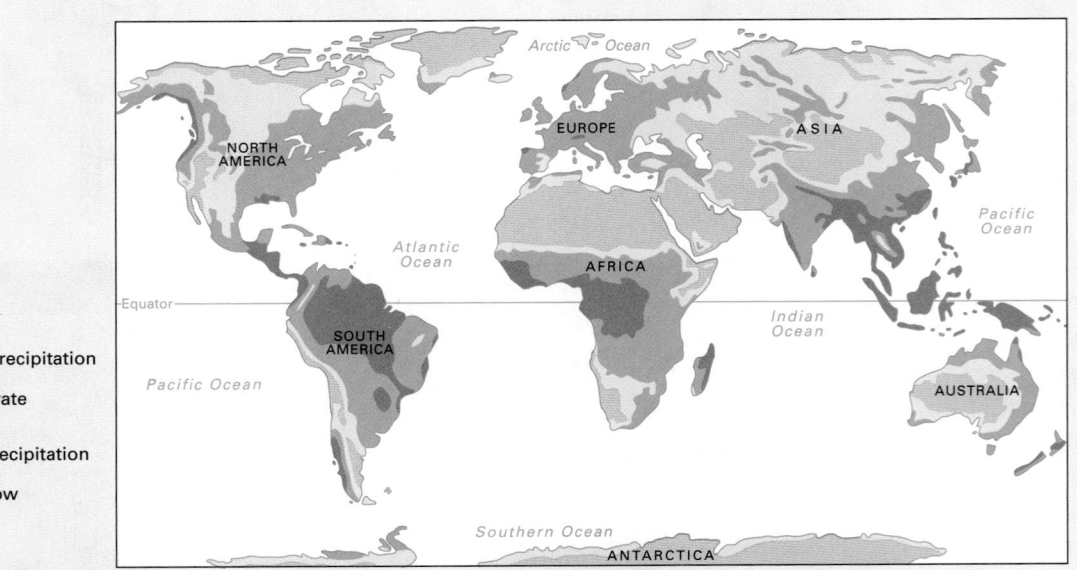

Areas with high precipitation

Areas with moderate precipitation

Areas with low precipitation

Areas with very low precipitation

This map shows the uneven distribution of precipitation around the world. Areas close to the equator and near coasts tend to receive the most precipitation. Areas near the poles or far from the oceans often receive less precipitation.

Future Water Supplies

Shortages of clean water for drinking, irrigation, aquaculture, and other critical uses are occurring worldwide, forcing governments to grapple with the difficult problems of managing, protecting, and cleaning up supplies.

In some parts of the United States, water-protection programs are being developed at federal, state, and local levels. In 1990, for example, New York City proposed new rules that would restrict construction in its watershed areas.

Water that is already polluted can be cleaned, even if at great cost, but the key to future availability of water is to prevent contamination by eliminating sources of pollution and controlling existing sources. Private citizens have an active role to play in this process. Proper water management today will meet the water needs of future generations.

SAVING WATER AT HOME

You and your family can reduce the amount of water you use. Here are some tips on how to cut your water consumption.

- Run only full loads in the dishwasher and washing machine.
- Soak pots and pans overnight if they are very dirty.
- Do not run water continually while brushing your teeth, washing your face, or shaving.
- Water the lawn early in the morning or at dusk to minimize water loss from evaporation.
- Use a commercial car wash instead of washing the car at home.
- Fix leaky faucets and faulty connections.
- Insulate hot water pipes to reduce the amount of water that must run before the water from the faucet gets hot.

TURNING SALTWATER INTO FRESH WATER

Thousands of facilities around the world are extracting fresh water from seawater—a process called *desalinization* or desalination. (See pages 568–569.) These facilities range from small household units to units that can supply individual hotels or huge plants serving entire communities. The water can be used for human consumption, industry, and irrigation.

The market for desalinization plants has grown steadily as freshwater supplies have become insufficient to meet the needs of growing populations and as arid and semiarid areas have been urbanized and brought under cultivation. Several methods are available.

- distillation (including multistage flash distillation and solar distillation)
- freezing
- membrane processes (including electrodialysis and reverse osmosis)

Which method is most suitable in a particular locale depends on the condition of the unpurified water, the type of energy that is available to power the desalinization plant, the amount of fresh water needed, and the sum of money that can be spent to build and maintain the plant.

ENERGY is what we use to do work. We use energy for operating machinery, heating and cooling buildings, cooking, and transporting people and goods. To develop energy systems that are in keeping with the needs of the biosphere, engineers and planners must consider efficiency, economy, and the environment.

Fossil Fuels

Most of the energy that modern people use comes from burning *fossil fuels*.

Dwindling Stores

Energy that is produced by businesses and governments and sold to the public is called *commercial energy*. About 85 percent of all commercial energy comes from petroleum, coal, and natural gas. These sources are called fossil fuels because they developed from the fossilized remains of prehistoric plants.

Increasing Demand. The amount of fossil fuel burned by people to produce energy has nearly doubled every 20 years since 1900. Developed and developing countries use vast amounts of energy, rapidly depleting the supply of fossil fuels. Society's dependence on fossil fuels has been blamed for global economic problems and wars.

Decreasing Supply. Earth contains a limited supply of fossil fuels. Someday, the supply will run out. Scientists and engineers are working to develop other sources of energy to replace the shrinking reserves of fossil fuels.

Environmental Costs. Burning fossil fuels causes environmental problems, including air pollution and acid rain. Such burning also releases large amounts of carbon dioxide and other greenhouse gases that contribute to global warming. (See also pages 670–671.)

HOW DOES THAT WORK ?

FOSSIL FUELS

1. A living thing dies.
2. The remains are buried with layers of sand and mud.
3. Over millions of years, the weight of these layers presses down on the remains.
4. The resulting pressure and heat, along with other natural processes, transforms the remains into fossil fuels.

MAIN SOURCES OF ENERGY

- Fossil fuels
- Nuclear energy
- Water power
- Hydrogen power
- Solar energy
- Wind power
- Geothermal power

Huge drilling rigs in the North Sea, as well as in more temperate waters, are used to pump petroleum from undersea pools.

ENERGY CRISIS

For more than a century, petroleum and its by-products have fueled the industrialized world. The so-called energy crisis of the 1970s was really an oil crisis: supply of available petroleum declined while prices skyrocketed.

When the Organization of Petroleum Exporting Countries (OPEC) cartel began to limit production, gasoline prices in the U.S. rose from about 30 cents a gallon to more than a dollar. Home heating bills also increased rapidly.

This energy crisis led engineers and others to take a hard look at the rate at which the industrialized world was gobbling up resources that nature had taken millions of years to produce.

U.S. ELECTRICTY PRODUCTION BY ENERGY SOURCE, 1960–2000

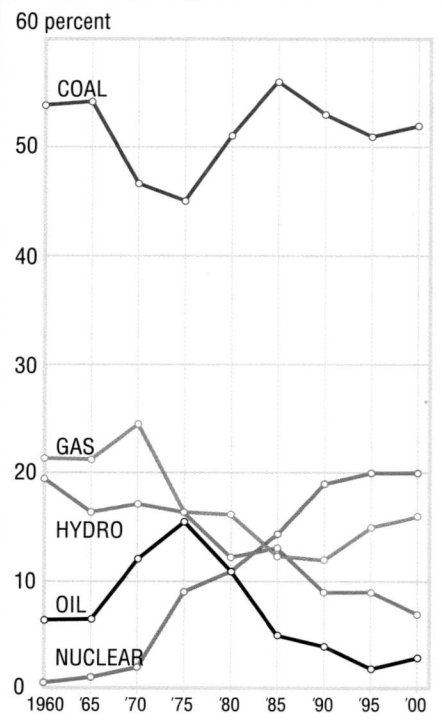

Coal is by far the most important energy source for electricity production in the United States. Oil has declined sharply as a source since energy problems of the 1970s.

NONRENEWABLE FUELS

Nonrenewable resources can't be replaced. Once they are used, they won't be replenished for millions of years.

- Coal
- Petroleum
- Natural gas

RENEWABLE FUELS

Renewable resources can be replaced. They exist in abundance because they are not depleted by daily use.

- Biofuels
- Solar energy
- Wind energy
- Hydrogen power

Nuclear Energy

Nuclear energy, also called atomic energy, is the powerful energy released by changes in the core of atoms. The heat and light of the sun result from nuclear energy. Scientists and engineers have found many uses for this energy, including the production of electric power, the explosion of nuclear weapons, and the diagnosis and treatment of medical conditions. (See pages 404–407.)

Nuclear Power in the Production Matrix

Yesterday. Some nuclear power plants have had accidents that have killed people, although not as many people as in other types of industrial accidents. The worst nuclear accident in the United States, at the Three Mile Island power plant in Pennsylvania, killed no one.

The worst nuclear accident ever, the Chernobyl explosion in Ukraine in 1986, killed dozens of people, but it may have affected many more in ways that will not be known for years.

Today. Almost all the world's electric energy is produced by hydroelectric and thermal power plants. Hydroelectric plants use the force of rushing water from a dam or waterfall to generate electric power. Thermal plants use the force of steam from boiling water. The great majority of thermal plants burn fossil fuels—coal, oil, and natural gas—to produce heat to boil water. The remaining thermal plants fission uranium.

Tomorrow. Few countries have enough water power to generate large amounts of hydroelectric power, and many regions have already fully exploited their hydroelectric capacity. Most countries depend mainly on fossil fuels. But fossil fuels are a nonrenewable resource, and burning them produces gases that can damage the environment. Therefore, many experts predict that nuclear power will become increasingly important.

Chain Reactions

In a nuclear reactor, chain reactions produce energy. The process happens when a mass of uranium or plutonium releases nuclear energy. That energy is created by a succession of nuclear fissions that continues automatically once it has been started. A fission is a splitting of an atomic nucleus.

Process. In a chain reaction, neutrons from the regular decay of uranium bump into other atoms of uranium and speed up the decay process. Each atom that decays produces more neutrons, so the number of atoms decaying increases with lightening speed. To produce nuclear power, the chain reaction is controlled by slowing down the neutrons.

Result. Like fire, a chain reaction produces heat. Unlike fire, it can do so without releasing chemicals into the air. When the heat from a chain reaction is used to produce electricity, the central heat-producing source is called a nuclear reactor. The entire complex is called a nuclear power plant.

 *Scientists first released nuclear energy on a large scale at the University of Chicago in 1942, 3 years after World War II began. This achievement led to the development of the atomic bomb. The first atomic bomb was exploded in the desert near Alamogordo, New Mexico, on July 16, 1945. In August, United States planes dropped bombs on Hiroshima and Nagasaki, Japan. The bombs largely destroyed both cities and helped end World War II.*

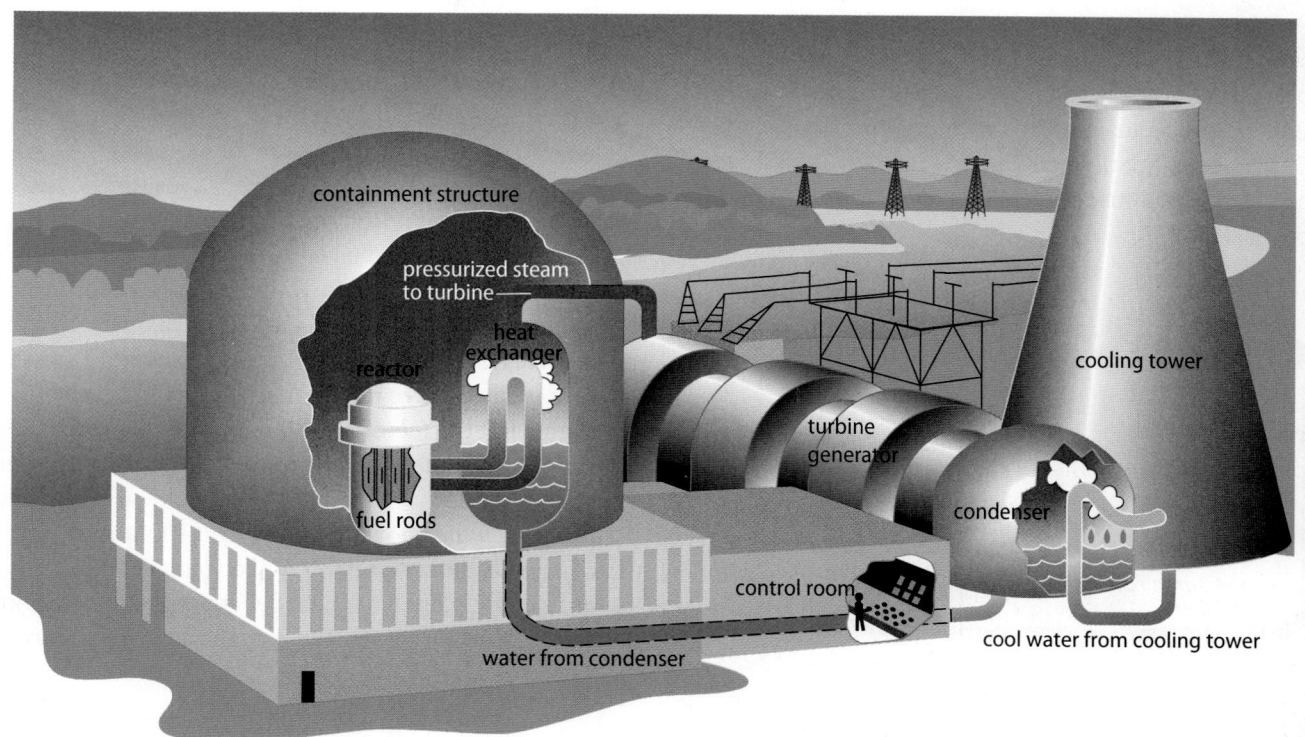

The following labels appear in the illustration:
containment structure, pressurized steam to turbine, heat exchanger, reactor, fuel rods, cooling tower, turbine generator, condenser, control room, water from condenser, cool water from cooling tower

The nuclear power plant shown here is typical of a pressurized water reactor. It has three separate water systems. Water used to cool the reactor passes through a heat exchanger, where water in the second system is changed into steam. This steam drives a turbine and then is changed back into water in a condenser that is cooled by water from a nearby water source.

Pros and Cons of Nuclear Power Plants

Advantages. Nuclear power plants have two main advantages over fossil fuel plants.

1. Nuclear plants are less expensive to operate than a fossil fuel plant. While a nuclear facility costs more to build, the fuel it uses is much cheaper, which leads to savings over the long term.

2. Uranium, unlike fossil fuels, releases no chemical or solid pollutants into the air during use.

3. It takes only a small amount of uranium to produce a large amount of energy. A chunk of uranium the size of a softball can release more energy than a trainload of coal that weighs 3 million times as much.

Disadvantages. Nuclear power plants have three major disadvantages. These disadvantages have slowed the development of nuclear energy in some countries.

1. Nuclear plants cost more to build than fossil-fuel plants.

2. Because of the need to assure that hazardous amounts of radioactive materials are not released, nuclear plants must meet certain government regulations that fossil-fuel plants do not have to meet.

3. Used nuclear fuel produces dangerous radiation long after it has been removed from the reactor. As a result, safe disposal of nuclear waste presents a challenge.

Water Power

SOUTHWESTERN

Water power is a valuable source of energy. When such fuels as coal, oil, and even nuclear fuels are burned up as a source of energy, they cannot be reused. But water used as a source of energy is not used up. Earth's constant flow of water can be harnessed to produce useful mechanical and electric power. (See pages 816–817.)

Turbines are classified as either impulse or reaction. Impulse turbines reverse the direction in which the water is flowing. Reaction turbines have blades that move at the same rate as the water.

Old Techniques

Wheels mounted on a frame over a river were the first devices used to harness water power. Blades around the outside of the wheels dipped into the river, and the flowing water striking the blades turned the wheels. The ancient Romans connected waterwheels to grinding stones and used the power to mill grain.

During the Industrial Revolution, large water wheels were used to run machinery in factories. The power was not completely reliable, however. Flood-waters created more power than was needed, and droughts left the factories without power. By the end of the 1800s, the steam engine had replaced water power in most factories.

The first water-powered plant for generating electricity was built in Appleton, Wisconsin, in 1882. This hydroelectric plant established water power as a major source of electric power. Hydroelectric power is now used all over the world.

WATER POWER AT WORK

Water flowing from a higher place to a lower place—as in a river, a waterfall, or a dam—is most often used to produce electric power. People use the effects of gravity pulling the water downward when they harness water for power. For example, in the customary system of measurement, a cubic foot of water weighs 62.4 pounds. The pull of gravity then creates a pressure of 6,240 pounds per square foot at the base of a body of water 100 feet tall. If this water were released from a nozzle at the bottom of its source, the stream of water would travel at a speed of about 80 feet per second. The force of this stream striking the blades of a water wheel would cause the wheel to turn, producing useful mechanical energy.

Hydroelectric power has become an important Canadian export to the United States. Shown here is a part of the vast James Bay hydroelectric project. ▶

New Techniques

Since the energy crisis of the 1970s, more importance has been placed on new approaches to using water power, tapping the energy of ocean waves or temperature differentials between layers of water.

Many researchers believe that the era of usable ocean energy will open the way to cheap and abundant power in the 21st century.

Concentrated Streams. Modern waterwheel technology employs pipes and nozzles to release concentrated streams of water to the wheel. This same principle is used for massive hydroelectric plants. Hydroelectric engineers must calculate supply and demand carefully to take maximum advantage of water availability. For example, during dry seasons, water is released from storage reservoirs.

Temperature Gradients. Another revolutionary scheme for using ocean power is the thermal energy, or temperature-gradient, concept. In the oceans, cool dense water tends to sink beneath currents of warm thin water. Experiments in the early part of the 20th century proved it was possible to extract energy from that temperature differential. But the amount of power produced was negligible, and the idea was dismissed in an era of cheap and abundant power.

Waves. Researchers are also developing several different technologies that can use waves to produce electric power. These technologies include devices that use the rise of waves to compress air that then turns a turbine, and floating devices that drive pistons as the water level rises and falls.

Using the Tides. Other researchers have tried to harness the tides of the oceans or river estuaries as sources of power. Since the 1960s, a sizeable tidal-power installa-

tion has been operating in the estuary of the Rance River near Saint-Malo, France. A large seawall built across the estuary contains reversible turbines.

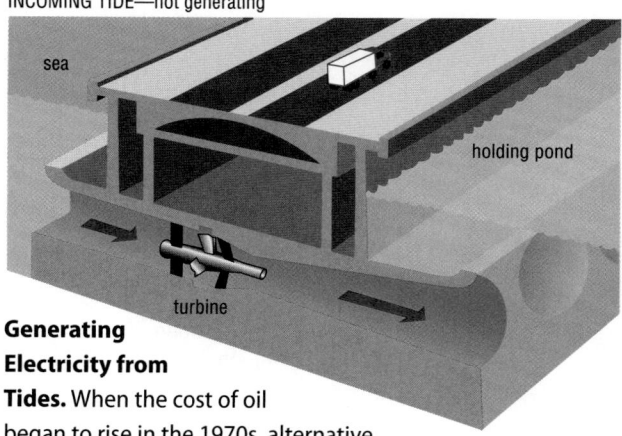

INCOMING TIDE—not generating

sea

holding pond

turbine

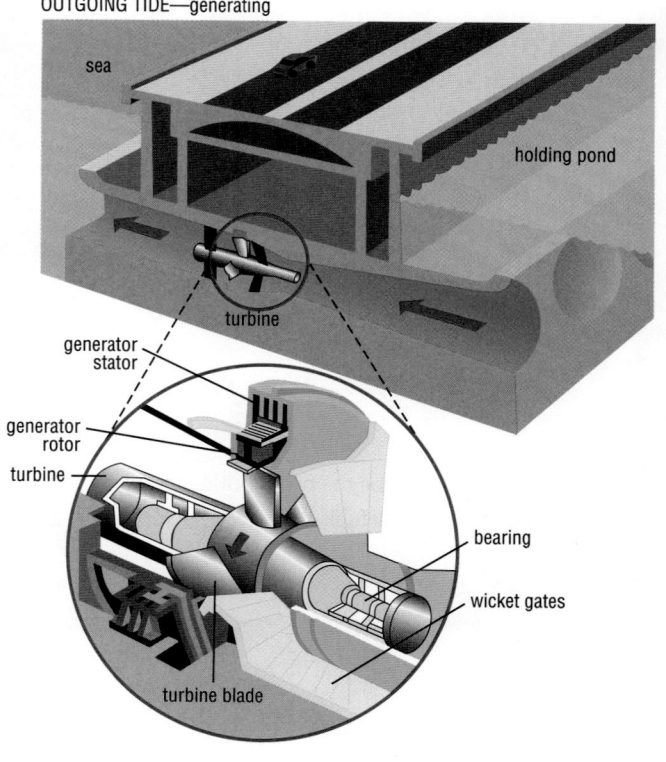

OUTGOING TIDE—generating

sea

holding pond

turbine

generator stator

generator rotor

turbine

bearing

wicket gates

turbine blade

Generating Electricity from Tides. When the cost of oil began to rise in the 1970s, alternative sources of energy became economically feasible. The power plant depicted here is similar to the one being tested in the Bay of Fundy in Canada. As the tide rises, seawater passes through the dam into the inlet behind. At high tide the wicket gates in the dam close, trapping the water. When the water in the bay outside has fallen about 5 feet, the gates open. The water rushing out spins the turbine to generate electricity. One of the drawbacks of this system is that it produces power for only about 6 hours during each 12.5-hour cycle.

Hydrogen Power

Someday, hydrogen could replace both gas and oil as a fuel. It burns easily, giving off huge amounts of heat. It is lightweight and efficient. In fact, it's such a good energy system that many people believe it will become an important fuel source in the future.

Fuel Cells

A *fuel cell* is a device that converts chemical energy to electrical energy. The chemical energy is produced from the chemical reaction between two combined substances—oxygen and hydrogen.

History. The concept of a fuel cell was developed in 1839, even before the rechargeable storage battery. Fuel cells were laboratory curiosities until the 1950s. After that, they were used in U.S. space programs as clean sources of power, with drinking water as a by-product.

Commercial fuel cells have been tested, with two large-scale tests taking place in New York City and Tokyo in the mid-1980s. The natural gas was first con-verted to hydrogen and carbon dioxide, so these fuel cells had carbon dioxide as a by-product as well as water. Concern about the contribution of carbon dioxide to global warming may limit the application of this process in the future.

Uses. Hydrogen can be used as a fuel. Many rockets burn hydrogen fuel with oxygen. Engine manufacturers can modify the internal combustion engines used in automobiles and other vehicles to burn hydrogen rather than gasoline. Some experts have suggested working to replace the use of fossil fuels, such as coal, oil, and natural gas, with more widespread use of hydrogen.

Interest in new energy sources invariably rises when oil becomes scarce. According to the Department of Energy, 94 percent of energy used in the U.S. comes from nonrenewable resources—most of them fossil fuels.

Hydrogen can also be used for other energy needs, such as electricity.

FUEL CELLS

1. When hydrogen and oxygen are in the presence of an appropriate chemical, they combine to form water.

2. In the process, electrons that can be directly siphoned off are released.

3. As long as enough hydrogen and oxygen are available, the fuel cell will keep producing power.

The fuel cell might be the best solution to our dependence on fossil fuels. ▶

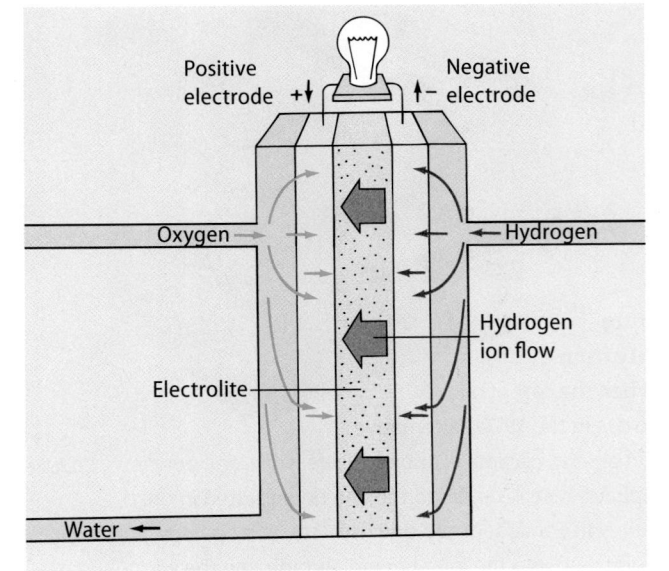

Advantages

- **Hydrogen power is efficient.** In most energy systems, electricity is made from steam-powered turbines turning a generator. Fuel cells, on the other hand, make energy directly. This is important because steam turbines produce only about 30 percent of the energy that is fed into them. A fuel cell, on the other hand, can make energy with an efficiency of 40 to 80 percent.

- **Hydrogen power is clean.** One advantage of hydrogen as a fuel is that its combustion with oxygen produces only water as a by-product, so such an engine doesn't pollute the environment. That means it doesn't produce emissions when it's used as fuel in cars.

- **Hydrogen is a renewable resource.** Oil, on the other hand, is a finite resource, which means it is completely used up when it's burned.

- **Hydrogen is plentiful and flexible.** It can be produced in a wide variety of ways.

Disadvantages

- **Hydrogen power requires huge amounts of hydrogen.** A fuel cell must constantly be fed a fuel and an oxidizer to produce power. An oxidizer is a substance that removes electrons in a chemical reaction. Ideally, it would be useful to have a pure source of hydrogen to run fuel cells.

- **Hydrogen is expensive.** Hydrogen is removed from water by a process called hydrolysis, which involves running an electric current through the water. But the process requires enormous amounts of electric power, making hydrogen a costly energy source.

- **Hydrogen is tricky to store.** A small amount of gas takes up a lot of space. Hydrogen can also be stored in liquid form, but it's too expensive to be practical.

- **There isn't a comprehensive distribution system in place.** This makes it difficult to make hydrogen widely available.

OBSTACLES TO PROGRESS

Hydrogen is, in many ways, a great source of energy. So why isn't it widely used yet?

The main obstacles are cost and durability. Fuel cells are expensive to use because they need a constant source of hydrogen. Also, the cells are very fragile, which makes them impractical for continuous use.

Researchers are hard at work to usher in the era of hydrogen fuel. Elias Greenbaum, a scientist at Oak Ridge National Laboratory, announced in 1985 that he had succeeded in making hydrogen by photosynthesis, the process that plants use to make starches and sugars. Greenbaum mixed chloroplasts, the plant parts in which photosynthesis takes place, with ultrafine particles of platinum. When exposed to sunlight, the combination split water into hydrogen and oxygen.

Although a long way from realization, this experiment raises the possibility that the sun could be the ultimate source of energy for fuel cells. Studies in this area continue today.

Eventually, the internal combustion engine that powers most cars could be replaced by hydrogen-burning engines. Such cars have already been built, but so far the costs have been prohibitive. If a cheap source of hydrogen became available, the situation might change.

To this end, the Department of Energy is currently working with various universities and national laboratories and partnering with industry leaders in the research and development of fuel cell systems.

Solar Energy

Solar energy is the direct use of sunlight to produce heat or electric power. The sun's energy is plentiful, but it is thinly distributed over a large area and must be collected and concentrated to produce usable power. (See pages 938–939.) As a result, solar energy is a more expensive power source than fossil fuels for most applications. Solar technology is improving rapidly, though. Someday, it may provide a clean and abundant source of power.

Harnessing the Sun's Energy

There are two main ways that sunlight is converted into electric power.

- directly, in a process called *solar cell conversion*
- indirectly, in a process called *solar thermal conversion*

Solar Cell Conversion. Devices called solar cells (also called photovoltaic cells) produce electric current directly from sunlight. This ability results from the *photovoltaic effect*, a phenomenon in which the energy in sunlight causes electric charges to flow through layers of a conductive material to produce a useful electric current.

Today, solar cells provide power for spacecraft and artificial satellites, handheld calculators, and wristwatches. Solar cells are also used for electric power generation in remote areas, where extending power lines would be difficult or costly. Most photovoltaic systems require a storage facility, which normally consists of batteries. Excess energy is stored in the batteries during the day and extracted as needed during the night.

fyi! *Nearly all the energy that we use is actually solar energy—energy from the sun. Solar energy stored in plants millions of years ago makes fossil fuels. The sun powers the air currents that cause the wind to blow. And there would be no moving water without the sun.*

Solar Thermal Conversion. Solar thermal conversion systems (also called solar concentrators) convert light to heat and then to electric power. They use one or more reflectors to concentrate solar energy to extremely high levels. There are three major kinds of systems.

- parabolic trough systems
- parabolic dish systems
- central receivers

Solar power, a renewable power source, only works in sunny climates. It is not so much the temperature of the air as the intensity and duration of sunlight that makes the difference. That's why solar energy can be a good source of energy in chilly areas like New England or the Pacific Northwest.

Solar Heating

Solar heating requires an efficient absorber to collect sunlight and convert it to heat. The absorber may be as simple as a coating of black paint, or it may be a textured, heat-absorbing ceramic. A good absorber collects 95 percent or more of the solar radiation while emitting 20 percent or less of the heat energy an ordinary hot surface would.

There are several methods of solar heating.

Flat-plate collectors are the simplest solar collectors. The sun shines on fixed plates at various angles as it moves. The sun heats fluid inside the plates to a temperature of up to 212°F (100°C). The hot fluid flows to a heat exchanger, a device like an automobile radiator through which water circulates, and transfers its heat to the water. The hot water is used to heat buildings and supply hot water.

Transpired solar collectors are designed specifically for heating air. They consist of flat or ridged plates pierced by an array of small holes. Air is drawn through the holes and is heated by the sun-warmed plates. As much as 80 percent of the solar energy collected by the plates is transferred to the airstream.

HOW DOES THAT WORK ?

SOLAR-HEATED HOMES

1. A solar-heated home has large south-facing windows that let in heat from the sun. The walls and floor absorb the heat during the day and release it at night.

2. A wood-burning stove can provide heat on cloudy days. Overhangs shade the windows in summer when the sun is high. Sunlight also heats collectors on the roof. Liquid inside the collectors flows to a heat exchanger in the basement, where water is heated for household use.

3. A flat-plate collector has a black plate that absorbs heat from sunlight. When the plate gets hot, it heats a liquid that flows in channels inside the collector. Glass or plastic sheets and insulation prevent heat loss.

Solar furnaces concentrate sunlight to produce temperatures high enough for use in industrial processes. Scientists use solar furnaces to

- process steel, ceramics, and other materials.
- provide energy for solid-state lasers.
- destroy hazardous wastes.

HEATING BUILDINGS

Building construction uses solar energy in two forms: passive and active.

Passive solar heating refers to heating in buildings that have been designed to take full advantage of the sun's rays.

Active solar heating happens when changes are made to an existing building. Those changes might include special pumps, ducts, rooftop solar collectors, or a new heat-distribution system.

◄ **Solar buildings** may have both active and passive components. It is possible to construct dwellings that are not only self-sufficient but also capable of generating power to share.

Other Energy Sources

Wind Power

Wind power is the energy associated with the air that moves over Earth's surface. The world's growing demand for energy threatens to exhaust the supply of such fuels as coal, oil, and natural gas. But wind is a renewable energy source that doesn't harm the environment. (See pages 518–519.)

Uses. People have harnessed the power of the wind to do work for thousands of years. Throughout history, wind power has been used primarily for mechanical purposes such as grinding grain, pumping water, or running sawmills.

Today, wind power turns windmills and propels sailboats. Private uses of the clean energy that is provided by wind occur all over the world. But wind power is commercially practical only in areas that have strong, steady winds.

Wind power is a renewable power source because it's always blowing somewhere on earth.

Windmills. Windmills probably originated in Persia, now Iran, around AD 600. Most early windmills used this rotational energy to operate machinery to grind grain. But a windmill can also be used to drive other devices, such as a pump to lift water from a well. Windmills generated electric power in some rural communities of the United States in the early 1900s.

Wind Turbines. Today, modern devices called wind turbines drive electric power generators. Wind power was first used to generate electric power in Denmark in the 1890s. By the 1990s, there were about 25,000 wind turbines operating in the world. However, these devices produced only about 0.1 percent of the world's electric power.

CONSERVING ENERGY

There are many simple ways you can conserve energy in your day-to-day life.

- Set your thermostat below 68°F in winter and above 78°F in summer.
- Turn off the lights when you leave a room.
- Use less hot water.
- Travel by bus, train, or car pool whenever possible.
- Recycle paper, aluminum, glass, and plastic.

 *Although the cost of wind power has declined dramatically over the last 20 years, it provides less than 2 percent of energy in the United States. This is a large drop from the mid-19th century, when wind power provided more than 10 percent of the nation's power.*

Disadvantages. Wind power isn't very reliable. While many areas have fairly steady winds, they do not blow at a constant speed. At times, they may die down completely, so it's not always possible to match supply with demand. To ensure a reliable supply of electric power, wind turbines must be combined with either an energy storage system or a backup generator that uses a different energy source.

Geothermal Power

Geothermal power is energy that comes from the heat of Earth. Most geothermal energy is converted to electric power.

Hot Rocks. Miners learned long ago that Earth's interior is hot. Geothermal power is generated wherever water comes in contact with hot rocks below Earth's surface. The rocks give off heat that makes the water hot enough to turn into steam. Power companies can drill wells and pump the hot water or steam to the surface, where it can be used to generate energy.

In areas where no underground water or steam exists naturally, engineers can pump water into the ground to be heated by hot rocks.

Advantages. Geothermal power plants have the potential to produce power more cheaply than plants that use oil, gas, or nuclear fuel. Rainwater that seeps back into the geothermal reservoir replenishes the fluid consumed by the geothermal plants. Thus, geothermal energy is considered a renewable energy source.

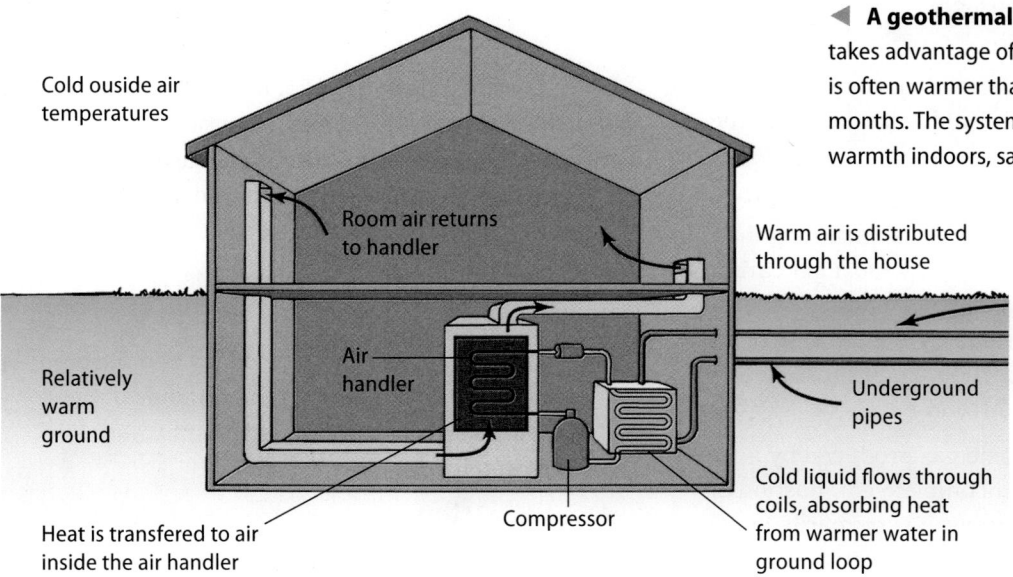

◀ **A geothermal home heating system** takes advantage of the fact that the ground is often warmer than the air during cold months. The system transfers that extra warmth indoors, saving heating fuel.

Cold ouside air temperatures

Room air returns to handler

Warm air is distributed through the house

Relatively warm ground

Air handler

Underground pipes

Heat is transfered to air inside the air handler

Compressor

Cold liquid flows through coils, absorbing heat from warmer water in ground loop

GEOTHERMAL POWER PLANTS

The production of geothermal energy can occur only in areas where hot rocks lie near Earth's surface. Geothermal power plants have been developed in

- El Salvador
- Greece
- Iceland
- Italy
- Japan
- Mexico
- New Zealand
- Philippines
- United States

Geothermal power taps into the heat that's inside of the earth. Iceland has used volcanoes as a power source to heat homes at low cost as well as to generate electricity.

abiotic factors the nonliving aspects of an environment, such as water, soil minerals, and atmospheric gases.

acid rain rain and other precipitation that is polluted by acids, particularly sulfuric acid and nitric acid.

aquifers underground formations filled with groundwater.

biome a major type of ecosystem; each type of biome shares common characteristics; biomes are scattered worldwide.

biotic factors the living aspects of an environment, such as producer organisms, consumer organisms, and reducer organisms.

biotic potential the inherent capacity or maximum rate at which a population could increase under the best of conditions.

carbon dioxide a colorless, odorless gas. It occurs in the atmospheres of many planets, including that of Earth. On Earth, all green plants must get carbon dioxide from the atmosphere to live and grow. Carbon dioxide is also created by the burning of any substance that contains carbon. Such substances include coal, gasoline, and wood.

carbon monoxide a toxic gas produced by any process that involves the incomplete combustion of carbon-containing compounds; it is primarily emitted in the exhausts of gasoline-powered vehicles.

carnivore an animal that feeds mainly on meat.

chlorofluorocarbons (CFCs) a family of synthetic, nontoxic chemicals used as refrigerants, solvents, aerosol propellants, and so on. Highly volatile, they are not destroyed in the lower atmosphere but drift into the upper atmosphere, where their chlorine atoms destroy ozone.

climate the weather of a place averaged over time.

commercial energy power that is produced by businesses and governments to be sold to the public.

community in ecology, a group of animals or plants living together; any group of mutually related organisms.

competition the simultaneous demand by different organisms for food, places for habitation, and other vital factors.

coniferous a type of tree that bears cones.

conservation the protection and improvement of natural resources such as forests and fossil fuels.

consumer in ecology, an organism in an ecosystem that does not obtain its energy directly, but acquires it secondhand from energy stored in green plants. Primary consumers feed directly on plants. Secondary consumers feed on other animals and thus receive their energy after it has been processed by two or more organisms.

DDT (dichlorodiphenyltrichloroethane) the first chlorinated hydrocarbon insecticide. It is quite persistent in the environment and causes harm as it accumulates in food chains. Its use in the United States has been restricted since 1972.

deciduous a type of tree that sheds its leaves each autumn.

decomposer organisms that decay and decompose organic matter by feeding on the remains of dead plants and animals; reducer organisms. Mainly bacteria and fungi.

desalinization the process of extracting fresh water from seawater.

desert a dry region where evaporation exceeds rainfall.

deep-well injection the practice of disposing of hazardous fluid wastes by injecting them into rock formations hundreds of feet below Earth's surface.

dispersal in ecology, the process by which members of a population spread out into unknown territory; helps to maintain a stable population.

domestication the transformation of animals or plants from wild to tame.

ecosystem a system made up of a group of living organisms and its physical environment, and the relationship between them.

endangered species living creatures threatened with extinction.

epiphytes plants that grow attached to larger plants without deriving nourishment from the hosts.

estuary a water passage where the tide meets a river current.

ethics the study of the standards of right and wrong.

extinction a state that occurs when every member of a species has died. Mass extinctions, or events in which large numbers of species suddenly become extinct, have occurred several times in Earth's history.

fallout radioactive material or other polluting particles that fall out of the atmosphere in dust or precipitation.

flocculants chemicals used in water treatment processes to improve the sedimentation or filterability of small particles.

food chain the pathways along which energy is transferred from one organism to another; a group of interrelated organisms; each member of the group feeds upon the one below it and is in turn eaten by the organism above it.

food web a group of interrelated food chains in an ecosystem.

fossil fuels coal, oil, and natural gas formed from the remains of organisms that lived millions of years ago.

fuel cell a device that converts chemical energy to electrical energy.

genotoxins pollutants that interfere with cell reproduction.

global warming an increase in the average temperature at Earth's surface. People often use the term global warming to refer specifically to the warming observed since the mid-1800s. Global surface temperatures have risen chiefly because of a process called the greenhouse effect.

greenhouse effect the absorption by gases in the atmosphere of heat energy radiated from Earth's surface, causing the atmosphere to become warmer.

greenhouse gases gases in Earth's atmosphere that absorb heat from the surface. The primary greenhouse gases are carbon dioxide, methane, nitrous oxide, and chlorofluorocarbons, or CFCs.

groundwater fresh water under the surface of Earth that fills aquifers and moves between soil particles and rock, supplying wells and springs. It is susceptible to contamination by leaching agricultural and industrial pollutants, by substances from leaking underground storage tanks, and so on.

habitat the kind of place in which an organism usually lives. A single habitat may satisfy the needs of many different types of organisms.

half-life a measure of radioactivity, different for each element or isotope, defined as the average time it takes for half the atoms of a sample to undergo radioactive decay. Half-lives vary from trillions of years to fractions of seconds. For example, the half-life of samarium-152 is 1,012 years; that of polonium-212 is $3 \times 10_{-7}$ seconds.

hazardous wastes wastes that may cause illness or death or pose other threats to human health or that may harm the environment.

herbivore an animal that feeds on plants.

hydrocarbons compounds in fossil fuels such as petroleum, natural gas, and coal that contain carbon and hydrogen; may be carcinogenic.

hydroponics the growing of plants without soil, by the use of water containing the necessary mineral nutrients.

incineration the destruction of waste products by fire in furnaces.

intercropping an agricultural technique in which two or more crops are grown side by side in alternating rows in combinations that increase soil fertility and crop yields.

Ecology Glossary

invasive species animals, plants, and other living things that spread rapidly after they are introduced into a new environment where there are few or no natural controls on their growth.

inversion an atmospheric condition caused by a layer of warm air that prevents the rise of cool air trapped underneath; this holds down pollutants that might otherwise be dispersed.

law of tolerance ecological law stating that in order to live, grow, and reproduce, all organisms have to fulfill certain basic requirements, such as sufficient space, air, food, and water.

leaching the process by which nutrient chemicals or contaminants are dissolved and carried away by water or are moved to a lower layer of the soil.

methane (CH_4) a component of natural gas; also produced during bacteria decomposition in rice paddies, cow guts, and other environments.

natural resources those products and features of Earth that permit it to support life and satisfy people's needs. Minerals, land, and water are natural resources, as are such biological resources as flowers, trees, birds, wild animals, and fish.

niche the function of an organism within its ecosystem.

nitrous oxide a gas produced from the breakdown of nitrogen-based fertilizers; a significant contributor to global warming.

nonpoint-source pollutants contaminants that cannot be easily traced to a single source.

nonrenewable resources materials that cannot be replaced.

nutrient a nourishing substance.

occupational hazard a danger that a person encounters in the course of doing his or her job. Many occupational hazards are the result of industrial pollutants.

overpopulation having more organisms than an ecosystem can support.

ozone (O_3) a form of oxygen present primarily in the stratosphere and responsible for blocking ultraviolet radiation; concentrations near Earth's surface contribute to smog.

ozone hole a region in the stratosphere of depleted ozone levels.

ozone layer the concentration of ozone in the stratosphere that protects Earth from ultraviolet radiation.

parasite an animal or plant that lives on or in another from which it gets its food, always at the expense of the host.

parasitism state in which members of one population feed upon members of another.

particulates dust, ash, smoke, mist, and other fine particles, either solid or liquid, that are found in emissions or in the atmosphere.

pesticide a chemical used to control pests, either by killing them or rendering them harmless.

photovoltaic effect a phenomenon in which the energy in sunlight causes electric charges to flow through layers of a conductive material to produce a useful electric current.

point-source pollutants contaminants that come directly from identifiable sources.

population the number of inhabitants occupying an area.

population density the number of organisms per unit area.

predator an animal that preys upon others.

producer in ecology, an organism in an ecosystem capable of capturing sunlight energy through the process of photosynthesis.

radiation energy given off in the form of waves or tiny particles of matter. There are two chief types of radiation. One type is called electromagnetic radiation. It consists only of energy. The other type is known as particle radiation or particulate radiation. It consists of tiny bits of matter.

recycling the process of using something over and over again or of converting discarded materials into new products.

reducer organisms decomposers; organisms that decay and decompose organic matter by feeding on the remains of dead plants and animals. Mainly bacteria and fungi.

renewable resources materials that can be replaced.

savanna a biome consisting of grassland; transitional area usually found between tropical rain forests and deserts.

senescence the state of being old; the growth phase in a plant or plant part from full maturity to death.

solar cell conversion a process that produces electric current directly from sunlight.

solar thermal conversion a process that concentrates solar energy using one or more reflectors.

sulfur dioxide a colorless, poisonous gas with a sharp odor. Sulfur dioxide forms naturally from volcanic activity and from the decay of organic matter. It can be manufactured by burning sulfur or heating metallic sulfur compounds. It is also released into the atmosphere by oil refineries, by some metal smelters, and by factories and electric power plants that burn coal or oil. Sulfur dioxide contributes to acid rain.

sustained yield a forest management procedure in which trees cut down in a forest are replaced by new plantings to ensure future lumber supplies; also, a fisheries management practice limiting fish catches to prevent depletion of fish populations.

symbiosis an association between two unlike organisms in which both organisms benefit.

synergistic effect a situation in which a combination of pollutants has a greater effect than would be expected from either pollutant alone.

territoriality a form of behavior in which an animal claims an area for itself and defends it from intrusion by others.

tertiary occurring in or being part of a third stage.

transuranic wastes waste consisting of any of the artificially produced elements, all having atomic numbers greater than 92 (that of uranium). Transuranium elements with atomic numbers up to 118 have been obtained.

trophic levels the various levels through which energy is transferred in a community.

tundra a biome consisting of vast, treeless, Arctic grassland.

ultraviolet (UV) radiation an invisible form of short-wave radiation emitted by the sun.

volatiles substances that are readily vaporizable at relatively low temperatures.

wetlands swamps, marshes, estuaries, and other areas that are regularly saturated by water, and whose vegetation is adapted for life in saturated soil conditions.

Physics

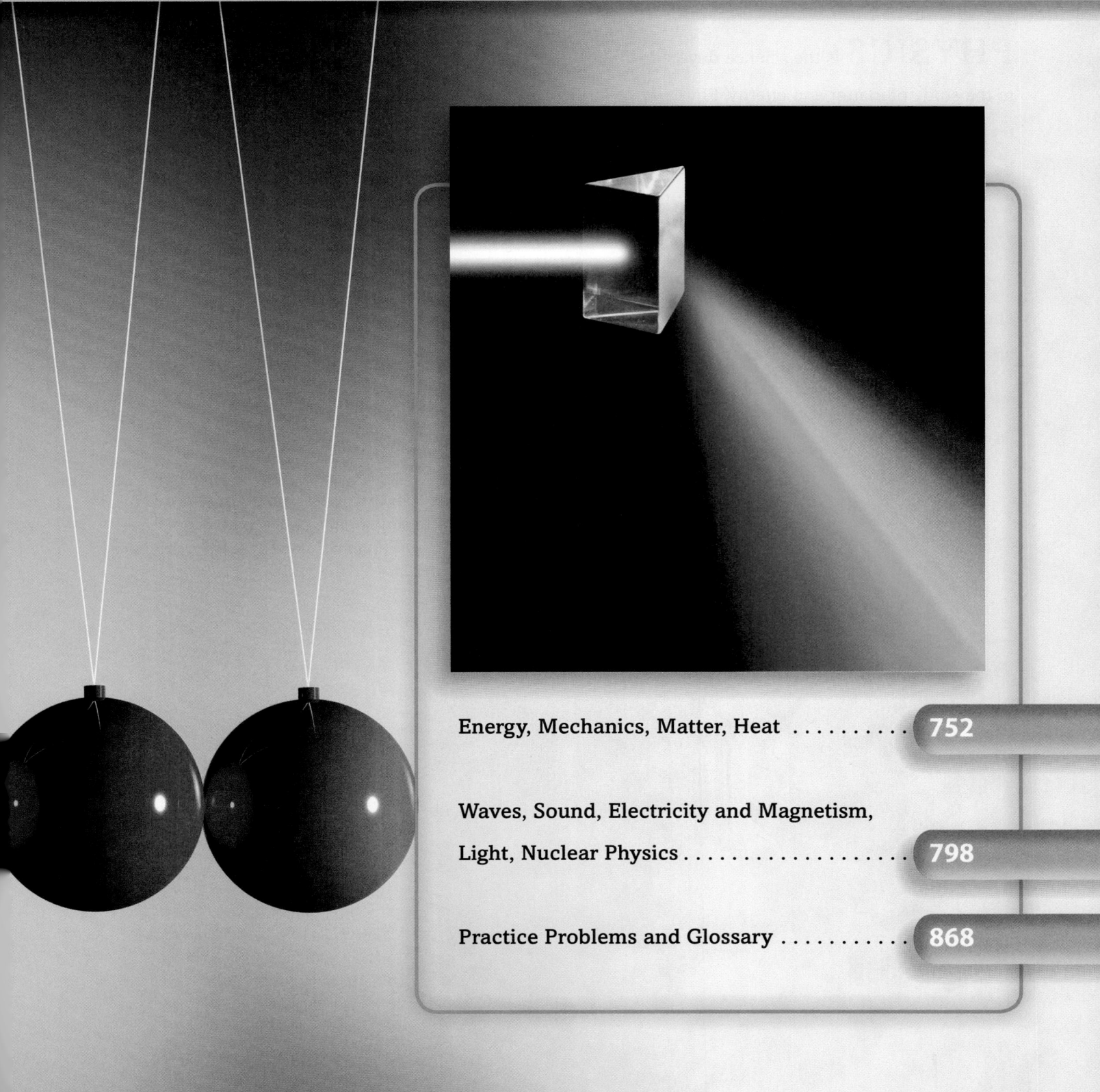

Energy, Mechanics, Matter, Heat **752**

Waves, Sound, Electricity and Magnetism,
Light, Nuclear Physics **798**

Practice Problems and Glossary **868**

PHYSICS is the science devoted to the study of matter and energy. Physicists try to understand what matter is and why it behaves the way it does. They seek to learn how energy is produced, how it travels from place to place, and how it can be controlled. Physicists are also interested in how matter and energy are related to each other and how they affect each other over time and through space.

What Is Physics?

Physics, once called natural philosophy, underpins many other branches of science.

- Astrophysics may be called the physics of the stars.
- Geophysics is the physics of Earth.
- Chemistry may be considered a branch of atomic physics.
- Engineering is often called applied physics.

Much of modern engineering is based on research performed in physics laboratories. For example, the X-ray machines, ultrasound imaging devices, radium, radioactive isotopes, computer-assisted tomography (CAT scanners), and electrocardiographs used in hospitals were discovered in physics laboratories.

Many of the conveniences in our homes—temperature controls, air conditioning, refrigerators, microwave ovens, and vacuum cleaners—are by-products of this same research.

GETTING OFF THE GROUND

Laws and theories of physics have enabled engineers and scientists to put satellites into orbit and to receive information from space probes that travel to distant regions of the solar system.

Before astronauts go into space, many calculations must be made. Scientists must determine the energy required for launching, the direction of launching, and the timing of the final boost to the vehicle in which they ride. The principles of physics help make these computations. (See pages 970–971.)

Milestones in Physics	
c. 200 BC	Archimedes observes and formulates the laws of levers and pulleys and determines weight and volume relationships.
1543	Nicolaus Copernicus formulates the theory that Earth and other planets move in circles around the sun.
1600	Galileo builds telescopes for studying the heavens and states several laws of mechanics.
1687	Sir Isaac Newton publishes his law of motion.
1690	Christiaan Huygens publishes the wave theory of light.
1803	John Dalton proposes his theory on the atomic structure of matter.
c. 1830	Michael Faraday and Joseph Henry independently produce electricity using magnetism.
c. 1860	James Clerk Maxwell predicts existence of electro-magnetic waves.
1895	Wilhelm Roentgen discovers X-rays.
1896	Antoine Bequerel discovers natural radioactivity.
1898	Marie and Pierre Curie isolate radioactive radium.
1900	Max Planck publishes his quantum theory.
1912	Ernest Rutherford and Niels Bohr propose "planetary system" models of the atom.
1915	Albert Einstein announces his theory of relativity.
1930	Paul Dirac predicts existence of positively charged electrons called positrons.
1932	John Cockcroft and Ernest Walton build the first particle accelerator.
1942	Enrico Fermi achieves the first controlled nuclear chain reaction.
1947	John Bardeen, Walter Brattain, and William Shockley invent the transistor.
1960	Theodore Maimon builds the first laser.
c. 1980	Ceramic superconductors are developed.
1995	Fermi National Accelerator Laboratory announces the discovery of a type of subatomic particle known as the top quark.
2000	Fermi researchers announce the first direct detection of a kind of subatomic particle called the tau-neutrino.

◄ Galileo

Christiaan Huygens ►

▲ Pierre and Marie Curie

▲ Enrico Fermi

◄ Theodore Maimon

Types of Physics

Physicists try to answer basic questions about the world, how it is put together, and how it changes. There are two main types.

- **Experimental physicists** perform experiments and compare their results to their predictions.
- **Theoretical physicists** develop laws and theories. These laws are usually expressed in mathematical terms.

The subjects studied by physicists include two broad categories: classical physics and modern physics.

Classical Physics

Classical physics deals with questions regarding motion and energy. There are five important areas.

Mechanics is the study of the effects of forces on bodies at rest or in motion. For example, it describes how force acts upon an object to produce acceleration.

Heat. The study of heat is called thermodynamics. It involves investigating how heat is produced, how it is transmitted, how it changes matter, and how it is stored.

Sound. The study of sound is called acoustics. Sound consists of vibrations that are produced by an object and that travel through a medium, such as air, water, or the walls of a building.

Electricity and magnetism deal with the characteristics of electric charges, currents, electric fields, and magnetic fields. The practical application of this knowledge led to the development of electric machinery and electronics.

Light. The study of light is called optics. Light is a form of electromagnetic radiation. Geometrical optics traces the paths of light rays through such devices as lenses and a variety of other optical instruments. Relatively recent developments in optics include lasers and fiber optics.

Modern Physics

Modern physics concentrates on scientific beliefs about the basic structure of the material world. There are five important areas.

Atomic, molecular, and electron physics are concerned with understanding the structures of molecules and atoms. In particular, these fields focus on the behavior, arrangement, motion, and energy states of the electrons that orbit atomic nuclei. Studies in this branch of physics have revealed much about the structure of matter.

Nuclear physics involves the study of the structure and properties of the atomic nucleus. It focuses on radioactivity, fission, and fusion. Radioactivity is the process by which certain nuclei spontaneously give off high-energy particles or rays. Radioactive materials are used

- to treat cancer and diagnose illness.
- to trace chemical processes.
- to trace physical processes.

Particle Physics. Physicists have discovered that the protons, neurons, and other particles within atomic nuclei are formed of still more elementary particles called quarks. Particle physicists conduct research by using devices called particle accelerators.

Solid-state physics is also called condensed-matter physics. Physicists who study solids are interested in how the properties of these materials are affected by such factors as temperature and pressure.

OTHER BRANCHES OF PHYSICS

- **Biophysics** applies the tools and techniques of physics to the study of living things and life processes.
- **Geophysics** is the study of Earth and its atmosphere and waters by means of the principles of physics.
- **Health physics** involves the protection of people who work with or near radiation.
- **Mathematical physics** is the study of mathematical systems that stand for physical phenomena.
- **Plasma physics** is concerned with the study of highly ionized gases—that is, gases that have been separated into positively and negatively charged particles.
- **Quantum physics** includes various areas of study based on quantum theory, which deals with matter and electromagnetic radiation and the interactions between them.

Fluid Physics. Understanding the behavior and movement of fluids is important for the design and construction of automobiles, ships, airplanes, and rockets, as well as for the study of weather.

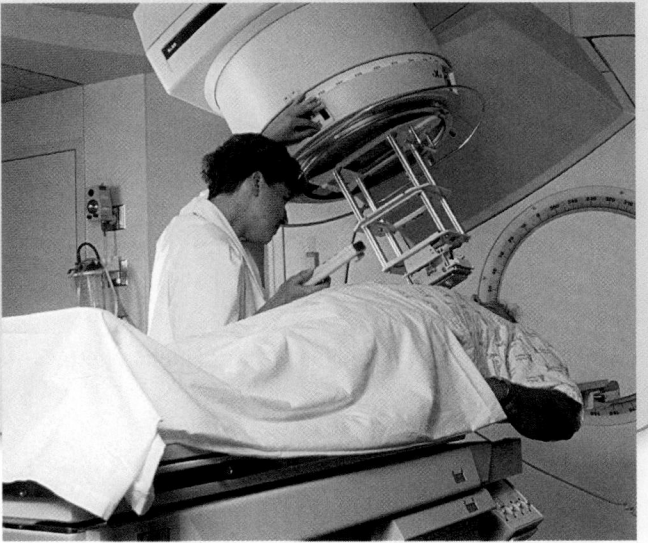

Nuclear physics helps physicians treat cancer by bombarding tumors with radiation.

ENERGY, in physics, is a quantity related to work. Energy has many forms. For example, you use mechanical energy to toss a ball. Heat energy warms a room. Electric energy makes a lightbulb glow. And chemical energy provides the driving force for an automobile.

Forms of Energy

Energy, the capacity for doing work, can exist in many forms. Two forms of energy are fundamental.

- **potential:** stored energy
- **kinetic:** energy of motion

All types of energy consist of kinetic energy, potential energy, or both. (See also pages 312–313.)

Potential Energy

Potential energy is the energy a body possesses by virtue of its location. Water in a reservoir, or a weight lifted to an elevated position, has potential energy that can be converted by a machine into a more desirable or convenient form.

Gravitational potential energy is the most common form. Since Earth's gravity attracts all bodies, work is required to elevate a body to a higher level. The work expended on the body represents energy that is stored and can be reconverted.

Kinetic Energy

Kinetic energy involves motion. A bird in flight, a spinning wheel, and a speeding car all possess kinetic energy. The amount of work a moving object can do while being brought to rest, or the work required to produce the velocity at which the body moves, is a measure of its kinetic energy.

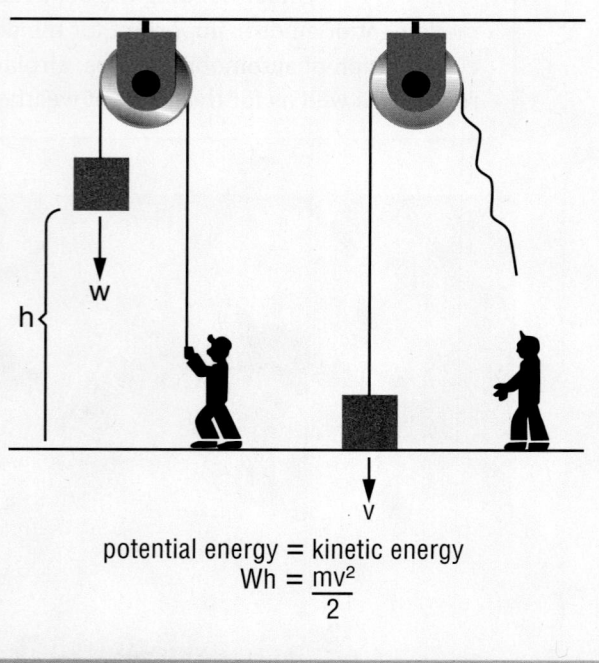

potential energy = kinetic energy
$$Wh = \frac{mv^2}{2}$$

The potential energy of the mass at rest becomes kinetic energy when the mass falls.

Energy Conversion

Energy can be converted from one form into another form. For example, a coal-burning power plant converts chemical energy to electric energy. The following description of that process will help you understand various forms of energy and how they can be converted.

1. The coal has potential energy in the form of chemical energy. That energy is stored in electrons of atoms that make up molecules in the coal. (Not pictured.)

2. When the coal burns, its molecules change as bonds break and other bonds form. As the molecules change, electrons release energy, which is immediately converted to heat energy. The hotter an object, the greater the kinetic energy of its atoms and molecules.

3. In the power plant, the molecular changes that occur when the coal burns create hot gases. In the next stage of the process, heat energy in the gases changes to heat energy in the metal that makes up a boiler, then to heat energy in molecules of water inside the boiler. As the water molecules absorb heat energy, they move more and more rapidly. Eventually, they move so rapidly that water turns to steam.

THE LAW OF CONSERVATION OF ENERGY

This law is fundamental to our understanding of energy. It states that in energy conversions, the total quantity of energy is conserved. The quantity of energy that exists at the end of a process is the same as the quantity that existed when the process began. That means that energy can never be created or destroyed.

4. The steam flows from the boiler through pipes to a device known as a steam turbine. The turbine has several wheels with fanlike blades. The steam rushes through the blades, pushing against them and thereby spinning the wheels. In this stage, heat energy of the steam is converted to mechanical energy of the turbine.

5. The turbine is connected to a machine called an electric generator. The generator converts mechanical energy of the spinning turbine to electric energy. That energy is partly kinetic and partly potential.

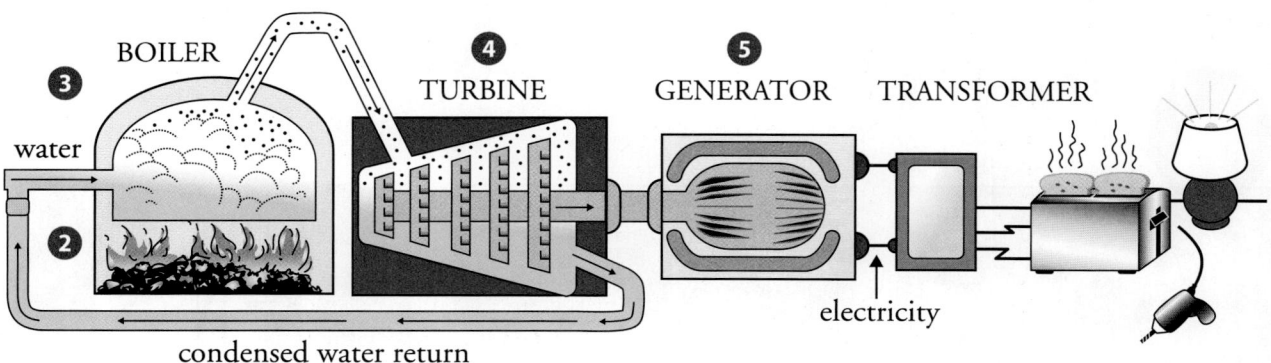

Mechanical Energy

Mechanical energy is the energy an object has from its position or motion. The study of mechanical energy is called *mechanics*. It looks at the effects of forces on bodies at rest or in motion. For example, it describes how force acts upon an object to produce acceleration.

Mechanics deals with force, motion, inertia, and energy. Of most interest are the laws governing the effect that a force—thought of as a push or a pull—will have on the form and motion of an object. Mowing a lawn, for example, requires a force to push the mower. A car engine exerts a pulling force to move its load.

Applications

The principles of mechanics are used in describing such types of motion as planetary orbits and the paths of other moving objects. They are also important to designers of bridges and other structures, containers, roads, and various kinds of vehicles.

Types

There are two main areas of study within mechanical energy.

- *Statics* is the area that deals with forces that are in equilibrium. This includes bodies that are at rest and bodies that are in motion at a constant speed in a constant direction.
- *Dynamics* deals with the production and causes of motion.

A third division called *kinematics* treats motion without regard to the forces that produce it.

Statics deals with a body at rest, or in motion at a constant speed and in a constant direction. Such a body is said to be in equilibrium because the forces acting on it cancel each other out.

Dynamics is the study of objects that change their speed or the direction of their motion because of forces acting upon them. The English scientist Isaac Newton expressed the relationship of these forces and changes in motion in his second law of motion. (See also pages 762–763.)

A book on a table or a bridge are bodies at rest. A car on the highway and a rocket being launched are both bodies in motion.

THE LAW OF MACHINES

The law of machines states that if friction and other resistances are ignored, the work input should equal the work output.

- An object that is moved exerts a force, the *resistance*, that must be overcome by the effort.

- The distance that the machine moves the resistance is the *resistance distance*.

- The work output is the product of the force of the resistance times the resistance distance.

- Machines can increase the effort that is applied to them, making work easier.

- This is usually accomplished by increasing the effort distance.

- The work done by a small effort over a large distance will equal the work done when a large resistance is moved over a small distance.

A system of pulleys enables the winch on his tow truck to lift the weight of an automobile.

Fixed pulley

Movable pulley

Pulley system

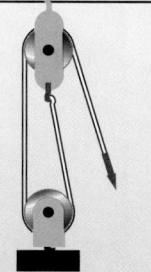

ARCHIMEDES: ANCIENT ENGINEER

Archimedes, a Greek, was a physicist and a mechanical engineer. In the Ancient World, he was best known as an inventor.

His inventions and discoveries included:

- proving the law of the lever.

- inventing the compound pulley.

- using a system of pulleys to move a ship fully loaded with passengers and freight .

- discovering that every object has a center of gravity.

- inventing a device known as the Archimedean screw that was used in ancient Egypt to drain and irrigate the land in the Nile Valley.

- inventing catapults.

In addition to being a mechanical engineer, Archimedes was the most original and profound mathematician of ancient times. ▶

MECHANICS is a science that studies the effects of forces on solids, liquids, and gases at rest or in motion. The principles of mechanics are used by engineers to design products that range in size from tiny computer parts to huge dams, and by physicists to study the motion of atomic particles.

Measurement

For the expression of physical quantities such as distance, mass, force, and time, scientists use the International System of Units (SI). It is the main system of measurement in all the technologically advanced nations of the world except the United States.

Scientists and many engineers in the United States use SI. For most commercial and everyday measurements, however, Americans use the inch-pound system.

Metric Units

SI units are related to one another in a simple, logical way that makes the metric system easy to use. Seven base units serve as the "building blocks" from which all the other units are constructed.

- meter (length)
- kilogram (mass)
- second (time)
- ampere (electric current)
- kelvin (thermodynamic temperature)
- candela (luminous intensity)
- mole (amount of substance)

Every unit in SI has a symbol. They are the same in all languages.

Units expressed in meters, kilograms, and seconds are also called mks *units. Since many scientists still use the centimeter, gram, and second for measurements, these units are called* cgs *units. In the United States, the foot, pound, and second, which are known as* fps *units, are still widely used.*

Length

Length is the base quantity for space measurement, and the meter is the base unit. Scientists define the meter as the distance traveled by light in a vacuum in 1/299,792,458 of a second.

Mass

The metric unit for mass is the kilogram. (In everyday language, mass is usually called weight.) Physicists define mass as a measure of *inertia*. Inertia is a property of all matter. Due to inertia, a motionless object tends to remain motionless.

Time

For the measurement of time, the second is the base unit. Track races are sometimes won by a margin of milliseconds. Calculations in a personal computer are performed in microseconds (millionths of a second).

Velocity (or speed) is distance traveled divided by the time required.

Acceleration is a change in velocity during a period of time.

Frequency measures how often a regularly repeating event occurs over time.

METRIC PREFIXES

These are standard SI prefixes. Attaching them to any SI unit increases or decreases the value of that unit.

Prefix	Increase or decrease in unit	Scientific Notation
yotta	1,000,000,000,000,000,000,000,000	1×10^{24}
zetta	1,000,000,000,000,000,000,000	1×10^{21}
exa	1,000,000,000,000,000,000	1×10^{18}
peta	1,000,000,000,000,000	1×10^{15}
tera	1,000,000,000,000	1×10^{12}
giga	1,000,000,000	1×10^{9}
mega	1,000,000	1×10^{6}
kilo	1,000	1×10^{3}
hecto	100	1×10^{2}
deka	10	1×10^{1}
deci	0.1	1×10^{-1}
centi	0.01	1×10^{-2}
milli	0.001	1×10^{-3}
micro	0.000001	1×10^{-6}
nano	0.000000001	1×10^{-9}
pico	0.000000000001	1×10^{-12}
femto	0.000000000000001	1×10^{-15}
atto	0.000000000000000001	1×10^{-18}
zepto	0.000000000000000000001	1×10^{-21}
yocto	0.000000000000000000000001	1×10^{-24}

KEEPING TIME

Timekeeping once was based on the rotation of Earth and the observation of the passage of a star through the crosshairs of a transit telescope. After astronomers discovered that the rotation of Earth is not constant, atomic clocks came into use as time standards. Atomic clocks like the one at left are more accurate than other clocks because they use the natural vibrations of atoms rather than a pendulum or oscillating crystal as the timekeeping device.

◀ **The U.S. Naval Observatory** in Washington, D.C., houses this atomic clock.

Motion

Motion is a change of position in space. Moving things surround us. When we catch a ball or safely cross a busy street, we use our understanding of motion. Physicists study motion to better understand the world.

Relativity

All motion is relative. That means that an object can only be described as moving or stationary in relation to another object. On an airplane in flight, for example, two passengers sitting in their seats are moving rapidly relative to the ground. But they are stationary relative to each other. This concept, called *relativity*, presents special challenges to our understanding of motion.

SIR ISAAC NEWTON

Sir Isaac Newton (1642–1727), an English scientist, astronomer, and mathematician, invented a new kind of mathematics, discovered the secrets of light and color, and showed how the universe is held together. He is sometimes described as one of the greatest names in the history of human thought because of his great contributions to mathematics, physics, and astronomy.

Newton did not enjoy the scientific arguments that arose from his discoveries. Many new scientific theories are opposed violently when they are first announced, and Newton's did not escape criticism. He was so sensitive to such criticism that his friends had to plead with him to publish his most valuable discoveries.

Newton was a bachelor who spent only part of his time on mathematics, physics, and astronomy. He studied and experimented with alchemy. He also spent a great deal of his time on questions of theology and Biblical chronology.

Although Newton's achievements were extremely important, he spoke modestly of himself shortly before his death, saying, "I do not know what I may appear to the world, but to myself I seem to have been only like a boy playing on the seashore, and diverting myself in now and then finding a smoother pebble or a prettier shell than ordinary, whilst the great ocean of truth lay all undiscovered before me."

Newton's Laws

In the 1600s, the relationship of force to motion was described in three laws formulated by Sir Isaac Newton. These laws can help us understand the kinds of motion we see every day.

First Law of Motion. Newton's first law is known as the principle of inertia. *Inertia* is the tendency of an object to continue moving if it is moving and to remain motionless if it is at rest.

Newton's first law has two important parts.

- A body at rest remains at rest unless acted on by an outside force.
- A body in motion continues to move at constant speed along a straight line unless acted on by an outside force.

Second Law of Motion. The second law states that a force acting on an object produces an acceleration equal to the force divided by the mass of the object. This relationship is usually written as the equation $F = ma$, where F is the force, m is the object's mass, and a is the acceleration.

- **Acceleration increases with force.** Imagine two people pulling two identical wagons. If one person exerts more force, that person's wagon will accelerate more. (See pages 764–765.)

- **Acceleration decreases with mass.** Imagine two people using the same amount of force to pull two identical wagons. One wagon is empty. The other is loaded with rocks. The full wagon will accelerate less than the empty wagon because the full wagon has more mass.

Third Law of Motion. The third law states that for every action or force, there is an equal and opposite reaction or force.

For example, rockets take off by expelling gases. The downward motion of the gases creates a reaction of the rocket upward. The reaction helps it overcome gravity and fly into space.

In the case of Earth, the planet tugs at the sun in reaction to the sun's pulling on it. But because the sun has much more mass than Earth does, the sun accelerates little in response.

Friction

Many kinds of motion we encounter every day are more complicated. Imagine, for example, rolling a ball across the ground. Newton's first law states that an object in motion will continue moving unless acted on by an outside force. However, we know from experience that the ball will eventually slow down and stop.

According to Newton's laws, some force must have acted on the ball. Physicists call this force *friction*. Friction occurs when one surface moves over another. As the ball rolls, its outer surface rubs against the ground. This rubbing generates a force of friction that slows the ball's movement.

The effects of friction complicated early efforts to understand motion. Newton developed his laws by studying planets. The planets experience almost no friction as they move through nearly empty space.

Friction is the reason why

- the tires of a car grip the road.

- a conveyor belt turns on pulleys without slipping.

- ice is more slippery than concrete.

EQUATIONS FOR LAWS OF MOTION AND GRAVITY

Second Law of Motion

$F = ma$ where F is force
m is mass
a is acceleration

$F = mv/t$ where F is force
m is mass
v is velocity
t is time

Third Law of Motion

$m_1v_1 = m_2v_2$ where m_1 is mass
m_2 is another mass
v_1 is the velocity of the first mass
v_2 is the velocity of the second mass

Law of Gravity

$f = G\dfrac{m_1 m_2}{r^2}$ where f is the attractive force
G is the gravitational constant (6.673×10^{-8} dyne-cm^2/g^2 in the cgs system)
m_1 is one mass
m_2 is another mass
r is the distance between masses

Motion of body falling to Earth

$v = v_0 + gt$ where v is velocity
v_0 is initial velocity
g is acceleration because of gravity (980 cm/s^2)
t is time

$s = v_0t + \frac{1}{2}gt^2$ where s is distance fallen
v_0 is initial velocity
t is time
g is acceleration because of gravity (980 cm/s^2)

Force

A *force* is a push or a pull. In your everyday life, you experience a variety of forces.

- You apply a force to a ball when you throw it up in the air.
- As the ball rises, the force of gravity slows it down.
- As the ball descends, gravity makes it fall more rapidly.
- When you catch the ball, it applies a downward force to your hands.
- Your hands apply an upward force to stop it.

Characteristics of Force

Size and direction are two essential characteristics of force. You might push a box across the floor with a force that has a size of 45 pounds (200 newtons) and is directed toward the south.

Because force has both a size and a direction, scientists call it a vector quantity. Physicists usually indicate a vector quantity by a letter with an arrow over it. Thus, $\vec{F}$ stands for force. Scientists also refer to the motion of a body in terms of a vector quantity—a combination of speed and direction known as *velocity*.

An action as simple as throwing a ball in the air involves many kinds of force.

EQUILIBRIUM

Equilibrium is a state of balance. It is achieved when the forces acting upon a body equal zero. With equilibrium, there is no change in motion. The body may be at rest or it may be moving in a straight line at a uniform speed.

A force is a push . . .

. . . or a pull.

Overcoming Inertia. A force acts by overcoming inertia, which is a property of all matter. Due to inertia, a body in motion continues to move with a constant velocity, while a motionless object tends to remain still.

Acceleration. Physicists refer to any change in motion—whether the change involves speed, direction, or both—as acceleration. The force necessary to accelerate an object by a given amount depends on the object's mass. The greater the mass, the greater the force must be.

Concurrent Forces. In most changes of velocity that we observe, more than one force is acting on the accelerated object. Such *concurrent forces* produce a single net force. Suppose you are part of a tug-of-war team. If your team pulls harder on the rope than the opposing team does, there will be a net force in your direction. But if the two teams pull equally hard, the forces will be in equilibrium. The rope will not move.

Concurrent forces are at work in this game of tug-of-war because the rope is being pulled in two different directions.

Kinds of Force

There are four fundamental forces.

Gravitation was the first of the fundamental forces to be understood scientifically. The force of gravity between objects arises from the attraction between the particles of matter that make up the objects. Gravity becomes weaker as the distance between two objects increases. (See next page.)

Electromagnetic force consists of two parts: the electric force and the magnetic force. The electric force is similar to the gravitational force. Both forces weaken as the square of the distance between objects.

The magnetic force that is used in everyday objects arises from two sources: the combined magnetic forces of "miniature magnets" and the movement of electrons through wires as electric current.

The strong force holds protons and neutrons together in atomic nuclei. The protons are so close to one another that there is a huge electric repulsion between them. The strong force overcomes this repulsion. If there were no strong force, only one chemical could exist—hydrogen, with one proton in its nucleus.

The weak force can change one type of particle into another. For example, in the main process by which the sun produces energy, the weak force changes a proton into a neutron. It does this by sending out a particle that carries off the proton's positive charge. The weak force also takes part in a kind of radioactivity known as beta decay.

Gravitation

Gravitation is the force of attraction that acts between all objects because of their mass. Gravitation results in some basic observations.

- An object that is near Earth falls toward the surface of the planet.
- An object that is already on the surface experiences a downward force due to gravitation.
- We experience this force on our bodies as our weight.

Gravitation also holds together the hot gases that make up the sun, and it keeps the planets in their orbits around the sun.

Predicting Motion

The principles of mechanics give us the ability to predict planetary motion. Each particle of matter attracts every other particle with a force, *F*, that is directly proportional to the product of their masses, m_1 and m_2, and inversely proportional to the square of the distance, *r*, between them.

$$F = G\frac{m_1 m_2}{r^2}$$

The most familiar example of universal gravitation is seen in the fall of an object when released. The amount of Earth's gravitation is different for different bodies, varying with their mass. This attraction is known as the weight of the body. Weight is proportional to mass; if the same force, gravitational attraction, produces the same acceleration on two bodies, the weights of the two bodies are equal. Since mass is the measure of quantity of matter, a quart of water, for example, must have twice the mass of a pint.

All bodies would fall with the same acceleration if there were no air resistance. One can prove this by dropping a feather and a metal pellet in an evacuated glass vessel. Both objects reach the bottom at the same time.

HALLEY'S COMET

Edmund Halley saw Halley's comet in 1682. It had been seen earlier, but he was the first to suggest it traveled a regular path. He said the comet would return in 1758 or 1759. It arrived on schedule, reinforcing the validity of Newton's theory of gravitation. (See pages 934–935.)

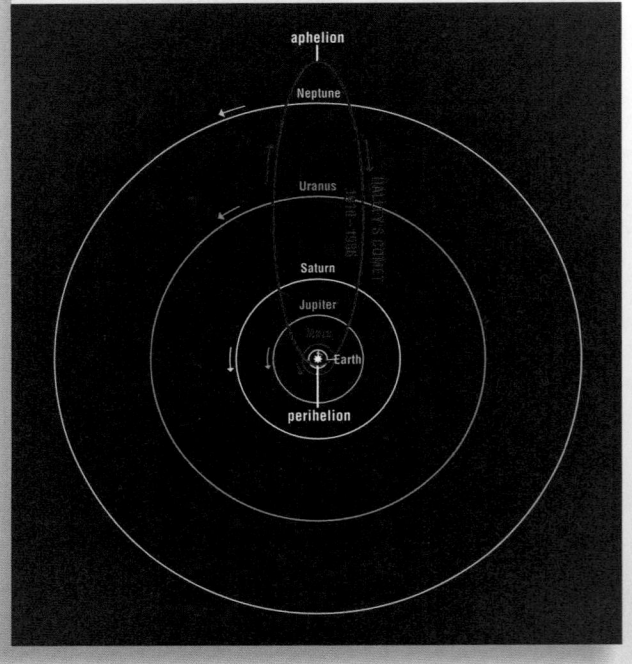

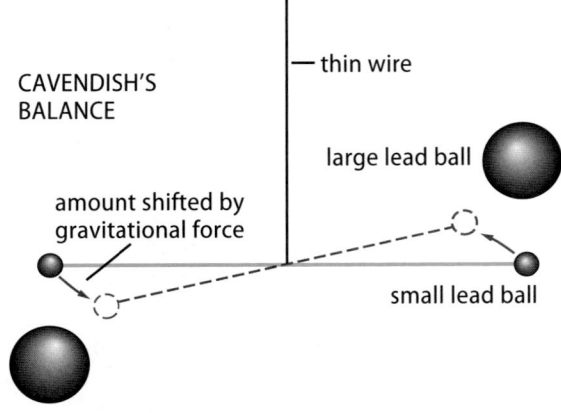

Henry Cavendish used a sensitive torsion balance to find the gravitational constant by measuring the attraction between two equal small masses and two equal large masses.

Newton's Law

Ancient astronomers measured the movement of the moon and planets across the sky, but they didn't understand those motions. In the late 1600s, Sir Isaac Newton described a connection between the movements of the celestial bodies and the gravitation that attracts objects to Earth.

In 1665, when Newton was 23 years old, a falling apple caused him to question how far the force of gravity reaches. Using the laws of planetary motion, Newton showed how the sun's force of gravity must decrease with the distance from the sun. He then assumed that Earth's gravitation decreases in the same way with the distance from Earth.

Newton knew that Earth's gravitation holds the moon in its orbit around Earth, and he calculated the strength of Earth's gravitation at the distance of the moon. Using his assumption, he calculated what the strength of that gravitation would be at Earth's surface.

NEWTON'S LAW OF GRAVITATION

Newton's law of gravitation says that the gravitational force between two objects is directly proportional to their masses. The larger either mass is, the larger is the force between the two objects.

Einstein's Theory

In 1915, the German-born physicist Albert Einstein announced his general theory of relativity, his theory of space, time, and gravitation. By expanding on Newton's law, it completely changed scientists' way of thinking about gravitation. (See pages 852–853.)

Einstein based his theory on two assumptions: space-time and the principle of equivalence.

Space-time. In the complex mathematics of relativity, time and space are not absolutely separate. Instead, physicists refer to space-time, a combination of time and the three dimensions of space—length, width, and height. Einstein assumed that matter and energy can change the shape of space-time, curving it. Gravitation is an effect of the curvature.

The principle of equivalence states that the effects of gravity are equivalent to the effects of acceleration. To understand this principle, suppose you were in a rocket ship so far from any planet, star, or other celestial object that the ship experienced virtually no gravitation. Imagine that the ship is traveling at a constant speed in a constant direction. If you held out a ball and released it, the ball would not fall. Instead, it would hover beside you.

BLACK HOLES

Einstein's theory predicts the existence of objects called black holes. A black hole is a region of space with a gravitational force that is so strong that not even light can escape from it. Researchers have found strong evidence that most very massive stars eventually evolve into black holes, and that most large galaxies have a gigantic black hole at their centers.

Torque

Torque

Torque is the amount of twisting effort that a force or forces exert on an object.

Motion. A body at rest or in uniform motion is in equilibrium. A body remains in equilibrium as long as all forces acting on the body pass through a common point and the sum of their vectors is zero. When the forces do not pass through a common point, the rotation and the linear motion will be changed. Torque is the force that produces rotation.

Equilibrium. When the vector sum of the forces acting on a body is zero, the body will not move in a linear manner, but rotation is still possible. Equilibrium is not assured unless a second condition is satisfied. That condition requires that the sum of the torques generated by the applied forces also be zero.

Calculation. The torque around any axis (or fulcrum) is calculated by multiplying the force by the distance between the line of force and the axis. The torque increases as the force moves farther from the axis. For this reason, a wheel turns more easily when the force is applied farther from the center.

The torque, L, about a selected axis is a product of the force, F, and the moment arm, s.

$$L = Fs$$

- The moment arm is the perpendicular distance from a selected axis to the line of the applied force.

- When combined into the single quantity torque, the magnitude of the force and the length of the moment arm are of equal importance.

- For a given moment arm, increasing the force increases the torque.

When two tugboats exert torque on a ship, it rotates.

Center of Gravity

Center of gravity is the point at which the entire weight of a body is concentrated. If an object is suspended from any point on the vertical line passing through its center of gravity, the object will remain stationary. But if the center of gravity is to one side of a point around which the object can pivot, the object will turn in that direction.

Stability. The location of the center of gravity can be important for stability. For example, a car with a center of gravity close to the road will not tip over as easily as a double-decker bus, which has a center of gravity that is much higher.

An object pivoted so that it is not balanced will turn until its center of gravity is at stable equilibrium (the lowest position possible). If the object is balanced with its center of gravity directly above the pivot, the slightest turn will cause the object to become unstable. An object balanced in this way is said to be in a position of unstable equilibrium.

Motion

- The force of gravity acts on all points in an object where there is mass (material), not simply at the center of gravity.

- When an object moves, the center of gravity moves as if all the mass of the object were concentrated there.

- The motion of an object moving under the force of gravity is described as the sum of the motion of the object's center of gravity and the object's rotation around its center of gravity.

- An object's center of mass is located at the same point as the object's center of gravity.

- The center of mass is used to calculate the motion of objects due to all kinds of forces, not only gravitational forces.

The center of gravity of a child's seesaw is at the center of the board when no one sits on it. If the seesaw is pivoted at its center, it will remain balanced.

When two people of different weights get on opposite ends of the seesaw, the force of gravity will be greater on one end. The center of gravity will then be between the center of the board and the end where the greater force is acting—that is, where the heavier person is.

If the heavier person moves toward the center of the seesaw, the center of gravity also moves toward the center of the board and it will again balance.

Work

Work, in physics, is a result of a force moving an object through a distance against a resistance.

Two factors determine the amount of work done.

- the amount of force applied
- the distance the object moves

When Is It Work?

Work occurs only when the force is sufficient to move the object. (See pages 764–765.) If the object does not move, no work is done. In other words, work is a measure of what is done, not the effort applied in attempting to move the object.

For example:

- A truck does not perform work when it holds a load of bricks.
- A truck does perform work when it moves the same load up a hill.
- People do work when lifting, pushing, or sliding an object from one place to another.
- They do no work when holding an object without moving it, even though they may become tired.

Work is done when an object moves in response to force.

Work is NOT done when an object doesn't move, even if force is applied.

Formulas

There are mathematical formulas for calculating work and power.

Work. The formula for work is

$$W = Fs$$

where W stands for work, F stands for force, and s stands for distance. Work is measured in foot-pounds and joules.

Power. The formula for power is

$$P = \frac{W}{t}$$

where P stands for power, W for work, and t for time. Power is measured in watts and horsepower.

MECHANICAL ADVANTAGE

Mechanical advantage is defined as the ratio of the force exerted by a machine to the force applied to the machine.

GEAR

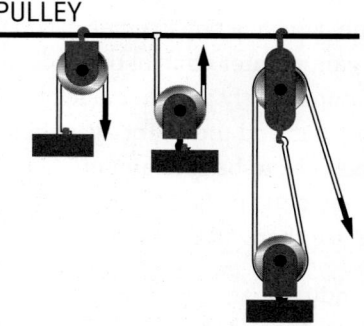

PULLEY

LEVER   fulcrum

With a lever, the mechanical advantage is the ratio between the lengths of the lever on either side of the fulcrum.

With gears, it is determined by the proportion of the teeth on each gear.

With pulleys, it is equal to the number of pulleys.

Power

Power is the rate at which work can be done. It's determined by dividing the amount of work involved by the time required to complete the work.

A task requires the same amount of work or energy whether it is done quickly or slowly. But the faster the task is done, the greater the power required. For example, to push a load of bricks 10 feet in 10 seconds takes twice as much power as does pushing the same load the same distance in 20 seconds.

POWER

The power needed to pull a wagon depends on its weight, and how far and how fast it is pulled.

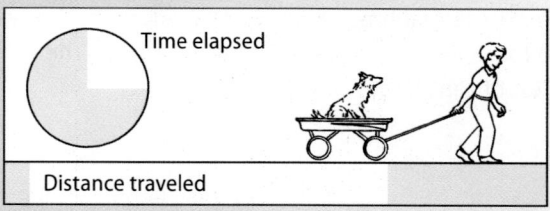

A boy uses a certain amount of power to pull a dog in a wagon over a given distance in a set time.

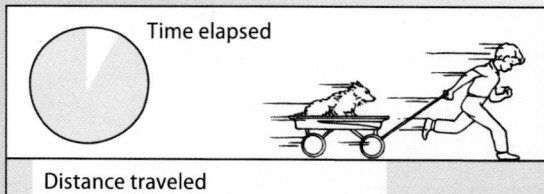

He must use twice as much power to pull the dog and wagon over the distance in half the time.

Machines

Machines are devices that we use to do work. Over time, we have constructed a wide variety of machines to gain greater control over our surroundings. For example, early people made stone axes that served as weapons and tools. Today, engineers design complex machines to be safe and efficient.

Since the purpose of machines is to make life easier, we use them all the time.

- Industries use drill presses, lathes, and grinding machines to make products.
- Businesses depend on computers, copy machines, and fax machines.
- People use automobiles, buses, and airplanes to travel swiftly over great distances.
- Farmers and other vendors use trucks, railroads, and ships to haul goods to and from markets.

Types of Simple Machines

There are six types of simple machines: levers, pulleys, wheels and axles, inclined planes, wedges, and screws. These machines help us do work by multiplying the force we put into them or by changing the direction of that force.

Levers. A lever consists of a bar that is supported at one position while a force is applied at another position. The place where the lever is supported is the fulcrum.

There are three basic types of levers, depending on where the effort is applied, the position of the load, and the position of the fulcrum.

- **First-class levers** have the fulcrum placed between the load and the effort, as in seesaws, crowbars, and balance scales.
- **Second-class levers** have the load between the effort and the fulcrum, as in wheelbarrows.
- **Third-class levers** have the effort placed between the load and the fulcrum, as in tweezers.

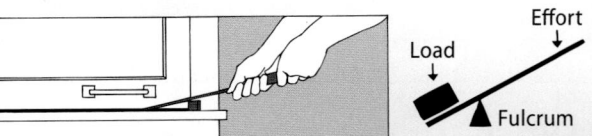

The lever is one of the earliest and simplest machines. Its advantage lies in the short distance between the fulcrum (pivotal point) and load, and in the long distance between the fulcrum and the point where effort is applied.

Wheels and Axles. The wheel and axle is a machine made of a large wheel attached to a smaller wheel (the axle) so that both wheels turn together. It is essentially a modified lever. It can move a load farther than a lever can, but the effort must move through a greater distance.

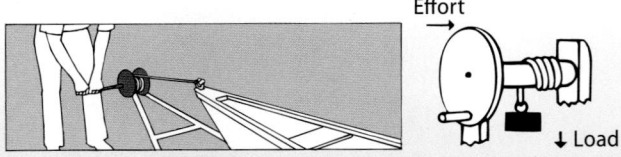

The wheel and axle has a rope attached to the axle to lift the load. The crank handle is the point where effort is applied. The effort is smaller than the load because it is at a greater distance from the axle, which is the fulcrum.

Pulleys. A pulley is a wheel over which a rope or belt is passed. It is a form of the wheel and axle. The simplest pulley is one that is fixed. This machine does not increase the force applied, but does allow a change in the direction of the force.

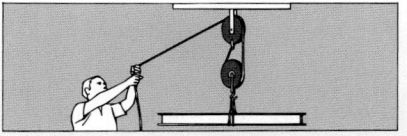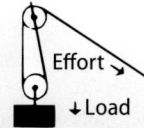

The pulley consists of a wheel with a grooved rim over which a rope is passed. It is used to change the direction of the effort applied to the rope. A block and tackle uses two or more pulleys to reduce the amount of effort needed to lift a load.

Inclined Planes. An inclined plane is a structure used to raise heavy loads with relatively small forces. For example, pushing a load up a ramp onto a platform requires less force than lifting the load onto the platform. In return, however, the load must be pushed farther.

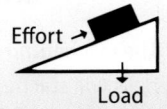

The inclined plane makes it easier to slide or skip a load upward than to lift it directly. The longer the slope, the smaller the effort required. The amount of work, however, is no less than if the load were lifted directly upward.

Wedges. The wedge is an adaptation of the inclined plane. The effectiveness of the wedge depends on the angle of the thin end. The smaller the angle, the less the force required to raise a given load.

- Wedges are used to raise loads like furniture and appliances over a short distance.
- A small wedge can be used to split a large log.
- Thin wedges called shims are used by carpenters to fasten wood pieces together.

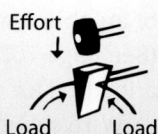

The wedge, when struck with a mallet or sledge, exerts a large force on its sides. A thin wedge is more effective than a thick one. The mechanical advantage of the wedge is of great importance.

Screws. A screw is an inclined plane wrapped around a post. The ridges of the screw are called the threads. The distance between threads is the pitch. The smaller the pitch of a screw, the more times it must be turned to fasten it in place. The number of turns equals the effort distance.

Screws have many practical applications, especially as fasteners. They also open and close vises, produce motion, and perform important operations in delicate and complex machinery.

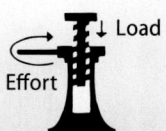

The screw is a spiral inclined plane. The jackscrew is a combination of the lever and the screw. It can lift a heavy load with relatively small effort. Therefore, it has a high mechanical advantage for practical purposes.

Momentum

Momentum is a measure of the motion of an object. The momentum of a moving object equals its mass (quantity of matter) multiplied by its velocity (speed in a given direction).

Momentum = mass × velcoity

or

$$P = mv$$

Newton's laws include the law of conservation of momentum. According to this law, the momentum of an object will change only if a net force acts on it. (See page 762.) A net force is a force that is not balanced by an opposing force.

With this basic fact in mind, the behavior of everyday objects can be studied and analyzed. When an internal force is applied to a system of bodies, the momentum of the system is altered, but some other set of bodies will gain or lose momentum equal to the loss or gain produced in the first system. This conservation of momentum can be expressed simply as momentum lost equals momentum gained.

MOMENTUM AT WORK

The law of conservation of momentum also applies to systems of objects. Consider a system made up of two equally massive bumper cars. Suppose each car is going 10 miles per hour, and the cars are moving directly toward each other. The two cars will have the same amount of momentum. However, the momentum of one will point in the direction opposite that of the other. The total momentum of the two cars will therefore be zero.

Suppose the cars collide head-on and bounce off each other at 9 miles per hour. The collision will change both cars' momentum. But, because no force from outside the system has acted on the cars, their total momentum remains zero.

MOMENTUM

The conservation of momentum can be demonstrated with pool balls.

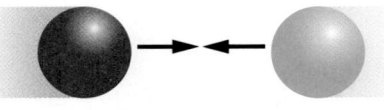

1. Two balls with equal velocity but traveling in opposite directions have a total momentum of zero.

2. After the head-on collision, the total momentum remains zero.

3. The momentum remains zero because the two pool balls will still be traveling in opposite directions with the same speed. If the two balls initially have different velocities, the total momentum is not zero. The total momentum will again be preserved after the collision. The slower ball will rebound with the speed the faster ball had before the collision, and vice versa. In other words, the balls exchange velocities.

Impulse

Impulse is equal to the change in momentum produced by the force. It is calculated by multiplying the average value of a force by the time during which that force acts.

Impulse and momentum are related concepts. Impulse may be defined in terms of momentum. Impulse is the average value of a force times the time during which it acts, and this product is equal to the change in momentum produced by force. While that might sound complex, impulse can be shown to be derived from the second law of motion.

Formulas. Newton originally stated his second law in terms of three factors: force, time, and momentum.

$$F = \frac{mv - mv_0}{t}$$

F is the force, *m* is the mass, *v* is the final velocity, v_0 is the starting velocity, mv and mv_0 are the terminal and initial momentums, and t is time.

This equation can be changed to its more familiar form by factoring out mass.

$$F = \frac{m(v - v_0)}{t}$$

Since

$$\frac{v - v_0}{t} = a$$

then

$$F = ma$$

By multiplying the above equation by *t*, it becomes

$$Ft = mv - mv_0$$

This is called the impulse equation. *Ft* is the impulse, and $mv - mv_0$ is the change in momentum.

Example. As an illustration of impulse, consider a hammer of mass *m* accelerating at a rate *a* to a velocity *v* and striking a nail with a force *F*.

- This force, which lasts for a fraction of a second, drives the nail into the wood by impulse.

- The hammer has supplied an impulse equal to its loss of momentum.

A hammer supplies an impulse equal to its loss of momentum.

fyi! *In the SI system, the unit of impulse is the newton-second. In the cgs system, the unit of impulse is the dynesecond. In the fps system, it is the pound-second.*

Density

Density is the amount of matter in a particular volume of a substance. Density has many uses in science and engineering. Earth scientists can identify minerals and other solids by measuring their density. Chemists can measure the density of a solution to determine the concentration of a particular substance.

Our everyday experience of density is closely related to weight. For two objects with the same volume or bulk, the denser object will be heavier.

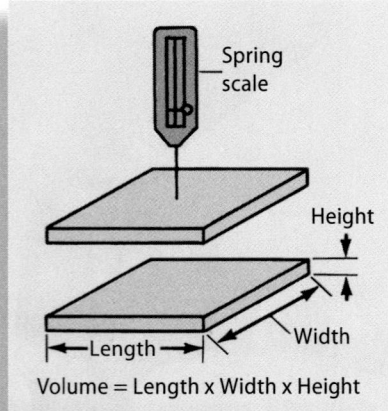

Volume = Length x Width x Height

To find the density of a regularly shaped object, measure its mass and use a formula to determine its volume. For example, to obtain the volume of a rectangular solid, multiply the length by the width by the height.

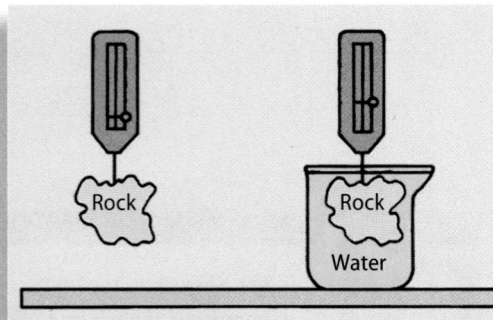

To find the density of an irregular object, measure its mass in air and then in water, subtract the second measurement from the first, and divide by the density of water.

Measurement

The density of a substance that is uniform (identical throughout) equals the substance's mass or weight divided by its volume.

$$p = \frac{m}{V}$$

Mass or weight can be measured on a scale or balance. The volume of a regularly shaped solid can be calculated by measuring its dimensions and applying a mathematical formula. It is harder to determine the volume of an irregularly shaped solid.

Specific Gravity

Specific gravity is a measure that compares a substance's density to that of water. It equals the density of the substance divided by the density of water.

Type of Matter	Substance	Specific Gravity
Solid	aluminum	2.7
	iron and steel	7.8
	copper	19.3
	gold	19.3
	concrete	2.3
	glass	2.6
	ice	0.917
Liquid	water (4°C)	1.0
	blood, plasma	1.03
	mercury	13.6
	alcohol, ethyl	0.79
	gasoline	0.68
Gas	air	1.29×10^{-3}
	helium	0.179×10^{-3}
	water (steam) (100°C)	0.598×10^{-3}

Pressure

Density varies with temperature and pressure. *Pressure* is often defined as force per unit area. In physics, the term is usually applied to gases and liquids. If a fluid is exposed to suitable forces, pressure is produced in it. The greater the force, the greater the pressure.

Measurement. Pressure is measured in pounds per square inch in the inch-pound system customarily used in the United States. In the metric system, the standard unit of pressure is the pascal; the nonstandard unit kilogram per square centimeter is also used.

Pressure is exerted whenever force is applied over an area. The smaller the area, the greater the pressure. For example, even a lightweight child can exert high pressure by applying his or her weight over a small area, like the heel of a shoe.

Fluids. If a fluid is at rest, pressure transmits equally to all its parts. At any one point, pressure is the same in all directions. This phenomenon is described by Pascal's law.

Fluids include both liquids and gases. The molecules in liquids are relatively close together; in gases, they are far apart.

Gases have a special ability to compress when pressure increases. The volume of liquids and solids also decreases when pressure increases, but by much smaller amounts than gases. Under ordinary conditions, the volume of a gas decreases by half when the pressure doubles. The law that describes how the volume of a gas changes when the pressure changes is called Boyle's law.

The ability of a gas to compress and expand has many practical uses. For example, air tires, air cushions, and air brakes are possible because of pressure.

Atmospheric pressure is produced by the weight of the air from the top of the atmosphere as it presses down upon the layers of air below it. At sea level, the average atmospheric pressure is 14.7 pounds per square inch (101.3 kilopascals). This decreases with altitude because of less air pressing from above.

PRESSURE AND ALTITUDE

Pressure changes the boiling point of water. The boiling point is that temperature at which the pressure of the steam is equal to the atmospheric pressure. At sea level, the two pressures are equal at 212°F (100°C). As height increases, the pressure decreases, and the boiling point becomes lower. This makes cooking at high altitudes difficult, because the cooking of food depends upon the temperature to which the food is heated, not on whether the surrounding water is boiling.

 *Wind is the movement of air from a point of high pressure to a point of low pressure. Pressure changes precede storms. Barometers detect storms by measuring such changes.*

MATTER is the substance of which all objects are made. Since ancient times, matter has been known to exist in three states: solids, liquids, and gases. The state of each body of matter is classified according to the power of its molecules to resist forces that may change its shape.

Solids

- Shape is fixed.
- Molecules cannot move freely.
- Difficult to compress
- Two types: amorphous and crystalline

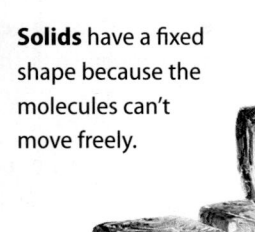

Solids have a fixed shape because the molecules can't move freely.

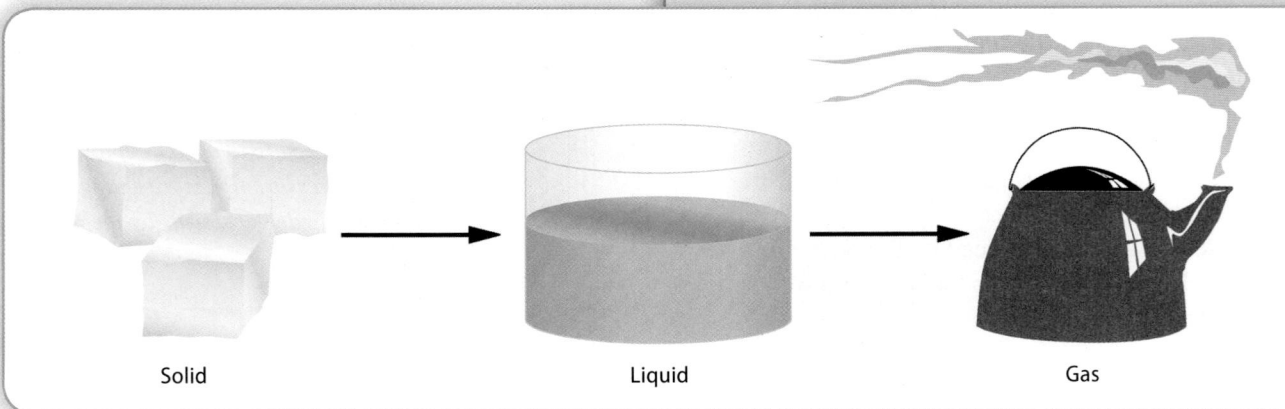

Solid   Liquid   Gas

Liquids

- Assume the shapes of their containers
- No definite shape
- Molecules move freely, but don't separate
- Difficult to compress
- Have surface tension and viscosity

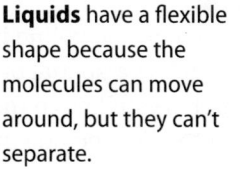

Liquids have a flexible shape because the molecules can move around, but they can't separate.

Gases

- Expand to fill their containers
- No definite shape
- Molecules that move freely and separately
- Easy to compress
- Particles move faster with heat

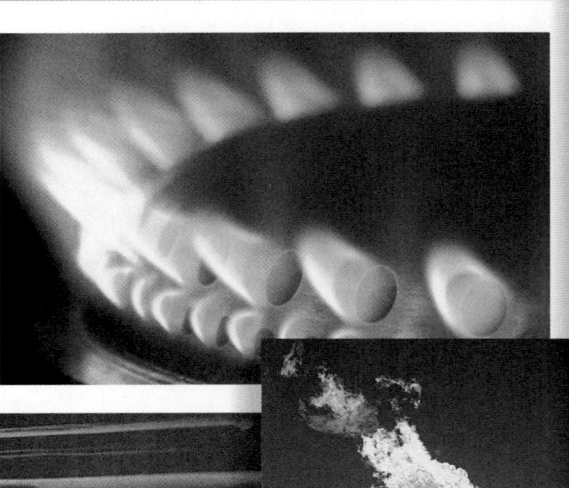

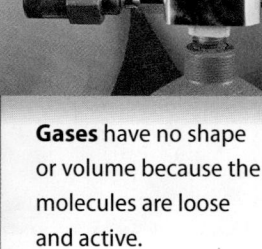

Gases have no shape or volume because the molecules are loose and active.

Solids

Matter is solid when it retains its shape and offers resistance to forces that try to deform it. A solid has a fixed shape and a fixed volume because its molecules cannot move freely. (See also pages 350–351.)

Solids can be divided into two groups:

- amorphous structures such as glass or asphalt.
- crystalline structures such as table salt or ice.

Amorphous Solids

Numerous solids are not crystalline in structure. Wood, for example, exhibits a spatial organization of its atoms, but it's not crystalline in the sense that metals are. Amorphous solids include glass and asphalt.

Properties. Amorphous solids are *isotropic*, which means their properties are the same in all directions.

- The atoms are not ordered.
- Glassy solids do not melt at defined temperatures.
- They gradually soften and become more fluid as the temperature rises.

In amorphous solids, the atoms are not ordered. They are usually glassy.

FRATERNAL TWINS: CARBON TWO WAYS

There are times when two or more crystalline substances occur for an element. For example, diamond and graphite have different crystal forms even though they are both pure carbon.

In the diamond, each carbon atom is surrounded by four other carbon atoms at the corners of a regular tetrahedron.

In graphite, the carbon atoms lie in planes or flat sheets, and each atom is attached to three others in this plane to form a series of hexagons. The flat sheets of atoms are relatively easy to separate or move over one another.

As a result of their respective structures, graphite acts as a lubricant, while diamond is the hardest naturally occurring substance.

Diamond

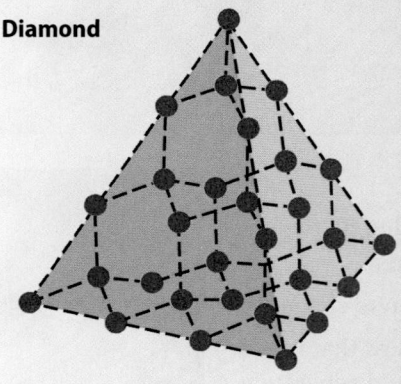

Graphite

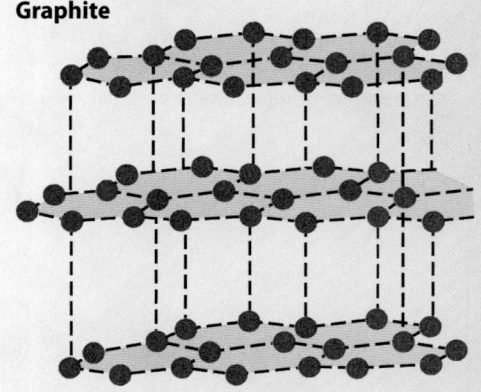

Crystalline Solids

Crystals are composed of atoms arranged in an orderly pattern. Most nonliving substances are made of crystals, including:

- metals
- rocks
- snowflakes
- sugar

Metals in the solid state are usually composed of many tiny crystals that interlock. A three-dimensional pattern of some type, called a unit cell, repeats itself regularly in all crystals. Different arrangements are found in different crystals.

Properties. Many crystalline solids are *anisotropic*, which means that their properties aren't the same in all directions.

- Heat conductivity and optical properties, such as the speed of light as it passes through, vary with the direction in which these properties are measured.
- Crystalline solids melt at clearly defined temperatures.
- Like amorphous solids, crystalline solids resist changes of shape and volume.

1. Table salt has a cubic structure. Ions in a unit are all placed at the corners of a cube.

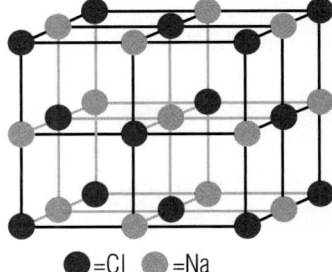

=Cl =Na

2. In quartz (silicon dioxide), the atoms are placed on hexagons. Such crystals have a hexagonal structure. The photo shows large quartz crystals that have been grown artificially. Crystals of such size rarely occur in nature.

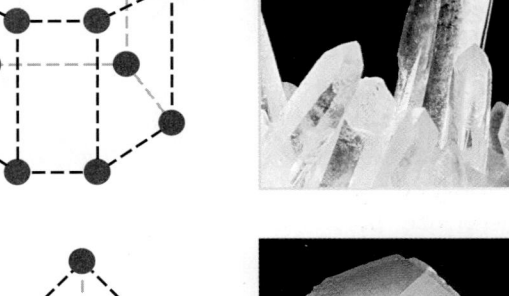

3. The atoms of calcite (calcium carbonate) are placed on the corners of a cube that has been stretched along a diagonal. The crystal is said to have a trigonal structure.

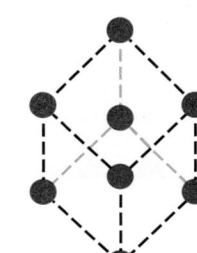

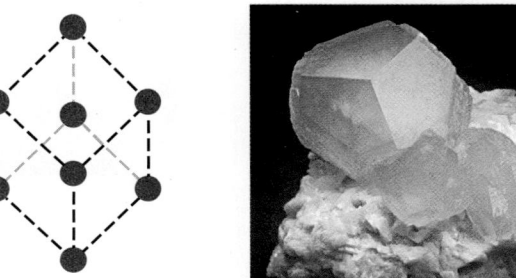

Crystals. The shape of crystals reflects the arrangement of atoms in the crystal lattice.

Liquids and Gases

Liquids and gases, the second and third types of matter, are both called fluids because they can flow to fit the shape of any container in which they are placed.

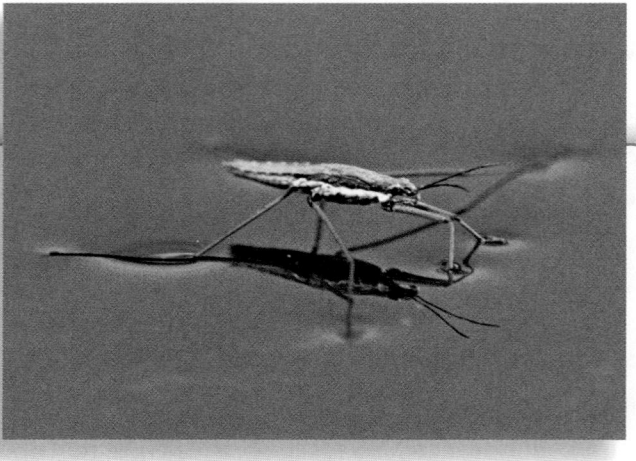

Molecular forces at the surface of water enable this water strider to walk on it.

Liquids

Liquids have molecules that move freely among themselves without separating. (See pages 352–353.) Liquids also

- flow freely.
- resist compression.
- change into a solid when cooled below a certain point.
- change into a gas when heated above a certain point.

Surface tension is the property that causes the surface of a liquid to behave as if it were covered by an elastic membrane under tension. The membrane is like a thin layer of skin.

Surface tension occurs because molecules near the boundary of a liquid experience different forces than the molecules near the interior. Deep inside the liquid, each molecule is attracted to other liquid molecules all around it. But molecules near the boundary also interact with molecules in the neighboring material.

Viscosity is the measure of the resistance of a fluid (liquid or gas) to flow. Fluids with high viscosity, such as molasses, flow more slowly than those with low viscosity, such as water. Changes in temperature affect the viscosity of liquids and gases.

When a liquid is heated, its molecules move apart, which decreases its viscosity. Heating a gas makes its molecules move more rapidly and collide more often, which increases its viscosity.

CAPILLARY ACTION

Capillary action is a phenomenon related to surface tension. The molecules of a liquid often have a greater attraction for other substances than they have for each other. For this reason, they will rise in narrow tubes above their own level.

Capillary action can be observed as the curvature of the surface of a liquid in a container or tube. For example, when water is contained in a glass tube, the attraction forces between the water molecules and the glass molecules (adhesion) will be greater than the forces between the water molecules themselves (cohesion). The surface of the water will bend in such a way to remain perpendicular to the resultant force.

If mercury were introduced to the glass tube, the cohesive forces would be greater than the adhesive forces. Therefore, the surface of the mercury curves upward.

Water is said to "wet" the surface of the glass.

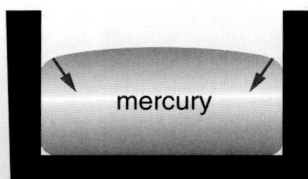

Mercury does not "wet" the surface of the glass.

Gases

A gas is a fluid that doesn't have shape or volume. (See pages 354–355.) Its molecules move freely and are not in contact with one another.

Gases are characterized by their sensitivity to changes in temperature and pressure.

Behavior. The behavior of gases is explained by what scientists call the kinetic theory. The kinetic theory states that

- All matter is made of constantly moving particles.
- The number of particles in a container the size of a pinhead is many millions of times as large as the number of people on Earth.
- Gas particles are so small that they occupy only a tiny amount of the space inside the container.
- The remaining space between the particles is empty.

Speed. Gas particles fly around in all directions at about the speed of sound. Their exact speed is determined by their weight and by the temperature of the gas. Gas particles move faster when the gas is hot than when it is cold. But light particles move faster than heavy ones at all temperatures. Each moving gas particle crashes into billions of other particles each second. Gas particles crashing into the walls of their container produce an effect called pressure.

Under special conditions, gases change into a fourth state of matter called a plasma. *Plasmas are formed by heating a gas to an extremely high temperature or by passing an electric current through it. Matter exists in a plasma state in stars and the regions between stars.*

Pressure. The idea that gas particles collide with the walls of a container was first expressed by Daniel Bernoulli in 1738.

- During each collision of a particle with the wall, the particle transfers momentum to the wall and exerts a tiny force.
- Because the number of particles bouncing off the wall is very large, the effect is that of a continuous force on the wall.
- This force per unit surface is defined as the gas pressure.

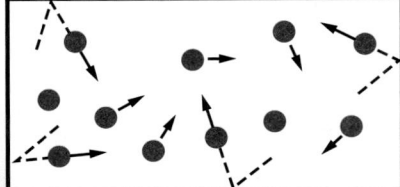

Low Temperature. The molecules move slowly, transferring only a small amount of momentum to the sides of the box. This results in less pressure.

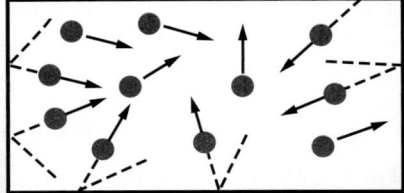

High Temperature. The molecules move faster, transferring more momentum to the sides of the box. This results in more pressure.

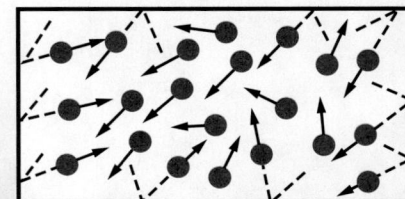

More Molecules. When more molecules hit the sides of the box, momentum and pressure increase.

HEAT is a form of energy. According to particle theory, all matter is made of particles that are always moving. Heat and energy are invisible, but you can see the work they do. For example, the burning of fuel in the engines of a jet creates hot gases. These gases expand and provide the power that moves the plane. (See also pages 378–379.)

Heat Energy

Heat is one of the most important forms of energy. We must have a carefully controlled amount of heat to live. If our body temperature rises too far above normal—or falls too far below normal—we can die.

No one knows how high temperatures may climb. The temperature inside the hottest stars is many millions of degrees. The lowest possible temperature, called absolute zero, is −459.67°F (−273.15°C).

Uses

Home. In our homes, we use heat in many ways.

- Heat cooks our food.
- It provides hot water.
- It warms chilly rooms.
- Heat dries the laundry.

Outdoors. Heat also runs our machinery.

- The heat from burning fuels in engines provides the power to move airplanes and automobiles.
- Heat causes the wheels of giant turbines to spin, driving generators that produce electric power.
- It also furnishes power to run all kinds of equipment—from electric pencil sharpeners to electric trains.

Industry. In industry, the uses for heat are almost endless.

- Heat is used to separate metals from their ores.
- Heat refines crude oil.
- It is used to melt, shape, and harden metals.
- Heat is also used to make or process foods, glass, and many other products.

Commercial kitchens use high-intensity burners to generate enough heat for such techniques as sautéing and searing.

HOW DO WE KNOW THAT?

The idea that heat is a form of energy was proven during the mid-1800s. The proof was developed largely by three men. They were Julius Robert von Mayer, a German physician and physicist; Hermann von Helmholtz, a German physicist; and James Prescott Joule, a British physicist.

- Mayer observed that people in warm and cold climates needed different amounts of food energy to maintain their normal body temperature. He presented his findings in 1842. But his ideas did not receive scientific recognition for many years.

- In 1847, Helmholtz completed a work on heat and energy. He stated that heat is a form of energy. The idea won rapid acceptance.

- In the 1840s, Joule measured the amount of mechanical energy needed to raise the temperature of a certain quantity of water. The relationship between mechanical energy and heat energy is called the mechanical equivalent of heat.

GOT TO KNOW

INSULATION

- **Insulation** is a way to control the movement of heat by keeping it in or out of a place.

- Certain materials, such as plastic and wood, make good **insulators** against the movement of heat by conduction.

- The movement of heat through the air by convection can be controlled by **blocking the space** between a hot and cold area with "dead air."

- Surfaces that reflect infrared rays can insulate heat traveling by **radiation**.

THE CALORIC THEORY OF HEAT

For a long time, people believed that heat was caused by an invisible fluid called *caloric*. This fluid was believed to have the power to act upon various materials in four ways.

- penetrate
- expand
- solidify
- dissolve

It was also thought to have the power of converting the materials from solid to liquid or from liquid to vapor. Caloric theory envisioned heat as flowing into a body when the body was heated and out of a body when it was cooled.

Although the caloric theory was accepted by many scientists, certain observations could not be explained by an invisible, weightless, all-pervading fluid. For instance, the generation of heat by friction when two mechanical objects rubbed against one another was attributed to a loss of caloric. (People thought the fluid was ground or squeezed out of the objects.) But many scientists of the late 18th century found this explanation inadequate.

In experiments conducted in a Bavarian arsenal, Benjamin Rumford demonstrated the inadequacy of this explanation and in so doing initiated the downfall of the caloric theory. Rumford had observed that when cannons were bored, a large temperature rise accompanied the boring. In his experiments, Rumford measured the heat generated by the boring process. He also attempted to measure the weight of the caloric fluid picked up by the hot cannon. Finding none, he concluded that the heat was some form of atomic motion.

Heat Sources

Anything that gives off heat is a source of heat. There are six main sources: the sun, Earth, electric power, chemical reactions, friction, and nuclear energy.

We control some of these sources. Others we do not. We use the sources we control, such as electric power and nuclear energy, to heat buildings and to do other work. But the sources we do not control also benefit us. For example, the sun provides the heat and light that make life possible.

The Sun

The sun is our most important source of heat. If the sun were to cool, Earth would become cold and lifeless. Only a tiny fraction of the heat produced in the sun strikes Earth. Yet it is enough to keep us—and all other organisms on Earth—alive.

The sun's heat is absorbed by the seas, the ground, plants, and the atmosphere. Heat can be collected by such devices as solar furnaces. These furnaces have mirrors that reflect the sun's light from a wide area onto one spot. Some solar furnaces can generate enough heat to melt steel. Smaller ones can gather enough heat to cook food.

UNITS OF HEAT

The three units most commonly used to measure heat are British thermal units (Btu), calories, and joules. Which unit is used usually depends on the context.

- One *Btu* is the quantity of heat needed to raise the temperature of 1 pound of water 1°F. The Btu is generally used in engineering.

- One *calorie* is the quantity of heat needed to raise the temperature of 1 gram of water 1°C. The calorie used to measure food energy is 1,000 times as large as this calorie. The calorie is used in the sciences.

- The *joule* can be used for measuring all forms of energy, including heat. One joule is the amount of energy used—or work done—when a force of 1 newton moves an object 1 meter in the direction of the force.

Much heat is contained deep inside Earth. Some of this heat escapes to the surface when a volcano erupts.

Earth

Earth itself contains much heat deep inside. When a volcano erupts, some of this heat escapes to the surface. The lava from a volcano is rock melted by the heat deep within Earth. Some of Earth's heat also escapes in geysers. These springs shoot forth boiling water that has been heated by hot rocks within Earth. People use Earth's heat to generate electric power and heat houses.

Electric Power

The flow of electric current through metals, alloys, and other conductors (substances that carry electric current) generates heat. People make use of this heat in the operation of many appliances. These appliances include electric furnaces, ovens, ranges, dryers, heaters, toasters, and irons.

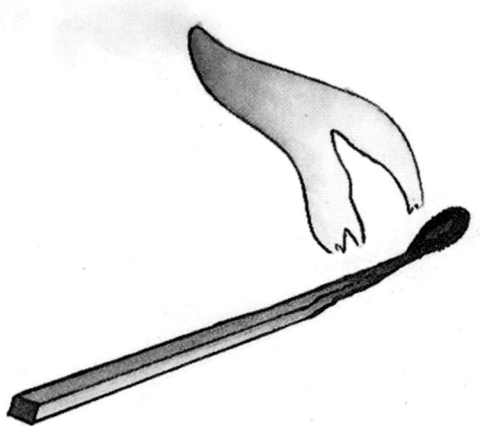

Chemical reactions produce heat by causing a chemical change in a substance. Fire is a chemical reaction in which oxygen rapidly combines with a substance, such as the wood of a match.

Chemical Reactions

Chemical reactions can produce heat in a number of ways. A chemical reaction in which a substance combines with oxygen is called *oxidation*. Rapid oxidation produces heat fast enough to cause a flame. When coal, wood, or any other fuel burns, substances in the fuel combine with oxygen in the air to form other compounds. This chemical reaction, known as combustion, produces heat—and fire.

The rusting of iron is also an example of oxidation. Unlike fire, however, rusting occurs so slowly that little heat and no flames are produced.

The mixing of certain kinds of chemicals also produces heat. For example, if sulfuric acid and water are combined, the mixture becomes boiling hot.

In all living things, food is changed into heat—as well as energy and living tissue—by the process of metabolism. *Metabolism* is a complicated series of chemical reactions carried out by living cells. (See pages 188–189.)

Friction—the rubbing of one object against another—produces heat. Scouts learn to start a fire with friction.

Friction

When one object rubs against another, heat is produced. Friction is usually an unwanted source of heat because it may damage objects. In a machine, for example, the heat created as the moving parts rub against one another may cause those parts to wear down. For this reason, oil is used between moving machinery parts. The oil reduces friction and so decreases the generation of heat.

Nuclear Energy

Nuclear energy can produce great quantities of heat. Nuclear weapons release so much heat so quickly that they destroy everything around them. Their heat cannot be put to useful work. But in a device called a *reactor*, heat can be produced from nuclear energy slowly enough to generate electric power. (See pages 404–407.)

Temperature

All things are made up of atoms or molecules, which are always moving. The motion gives every object internal energy.

Temperature is an indication of an object's internal energy level. It is important to recognize that heat and temperature are not the same thing. Temperature is an indication of the level of internal energy that an object has. Heat, on the other hand, is the passage of energy from one object to another.

Measurement

Temperature is expressed in degrees. The two most common scales are Fahrenheit and Celsius. The Kelvin scale and the Rankine scale are used to measure extreme temperatures that are very high or very low.

We use standards of references in temperature so readings from different scales can be compared. These reference points include

- the freezing point of water
- the boiling point of water
- the boiling and freezing points of certain other materials

ABSOLUTE ZERO

Absolute zero is the temperature at which substances would have no heat whatever, and all molecules would stop moving. Theoretically, it is the lowest temperature possible, 273.15 degrees Celsius or 459.67 degrees Fahrenheit.

Characteristics

- The level of an object's internal energy depends on how rapidly its atoms or molecules move. If they move slowly, the object has a low level of internal energy. If they move violently, it has a high level. Hot objects have higher internal energy levels than do cold objects.

- Heat passes only from an object at a higher temperature to an object at a lower one. The greater the difference in temperature between the two objects, the faster the heat will flow between them.

- The temperature of an object determines whether that object will gain or lose energy when it comes into contact with another object. When two bodies at different temperatures are brought together—such as when a hot steel bar is placed in a bowl of cool water—the hot body will begin to cool and the cool body will begin to warm. Soon both bodies will be at the same temperature.

- As the temperature of a substance changes, some of its chemical and physical properties also change. For example, substances may change in color, shape, or volume.

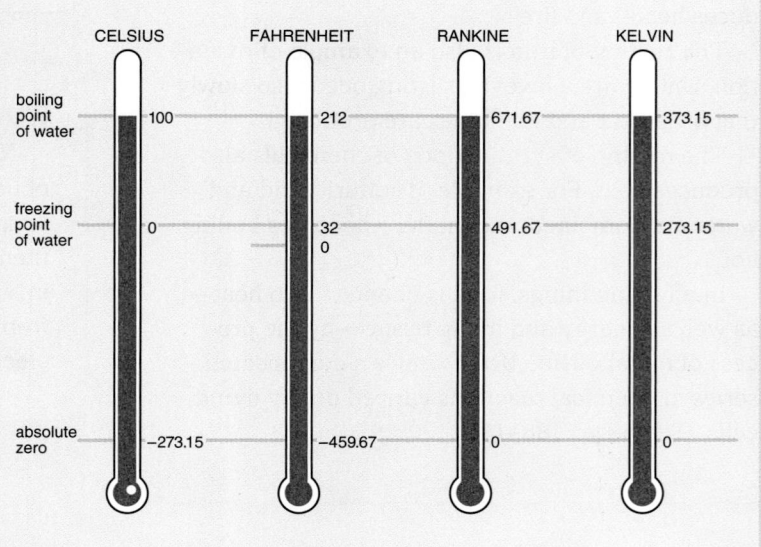

Melting and Boiling Points of Some Substances		
Substance	Melting Point (°C)	Boiling Point (°C)
Neon	−248	−246
Ethyl alcohol	−117.3	78.5
Chlorine	−101	−34.6
Water	0	100
Sodium	98	882.9
Sodium chloride	801	1,413
Silver	961.9	2,212
Copper	1,083	2,567
Iron	1,535	2,750

Thermometers

Thermometers are instruments that measure the temperature of gases, liquids, and solids. The five types of thermometers include thermal expansion, thermocouple, resistance, radiation, and liquid crystal.

Thermal expansion thermometers are the simplest and best-known type. They measure changes in the volume of a substance as its temperature changes. The most common types are liquid-in-glass thermometers, which are used for household tasks like cooking and measuring body temperature, and bimetallic and filled-system thermometers, which are used in manufacturing.

Thermocouple thermometers are often used in industry because they can measure a much greater range of temperatures than other thermometers can. They measure voltage between two wires of different metals using a voltmeter. The voltage can be converted to a temperature reading.

Resistance thermometers indicate temperature by measuring a material's electrical resistance—that is, its opposition to the flow of electric current. Temperature changes cause variations in the amount of a material's resistance. Generally, the greater the temperature change, the greater the change in resistance.

A bimetallic strip, consisting of two metals, can show temperature. As the temperature changes, the strip bends, indicating the temperature. This is an example of a thermal expansion thermometer.

Bimetallic thermometer

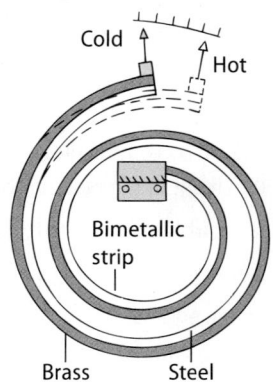

Cold
Hot
Bimetallic strip
Brass   Steel

HOW DOES THAT WORK **?**

LIQUID-IN-GLASS THERMOMETERS

1. When a thermometer is placed in hot water, it absorbs energy from the water.

2. The particles of the alcohol or mercury begin to move faster and move away from each other.

3. The mercury or alcohol expands up the tube, which is marked in increments of degrees.

Liquid-in-glass thermometer

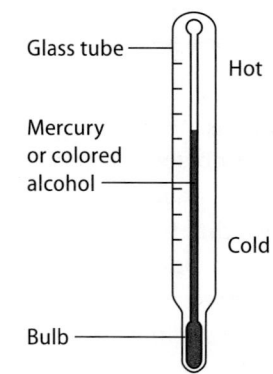

Glass tube
Hot
Mercury or colored alcohol
Cold
Bulb

A column of liquid shows the temperature in a liquid-in-glass thermometer. The liquid in most such thermometers is mercury or colored alcohol.

Radiation thermometers, also known as pyrometers, indicate temperature by detecting electromagnetic radiation (electric and magnetic energy). Every substance emits radiation in relation to its temperature. Radiation thermometers measure the radiation and convert the measurement to a temperature value.

Liquid crystal thermometers measure temperature by using liquid crystals, compounds that have properties of both liquids and solids. Some liquid crystals change color as the temperature changes. These color changes can be related to a temperature scale.

Thermodynamics

Thermodynamics is the study of how heat is produced, how it is transmitted from one place to another, how it changes matter, and how it is stored. It is based on three laws.

First Law

The first law of thermodynamics is the law of conservation of energy. It states that energy is never created or destroyed. (See page 381.)

Energy can change form. For example, internal energy can become mechanical motion. But the total quantity of energy in any system (group of things) remains the same.

Second Law

The second law of thermodynamics states that heat flows spontaneously from a hot object to a cool object, but never from a cool object to a hot object.

This law is important for engines that transform heat into mechanical work. They can produce only work if heat can flow from a hot reservoir to a cool reservoir, or heat sink. An automobile engine is a good example. It can work only when heat resulting from combustion is allowed to flow to a heat sink, the radiator.

Some of the heat from the radiator is used to warm the passenger compartment. Most of it is lost to the environment, so it can't be converted to mechanical work. No machine can convert heat energy completely into mechanical energy, because part of the heat energy is always lost.

Third Law

The third law of thermodynamics states that at absolute zero, the entropy of a system is zero. *Entropy* is a measure of the amount of disorder or randomness in a system.

While it is impossible for a substance to actually reach absolute zero, scientists have come extremely close.

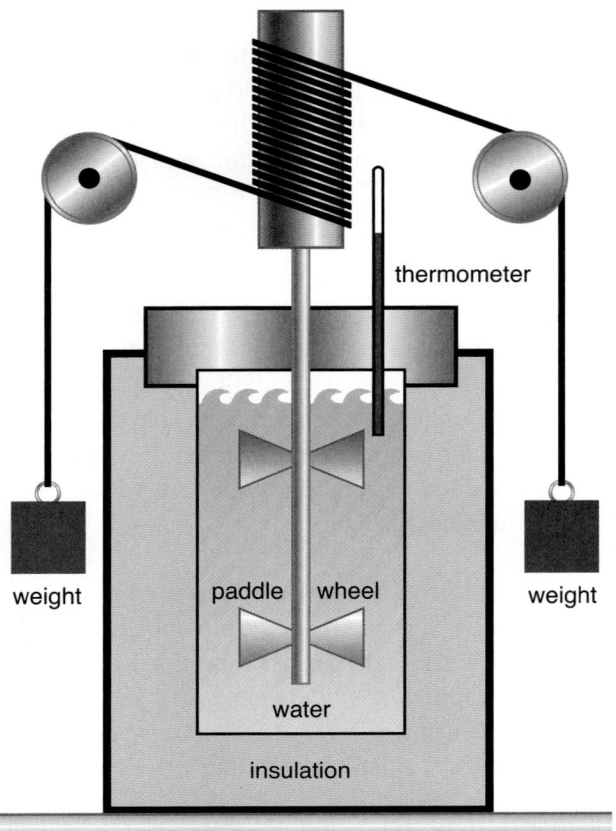

Joule's apparatus measures the amount of heat produced when the falling weights turn the paddles. It is named after the physicist who found that a fixed amount of mechanical work always produces a fixed amount of heat.

THERMAL EFFICIENCIES

The thermal efficiency of an engine relates the amount of heat that is converted to work to the amount that is released as waste heat. When an engine is said to be 40 percent efficient, it means that 40 percent of the heat created by combustion, for instance, has been used, and 60 percent of the heat has been wasted.

steam turbine	40%
diesel engine	38%
gasoline engine	25%
steam locomotive	8–12%

Laws of Thermodynamics in Action

Heat energy can be changed into other forms of energy. This diagram shows how heat is changed into electricity. Heat in a boiler creates steam that turns a turbine. The turbine drives an electric generator. A condenser changes the steam back to water, and the cycle is repeated.

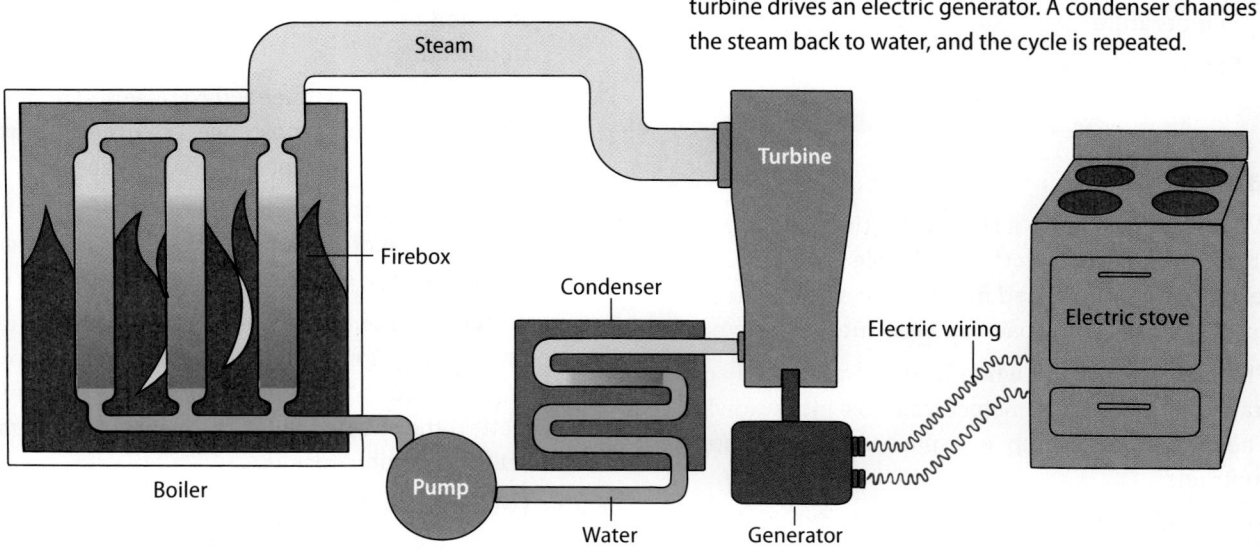

Changing Heat into Motion

Mechanical energy and heat energy are related. For example, mechanical energy is changed into heat by friction between the moving parts of a machine. Heat energy, in turn, can be changed into mechanical energy by heat engines.

There are two types of combustion engines: external and internal.

External-combustion engines produce hot gases that transfer heat energy to another fluid. The heat energy in this fluid, in turn, is changed into mechanical energy. For example, the heat from a steam turbine turns water into steam, which pushes the blades of a turbine.

Internal-combustion engines produce hot gases in which heat energy is changed directly into mechanical energy. An example is the gasoline engine in a car. Burning gasoline produces hot gases that expand and push down the pistons in the cylinders. The pistons move other parts of the car that turn the wheels.

Refrigeration

The temperature of an object can be lowered by bringing it into contact with a colder object. The temperature difference causes heat to flow from the warmer object into the colder one. For example, ice put in an insulated chest keeps food cold by removing heat from it.

A good way to remove heat from an object without using a colder object is mechanical refrigeration. It works by changing a substance called a refrigerant from a gas to a liquid back to a gas again.

In a refrigerator, for example, a compressor squeezes a gaseous refrigerant into a small space. The compression reduces the refrigerant's disorder so it becomes a liquid. The compressed liquid refrigerant then expands at a valve leading to pipes in the insulated part of the refrigerator. As the pressure falls, so does the temperature. The refrigerant absorbs heat from the foods in the refrigerator. As heat flows out of the foods, their temperatures fall. The warmed refrigerant becomes a gas and flows through pipes back to the compressor.

Heat Transfer

When heat passes into or out of a substance, it may change that substance in three ways.

- Size
- Temperature
- State

Changes in Size

- When heat flows into a substance, the motion of the atoms or molecules in the substance increases. As a result of their increased motion, the atoms or molecules take up more space and the substance expands.

- The opposite occurs when heat flows out of a substance. The atoms or molecules move more slowly. They therefore take up less space, and the substance contracts.

- All gases and most liquids and solids expand when heated. But they do not expand equally. If a gas, a liquid, and a solid receive enough heat to raise their temperatures the same amount, the gas will expand most. The liquid will expand much less. The solid will expand the least.

- Engineers can determine how much the length of any material will increase when its temperature rises.

Changes in Temperature

- Changes in temperature are one of the most common results when heat flows into or out of an object.

- The amount of heat needed to raise the temperature of 1 gram of a substance 1 degree Celsius is called the specific heat of the substance.

- Scientists use the specific heat of water, which is given a value of 1, as the standard for figuring the specific heat of all other substances.

- You can find out how much the temperature of a substance will rise when heat flows into it. To do so, you need to know how much mass (amount of matter) the substance has and what the specific heat of the substance is.

- Two substances with the same mass but different specific heats require different amounts of heat to reach the same temperature. The temperature of a substance with a low specific heat will increase more than that of a substance with a high specific heat if both substances receive the same amount of heat.

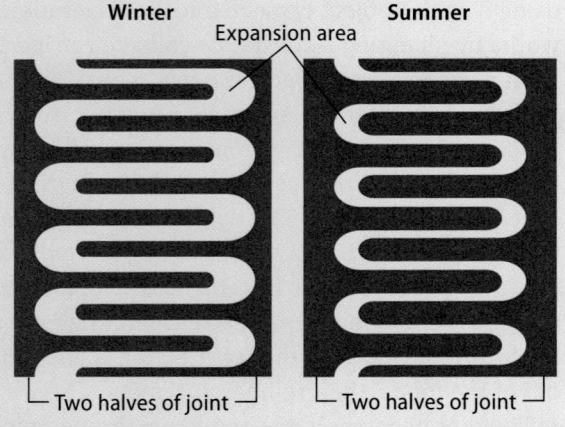

Winter **Summer**
Expansion area
Two halves of joint   Two halves of joint

EXPANSION JOINTS

Changes in temperature also cause the materials that are used in bridges, buildings, and other structures to expand and contract. This expansion and contraction can cause problems if the builders do not make allowances for it. For example, the steel beams used in a building will bend or break if they do not have room to expand.

An expansion joint allows the materials in bridges, buildings, and other structures to contract and expand without damaging the structure. The joint opens in winter, when the materials contract, and closes in summer, when they expand.

Changes in State

Ordinarily, the temperature of an object rises when heat flows into it. But under certain circumstances, the addition of heat causes no increase in an object's temperature. Instead, the disorder of the atoms or molecules in the object increases and causes the material to change state. For example:

- When heat is added to a block of ice that is colder than 0°C, the temperature of the ice will increase until it reaches 0°C, its melting point. Then the temperature will stop increasing for a time, even though more heat flows into the ice.

- The additional heat will increase the disorder of the molecules in the ice and cause the ice to melt. But until all the ice has melted, the water will remain at 0°C.

- As more heat flows into the water at 0°C, the temperature of the water will again rise until it reaches 100°C, its boiling point. Under normal atmospheric pressure, additional heat will not raise the temperature any further. Instead, some of the water will change into steam. All the water has to become steam in order for additional heat to cause the temperature to increase again.

Latent Heat. The heat needed to change a material from a solid to a liquid or from a liquid to a gas is called *latent heat*. It must be removed to change a gas back to a liquid or a liquid back to a solid.

Latent heat may also be associated with changes in the structure of the crystals that make up a solid substance. In general, much less latent heat is needed for such changes than for melting or vaporization.

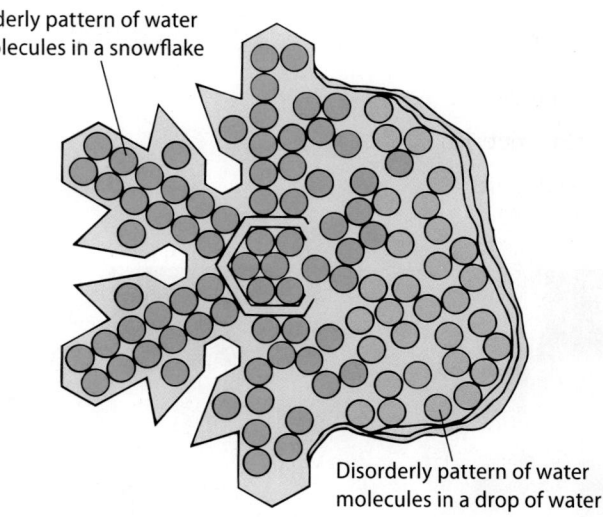

Orderly pattern of water molecules in a snowflake

Disorderly pattern of water molecules in a drop of water

Heat decreases the orderly arrangement of the atoms or molecules in an object. For example, the molecules of water in a snowflake are frozen in an orderly pattern. But as heat flows into the flake, its molecules move more rapidly. They become so disorderly that the snowflake begins to melt.

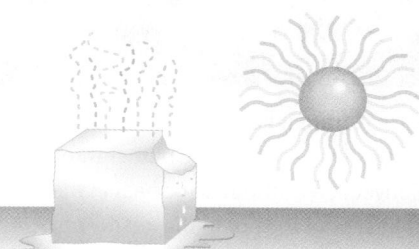

This phase diagram indicates the state of water at a given temperature and pressure. At certain combinations of temperature and pressure, ice changes directly to steam without becoming a liquid first. ▶

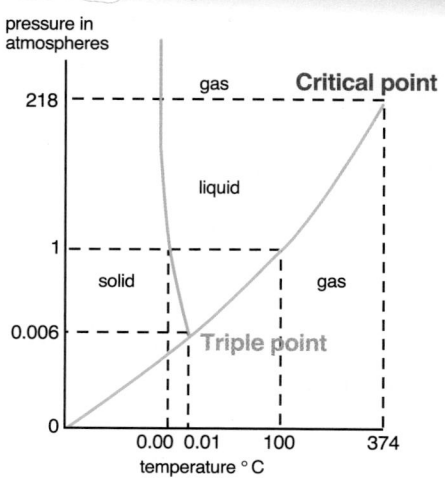

Heat Transfer Methods

Heat passes from one object or place to another by three methods.

- Conduction
- Convection
- Radiation

All three kinds of heat transfer are present in a pot of boiling water. Conduction transfers heat from the burner through the pot to the water. Convection distributes the heat in the water. Radiation transfers heat from the pot to the nearby objects.

Conduction

Conduction is the movement of heat through a material. When heat travels by conduction, it moves through a material without carrying any of the material with it. For example, the end of a copper rod placed in a fire quickly becomes hot. The atoms in the hot end begin to vibrate faster and strike neighboring atoms. These atoms then vibrate faster and strike adjoining atoms. In this way, the heat travels from atom to atom until it reaches the other end of the rod. But during the process, the atoms themselves do not move from one end to the other.

Conductors. Not all substances conduct heat equally well.

- Most metals conduct heat well.
- Glass, wood, and paper do not conduct heat well.

In general, solids that are poor conductors of electricity are also poor conductors of heat.

At identical temperatures, a piece of copper will feel much cooler to the touch than wood. Handles of cooking pans are usually made of materials that are poor conductors. The pan bottoms, by contrast, are made of metal with high thermal conductivity.

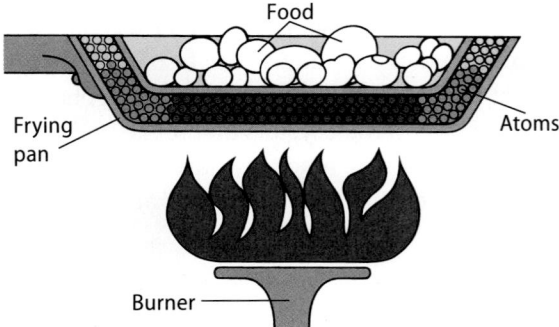

Conduction carries heat through an object. For example, heat from a burner makes the atoms on the underside of a frying pan vibrate faster. These atoms then strike atoms above them. In this way, heat passes through the pan to the food inside it.

Convection

Convection is the transfer of heat by the movement of a heated material. For example, a hot stove in a room heats the air around it by conduction. This heated air expands and so is lighter than the colder air surrounding it. The heated air rises, and cooler air replaces it. Then the cooler air near the stove becomes warm and rises. This movement of heated air away from a hot object and the flow of cooler air toward that object is called a convection current. The current of air carries heat to all parts of the room.

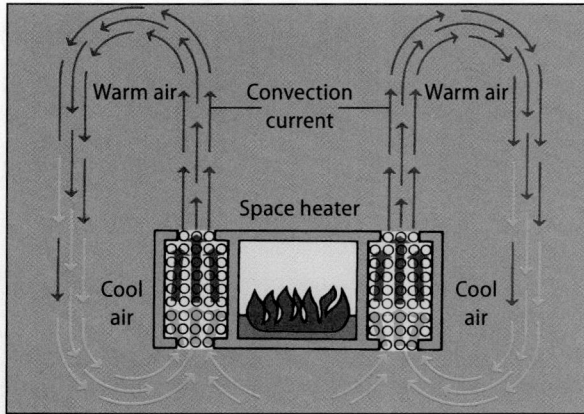

Convection carries heat by circulating a heated material. A space heater, for example, warms the air around it. This heated air rises and is replaced by cooler air. The movement of air creates a convection current that carries hot air through a room.

TYPES OF CONVECTION

- **Natural convection** occurs without any mechanical force. It occurs in boiling water when the buoyant force of gravity mixes the liquid.

- **Forced convection** occurs when mechanical means are used in convection, like with pumps or fans. Forced convection is used to cool car engines when a pump circulates water continuously along the cylinder walls to carry away excess heat.

Radiation

In conduction and convection, moving particles transmit heat. But in *radiation*, heat can travel through a vacuum, which has no particles.

In any object, the moving atoms or molecules create waves of radiant energy. These waves are also called *infrared rays*. Hot objects give off more infrared rays than cold objects do. Infrared rays travel through space in much the same way as water waves travel on the surface of a pond. When the radiant energy strikes an object, it speeds up the atoms or molecules in that object. Energy from the sun travels through space to Earth. These rays warm Earth's surface. (See pages 938–939.)

When heat radiation strikes a body, the radiation may be reflected, absorbed, or transmitted, depending on the frequency of the radiation and the properties of the surface of the body.

- Bright metallic surfaces like polished aluminum are good reflectors.

- Black, rough surfaces are usually good absorbers.

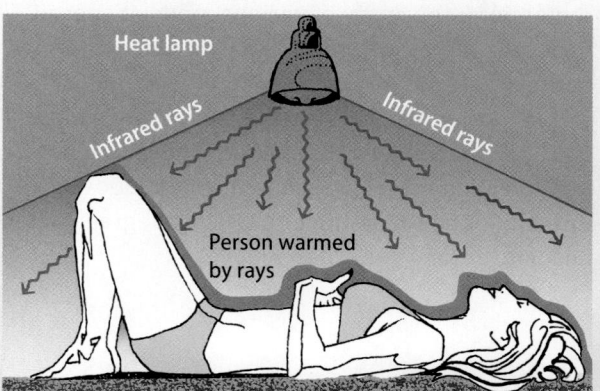

Radiation carries heat in the form of waves through space. A hot wire in a heat lamp gives off waves of radiant energy called infrared rays. When these rays strike someone, their energy warms that person.

Cryogenics

Cryogenics is the study of extremely low temperatures. It includes the development of techniques that produce and maintain such temperatures for industrial and scientific use.

- Temperatures of primary interest in cryogenics range from about −184°F (−120°C) to almost absolute zero, −459.67°F (−273.15°C).

- Cryogenic temperatures are usually given on the Kelvin scale, the standard for scientific temperature measurement.

Absolute Zero

Absolute zero is the temperature at which atoms and molecules have the least amount of heat possible. The atoms and molecules that make up matter are in constant motion relative to each other. What we think of as heat is actually a measure of the energy of this motion. If all the heat in a substance were removed, its molecular and atomic motion would virtually stop. The substance's temperature would then be absolute zero.

According to a widely accepted law of thermodynamics—the study of various kinds of energy, including heat—it is impossible for a substance to actually reach absolute zero.

Even so, scientists have come extremely close. In 2003, researchers at the Massachusetts Institute of Technology (MIT) reached 0.00000000045 K— one-half of one-billionth of a Celsius degree above absolute zero.

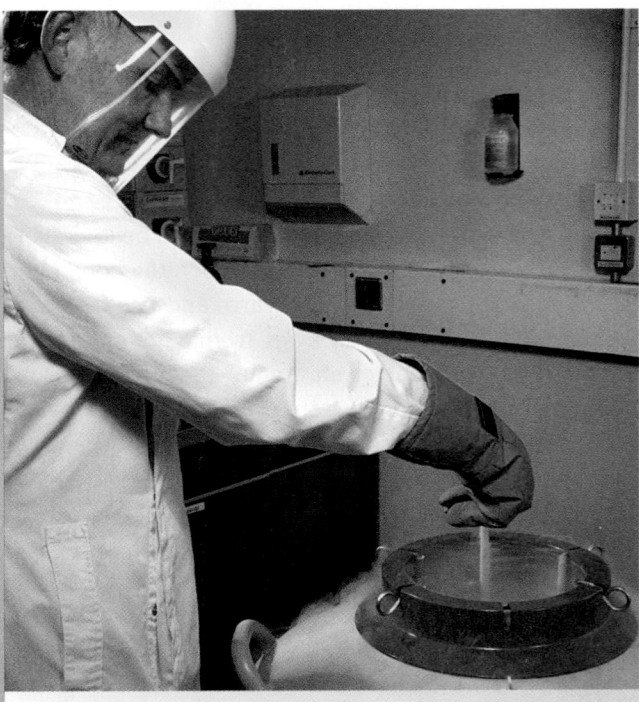

CRYOBIOLOGY

Cryobiology is the study of how extremely low temperatures affect living things. Its practitioners, cryobiologists, are chiefly concerned with freezing living matter to preserve it for future use. They use a liquid gas, usually nitrogen, to obtain temperatures far below normal freezing. The low temperature keeps the cells alive.

Cells kept cold in the gas stop working, but they stay alive and unchanged in a state of suspended animation. They can remain in this state without harm for long periods. After thawing, the cells resume their normal work almost at once.

The freezing of blood and tissues such as corneas and skin makes it possible to store these parts in facilities called biobanks. Doctors may use skin from such a bank to graft onto a badly burned patient. They use stored corneas to replace diseased or damaged ones. Frozen red blood cells can be stored for many years. Frozen sperm, eggs, and embryos are commonly used for animal breeding and sometimes for human in *in vitro* fertilization. Other tissue is stored as samples for scientific research.

In cryosurgery, surgeons use extreme cold to destroy diseased tissue. For example, surgeons can perform a "bloodless" operation using instruments equipped with freezing tips.

Superfluids

Ordinary liquids flow with an internal mechanical resistance called *viscosity*. A familiar example of a liquid with high viscosity—that is, a large amount of internal resistance—is molasses. When you pour molasses out of a jar, it moves slowly. Water, which has a low viscosity, flows more quickly.

Superfluids are liquids that have no viscosity, so they flow freely.

Other Properties. Superfluids have other unusual properties. For example, spinning a container of superfluid produces microscopic whirlpools called vortexes that will continue to spin as long as the liquid remains a superfluid. In addition, a superfluid can flow through a finely packed powder and conduct heat—that is, allow heat to pass through itself—at a tremendous rate.

Types. Scientists have found only two substances that can become superfluids. Both are isotopes (or forms) of helium that must be chilled to extremely low temperatures to become superfluids.

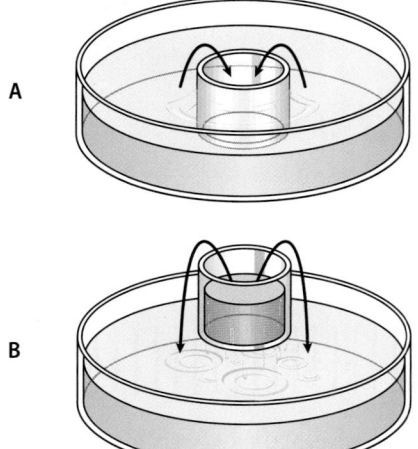

Two experiments show how a superfluid's lack of viscosity enables it to "crawl" up the side of a beaker. In figure A, an empty beaker sitting in a bowl of superfluid helium gradually fills. In B, the beaker is above the liquid, and the helium "crawls" back out.

Superconductors

Cryogenics also contributed to the discovery of superconductivity, the ability of some materials to conduct electric current at extremely low temperatures. These materials, called *superconductors*, have many useful properties. (See pages 832–833.)

- Electric current can flow through a superconductor without loss of energy.
- Superconductors can also produce powerful magnetic fields. Some are more than 400,000 times stronger than Earth's magnetic field.

The need for expensive, bulky cooling equipment limits the use of superconductors. However, they are used in magnetic resonance imaging (MRI) machines, which employ magnetic fields to produce images of tissue inside the body. Physics laboratories use superconducting magnets in devices called particle accelerators that enable scientists to study tiny bits of matter. Scientists and engineers are working to develop cheaper high-temperature superconductors for use in efficient power lines, high-speed electronic devices, and extremely sensitive magnetic field detectors.

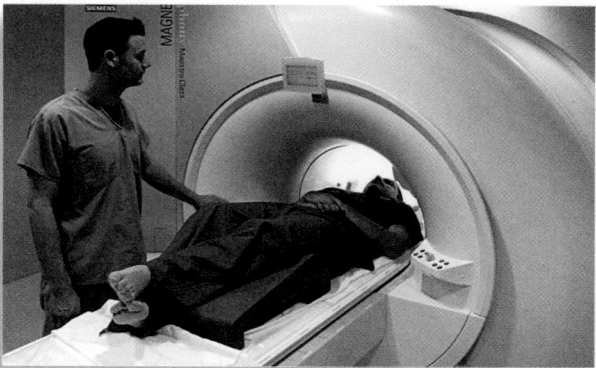

Superconductors are used in magnetic resonance imaging (MRI) machines, which use magnetic fields to produce images of tissue inside the body.

WAVES are disturbances in water, air, or another substance, or in an electric or magnetic field. Waves on water are a familiar example, but sound and light also travel in waves. Waves carry energy from place to place and can also transmit information.

Scientists call the material in which waves travel the *wave medium*. For example, water is the medium for water waves. Waves cause little overall displacement of their medium unless the disturbances become unusually large. For example, water waves travel horizontally across the surface of the water, but usually almost all the motion of the water itself is vertical.

Waves and Vibrations

Energy is often transmitted or transferred in the form of waves. The energy in a wave travels but the material that the wave travels through only vibrates.

For example, a boat bobs up and down as waves pass. The boat moves at right angles to the direction of the waves.

There are two main types of waves.

- *transverse waves*
- *longitudinal waves*

Transverse Waves

A transverse wave is one in which the medium moves perpendicular to the direction in which the wave travels. For example, imagine you are holding one end of a rope whose other end is tied to a doorknob. When you make a sharp up-and-down motion with your hand, a bump moves down the length of the rope. The rope itself does not move forward; only the bump does. The rope swings up and down across the direction of wave motion. This is a transverse wave.

Important examples of transverse waves are

- light
- television
- radio
- X-rays

TYPES OF WAVE MOTION

Transverse

Longitudinal

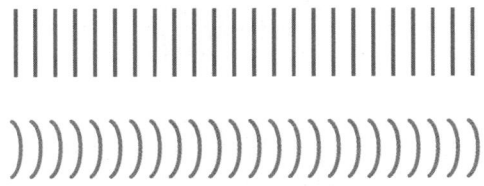

◄ **Waves.** Ocean waves are perhaps the most familiar type of wave, but sound and light also travel in waves.

Longitudinal Waves

Longitudinal waves are waves that travel in the same direction that the medium moves. Longitudinal waves require a medium that can be compressed. You can generate a longitudinal wave in a stretched spring by squeezing and then releasing a few coils at one end of the spring.

Important examples of longitudinal waves are

- sound waves
- some seismic (earthquake-generated) waves

Measuring Waves

We can determine the size of a wave by measuring the maximum distance that the wave medium moves from its usual position. Waves are usually measured by their amplitude, height, frequency, and wavelength.

- **Amplitude.** As rope waves travel through a rope, the rope forms a wavy line. The highest point on the line is called the *wave crest,* and the lowest point is the *wave trough.* The vertical distance from the crest to the level of the rope at rest is the *wave amplitude.*
- **Height.** *Wave height* is the vertical distance from the crest to the trough. This measurement is used when a wave's crest and trough are not the same distance.
- **Frequency.** The number of waves that pass a given point in a given time is called the *frequency* of the series of waves. By moving the free end of the rope up and down faster, for example, we increase the frequency of the waves because more waves pass any point in a given time.
- **Wavelength.** As the frequency is increased, the distance between the two adjacent wave crests or troughs is shortened. This distance is called *wavelength.* The shorter the wavelength, the higher the frequency.

How Waves Move

The simplest waves—*simple harmonic waves*—rise and fall with a fixed frequency and wavelength, but most wave motions are combinations of several waves with different frequencies and wavelengths.

- **Nondispersive waves** are combined waves in which the individual waves travel at the same speed. Water waves in shallow water are nondispersive waves.
- **Dispersive waves** are combined waves in which the individual waves travel at speeds that depend on their frequencies. Longer wavelengths race ahead of shorter ones, making the combined wave spread out. Water waves in deep water are dispersive. (See pages 576–577.)
- **Solitary waves** occur when the effects of dispersion and compression balance out. A solitary wave has a single humplike crest but no trough. They often form in shallow water channels.
- **Standing waves** are waves trapped in a medium. For example, if a rope is held at both ends and plucked, the energy in the waves cannot leave the rope at either end. Standing waves vibrate but do not move along the medium. The vibrations of guitar strings and violin strings are standing waves.

Wave Motion

Waves move in particular ways. When a pebble is dropped in the center of a pond, for instance, the waves move away from the point of impact in ever-widening circles.

When a wave moves from one medium to another, or when one wave meets another wave, wave motion changes. There are three main ways in which wave motion changes.

- *refraction*
- *diffraction*
- *interference*

CHRISTIAAN HUYGENS

Christiaan Huygens (1629–1695) was a Dutch physicist, astronomer, and mathematician. In 1678, Huygens proposed that light consists of series of waves. He used this theory in investigating the refraction (bending) of light.

Huygens's wave theory competed for many years with English scientist Isaac Newton's theory that light is made up of particles. Today, scientists believe that light behaves as both a particle and a wave.

Huygens also built the most powerful telescopes of his time, discovered Saturn's moon Titan, refined the value of *pi*, and invented a clock with a freely suspended pendulum.

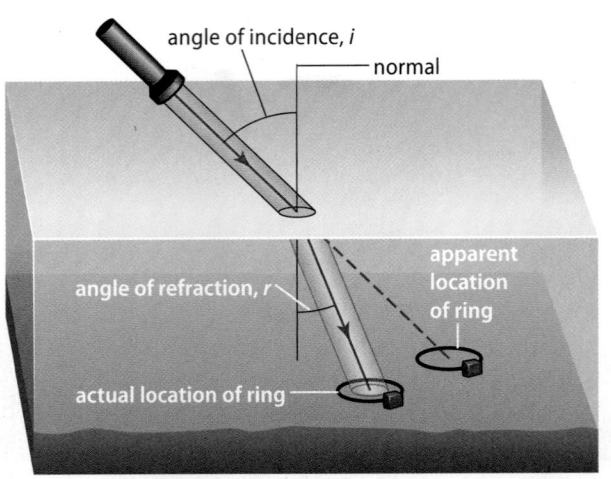

Refraction distorts the apparent location of a ring on the bottom of a pond. Light entering the water bends toward a line perpendicular to the surface.

Refraction

Refraction is a change in wave direction when waves pass from one medium into another. When waves leave one medium and enter another, some of the energy in the waves is reflected and some is transmitted to the new medium.

Angle of Incidence. The amount of energy reflected and transmitted depends on the *angle of incidence*— that is, the angle at which the incoming wave strikes the medium.

It also depends on the density and other properties of the two mediums.

Refracted Wave. The direction taken by the transmitted wave, called the *refracted wave*, also depends on the angle of incidence and the characteristics of the two mediums.

HOLOGRAMS

A *hologram* is a three-dimensional image stored on a photographic plate or other light-sensitive material. Holograms are created through the interference of light waves. Holograms have many uses, including artwork, advertising, and in credit cards to prevent counterfeiting.

Diffraction

Diffraction is the spreading out of waves as they pass through an opening or by the edge of an obstacle. Diffraction explains why water waves spread out in all directions after passing through a narrow channel in a breakwater. It also explains why sound can be heard around a corner even though no straight path exists from the source to the ear.

How It Happens. An expanding ring of water waves moves away from a stone dropped into a pond. As the ring becomes larger, any short part of the wave front (the outside edge of the ring) becomes a nearly straight line. However, if the wave front passes through a small slit in a barrier, the wave coming out the other side will spread out from the slit in a curve.

Diffraction occurs among all waves at all times, but it is only noticeable when the obstacle is about the same size as the wavelength diffracted.

Why It Happens. Diffraction occurs because each point on the surface of a wave is the source of small, curved waves called *wavelets* that move outward in all directions. The wavelets along the front combine to make the straight-line wave front. But the slit allows only a few wavelets through. The wavelets on either side of the slit are blocked, so the wave front is no longer straight.

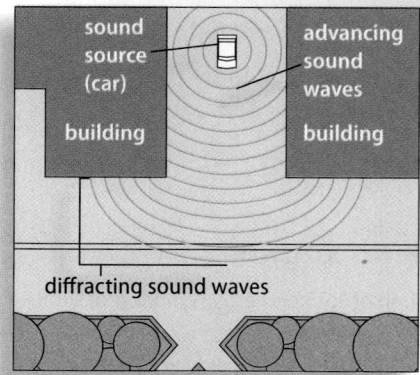

Diffraction enables the sound produced by a car to be heard around the corners of the buildings at the intersection.

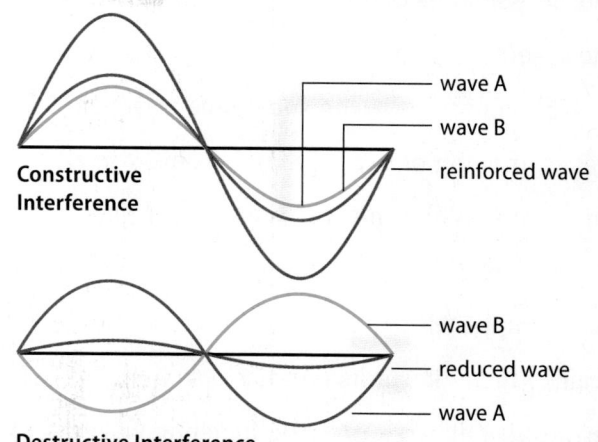

▲ **Interference.** In constructive interference, A and B combine to form a reinforced wave. In destructive interference, the difference between A and B forms a reduced wave.

Interference

Interference is an effect caused by two waves of the same kind passing through the same space. Interference causes the intensity of waves to be stronger in some locations than in others. There are two types of interference.

- *constructive interference*
- *destructive interference*

Constructive interference occurs where the crests of two waves with the same frequency pass the same point at the same time. The waves are said to be *in phase* with each other—that is, their crests and troughs coincide.

The two waves combine to produce a single wave with a larger amplitude. The amplitude of the combined wave equals the sum of the amplitudes of the two original waves.

Destructive interference occurs when the crest of one wave passes a point at the same time as the trough of the other. In destructive interference, the two waves combine to produce a wave with a smaller amplitude. The amplitude of the combined wave equals the difference between the amplitudes of the original waves.

SOUND originates in the vibration of an object. This vibration, in turn, makes the air—or some other substance surrounding the object—vibrate.

The vibrations in the substance travel as waves, moving outward from the object in all directions. When the waves enter our ears, our organs of hearing translate them into nerve impulses. The impulses travel to the brain, which interprets them as a sound. The term *sound* also refers to the traveling waves.

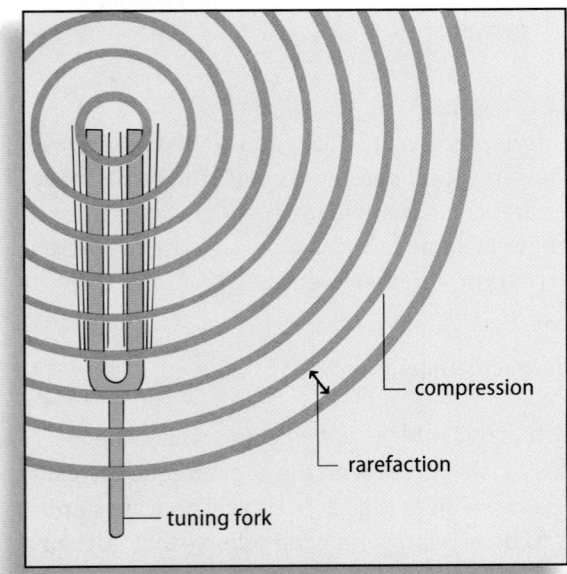

SOUND WAVES AND ENERGY

Sound waves move out on the surfaces of ever-growing spheres. Since the amount of energy carried by a single wave at the start remains with that wave throughout its existence, the amount of compression and rarefaction decreases as the area of the sphere increases.

In theory, the wave never disappears entirely. In actuality, the rubbing of air molecules against one another slowly absorbs all the initial energy and turns it into heat, so eventually the sound wave dissipates.

Sound Waves

Sound, like waves in the ocean, is three-dimensional. But the crests and troughs of sound do not rise and fall like water waves. They are high-pressure areas—*compressions*—and low-pressure areas—*rarefactions*—of the medium we know as air.

Springs of Air

Each compression forms the surface of an ever-growing sphere. Each following rarefaction is a slightly smaller sphere, just inside the pressure sphere, and is itself followed by another sphere of high pressure.

Water waves are examples of *transverse waves*. They rise and fall. Sound waves are *longitudinal waves*. To visualize sound waves, consider a spring. When you pull on the coils of a spring, you can watch the wave travel through it as the compressed coils bounce back and forth.

A sound wave is started by the vibration of an object.

1. When a musician hits a drum, the drumhead moves away from the stick, creating a partial vacuum in the layer of air touching the surface of the drum.
2. The surrounding air rushes in to fill this vacuum, leaving a partial vacuum just above the drumhead, and so on away from the surface.
3. The drumhead then returns from its depressed position and bounces to a level higher than normal.
4. This compacts the air immediately above the drum, and the high-pressure area in this space also moves out into the air immediately behind the rarefaction.
5. Thus, a wave is created by the back-and-forth motion of the drumhead.

ABSORBING SOUND

Dissipation of sound energy is more pronounced in enclosed areas than in wide-open spaces. In an auditorium, the sound waves initiated on the stage strike the walls, ceiling, and floor. While some of the sound is reflected back into the room, causing reverberations, the rest is absorbed by curtains, rugs, and clothing.

Loudness and Frequency

Sound has two important characteristics that affect how we hear noise.

- *intensity*
- *pitch*

Intensity of a sound wave is defined as the power transported by the wave per square meter. Intensity is expressed in watts per square meter, W/m². Intensity is related to loudness—the higher the intensity of a sound, the louder it sounds.

The human ear perceives sound intensities according to a logarithmic scale. For people to perceive that a sound is twice as loud as another requires a sound intensity 10 times higher. Intensity is measured in *decibels (dB),* and the scale begins at 0 dB, which is the faintest sound the human ear can perceive.

Intensity corresponds to the intensity of the pressure in the compression part of the wave and the reduction in pressure in the rarefaction. The greater the rise of pressure and the thinner the rarefaction, the louder the sound will seem.

Logarithmic Scale of Intensity
Unit: the decibel (dB)
A sound with an intensity of 0.468×10^{-12} W/m² is defined to have an intensity level of 0 dB.
10 dB corresponds to a sound intensity 10 times as large.
20 dB corresponds to a sound intensity 100 times as large.
30 dB corresponds to a sound intensity 1,000 times as large, and so on.
We usually cannot bear to hear sounds louder than 120 dB.

Pitch. The *frequency* of a sound is the number of waves that pass a given point each second. The more rapidly an object vibrates, the greater is the frequency of the sound that it makes. Scientists use a unit called the *hertz* to measure frequency. One hertz equals one *cycle* (vibration, or sound wave) per second.

The frequency of a sound determines its pitch—the degree of highness or lowness of the sound as we hear it. A high-pitched sound has a higher frequency than a low-pitched sound.

SOUND WAVE

Sound is a longitudinal vibration, which passes from place to place as alternate waves of compression and rarefaction of a material (most commonly for humans, the air). The same pattern can be seen in a coiled spring. (See page 799.)

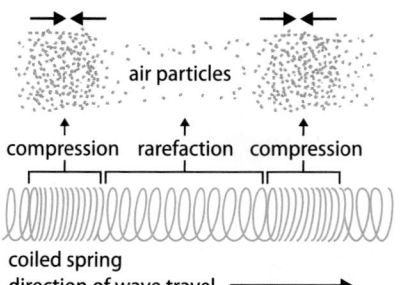

air particles

compression   rarefaction   compression

coiled spring
direction of wave travel ⟶

SOUND

Intensity of Sound	
Sound	**Decibels**
threshold of hearing	0
whisper	10–20
very soft music	30
average home	40–50
automobile	40–50
conversation	60–70
heavy street traffic	70–80
loud music	90–100
threshold of pain	120
jet airplane engine	170

Speed of Sound Through Various Substances		
Medium at 0°C	**ft./sec.**	**m/sec.**
air	1,090	332
alcohol	3,890	1,186
brass	11,480	3,499
carbon dioxide	846	258
copper	11,670	3,557
glass	16,500	5,029
iron	16,820	5,126
steel	16,820	5,126
water	4,794	1,461
wood (pine)	10,900	3,322

Sound Properties

The Speed of Sound

Velocity of sound depends on the density and compressibility of the *medium,* the material through which the sound waves travel. *Compressibility* is a measure of how easily a material can be squeezed into a smaller volume.

- If two mediums are equally dense, but one is more compressible than the other, sound will travel more slowly through the more compressible medium.

- If two mediums are equally compressible, but one is denser than the other, sound will travel more slowly through the denser medium.

Different Mediums. Regardless of the frequency of a wave, sound always travels through a given medium at the same speed. In general, liquids and solids are denser than air. But they are also much less compressible. Therefore, sound travels faster through liquids and solids than it does through air.

Sound Velocity			
Medium	Compressibility	Density	Velocity
Air	High	Low	334 m/sec. (1,100 ft./sec.)
Water	Lower	Higher	1,464 m/sec. (4,800 ft./sec.)
Steel	Low	High	4,877 m/sec. (16,000 ft./sec.)

THE SOUND BARRIER

When a jet flies at supersonic speeds—that is, flies faster than the speed of sound—it produces a shock wave called a *sonic boom*. A shock wave is a pressure disturbance that builds up around the supersonic jet. It results from a change in the airflow pattern around the plane's leading edges.

A sonic boom is loud. To a person on the ground, it may sound like a clap of thunder. Sonic booms cannot hurt people, but they may damage plaster walls and break windows.

Sonic Boom. An F/A-18 Hornet breaks the sound barrier, creating a shock wave and a loud noise like thunder. ▶

Resonance

Resonance is the phenomenon by which sound waves are reinforced so that they are perceived as sounding louder.

Sympathetic Vibration. If the handle of a vibrating tuning fork touches a table, the sound emanating from the tuning fork becomes louder. The reason for this is that the tuning fork causes the tabletop to vibrate. Thus, the tabletop also produces sound waves of the same frequency as the sound waves coming from the tuning fork. This particular type of resonance is called *sympathetic vibration.*

Wavelength

The distance between any point on one wave and the corresponding point on the next wave is the *wavelength*.

Wavelength is related to frequency: The greater the frequency of a wave, the shorter the wavelength.

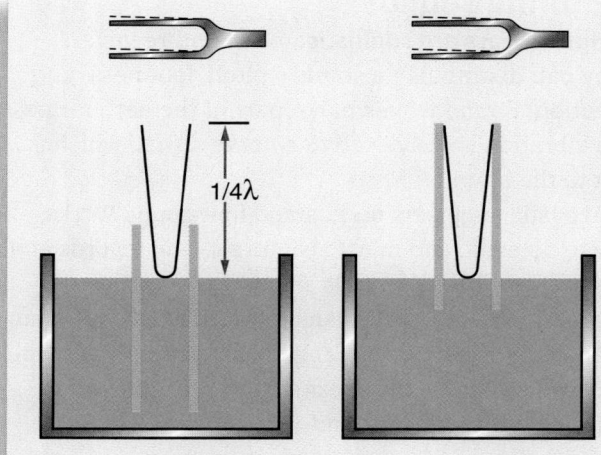

A RESONANT EXPERIMENT

Resonance can be illustrated by holding one end of a long cardboard tube in a bowl of water:

- A vibrating tuning fork is held near the open end of the tube.

- The tube is lowered slowly into the water.

- When the tube has reached the correct position, the sound will be amplified.

- For a certain length of the air column in the tube, that air column vibrates at the same frequency as the tuning fork.

Doppler Effect

When a person standing still listens to sound coming from a moving object, the observed frequency or pitch of the sound waves differs from the emitted frequency or pitch. This is called the *Doppler effect*.

Practical Applications. The Doppler effect has many uses, such as sonar devices to help submarines detect the speed and direction of surface vessels and other submarines. It is also used in astronomy, where the change in the frequency of light waves is measured to determine the velocities of distant galaxies.

HOW DOES THAT WORK

THE DOPPLER EFFECT

Consider sound waves coming from the siren of a fire truck traveling at high speed.

1. When the truck is moving toward you, the pitch of the siren is increased. Sound waves from the siren are compressed because the truck is moving in the same direction in which the waves are moving. Their wavelength is shorter. Therefore, their pitch is higher.

2. When the truck is even with you, the sound waves observed are equal in frequency and pitch to the sound waves emitted.

3. When the truck moves past you, waves traveling in the direction opposite to the movement of the truck are elongated, and the pitch drops.

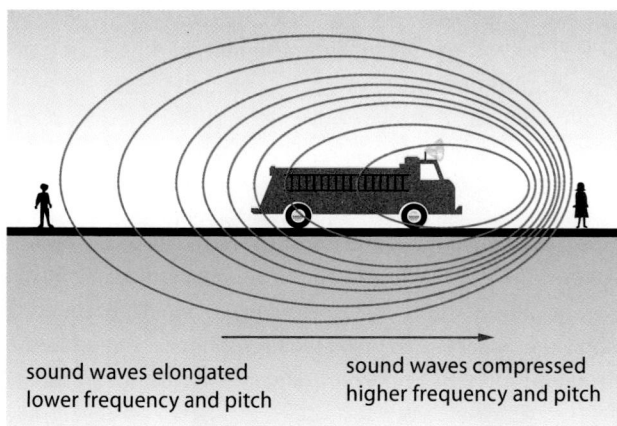

sound waves elongated
lower frequency and pitch

sound waves compressed
higher frequency and pitch

Acoustics

The branch of physics that deals with sound is called *acoustics*. It includes the study of how sound is produced, transmitted, detected, measured, and used. It is also concerned with the effect of sound on living things. Sound includes all mechanical vibrations that travel as waves through solid, liquid, or gas.

HOW DOES THAT WORK ?

HOW GUITARS MAKE SOUND

You know that to play a guitar you have to strum the strings, but how does the instrument actually make noise? The strings themselves do not make a lot of noise. They vibrate without causing a large disturbance in the air. But the strings cause the bridge to vibrate, and this in turn causes the body of the guitar to vibrate.

The vibrations of the guitar's body, and especially the sound board, cause air molecules to vibrate. Assuming the guitar player is skilled, these sound waves reach our ears as music. (See pages 802–803.)

Acoustic Guitar

- peg head
- tuning keys
- fingerboard
- frets
- body
- sound hole
- bridge
- soundboard

Capturing Sound

Human ears are sophisticated sound receivers. They can distinguish a sound's pitch, loudness, and direction. Sound waves make part of the ear vibrate. The vibration is converted to a nerve signal, which is sent to the brain.

Acoustic engineers understand how sound works, how to detect it, and how to capture it—on records and cassettes, then later on CDs and, more recently, on computer files—so that it can be played again and again.

Acoustic scientists and engineers use devices such as the microphone, the speaker, and the amplifier to record and reproduce sound.

Sound Recording

A microphone changes sound waves into electric signals that correspond to the patterns of the waves. The voltage of these signals oscillates in the same pattern as the pressure of the sound waves. Recording sound involves preserving the patterns of the oscillating voltage.

Recording Techniques. There are many ways to preserve the pattern of rising and falling voltage.

- The signal can move a pen back and forth over a moving strip of paper to create a jagged trace.
- The signal can drive a stylus back and forth as a soft plastic disk turns, leaving a wavy groove.
- The signal can power an electromagnet to create magnetized and reverse-magnetized areas on a strip of thin plastic tape coated with iron oxide particles.
- The voltage pattern can be stored as a series of digital numbers.

DIGITAL RECORDING

By electronically sampling the electric signal produced by a microphone thousands of times per second—typically between 44,000 and 55,000 times—one can create a stream of digital numbers that represent the amplitude fluctuations of the signal. For reproduction of the recorded sound, a special circuit converts the stream of numbers into the signal picked up by the microphone. The information can be stored on tape, disk, or software.

The advantage of digital recording is its purity of sound. Only the signal picked up by the microphone is reproduced. Sounds produced by the recording medium itself are absent.

HOW DOES THAT WORK

MICROPHONES

A microphone is a device that changes sound into electrical energy. Microphones work much as the ear does. A thin membrane in a microphone vibrates back and forth as the compressions and rarefactions impinge on it.

Moving-coil microphones have a metal disk called a *diaphragm*. When sound waves hit the diaphragm, it moves a coil of wire in a magnetic field to create an electric voltage.

Condenser microphones have two electrically charged metal plates set slightly apart. The plates act as a *capacitor*, a device that stores a charge. The back plate cannot move. Sound waves make the front plate vibrate, which causes variations in the electric current from the capacitor.

Earth, the Magnet. The magnetic lines of force are vertical at Earth's magnetic poles. Near the equator, the magnetic lines of force are nearly horizontal.

Amplifying the Signal. Once the sound is transformed into an electrical signal, which oscillates in voltage as sound waves do in pressure, it can then be amplified. The voltage is increased while the relative strengths of loud and soft signals are maintained.

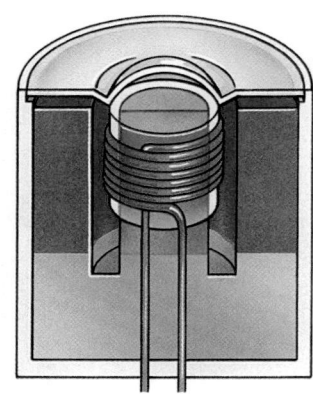

Moving-Coil Microphone

All these methods are used in modern sound recordings. The plastic disk is the master from which records are duplicated. The coated tape is used in tape recorders. Digital recordings are stored on CDs and mp3 files.

Sound Reproduction

Sound is recreated by reversing the recording process.

- In a tape recorder, an electromagnet senses the changing magnetism of the tape passing across its face and reproduces the original electrical signal.

- In a record player, a stylus rides in the groove of the record disk and moves back and forth. A tiny coil of wire placed in a magnetic field builds up a similarly varying voltage.

The electrical signal must then be amplified. It drives an electromagnet in the device's speaker. A *speaker cone* moves back and forth and reproduces a duplicate of the sounds originally recorded.

In Stereo

One of the advances in sound recording and reproduction is *stereophonic*, or *stereo*, sound

Direction Detection. The brain recognizes the direction from which sound comes by comparing the time of arrival and volume of the sound waves.

Imagine an orchestra with its brass section on your left and its percussion section on your right. The sound waves from the trumpets will reach your left ear a fraction of a second before the right ear. Those from the drums will reach the right ear before the left. By interpreting the time of arrival and the intensity, or volume, of the sound reaching each ear, your brain determines the locations of the musical instruments.

Direction Reproduction. To record in stereo:

- Two microphones are set a distance apart in front of the orchestra, one to record the sound waves from the left side, and one from the right.

- Electrical signals produced by each microphone are recorded on a separate channel or track.

- When the sound is reproduced through two separated speakers, each channel is reproduced only in the speaker on the corresponding side.

- The listener can sense the direction of the sound, experiencing a greater feeling of spaciousness and depth.

Acoustic Applications

Room Acoustics

Sound engineers face difficult challenges in designing concert halls. In planning Avery Fisher Hall at the Lincoln Center for the Performing Arts in New York City, studies were made of all the world's great concert halls. The goal was to duplicate the best characteristics of each hall.

- The hall contemplated for Lincoln Center would distribute music equally to all parts of the auditorium. There would be no seats where the music would be inaudible or overly loud.

- There would be no preferential treatment of some instruments at the expense of others. The piccolos would be heard as well as the bass drums.

- In addition, the *reverberation time,* the time it takes for all echoes of a note to die out, would have to be close to the ideal of 1.7 to 2.0 seconds.

Not all of this was accomplished in the initial design, but subsequent modifications have brought the hall closer to the original goal.

Avery Fisher Hall at New York City's Lincoln Center for the Performing Arts

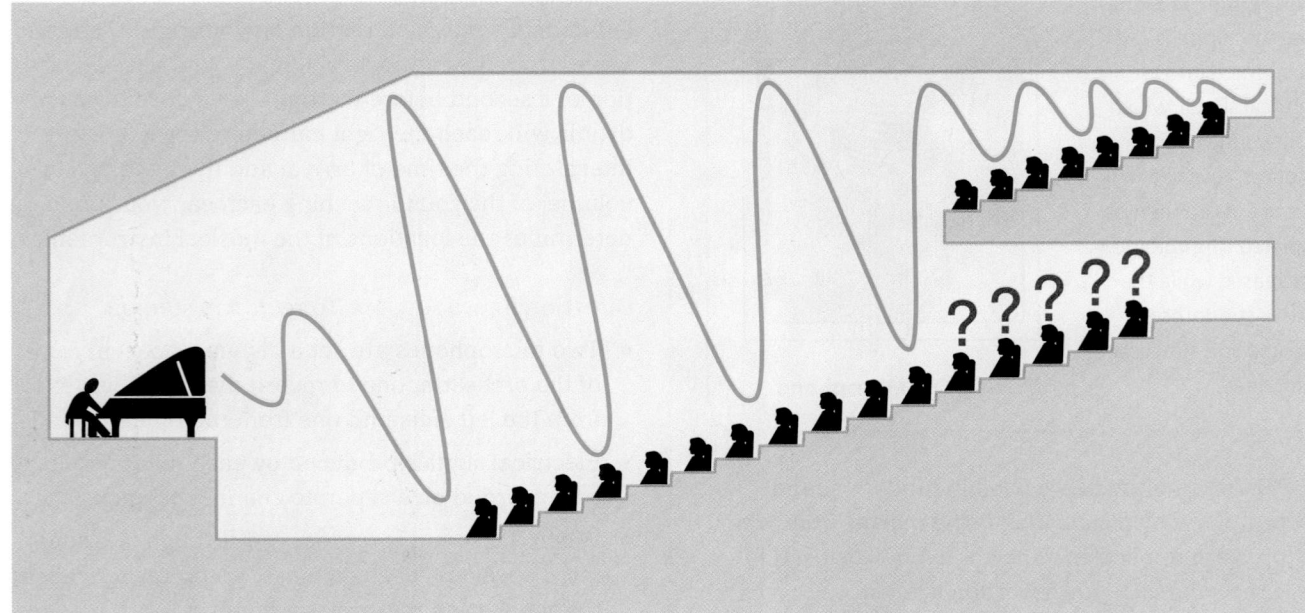

Acoustics are perhaps the most important factor in the design of a concert hall. Sound engineers use their knowledge of how sound waves behave to ensure that the music reaches every seat in the house.

Ultrasound

Ultrasonic frequencies of sound waves are frequencies above the range of human hearing, that is, greater than 20,000 cycles per second, or 20 kHz (kilohertz).

Many animals can hear and produce ultrasonic frequencies, or *ultrasound*. They use it to locate obstacles and to detect the movement of prey. Scientists and engineers have invented ultrasound devices, especially for medical and industrial uses.

Pitch and Frequency

- The *pitch* of a sound depends upon the frequency of vibration of the sound wave.

- *Frequency* is the number of cycles of vibration per second.

- Higher-pitched sounds have higher frequencies than do lower-pitched sounds.

- Scientists measure frequencies in *hertz*. One hertz is one cycle per second.

Piezoelectric Crystals

Certain crystalline materials—called *piezoelectric crystals*—change shape when an electric voltage is applied across their opposite faces. This change in dimension, although it is only a few thousandths of an inch, releases a sound wave in adjacent layers of air. Piezoelectric crystals are used in ultrasonic devices as sources of ultrasonic waves.

Some Widely Used Piezoelectric Crystals
quartz
Rochelle salt
lead zirconate titanate (PZT)
barium titanate

Uses of Ultrasound

- In medical devices that produce two- or three-dimensional images of internal structures of the body

- In devices such as automatic door openers and burglar alarms

- In industrial instruments that remove grease from tools and that sterilize surgical instruments

TINY BUBBLES

Cavitation is the creation and destruction of vapor bubbles by ultrasonic frequencies.

- When ultrasound moves through water, the sound wave's rarefaction portion thins out layers of water.

- This turns the water into a vapor, creating billions of tiny bubbles.

- Each vapor bubble lasts only a fraction of a second before a pressure wave snaps the bubble with a bang.

- It is believed that local pressures in the range of hundreds of thousands of pounds per square inch are generated in these collapsing bubbles.

Cavitation explains why high-speed ship propeller blades wear out faster than lower-speed propeller blades. The high pressure of the collapsing bubbles destroys the surfaces of the metal blades.

Ultrasound also kills a large number of fish in the sea. Their sensitive nerve cells cannot withstand the high-frequency sound.

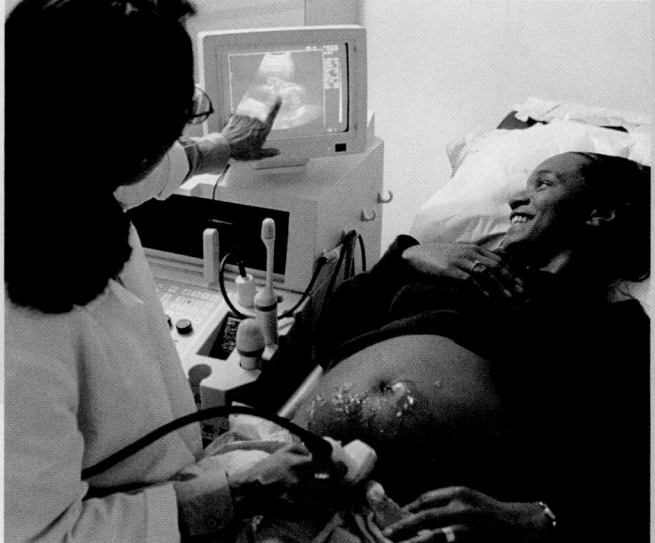

▲ **Ultrasonic waves,** unlike X-rays, are not harmful. They are used in medical devices to detect and evaluate cancer and to check the development of a fetus.

ELECTRICITY AND MAGNETISM are so closely

related that scientists often refer to the two of them together as *electromagnetism*.

Electromagnetism is the branch of physics that studies the relationship between electricity and magnetism. Electromagnetism is based on two facts: 1. An electric current or a changing electric field produces a magnetic field. 2. A changing magnetic field produces an electric field.

A combination of these effects produces electromagnetic radiation, which includes visible light, radio waves, and X-rays.

Electromagnetism has many applications, from junkyard cleanup, to storing information in a computer, to blaring music out of speakers.

Electromagnetism

The impact of electricity and magnetism on society has been far-reaching. Their many applications have made them familiar, but electricity and magnetism have been understood and harnessed only relatively recently in human history. This is true despite the fact that three natural manifestations of electricity and magnetism are readily observable.

1 electrical attraction
2. lightning
3. magnetism

Electrical Attraction

Records indicate the ancient Greeks knew that when a piece of ornamental amber was rubbed with wool or fur, it could be made to attract small bits of straw. The Greek name for amber was *electron*.

In 1600, William Gilbert discovered that many other substances could be made to exhibit the same effect. He called the effect "electric," from the word "electron."

Magnetism

Early Greek philosophers also knew of a third natural manifestation, involving magnetism. A *lodestone*—a piece of the mineral magnetite—was known to attract iron, and when suspended freely, to orient itself in a north-south direction.

The magnetizing of a steel needle by a lodestone and use of the needle as a compass were recorded by the Chinese at the beginning of the 12th century.

Lightning

Lightning, a second manifestation of electricity, has probably been observed since people first appeared on Earth.

A Shocking Storm. The fact that lightning is a form of electricity was not recognized until 1751. Benjamin Franklin performed experiments with electricity, flying a kite in a thunderstorm and noting that the kite and string became electrically charged. (See page 548.)

MAKING CONNECTIONS: AN ELECTROMAGNETISM TIME LINE

1820 Danish scientist Hans Oersted discovers that a conductor carrying an electric current is surrounded by a magnetic field. When he brought a magnetized needle near a wire in which an electric current was flowing, the needle moved.

1820s French physicist André Marie Ampère declares that electric currents produce all magnetism. He concludes that a permanent bar magnet has tiny currents flowing in it.

1831 English physicist Michael Faraday discovers electromagnetic induction. He finds that a varying magnetic field, such as one produced by a magnet moving inside a coil of wire, produces a current in the coil.

1864 James Clerk Maxwell, a British scientist, deduces that electric and magnetic fields act together to produce an electromagnetic field, or electro-magnetic waves of radiant energy.

1886–1888 German physicist Heinrich Hertz discovers electromagnetic waves, opening the way for the development of radio, television, and radar.

1897 J. J. Thomson, a British physicist, discovers the electron after experimenting with electrical discharges in evacuated glass tubes.

1912 American physicist Robert Millikan measures the charge of an electron.

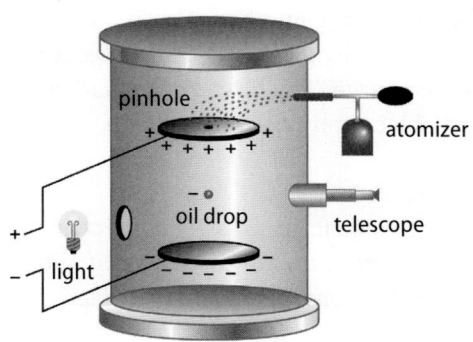

FLOATING OIL

Robert Millikan conducted a series of experiments on electricity in the early 1900s. In his famous oil-drop experiment of 1912, Millikan measured the charge of an electron.

Millikan's Experiment

- Millikan injected oil droplets between two plates with opposite electrical charges.

- By adjusting the charge on the plates, the droplets were held suspended between them.

- The charge necessary to suspend a droplet was always a multiple of a basic charge—that of the electron.

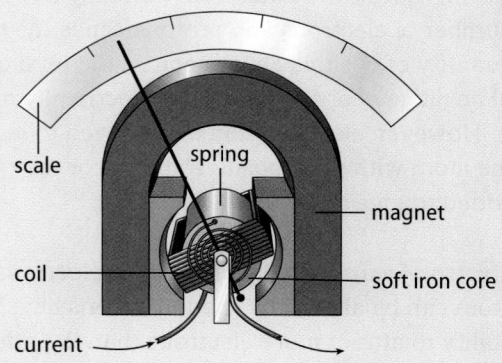

MEASURING CURRENT

André Ampère's discovery of the laws of electromag-netism in the 1820s led him to invent the galvanometer, an instrument for detecting and measuring electric currents. Ampère used the galvanometer to show that an electric current completes a circuit through the battery which produces the current.

Static Electricity

When a large number of atoms in an object gain or lose electrons, the entire object takes on an electric charge. The term *static electricity* describes when objects carry electric charge.

How It Works

Static electricity consists of electric charges at rest. Atoms contain three principal types of particles: protons, neutrons, and electrons.

- Each proton carries a specific amount of positive charge.
- Each electron carries the same amount of negative charge.
- Neutrons carry no electric charge and therefore are said to be electrically neutral.

Protons and neutrons are located together at the center of the atom to form the nucleus. Electrons move about the nucleus in tiny orbits.

Each proton or neutron has more than 1,800 times the mass of an electron. The number of protons and neutrons, and the number and arrangement of the orbiting electrons, are specific for each element. (See also pages 314–319.)

Normally Neutral. Each atom normally has the same number of electrons and protons. Since the total quantity of positive charge equals the total quantity of negative charge, the atom is electrically neutral.

However, electrons can be removed to leave the atom with a net positive charge, or they can be added to give a net negative charge.

Electron Exchange. The number of electrons in an atom can be altered by friction. Atoms have the ability to attract more electrons than the number normally moving about each nucleus. This attraction is of different strength for different materials.

When two substances of different attracting power rub together, some of the electrons in one will leave their orbits and move to new orbits in the other. One substance will then have a net positive charge, and the other will have a net negative charge.

COULOMB'S LAW

The French physicist Charles de Coulomb was the first to determine the forces between charged bodies. He found that the force between small charged spheres was inversely proportional to the square of the distance r between the two spheres and directly proportional to the product of the magnitudes q_1 and q_2 of the charges:

$$F = k\frac{q_1 q_2}{r^2}$$

Explanation

The constant k depends on the units that are used to express the force F and the charges. In SI units:

$$k = 8.99 \times 10^9 \left(\frac{Nm^2}{C^2}\right)$$

Here C is the *coulomb*, the SI unit of electrical charge. If two equal charges are separated by 1 cm and the repellent (or attracting) force between them is 1 *dyne*, the unit of force in the *cgs* system, then k equals one, and each charge is said to have the value of 1 electrostatic unit, abbreviated *esu*.

The unit of charge in the SI system is the coulomb. One coulomb equals 3 billion electrostatic units.

A torsion balance is a device for measuring small forces of push or pull. Charles de Coulomb invented the torsion balance and used it to establish Coulomb's law.

Static Forces

The presence of a force acting between two charged bodies a little distance apart can readily be demonstrated by suspending one charged body by a thread and approaching it with another charged body.

An uncharged bit of paper or straw is attracted to the charged body because a few of the electrons in the paper or straw are able to move about. Assume, for example, that a positively charged glass rod is brought near a bit of paper.

- Electrons drawn toward the rod will make the surface of the paper negatively charged and attract the paper to the rod.

- The more distant surface of the paper will be positive, but being farther away, will be repelled with less force, so the paper will be attracted.

- If the paper touches the rod, the movable electrons will go onto the rod, leaving the paper positively charged.

- The paper will then jump away.

Static Electricity Between Materials			
Rubbed Material	**Charge**	**Rubbing Material**	**Charge**
amber	−	fur or wool	+
rubber	−	fur or wool	+
glass	+	silk	−

▲ **Experimentation** with the materials in the chart will demonstrate the general law that like charges repel one another, and unlike charges attract one another.

STATIC ELECTRICITY

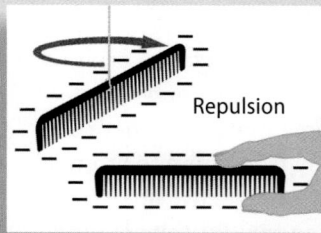

Repulsion

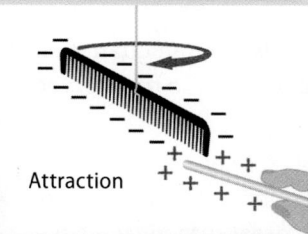

Attraction

We can demonstrate repulsive forces between charges of equal polarity by bringing a charged rubber comb near another comb suspended from a string.

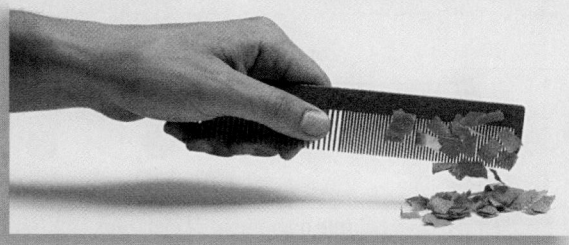

If a glass rod is brought close to the suspended rubber comb, it will be attracted because the charges are of opposite polarities. A charged comb can attract electrically neutral pieces of paper.

Static electricity is responsible for phenomena as powerful as a lightning strike and as harmless as a bad hair day.

Flowing Current

Electric charge moves through some materials better than others. Charge moves easily through substances called *conductors*. Materials known as *insulators* resist the movement of electric charge.

Conductors and Insulators

Rubbing a copper bar on wool or fur will not give it an electric charge. Unlike glass or amber, the electrons making up the electric charge of copper are free to move about in the material. They are able to flow away to Earth through your hand and body.

Copper is therefore a conductor, while amber and glass are insulators, of electricity. A stream of moving electric charges constitutes an *electric current.*

How Conductivity Works. The electrons orbiting about atomic nuclei are not all unchangeably fixed in their orbits. In some materials, there are electrons that move readily from atom to atom. If such a material is placed in an electric field, the free electrons will begin moving rapidly, thus creating an electric current.

- Generally speaking, metals contain quantities of such free electrons and are said to be good conductors.

- In most nonmetallic substances, electrons are tightly bound in their orbits and can move from atom to atom only with great difficulty. These substances are nonconductors, or insulators.

ELECTRIC FIELDS

If we place an electron near an electric charge, the electron experiences a force. This force will pull the electron toward the charge if the charge is positive, or push it away from the charge if the charge is negative. (See page 319.)

The space in which an electron or an electric charge experiences a force is called an *electric field*. Every electric charge has an electric field associated with it.

Resistance refers to a material's opposition to the passage of electric charges through it.

- Resistance occurs when electrons moving in the material collide with atoms and give up energy.

- The energy the electrons give up is converted into heat.

- Good conductors have low resistivity.

- Good insulators have very high resistivity.

- Plate glass has approximately 10^{19} times the resistivity of copper.

- Porcelain has approximately 10^{20} times the resistivity of copper.

- This enormous difference in resistivity between good insulators and good conductors makes efficient control and distribution of electricity possible.

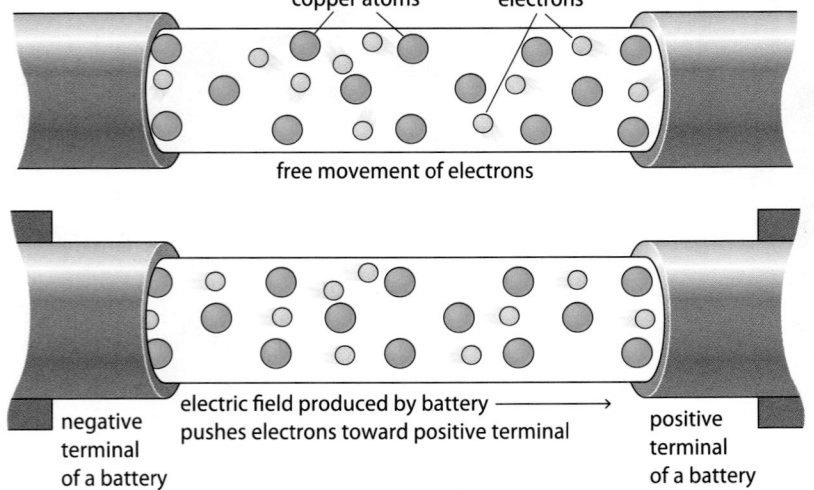

copper atoms   electrons

free movement of electrons

electric field produced by battery ⟶
pushes electrons toward positive terminal

negative terminal of a battery

positive terminal of a battery

Electric Current. Metals, such as copper wire, are good conductors because they have a large number of free electrons. If a copper wire is connected between the terminals of a battery, free electrons in the wire move from the negative to the positive terminal. This movement is defined as a flow of current.

Flowing Through Liquid. Some liquids are able to conduct electricity, principally water solutions of acids, bases, or salts.

- A portion of the molecules of the solute (the acid, base, or salt) split, or dissociate, into two parts.
- One part has an excess of electrons, the other a deficiency, so that they are respectively negatively and positively charged.
- Under the influence of an electric field between two conductors in the solution, these charged particles move, constituting a current.
- The solution is called an electrolyte, and the conductors are electrodes.

Pure water dissociates only to a slight extent and therefore is a poor electrolyte. However, outdoor swimming pools are dangerous in thunderstorms since the electrolytes in the water make it a good conductor of electricity.

CONDUCTIVITY OF METAL

- Of these metals, copper is the most widely used because it is relatively inexpensive and light in weight.
- High-power transmission lines frequently are constructed of stranded steel cable around which aluminum strands are spiraled.
- The combination of steel and aluminum is strong and lightweight, providing good conductivity at low total cost.

Metal	Conductivity (percent)
Copper	100
Silver	105
Gold	71
Aluminum	61
Iron	18
Low-carbon steel	8–13
Some alloy steels	2

Neon Light

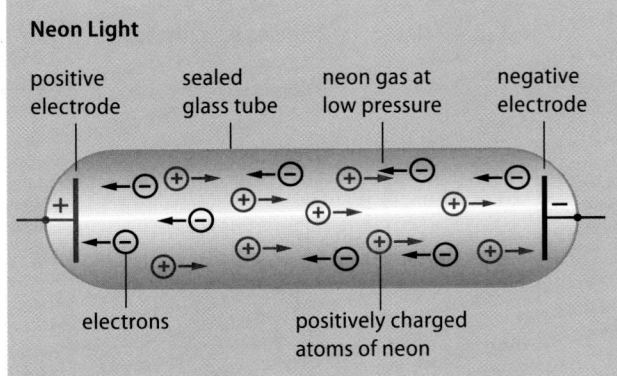

positive electrode · sealed glass tube · neon gas at low pressure · negative electrode

electrons · positively charged atoms of neon

Neon Lamps. When electricity is applied to a glass tube filled with neon gas, an electric discharge occurs, and the tube glows reddish-orange. A neon tube has two electrodes sealed within it. The neon forms a luminous band between these electrodes.

Conducting Gas. Under certain conditions, a gas can become a conductor. A neon light is an example.

- Under the influence of an electric field, atoms of neon in the glass tube become positively charged ions.
- These ions are drawn to the negatively charged conductor.
- At the same time, electrons that have left the neon atoms are drawn to the positive conductor.

A more spectacular example of an electric current through a gas—air—is a lightning flash. Lightning occurs when the electrical charge of a cloud is discharged to the earth or an oppositely charged cloud.

AC/DC

A flow of electric charge through a conductor is called electric current. Energy is associated with the flow of current. As current flows through electric devices, this energy may be converted to useful forms. The basic types of electric current are

- *direct current (DC).*
- *alternating current (AC).*

Direct Current

An electric current that flows steadily in one direction is called direct current. A stream of electrons flows past any one point in one direction. Batteries supply direct current.

Alternating Current

Alternating current alternates its direction, flowing past a point in one direction and then changing direction to flow in the opposite direction.

The frequency of an alternating current is its number of cycles per second. A complete cycle is the interval during which a current starts from zero, pulses to a maximum in one direction, drops back to zero, pulses to a maximum in the opposite direction, and returns to zero once again.

The current available in the home is alternating current. In the United States and Canada, household current reverses direction 120 times per second, completing 60 full cycles.

Current Conversion. Most electronic devices require direct current to operate, so television sets, stereo amplifiers, and personal computers contain special circuits that convert alternating current into direct current. The conversion of alternating current into direct current is called *rectification,* and the circuit for this process is called a *rectifier.*

Spotlight on... NIKOLA TESLA

1856–1943

Nikola Tesla was an inventor from Austria-Hungary. He received more than 100 patents for a variety of inventions.

Tesla is best known for his development of systems that produce alternating current (AC). To this day, Tesla's systems remain the heart of electric power in most of the world.

1884 Tesla moves to the U.S. and works for inventor Thomas Edison. Edison supports DC; has little interest in Tesla's AC.

1887 Tesla opens the Tesla Electric Company in New York City; produces three complete systems of AC machinery.

1888 Tesla sells his patents to U.S. industrialist George Westinghouse and works at the Westinghouse Electric Company to develop commercial uses of the AC system.

1893 Westinghouse uses Tesla's AC system to light the World's Columbian Exposition in Chicago.

1895 Westinghouse uses Tesla's generators and motors to harness the power of Niagara Falls and deliver power to Buffalo, New York, 22 miles from the falls.

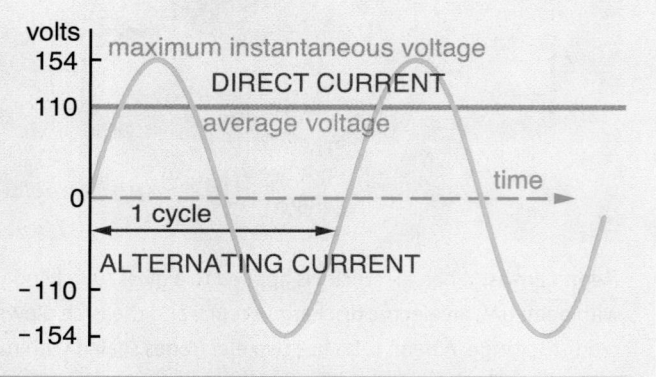

The voltage of direct current remains constant. In alternating current, voltage changes polarity 60 times per second.

Units of Measure

The names of units measuring electricity honor pioneers in the field: Charles de Coulomb, André Ampère, Alessandro Volta, and Georg Ohm.

Coulomb. The unit of quantity of electricity is the *coulomb*. One coulomb is equivalent to the charge carried by 6.24×10^{18} electrons.

Ampere. Electricity flowing at the rate of 1 coulomb per second is equal to a current of 1 *ampere*. Thus 1 ampere is equal to the passage through a given point of 6.24×10^{18} electrons per second.

Volts. The electric pressure, or *electromotive force—emf*—which causes the flow of current, is measured in *volts*. The intensity of an electric field may be expressed as volts per centimeter or volts per inch.

Ohms. The resistance of a conductor is measured in *ohms*. An emf of 1 volt applied to a resistance of 1 ohm will produce a current of 1 ampere.

OHM'S LAW

Ohm's law is a formula that expresses the relationship between the force, current, and resistance in a circuit. The law states that current is proportional to the voltage applied and inversely proportional to the resistance.

Ohm's law is stated in the form of an equation:

$$I = \frac{E}{R}$$

I – current in amperes; E – emf in volts; R – resistance in ohms

Production of Electric Current

Aside from the transient discharges of static electricity, the first production of electric current was by chemical means.

- Chemical production of current is still important, especially in battery-operated devices.
- Most electric power, however, is generated by *electromagnetic induction* in rotating machinery.
- *Photoelectric cells* are used to supply power in artificial satellites and certain small electronic devices, such as calculators.

Chemical Cells

When electrodes of two different materials, such as zinc and copper, are immersed in an electrolytic solution, one acquires a positive charge and the other a negative charge. They can then be connected externally by a wire, and a current will flow through the wire. This arrangement constitutes a *voltaic cell*.

How It Works. Chemical action between the electrolyte and the electrodes causes atoms of one electrode to go into solution. Each atom leaves behind one or more electrons. This leaves that electrode with a negative charge.

The electrolyte takes electrons from the other electrode, thus giving that electrode a positive charge. The electrons flow through the external wire from the negative electrode to the positive electrode. Voltaic cells connected together form a battery. (See pages 394–395.)

MAGNETISM is the force

that electric currents exert on other electric currents. Magnetism may be created by the motion of electrons in the atoms of certain materials, which are called *magnets*.

Magnetic force may also be produced by ordinary electric current flowing through a coil of wire, called an *electromagnet*.

The magnetic force may cause attraction or repulsion—that is, it may pull magnets together or push them apart.

Magnets: How They Work

A magnet always has two poles. When the magnet is free to move, the poles orient themselves along the north-south direction. The pole that orients itself toward the north pole of Earth is called the north pole. The other pole is called the south pole.

A magnet always retains its two poles. If you cut a magnet in two pieces, each piece will have a north pole and a south pole.

Push and Pull

Attraction and repulsion between magnets follow a set of principles similar to those that direct electro-static forces.

Poles. The ends of all magnets are called *poles*. Just as like electric charges repel and unlike electric charges attract each other, like poles repel one another, and unlike poles attract one another.

MAGNETIC FIELDS AND ELECTRIC CURRENT

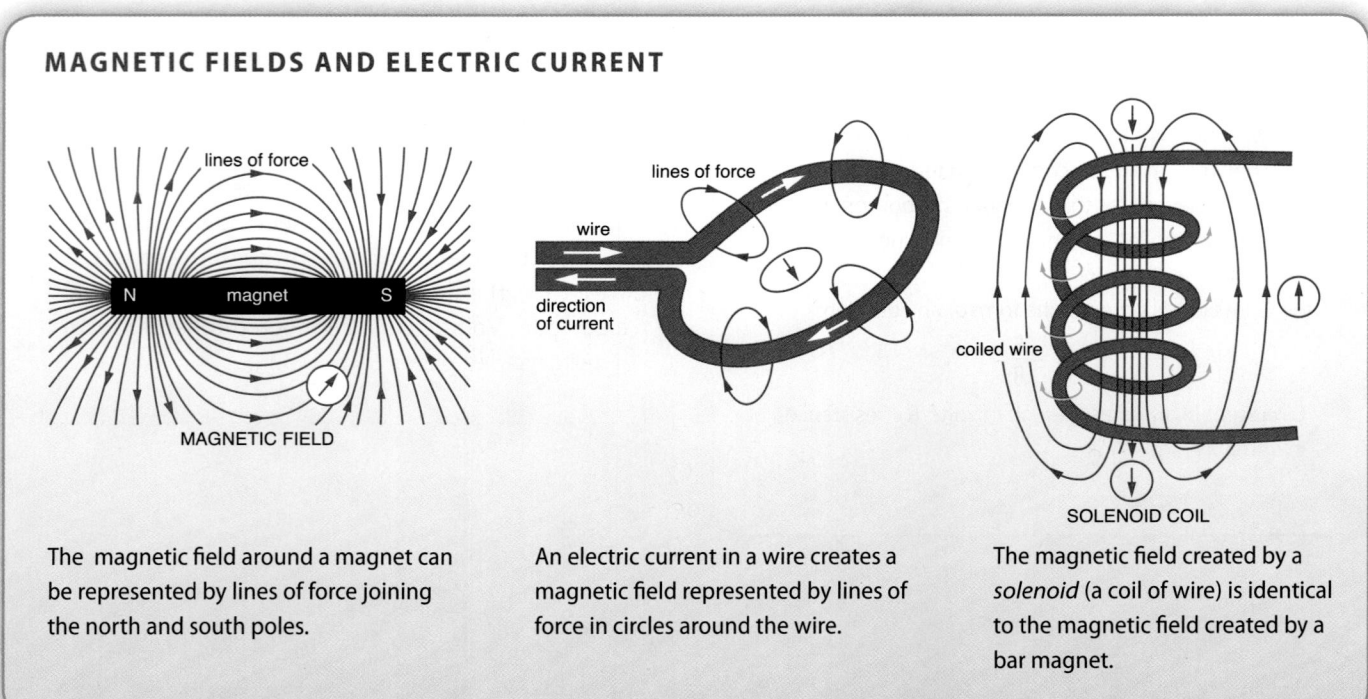

The magnetic field around a magnet can be represented by lines of force joining the north and south poles.

An electric current in a wire creates a magnetic field represented by lines of force in circles around the wire.

The magnetic field created by a *solenoid* (a coil of wire) is identical to the magnetic field created by a bar magnet.

Consider the familiar magnetic compass.

- A compass needle orients itself in a north-south direction.
- The end pointing north is marked N and the other end S.
- When another compass is brought near the first, the two needles deviate from their north-south direction and tend to point toward each other.
- The attracting and repelling forces reside in the ends of the needles, and ends that are marked alike repel one another.

Different Polarity, Same Strength. There is, however, an important difference between a magnetized bar and an electrically charged body.

- The charged body may carry the same polarity of charge over its entire surface.
- The magnetized bar always has two poles of unlike polarity and of equal strength.

Magnetic Fields

The region around a magnet where the force of magnetism can be felt is said to contain a *magnetic field*.

Lines of Force. Like an electric field, a magnetic field consists of *lines of force,* a line of force being a line along which a magnet pole tends to move.

The positive direction is that in which the N pole tends to move. Thus, a compass needle in a magnetic field will orient itself parallel with the lines of force, with the N pole pointing in the positive direction.

Closed Loops. There is an important difference, however, between the concepts of the magnetic field and the electric field. (See page 814.)

- The electric lines of force do not terminate at the S pole but continue unbroken through the magnet to emerge at the N pole.
- Magnetic lines of force exist only as closed loops and never cross.

LINES OF FORCE

A magnet such as the bar magnet shown below produces a magnetic field around it, a field that can be shown as lines of force.

When the north pole of one magnet is placed near the north pole of another, the lines of force interfere with each other, causing the magnets to repel one another.

When the north pole of one magnet is placed near the south pole of another, however, the lines of force work together to make the two magnets attract each other.

Magnetite, or lodestone, is a naturally occurring permanent magnet. It is a hard black rock that is attracted by magnets and acts as a magnet itself.

Electromagnets

Electromagnets are temporary magnets produced by electric currents. When a bar of soft iron is put inside a coil of wire and a current is then passed through the wire, the bar exhibits all the characteristics of a strong magnet. When the current is turned off, the magnetic properties of the bar disappear.

Solenoids

If a wire is bent into a closed loop and a current is passed through it, magnetic lines of force will form closed loops around the wire.

If a series of wire loops is joined to form a *helix,* or coil, lines of force will pass inside, parallel with the axis, and curving around outside to close upon themselves. Such a coil, which is called a *solenoid,* exhibits all of the characteristics found in a bar magnet.

Practical Electromagnetism

Discovery of the electromagnet and development of the chemical cell as a source of electricity opened the way for a series of inventions and practical uses.

- **Telegraph.** Samuel F. B. Morse invented the telegraph in 1837. A message was sent through a wire by varying the electric current. The movement of electromagnets would show the variations in the current, so that an operator at the other end could receive and decode the message.

- **Telephone.** Alexander Graham Bell invented the telephone in 1875. Magnets in the speakers of phone help change electrical impulses into sound.

- **Circuits and Valves.** Electromagnets are used in relays to open and close electric circuits, to operate valves, and to do a multitude of other mechanical tasks.

HOW DO WE KNOW THAT ?

ELECTROMAGNETISM

In 1820, Danish physicist Hans Christian Oersted was setting up a classroom experiment to teach his students when he made a startling discovery.

The experiment involved a compass needle, a battery, and some wires. Oersted noticed that when he ran an electric current through the wires, the compass needle moved away from its usual north-south orientation.

Oersted had discovered electromagnetism.

Further experimentation demonstrated that there is a magnetic field around an electric current. The lines of force of this magnetic field form closed loops encircling the conductor in planes perpendicular to the conductor.

The lines of force around two parallel wires carrying current produce a force between the two wires. They attract each other if the current flows in the same direction in both. They repel each other if the currents flow in opposite directions.

Hans Christian Oersted was a university professor who discovered that every conductor carrying an electric current is surrounded by a magnetic field.

Powerful electromagnets attached to cranes move scrap iron and steel and separate metals for recycling.

Ferromagnetic Materials
iron
nickel
cobalt
metal alloys made up of iron with nickel and cobalt
a few nonferrous metal alloys

Ferromagnetism

The magnetic characteristics exhibited when a core of soft iron is put into a solenoid are many times greater than those of a solenoid alone. The magnetic properties contributed by the iron are called *ferromagnetism,* and the iron is said to be *ferromagnetic*.

Orbiting Electrons. The source of ferromagnetic properties lies in the electrons orbiting about the atomic nuclei of the material. The electrons spin about as they orbit, producing a magnetic field along their axis.

In all materials other than ferromagnetic materials, electrons in each atom are so oriented that practically no magnetic field is produced outside the atom. In ferromagnetic materials, there is a net imbalance in each atom so that the atom has a magnetic field about it.

Domains. Thus, the ferromagnetic material can be thought of as being composed of a large number of tiny magnets. Large groups of these tiny magnets are lined up in one direction, forming *domains*. The domains are grouped together, forming closed loops, and no magnetic field appears outside the material.

Aligning Domains. Within a fairly small magnetic field, however, domains are altered until nearly all are oriented parallel with the magnetic field and add their own fields to it.

The total field of all the tiny magnets in the material may be many thousand times greater than the field required to line them up. When the external field is removed, the tiny magnets revert approximately to their former orientations, producing no outside field.

Permanent Magnets

In some ferromagnetic materials, the magnetic domains are reoriented with great difficulty, and a strong field is required to accomplish this. Moreover, when the field is removed, many of the domains do not revert to their initial orientations. The bar is said to be magnetized and is called a *permanent magnet*.

Uses. Early permanent magnets and compass needles were made of hardened carbon steel, but materials have recently been developed offering vastly improved permanent magnet characteristics.

Permanent magnets, when properly prepared and treated, exhibit great stability and are used in instruments that measure electricity and in loudspeakers. (See page 807.)

Current in a Coil

The generation of current in a coil by a varying magnetic field is called *electromagnetic induction*.

Generating Electricity

Electric generators make use of electromagnetic induction for the production of electricity. The current is created in coils mounted on an axis and moved through a magnetic field, thus generating electricity.

Producing Movement

Conversely, when a coil of conducting wire is placed in a magnetic field and a current is applied to the coil, the coil will undergo a force. Thus, in principle, the same device used for the generation of electricity from mechanical motion can also be used to produce mechanical motion from electricity.

Electric motors are, therefore, very similar in construction to electric generators, and many designs may be used interchangeably.

Producing Sound

The forces acting on a coil are also used to produce sound in a loudspeaker. A coil is attached to the diaphragm of the loudspeaker and placed inside the magnetic field of a strong permanent magnet. When the amplified sound signal flows through the coil, it will put the coil in motion and reproduce the sound waves that have been picked up by the microphone.

Transformers

A *transformer* is a device that is primarily used to change the alternating line voltage to a more useful one. It consists of two coils coupled closely, called the *primary* and the *secondary coils*.

- The primary coil is the coil to which the current is applied. It is connected to the source of the voltage to be changed.
- The secondary coil is the coil in which the current is induced. It is connected to the circuit to which the electricity is to be transferred.

A MAGNETIC DISCOVERY

English physicist Michael Faraday discovered electromagnetic induction in 1831. He found that a varying magnetic field, such as one produced by a magnet moving inside a coil of wire, produces a current in the coil.

Faraday also discovered that if two coils are wound around an iron core, an alternating current applied to one coil will induce an alternating current in the other coil.

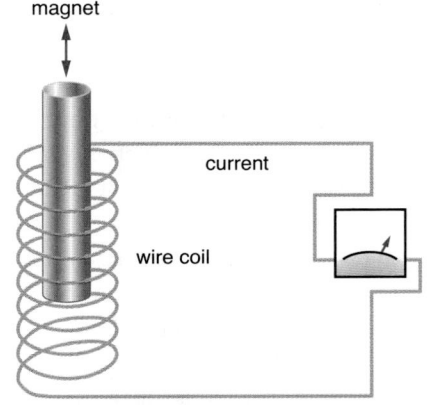

ELECTROMAGNETIC INDUCTION

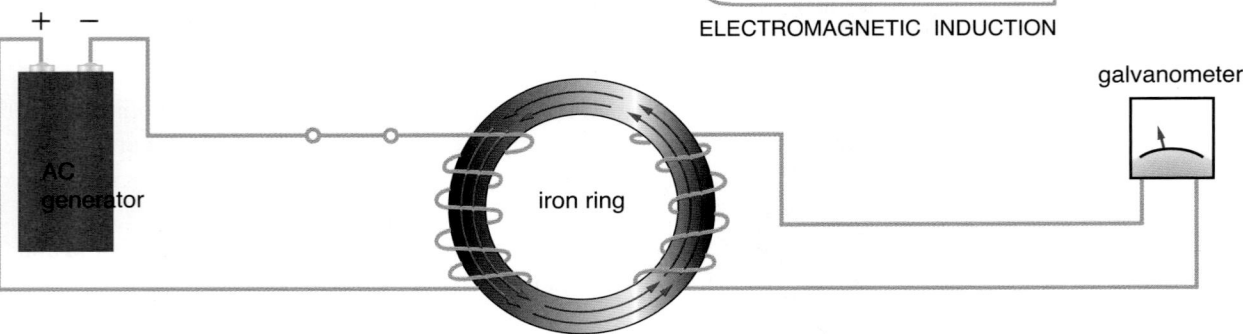

HOW DOES THAT WORK

TRANSFORMERS

- An electric current passing through a solenoid, or coil of wire, wrapped around an iron bar creates a magnetic field in the bar.

- If the current through the solenoid varies rapidly, the magnetic field in the bar will also vary.

- If another coil is wrapped around the iron bar, the varying magnetic field will create an electric current through this coil.

- Therefore, any voltage applied to the primary appears on the secondary in a proportionate level.

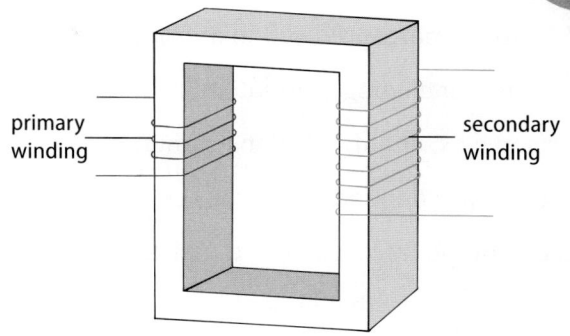

Transformers generally have cores made of insulated iron sheets. This prevents the induction of electric currents in the core itself and thus limits the losses in the transformer.

Transformers		
Number of Turns	**Voltage**	**Uses**
Equal in primary and secondary coils	Equal in both coils	To separate electric appliances from house current
More turns in primary coil than secondary coil	Higher in primary coil	Called step-down transformers; reduce high house voltage to a lower voltage suitable for appliance operation
More turns in secondary coil than primary coil	Higher in secondary coil	Called step-up transformers; used to generate high voltage. Large high-voltage transformers are used in long-distance transmission of electric power.

Electric Circuits

Electric devices may be interconnected in a variety of ways with respect to the circuits the current follows.

- In a series circuit, the current flows in sequence through one device after another. There is only one path. If a string of lights is on a series circuit, when one bulb burns out, the circuit is broken and all bulbs go out.

- In a parallel circuit, there are two or more paths. The current divides, and part flows simultaneously to each path. In a string of lights connected in parallel, the full supply voltage is applied to each bulb. The current through each bulb comes directly from the source and returns to it. Thus, when one bulb burns out, the other bulbs may not go out.

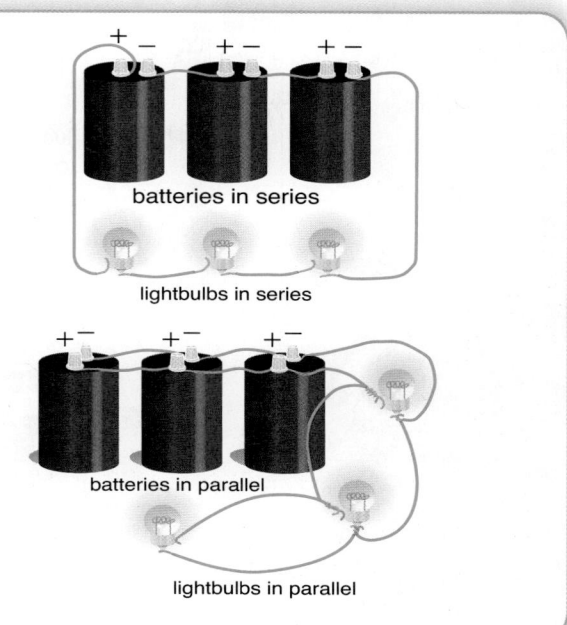

batteries in series

lightbulbs in series

batteries in parallel

lightbulbs in parallel

ELECTRONICS is a branch

of physics and engineering that involves controlling the flow of electric charges in certain devices for a useful purpose.

Electronic parts are used in a broad range of products, including computers, telephones, television sets, and medical instruments.

Electronics depend on certain highly specialized components, such as transistors and integrated circuits, that serve as parts of almost all electronic equipment. The value of such devices lies in their ability to manipulate signals extremely fast. Many components can respond to signals billions of times per second.

Electronic Development

Electronics is part of the broad field of electricity. Familiar uses of electricity include the furnishing of energy in homes and businesses to provide light and heat, and to drive motors. Electricity includes two important elements.

1. *electric current:* the flow of electric charges
2. *electric voltage:* a type of "pressure" or force that causes the charges to move in the same direction

Electronics deals chiefly with the use of current and voltage to carry *electric signals*. An electric signal is an electric current or voltage modified in some way to represent information. A signal may represent sound, pictures, numbers, letters, computer instructions, or other information.

History of Electronics

The discovery of the electron in 1897 by British physicist Joseph Thomson was a result of his study of the electric discharges in evacuated glass tubes. When the pressure is reduced in such a tube, the electric discharge causes the glass to glow with a faint greenish light. This green light is caused by invisible rays coming from the *cathode,* the negatively charged electrode. The light rays were called *cathode rays.*

electron gun

magnetic lens

electron beam

specimen

magnetic lenses

display screen

STEM detector

fluorescent screen

chamber for photographic plate or digital camera

Electron microscopes have been useful in studying the structure of matter and the nature of viruses.

ELECTRON MICROSCOPES

The electron microscope is a device in which a beam of electrons is used to produce magnified images of objects that are many times smaller than those the best light-beam microscope can see.

TEM. A transmission electron microscope (TEM) passes electrons from an electron gun through the specimen to a fluorescent screen. The microscope's operator can view the resulting image through a magnifier or record the image using a photographic plate or digital camera.

STEM. Adding an electron detector can enable the microscope to operate as an extremely powerful kind of microscope called a scanning transmission electron microscope (STEM).

Thomson's experiments with cathode rays led to the discovery of the electron. (See page 319.)

- Thomson showed that cathode rays were deflected both by magnetic and electrostatic fields.

- The rays were deflected toward positively charged plates, so Thomson concluded that they had to be negatively charged particles—electrons.

Electronic Emission. A very strong field is required to dislodge electrons from the atoms in the surface of a metal at room temperature. As the metal is heated, a temperature is reached at which electrons are emitted spontaneously. This is called *thermionic emission*.

The Photoelectric Effect. Electrons also are emitted at room temperature when light falls upon a metal. This is called the *photoelectric effect*.

Most metals exhibit this effect only under ultraviolet light, but such metals as rubidium and cesium emit electrons in visible light. The photoelectric effect is at the basis of the operation of the photodetector and the photomultiplier.

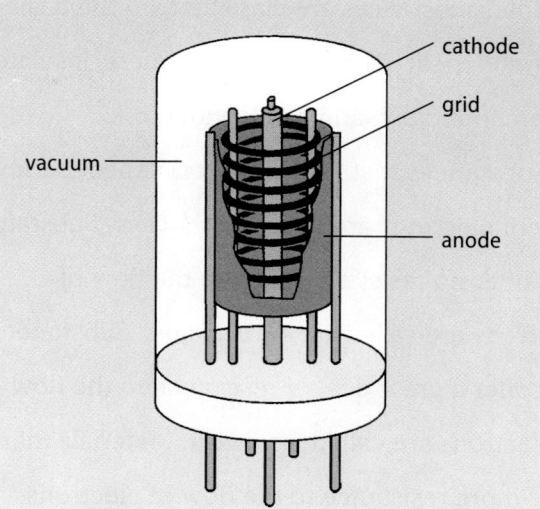

TRIODE VACUUM TUBE

A triode vacuum tube creates and controls a flow of electrons in a vacuum.

1. Electrons leave the cathode when a source of direct current is connected to the tube.

2. The electrons flow through the grid to the anode.

3. The voltage applied to the grid controls the number of electrons that reach the anode.

Vacuum Tubes

Electronic equipment once widely used vacuum tubes to create, strengthen, combine, or separate electrical signals. British scientist John Ambrose Fleming developed an early vacuum tube—the Fleming valve—from experiments with thermionic emission.

The Fleming valve consists of a wire filament surrounded by a metal cylinder inside a highly evacuated glass bulb. The filament is heated to incandescence by an electric current, and electrons are emitted from it.

- If the cylinder is made positive with respect to the filament, the electrons are drawn to it, constituting a current.

- If the cylinder is made negative, the electrons are repelled and no current flows.

Another Electrode. American inventor Lee De Forest advanced the Fleming valve in 1907 when he placed a wire grid between the valve's filament and plate.

De Forest called the new tube an *audion.* Such a tube also is called a *triode,* indicating the use of three electrodes.

Solid-State Devices. Since the late 1950s, transistors and integrated circuits, or *microchips,* have replaced vacuum tubes in most electronic devices. These devices are called *solid-state* because electronic signals flow through a solid material instead of a vacuum.

SEMI- AND SUPERCONDUCTORS

Solid substances are classified, on the basis of their electrical behavior, as conductors, insulators, superconductors, and semiconductors.

Substances that offer little resistance to the flow of electrons are called *conductors*. Substances that offer no resistance at all to the flow of electrons are called *superconductors*. Substances that offer a great deal of resistance to the flow of electrons are called *insulators*. Materials that offer more resistance to the flow of electrons than conductors, but offer less resistance than insulators, are called *semiconductors*.

Semiconductors

A semiconductor is a material that conducts electric current better than an insulator like glass, but not as well as a conductor like copper.

A computer chip is a piece of a semiconductor, usually silicon, that contains an electronic circuit. Solar cells that convert light energy to electric energy are made of semiconductors, as are some lasers.

Semiconductor Theory

To understand semiconductor theory, you must understand how electrons behave both in individual atoms and in groups of atoms.

In isolated atoms, electrons occupy stable orbits around the atomic nucleus. Each electron orbit corresponds to a fixed energy level of the electron.

In Grouped Atoms. When individual atoms are assembled in a crystal lattice (see Solids, pages 780–781), individual energy levels of the electrons merge into *energy bands*.

- Solids have several energy bands, which can be occupied by electrons.
- These energy bands are separated by gaps.
- Electrons require extra energy to pass from one band to another.

Silicon is the most widely used semiconductor. It is the main substance in computer chips, solar cells, transistors, and other electronic devices.

THE BASICS: SEMICONDUCTORS

- Semiconductors act as insulators at low temperatures.
- Their conductivity, contrary to that of conductors, increases with increasing temperature.
- This is because as the temperature rises, more electrons have enough energy to jump the forbidden gap.
- Conductivity increases with the addition of impurities or by creating missing electrons.
- Germanium and silicon are examples of semiconductors.

◀ **Germanium** is one of the most widely used semiconductors. Industry uses germanium in such semiconducting devices as diodes and solar batteries.

Electron Mobility

The electrical properties of solids can be described by the mobility of electrons in these energy bands. In electrical conductors, the outermost energy band is called the *conduction band*. This band is not completely filled, and its electrons can move easily from atom to atom.

The electrons in the conduction band are called *free electrons*. Free electrons account for the current in a conductor.

The valence band is the outermost energy level in an insulator. It is completely filled, and no electrons can move from atom to atom.

Insulators can conduct electricity under certain extreme conditions. If, for example, electrons acquire enough energy by acceleration in a very strong electric field, they can reach an energy band placed higher, and conduction can occur.

The gap between this higher energy band and the normally occupied valence band, called the *forbidden gap*, can only be bridged by highly energized electrons.

Bridging the Gap. In certain elements, the forbidden gap is quite narrow, so electrons can easily acquire energies to bridge the gap.

For example, semiconductors are solids that act as insulators at low temperatures. But an increase of temperature in a semiconductor energizes electrons enough to jump the forbidden gap.

Increasing Conductivity

In addition to raising the temperature, there are two other methods to increase a semiconductor's conductivity.

- adding minute amounts of different elements, called *impurities,* to the semiconductor material
- creating so-called *missing electrons* in the valence band

Impurities. Germanium has four electrons in its outermost shell and shares each one of them with the four neighboring germanium atoms in the crystal lattice, forming a completely filled valence bond.

Arsenic atoms have five electrons in their outer shell. When arsenic atoms are introduced into the germanium crystal lattice, four of the arsenic electrons will be shared with the four neighboring germanium atoms. The fifth arsenic electron will not find a place and will forcibly occupy a place in the conduction band.

These electrons flow through the material freely and can produce an electric current. Semiconductors of this type are called *n-type* semiconductors, the *n* indicating that the charge carriers are negative. The impurities are called *electron donors*.

Missing Electrons. Boron atoms have three electrons in their outermost shell and thus can share only three electrons with the four surrounding germanium atoms. The missing electron is called a *hole*.

Just as an electron can flow through a material, so can a hole. A hole can be filled up by a neighboring electron, which in turn leaves a hole. This new hole can be filled up by an electron, and so on. When the semiconductor is subjected to an electric field, holes behave as positive charge carriers.

Semiconductors containing holes are termed *p-type* semiconductors, with the *p* indicating that the charge carriers are positive. Impurities that produce holes are called *electron acceptors*.

Semiconductor Devices

Semiconductors had their first important application as rectifiers for low-frequency alternating currents. A rectifier is a circuit that converts an alternating current into a direct current.

Early Semiconductor Usage

- About 1904, semiconductors were used for their rectifying properties to provide a detector of the high-frequency currents set up in circuits by radio waves.

- The *crystal rectifier,* a fine metal wire in contact with crystalline lead sulfide or silicon, was the best detector of radio waves in the early days of radio.

- Vacuum tubes replaced such devices, and during World War II, metal point-contact silicon devices were used in radar.

SOLAR CELLS

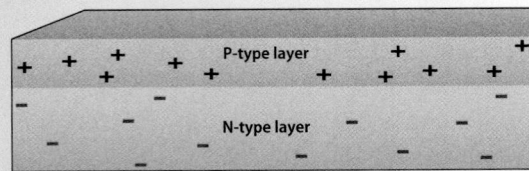

Solar cells are made of semiconductors—two layers of silicon with added impurities. Near their boundary, the p-type layer is negatively charged, so negative electrons (−) cannot enter it. The n-type layer is positively charged near the boundary, so positive holes (+) cannot enter it.

Sunlight frees additional charges (in circles below), some of which cross the boundary and then leave the cell as electric current.

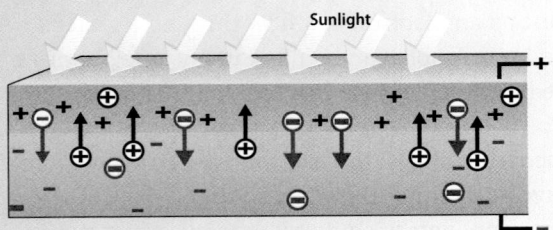

REMEMBER THIS... P-TYPE AND N-TYPE SEMICONDUCTORS

P-type semiconductors are semiconductors that carry positive charges. They are semiconductors that have a hole, or a missing electron, in their outermost shell. Impurities that produce holes in p-type semiconductors are electron acceptors. (See page 827.)

N-type semiconductors are semiconductors that carry negative charges. They are semiconductors that have an extra electron in their outermost shell—an electron that is not needed for bonding. These electrons flow through the material freely and can produce an electric current. Impurities that offer extra electrons in n-type semiconductors are electron donors.

P-N Junctions

It is possible to produce both an n-type region and a p-type region in a single crystal of semiconductor material. Such a combination, called a *p-n junction,* is the basis for many semiconductor devices.

- In the n-region, donor impurity atoms give up electrons in greater numbers than acceptor atoms contribute positive holes.

- In the p-region, holes are in excess compared with electrons.

Electrified Junction. Most of the electrons remain in the n-region, and most of the holes remain in the p-region. However, some electrons from the n-region diffuse into the p-region, leaving behind positive donor ions. Also, some holes from the p-region diffuse into the n-region, leaving negatively charged acceptor ions.

Due to the impurity ions, an electric field is established at the junction. This field inhibits additional electrons from diffusing out of the n-type material and additional holes from diffusing out of the p-type material.

DIODES

Diodes are electronic components that prevent current from flowing in one direction but not the other. A semiconductor diode consists of a piece of p-type semiconductor joined to a piece of n-type semiconductor, creating a p-n junction.

A diode is basically a switching device that allows current to flow in only one direction. The current is carried by the flow of holes and electrons. The direction (bias) of the applied voltage determines if the p-n junction blocks current or allows it to flow.

◀ **Light-Emitting Diode (LED)**

Forward-Biased P-N Junction

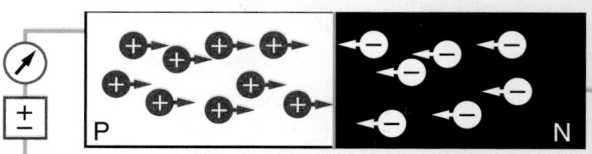

A forward bias allows current to flow through the junction.

Reversed-Biased P-N Junction

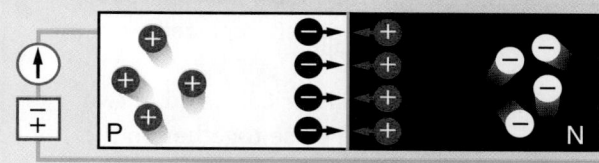

A reverse bias prevents most current from flowing through the p-n junction, though a small leakage current gets through.

Forward-Biased Junctions. A p-n junction is said to be *forward biased* when negative voltage is applied to the n-side and positive voltage is applied to the p-side. Forward-biased devices can carry large amounts of current.

- A forward-biased junction is created when a battery is connected with its negative terminal on the n-type material and its positive terminal on the p-type material.

- Electrons from the battery neutralize the positive ions on the n-side of the junction.

- Electrons enter the positive terminal of the battery from the p-region, thereby decreasing the negative charge on the p-side.

- As a result, the junction field is diminished and electrons can move from the n-type material through the junction to recombine with holes.

- The holes on the p-type side carry current from the positive battery terminal to the junction.

Reverse-Biased Junctions. In a *reverse-biased* p-n junction, negative voltage is applied to the p-side and positive voltage to the n-side.

- A field is present that causes the mobile holes and electrons to move away from the junction and one another toward the p-contact and n-contact, respectively.

- Electrons are added to the p-region and removed from the n-region by the battery.

- This leaves a wider region near the junction charged with immobile impurity ions but depleted of mobile charge carriers.

- The junction field is enhanced by reverse biasing, but because of the depletion of mobile charges, little current flows.

- The current that does flow is attributable to thermal excitation of holes and electrons in the junction region.

- These carriers contribute a small but finite reverse current.

Transistors

The most important development in the application of semiconductors is the *transistor*. A transistor is a tiny device that controls the flow of electric current in radios, television sets, computers, and almost every other kind of electronic equipment. Transistors vary in size from about 1/10,000 of a millimeter—approximately 1/500 the diameter of a human hair—to a few centimeters across.

Inventing the Transistor

The transistor was invented in 1947 by William Shockley, John Bardeen, and Walter H. Brattain at Bell Telephone Laboratories. By the late 1960s, transistors had almost completely replaced vacuum tubes in electronic devices.

The earliest type of transistor consisted of two metal-point contacts placed close together on the surface of a germanium crystal and a third soldered at its base. The point contacts are called the *emitter* and the *collector*. The soldered contact is called the *base*.

There are two main types of transistors.

- *junction transistors*
- *field effect transistors (FETs)*

Junction Transistors

Junction transistors are either *n-p-n junction transistors*—a thin section of p-type semiconductor between two parts of n-type semiconductor—or *p-n-p junction transistors*—a thin section of n-type semiconductor between two parts of p-type semiconductor.

While both n-p-n and p-n-p transistors are used commercially, only the n-p-n will be discussed here.

Structure. Two p-n junctions exist in an n-p-n transistor and share a common narrow p-region.

Three contacts are made to the three regions: the emitter, base, and collector.

- The emitter junction is the n-p junction between the emitter and the base. It is forward biased.
- The collector junction is the n-p junction between the collector and the base. It is reverse biased.

FUNCTION

A transistor has two basic functions.

1. to switch electric current on and off
2. to amplify, or strengthen, electric current

TINY CHIPS

The *integrated circuit*, also called a microchip, is a small chip of semiconductor—usually silicon—on which are deployed microminiaturized diodes, transistors, resistors, capacitors, and the needed insulation and connections. Thousands to millions of elements can be created on a single chip.

There are two main types of computer chips. *Microprocessors* carry out the instructions that make up computer programs. *Memory chips* hold computer programs and other data.

◀ **Many microchips** make up a computer motherboard—the circuit board that acts as the heart of a computer.

Electron Flow. Because the emitter junction is forward biased, electrons flow from the emitter contact through the n-region of the emitter to the emitter junction. There they are injected into the p-region.

These injected electrons diffuse as minority carriers across the thin p-base region and are collected by the reverse-biased collector junction.

The base region—the p-type semiconductor—should be thin so that practically all the injected electrons are drawn across to the collector. They are swept into the collector by the large junction field of the reverse-biased collector. Then they find their way to the base contact or recombine with holes. The emitter current also includes holes injected from the base into the emitter region.

By introducing impurities more heavily in the n-region of the base, the electron injection can be made to dominate as required for an efficient transistor.

Current Variation. When a signal voltage introduced at the input terminals varies the emitter current, there will be a corresponding variation of the collector current.

The collector impedance, or resistance, is high compared with the impedance of the forward-biased emitter. Therefore, a large-load resistor can be used in the output to accomplish voltage amplification or power amplification.

For example, if the impedances of the input and output circuits are 100 and 1,000,000 ohms respectively, there is a power gain and a voltage gain of about 10,000.

Field-Effect Transistors

In more recent years, the field-effect transistor, FET, has come into use. An FET operates by creating an electric field that changes how one of the transistor's semiconductor regions, the gate region, conducts electric current. Current flows when enough charge carriers—either electrons or holes—are attracted to the gate region.

An FET has three semiconductor regions—the *source,* the *gate region,* and the *drain.*

MOSFETs. The most common type of FET is the metal-oxide silicon FET (MOSFET). Its insulating layer of silicon oxide eliminates the need for physical isolation of the components.

Structure. In a MOSFET, the source and drain are made of the same type of semiconductor material—either n-type or p-type. The gate region, which lies between the source and the drain, is made of the opposite type of material. The gate region typically extends into the substrate, the underlying chip material. The source and drain are embedded in the substrate.

Current Flow. In normal operation, the drain is more positive than the source. Thus, current tends to flow from the source to the drain. Whether current actually flows depends upon whether the voltage to the gate is negative or positive.

A negative voltage to the gate permits current to flow in an n-channel MOSFET. A positive voltage has the same effect in a p-channel MOSFET. The voltage to the gate creates an electric field in the gate region. The field increases or reduces the number of charge carriers in that region, thus controlling current flow.

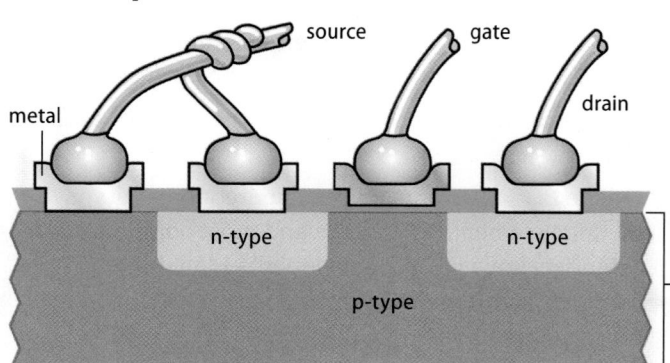

◀ **MOSFETs** are favored for use in high-frequency applications and integrated circuits.

Superconductors

Superconductivity is the ability of some materials to conduct electric current without resistance at extremely low temperatures. These materials, called *superconductors*, have many useful properties.

- Electric current can flow through a superconductor without loss of energy.
- Superconductors can also produce powerful magnetic fields.

Critical Temperature

A superconductor loses its resistance below a certain temperature, called the *critical temperature*. The critical temperature of many metallic superconductors is close to absolute zero (−273.15°C or 0 K). (See page 788.)

Different superconductors have different critical temperatures. For certain metals, the critical temperature is very close to absolute zero.

Critical Temperatures of Superconductors	
Mercury	−269°C (4 K)
Lead	−265.78°C (7.22 K)
Niobium germanium alloy	−249.8°C (23.2 K)
Niobium tin alloy	−255 °C (18 K)
Magnesium diboride	−234 °C (39 K)
Yttrium-barium-copper oxide	−180 °C (93 K)
Mercury-barium-calcium-copper oxide	−140 °C (133 K)

Explaining Superconductivity

A theory explaining one type of superconductivity was proposed in the mid-1950s by three American physicists—John Bardeen, Leon Cooper, and John Robert Schrieffer. Their theory is called the *BCS theory,* from the initials of their last names.

BCS Theory. Normal conductors consist of positive ions surrounded by free-moving electrons that can carry electric current. These electrons scatter off the positive ions, creating resistance.

In the BCS theory, superconductivity occurs when the electrons stop behaving as individual particles and begin to move in a more organized way.

Cooper Pairs. The organized state consists of electron pairs called *Cooper pairs,* named for Leon Cooper.

- Normally, negatively charged electrons repel each other.
- In superconductivity, a passing electron gently tugs nearby positive ions closer together, leaving behind a trail of slight positive charge.
- This short-lived charge attracts a second electron toward the first, forming a Cooper pair.
- When the electrons in a metal are linked as Cooper pairs, they no longer scatter off the positive ions.
- As a result, they move through the material without resistance.

The BCS theory describes superconductivity in metallic elements and alloys and most compounds. Scientists have not yet developed a model that explains superconductivity in copper oxides and some other compounds.

APPLICATIONS OF SUPERCONDUCTORS

The need for expensive, bulky cooling equipment limits the use of superconductors. However, several interesting applications of superconductivity exist.

Superconductor Uses	
Today	**Use**
magnetic resonance imaging (MRI) machines	Magnetic fields produce images of tissue inside the body.
particle accelerators	Superconducting magnets enable scientists to study tiny bits of matter.
In the Future	
high-efficiency power lines	
high-speed electronic devices	
extremely sensitive magnetic field detectors	

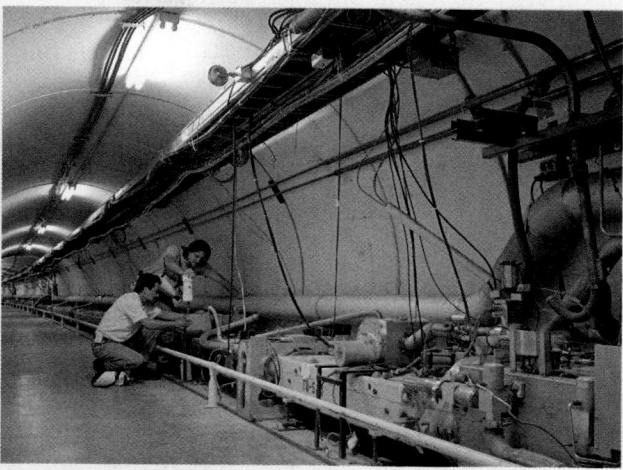

Superconducting magnets are used in particle accelerators, like this one in Fermilab, to speed up and collide ions and subatomic particles in order to study the particles and the forces that govern them.

High-Temperature Superconductors

In 1987, Swiss physicist Karl Alexander Muller and German physicist Georg Bednorz were awarded the Nobel Prize in Physics for their work on superconductivity. They had discovered materials that are superconductors at significantly higher temperatures than metallic superconductors.

In subsequent years, scientists discovered a large number of similar compounds with even higher critical temperatures. These newly discovered compounds are ceramics, not metals.

Superconducting Mystery. The structures of many of these superconducting compounds contain planes of copper and oxygen atoms. These planes form the layers that carry the superconducting charge carriers.

Scientists believe that paired electrons are responsible for the superconducting current. However, scientists have not yet been able to determine what forces are holding these pairs together.

Cheaper and Easier. These superconducting ceramic compounds offer important technical applications.

Normally, superconducting magnets have to be cooled to temperatures below 4 K using liquid helium, which is very expensive.

Many high-temperature superconductors, however, are superconducting above 77 K, the temperature at which liquid nitrogen—which is much cheaper—can be used for cooling.

The Main Difficulties. Several problems still have to be solved before high-temperature superconductors can be widely applied in technology.

- The brittleness of the material makes it difficult to shape into wires.
- The low current density—the amount of current high-temperature superconductors can carry—is very small compared with that of conventional superconductors.

Some superconductors can produce magnetic fields more than 400,000 times stronger than Earth's magnetic field!

LIGHT is a form of electromagnetic energy that can travel freely through space. This energy travels in patterns of electric and magnetic influence called electromagnetic waves. (See pages 810–811.)

There are many kinds of electromagnetic energy, including infrared rays, radio waves, ultraviolet rays, and X-rays. Human beings can see only a tiny part of all the different kinds of electromagnetic energy. This part is called visible light.

The Nature of Light

Light is dualistic in nature—it behaves both like a wave and like a particle traveling along a ray. Therefore, its properties must be explained by two separate and distinct theories.

- wave theory
- quantum theory

VISIBLE LIGHT AND THE ELECTROMAGNETIC SPECTRUM

A beam of white light passing through a prism is spread into a rainbowlike band of colors called the visible spectrum. Each color has a particular wavelength and frequency. The spreading occurs because the prism bends light of different wavelengths to varying degrees.

Light with shorter, or bluer, wavelengths bends the most. Light with longer, or redder, wavelengths bends the least.

All of the light that we can see makes up only a tiny portion of the full electromagnetic spectrum, as seen in the illustration.

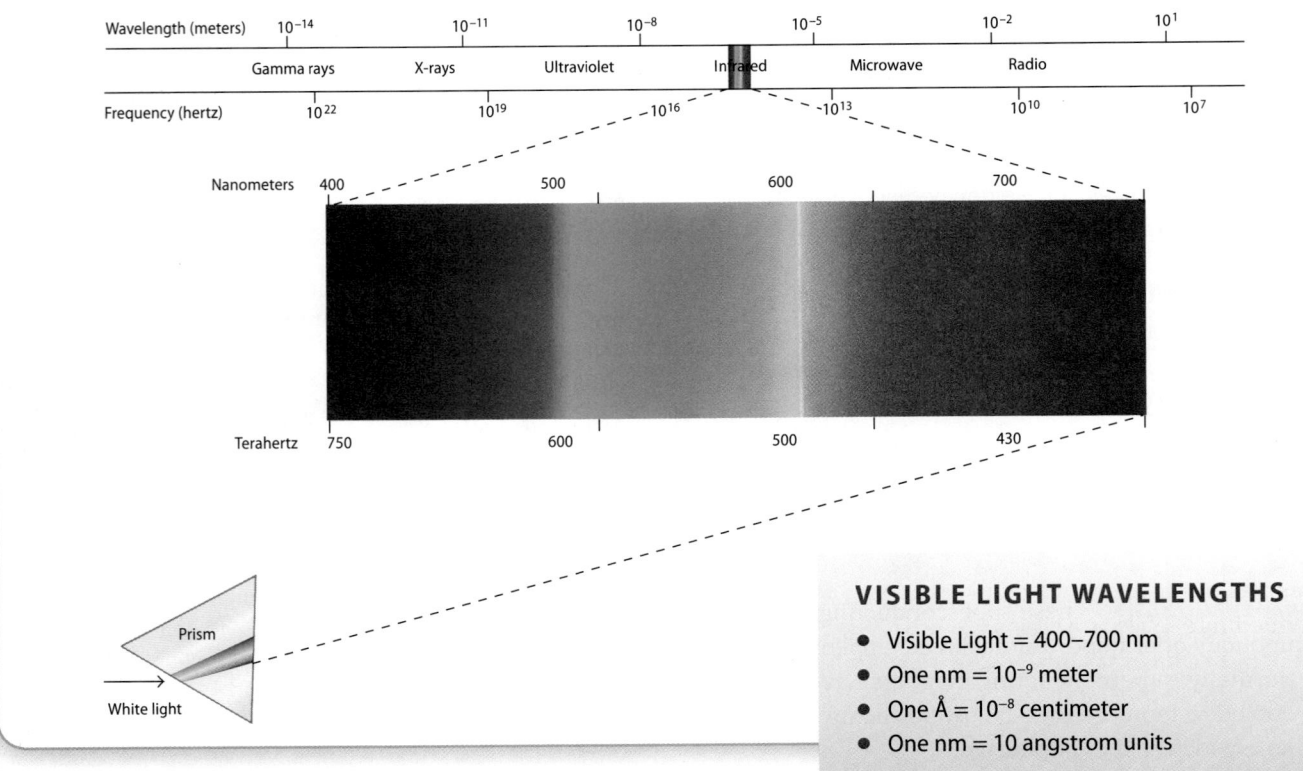

VISIBLE LIGHT WAVELENGTHS
- Visible Light = 400–700 nm
- One nm = 10^{-9} meter
- One Å = 10^{-8} centimeter
- One nm = 10 angstrom units

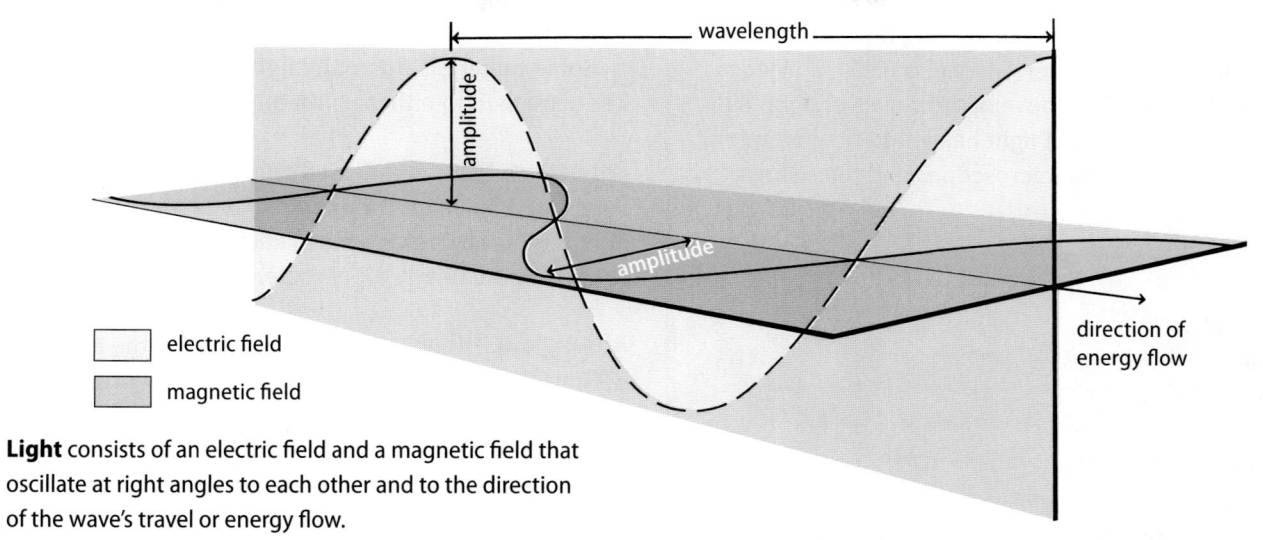

wavelength

amplitude

amplitude

direction of energy flow

☐ electric field

▨ magnetic field

Light consists of an electric field and a magnetic field that oscillate at right angles to each other and to the direction of the wave's travel or energy flow.

Wave Theory

Light is energy that travels in electromagnetic waves. These waves are *transverse waves,* meaning that light energy travels at right angles to the direction in which the waves travel.

Spherical Waves. In a luminous body, such as an incandescent bulb, the light waves travel out spherically, in three dimensions, from the bulb.

Electromagnetic waves can be depicted as follows.

- *A* represents the *amplitude* of the transverse wave— the maximum electric or magnetic intensity.

- The period, *T,* is the time it takes the wave to travel one wavelength, λ.

- Thus, λ equals velocity times time, or $λ = VT.$

- Velocity, therefore, equals wavelength divided by period, $V = λ/T.$

- Frequency is equal to $1/T$, so V can be equated to frequency times wavelength, $νλ.$

The Electromagnetic Spectrum. Electromagnetic waves are in the electromagnetic spectrum, which is divided into various regions. These regions, from long wavelengths to short, are radio waves, Hertzian waves or microwaves, infrared, visible light, ultraviolet rays, X-rays, and gamma rays.

The Visible Spectrum. In the visible light region, or *visible spectrum,* the waves are classified by the colors the human eye senses on receiving certain wavelengths. The wavelength is usually given in *nanometers* (nm). Wavelengths, especially in the visible region, are also denoted in *angstrom* (Å) units. Frequency is measured in *terahertz* (trillion hertz). One *hertz* equals one cycle per second.

Visible light has wavelengths from about 400 to 700 nm (4000 to 7000 Å). Its frequency ranges from about 430 to 750 terahertz.

Quantum Theory

Quantum theory explains light effects left unexplained by electromagnetic theory. It regards electromagnetic energy as traveling in small packets. A single packet is called a *quantum,* or *photon.*

The energy in a quantum is given by the expression $e = hv.$

- *e* is the energy in the photon

- *h* is a constant called Planck's constant

- *v* is the frequency

The existence of these discrete photons has been shown by the work of Niels Bohr, Albert Einstein, and Max Planck.

How Light Behaves

Scientists study light by observing how it interacts with itself and with matter. They use their knowledge of how light behaves to develop new uses of light in technology. The study of light has led to the invention of such instruments as microscopes and telescopes.

SPEED OF LIGHT

Light travels at a velocity of approximately 299,793 km per second (186,283 miles per second) in a vacuum and at practically the same speed in the atmosphere. The velocity is lower in all other transparent media.

- In water, the velocity of light is approximately 225,500 km per second (140,000 miles per second).

- The distance light travels in 1 second is roughly equivalent to seven times around Earth at the equator.

Reflection and Absorption

Some materials do not let light pass through them. They are said to either *reflect* the light or *absorb* it.

Reflection. Light is reflected when most of its energy is radiated back, as, for example, by a mirror. When light strikes such shiny metal surfaces as silver, gold, or aluminum, nearly all of the energy is reflected.

Absorption. When light strikes a surface, the amount of light that is not reflected is absorbed by the surface. A sheet of black paper does not reflect light, but absorbs it. Carbon black absorbs almost all the wavelengths of light, so it appears to us as black.

Refraction

When light passes into a denser medium from a less dense medium, its path is altered. This change in the direction of a light ray is called *refraction*. (See page 800.)

The velocity of light varies in different media, being greater in a less dense medium than in a denser medium. For example, the velocity of light is greater in air than in glass.

Refraction. Light slows as it moves from air into glass, causing it to bend toward the normal. The *angle of refraction,* measured between the normal and the refracted ray, is thus smaller than the angle of incidence. As light exits the glass, it travels faster, bending away from the normal.

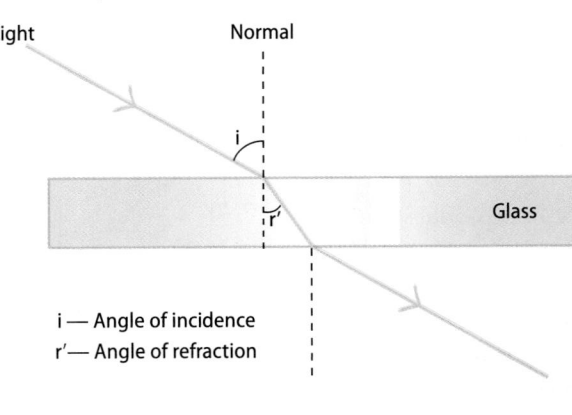

i — Angle of incidence
r' — Angle of refraction

Transmission. Glass is said to *transmit* light almost perfectly. That is, it allows significant amounts of light to pass through it. Only a small part of the transmitted light is absorbed.

Creating Color. Some materials absorb only a fraction of wavelengths and reflect light at other wavelengths.

A surface will appear as red if it absorbs all wavelengths but red light. A white surface does not absorb light in any specific wavelength range, so it reflects all the wavelengths it receives.

Reflection. A ray of light will reflect from a smooth surface, such as a mirror. The *angle of reflection* is measured in relation to the *normal,* an imaginary line perpendicular to the surface. The angle of reflection equals the *angle of incidence,* the angle formed by the normal and the incident (incoming) ray.

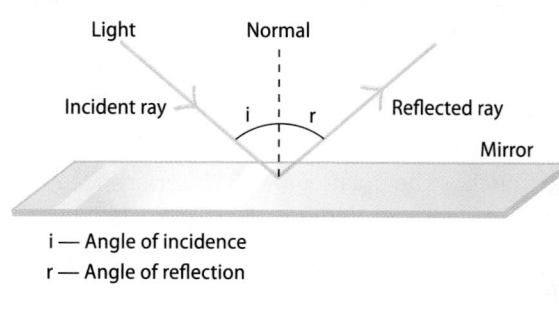

Light   Normal

Incident ray   i   r   Reflected ray

Mirror

i — Angle of incidence
r — Angle of reflection

Index of Refraction. Every material that transmits light is said to have an *index of refraction:* the velocity of light in a vacuum divided by the velocity of light at the same wavelength in the material.

The index of refraction, *n,* may be stated in the form of an equation:

$$n = \frac{\text{velocity of light in vacuum}}{\text{velocity of light in material}}$$

In the equation, the two velocities are for the same wavelength of light. The index of refraction depends, therefore, on the material and on the wavelength.

Density, More or Less. When a ray of light passes from a less dense medium into a more dense medium, the ray is bent toward the normal. Conversely, when the ray passes from a more dense medium into a less dense medium, it is bent away from the normal.

Snell's Law. The incident ray, the normal, and the refracted ray all lie in the same plane. For any given wavelength, the index of refraction of the first medium

multiplied by the sine of the angle of incidence is equal to the index of refraction of the second medium multiplied by the sine of the angle of refraction.

$$n_i \sin i = n_r \sin r$$

Dispersion

Since the index of refraction of a medium is different for different wavelengths of light, the component wavelengths of white light are bent by varying amounts when the light passes through a prism.

The light is separated into its component colors: red, orange, yellow, green, blue, indigo, and violet. This process is called *dispersion.*

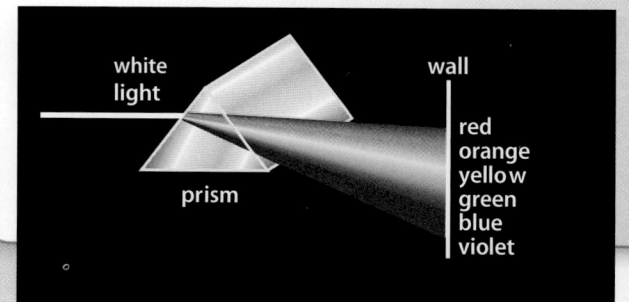

white light   wall

red
orange
yellow
green
blue
violet

prism

Interference and Diffraction

Interference

When two or more light waves cross, they interact. This interaction is called *interference*. (See page 801.)

Constructive Interference. Consider two light waves of the same frequency. If both waves are "in phase," that is, if the troughs and crests occur at the same time, the amplitudes of the waves will overlap and enhance each other.

This phenomenon is called *constructive interference*.

Destructive Interference. If two waves of equal frequency and equal amplitude are "out of phase," that is, if the trough of one wave matches the crest of the other wave, the amplitudes will cancel each other out, and the resultant amplitude will be zero.

This phenomenon is called *destructive interference*.

Fringes. When the combined light of the interfering waves strikes a surface, it forms an interference pattern of bright and dark regions called *fringes*.

- Regions of constructive interference often appear as bright lines or circles.
- Areas of destructive interference appear dark.

Interference in the World. The colors seen on a thin film of oil or a soap bubble are caused by interference effects at the surface of the medium.

- Light is reflected from the top and bottom surfaces of a film.
- Interference occurs at the top surface.
- The interference depends upon the wavelengths of the light, the index of refraction of the material, and the film thickness.

Diffraction

Light that passes through a small opening, such as a pinhole, will spread out in space. This spreading is called *diffraction*. (See page 801.)

Light also diffracts when it passes near a sharp edge. For example, careful measurements of the shadow of the sharp end of a razor blade show that light spreads at the shadow's edge.

How It Works

- When a beam of light passes through a slit to a screen beyond it, a number of alternate light and dark areas appear on the screen.
- These areas are similar to the light and dark areas produced by interference.
- The light has bent around the corners of the slit.
- This same diffraction effect takes place with all waves, such as sound and water waves.

The Diffraction Pattern. Light rays coming from the slit can be divided into two parts.

- rays coming from the upper part of the slit
- rays coming from the lower part

Depending on the angle, the upper and lower parts of the rays interfere constructively or destructively, thus forming the light and dark bands.

Gratings. Diffraction can serve a purpose in technology. A device called a *diffraction grating* can separate the colors in a beam of light for study. A diamond point is used to cut very narrow parallel slits on a piece of glass. The grating consists of thousands of thin slits that diffract light.

When a beam of parallel rays of white light strikes such a grating, the various wavelengths are spread out by the diffraction, and a spectrum is produced.

This is similar to the color spectrum produced by a prism, except that in the case of diffraction the longest wavelength is bent most. In the case of prism refraction, red light is bent least.

Interference. Light waves can interfere with one another in two ways: (1) constructive interference and (2) destructive interference.

Constructive interference occurs where the crest of one wave meets the crest of another—or where the trough of one wave meets the trough of another. The two waves reinforce each other, forming a bright region of light.

Destructive interference occurs where a crest meets a trough. The two waves cancel, leaving a dark region.

The diagram shows the pattern of interference formed by light waves from two slits. The photograph shows interference in water waves produced by two sources.

Grating Uses

- Used with a telescope, a grating can separate the colors in the light from a star, enabling scientists to learn what materials make up the star.

- Used with an optical fiber, a grating can combine many wavelengths of light so that the fiber can carry many signals on one small strand of glass.

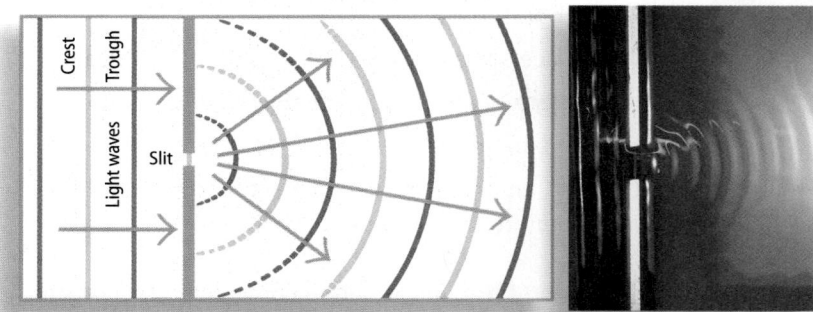

▲ **Diffraction.** Light and other waves usually travel in a straight line. But when waves meet certain obstacles or openings, they diffract, or spread out.

In this diagram, the crests and troughs of light waves are straight as they near a slit. The waves diffract at the slit, forming curved crests and troughs. The photograph shows this effect in water waves, where it is easier to see than in light.

SCATTERING

Another way that light behaves is called *scattering*. Scattering occurs when light rays strike atoms, molecules, other tiny particles, or rough surfaces. The particles send the rays of light off in new directions—that is, they cause the rays to scatter.

Most of a clear sky appears blue because air molecules scatter more higher-frequency, or bluer, rays of sunlight than they do lower-frequency, or redder, rays. As a result, we see blue light coming from nearly every direction in the sky. The red and orange light scatters less, and so it travels in a relatively straight path.

OPTICS is the branch of physics and engineering that is concerned with the properties of light. Optics deals with how light is produced, how it is transmitted, and how it can be detected, measured, and used.

There are three major branches of optics:

Geometrical optics traces the paths of light rays through such devices as lenses and a variety of other optical instruments.

Physical optics deals with light as a form of electromagnetic radiation.

Quantum optics studies the nature of light as individual particles called photons.

Prisms are an important part of many optical instruments, including spectrometers and other instruments that are used to measure the spectral composition of light.

Geometrical Optics

Geometrical optics is concerned with the study of light paths through optical systems, more specifically the laws governing reflection and refraction. The basic assumption of geometric optics is that light travels in rectilinear paths.

Reflecting Light

When a ray of light from an object strikes a plane mirror, it does not change. It merely travels in a new direction. The properties of reflected light result in certain constants in reflected images.

- When looking at a plane mirror, the eye sees a reflected image that is identical to the actual object.
- The reflected image appears to be at the same distance behind the mirror as the object is in front of the mirror.
- A line joining the object and the image would be perpendicular to the mirror.
- The image is said to be *virtual*. That is, the rays appear to be coming directly from the object, even though they are not.

Prisms

A prism is a solid with two parallel bases joined by three or more lateral surfaces. Transparent prisms are widely used in optics.

Reflecting prisms are used in optical instruments for a number of reasons.

1. to displace a beam of light through a certain distance
2. to deflect a beam of light through a known angle
3. to rotate an image
4. to invert an image formed by a lens before the image enters another lens

Prism Systems. Prisms are often combined into a prism system. For example, two prisms may be combined so that the rays entering and exiting the system are parallel, although laterally displaced.

Since the image formed by this system is inverted, binoculars use this system to reinvert the image formed by the objective lens and eyepiece.

Curved Mirrors

The physics of reflection are somewhat altered when the light is reflected off a curved surface. A spherical mirror is the simplest curved mirror. Its reflecting surface is a section of a sphere.

There are two main types of curved mirrors.

- *convex mirrors*
- *concave mirrors*

Convex mirrors are mirrors whose outer surface of the sphere segment is reflective. Parallel rays reflected by a convex mirror *diverge,* or spread apart.

Concave mirrors are mirrors whose inner surface of the sphere segment is reflective. Parallel rays reflected by a concave mirror *converge,* or come together.

The Focus. The point at which the rays converge is called the *focus* of the mirror.

A spherical mirror focuses well only those rays that are close to the *optical axis* of the mirror. The optical axis is the line perpendicular to the surface of the mirror and passing through its center.

Rays reflected off the mirror at some distance from the optical axis meet at a point closer to the mirror. This phenomenon is called *spherical aberration*.

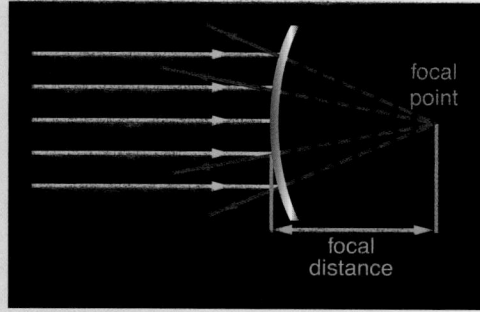

CONVEX MIRROR

In a convex mirror, parallel rays diverge from a point behind the mirror.

focal point

focal distance

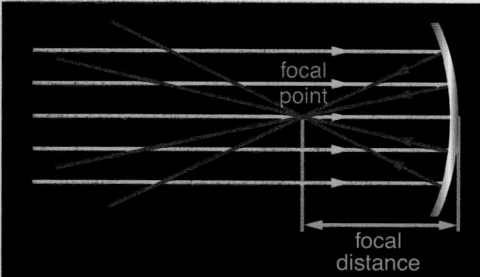

CONCAVE MIRROR

Parallel rays reflected by a concave mirror meet at a point called the focus.

focal point

focal distance

A parabolic mirror will focus a beam of parallel rays perfectly at one point. Because of the absence of aberration, parabolic mirrors are used extensively in optical telescopes and in radio telescopes.

THE BASICS: GEOMETRICAL OPTICS

The incident ray is a ray of light that strikes a surface.

The normal is a line drawn perpendicular to the surface at the point where the incident ray strikes the surface.

The angle of incidence is the angle between the incident ray and the normal.

The angle of reflection is the angle between the reflected ray and the normal.

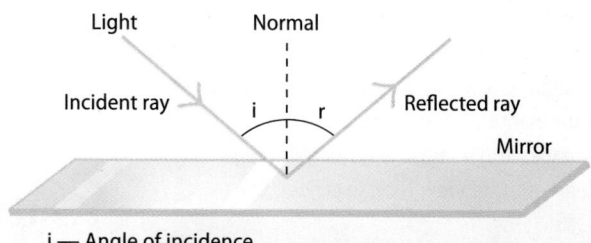

Light   Normal

Incident ray   i   r   Reflected ray

Mirror

i — Angle of incidence
r — Angle of reflection

The law of reflection states that when a ray of light is reflected from a surface, the incident ray, reflected ray, and normal all lie in the same plane.

The law of reflection also states that the angle of incidence is equal to the angle of reflection.

Lenses

A lens is made of a material that *transmits* light, or allows light to pass through it. Its surfaces are shaped so that when light passes through the lens, the light will be refracted.

Lenses, which are usually made to form images, are generally of two types:

- positive (convex)
- negative (concave)

Positive Lenses

The simplest positive lens manufactured is disk-shaped, and it bulges outward equally on both sides. The lens of the human eye has the same general shape, but the side that "faces the world" is slightly flatter than the back side. Any lens that bulges outward on both sides, equally or not, is a *double-convex* lens. *Convex* means *curving out.* Positive lenses are used in eyeglasses to correct farsightedness.

Negative Lenses

The simplest kind of negative lens is disk-shaped, and it curves inward equally on both sides. Any lens that curves inward on both sides is a *double-concave* lens. *Concave* means *curving in.* Other negative lenses have one flat side and one side that curves inward. Negative lenses are used in eyeglasses to correct myopia (nearsightedness).

LENSES

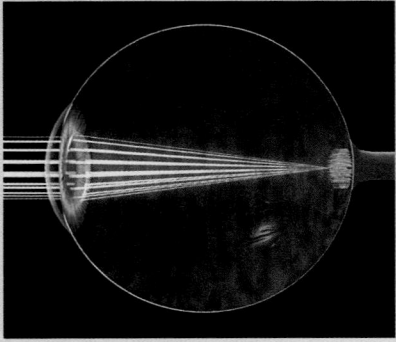

Positive (Convex) Lens

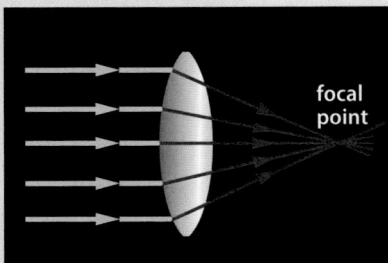

focal point

A positive lens is thicker in the middle than at the edges.

Negative (Concave) Lens

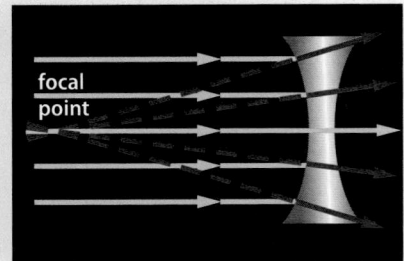

focal point

A negative lens is thinner in the middle than at the edges.

CORRECTIVE LENSES

Normally the lens of the eye focuses an image on the retina. (See pages 244–245.) The lens adjusts itself to the distance of the object being viewed. When viewing a faraway object, the lens is nearly flat. To view a close object, the lens thickens.

An eye that is nearsighted or farsighted is unable to focus an image properly on the retina. Corrective lenses, in the form of glasses or contact lenses, help bring the image into focus.

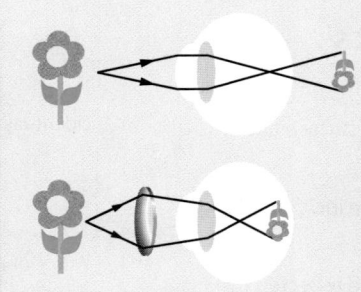

Farsighted Eye. The focal point is behind the retina. A positive lens causes the focal point to be moved forward so it rests on the retina.

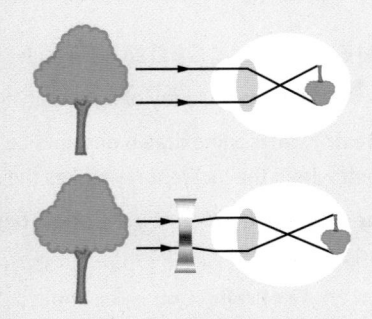

Nearsighted Eye. The focal point is in front of the retina. A negative lens causes the focal point to be moved back so it rests on the retina.

Creating an Image

A lens creates an image by *refraction*. Refraction is the bending of a light ray as it travels through the surface of a transparent material.

Real Images. It may be said that an image is *real* if it is on the side of the lens opposite to the object. That is, the image is real in the sense that if a screen is placed at the image distance, the image will be formed on the screen.

In the case of a slide projector, for example, the slide is the object; the lens becomes the projection lens; and on the screen is produced a real image of whatever is on the slide.

Image Inversion. The real image produced by a single lens is *inverted*, or upside down, and turned left for right, the right side of the object becoming, in effect, its left side in the image.

Virtual images only appear to be where they are seen. If a screen is placed at the point where the virtual image appears to be, no image is formed on the screen. However, to an eye looking through the lens, the image appears to be at that point.

Images Through a Positive Lens

- If the object is located between the first focus and the lens, the image is virtual, upright, and magnified. This is the principle of the simple magnifying glass.

- If the object is located at a distance greater than twice the focal length of the lens, the image is real, inverted, and reduced.

- If the object is located at a distance from the lens greater than once, but less than twice, its focal length, the image is real, magnified, and inverted.

- If the object is located at a distance equal to twice the focal length of the lens, the image will be real, inverted, and the same size as the object.

Images Through a Negative Lens

- For all positions of the object, the image is virtual, upright, and smaller.

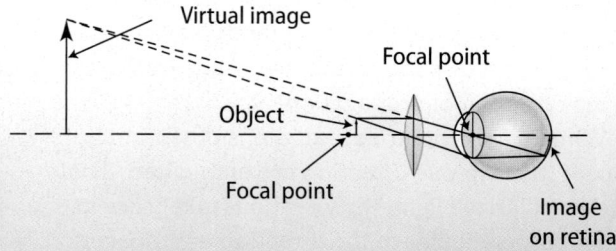

The eye's lens bends light rays, creating an image on the retina. When we view an object through a magnifying glass, the eye creates an image that is larger than the object.

LENS STRENGTH

Focal length determines a lens's power: the shorter the length, the greater the power. A lens's focal length is approximately the distance from its center to its *focal point*. This point is the focus of wave fronts that approach the lens as from the left in this diagram—perpendicular to the *optical axis,* a line through its center.

The linear magnification of a lens is the image height divided by the object height.

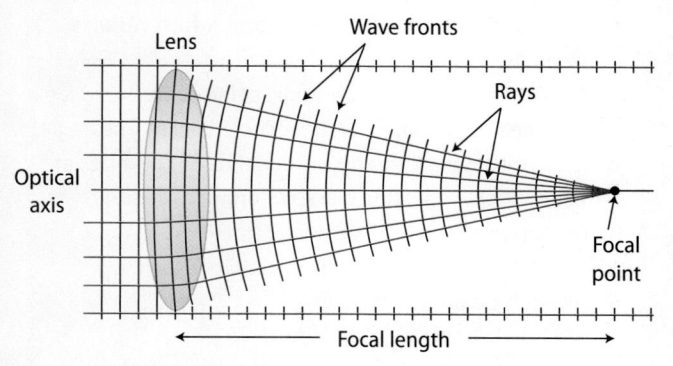

Polarized Light

Polarized light consists of light waves that vibrate in simple, regular patterns. In most of the light that we see, such as light from the sun or a lamp, the waves vibrate in many different directions. Such light is said to be *unpolarized*.

If the vibrations stay in the same direction or form the same shape for a long time, the light is said to be polarized.

How Polarization Works

Polarization is a phenomenon that depends not only on the fact that light travels as a wave but also on the fact that light waves are *transverse*. A transverse wave is one in which the medium—in this case, light—moves perpendicular to the direction in which the wave travels. For this reason, longitudinal waves, such as sound waves, cannot undergo polarization.

One-Way Vibrations. According to wave theory, light is an electromagnetic transverse wave. Ordinary light consists of waves whose vibrations take place in all possible directions, or planes, perpendicular to the direction of propagation.

When light is polarized, all paths of vibration except those in one direction are eliminated. Therefore, in polarized light, the vibrations take place in one plane perpendicular to the direction of propagation.

Linearly Polarized Light

Polarized light of this type, called linearly polarized or plane-polarized light, can be produced in a number of ways.

- Tourmaline, a transparent mineral containing aluminum, boron, silicon, and oxygen, transmits vibrations in only one plane.
- Polaroid, a man-made material developed in 1934 and consisting of transparent sheets resembling cellophane, possesses the same property.

Double Refracting Materials. Other crystalline materials, such as calcite and quartz, split an ordinary light beam into two beams. These two beams are plane-polarized light beams.

The planes of polarization in the two beams are at right angles to one another. Such crystalline materials are called double refracting.

Brewster's Law

The relationship between polarized light and the medium through which it passes was explained by Scottish physicist David Brewster in 1811.

Brewster's law states that a light ray will achieve its maximum polarization when a transparent medium is angled in such a way that the light ray is refracted at a 90° angle to the reflected ray.

POLARIZING SUNLIGHT

Reflection can polarize light, as when sunlight reflects off a car windshield. Sunlight is unpolarized—that is, its waves vibrate in many directions. The reflected light consists of more horizontally polarized light, which vibrates horizontally.

This is because, at a certain angle of incidence, vibrations in one plane predominate in the reflected beam. The angle of incidence at which this occurs depends on the index of refraction of the reflecting glass. For ordinary glass, this angle is approximately 57 degrees.

Vertically polarized sunglasses can block such horizontally polarized glare.

POLARIZING FILTERS

When a source of light is observed through a polarizing filter, such as a sheet of Polaroid, the eye cannot detect polarization, and the source appears as it would to the naked eye.

However, when the source of light is seen through two pieces of Polaroid whose transmitting planes of vibration are perpendicular to one another, the light source cannot be seen.

For any other angle between the transmission planes of the two sheets of Polaroid, some light from the source will reach the eye, with the maximum amount of light visible when the transmission planes are parallel.

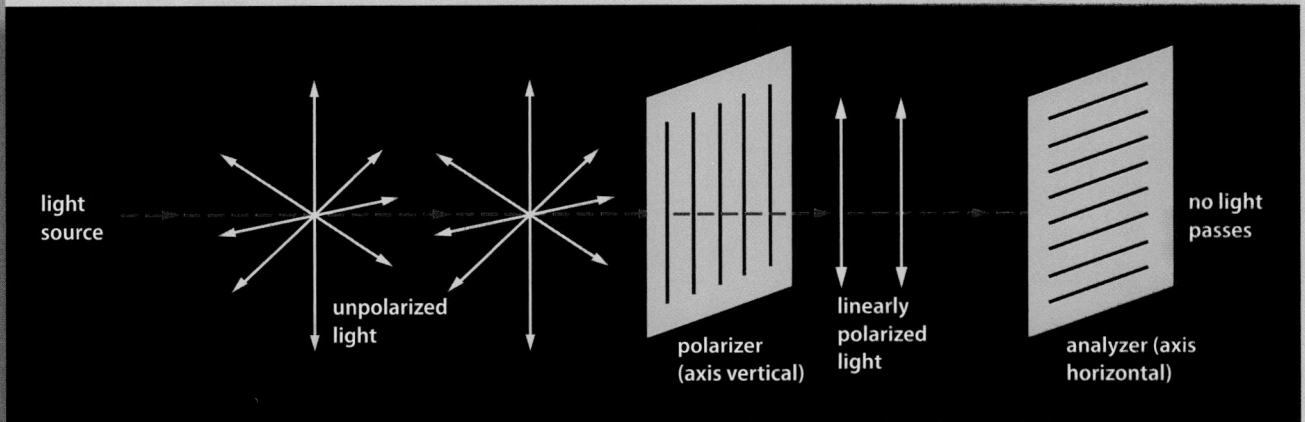

light source — unpolarized light — polarizer (axis vertical) — linearly polarized light — analyzer (axis horizontal) — no light passes

Rounded Polarization

In addition to plane polarization, light can also be *circularly polarized* and *elliptically polarized*.

In circular polarization, the plane of the vibration rotates and the maximum amplitude of the wave remains the same as the wave progresses.

In elliptical polarization, the plane of vibration rotates and the maximum amplitude of the wave varies as the wave progresses.

◀ **Polarized light** is made up of waves that vibrate in regular patterns. A wave consists in part of an electric field. The electric field oscillates as shown by the arrows, tracing out a shape as the wave travels. Vertically polarized light oscillates up and down. In circularly polarized light, the oscillations rotate in a circle.

Vertically Polarized Light — electric field — direction of travel

electric field

Circularly Polarized Light — direction of travel

Measuring Light

The definition of light is based on our visual awareness of radiation in a very narrow band of the electromagnetic spectrum, the visible region.

The eye is not equally sensitive to all visual light waves. Variation in sensitivity to wavelengths may be graphed as a *luminosity curve*.

Luminosity Curve

The luminosity curve for the average eye shows how the eye responds to equal amounts of energy at the various wavelengths within the visible region.

On the Curve

- Since the eye is more sensitive to wavelengths in the yellow region, yellows appear brighter than reds and blues.

- The most sensitive wavelength is at 555 nanometers (nm), and the curve is normalized by making the maximum ordinate at this point equal to 1.

- Above and below, the maximum curve falls off sharply. It drops to practically zero at 400 and 700 nm, the limits of the visible region.

Inverse Square Law

The inverse square law states that the illuminance on a surface varies inversely as the square of the distance from a point source.

For example, consider a surface whose illuminance is 1 lumen per square meter when it is at a distance of 1 meter from a point source. The illuminance on the surface will be ¼ lumen per square meter when the object is placed at a distance of 2 meters from the same source.

Uses

- The inverse square law makes it possible to compare the intensities of two point sources of light.

- Or, if one intensity is known, the other can be determined.

- In essence, the sources are so placed that the illuminance on the screen is the same from either source.

- In astronomy, the inverse square law is used to measure the distance of stars whose intrinsic luminosity is precisely known.

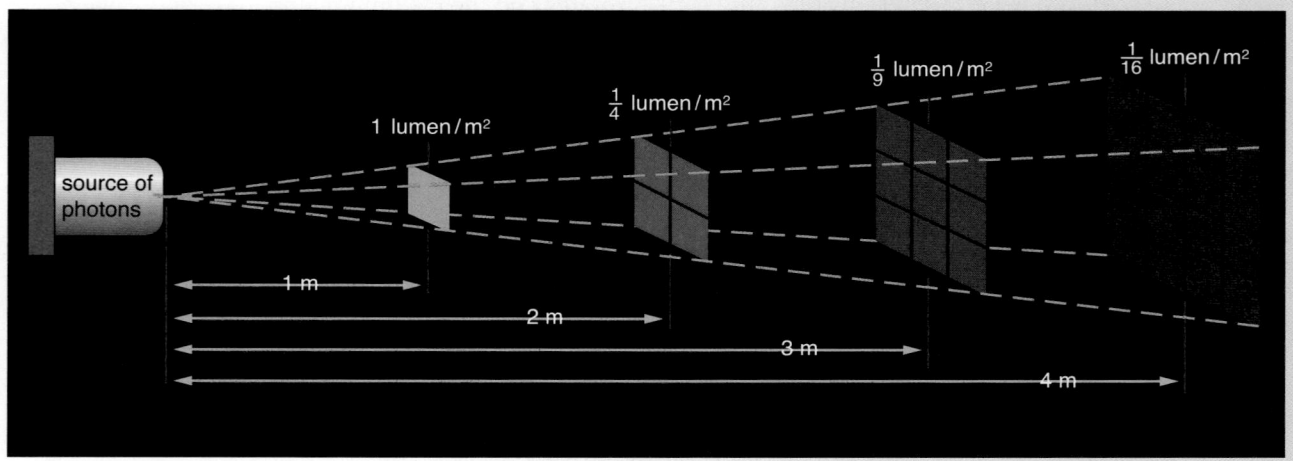

Radiant Units

Light is measured in two sets of units. There would be no need for two sets of units if the eye responded equally to all the visible wavelengths. If this were the case, only the purely physical radiometric units would be needed. The two sets of light units are:

- *luminous units*
- *radiometric units*

Luminous units, or *photometric units*, are units based on the visual interpretation of radiant energy.

Radiometric units are units based on the physical interpretation of radiation.

The candela, the standard unit of luminous intensity, gets its name from the fact that the light from a standard candle originally defined the unit.

Measuring Light					
Luminous Units			**Radiant Units**		
Unit	**Measures**	**Value**	**Unit**	**Measures**	**Value**
lumen	luminous flux or power		watt	radiant flux	at 555 nm, 1 watt equals 685 lumens
candela	luminous intensity	1 lumen per steradian	watts per steradian	watts per steradian	1 watt per steradian
illumination	luminous flux per unit area	1 foot-candela equals 1 lumen per sq. ft.	irradiance	watts per sq. ft.	
luminous emittance	total luminous flux per unit area (from an extended source rather than a point source)	lumens per square centimeter, lumens per square meter, lumens per square inch, lumens per square foot, and so on	radiant emittance	total radiant flux per unit area (from an extended source rather than a point source)	watts per square centimeter, watts per square meter, watts per square inch, watts per square foot, and so on
luminance	luminous intensity per unit area of the source (from an extended source rather than a point source)	candelas per square centimeter, candelas per square meter, candelas per square inch, and so on	radiance	radiant intensity per unit area of the source (from an extended source rather than a point source)	watts/steradians per square centimeter, watts/steradians per square meter, watts/steradians per square inch, and so on

Spectra and Atomic Structure

During the 19th century, scientists observing the light of a heated gas, such as a flame or an electrical discharge, through a spectroscope observed that the emitted radiation was concentrated in narrow regions of its spectrum.

Line Spectrum

These scientists found that for certain gases, only narrow colored lines were visible, instead of a continuous spectrum in which all colors are present. Such a spectrum was called a *line spectrum*, the lines were called *emission lines*.

If light with a continuous spectrum is sent through gas and then observed through a spectroscope, black lines, called *absorption lines,* appear in its spectrum.

Spectral Line Series. The Swiss mathematician Johann Balmer found in 1885 that the absorption and emission lines of hydrogen formed a series that could be represented by a simple formula.

WHAT'S A SPECTROSCOPE?

A spectroscope is an instrument for producing and examining the spectrum of a ray from any source. The spectrum produced by passing a light ray through a prism can be examined to determine the composition of the source of the ray.

Balmer's Equation

$$\frac{1}{\lambda} = R\left(\frac{1}{2^2} = \frac{1}{n^2}\right)$$

λ is the wavelength, R the *Rydberg constant,* and n an integral number with value 3, 4, 5, etc.

The Rydberg constant is a constant that describes the frequencies or wavelengths of light. It was developed by Swedish physicist Johannes Rydberg.

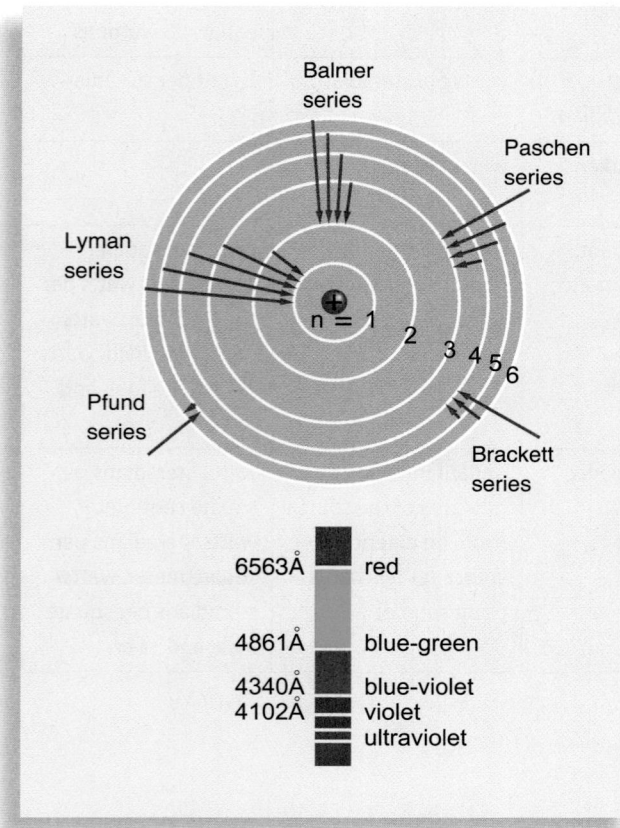

Atomic Structure and Line Spectra

An atom's electrons can only occupy certain stable orbits. Each orbit corresponds to an energy level of the atom. Electrons can jump from one orbit to another by absorbing or emitting energy in the form of a photon. (See pages 318–319.)

Photon Frequency. The energy of the emitted or absorbed photon, or the frequency of the associated wave, is proportional to the energy levels.

The lower and upper energy levels of the atom are designated E_1 and E_2. The frequency of the emitted photon will be given by the equation $(E_2 - E_1)/h$, where h is Planck's constant.

Each element has a characteristic line spectrum, so spectra are used to detect and identify chemical elements. For example, by studying the absorption lines present in sunlight, astronomers were able to determine the composition of the solar atmosphere.

◀ **An electron** can jump from one stable orbit to another by absorbing or emitting a photon with energy proportional to the energy difference between the two orbits. Photons thus emitted or absorbed produce a line spectrum.

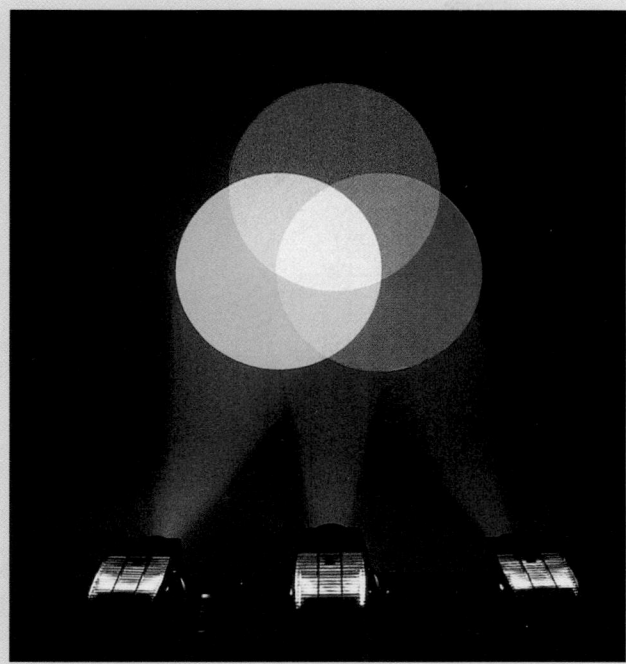

COLOR

The word *color* is used in various ways. It may refer to the sensation received in the brain when the retina is stimulated by light of a particular wavelength. It may be used to describe a property of an object, for example, a red barn.

Indeed, by definition, everything that is seen has a sensation of color associated with it. The only truly colorless things are those that are invisible, such as air.

The Visible Spectrum

When a beam of sunlight passes through a prism, the rays of different wavelengths are bent at different angles. The bending breaks up the sunlight into the visible spectrum. (See page 840.)

- Violet, at one end of the spectrum, consists of the shortest wavelengths of light that we can see.
- At the other end of the spectrum, the longest wavelengths of light that we can see appear deep red in color.

Black and White

- An object that reflects most of the light of all wavelengths in nearly equal amounts appears white.
- An object that absorbs most of the light of all wavelengths in nearly equal amounts appears black.

◄ **Primary Colors.** Red, green, and blue are the primary colors in light. They can be combined in various ways to form different colors. Combining all three primary colors results in white light.

Additive Process

Sunlight is essentially white light. If the colors of the spectrum are added in the same amounts in which they are known to appear in sunlight, white light will be produced. Sunlight is an *additive color mixture* of all the spectral colors.

Projecting Colors. When colors are projected on a screen simultaneously by two or more projectors, different colors are obtained in regions where the colored images overlap. Similarly, when a disk made up of different colored sectors is rotated rapidly in front of the eye, the eye sees a color different from that of any of the colored sectors.

Primary Colors. Since the greatest number of color variations can be produced by additively mixing red, green, and blue, they are called the primary colors.

Complementary Colors. In some cases, it is possible to produce white light by adding two colored lights instead of three. Such colors are called complementary colors. Purple and green, for example, are complementary.

Subtractive Process

When white light is passed through an optical filter, the filter transmits a percentage of the incident light at each particular wavelength in the visible region.

- If the filter is yellow, it transmits a greater percentage of yellow light than light of other wavelengths. A blue filter transmits a larger percentage of blue light, and so on.
- If the incident light passes a blue filter and yellow filter in combination, the light transmitted is of the wavelengths where the transmission curves of the two filters overlap.
- In the case of the blue and yellow filters, the greatest percentage of light transmitted is in the green region; thus, green light is observed through the two filters.

Since each filter subtracts a certain amount of energy from the incident light, this method is called the *subtractive method* of color mixing.

Lasers

A *laser*—Light Amplification by Stimulated Emission of Radiation—is a device that produces a very powerful beam of light. They are used in a large number of optical experiments and instruments, and in optical communication.

Laser Light

Light emitted by a laser has two main qualities that distinguish it from ordinary light.

1. It is *coherent.*
2. It is *monochromatic.*

Coherent light refers to the fact that the waves are in the same phase relation—their up/down motion is concurrent.

A typical light source, such as the glowing filament of a lamp, emits light in small wave packets in random directions and with no special phase relationships. This light is incoherent.

It is difficult to create interference phenomena with incoherent light. This is because light wave packets with random phase differences interfere with one another so that no clear-cut constructive or destructive interference is possible.

In coherent light, by contrast, all the wave packets are in phase. The amplitude of each wave packet goes through a crest and a trough at the same time.

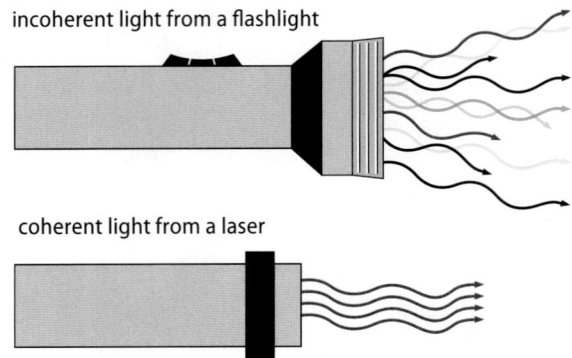

incoherent light from a flashlight

coherent light from a laser

Lasers produce coherent light. Waves of coherent light, unlike waves of incoherent light, move "in step" with one another. As a result, they spread out slightly—even over great distances.

Monochromatic light refers to the fact that the light is a single color, or there is only one wavelength.

Ordinary light consists of waves of many wavelengths—and colors. When all these waves are seen together at the same time, their colors appear white—like those from a lightbulb.

Light produced by most lasers consists of waves with a very narrow range of wavelengths, and so it appears to consist of a single color.

LASER FOCUS

One important use of lasers is LASIK surgery. LASIK surgery is a medical procedure used to correct certain eye defects that cause imperfect vision. LASIK stands for *l*aser-*a*ssisted in *si*tu *k*eratomileusis.

Fuzzy Focus. Eye defects called refractive errors prevent the eye from properly focusing light to create images. These defects include myopia (nearsightedness), hyperopia (farsightedness), and astigmatism.

Laser Surgery. During LASIK surgery, a surgeon cuts a thin flap on the surface of the cornea, the clear tissue that covers the eyeball and focuses light onto the retina at the back of the

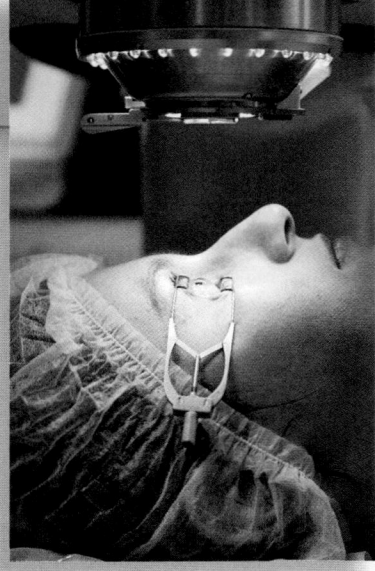

eye. The flap is folded back to expose the underlying corneal tissue. The surgeon applies a beam from a type of laser called an excimer laser to the eye. The excimer laser beam reshapes the cornea so that it can properly focus light. The doctor then carefully lays the flap back over the exposed cornea.

People who undergo LASIK surgery can reduce or even eliminate dependency on eyeglasses or contact lenses.

Producing Laser Light

Laser light results from changes in the amount of energy stored by the atoms in an active medium. The central process of a laser is called *stimulated emission*.

The Usual. Normally, atoms or molecules raised to a higher energy level—by the absorption of a photon, for example—fall down to a lower energy level spontaneously after a short time by emitting a photon. This process is called *spontaneous emission*.

Stimulated emission is when an atom or molecule raised to a higher energy level is induced to emit a photon when another photon with the same frequency interacts with the atom or molecule.

The emitted photon has exactly the same frequency, the same direction, and the same phase as the interacting photon. The creation of this extra photon underlies the amplifying principle of the laser.

Light Amplification. In a laser, a certain amount of matter, called the *active medium,* is used for light amplification. If the atoms are left undisturbed, most of them will be in the ground state. This means that the population of atoms in the ground state will be much larger than the population of atoms in an excited state.

In order to obtain light amplification by stimulated emission, the population of excited atoms must be made larger than the population of atoms in the ground state. This condition is termed *population inversion*.

Optical pumping is a process that can create a population inversion. In optical pumping, atoms are pumped to a higher energy level by light.

- When a beam of light enters a chamber containing atoms in which population inversion is achieved, the photons interact with the excited atoms.

- These atoms transmit photons of the same frequency and in the same direction as the incoming photons.

- Many of the newly created photons interact with other excited atoms, producing new photons in a manner resembling a chain reaction.

The optical cavity is a chamber containing the active medium placed between two parallel mirrors, one of them semitransparent.

- The light beam bounces between the two mirrors several times and becomes amplified each time it travels through the active medium.

- The beam finally emerges from the laser through the semitransparent mirror.

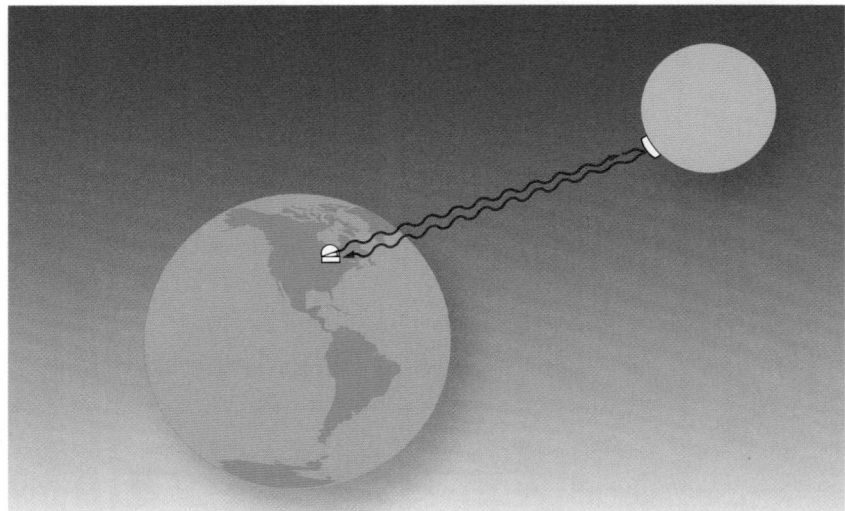

A laser beam sent from Earth can be used to measure the distance to the moon to an accuracy of 5 centimeters (2 inches). The beam bounces off a laser reflector that was placed on the moon by astronauts; then it returns to Earth. (See pages 922–923.)

THEORIES OF RELATIVITY

Einstein's theories of relativity explain the behavior of matter, energy, and even time and space. They are two of the "foundation blocks" upon which modern physics is built. The theories describe events so strange that people find it difficult to understand how they could possibly occur. For example, one person can observe that two events happen at the same time, while another person observes that they occur at different times. Matter can turn into energy, and energy can turn into matter.

Special and General Relativity

Until the beginning of the 20th century, scientists believed that Newton's laws of motion and of gravity offered a satisfactory basis for explaining the physical world. (See pages 762–763.) Then a series of experiments began to raise questions about motion, and about the behavior and speed of light.

Special Relativity

In 1905, Albert Einstein published a theory based on the notion that it is impossible to determine the absolute motion of a moving object.

Assumptions. Einstein's theory is based on the following assumptions.

- Absolute speed cannot be measured; only speed relative to some other object can be measured.
- The measured value of the speed of light in a vacuum is always the same no matter how fast the observer or light source is moving.
- The maximum velocity possible in the universe is that of light.

ALBERT EINSTEIN

1879–1955

Einstein was the most important physicist of the 1900s and one of the greatest and most famous scientists of all time. He was a theoretical physicist, a scientist who creates and develops theories of matter and energy.

- He was working as a patent clerk when he wrote three of his most famous theories.
- He left his native Germany due to anti-Semitic threats.
- In 1939, he warned the U.S. that Germany might be developing an atomic weapon. This led to the U.S. development of the atomic bomb.
- He became a United States citizen in 1940.
- A pacifist, he worked for international controls on nuclear energy and weapons after World War II.

Conclusions

From these assumptions, Einstein could show that when the velocity of a body increases, three things happen.

1. Its mass increases.
2. Its length changes: a body moving at high speed is shorter than a body at rest. However, these changes in mass and length will be perceived differently by observers moving at different speeds relative to each other.
3. Time slows at high speeds.

The Twin Paradox

The slowing of time can be demonstrated by the twin paradox: One twin takes off in a spaceship and makes a trip through space at a speed close to the velocity of light; the other twin stays on Earth. When the first twin comes back from his trip, he will be younger than the twin who stayed behind.

$E = mc^2$

One of the most important consequences of Einstein's theory is the equivalency of mass and energy, $E = mc^2$. This equation shows that whenever energy is created it is associated with a decrease in mass. In ordinary chemical reactions, the decrease in mass is not measurable, but in nuclear reactions, a sizable fraction of the mass of atoms is converted into energy.

◄ **Mass-to-energy conversion** is responsible for the tremendous destructive force of nuclear weapons.

General Relativity

Einstein developed the general theory of relativity to modify Newton's law of gravitation so that it would agree with special relativity.

Testing the Theory. Einstein suggested that astronomers could make certain observations to test the general theory of relativity. The most dramatic of these would be a bending of light rays by the sun's gravitation.

- In relativity, mass and energy are equivalent.
- Because light carries energy, it is also affected by gravity.
- The light-bending effect is small, but Einstein calculated that it could be observed during a solar eclipse.

In 1919, the British astronomer Arthur S. Eddington observed it, thereby making Einstein world-famous.

▲ **In general relativity theory,** matter and energy *distort* (change the shape of) space-time, and the distortion is experienced as gravity. A more common—but less precise—way of explaining the distortion is "mass curves space." This diagram shows how space curves around a mass.

NUCLEAR PHYSICS

is the study of atomic nuclei and the application of nuclear processes to technology. Nuclear physics began in about 1900 as the study of radioactive materials, such as radium and uranium. In the atoms of these materials, the nucleus changes, emitting particles and energy.

▲ **Hydrogen Atom.** In the atom of the commonest form of hydrogen, which is composed of one electron and one proton, the mass of the nucleus is 1,837 times greater than the mass of the region outside the nucleus.

Atomic Structure

An atom is about 10^{-10}, or 0.0000000001 meter (m) in diameter. An atom is incredibly small: a drop of water contains 6 sextillion (6 followed by 21 zeros) atoms. This tiny thing is made up of parts that are even smaller—*protons*, *neutrons*, and *electrons*.

The neutrons and protons of an atom form its nucleus. (See pages 314–319.)

- The nucleus is about 10^{-12} m in diameter.
- The neutron and the proton have almost identical masses, 1.67×10^{-27} kilogram.
- This is approximately 1,837 times the mass of an electron.

Nuclear Structure

The neutron and proton have virtually the same mass, but the proton carries an electrical charge, and the neutron does not. The electron has an electrical charge of the same magnitude as that of the proton, but its charge is negative.

The Forces at Work. The forces that keep an atom together can be explained by looking at an atom of the most common form of hydrogen.

- The nucleus of a hydrogen atom consists of one proton and therefore has a positive charge.
- The electron has a negative charge, so the net charge on the hydrogen atom is zero, because the positive charge is equal to but opposite the negative charge.
- The force holding the atom together, which binds the electron to the proton in some way, is the *coulomb force*, the attraction between positive and negative charges.

The Strong Force. Because the protons in a nucleus are so close to one another, and both carry positive charges, there is a huge electric repulsion between them. Yet do they not repel one another and cause the nucleus to fly apart. Why?

Another force, called the *strong force*, overcomes the repulsion. If there were no strong force, only one chemical element could exist—hydrogen, with one proton in its nucleus.

▲ **Helium Atom.** The next smallest atom after hydrogen is helium, which has two protons and two neutrons in the nucleus. This results in a net positive charge of two units. In order for helium to be electrically neutral, therefore, two electrons must orbit the nucleus. The forces holding the electrons in the atom are the *coulomb forces*.

Scattering experiments can help determine the size and shape of an unknown target. Rutherford used the apparatus shown below left to determine the size of the nucleus of an atom. Rays of alpha particles were directed onto a thin gold foil. The size of the nucleus could then be calculated by the way the alpha particles were scattered. ▼

SCATTERING EXPERIMENTS

Much of our knowledge of atomic nuclei comes from the scattering experiment, pioneered by Ernest Rutherford.

How They Work. In scattering experiments, neutrons, protons, electrons, gamma rays, and various other nuclear particles are accelerated to high energies and directed at a target. This target consists of atoms of a material to be studied. Detectors, or collectors, of various types are set up at positions around the target.

Knowns and Unknowns. Physicists use what they know to make deductions about the target's size and shape.

- They know what kind of accelerator they have.

- They know what the projectiles—the protons, neutrons, or other particles—look like.

- They know what the collectors do because they are built for a specific performance.

Identifying the Target. The right-hand side of the diagram illustrates how physicists might deduce the appearance of the target.

1. The dimensions of the target have to be about the distance from point A to E, because Balls (1) and (4) passed straight through the target area without deflection.

2. The surface of the target must be able to deflect Ball (2) to the left, and Ball (3) to the right.

3. A target shaped like the one shown would possibly be able to produce these results.

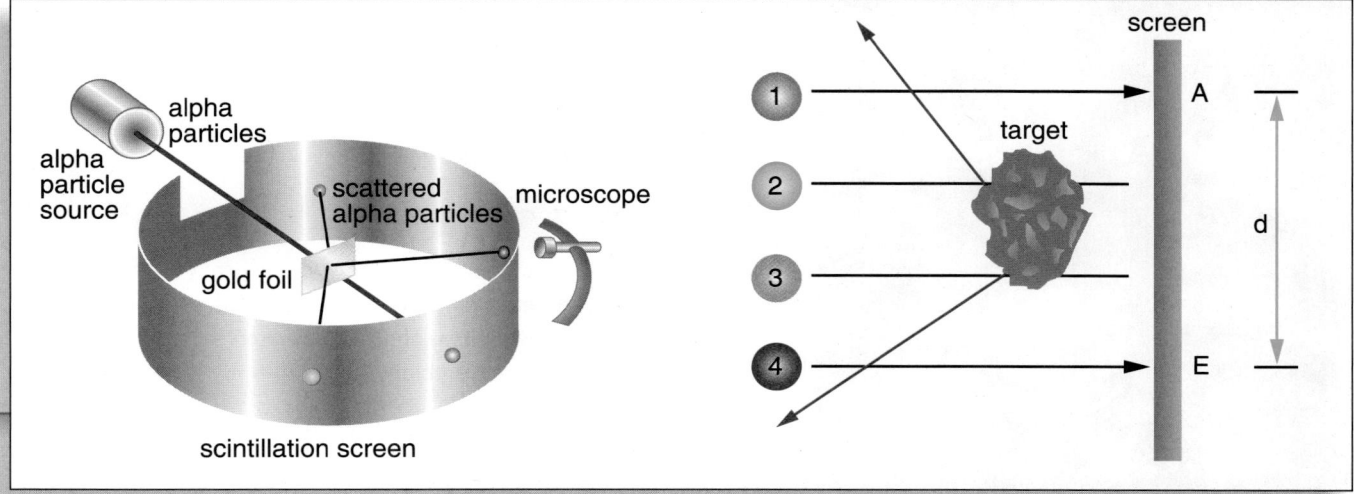

Accelerators

Physicists use accelerators to discover and study subatomic particles and the forces that govern them. Particle accelerators are devices that speed up the movement of tiny bits of matter.

These particles are either *ions* (electrically charged atoms) or electrically charged *subatomic particles*, objects that are smaller than an atom. The particles travel through an accelerator in a narrow beam. In accelerating the beam, the machine increases the particles' energy of motion.

Types of Accelerators

One of the first accelerators used in a nuclear physics experiment was a naturally radioactive element that emitted alpha particles. An alpha particle consists of two protons and two neutrons bound together—it is a helium atom, stripped of electrons.

Radium. Rutherford used radium as his accelerator to bombard thin foils of materials. (See Scattering Experiments, page 855.)

- The results indicated that some of the alpha particles were scattered backward, although most went through relatively untouched.

- Back-scattering could be explained only if the alpha particles were striking something with more mass than the alpha particles.

▲ **The Cockcroft-Walton accelerator,** a linear machine, was the first accelerator to break up atomic nuclei. Today's machines speed up protons, electrons, and ions. Most of them serve as beam sources for more powerful accelerators.

Modern Accelerators. The main types of accelerators include:

- the Cockcroft-Walton accelerator, invented by J. Douglas Cockcroft and Ernest Walton in 1932.
- the Van de Graaff accelerator, proposed by Robert Jeminson Van de Graaff in 1931.
- the cyclotron, built by Ernest O. Lawrence in 1930.
- the synchrotron.
- the linear accelerator.

In all these accelerators, the effect of electric and magnetic fields on charged particles is used to give the particles high velocities.

◄ **The Van de Graaff generator** can accelerate protons, electrons, and ions to about 15 MeV. Hundreds of such accelerators have been built, more than all other types combined.

HOW DOES THAT WORK

CYCLOTRONS AND SYNCHROTRONS

The cyclotron uses the effects of both electric and magnetic fields to produce an energetic beam of particles.

1. As shown in the diagram, charged particles (protons) are introduced at point A.

2. B and C are magnets, called *dees* because they resemble the letter "D" in shape.

3. An electrically charged particle is pushed on by the electric field, say, in the direction shown by the arrow.

4. The particle then enters the magnetic field of C. While in the magnet, it is turned in a circular path, as shown, and finally is ready to emerge from the magnet.

5. While the particle is completing the half circle, the voltage on the magnets is reversed. Once again the particle is accelerated, but now toward magnet B.

6. Once the particle enters B, it again is turned in a circular path. Upon emerging from B, the particle finds that the direction of the electric field has again been reversed to cause acceleration toward C. This process continues until the particle emerges from the cyclotron.

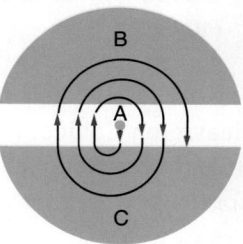

The first cyclotron used two D-shaped magnets (*right*) and the effect of electric and magnetic fields to accelerate the particles. Modern accelerators use large superconducting magnets (see photo) and can be as huge as 60 miles in circumference (*below*).

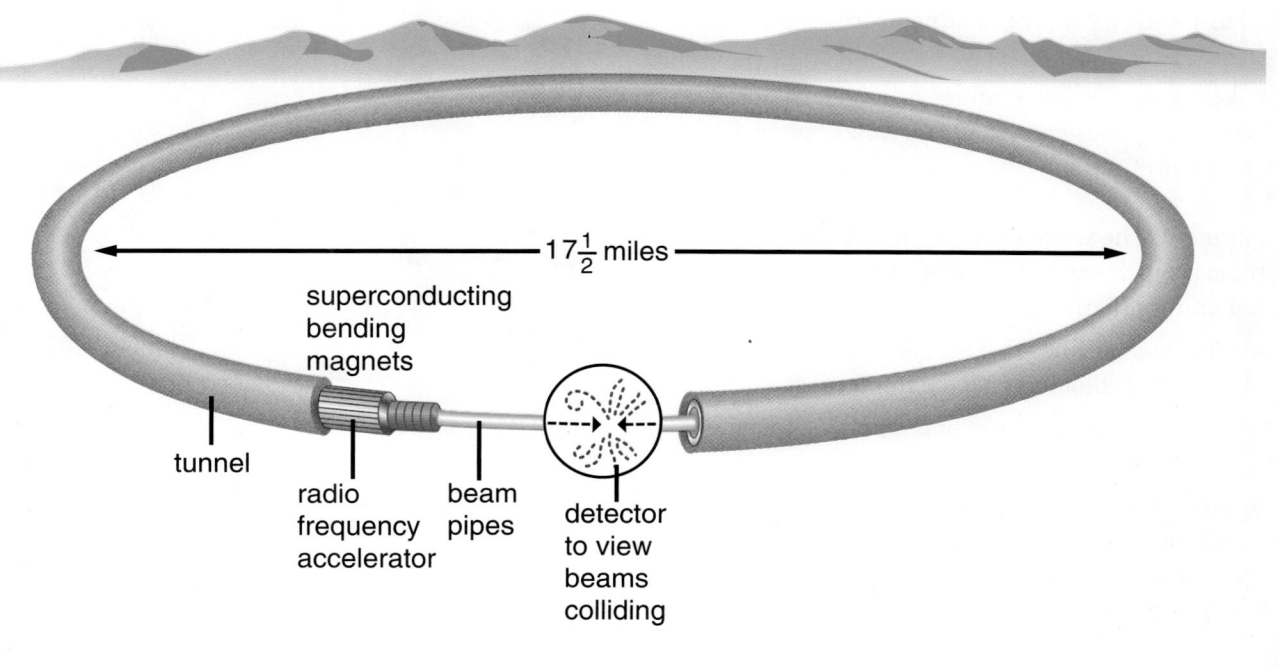

$17\frac{1}{2}$ miles

superconducting
bending
magnets

tunnel

radio
frequency
accelerator

beam
pipes

detector
to view
beams
colliding

Accelerators

Colliders and Supercolliders

Modern particle accelerators can be enormous structures, capable of accelerating protons near the speed of light.

The SSC. The construction of the Superconducting Super Collider (SSC) began in Texas during the early 1990s, but in 1993, Congress voted to cancel funding for the project.

- Its design consisted of two rings of pipe placed in a circular tunnel 53 miles (137 kilometers) across.

- In these rings, two beams of protons, highly accelerated in opposite directions, were to be controlled by superconducting magnets.

- They were to be aimed to meet head on, producing collisions with an energy of 40 billion electronvolts (40 GeV).

The RHIC. In 2000, a machine called the Relativistic Heavy Ion Collider (RHIC) began operating at Brookhaven National Laboratory on Long Island, New York.

- The RHIC accelerates gold ions through two tubes that are 2.4 miles (3.9 kilometers) in circumference.

- The machine is designed to operate at energies up to 100 GeV per proton or neutron.

- The collisions of gold ions conducted by the RHIC can produce temperatures around 4 trillion K (kelvins), more than 250,000 times hotter than the center of the sun.

Fermilab. The world's second most powerful accelerator is a synchrotron at the Fermi National Accelerator Laboratory (Fermilab) in Batavia, Illinois.

- This machine lies in a tunnel that measures 3.9 miles (6.3 kilometers) in circumference.

- In 1972, its first year of operation, the machine accelerated protons to 400 GeV.

- Since 1987, it has collided beams of protons with beams of antiprotons, antimatter counterparts of protons. Each beam can reach an energy of about 980 GeV.

THE LARGE HADRON COLLIDER

The Large Hadron Collider, abbreviated LHC, is the highest-energy particle accelerator in the world. The LHC is a type of ring-shaped particle accelerator known as a synchrotron.

- Particles in the LHC travel around a ring measuring nearly 17 miles (27 kilometers) in circumference.

- The collider accelerates high-energy subatomic particles called hadrons to nearly the speed of light.

- It guides the two particle beams into collisions at several places around the ring. At these locations, giant detectors record other particles produced by the collisions.

Because the detectors study the most energetic collisions ever observed, scientists hope that experiments at the LHC will lead to new discoveries in physics.

The LHC became operational in 2008. A malfunction then delayed operation until 2009. Over 100 countries have contributed to the $10 billion cost.

NEUTRON PRODUCTION

After accelerated particles emerge from the accelerators, one of two things happens:

- They are allowed to hit targets directly in order to study the targets themselves.

- They are allowed to hit targets in order to produce beams of a different type of particle.

For example, since neutrons have no charge, they cannot be accelerated or steered by electric and magnetic fields. Beams of neutrons must be produced by collisions of the primary beam with other targets.

Particle Detectors

In the early days of nuclear physics, nuclear events were observed on photographic plates. The use of photographic plates and their descendants, nuclear track plates, continues to this day.

These methods yield accurate and useful data, but they are slow, and the plates require developing and processing. This makes data collection and processing more complex and more difficult. As a result, several electronic techniques are also used.

Types of Particle Detectors		
Detector	**How It Works**	**What It Tells You**
Geiger counter	Uses the effect of energetic radiation in making an enclosed gas electrically conductive in order to measure nuclear processes.	Tells the user the number of nuclear events taking place. Details of the events are not visible, however.
Scintillation counter	These produce light when particles transfer energy to them. The light, in turn, strikes devices called phototubes or photodiodes, which then produce electric signals.	These devices measure the quantity of a certain type of event but do not give detailed information about the event.
Cloud chamber	A gas-filled chamber containing supersaturated vapor is exposed to radiation. The incoming particles cause the excess moisture to precipitate along the trail of the particle, creating a visible trace.	When used in conjunction with electric and magnetic fields and photographic films, the charge and momentum of the incident particles can be deduced. Relatively few events can be observed in a given time.
Bubble chamber	This chamber usually contains supersaturated liquid hydrogen, liquid xenon, or helium. Incoming radiation causes a row of bubbles along the trail of the incoming charged particle. When the liquid is supersaturated, a light is flashed to record events of interest on film.	Records more events than the cloud chamber, but it is relatively slow. Since the picture does not necessarily coincide with a particular type of event, it is not very selective.

Fission and Fusion

Three types of nuclear reactions release useful amounts of energy. The first type of reaction is *radioactive decay*. (See pages 404–405.) The other two reactions are *nuclear fission* and *nuclear fusion*. During each reaction, the matter involved loses mass. The mass is lost because it changes into energy.

Nuclear Fission Reactions

In nuclear fission reactions, the nucleus of a heavy isotope of an element ruptures into two segments of almost equal mass and releases large quantities of energy and of neutrons.

- The two segments into which the nucleus splits are the nuclei of other, lighter atoms.

- The rupture occurs when the nucleus absorbs a free neutron.

- The neutrons released during the fission process may, in turn, cause other atoms of the heavy isotopes to undergo fission in a chain reaction.

▲ **When a chain reaction is inhibited,** a controlled reaction takes place, and the same quantity of energy is liberated over a much longer period of time. This is what takes place in a nuclear reactor.

◀ **An uncontrolled fission reaction** releases vast amounts of energy over a very short period. This is what happened in the atomic bombs that were exploded over Hiroshima and Nagasaki, Japan, in 1945.

Under certain conditions, a fission reaction can be made to sustain itself in a chain reaction that involves a very large number of nuclei. This diagram shows how such a chain reaction can take place. ▶

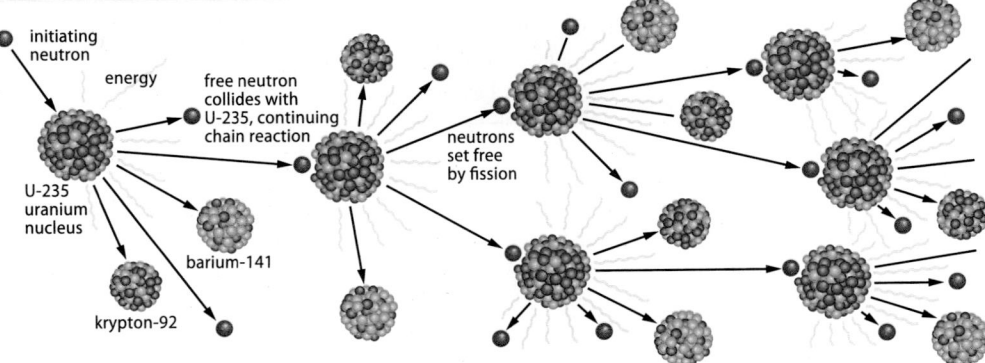

initiating neutron

energy

free neutron collides with U-235, continuing chain reaction

neutrons set free by fission

U-235 uranium nucleus

barium-141

krypton-92

Nuclear Fusion Reactions

A fusion reaction is virtually the exact opposite of a fission reaction. In a fusion reaction, the nuclei of two light atoms combine to form a somewhat heavier nucleus. This thermonuclear reaction results in the release of a tremendous amount of energy.

A controlled fusion reaction would become highly important as a commercial source of energy. Energy sufficient to meet the world's requirements for thousands of years would be readily available from the small amount of heavy hydrogen found in ordinary water. In addition, fusion reactions do not produce radioactive wastes.

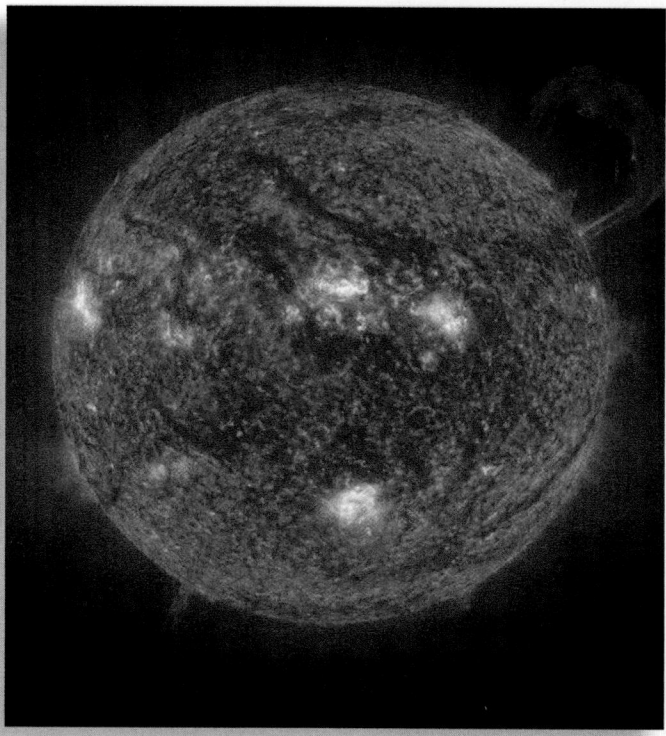

▲ **The Energy of the Sun.** Scientists believe that chains of uncontrolled nuclear fusion reactions produce the energy emitted by the sun and by other stars.

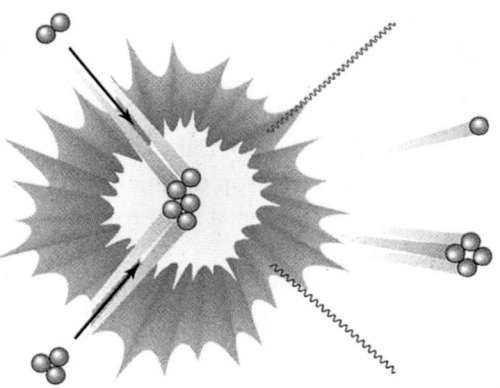

▲ **Fusion** occurs when the nuclei of two lightweight elements join to form the nucleus of a heavier one. In the example shown here, nuclei of deuterium and tritium unite and form a helium nucleus.

Controlling Fusion. Scientists hope that research, such as that being done at the Tokamak Fusion Test Reactor at Princeton University, will produce a controlled fusion reaction. The major difficulty to be overcome in obtaining a controlled release of fusion energy is the extremely high temperature that must be maintained for long periods of time to sustain the reaction. ▶

DANGER
HIGH VOLTAGE
13,800 VOLTS

SUBATOMIC PARTICLES

SUBATOMIC PARTICLES are units of matter smaller than an atom. They include the three major particles found in atoms: *protons*, which carry a positive electric charge; negatively charged *electrons*; and electrically neutral *neutrons*. Protons and neutrons form the nucleus of an atom. Electrons whirl about the nucleus. Electrons and several other subatomic particles are *elementary particles*—that is, they are not made up of smaller units of matter. Protons and neutrons are *composite particles*. They are made up of elementary particles called *quarks*.

▲ **Enrico Fermi** won the 1938 Nobel Prize in Physics for his work on nuclear processes. He also designed the first nuclear reactor and produced the first nuclear chain reaction in 1942.

New Particles

Until 1932, only the electron and the proton were known as the basic constituents of matter.

Neutrons and Neutrinos

In 1932, James Chadwick discovered the neutron, which was the missing link in explaining the stability of the atomic nucleus.

- Chadwick had previously observed that the electrons emitted in beta decay of radioactive nuclei did not have fixed values for their energy.
- The sum of the energy of the final particles—the proton and the electron—was less than the energy of the neutron at the beginning of the reaction.
- To explain this difference, Wolfgang Pauli proposed the existence of another particle that would be emitted during the reaction.

The Neutrino. Pauli's hypothetical particle was called the *neutrino*, the little neutron. In 1933, Enrico Fermi formulated a theory in which a neutron during beta decay is transformed into an electron, a proton, and a neutrino.

Since the neutrino barely interacts with matter, its existence was difficult to prove experimentally. In 1955, Clyde Cowan and Frederic Reines succeeded in showing the existence of neutrinos emitted by nuclear fission in a reactor.

ANTIPARTICLES

In the 1920s, British physicist Paul Dirac suggested the existence of positive electrons: particles with the mass of electrons, but with a positive charge. During 1932, the year of discovery of the neutron, Carl Anderson discovered Dirac's particles, called positrons, while studying cosmic rays in cloud chambers.

Scientists subsequently discovered that all the other known particles have corresponding antiparticles. Antineutrinos are the antiparticles of neutrinos, while antiprotons are the antiparticles of protons, and so forth. When a particle and its antiparticle collide, they annihilate each other—that is, their masses are converted into energy.

New Particles

Modern particle accelerators, which have much higher energies, have made possible the discovery of a large number of new elementary particles. Three groups of subatomic particles are the *leptons*, *baryons*, and *mesons*. (See pages 314–315.)

- Leptons are said to undergo weak interactions.
- There are six different leptons: the electron, muon, tau-particle, and three varieties of neutrinos.
- Unlike hadrons, leptons are considered to be true elementary particles, in that they are not believed to be composed of smaller constituents.
- Baryons and mesons, which together form the hadrons, undergo strong interactions.
- The most familiar baryons are the neutron and the proton.
- The pi-meson, a particle proposed by Hideki Yukawa to explain nuclear forces, is an example of a meson.

Doctors use antimatter widely in positron emission tomography (PET). A PET scan uses gamma rays given off by electron-positron pair annihilation to produce three-dimensional images of the brain or other body parts. ▼

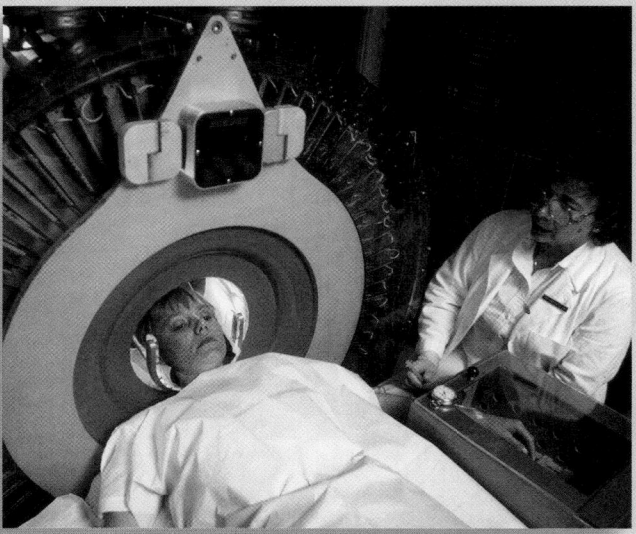

Quarks. By the early 1960s, so many hadrons had been discovered that it became clear they had to be composed of even smaller building blocks.

In 1963, two physicists at the California Institute of Technology, Murray Gell-Mann and George Zweig, proposed independently that all the hadrons would be made up of three even more fundamental particles. Gell-Mann named these particles *quarks*.

- The six types of quarks are designated by *u* (*up*), *d* (*down*), *s* (*sharp*), *b* (*bottom*), *c* (*charm*) and *t* (*top*). These are known as *flavors*.
- Quarks have a fractional charge: three of the quarks (d, s, and b) have 1/3 unit of negative charge. The other three—u, c, and t—have 2/3 unit of positive charge.
- Quarks combine in such a fashion as to form particles with a charge of 0, 1, or −1.

Antiquarks. Soon it became clear that antiquarks were required to explain the composition of hadrons. Baryons are now believed to consist of three quarks, and mesons to consist of a quark and an antiquark. To complete the scheme, colors were introduced in addition to flavors.

- Quarks may be red, green, or blue.
- Their corresponding antiquarks are given complementary colors: cyan, magenta, and yellow.

When quarks combine, the colors have to combine in such a way that white theoretically results. The proton is believed to consist of two u and one d quarks, with the condition that there is a quark of each color: red, green, and blue (their mixture results in white).

Forces and Grand Theories

Four fundamental forces exist in nature: gravity, electromagnetic force, the strong nuclear force (or strong interaction), and the weak nuclear force (or weak interaction).

- Gravity is the force of attraction between masses.
- Electromagnetic force refers to the attraction and repulsion forces between electric charges.
- The strong nuclear force holds the atomic nucleus together.
- The weak nuclear force is responsible for certain forms of radioactive decay.

How They Act. Subatomic particles interact with one another mainly through the last three forces. Strong and weak forces act only over very short distances, typically the distance between nucleons in nuclei. Over these short distances, however, the strong force is much stronger than gravitational or electromagnetic forces.

Grand Unification Theories

Several attempts have been made in recent years to explain the four fundamental forces by a single theory. These theories are called *unification schemes*. A theory that would unify the strong, weak, and electromagnetic forces is called a grand unified theory, or GUT.

Gravitation, the fourth fundamental force, is not included in GUTs. The effect of gravity on a single atom or nucleus is so weak that scientists have never been able to detect it.

Exchange Particles. One basic concept in these theories is that forces between particles are mediated by exchange particles. The mass of these particles should be inversely proportional to the range of the force. For example:

- Electromagnetic forces are transmitted by virtual photons—photons with a very short lifetime.
- Photons have no mass, which agrees with the fact that the electromagnetic force has an infinite range.
- The exchange particle for gravity, the hypothetical graviton, would also have zero mass, because gravitation is also a long-range force.

An experiment to test GUTs directly would require an energy about a trillion times higher than what is now available.

Hideki Yukawa first predicted the existence of the exchange particle for the strong force in 1935. The particle was found by a group at the University of Bristol, England, in 1947. Since the strong force is a short-range force, this exchange particle had to have a mass, which was confirmed to be 15 percent of that of the proton. ▶

The Electroweak Theory. In the early 1970s, Steven Weinberg, Abdus Salam, and Sheldon Lee Glashow formulated a theory that would unify the electromagnetic and the weak force. They called it the *electroweak theory*.

- They predicted that three particles, the W+, W−, and Z^0, would transmit the weak force in atomic nuclei.

- Since the weak force has a shorter range than the strong force, the masses of these particles had to be greater than the mass of the pi-meson, the Yukawa particle.

- They predicted that the two W particles would have a mass of 81 GeV, which is 80 times the mass of the proton, and that the mass of the Z particle would be 93.8 GeV.

- All three particles were discovered by Carlo Rubbia in 1983.

CERN. The W+, W−, and Z^0 particles were formed in collisions of protons and antiprotons in the huge proton-antiproton collider at the *Centre Européen de Recherche Nucléaire* (CERN), near Geneva, Switzerland. CERN is now home to the Large Hadron Collider. (See page 858.)

SUPERSYMMETRY AND SUPERSTRINGS

Some scientists are now trying to find a theory that would combine gravitation with GUTs. Because such a theory would explain all behavior of all forces and matter, it is termed a "theory of everything (TOE)." The concept of supersymmetry is one step in the direction of a TOE.

- Scientists divide subatomic particles into two major classes, fermions and bosons.

- Fermions are the particles that make up matter, such as quarks and electrons.

- Bosons are the particles that mediate forces, such as photons, pions, and the W and Z particles.

- Supersymmetry assumes that each fermion has a counterpart boson and each boson has a counterpart fermion.

The supersymmetric counterparts are denoted with an "s" or with the ending "-ino." For example, sleptons are the corresponding supersymmetric particles of leptons, squarks correspond with quarks, and photinos with photons.

Superstrings. By assuming that the most elementary building blocks of matter are not infinitely small points but extremely small strings—typically 10^{-35} long—scientists have been able to formulate theories that account for gravity. The combination of string theory with supersymmetry resulted in the superstring theory, which is today the most promising theory for giving a unified picture of all four fundamental forces.

Formulas and Constants

Basic Physics Formulas

In physics, laws and theories are almost always expressed in the language of mathematics. The following are 20 of the basic formulas of physics.

Acceleration	$a = \dfrac{(v_t - v_0)}{t}$	a = acceleration v_t = final velocity v_0 = initial velocity t = time
Acceleration of gravity	$w = mg$	w = force of weight m = mass g = acceleration due to gravity (always 32.2 feet per second²)
Centrifugal force	$F = \dfrac{mv^2}{r}$	F = force m = mass of moving object v = velocity r = radius of the orbit of mass
Coulomb's law	$F = k\,\dfrac{Q_a Q_b}{d^2}$	F = electrostatic force k = a constant of proportionality Q_a and Q_b = quantities of electrostatic charge d = distance between charges
Density	$D = \dfrac{m}{v}$	D = density m = mass v = volume
Electrical powers	$P = IV$	P = power (watts) I = electrical current (amperes) V = electrical potential (volts)
Energy-matter relationship	$E = mc^2$	E = energy m = mass c = velocity of light
Gravity inverse square law	$F = G\,\dfrac{Mm}{r^2}$	F = force G = gravitation constant M and m = masses of 2 objects r = distance between masses
Kinetic energy	$KE = \dfrac{1}{2}\,mv^2$	KE = kinetic energy m = mass of moving object v = velocity
Light inverse square law	$\dfrac{I_1}{I_2} = \left(\dfrac{d_2}{d_1}\right)^2$	I_1 = light intensity at distance d_1 I_2 = light intensity at distance d_2
Mass and weight relationship	$\dfrac{m_1}{m_2} = \dfrac{W_1}{W_2}$	m_1 and m_2 = 2 masses W_1 and W_2 = respective weights
Momentum	$p = mv$	p = momentum m = mass of object v = velocity

Newton's second law	$F = ma$	$F =$ force $m =$ mass of object $a =$ acceleration
Ohm's law	$R = \dfrac{V}{I}$	$R =$ electrical resistance (ohms) $V =$ electrical potential (volts) $I =$ electrical current (amperes)
Potential energy	$E = mgh$	$E =$ potential energy $m =$ mass of object $g =$ acceleration of gravity $h =$ distance to be traveled by m
Power	$P = \dfrac{W}{t}$	$P =$ power $W =$ work $t =$ time
Velocity	$v = \dfrac{d}{t}$	$v =$ velocity $d =$ distance $t =$ time
Wave equation	$V = nl$	$V =$ Velocity $n =$ frequency $l =$ wavelength
Weight	$W = mg$	$W =$ weight $m =$ mass $g =$ gravity
Work	$W = Fd$	$W =$ work $F =$ applied force $d =$ distance

Fundamental Constants

A constant is a numerical quantity that remains unchanged under different conditions. A constant can express a value, as of a physical substance, or a relation. In physics formulas, constants are represented by particular symbols. The symbols and values of some fundamental constants are given here.

Fundamental Constants		
Quantity	**Symbol**	**Value**
Avogadro's number	NA	6.022137×10^{23} mol^{-1}
Boltzmann's constant	k	$1.3806504 \times 10^{-23}$ J/K
Electron charge magnitude	e	$1.60217733 \times 10^{-19}$ C
Permeability of free space	μ_0	$4p \times 10^{-7}$ T $\cdot$ m/A
Permittivity of free space	ε_0	$8.854187817 \times 10^{-12}$ C^2 /(N $\cdot$ m^2)
Planck's constant	h	$6.6260755 \times 10^{-34}$ J $\cdot$ s
Mass of electron	me	$9.1093897 \times 10^{-31}$ kg
Mass of neutron	mn	$1.6749286 \times 10^{-27}$ kg
Mass of proton	mp	$1.6726231 \times 10^{-27}$ kg
Speed of light in a vacuum	c	2.99792458×108 m/s
Universal gravitational constant	G	6.67259×10^{-11} N $\cdot$ m^2/kg^2
Universal gas constant	R	8.314510 J/(mol $\cdot$ kg)

PRACTICE PROBLEMS

These problems are designed to give supplementary information and practice in applying the basic concepts of physics. Some of the information needed to solve some of these problems was not included in the section, so don't feel frustrated if you need to read the solutions on pages 878–891 before figuring it out. Be careful—many of the problems contain information that you won't need to solve the problem. Don't let unnecessary information confuse you as you consider the questions.

Physics Practice

1. Vectors. The Tennessee Titans have possession of the football, and they have a few new star players.

- Lee snaps the ball to the quarterback, Bob, south 2 yards from the line of scrimmage.
- Bob runs east with the ball for 8 yards, and then throws it northwest 15 yards to Dan, for a completed pass.

a) Draw the vector diagrams and give the magnitude and direction of the net displacement (i.e., from Lee to Dan) of the football.

b) Was this a first down (i.e., 10 yards north of the line of scrimmage)?

The movements of both a football and the football players across the playing field can be described using vectors. ▼

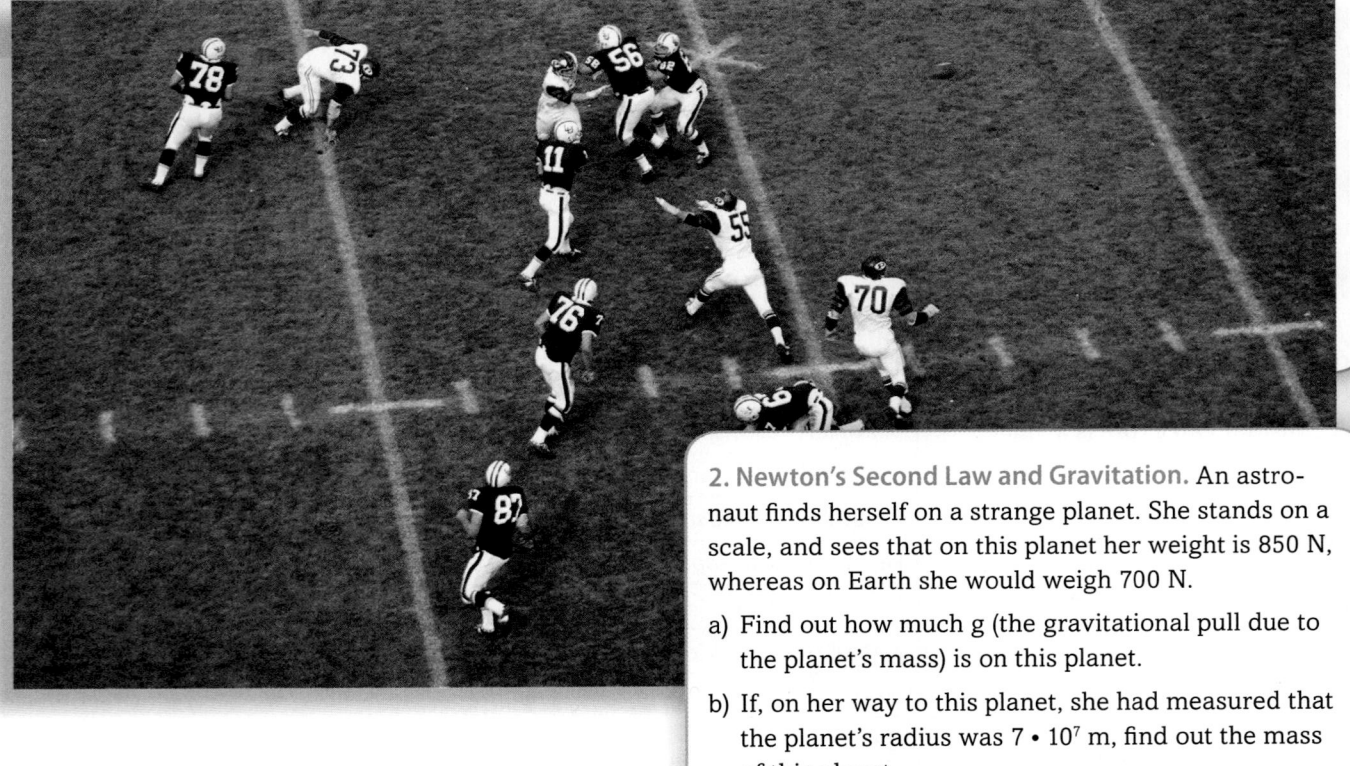

2. Newton's Second Law and Gravitation. An astronaut finds herself on a strange planet. She stands on a scale, and sees that on this planet her weight is 850 N, whereas on Earth she would weigh 700 N.

a) Find out how much g (the gravitational pull due to the planet's mass) is on this planet.

b) If, on her way to this planet, she had measured that the planet's radius was $7 \cdot 10^7$ m, find out the mass of this planet.

3. Kinematics and Friction. Susan and Elizabeth go skiing at Lake Louise and find a cool jump that they think they can use to clear a small tree. But first, they want to make sure that they will build up enough speed to fly that high.

Using the information and assumptions provided, find out the minimum distance up the hill from which each girl will need to start her descent.

Information:

- Decline of hill = 30°
- Incline of jump = 45°
- Coefficient of friction between skis and snow is $u_d = 0.2$
- Height of tree above base of jump = 5 m
- Air resistance = Negligible

Assumptions:

- Assume that Susan does not use any extra lift from jumping with her knees, as she takes off from the jump.
- Assume that Elizabeth jumps with her knees at the right time, giving her an additional 2.4 m/s of vertical velocity.
- Assume that the jumper's speed after going up the jump is the same as her max downhill speed.
- Assume that if Susan and Elizabeth can gain enough height to clear the tree, then they will make it (in other words, don't worry about horizontal displacement).

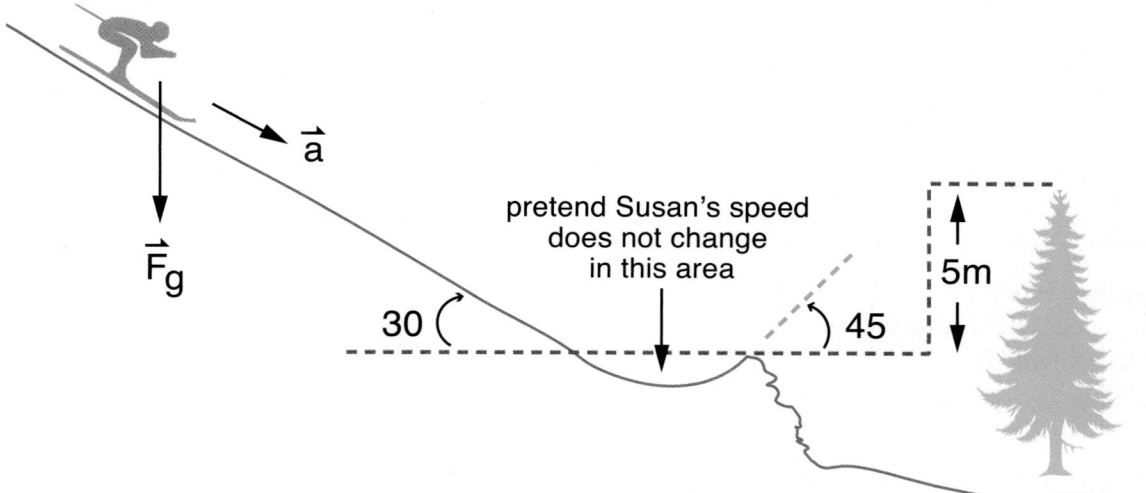

4. Friction and Circular Motion. James Bond is driving his BMW, pursued by his enemy's henchman. He takes an unbanked curve so fast that his car slides at 80 miles/hr. His pursuer's car flips instead of sliding, at the same speed, because it wasn't built as well.

What was the radius of the turn he took for the car to flip over, if the coefficient of friction between the tires and the road is 0.91?

5. Energy. Han Solo is flying the Millennium Falcon and is being pursued by a Star Destroyer. He's accelerating away from the giant ship until he can make the jump to light speed.

a) How much energy does it take to accelerate each spacecraft by 15 m/s² for a distance of 5 m in outer space, far from the gravitational pull of any other bodies?

b) How much energy does it take to make the jump to light speed?

Mass of the Millennium Falcon: 3,617 metric tons.
Mass of Star Destroyer: 180,000,000 metric tons.

6. Torque. Seth goes skiing in Aspen with his brother, Levi, who decides to snowboard for the day. If they have relatively the same ability on skis and a board, explain why it's easier for Levi to do a 360 off a jump, on a board, than it is for Seth, on skis.

Snowboarders and skiers rely on the concept of torque for any kind of rotation.

7. Energy. Rob is refereeing a Toronto Raptors basketball game. He throws the ball straight up to let the players jump for it.

- When he throws the ball, his hand is 1.5 m off the ground.
- He throws the ball at a speed of 5 m/s.
- Take the mass of the basketball to be 0.8 kg.

Using the concepts of kinetic and potential energy, find out the ball's maximum height. If the players miss the ball and it falls to the ground untouched, find its maximum speed.

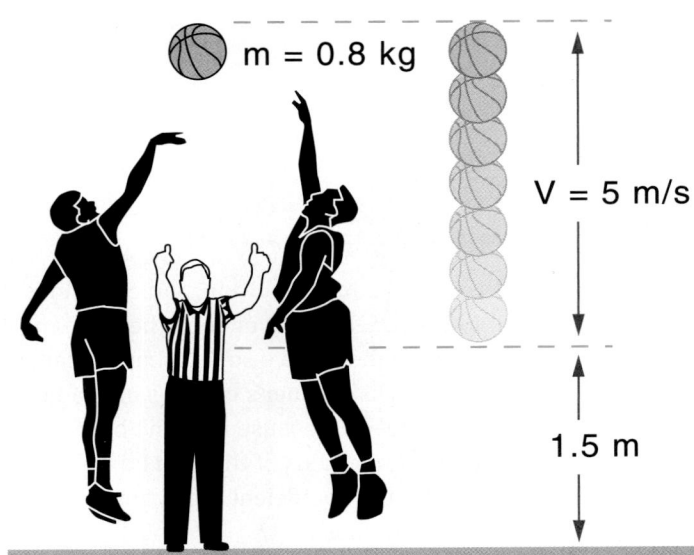

8. Collisions. Kyle and Paul, two NHL players, are playing hockey against each other. Kyle checks Paul on center ice. They hang on to each other so the collision is inelastic.

- Assume Kyle weighs 90 kg and Paul weighs 80 kg.

- Assume Kyle was skating at 5 m/s and Paul at 8 m/s.

Find their resultant speed and direction, if

a) They collide head on.

b) They collide at a 90° angle of incidence to each other.

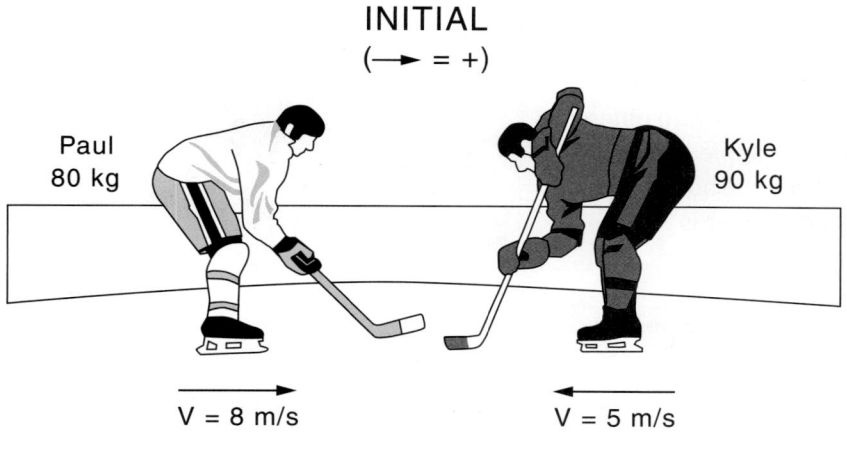

INITIAL

($\longrightarrow$ = +)

Paul
80 kg

Kyle
90 kg

V = 8 m/s   V = 5 m/s

9. Momentum and Impulse. Ron decides he's going to play Major League baseball. He steps up to the plate on his first-ever at bat.

- Tim pitches him a ball at 42 m/s (94.5 miles/hr).

- Ron gets a home run, the ball flying down centerfield and clearing the wall 400 feet away.

- The mass of a baseball is 0.145 kg.

   If the ball was flying at 55 m/s in the opposite direction, after Ron hit it, find the change in momentum of the ball and the impulse applied to it by the bat.

The impulse applied to an object such as a baseball is defined as a force acting on a body over a period of time.

10. Optics. Alex, a famous scientist, invents a laser that can be fired underwater. He wants to try his laser out by shooting at an apple that is above the water.

- Alex sits on the bottom of a 4-m-deep pool.
- The apple is perched on top of a pole, over the water, which is 3.5 m away from Alex.
- Alex knows that the pole is 6 m tall.

Where should he aim his laser, in relation to the apple, to hit it and still compensate for the change in direction that light makes when crossing two boundaries with different indices of refraction? The apple appears to be at an angle of 30° from the normal. The index of refraction of the water is 1.33.

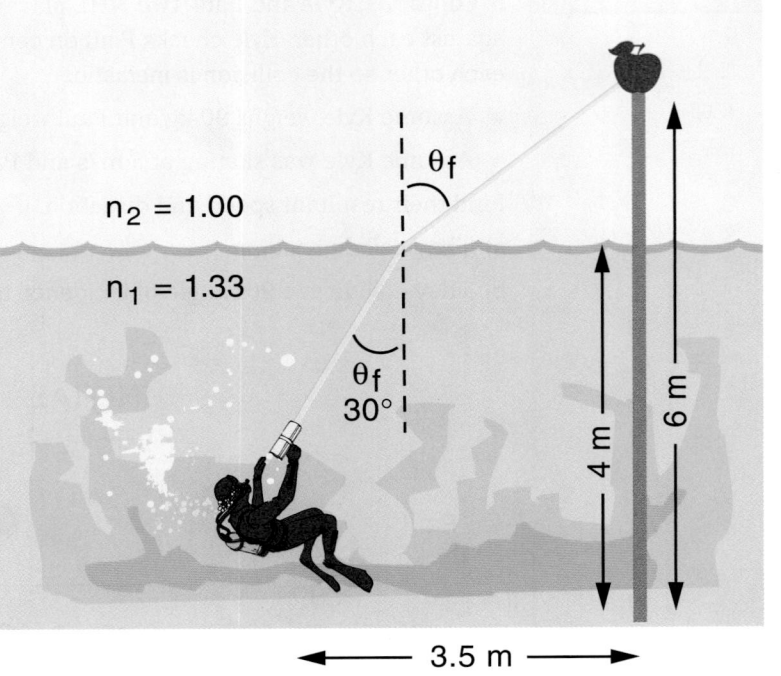

11. Optics. Nate and Tye go out to a dance club together. Nate is wearing red sunglasses, and Tye is wearing blue sunglasses. Explain why they see the world in different colors.

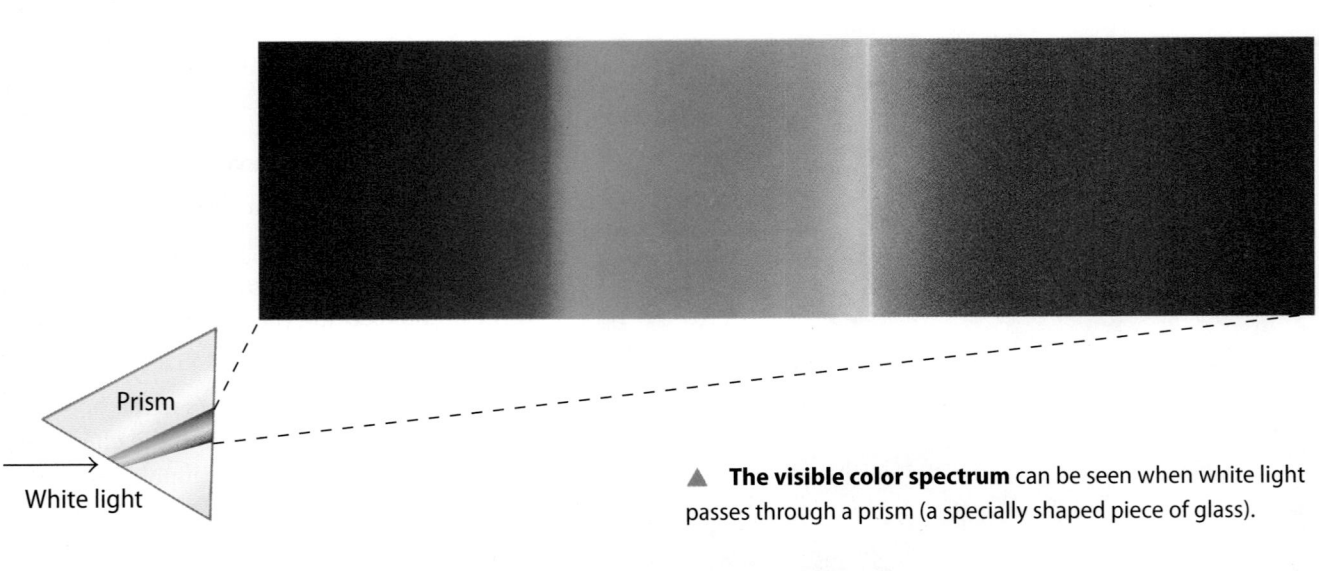

▲ **The visible color spectrum** can be seen when white light passes through a prism (a specially shaped piece of glass).

12. Optics. Kaci is using the underwater laser (from problem 10) and wants to shoot the evil kidnapper Jonas. The problem is, Jonas has placed his hostage, Eren, between himself and Kaci.

- Kaci and Eren are underwater, while Jonas is on the surface (see diagram).

- If Kaci shoots directly at Jonas, she risks hitting Eren.

- Kaci figures she'll shoot at the water surface, and use the concept of the critical angle to hit Jonas and free Eren.

  Find out at what angle she needs to aim her laser to hit Jonas.

Index of refraction of water: 1.33
Index of refraction of air: 1.00

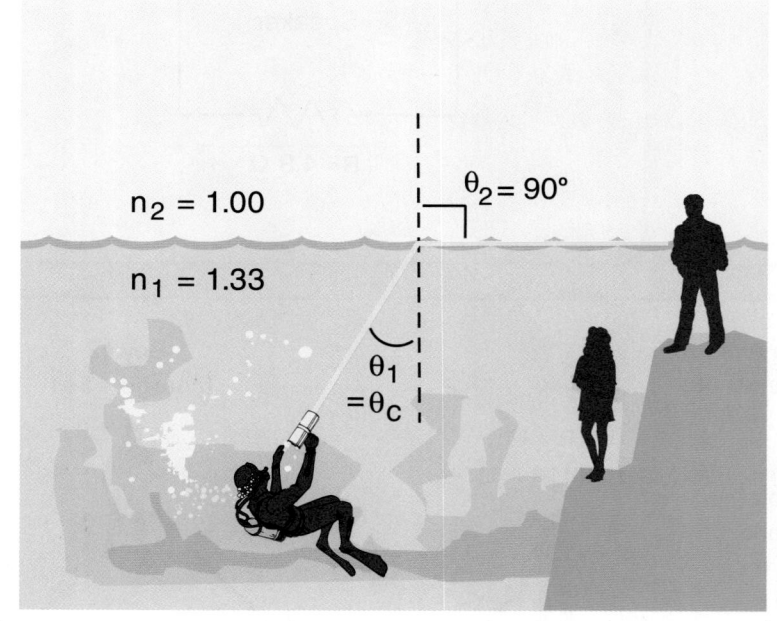

13. Circuits. Sean gave himself an electric shock by touching the wires in the circuit below. Luckily, his hands were dry, so his skin's internal resistance prevented a lot of the current from flowing into his body, but it still hurt to touch these wires.

Find out any unknown currents or resistances in the circuit below, so that Sean can realize why it hurt to touch the wires.

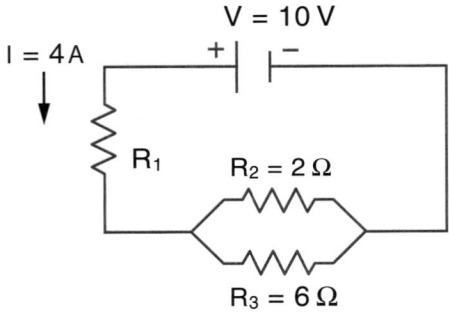

15. Voltage and Current. Amy is installing a new car stereo. The car battery (12 V) is used to power the car stereo. She's using a deck that supplies 30 W of power to a speaker.

- Find the current that goes through this load (the speaker), assuming that the battery's only load is this speaker.
- Then, find the speaker's internal resistance. (See the circuit diagram, pretending that the battery and the deck are the same source.) The deck acts as an amplifier, which supplies power from the battery to the speakers.

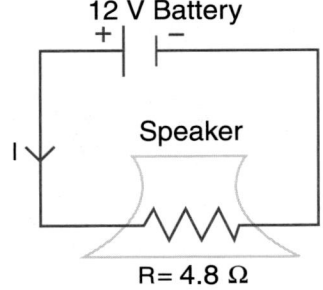

14. Electric Charge. Laura and Ingrid walk into a room where there are two boys, one each at opposite ends of the room. The diagram shows where Laura and Ingrid are in relation to the boys.

a) Pretend that Ingrid only has eyes for boy #1 on the left, and that she has $-e$ charge and mass, while he has $+e$ charge. Find the force of attraction on her and her acceleration toward him. (We are only using the electron's charge and mass for the sake of this example. Obviously in real life, people have a much higher mass and usually a neutral or close to neutral charge.)

b) Pretend Laura sees both guys. Find the force on her from each boy, and her net acceleration. Boy #2 has a +3e charge.

- Electron mass = $m_e = 9.11 \cdot 10^{-31}$ kg
- Electron charge = $e = 1.60 \cdot 10^{-19}$ C

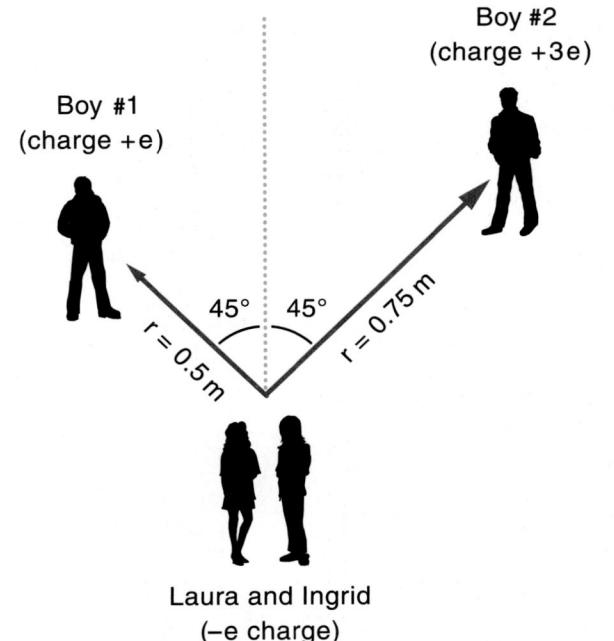

16. Energy and Power. Kyah wants to save money and decides to replace one of her 100 W lightbulbs with 60 W bulbs.

a) How much money does she save per week if the lamp is on for an average 30 hours/week, and she pays $0.12/kilowatt-hour (kWh)?

b) Kyah decides to buy halogen lightbulbs. A 60 W halogen bulb burns more brightly than an ordinary 100 W bulb, but uses less power. How much money does she save with this purchase over the course of the bulb's life, given the following:

- A regular 100 W bulb lasts 1,000 hours and costs $0.95/bulb.

- A halogen 60 W bulb lasts 3,000 hours and costs $7.45/bulb.

The energy consumed by different types of lightbulbs varies.

17. Sound and Doppler Effect. Colin is picking up his friend on their way to school and is playing loud music on his car stereo. His friend is outside waiting for him, so she hears the music as his car approaches.

If Colin hears the singer's voice on the stereo at a frequency of 320 Hz, and is approaching his friend at 30 m/s, at what frequency does she hear it? For the speed of sound in air, use 340 m/s.

Use the following symbols:
v = wave's velocity (usually in m/s)
λ = wavelength (Greek letter lambda)
f = frequency of the wave, in hertz, or Hz for short
Hz means cycles/second or, in our case, number of wave crests/second, with units of 1/s.

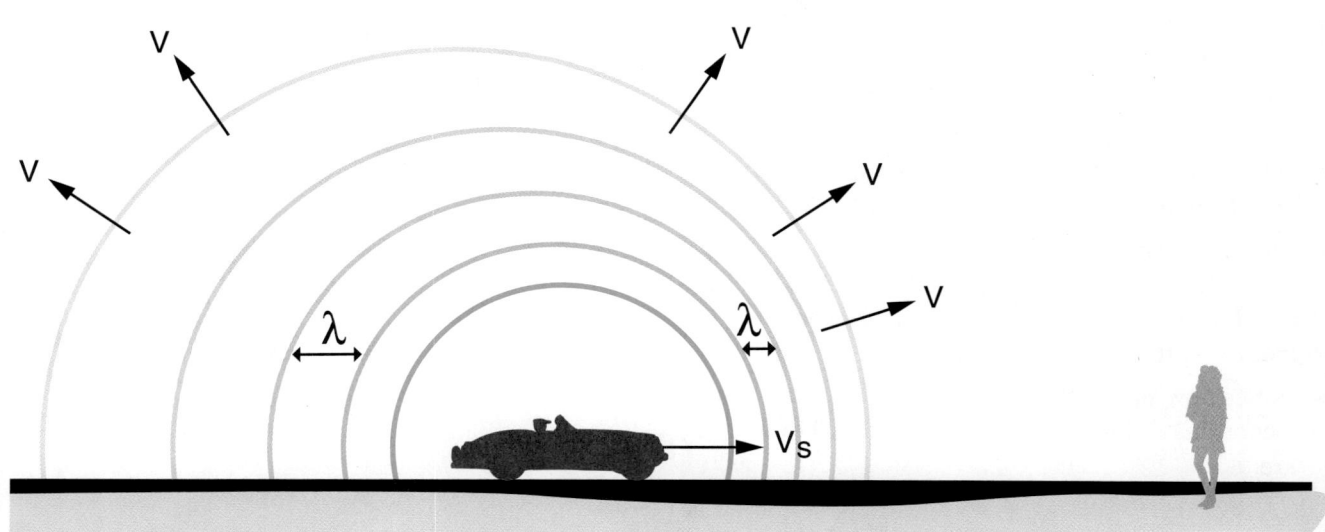

Radians

One very important concept that needs to be addressed is radians. The idea of radians is that someone has invented an alternate way to measure angles and revolutions. Just like distance can be measured in yards or meters, so can angles and rotations be measured in both degrees and radians.

Why Radians? "There are 360 degrees in a circle" is equivalent to saying, "There are 2π radians in a circle" (where π is approximately 3.1415…). Certain calculations, such as angular velocity and rotational kinetic energy, are just so much easier with radians.

The real simplicity of using radians becomes apparent when we have a circle with a radius of 1. In this situation, the angle is the same as the arc length, which the angle measures. (Notice that there are no units added to the "1" of this unit circle. Really, the units could be anything: meters, centimeters, miles. It does not matter, since the point is that it makes these numbers easier to work with.)

Using Radians. One useful tool to memorize would be the diagram here, showing the angles and coordinates of a unit circle (where the radius is 1). This can help us to know the sine and cosine relations for different angles. Also understand that if we use the x- and y-coordinates to draw this circle, then the sine and cosine of the angle give us the coordinates.

- If the circle is placed on a coordinate grid, each x-coordinate shows the value of $\cos(\theta)$ and each y-coordinate shows the value of $\sin(\theta)$.

- Notice that the x- and y-coordinates share the same values, with a different sign at times, and when one goes from 0 to 1, the other goes from 1 to 0.

- The angles shown are multiples of 30°, 45°, 60°, and 90° or $\pi/2$, $\pi/4$, $\pi/3$, and $\pi/2$ radians. These values are so common that you should understand and memorize them.

- Notice how simple the pattern is to memorize. The x-coordinates in the (+,+) quadrant from 0 to 90° are:

$1, \dfrac{\sqrt{3}}{2}, \dfrac{\sqrt{2}}{2}, \dfrac{1}{2}$, and 0, which is basically: $\dfrac{\sqrt{4}}{2}, \dfrac{\sqrt{3}}{2}, \dfrac{\sqrt{2}}{2}, \dfrac{\sqrt{1}}{2}, \dfrac{\sqrt{0}}{2}$

Converting Angles to Radians. To convert between angles and radians, remember that a circle has 360 degrees and 2π radians.

2π radians $= 360°$

$1 \text{ radian} = \dfrac{360°}{2\pi} = 57.3°$

$360° = 2\pi$ radians

$1° = \dfrac{(2\pi \text{ radians})}{360°} = 0.017 \text{ radians}$

$90° = \left(\dfrac{\pi}{2}\right) \text{rads}$

$180° = \pi \text{ rads}$

Most scientific calculators have a setting for degrees and radians. If your calculator is set to degrees, you will find:

$\sin(90) = 1$

If your calculator is set to radians, you will find:

$\sin\left(\dfrac{\pi}{2}\right) = 1$

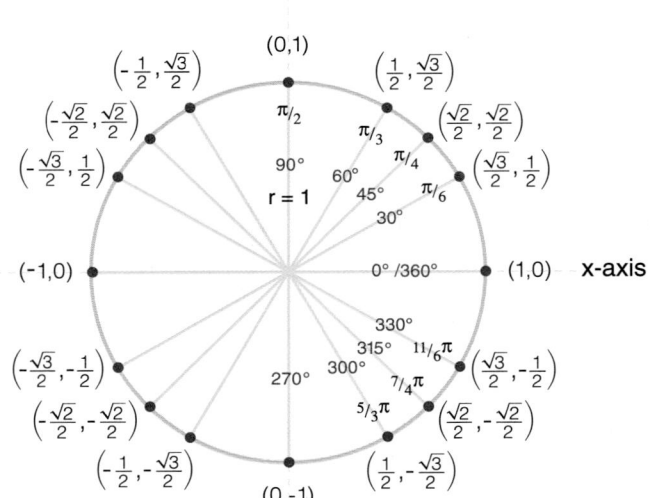

Rotational Kinetic Energy

One application of radians is in calculating *rotational kinetic energy*. If a ball is kicked, in addition to having gravitational potential energy and kinetic energy due to the ball's speed, it also has a rotational kinetic energy that comes from the ball's spin. Any object that is spinning has a rotational kinetic energy, given by

$K = \frac{1}{2} I\omega^2$, where

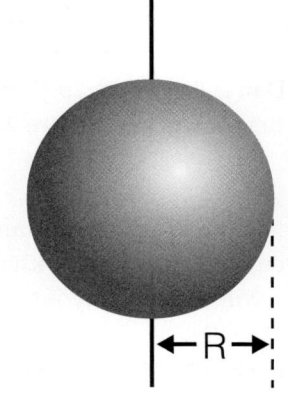

- ω (the Greek letter omega) is the angular velocity (number or radians rotated through per unit time).
- I is the body's moment of inertia, in units of kg/m².

Moment of inertia is similar to momentum, only it is a way to describe a body's momentum around its axis of rotation. Calculating I is different for different shapes of bodies; here we'll list just two.

- A solid sphere has

$$I = \frac{2}{5} mr^2$$

- A hollow sphere has

$$I = \frac{2}{3} mr^2$$

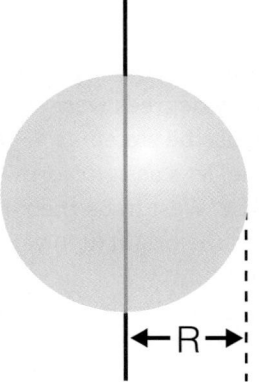

Notice that the rotational kinetic energy expression is analogous to the expression for the kinetic energy of a particle,

$K = \frac{1}{2} mv^2$

Using this information, a rotating body has a total kinetic energy of

$K = \frac{1}{2} mv^2 + \frac{1}{2} I\omega^2$

18. Rotational Kinetic Energy. Ruthy kicks a soccer ball that spins at 10 π/s. What is its rotational kinetic energy? Find the ball's total potential and kinetic energy, if the ball is flying at 10 m/s while being 5 m above the ground, has a mass of 0.5 kg, and has a radius of 20 cm.

Physics Practice—Answers

1. Vectors

a) If Dan was tackled right at the spot where he caught the pass from Bob, then the final displacement of the ball from Lee to Dan is 9.0 yards, 29.4° west of north.
b) There was no first down, since there was a gain of only 8.6 yards.

Explanation: Vectors are a very important concept in physics, and your ability to work with many other types of problems will depend on your understanding of vectors.

Remember that vectors have both magnitude and direction. In this case, the magnitude is how far the ball gets carried, and the direction is which way. (By convention, we'll use North, South, East, West, instead of forward, back, etc.) If a direction does not directly match N, S, NW, etc., then we can state the direction by saying how many degrees west of north it is, for example. NE can also be stated as 45° east of north.

For our example, let's assign North/South to be the y-axis, and East/West to be the x-axis. Then Lee snaps the ball from the origin (0,0) yards.

The first step is to draw the vector diagram:

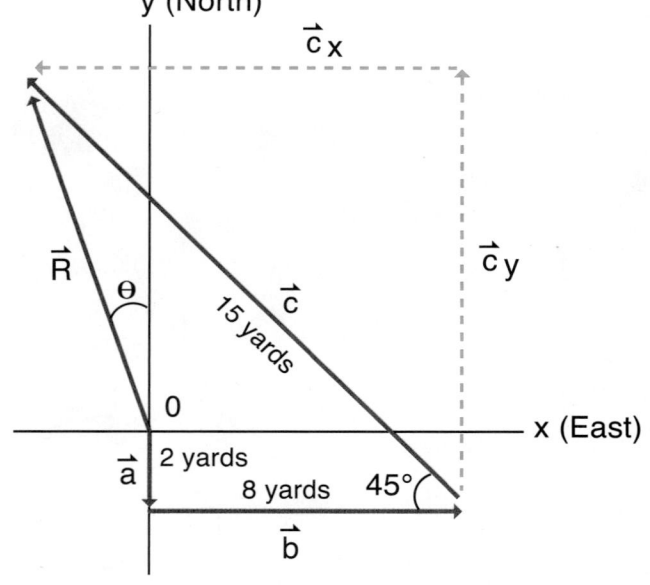

If R is the resultant displacement, and a, b, c, are the first, second, and third carries, then
$$R = a + b + c$$

And a, b, and c can be further broken down as:
$$a = a_x + a_y = (0, -2) \text{ yards}$$
$$b = b_x + b_y = (8, 0) \text{ yards}$$
$$c = c_x + c_y = (-10.6, 10.6) \text{ yards}$$

Or put another way:
$$R_x = a_x + b_x + c_x$$
$$R_y = a_y + b_y + c_y$$

Texts usually denote a vector by writing in boldface the letter that is used to represent it (e.g. **A**). Handwritten, they are usually denoted by an arrow above or a line underneath (e.g. **A**, $\vec{A}$, $\bar{A}$, $\underline{A}$). You can use whatever you like.

2. Newton's Second Law and Gravitation

a) 11.91 m/s²
b) 8.74 • 10²⁶ kg

Explanation: From NII (Newton's 2nd law), we know F = ma. We know that a body's mass does not change, so F′ = ma′ (where ′ is called *prime*, meaning new or different).

In this case,

$$a = g =$$
gravitational attraction of Earth = 9.81 m/s²

We also know that the weight is given by the force that the planet's gravitational pull exerts on the body, so

$$Fg = mg \ (= weight)$$

Two vertical lines around a vector, | |, are used to indicate magnitude only. $|a|$ means the distance that a carries the ball, and we don't care about direction. Now, to find c,

- we can use trigonometry relations, such as

$$\sin 45 = \frac{|c_x|}{|c|}$$

and

$$c_x = \sin 45 \cdot |c|$$

- or we can use Pythagoras:

$$|c|^2 = |c_x|^2 + |c_y|^2 = 2|c_x|^2$$

(since $|c_x| = |c_y|$)

to find that $c_x = (-10.6, 0)$ yards and $c_y = (0, 10.6)$. You can look at the diagram to make sure of the $+/-$ sign. So now we know that

$$R_x = +8 - 10.6 = -2.6 \text{ yards and}$$
$$R_y = -2 + 10.6 = 8.6 \text{ yards}$$

Let's redraw our diagram to fill in the values of R.

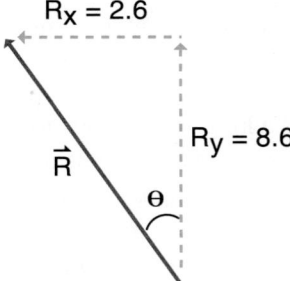

We can use Pythagoras again to find the magnitude of R, since

$R = R_x + R_y$, so
$|R|^2 = |R_x|^2 + |R_y|^2 =$
$2.61^2 + 8.61^2 = 80.86$, and so:

$$|R| = \sqrt{80.86} = 8.99 \text{ yards.}$$

Right away, you can see that this was not a first down, since R_y is less than 10 yards.

The direction can be found with the relation

$$\tan(\theta) = \left| \frac{R_y}{R_x} \right| = \frac{2.6}{8.6} \text{ and}$$

$$\theta = \tan^{-1}\left(\frac{2.6}{8.6} \right) = 29.4°$$

By isolating m in the two equations $F = ma$ and $F' = ma'$, we can see that

$$m = \frac{F}{a} = \frac{F'}{a'}$$

Then

$$a' = g \cdot \frac{F'}{F} = 9.81 \text{ m/s}^2 \cdot \frac{850N}{700N} = 11.91 \text{ m/s}^2.$$

So the acceleration due to gravity on this planet, g', is 11.91 m/s².

Note: Remember not to confuse G (the gravitational constant, which doesn't change, and equals

$$6.67 \cdot 10^{-11} \frac{Nm^2}{kg^2}$$

with g (the acceleration on a body due to the gravitational pull of the planet, which changes with the planet's mass and radius).

To find the mass of this planet, we can use Newton's law of gravitation.

$$F = G \cdot \frac{m_1 m_2}{r^2}$$

We want to find the mass of this planet, which we will call m_2. The astronaut will be the mass m_1. Then we have

$$m_2 = \frac{F_g \cdot r^2}{(G \cdot m_1)}$$

From part (a), we know that

$$\frac{F_g}{m_1} = a' = 11.91 \text{ m/s}^2$$

So:

$$m_2 = \frac{F_g}{m_1} \cdot \frac{r^2}{G}$$

$$= 11.91 \text{ m/s}^2 \cdot \frac{(7 \cdot 107m)^2 \text{ kg}^2}{6.67 \cdot 10^{11} \text{ Nm}^2}$$

$$= 8.74 \cdot 10^{26} \text{ kg}$$

3. Kinematics and Friction

Susan must start at 30.6 m up the hill; Elizabeth must start at 17.6 m.

Explanation: This is a long, tricky question, in that there are many separate issues to consider. But it can be broken down more simply into two parts: We need to find out how fast Susan needs to go to reach a height of 5 m; and we need to find out what her acceleration is going down the hill.

Susan. Let's start from the tree and work backwards. To reach a height of 5 m, we want to find the vertical velocity Susan must have. Assuming down is negative, we know:

$$a_y = g = -9.81 \text{ m/s}^2.$$

We can use the kinematics equation:

$$v_f^2 = v_0^2 + 2as$$

Where:
s = distance = 5 m
v_0 = initial velocity (what we're trying to find)
v_f = final velocity = 0 (Remember, only v_{fy} is actually 0 for her to clear the tree, but v_x does not become 0)

So we have:
$$v_0^2 = -2(-9.81 \text{ m/s}^2)\,(5\text{ m}) = \frac{98.1 \text{ m}^2}{\text{s}^2}$$

and $v_0 = \sqrt{98.1} = 9.9$ m/s.

Since this v_0 is v_{0y}, we can use this to find the overall speed (i.e., magnitude of the total velocity) that Susan needs to have.

Use $|v_0|^2 = |v_{0x}|^2 + |v_{0y}|^2 = 2 \cdot (9.9)^2$ to find

$$v_0 = 14 \text{ m/s}$$

(we know $|v_{0x}| = |v_{0y}|$ because the jump is at 45°),

or use
$$\cos 45 = \frac{v_{0x}}{v_0} \text{ to find } v_0 = \frac{9.9}{\cos 45} = 14.0 \text{ m/s.}$$

So now we have accomplished one big step of the problem, namely finding out how fast Susan must be on taking off from the jump. Now, to find the acceleration while going downhill, let's look at a diagram of all the forces acting on Susan.

(Note that we chose the x-axis to be parallel to the ski hill, whereas before we chose the y-axis to be vertical, same as the tree.)

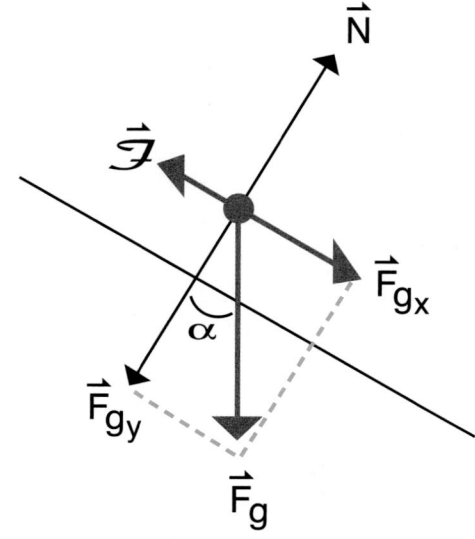

From the diagram, we can readily see that

$$F_{gx} = F_g(\sin(a)) \text{ and } F_{gy} = F_g(\cos(a)).$$

We know that $ma = F_{sum}$ (and our goal is to find this total acceleration).

$$
\begin{aligned}
ma = F_{sum} &= F_g + N + \mathcal{F} \\
&= F_{gx} + F_{gy} + N + \mathcal{F} \\
&= F_{gx} + \mathcal{F} \text{ (since the direction of motion is the x-axis)}
\end{aligned}
$$

F_g is simply the weight of the skier, so F_g = mg, and this gives us:

F_{gx} = mg sin (a) and

F_{gy} = mg cos (a).

We also know that $\mathcal{I}$ = Nu_d (frictional force)

(where u_d = 0.2 for a ski on snow).

And since

N = − F_{gy}, we have

N = −mg cos(a).

We can simplify our equation a little more now:

F_{sum} = mg sin(a) − mg cos(a) • u_d = ma.

Cancel m, which appears in each term, and we are left with:

$$a = g(\sin(a) - u_d\cos(a))$$
$$= 9.81 \text{ m/s}^2 (\sin 30 - 0.2\cos 30)$$
$$= 3.2 \text{ m/s}^2$$

From here on, we're basically home free. All we need to do now is use the same kinematics formula as we used at the beginning of the problem:

$$v_f^2 = v_0^2 + 2as$$

Where this time

v_0 = 0

a = 3.2 m/s²

v_f = 14.0 m/s

So s $= \dfrac{v_f^2}{2a}$ = 30.6m.

Friction causes resistance between a skier's skis and the snow beneath them. This affects the rate at which the skier will travel downhill.

Elizabeth. This part should be relatively painless, because it's almost the same question with one change. Elizabeth still needs a vertical velocity v_{0y}= 9.9 m/s on leaving the jump, but she gets 2.4 m/s extra lift from jumping. So really, all she needs before the jump is 7.5 m/s of vertical velocity.

Then we have

$$v_0 = \frac{7.5 \text{ m/s}}{\sin(45)} = 10.6 \text{ m/s}.$$

The acceleration downhill does not change, so we can again use

$$v_f^2 = v_0^2 + 2as$$

Where

v_0 = 0

a = 3.2 m/s²

v_f = 10.6 m/s

So s $= \dfrac{v_f^2}{2a} = \dfrac{10.6^2}{(2 \cdot 3.2)} = 17.6$ m.

Physics Practice—Answers

4. Friction and Circular Motion

The radius is smaller than 141.6 m.

Explanation: To solve this problem we need to introduce the concept of *centripetal acceleration*, which is basically acceleration toward the center of a curve. It is given by

$$a_{rad} = \frac{v^2}{R} \text{ where R = radius of the curve.}$$

- The subscript "rad" is used to remind us that the acceleration is toward the center of the curve.
- The car is rounding a turn, and so is accelerating inward.
- Remember, even if the speed isn't changing, the direction is, so the car is accelerating.

The acceleration toward the center of the curve must come from the force of friction between the tires and the road; without it, the car could not round the curve. The second figure shows a balance of all the forces acting on the car.

The force of friction causing the centripetal acceleration is given by

$$F = ma_{rad} = \frac{mv^2}{R}$$

You can surmise from this formula that the quicker the car moves around a given turn, the more force is needed to keep it accelerating to the center. The concept behind the car sliding around the curve is that there is a maximum friction force available, given by

$$F = u_s N = u_s mg$$

Now we are ready to solve our problem. We know that the car began to slide at

$$80 \text{ miles/hr} = 128 \text{ km/hr} = 35.6 \text{ m/s}$$

By equating $u_s mg = \frac{mv^2}{R}$, we get

$$R = \frac{mv^2}{u_s mg} = \frac{v^2}{u_s g} = \frac{(35.6 \text{ m/s})^2}{(0.91 \cdot 9.81 \text{ m/s}^2)}$$

$$= 141.6 \text{ m}$$

So if James Bond's car was sliding around this curve at 80 miles/hr, then we know that the curve must have a radius smaller than 141.6 m.

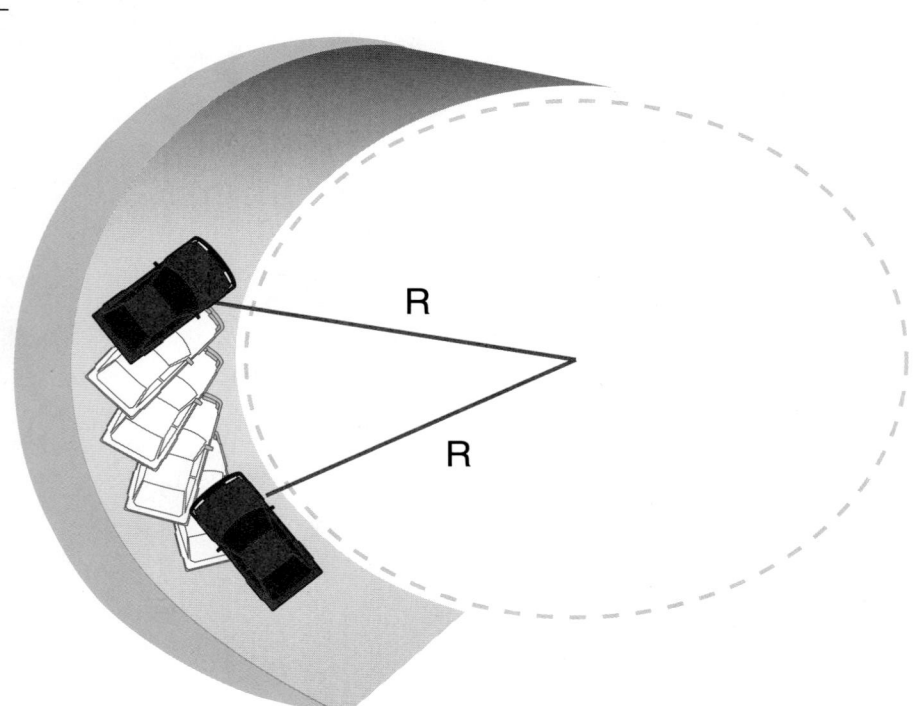

5. Energy

Millennium Falcon: 271 megajoules

Star Destroyer: $1.35 \cdot 10^7$ megajoules

Explanation: Asking how much energy was used is another way of phrasing, "How much work was done?" Work done is given by the formula:

$W = Fs$

$\quad = ma \cdot s$, where

$a = 15 \text{ m/s}^2$

$s = 5 \text{ m}$

So for the Millennium Falcon,

$W = 3617000 \text{ kg} \cdot 15 \text{ m/s}^2 \cdot 5\text{m}$

$\quad = 271275000 \text{ J (joules)}$

$\quad = 271 \text{ MJ (megajoules)}$

And for an Imperial Class Star Destroyer:

$W = 180,000,000,000 \text{ kg} \cdot 15 \text{ m/s}^2 \cdot 5 \text{ m}$

$\quad = 1.35 \cdot 10^{13} \text{ J}$

$\quad = 1.35 \cdot 10^7 \text{ MJ}$

So it takes the Star Destroyer approximately 50,000 times more energy than it took for the Millennium Falcon.

As for how much energy it takes to make the jump to hyperspace, given what we know now about physics, it would take an infinite amount of energy for either spacecraft to reach the speed of light. Obviously, the engineers and physicists in this galaxy far, far away have discovered and learned more than we have to date!

6. Torque

Explanation: This question did not ask for any number crunching, only for a description that indicates the concept is understood. Even so, it is best to back up an explanation with the correct formulae whenever possible.

Remember that torque is the force that tends to produce rotation, and is given by

$L = Fl$

where l is the distance of the applied force from the center of gravity of the object.

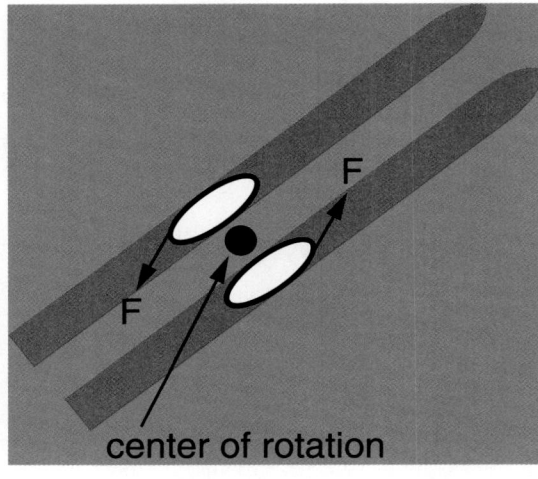

center of rotation

(Note that some texts use L to represent torque, some use τ, the Greek letter Tau. Different symbols are often used to represent different concepts. It doesn't really matter, as long as you understand the concept of how to find whatever you're looking for.)

Looking at this equation, you can see the following:

● When the distance of the force to the center of rotation is bigger, the torque is higher.

● When the distance of the force to the center of rotation is 0, there is no torque.

When a skier or a snowboarder jumps and tries to spin, his feet—pushing against the ground when he jumps—cause the torque. A snowboarder's feet are usually farther apart from the axis of rotation than a skier's feet, and so he has a greater potential for maximum torque. It's the same concept as pushing open a door by the handle, or right near the hinge.

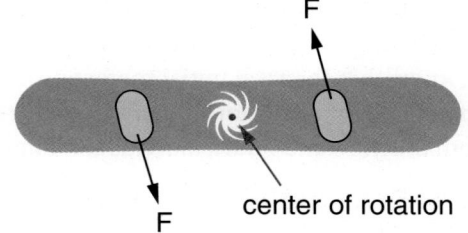

center of rotation

Physics Practice—Answers

7. Energy

Maximum height: 2.77 m
Maximum speed: 7.4 m/s

Explanation: We know that total energy is conserved, and the total energy is the combination of the kinetic and potential energy: $E_{tot} = U + K$.

(Usually potential energy is represented by U or by PE, and kinetic energy is represented by K or KE but again, this can vary.)

In our case, the potential energy is the gravitational potential energy, given by

$$U = mgy$$

and the kinetic energy is given by

$$K = \frac{1}{2}mv^2$$

So we have:

$$E_{tot} = K + U = \frac{1}{2}mv^2 + mgy$$

When Rob threw the basketball, we had

$v = 5$ m/s and

$y = 1.5$ m

Then $E = \frac{1}{2}(0.8 \text{ kg})(5\text{m/s})^2 +$
$(0.8 \text{ kg})(9.81 \text{ m/s}^2)(1.5 \text{ m})$
$= 21.77$ J

We can find the maximum height because we know the energy will be the same, but the kinetic energy will be 0 as the velocity becomes 0.

So $E = \frac{1}{2}mv^2 + mgy = mgy$

$$y = \frac{E}{mg}$$

$$y = \frac{21.77 \text{ J}}{(0.8 \text{ kg})(9.81\text{m/s}^2)} = 2.77 \text{ m}$$

We can now find the maximum speed of the ball because we know that when it hits the ground, the potential energy will be 0.

So $E = \frac{1}{2}mv^2 + mgy$

$\quad = \frac{1}{2}mv^2 + mg(0)$

$\quad = \frac{1}{2}mv^2$

$$v = \sqrt{\frac{2E}{m}} = \sqrt{\frac{2 \cdot 21.77 \text{ J}}{0.8\text{kg}}} = 7.4 \text{ m/s}$$

8. Collisions

a) 1.1 m/s, to the right (Paul's initial direction)
b) 4.60 m/s, in the direction of 35° up from the positive x-axis.

Explanation: We know that momentum is conserved, because there are no external forces acting on Kyle and Paul. From the conservation of momentum, we know that the total initial momentum P_i is equal to the final momentum P_f, and we know that P_i is the sum of Kyle's and Paul's individual momenta.

FINAL

m = 170 kg

a) Let's define the direction to the right as positive, and the left as negative. Then we have:

$$P_p = m_p v_p$$
$$= (80\text{kg})(8 \text{ m/s})$$
$$= 640 \text{ kg m/s}$$

(where the subscript $_p$ signifies Paul)

$$P_k = m_k v_k$$
$$= (90\text{kg})(-5 \text{ m/s})$$
$$= -450 \text{ kg m/s}$$

(where the subscript $_k$ signifies Kyle)

$$P_i = P_p + P_k$$
$$= (640 \text{ kg m/s}) + (-450 \text{ kg m/s})$$
$$= 190 \text{ kg m/s}$$

$$P_f = P_{pk} = m_f v_f$$

And we know that

$$m_f = m_k + m_p$$
$$= 90 \text{ kg} + 80 \text{ kg}$$
$$= 170 \text{ kg}$$

$$v_f = \frac{P_f}{m_f} = \frac{190 \text{ kg m/s}}{170 \text{ kg}} = 1.11 \text{ m/s}$$

So the final combined velocity is 1.11 m/s, and notice that since the resultant is a positive value, their direction is to the right, or the same as Paul's initial direction.

b) Let's have Paul going right (the x-axis) and Kyle traveling straight up (the y-axis).

The total final momentum is still the same as the total initial momentum, only this time we need to worry about both the x and the y momenta. Since the only x momentum before the collision is from Paul, and the only y momentum before the collision is from Kyle, we know that

$$P_{xi} = P_p = 640 \text{ kg m/s}$$
$$P_{yi} = P_k = 450 \text{ kg m/s}$$

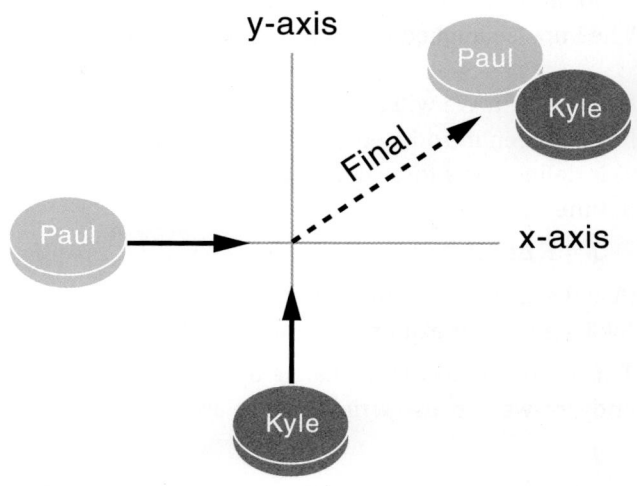

The conservation of momentum means that the x and y components of the momenta both need to be conserved. So, using the initial values above, and the total mass after the collision, let's find the x and y components of the velocity after the collision.

$$P_{xf} = m_f v_{xf}$$
$$V_{xf} = \frac{P_{xf}}{m_f} = \frac{(640 \text{ kg m/s})}{(170 \text{ kg})} = 3.76 \text{ m/s}$$

$$P_{yf} = m_f v_{yf}$$
$$V_{yf} = \frac{P_{yf}}{m_f} = \frac{(450 \text{ kg m/s})}{(170 \text{ kg})} = 2.65 \text{ m/s}$$

Now that we have the x and y components of the velocity, we can use Pythagoras to find the total velocity.

$$v_f = \sqrt{[(3.76 \text{ m/s})^2 + (2.65 \text{ m/s})^2]} = 4.60 \text{ m/s}$$

The angle of the direction is given by

$$\tan(\theta) = \frac{v_{yf}}{v_{xf}}$$

$$\theta = \tan^{-1}\left(\frac{2.65 \text{ m/s}}{3.76 \text{ m/s}}\right) = 35°$$

So the final velocity of Kyle and Paul is 4.60 m/s at an angle of 35° up from the positive x-axis.

Physics Practice—Answers

9. Momentum and Impulse

The impulse applied to the ball is 14.07 kg m/s.

Explanation: We will start by defining impulse, which has not been introduced before. Impulse (denoted by J) is defined as a force acting on a body over a period of time:

$$J = F \, \Delta t$$

(Δ is the Greek letter delta, and usually represents "change in." For example, in this case, Δt means $t_2 - t_1$.)

This is analogous to the change in momentum on a body, so we can also write impulse as

$$J = p_2 - p_1$$

Now we readily see what we must do:

$$p_1 = m_1 v_1 = (0.145 \text{ kg}) \cdot (-42 \text{ m/s})$$
$$= -6.09 \text{ kg m/s}$$

$$p_2 = m_2 v_2 = (0.145 \text{ kg}) \cdot (55 \text{ m/s})$$
$$= 7.98 \text{ kg m/s}$$

$$J = p_2 - p_1 = (7.98 \text{ kg m/s}) - (-6.09 \text{ kg m/s})$$
$$= 14.07 \text{ kg m/s}$$

So the impulse that was applied to the ball was 14.07 kg m/s. Remember, it doesn't matter which velocity we denote as negative and which one as positive, as long as they're different.

10. Optics

Alex needs to aim exactly where he sees the apple.

Explanation: When light passes between two different media at an angle, it is refracted (its path changes direction on entering the medium) or else reflected, and doesn't even leave the initial medium.

Snell's law gives us the ratio of the angles of incidence and the angle refraction to the indices of refraction (n) for media 1 and 2:

$$n^1 \sin\theta^1 = n^2 \sin\theta^2$$

Now we could plug in the values of n and θ to attempt this problem, but first we should realize that if the laser's light changes paths on leaving the water, then the light from the apple would change also on entering the water. Thus, to shoot the apple, Alex simply needs to aim at the apple as he sees it.

11. Optics

Explanation: Objects will appear in different colors to each boy because the differently colored glasses absorb all sorts of wavelengths and reflect only a few.

- Red lenses absorb a bunch of colors, but reflect red light, and also transmit red light through to Nate's eyes.

- Blue lenses absorb a bunch of colors, but reflect blue light, and transmit blue light through to Tye's eyes.

In essence, the red sunglasses act as a filter for light of any wavelength other than red. The blue glasses act the same. However, these glasses are not perfect filters. So when Nate looks around, he sees lots of red. He'll especially see things like white light in red (because white is an additive mixture of red and two other primary additive colors: green and blue), but he will also see colors that don't have any red in them.

If the glasses were perfect filters for red, Nate wouldn't see any colors but red—anything without red in it would appear black or gray. The same applies to Tye.

12. Optics

She must aim her laser at 48.75°.

Explanation: Snell's law states that

$$n_1 \sin\theta_1 = n_2 \sin\theta_2.$$

We will take medium 1 to be water and medium 2 to be the air. We know what both the indices of refraction are, and the critical angle θ_c is such that θ_2 is 90°. Since $\sin(90) = 1$, we have

$$n_1 \sin\theta_c = n_2 \sin 90 = n_2$$

$$\sin\theta_c = n_2 \sin 90 = n_2$$

$$\sin\theta_c = \frac{n_2}{n_1}$$

$$\theta_c = \sin^{-1}\left(\frac{n_2}{n_1}\right) = \sin^{-1}\left(\frac{1}{1.33}\right) = 48.75°$$

13. Circuits

Explanation: We need to find one unknown resistance, and two unknown currents. We notice that R_2 and R_3 are parallel resistors, and R_1 is in series with this combination. To recap the rules for finding the equivalent resistance when we see resistors in series or in parallel with each other, we have:

Series resistors:

$$R_{eq} = R_1 + R_2 + R_3 + \ldots$$

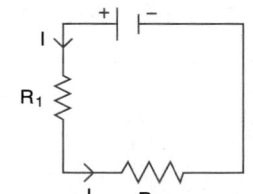

$$R_{eq} = R_1 \quad + \quad R_2 \quad + \quad R_3 \quad + \quad \cdots$$

Parallel resistors:

$$\frac{1}{R_{eq}} = \frac{1}{R_1} + \frac{1}{R_2} + \frac{1}{R_3} + \ldots$$

We can reduce the network to show the equivalent resistors,

$$\frac{1}{R_{eq}} = \frac{1}{R_2} + \frac{1}{R_3} + \frac{1}{2\,\Omega} + \frac{1}{6\,\Omega} = \frac{1}{3\,\Omega}$$

$$R_{23} = 1.5\,\Omega$$

13. (cont'd)

To find R_1, we have a simple series circuit where

$$R_{eq} = R_2 + R_{23} = R_1 + 1.5\,\Omega.$$

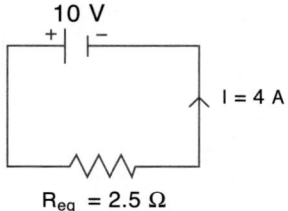

We know that $R_{eq} = V/I = 10\,V/4\,A = 2.5\,\Omega$. From Kirchhoff's rules, we know that over any closed loop

$$\Sigma V = 0$$

and that over any junction

$$\Sigma I = 0$$

$$V = IR_{eq} = IR_1 + IR_{23}$$

(We can write it as such since the current going through R_1 must be the same as the combined currents going through R_2 and R_3.)

The equivalent resistance for R_2 and R_3 is given by

$$\frac{1}{R_{23}} = \frac{1}{R_2} + \frac{1}{R_3}$$

$$\frac{1}{R_{23}} = \frac{R_2 R_3}{R_2 + R_3} = \frac{(2\,\Omega)(6\,\Omega)}{2\,\Omega + 6\,\Omega} = 1.5\,\Omega$$

$$R_1 = \frac{V - IR_{23}}{I} = \frac{10\,V - 4\,A \cdot 1.5\,\Omega}{4\,A} = 1\,\Omega$$

Now we can build the circuit back up and find the current passing through R_2 and R_3. Since the voltage drop over R_1 is $(4\,A)(1\,\Omega) = 4\,V$, we know that the voltage drop over R_2 and R_3 must be 6 V.

$V = IR = I_2 R_2 = I_3 R_3$ (where I_2 and I_3 represent the currents going through resistors 2 and 3, respectively).

So

$$I_2 = \frac{V}{R_2} = \frac{6\,V}{2\,\Omega} = 3\,A$$

and $I_3 = \dfrac{V}{R_3} = \dfrac{6\,V}{6\,\Omega} = 1\,A.$

So hopefully Sean touched the part of the circuit with resistor R_3.

Physics Practice—Answers

14. Electrical Charge

a) 10^{10} m/s²

b) Force: $F_{boy\#1} = (-6.51, +6.51) \cdot 10^{-28}$ N; $F_{boy\#2} = (+8.68, +8.68) \cdot 10^{-28}$ N

Net acceleration: 1,684 m/s² in a direction 8.13° clockwise from the + y-axis

Explanation: We can disregard any forces other than electrical attraction. Electrical force of attraction is given by

$$F_e = \frac{k(q_1q_2)}{r^2}$$

And $k = \dfrac{8.99 \cdot 10^9 Nm^2}{C^2}$

Therefore $F_e = \dfrac{8.99 \cdot 10^9 Nm^2}{C^2}$

$$\frac{(1.60 \cdot 10^{-19})(1.60 \cdot 10^{-19})}{(0.50m)^2}$$

$$= 9.21 \cdot 10^{-28} \text{ N}$$

(Be sure to check that the units match.)

$$F = ma$$

$$a = \frac{F_e}{m} = \frac{9.21 \cdot 10^{-28}N}{9.11 \cdot 10^{-31}kg} = 10^{10} \text{ m/s}^2$$

Notice how the force has a – sign. We have used, by convention, a + sign for a + force, and a – sign for a – force. This means that an attractive electrical force should be "negative" and a repulsive electrical force should be "positive."

We could have just as easily decided to use a different sign convention; all that matters is that we understand which direction the force is acting on a body. Since we know that in this example, the force of the boys on Laura and Ingrid is always an attracting force, we don't need to keep track of them.

Now for Laura. Since she's in the same spot as Ingrid, we know that $F_{boy\#1}$ is the same. We need to use the same method to find $F_{boy\#2}$ on her, and then add the two vectors to find the resultant force and acceleration. Remember that this time,

$$r = 0.75m, \text{ and } q_2 = 3e = 4.80 \cdot 10^{-19} \text{ C}$$

$$F_e = \frac{k(q_1q_2)}{r^2}$$

And $k = \dfrac{8.99 \cdot 10^9 Nm^2}{C^2}$

Therefore $F_e = \dfrac{8.99 \cdot 10^9 Nm^2}{C^2}$

$$\frac{(1.60 \cdot 10^{-19})(4.80 \cdot 10^{-19})}{(0.75m)^2}$$

$$= 1.23 \cdot 10^{-27} \text{N}$$

Already we see that boy #2 has a greater attractive force on Laura, so we know that she'll go more in his direction. Now, to find the net force on Laura and her acceleration, let's use coordinate notation to add the x and y components of the forces.

The fact that both boys are at 45° angles makes the math a little easier. We can use Pythagoras to find that

$$|F_e|^2 = |F_{ex}|^2 + |F_{ey}|^2 = 2|F_{x \, or \, y}|^2$$

(We've written $F_{x \, or \, y}$ to emphasize that the magnitudes of these two components of the force are the same.)

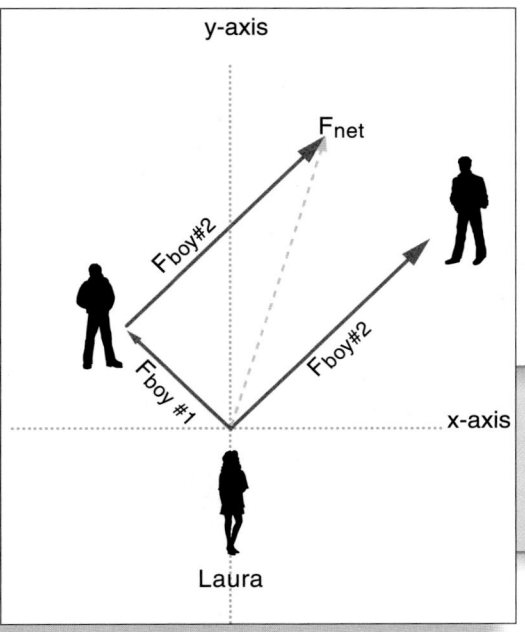

888

From Boy #1 we have:

$$F_x = \sqrt{\frac{|F_e|^2}{2}} = \sqrt{\frac{(9.21 \cdot 10^{-28})^2}{2}} = 6.51 \cdot 10^{-28}N$$

From Boy #2 we have:

$$F_x = \sqrt{\frac{|F_e|^2}{2}} = \sqrt{\frac{(1.23 \cdot 10^{-27})^2}{2}} = 8.68 \cdot 10^{-28}N$$

If we define the positive x-axis and the positive y-axis to be +, and the negative x-axis and the negative y-axis to be −, then our net forces would be:

$$F_{boy\#1} = (-6.51, +6.51) \cdot 10^{-28}N$$
$$F_{boy\#2} = (+8.68, +8.68) \cdot 10^{-28}N$$
$$F_{boy\#1} + F_{boy\#2} = (+2.17, +15.19) \cdot 10^{-28}N$$
$$F_{net} = \sqrt{(2.17 \cdot 10^{-28}N)^2 + (15.19 \cdot 10^{-28}N)^2} = 1.53 \cdot 10^{-27}N$$

The acceleration is given by F = ma, so

$$a = \frac{F}{m} = \frac{1.53 \cdot 10^{-27}N}{9.11 \cdot 10^{-31}kg} = 1,684 \text{ m/s}^2$$

And the direction is given by $\tan\theta = \dfrac{2.17}{15.19}$

$$\theta = \tan^{-1}\left(\frac{2.17}{15.19}\right) = 8.13°$$

Laura is attracted to both guys, but feels a stronger pull from boy #2. Her acceleration is more in his direction than in boy #1's direction, so eventually she'll hit him. Actually, she'll probably reach him pretty fast. Her initial acceleration is 1,684 m/s² in a direction 8.13° clockwise from the + y-axis.

Note that in order to figure out other things, such as the amount of time it takes these girls to reach their boys, we would need to use other means. Since the force of attraction is proportional to 1/r², it increases as they get closer. Since the force of attraction increases, the acceleration will increase also. In order to solve this, we would need to do an integral over the distance, but that is beyond the scope of this material.

15. Voltage and Current

Current: 2.5 A
Resistance: 4.8 Ω

Explanation: Solving this question is pretty straight-forward if you know which formulae and relations are needed.

We know that power is related to voltage and current by P = IV, so

$$I = \frac{P}{V} = \frac{30 \text{ W}}{12 \text{ V}} = 2.5$$

We also know that voltage and resistance are related by Ohm's law, V = IR, so

$$R = \frac{V}{I} = \frac{12 \text{ V}}{2.5 \text{ A}} = 4.8 \text{ Ω}$$

Resistance can either be placed in a circuit to control the current, or else it can be part of a load, such as speakers or lights.

Note that 2.5 A is an extremely high current (if this were a real system, that would probably short-circuit just about any stereo system). So if this were a real system, there would be other factors controlling the current that goes through the speakers.

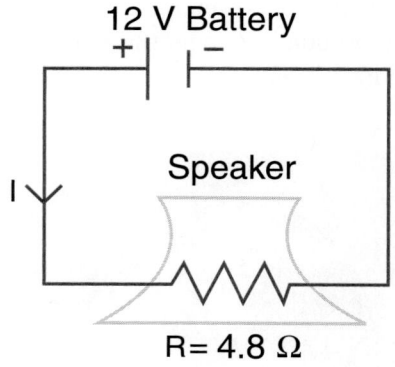

16. Energy and Power

a) Kyah saves about 14 cents/week by using the dimmer bulb.

b) Kyah saves $14.40 on her electrical bill over these 3,000 hours.

Explanation: Power is defined as the amount of work W done over a time t, and the units are given in watts, W, which stands for joules/second. (Don't confuse all these Ws.)

$$P = \frac{W}{t}$$

If you lift a heavy stone quickly, as opposed to slowly, you will be using the same amount of energy, but a lot more power. A kilowatt-hour (kWh) is a unit of energy or work (not power), which is usually used commercially. Again, another source of confusion is that even though the word watt is in the units, the "hour" signifies actually multiplying the kilowatt by an hour (3,600 s), and so the units are joules.

$$\begin{aligned} 1 \text{ kWh} &= 1{,}000 \text{ J/s} \cdot 3{,}600 \text{ s} \\ &= 3.6 \cdot 10^6 \text{ J} \\ &= 3.6 \text{ MJ} \end{aligned}$$

a) If Kyah uses a 60 W light bulb instead of a 100 W bulb, she saves 40 W of power. Let's find out how much power this equates to over the 30 hrs/week during which the light is on:

40 W • 60 s/min • 60 min/hr • 30 hr

$= 4{,}320{,}000$ W

$= 4.320$ MJ

She pays 12 cents/kWh, so she pays $0.12 to use each 3.6 MJ. For 4.320 MJ, she would have paid

$$\frac{4.32}{3.6} \cdot \$0.12 = \$0.14.$$

So Kyah saves about 14 cents/week by using the dimmer bulb.

b) To consider the real savings of the halogen bulb, first consider that it lasts at least 3 times as long. So we need 3 regular bulbs for $2.85 to cover each $7.45 halogen bulb. From part (a), we can figure the total energy saved over 3,000 hours.

40 W • 60 s/min • 60 min/hr • 3,000 hr

$= 4.32 \cdot 10^8$ J

$= 432$ MJ

and $\dfrac{432 \text{ MJ}}{3.6 \text{ MJ}} \cdot \$0.12 = \$14.40$

So Kyah saves $14.40 on her electrical bill over these 3,000 hours, but actually saves only

$14.40 − ($7.45 − $2.85) = $14.40 − $4.60 = $9.80

after you consider the cost of the bulb. (But remember that the other advantage to halogen bulbs is that there's less environmental waste.)

Halogen bulbs have a higher initial cost, but last longer and produce less environmental waste than standard lightbulbs.

17. Sound and Doppler Effect

She hears the singer's voice at a frequency of 351 Hz.

Explanation: The wavelength and frequency for any wave are related by $\lambda = v/f$. The sound waves travel at the same speed no matter which way they leave the car, since their speed depends on the medium through which they travel (e.g., air, water, etc.).

In this respect, sound travels differently than something like a baseball. If you were driving a car and decided to throw a baseball in the same direction as the car, you would add the car's speed relative to the ground, and the baseball's speed relative to the car, to find the baseball's ground speed. The speed of sound would not change no matter how fast the source is moving.

Since the speed of sound stays the same, but the source still moves, the wavelength changes: the distance between each wavecrest and the source changes as the car's speed changes.

From the diagram on page 975, you can see the following.

- The sound's wavelength is smaller when traveling in the same direction as the car, than in the opposite direction.
- To the right of the car, the wavelength is smaller than it would be if the car were not moving.

To find out how much smaller the wavelength is, we need to subtract from the wavelength the distance that the car traveled during one period of the wave's emission:

$$\lambda = \frac{v}{f_s} - \frac{v_s}{f_s}$$

(where v_s and f_s are the velocity and frequency of the source)

$$= \frac{(v - v_s)}{f_s}$$

$$= \frac{(340 \text{ m/s} - 30 \text{ m/s})}{320 \text{ Hz}}$$

$$= 0.97 \text{ m}$$

Now to find the frequency at which Colin's friend hears the sound, we can put our wavelength back into the original relation:

$$f = \frac{v}{\lambda}$$

$$= \frac{340 \text{ m/s}}{0.97 \text{ m}}$$

$$= 351 \text{ Hz}$$

So Colin's friend will hear a slightly higher-pitched voice than Colin does.

When both the listener and the source are moving, the formula for the actual frequency heard is a little more complicated. For the sake of completeness, we will show it here but not derive it.

$$f_l = \frac{(v + v_l)}{(v + v_s)} \cdot f_s$$

(where v_l and f_l mean the velocity and frequency of the listener)

18. Rotational Kinetic Energy

56.1 J

Explanation: Often, when angles are given in radians, you omit saying the word radians. You could say a ball is spinning at 180 degrees/s, or simply that it is spinning at π/s.

Careful: when you see $(10\pi)^2$ remember that this means $(10 \cdot 3.14)^2$.

$$E_{tot} = U + K$$

$$= mgy + \frac{1}{2}mv^2 + \frac{1}{2}I\omega^2$$

$$= mgy + \frac{1}{2}mv^2 + \frac{1}{2}\left(\frac{2}{3}mr^2\right)\omega^2$$

$$= (0.5 \text{ kg})(9.81 \text{ m/s}^2)(5 \text{ m})$$

$$+ \frac{1}{2}(0.5 \text{ kg})(10 \text{ m/s})^2$$

$$+ \frac{1}{2}\left[\left(\frac{2}{3}\right)(0.5 \text{ kg})(0.2 \text{ m})^2\right](10\pi/s)^2$$

$$= 24.525 \text{ J} + 25 \text{ J} + 6.58 \text{ J}$$

$$= 56.1 \text{ J}$$

Physics Glossary

absolute zero the temperature at which substances have no heat whatever, and all molecules stop moving. Theoretically, absolute zero is the lowest temperature, −273.15 degrees Celsius or −459.67 degrees Fahrenheit.

absorption in optics, the act of taking in, as opposed to reflecting back. A sheet of black paper does not reflect light but absorbs it.

acceleration an increase in velocity.

acoustics the branch of physics that deals with sound. It includes the study of how sound is produced, transmitted, detected, measured, and used.

alpha particle the nucleus of a helium atom, consisting of two protons and two neutrons. Alpha particles are emitted by radioactive materials.

amplitude the vertical distance from the crest of a wave to the wave at rest.

antiparticle elementary particle corresponding to a normal particle but opposite to it in electric and magnetic properties. When brought together with its counterpart, the result is their mutual annihilation.

atom the smallest unit of matter having the characteristics of an element. The atom is composed of a nucleus which contains neutrons with no electrical charge as well as positively charged protons and surrounded by revolving negatively charged electrons. Most of the mass of an atom is in its nucleus. The number of electrons (its atomic number) is equal to the number of protons it holds.

beta particle an electron emitted during radioactive decay of such substances as thorium and uranium. Positive beta particles are positrons; they are emitted during the radioactive decay of certain elements.

capacitor a device that stores a charge.

center of gravity the point at which the entire weight of a body is concentrated.

composite particle a particle made up of smaller elementary particles, such as quarks.

concave curved in, like the inside of a sphere or circle.

concurrent forces when more than one force acts on an accelerated object.

conduction the movement of heat through a material.

conductor a material through which electric charge moves easily.

constant a measurement or quantity that never changes.

convection the transfer of heat by the movement of a heated material.

convex curved out, like the outside of a sphere or circle.

Coulomb force the attraction between positive and negative charges that binds protons to electrons in an atom.

critical point the temperature at which the liquid and gaseous phases of a pure stable substance become identical.

cryogenics the study of extremely low temperatures.

deceleration a decrease in velocity, also called negative acceleration.

density the mass per unit of volume. The density of an object once determined is used to calculate specific gravity.

diffraction the spreading out of waves as they pass through an opening or by the edge of an obstacle.

diffusion the scattering of light in all directions during transmission or reflection. During transmission, diffusion is caused by light waves striking minute particles. During reflection, diffusion is caused by irregularities in the reflecting surface.

dispersion in optics, the separation of light into its component colors: red, orange, yellow, green, blue, indigo, and violet.

Doppler effect the change in frequency of sound, light, or radio waves caused by the relative motion of the source of the waves and their observer.

dynamics the study of objects that change their speed or the direction of their motion because of forces acting on them.

electric circuit the path followed by an electrical current.

electric current the flow of electric charge through a conductor. The current is measured in amperes; 1 ampere equals the flow of 1 coulomb (the unit of electric charge) per second.

electric field the space in which an electron or an electric charge experiences a force.

electric signal an electric current or voltage modified in some way as to represent information, such as sounds, pictures, numbers, or letters.

electric voltage a type of pressure or force that causes the charges to move in the same direction.

electrode a terminal, pole, or conductor that conveys a flow of electrons through a solid, a molten solution, a gas, or a liquid. Electrodes are either negatively or positively charged.

electrolysis the application of a direct electric current through the positive electrode (anode), electrolytes, and negative electrode (cathode) of an electrolytic cell to produce a chemical reaction. The components of the electrolyte become ionized. Reduction takes place at the cathode, and oxidation takes place at the anode. Depending on selection, the electrodes may participate in the reaction.

electrolyte in electrolysis, any substance (usually an acid, base, or soluble or molten salt) that dissociates into its respective cations (positive ions) and anions (negative ions) by the application of a direct electric current.

electromagnet a temporary magnet produced by electric currents.

electromagnetic force a force that consists of two parts: (1) the electric force and (2) the magnetic force. The electric force is an attraction or repulsion between objects that carry an electric charge. The magnetic force arises from two sources: (1) the combined magnetic forces of "miniature magnets" and (2) the movement of electrons through wires as electric current.

electromagnetic spectrum the entire range of wavelengths or frequencies according to which electromagnetic radiation is classified; the range is from about 10^{-14} meter (gamma rays) to about 10^7 meters (radio waves).

electromagnetic wave a wave of energy made up of an electric and a magnetic field, generated when an electric charge oscillates or is accelerated. The chief kinds of electromagnetic waves, ranging from longest to shortest wavelength, are long radio waves, short radio waves, infrared rays, visible light, ultraviolet light, X-rays, and gamma rays.

electromagnetism the branch of physics that studies the relationship between electricity and magnetism. Electromagnetism is based on two facts: (1) An electric current or a changing electric field produces a magnetic field and (2) A changing magnetic field produces an electric field.

electron a subatomic particle with negative charge that commonly occupies the outer region of the atom. An electron has a mass of about 1/1,800 that of a proton or about 9.11×10^{-31} kg. It is the electrons that provide valence.

elementary particles the particles that comprise all matter including subatomic particles. Early atomic understanding identified electrons and nucleus which consisted of protons and neutrons which have now been determined to be made of even smaller particles. Continuing research finds or postulates the existence of additional such particles. Quarks may be the smallest elementary particle.

Physics Glossary

energy in general, the capacity to do work. Types of energy include: potential (stored), kinetic (from motion), light, heat, chemical, electrical, nuclear. One kind of energy can be converted or transformed into another, but cannot be created or destroyed.

entropy a measure of the amount of disorder or randomness in a system.

equilibrium a state of balance; a condition in which opposing forces exactly balance or equal each other.

ferromagnetism a term that refers to the magnetic properties iron contributes when it is placed inside a solenoid.

fluid any substance that flows easily; includes all liquids and gases.

focus the point at which rays of light, heat, or other radiation converge after being reflected by a mirror.

force a push or pull.

frequency the number of times an event will take place in a given unit of time. Can be measured in cycles per second, revolutions per minute, pulses per second, and so on.

friction resistance that is produced when one object rubs against another.

gamma ray electromagnetic radiation of very short wavelength, typically 0.1 nanometer. Gamma rays penetrate matter easily and are emitted during radio-active decay.

grand unification theory (GUT) a theory that seeks to explain an underlying unity to three of the basic forces of the universe: the strong force, the weak force, and the electromagnetic force that bind electrons to the nucleus.

heat the energy that results from the vibrations, motions, reactions, and collisions of nuclear particles, atoms, and molecules.

impulse the change in momentum produced by a force.

inertia the tendency of an object to continue moving if it is moving and to remain motionless if it is at rest.

insulation a way to control the movement of heat by keeping it in or out of place.

insulator a material that resists the movement of electric charge.

interference an effect caused by two waves of the same kind passing through the same space. There are two types of interference: constructive interference (two waves combine to produce a single wave with larger amplitude) and destructive interference (two waves combine to produce a wave with smaller amplitude).

ion a charged particle that results when an atom or molecule gains or loses one or more electrons. A positive ion is an atom or molecule that has lost an electron; a negative ion is an atom or molecule that has gained an electron.

isotope atoms of the same element with the same number of protons (and thus identical atomic numbers), but with different numbers of neutrons (and thus different mass numbers).

kinetic energy energy of motion.

kinetic theory the theory that molecules of a gas are in a state of rapid motion, constantly colliding with the walls of any containing vessel and with one another, causing changes in their velocity and direction.

laser a device that produces a very powerful beam of light of only one wavelength going in only one direction; used in optical experiments, instruments, and communication; stands for Light Amplification by Stimulated Emission of Radiation.

latent heat the heat needed to change a material from a solid to a liquid or from a liquid to a gas.

lens a curved piece of glass or other material that allows light to pass through it, shaped so that the light is refracted as it passes through.

light a form of electromagnetic energy that acts on the retina of the eye, allowing sight; can travel freely through space in patterns of electric and magnetic influence called electromagnetic waves.

longitudinal waves waves that travel in the same direction that the medium moves. They require a medium that can be compressed. Examples include sound waves and some seismic (earthquake-generated) waves.

magnetic poles the ends of magnets. A magnet always has two poles, a north pole and a south pole. Like poles repel each other, and unlike poles attract each other.

mechanical advantage the ratio of the force exerted by a machine to the force applied to the machine.

mechanics the study of mechanical energy (energy that an object has from its position or motion).

magnetic field the region around a magnet where the force of magnetism can be felt is said to contain a magnetic field. It can also be thought of as a set of lines called lines of force.

meson any of the subatomic particles belonging to the hadrons, and whose mass lies between that of the electron and that of the proton. Mesons have electrical charges of 0, +1, or −1, and are unstable. They are found in cosmic rays and are produced in nuclear reactors.

momentum a measure of the motion of an object.

motion a change of position in space.

neutrino an elementary particle without mass or electrical charge, but with spin. It always travels at the speed of light, hardly interacts with matter, and is considered to be formed in nuclear reactions.

neutron electrically neutral particle, constituting with protons the nuclei of atoms. The mass of a neutron is almost equal to the mass of a proton. Isotopes occur with varying neutron counts.

nuclear fission a nuclear reaction in which the nucleus of an atom is split into two lighter nuclei. The total mass of the lighter nuclei is less than the mass of the original nucleus. This difference in mass, called mass defect, is converted entirely into energy.

nuclear fusion a nuclear reaction consisting of the combination of two light nuclei into one nucleus. The mass of the formed nucleus is less than the total mass of the nuclei before the reaction. This difference in mass, called mass defect, is converted entirely into energy.

optics the branch of physics and engineering that is concerned with the properties of light.

parallel circuit an electrical circuit with more than one path for current. Parts of the circuit can be changed or removed without affecting the entire circuit.

particle accelerator a device that speeds up the movement of tiny bits of matter. These particles are either ions (electrically charged atoms) or electrically charged subatomic particles, objects that are smaller than an atom. Types of particle accelerators include cyclotrons, synchrotrons, and linear accelerators.

piezoelectric crystals certain crystalline materials that change shape when an electric voltage is applied across their opposite faces.

plasma a highly ionized gas, consisting of almost equal numbers of free electrons and positive ions.

polarization in optics, the state in which the vibrations of waves of light take place only in one plane.

potential energy the energy a body possesses by virtue of its location.

prism a solid with two parallel bases joined by three or more lateral surfaces. A transparent prism, usually made of glass, separates white into the colors of the spectrum.

Physics Glossary

proton an electrically charged particle that, with neutrons, is contained in the nuclei of atoms. The proton has a positive electrical charge equal in magnitude to that of the electron. Its mass is equal to that of the neutron and is about 1,800 times as heavy as that of the electron.

quark one of the three families of particles that serve as "building blocks" of matter. Quarks are elementary particles—that is, they have no known smaller parts.

radiation the transfer of heat in the form of waves through space.

reflection light or other type of wave that is radiated back after striking a surface such as a mirror.

refraction a change in wave direction when waves pass from one medium into another.

relativity the idea that an object can only be described as in motion or stationary by comparing it to another object. Refers to either of two theories of physics developed by the German-born American physicist Albert Einstein. Those theories are (1) the special theory of relativity, and (2) the general theory of relativity.

resistance a material's opposition to the passage of electric charges through it.

resonance the phenomenon by which sound waves are reinforced, so that they are perceived as sounding louder.

semiconductor a material that conducts electric charge better than insulators but not as well as conductors. They act as insulators at low temperatures; their conductivity increases with temperature.

series circuit an electrical circuit with only one path for current. The current flows in sequence through one device after another. A change in any part of the circuit affects all circuit parts.

solenoid a cylindrical coil of wire through which current is passed, giving the coil all the properties of a bar magnet.

spectroscope an instrument used to produce and examine the spectrum of a ray from any source. The spectrum produced by passing a light ray through a prism can be examined to determine the composition of the source of the ray.

static electricity the term to describe a situation where an object is carrying an electric charge.

statics the study of bodies at rest or in motion at a constant speed and in a constant direction.

steradian the SI unit of solid angle, used to describe two-dimensional angular spans in three-dimensional space (much like the way *radian* describes angles in a plane).

strong force a force that binds protons and neutrons in an atomic nucleus. It also holds together the quarks that make up protons and neutrons.

subatomic particles a unit of matter smaller than an atom. Subatomic particles include the three major particles found in atoms: (1) protons, which carry a positive electric charge; (2) negatively charged electrons; and (3) electrically neutral neutrons. Protons and neutrons form the nucleus of an atom. Electrons whirl about the nucleus.

superconductor a material that can conduct electric current without resistance at extremely low temperatures.

superfluid a fluid, such as liquid helium, characterized by the complete disappearance of viscosity at temperatures near absolute zero.

surface tension the property that causes the surface of a liquid to behave like it's covered with a thin layer of skin.

temperature an indication of an object's internal energy level.

thermodynamics the study of heat.

torque the amount of twisting effort that a force or forces exert on a subject.

transformer a device that increases or decreases the voltage of alternating current. Transformers consist of two coils coupled closely—called primary and secondary coils. The primary coil is the coil to which current is applied. The secondary coil is the coil in which current is induced.

transverse wave a wave in which the medium moves perpendicular to the direction in which the wave travels. Examples include light, television, x-rays, and radio waves.

triple point the particular temperature and pressure at which the solid, liquid, and gaseous phases of a given substance are all at equilibrium with each other.

ultrasonic frequency sound waves with frequencies above the range of human hearing, that is, greater than 20,000 cycles per second, or 20 kHz (kilohertz). Also called *ultrasound*.

vacuum a space with nothing in it—not even air. Light can travel through a vacuum as waves, but sound cannot without a means of transmitting vibrations.

valence the potential number of outer electrons that an atom of a given element can either gain or lose in reacting chemically with another atom. For example, hydrogen can lose an outer electron and become electropositive (H^{+1}) or gain an electron and become electronegative (H^{-1}). Therefore, it has two possible valences, +1 and −1.

velocity a combination of speed and direction.

viscosity the measure of resistance of a fluid to flow.

watt per steradian the standard unit of radiant intensity.

wave a disturbance in water, air, or another substance, or in an electric or magnetic field. Waves carry energy from place to place and transmit information. The highest point on the wave is the wave crest, and the lowest point the wave trough.

wavelength the distance between any point on one wave and the corresponding point on the next wave. The shorter the wavelength, the higher the frequency.

wave medium the material, such as water or air, through which a wave is traveling.

work a result of a force moving an object through distance against a resistance.

X-ray electromagnetic radiation with wavelengths ranging from 0.0001 nm to 100 nm. In the electromagnetic spectrum, X-rays occupy the region between gamma rays and ultraviolet rays.

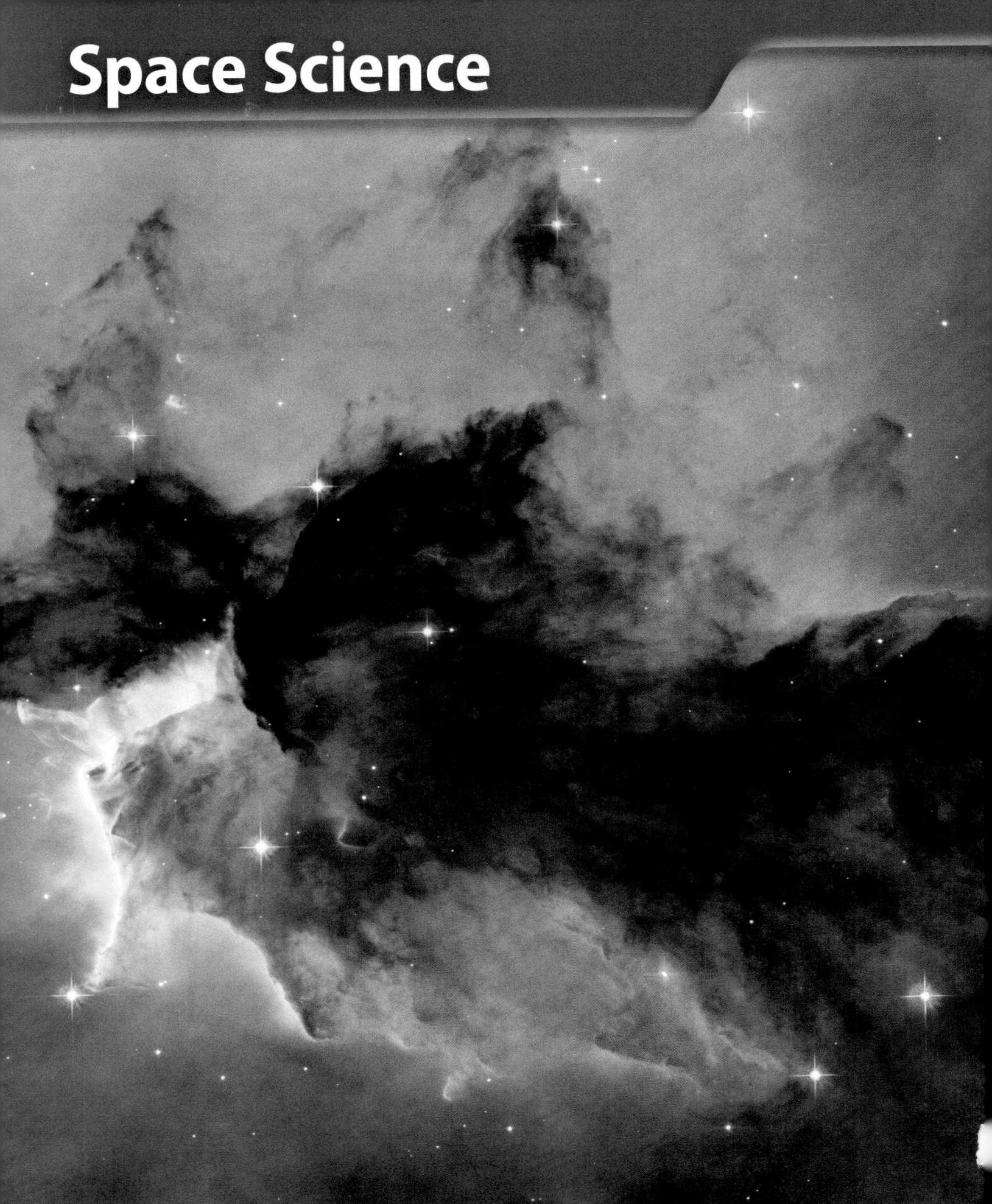

Space Science

Astronomy 900

The Universe 916

Exploration and Glossary 968

ASTRONOMY is the study of the universe and the objects in it. Astronomers observe the sky with telescopes of different kinds that gather not only visible light but also invisible forms of energy, such as radio waves.

Astronomers investigate nearby bodies, such as the sun, planets, and comets, as well as distant galaxies and other faraway objects. They also study the structure of space and the past and future of the universe.

Scientists have found bones, approximately 25,000 years old, in the Democratic Republic of the Congo that carry marks believed to be recordings of months and lunar phases.

History of Astronomy

To the ancients, the stars appeared as points of light attached to a large sphere that rotated slowly around Earth. This "celestial sphere" helped ancient civilizations know when to plant crops, develop calendars, and navigate the seas.

Wandering Stars

About 5,000 years ago, ancient peoples noticed that not all the stars appeared to be fixed to this sphere. Instead, a small number of them moved on more erratic paths and seemed to wander through the sky.

These stars became known as wandering stars or planets. The term "planet" is derived from the Greek verb *planan,* "to lead astray" or "to wander." The other stars became known as fixed stars.

The Stars to Guide Us

Early in prehistory, humans noticed the relationship between the path of the sun through the sky and the regularly recurring seasons.

The First Farmers. With the birth of agriculture about 12,000 years ago, it became necessary to keep track of time. Planting and harvesting had to be done at the right time of year. Early calendars were based on the phases of the moon or on the motion of the sun through the zodiac.

Early Astronomers		
Civilization	**Time Period**	**Knowledge**
Babylonians	About 1800 BC	Prepared the first known star catalogs and records of planetary motion. Used a number system with 60 as the base. Grouped patterns of stars into constellations.
Babylonians	About 450 BC	Began using the base-60 number system to indicate the position of stars.
Ancient Egyptians	c. 3000 BC–1000 BC	Used astronomical observations—especially of the stars that rose or set with the sun—for timekeeping and to create a calendar. Planted crops based on positions of certain stars. Grouped patterns of stars into constellations.
Ancient Chinese	c. 1500 BC–200 BC	Kept accurate records of astronomical events; many have been helpful to present-day astronomers. First record (in 240 BC) of the comet that would later be known as Halley's Comet. Reported several novas. Grouped patterns of stars into constellations.

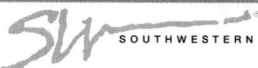
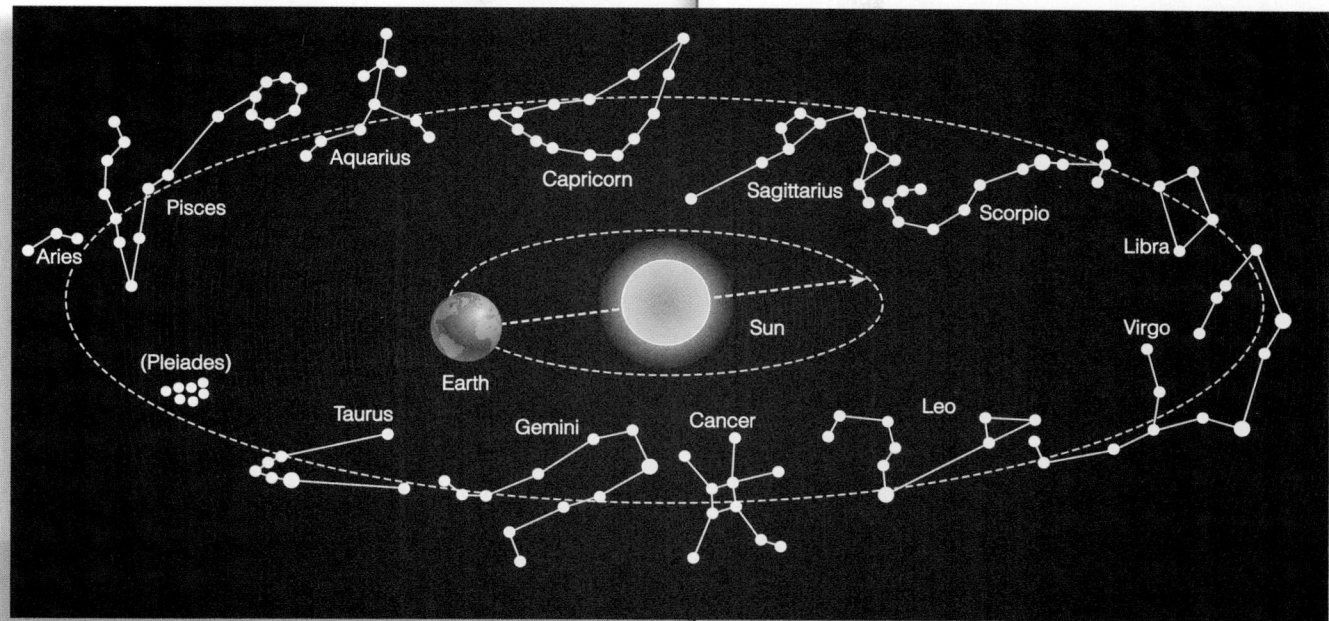

▲ **The zodiac** is the area in the sky through which the sun appears to travel. It is divided into 12 sections, each containing a constellation.

Lunar Calendar. The Babylonians created a calendar based on the phases of the moon.

- The Babylonians defined the month as the period from one new moon to the next.

- They divided the year into 12 lunar months.

- Their calendar was not in tune with the seasons (a solar year is 12 lunar months plus 11 days), so they inserted an extra month in sporadic years.

- The Babylonians were so accurate in administering their calendar that today we can trace historical events from 636 BC to AD 45 with a margin of error of just 1 day.

Solar Calendar. The Egyptians based their calendar on the position of the sun.

- The Egyptians used a calendar of 365 days and determined the time of year by observing the positions of stars at the spot where the sun would rise.

- The Egyptian calendar had a problem: after 4 years, it would be 1 day out of step with the seasonal variation of the sun's path.

- This is because the sun actually returns to its starting position in 365¼ days.

The Zodiac

Ancient peoples noticed that the sun seemed to wander against the background of fixed stars. These early astronomers

- followed the path of the sun in the sky throughout the year.

- perceived that the sun occupied a position in the same constellation after approximately 365 days.

- concluded that the sun had traveled a full circle in that time.

Circle of Animals. The path the sun describes on the celestial sphere (the *ecliptic*) passes through 12 constellations. Early astronomers and astrologers, especially the Assyrians, attached special importance to these constellations.

They named the constellations after mythical people and animals. The band across the sky that contains these constellations is called the *zodiac*, literally, "circle of animals."

Early Concepts of the Universe

A *cosmological model* is a mathematical or physical description of the structure of the universe. Early cosmological models were static, holding that the universe does not change with time. They generally placed Earth at the center of the universe.

New insights gained during the 17th century led scientists to replace the idea of an unchanging universe with the knowledge that the universe has undergone some form of development.

Early Cosmologies

While ancient civilizations were able to chart the movements of stars with relative accuracy, they misinterpreted much of what they saw in the heavens. Ancient peoples concluded that the sun, moon, and planets orbit a motionless Earth. In many places, religious teachings seemed to support this conclusion until the 1600s.

Pancake Earth. Concepts of the universe in the great civilizations of about 1000 BC were straightforward.

- Earth is flat and is covered by a large dome carrying the stars.
- The Babylonians believed that Earth floats on an ocean.
- The Egyptians and Chinese believed Earth to be square.
- The Egyptians believed that a god inhabits each star and travels with the star in a boat on celestial rivers.

Greek astronomer Ptolemy's 13-part book of observations and theories—Mathematike Syntaxis—was so admired that when Arabic scholars translated the work in the 9th century, they renamed it Almagest, *which means "the greatest" in Arabic.*

Cosmologies of Ancient Greece

The ancient Greeks carried forward ideas from the Babylonians and invented some of their own.

Pythagoras, a philosopher and scientist born around 580 BC, believed that Earth was spherical and that the sun, moon, and planets have movements of their own. He based his ideas on his observations.

- During an eclipse of the moon, Pythagoras observed the round form of Earth's shadow on the surface of the moon.
- Pythagoras also noticed that at sea the masts of a ship become visible before the hull.

Ptolemy was one of the greatest astronomers and geographers of ancient times.

Ptolemy's System of Astronomy

Most of our knowledge of Greek astronomy is from a book called *Mathematike Syntaxis,* or *Mathematical Composition.* It was written by Ptolemy (AD 127–180), an astronomer of the Alexandrian school in Egypt.

Ptolemy's book remained the standard text for astronomy throughout the Middle Ages.

Greek Synthesis. Most important, the *Syntaxis* contained the description of the *Ptolemaic system,* a synthesis of Ptolemy's ideas with those of other Greek scholars, including Aristotle, Pythagoras, and Hipparchus, who believed in a finite, geocentric universe.

Aristotle (384–322 BC), who became one of the most influential Greek scholars, taught that Earth is the center of the universe. His influence was so great that the idea of an Earth-centered, or *geocentric,* universe went practically unchallenged for the next 2,000 years.

Aristarchus (circa 310–230 BC) of Samos was an astronomer who challenged Aristotle. About 280 BC, Aristarchus suggested that Earth and other planets move around the sun, and that the sun occupies the center of the universe. A sun-centered universe is termed *heliocentric.*

In his book *On the Sizes and Distances of the Sun and Moon,* Aristarchus maintained that the moon shines because it reflects sunlight and that the sun is much larger than the moon, and is 18 to 20 times farther away.

These ideas were not widely accepted because he could not supply proof that Earth was moving.

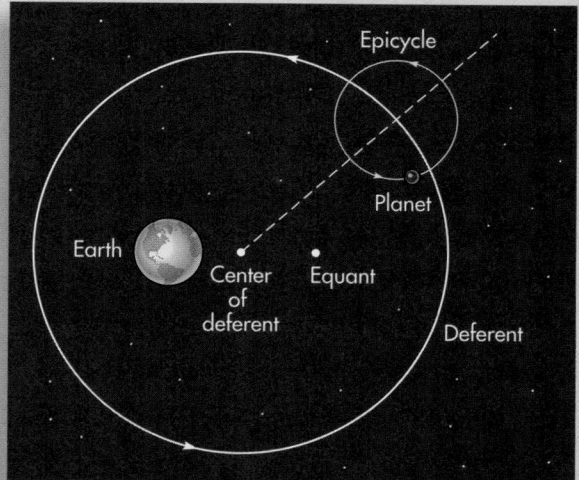

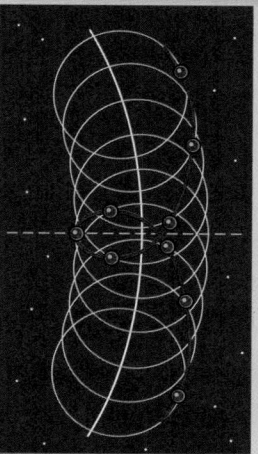

Ptolemy's Theory. According to the Ptolemaic system, Earth is at the center of the universe. The sun and moon move around Earth on perfect circles at a constant rate.

Ptolemy rejected the idea of Earth rotating around the sun. Like some previous Greek scholars, Ptolemy argued that if Earth orbited around the sun, the fixed stars would exhibit a small yearly shift, called *parallax.*

Parallax View. To understand parallax, imagine that you are on a merry-go-round. While going around, the buildings around you will appear to move to the right and then to the left for every turn of the merry-go-round.

Ptolemy could not observe the stellar parallax, so he concluded that Earth must be in a fixed position. However, he had underestimated the distance to the stars. They are so distant and the effect is so small that astronomers could not discover stellar parallaxes until 1838. (See page 941.)

Cloud Cover. Ptolemy also rejected the idea that Earth would rotate around its axis. He thought that if Earth did rotate, then all clouds would appear to move in one direction, opposite to the rotation of Earth.

THE PTOLEMAIC SYSTEM

The Planet Problem. Because of the planets' irregular and sometimes seemingly *retrograde* (moving backward) motion, Ptolemy determined that the planets could not move on perfectly circular orbits at a constant rate. His theory asserted several ideas.

- Each planet is on a small circular orbit, called an *epicycle.*
- The planet rotates on the epicycle around a point called the *deferent.*
- The deferent, in turn, rotates around Earth in a circular orbit.
- The combined motions of the planet on the epicycle and the rotation of the entire epicycle around Earth was held to explain the irregular motion of the planets.

The influence of Aristotle on scientific thinking throughout the Middle Ages was so great that most scholars contented themselves with teaching his theories and elaborating on them without attempting much innovation. Most of the teaching was in the hands of the Church, and religious thinkers believed that Aristotle's ideas were in accordance with the Holy Scriptures.

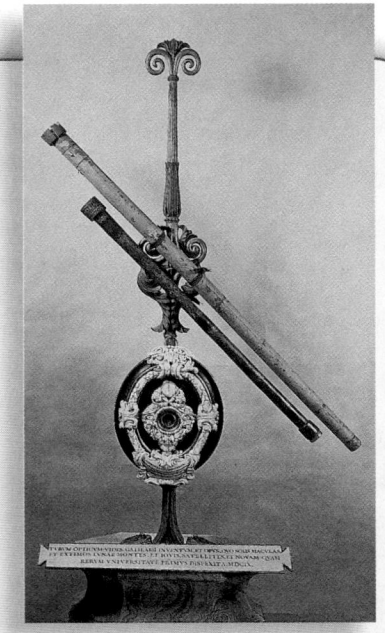

Galileo's telescopes were larger and more powerful than the telescopes that had been made previously.

Galileo

Galileo Galilei (1564–1642), an Italian physicist and astronomer, was a contemporary of Kepler. Galileo has been called the founder of modern experimental science. He discovered several new scientific laws and designed a variety of scientific instruments.

Galileo's Telescope. In 1609, while Galileo was staying in Venice, he heard about a system of lenses, invented in Holland, that magnifies distant objects. Galileo set about assembling his own instrument.

Galileo's Discoveries. When Galileo directed his telescope to the night sky, he made more discoveries than had been made by all the astronomers who had lived before him, discovering the craters on the moon, the moons of Jupiter, and the phases of Venus.

Copernicus

Around 1507, Nicolaus Copernicus (1473–1543), himself a church official, became convinced that Ptolemy's system was wrong. He proposed the idea that Earth, instead of being the fixed center of the universe, is a planet circling the sun.

Copernicus completed his famous book *De Revolutionibus Orbium Coelestium (Concerning the Revolutions of the Celestial Orb)* around 1533, but he postponed publication of it until 1543, shortly before his death, since he feared being accused of heresy.

Copernicus's System. Similar to Ptolemy's system, Copernicus's system uses perfect circles and deferents to describe the motions of the planets, with the difference that Earth revolves around the sun.

Discrepancies. Copernicus explained that the discrepancies between his model and actual observations were caused by observational errors. He tried to account for the errors by adding circles.

Brahe's Splendid Data

A great advance in observational astronomy came from the experimental skills of Danish astronomer Tycho Brahe (1546–1601). Brahe not only developed instruments of novel design that greatly increased observational accuracy, he also introduced sound observational procedures.

Brahe's Assistant. The improved determinations of stellar and planetary positions served as ideal material for Johannes Kepler (1571–1630), a German astronomer and mathematician whom Brahe appointed as his assistant not long before Brahe's death.

Elliptical Orbits. Kepler used Brahe's splendid data to devise a heliocentric system that would agree with the observations. His outstanding finding was that the true shape of the orbit of a planet around the sun is not a circle, but an ellipse with the sun at one of the foci of the ellipse, not at its center.

Kepler's Laws

Kepler used Brahe's observations of Mars to figure out three laws of planetary motion. Kepler developed his laws for the planets of our solar system, but astronomers have since realized that Kepler's laws are valid for all orbiting heavenly bodies. With these three laws, a planet's path and orbital velocity can be determined.

Kepler's first law states that the orbit of every planet is an ellipse with the sun at one focus.

Kepler's second law states that the *radius vector*, an imaginary line joining the sun to a planet, sweeps over equal areas in equal times.

Kepler's third law states that the square of the time any planet takes to complete its orbit is proportional to the cube of its distance from the sun. When a planet is closer to the sun, it moves faster. When it is farther from the sun, it moves more slowly.

UNIVERSAL GRAVITATION

Sir Isaac Newton discovered how the universe is held together through his theory of universal gravitation while he was staying in the country to avoid a plague outbreak.

Newton realized that one and the same force pulls an object to Earth and keeps the moon in its orbit. He found that the force of universal gravitation makes every pair of bodies in the universe attract each other. (See pages 766–767.)

The force depends on

1. the amount of matter in the bodies being attracted.

2. the distance between the bodies.

Sir Isaac Newton is sometimes described as "one of the greatest names in the history of human thought" because of his great contributions to mathematics, physics, and astronomy. ▼

Newton

If Kepler showed *how* the planets move, it was Isaac Newton (1642–1727), an English scientist, astronomer, and mathematician, who showed *why* they move in elliptical orbits.

Delaying Gravity. Before he was 24, Newton had deduced from Kepler's laws that the force keeping a planet in its orbit must be inversely proportional to the square of the distance between the planet and the center about which it revolves.

However, Newton did little with his result for almost 20 years. In 1684, the physicist Edmund Halley (1656–1742) urged him to publish his law of gravity.

The *Principia*. The resulting manuscript, *Philosophiae Naturalis Principia Mathematica* (the *Principia*), published in 1687, sets forth the physical principles for the motion of bodies under the influence of gravitational forces. Newton's work demonstrates mathematically that a body moving under a force inversely proportional to the square of the distance moves on an elliptical path.

The *Principia* is considered one of the greatest single contributions in the history of science.

Among the Stars

FINDING YOUR WAY IN THE STARS

Astronomers use two main systems to pinpoint objects on the celestial sphere.

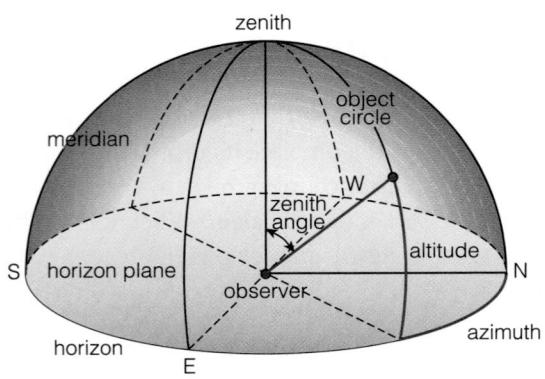

Horizon System

It is important to realize that angular distances between objects on the celestial sphere do not represent real distances between them. Two stars that appear close on the celestial sphere can actually be very far apart. The simplest coordinate system is called the *horizon system.*

- The observer projects the horizon onto the celestial sphere to form a great circle called the *astronomical horizon.*

- Starting from the zenith, one can draw an arc, called a *vertical circle,* that intersects the astronomical horizon.

- The height of the star in degrees on the vertical circle above the astronomical horizon is called the *altitude* or *elevation* of the star. The altitude of the zenith is precisely 90 degrees.

- The angle along the astronomical horizon from the direction of the North Pole to the vertical circle of the star is called the *azimuth* of the star.

- The azimuth is counted turning from north to east to south to west. For example, the azimuth of a star directly west is 270 degrees.

- The altitude and the azimuth together determine the position of the star on the celestial sphere.

Disadvantages. The horizon system has two disadvantages.

1. The position of the star depends on the location of the observer on Earth.

2. As Earth rotates, the coordinates of the star change continuously with time.

Equatorial System

Astronomers prefer to use equatorial coordinates, a system that is independent of the rotation of Earth and of the location of the observer on Earth.

- The celestial sphere is assumed to rotate around the same axis as Earth's axis.

- The *celestial poles* are the points around which the celestial sphere seems to rotate.

- The *celestial equator* is the projection of Earth's equator on the celestial sphere.

- The *ecliptic* is the apparent path of the sun around the celestial sphere.

- The ecliptic intersects the celestial equator in two points, called *equinoxes.*

- Starting from the celestial pole, an imaginary circle called an *hour circle* intersects the celestial equator.

- The *declination* of a star is its angular distance north or south of the celestial equator, measured along the hour circle passing through the star.

- The angular distance between the hour line of a star and the vernal equinox (the point the sun crosses the equator on the first day of spring) is called the *right ascension* of the star.

- The right ascension is measured, turning west-south, in hours, minutes, and seconds rather than arc degrees.

- The choice of time units is easily understandable if one remembers that it takes a star 24 hours to describe a full circle in the sky.

THE CONSTELLATIONS

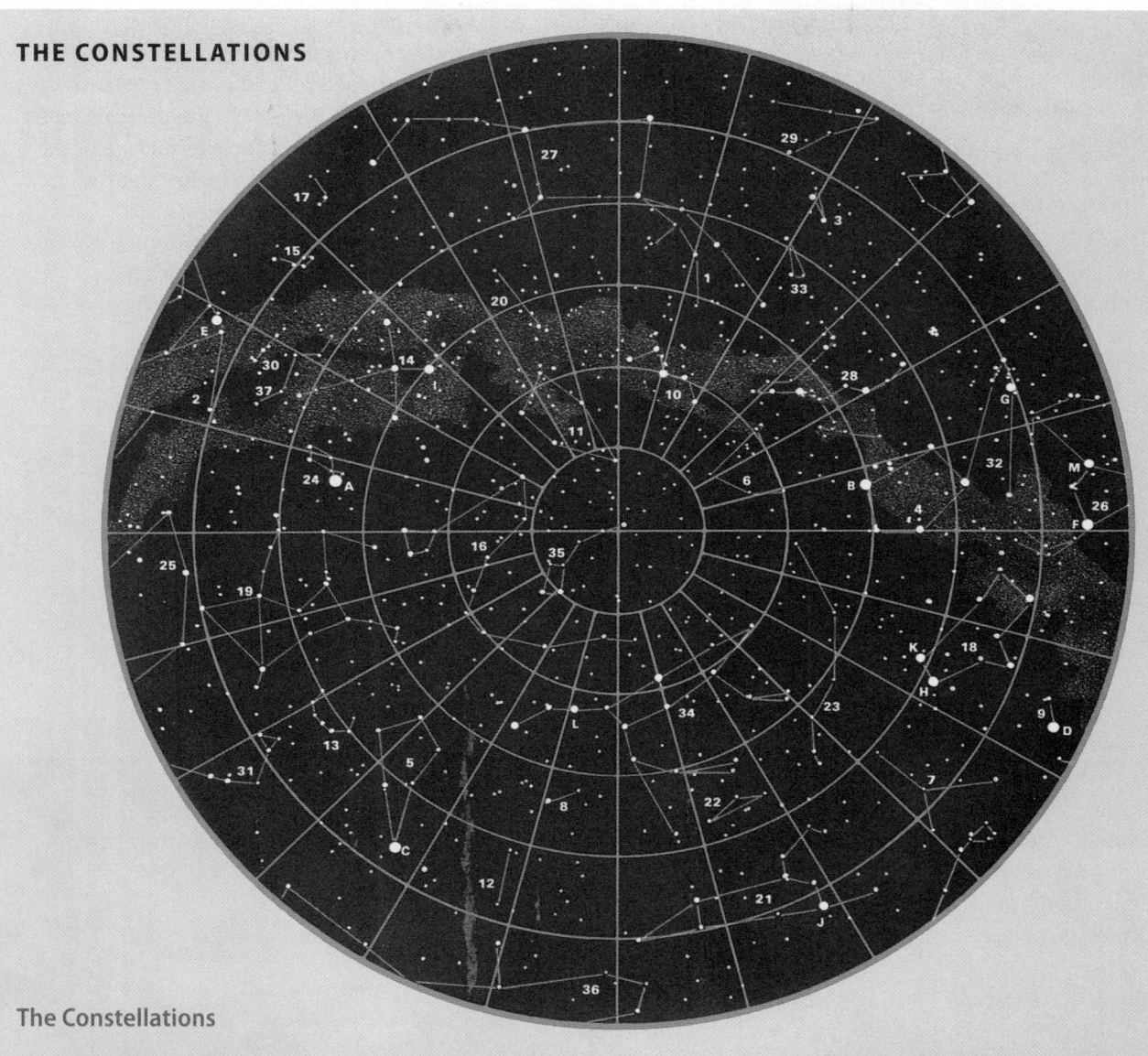

The Constellations

Latin Name	English Name	Latin Name	English Name	Latin Name	English Name	Brightest Stars
1. Andromeda	The Chained Lady	13. Corona Borealis	The Northern Cross	26. Orion	The Hunter	A. Vega
2. Aquila	The Eagle	14. Cygnus	The Swan	27. Pegasus	The Winged Horse Persons	B. Capella
3. Aries*	The Ram	15. Delphinus	The Dolphin	28. Perseus		C. Arcturus
4. Auriga	The Charioteer	16. Draco	The Dragon	29. Pisces*	The Fishes	D. Procyon
5. Boötes	The Herdsman	17. Equuleus	The Lesser Horse	30. Sagitta	The Arrow	E. Altair
6. Camelopardalis	The Giraffe	18. Gemini*	The Twins	31. Serpens	The Serpent	F. Betelgeuse
7. Cancer*	The Crab	19. Hercules	Hercules	32. Taurus*	The Bull	G. Aldebran
8. Canes Venatici	The Hunting Dogs	20. Lacerta	The Lizard	33. Triangulum	The Triangle	H. Pollux
9. Canis Minor	The Lesser Dog	21. Leo*	The Lion	34. Ursa Major	The Great Bear (The Big Dipper)	I. Deneb
10. Cassiopeia	The Lady in the Chair	22. Leo Minor	The Lesser Lion	35. Ursa Minor	The Little Bear (The Little Dipper)	J. Regulus
11. Cephus	Cassiopeia's Consort	23. Lynx	The Lynx	36. Virgo*	The Virgin	K. Castor
12. Coma Berenices	Bernice's Hair	24. Lyra	The Lyre	37. Vulpecula	The Fox	L. Alioth
		25. Ophiuchus	The Serpent Holder			M. Bellatrix

*Located in the Zodiac

ASTRONOMICAL INSTRUMENTS

Perhaps more than in any other science, advances in astronomy have been the direct consequence of the introduction of one new instrument: the telescope. Astronomers use telescopes to study the planets, stars, and other heavenly bodies.

Objects in space also give off many kinds of invisible radiation, such as radio waves, ultraviolet rays, and even X-rays. Astronomers use a technique called *spectroscopy*, as well as other kinds of telescopes equipped with electronic detectors, to form images with this radiation.

Telescopes

Telescopes vary in shape and size from handheld telescopes to bowl-shaped reflectors that measure up to 305 meters (1,000 feet) across. There are telescopes in large, dome-shaped buildings on the surface of the earth and telescopes in artificial satellites in orbit around the earth.

The most familiar telescopes are *optical telescopes*. These instruments work with visible light. In an optical telescope, a mirror or lens collects the light and uses it to form an image.

Large telescopes used by professional astronomers rarely contain an eyepiece for viewing the image. Instead, they record the image with an electronic sensor called a *charge-coupled device* or, less often, with photographic film.

The two main types of optical telescopes are

- *refracting telescopes*
- *reflecting telescopes*

TELESCOPES IN SPACE

Earth's atmosphere spoils the quality of the images of celestial objects. It also absorbs or blocks large parts of the radiation that reaches Earth, especially infrared and ultraviolet light. For this reason, astronomers have placed telescopes for observation in orbits around Earth.

The Hubble Space Telescope, the largest orbiting telescope to date, was launched in 1990. It is a reflecting telescope with a light-gathering mirror 240 centimeters (94 inches) in diameter.

Astronomers have used the Hubble Space Telescope to obtain images of celestial objects and phenomena in detail never before observed.

- pictures of stars surrounded by dusty disks that might someday evolve into planetary systems
- images of galaxies on the edge of the observable universe
- pictures of galaxies colliding and tearing each other apart
- evidence suggesting that most galaxies have massive black holes in their centers

▲ **The Hubble Space Telescope** orbits about 610 kilometers (380 miles) above Earth.

Refracting Telescope

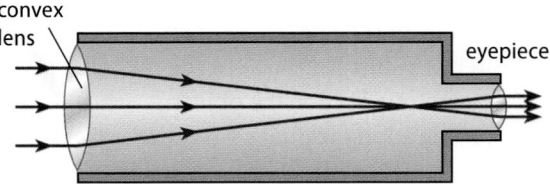

Newtonian Reflecting Telescope

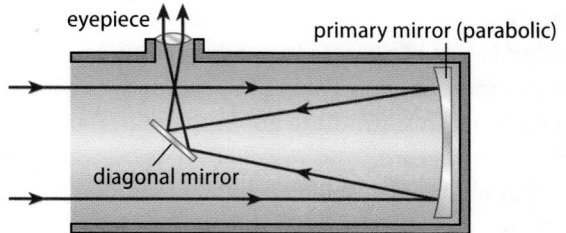

Refracting Telescopes

Refracting telescopes consist of a tube and two lenses: a large *objective lens* and an eyepiece. (See pages 840–843.)

The objective is a convex lens. When light from a star reaches the lens, it bends slightly toward the optical axis as it passes through. The curvature of the lens is designed so that all the light passing through the lens is bent toward a single spot behind the lens, called the *focus*. An observer sees the image formed by the objective in the focal plane with the eyepiece, which works like a magnifying glass.

Chromatic Aberration. The objective lens in early telescopes was a single lens. Since glass bends light of different colors differently, the objective lens will focus red light, for example, at a different point from blue light. This effect—called *chromatic aberration*—degrades the quality of images that can be obtained with a single-lens objective.

Achromatic Lenses. In 1729, the inventor Chester More Hall (1703–1771) eliminated chromatic aberration by combining two lenses of different types of glass. Such lenses are called *achromatic*.

Largest Refractors. Throughout the 18th and 19th centuries, large lenses were easier to produce than large mirrors. Most of the telescopes were refractors.

However, it is impractical to construct lenses larger than 1 meter (3 feet) in diameter. The thickness of the glass results in too much light absorption, and the lenses distort under their own weight. It is easier now to build large telescope mirrors, and today most large telescopes are reflectors.

Reflecting Telescopes

In a reflecting telescope, the light from a star passes down a tube to a mirror mounted at the bottom of the tube. The surface of the mirror is ground to a precise convex shape, which reflects the light back up the tube toward the *prime focus,* where all the light passes through a single point.

A Second Mirror. Because the focus is directly in the path of the incoming light, the image at the focus usually cannot be observed directly. A secondary mirror reflects the light inside the tube to bring the focus to a convenient location.

Flat vs. Curved. Issac Newton used a flat secondary mirror to reflect the light to one side of the tube. The eyepiece is mounted on the telescope tube at a right angle to the incoming light from a star.

French physician and scientist N. Cassegrain used a convex secondary mirror to reflect the light through a hole in the primary mirror to an eyepiece behind it.

Multiple-Mirror Designs. The primary mirrors of telescopes can be made much larger than objective lenses. However, problems arise in building telescopes with mirrors larger than 6 meters (19.5 feet) in diameter. The mirrors become deformed by their own weight.

One solution to this problem is to combine a number of smaller mirrors in one telescope. For example, the Keck telescope, installed on Mauna Kea, Hawaii, consists of thirty-six 1.8-meter (72-inch) mirrors that are individually aligned and focused. In unison, they work as a 9.82-meter (387-inch) mirror.

Spectroscopy

The most important source of information about a star is its light spectrum. *Spectroscopy* is the scientific study of how matter interacts with light and certain other forms of energy. In spectroscopy, scientists study the radiation given off, absorbed, or scattered by a material to learn more about the material's composition or structure.

For example, a scientist might study the light given off by a star to determine the chemical elements present in the star. Many kinds of spectroscopy make use of ultraviolet (UV) light, visible light, X-rays, and other forms of electromagnetic radiation.

Spectra of the Stars

The spectrum of a celestial body provides us with information on chemical composition and many other properties.

- the presence of magnetic fields
- temperature
- velocity in relation to Earth

Invisible Light. Spectra in electromagnetic radiation of other wavelengths, such as ultraviolet, infrared, and radio waves, have spectral lines that react similarly to visible light. These types of radiation also provide astronomers with important data.

The Doppler Effect

Spectroscopy can reveal the speed and direction of motion of a star. In the spectrum of any moving object, the spectral lines shift from where they would appear in the spectrum of a stationary object.

An object's motion produces a *Doppler effect* similar to the way a sound's pitch changes when the source moves toward or away from a listener. (See page 805.)

Red Shift. Knowing how the wavelength of the light of moving objects behaves has allowed astronomers to learn much about celestial bodies.

- When a light source is moving away from Earth, its light becomes shifted to longer wavelengths. The longer wavelengths appear as a wider band of red in the spectrum.

- When a light source is moving toward Earth, its light becomes shifted to shorter wavelengths. The shorter wavelengths appear as a wider band of blue in the spectrum.

Astronomers can detect these small shifts in the spectra of celestial bodies by comparing the spectra with spectra photographed on the same film.

Doppler shifts are used for measuring local velocities on celestial objects, such as the velocities of moving gas masses on the sun.

TIME LINE OF SPECTROSCOPY

late 1600s

Sir Isaac Newton begins the study of spectroscopy when he uses a glass prism to produce a rainbow spectrum: a band of colors ranging from the red to the blue.

Newton theorizes that white light is a mixture of all the colors of the rainbow.

1814

German optician Joseph von Fraunhofer (1787–1826) observes a large number of dark lines in the spectrum produced by a prism that receives sunlight through a narrow slit. These dark lines are later named absorption lines.

1859

German physicist Gustav Kirchhoff (1824–1887) notices that he can observe these dark lines when white light is passed through a gas. When a gas is heated so that it glows, it emits a spectrum of narrow bright lines, later named emission lines.

But gases under high pressures, liquids, and solids emit a continuous spectrum when brought to high temperatures. That is, they form a spectrum containing the colors of the rainbow without any dark or bright lines.

RED SHIFT

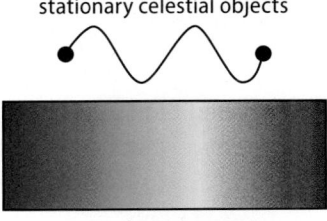

stationary celestial objects

normal spectrograph

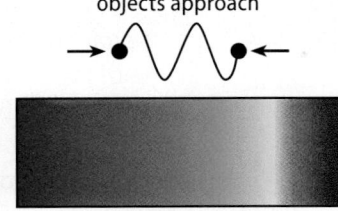

objects approach

shift to blue

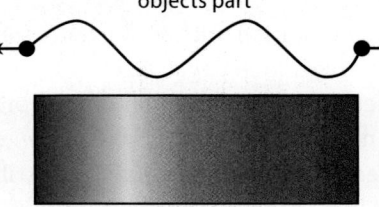

objects part

shift to red

A spectrograph provides information about the composition of celestial bodies by producing lines that mark the frequencies corresponding to particular elements found in the body under observation. Astronomers compare the pattern of these lines with reference patterns produced in a lab to determine the composition of the body.

- If an object is not moving toward or away from Earth, spectral lines will match up closely to those produced artificially.

- If the body is moving toward the observer, light waves are compressed, changing their frequency and shifting the object's spectral lines toward the blue end.

- If the body is moving away from the observer on Earth, the light waves become elongated, shifting the spectral lines toward the red end of the spectrum.

The Expanding Universe

The determination of red shifts in the spectra of galaxies has played a key role in establishing that the universe is expanding.

Receding Galaxies. In 1929, the American astronomer Edwin Hubble discovered that distant galaxies show red shifts in their spectra. Other scientists interpreted the red shifts as showing that the galaxies are receding, or moving farther away, from our own galaxy.

Cosmological Red Shift. Hubble also found that farther galaxies have higher red shifts, indicating that they are receding at higher rates.

Unlike the Doppler redshift, this *cosmological red shift*—which applies only to faraway objects—occurs because the universe is expanding. That is, every point in the universe is receding from every other point. Thus, astronomers can determine the distance of a galaxy by measuring its red shift.

1862
Kirchhoff completes the first map of the solar spectrum. He had earlier established that absorption and emission lines are indicators of elements present in a gas. Each element produces a number of absorption or emission lines at certain wavelengths.

By studying the lines in the solar spectrum, Kirchhoff and the German chemist Robert Wilhelm Bunsen (1811–1899) were able to identify a number of elements in the solar atmosphere.

1897
Dutch physicist Pieter Zeeman (1865–1943) discovers that the spectral lines of a gas placed in a magnetic field are split.

1908
American astronomer George Ellery Hale (1868–1938) discovered split absorption and emission lines in the spectra of sunspots, proving that sunspots are magnetic phenomena.

Invisible Astronomy

Visible light is an electromagnetic wave, as are the waves of radiation we can't see—radio waves, infrared radiation, ultraviolet radiation, X-rays, and gamma rays. (See pages 834–835.)

These forms of radiation differ from each other only in their wavelengths, which range from the smallest gamma rays—roughly 10-trillionths of a meter in length—to the longest radio waves—more than 10,000 kilometers (6,000 miles) in wavelength.

Most of what we know about the objects outside of Earth's atmosphere comes from the study of these invisible waves.

Absorption by the Atmosphere

Most of the infrared and ultraviolet sunlight that reaches Earth is absorbed by Earth's atmosphere. The atmosphere is transparent only to visible light, some infrared radiation, and most radio waves.

Absorbers. Ozone and other components of the atmosphere absorb ultraviolet radiation and X-rays almost completely. Water vapor and oxygen absorb large parts of infrared radiation and radio waves at wavelengths shorter than 1 millimeter.

Windows. The regions in the spectrum where the atmosphere is transparent are called *windows*. The radio window is largest.

- Radiation with wavelengths between 2 centimeters and 30 meters passes almost unhindered.
- Radio waves with wavelengths between 30 and 100 meters are partially reflected by the ionosphere.
- Waves above 100 meters are reflected completely.

Radio Astronomy

The introduction of sensitive radio technology revolutionized astronomy. This revolution began with two major discoveries. Both were the result of attempts by scientists at Bell Laboratories to pinpoint the sources of interference that disturb radio communications.

1931: the discovery that the Milky Way transmits radio waves

1965: the discovery of the existence of cosmic background radiation

Galactic Radio Waves. Between 1928 and 1930, the radio engineer Karl Jansky (1905–1949) was assigned by Bell Laboratories to track down the source of radio static that interfered with shortwave communications. By using a rotating directional antenna, he found that the static came from one area in the sky, the center of the Milky Way galaxy.

The Electromagnetic Spectrum		
Name	**Wavelength**	**Sources**
Radio waves	1 millimeter and up	Pulsars; quasars; gas clouds orbiting the center of the Milky Way
Infrared rays	700 nanometers* to 1 millimeter	Stars in the process of forming; relatively cool stars; planets
Visible light	400 to 700 nanometers	Planets; stars; galaxies; asteroids; comets
Ultraviolet rays	10 to 400 nanometers	Hydrogen gas between the stars; the sun
X-rays	0.1 to 10 nanometers	The sun's corona; disks of material around black holes; quasars
Gamma rays	up to 0.1 nanometer	Collapsed stars; matter-antimatter annihilations
*One nanometer is 1 billionth of a meter.		

Radio Telescopes. Because radio telescopes gather electromagnetic radiation of much longer wavelengths than light, the requirements for the exact shape of the dish are much less demanding than for the mirrors of an optical telescope.

- A typical modern radio telescope consists of a huge metal dish that functions like a mirror and an antenna placed in the focus of the dish.

- The largest single-dish radio telescope is at Arecibo, Puerto Rico. Its fixed metal mesh reflector is 304.8 meters (1,000 feet) in diameter, suspended horizontally in a circular valley.

The Images. By scanning an object, radio astronomers can construct an electronic image similar to the ones obtained by charge-coupled devices (CCDs) in optical telescopes. These images can be processed electronically, for example, by using colors to represent differing intensities.

VERY LARGE TELESCOPES

The Very Large Array telescope in Socorro, New Mexico, is operated by the National Radio Astronomy Observatory.

The Very Large Array is a *radio interferometer*—a setup of two or more radio telescopes operating in tandem. Computers can combine signals from the antennas to produce images with the detail that would be provided by a single telescope 22 miles across.

Even greater resolution can be achieved by combining existing radio telescopes at different places in the world. The Very Long Baseline Array (VLBA) consists of 10 telescopes, each 82 feet across, spread across one side of Earth. As an interferometer, the VLBA is equivalent to a single telescope with a diameter roughly that of Earth.

The Very Large Array consists of 27 movable dish antennas, each 25 meters (82 feet) in diameter, placed in a Y-shaped pattern. ▶

Outside the Atmosphere

By placing their instruments aboard satellites, astronomers can observe celestial objects at wavelengths that are absorbed by Earth's atmosphere.

Infrared Astronomy. IRAS, the first satellite devoted to infrared astronomy, completed a sky survey in 1983. Its 60-centimeter (24-inch) telescope was cooled by liquid helium to eliminate radiation from the telescope itself. A successor, the Infrared Space Observatory, was launched by the European Space Agency in 1995.

X-Ray Astronomy. In recent years, several important discoveries in astronomy, such as possible black holes, have been made with X-rays. The atmosphere entirely absorbs X-rays (rays with wavelengths between 0.1 and 100 angstroms). Thus, all observations have been made with instruments aboard rockets and satellites.

Gamma-Ray Astronomy. Gamma-ray photons are the most energetic of all. They are located through the use of detectors placed in satellites that resemble the instruments used by particle physicists: scintillation counters and spark chambers.

The first gamma-ray pulses from space were detected by a series of satellites that were designed to monitor nuclear explosions on Earth (a nuclear explosion produces a strong burst of gamma rays). By using triangulation methods (simultaneous detection by at least three satellites), the extraterrestrial origin of the pulses could be established.

Beyond the Telescope

Vast Distances

Many distances involved in astronomy are so huge that they are measured in special units. To get a sense of the vast sizes and distances involved in the study of space objects, consider the tables below.

Light-Years. One such unit is the *light-year*, the distance that light travels in a vacuum in a year.

- This distance equals about 9.46 trillion kilometers (5.88 trillion miles).
- The star nearest the sun, Proxima Centauri, is about 4 light-years from Earth.
- The Milky Way is about 100,000 light-years across.
- The sun is roughly 25,000 light-years from the center.
- The nearest large galaxy is the Andromeda Galaxy. It is about 2 million light-years away.
- Some galaxies are more than 10 billion light-years distant.

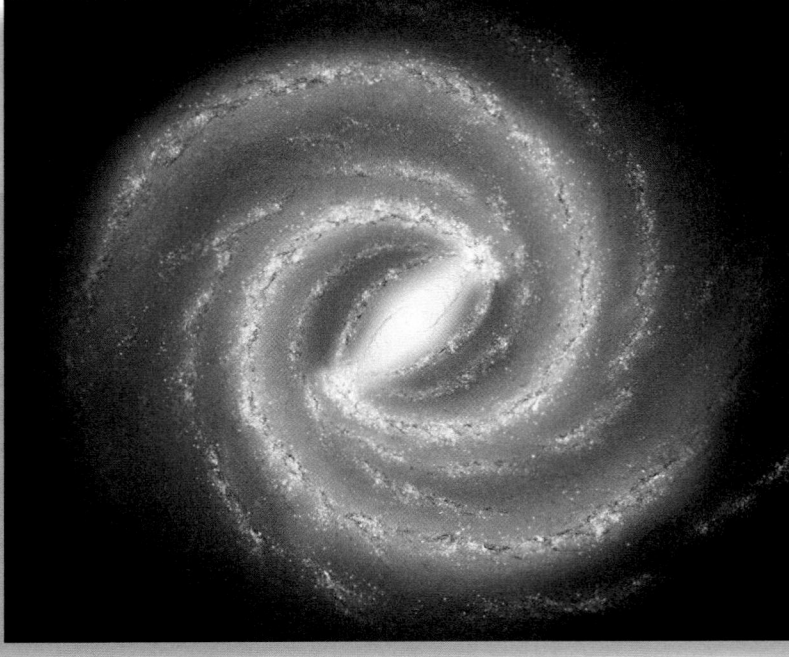

▲ **The Milky Way** measures about 100,000 light-years across.

Astronomical Units. Astronomers measure distances in the solar system in *astronomical units (AU)*.

- One AU is the average distance from Earth to the sun—about 93,000,000 miles (150,000,000 kilometers).
- This distance equals about 8 light-minutes.
- The average distance from the sun to Neptune, the farthest planet, is about 30 AU.

Parsecs. In their technical work with extremely long distances, astronomers use a unit called a *parsec*, rather than the light-year. The parsec is based on *parallax*, an angular measurement. One parsec equals about 3.26 light-years.

Sizes of Astronomical Objects		
Object	**Diameter**	**In Comparison**
Earth	12,700 km (7,900 mi.)	Jupiter, the biggest planet in the solar system, is more than 11 times as large.
The sun	1,390,000 km (864,000 mi.)	The sun is about 109 times as large as Earth. The largest stars are about 1,500 times as large as the sun.
The Milky Way	100,000 light-years	About 700 billion times as large as the sun
Markarian's Chain of galaxies	2.5 million light-years	About 25 times the diameter of the Milky Way, and located about 70 million light-years away

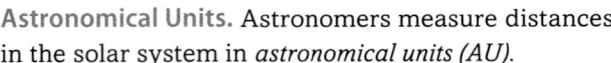

Units of Distance in Astronomy				
Unit	**Metric**	**English**	**In Comparison**	
Astronomical unit	150.0 million kilometers	93.0 million miles	0.0000158 light-years	0.00000485 parsecs
Light-year	9.46 trillion kilometers	5.88 trillion miles	63,200 astronomical units	0.307 parsecs
Parsec	30.9 trillion kilometers	19.2 trillion miles	206,000 astronomical units	3.26 light-years

Space Rocks

Direct sampling is the examination of pieces of material from celestial objects. In their examinations, scientists often use techniques of geology, including chemical analysis.

Meteorites. The most common samples are *meteorites,* rocks that fell through the atmosphere from farther out in our solar system.

Thousands of meteorites have been found. Most come from asteroids. A handful come from the moon or Mars. The best place to find meteorites is Antarctica. They show up on the polar ice much more clearly than they do among ordinary rocks elsewhere.

Moon Rocks. Scientists have also studied hundreds of kilograms of moon rocks brought to Earth by astronauts from 1969 to 1972.

Researchers have also analyzed bits of space dust collected by devices on high-altitude aircraft. They have determined that some of the dust came from beyond our solar system.

Computer Modeling

Astronomers use computers to build scientific models (sets of mathematical equations) that represent certain processes, such as the formation of a star. After entering the equations into a computer, an astronomer inserts numbers into the equations. The computer then simulates how the process would develop.

Speeding the Process. In some cases, the computer produces a moving picture on a computer screen. The picture can run much faster than the actual process. This kind of model can help astronomers because many important processes occur much too slowly for astronomers to observe.

Other important processes that can be simulated occur in inaccessible places, such as the interiors of stars.

CAPTURING PARTICLES

From 2001 to 2004, NASA's Genesis spacecraft gathered samples of the solar wind, a continuous flow of particles from the sun. Genesis returned to Earth in September 2004. (See page 938.)

Also in 2004, NASA's Stardust spacecraft passed near Comet Wild 2 and captured particles from its coma, a cloud of gas and dust surrounding the comet's core. Stardust dropped a capsule containing the samples to Earth in 2006.

◀ **The Eagle Nebula.** These gas pillars in the Eagle Nebula are about 7,000 light-years away from Earth. The pillars—made up of hydrogen gas and dust—are about 1 light-year (5.9 trillion miles) in length.

THE SOLAR SYSTEM

A solar system consists of a star and the planets and other objects orbiting around it.

Our own solar system includes the sun, Earth, and the other planets that orbit the sun. It also includes smaller objects that orbit the sun, such as dwarf planets, asteroids, and comets. More than 100 moons, or satellites, orbit the planets.

In addition, our solar system includes a cloud of gas and dust known as the interplanetary medium.

NINE PROPERTIES

There are nine important properties that a theory on the formation of the solar system has to account for. These major properties of the solar system must be explained in a way consistent with the estimated age of the solar system (4.6 billion years).

1. All planets orbit around the sun in almost circular orbits and in planes very close to the plane of the ecliptic (the plane that contains Earth's orbit).

2. The axis of the sun's rotation is approximately perpendicular to the plane of the ecliptic.

3. The planets all revolve around the sun in the same direction, which is also the direction of the sun's rotation.

4. The sun possesses more than 99 percent of the mass of the total system.

5. The planets possess the preponderant angular momentum of the system. (The sun rotates slowly in relation to the revolution and rotation of the planets.)

6. The majority of the planets rotate in a prograde direction around their axes.

7. Almost all the satellites of planets revolve around their primaries in the same direction as the primaries rotate around their axes.

8. A host of smaller objects, such as comets and meteoroids, often of low density, with orbits that are elongated, exist. The inclination of the orbits to the plane of the ecliptic varies widely.

9. The chemical composition of planets close to the sun (terrestrial planets) is different from those that are distant from the sun (gas giants).

Theories of Origin

The study of the origin of the solar system often is termed *cosmogony* (in contrast with *cosmology,* which refers to the study of the origin and evolution of the universe in its entirety).

Forming a Solar System

A theory of the origin and evolution of the solar system has to satisfy two requirements.

1. The theory must explain the dynamic (motion of the planets and sun), physical, and chemical properties of the solar system.

2. The theory has to explain the mechanisms for formation of planets from a contracting nebula.

▲ **Disk Star.** In 1977, astronomers discovered a star surrounded by a disklike structure with a diameter 20 times that of the star. This artist's depiction shows a star surrounded by a disk of dust that will eventually form planets.

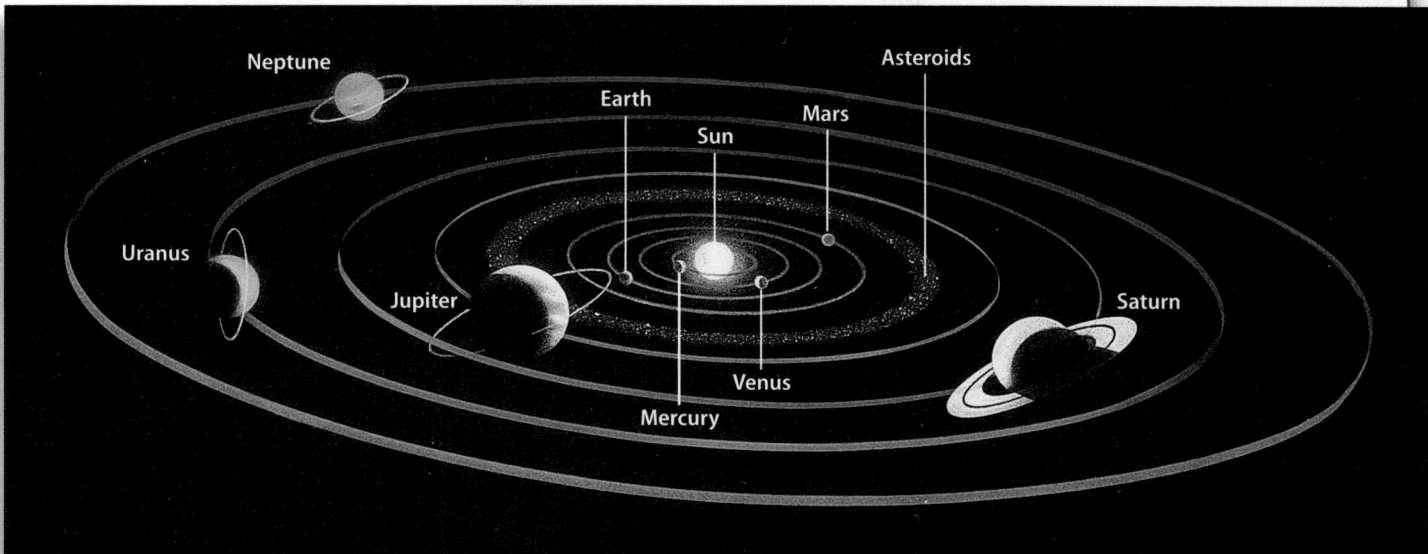

▲ **The solar system** includes many different objects that orbit the sun. These objects vary from planets much larger than Earth to tiny meteoroids and dust particles.

The Nebular Hypothesis

Many scientists believe that our solar system formed from a giant, rotating cloud of gas and dust known as the *solar nebula*. According to this theory, the solar nebula began to collapse because of its own gravity. Some astronomers speculate that a nearby *supernova* (exploding star) triggered the collapse. (See pages 948–949.)

Star Formation. The slowly rotating cloud contracted because of the mutual attraction between the particles making up the cloud. This process is termed *gravitational collapse* and is believed to be the initial stage of star formation. Because it preserves its angular momentum, the rotation speeds up. The rotation causes the cloud to flatten.

- Because gas heats up when compressed, the center region of the nebula, where the collapse was the strongest, began heating up and forming the sun.

- The increase in temperature caused the sun to stop contracting, now surrounded by a less dense cloud.

- The material in this cloud began to condense, forming small solid aggregations circling the sun.

Planet Composition. It is in this stage that the separation may have occurred to cause the difference in chemical composition between the terrestrial planets and the gas giants.

- Materials that are solid at high temperatures, such as iron, nickel, and magnesium silicate, condense in the hotter areas of the cloud, close to the sun.

- The volatile compounds, such as hydrogen and helium, condense at greater distances from the sun, forming the matter of the gas giants.

Protoplanets. The small solid aggregates formed larger ones under the influence of gravitation and collisions. These were the *protoplanets*.

The hot sun drove off volatile materials, such as hydrogen and helium, from the terrestrial planets, while the gas giants kept accumulating these compounds, thus increasing their mass and size.

Around the Sun

Planets move in two main ways. They travel around the sun in paths called *orbits*. Each planet also *rotates* on its *axis,* an imaginary line through its center.

Orbits

The planets of the solar system all move approximately in the same plane of orbit as Earth. Because of this, when seen from Earth, all the planets occupy positions near the ecliptic. The *ecliptic* is the apparent path of the sun around the celestial sphere.

Prograde Motion. Most of the time, the planets move westward across the sky slightly more slowly than the stars do. As a result, the planets seem to drift eastward relative to the background stars. This motion is called *prograde.*

Retrograde Motion. For a while each year, however, the planets seem to reverse their direction. This backward motion is called *retrograde.*

Retrograde motion occurs because Earth moves faster in its orbit than the planets that are farther from the sun. The planets that are closer to the sun move faster in their orbits than Earth travels in its orbit.

Retrograde motion occurs whenever Earth passes an outer planet traveling around the sun or an inner planet passes Earth.

OTHER ORBITERS

Besides the sun and the planets, several other types of celestial bodies make up the solar system: satellites (or moons) of planets, asteroids, comets, meteoroids, and interplanetary dust.

The Solar System

	Sun	Mercury	Venus	Earth	Mars	Jupiter
Distance from sun		57,910,000 km (35,980,000 mi.)	108,210,000 km (67,240,000 mi.)	149,600,000 km (92,960,000 mi.)	227,920,000 km (141,620,000 mi.)	778,570,000 km (483,780,000 mi.)
Length of year (in Earth days)	200 million yr.	87.969	224.701	365.256	686.980	4,332.589 (11.86 yr.)
Diameter	860,000 mi.	4,879 km (3,032 mi.)	12,104 km (7,521 mi.)	12,756 km (7,926 mi.)	6,792 km (4,221 mi.)	142,984 km (88,846 mi.)
Length of day	25 Earth days	59 Earth days	About 243 Earth days	23 hr., 56 min.	24 hr., 37 min.	9 hr., 55 min.
Mass relative to Earth	333,000	0.0553	0.815	1.00	0.107	317.83
Average surface temperature	10,000°F	332°F	750°F	59°F	−67°F	−128°F*
Atmosphere	Hydrogen, helium	Solar wind	Carbon dioxide, nitrogen	Nitrogen, oxygen, carbon dioxide, argon	Carbon dioxide, argon, nitrogen, water	Hydrogen, helium, methane, ammonia, water
Gravity relative to Earth		0.378	0.905	1.00	0.377	2.364
Number of moons		none	none	1	2	64 known

*Effective temperature, a measure of the amount of energy given off by the planet

Rotation

Planets rotate at different rates. One day is defined as how long it takes Earth to rotate once. Jupiter and Saturn spin much faster, in only about 10 hours. Venus rotates much more slowly, in about 243 Earth days.

Prograde Rotation. Most planets rotate in the same direction in which they revolve around the sun, with their axis of rotation standing upright from their orbital path.

A law of physics holds that such rotation does not change by itself. So astronomers think that the solar system formed out of a cloud of gas and dust that was already spinning.

Uncommon Motion. Uranus and Pluto (a dwarf planet) are tipped on their sides, however, so that their axes lie nearly level with their paths around the sun.

Venus is tipped all the way over. Its axis is almost completely upright, but the planet rotates in the direction opposite from the direction of its revolution around the sun. (See page 921.)

Most astronomers think that some other objects in the solar system must have collided with Uranus, Pluto, and Venus and tipped them.

IN RETROGRADE

The planets sometimes appear to change direction because of differences in orbital speed. In this diagram, each set of three numbers—for example, the three 5's—represents the same moment of time.

Earth orbits the sun more rapidly than does a more distant planet. As Earth passes a more distant planet, that planet's movement appears to briefly change direction as seen from Earth.

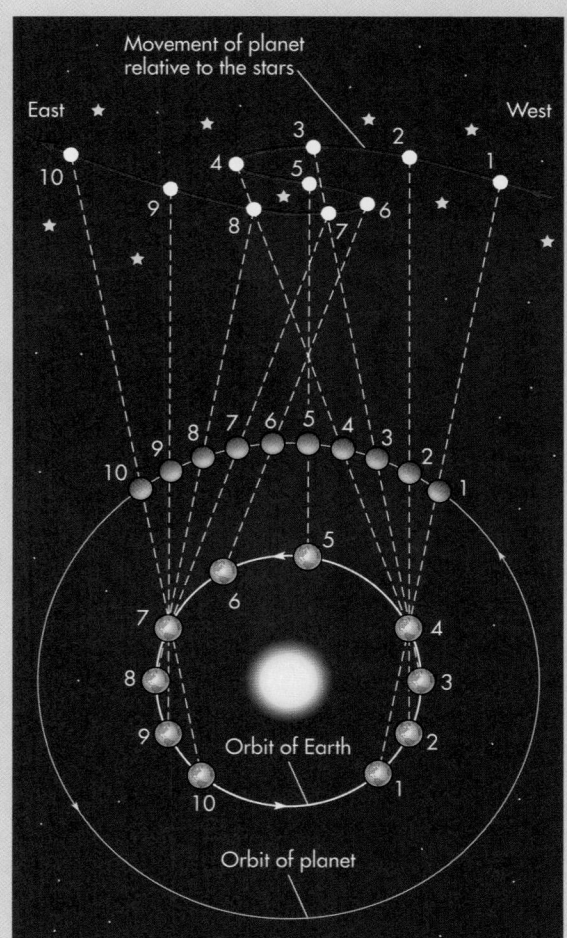

Saturn	Uranus	Neptune
1,433,530,000 km (890,750,000 mi.)	2,872,460,000 km (1,784,860,000 mi.)	4,495,060,000 km (2,793,100,000 mi.)
10,759.22 (29.46 yr.)	30,685.4 (84.01 yr.)	60,189 (164.79 yr.)
120,536 km (74,898 mi.)	51,118 km (31,763 mi.)	49,528 km (30,775 mi.)
10 hr., 33 min.	17 hr., 14 min.	16 hr., 7 min.
95.161	14.536	17.148
−148°F*	−344°F	−365°F
Hydrogen, helium, methane, ammonia	Hydrogen, helium	Hydrogen, helium, methane
1.07	0.905	1.14
62 known	27 known	13 known

TERRESTRIAL PLANETS

Because of certain similarities in their physical characteristics, the eight planets of our solar system are divided into *terrestrial (Earthlike) planets* and *gas giants,* or *Jovian planets.*

The terrestrial planets are Mercury, Venus, Earth, and Mars. They are rocky in nature, relatively small, and have high densities. Only Venus has a dense atmosphere.

Earth is the largest terrestrial planet. The other Earthlike planets have from 38 to 95 percent of Earth's diameter and from 5.5 to 82 percent of Earth's mass.

Mercury and Venus

Mercury

- Mercury is the planet closest to the sun.
- It has almost no atmosphere. Its surface temperature is 440K (332°F).
- It orbits around the sun with a period of 88 terrestrial days.
- By bouncing radar signals on its surface, astronomers have measured a rotational period of 59 Earth days.
- A day on Mercury lasts 176 Earth days.

Exploration. Mercury was explored in March 1974, by the Mariner 10 probe, which performed three flybys and returned images of its surface to Earth. Except for many elongated ridges, Mercury's surface features resemble the craters, basins, and plains found on the moon.

The Mariner probe also discovered that Mercury has an extremely tenuous atmosphere and a weak magnetic field, although stronger than the magnetic fields of Venus and Mars. This field hints of the existence of a large molten iron core.

The terrestrial planets are the four planets closest to the sun. They are significantly smaller than the gas giants. A group of *asteroids*—rocky or metallic space objects—called the Main Belt orbits between the terrestrial planets and the gas giants.

MISSION TO MERCURY

In August 2004, the Messenger mission to Mercury was launched. In 2008, it was announced that the probe had discovered water in Mercury's atmosphere during a flyby. It entered planetary orbit and began collecting data in 2011.

Venus

- Venus is the closest planet to Earth and the brightest object in the sky.

- Venus has a diameter of 12,102 kilometers (7,520 miles), about 644 kilometers (434 miles) smaller in diameter than Earth.

- It is nearly as massive and dense as Earth.

- Like Earth, Venus has an atmosphere; its cloud cover has long been known.

- Venus revolves around the sun in 224.7 Earth days.

- Its rotation is very slow—243 days—and retrograde.

- The Venusian day is equal to 118 Earth days.

- The Venusian atmosphere consists almost entirely (97 percent) of carbon dioxide (CO_2), some nitrogen and water, and minute amounts of hydrogen chloride (HCl) and hydrogen fluoride (HF).

- The atmosphere absorbs much of the infrared radiation from the planet's surface, causing the heating of the atmosphere known as the *greenhouse effect*.

- The cloud cover is at an altitude of 50 kilometers (31 miles) and consists of droplets of sulfuric acid.

- The upper clouds move at 350 kilometers (224 miles) per hour and circle the planet in 4 days.

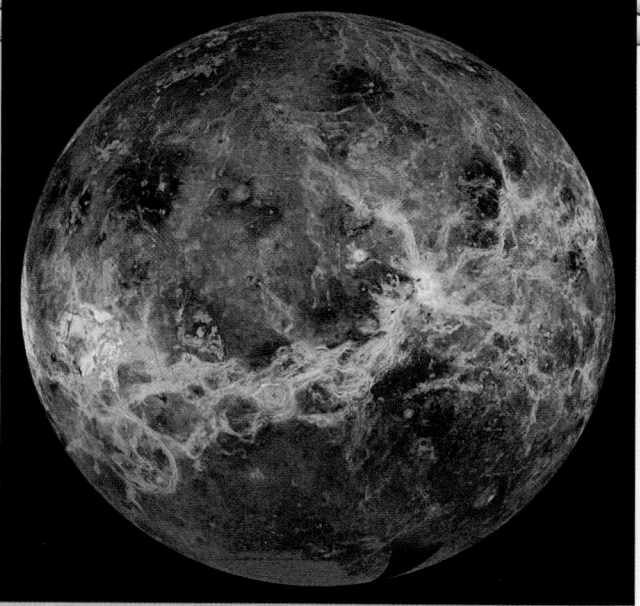

Surface of Venus. The U.S. space probe Magellan scanned the surface of Venus with radar waves to produce this image.

Exploration. Beginning in 1969, the Soviet Union launched a series of Venera probes that landed on the surface of Venus. Venera 9 and 10 returned the first pictures of the planet in 1975, showing a landscape resembling that of Mars.

In 1982, two more Venera probes sent back to Earth the most sophisticated and detailed analyses of the surface of Venus to date. Analyses of the soil of Venus showed that its chemical composition is similar to that of volcanic rock on Earth. (See pages 466–467.)

Pioneer Venus. In 1978, NASA launched the Pioneer Venus, which mapped 93 percent of the surface of Venus. The planet was shown to be very flat. About 60 percent of the surface has variations of less than half a mile in height, and nearly 80 percent has variations of less than a mile.

Magellan. On May 5, 1989, NASA launched the Venus orbiter Magellan, which began mapping the planet's surface by radar in September 1990.

Small craters indicate a volcanic past. Several large impact craters—one as wide as 275 kilometers (170 miles)—are visible. The number of craters per square kilometer corresponds roughly to that of Earth.

The Mariner 10 space probe visited both Venus and Mercury.

Earth's Satellite

Earth

- Earth is the third planet from the sun.
- Earth ranks fifth in size among the sun's planets.
- It has a diameter of about 13,000 kilometers (8,000 miles).
- Earth is about 150 million kilometers (93 million miles) from the sun.
- The planet has an atmosphere that is mostly nitrogen with some oxygen.
- Earth has oceans of liquid water and continents that rise above sea level.

For information on Earth's geology, biosphere, and other physical features, see Earth Science.

The Moon

The moon is Earth's only natural satellite and the only astronomical body other than Earth ever visited by human beings. The moon is the brightest object in the night sky but gives off no light of its own. Instead, it reflects light from the sun.

▲ **The near side of the moon** consists of two-thirds light-colored, highly cratered highlands and one-third dark, fairly smooth, less cratered plains. The plains are sometimes called *maria*—Latin for *seas*—because of their resemblance to bodies of water.

Moon Facts	
Age	Like Earth, the moon is about 4.6 billion years old.
Distance from Earth	Average—384,467 km (238,897 mi.)
	Shortest—363,300 km (225,740 mi.)
	Greatest—405,500 km (251,970 mi.)
Radius	1,737.1 km (1,079.4 mi.), about 27 percent of Earth's radius
Volume	22.0 billion cu. km (5.27 billion cu. mi.), about 1/50 the volume of Earth
Mass	7.35×10^{19} metric tons (8.10×10^{19} tons), about 1/81 the mass of Earth
Density	3.34 grams per cu. cm, about 3/5 the density of Earth
Surface gravity	About 1/6 that of Earth
Temperature at equator	−173° to +127°C (−280° to +260°F)
Atmosphere	An exosphere consisting of small amounts of various gases is present above the surface.
Revolution period around Earth	Relative to the stars: 27 days, 7 hours, 43 minutes; relative to the sun: 29 days, 12 hours, 43 minutes
Average speed around Earth	3,683 km (2,289 mi.) per hour

The Moon's Composition

From samples, scientists have determined that the moon's surface contains only igneous rock and no sedimentary rock. This indicates that at one time the moon's surface was completely molten and that no seas filled with water ever existed on the moon.

Based on seismographic measurements, scientists believe the moon's central core is molten.

The moon's gravity is not constant over its surface. Especially in large circular plains, there are *mascons*, concentrations of higher than normal density causing local increases of gravity.

Tiny Moonquakes. Very little geological activity, such as erosion or eruption, takes place in the lunar crust. Seismographs placed on the moon's surface by the Apollo crews registered "moonquakes" of 1 or 2 points on the Richter scale.

Lunar Exploration

Beginning in 1959, the Soviet Union and the United States sent a series of robot spacecraft to examine the moon in detail. Their ultimate goal was to land people on the moon. The United States reached that goal in 1969 with the landing of the Apollo 11 lunar module. (For more on the Apollo missions, see page 973.)

Twelve American astronauts have landed on the moon, performing experiments and returning a total of 382 kilograms (842 pounds) of rock. Three Soviet Luna spacecraft have brought back 310 grams (11 ounces) of soil.

THE FAR—BUT NOT NECESSARILY DARK— SIDE OF THE MOON

The moon's orbital period is 28 days. It also rotates around its axis once every 28 days. This means that the same hemisphere—the *near side*—is always facing Earth. The other side—the *far side*—is always facing away from Earth.

People sometimes mistakenly use the term *dark side* to refer to the far side. The moon does have a dark side—it is the hemisphere that is turned away from the sun. The location of the dark side changes constantly, moving with the dividing line between sunlight and dark.

WHERE DID IT COME FROM?

Radiocarbon dating of soil samples indicates that the moon is about 4.6 billion years old, but there is no certainty as to how or where the moon was formed.

Scientists believe that the moon formed as a result of a collision known as the Giant Impact. According to this idea, Earth collided with a planet-sized object 4.6 billion years ago. As a result of the impact, a cloud of vaporized rock shot off Earth's surface and went into orbit around Earth. The cloud cooled and condensed into a ring of small, solid bodies, which then gathered together, forming the moon.

▲ **The first people on the moon** were U.S. astronauts Neil A. Armstrong, who took this picture, and Edwin "Buzz" Aldrin, who is pictured next to a seismograph.

The United States lunar program started with the eight Pioneer spacecraft launched before 1960. Only one Pioneer was successful in flying past the moon and measuring particles and fields near that body.

The U.S. sent up lunar probes throughout the 1960s, taking pictures, testing soil, mapping the lunar surface, and selecting landing sites for the Apollo missions.

The Soviet Union started exploration of the moon's surface in the 1960s. Luna 9 made the first intact lunar landing on February 3, 1966.

In the early 1970s, Luna 17 carried a roving vehicle to study the moon that was operated via radio from a base on Earth.

Eclipses

An *eclipse* is the darkening of a heavenly body. It occurs when the shadow of one object in space falls on another object or when one object moves in front of another to block its light. There are two types of eclipses that are observable on Earth.

- *solar eclipse*
- *lunar eclipse*

Solar Eclipse

Solar eclipses occur when the moon's shadow sweeps across the face of Earth. The shadow usually moves from west to east across Earth at a speed of about 3,200 kilometers (2,000 miles) per hour.

People in the path of the shadow may see one of three kinds of eclipses: a *total eclipse,* an *annular eclipse,* or a *partial eclipse.*

A total solar eclipse occurs if the moon completely blots out the sun.

- The dark moon appears on the western edge of the sun and moves slowly across the sun.
- At the moment of total eclipse, a brilliant halo flashes into view around the darkened sun. This halo is the sun's outer atmosphere, the *corona.*
- The sky remains blue but darkens.
- Some bright stars and planets may become visible from Earth.
- After a few minutes, the sun reappears as the moon moves off to the east.
- The period when the sun is totally darkened may be as long as 7 minutes, 40 seconds, but it averages about 2.5 minutes.

The ancient Chinese thought solar eclipses occurred when a dragon in the sky tried to swallow the sun.

THE BASICS: ECLIPSES

- **A solar eclipse** takes place when the sun appears to become dark as the moon passes between the sun and Earth.
- **A lunar eclipse** occurs when the moon darkens as it passes through Earth's shadow.

A total eclipse of the sun is one of nature's most impressive sights. ▼

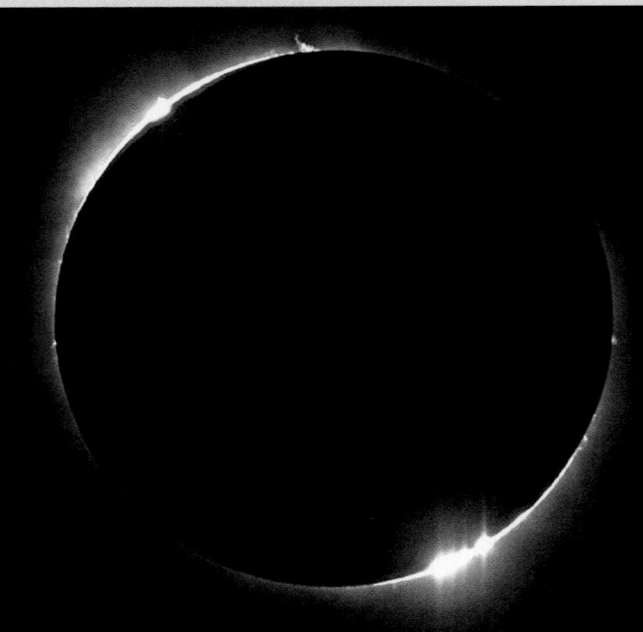

Path of Totality. A total solar eclipse can be seen only in certain parts of the world. These areas lie in the *path of totality,* the path along which the moon's shadow passes across Earth. The path of totality is never wider than about 274 kilometers (170 miles).

Annular Eclipse. If the moon is at its farthest point from Earth when a total eclipse occurs, the eclipse may be only an annular eclipse. In such an eclipse, the moon darkens only the middle of the sun, leaving a bright ring around the edges.

A partial eclipse occurs if the moon covers only part of the sun.

Lunar Eclipse

Lunar eclipses take place when the moon passes through the shadow of Earth.

A total lunar eclipse occurs if the entire moon passes through Earth's shadow. A total lunar eclipse may last up to 1 hour, 40 minutes.

A partial eclipse occurs if only part of the moon passes through the shadow.

Viewing a Lunar Eclipse. A lunar eclipse may be seen by most of the people on the night side of Earth. There is no danger in viewing a lunar eclipse.

The moon does not become completely dark during most lunar eclipses. In many cases, it becomes reddish. Earth's atmosphere bends part of the sun's light around Earth and toward the moon. This light is red because the atmosphere scatters the other colors present in sunlight in greater amounts than it does red.

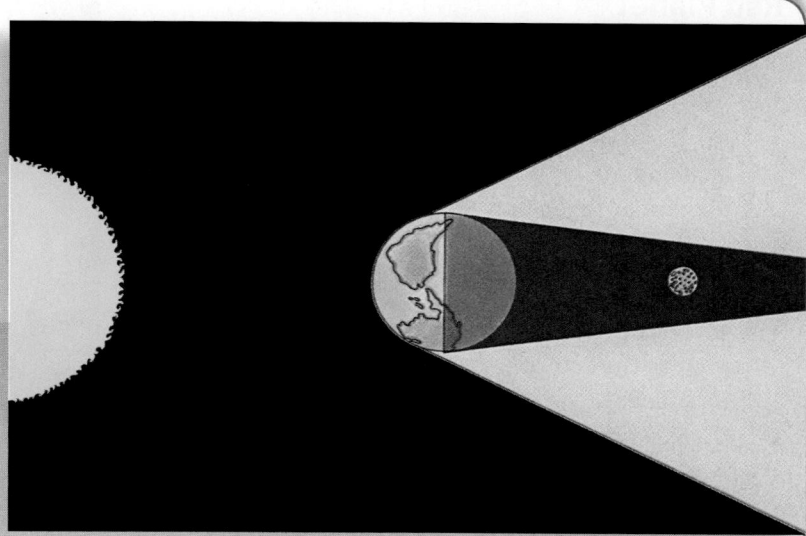

▲ **A lunar eclipse** is the darkening of the moon that occurs when Earth gets between the sun and the moon. Earth's shadow darkens the moon.

VIEWING A SOLAR ECLIPSE

Looking at the sun during a solar eclipse can be damaging to the eyes and must be done with special tools.

- A partial solar eclipse or a partial phase of a total eclipse should be viewed only with special filters that cut the solar light to a safe level. Sunglasses and smoked glasses do not provide enough protection.

- You can also view the sun indirectly with a pinhole projector—two pieces of cardboard, one with a small hole punched through it. Hold this piece so that sunlight passes through the hole and casts an image on the other piece.

- Spaces between tree leaves can also serve as pinholes, casting images on the ground.

- A total solar eclipse can be viewed safely without protection only when the disk of the sun is completely hidden and only the corona is visible. The corona is no brighter than a full moon.

What Eclipses Teach

- Astronomers have observed solar eclipses to determine the exact relative positions of Earth, the sun, and the moon.

- In 1939, astronomers observed that the moon's surface cooled extremely rapidly during a lunar eclipse. They theorized that a layer of fine dust covers the moon, a theory proven correct by space probes on the moon in the 1960s.

- Eclipses have allowed astronomers to study possible changes in the sun's size and strength of gravity.

Proving Einstein Right. Measurements of the sun's corona and certain kinds of other studies can be made the best during a total solar eclipse.

Albert Einstein claimed in his theory of general relativity that light from stars beyond the sun bends slightly from a straight path as it passes the sun.

Normally, the bright glare of the sun drowns out starlight passing near the sun. But this light can be photographed during a total solar eclipse. Photographs taken during an eclipse in 1919 strongly supported Einstein's theory. (See pages 852–853.)

Mars

Red Planet

- Mars is the fourth planet from the sun.
- Mars's diameter is 6,792 kilometers (4,221 miles).
- Mars has a very thin, transparent atmosphere consisting mainly of carbon dioxide, with about 2 percent nitrogen and 1.5 percent argon.
- Minute quantities of oxygen and water vapor are also present in the atmosphere.
- Weather on Mars includes clouds, winds, and tremendous dust storms that sometimes rage over the entire planet.
- Mars has two small satellites: *Phobos* is about 16 kilometers (10 miles) in diameter, and *Deimos* is about 10 kilometers (6 miles) in diameter.
- The surface of Mars has spectacular features, including a canyon system that is much deeper and much longer than the Grand Canyon.
- Mars also has mountains that are much higher than Mount Everest, Earth's highest peak.
- Viewed from Earth, Mars is a bright reddish-orange because of iron-rich minerals in its soil.

▲ **Mars,** like Earth, has clouds in its atmosphere and deposits of ice at its poles. The rustlike color of Mars comes from the large amount of iron in the planet's soil.

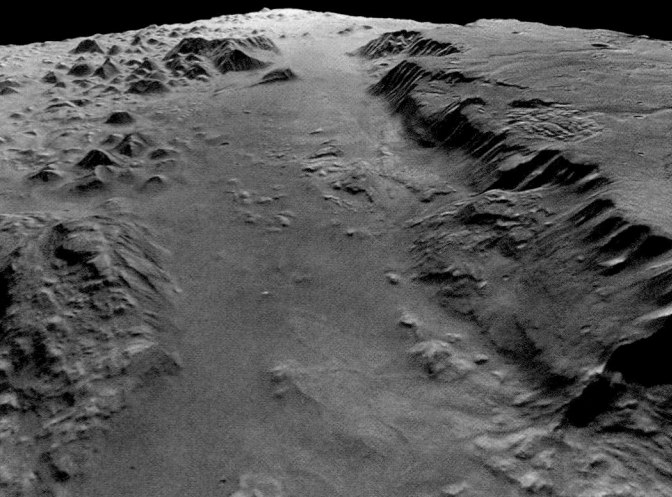

▲ **Valles Marineris Canyon** is wider and deeper than the Grand Canyon. Scientists believe that running water and winds formed the canyon over Mars's long history.

Exploration. Scientists have observed Mars through telescopes based on Earth and in space. Space probes have carried telescopes and other instruments to Mars.

Early probes were designed to observe the planet as they flew past it. Later, spacecraft orbited Mars and even landed there. But no human being has ever set foot on Mars.

Mariner 4, the first spacecraft to reach Mars, was launched on November 28, 1964. Mariner 6 in 1969 and Mariner 9 in 1971–1972 returned large numbers of images of the Martian surface.

Viking 1 and Viking 2, launched in 1975, each combined a 2,356-kilogram (5,190-pound) orbiter with a 1,180-kilogram (2,600-pound) lander. Both made safe landings on Mars in 1976, after a 10-month, 800-million-kilometer (496-million-mile) journey.

The orbiters photographed the surface and relayed data and commands between the landers and Earth. The landers reported the weather, analyzed the air and soil, photographed the terrain, and performed biological experiments in a search for life.

▲ **Martian Landscape.** Over half of the Martian surface is desertlike, and vast dust storms sometimes rage over the planet. These storms have probably been responsible for the development of the featureless type of terrain.

The Pathfinder mission was launched in 1997, delivering a lander and the rover Sojourner to the surface of Mars. The rover returned a massive amount of data during its 3 months of operation.

Spirit and Opportunity, two rovers launched in June 2003, landed on Mars in January 2004. They sent back data and dramatic images that have expanded scientific knowledge of Mars. Both rovers surpassed longevity expectations, operating for more than 5 years and sending a quarter-million images back to Earth.

The Phoenix Mars lander, launched in August 2007, operated in the north polar region from May to November 2008. The lander revealed the presence of various minerals in the soil. However, chief among its contributions was the confirmation of water ice just below the surface of the Martian soil.

A Weak Magnet. Instruments aboard the Mariner 4 measured a very weak magnetic field. But later data sent back from Mars Global Surveyor, launched in 1997, indicate that some of Mars's oldest rocks formed in the presence of a strong magnetic field. This suggests that Mars once had a molten core, which has since solidified.

THE SEARCH FOR LIFE

In 1877, the Italian astronomer Giovanni Schiaparelli (1835–1910) caused a sensation when he announced his discovery of a network of canals on Mars.

Thus was born the theory of Martian inhabitants, the canal builders. No canals have been revealed by photographs taken by space probes, but several large canyons are present.

Today, scientists believe Mars might once have harbored life, and living things might exist there even today. Mars almost certainly has three ingredients that scientists believe are necessary for life.

1. chemical elements such as carbon, hydrogen, oxygen, and nitrogen that form the building blocks of living things

2. a source of energy that living organisms can use

3. liquid water

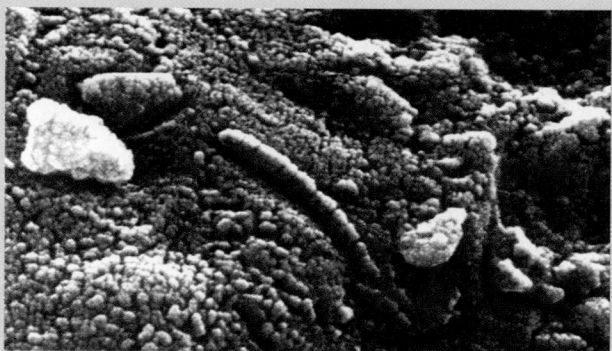

▲ **Possible Fossil.** Some scientists believe this curved, rodlike structure to be a fossilized Martian creature.

GAS GIANTS are the outer four planets—Jupiter, Saturn, Uranus, and Neptune. They are also called *Jovian,* or Jupiterlike, planets.

The gas giants are quite different from the terrestrial planets. They have gaseous atmospheres and no solid surfaces. They are quite large, with dense atmospheres and low densities.

All four Jovian planets consist mainly of hydrogen and helium. Jupiter, Saturn, and Neptune give off more energy than they receive from the sun. Scientists think the source of some of the energy is probably the slow compression of the planets by their own gravity.

Jupiter

Biggest Giant

- Jupiter is a giant planet, larger and heavier than all the other planets combined.
- It has a diameter of 143,000 kilometers (88,856 miles)—about 11 times larger than Earth's.
- Jupiter's volume is more than 1,000 times that of Earth and its mass 318 times that of Earth.
- Like the other Jovian planets, its density is very close to that of the sun.
- Its strong surface gravity enables it to hold an atmosphere many hundreds of miles deep.
- Jupiter's rotation period is 10 hours.
- The planet takes 11.9 years to complete one revolution around the sun.
- Multicolored bands of clouds and numerous red and brown spots are visible on Jupiter's surface. The largest of these, the Great Red Spot, is 25,000 kilometers (15,500 miles) long.

▲ **The space probe Voyager 2** was launched on August 20, 1977. Its path through the solar system is shown in red. Voyager 2 flew past and photographed Jupiter in 1979, Saturn in 1981, Uranus in 1986, and Neptune in 1989.

GREAT RED STORM

The Great Red Spot appears in high-resolution pictures to be a giant, long-lasting storm. The cloud's gas masses make a full rotation every 12 days, rotating even faster closer to the center. Several smaller red spots have been photographed, indicating to astronomers that the Great Red Spot is not unique.

▲ **Jupiter's colorful appearance** comes from bands of clouds in the planet's lower atmosphere. The large oval-shaped mark is the Great Red Spot.

When subjected to very high pressure, liquid hydrogen becomes metallic. Therefore, at a depth of about 25 percent of Jupiter's radius, there is an abrupt transition from the molecular liquid to the metallic liquid.

The Strongest Magnet. Jupiter has the strongest magnetic field of all planets, 20,000 times stronger than that of Earth. It is believed to be generated by electric currents in the zone of transition from liquid to metal.

Just as Earth's magnetic field traps charged particles, so does Jupiter's. Jupiter's radiation belts are 10,000 times stronger than Earth's. They pose a serious threat to visiting spacecraft. (See pages 502–503.)

Exploration. Data from flybys by Pioneer 10 and Pioneer 11 in 1973 and 1974, and from Voyager 1 and Voyager 2, which flew by in 1979, have provided detailed information about Jupiter and its moons.

Voyager 1 discovered Jupiter's ring system. NASA launched the Galileo spacecraft in 1989. It arrived at Jupiter on December 7, 1995, and relayed remarkable images and data back to Earth for more than 7 years.

Jovian weather, unlike Earth's weather, is internally driven. Jupiter radiates twice as much heat as it receives from the sun. The heat source may be energy left over from Jupiter's formation, or it may be due to slow contractions of the planet due to gravity.

Stellar Failure. Astronomers consider Jupiter to be a failed star: nuclear fusion would have started in its core if the planet had been 10 times more massive.

Transitioning to Metal. Instead of a solid surface, Jupiter transitions gradually from gas to the liquid, molecular hydrogen surface.

JUPITER'S MOONS

Jupiter has 64 known moons. The four largest are Io, Europa, Ganymede, and Callisto.

- Io has an unscarred surface but at least seven large active volcanoes.

- Europa has no craters but is crosshatched by narrow fractures hundreds of miles long.

- Ganymede is dotted with very large, ancient ringed craters.

- Callisto displays 10 times as many craters as Ganymede.

Io is the most colorful satellite in the solar system. Sulfur gases erupt from volcanoes, then drift to the surface as colored "snow." Sulfur dioxide settles as a white frost. ▶

Saturn

- Saturn is second only to Jupiter in size, mass, and speed of rotation.
- Its diameter is 120,500 kilometers (74,875 miles).
- Saturn's mass is 95 times that of Earth.
- The mean distance from the sun is 1,427 million kilometers (886.7 million miles).
- Its rotational period is 10 hours, 39.4 minutes.
- It orbits the sun in 29.5 years.
- Saturn is the least dense of all planets.
- Many features of Saturn's atmosphere and inner structure are similar to those of Jupiter.

Exploration. Much has been learned about Saturn from space probes. Pioneer 11 reached Saturn in September 1979 and approached within 20,880 kilometers (12,974 miles).

Voyager 1 reached the planet in November 1980, and Voyager 2 in August 1981. Voyager 1 passed close by Titan, Saturn's largest satellite. Voyager 2 continued its voyage to Uranus and Neptune.

SATURN'S RINGS

By far Saturn's most outstanding feature is its ring system. The seven main rings surround the planet at its equator but do not touch it. They consist mainly of pieces of ice, ranging from dust-sized grains to chunks more than 3 meters (10 feet) in diameter.

Many of the rings feature thin bands of varying brightness, called *ringlets*. Gaps of several thousand miles separate most of the major rings.

In 2009, scientists using the Spitzer Space Telescope discovered a diffuse doughnut-shaped ring far beyond the orbit of the previously known rings. The ring is centered around the orbit of the moon Phoebe. The ring is roughly 13 million kilometers (8 million miles) thick.

New Rings. The pictures of Saturn's ring system taken by the Pioneer and Voyager spacecraft count among the most spectacular ever obtained in astronomy. The F ring, never observed from Earth before, became visible in the photographs.

Spokes. In the B ring, are a number of *spokes*—radial darker zones—became visible. Voyager 2 performed measurements that showed that the ring system is very thin, at most 150 meters (490 feet) thick.

Orbiting Saturn. After traveling for 7 years, the Cassini-Huygens spacecraft became the first to orbit Saturn when it arrived in June 2004.

In January 2005, the Huygens probe, which had detached from the Cassini spacecraft, landed on Saturn's largest moon, Titan. Scientists believe conditions on Titan to be comparable to that of early Earth and hope that study of Titan will shed light on Earth's beginnings. Early photos from Titan indicated rain and rivers of methane.

Saturn's Rings	
Distance from center of Saturn to inner edge of ring.	
Name	**Distance in km (mi.)**
D	67,600 (42,000)
C	73,200 (45,500)
B	92,200 (57,300)
Cassini division	117,500 (73,000)
A	121,000 (75,200)
Encke division	133,600 (83,000)
F	140,700 (87,400)
G	170,600 (106,000)
E	209,200 (130,000)

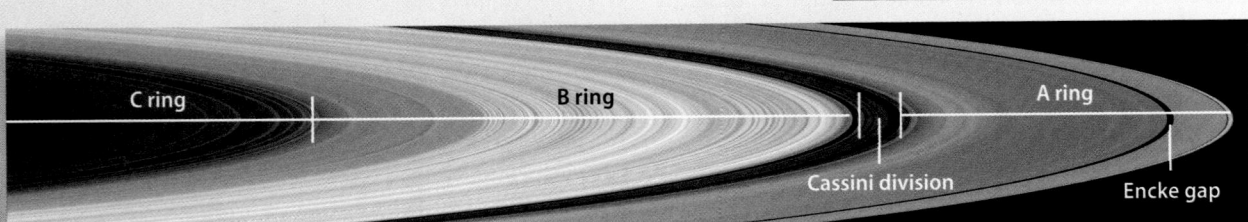

C ring B ring A ring Cassini division Encke gap

Saturn's Moons. With the discovery of new satellites by spacecraft, the total number of known moons of Saturn has grown to 62.

Saturn's largest moon, Titan, was discovered by Dutch astronomer Christiaan Huygens in 1655. Voyager photographs of Titan show that it is covered by a thick orange atmosphere mainly containing nitrogen. The atmospheric pressure is 1.6 times that of Earth.

Discoveries from the Cassini-Huygens mission include previously unknown moons, towering sand dunes and liquid seas on Titan, and an atmosphere on Enceladus. Additionally, partial rings have been noted orbiting two of Saturn's small inner moons.

▲ **Saturn,** in a photograph taken by the Cassini-Huygens spacecraft

Uranus

- With a magnitude of 5.5, Uranus is the farthest planet that can be seen without a telescope.

- Uranus is half the size of Saturn, with a diameter of 51,100 kilometers (31,690 miles).

- The mean distance from the sun is 2,871 million kilometers (1,784 million miles).

- Uranus orbits the sun in 84 years and rotates around its axis in 16.3 hours.

- Like Venus, Uranus rotates in retrograde, but its axis is tilted over 98° to its orbital plane. (See page 919.)

- Consequently, unlike the other planets, Uranus does not have day and night.

- Its northern and southern halves are pointed toward the sun alternately every 42 years.

- At the present, Uranus has been found to have 13 rings that are similar to Saturn's rings.

Exploration. Voyager 2 visited the planet in December 1985. Pictures taken then show that Uranus is covered by a thick atmosphere colored greenish blue by trace amounts of methane.

The planet's surface may be covered with water 8,000 kilometers (5,000 miles) deep. The central part of the planet may consist of a rocky core the size of Earth.

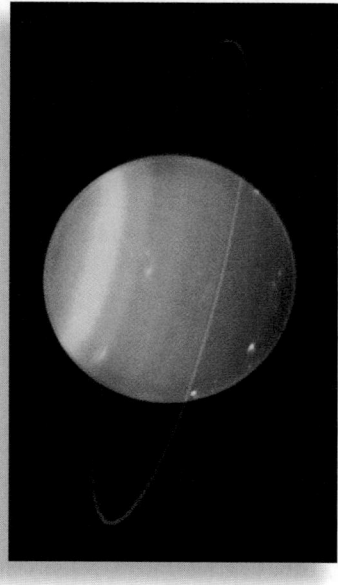

◄ **Uranus's atmosphere** features complex cloud patterns colored blue-green by methane gas.

Moons. Uranus has 27 known moons. The five largest moons are Ariel, Miranda, Oberon, Titania, and Umbriel. They consist of about 60 percent water ice and 40 percent rock.

Pictures of Miranda revealed structures never seen on other celestial bodies in the solar system. Rectangular and circular features cover large parts of its surface, hinting that Miranda never completed the process in which heavier elements sank to form the core and lighter elements formed the crust.

Neptune and Dwarf Planets

Neptune

- With a magnitude of 8, Neptune is invisible to the naked eye, but can be observed through binoculars.

- The average distance from the sun is 4,504 million kilometers (2,799 million miles).

- The planet completes an orbit around the sun in 164.8 years.

- Neptune's rotation period is 16 hours, 7 minutes.

- Its average temperature is −201°C (−330°F).

- The planet's atmosphere is made up of hydrogen, helium, methane, and acetylene.

- Neptune has at least 13 satellites.

Exploration. Voyager 2 reached Neptune in 1989. It detected Neptune's magnetic field and measured its rotational period, which is 16 hours, 7 minutes, and corresponds to the rotational period of the planetary core. The cloud formations rotate more slowly, with a period of more than 18 hours near the equator.

Voyager 2 discovered six new moons in addition to the previously known moons Triton and Nereid. Five more have since been discovered.

Voyager 2 also produced the first images of Neptune's system of six dim rings. All of these rings are much fainter and darker than the rings of Saturn. They appear to consist of particles of dust.

▲ **Neptune and Triton.** The blue clouds of Neptune are mostly frozen methane, the main chemical in natural gas.

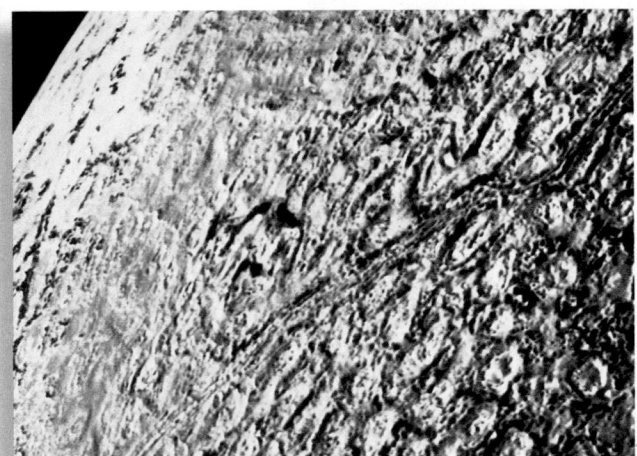

▲ **Trapped Comet.** Triton may once have been a large comet before being captured by Neptune's gravity.

HOW DO WE KNOW THAT ?

THE DISCOVERY OF NEPTUNE

Neptune was discovered mathematically before it was seen through a telescope. Astronomers thought Uranus was the most distant planet, but they noticed that it was not always in the position they predicted. The force of gravity of an unknown planet seemed to be influencing Uranus.

In 1843, English astronomer and mathematician John C. Adams began working to find the location of the unknown planet. Adams predicted the planet would be about 1.6 billion kilometers (1 billion miles) farther from the sun than Uranus. In 1845, Adams sent his remarkably accurate work to Sir George B. Airy, the Astronomer Royal of England. However, Airy did not look for the planet with a telescope. Apparently, he lacked confidence in Adams.

By mid-1846, French mathematician Urbain J. J. Leverrier also had predicted Neptune's position. He sent his predictions, which were similar to those of Adams, to the Urania Observatory in Berlin, Germany. On September 23, 1846, astronomers at the observatory found Neptune near the position predicted by Leverrier. Today, both Adams and Leverrier are credited with the discovery.

Dwarf Planets

A *dwarf planet,* also called a *plutoid,* is a celestial body that orbits the sun, is near-spherical in shape, is not a satellite, and, because of its small size, has not cleared the orbit in its neighborhood.

Pluto is the best known dwarf planet, having been considered the ninth planet for 76 years.

- Pluto's average distance from the sun is around 5,906,380,000 kilometers (3,670,050,000 miles).
- Pluto completes one orbit every 248 Earth years.
- For 20 years of each orbit, it comes closer to the sun than the orbit of Neptune. Pluto last entered Neptune's orbit in 1979 and remained there until 1999.
- Pluto rotates about once every 6 Earth days.
- Pluto has an estimated diameter of 1,460 miles (2,350 kilometers), only about two-thirds the diameter of Earth's moon.
- Pluto's surface is one of the coldest places in our solar system. Astronomers think the temperature on parts of Pluto is about −232°C (−385°F).

Crowded Orbit. Unlike a planet, a dwarf planet lacks the gravitational pull to sweep other objects from the region of its orbit. As a result, dwarf planets are found among populations of smaller bodies.

The dwarf planet Ceres, for example, orbits in the Main Belt of asteroids, between the orbits of Mars and Jupiter.

Other Plutoids. Other dwarf planets orbit primarily beyond Neptune in the Kuiper belt. Compared with the planets, KBOs tend to follow irregular, elongated orbits.

The first KBOs to be classified as dwarf planets include Eris, Haumea, Makemake, and Pluto.

THE PLUTO CONTROVERSY

Pluto was discovered in 1930 and for 76 years was considered a planet. But its small size and irregular orbit led many astronomers to question whether Pluto should be grouped with such worlds as Earth and Jupiter.

The debate intensified in the 1990s with the discovery of the Kuiper belt objects (KBOs), a band of icy, rocky objects in the outer regions of our solar system. KBOs have many similarities with Pluto.

In 2006, the International Astronomical Union (IAU) created a new category called dwarf planets. Pluto was reclassified and is now considered a dwarf planet.

PLUTO'S SURFACE

These images, taken by the Hubble Space Telescope, show Pluto's surface. The bright regions, which include Pluto's polar caps, are frozen nitrogen and methane. The dark areas may be methane frost that has been broken down chemically by the sun's radiation.

 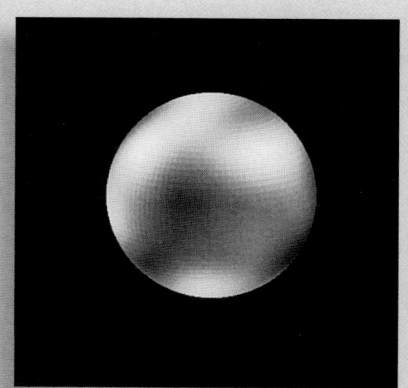

OTHER OBJECTS

Besides the sun and the planets, our solar system consists of other orbiting objects usually made up of such materials as rock, metal, and ice. They are found in two main areas of the solar system: the *Main Belt* and the *Kuiper belt*. The Main Belt is a belt of asteroids that orbits the sun between Mars and Jupiter. The Kuiper belt is a group of dwarf planets and cometlike bodies in orbit out beyond Neptune.

▲ **Comet Hale-Bopp** was visible to the naked eye for 18 months in 1997. It only came within 197 million kilometers (122 million miles) of Earth—not especially close for a comet—but its unusually large nucleus gave off a great deal of dust and gas, making it very bright.

Comets

A comet is a space object made up mostly of ice and rock. Most comets that are visible from Earth travel around the sun in long, oval orbits.

Classification. Astronomers classify comets according to how long they take to orbit the sun. *Short-period comets* need less than 200 years to complete one orbit. *Long-period comets* take 200 years or longer.

Small Bodies

Besides the large planets and dwarf planets, a host of smaller bodies circle the sun. These are now categorized as *small bodies*.

The small bodies are classified by size.

- *asteroids*
- *comets*
- *meteoroids*

Asteroids

Asteroids are the largest of the small bodies. They are found mainly between the orbits of Mars and Jupiter. This region is known as the Main Belt.

Rock and Metal. Millions of asteroids may exist. Astronomers think that most of them measure less than 10 kilometers (6 miles) in diameter. The majority of asteroids have a rocky composition. Some consist of metal or a mixture of metal and rock.

Origins. Astronomers believe that comets are leftover debris from the formation of the outer planets. A collection of gas, ice, rocks, and dust formed the outer planets about 4.6 billion years ago.

Some scientists believe that comets originally brought to Earth some of the water and the carbon-based molecules that make up living things.

Structure of Comets. Comets consist of a *nucleus, coma,* and *tail*.

- Based on spectroscopic analysis, the nucleus of a comet appears to contain water ice, carbon dioxide, formaldehyde, carbon monoxide, and nitrogen.
- The coma is a cloudy atmosphere of gas and dust that surrounds a comet's nucleus.
- At great distances from the sun, comets do not have a tail and appear as fuzzy spots in telescopes.
- As a comet approaches the sun, matter from the nucleus becomes heated and dissociates, forming the luminous and extensive tail.
- The tail shines by reflecting sunlight and by reradiated sunlight absorbed by gases in the coma.

Very Old Rocks. Scientists think that asteroids consist of material left over from the formation of the solar system. Such processes as erosion and volcanic activity have altered the planets and moons. But much of the material in asteroids is almost unchanged.

Asteroid Flyby. In 1991, the spacecraft Galileo, on its way to Jupiter, flew by the Gaspra asteroid at a distance of 1,600 kilometers (1,000 miles).

Images returned by the spacecraft show an irregular body of about 12 by 16 kilometers (7.5 by 10 miles) covered with impact craters.

Dinosaur Killer. In 2007, scientists reported that they had traced the asteroid that led to the dinosaurs' extinction back to a family of asteroids in the Main Belt called the Baptistina family. This asteroid family came from a single asteroid that broke apart during a collision about 160 million years ago. (See pages 496–497.)

The U.S. spacecraft Galileo took this photograph of the asteroid Ida and its tiny moon Dactyl. ▼

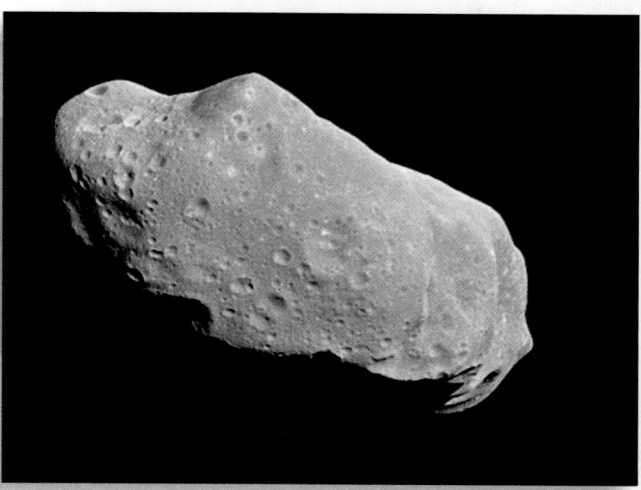

- A comet's tail always points away from the sun. This is because the solar wind and solar radiation push particles of gas and dust away from the sun.

Death of a Comet. With each new approach to the sun, some of the comet's material is driven away from its nucleus and left strewn along the comet's orbital path. Because of this, after many return trips, any comet that orbits close to the sun will eventually waste away entirely.

Comet Up Close. In 2005, the United States launched the Deep Impact spacecraft to Comet Tempel 1. The craft consisted of two smaller probes, one of which intentionally slammed into the comet's nucleus. Moments before the collision, the probe took unprecedented close-up photos of the comet's nucleus.

Scientists believe that analysis of collected data should lead to a better understanding of the formation of the solar system and the implications of comets colliding with Earth.

▲ **Arizona Meteor Crater** is the result of a prehistoric collision of Earth and a small asteroid.

METEOROIDS

A meteoric particle traveling in space is known as a meteoroid. The same particle, after it enters Earth's atmosphere and is made luminous by friction with the upper air, is called a *meteor*.

Meteors are visible as falling stars. They usually burn up before reaching Earth. Any part of a meteor that reaches Earth's surface is known as a *meteorite*.

Many meteors are the debris of comets and do not reach Earth's surface. The meteors that hit Earth are small asteroids composed largely of iron and nickel or stone, capable of withstanding the enormous heat of entry into Earth's atmosphere.

THE SUN AND STARS

are huge, shining spherical masses of gas in space that produce a tremendous amount of light and energy.

The stars look like twinkling points of light—except for the sun. The sun looks like a ball because it is much closer to Earth than any other star.

The sun and most other stars are made of gas and a hot, gaslike substance known as *plasma*. But some stars, called white dwarfs and neutron stars, consist of tightly packed atoms or subatomic particles. These stars are therefore much more dense than anything on Earth.

The Sun: A Typical Star

The sun, our own star, is an average, or typical, star, for it is about halfway between the faintest and the brightest and the smallest and the largest of known stars. The sun formed about 4.6 billion years ago.

The energy of the sun comes from nuclear fusion reactions that occur deep inside the sun's core. In a fusion reaction, two atomic nuclei join together, creating a new nucleus. Fusion produces energy by converting nuclear matter into energy.

The Solar Atmosphere
The solar atmosphere is made up of

- the *photosphere*
- the *chromosphere*
- the *corona*

 *The sun's mass makes up 99.8 percent of the mass of the solar system.*

The Sun	
Distance from Earth	*Average*, about 149,600,000 kilometers (92,960,000 miles)
Sunlight	Takes about 8 minutes to reach Earth, traveling at 299,792 kilometers (186,282 miles) per second
Radius	About 695,500 kilometers (432,000 miles)
Volume	About 14×10^{17} cu. km (33×10^{16} cu. mi.)
Mass	About 2×10^{27} metric tons (2.2×10^{27} tons)
Density	*Average*, about 1.4 grams per cu. cm (90 lb. per cu. ft.), roughly 1.4 times the density of water
Temperature	*Surface*, about 5,800K (5,500°C or 10,000°F); core, more than 15 millionK (15 million°C or 27 million°F)
Age	About 4.6 billion years
Chemical makeup	By mass: about 72% hydrogen; about 26% helium; other elements, roughly 2% By number of atoms: about 94% hydrogen; about 6% helium; other elements, about 0.1%
Luminosity	The rate at which the sun sends out energy: about 4×10^{26} watts
Solar constant	Amount of energy from the sun that arrives at the top of Earth's atmosphere: about 1,370 watts per sq. m
Rotation period	About 25 days at the equator; about 28 days at higher latitudes
Revolution period	(In the Milky Way Galaxy): about 250 million years

The **photosphere** is a layer of gas that makes up the lowest layer of the atmosphere.

The photosphere is about 500 kilometers (310 miles) thick. It has a temperature at the outer edge of 4,300K (7,280°F). The temperature at its inner boundary is 6,600K (11,420°F).

The photosphere consists of *granules,* which are caused by the convection of hot matter just under the visible layer. As in boiling water, hot gas elements rise to the surface while cooled elements sink. The small difference in temperature between the cool and hot elements is enough to cause a difference in brilliance that is easily observed from Earth.

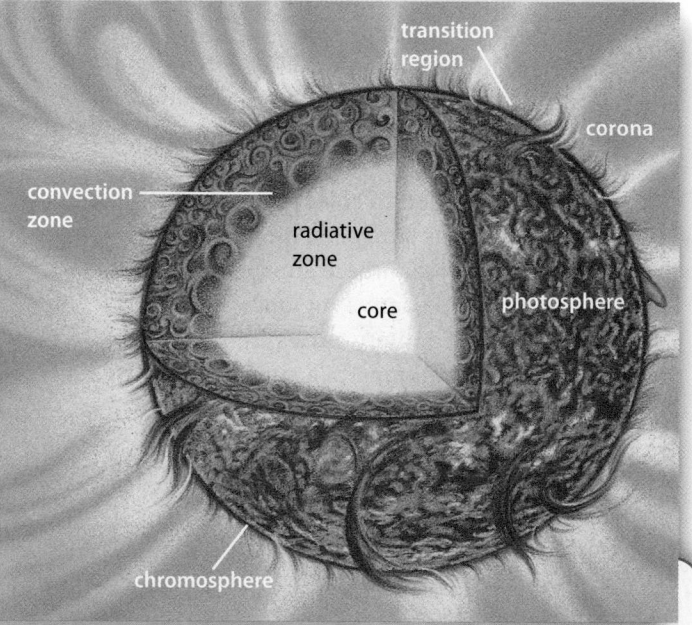

▲ **Solar Structure.** The sun and its atmosphere consist of several zones. Energy flows from the core through radiative and convection zones. The thin photosphere, the lowest part of the atmosphere, produces the light we see.

The **chromosphere** is the layer above the photosphere. The chromosphere extends from the photosphere to an altitude of several thousand kilometers. It consists of numerous gas jets, called *spicules.*

Spicules are typically 1,000 kilometers (620 miles) across and rise up to heights of 10,000 kilometers (6,200 miles). The gas masses rise upward with velocities of about 25 kilometers (15 miles) per second. Each mass has an average lifetime of about 15 minutes.

Going toward the outer edge of the chromosphere, the temperature of the gas rises from about 4,500K

(7,640°F) to 400,000K (720,000°F). The increase in temperature is caused by the increasing speed of the particles that are flowing away from the sun.

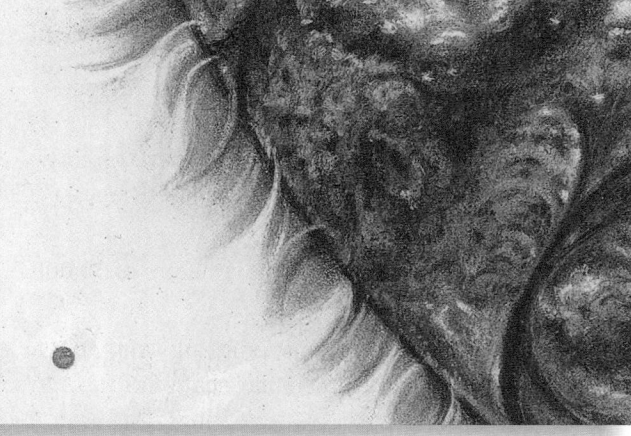

▲ **The sun** has a radius that is 109 times that of Earth. The sun's volume is about 1,300,000 times Earth's volume, and its mass is 333,000 times that of Earth.

The **corona** is a very thin envelope of gas surrounding the sun and extending far from the sun, a distance as great as several solar radii.

Because the corona gives off a million times less light than the photosphere, it can be observed with the naked eye only during an eclipse or with an instrument called a coronagraph.

The temperature in the corona is believed to reach 2,000,000K (3,600,000°F). The corona, however, radiates very little heat. The high temperature is only a measure of the high average speed of the individual particles. Because of the high temperature, the corona is a strong emitter of X-rays. (See page 835.)

Solar Activity

The sun, like Earth, is magnetic. The sun's magnetic fields rise through the convection zone and erupt through the photosphere into the chromosphere and corona.

The eruptions lead to solar activity, which includes such phenomena as sunspots, flares, and coronal mass ejections. Areas where sunspots or eruptions occur are known as active regions.

The amount of activity varies from a *solar minimum* at the beginning of a sunspot cycle to a *solar maximum* about 5 years later.

SOLAR WIND

A constant stream of particles, mainly electrons and protons, flows from the sun's corona into interplanetary space. This stream is known as the *solar wind*.

- Because of the high temperature in the corona, individual particles have enough energy to escape into space.
- The corona is replenished continuously by the gases escaping through the spicules in the chromosphere.
- Approximately 100 billion tons of particles escape from the sun every day; although this figure seems enormous, it would take at least 55 trillion years for the sun to evaporate.
- The solar wind particles reach Earth with a speed of 600 kilometers (375 miles) per second.
- The solar wind carries a magnetic field with it; it strongly influences the magnetosphere of Earth and other planets.

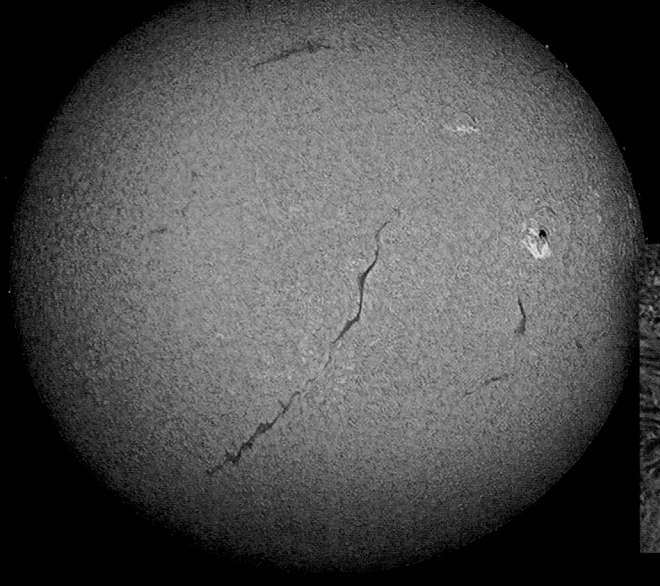

◀ **Sunspots** are slightly cooler than the rest of the surface of the sun. This sunspot is larger than Earth. The yellowish clumps outside the sunspot are granulation cells, which are about 1,000 kilometers (600 miles) across.

Sunspots

The most conspicuous markings on the sun are sunspots. Even without a telescope, sunspots can sometimes be observed at sunset.

Dark Spots. Sunspots appear as dark regions on the photosphere that start out as tiny specks and grow. Their lifetime is usually a few weeks to a few months, after which they gradually disappear.

A typical sunspot consists of a central dark region called the *umbra* surrounded by a brighter region called the *penumbra*.

- Sunspots sometimes grow to diameters of 50,000 kilometers (31,000 miles).
- They occur in pairs, groups, or strings and appear to move slowly across the sun because of the sun's rotation.
- The temperature in a spot is approximately 4,500K (7,640°F), or 2,000K (3,600°F), cooler than the surrounding photosphere.

Solar Flares

Solar flares are sudden, short-lived, spectacular outbreaks releasing large amounts of energy, sometimes equivalent to the explosion of 10 billion 1-megaton hydrogen bombs.

Radiated Waves. Flares transmit a large amount of ultraviolet light, X-rays, radio waves, and streams of charged particles. Flares often have strongly noticeable effects on Earth.

- The radiation causes disturbances in the ionosphere that result in auroras, disruptions of short-wave radio communications, and voltage surges in electrical transmission lines.

- The radiation can cause magnetic storms.

- It can pose radiation hazards to astronauts and planes flying at very high altitudes.

Nuclear Fusion

The nature of the sun's energy source remained a mystery until the development of nuclear physics in the years before World War II.

The American physicist Hans Bethe worked out the theory that nuclear fusion reactions furnish the enormous amounts of energy liberated by the sun.

The Process. In nuclear fusion, four hydrogen atoms combine into one helium atom and release energy.

This reaction can occur only under conditions of extremely high temperature (when the particles have high kinetic energy) and extremely high pressure (when the particles have a reasonable chance of colliding). (See Chemistry, page 405; Physics, page 861.)

Core Fusion. The fusion of hydrogen into helium occurs in the sun's core. The released energy is transported by radiation toward the outer layers.

Emitted Photons. The photons leaving the sun's core, however, are absorbed, reemitted, and scattered in the sun's interior on their path to the outer layers. It takes a million years for the photons to reach the outer layers of the sun.

The sun blazes with energy. On its surface, magnetic forces create loops and streams of gas that extend tens of thousands of miles into space. ▼

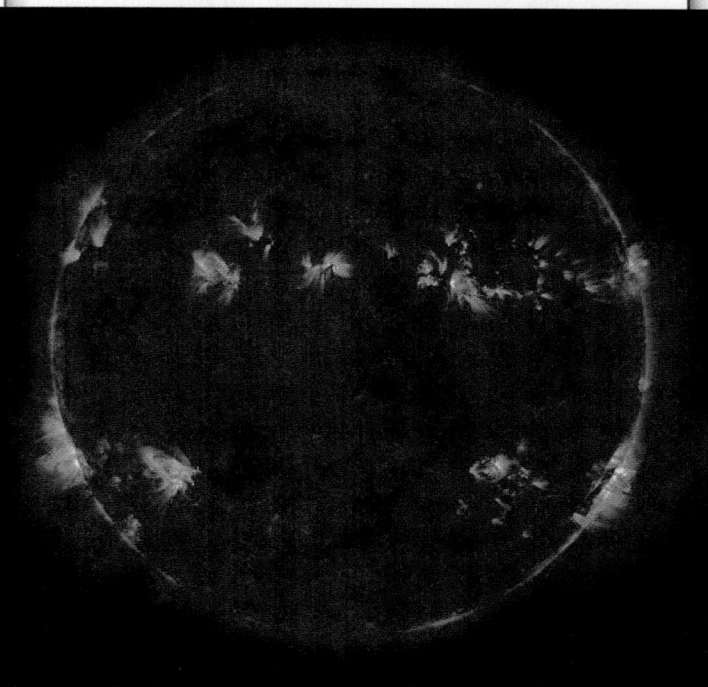

Neutrinos

The nuclear reactions in the core of the sun produce electrically neutral particles called *neutrinos*.

- Because they have no mass or electric charge, neutrinos pass almost unhindered through matter.

- In contrast to the photons produced in the sun's core, which take a million years to reach the photosphere, neutrinos pass through the sun instantly.

Detecting Neutrinos. Since neutrinos hardly interact with matter, they are difficult to detect. However, when they interact with chlorine-37 atoms, a radioactive argon atom is produced.

Deep Down. Neutrino detectors must be placed deep underground where other types of particles cannot penetrate. Scientists have found fewer neutrinos than expected in their detectors. Astronomers have not yet explained the discrepancy between predictions and experimental findings.

THE STARS

Like the sun, stars are huge spherical masses of gas that began radiating energy because of nuclear reactions occurring deep within their interiors.

Stars do, however, differ greatly in size, luminosity, temperature, and composition. The smallest stars have a radius of about 10 kilometers (6 miles). The largest have a radius of about 1 billion kilometers (650 million miles).

The nuclear reactions in the cores of stars can also be different. When the hydrogen in the core is depleted, stars can begin to convert helium into carbon and carbon into heavier elements.

Stellar Distance

Because stars are so far away, it is impractical to use kilometers, miles, or even astronomical units to express their distances. One of the units used is the *light-year*.

Light's Journey

One light-year is equal to the distance light travels in 1 year.

$$94,607 \times 10^9 \text{ kilometers } (5,878 \times 10^9 \text{ miles})$$

Near and Far. The closest star to the sun, Proxima Centauri, is about 4.5 light-years away, corresponding to 284,750 AU. The most distant stars in our galaxy are more than 50,000 light-years away.

Back in Time

It is interesting to note that when we look across huge distances, expressed in thousands of light-years, we also look back in time thousands of years.

For example, quasars are at distances of billions of light-years. When we examine them, we are observing phenomena that occurred not long after the big bang. (See page 962.)

▲ **A star forms** from a massive cloud of dust and gas. The cloud slowly rotates, collapsing in on itself due to its own gravity. As it shrinks, it rotates more rapidly, eventually forming a spherical clump, which continues to collapse.

STAR FORMATION

Stars begin their lives through the gravitational contraction of clouds of gas and dust.

- The collapsing mass heats up because the pressure increases. (This is exactly the same process that heats up the air in a bicycle pump when it is being used.)

- After a while, the mass of gas becomes spherical and glows red: a protostar is formed.

- As the gravitational contraction continues, the confined temperature and pressure at the center of the gaseous mass initiates the nuclear reactions that supply the energy of a fully formed star.

Star formation is an ongoing process in areas of the galaxy rich in dust and gas, such as the Orion nebula. The heated dust clouds radiate strongly in infrared light. Several areas of active star formation have been photographed by means of the IRAS satellite.

Measuring Stellar Distances

The basic way of measuring the distance to a star is by the *trigonometric parallax method.*

- As Earth moves around the sun, a star relatively nearby will appear to shift its position in the sky relative to more distant stars.

- The trigonometric parallax is half the total apparent shift of the star with respect to the background.

- The parallax of a star, then, is the angle formed at the star by the triangle formed between the star and each end of the radius of Earth's orbit.

- A parallax of 1 second of arc equals a distance of 1 parsec, or 3.26 light-years.

Spectroscopic Parallax. The intensity of light varies inversely as the square of the distance. When we look at two stars of the same intrinsic brightness, but one is twice as far away as the other, the more distant star will appear four times fainter than the closer one.

The intensity of certain absorption lines in stellar spectra depends strongly on the intrinsic brightness of the star. A star's distance can be derived by noting how bright or faint it appears.

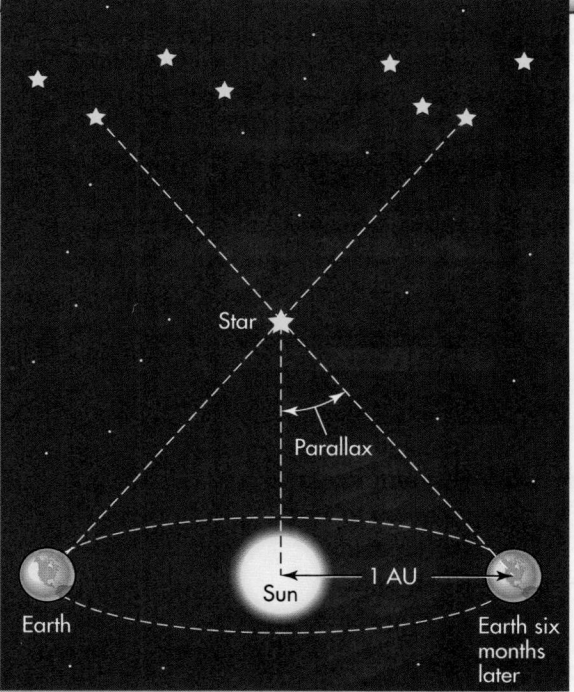

▲ **Parallax.** By definition, a parallax of 1 second of arc corresponds to a distance of 1 parsec (parallax of 1 second). The distance of a star in parsecs is thus 1/parallax. One parsec is equal to 3.26 light-years.

The Basics: Stars	
Number	Perhaps more than 10 billion trillion in the known universe
Age	Up to about 13 billion years. Most stars are from 1 million to 10 billion years old.
Composition	As determined by mass, at least 71 percent hydrogen and roughly 27 percent helium. Oxygen and carbon account for most of the remaining mass.
Mass	From about 1/10 of the mass of the sun to more than 100 times the mass of the sun
Largest known stars	Supergiant stars that have a radius of roughly 650 million miles (1 billion kilometers)—about 1,500 times the radius of the sun
Smallest known stars	Neutron stars that have a radius of approximately 6 miles (10 kilometers)
Colors	Ranging from reddish for the coolest stars to yellowish for warmer stars, to bluish for the hottest stars
Temperature	Surface: from about 2,500K (2,200°C or 4,000°F) for dark red stars to about 50,000K (50,000°C or 90,000°F) for the hottest blue stars
	Core: about 10 millionK (10 million°C or 18 million°F) in stars in which hydrogen is fusing to form helium, to nearly 10 billionK (10 billion°C or 18 billion°F) in collapsing stars that are about to produce supernova explosions
Energy source	Nuclear fusion that changes hydrogen into helium or similar fusion processes that produce heavier and heavier chemical elements up to iron

Star Light, Star Bright

How bright a star looks when viewed from Earth depends on two factors.

1. the actual brightness of the star—that is, the amount of light energy the star emits (sends out)

2. the distance from Earth to the star

A nearby star that is actually dim can appear brighter than a distant star that is really extremely brilliant.

Magnitude	
Object	**Apparent Magnitude**
The sun	−26.7
The moon	−12.6
Venus (at maximum brightness)	−4.0
Sirius	−1.4
Betelgeuse	−0.7
Rigel	0.12

Magnitude

In about 125 BC, the Greek astronomer Hipparchus categorized stars in six classes of brightness, the brightest having a magnitude of 1 and the dimmest a magnitude of 6.

ABSOLUTE MAGNITUDE

Because a star's apparent magnitude depends both on the intrinsic brightness and the distance of the star from Earth, astronomers introduced the concept of absolute magnitude: the magnitude a star would have if it were at a distance of 10 parsecs, or 32.6 light-years.

The Magnitude Scale. Astronomers have preserved this definition of the magnitude scale; in the middle of the 19th century, they agreed to a scale based on that of Hipparchus. Today, however, they measure both a star's *apparent magnitude*—its brightness as viewed from Earth—and its *absolute magnitude*—its actual brightness.

- The difference of 5 magnitudes corresponds exactly to a ratio of 100 in brightness.

- If five steps correspond to a ratio of 100, one step corresponds to the fifth root of 100, which is 2.5.

- Each step in the magnitude scale corresponds to a factor of 2.5 in brightness.

Astronomers have maintained this system because the response of photographic emulsion is also a logarithmic function of light intensity.

Extending the Scale. Astronomers have extended the magnitude scale to include objects brighter than the brightest stars: the planets, the sun, and the moon. For this, the scale has been extended to negative numbers.

When photometry became more accurate, it was found that the stars Sirius and Betelgeuse have negative magnitudes.

With good binoculars we can see stars with magnitudes of 9. The photographic limit of the Hale telescope is 24.

◀ **Pleiades** is a star cluster in the constellation Taurus. Some of its stars have magnitudes between 3 and 4.

Luminosity

Luminosity is the rate at which a star emits energy. The luminosity of a star depends directly on its size and on how brightly each unit of area shines.

luminosity = surface area ×
luminosity per unit area

Brightness and Size. A big star can appear bright even though it is relatively faint per unit area. A small, intensely brilliant star can appear as bright as an enormous but faint star.

The total luminosity of a star, therefore, reveals nothing of the star's size unless we also know the star's surface brightness. To find this, the star's temperature must be known.

◄ **Rigel** is the eighth brightest star in Earth's sky. Its bluish color indicates that it is an extremely hot star—about 12,000K.

Color and Temperature

Even without binoculars or a telescope, it is possible to see a range of color in the stars, from reddish to yellowish to bluish. For example, Betelgeuse looks reddish, Pollux—like the sun—is yellowish, and Rigel looks bluish.

The color of a star is a fairly good indicator of its surface temperature. The hotter the temperature, the bluer the color.

We can compare this to a piece of metal that is heated.

- At first, it glows a dull red.
- Then, as its temperature rises, it becomes brighter.
- It becomes, in turn, orange and then bright yellow.
- If the metal does not melt and vaporize, it will become green and then blue.

Stars, of course, are completely vaporized, but they still conform with the laws of radiation.

Stars by Color and Temperature		
Star	**Color**	**Temperature**
Arcturus	Orange-yellow	about 4,100K (6,900°F)
The sun	Yellow	about 5,800K (9,900°F)
Rigel	Bluish	about 12,000K (21,600°F)

Stellar Spectra. Like the sun, stars are surrounded by a gaseous atmosphere consisting mainly of hydrogen, a lesser amount of helium, and a small amount of other elements.

Absorption in this atmosphere produces the Fraunhofer lines that are superimposed on the continuous spectrum of the star. The spectra of hotter stars contain a smaller number of Fraunhofer lines than the spectra of cooler stars.

Classifying the Stars

Astronomers classify stars based on their characteristics. The main characteristics by which stars are classified are

- *luminosity*, the rate at which a star emits energy.
- surface temperature.
- *absolute magnitude,* the apparent magnitude a star would have if it were at a distance of 10 parsecs, or 32.6 light-years.

GRAPHING THE STARS

At the beginning of the 20th century, two astronomers—Ejnar Hertzsprung of Denmark and American Henry Russell—independently developed graphs to record the relationship between the color and absolute magnitude of a star.

Today, astronomers use one diagram—the Hertzsprung-Russell diagram—to display the main characteristics of stars.

Luminosity Classes

In the 1930s, American astronomers William W. Morgan and Philip C. Keenan invented what came to be known as the *MK luminosity classification system* to group different kinds of stars. Astronomers revised and extended this system in 1978.

In the MK system, the largest and brightest classes have the lowest classification numbers.

The MK classes are: Ia, bright supergiant; Ib, supergiant; II, bright giant; III, giant; IV, subgiant; and V, main sequence or dwarf.

Overlapping Classes. Because temperature also affects the luminosity of a star, stars from different luminosity classes can overlap. For example, Spica, a class V star, has an absolute magnitude of −3.2; but Pollux, a class III star, is dimmer, with an absolute magnitude of 0.7.

Spectral Classes

In the MK system, there are eight spectral classes, each corresponding to a certain range of surface temperature.

- From the hottest stars to the coolest, these classes are: O, B, A, F, G, K, and M.
- Each spectral class, in turn, is made up of 10 spectral types, which are designated by the letter for the spectral class and a numeral.
- The hottest stars in a spectral class are assigned the numeral 0; the coolest stars, the numeral 9.

A complete MK designation thus includes symbols for luminosity class and spectral type.

- The complete designation for the sun is G2V.
- Alpha Centauri A is also a G2V star.
- The complete designation for Rigel is B8Ia.

STELLAR CLASSIFICATION

Luminosity Classes	
Ia	bright supergiant
Iab	less bright supergiant
Ib	supergiant
II	bright giant
III	giant
IV	subgiant
V	main sequence
VI	subdwarf
VII	white dwarf

Spectral Classes		
Type	Temperature Range (Kelvin)	Color
O	100,000–30,000	blue-white
B	25,000–12,000	blue-white
A	11,000–8,000	white
F	7,800–6,200	creamy
G	6,000–4,600	yellow
K	4,900–3,350	orange
M	3,400–2,600	red

THE HERTZSPRUNG-RUSSELL DIAGRAM

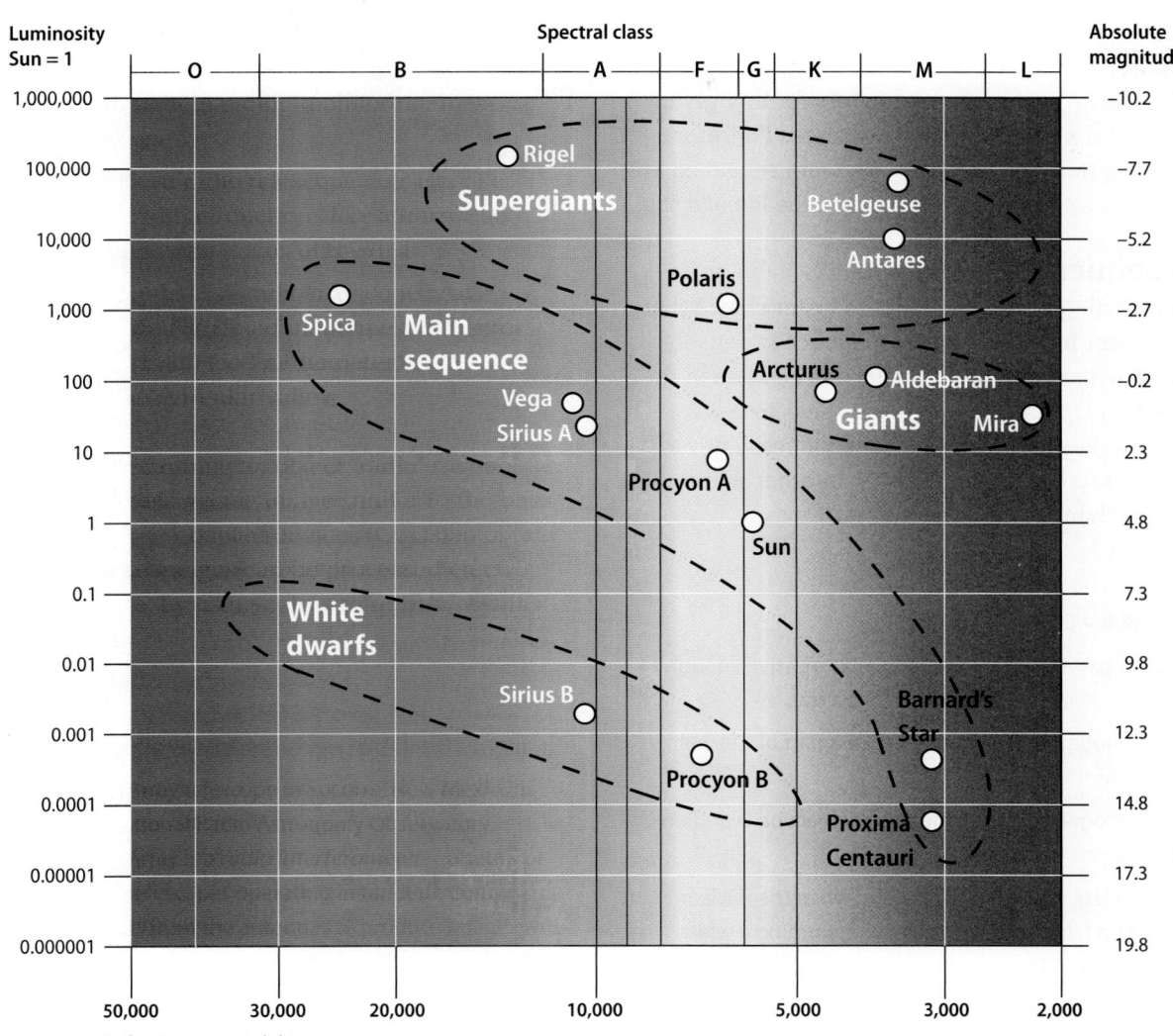

The Hertzsprung-Russell (H-R) diagram is one of the most important graphs of astrophysics. It shows that the great majority of stars fall on the *main sequence,* a nearly straight line running from highly luminous, hot, bluish stars down to faint, relatively cool, reddish stars. A given temperature and size go together. Thus, along the main sequence, any stars having the same temperature will also be of the same magnitude.

Mass-Luminosity Relation. Measurements of a small number of stars have shown that the luminosity L is proportional to the third power of the mass of a star. This relationship—the *mass-luminosity relation*—implies that for main sequence stars, the bright stars are much more massive than the faint stars.

Exceptions to the Rule. Spectral type does not always correspond to only one absolute magnitude. For example, Alpha Aurigae and Alpha Centauri are both G-type stars, but they differ strongly in absolute magnitude, 0.3 and 4.4, respectively.

Since the surface temperature has to be approximately the same, the much higher luminosity can only be explained by assuming that the star is much larger. Hertzsprung introduced the term *giant* for these large stars. The stars that lie above the main sequence in the H-R diagram include the red and yellow giants and the very large *supergiants.*

Similarly, there are groups of stars that are much fainter than their counterparts in the main sequence. These stars are much smaller and are called white dwarfs.

Life of a Star

When a star first develops from a primordial gas cloud, it becomes a member of the main sequence at a point appropriate to its mass.

By far the largest majority of stars for any given cluster are found in the main sequence. Therefore, astronomers think that stars in the main sequence are in the longest and most stable phase in the life of a star.

Main Sequence Phase

The H-R diagram of an old star cluster shows that only the lower half of the main sequence is densely populated with stars. (See page 945.) The stars in the upper half of the main sequence appear to have migrated to the right of the main sequence. They are cooling but retain their luminosity. In other words, they are evolving to become giants.

STELLAR EVOLUTION

A. A cloud of gas and dust contracts. If it is massive enough to support nuclear reactions, it becomes a star.

B. The star through most of its existence is part of the main sequence of stars.

C. As the hydrogen that fuels the nuclear reaction is depleted, the star begins to expand.

D. In a star of less than 1.4 solar masses, when the nuclear reactions end, the star again contracts, forming a white dwarf. Then, as it cools, it forms a black dwarf.

E. When a star is greater than 1.4 solar masses, a supernova occurs. If the remaining core is massive enough, the star becomes a black hole. Otherwise, it becomes a neutron star.

Bigger, Faster. These examples confirm the theory that more massive stars evolve faster than their less massive counterparts. This can be understood if one considers that the temperature in the cores of more massive stars becomes higher because of greater compression. Consequently, the nuclear reactions proceed much faster.

Tracking a Star's Evolution

The plot of the successive positions of an evolving star in the H-R diagram is called an *evolutionary track*.

- A *protostar*—a ball-shaped object that is no longer just a cloud of gas and dust, but is not yet a star— starts somewhere on the right of the main sequence and evolves rapidly toward the main sequence.

- Almost throughout its entire life, the star remains on the main sequence.

- When the hydrogen in its core is depleted, the star starts moving away and becomes a giant.

A star's ultimate fate depends on its mass.

- It can end up as a dwarf or as a neutron star.
- It can end its life by exploding as a supernova.
- It can become a black hole.

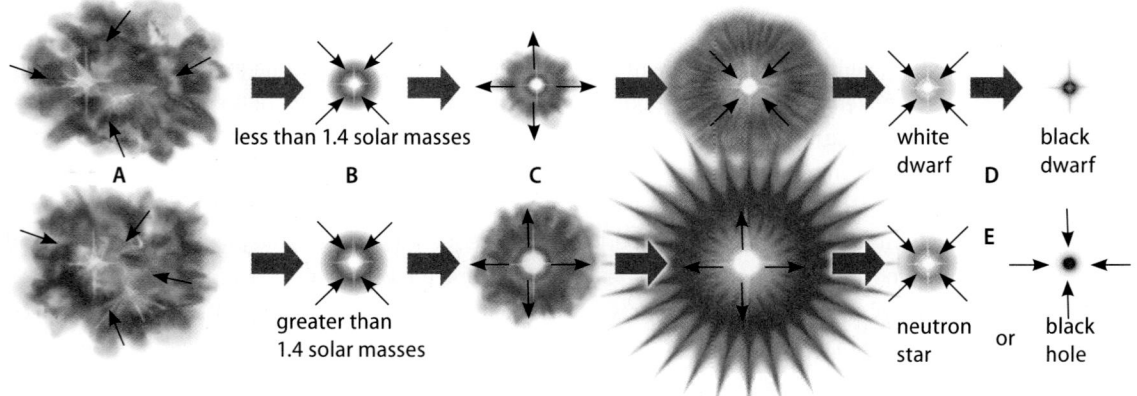

less than 1.4 solar masses
A   B   C   white dwarf   black dwarf   D

greater than 1.4 solar masses
E   neutron star   or   black hole

Different Paths

Depending on the initial mass of the protostar, the evolution of a star can take different courses.

False Starts. Protostars of less than 0.1 solar mass never become stars. The temperature in the core does not reach the required temperature and pressure for nuclear reactions.

These objects quickly fade away as faint red dwarfs and become invisible. Many astronomers consider Jupiter to be such a failed star.

Hot Enough. Protostars between 0.1 and 1.4 solar mass contract slowly until the core reaches a temperature of about 10,000,000K and the nuclear reactions begin.

In stars of lower mass, the proton-proton cycle is the most important mechanism for conversion of hydrogen into helium.

Hotter Still. In hotter stars, the carbon cycle is the more important reaction mechanism. When the hydrogen in the core is depleted, the star leaves the main sequence and begins to convert helium into carbon.

The star's volume increases enormously as the surface temperature decreases. Because of the increased volume, the star becomes much more luminous.

The giant phase is relatively short. It has been calculated that for the sun, it will last only 100 million years.

Even in the giant phase, the temperature in the core is not high enough for nuclear reactions beyond the formation of carbon and oxygen. When the nuclear fuel becomes exhausted, the star begins to contract.

Forming a White Dwarf. With no thermonuclear reactions to stave it off, gravitation wins the battle. The core of the star goes on contracting until a white dwarf is formed.

Final Stages

White dwarfs were first discovered as the fainter companions in double star systems.

Dog and Pup. The bright star Sirius, also known as the Dog Star, has a companion, Sirius B (sometimes called the Pup).

- Sirius B is a white dwarf.
- It has a mass similar to that of the sun but with a size smaller than that of Neptune.
- The density of the star is very high.
- In fact, the Pup is so dense that a cubic inch of it would weigh 10 tons on Earth.

Compressed Matter. A white dwarf can form only if the mass left over when the nuclear reactions end is less than 1.4 times the mass of the sun. Below that mass, the star will be held up by electron pressure.

In a white dwarf, compression of matter is so high that all allowed energy levels are fully occupied with electrons. There is no room for further compression.

A Common End. According to estimates, 99.9 percent of all stars end their careers as white dwarfs.

The white dwarfs continue to radiate energy and cool down slowly. They become fainter and fainter and become black dwarfs, huge chunks of crystalline and extremely dense matter unobservable from Earth.

▲ **Two white dwarfs** orbit each other about 1,600 light-years from Earth. Their gravity is so high that they orbit each other once every 321 seconds, even though they are about 80,000 kilometers (50,000 miles) apart.

Supernovas and Neutron Stars

Supernovas

A *supernova* is an exploding star that can become billions of times as bright as the sun before gradually fading from view. At its brightest, a supernova may outshine an entire galaxy.

When a Supernova Occurs. Only the 0.1 percent of stars that reach the 1.4 solar-mass limit become supernovas. Because of their greater mass, these stars spend less time as main sequence stars. In the giant phase, the core temperature becomes much higher.

When hydrogen is depleted, the star converts helium through fusion reactions.

The fusion reactions stop with iron because the fusion of iron into heavier elements would consume energy instead of producing it.

Fusion Reactions
helium → carbon and oxygen
carbon → neon
oxygen → silicon
silicon → nickel, cobalt, and iron

NOVAS

Novas are also explosions of stars, but they are less violent. Forty novas occur in a given year in our galaxy.

- A nova can brighten up to 9 magnitudes in a few days and can reach luminosities of 100,000 suns.
- Novas occur in double-star systems and may be caused when one star draws hydrogen-rich material from the other.
- The star receiving the matter heats up because of the additional gravitational contraction.
- Suddenly, new nuclear reactions begin in the star's core and cause the explosion.

One cubic centimeter of matter from a neutron star would weigh about 200 million tons on Earth.

How a Supernova Occurs. As soon as the nuclear reactions stop, the core collapses catastrophically in a fraction of a second.

- Gravity crushes the core together into a small sphere about 16 kilometers (10 miles) across.
- The pressure is so enormous that the electrons are forced to combine with protons to form neutrons.
- Neutron pressure eventually builds up to the point at which it can resist further gravitational collapse.
- The result is that the core is transformed into a neutron star or, if the remaining core exceeds about 2 solar masses, it is transformed into a black hole.

The Collapsing Core. During the resulting collapse of the core, the outer layers of the star are blown off by a shock wave traveling from the core outward.

Some astronomers believe that this phenomenon is the result of an enormous flux of neutrinos coming from the collapsing core and dispersing the outer layers of the star into space. (See page 862.)

Neutron Stars

Neutron stars are the smallest and densest type of star known.

- Matter is crushed to such a degree that the electron pressure is not sufficient to withstand the pressure.
- Electrons combine with protons to form neutrons.
- Matter in that form consists, then, of neutrons packed side by side.
- Its density is incredibly high, 10^{15} times the density of ordinary matter—about as dense as the nucleus of an atom.

Star Nucleus. There are 20 times more neutrons than protons in a neutron star. The star can be viewed as a huge atomic nucleus containing a very large number of nucleons. The neutrons form a rigid crystalline structure, making the star behave like a solid sphere.

▲ **The Crab Nebula** is a cloud of gas thrown off by a star in a supernova explosion. Chinese astronomers recorded the supernova in the year 1054. It is about 6,000 light-years from Earth in the constellation Taurus.

Two Types of Supernovas. The most luminous ones, type I, can reach a brightness as much as 10 million times that of the sun. During the explosion, a relatively small amount of mass is ejected into space.

Type II supernovas are less bright, up to only 1 million times the brightness of the sun. A much larger proportion of stellar mass is blown into space. It is believed that in type II supernovas, the remaining core collapses into a black hole.

Heavy Atoms. During the explosion, atoms are accelerated to such energies that they are able to combine to form the heavier elements. Astronomers believe supernovas are the source of the heavier elements found in stars like the sun and that constitute Earth, planets, and even living matter.

Pulsars are rapidly spinning neutron stars. They send regular bursts of electromagnetic radiation that are received on Earth. Most of this radiation takes the form of radio waves.

Pulsars provided astronomers with the first proof that neutron stars exist.

- Physicists predicted the existence of neutron stars in 1938.
- The prediction remained a theory until 1967, when radio telescopes in England picked up regular bursts of radio waves from an object in space.
- Scientists named these wave-emitting objects pulsars, and later concluded that they are actually neutron stars.

In 1968, a pulsar was discovered in the middle of the Crab nebula. The remnant of the supernova observed in the year 1054, it transmits radio pulses with a period of 30 milliseconds.

▲ **Pulsars** rotate extremely quickly. The fastest pulsar known has a period of 1.5 milliseconds. A pulsar has an extremely powerful magnetic field, and it emits regular bursts of electromagnetic radiation from its magnetic poles.

Black Holes and Binary Stars

Black Holes

A *black hole* is a region of space whose gravitational force is so strong that nothing can escape from it. A black hole is invisible because it even traps light.

Neutron Star Limits. Just as there is a limit to the mass of a dwarf star consisting of electron-degenerate matter, there is an upper mass limit to the existence of a neutron star. (See pages 946–947.)

This limit is estimated to be about 3 solar masses. Above that value, the stellar core of neutron-degenerate matter cannot support itself and begins collapsing even further into a black hole.

Relativity and Black Holes. The fundamental descriptions of black holes are based on equations in the theory of general relativity developed by the physicist Albert Einstein. Einstein's theory describes gravity as the degree of curvature of space-time.

Characteristics of Black Holes

- The gravitational force is strong near a black hole because all the black hole's matter is concentrated at a single point in its center—the *singularity*.

- The singularity of a black hole is believed to be much smaller than an atom's nucleus.

- A black hole is surrounded by a region around its singularity called the *event horizon*.

- At the event horizon, the pull of gravity becomes infinitely strong. An object can exist there for only an instant as it plunges inward at the speed of light.

- The radius of the event horizon depends on the amount of mass that has collapsed.

- Astronomers use the event horizon's radius to specify the size of a black hole.

Proving Their Existence. Astronomers have found compact objects that are likely black holes, but have not yet discovered a black hole for certain.

To prove that a compact object is a black hole, scientists would have to measure such effects as severe bending of a light beam and an extreme slowing of time.

▲ **A supermassive black hole** sucks in a swirling disk of matter, shooting out beams of particles in this artist's conception. A supermassive black hole has a mass from millions to billions of times that of the sun.

PROBABLE BLACK HOLE

There are two X-ray sources that may be black holes. The most promising candidate, discovered by the *Uhuru* satellite, is called Cygnus X-1. Other satellites have also discovered gamma rays coming from this object.

Cygnus X-1 is at a distance of 6,000 light-years from Earth and consists of a blue supergiant star of about 30 solar masses around which rotates a highly condensed object of about 14 solar masses.

Cygnus X-1 emits X-rays that astronomers think are produced by matter flowing from the supergiant to the black hole. The matter spirals in a disklike region around the black hole before being swallowed by it. As the matter swirls toward the black hole, it becomes more and more concentrated and heated, and it begins emitting X-rays.

Binary Stars

A *binary star*, or a *double star*, is a pair of stars that revolve around each other and are held together by gravity.

Bigger, Closer, Faster.
The orbital speed of binary stars depends mostly on two factors.

- **Mass:** The greater a star's mass, the stronger its gravity and the faster it pulls its companion around in orbit.

- **Proximity:** The closer the two stars are to each other, the faster they revolve.

Some are so close as to almost touch and can go around each other in just a few hours or minutes. Other pairs may be separated by many times the diameter of the solar system and take a million years to revolve around each other.

The Numbers.
Perhaps as many as 25 percent of the stars in our galaxy have a partner. Some stars have more than one partner. The "star" Castor in the Gemini constellation is at least six stars.

Approximately 50 percent of all stars belong to double or multiple star systems.

Contact Binaries.
The stars in some binaries are so close that they touch. In these *contact binaries,* the gravity of each star distorts its companion, causing enormous tides to form on the surfaces of both stars. Violent events can occur in such close pairs.

- One star may become an *X-ray pulsar,* a star that radiates X-rays in precisely timed bursts.

- Other close pairs radiate powerful radio waves.

- In others, one of the stars pulls matter to itself from the other star. This matter may explode in nuclear reactions, causing the star to flare brightly.

fyi! *The fastest binaries can complete an orbit in less than 6 minutes traveling at over 480 kilometers (300 miles) per second.*

Ghostly Binaries.
The star Algol, also called Beta Persei, derives its name from an Arabic word meaning *ghoul,* likely due to the star's unusual periodic brightening and dimming.

Algol appears to be a single star, but it is actually a type of double star called an *eclipsing binary.* In such a binary, a pair of stars revolve around each other so that one periodically blocks the light of the other. This action reduces the brightness of the double star as viewed from the earth.

Finding Binaries.
The existence of close binaries can be revealed by a spectrograph.

- When, in its motion, a component approaches Earth, its spectral lines are shifted by the Doppler effect toward the blue end of the spectrum and reduced in wavelength.

- Half a cycle later, when this component recedes from Earth, the lines shift toward the red and the wavelengths increase.

- This Doppler shift can easily be measured. It has led to the discovery of many spectroscopic binaries.

▲ **The binary star system Albireo** consists of two bright stars orbiting 380 light-years apart. They take about 75,000 years to orbit each other once.

THE MILKY WAY is the galaxy that contains the sun, Earth, and other objects in our solar system. It also includes hundreds of billions of stars besides the sun. Huge clouds of gas and dust lie throughout the galaxy, and they constantly form new stars. The Milky Way is so massive that about 10 smaller galaxies orbit it like satellites revolving around a planet.

The name *Milky Way* also refers to the part of the galaxy that can be seen with the unaided eye. On clear, dark nights, this portion of the galaxy appears as a broad, milky-looking band of starlight stretching across the sky.

▲ **Spiral Galaxy.** This galaxy—called NGC 3949 and located about 50 million light-years from Earth—has a similar shape and structure to that of the Milky Way.

A Spiral Galaxy

The Milky Way is shaped like a thin disk with a bulge in the center. To someone far above the galaxy, it would resemble a huge pinwheel. But our view of the Milky Way is dominated by the hazy light from a strip of nearby stars.

There are two reasons why we have this view.

1. We are inside the galaxy.
2. Interstellar dust (dust between the stars) partially blocks the starlight.

The Galaxy's Structure

From optical and radio observations made of our galaxy, and from comparisons with observations made of other galaxies, such as Andromeda, astronomers have been able to construct a precise image of the shape of the Milky Way.

- The galaxy is a huge disk about 100,000 light-years in diameter.
- The five or six spiral arms emerge from a central bulge.
- This bulge is a flattened spheroid about 6,000 light-years in diameter and 3,000 light-years thick.
- The central bulge surrounds the galactic nucleus and has a diameter of about 20 light-years.
- The entire galaxy is surrounded by the galactic halo, a spherical region with a diameter comparable to that of the galaxy.
- The halo contains very thin gas, mainly hydrogen, and globular clusters.
- The globular clusters are distributed quite evenly throughout the galaxy and the galactic halo.
- A giant cloud of gas called the *galactic corona* surrounds the galaxy and its halo. The corona is very thin, but has an estimated mass of more than 1 trillion solar masses.

The galaxy rotates very slowly. The sun travels around the galactic center at a speed of 250 kilometers (155 miles) per second and completes one revolution in 240 million years. In the sun's lifetime of 4.5 billion years, it has revolved 20 times around the galactic center.

The galactic nucleus is located in the direction of Sagittarius, hidden from Earth behind dense clouds of gas and dust. Astronomers have made observations of the nucleus using radio telescopes.

- A small region, about the size of Jupiter's orbit around the sun, produces strong radio waves from the galactic center.
- The same area also radiates strongly in infrared light.
- Taking all the radiation together, the nucleus emits as much radiation as would be emitted by 100 million suns.

Energy Source. The nature of the energy source in the galactic center is still a mystery.

The nucleus may be a massive black hole, perhaps formed by the sudden merging of millions of stars.

Or it may be a region of annihilation of matter and antimatter. Annihilation reactions produce gamma rays. This radiation coming from the nucleus has been detected by gamma ray telescopes aboard satellites.

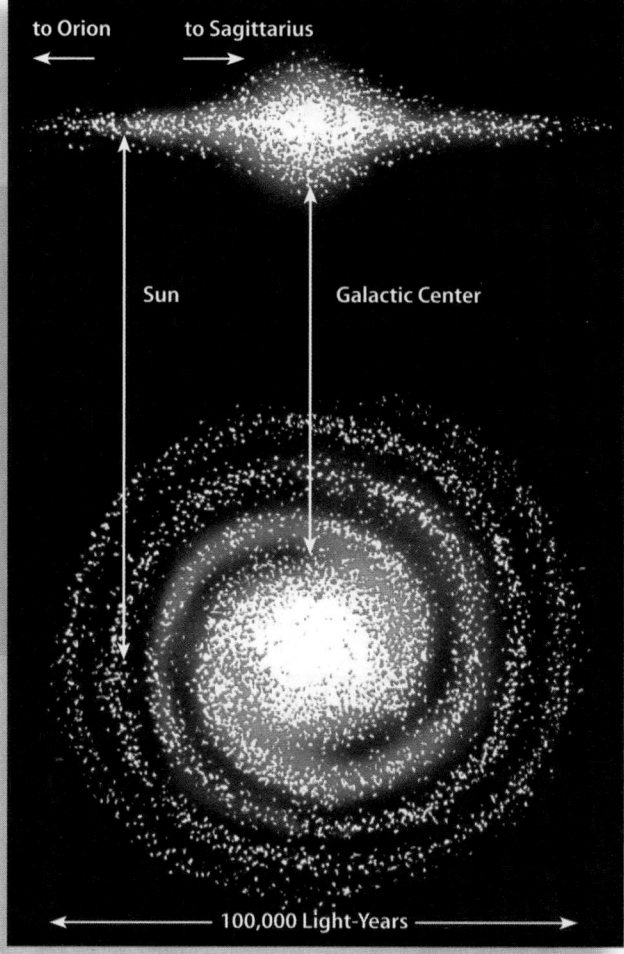

▲ **The Milky Way.** Our sun lies roughly 32,000 light-years from the galactic center.

THE SPIRAL ARMS

The spiral arms of galaxies are regions of active star formation. The newly formed stars and those formed within the last several billion years are known as *Population I* stars.

Older stars, whose histories go back to the early stages of the galaxy, are called *Population II* stars. Population II stars are found chiefly between the spiral arms, outside of the galactic plane, in globular clusters, and in the galactic nucleus.

Population I stars have on average a concentration of metals 100 times greater than Population II stars. The metals and heavy elements were formed in the first-generation stars, blown into galactic space by supernova explosions, and then recycled by Population I stars.

A Dusty Galaxy

On a clear night, the Milky Way can be seen as a whitish band of starlight spread across the sky. When observed through an entire year, this band appears to circle completely around us in the sky. Dark gaps in the band consist of clouds of gas and dust that block out light from the stars behind them.

Interstellar Matter

In fact, about 10 percent of the mass of our galaxy consists of gas and dust. Much of the dust absorbs light, thus obscuring large parts of our galaxy from the view of optical astronomers.

Extinction. The absorption and scattering of starlight by dust is called *extinction*. The extinction is not the same in all directions, but on the average it makes a star at a distance of 1,000 parsecs appear 1 magnitude fainter.

Galactic Nebulas. Some interstellar clouds are visible either because they reflect starlight or because they absorb ultraviolet light and reemit visible light.

- An example of the first type of cloud, a *reflection nebula,* is the nebula surrounding the Pleiades.
- The stars light up the gases in a way similar to that of automobile headlights illuminating dense fog.
- The second type of cloud is called an *emission nebula*. An example is the Great Orion Nebula (M42).
- Emission nebulas are irradiated by very hot stars that are located nearby, usually O-type and B-type.
- The nebulas emit light by *fluorescence*. Their spectra mainly contain hydrogen emission lines.

The dust particles of cosmic rays, it is estimated, are about 100 meters (300 feet) apart, but there are enough of them in line of sight to cause substantial extinction.

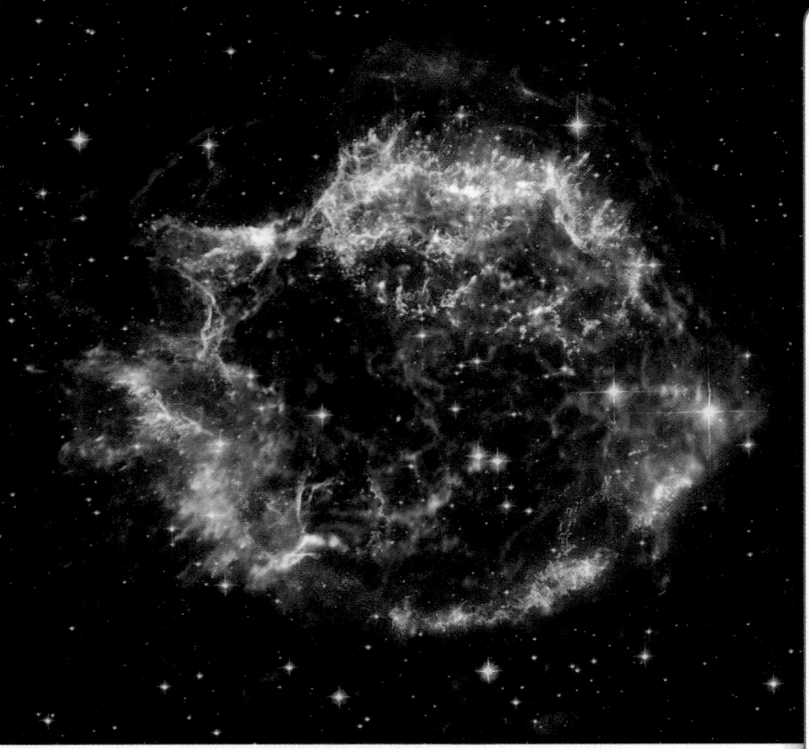

▲ **Cosmic rays** that strike Earth help astronomers study supernovas like Casseiopeia A, shown here in an image taken by the satellite observatory Chandra.

Cosmic Rays

Cosmic rays are electrically charged, high-energy particles that travel through space. They are subatomic particles, units of matter smaller than an atom. (See pages 862–863.)

Astronomers think that cosmic rays fill galaxies, including our own Milky Way, and cross vast stretches of intergalactic space (the space that separates the galaxies).

The Composition of Cosmic Rays	
hydrogen nuclei (protons)	89%
helium nuclei (alpha particles)	9%
electrons	1%
atomic nuclei of heavier elements, mainly those with atomic numbers less than 26 (iron), but some heavier elements	1%

Interstellar Organics. An important recent discovery is that a large number of more complex, and even organic, molecules exist in interstellar space. More than 40 such molecules have been discovered, including those of carbon monoxide, water, ammonia, hydrogen cyanide, ethanol, hydrogen sulfide, and formaldehyde.

The Composition of Interstellar Matter	
hydrogen	about 2/3
helium	about 1/3
heavier elements*	about 2%
*Few of the heavier elements have aggregated into dust particles.	

▲ **The Great Orion Nebula** is located close to the tip of Orion's sword and can be seen easily even with binoculars or a small telescope. It is an emission nebula that is composed of dust and ionized gases that emit their own light.

Studying Cosmic Rays

- Scientists study cosmic rays because these particles include the only matter that reaches Earth from outside the solar system.
- Studies of cosmic rays reveal conditions in intergalactic space and interstellar space.
- Scientists also study cosmic rays to learn about supernovas.

Abundance Distribution. Cosmic rays bombard Earth's atmosphere with about 1,000 protons per square meter (9 square feet) each second. The *abundance distribution,* that is, the relative amount of the elements, is similar to the abundance distribution of the sun and the solar system. The exceptions are the elements lithium, beryllium, and boron, which have much higher abundance distributions in cosmic rays.

Speed and Energy. Cosmic ray particles, which come toward Earth from all directions, possess relativistic velocities—velocities close to that of light. Some of the particles possess enormous energy, much higher than the energy imparted to particles by the largest particle accelerators on Earth. The most energetic particles possess the energy required to lift 2.5 kilograms (5.5 pounds) to a height of 1 meter (3.28 feet).

Primary and Secondary Radiation. Scientists divide cosmic rays into two types.

1. primary cosmic rays, or primaries, which originate in outer space
2. secondary cosmic rays, or secondaries, which originate in Earth's atmosphere

Colliding Rays. Secondaries form when primaries collide with atoms at the top of the atmosphere.

- The collision changes the primary and the atom into a shower of secondaries.
- Many secondaries then collide with other atoms, making more secondaries.
- Some secondaries reach the surface and even penetrate deep into the ground.
- No measurable amount of primaries reaches Earth's surface.

THE UNIVERSE is everything.

It consists of all matter and all light and other forms of radiation and energy. It includes everything that exists anywhere in space and time.

All stars, including the sun, are part of the universe. Some other stars also have planetary systems. In addition to planets, stars, and other bodies, the universe contains gas, dust, magnetic fields, and cosmic rays.

Galaxies

In the 1920s, the American astronomer Edwin P. Hubble discovered that the universe contains many other galaxies beyond our own. The observable universe includes billions, possibly even trillions, of galaxies. Each galaxy consists of from hundreds of thousands to trillions of stars.

Classification

Galaxies come in a variety of sizes and shapes.

- The smallest galaxies, called *dwarf galaxies,* are 2,000 parsecs in diameter and have a mass 10 million times that of the sun.
- The largest galaxies, the *giant ellipticals,* are some 100,000 parsecs in diameter and have a mass 1,000 billion times that of the sun.

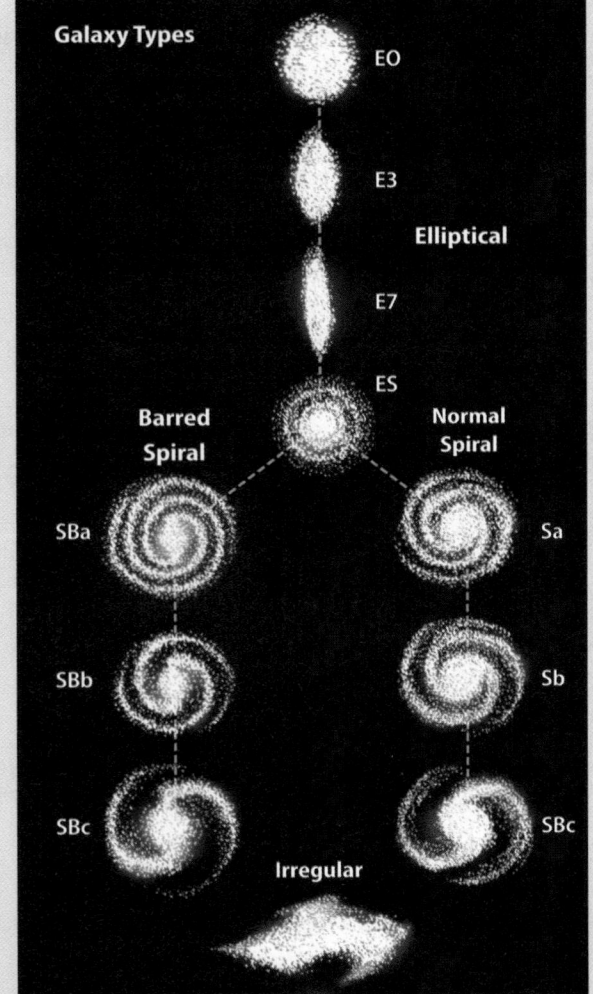

HUBBLE CLASSIFICATION

Edwin Hubble in 1925 introduced a classification system for galaxies based on their forms and structure.

Elliptical Galaxies

- These galaxies are designated with the letter E followed by an index suggesting the ellipticity of the galaxy.
- E0 is used for spherical galaxies.
- E7 is used for very elongated ellipses.

Spiral Galaxies

- Normal spiral galaxies are denoted with the letter S.
- Barred spirals are designated with SB.

Both types are subdivided as a, b, and c types.

- The a types have large and very bright nuclei or central bars.
- The b types have a less pronounced nucleus.
- The c types have most of their light coming from the spiral arms.

S0-type galaxies are an intermediate form between elliptical and spiral galaxies. They have a bright nucleus surrounded by an elliptical zone with little evidence of spiral arms. Spiral galaxies range in size from 50,000 to 200,000 light-years.

Spiral Galaxies. About 17 percent of galaxies that astronomers can observe through a telescope have a structure with spiral arms comparable to that of our own galaxy or to that of the Andromeda galaxy. However, among the 1,000 brightest galaxies, almost 70 percent have a spiral structure.

Elliptical Galaxies. Eighty percent of all galaxies are elliptical, with no spiral arms and little or no visible structure.

Irregular Galaxies. A small percentage of galaxies have irregular shapes. The Large and Small Magellanic Clouds are irregular galaxies.

Clean or Dusty. Spiral galaxies and irregular galaxies contain large amounts of interstellar gas and dust and large numbers of newly formed stars.

It is believed that supernovas, which occur much more frequently in elliptical galaxies, keep these galaxies clean of interstellar gas and dust and thus prevent the formation of new stars.

▲ **The Andromeda Galaxy** and our own galaxy—the Milky Way—are the largest galaxies in the cluster known as the Local Group.

Distribution

Few galaxies are truly isolated. Most galaxies, including our own, inhabit *groups,* containing dozens of galaxies, or *clusters,* containing from hundreds to thousands of members. Groups and clusters, in turn, reside in large *superclusters.*

The Local Group. Our galaxy has several neighbors, of which the Small and Large Magellanic Clouds are the closest. These galaxies are members of the so-called *Local Group,* which also includes the Andromeda galaxy and at least 25 smaller galaxies located in a sphere of 3 million light-years.

These galaxies are so close that they interact gravitationally. For example, the plane of the Andromeda galaxy is somewhat warped by the presence of two satellite galaxies and, under mutual gravitational attraction, it approaches our galaxy with a speed of 500 kilometers (310 miles) per second.

Galaxy Clusters

- Over 2,000 clusters of galaxies are known, and it is believed that billions exist.
- Most of the clusters contain at least 50 members.
- Regular clusters are generally spherical, with more galaxies toward the center.
- They contain mainly E and S0 galaxies and have a total mass 10,000 times the mass of our galaxy.

Irregular clusters are less symmetrical and contain fewer galaxies. They usually contain about 100 times the mass of our galaxy. Irregular clusters with a small number of galaxies generally contain spiral galaxies. Those with a large number of galaxies generally contain elliptical galaxies.

Supercluster. The Local Group, the Virgo Cluster, and the Coma Cluster are relatively close and form a supercluster. About 50 superclusters, which are clusters of clusters, have been identified in the universe.

Vast Distances

Today astronomers can observe some systems that are believed to be more than 10 billion light-years away. This means that light coming from these systems has taken 10 billion years—almost the entire lifetime of the universe—to reach us. Thus, we can see systems the way they looked shortly after the birth of the universe. (See Big Bang, page 962.)

The farthest galaxy yet discovered is also one of the oldest. These images, taken by the Hubble Space Telescope, show a galaxy named UFDj-39546284. Astronomers think the galaxy is about 13.2 billion light-years away. ▶

Determining Distances

Astronomers learn about the objects across such vast distances by studying the light and other forms of radiation that they emit.

Determining Distance	
Celestial Object	**How Astronomers Use It to Determine Distance**
Cepheid variable	• Cepheid variables are variable stars whose changes in brightness recur in a characteristic manner with a relatively short periodicity and may be due to expansion and contraction. • Cepheid variables are visible only in galaxies closer than 10 million light-years. • They play a role in proving the extragalactic nature of spiral galaxies.
O-type and B-type stars	• The very bright O- and B-type stars delineate the spiral arms in our galaxy. • They are clearly visible in other galaxies at distances up to 75 million light-years. • These stars have approximately the same absolute magnitude. • Thus, by measuring their apparent magnitude, astronomers are able to estimate the distances of the galaxies that contain them.
Supernovas	• Can be used to estimate distances beyond 75 million light-years • Supernovas are so bright that they can be observed in galaxies at enormous distances. • Supernovas occur sporadically, so they are not suitable for systematic determinations of distance in the universe.
Galaxy clusters	• It is reasonable to assume that in clusters the brightest or largest galaxies are comparable in brightness or size. • The distance of these clusters can be estimated by comparing the brightest or largest galaxies with those in clusters whose distance has been determined by other means.

Hubble's Law

One of the most important observations in the study of the structure and development of the universe was made by American astronomer Edwin P. Hubble in 1929. It has come to be known as Hubble's law.

Before the Law. In 1914, the American astronomer Vesto Melvin Slipher (1876–1939) studied the spectra of the spiral nebula to find out whether nebulas rotate. If they do, it was argued, the absorption lines in the spectra from one side of the galaxy would be shifted toward the red and those coming from the other side of the galaxy would be shifted toward the blue.

Slipher's Findings. Slipher found that the absorption lines were shifted to the red in almost every galaxy. He also found that this red shift was larger in the fainter galaxies.

Because the red shift is caused by the Doppler effect, Slipher concluded that the fainter, farther galaxies move away from us at higher speeds than brighter, closer ones.

Hubble's Findings. When Hubble compared his results with the red shifts measured by Slipher, he reached a surprising conclusion. The recession velocity of galaxies is directly proportional to their distance. In other words, the farther away a galaxy is from Earth, the faster it moves away from Earth.

The relationship between the recession velocity V and the distance D of a galaxy is given by Hubble's law:

$$V = H \times D$$

H is a constant called *Hubble's constant*. This constant indicates the increase in velocity with distance. Hubble initially found that the velocity of galaxies increases by 15 kilometers (9.3 miles) per second for each million light-years that they are farther away from us.

A New Understanding. Hubble's discovery led to a new method for measuring the distance of galaxies. Most importantly, it revolutionized the understanding of the structure of the universe. The fact that galaxies appear to move away from us in all directions became the basis of the theory of the expanding universe and the big bang.

EDWIN POWELL HUBBLE

1889–1953

Edwin Hubble was an American astronomer whose work revolutionized our understanding of the size and structure of the universe.

- **Early 1900s:** Many astronomers believe that all stars and other celestial objects are part of our galaxy—the Milky Way.

- **By 1919:** After studying 86 novas and 40 Cepheid variables, Hubble establishes the distance of about two dozen celestial bodies from their apparent magnitudes. These turn out to be separate galaxies.

- **1923:** Hubble proves that the Cepheid variables and the nebulas he is studying are located outside of the Milky Way, thus proving that other galaxies exist.

- **1929:** Hubble discovers that the farther apart galaxies are from each other, the faster they move away from each other. He concludes that the universe expands uniformly.

Quasars

A number of galaxies are said to be *active galaxies* because they are very powerful transmitters of radiation in certain ranges of the electromagnetic spectrum.

A *quasar* is an extremely luminous object at the center of some distant active galaxies.

Distance and Light

Quasars are among the most distant objects detected in the universe. The light from the farthest quasars traveled 13 billion light-years to reach Earth. Some quasars shine a trillion times brighter than the sun.

Radiation

Quasars give off tremendous energy in the form of visible light, ultraviolet light, infrared rays, X-rays, gamma rays, and in many cases, radio waves. They also release high-speed jets of protons and electrons.

The Early Universe. Radiation from quasars takes billions of years to reach Earth. For this reason, the study of quasars can yield information about the early history of the universe.

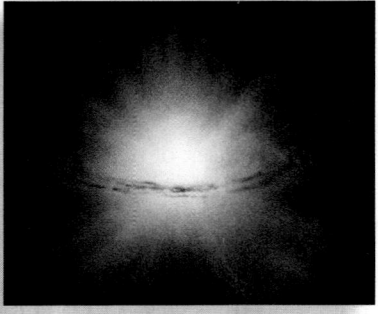

◄ **Quasars** are thought to be the most distant objects in the universe.

Nature of Quasars

- Astronomers think each quasar is powered by a giant black hole at the center of a galaxy.
- The black hole produces energy by swallowing clouds of gas from the surrounding galaxy.
- The mass of the central black hole tends to be about 0.5 percent of the mass of all the stars in the surrounding bulge at the center of the quasar galaxy.
- Scientists use this relationship to try to determine how galaxies and their central black holes formed in the early universe.
- Most astronomers agree that the black holes were created after the universe's first stars exploded in events called *supernovas*.

RADIO GALAXIES

During the early years of radio astronomy, shortly after World War II, astronomers discovered a number of strong radio sources in the sky. One of these sources is Centaurus A, a galaxy in the southern sky.

Centaurus A is only 16 million light-years away. It occupies an area in the sky several times that of the moon and can easily be observed with binoculars.

Observed at radio frequencies, the radiation comes from two huge lobes stretching over 9 degrees in the sky, about 20 times the width of the moon.

The lobes stretch out over 2.5 million light-years, making Centaurus A one of the largest radio galaxies known. The energy production at radio wavelengths is about 1,000 times that of our own galaxy.

Centaurus A is an example of an extended radio source.

◄ **Centaurus A** is one of the strongest radio galaxies known.

Gravitational Lenses

In 1979, a phenomenon was discovered that may help settle the issue of how far away quasars actually are. Astronomers found a pair of identical quasars separated by only 6 arc-seconds with similar spectra, red shift, and color.

The Problem. It seemed improbable that two quasars with identical red shifts and spectra could be found so close together as to be hard to separate even with the best telescopes under the best conditions.

The explanation is that the double quasar is really just one quasar, with the gravity of an intervening galaxy bending the light as a lens does, so astronomers see two images of the same quasar.

Halfway Point. If a gravitational lens—the intervening galaxy—is to produce two images, it should be approximately halfway between Earth and the quasar.

Absorption lines stemming from the intervening galaxy have been observed in the spectra of the two components. These absorption lines have a lower red shift than those of the quasar, showing that the galaxy is closer than the quasar. (See pages 910–911.)

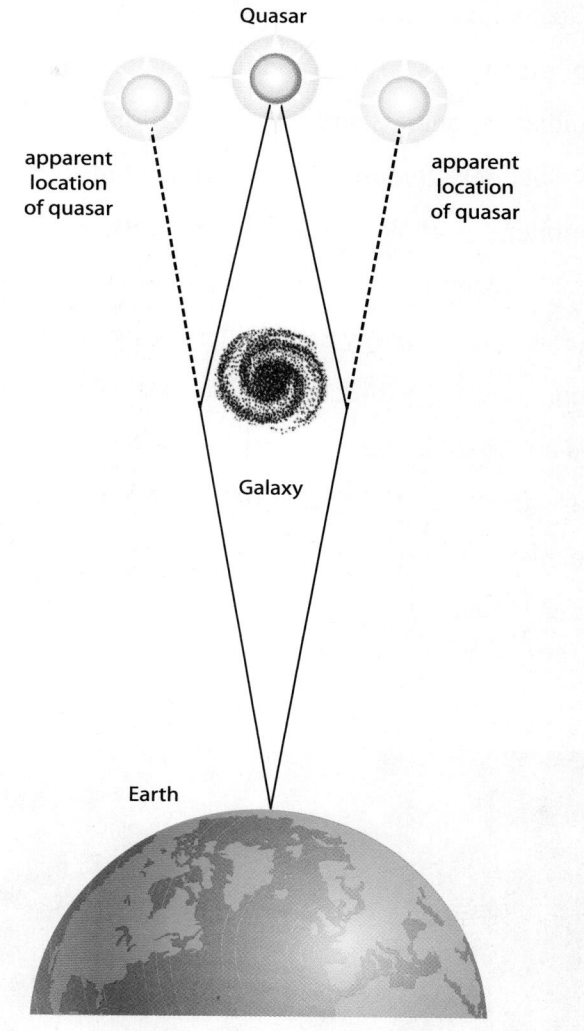

▲ **A galaxy's gravitation** can act as a lens, bending light and causing a distorted image.

SEYFERT GALAXIES

A group constituting 1 percent of spiral galaxies is called the *Seyfert galaxies,* after the American astronomer Carl Seyfert, who first identified them in 1943.

- Seyfert galaxies have bright, very compact nuclei that exhibit violent activity.

- In contrast with the nuclei of normal spiral galaxies, which contain only absorption lines, the spectra of the nuclei of Seyfert galaxies contain broad emission lines, indicating the presence of hot gas.

- The nuclei are powerful infrared transmitters and have been identified as X-ray sources.

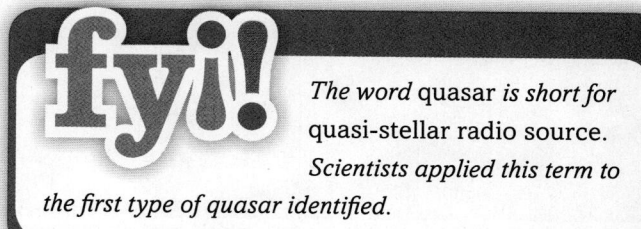

The word quasar *is short for* quasi-stellar radio source. *Scientists applied this term to the first type of quasar identified.*

COSMOLOGY is, as a branch of astronomy, the scientific study of the general structure, origin, and evolution of the universe. Cosmologists are concerned with the physics of the universe: space and time, matter, radiation, energy, and their interactions.

Six observations have contributed much to modern cosmology: (1) the sky is dark at night; (2) galaxies move away from one another; (3) a type of energy called microwave radiation comes from all directions in the sky; (4) helium is abundant in the universe; (5) the oldest stars are about 13 billion years old; and (6) distant exploding stars called supernovas appear fainter than expected.

▲ **Globular clusters** are groups of tens of thousands to several million stars that form a tight ball. Many globular clusters appear to have formed soon after the big bang, around 13 billion years ago.

Origins and Age

The discovery in the 1920s that other galaxies are moving away from the Milky Way at high speeds led to new theories about the origin and age of the universe.

The Big Bang

The big bang was a cosmic explosion that scientists think started the expansion of the universe. The big bang theory ranks as the most widely held scientific theory of the universe's origin.

According to the theory, the big bang occurred about 14 billion years ago. At that time, the universe was much hotter and denser than it is today. As the universe expanded, it grew cooler and less dense.

Hubble's Law. In 1929 came Hubble's publication of his research on the velocity-distance relationship of galaxies, with observational evidence that the universe is expanding. By 1936, based on the red shift, Hubble had enough data to give a numerical value to the distance of galaxies.

Age Discrepancy. Some problems with the big bang theory remained, however.

- According to Hubble's constant as calculated in 1936, the big bang took place 1.8 billion years ago.
- This, then, could be taken as the age of the universe: if it is known how fast the galaxies are flying apart (Hubble's constant), then it can be determined when the expansion began.
- But geologists have established that the oldest rocks on Earth are at least 3 billion years old.
- Clearly Earth could not be older than the universe. If the geologists were correct, something was wrong.

AN EXPLOSIVE THEORY

The big bang theory was first proposed in 1927 by the Belgian priest Georges Lemaître (1894–1966). Lemaître linked the observation of the red shift in distant nebulas by astronomers to a model of the universe based on relativity.

Lemaître proposed that the universe began with the explosion of a primeval atom.

The Age of the Universe

The discovery by German astronomer Walter Baade that there are two populations of stars helped to explain the discrepancy.

- Population I stars are the newly formed stars and those formed within the last several billion years.

- Population II stars are older stars whose histories go back to the early stages of the galaxy.

- Astronomers theorize that there are still older stars—Population III stars—but none have yet been found.

The Wrong Population. Baade studied the short-period variables used by Hubble to determine the distance from Earth to Andromeda and other galaxies. He determined that these stars are Population I stars rather than Population II stars. Therefore, they are twice as far away as first believed.

Brighter Stars. This implies that they are also twice as luminous as originally assumed. Consequently, all distance determinations based on the short-period variables were wrong by a factor of two. The galaxies in which they were observed are also twice as far away.

The Elderly Universe. Because the galaxies are much farther away than previously thought, they must have taken much longer to get where they are. Thus, the universe is much older than 1.8 billion years.

Current estimates by scientists place the age of the universe at about 13.7 billion years.

Newer Evidence. Studies of *cosmic microwave background (CMB) radiation* have provided further strong evidence supporting the big bang theory and provided this more accurate calculation for the age of the universe. (See page 964.)

IS THE UNIVERSE OPEN OR CLOSED?

Cosmologists over many years have tried several approaches to determine whether the universe is open, closed, or flat.

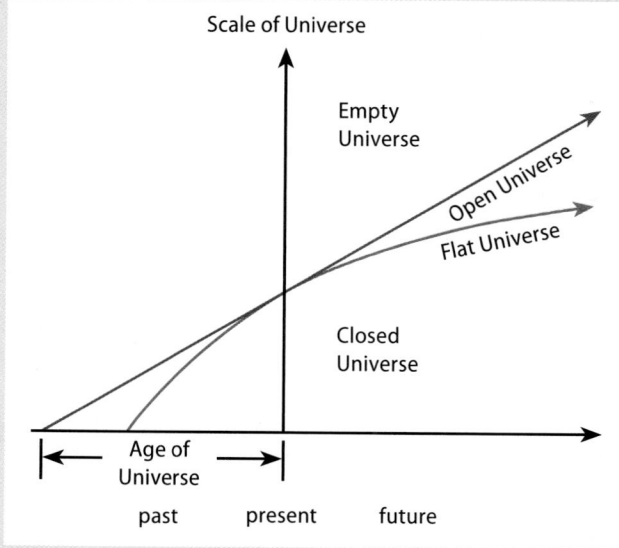

- In an *open universe,* the gravitational attraction between fragments that are flying in all directions is too small to slow them down, and the expansion of the universe will be expected to go on forever.

- In a *closed universe,* the average density of the universe is high enough that gravitational forces will slow the expansion down. Gravity will then pull fragments back together. The entire universe will collapse gravitationally, constituting a big bang in reverse: the big crunch.

- In a *flat universe,* the universe will expand forever, but at a lower rate than that expected in an open universe.

On the graph, the curved line represents *critical density*—the average density of matter in the universe below which the universe is open. The critical density is about 10^{-29} gram/cm^3, which corresponds to a few hydrogen atoms per cubic meter. If the density of the universe is above that value, the universe becomes closed.

Nature of the Universe

Until 1965, the only existing proof for the big bang theory was the red shift in the spectra of distant galaxies and quasars. However, the red shift of quasars was so great that some astrophysicists believed it was caused by some other, still unknown mechanism.

CMB Radiation

In 1965, astronomers detected faint microwave radiation coming from all directions in space. This radiation is known as the *cosmic microwave background (CMB) radiation*.

Shortly after the big bang, the heat of the early universe would have produced radiation that cooled as the universe expanded. CMB radiation closely matches predictions of how this radiation would appear today. (See pages 402–403.)

Educational Radiation. The CMB radiation originated about 13.3 billion years ago, when the universe was only 380,000 years old. Scientists study the radiation to learn about the universe at that time.

For example, the CMB radiation has nearly the same temperature in all directions. Accordingly, matter must have spread quite evenly throughout the early universe.

The apparent "smoothness" of the early universe once puzzled scientists because the universe now has a clumpy structure, with concentrations of galaxies separated by vast regions of empty space.

Clumpy Galaxies. Today scientists think the variations show that matter began to clump in the early universe. Over billions of years, the clumps grew into the galaxies that are observed today.

In 2010, scientists released the "7-year data set" of a satellite observatory that supported certain models of *inflation theory*, the idea that the early universe expanded at an accelerated rate.

DARK MATTER

Based on studies of the movement of galaxies, scientists estimate that about 85 percent of the matter in the universe consists of an invisible substance called *dark matter*.

Unlike ordinary matter, dark matter does not give off, reflect, or absorb light rays.

Most astrophysicists think that the majority of dark matter consists of undiscovered subatomic particles called WIMPs. *WIMP* is short for *weakly interacting massive particle*. WIMPs interact only through the force of gravity and through another fundamental force called the *weak nuclear force*.

Experiments. Scientists have devised many experiments to look for evidence of WIMPs.

- Unlike most particles from space, WIMPs can penetrate Earth, so researchers have placed particle detectors deep underground.
- Telescopes or other detectors look for particles that may be created when a pair of WIMPs come into contact and destroy each other.
- Physicists also hope to create WIMPs in particle accelerators, such as the Large Hadron Collider in Switzerland.

DARK ENERGY

Dark energy is a little-understood form of energy that apparently makes the universe expand more and more rapidly.

Critical Density

- By the late 1990s, astronomers had confirmed that the universe has *critical density*.
- This means there is just enough matter in it to decrease its rate of expansion.
- According to this idea, the universe has been expanding since the big bang—but more and more slowly.
- Astronomers found that matter accounts for about 30 percent of the universe's critical density.

Faster Expansion. However, they had also found that, several billion years ago, the rate of expansion began to speed up. According to relativity theory, energy also contributes to density.

Dark energy can account for the increase in the expansion rate if there is enough of it to account for the remaining 70 percent of critical density.

LISTENING TO THE BIRTH OF THE UNIVERSE

CMB radiation was discovered in the 1960s by two physicists from Bell Telephone, Arno H. Penzias and Robert W. Wilson. They were experimenting with a horn antenna installed in Holmdel, New Jersey. The antenna had been used for communications with Telstar satellites and was readied for use as a radio telescope.

Using a very sensitive receiver to test the sensitivity of the antenna, the researchers picked up a hiss at a wavelength of 7.35 centimeters with an intensity that seemed independent of the orientation of the antenna.

Penzias and Wilson first assumed that the radiation was produced by the antenna itself. The antenna had been a roosting place for pigeons, so it was possible that pigeon droppings were the source of the radio signal. (Any matter at a temperature above absolute zero emits radiation, known as black body radiation.)

After thorough cleaning of the antenna, the signal was still present and the two researchers concluded that the radiation came from the universe. The most puzzling fact was that this radiation appeared to be isotropic—coming from every direction in the universe with the same intensity.

Penzias and Wilson consulted the American physicist Robert H. Dicke. Dicke and several colleagues were searching for evidence of radiation that formed soon after the big bang. They determined that the noise the antenna picked up was this radiation.

▲ **Penzias and Wilson** shared half of the 1978 Nobel Prize in physics for the discovery of CMB radiation.

▲ **Dark Matter.** This star cluster's normal matter appears in pink. The blue areas hold most of the cluster's mass in invisible dark matter, which can be detected due to gravitational lensing.

Inflation Theory

Certain properties of the universe have been highly perplexing to cosmologists. One of them is the large-scale homogeneity of the universe.

Homogeneity in a system is usually considered to be the consequence of the exchange of matter or energy. However, this exchange of energy cannot have taken place everywhere in the universe. Some parts of the universe are so far from others that light has not had sufficient time to travel from one part to the others.

Early Moments. American physicist Alan H. Guth has proposed a model for the first moments following the big bang that would explain the large-scale uniformity of the universe.

Guth's model suggests that before the universe reached the age of 10−35 seconds, an enormously rapid expansion, or *inflation,* occurred. During the sudden expansion, any irregularities that would have prevented the universe from becoming uniform were smoothed out.

Ballooning Universe. Inflation theory also predicts that the universe is flat. The curvature of space can be compared to the curvature of the surface of a balloon. When a balloon suddenly inflates to a very large size, its surface becomes flatter.

Cosmologists believe that the sudden inflation of the universe right after the big bang caused space to become rigorously flat.

The Search for Life

Although astronomers have tried to find the artifacts of intelligent beings on other planets, an active search for extraterrestrial beings became possible only with the advent of radio astronomy. Because the operation of radio telescopes is expensive and each instrument is continually in demand for astronomical programs, it is mandatory that the search for extraterrestrial intelligence be based on scientific reasoning.

Conditions for Life

Scientists agree today that life in the universe will only be found in surroundings similar to our own.

- It would begin on a planet that circles a star very similar to the sun.

- A hotter star would radiate too much deadly ultraviolet radiation.

- A cooler star would not radiate enough energy, and processes basic to life, such as photosynthesis, would not occur.

- The planet would rotate fast enough so that its temperature would not vary too much between day and night.

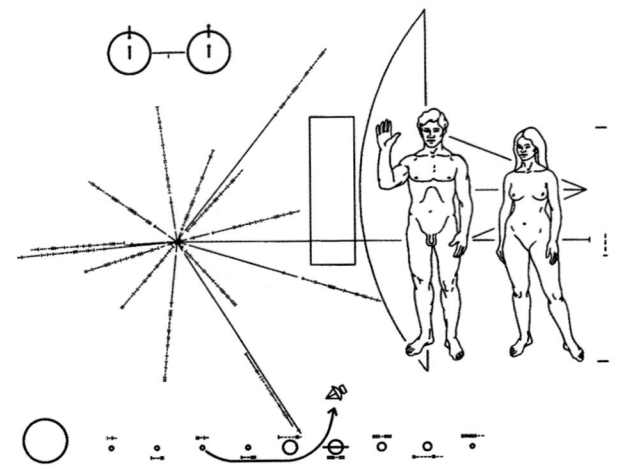

▲ **Making Contact.** Pioneer 10, a spacecraft launched by NASA in 1972 on a mission to Jupiter, carried this drawing, a message to alien life.

- The planet would have to be at the right distance from the star so that the temperature would not deviate too much from the 10° to 38°C (50° to 100°F) range—the optimal temperature range for the occurrence of complex chemical reactions.

- Molecules that make up living organisms, such as proteins, react very slowly at low temperatures and disintegrate at high temperatures.

▲ **Signs of Life?** In the late 1800s, astronomers believed they had found a network of canals on Mars, giving rise to the theory of alien life on Mars. The "canals" turned out to be shadows or nothing at all.

Main Sequence Stars. We know that a large number of stars similar to our sun exist in our galaxy. As a matter of fact, the sun belongs to the most common group of stars in our galaxy. These are the main sequence stars. (See page 945.)

Astronomers believe that many stars with planets have not yet been observed directly. Some stars appear to wiggle as they travel, indicating that both the star and an invisible companion are rotating around a common center of mass.

The Milky Way has hundreds of billions of stars in it. Even if the stars having planets that satisfy the conditions for life comprise an extremely small fraction of the total number of stars, their number could still be substantial.

The Allen Telescope Array is used to search for signs of intelligent life in the universe. Located in Hat Creek, California, the telescope began operating in October 2007 with 42 antennas. When completed, the telescope will consist of 350 antennas. ▼

The Search Is On

Since 1960, radio astronomers have pointed their radio telescopes at targets on the celestial sphere in the hope of detecting signals produced by intelligent beings. These signals would be expected to differ from radio waves transmitted naturally by celestial objects.

- Natural signals look much like the noise and static that interfere with radio reception.

- Signals from extraterrestrial life would have regular patterns, such as coded transmissions or transmissions similar to those produced on Earth.

- Some radars on Earth are powerful enough to be received by a civilization many light-years away.

Wavelength Range. For their search programs, radio astronomers have selected one portion of the radio spectrum: radio waves with wavelengths between 18 and 21 cm. That portion is relatively free of radio noise from natural cosmic sources.

Hydrogen and Water. More importantly, the hydroxyl radical (−OH), as found in water, emits radio waves with 18-cm wavelengths. Neutral hydrogen emits 21-cm waves.

These two wavelengths are used extensively in radio astronomy because they indicate the presence of hydrogen and water. It is considered likely that extraterrestrial civilizations would also be scanning or transmitting in these frequencies.

The SETI Institute is a research organization that searches for extraterrestrial life. The term *SETI* refers to the *search for extraterrestrial intelligence*.

SETI uses large radio telescopes and optical telescopes to search the sky for signals made by extraterrestrial technology. The institute uses facilities around the world.

SETI is also building its own radio telescope with the University of California at Berkeley. Known as the Allen Telescope Array, it is planned to consist of 350 small dish antennas working as one big antenna.

SPACE EXPLORATION

Humans have always been curious about the sky, the stars, the sun and the moon, and the galaxies. The first steps into space were short flights in the upper atmosphere and orbits around Earth. Then followed the longer journeys into space, and eventually humans landed on the moon.

Space exploration helps us see Earth in its true relation with the rest of the universe. Such exploration could reveal how the sun, the planets, and the stars were formed and whether life exists beyond our own world.

Rockets

A *rocket* is a type of engine that pushes itself forward or upward by producing thrust. Rocket engines do not need outside air, so they are able to operate in outer space, where there is almost no air.

Fathers of Space Flight

Three scientists working independently in the early 1900s addressed many of the technical problems of rocketry and space travel.

Russian physicist Konstantin Tsiolkovsky (1857–1935) was the first to investigate seriously the use of rockets for space travel. In 1903, he published an extensive work, *Exploration of Planetary Space by Means of Reaction-Powered Equipment.*

American physicist Robert H. Goddard (see below).

German physicist Hermann Oberth (1894–1989) published *The Rocket into Interplanetary Space* in 1923. This work discussed many technical problems of space flight and described what a spaceship would be like.

ROCKET MAN

The American physicist Robert H. Goddard (1882–1945) was a pioneer of rocket science. He experimented with solid- and liquid-propellant rockets between 1909 and 1945. His experiments led to the development of powerful boosters for intercontinental missiles and for spacecraft.

- In 1919, after years of experimenting with various explosive charges as propellants, Goddard published his revolutionary treatise, *A Method of Reaching Extreme Altitudes.*
- Goddard obtained more than 200 patents that embraced liquid-propellant-fed combustion chambers, thrust modulation, and staged-rocket vehicles.
- He ran rocket tests in a vacuum and proved that thrust and propulsion could take place in an airless environment.
- At Worcester, Massachusetts, in 1926, he first launched a rocket with such a liquid-propellant engine. The propellants were liquid oxygen and gasoline.

◀ **Robert H. Goddard** stands beside the first successful liquid-propellant rocket.

Rocket Research

Oberth was the president of the *Verein für Raumschiffahrt* (Society for Space Travel), which began rocket experiments with liquid oxygen and gasoline in 1927.

German army influence infiltrated the society in 1932, resulting in the development of the world's first large rocket missile, the V-2. It first flew in 1942. By the end of World War II, more than 3,000 had been produced.

The V-2 was to become the first tool for research beyond the atmosphere for the United States, the Soviet Union, France, and the United Kingdom.

Postwar Developments

After the war, both the United States and the Soviet Union instituted programs to develop long-range guided missiles. Both developed a series of missiles.

- First: intermediate-range missiles with typical ranges of 2,400 kilometers (1,500 miles)
- Then: intercontinental missiles with ranges over 10,000 kilometers (6,000 miles)

The Space Age. By 1960, both nations were well under way with programs of space exploration. Hundreds of satellites, space probes, and manned spacecraft were to be launched in the next decades.

The Basics: Space Exploration—Terms to Know	
Artificial satellite	a manufactured object that orbits Earth or any other body in space
Astronaut	a general term for any space traveler, particularly one from the United States
Booster	the rocket that provides most or all of the energy for the launch of a spacecraft
Cosmonaut	an astronaut from the former Soviet Union (now the Commonwealth of Independent States)
Entry	the phase of a space flight during which the vehicle is moving through a planet's atmosphere before landing
Escape velocity	the minimum speed a spacecraft must reach to overcome the pull of gravity
Heat shield	the part of a spacecraft designed to protect the vehicle from heat during atmospheric entry. The shield may consist of tiles or other types of insulation.
Launch window	the period when a spacecraft's target—such as a planet or a satellite—is properly lined up with the launch point, creating an efficient flight path
Mission control	a facility on the ground that supervises a space flight
Module	a section of a spacecraft that can be disconnected and separated from other sections
Orbital velocity	the minimum velocity needed to maintain an orbit around Earth or some other body
Oxidizer	the substance in a rocket propellant that provides the oxygen needed to make the fuel burn in the airlessness of space
Space probe	an unmanned spacecraft sent to explore other planets, celestial bodies, or interplanetary space
Space shuttle	a reusable space vehicle that takes off like a rocket and lands like an airplane
Space station	an orbiting spacecraft designed to be occupied by teams of astronauts or cosmonauts over a long period
Stage	a section of a rocket having its own engine
Thrust	the push given to a rocket by the expulsion of the gases created by burning fuel

Rocket Flight

Airplanes are not usable in space because the presence of air is necessary to create the forces on the wings that keep an airplane aloft and to supply the oxygen needed by its engine. The ability of a rocket to provide adequate thrust even when air is absent makes it a suitable propulsion system for space flight.

Rocket Engines

In its simplest form, a rocket engine consists of a combustion chamber and a nozzle. The fuel and the *oxidizer*—the substance that provides the oxygen needed to make fuel burn in space—are pumped into the combustion chamber and burned.

The hot, high-pressure gas produced by this combustion escapes through the nozzle at high velocity and forms the jet that provides *thrust.*

The thrust, or reaction force, produced by a rocket engine depends on the amount of gas ejected through the nozzle and the velocity of the gas particles. The conventional measure by which propellants are rated is *specific impulse,* which is defined as pounds of thrust produced per pound of propellant burned per second.

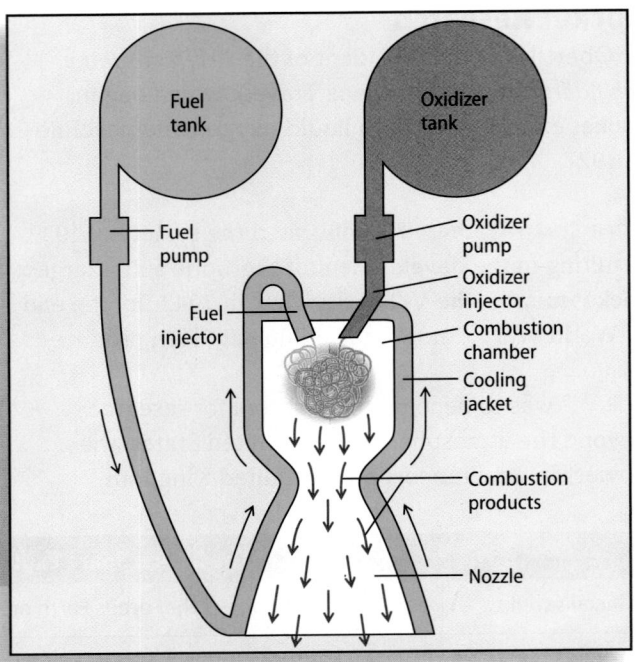

▲ **A liquid-propellant rocket** carries fuel and an oxidizer in separate tanks. The fuel circulates through the engine's cooling jacket before entering the combustion chamber. This circulation preheats the fuel for combustion and helps cool the rocket.

Rocket Fuels

Selection of a propellant for a specific application depends on several factors such as performance, storability, reliability, safety, servicing needs, and cost.

Solid propellants are made of a rubbery or plastic-like material called the *grain.* The grain consists of a fuel and an oxidizer in solid form. It is shaped like a cylinder with one or more channels or ports that run through it. The ports increase the surface area of the grain that the rocket burns.

Largely because they are simple and ready to go, solid rockets are useful for the propulsion of military missiles and as booster rockets.

Liquid propellants may be monopropellants like hydrazine or hydrogen peroxide, which decompose when a suitable catalytic agent is present to produce high-temperature gas.

Such systems are useful for controlling a spacecraft's motions, but their performance is not adequate for use as primary propulsion.

A bipropellant system provides the highest propulsion performance.

- Commonly used oxidizers are liquid oxygen and nitrogen tetroxide.
- The fuels include kerosene and ethyl alcohol.
- The most efficient fuel is liquid hydrogen, which powers the engines of the space shuttle.

Nuclear Propulsion. A test-stand version of a U.S. nuclear rocket has demonstrated much higher performance than chemical fuels.

However, nuclear rockets are not feasible for launching spacecraft from Earth because they would require shielding and be too bulky. They can be used for powering spacecraft already in orbit around Earth.

SATURN 5 ROCKET

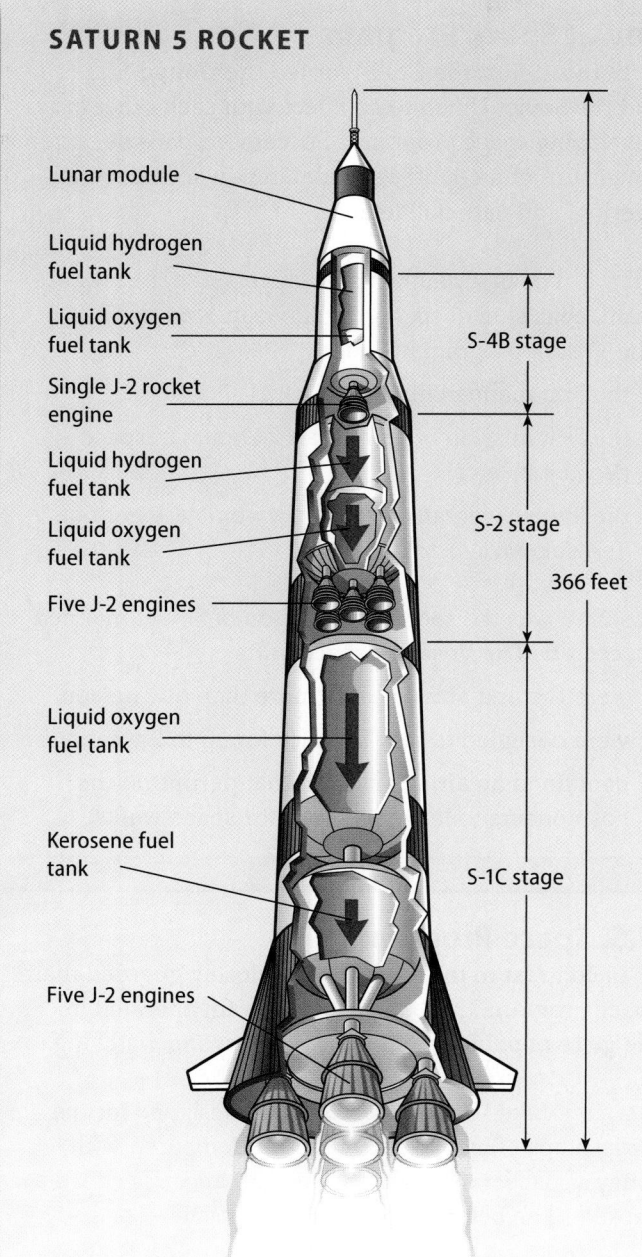

- Lunar module
- Liquid hydrogen fuel tank
- Liquid oxygen fuel tank
- Single J-2 rocket engine
- Liquid hydrogen fuel tank
- Liquid oxygen fuel tank
- Five J-2 engines
- Liquid oxygen fuel tank
- Kerosene fuel tank
- Five J-2 engines

S-4B stage

S-2 stage

366 feet

S-1C stage

◄ **The Saturn 5 rocket** carried the first astronauts to the moon. A rocket engine combines a fuel and an oxidizer. When the two are ignited, the resulting hot gases leave the combustion chamber at high speed, providing thrust.

Principles of Spaceflight

Isaac Newton suggested that if a projectile were shot fast enough from a mountain in a trajectory parallel with the surface of Earth, it would assume a circular orbit.

Orbital velocity is the velocity required to put a space vehicle in orbit around Earth.

- Orbital velocity close to Earth's surface is 27,360 kilometers (17,000 miles) per hour.
- At that velocity, the centrifugal force is balanced by gravity.
- Satellites placed in higher orbits have lower velocities because gravitational attraction diminishes with altitude.
- The moon orbits Earth with a velocity of 3,681 kilometers (2,287 miles) per hour.

Escape velocity is the velocity required to break free of the gravity of Earth or another celestial body.

- Escape velocity is determined by the kinetic energy required to overcome the gravitational field.
- Escape velocity for Earth is 11.2 kilometers (36,700 feet) per second.
- Escape velocity of the moon is much less because of the moon's lesser mass.

ISAAC NEWTON AND ROCKET THRUST

Newton's third law of motion describes how a rocket engine produces thrust.

- The law states that for every action there is an equal and opposite reaction.
- The way Newton's law works for gases can be seen in the flight of an inflated toy balloon when its stem is released.

Electric propulsion, like nuclear propulsion, is still in an experimental stage. A still higher specific impulse than with nuclear propulsion can be obtained by electric rockets.

In one design, an electric arc heats hydrogen or another gas to very high temperatures to obtain high exhaust-jet velocities.

HUMANS IN SPACE

The first manned spaceflight took place on April 12, 1961. Russian cosmonaut Major Yuri A. Gagarin went into orbit aboard the Soviet Vostok 1 spacecraft. Gagarin circled Earth once. His total flight time was 1 hour, 48 minutes.

On May 5, 1961, the United States sent its first astronaut, Alan B. Shepard, Jr., in a Mercury capsule, boosted by a Redstone rocket, for a 15-minute flight to an altitude of 188 kilometers (117 miles). The first American orbital flight was three circuits by John H. Glenn, Jr., in Mercury-Atlas 6 on February 20, 1962.

United States astronauts landed on the moon six times between 1969 and 1972. Here, Apollo 16 astronaut John W. Young salutes a U.S. flag on the moon's surface. ▼

The Space Race

Soviet Space Program

In the 1960s, the Cold War led the United States and the Soviet Union to compete with each other in developing space programs. Success in space became a measure of a country's leadership in science, engineering, and national defense.

Vostok. The first manned spaceflights, the Vostok program, consisted of six flights between 1961 and 1963. The Vostok program included

- the first manned flight (Vostok 1)
- the first mission of more than 24 hours in space (Vostok 2)
- the first spacecraft piloted by a woman, Valentina V. Tereshkova (Vostok 6)

Voskhod was the second generation of Soviet manned spacecraft. The Voskhod spacecrafts

- were the first able to carry more than one person.
- were designed to stay in space for up to 2 weeks.
- contained an airlock system that permitted the cosmonauts to leave the craft for space walks.

U.S. Space Program

In contrast to the Soviets, who closely guarded their space program, the U.S. space program operated in the glare of publicity, with the whole world watching.

Mercury. Like Vostok, Mercury was designed for the initial steps of manned spaceflight. Compared with today's spacecraft, Mercury was tiny and was called a capsule. The bell-shaped Mercury capsule

- was 2.9 meters (9 feet, 7 inches) long, and 2 meters (6 feet, 7 inches) wide at its widest point.
- weighed approximately 1,360 kilograms (3,000 pounds) and landed on water.
- completed six flights between 1961 and 1963, four of them orbital.

Gemini was the second generation of U.S. manned spacecraft. Gemini was designed for two-man crews.

The Soyuz spacecrafts became the third-generation manned space vehicles. The Soyuz spacecrafts

- were three-module spacecraft.
- were more than 10.4 meters (34 feet) long.
- weighed 5,900 kilograms (13,000 pounds).

Salyut Space Station. From 1971, Soyuz craft had the opportunity to dock with a space station, Salyut. The 19.8-meter (65-foot) space station had several compartments, including an airlock transfer tunnel.

Mir, a modernized version of Salyut 7, was launched on February 19, 1986. It was the first space station to be manned permanently.

After 15 years of service, which included 28 crews, a total of 104 people, and 17 expeditions, Mir was forced out of orbit and burned up during a flawless reentry to Earth's atmosphere on March 23, 2001.

Cosmonaut Yuri Gagarin became the first human to travel in space on April 12, 1961. ▶

The Gemini spacecraft consisted of two parts, a reentry module housing the crew and an adapter section containing fuel and equipment. Like Mercury, the Gemini spacecraft landed on water.

NASA launched the first Gemini on March 23, 1965, and the program continued through 10 manned flights. The last was launched November 11, 1966. The program included a number of highlights.

- the first orbital maneuvering by a manned spacecraft (Gemini 3)
- the first flight by an American crew of two, and the first American space walk (Gemini 4)
- a flight of exceptionally long duration for that time, 330½ hours (Gemini 7)
- the first rendezvous between two spacecraft (Gemini 6 and 7)
- the first docking in space (Gemini 8, with an unmanned capsule)

MISSION TO THE MOON

In 1961, President John F. Kennedy called on NASA to land a man on the moon and return him safely to Earth before the decade ended.

The Apollo program, beginning in 1969 and lasting until 1972, culminated in several landings on the moon.

The first manned lunar landing came on July 20, 1969, when Apollo 11 astronauts Neil A. Armstrong and Edwin E. "Buzz" Aldrin, Jr., set foot on the moon. Michael Collins waited for them in orbit.

Armstrong and Aldrin

- performed a solar wind experiment.
- set up a seismometer to measure surface vibrations.
- assembled a reflector to bounce back laser beams sent from Earth, enabling scientists to measure the distance between the moon and Earth to within inches.
- collected 22 kilograms (48 pounds) of surface material from the Sea of Tranquility, where they had landed.

The Final Frontier

Space Shuttles

The most versatile spacecraft designed by NASA is the space shuttle, a vehicle that can take off from Earth, execute its mission in orbit, reenter the atmosphere, and glide back to Earth.

Design. The space shuttle system consists of an *orbiter*—a winged spacecraft that returns to Earth—two reusable solid-fuel rocket boosters, and an external tank containing the ascent propellant.

On takeoff, the main liquid-fueled engines are assisted by the two solid-fuel rocket boosters. The spent boosters parachute into the ocean for recovery.

After reentry into the atmosphere, the orbiter becomes an 80-ton glider that can be maneuvered. It is not powered. It lands like a conventional airplane.

Missions. Many scientific experiments and observations have been performed during shuttle missions.

- Shuttle crews have placed satellites in orbit and retrieved satellites for repair.
- Several secret military missions commissioned by the Department of Defense have been flown.
- Experiments have been conducted assembling large aluminum structures in space, similar to those that will be used in future manned space stations.

▲ **Billows of smoke and steam** rise above Launch Pad 39A at NASA's Kennedy Space Center in Florida, alongside space shuttle Discovery as it races toward space on the STS-128 mission.

SHUTTLE TRAGEDIES

Two of the worst accidents in the history of manned spaceflight involved space shuttles.

- On January 28, 1986, the Challenger exploded 73 seconds after takeoff from the Kennedy Space Center in Florida. The crew, including teacher-observer Christa McAuliffe, perished.
- On February 1, 2003, the Columbia exploded during reentry minutes before a scheduled landing in Florida, killing the crew.

The International Space Station

The International Space Station is a joint undertaking of the United States, Russia, Canada, Japan, and nine member countries of the European Space Agency (ESA). The first modules of the station were launched and joined in 1998. Other construction followed; the first crew arrived in 2000.

The station functions as an observatory, laboratory, and workshop. Astronauts and cosmonauts live and work in cylindrical modules. Solar panels furnish the electric power for the station.

Current and Future Space Plans

Although the space station is NASA's biggest effort in space, several other space projects are in progress or planned.

Mars Global Surveyor, launched in 1996, is the first of a series of probes that will study Mars and send back information about the planet's atmosphere, climate, and geology.

The Cassini spacecraft, launched in 1997, is a joint venture led by NASA, the ESA, and the Italian Space Agency. Cassini rendezvoused with Saturn in 2004, beginning a 4-year survey of the planet and its satellites, particularly the moon Titan.

Cassini's Huygens probe began gathering data on Titan in January 2005. The mission will conduct 27 different studies and send back about 300,000 color photos of Saturn and its moons.

International Space Programs	
Canada	• Has a space research program and a communications satellite program • Took part in the U.S. space shuttle program by designing and building the Canadarm, the shuttle's robot arm • Canada also built a larger robot arm that was installed on the International Space Station.
China	• Sent its first satellite into space aboard a CZ-1 launcher in April 1970 • In the 1980s, developed space technology that included liquid-hydrogen engines, powerful Long March rockets, and recoverable satellites • Became the third nation to launch a person into space in October 2003 • Another spacecraft carried two astronauts into orbit on a 5-day mission in October 2005. • On the third piloted spaceflight in September 2008, two astronauts performed the country's first spacewalk.
European Space Agency (ESA)	• Formed in 1975; western European member nations combine their financial and scientific resources in the development of spacecraft, instruments, and experiments. • Supervised the construction of Spacelab, a laboratory carried into space by a space shuttle • Launched the space probe Giotto toward Halley's Comet • Built the Ulysses solar probe • Developed a series of Ariane booster rockets to launch communications satellites for paying customers • By the late 1980s, Ariane rockets were launching more commercial satellites than U.S. rockets were.
India	• The Indian Space Research Organisation builds boosters. • Launched a satellite into orbit in July 1980 • Launched the Chandrayaan-1 lunar orbiter in 2008. The orbiter carried and dropped an impactor on the moon, making India's space program the fifth program to reach the lunar surface.
Japan	• Launched a satellite in February 1970, becoming the fourth nation in space • Fired two probes toward Halley's Comet in 1985 • Developed a family of small, efficient space-boosters • Developed the H-1 rocket, a medium-sized booster with liquid-hydrogen fuel • Launched a lunar probe in 1990 • The H-2, a heavy-lifting booster, sent the Advanced Earth Observing Satellite into orbit in 1994. The satellite began to gather data on Earth's lands, seas, and atmosphere. • Developed a laboratory module for the International Space Station

The Deep Impact spacecraft traveled to comet Tempel 1, arriving on July 4, 2005, where it released a small impactor to create a crater in the comet. The objective of the mission was to discover and understand the inside of a comet to gain clues to the early formation of the solar system.

▲ **The International Space Station**

Time Line: 1900–1959

The challenges involved in studying space are great—massive distances and environments inhospitable to humans. But these challenges have been met, to an extent, by the human curiosity and ingenuity that fuels space exploration.

Use the legend, found on each two-page section, to identify the country that accomplished each achievement in space exploration. For example, milestones reached by the United States are identified by a blue circle.

Legend

● United States
● Soviet Union/Russia
● Germany
● Japan
● China
● European Space Agency
● India

1942–1943
● Germany launches thousands of V-2 rockets, each carrying a ton of high explosive, on London. Breakthrough achievements include liquid oxygen and alcohol producing 55,000 pounds of thrust and a ballistic trajectory of over 100 miles at supersonic speed.

1900   1910   1920   1930   1940

1903
● The Wright brothers launch man's dream of controlled flight with a 120-foot flight.

1912
An unnamed European balloon flight results in the discovery of cosmic rays.

1923
● Hermann Oberth becomes the leader of interest in rocket development in Germany by publishing *The Rocket to Interplanetary Space.*

1931
● The German Rocket Society develops a liquid-propellant rocket engine producing 110 pounds of thrust.

1946–1947
● The first captured V-2 rockets are fired at White Sands Proving Ground, New Mexico, under the direction of Werner von Braun and about 100 of his top engineers, who had surrendered to the U.S. Army in 1945.

1934
● German Rocket Society disbands as German army takes over rocket development. Werner von Braun develops the A-3 rocket with 660 pounds of thrust.

1919
● The Smithsonian Institution publishes Robert Goddard's *A Method of Reaching Extreme Altitudes.*

1926
● Goddard launches the first liquid propellant rocket at Auburn, Massachusetts. It travels 120 feet.

Oct. 4, 1957

● Sputnik 1, the first man-made Earth satellite, is launched by the Soviet Union. It circles Earth once every 96 minutes at a speed of 29,000 kph (18,000 mph) until it falls to Earth on January 4, 1958.

1958

● The National Aeronautics and Space Administration (NASA) is established to oversee and coordinate all U.S. space missions and activities.

1950	1958	1959

Nov. 3, 1957

● The Soviet Union launches Sputnik 2, which carries a dog named Laika, the first animal to soar into space. Laika survives the launch, but the technology does not yet exist to bring Sputnik 2 back safely to Earth. Laika does not survive the mission, but she proves that animals can survive a launch into space and the effects of microgravity.

Jan. 31, 1958

● The United States launches its first satellite—Explorer 1. Data from Explorer 1 leads to the discovery of the Van Allen belts, two bands of radiation that surround Earth high above its surface.

Nov. 17, 1958

● The U.S. launches its second satellite, Vanguard 1, which is a tiny sphere just 6.4 inches in diameter. Vanguard 1 relays information showing Earth is pear-shaped.

Jan. 2, 1959

● The Soviet Union launches Lunik 1. This satellite makes the first lunar flyby and sends back data that leads to the discovery of the solar wind.

Feb. 17, 1959

● The U.S. launches Vanguard 2, the first satellite to send back weather data.

May 28, 1959

● The U.S. launches two monkeys—a rhesus monkey named Able and a squirrel monkey named Baker—into space in the nose cone of a Jupiter missile. The monkeys return unhurt after a 300-mile-high suborbital flight.

Sept. 12, 1959

● The Soviet Union launches Lunik 2. Two days later, Lunik 2 becomes the first spacecraft to impact the moon's surface.

Oct. 4, 1959

● The Soviet Union launches Lunik 3 into a huge orbit around both Earth and the moon. Lunik 3 returns the first images of the moon's perpetually far side on October 7.

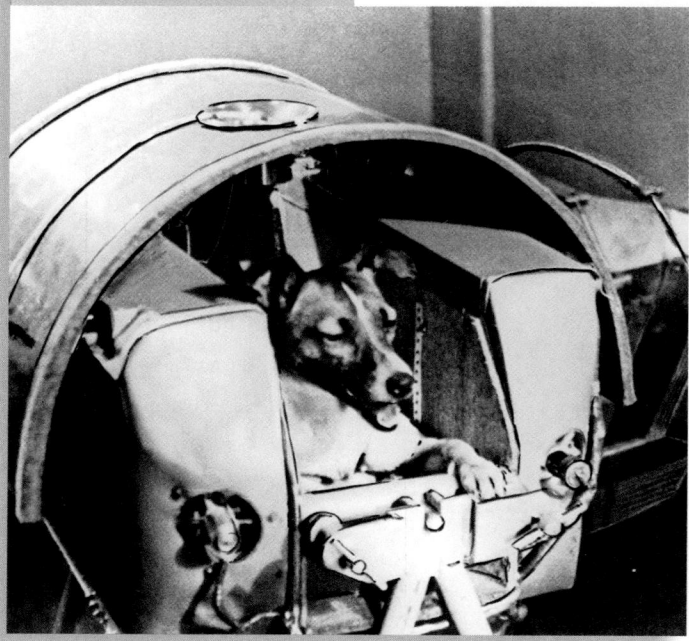

Aug. 19, 1960
● The Soviet Union launches Sputnik 5, the first satellite to carry plants and animals and return them alive after 24 hours.

Oct. 4, 1960
● The U.S. launches Courier 1-B, the first satellite to record the communications it receives and retransmit them to Earth.

Jan. 21, 1961
● A chimpanzee named Ham is sent into suborbital flight by the U.S. in a Mercury spacecraft. Ham returns safely to Earth.

Ham, the first chimpanzee in space, returned safely to Earth in the Mercury capsule about 18 minutes after launch. ▶

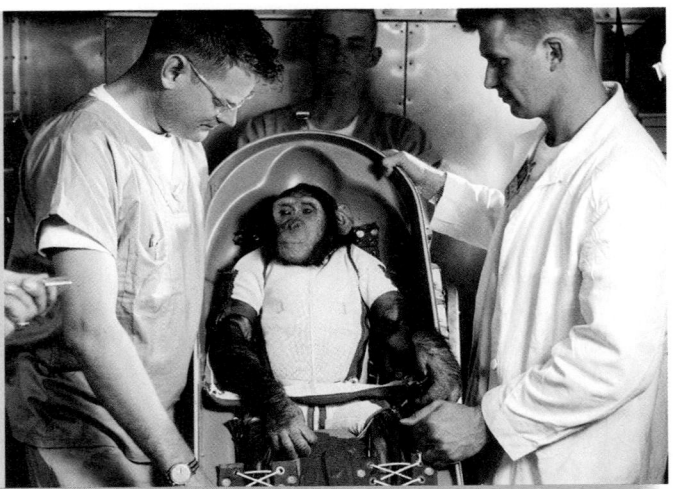

| 1960 | 1961 | 1962 | 1963 |

Nov. 11, 1960
● The U.S. launches Pioneer 5. The satellite sends back data from 22 million miles. Also called Solar Monitor, Pioneer 5 is currently in solar orbit.

April 12, 1961
● Yuri Gagarin becomes the first human to orbit Earth in the Soviet Vostok 1.

July 21, 1961
● The U.S. sends a second astronaut into space: Virgil "Gus" Grissom. The Mercury 4's capsule, called Liberty Bell 7, sank after Grissom's recovery at sea.

Dec. 14, 1962
● The Mariner 2, an unmanned U.S. space probe, flies to within 22,000 miles of Venus. It returns the first data from another planet.

May 5, 1961
● Astronaut Alan Shepard becomes the first American in space aboard the Mercury 3. He completes a suborbital flight launched from Cape Canaveral in a capsule named Freedom 7.

Aug. 6–7, 1961
● The Soviet Union sends up Vostok 2, the first spaceflight to exceed 24 hours.

May 7, 1963
● Telstar 2 is sent into orbit by the U.S. The successful communications satellite permits relaying black-and-white and color television signals between Europe and the U.S.

Feb. 20, 1962
● John Glenn becomes the first American to orbit Earth. He completes three orbits in Mercury 6's capsule Friendship 7.

May 25, 1961
● President John F. Kennedy gives a speech before a special joint session of Congress announcing an ambitious goal: "I believe that this nation should commit itself to achieving the goal, before this decade is out, of landing a man on the moon."

April 23, 1962
● Ranger 4 is launched. On April 26, it becomes the first U.S. spacecraft to reach the moon when it is purposefully crashed on the lunar surface.

Legend
● United States
● Soviet Union/Russia
● Germany
● Japan
● China
● European Space Agency
● India

June 16–19, 1963
● Valentina Tereshkova becomes the first woman in space. Tereshkova makes 48 revolutions around Earth in the Soviet Volstok 6 spacecraft. Her flight lasts 70 hours, 50 minutes.

Dec. 4–18, 1965
● On Gemini 7, Americans Frank Borman and James Lovell remove their space suits in orbit. Their 14-day, 206-orbit mission includes a rendezvous in space with Gemini 6, piloted by Walter Schirra and Thomas Stafford, 185 miles above Earth in close (less than 6 feet) formation.

1964   **1965**   **1966**

July 31, 1964
● The U.S. spacecraft Ranger 7 sends over 4,000 photographs of the lunar surface back to Earth before crashing into the lunar surface.

Feb. 16, 1965
● The U.S. launches the Pegasus 1 satellite, designed to detect micrometeoroids with deployed 96-foot wings as sensors.

Aug. 21–29, 1965
● American astronauts Gordon Cooper and Charles Conrad set an endurance record for manned spacecraft aboard Gemini 5. Their mission lasted 8 days and consisted of 120 orbits, in time and distance equivalent to a round trip to the moon.

March 16, 1966
● Neil Armstrong and David Scott pilot Gemini 8 in the first successful docking with another space vehicle, although a thruster malfunction cut the total mission short.

Oct. 12–13, 1964
● The Soviet Union places a three-man crew in orbit in the Voskhod 1, the first spacecraft to carry more than one person.

March 18, 1965
● Soviet cosmonaut Alexei Leonov makes the first space walk from the Voskhod 2.

June 2, 1966
● The U.S. Surveyor 1 makes the first soft landing on the moon. The craft sends back television pictures showing a surface strong enough to support an astronaut.

Nov. 28, 1964
● U.S. craft Mariner 4 is launched. It photographs Mars from a distance 6,000 miles away on July 14, 1965.

June 3–7, 1965
● U.S. astronauts James McDivitt and Edward White are sent up in the Gemini 4. White completes the first U.S. space walks.

Edward White made the first U.S. space walk on June 3, 1965. ▶

Jan. 27, 1967
● During preparations for the Apollo 1 flight, a fire breaks out inside the command module, killing the crew of Virgil Grissom, Edward White, and Roger Chaffee. NASA delays the Apollo program for 18 months.

July 20, 1969
● Apollo 11 becomes the first mission to land astronauts on the moon. It blasts off on July 16, carrying Neil Armstrong, Edwin "Buzz" Aldrin, and Michael Collins, and touches down on a flat lowland called the Sea of Tranquility on July 20. Armstrong and Aldrin become the first men to walk on the moon, while Collins stays with the command module orbiting the moon.

1967   **1968**   **1969**

Feb.–Nov. 1967
● NASA flies a series of five Surveyor missions to determine the best moon landing site. The missions culminate in Surveyor 6 accomplishing a soft landing, liftoff, and relanding several feet away.

Oct. 11–22, 1968
● Apollo 7 becomes the first manned Apollo mission, crewed by Walter Schirra, Donn Eisele, and Walter Cunningham. Highlights are transmitted live on TV from the spacecraft and of successful docking maneuvers with the lunar module.

April 23, 1967
● The Soviet spacecraft Soyuz 1 crashes after reentering Earth's atmosphere, killing cosmonaut Vladimir Komarov.

Dec. 21–27, 1968
● The first manned mission to the moon—Apollo 8—is flown. Frank Borman, James Lovell, and William Anders make 10 lunar orbits.

Jan. 16, 1969
● The Soviet Soyuz 4 and 5 make the first transfer of crew members from one spacecraft to another.

Feb. 25 and March 27, 1969
● U.S. crafts Mariner 6 and 7 are launched. They pass less than 2,200 miles from Mars on July 30, sending back numerous photographs.

June 14, 1967
● U.S. craft Mariner 5 is launched. It passes within 2,500 miles of Venus on October 19.

Nov. 14, 1969
● As part of the Apollo 12 mission, Charles Conrad, Richard Gordon, and Alan Bean touch down on the moon. Conrad and Bean become third and fourth men on the moon.

Nov. 9, 1967
● In preparation for the moon landing, the U.S. successfully launches the Saturn 5 reusable rocket as an unmanned test vehicle.

Legend
● United States
● Soviet Union/Russia
● Germany
● Japan
● China
● European Space Agency
● India

April 16, 1972
● The Apollo 16 mission flies to the moon. The crew is John Young, Charles Duke, and Thomas Mattingly. Young and Duke spend 3 days on the moon's surface collecting and experimenting.

Nov. 1970
● In the Lunik 17 mission, the Soviet Union lands an unmanned spacecraft on the moon and deploys the automated Lunokhod 1 lunar rover.

May 30, 1971
● The unmanned U.S. probe Mariner 9 is launched on a mission to Mars. It reaches Mars on November 13, orbits the planet, and photographs most of its surface.

Feb. 11, 1970
● Japan launches its first satellite, called Ohsumi, into orbit.

July 23, 1972
● First of the Earth Resources Technology Satellites (ERTS-1) sends back detailed photos of Earth's resources.

1970   **1971**   **1972**

April 11–17, 1970
● The Apollo 13 mission, which is supposed to be the manned third lunar landing, almost ends in disaster. An explosion cripples the spacecraft, but the crew—James Lovell, John Swigert, and Fred Haise—is able to circle the moon and return to Earth safely.

Jan. 31–Feb. 9, 1971
● Alan Shepard, Edgar Mitchell, and Stuart Roosa fly the Apollo 14 mission. Shepard and Mitchell make a successful moon landing, bringing back 100 pounds of moon rocks for study. The exploration of the lunar surface lasts 9 hours.

July 26–Aug. 7, 1971
● U.S. astronauts David Scott, James Irwin, and Alfred Worden fly mission Apollo 15. Scott and Irwin make a successful moon landing highlighted by travel on the surface via lunar rover and the collection of the "Genesis" rock (a fragment of the moon's original crust found to be 4 billion years old).

Dec. 7–19, 1972
● The Apollo 17 mission makes a record 75-hour lunar stay. Eugene Cernan and Harrison Schmitt land in the Taurus Mountains on the last Apollo moon mission to touch down on the moon. The highlight of the mission is the discovery of orange soil that could indicate volcanic activity.

April 24, 1970
● China launches its first satellite—China 1—into orbit.

April 19, 1971
● The Soviet Union launches the first space station, Salyut 1. George Dobrovolsky, Victor Patseyev, and Vladislav Volkov man the station for 23 days (June 6–30). All three men are killed when air leaks out of the spacecraft on the return flight.

March 3, 1972
● U.S. probe Pioneer 10 is launched on a path to pass Jupiter and become the first man-made object to leave the solar system.

Aug. 17, 1970
● The Soviet Union lands Venera 7 on Venus, the first successful landing of a spacecraft on another planet.

April 6, 1973
- The U.S. space probe Pioneer 11 leaves the solar system after flybys of Jupiter and Saturn.

July 28–Sept. 25, 1973
- Alan Bean, Owen Garriot, and Jack Lousma rendezvous with Skylab for repairs and experiments.

June 1975
- The Soviet Union sends out Venus 9 and 10, two successful missions to Venus that transmit pictures of the surface for over an hour.

Dec. 10–March 16, 1978
- Soviet cosmonauts on the Soyuz 26 mission board the Salyut 6 space station and set a 96-day endurance record.

May 14, 1973
- The first U.S. space station, Skylab, is launched into orbit. It suffers damage in the process, losing most of its thermal insulation and one of its two solar panels.

Nov. 3, 1973
- The U.S. space probe Mariner 10 completes a flyby of Venus on the way to Mercury, which it reaches in March 1974.

July 17, 1975
- The United States and Soviet Union perform the first international docking in space. An Apollo capsule successfully links up with a Soviet Soyuz capsule.

1978–1983
- The Soviet Union flies the Venera 11–16 missions, continuing its study of Venus.

1973　　**1974**　　**1975**　　**1978**

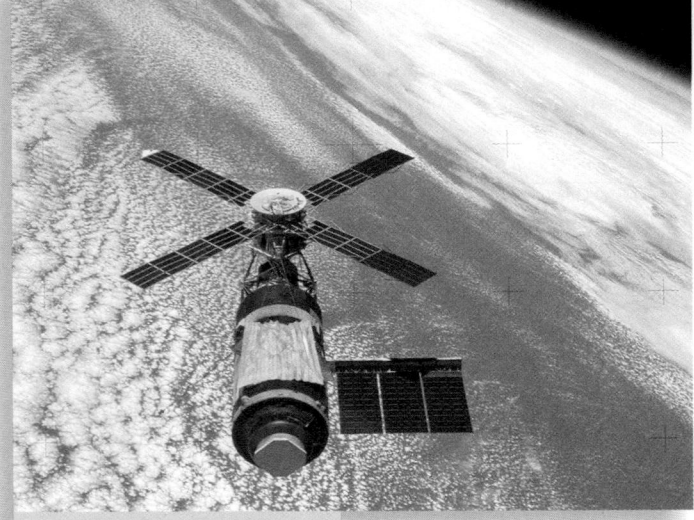

Aug. 20, 1975
- The U.S. launches the Viking 1 probe. Viking 1 and a second probe called Viking 2 land on Mars in 1976 and send back photos and data.

Sept. 20, 1977
- The U.S. space probe Voyager 2 is launched. The unmanned mission passes Jupiter in 1979, Saturn in 1981, Uranus in 1986, and Neptune in 1989, sending back photos and data from each.

July 11, 1979
- Skylab reenters Earth's atmosphere and breaks up over the Indian Ocean and Australia, showering 77 tons of debris, but no injuries are reported.

May 25–June 22, 1973
- Charley Conrad, Joseph Kerwin, and Paul Weitz become the first crew to visit Skylab. They work outside the station to complete repairs on the 28-day expedition.

Nov. 11, 1973–Feb. 8, 1974
- A third crew of astronauts visits Skylab and occupies it successfully for 84 days.

Legend
- United States
- Soviet Union/Russia
- Germany
- Japan
- China
- European Space Agency
- India

Feb. 14, 1980
- The U.S. launches the Solar Maximum Mission, a 1,500-lb. satellite sent to study solar flares.

Aug. 25, 1981
- Voyager 2 flies within 63,000 miles of Saturn and sends back data showing thousands of rings.

April 9–Oct. 11, 1980
- The Soviet mission Soyuz 35 sets a new endurance record at 185 days.

May 13–Dec. 10, 1982
- The Soviet mission Salyut 7 sets a 211-days-in-space endurance record.

June 18–24, 1983
- Sally Ride becomes the first U.S. woman astronaut in space aboard the space shuttle Challenger.

Aug. 30–Sept. 5, 1984
- The third space shuttle, Discovery, makes its maiden flight. Judith Resnick becomes second woman in space.

1980   1982   1983   1984

Nov. 12, 1980
- Three years after its launch, Voyager 1 flies within 77,000 miles of Saturn and finds more rings than previously identified, as well as three new moons, bringing known total to 15.

Nov. 11–16, 1982
- The first operational space flight of Columbia places two satellites in orbit.

Feb. 7, 1984
- On a Challenger mission, Bruce McCandless (*pictured*) and Robert Stewart become the first humans to float in space without lifelines connected to the spacecraft. Instead, they maneuver with jet packs.

Oct. 18, 1984
- On a Challenger mission, Dr. Kathryn Sullivan becomes the first woman to complete a space walk.

April 12–14, 1981
- U.S. astronauts John Young and Robert Crippen man the first flight of Columbia, the first reusable space shuttle.

Nov. 12–14, 1984
- On a Discovery mission, Joseph Allen and Dale Gardner complete the first space salvage operation with retrieval of two nonfunctioning satellites.

Jan. 28, 1986

● An explosion barely a minute after liftoff of the space shuttle Challenger kills the entire crew: (*Front row*) Michael Smith, Francis Scobee, Ronald McNair; (*Back row*) Ellison Onizuka, Christa McAuliffe, Gregory Jarvis, Judith Resnick.

1984–1985

● The Soviet Union launches the Vega 1 and Vega 2 mission. These two dual purpose missions continue information gathering on Venus and also investigate Halley's Comet.

1985   **1986**   **1989**   **1990**

July 2, 1985

● The European Space Agency (ESA) launches Giotto, an unmanned probe that passes within 335 miles of Halley's Comet nucleus on March 14, 1986, sending back photographs and data of the nucleus. The probe is then put in hibernation for later use.

Jan. 24, 1986

● The U.S. probe Voyager 2 flies within 51,000 miles of Uranus, discovering new moons and the rings and first evidence of a magnetic field.

Feb. 20, 1986

● The Soviet Union launches the Mir space station.

June 1987

● Dr. Mae Carol Jemison is selected for the NASA astronaut program, becoming the first black female astronaut. In September 1992, Jemison makes an 8-day spaceflight on the space shuttle Endeavour.

Dec. 21, 1988–Dec. 21, 1989

● Soviet cosmonauts Vladimir Titow and Musa Manarov set an endurance record of 366 days in space at the Mir space station.

May 4, 1989

● The U.S. space probe Magellan is launched from the shuttle Atlantis. In August 1990, Magellan begins sending back photos and data from Venus showing active volcanoes and landscapes not previously seen in the solar system.

Oct. 18, 1989

● The U.S. launches the Galileo probe from Atlantis on a 6-year journey to Jupiter.

April 25, 1990

● ● The U.S. and ESA launch the Hubble Space Telescope into orbit. It provides sharper images of celestial bodies than other telescopes.

Oct. 6, 1990

● The U.S. launches the Ulysses probe from the shuttle Discovery. In 1994, Ulysses begins to survey the southern hemisphere of the sun from a solar orbit achieved via a 500-million-mile trip to Jupiter to use the planet's gravity.

April 7, 1991

● The U.S. launches the Gamma Ray Observatory to study gamma ray emissions from collapsing stars and other violent space explosions.

Aug. 31, 1991

● ● Japan, the U.S., and the United Kingdom launch Yohkoh, a solar probe sent to study high-energy radiation from solar flares.

Dec. 7, 1995
- The U.S. probe Galileo enters orbit around Jupiter as planned after a 6-year journey, which began October 1989.

Jan. 17, 1997
- Galileo sends back data suggesting that Jupiter's moon Europa may be the only other place besides Earth in the solar system with a large amount of liquid water.

Oct. 9, 1992
- The U.S. probe Pioneer 12 ceases operations after 14 years observing Venus (only 1 year of service had been expected).

March 22, 1995
- Russian cosmonaut Valery Polyakov completes a record 438 days in space aboard Mir.

Dec. 12, 1995
- ● The ESA and U.S. launch the Solar and Hemispheric Observatory (SOHO), designed to study the internal structure of sun.

1992   **1995**   **1996**   **1997**

Sept. 3, 1993
- ● ● The U.S. and Russia agree to build the International Space Station, a jointly manned space station.

June 27–July 7, 1995
- The shuttle Atlantis flies the 100th manned U.S. space mission. Atlantis docks with Mir to pick up Nathan Thagard from his extended stay on the space station.

Dec. 4, 1996
- The U.S. probe Pathfinder is launched to reach Mars and deploy a rover, Sojourner.

Oct. 15, 1997
- ● ● The U.S. launches the Cassini probe on a 7-year trip to Saturn and its moons. Cassini carries the ESA probe Huygens with it.

Dec. 2–10, 1993
- A crew aboard the shuttle Endeavour repairs and updates the Hubble Space Telescope during a record five space walks.

Legend
- ● United States
- ● Soviet Union/Russia
- ● Germany
- ● Japan
- ● China
- ● European Space Agency
- ● India

Time Line: 1998–2009

Feb. 7, 1999
● Stardust, a NASA spacecraft about the size of a desk, is launched. The unmanned probe is collecting and analyzing samples from three different comets.

Dec. 1999
● The Terra EOS (Earth Observing System) satellite collects data to enable scientists to examine Earth's climate system. Terra's objective is to determine how life on Earth affects, and is affected by, climate system changes.

Oct. 29, 1998
● John Glenn, now a U.S. Senator, orbits Earth again, thus becoming the oldest astronaut at age 77.

July 23, 1999
● Eileen Collins becomes the first woman commander of a space shuttle (Columbia) and crew. The mission places the Chandra X-ray observatory into orbit around Earth.

1998   **1999**   **2000**   **2003**

Dec. 4, 1998
● Shuttle Endeavour attaches the first American-built module to the International Space Station, marking the beginning of a 5-year construction period.

July 1999
● The Chandra Orbiting X-ray Observatory reveals images of exploding stars, falling stars, and a small galaxy being eaten by a larger one. Chandra has 8 times greater resolution than any previous X-ray telescope.

Nov. 2000
● ● The first crew to live aboard the International Space Station arrives. They spend more than 138 days at the station. Expeditions to the space station continue.

March 2001
● ● After 15 years of service, including joint Russian-American missions, Mir is deemed to be at the end of its usefulness. A final docking mission supplies fuel and a check of control mechanisms. A final thrust deorbits the space station and a controlled operation guides its reentry into the Pacific Ocean.

Feb. 1, 2003
● The U.S. shuttle Columbia is destroyed in an accident occurring during reentry, killing the entire crew: Rick Husband, David Brown, Laurel Clark, Kalpana Chawla, Michael Anderson, William McCool, and Ilan Ramon (the first Israeli in space).

Sept. 21, 2003
● A controlled crash into Jupiter ends Galileo's research mission, thus avoiding the possibility of a crash with the moon Europa. Such a crash could have caused contamination and jeopardized further studies of possible life there.

◄ **Chandra and Hubble.** This image of a dwarf starburst galaxy was created from data gathered from the Chandra Orbiting X-ray Observatory and the Hubble Space Telescope.

Oct. 14, 2003

● China's first manned space mission—Shenzhou 5—is a success, making China only the third country to send a person into orbit.

Jan. 2004

● The Spirit and Opportunity rovers begin explorations of the surface of Mars, sending back geologic data and dramatic photographs.

March 7, 2009

● NASA launches Kepler, a space telescope designed to look for Earthlike planets beyond our solar system.

2004   2007   2008   2009

March 2, 2004

● The ESA launches the Rosetta mission. Rosetta is scheduled to rendezvous with the comet Churyumov-Gerasimenko in November 2014.

July 4, 2005

● The NASA craft Deep Impact shoots an impactor into the comet Tempel 1 to probe the comet's interior.

Sept. 14, 2007

● The Japanese lunar orbiter mission SELENE is launched to gather data for study of the origin, evolution, and tectonics of the moon, as well as to measure the moon's gravitational field.

Oct. 24, 2007

● China launches the Chang'e 1 mission, the first of a planned series of lunar missions, to orbit the moon for a year, testing spacecraft technology for future missions and studying the lunar environment, analyzing minerals of the lunar surface, and mapping the lunar surface.

May 25, 2008

● The U.S. probe Phoenix lands on the north pole of Mars. The probe begins a 3-month mission, digging through to the ice layer below the surface, baking and sniffing soil, searching for and finding what appears to be nutrients necessary to support life.

Nov. 14, 2008

● India sends its lunar probe Chandrayaan-1 to the moon. The 2-year mission includes chemical and mineral mapping of the entire surface and preparation of a three-dimensional atlas. This will help determine location of a future NASA outpost.

Legend

● United States
● Soviet Union/Russia
● Germany
● Japan
● China
● European Space Agency
● India

Jan. 14, 2008

● The U.S. spacecraft Messenger performs the first flyby of Mercury since 1974, taking photographs and collecting data. Messenger is the first spacecraft designed to orbit Mercury.

absolute magnitude the apparent magnitude that a star would have if it were observed from a distance of 10 parsecs (32.6 light-years).

active galaxy any galaxy that is a very powerful transmitter of radiation in certain ranges of the electromagnetic spectrum.

annular eclipse an eclipse in which the moon darkens only the middle of the sun, leaving a bright ring around the edges.

asteroid a rocky or metallic object smaller than a planet that orbits the sun.

astronomical unit the average distance from Earth to the sun—about 150,000,000 kilometers (93,000,000 miles); used as a unit in measuring the distances between stars and planets.

astronomy the study of the universe and the objects in it.

azimuth the angle along the astronomical horizon from the direction of the North Pole to the vertical circle that passes through a star.

big bang the initial explosion of a very high concentration of matter and energy that scientists think started the expansion of the universe. The big bang theory ranks as the most widely held scientific theory of the universe's origin. According to the theory, the big bang occurred about 14 billion years ago.

binary star a pair of stars that revolve around each other and are held together by gravity.

black hole a region of space whose gravitational force is so strong that nothing can escape from it; it is invisible because it traps light as well.

celestial poles the points around which the celestial sphere appears to rotate.

celestial sphere the imaginary sphere that rotates around Earth. The stars, planets, and other celestial bodies appear to be fixed on the celestial sphere.

Cepheid variable variable star whose changes in brightness recur in a characteristic manner with a relatively short periodicity, and may be due to expansion and contraction.

chromosphere the layer of the sun's atmosphere above the photosphere; extends to an altitude of several thousand kilometers.

closed universe one of three possibilities that cosmologists use to describe the nature of the universe (the others being *open* and *flat*). In a closed universe, the average density of the universe is high enough that gravitational forces will slow and eventually reverse expansion, and the universe will collapse on itself.

cluster an association of stars. *Globular clusters* are spherical associations of stars found in galaxies that contain up to several hundred thousand stars. Large associations of galaxies are also called clusters.

corona a thin envelope of gas surrounding the sun and extending far from the sun to a distance as great as several solar radii.

cosmic microwave background (CMB) radiation energy left over from the early universe coming from all directions in the universe; believed to be remnants from the big bang.

cosmic rays electrically charged, high-energy subatomic particles moving at very high speeds that reach Earth from all directions, coming from the sun and from interstellar space.

cosmogony the study of the origin of the solar system.

cosmological model a mathematical or physical description of the structure of the universe.

cosmology the scientific study of the general structure, origin, and evolution of the universe.

dark energy a theoretical form of energy that apparently makes the universe expand more and more rapidly.

dark matter invisible matter that does not give, reflect, or absorb light rays; believed by scientists to make up about 85 percent of the matter in the universe.

declination a star's angular distance north or south of the celestial equator, measured along the hour circle passing through the star.

Doppler effect the apparent change in wave frequency when either the source of waves or the observer moves toward or away from the other.

dwarf planet a celestial body that orbits the sun, is near-spherical in shape, is not a satellite, and, because of its small size, has not cleared the orbit in its neighborhood; also called a plutoid.

eclipse the obscuring of light from one celestial body by another. In a *solar eclipse,* the moon moves between the sun and Earth so as to obscure the sun as seen from Earth. In a *lunar eclipse,* Earth moves between the sun and the moon so that the moon is in Earth's shadow.

ecliptic the apparent path of the sun around the celestial sphere.

equinox one of two points where the ecliptic intersects the celestial sphere.

event horizon the boundary of the region around a black hole from which no light or matter can escape. At the event horizon, the pull of gravity becomes infinitely strong.

extinction In astronomy, the absorption and scattering of starlight by dust.

flat universe one of three possibilities that cosmologists use to describe the nature of the universe (the others being *open* and *closed*). In a flat universe, the universe will expand forever, but at a lower rate than that expected in an open universe.

gas giant any one of the four planets with orbits beyond that of Mars. They are Jupiter, Saturn, Uranus, and Neptune. The gas giants have no solid surface, and they consist mostly of hydrogen and helium. Also called the Jovian planets.

geocentric Earth-centered; early astronomers believed the universe to be geocentric.

globular cluster a tightly packed spherical collection of stars found in galaxies that contain up to several hundred thousand stars.

heliocentric sun-centered; early astronomers believed the universe to be heliocentric.

inflation theory theory that holds that the early universe went through an extremely brief period of particularly rapid expansion.

Jovian planet any one of the four planets with orbits beyond that of Mars. They are Jupiter, Saturn, Uranus, and Neptune. Jovian planets have no solid surface, and they consist mostly of hydrogen and helium. Also called gas giants.

Kuiper belt objects a band of icy, rocky objects in the outer regions of the solar system.

light-year the distance that light travels in a vacuum in a year; used as a unit to measure astronomical distances.

Local Group a concentration of galaxies that includes our own galaxy—the Milky Way—as well as many nearby galaxies.

luminosity the rate at which a star emits energy; a star's luminosity depends directly on its size and on how brightly each unit of area shines.

lunar eclipse an eclipse in which Earth moves between the sun and the moon so that the moon is in Earth's shadow.

magnitude the measure of the brightness of a star. *Apparent magnitude* is the brightness of a star as it appears to an observer on Earth. *Absolute magnitude* is the apparent magnitude that a star would have if it were observed from a distance of 10 parsecs.

Main Belt a belt of asteroids that orbits the sun between Mars and Jupiter.

main sequence star a star that produces nearly all of its energy by combining hydrogen nuclei to form helium nuclei in its core.

meteor a mass of stone or metal that enters Earth's atmosphere from outer space with enormous speed; meteors are visible in the sky as falling stars.

meteorite the portion of a meteoroid that survives as it passes through Earth's atmosphere and reaches the surface.

Space Science Glossary

meteoroid any mass of rock in the solar system. When a meteoroid enters Earth's atmosphere, it can be observed as a meteor.

Milky Way the galaxy that contains our solar system as well as hundreds of billions of stars.

nebula a mass of dust particles and gases or a cloud-like cluster of stars in space. A nebula may be either luminous or dark in appearance. *Galactic nebulae* are clouds of luminous gas and dust particles within our galaxy and comparable in size with it. *Extragalactic nebulae* are clusters of stars outside our Milky Way.

neutrino an electrically neutral particle produced by nuclear reactions in the sun's core.

neutron star the smallest and densest type of star known; composed solely of neutrons packed vary closely together.

nova a star that flares from obscurity to great brilliance and then sinks back to obscurity.

open universe one of three possibilities that cosmologists use to describe the nature of the universe (the others being *closed* and *flat*). In an open universe, the gravitational attraction between fragments that are flying in all directions is too small to slow them down, and the expansion of the universe will be expected to go on forever.

optical telescope an instrument that uses a mirror or lens to collect visible light and use it to form an image, making distant objects appear nearer and larger.

oxidizer the substance in a rocket that provides the oxygen needed to make fuel burn in space.

parallax the apparent change of position of a celestial body against the celestial sphere when viewed from two different points in Earth's orbit.

parsec a unit of distance used in computing the distance of stars, equal to about 30.9 trillion kilometers (19.2 trillion miles), or 3.26 light-years. The measurement is equal to the distance of a star whose annual parallax is 1 second of arc.

partial eclipse an eclipse in which the moon covers only part of the sun or in which only part of the moon passes through Earth's shadow.

photosphere a layer of gas that makes up the lowest layer of the sun's atmosphere; the layer of the sun that gives off light.

plasma a gas that is almost completely ionized. That is, one or more electrons are split off each atom. The sun and most of the stars are made of plasma.

plutoid a celestial body that orbits the sun, is near-spherical in shape, is not a satellite, and, because of its small size, has not cleared the orbit in its neighborhood; also called a dwarf planet.

Population I star newly formed stars and those stars formed within the last several billion years.

Population II star old stars that formed in the early stages of the galaxy.

Population III star the oldest generation of stars; Population III stars are theoretical: astronomers have not yet found any.

protostar a ball-shaped object that is no longer just a cloud of gas and dust, but is not yet a star.

pulsar a rapidly spinning neutron star that sends regular bursts of electromagnetic radiation that are received on Earth.

quasar an extragalactic system with the appearance of a star but exhibiting a large red shift. Quasars are believed to be at very great distances and to emit very large amounts of radiation.

radio galaxy a galaxy that emits radio waves.

radio interferometer a setup of two or more radio telescopes operating in tandem. Computers combine signals from the antennas to produce detailed images.

red shift a shift of the light of stars, nebulas, and other luminous bodies toward the red end (the longest wavelengths of the spectrum), indicating movement outward at increasing speed, and leading to the theory that the universe is constantly expanding at an ever greater rate of speed.

retrograde motion the apparent motion of a planet from west to east among the stars, caused by a combination of its true motion with the motion of Earth.

retrograde rotation rotation around the axis of a celestial object in the clockwise direction as viewed from north of the ecliptic.

right ascension the angular distance between the hour line of a star and the vernal equinox.

rocket a type of engine that pushes itself forward or upward by producing thrust.

singularity a hypothetical point in space at which an object becomes compressed to infinite density and infinitesimal volume.

solar eclipse an eclipse in which the moon moves between the sun and Earth so as to obscure the sun as seen from Earth.

solar flare a sudden, short-lived eruption of hydrogen on the surface of the sun, usually associated with sunspots, accompanied by a burst of ultraviolet radiation that travels toward Earth. Solar flares cause ionization in the upper atmosphere and the fading of high-frequency radio reception.

solar system a group of celestial bodies that consists of a star and planets and other objects orbiting around it.

solar wind a constant stream of particles, mainly electrons and protons, that flows from the sun's corona into interplanetary space.

specific impulse in a rocket engine, the pounds of thrust produced per pound of propellant burned per second.

spectroscopy the study of how matter interacts with light and certain other forms of energy. In spectroscopy, scientists study the radiation given off, absorbed, or scattered by a material to learn more about the material's composition or structure.

star a celestial body made up of hot gases held together by its own gravity and emitting light and heat resulting from its internal nuclear reactions.

sunspot one of the dark spots that appear at regular intervals in certain zones of the surface of the sun. Disturbances of Earth's magnetic field often occur when sunspots appear.

supergiant any one of various extremely large and brilliant stars, ranging in luminosity from 100 to 10,000 or more times that of the sun.

supernova an exceptionally bright nova; considered to be the explosion of a star during the final stage of its development.

terrestrial planet a small, rocky planet, similar in size to Earth; any one of the four planets closest to the sun and close together in size. They are Mars, Earth, Venus, and Mercury.

total eclipse an eclipse in which the moon completely blots out the sun or in which the entire moon passes through Earth's shadow.

white dwarf a white star of low luminosity, small size, and great density.

zodiac a band on the celestial sphere extending about 9 degrees on either side of the ecliptic that ontains the orbits of the sun, moon, and all eight planets. The zodiac is divided into 12 sections, each containing a constellation.

Photo and Illustration Credits

10–11   blickwinkel/Alamy; Martin Shields/Alamy; Scott Camazine/Alamy

12–13   Phil Degginger/Alamy; Sciencephotos/Alamy; Westend61 GmbH/Alamy

14–15   David J. Slater/Alamy; Stockfolio/Alamy; ClassicStock/Alamy

16–17   World History Archive/Alamy; ImageState/Alamy; NASA; NASA

18–19   Denis Balibouse/Reuters/Corbis; NASA

20–21   World Book illustration; National Geographic/Getty Images; National Geographic/Getty Images; Popperfoto/Getty Images; Bettmann/Corbis; A. Barrington Brown/Photo Researchers, Inc.

22–23   Travelpix Ltd./Getty Images; Shutterstock; World Book illustration

24–25   Getty Images; The Granger Collection, NYC; The Granger Collection, NYC; The Granger Collection, NYC; Shutterstock

26–27   David Stuckel/Alamy; Richard Heinzen/SuperStock; Peter Stone/Alamy; Marka/SuperStock; Ace Stock Limited/Alamy; NASA

28–29   Peter Arnold, Inc./Alamy; David Stuckel/Alamy

30–31   Professor Pietro M. Motta/Photo Researchers, Inc.; Alan Sirulnikoff/Photo Researchers, Inc.

32–33   Shutterstock; Shutterstock; The Southwestern Company illustration

34–35   Gary Bell/Getty Images; Steve Bloom Images/Alamy; Mark Conlin/Alamy; Shutterstock; Shutterstock; Shutterstock; Shutterstock; Shutterstock

36–37   Science Source/Photo Researchers Inc.; Shutterstock

38–39   Jim Richardson/Getty Images; Joe McDonald/Corbis

40–41   Shutterstock; Shutterstock

42–43   Shutterstock; Shutterstock

44–45   The Southwestern Company illustration; Digital Vision/Getty Images; Kenneth Eward/Photo Researchers, Inc.

46–47   The Southwestern Company illustration; Ralph White/Corbis; The Southwestern Company illustration

48–49   Michael Abbey/Photo Researchers, Inc.; Dr. Keith Wheeler/Photo Researchers, Inc.; Rob Atkins/Getty Images; Eye of Science/Photo Researchers, Inc.; Michael Abbey/Photo Researchers, Inc.

50–51   World Book illustration; World Book illustration

52–53   The Southwestern Company illustration; The Southwestern Company illustration; The Southwestern Company illustration; The Southwestern Company illustration

54–55   Shutterstock; The Southwestern Company illustration; Spike Walker/Getty Images; Kevin Schafer/Getty Images; Digital Stock

56–57   The Southwestern Company illustration; The Southwestern Company illustration

58–59   The Southwestern Company illustration; The Southwestern Company illustration

60–61   World Book illustration; Dr. Kessel & Dr. Kardon/Tissues & Organs/Getty Images; Dr. David M. Phillips/Getty Images; Scientifica/Getty Images

62–63   The Southwestern Company illustration

64–65   Randy Allbritton/Getty Images; The Southwestern Company illustration; Lawrence Lawry/Getty Images; The Southwestern Company illustration

66–67   World Book illustration; World Book illustration; World Book illustration; World Book illustration

68–69   Science VU/Getty Images; Lester V. Bergman/Corbis

70–71   Christopher McGowan/Alamy; Getty Images; Shutterstock; World Book illustration; World Book illustration

72–73   The Southwestern Company illustration; The Southwestern Company illustration; The Southwestern Company illustration; Shutterstock; David Maitland/Getty Images; The Southwestern Company illustration

74–75   World Book diagram; The Southwestern Company illustration

76–77   World Book diagram; Eric Crichton/Corbis; World Book diagram

78–79   Getty Images; The Southwestern Company illustration

80–81   The Southwestern Company illustration; Dr. David M. Phillips/Getty Images; Redmond Durrell/Alamy; CMSP/J. L. Carson/Getty Images; Max Oppenheim/Getty Images; The Southwestern Company illustration

82–83   World Book diagram; Juniors Bildarchiv/Alamy; World Book diagram

84–85   World Book diagram; Dr. Kessel & Dr. Kardon/Tissues & Organs/Getty Images; Shutterstock; World Book diagram

86–87   World Book diagram; World Book diagram

88–89   World Book diagram; World Book diagram

90–91   Maria Platt-Evans/Photo Researchers, Inc.; Steve Gschmeissner/Photo Researchers, Inc.

92–93   Shutterstock; Steve Taylor/Getty Images; G. Wanner/Getty Images; Kallista Images/Getty Images

94–95   Cornforth Images/Alamy; Wim van Egmond/Getty Images; The Southwestern Company illustration; Peter Barritt/Alamy; C. Boisvieux/Explorer/Photo Researchers, Inc.; Valentyn Volkov/Alamy; Phil Degginger/Getty Images

96–97   Digital Stock; Shutterstock; Shutterstock; Shutterstock

98–99   Michael Snell/Alamy; Li Ziheng/Xinhua Press/Corbis

100–101   Amana Images, Inc./Alamy; World Book illustration

102–103   Gerard Fritz/Getty Images; Mary Evans Picture Library/Alamy; The Southwestern Company illustration

104–105   Visual Language Library; Visual Language Library

106–107   Etienne Morasse EtienneM/Alamy

108–109   Eastcott Momatiuk/Getty Images; Mark Conlin/Alamy

212–213 Dreamstime; Bettmann/Corbis

214–215 Visuals Unlimited, Inc./Eric Tourneret/Getty Images; Shutterstock; Shutterstock

216–217 GM Photo Images/Alamy; Images of Africa Photobank/Alamy; Gail Shumway/Getty Images; Dreamstime

218–219 World Book illustration; Shutterstock; Shutterstock; Pete Oxford/Getty Images

220–221 The Southwestern Company illustration; World Book illustration

222–223 Shutterstock; Kenneth Love/Getty Images; Getty Images

224–225 Tina Manley/Alamy; Shutterstock

226–227 World Book illustration; World Book illustration

228–229 World Book illustration; World Book illustration; World Book illustration

230–231 Shutterstock; World Book illustration; World Book illustration

232–233 World Book illustration; World Book illustration; The Southwestern Company illustration

234–235 World Book illustration; World Book illustration; World Book illustration; Shutterstock

236–237 Medicalpicture/Alamy; World Book illustration; World Book illustration

238–239 Phototake Inc./Alamy; World Book illustration; World Book illustration

240–241 The Southwestern Company illustration; World Book illustration

242–243 World Book illustration; Shutterstock; Phototake, Inc./Alamy

244–245 World Book illustration; World Book illustration

246–247 World Book illustration; World Book illustration; Avatra images/Alamy; Shutterstock

248–249 The Southwestern Company illustration; The Southwestern Company illustration

250–251 The Southwestern Company illustration; The Southwestern Company illustration

252–253 The Southwestern Company illustration; The Southwestern Company illustration

254–255 The Southwestern Company illustration; The Southwestern Company illustration

256–257 The Southwestern Company illustration; The Southwestern Company illustration

258–259 Washington Post/Getty Images; U.S. Department of Agriculture

260–261 Shutterstock

262–263 Shutterstock; Shutterstock; Shutterstock

264–265 Universal Images Group Limited/Alamy

266–267 Ian O'Leary/Getty Images

268–269 Shutterstock

270–271 Getty Images

272–273 Shutterstock

274–275 The Southwestern Company illustration

280–281 Explorer/Photo Researchers, Inc.; Dreamstime

282–283 World Book illustration

286–287 Science Source/Photo Researchers, Inc.; P-59 Photos/Alamy

288–289 Dreamstime; Dreamstime; JLP/Jose L. Pelaez/Corbis; Picture Partners/Alamy

290–291 Jochen Tack/Alamy; Tetra Images/Corbis

292–293 Louise Gubb/Corbis

294–295 World Book illustrations; World Book illustrations; Oleksiy Maksymenko/Alamy

296–297 World Book illustration; Marc F. Henning/Alamy

300–301 Thomas Deerinck, NCMIR/Photo Researchers, Inc.

302–303 World Book illustration; World Book illustration; World Book illustration

310–311 Dreamstime; Richard Heinzen/SuperStock

312–313 The Southwestern Company illustration; David R. Frazier Photolibrary, Inc./Alamy; Martin Bennett/Alamy

314–315 The Southwestern Company illustration; World Book illustration; Shutterstock; World Book illustration

316–317 The Southwestern Company illustration; The Southwestern Company illustration; World Book illustration; The Southwestern Company illustration; The Southwestern Company illustration

318–319 Alexander Tsiaras/Photo Researchers, Inc.; World Book illustration; World Book illustration; World Book illustration; World Book illustration

320–321 The Southwestern Company illustration; Baldwin H. Ward & Kathryn C. Ward/Corbis

322–323 The Southwestern Company illustration

324–325 The Southwestern Company illustration

344–345 The Southwestern Company illustration; Nigel Cattlin/Photo Researchers, Inc.

346–347 World Book illustration; The Southwestern Company illustration; The Southwestern Company illustration; World Book illustration

348–349 Neil Fraser/Alamy; James M. Bell/Photo Researchers, Inc.; Volker Steger/Photo Researchers, Inc.

350–351 Shutterstock; Shutterstock; Shutterstock; The Southwestern Company illustration; Shutterstock

352–353 Shutterstock; Shutterstock; World Book illustration; The Southwestern Company illustration

354–355 World Book illustration

356–357 The Southwestern Company illustration

358–359 Nigel Cattlin/Photo Researchers, Inc.; Andrew Lambert Photography/Photo Researchers, Inc.; Phototake, Inc./Alamy; Shutterstock

360–361 Shutterstock; World Book illustration

362–363 Alan Pembleton/Alamy

364–365 The Southwestern Company illustration; David Taylor/Photo Researchers, Inc.

368–369 Popperfoto/Getty Images; The Southwestern Company illustration; Clive Streeter/Getty Images

370–371 Roger Viollet/Getty Images; Dorling Kindersley/Getty Images

372–373 World Book illustration; The Southwestern Company illustration

376–377 Mary Evans Picture Library/Alamy

378–379 SSPL/Getty Images; Shutterstock

380–381 Getty Images

382–383 The Southwestern Company illustration

384–385 Hulton-Deutsch Collection/Corbis; World Book illustration

386–387 JTB Photo/SuperStock; Wildlife GmbH/Alamy

390–391 Shutterstock; The Southwestern Company illustration

392–393 Science Source/Photo Researchers, Inc.; The Southwestern Company illustration

394–395 Interfoto/Alamy; World Book illustration

396–397 Shutterstock

398–399 Biophoto Associates/Photo Researchers, Inc.

400–401 The Southwestern Company illustration; The Southwestern Company illustration; Manfred Kage/Getty Images; David J. Green/Alamy

402–403 X-ray: NASA/CXC/Caltech/D. Fox et al.; Illustration: NASA/D. Berry; Library of Congress/digital version by Science Faction/Getty Images

404–405 NASA; The Southwestern Company illustration

406–407 World Book illustration; SuperStock/Getty Images

408–409 Interfoto/Alamy; Shutterstock

410–411 Shutterstock; The Southwestern Company illustration; The Southwestern Company illustration

412–413 Shutterstock

414–415 The Southwestern Company illustration; The Southwestern Company illustration

416–417 Kallista Images/Getty Images; World Book illustration

418–419 Scott Camazine/Alamy; SPL/Photo Researchers, Inc.; The Southwestern Company illustration; The Southwestern Company illustration

420–421 World Book illustration; Laguna Design/Photo Researchers, Inc.; SPL/Photo Researchers, Inc.

422–423 Will & Deni McIntyre/Photo Researchers, Inc.; The Southwestern Company illustration

424–425 Corbis; Corbis; BSIP/Photo Researchers, Inc.

440–441 Larry Lilac/Alamy; Peter Stone/Alamy

442–443 Arctic Images/Alamy; The Southwestern Company illustration; The Southwestern Company illustration; The Southwestern Company illustration

444–445 Shutterstock; The Southwestern Company illustration

446–447 Shutterstock; World Book illustration; Marvin Dembinsky Photo Associates/Alamy

448–449 World Book map; Mary Evans Picture Library/Alamy; World Book map; NOAA

450–451 The Southwestern Company illustration; Jeff Schmaltz, MODIS Rapid Response Team, NASA/GSFC; World Book illustration; The Natural History Museum/The Image Works

452–453 Classic Image/Alamy; FLPA/Alamy; World Book illustration; World Book map

454–455 Shutterstock; World Book Illustration; Jaques Descloitres, MODIS Rapid Response Team, NASA/GSFC; World Book Illustration

456–457 The Southwestern Company illustration; Ivan Alvarado/Reuters/Corbis; World Book Illustration; The Southwestern Company illustration

458–459 The Southwestern Company illustration; World Book Illustration; World Book map; Shutterstock

460–461 Shutterstock; Shutterstock; The Southwestern Company illustration; U.S. Geological Survey; U.S. Geological Survey

462–463 Danilo Calilung/Corbis; Hubert Stadler/Corbis; Shutterstock; Shutterstock; Julian Nieman/Alamy; World Book illustration

464–465 Shutterstock; The Southwestern Company illustration; Shutterstock; Shutterstock; Shutterstock

466–467 Shutterstock; Shutterstock; Ashley Cooper/Corbis

468–469 John Carnemolla/Corbis; Shutterstock; Yonhap/epa/Corbis

470–471 Shutterstock; PhotoDisc, Inc.; PhotoDisc, Inc.; The Southwestern Company illustration; PhotoDisc, Inc.

472–473 The Southwestern Company illustration; Shutterstock; World Book map

474–475 Mary Evans Picture Library/Alamy; The Southwestern Company illustration

476–477 Shutterstock; Joel Arem/Photo Researchers, Inc.; Francois Gohier/Photo Researchers, Inc.

478–479 Shutterstock; Shutterstock; Associated Press

480–481 Shutterstock; The Southwestern Company illustration; Shutterstock

482–483 Shutterstock

484–485 World Book illustration; Gordon Wiltsie/National Geographic Stock; Jason Edwards/Getty Images; Sinclair Stammers/Photo Researchers, Inc.

486–487 Shutterstock; Marvin Dembinsky Photo Associates/Alamy; Mark A. Schneider/Photo Researchers, Inc.

488–489 Wildlife GmbH/Alamy; Mark Schneider/Visuals Unlimited, Inc./Getty Images; Kaj R. Svensson/Photo Researchers, Inc.; James Randklev/Getty Images; Shutterstock

490–491 Martin Sheilds/Photo Researchers, Inc.; Dreamstime; Laurie O'Keefe/Photo Researchers, Inc.; World Book illustration

492–493 World Book map; National Geographic Society/Corbis; Friedrich Saurer/Photo Researchers, Inc.; Richard Bizley/Photo Researchers, Inc.; Ken Lucas/Getty Images

494–495 World Book illustration; World Book illustration; World Book illustration; World Book illustration; World Book map; World Book illustration; Joe Tucciarone/Photo Researchers, Inc.

496–497 World Book illustration; World Book map; Dreamstime; Mike Agliolo/Corbis

498–499 World Book illustration; World Book map; Shutterstock; Shutterstock; World Book map

500–501 World Book illustration; Imagebroker/Alamy; The Natural History Museum/Alamy

502–503 World Book illustration; Shutterstock; The Southwestern Company illustration

504–505 Shutterstock; World Book map; World Book map; Dreamstime

506–507 Jason Langley/Alamy; Michael P. Gadomski/Photo Researchers, Inc.; Calkins/U.S. Geological Society

508–509 Panoramic Images/Getty Images; Shutterstock; Shutterstock

510–511 The Southwestern Company illustration; Shutterstock; The Southwestern Company illustration

512–513 Karen Kasmauski/Getty Images; Shutterstock

514–515 Worldsat International/Photo Researchers, Inc.; Dreamstime; Marilyn Dunstan Photography/Alamy

516–517 PhotoDisc, Inc.; The Southwestern Company illustration; Derek Croucher/Alamy; The Southwestern Company illustration

518–519 PhotoDisc, Inc.; The Southwestern Company illustration; PhotoDisc, Inc.

520–521 David Boag/Alamy; PhotoDisc, Inc.

522–523 The Southwestern Company illustration; The Southwestern Company illustration

524–525 Thomas Hallstein/Alamy; World Book illustration; John Elk III/Alamy

526–527 U.S. Geological Survey; The Southwestern Company illustration; Dennis Flaherty/Getty Images; The Southwestern Company illustration; Shutterstock; The Southwestern Company illustration

528–529 Dreamstime

530–531 World Book photo; Shutterstock; World Book illustration

532–533 Associated Press; Shutterstock

534–535 World Book illustration

536–537 The Southwestern Company map; The Granger Collection, NYC

538–539 World Book Illustration; Cephas Picture Library/Alamy

540–541 The Southwestern Company illustration; Shutterstock

542–543 The Southwestern Company illustration; The Southwestern Company illustration; The Southwestern Company illustration; The Southwestern Company illustration

544–545 World Book Illustration; NASA

546–547 Jim Reed/Getty Images; PhotoDisc, Inc.; Ilene MacDonald/Alamy

548–549 Jim Reed/Corbis; Shutterstock; Don Farrall/Getty Images; World Book Illustration

550–551 National Weather Service, NOAA; Shutterstock; World Book illustration

552–553 Scott Camazine/Alamy; SSPL/Getty Images; Shutterstock; Visuals Unlimited/Corbis

554–555 World Book illustration; The Southwestern Company illustration

556–557 Shutterstock; World Book map; Dreamstime

558–559 Dreamstime

560–561 Shutterstock

562–563 Louise Murray/Alamy; The Southwestern Company illustration; World Book Illustration

564–565 World Book illustration; Shutterstock

566–567 Peter Horree/Alamy; Maria Stenzel/National Geographic Stock; Marek Zuk/Alamy

568–569 Steve Bloom Images/Alamy; Richard Ellis/Photo Researchers, Inc.

570–571 World Book map

572–573 World Book map; Michael Patrick O'Neill/Alamy; World Book map

574–575 World Book map; World Book illustration

576–577 World Book illustration; Dreamstime

578–579 Francois Gohier/Photo Researchers, Inc.; World Book illustration

580–581 Mark Conlin/Alamy; Alexis Rosenfeld/Photo Researchers. Inc.

588–589 Jan Wlodarczyk/Alamy; Marka/SuperStock

590–591 PhotoDisc, Inc.; Philip Schermeister/Getty Images; Alex Segre/Alamy

592–593 The Southwestern Company illustration; Shutterstock; Dr. Tony Brain/Photo Researchers, Inc.

594–595 Shutterstock; Photos.com; The Southwestern Company illustration

596–597 Rand McMeins/Getty Images; Ted Kinsman/Photo Researchers, Inc.; Shutterstock; M. Timothy O'Keefe/Alamy; Science Picture Co./Getty Images; www.isleroyalewolf.org

598–599 Ted Kinsman/Photo Researchers, Inc.; F1online digitale Bildagentur GmbH/Alamy; Wesley Hitt/Alamy; Nigel Cattlin/Alamy; Shutterstock; Shutterstock

600–601 Peter Arnold, Inc./Alamy; Federico Veronesi/Getty Images; Shutterstock; Biophoto Associates/Photo Researchers, Inc.

602–603 Shutterstock; Shutterstock; The Southwestern Company illustration; The Southwestern Company illustration

604–605 The Southwestern Company illustration; World Book Illustration

606–607 The Southwestern Company illustration; The Southwestern Company illustration; World Book illustration

608–609 Images & Stories/Alamy

610–611 World Book illustration; World Book photo

612–613 Gregory G. Dimijian, M.D./Photo Researchers, Inc.; Per Karlsson-BKWine.com/Alamy; WorldFoto/Alamy; Prisma Bildagentur AG/Alamy

614–615 World Book illustration; Norbert Wu Productions; World Book illustration; Shutterstock; World Book illustration; World Book illustration; World Book illustration; World Book illustration; World Book illustration

616–617 World Book illustration; Cro Magnon/Alamy; World Book photo

618–619 PhotoDisc, Inc.

620–621 Thomas & Pat Leeson/Photo Researchers, Inc.; Shutterstock

622–623 Clint Farlinger/Alamy; All Canada Photos/Alamy; Greg Dimijian/Photo Researchers, Inc.; Ron and Patty Thomas/Getty Images; Paul Thompson Images/Alamy; Richard Susanto/Getty Images; Prisma Bildagentur AG/Alamy

624–625 Philippe Psaila/Photo Researchers, Inc.; Bob Gibbons/FLPA/Photo Researchers, Inc.

626–627 World Book photo; John Doebley; Mike Grandmaison/Corbis

628–629 Inga Spence/Photo Researchers, Inc.; Alternative Garden Supply

630–631 William Leaman/Alamy; Shutterstock; World Book illustration; Keren Su/Getty Images; World Book illustration

632–633 Chris Howes/Wild Places Photography/Alamy; PhotoDisc, Inc.; The Southwestern Company illustration; Oxford Scientific/Photolibrary/Getty Images

634–635 Digital Stock; The Southwestern Company illustration; Karen Kasmauski/Science Faction/Corbis

636–637 Getty Images; World Book map

638–639 National Geographic/Getty Images; Shutterstock

640–641 Jeffrey Lepore/Photo Researchers, Inc.; Shutterstock

642–643 National Geographic/Getty Images; Shutterstock; Getty Images

644–645 U.S. Department of Energy; Shutterstock

646–647 Shutterstock; U. Bellhaeuser/Getty Images; Shutterstock

648–649 Alfred Pasieka/Photo Researchers, Inc.; Getty Images; World Book map

650–651 Photos.com; Shutterstock

652–653 Medioimages/PhotoDisc/Getty Images; Karen Kasmauski/Science Faction/Corbis; Karen Kasmauski/Corbis

654–655 Kevin McNeal/Getty Images; Bettmann/Corbis

656–657 PhotoDisc, Inc.; Luis Veiga/Getty Images

658–659 Washington Post/Getty Images; Shutterstock

660–661 Getty Images; Arctic-Images/Corbis

662–663   AFP/Getty Images; Nick Suydam/ Alamy; Sheila Terry/Photo Researchers, Inc.

664–665   Photos.com; The Southwestern Company illustration; Photos.com; Car Culture/Corbis

666–667   World Book diagram; The Southwestern Company illustration; PhotoDisc, Inc.

668–669   Ryan McGinnis/Getty Images; Panoramic Images/Getty Images; Time & Life Pictures/Getty Images

670–671   The Southwestern Company illustration; Shutterstock

672–673   Nigel Cattlin/Alamy; NASA/ National Snow & Ice Data Center; Christopher Pillitz/Getty Images

674–675   Visions of America, LLC/ Alamy; Corbis Nomad/Alamy; Shutterstock; AFP/Getty Images

676–677   Kendra Luck/San Francisco Chronicle/Corbis; Peter Arnold, Inc./Alamy; Wolfgang Flamisch/ Corbis

678–679   Ted Spiegel/Corbis; NASA/ Goddard Space Flight Center

680–681   Alex Segre/Alamy; Shutterstock; Shutterstock

682–683   World Book illustration; Sascha Pflaeging/Getty Images

684–685   Mitchell Funk/Getty Images; Antony Nettle/Alamy; Shutterstock; Shutterstock

686–687   Jochen Tack/Alamy; Alberto Incrocci/Getty Images

688–689   The Southwestern Company illustration; PhotoDisc, Inc.; Getty Images

690–691   Associated Press; World Book illustration; Imagebroker/Alamy; John Lund/Getty Images

692–693   The Southwestern Company illustration; Shutterstock; Bloomberg/Getty Images

694–695   Michel Philippot/Sygma/Corbis; Getty Images

696–697   PhotoDisc, Inc.; Getty Images; John Gaffen/Alamy

698–699   Roger Ressmeyer/Corbis; Picture Contact BV/Alamy; Getty Images

700–701   World Book illustration; Mark Newman/Photo Researchers, Inc.

702–703   World Resources Institute

704–705   World Book illustration; World Book illustration; World Book illustration; World Book illustration; Shutterstock

706–707   Imagebroker/Alamy; Shutterstock; PhotoDisc, Inc.; Shutterstock

708–709   The Southwestern Company illustration; Shutterstock

710–711   PhotoDisc, Inc.; PhotoDisc, Inc.

712–713   The Southwestern Company illustration; Shutterstock

714–715   Arterra Picture Library/Alamy; Shutterstock; Peter Titmuss/ Alamy; Dr. George Wilder/Visuals Unlimited/Corbis

716–717   PhotoDisc, Inc.; World Book photo

718–719   The Southwestern Company illustration; PhotoDisc, Inc.; PhotoDisc, Inc.

720–721   World Book illustration; World Book illustration

722–723   PhotoDisc, Inc.; The Southwestern Company illustration

724–725   Getty Images

726–727   The Southwestern Company illustration; National Geographic/ Getty Images; Tyrone Turner/ Getty Images

728–729   The Southwestern Company illustration

730–731   PhotoDisc, Inc.; World Book illustration; World Book illustration; World Book illustration

732–733   World Book Map; Shutterstock

734–735   PhotoDisc, Inc.

736–737   The Southwestern Company illustration

738–739   Photos.com; The Southwestern Company illustration

740–741   World Book illustration

742–743   PhotoDisc, Inc.; PhotoDisc, Inc.

744–745   PhotoDisc, Inc.; World Book illustration; PhotoDisc, Inc.

750–751   artpartner-images.com/Alamy; Ace Stock Limited/Alamy

752–753   NASA; National Geographic Society/ Corbis; Stefano Bianchetti/Corbis; Corbis; Getty Images; Bettmann/ Corbis

754–755   Shutterstock; Shutterstock; blickwinkel/Alamy; Dreamstime; Lawrence Lawry/Photo Researchers, Inc.; Doug Martin/ Photo Researchers, Inc.

756–757   The Southwestern Company illustration; The Southwestern Company illustration

758–759   The Southwestern Company illustration; The Southwestern Company illustration; Nick Clements/Getty Images; The Southwestern Company illustration; Hulton-Deutsch Collection/Corbis

760–761   Getty Images

762–763   Bettmann/Corbis

764–765   Ilene MacDonald/Alamy; Shutterstock; Ilene MacDonald/ Alamy; Flirt/SuperStock

766–767   The Southwestern Company illustration; The Southwestern Company illustration; NASA

768–769   The Southwestern Company illustration; World Book illustration; World Book illustration; World Book illustration

770–771   Blend Images/SuperStock; Blend Images/SuperStock; The Southwestern Company illustration; World Book illustration

772–773   World Book illustration; World Book illustration; World Book illustration; World Book illustration; World Book illustration

774–775   The Southwestern Company illustration; Shutterstock

776–777   World Book illustration; Shutterstock

778–779   Shutterstock; Shutterstock; Shutterstock; Shutterstock; Shutterstock; The Southwestern Company illustration; Shutterstock; Dreamstime; Shutterstock; Shutterstock; Shutterstock; Flirt/ SuperStock; Shutterstock; Bryan and Cherry Alexander/Photo Researchers, Inc.; Doug Martin/ Photo Researchers, Inc.

780–781   Shutterstock; The Southwestern Company illustration; The Southwestern Company illustration; The Southwestern Company illustration; The Southwestern Company illustration; The Southwestern Company illustration; John E. Fletcher/Getty Images; Mark Schneider/Getty Images; Mark van Aardt/Getty Images

782–783   Steve Maslowski/Getty Images; The Southwestern Company illustration; The Southwestern Company illustration

784–785   Tetra Images/SuperStock

786–787   World Book illustration; World Book illustration; World Book illustration; World Book illustration

788–789   The Southwestern Company illustration; World Book illustration; World Book illustration

790–791   The Southwestern Company illustration; World Book illustration

792–793   World Book illustration; World Book illustration; The Southwestern Company illustration

794–795 Shutterstock; World Book illustration; World Book illustration; World Book illustration

796–797 Health Protection Agency/Photo Researchers, Inc.; World Book illustration; Spencer Grant/Photo Researchers, Inc.

798–799 The Southwestern Company illustration; Shutterstock

800–801 PSL Images/Alamy; World Book illustration; World Book illustration; World Book illustration

802–803 World Book illustration; The Southwestern Company illustration

804–805 U.S. Department of Defense; The Southwestern Company illustration; The Southwestern Company illustration

806–807 World Book illustration; Dorling Kindersley/Getty Images

808–809 The Southwestern Company illustration; Gail Mooney/Corbis; PhotoDisc, Inc.

810–811 Paul Ridsdale/Alamy; Scenics & Science/Alamy; Shutterstock; The Southwestern Company illustration; World Book illustration

812–813 SSPL/Getty Images; Shutterstock; The Southwestern Company illustration; Mike Dunning/Getty Images

814–815 World Book illustration; The Southwestern Company illustration

816–817 Library of Congress/digital version by Science Faction/Getty Images; The Southwestern Company illustration

818–819 The Southwestern Company illustration; The Southwestern Company illustration; Sciencephotos/Alamy

820–821 Prisma Archivo/Alamy; Stockbyte/Getty Images

822–823 The Southwestern Company illustration; World Book illustration; The Southwestern Company illustration

824–825 World Book illustration; World Book illustration

826–827 Shutterstock; Charles D. Winters/Photo Researchers, Inc.

828–829 World Book illustration; World Book illustration; The Southwestern Company illustration; GIPhotoStock/Photo Researchers, Inc.; The Southwestern Company illustration

830–831 Photos.com; Universal Images Group Limited/Alamy

832–833 Interfoto/Alamy; Science Source/Photo Researchers, Inc.

834–835 World Book illustration; World Book illustration

836–837 World Book illustration; World Book photo; World Book illustration; World Book photo; The Southwestern Company illustration

838–839 World Book illustration; World Book photo; World Book illustration; World Book photo

840–841 GIPhotoStock/Photo Researchers, Inc.; The Southwestern Company illustration; The Southwestern Company illustration; World Book illustration

842–843 Purestock/Getty Images; The Southwestern Company illustration; The Southwestern Company illustration; The Southwestern Company illustration; The Southwestern Company illustration; World Book illustration; World Book illustration

844–845 World Book illustration; The Southwestern Company illustration; World Book illustration

846–847 The Southwestern Company illustration; Shutterstock

848–849 The Southwestern Company illustration; World Book photo

850–851 World Book illustration; Olivier Voisin/Photo Researchers, Inc.; World Book illustration

852–853 Getty Images; Library of Congress; Victor de Schwanberg/Photo Researchers, Inc.

854–855 Russell Kightley/Photo Researchers, Inc.; Russell Kightley/Photo Researchers, Inc.; The Southwestern Company illustration

856–857 SuperStock/Getty Images; Everett Collection/SuperStock; The Southwestern Company illustration; Time & Life Pictures/Getty Images

858–859 Daily Mail/Rex/Alamy

860–861 PhotoDisc, Inc.; The Southwestern Company illustration; PhotoDisc, Inc.; World Book illustration; ESA/NASA/SOHO; U.S. Department of Energy

862–863 Bettmann/Corbis; Hank Morgan/Photo Researchers, Inc.

864–865 Bettmann/Corbis; CERN

868–869 ClassicStock/Alamy; The Southwestern Company illustration

870–871 Shutterstock; The Southwestern Company illustration; The Southwestern Company illustration; Shutterstock

872–873 World Book illustration; The Southwestern Company illustration; The Southwestern Company illustration

874–875 The Southwestern Company illustration; The Southwestern Company illustration; The Southwestern Company illustration; The Southwestern Company illustration; Shutterstock

876–877 The Southwestern Company illustration; The Southwestern Company illustration; Shutterstock

878–879 The Southwestern Company illustration; The Southwestern Company illustration

880–881 The Southwestern Company illustration; Shutterstock

882–883 The Southwestern Company illustration; The Southwestern Company illustration; The Southwestern Company illustration

884–885 The Southwestern Company illustration; The Southwestern Company illustration

886–887 Shutterstock; The Southwestern Company illustration; The Southwestern Company illustration; The Southwestern Company illustration

888–889 The Southwestern Company illustration; The Southwestern Company illustration

890–891 Dreamstime

898–899 NASA, ESA, and The Hubble Heritage Team (STScI/AURA); NASA

900–901 The Southwestern Company illustration

902–903 The Granger Collection, NYC.; World Book illustration; World Book illustration

904–905 SuperStock; Bettmann/Corbis

906–907 The Southwestern Company illustration; The Southwestern Company illustration; The Southwestern Company illustration

908–909 NASA; The Southwestern Company illustration; The Southwestern Company illustration

910–911 World Book illustration; The Southwestern Company illustration

912–913 Shutterstock

914–915 NASA/JPL-Caltech; PhotoDisc, Inc.

916–917 NASA/JPL; World Book illustration

918–919 World Book illustration

920–921 World Book illustration; NASA/JPL; NASA

922–923 Stocktrek Images, Inc./Alamy; NASA

924–925 Laurent Laveder/Photo Researchers, Inc.; World Book illustration

926–927 ESA/DLR/FU Berlin (G. Neukum)/ epa/Corbis; NASA/JPL/Malin Space Science Systems; NASA/ JPL-Caltech/ASU; NASA/JSC

928–929 World Book illustration; NASA/ JPL/Space Science Institute; NASA

930–931 NASA/JPL/Space Science Institute; NASA/JPL/Space Science Institute; NASA/JPL/STScl

932–933 NASA/JPL; NASA/JPL; NASA

934–935 D. Nunuk/Photo Researchers, Inc.; NASA/JPL; Francois Gohier/Photo Researchers, Inc.

936–937 World Book illustration; World Book illustration

938–939 Greg Piepol/Photo Researchers, Inc.; Greg Piepol/Photo Researchers, Inc.; NASA/Trace

940–941 NASA/STSi; World Book illustration

942–943 NASA/STScl Digitized Sky Survey/ Noel Carboni; NASA/JPL-Caltech/ J. Stauffer (SSC/Caltech)

944–945 World Book illustration

946–947 The Southwestern Company illustration; Tod Strohmayer (GSFC), CXC, NASA, Illustration: Dana Berry (CXC)

948–949 NASA/GSFC; NASA

950–951 NASA; Richard Yandrick/ CosmicImage

952–953 NASA/ESA/Hubble Heritage Team; JPL/NASA; The Southwestern Company illustration

954–955 NASA/CXC/Umass Amherst/ M.D.Stage et al.; John Chumack/ Photo Researchers, Inc.

956–957 Mount Wilson and Palomar Observatories; NASA/JPL/ California Institute of Technology

958–959 NASA, ESA, G. Illingworth and R. Bouwens (University of California, Santa Cruz), and the HUDF09 Team; Time & Life Pictures/ Getty Images

960–961 X-ray: NASA/CXC/CfA/R. Kraft et al.; Submillimeter: MPlfR/ESO/ APEX/A. Weiss et al.; Optical: ESO/WFl; Digital Stock; The Southwestern Company illustration

962–963 AURA/STScl/NASA; The Southwestern Company illustration

964–965 NASA/CXC/CfA/M. Markevitch et al./ESO WFI/Magellan/U. Arizona/D. Clowe et al.; Roger Ressmeyer/Corbis

966–967 World Book illustration; The Southwestern Company illustration; Dr. Seth Shostak/ Photo Researchers, Inc.

968–969 Time & Life Pictures/Getty Images

970–971 World Book illustration; The Southwestern Company illustration

972–973 NASA; Bettmann/Corbis

974–975 NASA/Sandra Joseph and Kevin O'Connell; NASA

976–977 Bettmann/Corbis; SPL/Photo Researchers, Inc.; Bettmann/ Corbis; NASA

978–979 NASA; NASA; Hulton-Deutsch Collection/Corbis; NASA

980–981 NASA; NASA/JPL; NASA

982–983 NASA; NASA; NASA; NASA

984–985 NASA; NASA; NASA

986–987 X-ray (NASA/CXC/Virginia/A. Reines et al); Radio (NRAO/AUI/ NSF); Optical (NASA/STScl); NASA; NASA/Kepler mission/ Wendy Stenzel; NASA/JPL

Index

A

aa, 527, 582
abiotic factors in ecosystems, 600, 746
ABO blood group system, 76
abrasion, 510, 516
abscisic acid, 143, 144, 145
abscission layer, 127
absolute magnitude, 942, 943, 988
absolute temperature scale, 357, 788, 796
absolute zero, 357, 788, 790, 796, 892
absorbers of radiant energy, 795, 912
absorption
  defined, 892
  light, 836
  sound, 802
  water transport in plants, 133
abundance distribution, 955
abyssal plains, 475, 579, 614
acacias, 610, 619
acanthodians, 488
acaricides, 713
Acatama Desert, 611
acceleration
  deceleration, 892
  defined, 892
  force, 765
  formula, 866
  second law of motion, 762–763
  time measurement, 761
accelerators, particle. *See* particle accelerators
accommodation (optical), 245
acetaldehyde, 413
acetic acid, 413
acetylcholine, 230
acetylene (ethyne), 409, 411, 412
Achilles' tendon, 229, 255
achromatic lenses, 909
acid dissociation constant, 389
acid rain, 633, 666–669, 746

acids, 386–389
  acidic solutions, 388
  defined, 436
  hazardous wastes, 694
  naming, 360, 361
  neutralization reactions, 359
  organic, 418, 438
  pH scale, 388–389, 666
  properties, 386
acoustics, 754, 806–809, 892
actinide metals, 322, 326
actinium
  alphabetical guide to the elements, 327
  periodic table of the elements, 322
  symbol and atomic number, 324
activation energy, 368
active galaxies, 960, 988
active medium, 851
active transport, 53
acupuncture, 102
acute retroviral syndrome, 301
adaptation (vision), 245
adder's tongue fern (*Ophioglossum reticulatum*), 142
addiction to drugs, 299
addition reactions, 413, 436
additive method of color mixing, 849
adductor longus muscle, 254
adductor magnus muscle, 255
adenine, 65, 66, 304, 414–415
adenosine diphosphate (ADP), 137, 304
adenosine triphosphate (ATP)
  animal metabolism, 189
  cells manufacture, 53, 417
  defined, 304
  DNA replication, 65
  fatty acids, 417
  mitochondria, 51, 119
  plant respiration, 136, 137
Adirondack Mountains, 666, 668
adolescence, 289
adrenal glands, 240, 241, 257
adrenalin, 240

adrenocorticosteroids (corticoids), 240
aerobic exercises, 281
Africa
  deforestation, 703
  Gondwanaland, 448, 449
  Great Rift Valley, 501
  human origins, 163
  Jurassic period, 494
  middle latitude climate zone, 561
  Paleogene and Neogene periods, 498, 499
  population growth, 636
  savanna, 590, 600
  tropical climates, 559
  tropical rain forest, 608
  world population density, 637
  world precipitation distribution, 732
agar, 109
Age of Exploration, 104
aggregate fruits, 130
aggression, animal, 216–217
aging. *See* senescence (aging)
agnaths (Agnatha), 155, 178
agriculture, 708–717
  See also irrigation
  astronomy, 900
  climate change, 674, 675, 677
  domestication of animals, 616
  domestication of plants, 624–625
  early technology for controlling plants, 626
  Green Revolution, 717
  modern technology for controlling plants, 627–629
  origins, 102
  recycling organic wastes, 692
  water conservation, 732
  water pollution, 723
  wetland destruction, 700
A horizon, 532, 708
AIDS
  discovery of virus, 23
  HIV (human immunodeficiency virus), 301, 411
  sexually transmitted diseases, 301

air

See also atmosphere

air masses, 542–543, 582

animal movement, 185

density, 776

hot air rises, 536

indoor pollution, 650–651

pollution, 660–665

"pure," 660

sound velocity, 804

airplane noise pollution, 684, 687

Aiton, William, 105

alanine, 419

Alaska National Interest Lands Conservation Act (1980), 657

Albireo (star system), 951

alcohol abuse, 298

alcoholic beverages

alcoholism, 298

diet and cancer, 267

general dietary guidelines, 266

yeasts in fermentation, 150

alcoholism, 298

alcohols

See also ethanol (ethyl alcohol)

defined, 436

glycerol, 262, 416, 417

methanol, 358

Aldrin, Edwin "Buzz", 923, 973, 980

Aleutian Islands, 451

algae

See also brown algae (Phaeophyta); cyanobacteria (blue-green algae); green algae (Chlorophyta); red algae (Rhodophyta)

Cretaceous period, 497

eukaryotic cells, 47

healthy water systems, 720

kingdom Protista, 94

lichens, 95

photosynthesis, 134

Algol (Beta Persei), 951

alicyclics, 409, 411, 436

alimentary canal, 236–237

aliphatics, 408–409

defined, 436

reactions, 412

structure and names, 410–411

alkali metals

alphabetical guide to the elements, 326

defined, 436

periodic table of the elements, 320, 322

alkaline dry cells, 395

alkaline earth metals

alphabetical guide to the elements, 326

periodic table of the elements, 320, 322

alkaloids, 137

alkanes, 408

defined, 436

structure and names, 409, 410

alkenes, 408

defined, 436

naming, 410–411

reactions, 412

structure, 409

alkyls, 412, 418

alkynes, 409

defined, 436

naming, 411

reactions, 412

Allegheny Mountains, 473

alleles, 71, 75, 76, 143, 304

Allen Telescope Array, 967

alleopathy, 619

allergens, 303

allergies, 303

Allosaurus, 158, 159, 161

alluvial fans, 513, 582

Alpha Aurigae, 945

Alpha Centauri, 944, 945

alpha particles

defined, 436, 892

nuclear reactions, 406

particle accelerators, 856

radioactivity, 402, 682

symbol and properties, 404

alpine glaciers, 514

Alps, 517, 525, 613

alternating current (AC), 816

alternation of generations, 111, 112

alternative arrangement of leaves, 126

altitude, climate and, 554–555

altitude (elevation) of a star, 906

altocumulus clouds, 540

altostratus clouds, 540

altruism, 218

aluminum

alphabetical guide to the elements, 327

density, 776

Earth's crust, 447

electrical conductivity, 815

main group elements, 398

nuclear reactions, 406

ores, 529

periodic table of the elements, 323

recycling, 693

states of matter, 350

symbol and atomic number, 324

alveoli, 234

Alzheimer's disease, 293, 297

Amanita muscaria, 95

Amanita phalloides, 151

Amazon rain forest, 704

amber, 478, 810, 813

American chestnut trees, 598

americium

alphabetical guide to the elements, 327

periodic table of the elements, 322

symbol and atomic number, 324

amine group, 418

aminoacetic acid, 413

amino acids, 418–419

adenosine triphosphate (ATP) production, 417

animal metabolism, 189

classification of animals, 171

polypeptide chains, 66

proteins, 67, 260, 414, 418–419

vegetarian diet, 267

ammonia

animal waste products, 201

common compounds, 358

Haber process, 349, 371
hydrides, 399
molar mass, 374
molecules, 346
pH, 389
substitute for ozone-destroying
    chemicals, 681
ammonites, 159, 489
amoebas, 98, 153
amorphous solids, 350,
    778, 780
Ampère, André Marie, 811, 817
amperes, 817
amphibians (Amphibia)
    See also frogs
    Age of Amphibians, 157
    Aristotle's classification of
        animals, 164
    chordates, 97, 178, 179
    circulatory system, 192
    cold-blooded animals, 203
    dependence on aqueous
        environment, 172
    eyes, 204
    life span, 207
    lobe-fins, 156
    metamorphosis, 187
    Pennsylvanian epoch, 491
    reproduction, 186
    respiratory system, 194
    waste nitrogen, 201
amphiboles, 466
amplification of sound, 807
amplitude (waves), 799, 892
amylases, 137
anagenesis, 36
analogy, 170, 304
anaphase (mitosis), 56, 59, 197
anatomy
    animals, 166–167, 180–182
    fungi, 148
    history of science, 22
    human, 224–257
    organ systems, 60
    plants, 99, 105, 118–131
Andes Mountains, 496
Andromeda Galaxy, 914, 957

angiosperms (flowering plants),
    116–117
    classification of plants, 96, 107
    Cretaceous period, 497
    defined, 304
    early land plants, 101
angle of incidence, 800, 836, 841
angle of reflection, 837, 841
angle of refraction, 800, 836
angstrom units, 835
anhydrite, 465
animal ecology, 588
Animalia. *See* animals (Animalia)
animal rights, 617
animals (Animalia), 152–225
    See also amphibians (Amphibia);
        arthropods (Arthropoda);
        birds (Aves); chordates
        (Chordata); cnidarians
        (coelenterates); fishes;
        flatworms (Platyhelminthes);
        mammals (Mammalia);
        mollusks (Mollusca); reptiles
        (Reptilia); roundworms
        (Nematoda); segmented
        worms (Annelida); sponges
        (Porifera)
    acid rain, 668
    anatomy, 166–167, 180–182
    Aristotle's classification, 164–165
    behavior, 208–223
    Cambrian period, 154, 483, 486
    cells, 44, 48, 51
    climate change, 675
    consumer organisms, 601
    deserts, 611
    Devonian period, 489
    differences between plants
        and, 152
    emergence, 154, 485
    endangered species, 638–643
    eukaryotic cells, 47
    fat, 262, 263
    first life on Earth, 152–157
    fruit dispersal, 130
    genetic diversity, 716–717
    gradations among phyla, 172

    and humans, 616–617
    infectious disease spread, 292
    kingdom Animalia, 97, 172
    life cycles, 186–187
    life spans, 188, 206–207
    Linnaean classification, 90, 165
    modern classification, 91,
        170–179
    morphology, 180–187
    movement, 184–185
    move to land, 155
    natural resources, 638
    number of species catalogued,
        164, 188
    oil spills, 724
    physiology, 188–207
    savanna, 610
    size and shape, 183
    size range, 172
    smog's effects, 665
    social behavior, 214–219
    tundra, 614
    ultraviolet radiation's effects, 680
    water pollution, 726
    weathering of rock, 507
    wildlife conservation, 642–643
Animal Welfare Act (1985), 617
anions, 315, 436
anisotropic solids, 781
Ankylosaurus, 161
Annelida. *See* segmented worms
    (Annelida)
annual plants, 147
annual rhythms, 209
annular eclipses, 924, 988
anodes, 391
anorexia nervosa, 284
Antarctica
    climate change, 672, 673
    Gondwanaland, 448
    ice sheet, 514, 573
    meteorites, 915
    nature reserve, 706
    ozone layer, 678, 679
    Paleogene and Neogene
        periods, 498
    polar climate, 562

world precipitation distribution, 732

Antarctic Treaty (1961), 706

anterior tibial artery and vein, 253

anthers, 128

Anthophyta, 96, 107, 117

anthrax, 93

antibiotics
    defined, 304
    fungi, 150
    penicillin, 23, 24, 150, 151

antibodies
    genes in production of proteins, 66
    immune system, 302
    proteins, 260
    vaccines, 291

anticlines (upfolds), 522, 523, 582

anticodons, 66

antigens, 302–303

antimatter
    annihilation, 953
    antiparticles, 753, 858, 862, 892

antinoise technology, 687

antinomy
    alphabetical guide to the elements, 327
    periodic table of the elements, 323
    symbol and atomic number, 325

antiparticles, 753, 858, 862, 863, 892

antiquarks, 863

ants, 186, 219

anus, 174, 176, 257

anvil (cloud formation), 541, 549

anvilcirrus clouds, 540

anxiety, 281

aorta, 232, 253

aortic arch, 257

apatite, 461, 463, 528

Apatosaurus, 160

apes
    See also chimpanzees
    brain, 221
    gorillas, 97, 184

orangutans, 641, 642

Paleogene and Neogene periods, 499

primates, 163

social distance, 594

aphids, 186, 599

apical dominance, 144

apical meristems, 120, 138

Aplacophora, 176

Apollo space program, 973
    Apollo 1, 980
    Apollo 11, 23, 923, 973, 980
    Apollo 12, 980
    Apollo 13, 981
    Apollo 16, 972

Appalachian Mountains, 157, 491

apparent magnitude, 942, 989

appendicular skeleton, 226

appendix (anatomy), 256

aquarium fish, 615

aquatic environments, 614–615

aquifers, 564, 565, 582, 728, 746

Arabian Desert, 559, 611

arachnids
    See also spiders
    acaricides, 713
    kingdom Animalia, 97, 177
    respiratory system, 195

arapaimas, 615

Archaea, 92
    defined, 304
    modern classification of plants and animals, 91
    prokaryotic cells, 46, 91

Archaeopteryx, 159, 495

Archean eon, 483

Archimedes, 22, 753, 759

Arctic, the, 562, 614

Arctic Ocean, 571

aretes, 516, 517

arginine, 419

argon
    air, 660
    alphabetical guide to the elements, 327
    chemical bonds, 344
    noble gases, 399

periodic table of the elements, 323
    symbol and atomic number, 324

Aristarchus, 903

Aristotle
    astronomy, 902–903, 904
    classification of plants and animals, 90, 164
    first cause, 43

Arizona Meteor Crater, 935

arkose sandstone, 468

arms, 226, 228

Armstrong, Neil A., 923, 973, 980

aromas, 248

aromatic hydrocarbons, 409, 412, 436

Arrhenius, Svante, 384, 386

arsenic
    alphabetical guide to the elements, 327
    periodic table of the elements, 323
    semiconductors, 827
    symbol and atomic number, 324

arteries
    atherosclerosis, 264, 265, 293, 294
    carotids, 253, 256, 265
    human circulatory system, 233, 253
    hypertension, 295
    plaque, 265, 294

arterioles, 295

artesian wells, 564, 565

arthritis, 282, 293

arthropods (Arthropoda)
    See also arachnids; crustaceans; insects; trilobites
    adapted to land, 172
    centralized nervous system, 220
    kingdom Animalia, 97, 177
    number of species catalogued, 164
    oldest terrestrial fossils, 155
    Pterygotus, 155

artificial colors, 274

artificial flavors, 274

artificial transmutation, 403, 406

Artiodactyla, 179

asbestos, 651

asexual reproduction
animals, 186
cell cycle, 54
cell division, 55
defined, 304
reproduction, 196, 198, 199
types, 55

Asia
deforestation, 703
deserts, 611
Laurasia, 448
medicinal plants, 102
middle latitude climate zone,
560, 561
Ordovician period, 487
Paleogene and Neogene
periods, 498
Pleistocene epoch, 500
polar climate, 562
population growth, 636
temperate deciduous forest, 612
tropical climates, 559
tropical rain forest, 608
world precipitation distribution,
732

asparagine, 419

aspartic acid, 419

astatine
alphabetical guide to the
elements, 328
halogenation of hydrocarbons,
412
periodic table of the elements,
323
symbol and atomic number, 324

asteroids, 934–935
Cretaceous period mass
extinction, 496, 497
defined, 988
Main Belt, 920, 933, 934, 935, 989

asthenosphere, 443, 445, 449, 582

astronauts, 969

astronomical horizon, 906

astronomical units (AU), 914, 988

astronomy, 900–967
See also universe
computer modeling, 915
defined, 988
history, 22–23, 900–901
instruments, 908–915
inverse square law for
illuminance, 847
observations by Egyptians and
Babylonians, 24
Ptolemaic, 22, 902–903, 904

astrophysics, 752

atherosclerosis, 264, 265, 293, 294

Atlantic Ocean
Cretaceous period, 496
Gulf Stream, 556, 572
hurricanes, 547
Paleogene and Neogene
periods, 498
temperature and density, 571
thermohaline circulation, 574
widening, 451

atmosphere
atmospheric circulation, 557
biosphere, 630
defined, 582
formation during Precambrian
time, 484
layers, 534–535
Oparin-Haldane hypothesis of
origin of life, 32, 33
oxygen in Cambrian period, 154
ozone layer, 412, 486, 585,
678–681, 748
plants respire oxygen, 99, 134

atmospheric pressure, 355, 436,
555, 777

atomic bombs
Einstein, 852
first nuclear reaction, 23, 736
Hiroshima and Nagasaki, 407, 860
nuclear fission, 404, 860

atomic clocks, 318, 761

atomic mass units, 356, 357, 436

atomic number, 314, 320, 436

atomic physics
See also nuclear physics

chemistry, 752
types of physics, 755

atomic weight, 317

atoms, 314–319
See also electrons; nucleus
(atomic)
Bohr model, 316–317, 318,
349, 753
chemical bonds, 344–345
chemical equations, 363
Dalton's atomic theory, 316, 349,
376, 753
defined, 436, 892
electron cloud model, 318–319
helium, 855
hydrogen, 854
line spectra and atomic
structure, 848
molecules, 346–349
parts, 314
periodic properties, 321
relative atomic mass, 372
Rutherford model, 23, 316,
317, 753
size, 315, 854
structure, 316–317

ATP. *See* adenosine triphosphate
(ATP)

atria (heart), 232

audions, 825

Audubon, John J., 655

auricle (ear), 246

Australia
deforestation, 703
Gondwanaland, 448, 449
grasslands, 613
Great Barrier Reef, 706
Kakadu National Park, 707
Ordovician period, 487
Paleogene and Neogene
periods, 498
population growth, 636
Quaternary period, 501
rabbits as environmental
boomerang, 632
savanna, 610
temperate deciduous forest, 612

tropical climates, 559
world population density, 637
world precipitation distribution, 732

automobiles
acid rain, 669
air pollution, 663, 665
conserving fossil fuels, 644
heat, 784
hybrids, 659
hydrogen power, 741
noise pollution, 684
recycling wastes, 692
reflecting windshields, 681
second law of thermodynamics, 790
wastes, 689
autonomic nervous system, 202–203, 230
autotrophs, 152
auxins, 127, 138, 139, 143, 144, 304
avalanches, 520–521, 582
Avery Fisher Hall (New York City), 808
avocados, 624
Avogadro, Amedeo, 349, 357
Avogadro's constant, 356, 357, 374, 390, 436, 867
axial skeleton, 226
axillary artery and vein, 253
axis of the Earth, 502
axons, 230, 231
azimuth, 906, 988

B

Baade, Walter, 963
Babylonian astronomy, 900, 901, 902
backbone (vertebral column), 178
bacteria
See also cyanobacteria (blue-green algae)
Age of Bacteria, 152
biotic potential, 592
Cambrian period, 486
cells, 44
defined, 304
designer life forms, 80
disease caused, 93, 292
flagella, 42, 43
indoor pollution, 651
kingdom Bacteria, 93
modern classification of plants and animals, 91
phospholipids, 416
plant ancestors, 98
prokaryotic cells, 46, 91
reducer organisms, 601
surface-to-volume ratio, 183
unicellular organisms, 44
Baikal, Lake, 706
baker's yeast, 150
balance, 246
balanced diet, 266
Balanced Rock (Colorado), 473
balance of nature, 631
balancing equations (chemistry), 364–365, 397, 436
balloons, 375
Balmer, Johann, 848
Balmer's equation, 848
Bangladesh, 673
Baptistina family, 935
Bardeen, John, 753, 830, 832
barite, 461
barium
alphabetical guide to the elements, 328
nuclear fission, 405, 860
periodic table of the elements, 322
superconductors, 832
symbol and atomic number, 324
barium fluoride, 358
barley, 624
barometric pressure, 777
bars (rivers and streams), 512, 582
Bartlett, Neil, 399
baryons, 863
basal layer (epidermis), 242
basalt, 452, 467
base pairing, 415
bases (chemistry), 386–389
defined, 436
neutralization reactions, 359
pH scale, 388–389, 666
properties, 386
basic solutions, 388
Basidiomycota, 95
basilar membrane, 246
basilic vein, 253
Basin and Range region, 524
bathyl region, 614
batteries, 394–395, 817
battery jars, 394
bauxite, 529
BCS theory, 832
beaches, 509, 519
Beadle, George, 63
Beagle, H.M.S., 22
beans
balanced diet, 266
carbohydrates, 260
domestication, 624
food pyramid, 259
bears, 630, 675
Becquerel, Antoine, 753
bed load, 511, 582
Bednorz, Georg, 833
bee hummingbirds, 188
bees
castes in honeybees, 219
contact species, 594
domestication of honeybee, 616
metamorphosis, 187
parthenogenesis, 186
pheromones in communication, 214
pollination, 129
beetles, 187
behavior, animal, 208–223
Bell, Alexander Graham, 820
Bémont, Gustave, 23
benthic environment, 580, 581
benzene, 409, 411, 651, 694
beriberi, 268
berkelium
alphabetical guide to the elements, 328
periodic table of the elements, 323
symbol and atomic number, 324

berries, 130
beryllium
  alphabetical guide to the
    elements, 328
  periodic table of the
    elements, 322
  symbol and atomic
    number, 324
beryllium oxide, 398
Berzelius, Jons J., 349
beta-carotene, 267
beta particles
  Chadwick on emitted
    electrons, 862
  defined, 436, 892
  nuclear reactions, 406
  radioactivity, 402, 682
  symbol and properties, 404
  weak force, 765
Beta Persei (Algol), 951
Betelgeuse, 942
beverages, 276
Bhopal, India, disaster, 649
B horizon, 532, 533, 708
biceps brachii muscles, 228, 254
biceps femori muscle, 255
bicycles, 645
biennial plants, 147
Big Bang, 962–965, 988
bilateral symmetry, 172, 220
bile, 237
bimetallic thermometers, 789
binary (double) stars, 951, 988
binomial nomenclature, 91, 171
biobanks, 796
biodegradability, 720
biofuels, 735
biogas, 692
biological clock, 140
**biological control of invasive
    species,** 599
biological oceanography, 568, 580
biological pest control, 714
biology, 28–311
  See also botany; ecology; life;
    zoology
  cryobiology, 796

  glossary, 304–309
  history of science, 22–23
biomedical research, 617
biomes, 608
  defined, 746
  North American, 622–623
biophysics, 755
biosphere, 630–631
Biosphere 2 (Arizona), 633
biotechnology, 78–79
biotic factors in ecosystems,
    600, 746
biotic potential, 592, 746
biotic pyramids, 604
biotite mica, 466
bipedalism, 184
birds (Aves)
  Archaeopteryx, 495
  Aristotle's classification of
    animals, 164
  brain, 221
  chordates, 97, 178, 179
  circulatory system, 193
  courtship behavior, 217
  digestive system, 191
  Everglades, 701
  flight, 185
  hollow bones, 183
  homologous structures with
    pterosaurs, 170
  imprinting, 212
  life span, 207
  magnetoreceptors, 205
  mating, 218
  migratory, 205, 209, 707
  oil spills, 724
  pair-bonding, 218
  poisonous hooded pitohui, 188
  relation to dinosaurs, 494
  respiratory system, 194
  songs, 215
  territoriality, 217
  thermoregulation, 203
  warm-blooded animals, 203
  waste nitrogen, 201
  water pollution, 726
  wetlands, 700

birthrate reduction, 595, 637
bismuth
  alphabetical guide to the
    elements, 328
  particle emission and half-life of
    bismuth 212, 404
  periodic table of the
    elements, 323
  symbol and atomic number, 324
bison, 642
bitterness, 249
bivalves
  Cambrian period, 486
  defined, 304
  Ordovician period, 487
  Pennsylvanian epoch, 491
  phylum Mollusca, 176
black dwarf stars, 946
black holes, 950
  defined, 988
  Milky Way galaxy, 953
  relativity predicts, 767, 950
  stellar evolution, 946
  type II supernovas, 949
black lung disease, 653, 654
blackness, 849
bladder (urinary), 241, 256, 257
blade (leaves), 126, 127, 138
blastoids, 490
block fields, 506
blood
  See also blood circulation;
    circulatory system
  cells, 44
  clotting, 42, 268
  components, 233
  density, 776
  fats in, 264
  human urinary system, 241
  pH, 389
  typing, 76
blood circulation
  See also blood; circulatory system
  animals, 192–193
  discovery, 22, 25, 166
  human, 232–233
blood pressure, high, 282, 293, 295

blood vessels
   See also arteries
   human circulatory system, 233
   thermoregulation, 203
blue-green algae. *See* cyanobacteria
   (blue-green algae)
blue-white stars, 944
B lymphocytes, 302
body mass index (BMI), 282
bogs, 621
Bohr, Niels, 316–317, 318, 349,
   753, 835
bohrium
   alphabetical guide to the
      elements, 328
   periodic table of the
      elements, 322
   symbol and atomic number, 324
boiling point, 354, 777, 788
Boltzmann's constant, 867
bond angle, 346
bond-dissociation energy, 378,
   380–381
bond energy, 345
bond lengths, 347
bone marrow, 227, 302, 303
bones
   animal anatomy, 182
   birds, 183
   broken, 227
   cells, 44
   early land animals, 156
   human skeletal system, 226–227
   minerals, 268, 272
   osteoporosis, 281, 293
   tendons, 229
bony fishes (Osteichthyes)
   chordates, 97, 179
   galvanoreceptors, 205
   lobe-fins, 156
book lungs, 194, 195
booster rockets, 969
boreal coniferous forests, 613
boron
   alphabetical guide to the
      elements, 328
   mineral nutrients, 607

   periodic table of the
      elements, 323
   plant nutrients carried by
      water, 134
   seawater composition, 569
   symbol and atomic number, 324
bosons, 865
botanical gardens, 105
botany, 98
   See also plants
   ancient Greece and Rome, 103
   branches, 99
   defined, 304
   International Rules of Botanical
      Nomenclature, 107
   and pharmacology, 102
   rebirth of European, 104–105
bowerbirds, 217
Boyle, Robert, 356
Boyle's law, 356, 370, 777
brachial artery and vein, 253
brachial plexus, 252
brachiation, 184
brachiopods (Brachiopoda), 175, 487
Brachiosaurus, 160
bracioradialis muscle, 254, 255
Brahe, Tycho, 905
braided streams, 512
brain, 250
   animal, 220–221
   central nervous system, 202, 230
   hearing, 246
   human, 163, 221, 231
   magnetic resonance imaging
      (MRI), 425
   olfaction, 248
   respiration, 235
   taste, 249
   touch, 247
   vision, 245
brain stem, 231, 250, 304
Brattain, Walter, 753, 830
breads
   balanced diet, 266
   calories and fats, 278
   carbohydrates, 260
   fiber, 261

breakers (surf waves), 577
breathing. *See* respiration
breccia, 468
breeder reactors, 404, 406, 436
breeding
   animals by humans, 617
   plants, 627
   programs for endangered species,
      642, 643
Brewster's law, 844
bristletails, 155
Brödel, Max, 250
broken bones, 227
bromine
   alphabetical guide to the
      elements, 329
   halogenation of hydrocarbons,
      412
   periodic table of the elements,
      323
   seawater composition, 569
   symbol and atomic
      number, 324
bronchi, 234, 257
Brønsted-Lowry theory, 387
Brookhaven National Laboratory,
   858
brown algae (Phaeophyta), 109
   classification of plants, 107
   kingdom Protista, 94
   Thallophyta, 108
brown lung disease (byssinosis),
   653
Bryce Canyon (Utah), 518
Bryophyta, 96, 107, 110–111
bubble chambers, 859
buckminsterfullerene (buckyballs),
   349, 411
budding in yeasts, 149
buffers (chemical), 389
Buffon, Georges-Louis Leclerc de,
   165
bulbs (plants), 125
bulimia nervosa, 284
Bunsen, Robert Wilhelm, 911
butadiene, 411
butane, 346, 410, 412

Index

butene, 410
butterflies, 129, 187
buttocks muscles, 228
butyne, 411
B vitamins, 268, 271, 401, 421
byssinosis (brown lung disease), 653

C

cabbage loopers, 717
cadmium
    alphabetical guide to the elements, 329
    periodic table of the elements, 323
    symbol and atomic number, 324
    water pollution, 726
calcaneum, 251
calcite, 463, 465, 469, 530, 781, 844
calcium
    alphabetical guide to the elements, 329
    bones, 268
    Earth's crust, 447
    macrominerals, 268, 272
    main group elements, 398
    mineral nutrients, 607
    periodic table of the elements, 322
    plant nutrients carried by water, 134
    seawater composition, 569
    symbol and atomic number, 324
calcium chloride, 385
calculus, 26
calderas, 567, 582
caliche, 582
California, 450, 458, 459
California condor, 641
californium
    alphabetical guide to the elements, 329
    periodic table of the elements, 323
    symbol and atomic number, 324
caloric theory of heat, 785

calories
    calorimeters, 378
    "creeping obesity," 283
    "empty," 260, 284
    exercise expends, 280
    fast foods, 285
    fats, 263
    general dietary guidelines, 266
    joules' relation to, 378
    nutrition information, 274
    reducing, 283
    in various foods, 276–279
calorimeters, 378
calyx, 128, 304
cambium, 105, 124
Cambrian period, 486
    animals, 154
    Cambrian Explosion, 154, 483, 486, 582
    geologic time scale, 483
camels, 616
Camerarius, Rudolph Jacob, 105
Camptosaurus, 159, 161
Canada. *See* North America
Canadian Shield, 473
canals of Mars, 927, 966
cancer, 296
    diet and, 267
    hazardous wastes, 694
    noninfectious disease, 293
    obesity as risk, 282
    occupational hazards, 652, 654
    ozone hole and skin, 680
candelas, 846, 847
canyons, submarine, 579
capacitors, 807, 830, 892
capillaries, 233
capillarity (capillary action), 353, 782
capsids, 181
carbohydrate metabolism. *See* respiration
carbohydrates
    animal building blocks, 180
    animal metabolism, 188
    calories, 263
    defined, 304

    fast foods, 285
    general dietary guidelines, 266
    human digestive system, 236
    nutrition, 260
carbon
    See also carbon 14; hydrocarbons
    alphabetical guide to the elements, 329
    Avogadro's number, 374
    buckminsterfullerene, 349, 411
    cycle in ecosystems, 606
    isotopes, 315
    mineral nutrients, 607
    organic compounds, 360, 361, 408
    periodic table of the elements, 323
    plant nutrients carried by water, 134
    relative atomic mass, 372
    seawater composition, 569
    symbol and atomic number, 324
    two minerals, 460, 780
carbon 14
    nuclear reactions, 406
    particle emission and half-life, 404
    radiocarbon dating, 403, 476, 480
carbonate minerals, 465
carbon dioxide
    air pollution, 662
    atmosphere, 534
    combustion, 359
    defined, 746
    global warming, 657
    greenhouse effect, 670, 677
    human respiratory system, 235
    molecules, 346, 347
    naming inorganic compounds, 360
    photosynthesis, 134, 135
    production during Precambrian time, 484
    "pure" air, 660
    reducing emissions, 657, 659
    relative molecular mass, 373
carbonic acid, 386, 666
Carboniferous period, 490–491
    Age of Amphibians, 157

forests of vascular plants, 100
geologic time scale, 483
carbon monoxide
air pollution, 662
bond-dissociation energy, 381
defined, 746
indoor pollution, 651
carbon tetrachloride, 679, 681
carboxylic acid group, 418
carcinogens, 296
cardiac end of stomach, 257
cardiac muscle, 229
Carnivora, 179
carnivores (secondary consumers)
biotic pyramids, 604
consumer organisms, 601
defined, 746
energy-flow in ecosystems, 603
energy pyramid, 603
food chains and food
webs, 604
carotene, 416
carotid arteries, 253, 256, 265
carpels, 116, 128, 304
carpus, 226, 251
carrageenan, 109
carrier molecules, 53
**carrying capacity of an
ecosystem,** 592, 619
Carson, Rachel, 655, 656
cartilage
animal anatomy, 182
human skeletal system, 227
vertebrate skeletons, 156
Cassegrain telescopes, 909
Casseiopeia A (supernova), 954
Cassini-Huygens (spacecraft), 930,
974, 985
Castor (star), 951
catalysts
defined, 436
enzymes, 420
inorganic reactions, 368, 369
organic reactions, 413
catalytic converters, 369, 663
catastrophism, 168
cathode rays, 824–825

cathodes, 391, 824
cations, 315
cats
biomedical research, 617
brain, 221
breeding, 617
cloning, 78
domestication, 616
life span, 206
lions, 219, 610, 641
saber-tooth, 162, 500, 501
tigers, 640, 641
cattails, 630
cattle
breeding, 617
domestication, 616
methane production, 670, 671
overgrazing and soil erosion,
709, 710
Texas longhorns, 716
Cavendish, Henry, 354, 766
caves, 508
cavitation, 809
celestial equator, 906
celestial poles, 906, 988
celestial sphere, 900–901, 988
cell body (neurons), 230, 231
cell colonies, 153
cell-mediated immune response,
302–303
cells (biological), 44–61
animal, 181
blood, 233
cancer, 296
cryobiology, 796
cycle, 54
defined, 304
discovery, 167
division, 54–59
functions, 52–53
genes, 62
inside, 48–49
multicellular organisms, 60–61
plant, 44, 48, 50, 118–119
protistan, 94
Schwann's drawings, 22, 167
successful scientific theories, 27

theory, 44–45
types, 46–47
cellulose, 48, 118, 261
cell wall, 48, 118
Celsius temperature scale, 788
cement, 530
Cenozoic era, 498–501
Age of Mammals, 162–163
angiosperms, 101
geologic time scale, 483
Centaurus A (galaxy), 960
center of gravity, 769, 892
center of mass, 769
center veined leaves, 126
centipedes, 491
Central America
savanna, 610
tropical climates, 559
central nervous system, 230
See also brain
regulating animal body, 202
centrifugal force, 866
centrioles, 51, 181, 197, 304
centromere, 62
cephalic artery and vein, 253
cephalopods
aquatic environments, 614
Aristotle's classification of
animals, 164
Cambrian period, 486
circulatory system, 193
eyes, 204
Ordovician period, 487
phylum Mollusca, 176
Cepheid variable stars, 958,
959, 988
cereals
See also grains
balanced diet, 266
calories and fats, 279
carbohydrates, 260
fiber, 261
phosphorus, 268
cerebellum, 231, 250, 304
cerebral cortex, 221, 249
cerebrum, 231, 250
Ceres (dwarf planet), 933

cerium
  alphabetical guide to the
    elements, 329
  periodic table of the elements,
    322
  symbol and atomic number, 324
CERN (Centre Européen de
    Recherche Nucléaire), 865
cervical plexus, 252
cervical vertebrae, 226, 251
cervix (uterine), 239, 257
cesium
  alphabetical guide to the
    elements, 330
  periodic table of the elements,
    322
  symbol and atomic number, 324
Cetacea, 179
CFCs. *See* chlorofluorocarbons
    (CFCs)
Chadwick, James, 862
Chain, Ernst Boris, 151
chain reaction (nuclear)
  controlled versus uncontrolled,
    860
  defined, 436
  first controlled, 23, 736, 753, 862
  nuclear energy, 736
  nuclear fission, 404, 405
chalcopyrite, 529
Challenger (space shuttle), 974, 983,
    984
chameleons, 188
**Chandra Orbiting X-ray
    Observatory,** 986
chaparral, 612
Chargaff, Erwin, 63
charge-coupled devices, 908, 913
Charles, Jacques Alexandre Cesar,
    356, 375
Charles's law, 356, 375
checkups (medical), 290
cheese. *See* milk and milk products
cheetahs, 641
chemical bonds, 344–349
  See also covalent bonds; ionic
    bonds

bond-dissociation energy, 378,
    380
chemical change, 313, 436
chemical compounds, 358–367
  acids and bases, 386–389
  defined, 437
  inorganic, 398–399
  naming, 360–361
  plant chemical warfare, 619
**chemical control of invasive
    species,** 599
chemical elements, 320–343
  See also periodic table of the
    elements
  defined, 320
  isotopes, 315
  main group elements, 398
  radioactive, 403
chemical evolution, 32, 304
chemical oceanography, 568
chemical properties of matter,
    313, 436
chemical reactions
  balancing equations, 364–365,
    397, 436
  defined, 362, 437
  electrochemical, 390–395
  equations, 362–365
  equilibrium, 370–371
  heat sources, 787
  organic, 412–413
  reaction rates, 368–369
  stoichiometry, 376–377
  types, 359
chemical rocks, 468, 469
chemical weathering, 472, 506,
    508, 582
chemistry, 310–439
  See also chemical bonds;
    chemical compounds;
    chemical elements; inorganic
    chemistry; organic chemistry
  atomic physics, 752
  defined, 312
  electrochemistry, 390–395
  glossary, 436–439
  history of science, 22–23

important dates, 349
  measurement, 372–377
  nuclear, 402–407
  problems, 426–435
  solutions, 382–385
  thermochemistry, 378–381
  tools, 422–425
chemoreceptors, 204
chemotherapy, 296
Cheney, Dorothy, 222
Chernobyl disaster, 649, 736
chestnut blight, 598
chickens, 44, 616, 636
Chihuahuan Desert, 623
chimpanzees
  division from humans, 163
  hunting, 223
  insight, 213
  intelligence, 222–223
  life span, 206
  movement, 184
  number left in the world, 617
  space exploration timeline, 978
China
  ancient astronomy, 900, 902, 924
  earthquakes, 458
  space program, 975, 981, 987
  traditional medicine, 102
chinooks, 555
chiropractors, 291
Chiroptera, 179
chitin, 177, 188
chitons (Polyplacophora), 176
chlamydia, 300
chlamydomonas, 94
chlorine
  alphabetical guide to the
    elements, 330
  halogenation of hydrocarbons, 412
  macrominerals, 268
  melting and boiling points, 788
  mineral nutrients, 607
  molar mass, 374
  periodic table of the elements,
    323
  plant nutrients carried
    by water, 134

salt, 345
seawater composition, 569
symbol and atomic number, 324
chloroacetic acid, 413
chlorofluorocarbons (CFCs)
defined, 746
greenhouse gases, 670
international agreement to cease
production, 657
oxidation, 412
ozone hole, 412, 678, 679
chlorophyll
Chlorophyta (green algae), 108
coordination compounds, 401
photosynthesis, 135, 602, 604
Chlorophyta. *See* green algae
(Chlorophyta)
chloroplasts
leaves, 127
photosynthesis, 50, 135, 741
plastids, 50, 119
cholera, 726
cholesterol, 264–265
defined, 304
general dietary guidelines, 266
cholinesterase, 244
Chonrichthyes, 179
chordates (Chordata)
See also vertebrates
adapted to land, 172
kingdom Animalia, 97, 172,
178–179
chorda tympani nerve, 248
C horizon, 532, 533, 708
chromatic aberration, 909
chromatids, 62
chromatin, 49, 304
chromite, 528
chromium
alphabetical guide to the
elements, 330
microminerals, 269, 273
periodic table of the
elements, 322
symbol and atomic
number, 324
chromoplasts, 50, 119

chromosomes, 64–65
animal building blocks, 180
cell cycle, 54
cell nucleus, 49
defined, 304
DNA, 49, 64, 180, 415
eukaryotic cells, 47
genes, 49, 62, 73
genetics terms to know, 75
heredity, 38, 239
independent assortment law, 69,
72,.73, 77
meiosis, 57, 59
mitosis, 56, 58, 196–197
mutations, 68
plant growth, 142
pollutants damage, 648
recombination, 69
sexual reproduction, 55
chromosphere, 937, 988
chrysalis, 187
Chrysophyta, 94
chyme, 190
Cicero, Marcus Tullius, 43
cilia
Chlorophyta (green algae), 108
human respiratory system, 235
nasal passages, 248
rotifers, 174
ciliary body, 244, 245
ciliates, 49
cinder cone volcanoes, 526
cinnabar, 465
circadian rhythms, 208, 209
circular polarization, 845
circulatory system
See also blood circulation; blood
vessels; heart
animal anatomy, 182, 192–193
human anatomy, 225, 232–233,
253
noise risks, 687
organ systems, 61
cirques, 516, 517
cirrhosis of the liver, 298
cirrocumulus clouds, 540
cirrostratus clouds, 540

cirrus clouds, 540
cities
noise pollution, 684
urban wetlands, 701
cladistic systematics, 171, 304
cladogenesis, 36
classes (biological), 91, 171
classification of data, 24
**classification of plants and
animals,** 90–97
animals, 164–165, 170–179
biochemical analysis, 171
early modern European
botany, 104
history of science, 22
Linnaean, 22, 90, 104, 165
modern, 91, 171
plants, 106–117
taxonomy defined, 309
clastic rocks, 468, 582
clavicle (collarbone), 226, 251
clay, 533
clay-life hypothesis, 30, 33
Clean Air Act (1970), 656, 663
cleanliness, 258
cleavage (minerals), 460, 462, 582
climate, 554–563
See also climate change
climates of the world, 563
defined, 582, 746
Earth's orbit and, 563
factors affecting, 554–557
stimulus and response in
plants, 141
zones, 558–563
climate change, 672–677
See also global warming
Intergovernmental Panel on
Climate Change, 657
slowing, 676–677
climatology, 677
climax communities, 620, 621
clitoris, 257
cloning, 79
cats, 78
ethical concerns, 79
sheep, 63, 79

closed circulatory systems, 192

closed universe, 963, 988

cloud chambers, 859

clouds
   formation, 540
   hydrologic cycle, 538
   lightning, 548
   precipitation, 540–541
   seeding, 551
   storm clouds, 541
   tornadoes, 549
   types, 540

club mosses (Lycophyta), 100,
   107, 112

clusters (galactic), 957, 958, 988

cnidarians (coelenterates)
   See also coral; jellyfish
   digestive system, 190
   kingdom Animalia, 97, 173
   radial symmetry, 172
   reproduction, 186

coal
   acid rain, 667
   Carboniferous period, 490, 491
   commercial energy, 734
   energy conversion, 757
   Jurassic period, 495
   natural resources, 531
   nonrenewable fuels, 735
   organic rocks, 469
   U.S. electricity production, 735

coarse-grained rocks, 467

coastal regions, 578

cobalt
   alphabetical guide to the
      elements, 330
   ferromagnetism, 821
   particle emission and half-life of
      cobalt 16, 404
   periodic table of the elements, 322
   symbol and atomic number, 324

cocaine, 299

coccygeal plexus, 252

coccyx, 178, 251

cochlea, 246

cochlear duct, 246

Cockcroft, John, 753, 856

Cockcroft-Walton accelerator,
   753, 856

cockroaches, 491

coconut crabs, 188

codons, 66

coefficients (chemical equations),
   363, 364, 437

coelacanths, 156

coelem, 172, 175

coelenterates. *See* cnidarians
   (coelenterates)

coenzymes, 421

cogeneration of electricity, 645

cognitive ethology, 222

coherent light, 850

**cold-blooded (ectothermic)
   animals,** 203

cold fronts, 543

collagen, 227, 305

collenchyma, 121

colliders (particle accelerators), 858

Collins, Eileen, 986

Collins, Michael, 973, 990

colon. *See* large intestines

color
   absorption of light, 837
   artificial in foods, 274
   human eye, 244
   interference effects, 838
   minerals, 460, 461
   spectra, 849

color (quarks), 863

Colorado River, 510, 566

color blindness, 77

Columbia (space shuttle), 23,
   974, 986

Columbia River, 722, 726

columnar joints, 523

coma (comets), 934

Coma Cluster, 957

combination reactions, 359

combustion, 362
   See also fire
   combustion reactions, 359
   engines, 791
   Hindenburg disaster, 368
   Lavoisier, 22, 349

comets, 934–935
   Halley's comet, 766, 984
   Tempel 1, 935, 975

commercial energy, 734, 746

common ancestry, 37

common carotid artery, 253, 256

**common extensor of
   fingers,** 255

common iliac artery and vein,
   253

common peroneal nerve, 252

communication
   animal, 214–215
   of scientific knowledge, 21

communities (ecological), 596–599
   defined, 746
   interaction, 596–597
   invasive species, 598–599
   plants, 619

comparative anatomy, 166

compasses, 463, 503, 811, 819

competition
   animal behavior, 216–217
   defined, 746
   how species become
      endangered, 639
   interactions within an
      ecosystem, 596
   natural selection, 36, 39
   plants, 618–619

competitive exclusion, 618

complementary colors, 849

complex carbohydrates, 260

complexity argument, 41

complex lipids, 416

complex tissues, 60

composite particles, 862, 892

composite volcanoes, 527

compound eyes, 177, 205

compound fruits, 130

compound ores, 529

compounds, chemical.
      See chemical compounds

Compsognathus, 161

computers
   microchips, 830
   modeling in science, 27, 915

semiconductors, 826

weather prediction, 27, 553

concave mirrors, 841, 892

concentration

equilibrium, 370, 371

reaction rates, 368, 369

solutions, 382, 383, 384, 385

concert halls, 808

conchae (turbinates), 248

concrete, 530, 776

concurrent forces, 765, 892

condensation

defined, 582

hydrologic cycle, 538–539

condensation nuclei, 540

condenser microphones, 807

conditioning, 213

condoms, 300

conduction (heat), 794, 892

conduction band, 827

conductivity (electricity)

See also semiconductors

electrical current, 814

solutions, 384

superconductors, 411, 753, 797, 832–833

cones (eye), 244

conflict, animal, 216–217

conglomerates (geology), 468

conidiophores, 148

conifers (Pinophyta), 115

classification of plants, 96, 107

coniferous forests, 613, 623, 702

defined, 582, 746

gymnosperms, 114

Triassic period, 493

conjugate acid-base pairs, 387

conjugate base strength, 387

conjunctiva, 244, 245

connective tissues, 182

consensus, knowledge through, 21

conservation of energy, law of, 312, 362, 379, 437, 757, 790

conservation of mass, law of, 312, 349, 362, 364, 438

conservation of momentum, law of, 774

conservation of natural resources, 638–647

See also recycling

defined, 746

forests, 704–705

fossil fuels, 644–647, 676

water, 732–733

wildlife, 642–643

conservation tillage, 629

constants

defined, 892

fundamental physics, 867

constellations, 901, 907

constriction (animal movement), 184

construction materials, 530

constructive interference, 801, 838, 839

consumer organisms, 601, 603, 746

contact binary stars, 951

contact dermatitis, 243

contact species, 594

continental climate, 561

continental drift, 448–449

defined, 582

fossil evidence, 481

continental margins, 578

continental polar air masses, 542

continental rises, 475, 578, 579

continental shelves, 578

neritic zone, 580, 615

ocean basins, 579

sublittoral region, 581

width, 475

continental slopes, 475, 578, 579

continental tropical air masses, 542

continents

See also continental drift

Cambrian period, 486

Earth's crust, 443, 444, 445, 450

emergence during Precambrian time, 484

Gondwanaland, 448, 488, 489, 491, 494, 496

height and sea-level change, 475

Laurasia, 448, 488, 489, 494, 496

Ordovician period, 487

Paleogene and Neogene periods, 498

Pangaea, 157, 448, 492, 493, 494, 496

Pennsylvanian epoch, 491

Permian period, 492

Silurian period, 488

contour plowing, 710

controlled-environment agriculture, 629

convection

air masses, 542, 582

heat, 794, 795, 892

Convention on Desertification (1994), 657

Convention on International Trade in Endangered Species of Wild Fauna and Flora (CITES), 707

Convention on Long Range Transboundary Air Pollution (1979), 656

Convention on Protecting Species and Habitats (1992), 657

convergent plate boundaries, 450, 453

convex mirrors, 841, 892

Cooper, Leon, 832

cooperation (animal), 218–219

Cooper pairs, 832

coordination compounds, 401

Copernicus, Nicolaus, 22, 753, 904

copper

alphabetical guide to the elements, 330

density, 776

electrical conductivity, 814, 815

galvanic cells, 392, 817

melting and boiling points, 788

microminerals, 269, 273

mineral nutrients, 607

ores, 529

periodic table of the elements, 323

plant nutrients carried by water, 134
relative atomic mass, 372
symbol and atomic number, 324
coracobrachialis muscle, 254
coral
asexual reproduction, 186
Ediacaran period, 485
Ordovician period, 487
phylum Cnidaria, 173
radial symmetry, 172
reefs, 173, 615, 706
Silurian period, 488
Coriolis effect, 547
cork, 121, 124
corms, 125
corn, 624, 626, 628, 717
cornea, 244, 245
corn-leaf blight, 628, 716
corolla, 128, 305
corona (solar), 937, 988
corpus callosum, 250
corrective lenses, 842
cortex (plants), 120, 123, 124, 305
corundum, 463
Corythosaurus, 158, 161
cosmic background radiation, 912, 962, 963, 964–965, 988
cosmic dust, 661
cosmic rays, 661, 954–955, 976, 988
cosmogony, 988
cosmology, 962–967
See also universe
cosmological models, 902, 988
defined, 988
cosmonauts, 969
cotton bollworms, 714
cotyledons, 117, 146
Coulomb, Charles de, 812, 817
coulomb force, 854, 855, 892
coulombs, 812, 817
Coulomb's law, 812, 866
courtship behavior, 217
covalent bonds, 345
covalent crystals, 351
defined, 437

electronegativity, 380
hydrocarbons, 408, 410
types of chemical bond, 344
covalent crystals, 350, 351
cover cropping, 710
Cowan, Clyde, 862
Cowper's gland, 257
coyotes, 593
Crab Nebula, 949
cranial nerves, 249
Crater Lake (Oregon), 567
craters (volcanic), 453, 526
creamy stars, 944
creationism, 40–43
defined, 305
theories of origin of life, 31
creation stories, 32
"creeping obesity," 283
crest of a wave, 576, 582
Cretaceous period, 496–497
geologic time scale, 483
mass extinction, 159, 496, 497, 935
Rocky Mountains rise, 482
crevasses, 516, 517
Crick, Francis, 23, 63, 414, 415
crinoids, 487, 490, 491
cristae, 51
critical density (cosmology), 963, 964
critical point, 793, 892
critical temperature, 354, 832
crocodilians, 495
crop rotation, 626, 712
cross breeding, 74–77
crossing over, 55, 69, 199
cross-pollination, 129
crust (Earth's), 444
chemical composition, 447
defined, 582
Earth's layers, 443, 445
lithosphere, 506
plate tectonics, 450
shifting, 522–527
crustaceans
Aristotle's classification of animals, 164

compound eyes, 177, 205
Jurassic period, 495
kingdom Animalia, 97, 177
cryobiology, 796
cryogenics, 796–797, 892
cryosurgery, 796
crystalline solids, 350–351, 781
defined, 437
minerals, 461, 582
types of solids, 350, 778, 780
crystallization, 382
crystal rectifiers, 828
cud, 191
cumulonimbus clouds, 540
cumulus clouds, 540
Curie, Marie, 23, 403, 753
Curie, Pierre, 23, 403, 753
curium
alphabetical guide to the elements, 330
periodic table of the elements, 323
symbol and atomic number, 324
Curl, Robert F., Jr., 349
current, electric. *See* electric current
currents (ocean), 556, 572–574
curved mirrors, 841
Cuvier, Georges, 166, 168
Cuyahoga River, 655
cyanobacteria (blue-green algae)
Age of Bacteria, 152
domain Bacteria, 46
kingdom Bacteria, 93
Precambrian fossils, 485
Cycadophyta (cycads), 96, 107, 114, 493
cyclohexane, 411, 423
cyclohexene, 411
cyclones, 542, 544
cyclotrons, 856, 857
Cygnus X-1, 950
cysteine, 419
cytokinesis, 54, 56, 305
cytokinins, 143, 144, 145
cytology
See also cells (biological)

botany, 99, 105
defined, 44
cytoplasm, 49
animal building blocks, 180
cell theory, 45
defined, 305
inside cells, 48, 119, 181
organelles in, 50–51
cytosine, 65, 66, 305, 414–415

D

dairy products. *See* milk and milk products
Dalton, John, 316, 349, 376, 753
Dalton's law of partial pressure, 355
dams
hydroelectric power, 646, 736, 738–739
water supply, 729
damselflies, 187
Daniell, John F., 394
dark energy, 964, 988
dark matter, 964, 965, 988
darmstadtium
alphabetical guide to the elements, 331
periodic table of the elements, 323
symbol and atomic number, 324
Darwin, Charles, 169
natural selection, 39, 168
observes nature on *Beagle* voyage, 24
The Origin of Species, 23, 169
dating
fossils, 480–481
radiocarbon, 403, 476, 480
rocks, 476–477
day-neutral plants, 141
DDT (dichlorodiphenyltrichloro ethane), 632, 643, 656, 713, 746
death
See also extinction (biology)
plant life cycle, 147
reducer organisms, 601

de Broglie, Louis, 318
debt-for-nature swaps, 705
decane, 410
deceleration, 892
decibel scale, 685, 686, 803
deciduous trees
conifers, 115
deciduous rain forest, 609
defined, 746
falling leaves, 127, 612
temperate deciduous forest, 612, 622, 702
declination of a star, 906, 988
decomposers
defined, 305, 746
fungi, 148, 150
reducer organisms, 601
rotifers, 174
decomposition (biological)
See also decomposers
landfills, 690
mineral nutrient cycle, 607
mycorrhizal associations, 608
decomposition reactions, 359
deep femoral artery and vein, 253
Deep Impact (spacecraft), 935, 975, 987
deep peroneal nerve, 252
deep-sea zone, 215, 581, 614
Deepwater Horizon oil rig, 725
deep-well injection, 695, 746
deer, 593, 604, 616
deferent, 903
definite proportions, law of, 376
De Forest, Lee, 825
deforestation, 703
deformation, 582
Deimos (satellite of Mars), 926
Deinonychus, 161
de la Brosse, Guy, 105
Delaware River, 674
deltas (river), 513, 582
deltoid muscles, 228, 254, 255
De Materia Medica (Dioscorides), 103
dendrites, 230, 231

dendrochronology, 480
density, 776–777
defined, 892
formula, 866
ocean currents, 572
refraction of light, 837
seawater, 570, 571
dental care, 258, 291
deoxyribonucleic acid. *See* DNA (deoxyribonucleic acid)
deoxyribose, 65, 66, 414
depth perception, 245
dermatitis, 243
dermis, 182, 242, 243
desalinization of water, 733, 746
Descartes, René, 22
desertification, 657, 709
deserts, 611
Convention on Desertification, 657
defined, 746
geographical barriers to plants, 620
middle latitude, 561
North American, 623
tropical, 559
designer life forms, 80
desmids, 94
desserts and snacks, 279
destructive interference, 801, 838, 839
deuterium, 406, 861
Deuteromycota, 95
developing countries
debt-for-nature swaps, 705
environmentalism, 656
population growth, 635
developmental disease, 293
Devonian period, 483, 489
de Waal, Frans, 222
dew point, 582
D horizon, 532
diabetes, 282, 283, 293, 297
diaghragm (anatomy), 228, 245
diamonds, 460, 462, 463, 780
diatomic molecules, 315

Index

diatoms
- defined, 305
- phylum Chrysophyta, 94
- plant ancestors, 98
- respiration, 194

Dicke, Robert H., 965

dicotyledons (dicots)
- angiosperms, 117
- classification of plants, 96
- defined, 305
- seeds, 131

diet. *See* nutrition

diethyl ether, 413

dieting, 283

diffraction, 800, 801, 838–839, 892

diffraction gratings, 838–839

diffraction patterns, 838–839

diffusion (biology), 52, 305

diffusion (light), 892

digestion
- *See also* digestive system
- defined, 305
- plant physiology, 134, 137

digestive system
- *See also* liver; stomach
- animal anatomy, 182, 190–191
- Archaea in human, 92
- human anatomy, 225, 236–237
- organ systems, 61

digital recording, 806–807

dihybrid crosses, 77

dilute solutions, 382

Dimetrodon, 157

dinoflagellates, 94

dinosaurs
- Age of Reptiles, 158–159
- Cretaceous period mass extinction, 159, 496, 497, 935
- imprint fossils, 479
- Jurassic period, 159, 494–495
- relation to birds, 494
- Triassic period, 159, 493
- two major groups, 158
- varieties, 160–161

diodes, 829

Dioscorides, 103

dioxins, 694, 695

Diplodocus, 159

diploid cells, 58, 305

dipole forces, 346

dipoles (polar molecules), 347

Dirac, Paul, 753, 862

direct current (DC), 816

disasters, environmental, 649

diseases, 292–301
- *See also* AIDS; cancer; heart disease
- bacteria cause, 93, 292
- cholesterol and, 264
- diet and health, 266–273
- dust diseases, 653
- fats and, 263
- fungi cause, 95, 151
- germ theory, 23, 27
- immunity, 302–303
- prevention, 290
- sex-linked disorders, 77
- viruses cause, 292
- vitamin deficiency, 268, 270
- water pollution causes, 726

dispersal
- defined, 746
- fruits, 130
- fungi spores, 149
- population regulating factors, 595

dispersion (optics), 837, 892

dispersion forces (London forces), 346–347

dispersive waves, 799

disposable products, 689

disrupted order, 41

dissolved load, 511, 582

distillation, 385, 437

divergent plate boundaries, 450, 453

diversity, genetic, 716–717

DNA (deoxyribonucleic acid), 64–65
- animal building blocks, 180
- asexual reproduction, 55, 198
- bases, 65
- chromosomes, 49, 64, 180, 415
- classification of animals, 171
- defined, 305

- extracting, 78
- fingerprinting, 78, 81
- first successful recombinant DNA procedure, 23
- genes, 62
- genetics timeline, 63
- genetic technology, 78–79
- meiosis, 57
- mitosis, 196, 197
- mutations, 38, 68
- polymers, 414–415
- profiling, 78–79, 80, 81
- prokaryotic cells, 46
- recombinant DNA, 80, 308
- sexual reproduction, 55, 57
- structure, 23, 63, 64, 414

doctors, selection of, 291

dogs
- biomedical research, 617
- breeding, 617
- domestication, 616
- first animal in space, 977
- noncontact species, 594
- sizes of breeds, 616

Dog Star (Sirius), 942, 947

doldrums, 536, 537, 583

Dolly (sheep), 63, 79

dolomite, 465

dolphins, 170, 179, 184

domains (biological), 91

domains (magnetic), 821

domestication of plants and animals
- animals, 616
- defined, 746
- life spans of animals, 206
- plants, 624–625

dominance hierarchies, 216, 595

dominant genes, 71, 75, 143, 305

Doppler
- effect, 804, 892, 910, 951, 959, 989
- radar, 551

dormancy
- animals, 209
- defined, 305
- seeds, 131

dorsal nerve cord, 178
double chemical bonds, 345
double helix structure of DNA, 23, 63, 64, 414
double (binary) stars, 951, 988
downfolds (synclines), 522, 523, 586
Down syndrome, 68
dragonflies, 187, 491
drives, 210
drone bees, 219
droughts
    climate change, 672
    soil erosion, 709
    water table, 719
drug abuse, 299
drumlins, 516, 517
drupes, 130
dry cell batteries, 394
dry fruits, 130
dubnium
    alphabetical guide to the elements, 331
    periodic table of the elements, 322
    symbol and atomic number, 324
ducks, 212, 217, 218
dumping waste, 690, 727
Dunkleosteus, 156
duodenum, 237, 256
dust
    air pollution, 661
    interstellar, 954–955
    storms, 518
Dust Bowl of 1930s, 519
dust diseases, 653
dwarf galaxies, 956
dwarf planets (plutoids), 933, 989, 990
dwarf stars, 944, 946, 947, 950
dyes, synthetic, 349
dynamics, 758, 892
dysprosium
    alphabetical guide to the elements, 331
    periodic table of the elements, 323
    symbol and atomic number, 324

E

Eagle Nebula, 915
eagles, 183, 597, 643
eardrum, 246
ears, 188, 246
Earth
    See also continents; crust (Earth's); Earth science; poles (Earth's)
    amount of water, 718
    average radius, 442
    axis, 502
    biosphere, 630–631
    Cambrian period, 486
    changing surface, 22, 474–475
    creationism on surface features, 41, 42
    density, 446–447
    diameter, 914
    early concepts of universe, 902–903
    formation during Precambrian time, 484
    future, 501
    geotropism, 139
    heat sources, 786
    interior, 442–445
    layers, 443, 444–445
    magnetic field, 502–503
    mapping, 504–505
    orbit, 563
    pressure in interior, 447
    rotation, 502, 572
    solar system, 918
    in space, 502–505
    temperature, 446
    terrestrial planets, 921
Earth Day, 656
earth flows, 520, 521
earthquake-resistant buildings, 458
earthquakes, 456–461
    causes, 456
    defined, 583
    measuring, 457, 586
    mid-ocean ridges, 579
    most powerful recent, 457
    predicting, 459
    transform plate boundaries, 450
    zones, 458
Earth science, 440–587
    See also geology; physical geography
    glossary, 582–587
earthworms, 176, 191, 192, 607
easterly waves, 544
eating disorders, 284
echinoderms (Echinodermata), 97, 178, 487
eclipses, 924–925, 989
eclipsing binary stars, 951
ecliptic, 901, 906, 989
ecology, 588–749
    See also ecosystems; environment
    animals and humans, 616–617
    botany, 99
    communities, 596–599
    division, 588
    energy, 734–745
    glossary, 746–749
    multidisciplinary approach, 591
    plants and humans, 624–629
    plants and the world, 618–623
    populations, 592–595
    restoration ecology, 705
ecosystem management, 599
ecosystems, 600–615
    See also deserts; forests; grasslands; tundra
    carbon cycle, 606
    classification of major, 608–615
    components, 600
    defined, 746
    energy flow, 602–603
    nitrogen cycle, 607
    people and, 632
    trophic levels, 596, 604–605
    ultraviolet radiation's effects, 680
    water cycle, 606
ecstasy (drug), 299
ectoderm, 172
Edaphosaurus, 157
Eddington, Arthur S., 853

Index

Edentata, 179
Ediacaran period, 485
Edison, Thomas, 816
EDNOS (eating disorder not
    otherwise specified), 284
E=mc², 27, 404, 853, 866
egg cells (ova)
    angiosperms ovules, 116, 128
    animal reproduction, 186
    defined, 305
    human reproductive system,
        238, 239
    meiosis, 57
    sexual reproduction, 55
eggs (food)
    calories and fats, 277
    cholesterol, 265
    fats, 263
    lipids, 416
    pH, 389
    protein, 419
Egypt, ancient
    astronomy, 900, 901, 902
    medicinal plants, 102
Ehrlich, Paul, 23, 655, 656
eighteen-electron rule, 400
Einstein, Albert
    E=mc², 27, 853
    general theory of relativity, 753,
        767, 853
    gravitation, 767, 950
    photons, 835
    special theory of relativity, 23,
        852–853
einsteinium
    alphabetical guide to the
        elements, 331
    periodic table of the elements,
        323
    symbol and atomic number, 324
electric circuits, 823
    See also electronics
    defined, 892
    parallel and series, 823, 895
electric current, 814–815
    AC and DC, 816
    defined, 892

electronics, 824
and magnetic fields, 818
measuring, 811
producing, 817
transistors, 830
electric fields
    defined, 893
    light, 835
    particle accelerators, 856, 857
electricity, 810–817
    See also electric circuits; electric
        current; electric fields; nuclear
        power
    batteries, 394–395
    electric energy, 312
    electrochemistry, 390–395
    electromagnetic induction for
        generating, 822
    electromagnetism, 810, 893
    fossil fuels in U.S. production, 735
    galvanoreceptors, 205
    geothermal power, 745
    heat sources, 786
    hydroelectric power, 646, 736,
        738–739
    lightning, 22, 810
    physics, 754
    rocket propulsion, 971
    solar energy, 647, 676, 742–743
    static, 812–813, 896
    superconductors, 753, 797
    tidal generation, 739
    units of measure, 817
    wind power, 647, 744
electric signals, 824, 893
electric voltage, 824, 893
electrochemical cells, 390–395,
    817
electrochemistry, 390–395
electrodes, 391, 893
electrolysis, 390–391, 893
electrolytes, 390, 437, 893
electrolytic dissociation
    (ionization), 384
electromagnetic force
    defined, 893
    electroweak theory, 865

exchange particles, 864
fundamental forces, 765, 864
electromagnetic radiation
    See also light; radio waves
    defined, 583
    harmful radiation, 682, 683
    Maxwell, 811
    radiation thermometers, 789
    spectra of stars, 910–911
electromagnetism, 810–811
    See also electricity;
        electromagnetic force;
        electromagnetic radiation;
        magnetism
    defined, 893
    discovery, 811, 820
    electromagnetic induction, 811,
        817, 822–823
    electromagnetic spectrum, 834,
        835, 893, 912
    electromagnetic waves, 811,
        835, 893
    electromagnets, 818, 820–821
    Maxwell's theory, 23, 753, 811
    practical applications, 820
electromagnets, 818, 820–821, 893
electromotive force, 817
electron acceptors, 827
electron cloud model of the
    atom, 318–319
electron donors, 827
electronegativity, 344, 345,
    380, 437
electronics, 824–833
    See also solid-state devices
    history, 824–825
electron microscopes, 824
    bacteria, 93
    cells, 45
    molecules, 349
electron physics, 755
electrons, 319
    atomic structure, 316–317
    charge, 314, 811, 867
    chemical bonds, 344–345
    defined, 437, 893
    discovery, 811, 824

fermions, 865
ferromagnetism, 821
leptons, 863
line spectra and atomic structure, 848
mass, 319, 867
parts of atoms, 314–315, 854
static electricity, 812
subatomic particles, 862

electron shells, 318, 319

electroplating, 391

electroweak theory, 865

elementary particles, 862, 863, 893

elements
See also chemical elements
defined, 437

elephants
See also mammoths
birthrate reduction, 595
body weight, 189
endangered species, 641
largest ears, 188
life span, 206
poaching, 643
Proboscidea, 179

elevation (above sea level), 583

elliptical galaxies, 956, 957

elliptical polarization, 845

El Niño, 573, 583

embryogenesis, 181

embryos
bilateral animals, 172
defined, 305
seeds, 131

emeralds, 462

emigration, 592

emission nebulas, 954

emotional health, 288–289

empirical formulas, 358

endangered species, 638–643
defined, 746
International Union for the Conservation of Nature and Natural Resources, 707

Endangered Species Act (1973), 656

endemic infectious diseases, 292, 305

endocrine system
animal anatomy, 182
human anatomy, 225, 240
organ systems, 61

endoderm, 172

endonucleases, 78

endophytes, 715

endoplasmic reticulum, 50

endosteum, 227

endothelial tissues, 182

endothermic (warm-blooded) animals, 183, 203

endothermic processes, 353, 437

endothermic reactions, 312, 363, 381, 437

energy, 734–745
See also electricity; heat; mechanical energy; nuclear energy
alternative sources, 646–647
carbohydrates, 260
cells manufacture, 53
chemical reactions, 363
chemistry, 312–313
conservation law, 312, 362, 379, 437, 757, 790
conversion, 757
crisis of 1970s, 735
dark energy, 964, 988
defined, 437, 894
ecosystem components, 600, 602–603
$E=mc^2$, 27, 853, 866
exercise, 280
fats, 262
fatty acids, 417
forms, 312, 756
fossil fuels, 644–647
kinetic, 312–313, 437, 756, 866, 894
mechanical, 758–759
physics, 756–759
potential, 312–313, 438, 756, 867, 895
pyramid, 603

quanta, 835
stored in molecules, 378
thermodynamics, 381
U.S. consumption compared to rest of world, 644

energy efficiency, 645

energy levels, 318, 826, 827

engineering
applied physics, 752
genetic, 80, 628, 715, 171

engines
combustion, 791
rocket, 970
thermal efficiency, 790

enthalpy, 363

entropy, 381, 790, 894

entry phase of space flight, 969

environment, 630–733
See also agriculture; environmentalism; habitats; natural resources; pollution
changing, 632–633
and health, 648–653
and heredity, 63
human population explosion, 634–637
natural selection, 39

environmental diseases, 293

environmentalism, 654–658
See also conservation of natural resources
conservationists and environmentalists, 655
economic costs and benefits, 659
history, 654–657
milestones, 656
what you can do, 658–659

Environmental Protection Agency (EPA), 658, 659, 695

environmental resistance, 592

enzymes, 420–421
catalysts, 369
defined, 305, 437
fungi digestion, 149
genes in production of proteins, 66
genetics, 63

human digestive system, 236
infectious disease, 292
plant digestion, 137
proteins, 260, 420
shape, 419
Eocene epoch, 483
ephedra, 114
ephemeral vegetation, 611
epicenter of an earthquake, 456
epicotyl, 146
epicycles, 903
epidemics, 292
epidermis
defined, 305
human integumentary system,
182, 242
leaves, 127
plants, 120
roots, 123
stems, 124
epididymis, 238, 257
epinephrine, 240
epiphytes, 112, 609
epithelial tissues, 182
equations (chemical), 362–365, 436
equator
climate and, 554
defined, 583
latitude, 504
tropical climates, 558
equatorial system, 906
equilibrium (chemical), 370–371,
436
equilibrium (physical), 764,
768, 894
equilibrium constant, 370, 388
equinoxes, 906, 989
equivalence, principle of, 767
erbium
alphabetical guide to the
elements, 331
periodic table of the elements,
323
symbol and atomic number, 324
erosion
acid rain, 669
defined, 583

deforestation, 703
glacial, 514–517
soil, 532, 709–711
streams and rivers, 510–513
trees prevent, 702
weathering, 506–509
wind, 518–519
Eryops, 157
escape velocity, 969, 971
eskers, 516, 517
esophagus
animal digestive systems,
190, 191
human digestive system, 236, 237
essential amino acids, 260
essential fatty acids, 262
estivation, 209
ethane, 409, 410, 412
ethanol (ethyl alcohol)
alternative energy sources, 647
formula, 358
melting and boiling points, 788
organic reactions, 413
specific gravity, 776
ethene. *See* ethylene (ethene)
ethics
cloning, 79
defined, 747
DNA profiling, 79
treatment of animals, 617
ethnobotany, 99
ethology, 210
ethyl alcohol. *See* ethanol (ethyl
alcohol)
ethylene (ethene)
alkenes, 409
naming, 410
plant growth inhibitor, 143,
144, 145
reactions, 413
structure, 409
ethyne (acetylene), 409, 411, 412
eudicotyledons (eudicots), 117, 305
euglenas (Euglenophyta), 94, 98
Eukaryota, 91
eukaryotic cells, 47
cell size, 44

cell types, 46
cell wall, 48
defined, 305
domain Eukaryota, 91
early plant ancestors, 98
emergence, 152
mitosis, 196–197
eulittoral region (intertidal zone),
581
euphotic zone, 614
Europa (satellite of Jupiter), 985, 986
Europe
coniferous forests, 613
deforestation, 703
Devonian period, 489
European Union pollution
register, 657
grasslands, 613
human migration, 163
Jurassic period, 494
Laurasia, 448
middle latitude climate zone,
560, 561
Mississippian epoch, 490
Ordovician period, 487
Paleogene and Neogene periods,
498, 499
Pleistocene epoch, 500
polar climate, 562
population growth, 636
scrub forests, 612
Silurian period, 488
temperate deciduous forest, 612
world population density, 637
European Space Authority (ESA),
975, 984, 985, 987
europium
alphabetical guide to the
elements, 331
periodic table of the elements,
322
symbol and atomic number, 324
euryptids (sea scorpions), 488
Eustachian tube, 246
evaporation
defined, 583
evaporates in dissolved load, 511

heat of evaporation, 379
hydrologic cycle, 538–539
salinity of seawater, 569
water cycle in ecosystems, 606
evaporite, 530, 583
event horizon, 950, 989
Everest, Mount, 177
Everglades, 701
evergreens, 115
evolution
See also natural selection
basics, 37
Buffon, 165
complexity, 41
Darwin observes nature on *Beagle* voyage, 24
Darwin's *The Origin of Species,* 23, 169
defined, 305
development of life, 30
evidence for, 30, 37
fossil evidence, 30, 31, 481
Lamarckian, 168
synthesis with genetics, 169
evolutionary track (stellar), 946
exchange particles, 864
excited state of an electron, 317
excretory system
See also kidneys
animal anatomy, 182
homeostasis, 200
organ systems, 61
exercise, 280–281
health, 258
respiration, 235
sleep improved, 287
exfoliation of rock, 507
exocrine glands, 240
exoskeletons, 97, 177, 188
exothermic processes, 353, 437
exothermic reactions, 312, 363, 381, 437
expanding universe, 911
expansion joints, 792
experimental physics, 754
experiments, 25
expiration (breathing), 195, 234

external auditory canal, 246
external carotid artery, 253
external-combustion engines, 791
external fertilization, 186
external iliac artery and vein, 253
external jugular vein, 253
external oblique muscle, 254, 255
extinction (biology)
Cretaceous period mass extinction, 159, 935, 496, 497
defined, 747
end of final Ice Age, 500
Lamarck, 168
natural selection, 39
number of extinct organisms, 90
Ordovician period mass extinction, 487
Permian period mass extinction, 157, 492, 493
rates, 638
extinction (of starlight), 954, 989
extractive metallurgy, 529
extraterrestrial life, 966–967
extrusive igneous rocks, 466
Exxon Valdez **oil spill,** 724
eye of a hurricane, 544, 545
eyes
animal, 204
arthropods, 177
human sense organs, 244–245
largest animal, 188
Eyjafjallajokull glacier volcano, 661

F

face muscles, 228
facial artery and vein, 253
factory farms, 636
Fahrenheit temperature scale, 788
falling bodies, 763, 766
falling leaves, 127, 145
Fallopian tubes, 239, 257
fallout, 649, 747
families (biological), 91, 171

Faraday, Michael, 390, 753, 811, 822
Faraday constant, 390
farsightedness, 842
fascicles, 115
fast foods, 284–285
fats, 262–263
added in foods, 274
animal building blocks, 180
dividing, 266
"empty" calories, 260
fast foods, 285
general dietary guidelines, 266
lipids, 416
sterols, 264
in various foods, 276–279
fat-soluble vitamins, 268, 270
fatty acids, 417
animal metabolism, 189
essential, 262
fats, 262–263
fault-block mountains, 524
faults (geological), 523
defined, 583
earthquakes, 456–457
lake basin formation, 567
ocean floor, 579
San Andreas fault, 450, 458
types, 458
favorable traits, 38
feet (anatomy), 251
feldspars, 464, 466, 468
femoral nerve, 252
femur, 226, 251
fermentation, 150
Fermi, Enrico, 23, 753, 862
Fermi National Accelerator Laboratory (Fermilab), 858
fermions, 865
fermium
alphabetical guide to the elements, 331
periodic table of the elements, 323
symbol and atomic number, 324
ferns, 112–113
classification of plants, 96

Pennsylvanian epoch, 491
Triassic period, 493
tropical rain forest, 609
ferrets, 641, 643
ferrocene, 400
ferromagnesian minerals, 466
ferromagnetism, 821, 894
Fertile Crescent, 625
fertilization
   animal reproduction, 199
   defined, 305
   evolutionary change, 38
   external, 186
   flowering plants, 129
   human reproductive system, 238, 239
   internal, 186
   in vitro, 796
fertilizers, 530, 626, 632, 712, 728
fiber (dietary)
   diet and cancer, 267
   fast foods, 285
   general dietary guidelines, 266
   nutrition, 261
fibrillation, 294
fibrous root systems, 122
fibula, 226, 251
fiddlehead ferns, 113
fiddler crabs, 208
field-effect transistors, 830, 831
fighting, 216
"fight or flight" hormone, 240
Fig Tree Formation, 485
filaments (flowers), 128
filters, polarizing, 845
finches, 169
fine-grained rocks, 467
fire
   air pollution, 661
   incineration of waste, 691, 695, 747
fireweed, 620
first aid, 290
first cause, 43
first-class levers, 772
first law of motion, 762
first law of thermodynamics, 381, 790

fir trees, 115
fish (food)
   balanced diet, 266
   calories and fats, 276
   cholesterol, 265
   fats, 263
fishes
   acid rain, 666, 668
   Age of Fishes, 155
   analogous features with dolphins, 170
   aquatic environments, 614–615
   Aristotle's classification of animals, 164
   brain, 221
   circulatory system, 192, 193
   cold-blooded animals, 203
   continental margins, 578
   Devonian period, 489
   eyes, 204
   food chain, 604
   freshwater environments, 615
   gills, 192, 195
   homeostasis, 201
   life span, 207
   movement in water, 184
   ocean's cycle of life, 605
   reproduction, 186
   respiratory system, 194, 195
   Silurian period, 488
   sublittoral region, 581
   ultrasound kills, 809
   unhealthy water systems, 720
   upwellings, 573
   vertebrates, 178
   waste nitrogen, 201
   water pollution, 722
   wetlands, 700
fission (cellular), 198
fission, nuclear. *See* nuclear fission
fitness (physical), 280–285
   See also exercise
   stress relieved, 287
fitness (reproductive), 36, 39
fixed action patterns, 211, 212, 305
fixed laws, 41

fjords, 515
flagella, 42, 43
flat universe, 963, 965, 988, 989
flatworms (Platyhelminthes)
   bilateral symmetry, 172
   head ganglion, 220
   kingdom Animalia, 97, 174
   photoreceptors, 205
   reproduction, 186
flavonoids, 137, 305
fleas, 593
Fleming, Sir Alexander, 23, 24, 151
Fleming, John Ambrose, 825
Fleming valve, 825
fleshy fruits, 130
flexor carpi radialis muscle, 254
flexor carpi ulnaris muscle, 254
flies, 185
flight
   birds, 185
   dinosaurs, 495
   insects, 185
   Wright brothers, 976
floating ribs, 251
floating sorrel, 641
flood, the, 40, 41, 168
floodplains, 512, 583
floods
   climate change, 674, 677
   trees prevent, 702
Florey, Lord, 151
Florida panther, 701
florigen, 144
flowering plants. *See* angiosperms (flowering plants)
flowers, 128–129
   angiosperms, 116
   defined, 305
   flowering hormone, 144
   monocots and dicots, 117
   plant growth, 143
   plant life cycle, 147
fluidity, 352
fluid physics
   See also fluids
   types of physics, 755

fluids

See also gases; liquids

defined, 894

pressure, 777

viscosity, 352, 353, 779, 782, 797

flukes (flatworms), 174, 593

fluorescence, 954

fluorine

alphabetical guide to the elements, 331

halogenation of hydrocarbons, 412

microminerals, 269, 273

periodic table of the elements, 323

seawater composition, 569

symbol and atomic number, 324

valence shell of atom, 319

fluorite, 462, 463, 465

focal length, 843

focal point, 843

focus (of an earthquake), 456

focus (optics)

lens, 909

mirror, 841, 894

focusing (eye), 245

foehn winds, 555

folded mountains, 525

folds (geology), 522, 523

foliated rocks, 470, 583

folic acid, 271

food

See also agriculture; digestion; nutrition

amino acids, 419

consumer organisms, 601

eating disorders, 284

feeding ladder, 596

fungi, 150

genetically modified organisms (GMOs), 80

historical regulation, 275

human population explosion, 636

infectious disease spread, 292

photosynthesis, 134–135

population limited by lack, 593

producer organisms, 601

taste, 249

waste, 689

Food and Drug Administration (FDA), 274

food chains, 596, 604, 747

food pyramid, 259, 266

food storage tissue, 131

food webs, 604, 747

fool's gold (pyrite), 461, 465

forbidden gap, 827

force, 764–765

defined, 894

dynamics, 758

fundamental, 765, 854, 864

second law of motion, 762–763

third law of motion, 763

torque, 768–769

forced convection, 795

forensic science, 78

forests

See also rain forest

coniferous forest, 613, 623, 702

deciduous rain forest, 609

habitats in peril, 702–703

North American southern forest, 622

Pennsylvanian epoch, 491

reforestation, 676, 705

scrub forest, 612

temperate deciduous forest, 612, 622, 702

types, 702

forforaminiferans, 490

formulas (chemical), 358

formula weight, 373

forward-biased p-n junctions, 829

Fossey, Dian, 222

fossil casts, 478

fossil fuels, 734–735

See also coal; petroleum (oil); natural gas

conserving, 644–647, 676

defined, 747

Industrial Revolution, 654

natural resources, 531

fossil molds, 478

fossils, 478–482

African and South American, 449, 474

annelids, 176

Cambrian period, 486

Cretaceous period, 497

dating, 480–481

defined, 305, 583

Ediacaran, 485

evidence for evolution, 30, 31, 481

first of living organism, 152

geologic time scale, 482

Jurassic period, 495

Leonardo da Vinci observes, 474

Martian, 927

Mississippian epoch, 490

oldest terrestrial animal, 155

Ordovician, 487

Paleogene and Neogene periods, 499

Pennsylvanian epoch, 491

Precambrian time, 485

scientific creationism on, 41

Silurian period, 488

Tiktaalik, 36

Triassic period, 493

zoology, 168

fovea centralis, 244, 245

foxes, 631

fracture (minerals), 460

fracture callus, 227

fracture zones, 579

fragmental rocks, 467

fragmentation (botany), 109

francium

alphabetical guide to the elements, 332

particle emission and half-life of francium 229, 404

periodic table of the elements, 322

symbol and atomic number, 324

frankenfoods, 80

Franklin, Benjamin, 22, 810

Franklin, Rosalind, 63

Fraunhofer, Joseph von, 910

Index

freezing point
    depression, 384, 385
    seawater, 570
freezing rain, 541
frequency
    defined, 894
    sound, 803, 809
    time measurement, 761
    waves, 799
freshwater environments, 615
Freud, Sigmund, 23
friction
    caloric theory of heat, 785
    defined, 894
    heat sources, 787
    Newton's laws of motion, 763
fringes (optics), 838
frogs
    digestive system, 191
    egg cells, 44
    life span, 207
    metamorphosis, 187
    reproduction, 186
Frohse, Franz, 250
fronds, 113
frontal bone, 251
fronts (weather), 542–543, 583
frost, 141
frost wedging, 507, 583
fruit fly (*Drosophila melanogaster*), 64, 73, 81
fruits, 130–131
    angiosperms, 116
    balanced diet, 266
    calories and fats, 277
    carbohydrates, 260
    defined, 306
    diet and cancer, 267
    fiber, 261
    general dietary guidelines, 266
    USDA guidelines, 259
fuel cells, 395, 740–741, 747
fuel oil, 412
fuel rods (nuclear), 697, 698
fuels. *See also* fossil fuels
    hydrocarbons, 412
    rocket, 970

Fuji, Mount, 527
fumaroles, 579, 583
functional MRI, 425
fungi, 148–151
    Cambrian period, 486
    corn-leaf blight, 628
    defined, 306
    diseases caused by, 95, 151
    eukaryotic cells, 47
    fungicides, 713
    indoor pollution, 651
    kingdom Fungi, 95
    modern classification of plants and animals, 91
    mycologists, 148, 307
    mycorrhizal associations, 608
    plant ancestors, 98
    reducer organisms, 601
    reproduction, 198
fungicides, 713
funnel clouds, 549
fusion, nuclear
    See nuclear fusion

G

gadolinium
    alphabetical guide to the elements, 332
    periodic table of the elements, 323
    symbol and atomic number, 324
Gagarin, Yuri A., 972, 973, 978
gaining weight, 283
galactic corona, 952
Galapagos Islands, 169
galaxies, 956–957
    See also Milky Way galaxy
    active, 960, 988
    farthest away, 958
    formation, 964
    moving apart, 911, 959, 962
    Seyfert, 961
Galdikas, Birute, 222
galena, 465, 529
Galen of Pergamum, 22, 166
Galileo, 26, 753, 904

Galileo (spacecraft), 935, 984, 985, 986
gallbladder
    animal digestive systems, 190, 191
    human digestive system, 236, 237, 256
gallium
    alphabetical guide to the elements, 332
    periodic table of the elements, 323
    symbol and atomic number, 324
Gallup, Gordon, 222
Galvani, Luigi, 392
galvanic cells, 392–393
galvanometer, 811
galvanoreceptors, 205
gametes (sex cells)
    See also egg cells (ova); sperm cells (spermatozoa)
    angiosperms, 116, 128
    defined, 306
    fungi, 149
    germinal mutations, 68
    independent assortment law, 69
    meiosis, 57
    sexual reproduction, 55, 198
gametophytes, 111, 112
gamma rays, 682
    defined, 437, 894
    electromagnetic spectrum, 835, 912
    gamma-ray astronomy, 913
    Gamma Ray Observatory, 984
    Milky Way galaxy, 953
    nuclear weapons, 407
    PET scans, 863
    radioactivity, 402, 682
gases, 354–357, 783
    See also noble gases
    Avogadro, 349, 356, 357
    defined, 437
    density, 776
    electrical conductivity, 815
    heat transfer, 792
    molecules, 349, 350, 779, 783

phase changes, 353
physical properties, 779
plasmas, 355
pressure, 355, 777
solutions, 382
states of matter, 312
stored energy, 378
universal gas constant, 357, 867
gas giants, 928–933
See also Jupiter; Neptune;
Saturn; Uranus
defined, 989
gas laws, 356–357
gasoline, 412, 776
gastric juice, 190
gastrocnemius muscle, 254, 255
gastroenteritis, 726
gastropods
Ordovician period, 487
Pennsylvanian epoch, 491
phylum Mollusca, 176
gauss units, 425
Geiger counters, 859
gel electrophoresis (DNA
fingerprinting), 78, 81
Gell-Mann, Murray, 863
Gemini space program,
972–973, 979
gems, 462
gene expression, 63
genera
modern classification of plants
and animals, 91, 171
scientific names, 91, 107
general theory of relativity, 753,
767, 853, 895, 925
genes, 62–63
See also genetic disorders;
genetics; mutations (genetic)
chromosomes, 49, 62, 73
defined, 306
diversity, 716–717
dominant and recessive, 71, 75
genetics terms to know, 75
genetic variation, 68–69
heredity, 38, 70, 72
mapping, 80–81

plant growth, 142–143
production of proteins, 66
sex-linked, 77
Genesis (Bible), 31, 40
"Genesis" rock, 981
genetically modified organisms
(GMOs), 80
genetic disorders
Down syndrome, 68
noninfectious disease, 293
sex-linked disorders, 77
genetic diversity, 716–717
genetic engineering (gene splicing),
80, 628, 715, 717
genetics, 62–89
See also genes; heredity
basics, 63
botany, 99, 105
classical, 70–71
history of science, 22–23
practice problems, 82–89
synthesis with evolution, 169
technology, 78–79
terms to know, 75
timeline, 63
genomes
defined, 64, 306
gene mapping, 80–81
Human Genome Project, 23,
63, 81
genotoxins, 648, 747
genotypes, 71, 306
genus. *See* genera
geocentric theory, 22, 902–903,
989
geographically isolated groups,
30, 36
geological oceanography, 568, 578
geologic time, 476–501
geology, 440–501
See also Earth; physical geology
catastrophism, 168
defined, 583
historical, 474–501, 583
history of science, 22
uniformatarianism, 168
geometrical optics, 840–841

geometry, 22
geophysics, 752, 754
geosynclines, 496, 583
geothermal energy, 647, 745, 786
geothermal gradient, 446, 583
geotropism, 139, 306
germanium
alphabetical guide to the
elements, 332
periodic table of the
elements, 323
semiconductors, 826, 827
superconductors, 832
symbol and atomic number, 324
German Rocket Society, 969, 976
germinal mutations, 68
germination
defined, 306
plant growth, 143
plant life cycle, 146
temperature, 141
germ theory of disease, 23, 27
Gesner, Conrad, 165
geysers, 565
defined, 583
heat sources, 786
Yellowstone National Park, 454
giant elliptical galaxies, 956
giant squids, 188
giant stars, 944, 946, 947
giardiasis, 726
gibberellins, 143, 144, 145
gibbons, 184
Gibbs free energy, 393
gill grooves, 178
gills, 192, 195
Ginkgophyta (ginkgos), 96, 107, 114
Giotto probe, 984
giraffes, 168, 217, 588, 610
gizzards, 191
glacial striations, 516, 517
glacial surges, 515
Glacier National Park, 516
glaciers, 514–517
defined, 583
ice ages, 500
ice sheets, 514, 573, 584, 675

lake formation, 567
Mississippian epoch, 490
sea-level change, 475
water supply, 718

glands
See also endocrine system
cells, 44
human endocrine system, 240

Glashow, Sheldon Lee, 865

glass
density, 776
electrical resistance, 814
heat conduction, 794
recycling, 693
static electricity, 813
transmission of light, 837
vitrification of radioactive
waste, 698
waste, 647

glassy rocks, 467

Glenn, John H., Jr., 972, 978, 986

Global Positioning System (GPS),
504, 583

global warming, 672–677
defined, 747
deforestation, 703
evidence, 677
fossil fuels, 734
human population explosion, 636
Intergovernmental Panel on
Climate Change, 657
regulating emissions, 657, 659

globular clusters, 952, 953, 962,
988, 989

glomeruli, 241

glossopharyngeal nerve, 248

glucagon, 240

glucose
animal metabolism, 188, 189
common compounds, 358
defined, 306
diabetes, 297
human digestive system, 236
photosynthesis, 134, 602
respiration, 136

glutamate, 249

glutamic acid, 419

glutamine, 419

gluteus maximus muscle, 228, 255

gluteus medius muscle, 228

glycerin, 262

glycerol, 189, 262, 416, 417

glycine, 419

glycolipids, 416

glycolysis, 189

gneiss, 470, 471

Gnetophyta, 107, 114

goats, 616, 671

Gobi Desert, 611

Goddard, Robert H., 968, 976

gold
alphabetical guide to the
elements, 332
electrical conductivity, 815
ores, 529
periodic table of the elements, 323
specific gravity, 463
streak, 461
symbol and atomic number, 324

Golgi apparatus, 51, 181, 306

Gombe Stream National Park
(Tanzania), 223

gonads
See also ovaries; testes
human endocrine system, 240

Gondwanaland, 448, 488, 489, 491,
494, 496

gonorrhea, 300

Goodall, Jane, 222–223

gorillas, 97, 184

gourds, 624

GPS (Global Positioning System),
504, 583

gracilis muscle, 254

gradualism, 37

gradual metamorphosis, 187

grains
See also cereals
calories and fats, 278
diet and cancer, 267
domestication, 624
general dietary guidelines, 266
lipids, 416
USDA guidelines, 259

Grand Canyon, 510

grand unified theories (GUTs),
864–865, 894

granite, 467, 528

granular layer (epidermis), 242

granules (solar), 937

graphite, 460, 780

grasshoppers, 187, 714

grasslands, 613
See also savanna
North American, 622
soil, 708

gravitation, 766–767
See also gravity
Einstein's theory, 767, 950, 853
exchange particles, 864
fundamental forces, 765, 864
grand unified theories, 864
inverse square law, 866
Newton's theory, 26, 763, 767,
904–905
open or closed universe, 963, 988
"theory of everything," 865
WIMPs (weakly interacting
massive particles), 964

gravitational collapse, 917

gravitational constant, 766,
866, 867

gravitational lenses, 961

gravitons, 864

gravity
See also gravitation
animal size limited by, 183
defined, 583
Earth's interior, 447
formula for acceleration, 866
geotropism, 139
moon, 923

gravity cells, 394

Great Barrier Reef, 706

Great Lakes, 514, 519, 567, 598

Great Orion Nebula (M42),
954, 955

Great Red Spot (Jupiter),
928, 929

Great Rift Valley, 501

Great Salt Lake (Utah), 566

great saphenous vein, 253
Greece, ancient
    astronomy, 902–903
    botany, 103
green algae (Chlorophyta), 108–109
    classification of plants, 107
    first plants, 99
    kingdom Protista, 94
    Thallophyta, 108
Greenbaum, Elias, 741
greenhouse effect, 670–677
    See also climate change
    atmosphere, 535
    defined, 747
    Kyoto Protocol, 657, 677
    Venus, 921
Greenland
    climate change, 672, 673
    ice sheets, 514, 562, 574
    Jurassic period, 494
    Laurasia, 448
    world population density, 637
    world precipitation distribution,
        732
green manuring, 712
green pitcher plant, 640
Green Revolution in agriculture,
    717
Greenwich time, 505
Grew, Nehemiah, 105
Griffin, Donald, 222
Grissom, Virgil "Gus," 978, 980
ground meristems, 120
ground sloths, 162, 500, 501
ground state of an electron, 317
groundwater
    defined, 583, 747
    hydrosphere, 564–565
    pesticides contaminate, 713
    septic tanks contaminate, 730
    water supply, 718
growth
    human body, 224
    plant physiology, 134, 142–147
growth rings, 124, 125
guanine, 65, 66, 306, 414–415
guayale, 619

guinea pigs, 616
Gulf of Mexico oil spill, 724, 725
Gulf Stream, 556, 572
gums, 261
Gustav (hurricane), 547
Guth, Alan H., 965
guyots, 579
gymnosperms (Gymnospermosida;
        naked seed plants), 114–115
    See also conifers (Pinophyta)
    classification of plants, 96, 107
    defined, 306
    early land plants, 101
gypsum, 461, 463, 465, 530
gyres, 572, 573, 583

H

Haber, Fritz, 349, 371
habitats
    defined, 747
    extent, 630
    Industrial Revolution in
        destruction, 654
    invasive species alter, 598
    loss, 639, 640
    ocean life, 580
    in peril, 700–717
    plant, 618–619
    population limited by loss, 593
    protecting, 706–707
habituation, 212, 306
Hadean eon, 483
hadrons, 863
hadrosaurs, 496
hafnium
    alphabetical guide to the
        elements, 332
    periodic table of the elements, 322
    symbol and atomic number, 324
hagfishes, 97, 178
hail, 541
hair
    See also cilia
    human integumentary system,
        182, 242
    organ of Corti, 246

Haldane, J. B. S., 32
Hale-Bopp, Comet, 934
Hales, Stephen, 105
half-life, 403, 437, 476, 583, 696,
    747
half reactions, 396, 397
halide minerals, 465
halite, 461, 463, 465, 469, 530
Halley, Edmund, 904
Halley's comet, 766, 984
halogenation, 412
halogens, 320
halophytes, 611
hamstring muscles, 228
hands, 247, 251
haploid cells, 59, 306
happy accidents, 24
hardness
    minerals, 460, 462–463
    water, 730
Harvey, William, 22, 25, 166
hassium
    alphabetical guide to the
        elements, 332
    periodic table of the
        elements, 322
    symbol and atomic
        number, 324
Hawaiian Islands, 453, 455
Hayes, Denis, 656
hazardous wastes, 694–699, 747
hazmat suits, 695
head ganglion, 220–221
health, 258–303
    See also diseases; medicine
    defined, 258
    and the environment, 648–653
    fitness, 280–285
    issues, 290–303
    mental, 286–289, 687
    nutrition, 258–279
    regulation of claims about, 275
Health Canada, 274
health physics, 755
hearing
    human ears, 246
    mechanoreceptors, 205

Index

noise pollution, 685
sense receptors, 230
heart
  See also heart disease
  amphibians and reptiles, 192
  birds and mammals, 193
  cardiac muscle, 229
  cephalopods, 193
  cholesterol, 264
  fish, 192
  Harvey on blood circulation, 166
  human, 224, 232, 253
  human organs illustration, 256
heart attacks (myocardial
    infarction)
  cholesterol, 264, 265
  diet and, 266
  diseases associated with aging, 293
  exercise reduces risk, 281
heart disease, 294–295
  See also heart attacks (myocardial
    infarction)
  noninfectious disease, 293
  obesity as risk, 282
  stress as risk factor, 286
heat, 784–797
  See also specific heat;
    thermodynamics
  caloric theory, 785
  defined, 437, 894
  and entropy, 381
  heat energy, 312
  high-temperature
    superconductors, 833
  hot air rises, 536
  rock cycle, 472
  sensing, 204
  sources, 786–787
  thermal metamorphism, 471
  thermal pollution of water, 722
  thermochemistry, 378–381
  thermodynamics, 381, 754
  transfer, 792–795
heat capacity, 378, 437
heating
  geothermal, 745
  solar, 743

heat of evaporation, 379
heat of fusion, 379
heat of reaction, 363
heat shields, 969
height (waves), 799
height and weight tables, 282
helicase, 65
heliocentric theory, 22, 26, 27, 903,
    904, 989
helium
  alphabetical guide to the
    elements, 333
  atom, 855
  chemical bonds, 344
  density, 776
  interstellar matter, 955
  noble gases, 399
  periodic table of the
    elements, 323
  stars, 943, 948
  superfluidity, 797
  symbol and atomic number, 324
Helmholtz, Hermann von, 785
Helmont, Jan Baptista van, 354
hematite, 465, 528, 529
hemicellulose, 261
hemoglobin
  classification of animals, 171
  coordination compounds, 401
  iron and copper, 269
  sickle cell anemia, 69
hemophilia, 77
Henry, Joseph, 753
hepatitis A, 726
heptane, 410
herbaceous stems, 124–125
herbals (books), 104
herbicides, 648, 713
herbivores (primary consumers)
  biotic pyramids, 604
  consumer organisms, 601
  defined, 747
  energy-flow in ecosystems, 603
  energy pyramid, 603
  food chains and food webs, 604
heredity
  chromosomes, 49, 239

  defined, 306
  genes, 38, 70, 72
  genetics, 62–81
  Mendel, 22, 23, 63, 70–73,
    167, 169
  Mendelian crosses, 74–77
  plant breeding, 627
  plant growth, 142–143
hermaphrodites, 186
Herodotus, 474
heroin, 299
herpes, genital, 300
hertz, 803, 809, 835
Hertz, Heinrich, 811
Hertzsprung-Russell (HR)
    diagram, 944, 945, 946
Hess, Harry, 451
Heterodontosaurus, 160
heterogeneous mixtures, 382
heterotrophs, 152
heterozygosity, 74, 75, 306
hexane, 410
hexene, 410
hexyne, 411
hibernation, 203, 209, 306
high-density lipoprotein (HDL),
    264
high-yield crops, 628, 708, 717
Himalaya Mountains, 444,
    451, 501
Hindenburg disaster, 368
Hipparchus, 942
Hippocrates, 22
Hiroshima bomb, 407, 860
histadine, 419
histology
  See also tissues
  botany, 99
  defined, 44
histones, 64
historical geology, 474–501
  defined, 583
  geologic time, 482–501
HIV (human immunodeficiency
    virus), 301, 411
holdfast, 109
hollow-shaft principle, 183

Holmes, Arthur, 449

holmium
> alphabetical guide to the
> > elements, 333
> periodic table of the elements,
> > 323
> symbol and atomic number, 324

Holocene epoch, 483, 500, 501

holograms, 800

homeostasis, 200–201, 306

homeothermic animals, 203

hominids
> *See also* human beings
> defined, 306
> emergence, 163

Homo, 163

Homo erectus, 163, 306

homogeneous mixtures, 382

Homo habilis, 163, 306

homologous chromosomes, 75

homology, 170, 306

Homo sapiens. See human beings

homozygosity, 74, 75, 306

honey mushroom (*Armillaria
> ostoyae*), 148

hoofed mammals, 499

Hooke, Robert, 22, 47, 107, 167

hookworms, 175

horizon system, 906

horizontal faults, 523

hormones
> cellular communication, 200
> defined, 306
> female sex hormones, 239
> genes in production of
> > proteins, 66
> human endocrine system, 240
> lipids, 416
> male sex hormones, 238
> plant growth, 143, 144–145
> proteins, 260
> regulating animal body, 202

hornfels, 470

horns (landforms), 516, 517

hornworts, 110, 111

horny layer (epidermis), 182, 242

horse latitudes, 493, 536

horses, 171, 616, 617

horsetails (Sphenophyta), 100,
> 107, 113

hot spots, 453, 454–455, 583, 647

hot springs, 565

hour circle, 906

Hubble, Edwin, 911, 956, 959, 962

Hubble's constant, 959, 962

Hubble's Law, 911, 959, 962

Hubble Space Telescope, 908, 958,
> 984, 985, 986

human beings, 224–303
> anatomy, 224–257
> animals and humans, 616–617
> Aristotle's classification of
> > animals, 164
> brain, 163, 221
> cloning, 79
> and ecosystems, 632
> health, 258–303
> *Homo sapiens* defined, 306
> Linnaeus names them *Homo
> > sapiens,* 165
> number of cells in body, 45
> number of chromosomes, 64
> nutrition, 258–279
> plants and people, 102–105,
> > 624–629
> population explosion, 634–637
> primates, 163
> Quaternary period, 500
> scientific creationism, 41
> scientific name, 91
> sex-linked disorders, 77
> smog's effects, 665
> in space, 972–975
> Vesalius on anatomy, 166

Human Genome Project, 23, 63, 81

humanities, 21

humerus, 226, 251

humidity, 538, 583, 585

hummingbirds, 37, 188

humoral immune response, 302

humus, 583

hunting
> *See also* predation
> animal cooperation, 218

> by chimpanzees, 223
> environmentalism, 654
> by humans, 616
> by lions, 219
> overhunting, 639

hurricanes, 544–547
> defined, 584
> tracking, 552

Hutton, James, 166, 474

Huygens, Christiaan, 753, 799, 931

hybrid automobiles, 659

hybridization (agriculture), 627, 628

hybridization probes, 81

hydras
> digestive system, 190
> vegetative reproduction, 55, 196,
> > 198, 199

hydration, 507

hydraulic action, 510

hydrides, 398, 399

hydrocarbons, 408–411
> *See also* amino acids; enzymes;
> > fossil fuels; nucleic acids
> air pollution, 663
> defined, 437, 747
> fatty acids, 262–263, 417
> lipids, 414, 416
> oil and natural gas, 531
> organic reactions, 412–413
> smog, 664

hydrochloric acid
> adding to calcium carbonate,
> > 364–365
> conjugate base, 387
> human digestive system,
> > 236, 386
> hydrogen chloride, 399

hydrochlorofluorocarbons
> (HCFCs), 681

hydrocyanic acid, 387

hydroelectric power, 646, 736,
> 738–739

hydrogen
> abundance, 354
> alphabetical guide to the
> > elements, 333
> atom, 854

Index

atomic weight, 317
discovery, 354
Earth's crust, 447
Hindenburg disaster, 368
hydrocarbons, 408–411
interstellar matter, 955
ions, 386, 388
mineral nutrients, 607
nonmetals, 398
nucleus of atom, 314
periodic table of the elements, 322
photosynthesis, 135
plant nutrients carried by
        water, 134
power, 735, 740–741
producing from water, 349
renewable fuels, 735, 741
seawater composition, 569
stars, 943, 948
symbol and atomic number, 324
water, 345, 346, 362
hydrogen bombs. *See* nuclear
        bombs
hydrogen bonds, 346–347, 352,
        415, 418
hydrogen chloride, 399
hydrogen fluoride, 399
hydrogen peroxide, 358, 398
hydrogen sulfide, 358, 399
hydrologic cycle, 538–541, 584
hydrolysis, 508
hydroponic gardening, 629, 747
hydrosphere, 564–581
        See also groundwater; lakes;
                oceans; streams
        defined, 564, 584
hydrotropism, 139
hydroxide ions, 386, 388
hyperglycemia, 297
hypertension (high blood pressure),
        282, 293, 295
hyperthyroidism, 283
hyphae, 148
hypocenter of an earthquake, 456
hypocotyl, 146
hypothalamus, 202
hypotheses, 26

I

ice
        See also glaciers
        changes in state, 793
        density, 776
        freezing rain, 541
        frost wedging, 507, 583
        hydrogen bonds, 352
        melting, 379
ice ages, 500, 584
ice caps
        climate change, 672
        defined, 584
        polar climates, 562
        water supply, 718
"ice-minus" bacteria, 717
ice sheets, 514, 573, 584, 675
ichthyosaurs, 158, 493
Ichthyostega, 157
ideal gases, 355, 375
ideal gas law, 356, 357
identity (personal), 289
igneous rocks, 466–467
        dating, 476
        defined, 584
        Hutton, 474
        metal ores, 528
        North America, 473
        rock cycle, 472
Iguanodon, 161
iliacus muscle, 254
iliohypogastric nerve, 252
ilium, 226, 251
illumination, 846
image inversion, 843
imbibition, 146
immigration, 592
immune system, 302–303
        disorders, 293
        irreducible complexity
                argument, 42
        ultraviolet radiation's effects, 680
immunity to disease, 302–303
immunization, 290, 291
immunoglobulins, 302
imperfect spores, 149

imprinting (behavior), 212
imprints (fossils), 479
impulse (physics), 775, 894
incident rays, 837, 841
incineration of waste, 691,
        695, 747
inclined planes, 773
incomplete dominance, 76
incus (anvil), 246
independent assortment, law of,
        69, 72, 73, 77
index fossils, 481, 482
index of refraction, 837
India
        Gondwanaland, 448, 449
        monsoon forests, 609
        monsoons, 557
        Paleogene and Neogene
                periods, 498
        savanna, 610
        space program, 975, 987
Indiana limestone, 490
Indian Ocean, 571, 574
indium
        alphabetical guide to the
                elements, 333
        periodic table of the elements,
                323
        symbol and atomic
                number, 324
Indonesia, 452, 457
indoor pollution, 650–651
induction (electromagnetic), 811,
        817, 822–823
industrial chemicals
        air pollution, 662
        Bhopal disaster, 649
        genotoxins, 648
        occupational hazards, 652
        water pollution, 722
Industrial Revolution, 654
industry
        See also industrial chemicals
        heat, 784
        machines, 772
        water conservation, 732
        water pollution, 722

inert gases. *See* noble gases

inertia
    defined, 894
    first law of motion, 762
    force overcoming, 765

infectious diseases, 292

inferior vena cava, 253, 257

inflation theory (cosmology), 964, 965, 989

infraorbital nerve, 252

infrared radiation
    electromagnetic spectrum, 835, 912
    infrared astronomy, 913
    infrared rays, 795
    Milky Way galaxy, 953

infraspinalis muscle, 255

ingredient listings, 274

inherited diseases. *See* genetic disorders

innate behaviors, 210–211

inner core (Earth), 443, 445, 584

inner ear, 246

inorganic chemistry, 396–407
    compounds, 398–399
    defined, 437
    naming compounds, 360
    nuclear chemistry, 402–407

inositol, 416

insecticides, 713

Insectivora, 179

insects
    See also bees
    Aristotle's classification of animals, 164
    compound eyes, 177, 205
    courtship behavior, 217
    Cretaceous period, 497
    Devonian period, 489
    flight, 185
    fossils, 478
    insecticides, 713
    kingdom Animalia, 97, 177
    metamorphosis, 187
    number of species classified, 97
    Pennsylvanian epoch, 491

    pheromones in communication, 214
    pollination, 129
    reproduction, 186
    respiratory system, 194, 195
    societies, 219
    sounds, 215
    taxis, 211
    waste nitrogen, 201
    wings, 183

insight, 213, 306

insolation, 584

inspiration (breathing), 195, 234

instinct, 210

insulation
    electrical current, 814, 826
    heat, 785, 894

insulators (electrical), 814, 894

insulin, 80, 240, 297

integrated circuits (microchips), 830

integrated pest management, 629, 715

integumentary system
    See also skin
    animal anatomy, 182
    human anatomy, 225, 242–243
    organ systems, 61

intelligence
    animal, 220–223
    extraterrestrial, 967
    great apes, 222–223
    insight, 213

intelligent design, 42–43
    creationism, 40
    defined, 306
    theories of origin of life, 31

intensity of sound waves, 803

interaction
    animal, 214–215
    within an ecosystem, 596–597

intercropping, 629, 747

interference (waves), 800, 801, 838–839, 894

interglacial periods, 500, 501

intermolecular forces, 346, 352, 415

internal carotid artery, 253

internal-combustion engines, 791

internal fertilization, 186

internal iliac artery and vein, 253

internal jugular vein, 253, 256

internal senses, 207, 244

International Geophysical Year (1957–1958), 449

International Migratory Bird Treaty (1918), 707

International Rules of Botanical Nomenclature, 107

International Space Station, 974, 985, 986

International System of Units (metric system), 374, 760–761, 775

International Union for the Conservation of Nature and Natural Resources (IUCN), 707

International Whaling Commission, 657

internists, 291

interphase (mitosis), 56, 59, 196

intertidal zone, 581

intertropical convergence zones, 544

intestines
    human digestive system, 236, 237, 256
    smooth muscles, 229

intrusive igneous rocks, 466

invasive species, 598–599, 747

inverse square law
    gravity, 866
    illuminance, 847, 866

inversion (atmospheric), 664, 747

invertebrates
    Cambrian period explosion, 154
    cold-blooded animals, 203
    defined, 306, 584
    kingdom Animalia, 97
    Ordovician period, 487
    Pennsylvanian epoch, 491

in vitro fertilization, 796

involuntary muscles, 229

iodine
  alphabetical guide to the
    elements, 333
  halogenation of hydrocarbons,
    412
  microminerals, 269, 273
  particle emission and half-life of
    iodine 131, 404
  periodic table of the elements,
    323
  seawater composition, 569
  symbol and atomic number, 324

ionic bonds, 345
  defined, 437
  types of chemical bond, 344

ionic compounds, 345
  chemical formulas, 358
  formula weight, 373
  inorganic compounds, 398
  naming, 360
  types of chemical bond, 344

ionic crystals, 350, 351

ionization, 384

ions, 315
  defined, 437, 894
  solutions, 384

iridium
  alphabetical guide to the
    elements, 333
  Cretaceous-Tertiary boundary,
    159, 497
  periodic table of the elements,
    322
  symbol and atomic number, 324

iris (eye), 244, 245

Irish moss (*Chondrus crispus*), 109

iron
  alphabetical guide to the
    elements, 334
  deficiency, 268
  density, 776
  Earth's crust, 447
  Earth's interior, 446
  electrical conductivity, 815
  ferromagnesian minerals, 466
  ferromagnetism, 821

melting and boiling points, 788
  microminerals, 269, 273
  mineral nutrients, 607
  ores, 528, 529
  periodic table of the elements,
    322
  plant nutrients carried by
    water, 134
  rust, 360
  seawater composition, 569
  stars, 948
  symbol and atomic number, 324

**irradiation in biological pest
    control,** 714

irreducible complexity, 31, 42

irregular clusters, 957

irregular galaxies, 956, 957

irrigation, 711
  agricultural efficiency, 708
  droughts, 675
  early agricultural technology, 626
  erosion affects, 709
  water conservation, 732

ischium, 226, 251

islets of Langerhans, 240

isobutane, 410

isoleucine, 419

isomers, 410

isopentane, 410

isotopes, 315
  defined, 437, 894
  masses, 372
  radioactive, 402, 403, 404, 406

Isthmus of Panama, 499

J

Jakobshavn Glacier, 672

Jansky, Karl, 912

Japan
  earthquakes, 458
  Mount Fuji, 527
  recycling, 692
  space program, 975, 981,
    984, 987
  temperate deciduous
    forest, 612

Japan Current, 609

Jardins des Plantes Medicinales
    (Paris), 105

jaws, 156, 251

jellyfish
  Aristotle's classification of
    animals, 164
  digestive system, 190
  Ediacaran period, 485
  galvanoreceptors, 205
  phylum Cnidaria, 173
  radial symmetry, 172

Jemison, Mae Carol, 984

jet stream, 537, 584

joints (anatomy), 227

joints (geology), 523, 584

Joliot-Curie, Frédéric, 403, 406

Joliot-Curie, Irène, 403, 406

Jolly, Alison, 222–223

Joule, James Prescott, 785

joules, 357, 378

Joule's apparatus, 790

journals (scientific), 21

Jovian planets. *See* gas giants

jugular vein, 253, 256

juice percentages, 274

junction transistors, 830–831

Jungle, The (Sinclair), 275

junk DNA, 81

junk food, 260

Jupiter, 928–929
  failed star, 929, 947
  moons, 904, 929, 985, 986
  properties, 918
  rotation, 919
  space exploration, 929, 981, 982,
    984, 985, 986

Jurassic period, 494–495
  dinosaurs, 159, 493
  geologic time scale, 483

K

Kakadu National Park (Australia),
    707

Kalahari Desert, 559

kaolinite, 463

Kaposi's sarcoma, 301
karyotyping, 64
Keck telescope, 909
Kelvin temperature scale, 788, 796
Kepler, Johannes, 22, 904, 905
Kepler space telescope, 987
keratin, 242
keratinocytes, 242
keratohyaline, 242
ketones, 260, 437
kettles, 516, 517
kidneys
    animal digestive systems, 191
    homeostasis, 200
    human, 224, 241, 257
    renal arteries and veins, 253
kinematics, 758
kinesis, 210, 306
kinetic energy, 312–313, 437, 756, 866, 894
kinetic theory of chemical reactions, 368
kinetic theory of gases, 354, 355, 437, 783, 894
kingdoms (biology), 90, 91, 171
Kirchhoff, Gustav, 910
koalas, 630
Koch, Robert, 93
Koelreuter, Joseph Gottlieb, 105
Kohler, William, 213
Krakatoa, 452
Kroto, Harold W., 349
krypton
    alphabetical guide to the elements, 334
    chemical bonds, 344
    compounds, 399
    noble gases, 399
    nuclear fission, 405, 860
    periodic table of the elements, 323
    symbol and atomic number, 324
Kuiper belt objects (KBOs), 933, 934, 989
Kyoto Protocol, 657, 677

L

labia major, 257
labia minor, 257
La Brea Tar Pits, 478, 479
lacteals, 233
lacto-ovo-vegetarian diet, 266
lacto-vegetarian diet, 266
lady's slippers, 596
Lagomorpha, 179
lakes, 566–567
    acid rain, 668
    balance of nature, 631
    defined, 584
    Great Lakes, 514, 519, 567, 598
    healthy and unhealthy systems, 720
Lamarck, Jean-Baptiste, 168
lampreys, 97, 178, 207
lampshells, 175
lancelets, 178
landfills
    land pollution, 688
    methane production, 670, 690
    waste disposal, 690
land pollution, 688–699
language, 163
lanthanide metals
    alphabetical guide to the elements, 326
    inorganic compounds, 401
    periodic table of the elements, 322
lanthanum
    alphabetical guide to the elements, 334
    periodic table of the elements, 322
    symbol and atomic number, 324
Large Hadron Collider (LHC), 20, 858, 865, 964
large intestines, 190, 236, 237, 256
Large Magellanic Cloud, 957
larval stage, 187
larynx, 234, 307
lasers, 753, 850–851, 894
LASIK surgery, 850

latent heat, 379, 793, 894
lateral femoral cutaneous nerve, 252
lateral moraines, 517, 584
lateral plantar nerve, 252
lateritic soil, 533
latissimus dorsi muscle, 254, 255
latitude, 504
    climate and, 554
    defined, 584
    parallels of latitude, 504, 585
launch window, 969
Laurasia, 448, 488, 489, 494, 496
lava, 452, 453, 455, 466
Lavoisier, Antoine, 22, 349
law of... *See under substantive words, for example,* conservation of energy, law of
Lawrence, Ernest O., 856
lawrencium
    alphabetical guide to the elements, 334
    periodic table of the elements, 323
    symbol and atomic number, 324
leaching, 668, 690, 747
lead
    air pollution, 663
    alphabetical guide to the elements, 334
    galena, 465
    indoor pollution, 651
    ores, 529
    periodic table of the elements, 323
    symbol and atomic number, 325
    water pollution, 726, 727
lead-acid batteries, 394, 395
learning, animal, 212–213
leaves, 126–127
    defined, 307
    falling, 127, 145, 612
    water transport in plants, 134
Le Châtelier's principle, 370, 371
Leclanche, Georges, 394, 395
leeches, 176
Leeuwenhoek, Anton van, 45, 167
leeward side, 555

Index

legs, 184, 226

legumes

See also beans

carbohydrates, 260

magnesium, 268

vegetarian diet, 266

Lemaître, Georges, 962

lemurs, 163

length

metric measurement, 761

special theory of relativity, 853

lens (eye), 244, 245

lenses (optics), 842–843

defined, 894

telescopes, 909

Leonardo da Vinci, 22, 474

leptons, 863

leucine, 419

leucoplasts, 50, 119

levees, 512, 584

levers, 772

Lewis, Gilbert N., 349

Lewis bases, 400

Lewis diagrams, 344–345

lianas, 609

Libby, W. F., 480

lichens, 95, 109, 614

life, 28–111

See also animals (Animalia);

Archaea; bacteria; evolution;

fungi; plants (Plantae); Protista

appearance during Precambrian

time, 484

biosphere, 630–631

carbon compounds, 360, 361

cells, 44–61

classification of plants and

animals, 90–97

extraterrestrial, 966–967

first life on Earth, 152–157

genetics, 62–89

interdependence of living

things, 590

largest-known living organism,

148

oldest forms, 46, 92

origins, 30–33

life cycle

animal, 186–187

plant, 143, 146–147

life expectancy, 258

life spans, animal, 188, 206–207

ligaments, 182, 227, 229

ligands, 400

light, 834–837

See also optics; photons; sunlight

behavior, 836–839

defined, 895

general theory of relativity, 353

human eye, 244, 245

insects attracted to, 211

inverse square law, 847, 866

lanthanide metals, 401

measuring, 846–847

Newton's theory, 26, 800, 910

particle theory, 800

photoelectric cells, 817

phototropism, 138

polarized, 844–845, 895

quantum theory, 834, 835

speed, 836, 852, 867

stellar brightness, 942–943

visible light and electromagnetic

spectrum, 834

wave theory, 753, 798, 800,

834–835

light amplification, 851

light-emitting diodes

(LEDs), 829

lighting, neon, 815

lightning

electricity, 22, 810

Oparin-Haldane hypothesis of

origin of life, 32, 33

plasmas, 355

static electricity, 812

thunderstorms, 548

light-years, 914, 940, 989

lignin, 118, 261

limestone

acid rain, 669

building materials, 530

chemical rocks, 469

folded mountains, 525

Mississippian period, 490

Paleogene period, 499

limonite, 528

linear accelerators, 856

lines of force, 819

line spectra, 316, 317, 848

linked genes, 69, 72

Linnaeus, Carolus, 22, 92, 93,

106, 165

lions, 219, 610, 641

lipases, 137, 420

lipids, 416

animal metabolism, 189

biological polymers, 414

defined, 307

plant digestion, 137

lipoproteins, 264

liquefaction, 354

liquid crystals, 348, 789

liquid-in-glass thermometers, 789

liquid-propellant rocket engines,

968, 970, 976

liquids, 352–353, 782

defined, 438

density, 776

electrical conductivity, 815

heat transfer, 792

molar volume, 375

molecules, 348, 350, 779, 782

phase changes, 353

physical properties, 779

solutions, 382

states of matter, 312

superfluids, 797

lithium

alphabetical guide to the

elements, 334

normal and ionized, 315

particle emission and half-life of

lithium 8, 404

periodic table of the elements,

322

seawater composition, 569

symbol and atomic number, 324

lithium hydride, 398

lithosphere, 506–521

defined, 584

Earth's layers, 445
plate movement, 450
lithospheric plates, 448, 584
littoral zone, 581
liver
  animal digestive systems, 190, 191
  cholesterol, 264
  cirrhosis, 298
  human digestive system, 236, 237, 256
liverworts, 110, 111
lizards, 179, 203, 221
lobe-fins, 156
Local Group of galaxies, 957, 989
loci (genetics), 75, 307
locomotion, animal, 184–185
locusts, 189
lodes, 528
lodestone. *See* magnetite (lodestone)
logging, 704
logic, 25
London forces, 346–347
long adductor of thumb, 255
long-day plants, 141
longitude, 505, 584, 585
longitudinal waves, 798, 799, 895
long-period comets, 934
long radial extensor of wrist, 255
Lorenz, Konrad, 212
losing weight, 283
loudness, 803
Love Canal, 694
low-density lipoprotein (LDL), 264
lower plants, 108–109
lower respiratory tract, 234
low pressure systems, 542
lumbar plexus, 252
lumbar vertebrae, 226, 251
lumens, 846
luminance, 846, 847
luminosity (stellar), 943, 944, 945, 963, 989
luminosity curve, 846
luminous emittance, 846
luminous units, 847
lunar calendar, 901

lunar eclipses, 924, 925, 989
lungfish, 156, 207, 209
lung(s)
  animal respiratory systems, 195
  cancer, 296
  human respiratory system, 234–235, 256
  surface area, 183
luster, 460, 462, 584
lutetium
  alphabetical guide to the elements, 335
  periodic table of the elements, 323
  symbol and atomic number, 324
Lycophyta (club mosses), 100, 107, 112
lycopods, 491
Lyell, Charles, 22, 166
lymph, 233, 307
lymphatic ducts, 233
lymphatic system, 233
lymph capillaries, 233
lymph nodes, 233, 307
lymphocytes, 302
lymphokines, 303
lymph vessels, 233
lysine, 419
lysosomes, 51, 181, 307

M

machines
  law of, 759
  mechanics, 772–773
MacNeish, Richard, 625
macrominerals, 268, 272
macronutrients, 712
macula lutea, 244, 245
Magellan (spacecraft), 921, 984
magma
  defined, 584
  hot spots, 454, 455
  igneous rocks, 466, 472
  metal ores, 528
  metamorphic rocks, 470, 471
  volcanoes, 452–453

magnesium
  alphabetical guide to the elements, 335
  Earth's crust, 447
  ferromagnesian minerals, 466
  macrominerals, 268, 272
  mineral nutrients, 607
  periodic table of the elements, 320, 322
  plant nutrients carried by water, 134
  seawater composition, 569
  superconductors, 832
  symbol and atomic number, 324
magnetic fields, 819
  defined, 895
  Earth's, 502–503
  and electric current, 818
  Jupiter, 929
  light, 835
  magnetic field reversal, 503
  magnetoreceptors, 205
  particle accelerators, 856, 857
  superconductors, 797, 833
magnetic north pole, 503
magnetic poles, 503, 584, 895
magnetic resonance imaging (MRI), 422, 424–425, 797, 833
magnetic sector mass spectrometers, 423
magnetic south pole, 503
magnetism, 818–823
  See also magnetic fields
  electromagnetism, 810, 811, 893
  how magnets work, 818–819
  magnetic resonance imaging (MRI), 422, 424–425, 797, 833
  magnetite, 463, 465
  physics, 754
  superconducting magnets, 797, 833
magnetite (lodestone)
  iron ores, 528, 529
  magnetism, 463 , 503, 811, 819
  nonsilicates, 465
magnetoreceptors, 205

Index

magnetosphere, 502, 584

magnets. *See* magnetism

magnitude (stellar), 942, 989

Maimon, Theodore, 753

Main Belt, 920, 933, 934, 935, 989

main group elements, 398

main sequence stars, 944, 945, 946, 966, 989

maize (corn), 624, 626, 628, 717

major histocompatibility complex (MHC), 303

malaria, 292

malleus (hammer), 246

Malpighi, Marcello, 105, 167

mammals (Mammalia)
  See also cats; cattle; dogs; elephants; primates (Primata); sheep; wolves
  advantages, 162
  Age of Mammals, 162–163
  Aristotle's classification of animals, 164
  chordates, 97, 178, 179
  circulatory system, 193
  common ancestor, 37
  Cretaceous period mass extinction, 159
  defined, 307
  eyes, 204
  hibernation, 203, 209
  life spans, 206
  mating, 218
  Paleogene and Neogene periods, 498–499
  Permian period ancestor, 492
  Quaternary period, 500
  reproduction, 186
  respiratory system, 194
  thermoregulation, 203
  Triassic period, 493
  warm-blooded animals, 203
  waste nitrogen, 201

mammoths
  extinction, 162
  fossils, 478
  Quaternary period, 500, 501

mandible, 251

mandrake plant, 103

manganese
  alphabetical guide to the elements, 335
  microminerals, 269, 273
  mineral nutrients, 607
  periodic table of the elements, 322
  plant nutrients carried by water, 134
  symbol and atomic number, 325

mangroves, 622

mantle (Earth), 443, 445, 450, 584

maple trees, 622

mapping the Earth, 504–505

maquis, 612

marble, 470, 471, 669

margin of error, 553

marijuana, 299

marine life
  See also fishes
  animal movement, 184
  animal respiratory system, 194
  aquatic environments, 614–615
  Cambrian period, 486
  deep-sea, 215, 581
  dumping waste in oceans, 691
  gills, 195
  ichthyosaurs, 158, 493
  Jurassic period, 495
  Mississippian epoch, 490
  ocean life, 580–581
  Ordovician period, 487
  organic rocks, 469
  Permian period mass extinction, 157, 492
  plesiosaurs, 158, 497
  Precambrian time, 485

Mariner (spacecraft), 920, 921, 926, 978, 980

marine west coast climate, 561

marine worms, 176

maritime polar air masses, 542

maritime tropical air masses, 542

Markarian's Chain of galaxies, 914

Mars, 926–927
  canals, 927, 966
  moons, 926

  properties, 918
  space exploration, 926–927, 979, 980, 981, 983, 985, 987

Mars Global Surveyor, 927, 974

Marsh, George Perkins, 656

Marsupialia, 179

mascons, 923

mass
  atomic mass units, 356, 357, 436
  conservation law, 312, 349, 362, 364, 438
  defined, 438
  $E=mc^2$, 27, 853, 866
  formula for weight relationship, 867
  gravitation, 766–767
  matter, 312
  metric measurement, 761
  molar, 356, 374–375, 438
  relative atomic mass, 372
  relative molecular mass, 373
  second law of motion, 762–763
  special theory of relativity, 853

masseter muscle, 254

mass-luminosity relation, 945

mass movement, 520–521, 584

mass number of an atom, 314, 438

mass spectrometry, 373, 422–423, 438

mastodons, 500, 501

mathematical physics, 755

mathematics, 22, 26

mating, 218
  See also reproduction
  courtship behavior, 217
  sexual imprinting, 212

matorral, 612

matter
  See also atoms; molecules; states of matter
  chemistry, 312–320
  dark matter, 964, 965, 988
  defined, 438
  molecules and, 348–349
  physical properties, 778–783

Matterhorn, 517

maturation, 143, 147

maxilla, 251

Maxwell, James Clerk, 23, 753, 811

Mayer, Julius Robert von, 785

M-discontinuity, 444, 445, 447, 584

meanders, 512, 584

measurement
    chemistry, 372–377
    earthquakes, 457
    light, 846–847
    mechanics, 760–761
    metric system (International System of Units), 374, 760

meat
    balanced diet, 266
    calories and fats, 276
    cholesterol, 265
    diet and cancer, 267
    fats, 263
    phosphorus, 268
    proteins, 260, 419
    USDA guidelines, 259

Meat Inspection Act (1906), 275

mechanical advantage, 770, 895

mechanical control of invasive species, 599

mechanical energy, 758–759
    changing heat into motion, 791
    forms of energy, 312
    mechanical equivalent of heat, 785

mechanical equivalent of heat, 785

mechanical weathering, 506, 507, 584

mechanics, 760–778
    defined, 895
    force, 764–765
    gravitation, 766–767
    laws of motion, 762–763
    machines, 772–773
    mechanical energy, 758
    momentum, 774–775
    torque, 768–769
    work, 770–771

mechanoreceptors, 205

medial cutaneous nerve, 252

medial moraines, 517, 584

medial plantar nerve, 252

median nerve, 252

medicine
    biomedical research, 617
    cryosurgery, 796
    enzymes, 421
    health, 258
    history of science, 22–23
    important health care providers, 291
    LASIK surgery, 850
    magnetic resonance imaging (MRI), 422, 424–425, 797, 833
    medical waste, 689, 694
    nuclear physics, 755
    plants, 102–103
    positron emission tomography (PET), 863
    radioactive waste, 697
    regular checkups, 290
    traditional Chinese, 102
    ultrasound, 809

Mediterranean Sea
    earthquake zone, 458
    middle latitude climate zone, 560, 561
    Paleogene and Neogene periods, 498, 499
    scrub forests, 612

medulla, 249

medulla oblongata, 250

megadose vitamins, 269

meiosis, 56–59
    defined, 307
    independent assortment law, 69
    sexual reproduction, 55, 198–199

meitnerium
    alphabetical guide to the elements, 335
    periodic table of the elements, 322
    symbol and atomic number, 325

melanin, 242

melanocytes, 182, 242

melting point, 379, 788

membrane (cell), 45, 47, 48, 52, 181

memory chips, 830

Mendel, Gregor, 22, 23, 63, 70–73, 167, 169

Mendeleev, Dmitri, 23, 24, 321, 349

mendelevium
    alphabetical guide to the elements, 335
    periodic table of the elements, 323
    symbol and atomic number, 324

Mendelian crosses, 74–77

menstrual cycle, 209

mental health, 286–289, 687

mental illness, 284, 288

mental nerve, 252

mercury (element)
    alphabetical guide to the elements, 335
    capillary action, 782
    density, 776
    periodic table of the elements, 323
    superconductors, 832
    symbol and atomic number, 324
    water pollution, 722

Mercury (planet), 920
    properties, 918
    space exploration, 920, 982, 987

Mercury space program, 972, 978

meridians of longitude, 505, 584

mesoderm, 172

mesons, 863, 895

mesopause, 534

mesophyll, 127, 307

mesosphere (atmosphere), 534–535

mesosphere (Earth's interior), 443, 445, 585

Mesozoic era, 493–497
    Age of Dinosaurs, 158–159, 495
    geologic time scale, 483
    gymnosperms, 101

messenger RNA (mRNA), 51, 66, 67

Index

Messenger (spacecraft), 987

Messenger space mission, 920

metabolic diseases, 293

metabolic rate, 189

metabolism
    animals, 188–189
    defined, 307
    heat sources, 787
    life span, 206
    thermoregulation, 203

metacarpus, 226, 251

metallic bonds, 351

metallic crystals, 350, 351

metalloids, 321

metal-oxide silicon field-effect transistor (MOSFET), 831

metals
    See also aluminum; iron; steel; *and others by name*
    conduction of heat, 794
    crystals, 350, 781
    defined, 437
    electrical conductivity, 814, 815
    group 1, 398
    inorganic compounds, 398
    main group elements, 398
    molar volume, 375
    ores, 528–529
    periodic table of the elements, 321
    recycling, 693
    waste, 689

metamorphic rocks, 470–471
    dating, 477
    defined, 585
    North America, 473
    rock cycle, 472

metamorphism, 470–471

metamorphosis, 187

metaphase (mitosis), 56, 59, 197

metastasizing cancers, 296

metatarsus, 226, 251

meteorites, 915
    atmosphere protects against, 535
    dating, 485
    defined, 989
    meteoroids, 935

Permian period mass extinction, 157, 492
    Triassic period sea level drop, 493

meteorology, 536
    See also weather
    computer models, 27, 553
    defined, 585
    predicting weather, 550–553

meteors, 535, 935, 989

meteroids, 935, 989

methamphetamine, 299

methane
    alkanes, 408, 409, 410
    combustion, 362
    defined, 748
    fuel, 412
    greenhouse effect, 670, 677
    landfills, 670, 690
    molecular compounds, 358
    recycling organic wastes, 692
    structure, 410

methanol, 358

methionine, 419

methyl chloroform, 679, 681

metric system (International System of Units), 374, 760–761, 775

Meyer, Julius Lothar, 349

micas, 464, 466

mice, 630

microchips (integrated circuits), 830

microfilaments (fibrils), 50

microminerals, 269, 273

micronutrients, 134, 712

microphones, 806–807

microprocessors, 830

microscopes
    See also electron microscopes
    anatomy, 167
    history of science, 22

microtubules, 50

microwave background radiation, 912, 962, 963, 964–965, 988

microwaves (Hertzian waves), 835

middle cutaneous nerve, 252

middle ear, 246

Middle East
    deserts, 611
    domestication of plants, 625
    tropical climates, 559

middle latitude climate zone, 560–561

mid-ocean ridges, 449, 451, 475, 525, 579, 585

midrib (leaves), 127

Miescher, Friedrich, 63

milk and milk products
    balanced diet, 266
    calcium, 268
    carbohydrates, 260
    cholesterol, 265
    fats, 263
    lipids, 416
    mammals, 162
    pH, 389
    proteins, 419
    USDA guidelines, 259

Milky Way galaxy, 952–955
    defined, 990
    diameter, 914, 952
    Local Group of galaxies, 957, 989
    stars with planets, 966
    static, 912

Miller-Urey experiments, 30, 33

millet, 624

Millikan, Robert, 811

minerals (dietary), 268–269
    human body, 272–273
    mineral nutrient cycle, 607

minerals (geology), 460–465
    defined, 585
    hardness of water, 730
    properties, 460–461

Miocene epoch, 483

Mir (space station), 973, 984, 985, 986

Miranda (satellite of Uranus), 931

mirrors, telescopic, 909

mirror self-recognition, 222

mission control, 969

Mississippian (Early Carboniferous) epoch, 483, 490

Mississippi River, 513

mitochondria, 51, 119, 181, 189, 307, 417

mitochondrial DNA, 79

mitosis, 48, 56–59, 196–197, 307

mixtures, 312, 313, 382, 438

MK luminosity classification, 944

mks units, 760

mobility in multicellular organisms, 153

models (scientific), 27

modules (spacecraft), 969

Mohl, Hugo von, 105

Mohorovicic, Andrija, 444

Mohs' hardness scale, 463

Mojave Desert, 623

molality, 383, 384, 385

molar heat capacity, 378

molarity, 383, 384, 385

molar mass, 356, 374–375, 438

molar volume, 375

molds (fungi), 148–151, 198

mole (chemical measure), 356, 374, 438

molecular compounds, 400

molecular crystals, 350, 351

molecular formulas, 358

molecular physics, 755

molecules, 346–349

  animal building blocks, 180

  atoms, 315

  covalent bonds, 344

  gases, 349, 350, 779, 783

  geometry, 346–347

  liquids, 348, 350, 779, 782

  and matter, 348–349

  relative molecular mass, 373

  solids, 348, 350, 778

  stored energy, 378

  temperature, 788

mole fraction, 383

mole ratio, 376

mollusks (Mollusca)

  See also bivalves; cephalopods

  Aristotle's classification of animals, 164

  head ganglion, 221

  kingdom Animalia, 97, 176

molybdenum

  alphabetical guide to the elements, 335

  microminerals, 269, 273

  mineral nutrients, 607

  periodic table of the elements, 322

  plant nutrients carried by water, 134

  symbol and atomic number, 325

momentum, 774–775, 867, 895

monkeys

  altruism, 218

  Costa Rican reforestation, 705

  dominance hierarchies, 216

  intelligence, 222

  physical contact, 215

  primates, 163

  space exploration timeline, 977

monochromatic light, 850

monocotyledons (monocots)

  angiosperms, 117

  classification of plants, 96

  defined, 307

Monoplacophora, 176

monosaccharide, 188

Monotremata, 179

monounsaturated fats, 263, 266

monsoon forests, 609

monsoons, 557, 585

montane coniferous forests, 613

months, solar and lunar, 901

moon, the, 922–923

  animal behavior affected, 208, 209

  Apollo 11 mission, 23, 923, 973, 980

  Apollo 12 mission, 980

  Apollo 16 mission, 972

  Apollo program, 973

  apparent magnitude, 942

  dating rocks, 485

  eclipses, 924, 925, 989

  far side, 923, 977

  lunar calendar, 901

  origin, 923

  rocks, 485, 915, 923, 981

  space exploration timeline, 977–987

  tides, 208, 575

moonquakes, 923

moose, 590, 591, 596, 597

moraines, 517, 585

Morgan, Thomas Hunt, 73

morphology

  animal, 180–187

  plant, 99, 105

Morse, Samuel F. B., 820

mortar, 530

mosasaurs, 158

moss animals (bryozoans), 487

mosses (Musci)

  Bryophyta, 111

  classification of plants, 96

  defined, 307

  early land plants, 100

  Silurian period, 155

  tundra, 614, 622

moths, 129

motion

  center of gravity, 769

  defined, 895

  dynamics, 758

  electromagnetic induction for generating, 822

  mechanics, 762–763

  momentum, 774–775

  Newton's laws, 753, 762–763

  planetary, 905, 918–919

  waves, 800–801

motor end plates, 230

motor neurons, 230

mountains

  See also Rocky Mountains

  Alps, 517, 525, 613

  Andes Mountains, 496

  Appalachians, 157, 491

  building, 524–527

  geographical barriers to plants, 620

  Himalayas, 444, 451, 501

  Hutton on formation, 474

  mid-ocean ridges, 525, 579

Index

plate tectonics, 449

Sierra Nevada range, 494, 496, 613

volcanoes, 452

mouth, 190, 236, 237

moving-coil microphones, 807

Mowat, Farley, 655

MRI (magnetic resonance imaging), 422, 424–425, 797, 833

mucous membranes, 248, 249

mucus, 235, 240

mudflows, 520, 521

Muller, Karl Alexander, 833

multicellular organisms, 60–61

appearance during Precambrian time, 485

cells, 44, 181

defined, 307

earliest traces, 154

eukaryotic cells, 47

first life, 153

multifactorial mutations, 68

multiple fruits, 130

multiple proportions, law of, 376

muons, 863

muscles

See also muscular system

cells, 44

eye, 245

tendons, 229

muscovite, 464, 466

muscular dystrophy, 77

muscular system

animal anatomy, 182

human anatomy, 225, 228–229, 254–255

organ systems, 61

musculocutaneous nerve, 252

mushrooms

fungi, 148–151

phylum Basidiomycota, 95

reproduction, 198

musk oxen, 218

mutations (genetic), 68

defined, 307

DNA replication, 65

evolution, 30, 37, 38, 169

mutualism in plants, 619

mycellium, 148

mycologists, 148, 307

Mycomycota, 95

mycoplasma, 45

mycorrhizal associations, 608

mycoses, 151

myocardial infarction. *See* heart attacks (myocardial infarction)

N

Nader, Ralph, 655

Nagasaki bomb, 407, 860

naiads, 187

nails (anatomy), 242

naming hurricanes, 547

naming hydrocarbons, 410–411

naming organisms, 91, 107

NASA (National Aeronautics and Space Administration), 977

nasal passages, 248

nastic movements, 140, 307

national parks, 654, 656, 704

native metals, 461, 529, 585

natural convection, 795

natural gas

commercial energy, 734

natural resources, 531

nonrenewable fuels, 735

Natural History (Pliny the Elder), 103

natural killer cells, 303

natural resources, 528–533

See also conservation of natural resources; fossil fuels; water supply

defined, 585, 748

fighting over limited, 637

natural selection, 39

basics, 168

defined, 307

evolutionary change, 30, 36, 37, 38, 169

nature reserves, 706–707

neap tides, 575, 585

nearsightedness, 842

nebular hypothesis, 917

nebulas

Crab Nebula, 949

defined, 990

galactic, 954

solar, 917

neck ligament, 251

nectar, 128, 129

negative feedback, 202

negative lenses, 842, 843

Nelson, Gaylord, 656

Nematoda. *See* roundworms (Nematoda)

nenes, 630

neodymium

alphabetical guide to the elements, 336

periodic table of the elements, 322

symbol and atomic number, 325

Neogene period, 483, 498–499

neon

alphabetical guide to the elements, 336

chemical bonds, 344

electrical conductivity, 815

melting and boiling points, 788

periodic table of the elements, 323

symbol and atomic number, 325

valence shell of atom, 319

neopentane, 410

nephrons, 241

Neptune, 932

discovery, 26, 932

properties, 919

space exploration, 932, 982

neptunium

alphabetical guide to the elements, 336

periodic table of the elements, 322

symbol and atomic number, 325

neritic zone, 580, 615

nerves

See also nervous system

cells, 44

neurons, 202, 221, 231, 307

nervous system

> *See also* central nervous system

> animal anatomy, 182

> human anatomy, 225, 230–231, 252

> organ systems, 61

> regulating animal body, 202

neurons

> defined, 307

> human brain, 221

> human nervous system, 230, 231

> regulating animal body, 202

neurosis, 288, 307

neurotransmitters, 202

neutralization reactions, 359

neutral solutions, 388

neutrinos, 862

> defined, 895, 990

> detecting, 939

> leptons, 863

> sun, 939

> supernovas, 948

> tau-neutrino, 753

neutrons

> baryons, 863

> charge, 314

> defined, 438, 895

> mass, 314, 854, 867

> mass number, 314

> neutron stars, 948

> nuclear chemistry, 404, 405

> particle accelerators, 859

> parts of atoms, 314–315, 854

> radioisotope production, 403

> static electricity, 812

> subatomic particles, 862

neutron stars, 946, 948–949, 950, 990

Newton, Sir Isaac

> gravitation, 26, 763, 767, 904–905

> history of science, 22

> laws of motion, 753, 762–763, 867, 971

> light, 26, 800, 910

> mathematics used by, 26

> momentum, 774–775

planetary orbits, 904

spectroscopy, 910

New Zealand

> deforestation, 703

> Gondwanaland, 448

> grasslands, 613

> population growth, 636

> world population density, 637

> world precipitation distribution, 732

NGC 3949 (galaxy), 952

niches (ecological), 619, 748

nickel

> alphabetical guide to the elements, 336

> Earth's interior, 446

> ferromagnetism, 821

> periodic table of the elements, 323

> symbol and atomic number, 325

nickel-cadmium batteries, 395

nimbostratus clouds, 540

niobium

> alphabetical guide to the elements, 336

> periodic table of the elements, 322

> superconductors, 832

> symbol and atomic number, 325

nitrates, 530

nitric acid

> acid rain, 667

> conjugate base, 387

> Lewis diagrams, 344–345

nitric oxide, 662

nitrogen

> air, 660

> alkaloids, 137

> alphabetical guide to the elements, 336

> amino acids, 418

> animal waste products, 201

> atmosphere, 534

> cycle in ecosystems, 607

> discovery, 354

> mineral nutrients, 607

> nuclear reactions, 406

particle emission and half-life of nitrogen 13, 404

> periodic table of the elements, 323

> plant nutrients carried by water, 134

> seawater composition, 569

> symbol and atomic number, 325

nitrogen dioxide, 664

nitrogen oxides, 651, 667

nitrosamines, 267

nitrous oxide

> defined, 748

> greenhouse effect, 670, 677

> ozone layer, 679

nobelium

> alphabetical guide to the elements, 336

> periodic table of the elements, 323

> symbol and atomic number, 325

noble gases

> alphabetical guide to the elements, 326

> chemical bonds, 344

> defined, 438

> inorganic compounds, 399

> periodic table of the elements, 320, 323

nociceptors, 247

Noise Control Act (1972), 656

noise pollution, 684–687

nonane, 410

noncontact species, 594

nondispersive waves, 799

nonfoliated rocks, 470

noninfectious disease, 293

nonmetals

> alphabetical guide to the elements, 326

> inorganic compounds, 399

> main group elements, 398

> periodic table of the elements, 321, 323

nonpoint sources of pollution, 721, 723, 748

nonpolar covalent bonds, 345

Index

nonpolar molecules, 347

nonrenewable resources, 735, 740, 748

nonsilicates, 465, 585

nonunion fractures, 227

nonvascular plants
bryophytes, 96, 110
classification of plants, 106
defined, 307

norepinephrine, 240

normal, the (optics), 837, 841

normal faults, 458, 524

North America
See also Rocky Mountains
biomes, 622–623
Cambrian period, 486
Canadian Shield, 473
coniferous forests, 613, 623
continental ice sheet, 562
Cretaceous period, 496
deciduous rain forest, 609
deforestation, 703
deserts, 611, 623
Devonian period, 489
earliest known humans, 501
fossils, 481
grasslands, 613, 622
Great Lakes, 514, 519, 567, 598
jet stream, 537
Jurassic period, 494
Laurasia, 448, 449
middle latitude climate zone, 560, 561
Mississippian epoch, 490
Ogallala Aquifer, 729
Ordovician period, 487
Paleogene and Neogene periods, 498
Pennsylvanian epoch, 491
Permian period, 492
Pleistocene epoch, 500
polar climate, 562
population growth, 636
Quaternary period, 500
rocks, 473
scrub forests, 612, 623
Silurian period, 488

southern forest, 622
temperate deciduous forest, 612, 622
Tornado Alley, 549, 587
Triassic period, 493
tropical climates, 559
tundra, 622
world population density, 637
world precipitation distribution, 732
Yellowstone National Park, 88, 454, 565, 654, 656

North Atlantic Drift, 556

North Pole, 503

nose, 234, 248

nostrils, 248

notochord, 178

novas
See also supernovas
defined, 990

n-p-n junction transistors, 830

n-type semiconductors, 827, 828

nuclear bombs, 407
See also atomic bombs
harmful radiation, 683
mass-to-energy conversion, 853
nuclear fusion, 404, 405
radioactive waste, 697

nuclear chemistry, 402–407

nuclear energy, 404–405
See also nuclear power; nuclear reactions
$E=mc^2$, 27, 404
heat sources, 787

nuclear fission, 404
chain reaction, 405
defined, 438, 895
Hiroshima and Nagasaki bombs, 407
nuclear physics, 860
nuclear power, 646
types of nuclear reaction, 406

nuclear fusion, 405
defined, 438, 895
nuclear physics, 861
nuclear power, 646
stars, 948

sun, 861, 939
types of nuclear reaction, 404, 406

nuclear magnetic resonance (NMR), 424

nuclear physics, 854–861
See also particle accelerators
nuclear reactions, 860–861
nuclear structure, 854–855
particle detectors, 859
types of physics, 755

nuclear power, 646, 736–737
Chernobyl disaster, 649, 736
decommissioned plants, 699
harmful radiation, 683
nuclear energy, 787
nuclear fission, 860
occupational hazards, 652
radioactive waste, 697
rockets, 970
Three Mile Island accident, 736
water pollution, 723

nuclear reactions, 404
See also nuclear fission; nuclear fusion
first controlled, 23, 736, 753, 862
nuclear physics, 860–861
types, 406

nuclear reactors
See also nuclear power
breeder reactors, 404, 406, 436
defined, 438
first, 862
nuclear fusion, 861
pressurized water, 737
radioactive waste, 697, 698
types of nuclear reactions, 406

nucleic acids
animal building blocks, 180
defined, 438
discovery, 63
polymers, 413, 414–415

nucleoid, 46

nucleolus, 49

nucleotides, 65, 307

nucleus (atomic)
See also neutrons; protons

atomic structure, 316–317

mass number, 314

neutron stars, 948

nuclear chemistry, 402–407

nuclear physics, 854–861

parts of atoms, 314

size, 854

strong force, 765, 854, 863, 864, 896

structure, 854–855

weak force, 765, 863, 864, 865, 964

nucleus (cell), 49

animals, 181

cell basics, 45

cloning, 79

defined, 307

eukaryotic cells, 46, 47

nuclear division, 54

plants, 119

prokaryotic cells, 46

nucleus (comets), 934

numbers pyramids, 604

nutrias, 599

nutrients

competition for, 618

content claims on food packaging, 275

defined, 748

ecosystem components, 600

healthy water systems, 720

listings on food packaging, 274

macronutrients, 712

micronutrients, 134, 712

nutrition, 258–279

See also nutrients

balanced diet, 266

defined, 258

diet and health, 266–273

information, 274–275

Nutrition Labeling and Education Act (1990), 274

nutrition panels on packages, 274

nuts

balanced diet, 266

fats, 263

fiber, 261

magnesium, 268

vegetarian diet, 266

nymphs, 187

O

oak trees, 116

Oberth, Hermann, 968, 969, 976

obesity, 282–283

diabetes, 297

hypertension, 295

objective lens, 909

observation, 24

obsidian, 462

occipital bone, 251

occipital muscle, 255

occipital nerve, 252

occluded fronts, 543

occupational diseases, 293

occupational hazards, 652–653, 748

oceanic zone, 580

oceanography, 568, 585

oceans, 569–581

See also Atlantic Ocean; Pacific Ocean; seafloor; sea level

basins, 475, 579

climate affected, 556

currents, 556, 572–574

cycle of life, 605

dumping waste, 691

Earth's crust, 443, 444, 445, 450

geographical barriers to plants, 620

life, 580–581, 614–615

mountains, 525

oil pollution, 724–725

one great sea, 568

Oparin-Haldane hypothesis of origin of life, 32

physical oceanography, 570–571

salts cause air pollution, 661

seawater composition, 568–569

temperature layers, 570

thermal energy, 739

tides, 574–575

water motion, 572–573

waves, 574, 576–577, 587, 739

octane, 358, 410

octet rule, 319, 344

odors, 248

Oersted, Hans Christian, 811, 820

offshore drilling, 724, 725, 735

Ogallala Aquifer, 729

Ohm, Georg, 817

ohms, 817

Ohm's law, 817, 867

oil (petroleum). *See* petroleum (oil)

oil-drop experiment, 811

oil pollution, 724–725

oils (edible)

See also fats

added in foods, 274

cholesterol, 265

oil spills, 421, 655, 724–725

Okeechobee, Lake, 701

Oken, Lorenz, 45

olfaction, 248

chemoreceptors, 204

sense receptors, 230

and taste, 249

olfactory bulb, 248

olfactory nerve receptors, 248

Oligocene epoch, 483

olivine, 466

ommatidia, 205

omnivores, 604

omohyoideus muscle, 254

one gene-one polypeptide hypothesis, 63

Onnes, Kamerlingh, 832

Oparin, Alexander I., 32

Oparin-Haldane hypothesis, 30, 32, 33

open circulatory systems, 192

open growth, 120

open universe, 963, 990

operant conditioning, 213

Opportunity rover, 925, 987

opposite arrangement of leaves, 126

optical axis, 841, 843

optical cavity, 851

optical pumping, 851

optical telescopes, 908, 990

Index

optic nerve, 244, 245
optics, 840–851
  See also lenses; light
  defined, 895
  geometrical, 840–841
  history of science, 22
  lasers, 753, 850–851
  spectra, 848–849
  types of physics, 754
orange stars, 944
orangutans, 641, 642
orbicularis oculi muscle, 254
orbicularis oris muscle, 254
orbitals, 318, 319
orbital velocity, 969, 971
orbits (electrons), 316
orbits (planetary), 904, 905, 918
orchids, 116
orders (biological), 91, 171
Ordovician period, 155,
    483, 487
ores
  defined, 585
  metal, 528–529
organelles, 50–51
  animal building blocks, 180
  eukaryotic cells, 47, 48
  nucleus, 49
  prokaryotic cells, 46, 48, 152
  types, 119
organic acids, 418, 438
organic chemistry, 408–421
  See also amino acids; enzymes;
    nucleic acids
  carbon, 360, 361, 408
  compounds form during
    Precambrian time, 484
  defined, 438
  fatty acids, 262–263, 417
  hydrocarbons, 408–411
  interstellar organics, 955
  lipids, 416
  reactions, 412–413
  Wöhler, 349, 408
organic farming, 712
organic rocks, 468, 469
organ of Corti, 246

organs
  See also organ systems
  animal, 182
  defined, 307
  endothelial tissues, 182
  human, 224, 256–257
  multicellular organisms, 60
  plant, 119, 122–131
organ systems
  See also circulatory system;
    digestive system; endocrine
    system; excretory system;
    integumentary system;
    muscular system; nervous
    system; reproductive system;
    respiratory system; skeletal
    system; urinary system
  development in bilateral animals,
    172
  multicellular organisms, 60, 61
***Origin of Species,** The* (Darwin), 23,
  169
ornithischians, 158, 495
Ornitholestes, 161
Ornithomimus, 161
orthoclase, 463
OSHA (Occupational Safety and
  Health Administration), 653
osmium
  alphabetical guide to the
    elements, 336
  periodic table of the
    elements, 322
  symbol and atomic
    number, 325
osmosis
  cell functions, 52
  defined, 307
  water transport in plants, 132–133
osteoblasts, 227
osteoclasts, 227
osteocytes, 227
osteopaths, 291
osteoporosis, 281, 293
ostracoderms, 487
ostriches, 218
Oswald, Avery, 63

other metals
  alphabetical guide to the
    elements, 326
  periodic table of the elements,
    323
outer core (Earth), 443, 445, 585
outer ear, 246
outwash plains, 516
ova. *See* egg cells (ova)
oval window (ear), 246
ovaries
  defined, 307
  human reproductive system, 238,
    239, 257
overgrazing, 708, 710
overhunting, 639
overpopulation, 594, 748
ovo-vegetarian diet, 266
ovules, 116, 128
ovum. *See* egg cells (ova)
oxidation
  catalytic converters, 369
  defined, 438, 585
  heat sources, 787
  hydrocarbons, 412
  rusting, 362
  weathering of rock, 508
oxidation numbers, 397
oxidation-reduction (redox)
    reactions, 359, 396–397, 438
oxides
  metal, 398
  metal ores, 529
  minerals, 465
oxidizers, 969, 990
oxidizing agents, 393, 396
oxyacids, 399
oxyanions, 360, 399
oxygen. *See also* ozone
  air, 660
  alphabetical guide to the
    elements, 337
  amino acids, 418
  animal respiratory systems,
    194–195
  atmosphere, 534
  blood flow, 232

Cambrian period atmosphere, 154
combustion, 362
discovery, 22, 349, 354
Earth's crust, 447
freshwater environments, 615
healthy and unhealthy water
systems, 720, 721
human respiratory system,
234–235
mineral nutrients, 607
oxyanions, 360
periodic table of the elements,
323
photosynthesis, 134, 602
plant nutrients carried by
water, 134
plants respire, 99, 105, 134, 702
seawater composition, 569
symbol and atomic number, 325
water, 345, 346, 362
ozone
See also ozone layer
defined, 748
ozone layer
Cambrian layer, 486
chlorofluorocarbons (CFCs),
412, 657
defined, 585, 748
ozone hole, 678–681, 748

P

Pacific Ocean, 636
El Niño, 573
Hawaiian Islands, 453, 455
"Ring of Fire" on rim, 453, 458
shrinkage, 451
temperature and density, 571
thermohaline circulation, 574
pahoehoe, 527, 585
pain, 247
pair-bonding, 218
paleobotany, 98, 99
Paleocene epoch, 483
Paleogene period, 483, 498–499
paleoseismology, 459
Paleozoic era, 155, 483, 486–492

Paley, William, 43
palisade tissue, 127, 135
palladium
alphabetical guide to the
elements, 337
periodic table of the elements,
323
symbol and atomic number, 325
palmaris longus muscle, 254
palmately veined leaves, 126
pampas, 613
pancreas
animal digestive systems,
190, 191
human digestive system, 236, 237
human endocrine system, 241
human organs illustration, 257
lipases, 137, 420
pandas, 631, 641
pandemics, 292, 307
Pangaea, 157, 448, 492, 493,
494, 496
panning for gold, 463
panspermia hypothesis, 30,
33, 308
Panthalassa, 494
panting, 203
paper
conduction of heat, 794
recycling, 676, 692, 705
waste, 689
water in making, 718
papillae (tongue), 249
parabolic mirrors, 841
parallax, 902–903, 914, 941, 990
parallel circuits, 823, 895
parallels of latitude, 585
parallel veined leaves, 126
paramecium, 91
parasites
defined, 748
flatworms, 174
fungi, 149, 151
organism interactions, 597
population growth limited by,
593, 597
roundworms, 175

**parasympathetic nervous
system,** 202
parathormone, 240
parathyroid glands, 240
parenchyma
defined, 308
leaves, 127
plants, 120
stems, 124
parietal bone, 251
parrots, 638, 641
parsecs, 914, 990
parthenogenesis, 186
partial eclipses, 924, 990
particle accelerators, 856–859
defined, 895
first, 753
Large Hadron Collider (LHC),
20, 858, 865, 964
new particles discovered, 863
superconducting magnets,
797, 833
types, 856
particle detectors, 859
particle physics
See also subatomic particles
types of physics, 755
particulates, 660, 662, 663, 748
pasta, 260, 266
Pasteur, Louis, 23, 93
Patagonia, 500
patella, 251
Pathfinder probe, 927, 985
path of totality, 924
pathogens, 292, 302
Pauli, Wolfgang, 862
Pauling, Linus, 63, 380
Pavlov, Ivan, 213
PCBs (polychlorinated biphenyls),
694, 695
peacocks, 217
peas, 70–71, 624
peat moss, 110, 111
pectin, 118, 261
pectineus muscle, 254
pectoralis major muscle, 254
pectoralis minor muscle, 254

pedalfer, 533

pediatricians, 291

pedigree charts, 77

pedocal soil, 533

peer review, 21

pelagic environment, 580

pellagra, 268

pelvis, 226

pelycosaurs, 492

penguins, 189, 218, 594, 680, 706

penicillin

    discovery, 23, 24, 151

    fungi, 150

    phylum Deuteromycota, 95

penis, 238, 257

Pennsylvanian (Late Carboniferous) epoch, 483, 491

Pentaceratops, 161

pentane, 410

pentene, 410

pentyne, 411

Penzias, Arno H., 965

pepsin, 236

peptide bonds, 418

peptide-MHC complexes, 303

percentage by weight, 383

percent daily values, 269, 274–275

perception

    See also senses

    animal, 204–205

perchloric acid, 387

perennial plants, 147

perfect flowers, 129

pericardium, 256

pericycle, 123

periodicities, biological, 208–209

periodic table of the elements, 320–323

    atomic number, 314, 320

    defined, 438

    Mendeleev, 23, 24, 321, 349

    structure, 320–321

period of a wave, 576

periosteum, 227

peripheral nervous system, 230

Perissodactyla, 179

Perkin, Sir William H., 349

permafrost, 614

permanent magnets, 821

permeability of cell membranes, 52

permeability of free space, 867

Permian period, 492

    geologic time scale, 483

    mass extinction, 157, 492, 493

    reptiles, 157

permittivity of free space, 867

peroneal artery and vein, 253

peroneus longus muscle, 254, 255

pesticides

    agriculture, 713–715

    chemical control of invasive species, 599

    DDT, 632, 643, 656, 713, 746

    defined, 748

    genotoxins, 648

    hazardous wastes, 694

    indoor pollution, 651

    water pollution, 720, 728

PET (polyethylene terephthalate), 693

PET (positron emission tomography), 863

petioles, 126

petrification, 478, 479, 585

Petrified Forest National Park, 478, 479

petrochemicals, 409, 412

petroleum (oil)

    Carboniferous period, 490

    commercial energy, 734

    natural resources, 531

    nonrenewable fuels, 735

    oil spills, 421, 655, 724–725

    sulfur dioxide from refining, 396

petrology, 466, 585

Phaeophyta. *See* brown algae (Phaeophyta)

phagocytes, 302, 303, 308

phagocytosis, 53

phalanges, 226, 251

Phanerozoic eon, 482, 483, 486–491

pharmacology, 102

pharynx, 191, 234, 308

phase changes, 350, 352, 379, 438, 793

phase diagrams, 353, 793

phelloderm, 124

phenetic systematics, 171, 308

phenotypes, 71, 308

phenylalanine, 419

pheromones, 200, 214, 308, 714

phloem, 121

    defined, 308

    leaves, 127

    photosynthesis, 135

    primary, 120

    roots, 123

    secondary, 124

    stems, 124

    vascular plants, 106

Phobos (satellite of Mars), 926

Phoenix Mars lander, 927, 987

phosphate, 65, 66, 530

phosphine, 399

phospholipids, 416

phosphorus

    alphabetical guide to the elements, 337

    bones, 268

    macrominerals, 268, 272

    mineral nutrients, 607

    nuclear reactions, 406

    periodic table of the elements, 323

    plant nutrients carried by water, 134

    polyatomic molecules, 315

    radioactivity, 403

    seawater composition, 569

    symbol and atomic number, 325

photochemical smog, 664–665

photoelectric cells, 817

photoelectric effect, 825

photons

    bosons, 865

    exchange particles, 864

    lasers, 851

    line spectra and atomic structure, 848

    quantum theory of light, 835

photoreceptors, 205
photosphere, 936–937, 990
photosynthesis, 134–135
    Archaea, 92
    carbon dioxide production during
        Precambrian time, 484
    chloroplasts, 50, 135, 741
    cyanobacteria, 93
    defined, 308
    energy flow in ecosystems, 602
    food chains and food webs, 604
    hydrogen from, 741
    leaves, 127
    plant physiology, 134
    producer organisms, 601
    reverse respiration, 136
    ultraviolet radiation's effects, 680
phototropism, 138, 308
photovoltaic cells, 647, 742, 748
phrenic nerve, 252
pH scale, 388–389, 666
phycoerythrin, 109
phylogeny, 90
phylum, 91, 171
physical change, 313, 438
physical contact, 215
physical geography, 502–581
    See also atmosphere; climate;
        crust (Earth's); hydrosphere;
        natural resources; weather
    defined, 585
physical geology, 442–473
    See also minerals (geology); plate
        tectonics; rocks
    defined, 585
    Earth's density, 446–447
    Earth's interior and layers,
        442–445
    plate tectonics, 448–459
physical oceanography, 570–571
physical properties of matter,
    313, 438
physics, 750–897
    See also electromagnetism;
        mechanics; nuclear physics;
        optics; particle physics;
        quantum theory; relativity

basic formulas, 866–867
classical, 754
energy, 756–759
fundamental constants, 867
glossary, 892–897
history of science, 22–23
milestones, 753
practice problems, 868–891
types, 754–755
unification theories, 864–865
what it is, 752–753
physiology
    animals, 188–207
    cells, 44
    fungi, 148–149
    organ systems, 60
    plants, 99, 105, 132–141
phytogeography, 99
phytopathology, 99
phytoplankton, 604, 605, 680
phytosaurs, 493
phytosociology, 99
piezoelectric crystals, 809, 895
pigs, 616
pi-mesons, 863
pineal body, 250
pine trees, 96, 115
pinnately veined leaves, 126
pinocytosis, 53, 308
Pinophyta. *See* conifers
    (Pinophyta)
pioneer communities, 620, 621
Pioneer (spacecraft), 923, 966, 981,
    982, 985
Pioneer Venus (spacecraft), 921
pions, 865
pistils, 128, 129, 308
pitch (sound), 803, 809
pith, 120
pitohui, hooded, 188
pituitary gland, 240, 241, 250
placenta, 239
placental mammals, 162
placoderms, 156
planarians, 199
Planck, Max, 23, 753, 835
Planck's constant, 835, 848, 867

planets
    See also gas giants; terrestrial
        planets
    dwarf planets, 933, 989, 990
    formation, 485
    gravitation and planetary
        movement, 767
    Kepler, 905
    motion, 918–919
    nebular hypothesis, 917
    orbits, 904, 905, 918
    origin of term, 900
    other stars, 966
    retrograde motion, 903, 918,
        919, 990
    rotation, 919
plankton
    defined, 308
    phytoplankton, 604, 605, 680
    zooplankton, 604, 605
Plantae. *See* plants
**plantar arterior and venous
    arch,** 253
Plante, Gaston, 394
plant ecology, 588
plant growth regulators, 629
plants (Plantae), 98–147
    See also angiosperms (flowering
        plants); gymnosperms
        (Gymnospermosida; naked
        seed plants); mosses
        (Musci); vascular plants
        (Tracheophyta)
    acid rain, 668
    anatomy, 118–131
    ancestors, 98
    ancient, 98–99
    appearance during Precambrian
        time, 485
    asexual reproduction, 55
    breeding, 627
    Cambrian period, 486
    cells, 44, 48, 50, 118–119
    classification, 106–117
    climate change, 675
    colonize dry land, 155
    competition among, 618–619

coniferous forests, 613
consumer organisms, 601
deserts, 611
Devonian period, 489
differences between animals and, 152
domestication, 624–625
early land plants, 100–101
ecological succession, 620
energy storage, 604
eukaryotic cells, 47
fats, 262, 263
first true plants, 99
genetic diversity, 716–717
genetic engineering, 628
geographical barriers, 620
grasslands, 613
growth, 142–147
habitat, 618–619
and humans, 102–105, 624–629
indoor pollution reduction, 651
kingdom Plantae, 96
Linnaean classification, 90
minerals, 268
modern classification, 91, 107
natural resources, 638
organs, 119, 122–131
oxygen production, 99, 105, 134, 702
photosynthesis, 134, 602
physiology, 132–141
producer organisms, 601
savanna, 610
scrub forests, 612
Silurian period, 155
smog's effects, 665
subkingdoms, 108
temperate deciduous forest, 612
tissues, 119, 120–121
tropical rain forest, 609, 618
tundra, 614
water cycle in ecosystems, 606
plaque (arterial), 265, 294
plasma (blood), 233, 308
plasma (state of matter), 355, 783, 895, 990

plasma physics, 755
plasmids, 80
plastics
ocean dumping, 691
polymers, 412, 413
recycling, 693
waste, 689
plastids, 50, 119
platelets (thrombocytes), 233
Plateosaurus, 160
plate tectonics, 448–459
See also continental drift
defined, 585
plate movement, 450–451
the plates, 449
when plates collide, 451
platinum
alphabetical guide to the elements, 337
periodic table of the elements, 323
symbol and atomic number, 325
Plato, 43, 90
Platyhelminthes. *See* flatworms (Platyhelminthes)
platypuses, 179, 188, 205
platysma muscle, 254
Pleiades, 943, 954
Pleistocene epoch
climate change, 162, 500
geologic time scale, 483
Quaternary period, 500
plesiosaurs, 158, 497
pleura, 234, 257
Pliny the Elder, 103
Pliocene epoch, 483
Pluto, 919, 933
plutoids (dwarf planets), 933, 989, 990
plutonium
alphabetical guide to the elements, 337
atomic weight, 317
half-life, 696
particle emission and half-life of plutonium 239, 404
periodic table of the elements, 322
symbol and atomic number, 325

Pneumocystis carinii **pneumonia,** 301
p-n junctions, 828, 829
p-n-p junction transistors, 830
poaching, 643
podzol, 533
point mutations, 68
point sources of pollution, 721, 723, 748
poison ivy, 243
poisons
enzymes destroyed, 421
fungi, 151
hooded pitohui, 188
polar bears, 630, 675
polar climate, 562
polar covalent bonds, 345, 347
polar easterlies, 536, 557
polar front, 542
polarized light, 844–845, 895
polar molecules (dipoles), 347
Polaroid, 844
polar troughs, 544
poles (Earth's)
climate, 554
continental polar air masses, 542
maritime polar air masses, 542
polar climate, 562
polar easterlies, 536
poles (magnets), 818–819
polio vaccine, 23, 291
pollen, 129, 651
pollen tubes, 129
pollination, 129, 308
pollution, 660–699
acid rain, 633, 666–669
air, 660–665
environmental disasters, 649
European Union pollution register, 657
health and the environment, 648–653
indoor, 650–651
land, 688–699
noise, 684–687
oil spills, 421, 655
ozone, 678

people and ecosystems, 632

radiation, 682–683

tall smokestacks as environmental boomerang, 633

water, 718–731

Pollux (star), 944

polonium

alphabetical guide to the elements, 337

periodic table of the elements, 323

symbol and atomic number, 325

polyatomic molecules, 315, 438

polychlorinated biphenyls (PCBs), 694, 695

polyethylene, 413

polyethylene terephthalate (PET), 693

polygenetic traits, 71, 77

polymerase chain reaction (PCR), 78

polymerization, 349, 438

polymers

biological, 413, 414–415

defined, 438

plastics, 412, 413

polypeptide chains, 66, 67, 418

polysaccharides, 188, 191

polyterpenes, 137

polyunsaturated fats, 263, 266

polyvinyl chloride (PVC), 413

pomes, 130

ponds, 631, 632

pond scum (spirogyra), 94, 109

Ponnamperuma, Cyril, 33

pons, 250

popliteal artery and vein, 253

Population I stars, 953, 963, 990

Population II stars, 953, 963, 990

Population III stars, 963, 990

population density, 594, 637

population genetics, 78

population inversion, 851

population(s), 592–595

controls, 594

defined, 748

human population explosion, 634–637

limitations on growth, 593

noise pollution, 684

plants, 619

regulating factors, 595

Porifera. *See* sponges (Porifera)

porphyritic rocks, 467

portal vein, 253

Portuguese man-of-war, 173, 186

positive lenses, 842, 843

positron emission tomography (PET), 863

positrons, 404, 753, 862

posterior cutaneous nerve, 252

posterior tibial artery and vein, 253

post-traumatic stress disorder (PTSD), 287

potassium

alphabetical guide to the elements, 338

Earth's crust, 447

fertilizers, 530

macrominerals, 268, 272

mineral nutrients, 607

particle emission and half-life of potassium 42, 404

periodic table of the elements, 322

plant nutrients carried by water, 134

seawater composition, 569

symbol and atomic number, 324

potatoes, 624

potato famine of 1840s, 716

potential energy, 312–313, 438, 756, 867, 895

poultry, 265, 266, 276

power (physics), 771, 866, 867

prairie, 613, 622, 708

prairie dogs, 218, 639

praseodymium

alphabetical guide to the elements, 338

periodic table of the elements, 322

symbol and atomic number, 325

praying mantises, 97

Precambrian time, 482, 483, 484–485

precipitation (meteorology), 540–541

See also rain

climate change, 672

defined, 585

ground water, 564

salinity of seawater, 569

trees soak up, 702

world distribution, 732

precipitation reactions, 359

predation

See also hunting

animal interaction, 597

defined, 748

invasive species, 598

populations limited by predators, 593

predicting weather, 550–553

pregnancy, human, 239

pressure, 777

altitude, 777

atmospheric, 355, 436, 555, 777

chemical equilibrium, 370, 371

Earth's interior, 447

gases, 355, 777, 783

kinetic theory of gases, 354

low pressure systems, 542

refrigeration, 791

regional metamorphism, 471

solubility, 383

touch, 247

pride of lions, 219

Priestly, Joseph, 22, 107, 349, 354

primary batteries, 394

primary care physicians, 291

primary colors, 849

primary roots, 122, 123, 146

primates (Primata)

See also apes; human beings; monkeys

animal movement, 184

biomedical research, 617

chordates, 179
emergence, 163
physical contact, 215
vision as primary sense, 205
prime focus, 909
prime meridian, 585
principal energy levels, 318
principal quantum number, 316
Principia Mathematica (Newton),
    904–905
prisms, 840, 895, 910
Proboscidea, 179
    See also elephants
procambium, 120
Procompsognathus, 160
producer organisms, 601, 603, 748
products of a chemical reaction,
    359, 363, 438
prograde motion, 918, 919
projecting colors, 849
prokaryotic cells, 46
    cell size, 44
    cell types, 46
    cell wall, 48
    defined, 308
    domains Archaea and Bacteria,
        46, 91
    first fossils of living organism, 152
    first life, 98
proline, 419
promethium
    alphabetical guide to the
        elements, 338
    periodic table of the elements,
        322
    symbol and atomic number, 325
propane, 358, 410, 412, 681
propene, 409, 410
proper volar digital, 252
prophase (mitosis), 56, 59, 197
propyne, 409, 411
prosimians, 163
prosthetic groups, 421
prostrate gland, 257
protactinium
    alphabetical guide to the
        elements, 338

periodic table of the elements, 322
    symbol and atomic number, 325
proteases, 137
proteins
    amino acids, 67, 260, 414,
        418–419
    animal building blocks, 180
    animal metabolism, 189
    calories, 263
    classification of animals, 171
    defined, 308
    enzymes, 260, 420
    fast foods, 285
    functions, 419
    genes in production of, 66–67
    human digestive system,
        236, 237
    lipoproteins, 264
    nutrition, 260
    photosynthesis, 135
    polymers, 413, 414
    shapes, 419
    USDA guidelines, 259
    vegetables, 260, 267
Proterozoic eon, 483
Protista, 94
    See also brown algae
        (Phaeophyta); green algae
        (Chlorophyta); protozoans;
        red algae (Rhodophyta)
    modern classification of plants
        and animals, 91
    plant ancestors, 98
protoderm, 120
proton-proton cycle, 947
protons
    baryons, 863
    Brønsted-Lowry theory, 387
    charge, 314
    defined, 438, 896
    mass, 314, 854, 867
    mass number, 314
    nuclear chemistry, 404
    parts of atoms, 314–315, 854
    static electricity, 812
    subatomic particles, 862
protoplanets, 917

protoplasm, 45, 180
protostars, 946, 947, 990
protozoans
    cells, 48–49
    kingdom Protista, 94
    reproduction, 48
Proxima Centauri, 914
pseudopods, 153
Psilophyta. *See* whisk ferns
    (Psilophyta)
psoas major muscle, 254
psychoanalysis, 23
psychology, 23
psychosis, 288, 308
Pteridopsida, 96
Pterophyta, 100, 107, 113
pterosaurs, 159, 165, 170, 495, 497
Pterygotus, 155
Ptolemy, 22, 902–903, 904
p-type semiconductors, 827, 828
pubis, 226, 251
publications (scientific), 21
puffballs, 198
pulleys, 759, 773
pulmonary artery, 232, 257
pulmonary vessels and
    bronchi, 257
pulsars, 949, 951, 990
pumas, 189
pumice, 468
punctuated equilibrium, 37
Punnett Square, 74, 77
pupal stage, 187
pupil (eye), 245
pure food laws, 275
pure substances, 312, 313, 439
purine bases, 65
PVC (polyvinyl chloride), 413
P-waves (primary waves), 442–443,
    456, 585
pyrimidine bases, 65
pyroclastic material, 452
Pyrolobus fumarii, 46
pyrometers, 789
pyroxines, 466
Pyrrophyta, 94
Pythagoras, 902

Q

quadriceps femoris muscle, 229, 254

quantum theory
Bohr's model of atom, 316, 318–319
defined, 439
light, 834, 835
Planck, 23, 753
types of physics, 755

quarks, 863
defined, 896
discovery of top, 753
fermions, 865
subatomic particles, 862

quarrying (glacial erosion), 516

quarrying (mineral extraction), 530

quartz
beaches, 509
color, 461
crystalline solids, 781
double refracting material, 844
igneous rocks, 466
Mohs' hardness scale, 463
piezoelectric crystals, 809
silicates, 464

quasars (quasi-stellar radio sources), 960–961, 990

Quaternary period, 483, 500–501

queen bees, 219

quillwort, 112

R

rabbits, 594, 631, 632

radar, 550–551, 585

radial artery and vein, 253

radial nerve, 252

radial symmetry, 172

radian, 896

radiation
See also electromagnetic radiation; radioactivity; ultraviolet (UV) radiation; X-rays
defined, 748, 896
harmful, 682–683
heat, 795
quasars, 960
Van Allen belts, 977

radiation thermometers (pyrometers), 789

radicle, 146

radio
See also radio waves
crystal rectifiers, 828

radioactivity, 402–403
air pollution, 661
Chernobyl disaster, 649
chromosome damage, 648
defined, 439
discovery, 23, 403, 753
Earth's temperature, 446
half-life, 403, 437, 476, 583, 696, 747
harmful radiation, 682, 683
hazardous waste, 696–699
nuclear physics, 755
nuclear power, 737
nuclear reactions, 406
occupational hazards, 652
particle detectors, 859
rock dating, 476–477
weak force, 864

radio astronomy, 912–913

radiocarbon dating, 403, 476, 480

radio galaxies, 960, 990

radio interferometers, 913, 990

radioisotopes, 402, 403, 404, 406

Radiolaria, 49

radiometric units, 847

radio waves
electromagnetic spectrum, 835, 912
Milky Way galaxy, 953
pulsars, 949
radio galaxies, 960, 990
transverse waves, 798

radium
alphabetical guide to the elements, 338
isolation, 753
periodic table of the elements, 322
scattering experiments, 856
symbol and atomic number, 325

radius (bone), 226, 251

radius vector, 905

radon
alphabetical guide to the elements, 338
chemical bonds, 344
indoor pollution, 650, 651
noble gases, 399
periodic table of the elements, 323
symbol and atomic number, 325

rain, 541
acid rain, 633, 666–669
coniferous forests, 613
deserts, 611
grasslands, 613, 622
hurricanes, 546
monsoons, 557
savanna, 610
temperate deciduous forest, 612
tropical rain forest, 608
tundra, 614
water cycle in ecosystems, 606

rain forest
deciduous, 609, 702
tropical, 559, 608–609, 618, 657, 702

Rankine temperature scale, 788

rare earth elements, 322

rats, 221

reactants, 359, 363, 439

reaction rates (chemistry), 368–369

reactors, nuclear. *See* nuclear reactors

recapitulation, 308

recessive genes, 71, 75, 143, 308

rechargeable batteries, 394, 395

recombinant DNA, 80, 308

recombination (genetic), 38, 69

recording sound, 806–807

rectification, 816

rectifiers, 816, 828

Index

rectum, 190, 237, 257

rectus abdominus muscle, 254

rectus femoris muscle, 254

recycling, 658, 676, 689, 692–693, 705, 748

red algae (Rhodophyta), 109
    classification of plants, 107
    kingdom Protista, 94
    Thallophyta, 108
    tissues, 120

red blood cells (erythrocytes), 167, 233

redox reactions, 359, 396–397, 438

red shift, 910–911, 959, 962, 990

red stars, 944, 947

red tides, 94

reducer organisms, 601, 603, 748

reducing agents, 393, 396, 398

reduction (chemistry), 393, 439

reduction potentials, 393

redwood trees, 115, 623

reefs (coral), 173, 615, 706

reflecting telescopes, 908, 909

reflection nebulas, 954

reflection of light, 836
    defined, 896
    geometrical optics, 840–841
    law of reflection, 841

reflectors of radiant energy, 795

reflexes, 211, 308

reforestation, 676, 705

refracting telescopes, 908, 909

refraction
    defined, 896
    double refracting material, 844
    human eye, 245
    lenses, 843
    light, 836–837
    waves, 800

refrigeration, 791

regeneration (biological), 55, 173, 178, 198

regional metamorphism, 471

regoliths, 585

regulating animal body, 202–203

reindeer, 616

Reines, Frederic, 862

relative atomic mass, 372

relative humidity, 538, 585

relative molecular mass, 373

Relativistic Heavy Ion Collider (RHIC), 858

relativity, 852–853
    black holes predicted, 767, 950
    defined, 896
    general theory, 753, 767, 853, 895, 925
    motion, 762
    special theory, 23, 852–853, 895

relaxation techniques, 287

relief (geography), 586

remoras, 596

rems (radiation), 683

renal arteries and veins, 253

renal pelvis, 241

renewable resources, 735, 741, 748

rennin, 236

replication, DNA, 65

representative elements, 321

reproduction
    See also asexual reproduction; reproductive system; sexual reproduction
    alternation of generations, 111, 112
    animal life cycles, 186
    animals, 196–199
    annual rhythms, 209
    cells, 44
    dominance hierarchies, 595
    flowering plants, 129
    fungi, 149

reproductive isolating factors, 30, 37

reproductive organs
    See also reproductive system
    flowers, 128
    plants, 122

reproductive system
    See also gonads
    animal anatomy, 182, 196–197
    female human, 237
    human anatomy, 225, 238–239

    male human, 239
    organ systems, 61

reptiles (Reptilia)
    See also dinosaurs; snakes
    Age of Reptiles, 158–159
    Aristotle's classification of animals, 164
    chordates, 97, 178, 179
    circulatory system, 192
    cold-blooded animals, 203
    Cretaceous period, 497
    dormancy, 209
    Jurassic period, 495
    life span, 207
    Pennsylvanian epoch, 491
    Permian period, 157
    reproduction, 186
    respiratory system, 194
    Triassic period, 493
    waste nitrogen, 201

reservoir rocks, 531

reservoirs, 729

resinous shrubs, 611

resistance
    electrical current, 814, 896
    law of machines, 759
    work, 770

resistance distance, 759

resonance, 804–805, 896

respiration
    See also respiratory system
    amount of air breathed per day, 661
    cellular, 189, 194
    defined, 308
    enzyme catalyst, 369
    human respiratory system, 234–235
    nose, 248
    plant physiology, 134, 136

respiratory system
    See also lungs
    amphibians, 157
    animal anatomy, 182, 194–195
    dust diseases, 653
    human anatomy, 225, 234–235
    organ systems, 61

restoration ecology, 705
resurrection plant, 112
retina, 244, 245
retrograde motion, 903, 918,
    919, 990
retrograde rotation, 911, 990
reverberation time, 808
reverse-biased p-n junctions, 829
reverse faults, 458
rhenium
    alphabetical guide to the
        elements, 338
    periodic table of the elements,
        322
    symbol and atomic number, 325
rhinoceros, 641, 642
rhizoids, 110
rhizomes, 125
rhodium
    alphabetical guide to the
        elements, 339
    periodic table of the elements,
        322
    symbol and atomic number, 325
rhodonite, 461
Rhodophyta. *See* red algae
    (Rhodophyta)
rhomboideus major muscle, 255
Rhyniophyta, 100
rhyolite, 452, 467
rhythms (biological), 208–209
ribonucleic acid. *See* RNA
    (ribonucleic acid)
ribose, 66
ribosomes, 46, 51, 67, 181, 308
ribs (anatomy), 226, 251
rice
    balanced diet, 266
    carbohydrates, 260
    domestication, 624
    high-yield varieties, 628
    methane from cultivation, 670
    paddies, 626
Richter scale, 457, 586
rickets, 268
Ride, Sally, 983
rift valleys, 493, 586

Rigel (star), 942, 944
right ascension of a star, 906, 990
"Ring of Fire," 453, 458
rivers, 566
    acid rain, 668
    deltas, 582
    erosion of rock, 510–513
    fertilizer runoff, 712
    healthy and unhealthy systems,
        720
    Mississippi River, 513
    salinity of seawater, 569
    wetlands absorb runoff, 700
RNA (ribonucleic acid)
    animal building blocks, 180
    defined, 308
    enzymes, 420
    parts, 66
    polymers, 414, 415
roadbeds, 530–531
rockets, 968–971
    defined, 991
    Saturn 5, 971, 980
    space exploration timeline,
        976–987
    V-2, 969, 976
rock falls, 520, 521
rocks, 466–473
    See also igneous rocks;
        metamorphic rocks;
        sedimentary rocks
    crystals, 350, 781
    dating, 476–477
    defined, 586
    minerals, 464–465
    moon, 915, 923, 981
    North American, 473
    oldest, 962
    Precambrian, 484, 485
    rock cycle, 472
    salinity of seawater, 569
    types, 466
    weathering, 506–509
rock salt, 530
rock slides, 520, 521
Rocky Mountains
    coniferous forests, 613, 623

    Cretaceous period, 482, 496, 497
    Pennsylvanian epoch, 491
    rocks, 473
Rodentia, 179
rodenticides, 713
rods (eye), 244
Roentgen, Wilhelm Conrad,
    227, 753
roetgenium
    alphabetical guide to the
        elements, 339
    periodic table of the elements,
        323
    symbol and atomic number, 325
room acoustics, 808
Roosevelt, Theodore, 655, 656
root caps, 123
root hairs, 123
roots (plants), 122–123
    defined, 309
    geotropism, 139
    water transport, 132
    weathering of rock, 507
root wedging, 532, 586
rotation
    Earth, 502, 572
    planets, 919
    sun, 936
rotifers, 172, 174, 186
rounded polarization, 845
roundworms (Nematoda)
    bilateral symmetry, 172
    circulatory system, 192
    kingdom Animalia, 97, 175
Royal Botanic Gardens (Kew,
    England), 105
rubber, 693, 813
rubidium
    alphabetical guide to the
        elements, 339
    periodic table of the elements,
        322
    seawater composition, 569
    symbol and atomic number, 325
rubies, 462
rumen, 191
Rumford, Benjamin, 785

Index

ruminants, 191, 671
runners (plants), 125
running buffalo clover, 641
rust, 360, 787
ruthenium
    alphabetical guide to the
      elements, 339
    periodic table of the elements,
      322
    symbol and atomic number, 325
Rutherford, Daniel, 354
Rutherford, Ernest, 23, 316, 317,
    403, 753, 855, 856
rutherfordium
    alphabetical guide to the
      elements, 339
    periodic table of the elements,
      322
    symbol and atomic number, 325
Rydberg, Johannes, 848

S

S0 galaxies, 956
saber-tooth cats, 162, 500, 501
saccule, 246
sacral plexus, 252
sacrum, 226, 251
Safe Drinking Water Act (1974),
    656
sagebrush, 623
Sahara Desert, 559, 611
St. Helens, Mount, 520, 526
Salam, Abdus, 865
salinity
    climate change and increased
      ocean, 674
    defined, 586
    salinization from irrigation, 711
    seawater, 568, 569
salinization, 711
salivary glands, 236, 237, 240
Salk, Jonas, 23
salmon, 722
salt (sodium chloride)
    crystals, 350, 351, 781
    empirical formula, 358

"empty" calories, 260
    formula weight, 373
    general dietary guidelines, 266
    halite, 461, 463, 465, 469
    heat and entropy in dissolving,
      381
    hypertension, 295
    ionic compounds, 345, 373
    melting and boiling points, 788
saltation, 511
salt bridges in galvanic cells, 392
saltiness, 249
salt lakes, 566
salts (chemical compounds)
    See also salinity
    air pollution, 661
    defined, 439
    formation, 387
    homeostasis, 200–201
    neutralization reactions, 359
    salinity of seawater, 568, 569
    salt bridges in galvanic cells, 392
    weathering of rock, 507
saltwater environments, 614
Salyut Space Station, 973, 981,
    982, 983
samarium
    alphabetical guide to the
      elements, 339
    periodic table of the elements, 322
    symbol and atomic number, 325
San Andreas fault (California),
    450, 458
sand, 509, 518
sand dollars, 178
sand dunes, 519, 586
sandstone, 468, 494
Sanio, Karl Gustav, 105
saphenous nerve, 252
sapphires, 462
saprophytes, 149
Sarcodina, 49
sartorius muscle, 228, 254
satellites (artificial)
    agricultural monitoring, 629
    basic terms of space exploration,
      969

Soviet union launches first,
    23, 977
    space exploration timeline,
      977–987
    weather prediction, 552
saturated fats, 263, 266, 267
saturated fatty acids, 263, 417
saturated hydrocarbons, 408
saturated solutions, 383
saturated zone, 564, 565
Saturn, 930–931
    moons, 931
    properties, 919
    rings, 930
    rotation, 919
    space exploration, 930, 982,
      983, 985
Saturn 5 rocket, 971, 980
saurischians, 158, 495
savanna, 610
    climate zones, 559
    defined, 748
    eastern African, 590
    grazing herds, 600
scala naturae, 164
scandium
    alphabetical guide to the
      elements, 339
    periodic table of the
      elements, 322
    symbol and atomic number, 325
**scanning transmission electron
    microscopes,** 824, 825
scanning tunneling microscopes,
    349
scaphopods (tooth shells), 176
scapula (shoulder blade), 226, 251
scattering experiments, 855
scattering of light, 839
Scelidosaurus, 160
Scheele, Carl, 22, 349, 354
Schiaparelli, Giovanni, 927
schist, 470, 471
Schizophyta, 93
Schleiden, Matthias Jakob,
    45, 167
Schrieffer, Robert, 832

Schrödinger, Erwin, 318
Schrödinger equation, 318
Schwann, Theodor, 22, 47, 167
sciatic nerve, 252
science
See also biology; chemistry; Earth
science; ecology; physics;
space science
history, 22–23
limits, 21
methods, 24–27
nature, 20–27
scientific creationism, 31, 40, 41
scintillation counters, 859
sclera, 244, 245
sclerenchyma, 121
sclerids, 121
scorpions, 176
screws, 773
screwworm flies, 714
scrotum, 238, 257
scrub forests, 612, 623
scurvy, 268, 270
sea anemones
digestive system, 190
habituation, 212
phylum Cnidaria, 173
radial symmetry, 172
seaborgium
alphabetical guide to the
elements, 340
periodic table of the
elements, 322
symbol and atomic
number, 325
sea cucumbers, 178
seafloor, 578–579
See also seafloor spreading
ocean's cycle of life, 605
seafloor spreading, 450
defined, 586
Earth's future, 501
evidence, 449, 451
plate tectonics, 448
sea level
changes, 474–475
climate change, 673

Paleogene and Neogene
periods, 498
Pleistocene epoch, 500
Triassic period, 493
seamounts, 579
sea pens, 485
seas. See also oceans
salty, 568–569
sea scorpions, 488
sea stars, 55
sea turtles, 572, 641
sea urchins, 178
seawage, 723
seawater composition, 568–569
seaweed, 94
sebaceous glands, 182
secondary batteries, 394
secondary roots, 122, 123
second-class levers, 772
second law of motion, 762–763,
775, 867
second law of thermodynamics,
381, 790
sediment
See also sedimentary rocks
abyssal plains, 579
defined, 586
soil erosion, 709
stream erosion, 510–513
wind erosion, 518
sedimentary rocks, 468–469
dating, 477
defined, 586
folded mountains, 525
fossils, 478, 482
geologic time scale, 482
law of superposition, 481, 482
North America, 473
oil and natural gas, 531
rock cycle, 472
seed-bearing plants
angiosperms, 96
early land plants, 101
gymnosperms, 96
seed coat, 131
seeding clouds, 551
seedlings, 143, 146

seeds
See also nuts
ancient plants, 625
angiosperms, 96, 116, 117
carbohydrates, 260
defined, 309
dormancy, 131
fats, 262
fruits, 130, 131
genetic diversity, 716
gymnosperms, 96
parts, 131
segmented worms (Annelida)
earthworms, 176, 191, 192, 607
kingdom Animalia, 97, 176
reproduction, 186
segregation, law of, 72
seismic waves
defined, 586
earthquakes, 456
study of Earth's interior, 442–443
seismographs, 442, 457, 586
seismometers, 457, 586
seismosaurus, 494
selenium
alphabetical guide to the
elements, 340
microminerals, 269, 273
periodic table of the elements,
323
symbol and atomic number, 325
self-esteem, 289
self-pollination, 129
Selye, Hans, 286
semen, 238
semicircular canals (ear), 246
semiconductors, 826–831
crystals, 351
defined, 896
devices, 828–829
semimembranosus muscle, 255
semimetals, 398
seminal vesicles, 257
semispinalis capitis muscle, 255
semitendinosus muscle, 255
senescence (aging)
diabetes, 297

diseases associated with, 293
hypertension, 295
plant growth promoters, 145
plant life cycle, 147
sense organs
five main organs, 207, 244
front of organism, 220
human anatomy, 225, 244–249
senses
See also hearing; olfaction; sense
organs; taste; touch; vision
(sight)
animal, 204–205
human, 225
sense receptors, 230, 244
sensory neurons, 211, 230
sepals, 128
Sepik River, 609
septic tanks, 730
septum (heart), 232
septum (nose), 248
series circuits, 823, 896
serine, 419
serpentine, 470
serratus anterior muscle, 254
serving sizes, 274
SETI (search for extraterrestrial
intelligence), 967
sewage treatment, 670, 731
sex cells. *See* gametes (sex cells)
sex-linked traits, 77
sexually transmitted diseases,
300–301
sexual reproduction
See also meiosis
animals, 186
cell division, 54
defined, 309
reproduction, 198–199
sexual imprinting, 212
Seyfarth, Robert, 222
Seyfert galaxies, 961
shale, 468, 494
sharks, 156, 179, 205, 221, 596
sheep
breeding, 617
cloning, 63, 79

domestication, 616
life span, 206
methane production, 671
shellfish
calories and fats, 276
cholesterol, 265
Cretaceous period, 497
organic rocks, 469
Shenzhou 5 (spacecraft), 987
Shepard, Alan B., Jr., 972, 978, 981
shield volcanoes, 527
shivering, 203
Shockley, William, 753, 830
shock waves, 456
short-day plants, 141
short extensor of thumb, 255
short-period comets, 934
short radial extensor of wrist,
255
shoulder blade (scapula), 226, 251
shoulder girdle, 226
shoulder muscles, 228
shrews, 183, 189
sickle cell anemia, 69, 293
Sierra Nevada range, 494, 496, 613
sieve tubes, 123
sight. *See* vision (sight)
signals (electric), 824, 893
silica (silicon dioxide)
See also quartz
magma, 452
seawater composition, 569
silicates, 464, 466, 586
silicon
alphabetical guide to the
elements, 340
Earth's crust, 447
periodic table of the elements,
323
semiconductors, 351, 826
symbol and atomic number, 325
silicosis, 653
silk moths, 616
Silurian period, 155, 483, 488
silver
alphabetical guide to the
elements, 340

electrical conductivity, 815
electroplating, 391
melting and boiling points, 788
ores, 529
particle emission and half-life of
silver 106, 404
periodic table of the elements, 323
symbol and atomic number, 324
simple carbohydrates, 260
simple fruits, 130
simple harmonic waves, 799
simple lipids, 416
simple machines, 772–773
simple tissues, 60
simulation (scientific), 27
Sinclair, Upton, 275
single chemical bonds, 345
single replacement reactions, 359
**single-stranded binding
proteins,** 65
singularities, 950, 991
Sirenia, 179
Sirius (Dog Star), 942, 947
skateboarding for exercise, 281
skeletal system
animal anatomy, 182
echinoderms, 178
evolution of internal skeleton, 156
human anatomy, 225, 226–227,
251
organ systems, 61
percentage of animal mass, 183
skeletal muscles, 228
skin
epithelial tissues, 182
human integumentary system,
182, 225, 242–243
human sense organs, 247
respiration by diffusion through,
194
sense receptors, 230
Skinner, B. F., 213
skull
eye socket, 244
Homo habilis and *Homo erectus,* 163
human, 251
sky, blueness of, 534

Skylab, 982

slate, 470, 471, 530

sleep
>health, 258
>respiration, 235
>stress and, 286, 287

sleptons, 865

slip face, 586

Slipher, Vesto Melvin, 959

Smalley, Richard E., 349

small intestines, 190, 236, 237, 256

Small Magellanic Cloud, 957

smallpox, 181

small saphenous vein, 253

smell, sense of. *See* olfaction

smelting, 529

smog, 649, 664–665

smokestacks, 633

smoking
>cancer, 296
>hypertension, 295
>indoor pollution, 650, 651

smooth muscles, 229

snakeroot, 641

snakes
>Aristotle's classification of
>>animals, 164
>eyes, 204
>fighting, 216
>infrared vision, 204
>life span, 207
>movement, 184
>paradise tree snake, 192
>respiratory system, 194

snapdragons, 117

Snell's law, 837

snowflakes, 781, 793

snow leopards, 641, 642

social behavior, animal, 214–219

social distance, 594

social support, 287, 288

societies, animal, 219, 594

socket (eye), 244

sodium
>*See also* salt (sodium chloride)
>alphabetical guide to the
>>elements, 340

Earth's crust, 447

fast foods, 285

hypertension, 295

macrominerals, 268

main group elements, 398

melting and boiling points, 788

nuclear reactions, 406

oxides, 398

periodic table of the elements,
>322

physiological function, 268

seawater composition, 569

symbol and atomic number, 325

valence shell of atom, 319

sodium chloride. *See* salt (sodium
>chloride)

soil, 532–533
>acid rain, 668
>agriculture, 708–714
>defined, 586
>erosion, 532, 709–711
>forests, 702
>mineral nutrients, 607
>mosses in building, 100
>roots protect, 123
>temperate deciduous forest, 612
>tropical rain forest, 608
>tundra, 614
>water cycle in ecosystems, 606

soil creep, 521, 586

soil profile, 532

Sojourner rover, 927, 985

**Solar and Hemispheric
>Observatory** (SOHO), 985

solar calendar, 901

solar cell conversion, 742, 748

solar cells, 828

solar eclipses, 924, 925, 991

solar energy, 647, 742–743
>classification of energy, 312
>renewable fuels, 735
>slowing climate change, 676
>solar cells, 828
>space stations, 974

solar flares, 939, 983, 991

solar maximum, 938

Solar Maximum Mission, 983

solar minimum, 938

solar nebula, 917

solar system, 916–935
>*See also* moon, the; planets;
>>sun, the
>defined, 991
>diagram, 917
>origins, 916–917
>other objects, 934–935

solar thermal conversion,
>742, 749

solar wind, 502, 915, 938, 977, 991

solenoids, 820, 823, 896

soleus muscle, 255

solid-propellant rocket engines,
>970

solids, 350–351, 780–781
>defined, 439
>density, 776
>heat transfer, 792
>molar volume, 375
>molecules, 348, 350, 778
>phase changes, 353
>physical properties, 778
>solutions, 382
>states of matter, 312
>types, 350, 778, 780

solid-state devices
>electronics, 825
>transistors, 753, 830–831

solid-state physics, 755

Solid Waste Disposal Act (1965),
>656

solifluction, 521, 586

solitary waves, 799

solubility, 382, 383

solutes, 382, 439

solutions (chemical), 382–385
>defined, 439
>pH, 388
>stream erosion, 510
>weathering of rock, 508

solvents, 382, 439

somatic cell nuclear transfer
>(SCNT), 79

somatic cells, 64

somatic mutations, 68

Index

sonar, 804
sonic booms, 804
Sonoran Desert, 611
sound, 802–809
    acoustics, 754, 806–809
    animal communication, 215
    decibel scale, 685, 686, 803
    diffraction, 801
    electromagnetic induction, 822
    human ear, 246
    noise pollution, 684–687
    properties, 804–805
    speed, 804
    waves, 799, 802–803
sound barrier, 804
sound recording and reproduction, 806–807
sourness, 249
South America
    Cretaceous period, 496
    deforestation, 703
    deserts, 611
    Devonian period, 489
    Gondwanaland, 448, 449
    grasslands, 613
    Jurassic period, 494
    middle latitude climate zone, 561
    Ordovician period, 487
    population growth, 636
    savanna, 610
    scrub forests, 612
    temperate deciduous forest, 612
    tropical climates, 559
    tropical rain forest, 608, 657
    world population density, 637
    world precipitation distribution, 732
Southern blotting, 81
Southern Ocean, 571, 574
South Pole, 503
Soyuz space program, 972, 980, 982, 983
space exploration, 968–987
    See also satellites (artificial); space shuttles; space stations
    basic terms, 969
    humans in space, 972–975

    international space programs, 975
    Jupiter, 929, 981, 982, 984, 985, 986
    Mars, 926–927, 979, 980, 981, 983, 985, 987
    Mercury, 920, 982, 987
    moon, 923, 973, 977–987
    Neptune, 932, 982
    rockets, 968–971
    Saturn, 930, 982, 983, 985
    timeline, 976–987
    Uranus, 931, 982, 984
    Venus, 921, 978, 980, 981, 982, 984, 985
space probes, 969
space race, 972–973
space science, 898–991
    See also astronomy; space exploration
space shuttles, 974
    basic terms of space exploration, 969
    Challenger, 974, 983, 984
    Columbia, 23, 974, 983
    Discovery, 983
    first flight, 23
    physics principles, 752
    tragedies, 974
space stations
    basic terms of space exploration, 969
    International Space Station, 974, 985, 986
    Mir, 973, 984, 985, 986
    Salyut, 973, 981, 982, 983
    Skylab, 982
space-time, 767, 853
space walks, 972, 973, 979, 983
spawning, 186
speaker cones, 807
special theory of relativity, 23, 852–853, 895
speciation, 30, 36, 37, 309
species
    See also endangered species
    anagenesis and cladogenesis, 36
    Aristotle originates term, 164

    classification of plants and animals, 90, 91, 171
    defined, 309
    distribution, 37
    evolution of new, 30, 37
    invasive, 598–599
    mutations change, 38
    scientific names, 91, 107
    total number known, 164
specific gravity
    defined, 586
    minerals, 460, 463
specific heat
    capacity, 378
    defined, 586
    heat transfer, 792
    salinity and, 570
    water versus land, 556
specific impulse, 970, 991
specified complexity, 31, 43
spectra, 848–849
    electromagnetic spectrum, 834, 835, 893, 912
    line spectra, 316, 317, 848
    stars, 910–913, 943
    visible spectrum, 835, 849
spectrometers
    See also mass spectrometry
    defined, 439
    prisms, 840
spectroscopic parallax, 941
spectroscopy, 910–913
    defined, 991
    spectroscopes, 848, 896
speech, 249
speed of light, 836, 852
speed of sound, 804
sperm cells (spermatozoa)
    angiosperms, 116
    animal reproduction, 186
    defined, 309
    human reproductive system, 238
    meiosis, 57
    phospholipids, 416
    sexual reproduction, 55
Sphagnum, 110, 111
sphalerite, 465, 529

spherical waves, 834

sphygmomanometer, 295

Spica (star), 944

spices, 274

spicules, 937

spiders
    arthropods, 177
    courtship behavior, 217
    hollow appendages, 183
    Pennsylvanian epoch, 491
    respiratory system, 194, 195
    water spiders, 172

spinal cord, 202, 230

spinal reflexes, 230

spindle fibers, 56, 57, 58, 59, 197

spine (spinal column), 226

spinous layer (epidermis), 182, 242

spiral galaxies, 952–953, 956, 957, 961

Spirit rover, 925, 987

spirogyra (pond scum), 94, 109

spleen, 191, 257

splenius capitis muscle, 255

sponges (Porifera)
    Aristotle's classification of animals, 164
    Cambrian period, 486
    digestion, 190
    Ediacaran period, 485
    first life, 153
    kingdom Animalia, 97, 172, 173
    ocean's cycle of life, 605
    Ordovician period, 487
    reproduction, 186
    separate subkingdom, 172

spongy body, 257

spongy tissue (leaves), 127, 135

spontaneous combustion, 362

spontaneous emission, 851

sporangia, 148

spores
    asexual reproduction, 55, 198
    defined, 309
    ferns and fern allies, 112, 113
    fungi, 148, 149
    mosses, 111

sporophytes, 111, 112

springs (water source), 565, 586

spring tides, 575, 586

sprouting conditions for seeds, 131

Sputnik, 977

squash, 865

squash, 624

squirting cucumber (*Ecballium elaterium*), 131

stability, 769

stages (rockets), 969

stamens, 116, 128, 309

standard reduction potentials, 393

standing waves, 799

stapes (stirrup), 246

starches, 413

Stardust (spacecraft), 915, 986

starfish, 178, 198

stars, 940–951
    See also sun, the
    basic facts, 941
    brightness, 942–943
    classifying, 944–945
    color and temperature, 943
    defined, 991
    evolution, 946–947
    finding locations, 906–907
    formation, 917, 940, 946
    Jupiter as failed star, 929, 947
    nuclear fusion, 948
    oldest, 962
    parallax, 902–903, 914, 941, 990
    planets, 966
    planets versus fixed, 900
    plasmas, 355
    spectra, 910–913, 943
    stellar distances, 940–941
    thermonuclear fusion reactions, 404

states of matter, 350–357
    See also gases; liquids; solids
    chemical equations, 363, 365
    phase changes, 350, 352, 379, 438, 793
    plasmas, 355, 783, 895, 990
    three main states, 312

static electricity, 812–813, 896

statics, 758, 896

stationary fronts, 543

steam, 776, 793

steel
    density, 776
    electrical conductivity, 815
    producing from scrap, 693
    sound velocity, 804

Stegosaurus, 159, 160

stele, 123

stems (plant), 124–125, 309

steppe, 559, 613

steradian, 896

stereophonic sound, 807

sternocleidomastoideus muscle, 254, 255

sternohyoideus muscle, 254

sternum (breastbone), 226, 251

steroids, 240, 416

sterols, 264

stigma (flowers), 128, 129

stills (apparatus), 385

stimulated emission, 851

stimulus and respsonse
    conditioning, 213
    plant physiology, 134, 138–141

stoichiometry, 376–377

stomach
    animal digestive systems, 190, 191
    human digestive system, 236, 237, 256
    ruminants, 191
    smooth muscles, 229

stomata, 127, 135

stone
    See also limestone
    granite, 467, 528
    natural resources, 530
    slate, 470, 471, 530

storm chasers, 548

storms
    clouds, 541
    cyclones, 542
    dust, 518
    hurricanes, 544–547, 584

thunderstorms, 548, 587
tornadoes, 549, 587
westerlies, 537
straight sinus, 250
stratocumulus clouds, 540
stratopause, 534
stratosphere, 534–535, 586
stratus clouds, 540
streak (minerals), 460, 461, 586
streams (hydrosphere), 566
See also rivers
defined, 586
erosion of rock, 510–513
stress, 202, 286–287, 687
stretching exercises, 281
striations (muscle), 229
strict creationism, 31, 40
strike-slip (transform) faults,
458, 524
string theory, 865
strip cropping, 710
stroma tissues, 182
stromatolites, 486
strong force, 765, 854, 863, 864,
896
strontium
alphabetical guide to the
elements, 341
periodic table of the elements,
322
seawater composition, 569
symbol and atomic number, 325
structural proteins, 419
style (flowers), 128, 129
styrene, 651
subarctic climate, 561
subatomic particles, 862–865
See also particle accelerators; *and*
particular particles
defined, 896
fermions and bosons, 865
parts of atoms, 314–315
subclavian artery and vein,
253, 256
subcutaneous tissues, 182, 242,
243, 309
subduction, 450, 586

subdwarf stars, 944
suberin, 121
subgiant stars, 944
sublittoral region, 581
subscapularis muscle, 254
subsoil, 532, 533, 708
subspecies, 171
substitution reactions, 413
subtractive method of color
mixing, 849
subtropical climate, 561
succession (ecological), 620–621
succulents, 611
sucrose, 358
sugar
See also glucose
animal metabolism, 188
crystals, 781
"empty" calories, 260
fast foods, 285
general dietary guidelines, 266
human digestive system, 236, 237
insulin, 240
molar mass, 374
photosynthesis, 134, 135
sucrose, 358
sulfate minerals, 465, 569
sulfide minerals, 465, 529
sulfur
alphabetical guide to the
elements, 341
macrominerals, 268
mineral nutrients, 607
periodic table of the elements,
323
polyatomic molecules, 315
symbol and atomic number, 325
sulfur dioxide
acid rain, 667, 669
air pollution, 662
common indoor pollutants, 651
defined, 749
oxidation-reduction reactions,
396
volcanoes, 452
sulfuric acid, 387
Sumner, James B., 421

sun, the, 936–939
See also solar energy; solar
system; sunlight
activity, 938–939
apparent magnitude, 942
atmosphere, 936–937
color and temperature, 943
diameter, 914
distance from center of Milky
Way, 914
distance from Earth to, 914, 936
eclipses, 924, 925, 991
giant phase, 947
heat sources, 786
hydrologic cycle, 538
Milky Way galaxy, 953
nuclear fusion, 861, 939
plasmas, 355
radiation of heat, 795
solar calendar, 901
solar wind, 502, 915, 938,
977, 991
sunspots, 938, 991
thermonuclear fusion reactions,
404, 405
time light takes to travel to
Earth, 21
weather, 536
sunbeans, 628
sunlight
additive color mixture, 849
blueness of sky, 534
cancer, 296
energy-flow in ecosystems, 603
middle latitude climate zone,
560, 561
photosynthesis, 134, 601, 602,
604
polarizing, 844
solar energy, 647, 742–743
stimulus and response in plants,
138, 141
sunspots, 938, 991
superclusters, 957
supercolliders, 858
Superconducting Super Collider
(SSC), 858

superconductors, 411, 753, 797, 832–833, 896
supereruptions (volcanic), 454
superficial peroneal nerve, 252
superficial temporal artery and vein, 253
superfluids, 797, 896
Superfund, 695
supergiant stars, 944, 945, 991
superior gluteal nerve, 252
superior mesenteric artery and vein, 253
superior saggital sinus, 250
superior vena cava, 256, 257
supernatural phenomena, 21
supernovas, 948–949
   Casseiopeia A, 954
   cosmology, 962
   defined, 991
   estimating vast distances, 958
   nebular hypothesis, 917
   stellar evolution, 946
superposition, law of, 481, 482, 584
superstrings, 865
supersymmetry, 865
supraclavicular nerve, 252
supralittoral region, 581
supraorbital nerve, 252
Supreme Being, 31, 40–41
suralis nerve, 252
surface tension, 352, 439, 779, 782, 896
surface-to-volume ratio, 183
surface waves (seismic waves), 456, 586
Surtsey, 452
suspended load, 511, 586
sustained yield management, 704, 749
Svalvard (Norway), 515
swamps
   Pennsylvanian epoch, 491
   Silurian period, 488
   water table, 719
S-waves (secondary waves), 442–443, 456, 586

sweat glands, 182, 240, 242, 243
sweetness, 249
swells (waves), 577
symbiosis, 596, 749
sympathetic nervous system, 202
sympathetic vibration, 804
synapses, 230
synchrotrons, 856, 857, 858
synclines (downfolds), 522, 523, 586
synergistic effect, 648, 749
synodic rhythms, 209
Syn-Roc, 698
syphilis, 300
systematics, 90, 170

T

tactile corpuscles, 247
tactile sense. *See* touch
tactile signaling, 215
tadpoles, 187
taiga, 613
tailings (mining), 697, 698
tails (anatomy), 178
tails (comets), 934
talc, 463
tallgrass prairie, 622
talus, 251
tannins, 137, 309
tantalum
   alphabetical guide to the elements, 341
   periodic table of the elements, 322
   symbol and atomic number, 325
tapeworms, 174, 186, 593, 597
taproots, 122
tarns, 516, 517
tarsiers, 163
tarsus, 226, 251
taste
   chemoreceptors, 204
   human sense organs, 249
   sense receptors, 230
   and smell, 249
taste buds, 249

Tatum, Edward, 63
tau-particles, 863
taxis (movement), 211, 309
taxonomy, biological. *See* classification of plants and animals
T cells, 302, 303
tear glands, 240
technetium
   alphabetical guide to the elements, 341
   periodic table of the elements, 322
   symbol and atomic number, 325
technology
   agricultural, 626, 627
   antinoise, 687
   genetic, 78–79
tectorial membrane, 246
telegraphy, 820
telephones, 820
telescopes, 908–909
   Allen Telescope Array, 967
   Galileo, 904
   Hubble Space Telescope, 908, 958, 984, 985, 986
   Kepler space telescope, 987
   milestones in physics, 753
   optical, 908, 990
   radio, 913
   in space, 908
television waves, 798
tellurium
   alphabetical guide to the elements, 341
   periodic table of the elements, 323
   symbol and atomic number, 325
telomere, 62
telophase (mitosis), 56, 59, 197
Telstar, 978
Tempel 1, Comet, 935, 975
temperature, 788–789
   See also global warming; heat
   absolute temperature scale, 357, 788, 796
   altitude, 555

Index

changing states of matter, 349
chemical equilibrium, 370, 371
chemical reaction rates, 368, 369
climate change, 673
cold fronts, 543
cryogenics, 796–797
defined, 896
Earth's interior, 446
heat transfer, 792–795
hot air rises, 536
kinetic theory of gases, 354, 783
ocean currents, 572
seawater, 570, 571
skin in control of internal, 243
skin in sensing, 247
solubility, 383
stellar color and, 943
stimulus and response in plants, 141
thermoregulation in animals, 203
warm fronts, 543
wind chill, 537
temporal bone, 251
tendons, 182, 229
tendrils (plants), 125
Tengusa (*Gelidium corneum*), 109
terahertz, 835
terbium
alphabetical guide to the elements, 341
periodic table of the elements, 323
symbol and atomic number, 325
Tereshkova, Valentina V., 972, 979
teres major muscle, 254, 255
teres minor muscle, 255
terminal moraines, 517, 586
terpenes, 137, 416
terracing, 626, 709
Terra EOS, 986
terrestrial planets, 920–927
See also Earth; Mars; Mercury; Venus
defined, 991
territoriality, 217, 595, 749
Tertiary period, 498
Tesla, Nikola, 816

tesla units, 425
testability, 21
test crossing, 74
testes (testicles), 238, 257
testosterone, 238
tetrads, 57, 59, 199
tetrapods, 157, 489
Texas longhorn cattle, 716
texture in igneous rocks, 467
thalamus, 249, 250
thalli, 111
thallium
alphabetical guide to the elements, 341
periodic table of the elements, 323
symbol and atomic number, 325
Thallophyta, 108
Theophrastus, 103
theoretical physics, 754
theories (scientific), 20
constantly changing, 21
successful, 27
what theories are, 26
"theory of everything," 865
therapsids, 162, 492
thermal efficiency of an engine, 790
thermal energy, 739
thermal expansion thermometers, 789
thermal gradients, 739
thermal metamorphism, 471
thermal pollution of water, 722
thermionic emission, 825
thermochemistry, 378–381
thermocouple thermometers, 789
thermodynamics, 381
defined, 378, 896
Gibbs free energy, 393
heat, 790–791
laws, 381
types of physics, 754
thermohaline circulation, 574, 587
thermometers, 789
thermonuclear fusion reactions, 404, 405, 439

thermoregulation, 203
thermosphere, 587
thigh muscles, 228
thigmonasty, 140
thigmotropism, 139
third-class levers, 772
third law of motion, 763, 971
third law of thermodynamics, 790
Thomson, J. J., 316, 811, 824–825
thoracic vertebrae, 226, 251
Thoreau, Henry David, 655
thorium
alphabetical guide to the elements, 342
nuclear reactions, 406
periodic table of the elements, 322
radioactivity, 403
symbol and atomic number, 325
thorn forest, 610
threat displays, 216
Three Mile Island accident, 736
threonine, 419
thrust, 969, 970
thrust faults, 525
thulium
alphabetical guide to the elements, 342
periodic table of the elements, 323
symbol and atomic number, 325
thunder, 548
thunderheads, 541
thunderstorms, 548, 587
thymine, 65, 66, 309, 414–415
thymus gland, 240, 256
thyroid cartilage, 257
thyroid gland, 240, 241, 256
thyroxin, 240
tibeal nerve, 252
tibia, 226, 251
tibialis anterior muscle, 254
tides, 208, 574–575, 587, 739
tigers, 640, 641
Tiktaalik, 36
till, 517, 587

time
 atomic clocks, 318, 761
 determining longitude with a
  clock, 505
 geologic time, 476–501
 light-years, 914, 940
 metric measurement, 761
 space-time, 767, 853
Times Beach (Missouri), 649
tin
 alphabetical guide to the
  elements, 342
 periodic table of the elements,
  323
 symbol and atomic number, 325
Tiros 1 (satellite), 552
tissues
 animal, 182
 defined, 309
 histology, 44
 multicellular organisms, 60
 plant, 119, 120–121
Titan (satellite of Saturn),
  931, 974
titanium
 alphabetical guide to the
  elements, 342
 Earth's crust, 447
 periodic table of the elements,
  322
 symbol and atomic number, 325
toads, 213
toadstools, 95
Tokamak Fusion Test Reactor,
  861
tolerance, law of, 593, 747
toluene, 409
tongue, 249
tooth shells (scaphopods), 176
topaz, 463
topographic maps, 522, 587
topography
 climate and, 554, 555
 defined, 587
topsoil, 708
Tornado Alley, 549, 587
tornadoes, 549, 587

torque, 768–769, 896
torso muscles, 228
tortoises, 216
total eclipses, 924, 991
touch
 mechanoreceptors, 205
 skin, 247
 tactile signaling, 215
 thigmotropism, 139
touch-me-not (*Mimosa pudica*), 140
tourmaline, 844
toxic waste, 649
toxins, 292, 302
Toxoplasma, 49
trace minerals, 268–269, 273, 421
Trachaeophyta. *See* vascular plants
  (Tracheophyta)
trachea (windpipe)
 animal respiratory systems, 194,
  195
 defined, 309
 human respiratory system, 234,
  257
traction (stream transport), 511
trade winds, 557
traits
 coding for, 66
 expression, 71
 favorable and unfavorable, 38
 heredity, 62
 sex-linked, 77
transcription (protein
  synthesis), 66
transformers, 822–823, 897
transform plate boundaries, 450
transgenic organisms, 80
transistors, 753, 830–831
transition metals
 alphabetical guide to the
  elements, 326
 inorganic compounds, 400
 periodic table of the elements,
  321, 322
translation (protein synthesis), 66
translocation (mutation), 68
transmission electron
  microscopes, 824

transmission of light, 837
transmutation (chemical), 23, 403,
  406, 439
transpiration
 defined, 309
 hydrologic cycle, 538–539
 water transport in plants, 134
transuranic wastes, 696,
  699, 749
transverse colon, 256
transverse waves, 798, 834,
  844, 897
trapezius muscle, 255
tree-ring counting, 480
trees
 See also forests
 American chestnut, 598
 carbon dioxide absorption,
  676, 702
 dominance among, 618
 oxygen production, 702
 redwoods, 115, 623
tree shrews, 163
trenches, ocean, 579
Triassic period, 493
triceps brachi muscles,
  228, 255
Triceratops, 159, 496
Trichinella spiralis, 175
trichinosis, 175
trichloroethylene, 652, 694
triglycerides, 262, 264, 309,
  416, 417
trigonometric parallax method,
  941
triiodothyronine, 240
trilobites
 Cambrian period, 154, 486
 compound eyes, 177, 205
 extinction, 157, 487
 index fossils, 481
Trimerophyta, 100
triode vacuum tubes, 825
triple chemical bonds, 345
triple point, 897
tritium, 406, 861
Triton (satellite of Neptune), 932

tRNA (transfer RNA), 66, 67
trophic levels, 596, 604–605, 749
tropical climates, 558–559
tropical depressions, 545
tropical disturbances, 545
tropical hardwoods, 705
tropical storms, 545
tropics
   climate, 558–559
   continental tropical air masses, 542
   maritime tropical air masses, 542
   tropical rain, 541
tropisms, 138–139, 309
tropopause, 534
troposphere, 534–535
   defined, 587
   temperature, 555
trough of a wave, 576, 587
truffles, 95
tryptophan, 419
Tsiolkovsky, Konstantin, 968
tsunamis, 457, 577, 587
tube feet, 178
tubers, 125
tubulin, 50
tumors, 296
tundra, 614
   defined, 749
   North American, 622
   polar climates, 562
tungsten
   alphabetical guide to the elements, 342
   periodic table of the elements, 322
   symbol and atomic number, 325
tunicates, 178
turbines, 738, 744, 784
turgor pressure, 140
turtles, 572, 641, 726
twin paradox, 853
typhoid fever, 726
typing blood, 76
Tyrannosaurus rex, 159, 161, 494, 496, 497
tyrosine, 419

U

ulcers (peptic), 236
ulna, 226, 251
ulnar artery and vein, 253
ulnar nerve, 252
ultrasound, 809, 897
ultraviolet (UV) radiation
   atmosphere blocks, 535
   defined, 749
   electromagnetic spectrum, 835, 912
   harmful radiation, 682
   health effects, 680
   ozone layer, 486, 680, 681
   ultraviolet astronomy, 913
umami, 249
UN Conference on the Human Environment (1972), 656
unfavorable traits, 38
unicellular organisms
   cells, 44
   chemoreceptors, 204
   defined, 309
   development of multicellular organisms, 61
   prokaryotic cells, 46
unification theories, 864–865
unified atomic mass units, 372
uniformatarianism, 168
uniramians, 177
United States. *See* North America
universal gas constant, 357, 867
universal gravitational constant, 766, 866, 867
universe, 956–961
   See also galaxies; solar system; stars
   age, 962–963
   distances, 958–959
   early concepts, 902–903
   expanding, 911, 959, 962
   extraterrestrial life, 966–967
   intelligent design, 43
   nature of, 964–965
   open or closed, 963, 988, 990
   origins, 962

unsaturated fats, 263
unsaturated fatty acids, 263, 417
unsaturated hydrocarbons, 409, 439
unsaturated zone, 564
upfolds (anticlines), 522, 523, 582
upper mantle (Earth), 443, 445, 506
upper respiratory tract, 234
upwellings, 573, 587, 605
uracil, 66, 415
Ural Mountains, 157
uranium
   alphabetical guide to the elements, 342
   harmful radiation, 683
   nuclear fission, 405, 860
   nuclear power, 646, 737
   nuclear reactions, 406
   occupational hazards, 652
   particle emission and half-life of uranium 238, 404
   periodic table of the elements, 322
   radioactive dating, 480
   radioactivity, 403
   symbol and atomic number, 325
Uranus, 931
   axis, 919
   discovery of Neptune, 26
   properties, 919
   space exploration, 931, 982, 984
urea, 201, 408
urease, 421
ureters, 241, 257
urethra, 241, 257
urinary system
   See also kidneys
   human, 225, 241
urine, 201, 241
uterus, 239, 257
utricle, 246

V

vaccines, 291, 717
vacuoles, 50, 119
vacuum, 897

vacuum tubes, 825, 828, 830

vagina, 239, 257

valence electrons, 319, 320, 439, 827, 897

valine, 419

Valles Marineris Canyon (Mars), 926

vanadium
    alphabetical guide to the elements, 343
    periodic table of the elements, 322
    symbol and atomic number, 325

Van Allen belts, 977

Van de Graaff accelerators, 856

van der Waals forces, 348, 349, 351

vapor pressure, 384, 570, 587

variable stars, 958

variation (genetic), 39, 142, 309

vascular cylinder, 123

vascular plants (Tracheophyta)
    classification of plants, 96, 106
    early land plants, 100–101
    ferns and fern allies, 112–113
    Silurian period, 488

vascular system
    botany, 105
    leaves, 127
    photosynthesis, 134

vas deferens, 238, 257

vastus intermedius muscle, 254

vastus lateralis muscle, 254, 255

vastus medialis muscle, 254

Vega (spacecraft), 984

vegetables
    balanced diet, 266
    calories and fats, 278
    carbohydrates, 260
    diet and cancer, 267
    fats, 263
    fiber, 261
    general dietary guidelines, 266
    proteins, 260, 267
    USDA guidelines, 259

vegetarian diet, 266–267

vegetation. *See* plants

vegetative organs, 122

vegetative reproduction, 55, 196, 198

vein patterns of leaves, 126

veins, 233

veldt, 613

Velociraptor, 161

velocity
    defined, 897
    escape velocity, 969, 971
    formula, 867
    light, 836, 852, 867
    orbital velocity, 969, 971
    sound, 804
    time measurement, 761

Venera probes, 921, 981, 982

ventricles, 232, 294

Venus, 921
    apparent magnitude, 942
    axis, 919
    properties, 918
    rotation, 919
    space exploration, 921, 978, 980, 981, 982, 984, 985

Venus's-flytrap, 140

vernalization, 141

vertebrae, 226, 251, 309

vertebral artery, 253

vertebrates
    brain, 221
    chemoreceptors, 204
    defined, 309, 587
    kingdom Animalia, 97, 172, 178–179
    number of species catalogued, 164
    Ordovician period, 487
    reach dry land, 156–157
    reproduction, 186
    Silurian period, 488

vertical circles, 906

vertical faults, 523

Very Large Array telescopes, 913

Very Long Baseline Array (VLBA), 913

Vesalius, Andreas, 22, 166

vessels (roots), 123

vestibule (ear), 246

vestigial organs, 309

vetiver grass, 710

vibrations. *See* waves

Viking (spacecraft), 926, 982

villi (intestinal), 237

Virgo Cluster, 957

virions, 181

virtual images, 840, 843

viruses, 181
    defined, 309
    disease caused, 292
    DNA and RNA, 414
    HIV (human immunodeficiency virus), 301, 411
    indoor pollution, 651

viscosity, 352, 353, 779, 782, 797, 897

visible spectrum, 835, 849, 912

vision (sight)
    animal, 204–205
    color, 244
    corrective lenses, 842
    history of science, 22
    human eyes, 244–245
    LASIK surgery, 850
    luminosity curve, 846
    sense receptors, 230
    visual signals, 215

vitamin A (retinol), 268, 270, 416

vitamin B_1 (thiamin), 271

vitamin B_2 (riboflavin), 271

vitamin B_3 (niacin; nicotinamide; nicotinic acid), 271

vitamin B_6 (pyridoxine; pyridoxal), 271

vitamin B_{12} (cobalamin), 271, 401

vitamin C (ascorbic acid), 267, 268, 270, 271

vitamin D (calciferol), 268, 270, 416

vitamin deficiency diseases, 268

vitamin E (alphatocopherol), 268, 270, 416

vitamin K, 268, 270, 416

vitamins, 268–271
    defined, 309
    enzymes, 421
    photosynthesis, 135

vitreous humor, 244, 245
vitrification, 698
volcanic ash, 518
volcanoes, 452–455
    air pollution, 661
    balance of nature, 631
    defined, 587
    heat sources, 786
    Mount St. Helens, 520, 526
    mudflows, 520
    seamounts, 579
    volcanic lakes, 567
    volcanic mountains, 526–527
Volta, Alessandro, 392, 394, 817
voltaic pile, 394, 817
volts, 817
volume
    chemical equilibrium, 370, 371
    gas laws, 356–357
    molar, 375
voluntary muscles, 228
von Braun, Wernher, 976
vortexes, 797
Vorticella, 49
Voskhod space program, 972, 979
Vostok space program, 972, 978
Voyager (spacecraft), 928, 929, 930, 932, 983, 984
V-2 rocket, 969, 976
vulva, 239

W

walking for exercise, 281
Walton, Ernest, 753, 856
warm-blooded (endothermic) animals, 183, 203
warm fronts, 543
Washoe (chimpanzee), 222
waste products
    disposal, 690–691
    dumping waste, 690, 727
    hazardous, 694–699, 747
    human population explosion, 634, 635
    land pollution, 688–689
    nuclear power, 646, 737

    oil, 724
    recycling, 658, 676, 689, 692–693, 705, 748
    sources, 689
    water pollution, 722–723, 724
watchmaker argument, 43
water
    See also hydrosphere; ice; irrigation; precipitation (meteorology); water supply
    amount on Earth, 718
    animal movement, 184
    aquatic environments, 614–615
    average daily consumption in U.S., 718
    capillary action, 782
    changes in state, 793
    climate and distance from, 556
    climate change and supplies, 674
    combustion, 359
    common compounds, 358
    conductivity, 384
    cycle in ecosystems, 606
    density, 776
    erosion of rock, 510–513
    Europa, 985
    homeostasis, 200–201
    hydrides, 399
    hydroelectric power, 646
    hydrologic cycle, 538–541
    hydroponic gardening, 629
    hydrotropism, 139
    infectious disease spread, 292
    liquid, 352
    melting and boiling points, 788
    mineral nutrients, 607
    molar mass, 374
    molecular geometry, 346
    mole ratio for reaction forming, 376
    pH, 389
    photosynthesis, 134, 135
    polar covalent bonds, 345
    pollution, 718–731
    ponds, 631
    quantity on Earth, 539
    seawater composition, 569

    sound velocity, 804
    uses, 719
    vapor in air, 660
    water transport in plants, 132–133
water chestnuts, 624
waterfalls, 513
water power, 719, 738–739
water-soluble vitamins, 268, 271
water spiders, 172
water striders, 782
water supply, 718–719
    See also groundwater
    aquifers, 564, 565, 582, 729, 746
    conservation, 732–733
    protecting, 728–731
    water table, 564–565, 587, 719
water table, 564–565, 587, 719
water transport (plants), 132–133
water treatment, 730
waterwheels, 738, 739
Watson, James, 23, 63, 414, 415
watt per steradian, 897
wave crest, 799
wavelength
    defined, 587, 897
    Doppler effect, 805
    measuring waves, 799
    ocean waves, 576
    sound waves, 804
    spectroscopy, 910–913
wavelets, 801
wave medium, 798, 897
waves, 798–801
    See also wavelength
    defined, 897
    electromagnetic, 835, 893
    light, 753, 798, 800, 834–835
    motion, 800–801
    ocean, 574, 576–577, 587
    power, 739
    sound, 799, 802–803
    types, 798
wave trough, 799
waxes, 416
weak force, 765, 863, 864, 865, 964
weakly interacting massive particles (WIMPs), 964

weather, 536–557
   See also climate; precipitation
      (meteorology); storms; wind
   air masses, 542–543
   changing, 551
   defined, 587
   hydrologic cycle, 538–541
   predicting, 550–553
   satellites, 977
   wind systems, 536–537
weathering, 506–513
   See also erosion
   mass movement, 520–521, 584
   rate, 509
   rock cycle, 472, 582
weaver birds, 210
wedges, 773
Wegener, Alfred, 448
weight (physics), 766, 867
weight control, 281, 282–283
weight pyramids, 604
Weinberg, Steven, 865
wells, 564, 565, 587
Welwitschia, 114
westerlies, 536, 537, 557
wet cell batteries, 394
wetlands
   See also swamps
   defined, 749
   draining as environmental
      boomerang, 633
   in peril, 700–701
whales, 179, 641, 657
wheat, 624, 625, 628, 717
wheels and axles, 772
whisk ferns (Psilophyta), 113
   classification of plants, 107
   early land plants, 100
   Silurian period, 488
white blood cells (leukocytes), 233
whitecaps, 577
White Cliffs of Dover, 469
white dwarf stars, 944, 945, 946,
   947, 991
whiteness, 849
white stars, 944
whooping cranes, 643

whorled pattern of leaves, 126
Wien, Wilhelm, 25
wildlife conservation, 642–643
wildlife refuges, 642, 654
wildlife trade, 639, 707
Wilkins, Maurice, 63
Wilmut, Ian, 63
Wilson, E. O., 638
Wilson, Robert W., 965
WIMPs (weakly interacting massive
   particles), 964
wind
   atmospheric circulation, 557
   belts, 536
   defined, 587
   erosion, 518–519
   hurricanes, 546–547
   leeward side of mountains, 555
   monsoons, 557, 585
   ocean currents, 572
   systems, 536–537
   tornadoes, 549
   wind power, 647, 744
windbreaking, 710
wind chill, 537
windmills, 744
windows (astronomy), 912
windpipe. *See* trachea (windpipe)
wind power, 647, 735, 744
wind turbines, 647, 744
windward side, 555
wings, insect, 177
withdrawal symptoms, 298, 299
wiwaxia, 154
Wöhler, Friedrich, 349, 408
wolves
   altruism, 218
   communication, 215
   endangered species, 641
   feeding ladder, 596
   predation, 597
   subspecies, 171
wood
   conduction of heat, 794
   energy source, 647
   tropical hardwoods, 705
   waste, 647

woodchucks, 203
woodpeckers, 630
woody stems, 124–125
work (physics), 770–771
   defined, 897
   formula, 867
   power, 771
worker bees, 219
World Wide Web, 23
worms. *See also* flatworms
   (Platyhelminthes);
     roundworms (Nematoda);
     segmented worms (Annelida)
   Ediacaran period, 485
   marine, 176
W particles, 865
Wright brothers, 976
Wundt, Wilhelm, 23

X

xenon
   alphabetical guide to the
     elements, 343
   chemical bonds, 344
   compounds, 399
   noble gases, 399
   periodic table of the elements,
     323
   symbol and atomic number, 325
xerophytic plants, 611, 623
X-rays
   atmosphere protects against, 535
   bones, 227
   cancer, 296
   Chandra Orbiting X-ray
     Observatory, 986
   defined, 897
   discovery, 227, 753
   electromagnetic spectrum,
     835, 912
   harmful radiation, 682
   pulsars, 951
   sun emits, 937, 939
   waves, 798
   X-ray astronomy, 913
   X-ray sources, 950

xylem, 121
  defined, 309
  leaves, 127
  primary, 120, 124
  roots, 123
  secondary, 124
  stems, 124
  vascular plants, 106

Y

year, solar and lunar, 901
yeasts, 149, 150
yellow stars, 944
Yellowstone National Park, 88,
    454, 565, 654, 656
ytterbium
  alphabetical guide to the
    elements, 343
  periodic table of the elements,
    323
  symbol and atomic number, 325
yttrium
  alphabetical guide to the
    elements, 343
  particle emission and half-life of
    yttrium 88, 404
  periodic table of the elements,
    322
  superconductors, 832
  symbol and atomic number, 325
Yukawa, Hideki, 864

Z

Zea mays, 626
zebra mussels, 598
zebras, 179, 600, 610
Zeeman, Pieter, 911
zero gravity, 447
zinc
  alphabetical guide to the
    elements, 343
  galvanic cells, 392, 817
  microminerals, 269, 273
  mineral nutrients, 607
  ores, 529

  periodic table of the
    elements, 323
  plant nutrients carried by
    water, 134
  symbol and atomic number, 325
zircon, 461
zirconium
  alphabetical guide to the
    elements, 343
  periodic table of the elements,
    322
  symbol and atomic number, 325
zodiac, 901, 991
zoology
  See also animals
  ethology, 210
  history, 164–169
zooplankton, 604, 605
zoos, 642
Zosterophyllophyta, 100
Z particles, 865
Zweig, George, 863
zygotes, 187, 199, 309

www.SWadvantage.com

How to Use Science Advantage

Strand/Subject color bars and names

Strand/Subject color bar

BIOLOGY

CHEMISTRY

EARTH SCIENCE

ECOLOGY

PHYSICS

SPACE SCIENCE

CELLS are the basic units of all life. Every living organism consists of either a single cell or a collection of many interdependent cells. Bacteria are examples of single-celled, or *unicellular*, organisms. *Multicellular* organisms, composed of many cells, include most plants, fungi, and animals.

While some cells—frog eggs and certain nerve cells, for example—can be seen with the naked eye, most cells can only be seen using a microscope. It would take about 40,000 red blood cells to fill this letter *O*. It takes millions of cells to make up the skin on the palm of your hand.

Cell Theory

Human beings, and every multicellular organism, develop from a single cell. That cell grows to a certain size and then divides. Each new cell grows and divides, over and over again, until it forms a complete organism.

The theory that every form of life is made up of cells was developed in the 1800s. Cell theory consists of three basic principles:

1. The cell is the fundamental unit of all life.
2. All living organisms are made up of cells.
3. Every cell is the product of the division of a previously existing cell.

Today, many different scientific specialists study the cell. Cell biologists deal with cells on every level. Cytologists study cell structure. Biochemists and biophysicists investigate cell *physiology*, or function. Histologists study tissues, which are collections of similar cells, such as muscles and blood.

BLOOD CELLS
red blood cells

MUSCLE CELLS
striated (voluntary)

BONE CELL

smooth (involuntary)

white blood cells

basophil

cardiac

REPRODUCTIVE CELL

eosinophil

lymphocyte

NERVE CELL

monocyte

GLAND CELL

neutrophil

Cell Size	
human nerve cell	up to 2 m in length
chicken egg cell	approx. 30 mm in diameter
frog egg cell	approx. 1 mm in diameter
human egg cell	approx. 100 µm* in diameter
human red blood cell	approx. 8 µm in diameter
average eukaryotic cell	approx 10–100 µm in diameter
average plant body cell	approx. 30–50 µm in diameter
average animal body cell	approx 10–20 µm in diameter
average true bacteria	approx. 1 µm in diameter
average prokaryotic cell	approx. 1–10 µm in diameter
mycoplasma	approx. 0.16 µm in diameter

*µm = micron (one micron = 0.000001 meters)